Plan.Map.Go.

TripTik® Travel Planner

Where premier mapping technology meets complete travel information:

- Map your trips using roads you prefer.
- Find AAA Approved places to stay and dine.
- Locate AAA recommended sights and activities.
- Book hotels at low AAA member rates.
- Create MyPlaces maps with places you select.
- Find local gas stations and prices.

Before and during your travels, turn to AAA.com.

Arkansas, Kansas, Missouri & Oklahoma

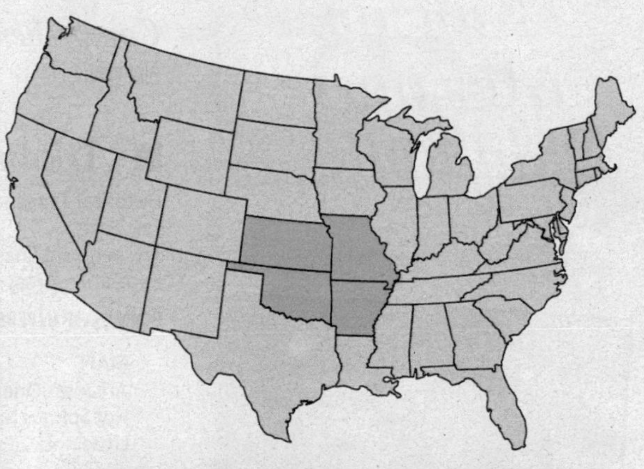

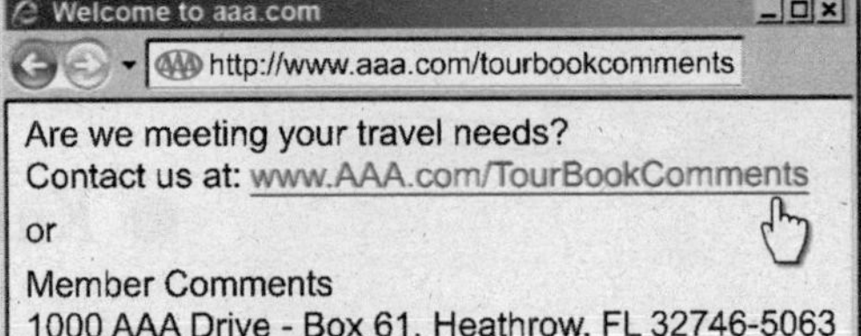
Welcome to aaa.com
http://www.aaa.com/tourbookcomments
Are we meeting your travel needs?
Contact us at: www.AAA.com/TourBookComments
or
Member Comments
1000 AAA Drive - Box 61, Heathrow, FL 32746-5063

Published by AAA Publishing
1000 AAA Drive, Heathrow, FL 32746-5063

Advertising Rate and Circulation Information: (407) 444-8280

Printed in the USA by Worldcolor, Buffalo, NY

Photo Credit: (Cover & Title Page)
Monument Rocks, Oakley, KS
© Chuck Haney / Danita Delimont Stock Photography

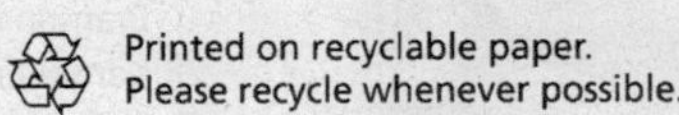
Printed on recyclable paper.
Please recycle whenever possible.

Stock #4603

Mixed Sources
Product group from well-managed forests and other controlled sources
www.fsc.org Cert no. SW-COC-002550
© 1996 Forest Stewardship Council
FSC

Arkansas, Kansas, Missouri & Oklahoma

Arkansas

Kansas

Missouri

Oklahoma

Featured Information

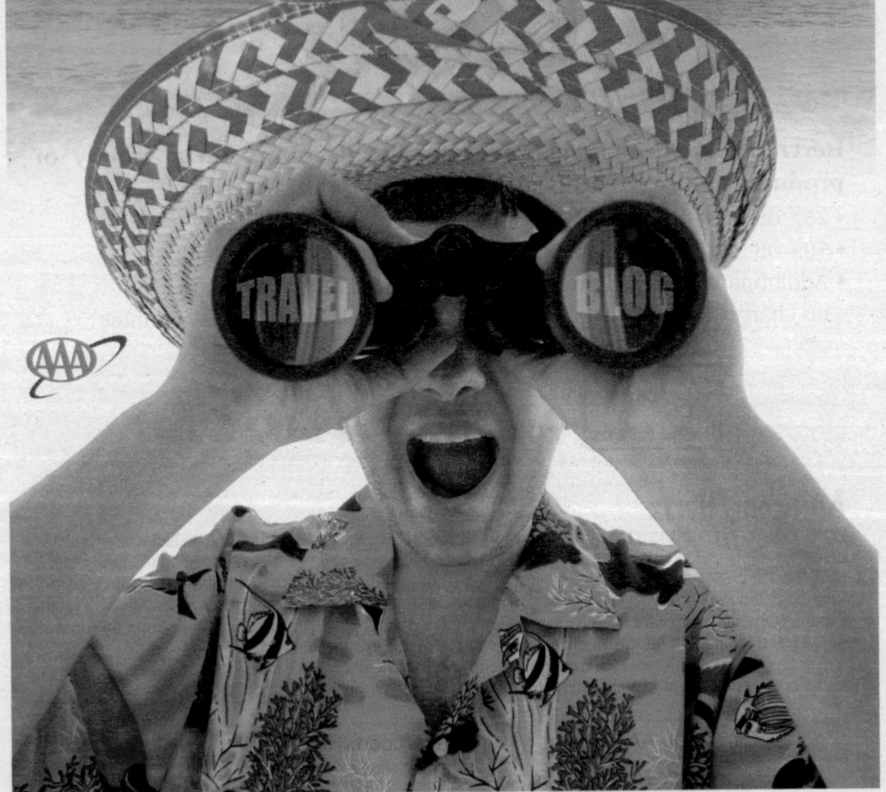
TRAVEL
BLOG
AAA

USING YOUR GUIDE

Attractions, lodgings and restaurants are listed on the basis of merit alone after careful evaluation and approval by one of AAA/CAA's full-time, professionally trained inspectors. Evaluations are unannounced to ensure that we see an establishment just as you would see it.

An establishment's decision to advertise in the TourBook guide has no bearing on its evaluation or rating. Advertising for services or products does not imply AAA endorsement.

Information in this guide was believed accurate at the time of publication. However, since changes inevitably occur between annual editions, we suggest you work with your AAA travel professional or check on AAA.com to confirm prices and schedules.

How the TourBook Guide is Organized

The TourBook guide is organized into three distinct sections.

The **Points of Interest** section helps you plan daily activities and sightseeing excursions and provides details about the city or attraction you are visiting.

The **Lodgings and Restaurants** section helps you select AAA Approved accommodations and dining facilities meeting your specific needs and expectations.

The **Reference** section provides indexes for locating information within this guide and items to aid the trip planning process.

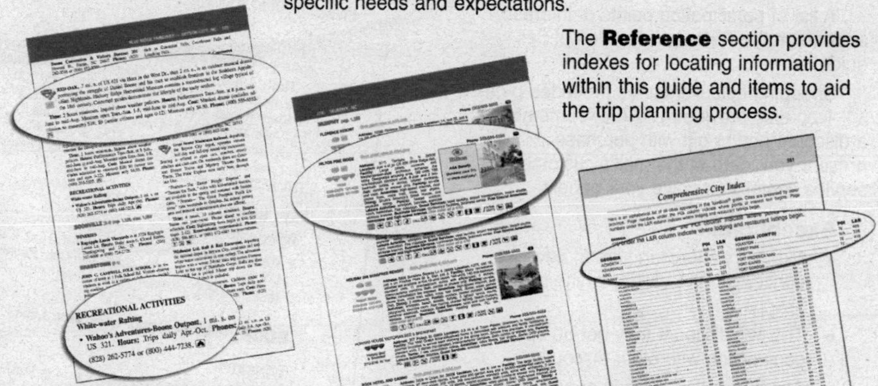

Locating the Attractions, Lodgings and Restaurants

Attractions, lodgings and restaurants are listed under the city in which they physically are located - or in some cases under the nearest recognized city. Most listings are alphabetically organized by state, province, region or island, then by city and establishment name.

A color is assigned to each state or province so that you can match the color bars at the top of the page to switch from the **Points of Interest** section to the **Lodgings and Restaurants** section.

Spotting maps help you physically locate points of interest, lodgings and restaurants in the major destinations.

The Comprehensive City Index located in the **Reference** section contains an A-to-Z list of cities.

Destination Cities and Destination Areas

Destination cities, established based on government models and local expertise, include metropolitan areas plus nearby vicinity cities. **Destination areas** are regions with broad tourist appeal; several cities will comprise the area.

If a city falls within a destination's vicinity, the city name will appear at its alphabetical location in the book, and a cross reference will give you the exact page on which listings for that city begin.

An Orientation map appears at the beginning of each destination section to familiarize you with that destination.

Understanding the Points of Interest Listing

GEM Designation

A GEM indicates the attraction has been rated a AAA GEM, a "must see" point of interest that offers a *Great Experience for Members®*. These attractions have been judged to be of exceptional interest and quality by AAA inspectors.

Discount Savings

The SAVE icon denotes those attractions offering AAA/CAA, AAA MasterCard, AAA VISA or international Show Your Card & Save discount cardholders a discount off the attraction's standard admission. Present your card at the attraction's admission desk.

A list of participating points of interest appears in the Reference section of this guide.

Shopping establishments preceded by a SAVE icon also provide to AAA/CAA members a discount and/or gift with purchase; present your card at the mall's customer service center to receive your benefit.

Exceptions

- Members should inquire in advance concerning the validity of the discount for special rates.
- The SAVE discount may not be used in conjunction with other discounts.
- Attractions that already provide a reduced senior or child rate may not honor the SAVE discount for those age groups.
- All offers are subject to change and may not apply during special events, particular days or seasons or for the entire validity period of the TourBook guide.

Adventure Travel

There are inherent risks with adventure travel activities like air tours, hiking, skiing and white-water rafting. For your own safety, please read and adhere to all safety instructions. Mentions of these activities are for information only and do **not** imply endorsement by AAA.

BLUE RIDGE

Boone Convention & Visitors Bureau: 208 Howard St., Boone, NC 28607 **Phones:** (828) 555-5555 or (800) 555-5555

GEM SAVE **RED OAK,** .7 mi. n. of US 421 via Horn in the Wes struggle of Daniel Boone and his men to establish Hickory Ridge Homestead Museum contains a rec Costumed guides demonstrate the lifestyle of the e

Time: 2 hours minimum. Inquire about weather policies June to mid-Aug. Museum open Tues.-Sun. 1-8, mid-Jun mission to museum) $18; $9 (senior citizens and ages 0 **Phone:** (800) 555-5555.

onstrate the lifestyle of the early settlers.

Time: 2 hours minimum. Inquire about weather policies. **Hours:** Performances Tues.-Sun. at 8 p.m., mid-June to mid-Aug. Museum open Tues.-Sun. 1-8, mid-June to mid-Aug. **Cost:** Musical drama (includes admission to museum) $18; $9 (senior citizens and ages 0-12). Museum only $4.50. **Phone:** (800) 555-5555.

RECREATIONAL ACTIVITIES

White-water Rafting

- **Wahoo's Adventures-Boone Outpost,** 1 mi. s. on US 321. **Hours:** Trips daily Apr.-Oct. **Phones:** (828) 555-5555 or (800) 555-5555.

BOONVILLE (B-4) pop. 1,138, elev. 1,066'

WINERIES

- **RagApple Lassie Vineyards** is at 3724 RagApple Lassie Ln. **Hours:** Daily noon-6. Closed Easter, Thanksgiving and Dec. 25. **Phones:** (336) 555-5555 or (866) 555-5555.

BRASSTOWN (F-1)

JOHN C. CAMPBELL FOLK SCHOOL is in the center of town at 1 Folk School Rd. Visitors observe students at work in a variety of folk classes inclu ing cooking, ... pottery

RECREATIONAL ACTIVI

White-water Rafting

- **Wahoo's Adventures-Boon** US 321. **Hours:** Trips da (828) 555-5555 or (800) 55

— BRYSON CITY, NC 129
: Falls, Courthouse Falls and
f Commerce
utdoor musical drama portraying the
he Southern Appalachian Highlands.
g village typical of the 18th century.
formances Tues.-Sun. at 8 p.m., mid-
g. Cost: Musical drama (includes ad-
m only $4.50. Cards: AX, MC, VI.
Bryson City, NC 28713
555-5555 or (800) 555-5555.
Smoky Mountains Railroad, departing
Bryson City depot, operates various
lay and full-day round-trip excursions.
fered in open cars, coaches, crown
lub cars. On weekends there are Gour-
Trains and Mystery Theatre Dinner
Polar Express runs early Nov. through
-The Easter Beagle Express" and
Tank," rides with kid-oriented themes,
in the spring and summer with limited
nuts— The Great Pumpkin Patch Ex-
weekends in October. An animal petting
usical entertainment also are offered.
4 hours, 30 minutes minimum. Hours:
year-round. Phone ahead to confirm
Cost: Sightseeing fares begin at $34; $19
2). Reservations: recommended. Phone:
-5555, or (800) 555-5555 for reservations.
er Ltd. Raft & Rail Excursion, departing
ad depot in Bryson City, combines rail and
ater excursions in one outing. The adventure
ith a scenic 2-hour train trip across Fontana
the top of Nantahala Gorge. Rafts are then
for a guided 3-hour trip down the Nan-
Lunch is included.
minimum. Children under 60
Hours: Trips daily mid-
times vary. Cost: Fares
-12). Phone: (828)
ES
st, 1 mi. s. on
-Oct. Phones:
3 mi. s.w. on US
daily 8-8, Apr.-Oct.
ec. 25. Phones: (828)
555.

Directions

Unless otherwise specified, directions are given from the center of town, using the following highway designations:

- **I**=interstate highway
- **SR**=state route
- **FM**=farm to market
- **Mex.**=Mexican highway
- **US**=federal highway
- **CR**=county road
- **FR**=forest road
- **Hwy.**=Canadian or Caribbean highway

Prices and Dates of Operation

Admission prices are quoted without sales tax. Children under the lowest age specified are admitted free when accompanied by an adult. Days, months and age groups written with a hyphen are inclusive.

Prices pertaining to points of interest in the United States are quoted in U.S. dollars; points of interest in Canada are quoted in Canadian dollars; prices for points of interest in Mexico and the Caribbean are quoted as an approximate U.S. dollar equivalent.

Schedules and admission rates may change throughout the validity period of this guide. Check AAA.com for the most current information.

Credit Card Information

Most establishments accept credit cards, but a small number require cash. If you want to use a specific credit card, call ahead to ensure it's accepted.

Icons

Attraction icons represent some of the services and facilities offered:

- Camping facilities available
- Food available on premises
- Recreational activities available
- Pets on leash allowed
- Picnicking permitted

Bulleted Listings

Gambling establishments within hotels are presented for member information regardless of whether the lodging is AAA Approved.

Recreational activities of a participatory nature (requiring physical exertion or special skills) are not inspected.

Wineries are evaluated by AAA inspectors to ensure they meet listing requirements and offer tours.

All are presented in an abbreviated bulleted format for informational purposes.

Understanding the Lodging Listing

Local Member Value

AAA or CAA and SAVE identify hotels that offer members a rate guarantee and up to two free special amenities as part of their Official Appointment partnership with AAA. Rate guarantee: Discounted standard room rate (usually based on last standard room availability) or the lowest public rate available at time of booking for dates of stay. Free special amenity options such as breakfast, local telephone calls, newspaper, room upgrade, preferred room or high-speed Internet are included in the listing.

Diamond Rating

The number of Diamonds informs you of the overall complexity of a lodging's amenities and service. Red indicates an Official Appointment lodging. An fyi in place of Diamonds indicates the property has not been rated but is included as an "information only" service. A detailed description of each rating level appears on page 18.

Classification

All Diamond Rated lodgings are classified using three key elements: style of operation, overall concept and service level. See pages 20-21 for details on our classifications.

Rates

The property's standard 2-person rates and effective dates are shown.

Rates provided to AAA for each lodging represent the publicly available rate or ranges for a standard room. Rates are rounded to the nearest dollar and do not include taxes. U.S., Mexican and Caribbean rates are in U.S. dollars; rates for Canadian lodgings are in Canadian dollars.

Information about cancellation and minimum stay policies is provided in the **Terms** section of the property's listing.

Online Reservations

This notation indicates AAA/CAA members can conveniently check room availability, validate room rates and make reservations for this property in a secure online environment at AAA.com.

Service Availability

Unit types, amenities and room features preceded by the word "Some" indicate the item is available in **some units**, potentially within only one unit. The term "fee" appearing beside an amenity indicates an extra charge applies.

Nationwide Member Value

The blue box in the listing identifies hotel brands that offer an everyday member benefit at all AAA Approved locations. (See page 17 for additional program benefits.)

Spotting Symbol

Black ovals with white numbers are used to locate, or "spot," lodgings on maps we provide for larger cities.

Credit Card Information

Most establishments accept credit cards, but a small number require cash. If you want to use a specific credit card, call ahead to ensure it's accepted.

Icons

Lodging icons represent some of the member values, services and facilities offered. The term "FEE" appearing to the left of an amenity icon indicates an extra charge applies.

The ECO icon indicates lodgings that have been certified by well-established government and/or private eco-certification organizations. For more information about these organizations and their programs, visit AAA.com/eco.

Discounts

- May offer discount

Member Services

- Airport transportation
- Pets allowed (call property for restrictions and fees)
- Restaurant on premises
- Restaurant off premises (walking distance)
- 24-hour room service
- Full bar
- Child care
- Accessible features (call property for available services and amenities)

Leisure Activities

- Full-service casino
- Pool
- Health club on premises
- Health club off premises
- Recreational activities

In-Room Amenities

- Designated non-smoking rooms
- Movies
- Refrigerator
- Microwave
- Coffee maker
- No air conditioning
- No TV
- No cable TV
- No telephones

Safety Features

(see page 22)
(Mexico and Caribbean only)

- S Sprinklers
- D Smoke detectors

Understanding the Restaurant Listing

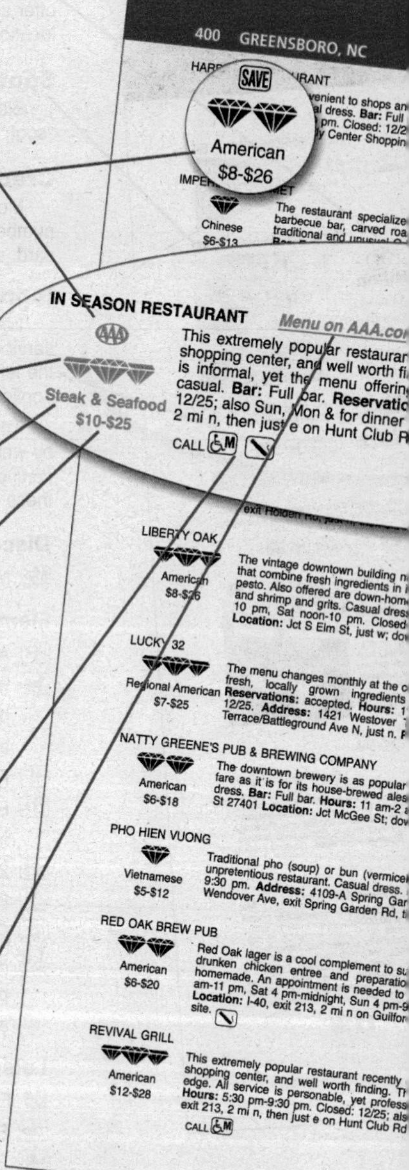

Official Appointment

AAA or CAA indicates Official Appointment (OA) restaurants. The OA program permits restaurants to display and advertise the AAA or CAA emblem. These establishments are highlighted in red to help you quickly identify them. The AAA or CAA Approved sign helps traveling members find restaurants that want member business.

Local Member Value

SAVE identifies restaurants that offer a Show Your Card & Save® discount to AAA/CAA members.

Diamond Rating

The number of Diamonds informs you of the overall complexity of food, presentation, service and ambience. Red indicates an Official Appointment restaurant. A detailed description of each Diamond level appears on page 19.

Cuisine Type

The cuisine type helps you select a dining facility that caters to your individual taste. AAA currently recognizes more than 120 different cuisine types.

Prices

Prices shown represent the minimum and maximum entree cost per person. Exceptions may include one-of-a-kind or special market priced items. Prices are rounded to the nearest dollar and do not include taxes. U.S., Mexican and Caribbean prices are in U.S. dollars; prices for Canadian restaurants are in Canadian dollars.

Icons

Icons provide additional information about services and facilities.

- AC No air-conditioning
- &M Accessible features offered (call property for available services and amenities)
- Designated smoking section available

Menus

This notation indicates AAA/CAA members can conveniently view the restaurant's menu in a secure online environment at AAA.com.

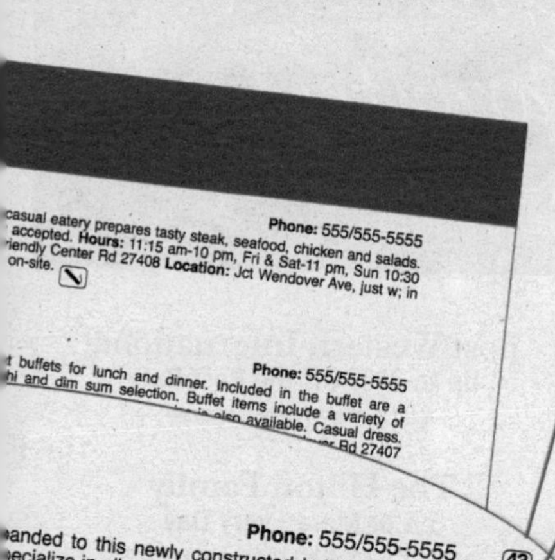

Spotting Symbol

White ovals with black numbers serve as restaurant locators and are used to locate, or "spot," restaurants on maps for larger cities.

Classifications

If applicable, a restaurant may be defined as:

Classic - renowned and/or landmark restaurant in business longer than 25 years, known for unique style and ambience.

Historic - establishments must meet one of the following criteria:

- Listed on the National Register of Historic Places
- Designated a National Historic Landmark
- Located in a National Register Historic District

Separate criteria designate historic properties in Canada, Mexico and the Caribbean.

Credit Card Information

Most establishments accept credit cards, but a small number require cash. If you want to use a specific credit card, call ahead to ensure it's accepted.

AAA/CAA members can generally expect to pay no more than the maximum regular rate printed in the TourBook guide in each rate range for a standard room. On rare occasions AAA receives or inadvertently publishes incorrect rates.

Obtain current AAA/CAA member rates and make reservations at AAA.com. Rates may vary within the range, depending on season and room type. Listed rates are usually based on last standard room availability.

Discounts

Member discounts, when offered, will apply to rates quoted within the rate range and are applicable at the time of booking. Special rates used in advertising, as well as special short-term promotional rates lower than the lowest listed rate in the range, are not subject to additional member discounts.

Exceptions

Rates for properties operating as concessionaires for the U.S. National Park Service are not guaranteed due to governing regulations. Rates in the Mexico TourBook are not guaranteed and may fluctuate based on the exchange rate of the peso.

Lodgings may temporarily increase room rates, not recognize discounts or modify pricing policies during special events. Examples of special events range from Mardi Gras and the Kentucky Derby (including pre-Derby events) to college football games, holidays, holiday periods and state fairs. Although some special events are listed in AAA/CAA TourBook guides and on AAA.com, it is always wise to check in advance with AAA travel professionals for specific dates.

Meeting Your Travel Needs

AAA is proud to stand behind the Approved hotels, restaurants, attractions and campgrounds listed in the TourBook and CampBook guides. If, however, your visit doesn't meet your expectations, now you can tell us about it immediately. Visit AAA.com/TourBookComments to complete an easy online form, or send written comments to: AAA Member Comments, 1000 AAA Dr., Heathrow, FL 32746.

Get the Room You Reserved

When making your reservation, identify yourself as a AAA or CAA member and request written confirmation to guarantee: type of room, rate, dates of stay, and cancellation and refund policies. At registration, show your membership card.

When you find your room is not as specified, and you have written confirmation of reservations for a certain type of accommodation, you should be given the option of choosing a different room or finding one elsewhere. Should you choose to go elsewhere and a refund is refused or resisted, submit the matter to AAA/CAA within 30 days, along with complete documentation, including your

reasons for refusing the room and copies of your written confirmation and any receipts or canceled checks associated with this problem.

If you are charged more than the maximum rate listed in the TourBook guide for a standard room, question the additional charge. If management refuses to adhere to the published rate, pay for the room and submit your receipt and membership number to AAA/CAA within 30 days. Include all pertinent information: dates of stay, rate paid, itemized paid receipts, number of persons in your party and the room number you occupied, and list any extra room equipment used. A refund of the amount paid in excess of the stated maximum will be made if our investigation indicates that unjustified charging occurred.

Deposit, Refund and Cancellation Policies

Most establishments give full deposit refunds if they have been notified at least 48 hours before the normal check-in time. Listing prose will note if more than 48 hours' notice is required for cancellation. Some properties may charge a cancellation or handling fee. When this applies, "cancellation fee imposed" will appear in the **Terms** section of the listing. If you cancel too late, you have little recourse if a refund is denied.

When an establishment requires full or partial payment in advance and your trip is cut short, a refund may not be given.

When canceling a reservation, phone the lodging immediately. Make a note of the date and time you called, the cancellation number if there is one, and the name of the person who handled the cancellation. If your AAA/CAA club made your reservation, allow them to make the cancellation for you as well, so you will have proof of cancellation.

Check-in and Check-out Times

Check-in and check-out times are shown in the lodging listings, under **Terms**, only if they are before 3 p.m. or after 10 a.m. respectively.

Members Save With Our Partners

These Show Your Card & Save® partners provide the listed member benefits. Visit AAA.com/Discounts to discover all the great Show Your Card & Save® discounts in your area. Even greater discounts on theme park tickets may be available at your local AAA/CAA club. Discounts apply to a maximum of six tickets for Amtrak, Gray Line and the theme parks. Restaurant savings apply to AAA/CAA members and up to five guests.

SeaWorld, Busch Gardens, Sesame Place

WORLDS OF DISCOVERY

- Save on admission at the gate, at participating offices or online AAA.com/SeaWorld
- Save 10% on up-close dining; visit Guest Relations for details

Six Flags

- Save on admission at the gate, at participating offices or online AAA.com/SixFlags
- Save 10% on merchandise purchases of $15 or more at in-park stores

Universal Orlando Resort and Universal Studios Hollywood

- Save on admission at the gate, at participating offices or online AAA.com/Universal

- Save 10% at select food and merchandise venues in-park and at Universal CityWalk®

Universal Studios Hollywood
The Entertainment Capital of L.A.

Hard Rock Cafe

- Save 10% on food, non-alcoholic beverages and merchandise at all U.S., Canadian and select international locations

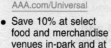

Hard Rock Cafe

Landry's Seafood House, The Crab House, Chart House, Saltgrass Steak House, Muer Seafood Restaurants and Aquarium Restaurants

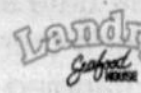

Muer Seafood Restaurants

- Save 10% on food and non-alcoholic beverages at all of the above restaurants
- Save 10% on merchandise at Aquarium and Downtown Aquarium restaurants

Amtrak

AMTRAK

- 10% discount on rail fare when booked at least 3 days in advance of travel date

EagleRider

- We Rent Dreams® 12% off motorcycle rentals 1-877-869-5023

Fetch! Pet Care

- Save 10% off pet-sitting and dog-walking services AAA.com/Fetchpetcare 1-877-533-8242 code AAAPETS

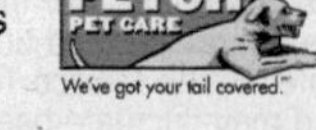

Grand Canyon Railway

- Save up to 20% on rail fare, hotel accommodations, restaurant and gift shop purchases sold outside of Grand Canyon National Park

GRAND CANYON Railway

Gray Line

AAA.com/GrayLine

- Save 10% on sightseeing tours of 1 day or less worldwide

Hertz

- Exclusive AAA member savings on daily, weekend, weekly and monthly rentals AAA.com/hertz or 1-800-654-3080

Tanger Outlet Centers www.tangeroutlet.com

- Save up to 20% on total purchase at select merchants with FREE coupon booklet
- Member BONUS: FREE $5 gift card for each additional Tanger Outlet Center visited after first within same calendar year

- Show membership card and register at the AAA customer service desk when you visit

Preferred Hotels

AAA Preferred Lodging Partners

EXPECT SAVINGS, SELECTION, AND SATISFACTION

- **Best AAA/CAA member rates for your dates of stay.** Provide a valid membership number when placing your reservation and show your card at hotel check-in.
- **Satisfaction guarantee.** Notify the property if you are dissatisfied with any part of your stay. If the matter cannot be resolved, you may be entitled to compensation (see page 15).
- **Seasonal promotions and special member offers.** Visit AAA.com to view current offers.
- **Everyday member benefit.** Look for the blue boxes in the TourBook listings for everyday values offered at all AAA Approved locations. *Offer good at time of publication: Chains and offers may change without notice. Preferred Hotel Partner discounts may vary in Mexico and the Caribbean.*

10% Off Best Available Rates
Best Western International

5% or More Off Best Available Rates
Conrad, DoubleTree, Embassy Suites, Hampton, Hilton, Hilton Garden Inn, Hilton Grand Vacations, Home2 Suites, Homewood Suites, and Waldorf=Astoria Collection

10% Off Best Available Rates
ANdAZ, Grand Hyatt, Hyatt Place, Hyatt Regency, Hyatt Summerfield Suites, and Park Hyatt

5% or More Off Best Available Rates
Courtyard, Fairfield Inn, JW Marriott, Marriott, Renaissance Hotels & Resorts, Residence Inn, SpringHill Suites, and TownePlace Suites

5-15% Off Best Available Rates
aloft, element, Four Points, Le Meridien, Sheraton, St. Regis, The Luxury Collection, Westin, and W Hotels

Understanding the Diamond Ratings

AAA/CAA inspectors have evaluated and rated each of the 58,000 lodging and restaurant establishments in the TourBook series to ensure quality travel information for our members. All properties must meet AAA's minimum requirements (for lodgings) concerning cleanliness, comfort and security - or - AAA's minimum requirements (for restaurants) pertaining to cleanliness, food preparation and service.

Eligible applicants receive an unannounced evaluation by a AAA/CAA inspector that includes two distinct components:

- **AAA Approval:** The inspector first must determine whether the property meets the criteria required to be AAA Approved. Every establishment that meets these strict guidelines offers AAA members the assurance that, regardless of the Diamond Rating, it provides acceptable quality, cleanliness, service and value.
- **AAA Diamond Rating:** Once an establishment becomes AAA Approved, it is then assigned a rating of one to five Diamonds, indicating the extensiveness of its facilities, amenities and services, from basic to moderate to luxury. These Diamond Ratings guide members in selecting establishments appropriately matched to their needs and expectations.

LODGINGS

1 Diamond 

One Diamond lodgings typically appeal to the budget-minded traveler. They provide essential, no-frills accommodations and basic comfort and hospitality.

2 Diamond 

Two Diamond lodgings appeal to travelers seeking affordable yet more than the basic accommodations. Facilities, decor and amenities are modestly enhanced.

3 Diamond 

Three Diamond lodgings offer a distinguished style. Properties are multi-faceted, with marked upgrades in physical attributes, amenities and guest comforts.

4 Diamond 

Four Diamond lodgings are refined and stylish. Physical attributes are upscale. The fundamental hallmarks at this level include an extensive array of amenities combined with a high degree of hospitality, service and attention to detail.

5 Diamond 

Five Diamond lodgings provide the ultimate in luxury and sophistication. Physical attributes are extraordinary in every manner. Service is meticulous, exceeding guest expectations and maintaining impeccable standards of excellence. Extensive personalized services and amenities provide first-class comfort.

The lodging listings with [fyi] in place of Diamonds are included as an *information only* service for members. The icon indicates that a property has not been rated for one or more of the following reasons: too new to rate, under construction, under major renovation, not evaluated, may not meet all AAA requirements.

A property not meeting all AAA requirements is included for either its member value or because it may be the only accommodation available in the area. Listing prose will give insight as to why the [fyi] designation was assigned.

RESTAURANTS

1 Diamond 

One Diamond restaurants provide simple, familiar specialty food (such as burgers, chicken, pizza or tacos) at an economical price. Often self-service, basic surroundings complement a no-nonsense approach.

2 Diamond 

Two Diamond restaurants offer a familiar, family-oriented experience. Menu selection includes home-style foods and family favorites, often cooked to order, modestly enhanced and reasonably priced. Service is accommodating yet relaxed, a perfect complement to casual surroundings.

3 Diamond 

Three Diamond restaurants convey an entry into fine dining and are often positioned as adult-oriented experiences. The atypical menu may feature the latest cooking trends and/or traditional cuisine. Expanded beverage offerings complement the menu. The ambience is well coordinated, comfortable and enhanced by a professional service staff.

4 Diamond 

Four Diamond restaurants provide a distinctive fine-dining experience that is typically expensive. Surroundings are highly refined with upscale enhancements throughout. Highly creative chefs use imaginative presentations to augment fresh, top-quality ingredients. A proficient service staff meets or exceeds guest expectations. A wine steward may offer menu-specific knowledge to guide selection.

5 Diamond 

Five Diamond restaurants are luxurious and renowned for consistently providing a world-class experience. Highly acclaimed chefs offer artistic menu selections that are imaginative and unique, using only the finest ingredients available. A maitre d' leads an expert service staff in exceeding guest expectations, attending to every detail in an effortless and unobtrusive manner.

The restaurants with fyi in place of Diamonds are included as an *information only* service for members. These listings provide additional dining choices but have not yet been evaluated.

Understanding the Lodging Classifications

To ensure that your lodging needs and preferences are met, we recommend that you consider an establishment's classification when making your travel choices. While the quality and comfort at properties with the same Diamond Rating should be consistent (regardless of the classification), there are differences in typical decor/theme elements, range of facilities and service levels.

Lodging Classifications

Bed & Breakfast

Typically smaller scale properties emphasizing a high degree of personal touches that provide guests an "at home" feeling. Guest units tend to be individually decorated. Rooms may not include some modern amenities such as televisions and telephones, and may have a shared bathroom. Usually owner-operated with a common room or parlor separate from the innkeeper's living quarters, where guests and operators can interact during evening and breakfast hours. Evening office closures are normal. A continental or full, hot breakfast is served and is included in the room rate.

1884 Paxton House Inn
Thomasville, GA

Cabin

Vacation-oriented, typically smaller scale, freestanding units of simple construction—roughly finished logs or stone—and basic design or décor. Often located in wooded, rural, or waterfront locations. As a rule, basic cleaning supplies, kitchen utensils, and complete bed and bath linens are supplied. The guest registration area may be located off site.

Greenbrier Valley Resorts
Gatlinburg, TN

Condominium

Vacation-oriented—commonly for extended-stay purposes—apartment-style accommodations of varying design or décor. Routinely available for rent through a management company, units often contain one or more bedrooms, a living room, full kitchen, and an eating area. Studio-type models combine the sleeping and living areas into one room. As a rule, basic cleaning supplies, kitchen utensils, and complete bed and bath linens are supplied. The guest registration area may be located off site.

Sands of Kahana
Kahana, Maui, HI

Cottage

Vacation-oriented, typically smaller scale, freestanding units with home style enhancements in architectural design and interior décor. Often located in wooded, rural, or waterfront locations. Units may vary in design and décor. As a rule, basic cleaning supplies, kitchen utensils, and complete bed and bath linens are supplied. The guest registration area may be located off site.

Paradise Villas, Little Cayman Island

Country Inn

Although similar in definition to a bed and breakfast, country inns are usually larger in scale with spacious public areas and offer a dining facility that serves—at a minimum—breakfast and dinner.

Greenville Inn, Greenville, ME

Hotel

Commonly, a multistory establishment with interior room entrances offering a variety of guest unit styles. The magnitude of the public areas is determined by the overall theme, location and service level, but may include a variety of facilities such as a restaurant, shops, fitness center, spa, business center, and/or meeting rooms.

The Grand America Hotel
Salt Lake City, UT

Motel

Commonly, a one- or two-story establishment with exterior room entrances and drive up parking. Typically, guest units have one bedroom with a bathroom of similar décor and design. Public areas and facilities are often limited in size and/or availability.

Best Western Deltona Inn, Deltona, FL

Ranch

Typically a working ranch with an obvious rustic, Western theme featuring equestrian-related activities and a variety of guest unit styles.

Lost Valley Ranch, Deckers, CO

Vacation Rental House

Vacation-oriented—commonly for extended-stay purposes—typically larger scale, freestanding, and of varying design or décor. Routinely available for rent through a management company, houses often contain two or more bedrooms, a living room, full kitchen, dining room, and multiple bathrooms. As a rule, basic cleaning supplies, kitchen utensils, and complete bed and bath linens are supplied. The guest registration area may be located off site.

ResortQuest, Hilton Head Island, SC

Lodging Sub-classifications

The following are sub-classifications that may appear along with the classifications listed previously to provide a more specific description of the lodging.

Boutique

Often thematic and typically an informal, yet highly personalized experience; may have a luxurious or quirky style which is fashionable or unique.

Casino

Extensive gambling facilities are available, such as: blackjack, craps, keno, and slot machines. **Note:** This sub-classification will not appear beneath its Diamond Rating in the listing. It will be indicated by a icon and will be included in the row of icons following the lodging listing.

Classic

Renowned and landmark properties, older than 50 years, well-known for their unique style and ambience.

Contemporary

Overall design and theme reflects characteristics of the present era's mainstream tastes and style.

Extended Stay

Offers a predominance of long-term accommodations with a designated full-service kitchen area within each unit.

Historic

These properties are typically over 75 years of age and exhibit many features of a historic nature with respect to architecture, design, furnishings, public record, or acclaim. Properties must meet one of the following criteria:

- Maintain the integrity of the historical nature
- Be listed on the National Register of Historic Places
- Have a National Historic Landmark designation or be located in a National Register Historic District

Separate criteria designate historic properties in Canada, Mexico and the Caribbean.

Resort

Recreation-oriented, geared to vacation travelers seeking a specific destination experience. Travel packages, meal plans, themed entertainment, and social and recreational programs are typically available. Recreational facilities are extensive and may include spa treatments, golf, tennis, skiing, fishing, or water sports. Larger resorts may offer a variety of guest accommodations.

Retro

Overall design and theme reflect a contemporary design reinterpreting styles from a bygone era.

Vacation Rental

Typically houses, condos, cottages or cabins; these properties are a "home away from home" offering more room and greater value for the money. In general, they provide the conveniences of home, such as full kitchens and washers/dryers. Located in resort or popular destination areas within close proximity to major points of interest, attractions, or recreation areas, these properties may require a pre-arranged reservation and check-in at an off-site location. Housekeeping services may be limited or not included.

Vintage

Offers a window to the past and provides an experience reflecting a predominance of traits associated with the era of their origin.

Guest Safety

Room Security

In order to be approved for listing in AAA/CAA TourBook guides for the United States and Canada, accommodations must have deadbolt locks on all guest room entry doors and connecting room doors.

If the area outside the guest room door is not visible from inside the room through a window or door panel, viewports must be installed on all guest room entry doors. Bed and breakfast properties and country inns are not required to have viewports. Ground floor and easily accessible sliding doors must be equipped with some type of secondary security locks.

Even with those approval requirements, AAA cannot guarantee guest safety. AAA inspectors view a percentage of rooms at each property since it is not feasible to evaluate every room in every lodging establishment. Therefore, AAA cannot guarantee that there are working locks on all doors and windows in all guest rooms.

Fire Safety

Because of the highly specialized skills needed to conduct professional fire safety inspections, AAA/CAA inspectors cannot assess fire safety.

Properties must meet all federal, state/province and local fire codes. Each guest unit in all U.S. and Canadian lodging properties must be equipped with an operational, single-station smoke detector. A AAA/CAA inspector has evaluated a sampling of the rooms to verify this equipment is in place.

Mexico and the Caribbean

Requirements for some features, such as door locks and smoke detectors/sprinkler systems, differ in Mexico and the Caribbean. If a property met AAA's security requirements at the time of the evaluation, the phrase "Meets AAA guest room security requirements" appears in the listing.

Service Animals

The Americans with Disabilities Act (ADA) prohibits U.S. businesses that serve the public from discriminating against persons with disabilities. Some businesses have mistakenly denied access to persons who use service animals. Businesses must permit entry to guests and their service animals, as well as allow service animals to accompany guests to all public areas of a property.

A property is permitted to ask whether the animal is a service animal or a pet, and whether the guest has a disability. The property may not, however, ask questions about the nature of the disability, the service provided by the animal, or require proof of a disability or certification that the animal is a service animal. These regulations may not apply in Canada, Mexico or the Caribbean.

No fees or deposits, even those normally charged for pets, may be charged for service animals. Service animals fulfill a critical need for their owners—they are not pets.

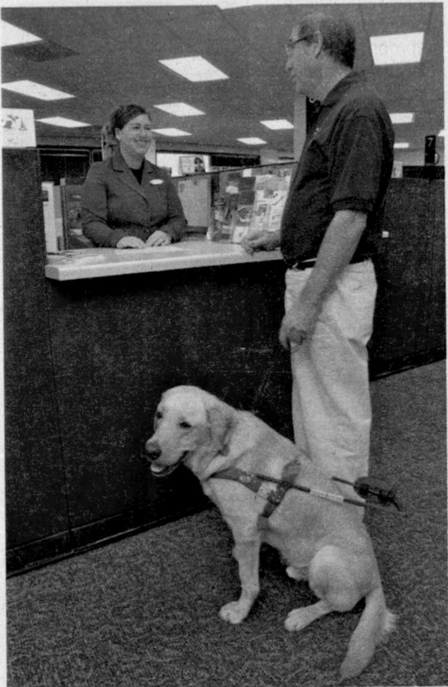

Frank Frand with his seeing eye dog, Cardinal.

Arkansas
Where the West Begins
Frontier spirit of the West blended with Southern hospitality
"Diamonds Are a Girl's Best Friend"
Search for new friends at Crater of Diamonds State Park—and it's finders keepers
Arkansas Architecture
Frontier log cabins, Victorian homes and Thorncrown Chapel
Yellowstone's Big Brother
Hot Springs National Park preserves access to "therapeutic" springs
19th-century Spa
Eureka Springs now is a resort area and center of holistic healing

The Old Mill at T.R. Pugh Memorial Park, North Little Rock
© Dennis Flaherty
Jaynes Gallery / Danita Delimont Stock Photography

Garvan Woodland Gardens, Hot Springs
Arkansas Department of Parks and Tourism

When evaluating a diamond, it's essential to keep the four "C's" in mind: Cut, color, clarity and carat highlight the qualities of the stone and define its natural beauty.

Like the gem, Arkansas also boasts four "C's." Clear lakes and streams, caves and colorful countryside accentuate the beauty of the Diamond State. And let's not forget Bill Clinton.

Waves calmly lap the shores of Bull Shoals Lake and lakes Norfork and Ouachita. The Arkansas and White rivers meander across the state, joining with the great Mississippi.

Underground caves offer a different view of Arkansas—from the bottom up. And if you're feeling lucky, you may unearth a jewel of your own at Crater of Diamonds State Park; a 16-carat diamond was found here in 1975.

Arkansas' countryside adds a splash of color. Sunsets on the rivers are known to mix shades of pinks, reds and yellows; trees among some 17 million acres of national forests don a rust-colored coat in the fall.

Fans of our 42nd president will find monuments to William Jefferson Clinton in Hope, Hot Springs and Little Rock. Walking tours in these cities point out numerous stops on his path to the presidency.

Come appraise the Diamond State. You're sure to find it full of wealth.

French explorers first started the Arkansas name game. Scouting the area now designated as the Diamond State, they met the Ugukhpah Indians, also known by the sobriquets Quapaw, Arkansas and Arkansa. One of these was adopted to identify the territory. Simple enough, right?

Well, not really. When Jacques Marquette and Louis Joliet explored the Mississippi and Arkansas rivers in 1673, the name appeared as *Akansea* in their journal. René-Robert Cavelier, sieur de La Salle, recorded his 1680 trip on a map showing *Acansa*. Another map drawn 1718-22 by Bénard de la Harpe referred to the territory as *Arkansas* and the inhabitants as *Les Arkansas*. Still later, Zebulon Pike spelled it *Arkansaw.*

You get the general idea. But how to pronounce it? Early senators were at odds; one was reputed to have introduced himself as the senator from Ar-*kansas;* the other called his home state Arkan-*saw.* To squelch any future confusion, the General Assembly passed a resolve in 1881 that the state name be spelled Arkansas, but pronounced Arkan*saw.*

Clearly, the evolving name game was much like finding a diamond in the rough—a jewel of an idea that just needed a little polishing to reveal its brilliance. The final decision conveys a melding of its cultural origins—the pronunciation respects the heritage of the land's earliest inhabitants, while the French spelling adds a bit of panache.

What's in a Name?

Little Rock, ironically the largest city in the state, also had French origins. The same man who dubbed the state *Arkansas* also is credited with naming its capital. After hearing from American Indians that a large "emerald stone" sat along the Arkansas River, de la Harpe and his party sought the treasure but found only a small rock, greenish in hue. He called it *"la petite roche,"* and the name stuck.

Nowadays, the capital is anything but a small green rock. The swiftly moving waters of the Arkansas reflect both the glitter of Little Rock's contemporary skyline and its success as a primary river port. Reminders of early days float right by you in the form of barges, still traversing the river.

Petit Jean Mountain, the centerpiece of Petit Jean State Park, is named for a French girl who dressed as a boy to be with her beau. But the park has more than a nifty name—lush foliage surrounds Cedar Falls, which

Arkansas Historical Timeline

1541 Exploration of the region begins under Hernando de Soto's leadership.

Library of Congress

1686 Henry de Tonty establishes the Mississippi Valley's first permanent European settlement.

1763 Spain gains control of the area but 37 years later returns it to France.

1803 The United States acquires the region as part of the Louisiana Purchase, which includes most of the land between the Mississippi River and the Rockies.

1836 Arkansas enters the Union as a slave-holding state.

drops almost 100 feet into a rocky pool. And from the top of the peak, you can see both the Ozark and Ouachita mountain ranges.

Rising steam from more than 40 boiling springs coined the name of Hot Springs, once known as the Valley of the Vapors. Literally a hot spot for centuries, Indians were drawn to the area for what they believed were healing potions bestowed by the Great Spirit. Rumors of "magic waters" spread, and after Hernando de Soto stumbled across the area in 1541, those suffering from rheumatism frequented bathhouses in hope of a cure.

The terrain, now a national park and health resort, still attracts visitors for its therapeutic aura, but it also has a more recent claim to fame—as the boyhood home of our 42nd president. A walking tour through downtown Hot Springs identifies noteworthy places in Bill Clinton's pre-presidential existence.

There are a few reasons why Arkansas is called the Diamond State: The 40-carat Uncle Sam, the 16-carat Amarillo Starlight, the 34-carat Star of Murfreesboro and the 15-carat Star of Arkansas rank high on the list of sensational finds at Crater of Diamonds State Park near Murfreesboro. The only public diamond mine in the country, visitors keep what they find.

And the hamlet of Mount Ida in the Ouachita Mountains offers more than outstanding scenery; clear quartz crystals hide in red clay, waiting to be unearthed by rockhounds. Once shaped and used by Indians as arrowheads, the crystals are believed by some to have healing powers.

Going Down Under

Exploring Arkansas' caverns is a way to discover some objects with interesting names. Once secret hideaways for Indians, dark and chilly caves throughout the state sport funky formations, subterranean lakes, mazes and tunnels.

Most cave deposits are named after things they resemble: You can see a pipe organ, a witch's fireplace, soda straws, popcorn, frozen waterfalls and a friendly dragon—all hidden beneath the earth in grottoes that date back almost 350 million years.

In Arkansas, it's easy to play the name game. Visit and you may coin some terms of your own—rich, serene, sparkling...

You name it.

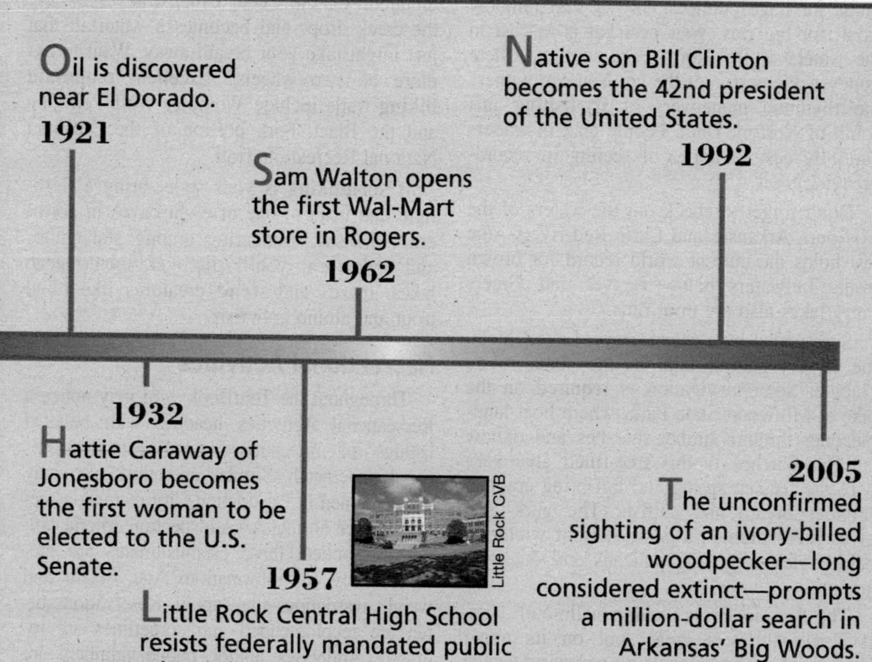
Oil is discovered near El Dorado.
1921
Sam Walton opens the first Wal-Mart store in Rogers.
1962
Native son Bill Clinton becomes the 42nd president of the United States.
1992
1932
Hattie Caraway of Jonesboro becomes the first woman to be elected to the U.S. Senate.
1957
Little Rock CVB
Little Rock Central High School resists federally mandated public school desegregation.
2005
The unconfirmed sighting of an ivory-billed woodpecker—long considered extinct—prompts a million-dollar search in Arkansas' Big Woods.

Recreation

The harnessing of rivers in Arkansas for water power and flood control has created a haven for anyone who enjoys being in, on or near the water. Be sure to include fishing poles, flippers, water wings, paddles and bathing suits on your packing list.

Gone Fishin'

Fishing holes throughout the state lure anglers to reservoirs, natural lakes and streams for a variety of good catches. Lake Norfork is best known for its lunker and striped bass. Nearby Bull Shoals Lake, which stretches across five counties in northern Arkansas, is fantastic for catfish, crappie, lunker bass, trout and walleye.

An annual stocking program helps ensure plentiful bites in both lakes, where bass swim alongside trout. **Night fishing** in summer increases your chance for hooking white bass and crappie. Daytime fishing is best in deeper waters. **Spearfishing** is permitted in both Bull Shoals and Lake Norfork; interested parties should contact the Arkansas Game and Fish Commission.

Looking for trout? Head north. The White River, a world-class cold trout stream, is famous for huge cutthroat, brown and rainbow trout; for big fins, your best bet is to cast in the waters of the North Fork section, where honeysuckle perfumes the air. You can witness the rhythmic maneuvers of **fly-fishing** just south of Norfork Dam. People clad in waders carefully cast in hopes of reeling in record-breaking trout.

Don't forget to check out the waters of the Missouri, Arkansas and Little Red rivers—the last holds the current world record for brown trout. Tailwaters below Beaver and Greers Ferry lakes also are trout runs.

Surrounded by a pecan grove, Lake Chicot, the largest natural lake in the state, offers crappie. Some navigation is required on the lake at Millwood State Park, where boat lanes meander through timber marshes and oxbow cutoffs. Catches in this tree-filled area vary with the season; spring and fall bring crappie, summer bream and catfish. The park also gives **birdwatchers** a good view of wintering bald eagles, migrating pelicans and ducks in autumn.

The Buffalo River yields smallmouth bass. It also features a great spot on its upper reaches where brave souls go **canoeing** on the challenging white water. Experienced canoeists and **kayakers** take on the rough waters in the rocky canyon where the Cossatot River plummets to form Cossatot Falls. Limestone bluffs provide a dramatic backdrop for a float down the Buffalo National River in the central Ozarks. Canoes also dot the White River from Fayetteville to Brashears.

The waters of Lake Norfork are wonderful for **boating, swimming** and **water skiing.** For **scuba diving,** head to limpid Lake Ouachita. Gigantic Bull Shoals Lake is called the "Caribbean of the Midwest" for a good reason: The blue, crystal-clear depths provide amazing visibility and an open invitation for diving and scavenging.

Take A Hike

Pinnacle Mountain State Park, within the Ouachita National Forest, offers many **hiking** trails that will afford visitors countless hours of pleasure. Nature enthusiasts will appreciate the varied wildlife and array of plant life while exploring the trails, which range from easy to strenuous in terms of difficulty. It is said that the view from atop Pinnacle Mountain is breathtaking.

At Petit Jean State Park, trails lead you past forests, canyons, streams, meadows and mountainsides to Cedar Creek Canyon, where the creek drops and becomes a waterfall that just might take your breath away. Want to explore on two wheels? Excellent **mountain biking** trails include Womble, Wolf Pen Gap and the Black Fork portion of the Ouachita National Recreation Trail.

If **spelunking** is your style, bring a flashlight and head to one of eight caves in northern Arkansas. Wandering among stalagmites and stalactites, you'll discover subterranean lakes, mazes and weird creatures like blind trout and albino crawfish.

Recreational Activities

Throughout the TourBook, you may notice a Recreational Activities heading with bulleted listings of recreation-oriented establishments listed underneath. Similar operations also may be mentioned in Destination City recreation sections. Since normal AAA inspection criteria cannot be applied, these establishments are presented only for information. Age, height and weight restrictions may apply. Reservations often are recommended and sometimes are required. Addresses and/or phone numbers are provided so visitors can contact the attraction for additional information.

Fast Facts

POPULATION: 2,673,400.

AREA: 51,945 square miles; ranks 29th.

CAPITAL: Little Rock.

HIGHEST POINT: 2,753 ft., Mount Magazine.

LOWEST POINT: 55 ft., Ouachita River.

TIME ZONE(S): Central. DST.

TEEN DRIVING LAWS: The minimum age for an unrestricted driver's license is 18. Drivers ages 16-18 holding intermediate licenses are not permitted to drive between 11 p.m. and 4 p.m. unless accompanied by a licensed driver age 21 or older. Phone (501) 682-4692 for more information about Arkansas driver's license regulations.

SEAT BELT/CHILD RESTRAINT LAWS: Seat belts are required for driver and front seat passengers 15 and older. Children ages 6 until 15 or at least 60 pounds are required to be in a child restraint or seat belt; child restraints required for under 6 years and less than 60 pounds.

CELL PHONE RESTRICTIONS: All drivers under age 21 are not permitted to use handheld cell phones while driving.

HELMETS FOR MOTORCYCLISTS: Required for riders under 21.

RADAR DETECTORS: Permitted.

MOVE OVER LAW: Driver is required to slow down and vacate the lane nearest stopped police, fire, rescue, recovery and tow truck vehicles using audible or flashing signals.

FIREARMS LAWS: Vary by state and/or county. Contact the Arkansas Attorney General's Office, 323 Center St., Little Rock, AR 72201; phone (501) 682-2007.

HOLIDAYS: Jan. 1; Martin Luther King Jr. Day/Robert E. Lee's Birthday, Jan. 19; Washington's Birthday, Feb. (3rd Mon.); Memorial Day, May (last Mon.); July 4; Labor Day; Veterans Day, Oct. (4th Mon.); Election Day; Thanksgiving; Christmas, Dec. 25.

TAXES: Arkansas' gross receipts tax is 6 percent with local options to impose additional increments. A 2 percent tourism gross receipts tax is levied on lodgings statewide; some cities may levy an additional 1 percent.

INFORMATION CENTERS: State welcome centers are 3 mi. n. of Bentonville on US 71; n. of Harrison on US 65; in Mammoth Spring on US 63N; 5 mi. s. of the Missouri state line on I-55S at Blytheville; 6 mi. n. of Corning on US 67N; 2 mi. e. of the Oklahoma state line on I-40W at Fort Smith/Van Buren; 5 mi. n. of the Louisiana state line on US 167S/SR 7 at junction with US 82 at El Dorado; on US 49 Bypass at Helena; 10 mi. w. of the Mississippi state line off US 82 at Lake Village; on I-30 in Texarkana; on US 71 on the Red River n. of Texarkana; on US 412W at Siloam Springs; 3 mi. w. of West Memphis on I-40; and at One Capitol Mall in Little Rock.

The centers are open daily 8-6, Memorial Day weekend-Labor Day; 8-5, rest of year. Helena and Red River are open daily 8-5, Memorial Day weekend-Labor Day; 8-4, rest of year. Centers are closed Jan. 1, Easter, Thanksgiving and Dec. 25.

FURTHER INFORMATION FOR VISITORS:

Arkansas Department of Parks & Tourism
One Capitol Mall
Little Rock, AR 72201
(800) 628-8725
TTY (501) 682-7777
See color ad p. 36 & p. 147.

FISHING AND HUNTING REGULATIONS:

Game and Fish Commission
2 Natural Resource Dr.
Little Rock, AR 72205
(501) 223-6300
(800) 364-4263

NATIONAL FOREST INFORMATION:

USDA Forest Service: Southern Region
1720 Peachtree Rd., Suite 700
Atlanta, GA 30309
(404) 347-4243
(877) 444-6777 (reservations)

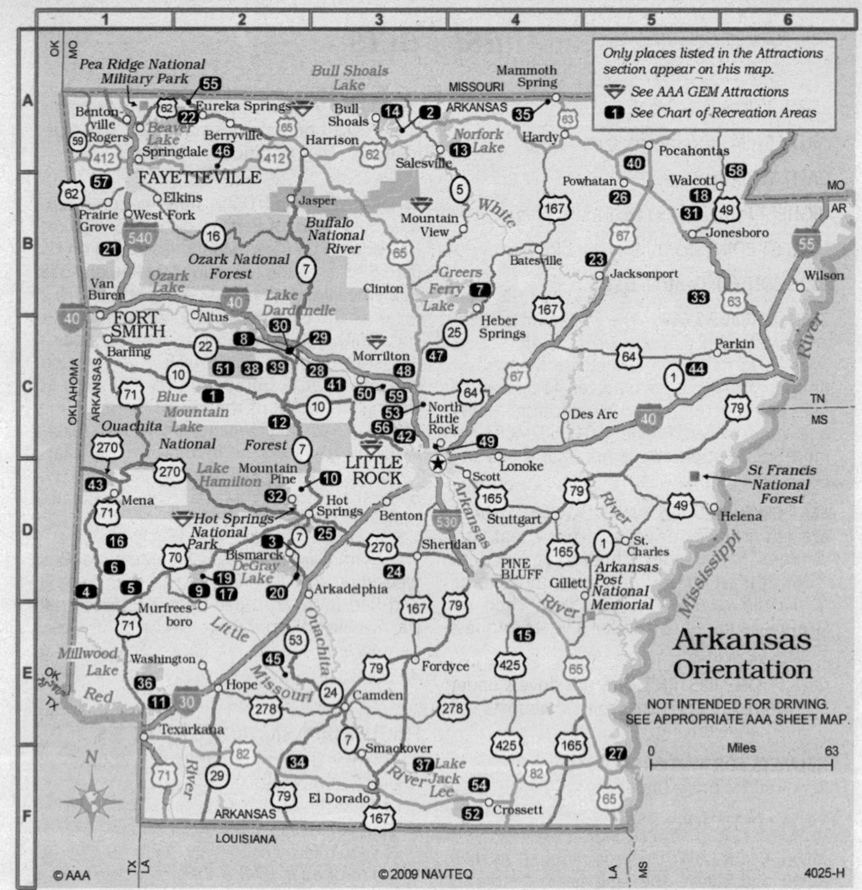

Arkansas Temperature Averages Maximum/Minimum

From the records of The Weather Channel Interactive, Inc.

	JAN	FEB	MAR	APR	MAY	JUN	JUL	AUG	SEP	OCT	NOV	DEC
Fort Smith	48	55	64	73	80	88	93	93	85	75	61	51
	28	33	41	49	59	67	71	70	63	51	40	31
Little Rock	50	56	64	73	81	89	93	92	85	75	62	53
	31	35	43	50	59	68	72	71	64	51	42	34
Texarkana	53	60	68	75	82	89	93	93	86	77	64	56
	36	39	46	54	62	69	73	72	65	55	45	38

RECREATION AREAS

	MAP LOCATION	CAMPING	PICNICKING	HIKING TRAILS	BOATING	BOAT RAMP	BOAT RENTAL	FISHING	SWIMMING	PETS ON LEASH	BICYCLE TRAILS	WINTER SPORTS	VISITOR CENTER	LODGE/CABINS	FOOD SERVICE
NATIONAL PARKS *(See place listings)*															
Hot Springs (D-2) 5,839 acres.		●	●	●						●			●		
NATIONAL FORESTS *(See place listings)*															
Ouachita 1,613,120 acres. West-central Arkansas and southeastern Oklahoma. Horse trails.		●	●	●	●	●	●	●	●	●	●		●	●	●
Ozark 1,123,079 acres. Northwestern Arkansas. Horse trails.		●	●	●	●	●	●	●	●	●	●		●	●	
St. Francis 20,977 acres. East-central Arkansas.		●	●	●	●	●	●	●	●	●					
NATIONAL RIVERS *(See place listings)*															
Buffalo River (B-3) 95,730 acres. Northwestern Arkansas.		●	●	●	●	●	●	●	●	●			●	●	●
ARMY CORPS OF ENGINEERS															
Blue Mountain Lake (C-2) 17,000 acres 1.5 mi. s.w. of Waveland on SR 10. Scuba diving, water skiing.	1	●	●		●	●		●	●	●					
Bull Shoals Lake (A-3) 101,196 acres 8 mi. w. of Mountain Home on SR 178. Sailing, scuba diving, water skiing.	2	●	●	●	●	●	●	●	●	●					●
DeGray Lake (D-2) 31,800 acres. Sailing, scuba diving, water skiing. *(See Bismarck p. 37)*	3	●	●	●	●	●	●	●	●	●			●	●	●
DeQueen Lake (D-1) 7,150 acres 4 mi. n.w. of DeQueen on SR 71. Scuba diving, water skiing.	4	●	●		●	●		●	●	●					
Dierks Lake (D-1) 8,100 acres 5 mi. n.w. of Dierks on SR 70. Scuba diving, water skiing.	5	●	●		●	●	●	●	●	●					
Gillham Lake (D-1) 9,000 acres 6 mi. n.e. of Gillham on SR 71. Scuba diving, water skiing.	6	●	●		●	●		●	●	●					
Greers Ferry Lake (B-4) 40,914 acres. Sailing, scuba diving, water skiing. *(See Heber Springs p. 44)*	7	●	●	●	●	●	●	●	●	●			●		●
Lake Dardanelle (C-2) 52,570 acres 4 mi. w. of Russellville on SR 7.	8	●	●		●	●	●	●		●			●		●
Lake Greeson (D-2) 15,842 acres 7 mi. n. of Murfreesboro on SR 19. Sailing, scuba diving, water skiing; motorcycle trails.	9	●	●	●	●	●	●	●	●	●				●	●
Lake Ouachita (D-3) 82,373 acres 12 mi. n. of Mountain Pine on SR 227. Sailing, scuba diving, water skiing.	10	●	●	●	●	●	●	●	●	●			●	●	●
Millwood Lake (E-1) 101,790 acres 9 mi. e. of Ashdown on SR 32.	11	●	●		●	●	●	●	●	●					
Nimrod Lake (C-2) 24,840 acres on SR 60 w. of SR 7 at Fourche Junction. Scuba diving, water skiing.	12	●	●	●	●	●	●	●	●	●	●				
Norfork Lake (A-4) 54,000 acres. Sailing, scuba diving, water skiing. *(See Salesville p. 57)*	13	●	●	●	●	●	●	●	●	●					●
STATE															
Bull Shoals-White River (A-3) 663 acres 6 mi. n. of Mountain Home on SR 5, then 8 mi. w. on SR 178. Scuba diving, trout fishing, water skiing.	14	●	●	●	●	●	●	●		●		●	●		
Cane Creek (E-4) 2,053 acres 4 mi. e. of Star City on SR 293.	15	●	●	●	●	●		●		●		●	●		
Cossatot River (D-1) 5,484 acres 9 mi. e. of Vandervoort on SR 246. Natural area. Canoeing, kayaking.	16		●	●				●	●	●			●		
Crater of Diamonds (D-2) 887 acres. Diamond hunting. *(See Murfreesboro p. 53)*	17	●	●	●						●		●	●		●
Crowley's Ridge (B-5) 270 acres. *(See Walcott p. 59)*	18	●	●	●	●	●	●	●	●	●		●	●	●	●
Daisy (D-2) 272 acres .2 mi. s. of Daisy off US 70.	19	●	●	●	●	●		●	●	●	●	●	●		
DeGray Lake Resort (D-2) 938 acres. Golf (18 holes), sailing, scuba diving, tennis, water skiing. *(See Bismarck p. 37)*	20	●	●	●	●	●	●	●	●	●	●	●	●	●	●
Devil's Den (B-1) 2,000 acres 17 mi. s.w. on SR 170. Canoe, pedal boats, tandem kayaks and water bicycle rentals; swimming pool. Scenic. *(See West Fork p. 60)*	21	●	●	●	●		●	●	●	●	●	●	●	●	●
Hobbs State Park-Conservation Area (A-2) 38,045 acres 10 mi. e. of Rogers on SR 12. Bridle/multi-use trails, firing range, interpretive programs, primitive campsites; hunting. *(See Rogers p. 56)*	22	●	●	●	●	●	●	●	●	●	●				
Jacksonport (B-5) 157 acres. *(See Jacksonport p. 47)*	23	●	●	●	●	●		●	●	●		●	●		
Jenkins' Ferry (D-3) 40 acres 13 mi. s. of Sheridan on SR 46.	24		●					●	●	●					

RECREATION AREAS

RECREATION AREAS	MAP LOCATION	CAMPING	PICNICKING	HIKING TRAILS	BOATING	BOAT RAMP	BOAT RENTAL	FISHING	SWIMMING	PETS ON LEASH	BICYCLE TRAILS	WINTER SPORTS	VISITOR CENTER	LODGE/CABINS	FOOD SERVICE
Lake Catherine (D-3) 2,180 acres 15 mi. n.w. of Malvern on SR 171.	25	•	•	•	•	•	•	•	•	•		•	•	•	•
Lake Charles (B-5) 140 acres 8 mi. n.w. of Hoxie on US 63, then 6 mi. s.w. on SR 25.	26	•	•	•	•	•		•	•	•		•	•		•
Lake Chicot (F-5) 132 acres 8 mi. n.e. of Lake Village on SR 144.	27	•	•	•	•	•	•	•	•	•		•	•	•	•
Lake Dardanelle															
Dardanelle (C-3) 90 acres 4 mi. w. of Dardanelle. Scuba diving, water skiing.	28	•	•	•	•	•	•	•		•					
Ouita (C-3) 20 acres .7 mi. e. of Russellville on SR 326. Scuba diving, water skiing.	29	•	•		•	•		•		•					
Russellville (C-2) 184 acres 4 mi. s. of Russellville on SR 326. Miniature golf, scuba diving, water skiing.	30	•	•	•	•	•	•	•	•	•	•	•	•		
Lake Frierson (B-5) 114 acres 10 mi. n. of Jonesboro on SR 141.	31	•	•	•	•	•	•	•		•		•			
Lake Ouachita (D-2) 370 acres. Scuba diving, water skiing. *(See Mountain Pine p. 52)*	32	•	•	•	•	•	•	•	•	•		•	•	•	•
Lake Poinsett (B-5) 111 acres 1 mi. e. of Harrisburg on SR 14, then 3 mi. s. on SR 163.	33	•	•	•	•	•	•	•		•		•	•		
Logoly (F-2) 345 acres .7 mi. e. of McNeil on CR 47. Playground.	34	•	•	•				•							
Mammoth Spring (A-4) 62 acres. Scenic. Historic. *(See Mammoth Spring p. 51)*	35		•	•				•		•			•		
Millwood (E-1) 823 acres 9 mi. e. of Ashdown on SR 32.	36	•	•	•	•	•	•	•	•	•		•	•		
Moro Bay (F-3) 117 acres 20 mi. n.e. of El Dorado on SR 15.	37	•	•	•	•	•	•	•	•	•		•	•		
Mount Magazine (C-2) 2,200 acres 17 mi. s. of Paris on SR 309.	38	•	•	•						•	•		•		
Mount Nebo (C-2) 2,812 acres 7 mi. w. of Dardanelle on SR 155. Tennis.	39	•	•	•					•	•	•		•	•	
Old Davidsonville (A-5) 173 acres. Historic. *(See Pocahontas p. 55)*	40	•	•	•	•	•	•	•		•		•	•		
Petit Jean (C-3) 2,896 acres. Scenic. Tennis. *(See Morrilton p. 52)*	41	•	•	•	•	•	•	•	•	•		•	•	•	•
Pinnacle Mountain (C-3) 2,000 acres 13 mi. w. of Little Rock on SR 10, then 2 mi. n. on SR 300. Arboretum. Interpretive programs. Scenic.	42		•	•	•	•		•		•		•	•		
Queen Wilhelmina (D-1) 460 acres.	43	•	•	•						•				•	•
Village Creek (C-5) 6,909 acres 13 mi. n. of Forrest City on SR 284. Tennis.	44	•	•	•	•	•	•	•	•	•	•	•	•	•	
White Oak Lake (E-2) 666 acres 2 mi. s.e. of Bluff City on SR 387.	45	•	•	•	•	•	•	•	•	•		•	•		
Withrow Springs (A-2) 786 acres 5 mi. n. of Huntsville on SR 23. Tennis. Canoe shuttle service and rental, playground, pool.	46	•	•	•	•		•	•	•	•		•	•		•
Woolly Hollow (C-3) 399 acres 12 mi. n. of Conway on US 65, then 6 mi. e. on SR 285.	47	•	•	•	•	•	•	•	•	•		•	•		•
OTHER															
Beaverfork Lake (C-3) 900 acres 3 mi. n. of Conway off US 65 or SR 25.	48		•		•			•	•	•					
Burns Park (C-4) 1,575 acres. *(See North Little Rock p. 53)*	49	•	•	•	•	•		•		•			•		
Cadron Settlement (C-3) 80 acres 5 mi. w. of Conway on US 64, then 1.5 mi. s. on SR 319.	50		•	•	•	•		•		•			•		
Cove Lake (C-2) 160 acres s.e. of Paris on SR 309 near Mount Magazine.	51	•	•	•	•	•		•	•	•					
Crossett Harbor (F-4) 300 acres 8 mi. w. of Crossett.	52	•	•		•	•		•		•			•		•
Lake Conway (C-3) 6,700 acres 3 mi. s. of Conway on SR 365.	53	•	•		•	•	•	•							
Lake Georgia-Pacific (F-4) 1,700 acres 10 mi. n.w. of Crossett.	54	•	•		•	•	•	•		•					
Lake Leatherwood (A-2) 1,600 acres 2 mi. w. of Eureka Springs off US 62. Canoe and paddleboat rental.	55	•	•	•	•	•	•	•	•	•	•			•	
Lake Maumelle (C-3) 8,900 acres 12 mi. w. of Little Rock on SR 10.	56		•	•	•	•	•	•							
Lake Wedington (B-1) 139 acres 13 mi. w. of Fayetteville on SR 16. Canoeing.	57	•	•	•	•	•	•	•	•	•				•	
Reynolds Park (A-6) 80 acres on n. edge of Paragould.	58	•	•			•		•	•						
Toad Suck Park (C-3) 78 acres 5 mi. w. of Conway on SR 60 on the Arkansas River.	59	•	•		•	•		•		•			•		

Points of Interest

ALTUS (C-2) pop. 817, elev. 538′

ST. MARY'S CATHOLIC CHURCH is atop Mount Bethel, 5 mi. s. of I-40 exit 41 on SR 186. This basilica-type church was dedicated in 1879 and is known for its original paintings by German artist Fridolin Fuchs. Four bells, weighing a total of nearly 6,400 pounds, hang in a 120-foot tower, and 29 stained-glass windows grace the interior. The altar and frescoes are covered in gold leaf. **Hours:** Open daily 7-7. **Cost:** Free. **Phone:** (479) 468-2585.

WINERIES

- **Post Familie Vineyards & Winery** is 1 blk. n. of US 64 on SR 186. **Hours:** Tasting room open Mon.-Sat. 9:30-6, Sun. noon-5. Guided 20-minute winery tours Mon.-Sat. 11-3; reservations are required. **Phone:** (479) 468-2741.
- **Wiederkehr Wine Cellars** is 4 mi. s. on SR 186, off I-40 exit 41. **Hours:** Guided 25-minute tours and tastings every 45 minutes Mon.-Sat. 9-4:30, Sun. noon-4:30. Last tour begins at 4:30. Phone ahead to confirm schedule. **Phone:** (479) 468-9463.

ARKADELPHIA (D-3) pop. 10,912, elev. 189′

Founded in 1839 and built along the bluffs of the Ouachita Valley, Arkadelphia was a river port during the steamboat days. The town is an agricultural and light industrial center producing aluminum, boats, clothing and wood products. It also has two colleges: Henderson State University has 5,000 students; Ouachita Baptist College's enrollment is 3,000.

Arkadelphia Area Chamber of Commerce: 700 Clay St., P.O. Box 38, Arkadelphia, AR 71923. **Phone:** (870) 246-5542.

Self-guiding tours: The Arkadelphia Historic Homes Tour is a driving tour featuring several homes dating from the 1840s. A brochure with a map of the path and descriptions of the homes is available from the chamber of commerce.

DeGRAY DAM VISITOR CENTER is 7 mi. n. on SR 7, then 2 mi. w. on entrance road. Displays and 3-D models illustrate the dam's construction and operational features. The center also features a wildlife exhibit and Caddo Indian artifacts. *See Recreation Chart and the AAA South Central CampBook.* **Hours:** Daily 8-4:15. Closed Jan. 1 and Dec. 25. **Cost:** Free. **Phone:** (870) 246-5501.

DeGRAY LAKE RESORT STATE PARK— *see Bismarck p. 37*

ARKANSAS POST NATIONAL MEMORIAL (D-5)

On SR 169, 7 miles south of Gillett along the lower Arkansas River, the Arkansas Post National Memorial occupies 389 acres. Erected as a fort by the French in 1686, Arkansas Post was the first permanent European settlement in the lower Mississippi Valley. Ownership passed to Spain 1765-1800, then briefly reverted to France. With the Louisiana Purchase the post became a frontier village.

Arkansas Post was the home of Arkansas' first newspaper, the *Gazette,* and the first capital of the Arkansas Territory. In 1821 both the newspaper and the capital moved to Little Rock. The site continued as a river port until the Civil War, when it became the scene of one of the state's major battles.

A visitor center and museum contain historical exhibits. Visitors can tour the town site, hike nature trails and fish, as well as enjoy bird-watching opportunities available due to the memorial's location along the Mississippi Flyway. Memorial open daily 8-dusk. Visitor center daily 8-5; closed Jan. 1, Thanksgiving and Dec. 25. Free. Phone (870) 548-2207.

BARLING (C-1) pop. 4,176, elev. 404′

JANET HUCKABEE ARKANSAS RIVER VALLEY NATURE CENTER is on Wells Lake at 8300 Wells Lake Rd. The nature center, on 170 acres that were part of the Fort Chaffee Army base, has interactive exhibits that provide information about the Ouachita and Ozark mountains, an aquarium with fish from the Arkansas River and a representation of a giant oak tree.

Several nature trails surround the visitor center, providing opportunities to see wildlife such as beavers, raccoons and deer. **Time:** Allow 45 minutes minimum. **Hours:** Tues.-Sat. 8:30-4:30, Sun. 1-5. Closed Jan. 1, Thanksgiving and Dec. 24-26. **Cost:** Free. **Phone:** (479) 452-3993.

BATESVILLE (B-4) pop. 9,445, elev. 338′

MARK MARTIN MUSEUM is at 1601 Batesville Blvd. This museum at Martin's Ford Mercury dealership features racing memorabilia, trophies and vehicles from his NASCAR career. Video displays tell the racing history of the cars he drove to win a record-setting 47 Busch Series victories and five IROC titles in one year. **Hours:** Mon.-Fri. 8-5, Sat. 9-5. **Cost:** Free. **Phone:** (870) 793-4461 or (800) 566-4461.

BENTON (D-3) pop. 21,906, elev. 416′

GANN MUSEUM OF SALINE COUNTY is at 218 S. Market St. Built in 1893, this structure is said to be the only known building in the world constructed of bauxite, or aluminum ore. Once the medical office of Dr. Dewell Gann Sr., the building was erected by his patients who could not afford to pay their bills. Exhibits also include a collection of

Niloak pottery. **Time:** Allow 30 minutes minimum. **Hours:** Tues.-Thurs. 10-4 or by appointment. Closed July 4, Thanksgiving and Dec. 24-25. **Cost:** Donations. **Phone:** (501) 778-5513.

BENTONVILLE (A-1)

pop. 19,730, elev. 1,280′

THE PEEL MANSION & HERITAGE GARDENS is at 400 S. Walton Blvd. Col. Samuel West Peel, a pioneer businessman, Indian agent, Confederate soldier, and congressman, built this Italianate mansion in 1875. He and his wife, Mary Emaline Berry Peel, raised nine children here. The house is furnished in period. A garden comprising historic roses, perennials and native plants also is on site. The mansion is available for viewing by guided tour only.

Time: Allow 30 minutes minimum. **Hours:** Tues.-Sat. 10-3, Mar.-Dec. Closed Christmas week. **Cost:** $3; $1 (ages 6-12). **Phone:** (479) 273-9664.

BERRYVILLE (A-2) pop. 4,433, elev. 1,246′

The "Turkey Capital of Arkansas," Berryville raises more than 500,000 turkeys each year. North on US 62 is a scenic drive through the Ozarks.

Berryville Chamber of Commerce: 506 S. Main St., P.O. Box 402, Berryville, AR 72616. **Phone:** (870) 423-3704.

CARROLL COUNTY HERITAGE CENTER MUSEUM is at 403 Public Sq. Three floors of displays in the 1889 Carroll County Courthouse include a pioneer-era schoolroom and funeral parlor, moonshine still, miniature train room, clock collection and genealogy department. **Time:** Allow 1 hour minimum. **Hours:** Mon.-Fri. 9-4. **Cost:** $2; $1 (ages 0-12). **Phone:** (870) 423-6312.

COSMIC CAVERN is just n.e. off SR 21. Guided 75-minute tours into this former onyx mine cover one-third mile and travel to such features as two underground lakes and a 9-foot-long soda straw stalactite. The cave maintains a constant temperature of 62 F.

Time: Allow 1 hour, 30 minutes minimum. **Hours:** Tours depart daily every 25 minutes 9-6, Memorial Day-Labor Day; every 45 minutes daily 9-5, rest of year (weather permitting). Last tour begins 10 minutes before closing. Phone to verify winter schedule. Closed Thanksgiving and Dec. 25. **Cost:** Fee $14; $7.50 (ages 5-12). **Phone:** (870) 749-2298.

SAUNDERS MEMORIAL MUSEUM is 1 blk. e. of Main St. at 113-115 Madison Ave. Col. C.B. Saunders' collection of pistols and revolvers includes a Chinese pistol more than 500 years old and side arms that belonged to Jesse James, Wild Bill Hickok, Pancho Villa and Annie Oakley. The museum also contains antique furniture, Persian rugs, European and American silverware and an Arabian sheik's tent.

Time: Allow 1 hour minimum. **Hours:** Mon.-Sat. 10:30-5, Apr. 15-early Nov. **Cost:** $5; $2.50 (ages 6-12). **Phone:** (870) 423-2563.

BISMARCK (D-2) elev. 531′

In the foothills of the Ouachita Mountains, 13,800-acre DeGray Lake is one of the state's most popular recreation destinations *(see Recreation Chart)*. The Army Corps of Engineers created this clear body of water in 1972 with completion of the DeGray Dam and Power Plant; the visitor center is on the southern end of the lake near Arkadelphia *(see attraction listing p. 35)*.

DEGRAY LAKE RESORT STATE PARK is off I-30 exit 78, then 6 mi. n. on SR 7. Interpretive programs at this 938-acre park include guided lake cruises, snorkeling and kayaking trips, trail hikes and wildlife demonstrations. Eagles Et Cetera in January spotlights the park's American bald eagles and other birds of prey. Facilities include an 18-hole championship golf course, a lodge and campsites, a swimming beach, picnic facilities and a marina that rents fishing tackle, boats, canoes and personal watercraft. *See Recreation Chart and the AAA South Central CampBook.*

Hours: Park open daily dawn-10 p.m. Visitor facilities open daily 8-8, Memorial Day-Labor Day; Mon.-Thurs. 8-5, Sat.-Sun. 8-8, rest of year. **Cost:** Free. Boat tours $8.50; $4.50 (ages 6-12). **Phone:** (501) 865-2801 for the park, or (501) 865-2811 for the marina.

BUFFALO NATIONAL RIVER (B-3)

Reached via US 65 or SRs 7, 14 or 21 in northwestern Arkansas, Buffalo National River stretches through the rugged Ozark Mountains. While the Buffalo River courses 150 miles through the Ozarks, only its lower 135 miles and adjacent land are designated a national river. To protect the natural beauty of this area, Congress declared it a national river in 1972, thereby preserving it from development and population encroachment.

A variety of wildlife, including bears, whitetail deer, bobcats, raccoons, opossums, beavers and minks, as well as geological features as distinct as caves, sinkholes, waterfalls, springs and bluffs, combine to provide a tranquil setting for hiking, fishing, camping and canoeing. More than 100 miles of hiking trails are available, and some allow horseback riding.

Interpretive programs are offered throughout the spring, summer and fall and include such activities as campfire programs, guided walks and hikes, canoe and float trips, and craft and folk music demonstrations. Backpacking is popular in the three wilderness areas. Hunting is permitted in season. Tyler Bend, the main visitor center, is 9 miles north of Marshall on US 65.

The national river is accessible daily 24 hours; Tyler Bend Visitor Center is open daily 8:15-4:45.

The visitor center is 11 miles north of Marshall off US 65. There is no admission charge but camping fees are imposed at Buffalo Point campground. For information contact the Superintendent, Buffalo National River, P.O. Box 1173, Harrison, AR 72602-1173; phone (870) 741-5443. *See Recreation Chart and the AAA South Central CampBook.*

BULL SHOALS (A-3) pop. 2,000, elev. 800′

Bull Shoals is a rural resort area on the shores of Bull Shoals Lake. This 101,196-acre reservoir offers fishing, camping, boating, picnicking and other recreational opportunities. *See Recreation Chart and the AAA South Central CampBook.*

Bull Shoals Lake-White River Chamber of Commerce: SR 178, P.O. Box 354, Bull Shoals, AR 72619. **Phone:** (870) 445-4443 or (800) 447-1290.

MOUNTAIN VILLAGE 1890 is at 1011 C.S. Woods Blvd., just off SR 178 following signs. This historic re-creation of an Ozark town is a living tribute to the pioneers who settled in this remote part of the country. Many of the buildings contain original furnishings.

Time: Allow 1 hour, 30 minutes minimum. **Hours:** Daily 9-6, June 1-Aug. 15; Wed.-Sun. 10-5, mid-Mar. through May 15; daily 9-5, May 16-31 and Aug. 16-Labor Day; Thurs.-Mon. 10-5, day after Labor Day-Oct. 31; Fri.-Sun. 10-4, in Nov. **Cost:** $11; $6 (ages 6-11). Combination for village and caverns $18; $10.80 (ages 6-11). **Phone:** (870) 445-7177.

Bull Shoals Caverns is in Mountain Village 1890 at 1011 C.S. Woods Blvd., just off SR 178 following signs. Guided 45-minute tours take visitors through caverns formed 350 million years ago. **Time:** Allow 1 hour minimum. **Hours:** Daily every half-hour 9-6, June 1-Aug. 15; Wed.-Sun. 10-5, mid-Mar. through May 15; daily 9-5, May 16-31 and Aug. 16-Labor Day; Thurs.-Mon. 10-5, day after Labor Day-Oct. 31; Fri.-Sun. 10-4, in Nov. Last tour departs 45 minutes before closing. **Cost:** Tour $11; $6 (ages 6-11). Combination for village and caverns $18; $10.80 (ages 6-11). **Phone:** (870) 445-7177.

TOP O' THE OZARKS TOWER is atop Bull Mountain, 1 mi. w. on SR 178 at Tower Rd. This 20-story-high tower offers a view of Bull Shoals Lake and Dam and the White River as well as the surrounding Ozark hill country, lakes, rivers and streams. **Time:** Allow 30 minutes minimum. **Hours:** Daily 9-5, Mar. 15-Labor Day. **Cost:** $5; $2.50 (ages 7-12). **Phone:** (870) 445-4302.

CAMDEN (E-3) pop. 13,154, elev. 149′

Camden, overlooking the Ouachita River, was an ancient American Indian trail crossing. Early French settlers named the town Fabre's Hill. American pioneers arrived during the 1820s, and soon a thriving cotton-growing industry was established. The proximity of the river made easy the transport of up to 40,000 bales a season. Wiped out by the Civil War, the cotton industry was replaced by timber production.

River Drive and Sandy Beach Park offer good views of the river; the latter also provides a boat ramp. Nearby White Oak Lake State Park provides camping, swimming, canoes, rental boats and fishing *(see Recreation Chart and the AAA South Central CampBook).*

Camden Area Chamber of Commerce: 314 S. Adams, P.O. Box 99, Camden, AR 71701. **Phone:** (870) 836-6426.

McCOLLUM-CHIDESTER HOUSE is .5 mi. w. on SR 4 at 926 Washington St. This 1847 house was an early stage stop and was occupied by a Union commander during the Civil War. Original furnishings are displayed, and bullet holes are visible in the upstairs walls. **Time:** Allow 1 hour minimum. **Hours:** Wed.-Sat. 9-4. Closed Jan. 1, Thanksgiving and Dec. 24-25. **Cost:** $5; $2 (ages 6-17). **Phone:** (870) 836-9243.

CROSSETT (F-4) pop. 6,097, elev. 159′

The Crossett division of Georgia-Pacific Corp. has gained national recognition for its tree-farming methods. Its large, scientifically managed prime forest supports plywood, paper and chemical plants. The company's Levi Wilcoxon Demonstration Forest, 15 miles east of Crossett, contains a series of marked trails with trees and plants identified by signs.

Felsenthal National Wildlife Refuge, 7 miles west on US 82, offers camping, picnicking, hiking trails, boating and fishing.

Crossett Area Chamber of Commerce: 101 W. First Ave., Crossett, AR 71635. **Phone:** (870) 364-6591.

DES ARC (C-4) pop. 1,933, elev. 202′

Settled in the early 1800s by fur traders, Des Arc sits on a bend of the White River. Its name in French refers to that curve. Farming is one of the area's chief industries, with rice the major crop.

LOWER WHITE RIVER MUSEUM STATE PARK is at the w. end of Main St. Arkansas rivers and associated lifestyles are the focus of this museum, with displays depicting life and the river-based economy, mainly from 1831 to 1931. Various mussels, which were used for trade as well as to make buttons and jewelry and for food, are exhibited. **Hours:** Tues.-Sat. and Mon. holidays 8-5, Sun. 1-5. Closed Jan. 1, Thanksgiving and Dec. 24-25. **Cost:** $3.25; $2 (ages 6-12); $10 (family). **Phone:** (870) 256-3711.

EL DORADO (F-3) pop. 21,530, elev. 250′

Until 1921 the town of El Dorado was quiet and peaceful. In that year, however, oil was discovered, and the once tranquil city was transformed into a boomtown whose population increased tenfold in a

4-year span. Gamblers and moonshiners soon arrived, as did H.L. Hunt, who began his oil empire in El Dorado after winning an interest in an oil well in a poker game.

The oil business is still important, but it has been joined by timber, poultry production and chemical manufacturing to form a more diverse economic base.

El Dorado Chamber of Commerce: 111 W. Main, El Dorado, AR 71730. **Phone:** (870) 863-6113.

SOUTH ARKANSAS ARBORETUM is 1 mi. n. off SR 82B at 501 Timberlane. This 13-acre site features plants native to the state's Gulf Coastal Plain region as well as other species such as azaleas and camellias. Botanist-led guided tours may be arranged in advance. **Time:** Allow 1 hour minimum. **Hours:** Daily 8-5; closed state holidays. **Cost:** Free. **Phone:** (870) 862-8131, ext. 188.

ELKINS (B-1) pop. 1,251, elev. 1,217′

TERRA STUDIOS is just s. of jct. SR 16 at 12103 Hazel Valley Rd. Visitors to the glassblowing and pottery studios can stroll through a sculpture garden and watch craftsmen create the glass Bluebird of Happiness figurines for which the studios are known. **Time:** Allow 30 minutes minimum. **Hours:** Daily 9-5. Closed major holidays. **Cost:** Free. **Phone:** (479) 643-3185 or (800) 255-8995.

EUREKA SPRINGS (A-2)

pop. 2,278, elev. 1,130′

The waters around Eureka Springs had been touted for alleged medicinal powers by American Indians and settlers alike long before Dr. Alvah Jackson established a clinic in the area in 1850. By the late 1870s a busy resort had developed; the arrival of the railroad in 1883 made the spa more accessible, and the sick and weary came great distances to be healed.

Modern medicine caused a drastic decline in the use of the springs, but recreational and artistic businesses have kept the city alive. Eureka Springs offers a variety of activities that cater to both body and mind. Country music shows abound throughout the year. The annual Eagle Watch, the last weekend in January, draws thousands of visitors from a four-state region.

A European-style farmer's market is held Sunday 9-4 early May through mid-October in a parking lot at One North Main St. Offerings range from produce to arts and crafts works to antiques and flea-market finds. Capping the day is the Lucky 13 Starlight Outdoor Cinema showing of films on a 17-by-25-foot screen painted on an outside wall of a building in the parking lot. Live entertainment before the screening is appropriate to the theme of the film, and audience members are encouraged to dress in garb in keeping with the film being shown.

Eureka Springs Visitor Information Center: 516 Village Circle Dr., Eureka Springs, AR 72632. **Phone:** (479) 253-8737 or (800) 638-7352.

Self-guiding tours: Elegant Victorian houses built at the turn of the 20th century can be seen in the city's historic district. Brochures outlining walking tours of Eureka Springs are available from the chamber of commerce.

Shopping areas: Pine Mountain Village, 1 mile north on US 62E is a Victorian-style shopping and entertainment complex with stores that specialize in local crafts. About 125 gift shops and restaurants are concentrated in the historic downtown district near the intersection of SRs 62 and 23N/Main Street.

BELLE OF THE OZARKS can be reached off SR 187 at 354 CR 146; take Mundell Rd. 4 mi. into Starkey Park and after the gatehouse turn right to lower-level parking, following signs. This 12-mile, 75-minute excursion of Beaver Lake features sightseeing of Beaver Dam, White House Bluffs, the Ozark Bluff Dweller's burial ground, the Lost Bridge area and a 200-acre game preserve island.

Time: Allow 1 hour, 30 minutes minimum. **Hours:** Cruises depart Fri.-Wed. at 11, 1 and 3, May-Oct. **Cost:** Fare $18.50; $7.50 (ages 2-11). **Phone:** (479) 253-6200 or (800) 552-3803.

BLUE SPRING HERITAGE CENTER is 5.5 mi. w. off US 62, following signs. The 33-acre complex, which features informal meadow, rock and wildflower gardens, also includes one of the largest natural springs in the Ozark Mountains. Several million gallons of water flow here each day. A 20-minute, three-screen presentation offers information about the area's history. **Time:** Allow 1 hour minimum. **Hours:** Daily 9-6, Apr.-Oct.; 9-5, in Mar. and Nov. **Cost:** $7.25; $4 (ages 10-17). **Phone:** (479) 253-9244.

EUREKA SPRINGS AND NORTH ARKANSAS RAILWAY departs from the town's original depot at 299 N. Main St. Narrated 45-minute rides are offered aboard a restored steam train. Lunch and dinner trips also are available. **Hours:** Departures Tues.-Sat. 10-4, early Apr.-late Oct. **Cost:** Fare $12; $6 (ages 4-9). Reservations are suggested for meal trips. **Phone:** (479) 253-9623 or (479) 253-9677.

EUREKA SPRINGS HISTORICAL MUSEUM is at 95 S. Main St. Exhibits chronicling Eureka Springs' history occupy three floors of an 1889 stone house. **Time:** Allow 1 hour minimum. **Hours:** Mon.-Sat. 9:30-4, Sun. 11-4. Closed Jan. 1, Thanksgiving and Dec. 25. **Cost:** $5; free (ages 5-18). **Phone:** (479) 253-9417.

GEM **"THE GREAT PASSION PLAY"** is 1 mi. e. off US 62, following signs. This production depicts the days leading to Christ's death, followed by the resurrection and the ascension. A cast of 250 actors accompanied by live animals performs in a 4,100-seat amphitheater. The 550-foot stage represents the streets of Jerusalem at the time of Christ. Prior to the play, guests may enjoy a meal at a dinner theater while listening to live gospel music.

Visitors also may view live re-enactments of Old and New Testament stories on the Living Bible Tour. At the Earth History Museum, exhibits explain the connection between dinosaurs and biblical history from a creationist perspective.

Hours: Curtain time Mon.-Tues. and Thurs.-Sat. at 8:30 p.m., May 1-Aug. 15 and Aug. 27-Sept. 6; Thurs.-Sat. at 7:30 p.m., day after Labor Day-Oct. 24. Special performances are presented at 8:30 p.m. on the Sundays before Memorial Day and Labor Day. Dinner theater seating 4:30-5. **Cost:** Play $25; $12 (ages 6-11); free (ages 0-5 on lap). Dinner theater $22; $10 (ages 6-15). **Phone:** (479) 253-9200 for information, or (800) 882-7529 for reservations.

Bible Museum is on the lower level of Smith Memorial Chapel, 1 mi. e. on US 62, then 1.2 mi. n. on Statue Rd. The museum contains more than 6,000 Bibles in 625 languages and dialects as well as a large collection of parchments and artifacts.

Hours: Mon.-Tues. and Thurs.-Sat. 10-8, May 1-Aug. 15 and Aug. 27-Sept. 6; Mon.-Tues. and Thurs.-Sat. 10-7, day after Labor Day-Oct. 24. **Cost:** $5. Combination with Living Bible Tour, Earth History Museum and Sacred Arts Center $15; $10 (ages 6-11). **Phone:** (479) 253-8559.

The Christ of the Ozarks is 3 mi. e. on US 62, then 1.5 mi. n. on Passion Play Rd. Towering seven stories above Magnetic Mountain and weighing more than 500 tons, the statue has outspread arms which measure 65 feet across, giving it the appearance of an immense cross when viewed from a distance. **Hours:** Daily 24 hours. **Cost:** Free.

Sacred Arts Center is 1 mi. e. on US 62, then 1.2 mi. n. on Statue Rd. The center displays more than 1,000 pieces of biblical art in 64 media, including sculptured marble, mosaics and needlepoint. **Hours:** Mon.-Tues. and Thurs.-Sat. 10-8, May 1-Aug. 15 and Aug. 27-Sept. 6; Mon.-Tues. and Thurs.-Fri. 10-7, Sat. 10-7:30, day after Labor Day-Oct. 24. **Cost:** $5. Combination with Bible Museum, Earth History Museum and Living Bible Tour $15; $10 (ages 6-11).

HOBBS STATE PARK-CONSERVATION AREA—
see Rogers p. 56.

ONYX CAVE PARK is 3 mi. e. on US 62, then 3.5 mi. n. on Onyx Cave Rd. Self-guiding 30-minute tours feature taped narration. The site includes the free Gay '90s Button and Doll Museum. **Hours:** Daily 9-5, May-Sept.; 9-4 in Apr. and Oct.-Nov. (weather permitting). **Cost:** $5; $2.50 (ages 4-13). **Phone:** (479) 253-9321.

ST. ELIZABETH CHURCH is just off US 62B on Crescent Dr. The church is unusual in that it is entered through the bell tower. Along the walkway are the Stations of the Cross. A prayer garden at the side of the church provides a good view of the "Christ of the Ozarks" statue nearby. **Hours:** Daily 8:30-6. **Cost:** Free. **Phone:** (479) 253-9853.

THORNCROWN CHAPEL is just w. off US 62. This modern glass and wood chapel is noted for its innovative architecture. Woods and trails surround the chapel, which is open for Sunday services and weddings. **Hours:** Daily 9-5, Apr.-Nov.; 11-4, in Mar. and Dec. Hours may vary Sat.-Sun.; phone to confirm schedule. **Cost:** Donations. **Phone:** (479) 253-7401.

TURPENTINE CREEK WILDLIFE REFUGE is at 239 Turpentine Creek Ln. This animal rescue center specializes in large exotic cats—cougars, leopards, lions and tigers—although visitors can see monkeys, bears and other assorted wildlife as well. The refuge's Education Station features exhibits about the biology of big cats including several hands-on displays. Brief descriptions are posted at each animal's enclosure recounting its life and how it came to be at the refuge. Guided tours of the natural-looking enclosures are available.

Time: Allow 30 minutes minimum. **Hours:** Open daily 9-6, Memorial Day-Labor Day; 9–5 rest of year. Guided tours depart on the hour 11-4, Memorial Day-Labor Day; on the hour 11-2 rest of the year. Closed Dec. 25. **Cost:** $15; $10 (ages 3-12 and 65+); free (ages 0-2). **Phone:** (479) 253-5841.

FAYETTEVILLE (B-1)

pop. 58,047, elev. 1,416'

Lots first were sold in Fayetteville in 1828, and the town soon became known for an interest in education. Several small colleges were founded in the 1840s and '50s. Arkansas Industrial University, established in 1871, became the University of Arkansas with an enrollment in excess of 14,000.

Walton Arts Center is home to the North Arkansas Symphony, which presents several concerts throughout the year; phone (479) 443-5600.

Guided walking tours of the Washington-Willow Historic District, a neighborhood with Victorian houses and large shade trees, can be arranged through the Washington County Historical Society. The society also offers living history tours of the 1853 Headquarters House Museum by appointment; phone (479) 521-2970. Nearby Lake Wedington offers camping, cabins, a boat ramp, boat rental and fishing *(see Recreation Chart and the AAA South Central CampBook)*.

The Battle of Fayetteville Re-enactment is held on a weekend close to the anniversary of the April 18, 1863, engagement; living-history demonstrations include battle camp cooking, weaving, quilting and other crafts of the Civil War period. The 4-day Bikes, Blues & BBQ Motorcycle Rally brings some 250,000 visitors into town in late September or early October; phone (479) 527-9993.

Fayetteville Convention & Visitors Bureau: 21 S. Block St., Fayetteville, AR 72701. **Phone:** (479) 521-5776 or (800) 766-4626.

ARKANSAS AIR MUSEUM is 5 mi. s. on US 71 next to the Fayetteville Municipal Airport. The museum houses racing planes of the 1920s and '30s, open cockpit biplanes and early aircraft engines. Most of the planes are maintained in flying condition. Various exhibits trace the history of manned flight. Antique airplanes are restored in the museum's shop. **Time:** Allow 30 minutes minimum. **Hours:** Sun.-Fri. 11-4:30, Sat. 10-4:30. Closed major holidays. **Cost:** $8; $4 (ages 6-12). **Phone:** (479) 521-4947.

BOTANICAL GARDEN OF THE OZARKS is at 4703 N. Crossover Rd. (SR 265), just n. of jct. Zion Rd. Visitors can experience nine themed gardens with plantings common to the Ozarks as they progress along a circular walkway. Water features and statues enhance the landscape and the rock and water, Japanese, vegetable and herb, children's, four seasons, shade, Ozark native, sensory, and rose and perennial gardens.

Time: Allow 45 minutes minimum. **Hours:** Tues.-Sun. 9-5 (also Tues.-Fri. 5-8), Memorial Day-Labor Day; Tues.-Sun. 9-5, Feb. 1-day before Memorial Day, day after Labor Day-Oct. 31 and Nov.-Dec. Closed Thanksgiving and Dec. 25. **Cost:** $5; $2.50 (ages 5-13); free (Sat. 9-noon). **Phone:** (479) 750-2620.

FINE ARTS CENTER is on the University of Arkansas campus at 1125 Maple St. Theatrical and musical performances are presented in its theater and concert hall. An art gallery also is part of the center. **Hours:** Most events are held during the school year. Art gallery open Mon.-Fri. 10-4. **Cost:** Many events are free. Gallery free. **Phone:** (479) 575-5202 for gallery information, (479) 575-4701 for concert information, or (479) 575-4752 for theater schedule.

FORDYCE (E-3) pop. 4,799, elev. 285'

From the age of 10, legendary football coach Paul "Bear" Bryant grew up in Fordyce. In 1927, when Bryant was 13 or 14, a promoter at the Fordyce Theatre offered a dollar to anyone who would wrestle a bear—Bryant took him up on the offer, thereby earning his nickname. The mainstays of the local economy are logging and wood products.

There are 18 Craftsman-style houses in the Charlotte Street Historic District of Fordyce, some designed by Charles Thompson in the early 1900s. The First Presbyterian Church on West 4th Street has 36 stained-glass windows.

Fordyce Chamber of Commerce: 119 W. 3rd St., Fordyce, AR 71742. **Phone:** (870) 352-3520.

DALLAS COUNTY HISTORICAL MUSEUM is at 221 S. Main St. The museum traces the history of the county. Exhibits include tools and housewares from the early 1900s and photographs of legendary football coach Paul "Bear" Bryant, who attended high school in Fordyce. **Time:** Allow 30 minutes minimum. **Hours:** Tues.-Fri. 11-4, Sat. 10-1. Closed major holidays. **Cost:** Free. **Phone:** (870) 352-5262.

FORT SMITH (C-1) pop. 80,268, elev. 439'

In 1817 Maj. Stephen H. Long selected a site at the confluence of the Arkansas and Poteau rivers as the location for the region's first military fort. Named for Gen. Thomas Smith, the fort prompted settlement and the resultant town shared the fort's name. With the discovery of natural gas in nearby Mansfield, a large and diverse manufacturing industry developed; Fort Smith remains one of Arkansas' leading manufacturing cities.

A navigation channel on the Arkansas River connects Fort Smith with other ports. Fort Smith is a convenient starting point for picturesque drives through the Ozark, Ouachita and Kiamichi mountains and the Cookson Hills via two of the state's scenic highways, US 71 and I-40.

Fort Smith Chamber of Commerce: 612 Garrison Ave., Fort Smith, AR 72901. **Phone:** (479) 783-6118.

ARKANSAS AND MISSOURI RAILROAD—
see Van Buren p. 58.

THE CLAYTON HOUSE is at 514 N. 6th St. William Henry Harrison Clayton, district attorney under Judge Isaac C. Parker, purchased this antebellum house in the 1880s and added onto it. Clayton lived there until 1897. Restored and furnished in period, this example of Classic Revival Victorian architecture contains Clayton belongings, artifacts and other memorabilia.

Time: Allow 30 minutes minimum. **Hours:** Wed.-Fri. 10-4, Sat. noon-4, Sun. 1-4, June 1-Labor Day; Wed.-Sat. noon-4, Sun. 1-4, rest of year. Closed Jan. 1, Thanksgiving and Dec. 25. Phone ahead to confirm schedule. **Cost:** $2.50; $1 (ages 12-18). **Phone:** (479) 783-3000.

THE DARBY HOUSE is at 311 General Darby St. This was the boyhood home of Brig. Gen. William O. Darby, the organizer and commander of the U.S. Army's 1st Ranger Battalion. Two rooms are open to the public: the living room, restored to its appearance when Darby's parents were informed of his death on May 1, 1945, and another room containing memorabilia and tributes. **Time:** Allow 30 minutes minimum. **Hours:** Mon.-Fri. 8-1, Sat.-Sun. by appointment. Closed major holidays. **Cost:** Free. **Phone:** (479) 782-3388.

FORT SMITH ART CENTER is at 423 N. 6th St. The center, which occupies a restored Victorian house built about 1870, contains permanent displays of works by local artists and a variety of traveling exhibits. **Note:** The center is scheduled to relocate to 1601 Rogers Ave. on July 1, 2010. **Time:** Allow 1 hour minimum. **Hours:** Open Thurs.-Sat. 9:30-4:30 until reopening at new location on July 1. Open Tues.-Sat. 9:30-4:30 after June 30. Closed July 4, Thanksgiving and Dec. 25-Jan. 1. **Cost:** Free. **Phone:** (479) 784-2787.

FORT SMITH MUSEUM OF HISTORY is at 320 Rogers Ave. Chronicling the development of Fort

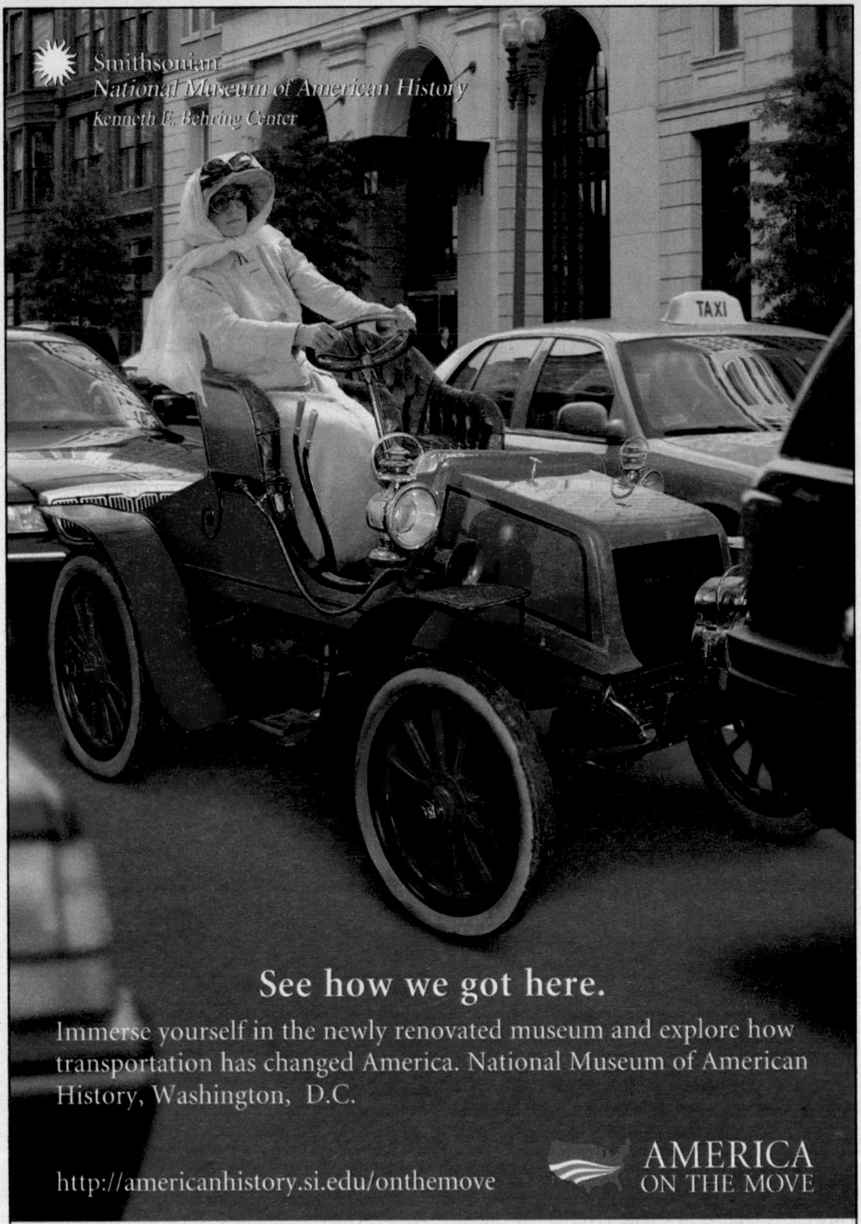

Smith, museum collections include an early 20th-century pharmacy and soda fountain, the area's first steam-powered fire pump and memorabilia of World War II hero Brig. Gen. William O. Darby. Weaving demonstrations are given on weekends. A restored trolley offers trips through the historic district; tokens may be purchased at the museum.

Time: Allow 2 hours minimum. **Hours:** Tues.-Sat. 10-5, Sun. 1-5. Closed Jan. 1, Thanksgiving and Dec. 24-25. **Cost:** Museum $5; $2 (ages 6-15). Trolley fare $2; $1 (ages 0-12). **Phone:** (479) 783-7841 or (479) 783-1237.

FORT SMITH NATIONAL CEMETERY is at 522 Garland St. at S. 6th St. Established in 1867, the cemetery contains the graves of many who were important to the area, including Brig. Gen. William O. Darby, organizer of Darby's Rangers; Maj. William C. Bradford, who established the first fort; and Judge Isaac C. Parker, who held court in Fort Smith during the years of the Indian Territory days. **Hours:** Gates open daily 24 hours. Office open Mon.-Fri. 8-4:30. Closed major holidays. **Cost:** Free. **Phone:** (479) 783-5345.

FORT SMITH NATIONAL HISTORIC SITE is at 3rd and Garland sts. Incorporating the remains of two successive frontier forts, the site chronicles the frontier years 1817-96. Themes include military history, westward expansion, Indian Removal along the Trail of Tears, the Indian Territory, law and order in the late 19th century and the diverse people who lived in the region.

Seventy-nine felons were hanged at the fort during Judge Isaac C. Parker's 21 years on the bench of the U.S. District Court for Western Arkansas—outlaws dubbed him the "hanging judge." The fort's visitor center in his restored courtroom features original furnishings and exhibits, a 15-minute DVD program about the fort's history and a reproduction of the gallows.

Hours: Daily 9-5. Closed Jan. 1 and Dec. 25. **Cost:** Site admission free. Visitor center $4; free (ages 0-15). **Phone:** (479) 783-3961.

JANET HUCKABEE ARKANSAS RIVER VALLEY NATURE CENTER—*see Barling p. 35.*

MISS LAURA'S VISITORS CENTER is at 2 N. B St. This turn-of-the-20th-century brothel eventually became one of the most celebrated bordellos in the Southwest. Laura Ziegler owned the establishment that now is furnished in period. Transoms show the names of women who worked there. **Time:** Allow 30 minutes minimum. **Hours:** Guided 30-minute tours of the house are offered as necessary Mon.-Sat. 9-4, Sun. 1-4:30. Last tour begins 30 minutes before closing. Closed major holidays. **Cost:** Donations. **Phone:** (479) 783-8888 or (800) 637-1477.

GILLETT (D-4) pop. 819, elev. 188'

ARKANSAS POST STATE MUSEUM is at jct. US 165 and SRs 1 and 169. Five buildings house artifacts illustrating local history. **Hours:** Tues.-Sat. and Mon. holidays 8-5, Sun. 1-5. Closed Jan. 1, Thanksgiving and Dec. 24-25. **Cost:** $3; $2 (ages 6-12); $10 (family, two adults and children ages 0-18). **Phone:** (870) 548-2634.

HARDY (A-4) pop. 578, elev. 358'

Hardy is set in the Ozark Mountain foothills along the banks of Spring River. The river provides white-water canoeing and fishing, while the town serves up its own brand of entertainment—music. Country sounds abound in musical productions, music theaters and weekly outdoor jam sessions. The downtown district has remained virtually unchanged since the 1920s and features 43 historic buildings.

GOOD OLD DAYS VINTAGE MOTORCAR MUSEUM is at 301 W. Main St. More than 50 rare and vintage cars, trucks, motorcycles and bicycles are displayed. A large collection of cars from the 1915-29 era also is featured. Some vehicles still have all their original parts. The museum's collection is constantly changing. **Time:** Allow 30 minutes minimum. **Hours:** Mon.-Fri. 9:30-4, Sat. 9-5, Sun. noon-5, Memorial Day-Labor Day; Sat. 9-5, Sun. noon-5, rest of year. **Cost:** $8.50; $4.50 (ages 1-12). **Phone:** (870) 856-4884.

HARRISON (A-3) pop. 12,152, elev. 1,061'

The "Crossroads of the Ozarks," Harrison is the center of a rustic resort community in the valley of Crooked Creek, one of the most scenic sections of the Arkansas Ozarks. The town is home to the two-year North Arkansas College.

Running from the state's northern border through Hot Springs National Park *(see place listing p. 46)* and ending in Arkadelphia, SR 7 encompasses lofty mountains and numerous lakes and rivers. The road is popular for leisurely drives and photographic opportunities. En route to Hot Springs, SR 7 crosses two national forests, the Ozark *(see place listing p. 54)* and the Ouachita *(see place listing p. 54)*, and the Buffalo National River *(see place listing p. 37)*. *See Recreation Chart and the AAA South Central CampBook.*

Harrison Convention & Visitors Bureau: 122 E. Rush St., P.O. Box 940, Harrison, AR 72601. **Phone:** (870) 741-1789 or (888) 283-2163.

BOONE COUNTY HERITAGE MUSEUM is at 110 S. Cherry St. This three-story museum features large collections of railroad memorabilia and antique clocks, a room devoted to medical instruments of the past, American Indian artifacts and World Wars I and II memorabilia. A genealogy library also is available. **Time:** Allow 1 hour minimum. **Hours:** Mon.-Fri. 10-4, Mar.-Nov.; Thurs. 10-4, rest of year. Closed major holidays. **Cost:** $2; free (ages 0-11 with adult). **Phone:** (870) 741-3312.

MARINE CORPS LEGACY MUSEUM is on the n.w. corner of the town square at 125 W. Rush Ave. Using displays of uniforms, weapons and equipment, this museum traces the history of marine forces from 400 BC through the founding of the United States Marine Corps in 1775, to the present. **Time:** Allow 1 hour minimum. **Hours:** Tues.-Sat. 10-5. Closed major holidays. **Cost:** $8; $3 (ages 0-11). **Phone:** (870) 743-1680.

MYSTIC CAVERNS is 8 mi. s. on SR 7. Guided 70-minute tours feature two Ozark caverns with well-lighted walkways and wide steps. The temperature in the caves is a constant 59 F. A jacket is advised. **Time:** Allow 30 minutes minimum. **Hours:** Tours Mon.-Sat. every 40 minutes 9-5:30, June-Aug.; Mon.-Sat. 9-5, Mar.-May and Sept.-Oct.; Mon.-Sat. 9-4, Nov.-Dec. Last tour begins at closing. Closed Thanksgiving and Dec. 25. **Cost:** Tour $14.99; $13.99 (ages 62+); $6.99 (ages 4-12). **Phone:** (870) 743-1739 or (888) 743-1739.

HEBER SPRINGS (C-4) pop. 6,432, elev. 348'

The hallmark of Heber Springs, at the foot of Round Mountain, is water. The springs for which the town is named are downtown. Other waters also are important to the community; the Little Red River offers excellent fishing for rainbow trout, thanks to stocking by the federal trout hatchery just north of Greers Ferry Dam.

Heber Springs Area Chamber of Commerce: 1001 W. Main St., Heber Springs, AR 72543. **Phone:** (501) 362-2444.

GREERS FERRY DAM AND LAKE is 3.5 mi. n.e. on SR 25. Completed in 1962, the dam is part of the White River Basin power and flood control project. Sugar Loaf Mountain in the middle of Greers Ferry Lake has hiking and nature trails. Opportunities for fishing and other aquatic activities are available. The visitor center at the west end of the dam offers historical exhibits and a 20-minute presentation. A trout hatchery and an aquarium are 1.5 miles north of the dam off SR 25N. *See Recreation Chart and the AAA South Central CampBook.*

Hours: Visitor center open daily 10-6, May-Sept.; Thurs.-Mon. 10-6, in Apr. and Oct. Trout hatchery and aquarium open daily 7-3. **Cost:** Free. **Phone:** (501) 362-9067, or (501) 362-3615 for the hatchery and aquarium.

HELENA (D-6) pop. 6,323

Founded in 1820, Helena enacted early laws that set the speed limit at a trot or pace and required that guns be fired within town limits only with just cause. Such cause was found on July 4, 1863, during the bloody Battle of Helena, when Confederate troops tried in vain to recapture the town from occupying Union forces.

Helena now is a river port; it also was the hometown of lyric soprano Frances Greer; country singer Harold Jenkins, better known as Conway Twitty; and blues singer Sonny Boy Williamson II. A mural depicting musicians stretches for a block beginning at 95 Missouri St., on the levee walk.

The Wild Hog Music Festival & Motorcycle Rally zooms into town in April. The Delta Cultural Center retells the story of the Delta region and its people and hosts the late May Arkansas Delta Family Gospel Festival; phone (870) 338-4350 or (800) 358-0972. The town celebrates its musical talent again in October with the 4-day, well-known Arkansas Blues and Heritage Festival, formerly the King Biscuit Blues Festival; phone (870) 338-8327.

Guided tours of some of Helena's historic houses are available year-round by appointment. For further information contact the chamber of commerce.

Phillips County Chamber of Commerce: 111 Hickory Hill Dr., P.O. Box 447, Helena, AR 72342. **Phone:** (870) 338-8327.

CONFEDERATE MILITARY CEMETERY is n. off US 49 Bus. Rte. to Columbia St., 2 blks. e. on McDonough St. to Holly St., then 4 blks. n. to Maple Hill Cemetery, following signs. This cemetery contains approximately 100 marked and unmarked graves of Confederate soldiers. The site offers views of the Mississippi River. **Hours:** Daily 9-5. **Cost:** Free. **Phone:** (870) 338-8327.

PHILLIPS COUNTY LIBRARY AND MUSEUM is 2 blks. e. of US 49 Bus. Rte. at Porter and Pecan sts. The museum displays memorabilia from the Spanish-American and Civil wars as well as artworks and period costumes. The library is among the oldest in the state. **Hours:** Free guided 1-hour tours of the library depart on demand Mon.-Fri. 7-5. Museum open Tues.-Sat. 10-4. Last tour begins 1 hour before closing. Closed major holidays. **Cost:** Free. **Phone:** (870) 338-7790.

HOPE (E-2) pop. 10,616, elev. 355'

Known as the birthplace of Bill Clinton, Hope was settled in 1852 and named after the daughter of a railroad commissioner. Local growers began cultivating watermelons for rail shipment in the early 1900s and soon began breaking world records for giant-sized melons. Today's entries regularly tip the scales at 250 pounds. The Watermelon Festival in August features an arts and crafts show, a 5K race, a fishing tournament, the Watermelon Olympics and watermelon-eating and seed-spitting contests.

Hope-Hempstead County Chamber of Commerce: 200 S. Main St., P.O. Box 250, Hope, AR 71802. **Phone:** (870) 777-3640.

PRESIDENT BILL CLINTON'S 1ST HOME MUSEUM is 1.4 mi. s.e. of I-30 on SR 278B to 117 S. Hervey St. This 2-story house was the first home of William Jefferson Clinton, 42nd president of the United States, and is furnished to reflect his boyhood years in the 1940s and '50s. An exhibit center features photographs of Clinton's childhood. Parking and the main entrance are located behind the museum. **Hours:** Mon.-Sat. 10-5. **Cost:** Donations. **Phone:** (870) 777-4455.

HOT SPRINGS (D-3) pop. 35,750, elev. 632'

Hot Springs is a year-round health and pleasure resort adjacent to Hot Springs National Park *(see place listing p. 46)*. The city sponsors a variety of events, including the Miss Arkansas Pageant in July and the Hot Springs Documentary Film Festival in October. In mid-April, Arkansas Derby Day takes place at Oaklawn Park as part of its thoroughbred racing season, January through April; phone (800) 625-5296.

Note: Policies concerning admittance of children to pari-mutuel betting facilities vary. Phone for information.

The Hot Springs region is well-known for its three nearby lakes—Lake Hamilton, Lake Ouachita and Lake Catherine—and for being rich in quartz crystals of superior hardness and brilliance; the finest are in the veins of Crystal Mountain.

Hot Springs Convention and Visitors Bureau: 134 Convention Blvd., Hot Springs, AR 71901. **Phone:** (501) 321-2277 or (800) 772-2489.

Shopping areas: Temperance Hill Square, SR 7 at Central Avenue, features specialty stores including Bon Worth and Tuesday Morning. Cornerstone Mall, off the US 270/70 Bypass, includes Chico's, Old Navy and Pier 1.

ARKANSAS ALLIGATOR FARM AND PETTING ZOO is at 847 Whittington Ave. Four ponds are stocked with alligators of different sizes. A petting zoo also is featured. **Hours:** Daily 9:30-5. Feeding time is Thurs. and Sat.-Sun. at noon. **Cost:** $6.50; $5.50 (ages 3-12). **Phone:** (501) 623-6172.

ART CENTRAL is at 405 Park Ave. The center presents changing exhibitions and special events. **Hours:** Center open Mon.-Fri. 10-2. **Cost:** Free. **Phone:** (501) 625-3992.

BELLE OF HOT SPRINGS departs from 5200 Central Ave. The 220-passenger riverboat offers narrated 75-minute daytime and 2-hour evening sightseeing cruises on Lake Hamilton. Lunch and dinner cruises also are available.

Hours: Departures daily at 1 and 7 (also Sat. at 3, 5:30 and 8:30, July-Aug.), Memorial Day-Labor Day; at 1 and 6, day after Labor Day-Oct. 31; at 1 and 5, in Nov.; at 1 and 7, Feb. 1-day before Memorial Day; schedule varies rest of year. Phone ahead to confirm schedule. **Cost:** Evening fare $16.99; $15.99 (ages 55+); $8.99 (ages 2-12). Daytime fare $15.99; $14.99 (ages 55+); $7.99 (ages 2-12). **Phone:** (501) 525-4438.

GARVAN WOODLAND GARDENS is at 550 Arkridge Rd. This 210-acre botanical garden features almost 2 miles of walking trails that provide visitors access to a variety of plant collections, flower borders, rock and antique rose gardens, waterfalls, pools and a bird sanctuary. A welcome center also is on-site.

Time: Allow 1 hour, 30 minutes minimum. **Hours:** Daily 9-8, Memorial Day-Labor Day; noon-9, Thanksgiving week-Dec. 31; 9-6, rest of year. Closed Thanksgiving and Dec. 25. **Cost:** $8.75; $7.75 (ages 56+); $4.50 (ages 6-12). Pets on leash $4.50. **Phone:** (501) 262-9300 or (800) 366-4664.

JOSEPHINE TUSSAUD WAX MUSEUM is at 250 Central Ave. Representations of historical figures range from 16th-century explorer Hernando de Soto to former president Bill Clinton. **Hours:** Mon.-Thurs. 9-8, Fri.-Sat. 9 a.m.-10 p.m., Memorial Day weekend-Labor Day; daily 10-5, rest of year. Closed Jan. 1, Thanksgiving and Dec. 25. **Cost:** $10; $7 (ages 3-12). **Phone:** (501) 623-5836.

MAGIC SPRINGS & CRYSTAL FALLS is 2 mi. e. at 1701 US 70E. This theme and water park offers more than 25 rides, including the Arkansas Twister, a 100-foot-high, 3,500-foot-long out-and-back-style wooden roller coaster; The Gauntlet, a suspended looping coaster 110 feet high and 2,260 feet long; and the X-Coaster, a corkscrewing drop from 150 feet at 65 miles per hour. The water park offers a wave pool, a lazy river, four slides and an interactive splash zone.

Time: Allow 3 hours minimum. **Hours:** Magic Springs open Sun.-Thurs. 11-8, Fri.-Sat. 11-10, late June-early Aug.; Sun.-Thurs. 11-7, Fri.-Sat. 11-10, Memorial Day weekend-late June; Fri.-Sat. 11-10, Sun. 11-7, early Aug. to mid-Aug.; Sat.-Sun. 11-7, early Apr.-day before Memorial Day weekend and mid-Aug. to late Sept. Crystal Falls open Sun.-Thurs. 11-6, Fri.-Sat. 11-8, Memorial Day weekend to mid-Aug.; Sat.-Sun. 11-6, early May-day before Memorial Day weekend and mid-Aug. to late Sept. Schedule may vary before Memorial Day and in Sept.; phone ahead. Gates open 1 hour before attractions.

Cost: $45.99; $35.99 (ages 55+ and children under 52 inches tall). Phone ahead to verify schedules and prices. **Parking:** $10. **Phone:** (501) 624-0100.

MID-AMERICA SCIENCE MUSEUM is on SR 227, 1 mi. n. of US 270 at 500 Mid-America Blvd. This museum offers participatory exhibits that explore such subjects as perception, energy, sound, light and gravity. Visitors can launch a hot-air balloon, generate electricity and create rivers and mountains in a land model. The museum also offers a laser show and virtual reality simulator.

Time: Allow 2 hours minimum. **Hours:** Daily 9:30-6, Memorial Day weekend-Labor Day; Tues.-Sun. 10-5, rest of year. Closed Jan. 1, Thanksgiving and Dec. 24-25. **Cost:** $8; $7 (ages 2-12 and 62+). Pricing may vary with special events. Laser show $2 additional. Virtual reality simulator $3 additional. **Phone:** (501) 767-3461.

MOUNTAIN VALLEY WATER SPRING VISITOR CENTER is at 150 Central Ave. The center offers samples, self-guiding tours and exhibits. Built beginning in 1910, this historically restored building also

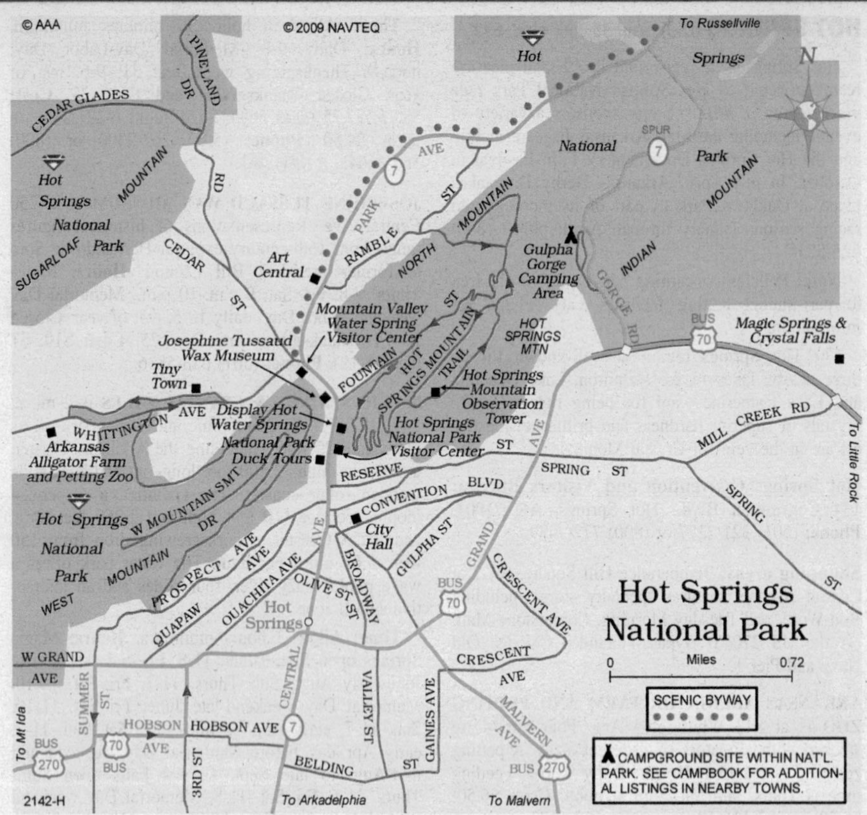

houses a museum and the mineral water company's headquarters. **Time:** Allow 30 minutes minimum. **Hours:** Mon.-Fri. 9-4:30, Sat. 10-4, Sun. noon-4. Closed Jan. 1, Thanksgiving and Dec. 25. **Cost:** Free. **Phone:** (501) 623-6671 or (800) 643-1501.

TINY TOWN is at 374 Whittington Ave. The handiwork of one family, this miniature village consists of animated replicas at one-quarter scale. Settings include a farm, sawmill, American Indian village, Wild West town, blacksmith shop and park. **Hours:** Mon.-Sat. 10-3, Mar.-Oct. **Cost:** $4; $3 (ages 4-12). **Phone:** (501) 624-4742.

GEM HOT SPRINGS NATIONAL PARK (D-2)

Elevations in the park range from 600 ft. at the corner of Central and Reserve aves. to 1,420 ft. at Music Mountain. Refer to AAA maps for additional elevation information.

Hot Springs National Park, in western Arkansas, can be reached from the north and south via scenic SR 7, as well as via US 70 from the east and US 270 from both the east and west.

In the picturesque Ouachita (WASH-i-taw) Mountains, Hot Springs differs sharply from the country's other scenic national parks in that portions of it are nearly surrounded by a sizable city. Its 5,839 acres occupy the slopes of Hot Springs, Music, North, West, Sugarloaf and Indian mountains.

The thermal water that flows from the springs is naturally sterile. It begins as rainwater, is absorbed into the mountains northeast of the park and is carried 4,000-8,000 feet underground, where the earth's extreme heat raises its temperature to 143 F. The purified water makes its way back to the surface through cracks and pores in the rock in the form of hot springs. The entire process takes about 4,000 years.

The first European to visit the hot springs is believed to have been Hernando de Soto in 1541. According to legend, the beneficial qualities of the water were known to the American Indians long before the Spaniards arrived. It is said that they declared this area neutral ground, available to all on peaceful terms.

In 1832, because of tourism brought on by the water's perceived medicinal properties, the federal government set aside the springs and surrounding area as the country's first park-type federal reservation. In 1921 Hot Springs became a national park, the country's eighteenth. Numerous bathhouses, eight of which still stand along a portion of Central Avenue known as Bathhouse Row, catered to thousands of health seekers. The popularity of the springs began to decrease in the 1950s, but the springs still attract many visitors.

General Information and Activities

The springs are found along the west slope of Hot Springs Mountain. Within about 10 acres there are 47 springs with a daily flow that varies from 750,000 to 950,000 gallons. The water is collected into one central system and distributed to bathhouses and the drinking and jug fountains near the corner of Central and Reserve. The standard tub baths can be taken by applying at any of the bathhouses. Options, at no extra cost, include showers, sitz tubs, vapor cabinets and hot packs.

Prescription baths may be taken only by application to a registered physician. Three bathhouses, the Buckstaff, Fordyce and the Libbey Memorial Physical Medicine Center, operate within the park; the latter has pools and specialized equipment and offers pool baths and prescribed physical therapy. Other bathhouses in the park are managed in connection with city hotels; prices vary according to equipment and available accommodations.

The park has 10 miles of good mountain roads for sightseeing by car, as well as extensive walking and horse trails for outdoor enthusiasts; the trails are open daily year-round. Interpretive programs are presented from mid-June to mid-August; phone for schedule. **Note:** Because of sharp switchbacks, vehicles more than 30 feet long cannot negotiate Hot Springs Mountain Drive.

Fall and spring offer displays of flowering trees, shrubs and colorful foliage. Limited programs are available at these times. Nearby Catherine, Hamilton and Ouachita lakes offer fishing. *See Recreation Chart and the AAA South Central CampBook.*

ADMISSION to the park is free.

PETS are permitted in the park only if they are leashed, crated or otherwise physically restricted at all times.

ADDRESS inquiries to the Park Superintendent, P.O. Box 1860, Hot Springs National Park, AR 71902; phone (501) 624-3383.

Points of Interest

DISPLAY HOT WATER SPRINGS is behind Maurice Bathhouse at 369 Central Ave. These are the two thermal springs in Hot Springs National Park from which water still issues in open view. A thermal water cascade is on the Arlington Lawn at the north end of Bathhouse Row. **Hours:** Daily 24 hours. **Cost:** Free.

HOT SPRINGS MOUNTAIN OBSERVATION TOWER is off Fountain St. at 401 Hot Springs Mountain Dr. This 216-foot tower provides scenic views of the park, city and vicinity. Several towers have stood on the site, including the original wooden fire tower that was destroyed by lightning.

Note: Because of sharp switchbacks, vehicles more than 30 feet long cannot negotiate Hot Springs Mountain Drive. **Time:** Allow 30 minutes minimum. **Hours:** Daily 9-9, Memorial Day-Labor Day; 9-6, Mar. 1-day before Memorial Day and day after Labor Day-Oct. 31; 9-5, rest of year. Closed Jan. 1, Thanksgiving and Dec. 24-25. **Cost:** $7; $6 (ages 55+); $4 (ages 5-11). **Phone:** (501) 623-6035.

HOT SPRINGS NATIONAL PARK VISITOR CENTER is on Bathhouse Row. Housed in the historic Fordyce Bathhouse, the center offers displays about area history. The 1915 Spanish Renaissance-style building has marble and mosaic tile floors, stained-glass ceilings and ceramic fountains. Self-guiding and limited 45-minute guided tours are available. A movie is shown every 20 minutes. **Hours:** Open daily 9-5. Guided tours are given by volunteers; phone ahead for an appointment/reservation. Closed Jan. 1 and Dec. 25. **Cost:** Free. **Phone:** (501) 624-2701.

NATIONAL PARK DUCK TOURS depart 418 Central Ave., across from Historic Bath House Row in downtown. A 75-minute narrated sightseeing tour aboard amphibious vehicles takes visitors around St. John's Island and Lake Hamilton. **Time:** Allow 1 hour minimum. **Hours:** Daily 9:30-7:30, Memorial Day-Labor Day; 9:30-6, day after Labor Day-Oct. 31; 11-6, Mar. 1-day before Memorial Day; as weather permits, rest of year. **Cost:** Fare $15; $10 (ages 3-12); $2 (ages 0-2). Phone ahead to confirm rates. **Phone:** (501) 321-2911.

JACKSONPORT (B-5) pop. 235, elev. 229'

Once a river port for paddlewheelers from New Orleans, Memphis and St. Louis, Jacksonport is just below the confluence of the White and Black rivers. Although the venerable paddlewheelers no longer dock at Jacksonport, the town remains a river port.

JACKSONPORT STATE PARK is .8 mi. n. at 310 Adams St., between SR 69 and the White River. Swimming, boating, hiking and fishing are permitted. *See Recreation Chart and the AAA South Central CampBook.* **Hours:** Daily 8-5. **Cost:** Free. **Phone:** (870) 523-2143.

Jacksonport Courthouse Museum is in Jacksonport State Park, .8 mi. n., between SR 69 and the White River. This building dates from 1872. Museum tours offer a look back in history at the steamboat town of Jacksonport. Artifacts and exhibits interpret the use and operation of the courthouse in the 1800s as well as the life of the local citizens.

Hours: Tues.-Sat. 8-5, Sun. 1-5, during DST; Wed.-Sat. 8-5, rest of year. **Cost:** $3.25; $1.75 (ages 6-12). Combination ticket with *Mary Woods No. 2* Sternwheel Paddleboat $5.50; $3 (ages 6-12). **Phone:** (870) 523-2143.

Mary Woods No. 2 **Sternwheel Paddleboat** is in Jacksonport State Park, .8 mi. n. of Jacksonport, between SR 69 and the White River. This 1930s vessel moved barges of lumber to mills along the lower White River. Now a floating museum, it features exhibits and furnished cabins and common areas that tell the story of the working crew. **Hours:** Open Tues.-Thurs. 10-5, Fri.-Sat. 9-5, Sun. 1-5, Apr.-Oct. **Cost:** $3.25; $1.75 (ages 6-12). Combination ticket with Jacksonport Courthouse Museum $5.50; $3 (ages 6-12). **Phone:** (870) 523-2143.

JASPER (B-2) pop. 498, elev. 834'

Jasper, 4 miles south on the Little Buffalo River, an offshoot of the scenic Buffalo River, took its name from the jasper-green color of the waters of that stream. Passing through town, SR 7 is a Scenic Byway from Harrison north of Jasper to Hot Springs National Park.

In 1972 the Buffalo River, which travels 150 miles through bluffs as high as 440 feet and past wooded hillsides and cultural sites dating back 10,000 years, was designated the country's first National River. Waters range from relatively slow-moving to white-water upriver of Pruitt; the upriver section is generally floatable only in winter and spring. The many hiking trails along the river range from short day-use trails to routes for which a guide is suggested. Canoe rentals are available in Jasper. *See Recreation Chart and the AAA South Central CampBook.*

Jasper/Newton County Chamber of Commerce: 204 North Spring, P.O. Box 250, Jasper, AR 72641. **Phone:** (870) 446-2455 or (800) 670-7792.

JONESBORO (B-5) pop. 55,515, elev. 302'

More than 15,000 students attend Jonesboro's Arkansas State University. The school's 79,000-square-foot Fowler Center houses a 975-seat concert hall noted for its acoustics, a 344-seat theater and the 5,200-square-foot Bradbury Gallery of art.

ARKANSAS STATE UNIVERSITY MUSEUM is 2 mi. e. in the center of campus off Aggie Rd. at 110 Cooley Dr. Extensive displays relate to Arkansas' prehistory, native cultures, wildlife, pioneer era and military history. The museum also displays decorative glassware and changing exhibits. A historical library and reading room are open to visitors and the 10,000 students. **Time:** Allow 1 hour, 30 minutes minimum. **Hours:** Tues.-Fri. 9-4 (also Tues. 4-7), Sat. 9-5, Sun. 1-5. Closed major holidays and the week of Dec. 25. **Cost:** Free. **Phone:** (870) 972-2074.

FORREST L. WOOD CROWLEY'S RIDGE NATURE CENTER is 3.5 mi. s. on SR 141 to 600 E. Lawson Rd. Opened in 2004, this center focuses on the natural history of the 200-mile-long Crowley's Ridge, and the wildlife that inhabits it. Trails explore wetlands, forest and prairie areas. *See also Crowley's Ridge State Park p. 59.* **Time:** Allow 30 minutes minimum. **Hours:** Tues.-Fri. 8:30-4:30, Sat. 9-6, Sun. 1-5. Closed Jan. 1, Thanksgiving and Dec. 24-25. **Cost:** Free. **Phone:** (870) 933-6787.

LITTLE ROCK (D-3) pop. 183,133, elev. 300'

The profusion of roses in its residential areas has earned Little Rock, capital of Arkansas, the nickname "City of Roses." Settled in 1814 on a rocky bluff overlooking the Arkansas River, Little Rock became the seat of territorial government in 1821 when its population was less than 20. Except for a period during the Civil War when Federal troops under Gen. Fredrick Steele captured the city, it has remained the capital. It also is the state's largest city.

The oldest section of Little Rock is known as the Quapaw Quarter, a 9-square-mile area encompassing the city's central business district and adjacent residential neighborhoods. It includes many examples of Victorian and antebellum architectural styles. Of particular interest is the 1881 English-Gothic-style Cathedral of St. Andrew on the corner of Sixth and South Louisiana streets, with its stained-glass windows by the New York branch of Mayer of Munich; phone (501) 374-2794 for hours of accessibility.

Although no longer open to the public, the Villa Marre at 1321 S. Scott St. can be viewed as part of a driving or walking tour. Built in 1881 this combination Second Empire- and Italianate-style house gained fame in the 1980s when television producers and former Arkansas residents Harry Thomason and Linda Bloodworth-Thomason used the house's exterior to portray the Sugarbaker design firm on the CBS television series "Designing Women."

Riverfront Park comprises 17 acres containing walkways, terraces, plazas, recreation space, a 1,200-seat amphitheater, an activity center and a historical pavilion. The "little rock" for which the city was named is marked by a bronze plaque. Murray Lock and Dam and Murray Park are among the other popular riverbank attractions. The Henry Moore sculpture "Knife's Edge" graces a public plaza downtown at Main and Capitol streets.

River Rail Streetcars connect Little Rock and North Little Rock, with eight stops along the way. Stops include the Historic Arkansas Museum, the Museum of Discovery and the two chambers of commerce.

There are a variety of recreational offerings in the Little Rock area. A notable city event is Riverfest, held Friday through Sunday of Memorial Day weekend. Little Rock's visitor information center is in a historic antebellum building, circa 1842, called the Walters-Curran-Bell home but is commonly known as Curran Hall.

The Little Rock Visitor Information Center at Historic Curran Hall: 615 E. Capitol Ave., Little Rock, AR 72202. **Phone:** (501) 370-3290 or (877) 220-2568.

Self-guiding tours: Brochures describing three self-guiding walking tours of historic areas of Little Rock are available from the visitor information center. Highlights of the MacArthur Park neighborhood,

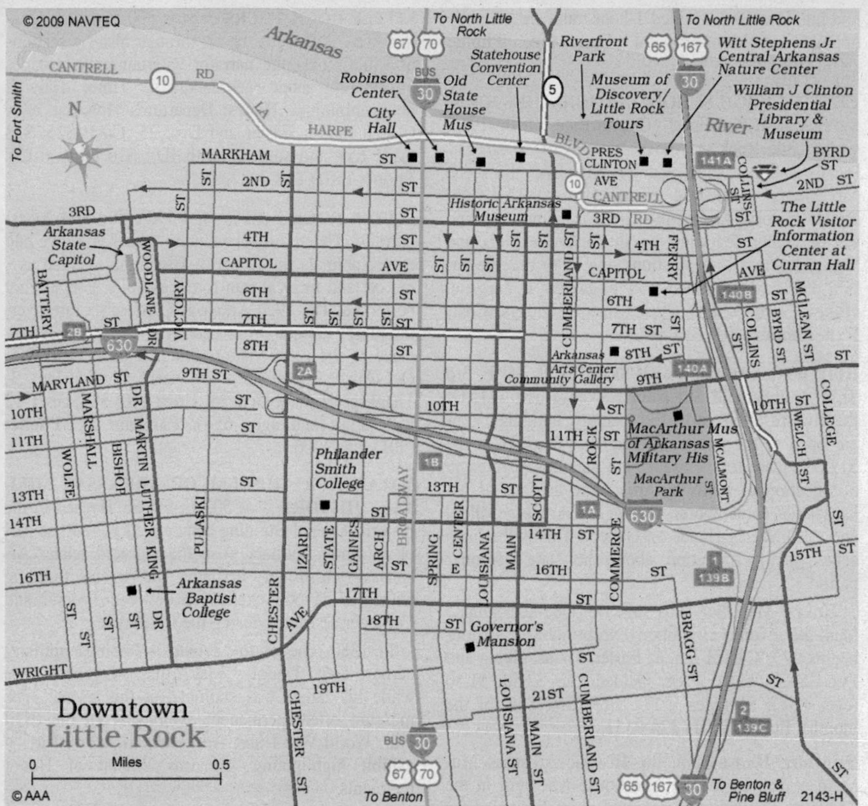

the downtown riverfront district and the governor's mansion area are covered in the tours, each of which can be completed in less than an hour.

Shopping areas: Park Plaza Shopping Center on University Avenue is anchored by Dillard's. The River Market District, on President Clinton Avenue, offers visitors an array of diverse shops, galleries, eateries and nightlife entertainment venues.

AEROSPACE EDUCATION CENTER is at 3301 E. Roosevelt at the Little Rock National Airport. The center features a NASA-sponsored exhibit, several historical aircraft and an aerospace library. The state-of-the-art, 150-seat EpiSphere theater presents planetarium shows and other immersive digital programs using a 360-degree domed screen and a cutting-edge surround sound system. The center's Giant Screen theater shows high-resolution, large-format films on a screen six stories high.

Hours: Tues.- Fri. 9:30-2 (also Fri. 6-9 p.m.), Sat. 11:30-8:15. Phone for titles and times of films and planetarium shows. Closed major holidays. **Cost:** Museum $5 (ages 17+). Museum and EpiSphere $7.75; $6.75 (ages 60+); $5.75 (ages 0-12). Museum, EpiSphere and Giant Screen theater $9.75; $8.75 (ages 60+); $5.75 (ages 0-12). Giant Screen theater $5.75. EpiSphere theater $5.75. **Phone:** (501) 371-0331.

ARKANSAS ARTS CENTER is in MacArthur Park at 9th and Commerce sts. The center contains nine galleries, a children's theater, a museum school and a decorative arts museum. Permanent exhibits include American and European paintings, drawings and sculpture from the 16th century to the present. Food is available 11-2. **Hours:** Center open Tues.-Sat. 10-5, Sun. 11-5. Closed major holidays. **Cost:** Free. **Phone:** (501) 372-4000.

Arkansas Arts Center Community Gallery is at 7th and Rock sts. Changing exhibits in this restored 1839 house feature works in various styles and media by local and regional artists and students. **Time:** Allow 1 hour minimum. **Hours:** When exhibitions are mounted the gallery is open Tues.-Sat. 10-5, Sun. 11-5; closed major holidays and between exhibitions. **Cost:** Donations. A fee may be charged for traveling exhibitions. **Phone:** (501) 372-4000, ext. 357, to verify the gallery is open.

ARKANSAS STATE CAPITOL is on W. Capitol Ave. Made of Arkansas white marble and granite, the building is patterned after the U.S. Capitol in Washington, D.C. An information desk is on the first floor. Exhibits include a mineral display; videotape programs are available. **Tours:** Guided tours are available. **Hours:** Open Mon.-Fri. 8-5, Sat.-Sun.

and holidays 10-3. Guided 1-hour tours are given by appointment Mon.-Fri. 9-4. **Cost:** Free. **Phone:** (501) 682-5080.

CENTRAL HIGH SCHOOL NATIONAL HISTORIC SITE is at 2125 Daisy L. Gatson Bates Dr. In 1957, while Little Rock was in the process of desegregating its public schools, Central High was the scene for events considered pivotal in national Civil Rights history. Across the street is a museum and visitor center featuring an interactive exhibit and two audiovisual presentations related to the integration crisis. A commemorative garden is on site. **Hours:** Daily 9-4:30. Closed major holidays. **Cost:** Free. **Phone:** (501) 374-1957.

HISTORIC ARKANSAS MUSEUM is at 200 E. 3rd St. at Cumberland St.; from I-30 take exit 141. Of the five restored early-19th-century buildings, four are open to the public. Among the offerings in the 51,000-square-foot museum are galleries devoted to a collection of items by artists and artisans of Arkansas, a contemporary Arkansas Artists' Gallery and a Children's Hands-on Gallery. This is the main center of interpretation about the state's frontier period.

Hours: Mon.-Sat. 9-5, Sun. 1-5. One-hour guided tours are given on the hour (except noon). Last tour begins at 3. Closed Jan. 1, Easter, Thanksgiving and Dec. 24-25. **Cost:** Free. Guided tour $2.50; $1.50 (ages 65+); $1 (ages 0-17); free (first Sun. of the month). **Phone:** (501) 324-9351.

Brownlee House is in the Historic Arkansas Museum at 200 E. 3rd St. The house was built in the 1840s by Scottish stonemason Robert Brownlee for his brother, James. The builder recuperated in the house from a mining accident before leaving for the California gold rush. The marbleized mantels are of particular interest.

Hinderliter Grog Shop is in the Historic Arkansas Museum at 200 E. 3rd St. Built of logs in the late 1820s, the shop was an important social institution—the settlement tavern where men gathered to talk, drink and gamble. Jesse Hinderliter and his family lived upstairs until 1834 in this, the oldest house in Little Rock. Legend has it that the last Territorial Legislature convened in the large log structure in 1835.

McVicar House is in the Historic Arkansas Museum at 200 E. 3rd St. Built in the 1840s by James McVicar, warden of the state prison, the house exemplifies the smaller Southern house of its time. The house is held together by white oak pegs and is furnished in period.

Woodruff Print Shop is in the Historic Arkansas Museum at 200 E. 3rd St. The site includes a house built in 1824 by William E. Woodruff, founder of the *Arkansas Gazette,* the oldest newspaper west of the Mississippi River. A reproduction 1820s print shop includes original furniture and a replica of the press Woodruff rafted up the Arkansas River.

LITTLE ROCK TOURS departs 500 President Clinton Ave. As the bus travels through historic sections of Little Rock, the narrator entertainingly provides information about each landmark. **Time:** Allow 2 hours minimum. **Hours:** Departures Mon.-Sat. at 1. Closed Jan. 1, Easter and Dec. 25. **Cost:** $25; $23 (ages 65+ and students with ID); $10 (ages 6-12). **Phone:** (501) 868-7287.

LITTLE ROCK ZOO is off I-630 exit 4 at 1 Jonesboro Dr. The zoo displays more than 725 native and exotic animals on 40 acres. Highlights include ape, big cat and tropical rain forest exhibits. Pets are not permitted. The 1924 Arkansas Carousel, a rare over-the-jumps antiquity, has been restored as the centerpiece of the zoo's visitor center. **Hours:** Daily 9-5, Oct.-Apr.; 9-4:30, rest of year. Closed Jan. 1, Thanksgiving and Dec. 25. **Cost:** $10; $8 (ages 1-12 with adult and ages 65+). **Parking:** $2. **Phone:** (501) 666-2406.

MacARTHUR MUSEUM OF ARKANSAS MILITARY HISTORY is at 503 E. 9th St. Housed in the historic Arsenal Building constructed in 1840 as part of a frontier military post, the museum relates Arkansas' rich military heritage. The Arsenal Building witnessed pivotal exchanges between Federal and Confederate forces during the Civil War.

In 1880, one of the country's foremost military heroes, Gen. Douglas MacArthur, was born here while his father was stationed at the arsenal. The museum offers permanent exhibits about the Civil War, World War I and World War II, as well as an exhibit highlighting Arkansas' Medal of Honor recipients.

Time: Allow 30 minutes minimum. **Hours:** Tues.-Fri. 9-4:30, Sat. 10-4, Sun. 1-4, Memorial Day-Labor Day; Tues.-Sat. 10-4, Sun. 1-4, rest of year. **Cost:** Donations. **Phone:** (501) 376-4602.

MUSEUM OF DISCOVERY is at 500 President Clinton Ave., Suite 150, in the historic riverfront district. Science and history displays are featured in such exhibit areas as Bug Zoo, Arkansas Indians, Passport to the World, Health Hall, Imagination Station, World of the Forest and Zoom Zone. Changing exhibits also are offered. **Note:** The museum will be closed for renovations beginning in late 2009; phone for scheduled reopening date. **Hours:** Mon.-Sat. 9-5, Sun. 1-5. Closed Jan. 1, Easter, Thanksgiving and Dec. 24-25. **Cost:** $8; $7 (ages 1-12 and 65+); free (second Sun. of the month). **Phone:** (501) 396-7050 or (800) 880-6475.

OLD STATE HOUSE MUSEUM is at 300 W. Markham at Center St. One of the finest examples of Doric architecture in the South, the house includes two chambers once used by the state legislature and supreme court. Designed by Gideon Shryock, it was begun in 1833 and completed in 1842; additions were made in 1885. When Arkansas became a state in 1836, the building served as the capitol. Displayed are items of state historical interest.

Hours: Mon.-Sat. 9-5, Sun. 1-5. Closed Jan. 1, Thanksgiving and Dec. 24-25. **Cost:** Free. **Phone:** (501) 324-9685.

WILLIAM J. CLINTON PRESIDENTIAL LIBRARY AND MUSEUM is at 1200 President Clinton Ave., just e. of I-30 exit 141A. This dramatic glass building cantilevers over the Arkansas River, representing a "bridge to the 21st century." State-of-the-art exhibits chronicle 8 years of the Clinton Administration.

Included in the 20,000 square feet of exhibition space are video stations, interactive displays, a collection of gifts the Clintons received in the White House and full-scale reproductions of the Oval Office and the Cabinet Room. The former president often stays in the modern penthouse suite above the museum.

Time: Allow 3 hours minimum. **Hours:** Mon.-Sat. 9-5, Sun. 1-5. Closed Jan. 1, Thanksgiving and Dec. 25. **Cost:** $7; $5 (ages 62+, retired military and college students with ID); $3 (ages 6-17); free (active-duty military with ID and to all on President's Day, July 4, Aug. 14, and Nov. 18). **Phone:** (501) 374-4242.

WITT STEPHENS JR. CENTRAL ARKANSAS NATURE CENTER is at 620 President Clinton Ave. The 16,232-square-foot building beside the Arkansas River in the River Market district features aquariums, a theater and exhibits promoting fish and wildlife management. A self-guiding tour begins with a 10-minute multimedia presentation about conservation. **Hours:** Tues.-Sat. 8:30-4:30, Sun. 1-5. Closed Jan. 1 and Dec. 24-25. **Cost:** Free. **Phone:** (501) 907-0636.

LONOKE (D-4) pop. 4,287, elev. 242′

JOE HOGAN STATE FISH HATCHERY is 1 mi. s. on US 70 at 23 Joe Hogan Ln. Considered the largest state-owned warm-water fish hatchery in the country, the facility has 56 ponds producing nearly 4 million fish annually for stocking public lakes and streams. The main species are largemouth bass, black and white crappie, bluegill and channel catfish. Spawning season is April through July. A visitor center features an aquarium and an observation platform.

Time: Allow 1 hour minimum. **Hours:** Daily 8-4:30. **Cost:** Free. **Phone:** (501) 676-6963.

MAMMOTH SPRING (A-4) pop. 1,147, elev. 515′

Named for its size, Mammoth Spring is the outlet of a subterranean river beginning far to the north. American Indian legend has it that the spring erupted as a chief dug a grave for his son, who had died searching for water. The Spring River, formed by the underground spring, is a popular spot for trout fishing and rafting.

MAMMOTH SPRING STATE PARK is on US 63 at jct. SR 9. The park contains Mammoth Spring, one of the nation's larger single springs. Water flow is estimated at 9 million gallons per hour. Some of the flow is stored in a nearby scenic lake. A restored 1886 train depot houses railroad memorabilia and local historical artifacts. Outside the depot stands a Frisco Railroad caboose. Paddleboat rides are available for a fee. *See Recreation Chart.*

Hours: Park open daily 8-dusk. Visitor information center open daily 8-6, Memorial Day weekend-Labor Day; 8-5, rest of year. Depot open Wed.-Sun. Phone to verify depot schedule. Closed Jan. 1 and Dec. 25. **Cost:** Park free. Depot $2.75; $1.50 (ages 6-12). Paddleboats and solo kayaks $4 for 30 minutes; $6 for 1 hour. Tandem kayaks $6 for 30 minutes; $8 for 1 hour. Fees are per boat, not per person. **Phone:** (870) 625-7364.

Mammoth Spring National Fish Hatchery and Aquarium is at 302 Fish Hatchery Ln. in Mammoth Spring State Park at jct. US 63 and SR 9. Established in 1903, the federal hatchery is one of the oldest in the country. The aquarium displays fish and marine life indigenous to the state, including paddlefish, sturgeon, Gulf Coast striped bass, rainbow trout and freshwater mussels. **Hours:** Daily 7-3:30. **Cost:** Free. **Phone:** (870) 625-3912.

MENA (D-1) pop. 5,637, elev. 1,145′

Bordering the Ouachita National Forest, Mena owes its growth to a resort built on Rich Mountain in 1896 by the Kansas City, Pittsburgh and Gulf Railroad. The resort and nearby Lake Wilhelmina were named after Queen Wilhelmina in honor of the railroad's Dutch ownership.

Talimena Scenic Drive (SR 88) begins in Mena and follows the high ridges of the Ouachita Mountains 54 miles west to Talihina, Okla. A number of overlooks along the route afford panoramas of the area.

Along the scenic drive, 13 miles northwest of Mena atop Rich Mountain, is Queen Wilhelmina State Park. At 2,681 feet, the park occupies one of the highest elevations in the state and features a lodge, restaurant and campsites. Phone (479) 394-2863 for park information, (800) 264-2477 for lodge reservations, or (479) 394-2864 for campsite reservations.

Mena/Polk County Chamber of Commerce: 524 Sherwood Ave., Mena, AR 71953. **Phone:** (479) 394-2912.

JANSSEN PARK is at 7th St. and Janssen Ave. The 10-acre park has two spring-fed lakes and a deer enclosure. Highlights include an 1851 log cabin. **Hours:** Daily dawn-dusk. **Cost:** Free.

MENA DEPOT CENTER is at 524 Sherwood Ave. The restored rail station houses a variety of artifacts and displays. Highlights include railroad memorabilia and arts and crafts exhibits. **Hours:** Mon.-Fri. 10-4. Closed major holidays. **Cost:** Free. **Phone:** (479) 394-2912.

MORRILTON (C-3) pop. 6,550, elev. 367′

Morrilton was built along the Little Rock & Fort Smith Railroad in the 1870s. The town's early trading business expanded after a highway bridge built over the Arkansas River increased Morrilton's accessibility. Local industries include plastics, clothing, food and automotive products.

Morrilton Area Chamber of Commerce: 120 N. Division St., P.O. Box 589, Morrilton, AR 72110. **Phone:** (501) 354-2393.

THE MUSEUM OF AUTOMOBILES is 16 mi. s.w. via SRs 9 and 154 on Petit Jean Mountain. More than 50 antique and classic automobiles are displayed. **Time:** Allow 30 minutes minimum. **Hours:** Daily 10-5. Closed Dec. 25. **Cost:** $7; $6.50 (ages 65+); $3.50 (ages 6-17); free (ages 0-5 with adult). **Phone:** (501) 727-5427.

GEM **PETIT JEAN STATE PARK** is 9 mi. s. on SR 9, then 12 mi. w. on SR 154 to Petit Jean Mountain Rd. Perched on flat-topped Petit Jean Mountain, the park boasts an array of natural features including 95-foot Cedar Falls, Indian Cave, Bear Cave, Rock House Cave and two gravel scenic drives overlooking Cedar Creek Canyon, Red Bluff Drive and the Palisades. The Seven Hollows region contains the unusual Turtle Rocks, the Grotto and the Petit Jean Natural Bridge.

The mountain's name is taken from the legend of a French girl who disguised herself as a boy and accompanied her sailor sweetheart to America. Many points of interest are reached by foot trails. *See Recreation Chart and the AAA South Central CampBook.*

Hours: Park open daily dawn-dusk. Visitor center open daily 8-8, Memorial Day weekend-Labor Day; Sun.-Thurs. 8-5, Fri.-Sat. 8-7, Mar. 1-day before Memorial Day weekend and day after Labor Day-Oct. 31; daily 8-5, rest of year. Closed Dec. 25. **Cost:** Free. **Phone:** (501) 727-5441.

MOUNTAIN PINE (D-2) pop. 772, elev. 470′

The town of Mountain Pine is so named because its economy is based on pine trees. The local lumber mill is the major industry.

LAKE OUACHITA STATE PARK is 12 mi. n. via SR 227 and Mountain Pine Rd. This 370-acre recreation area is on the shore of Arkansas' largest man-made body of water, Lake Ouachita. *See Recreation Chart and Hot Springs in the AAA South Central CampBook.* **Hours:** Park and visitor center open daily 8-8, Memorial Day weekend-Labor Day; 8-5, rest of year. Closed Thanksgiving and Dec. 25. **Cost:** Free. **Phone:** (501) 767-9366.

MOUNTAIN VIEW (B-3) pop. 2,876, elev. 770′

One of the Ozarks' most active crossroads is Mountain View, whose lively cultural heritage is evident in its community events. The annual GEM Arkansas Folk Festival and the Southern Regional Mountain and Hammer Dulcimer Workshop and Contest are held in April; mid-September brings the Arkansas Old-Time Fiddlers Association State Championship Competition; and mid-October brings the Fall Harvest Festival.

Mountain View Tourist Information Center: Court Square, P.O. Box 133, Mountain View, AR 72560. **Phone:** (870) 269-8068.

GEM **BLANCHARD SPRINGS CAVERNS** is 15 mi. n.w. on SR 14. Guided tours include three underground passageways. A visitor center has an exhibit hall and shows a 20-minute movie every half-hour.

The half-mile Dripstone Trail tour lasts 1 hour and covers a variety of cave formations in the upper level of the cave. The 1.2-mile Discovery Trail tour lasts 90 minutes and follows a cave stream and water-carved passages into the caverns' middle level. This trail has many steps and is not recommended for those with limited mobility or respiratory problems. For the more adventurous, the strenuous 4-hour, 2-mile Wild Cave tour explores the undeveloped reaches of the underground system. Cave gear is provided. The caverns are 58 degrees Fahrenheit and damp, and the floors tend to be wet; dress appropriately.

Hours: Dripstone Trail tour departs approximately every hour daily 9:30-5. Last tour begins at 4:15. Discovery Trail tour departs approximately every hour daily 9:30-4:30, Memorial Day weekend-Labor Day. Wild Cave tour departs daily at 10. Visitors are advised to arrive 30 minutes before departure. Visitor center open daily 9:30-6. Closed Jan. 1, Thanksgiving and Dec. 25.

Cost: Fee for trail tours $10; $5 (ages 6-15 and holders of National Forest Senior and National Parks Access passes). Fee for Wild Cave tour $75. A $25 non-refundable deposit is required. Ages 10-12 must be with an adult. Under 10 are not permitted. Reservations are suggested for the Dripstone Trail and Discovery Trail tours. Reservations are required for the Wild Cave tour. **Phone:** (870) 757-2211, or (888) 757-2246 for reservations or to verify tour times or fees.

GEM **OZARK FOLK CENTER** is 1.5 mi. n. via SRs 9/5/14, then 1 mi. w. on SR 382. The center focuses on the crafts, music, dance and oral history of an existing mountain folk culture. Local artisans demonstrate such skills as weaving and candle-making. Special events take place throughout the year.

Hours: Craft demonstrations are featured Wed.-Sat. 10-5, Apr.-Oct. Musical programs are presented in the auditorium at 7 p.m. on days when craft demonstrations are featured. The center is open on a limited schedule rest of year for workshops, special events and holiday offerings. **Cost:** For craft area or for musical program $10; $6 (ages 6-12). Combination crafts and musical program $17.50; $8.25 (ages 6-12); $40 (family, two adults and children ages 0-17). **Phone:** (870) 269-3851.

MURFREESBORO (E-1)

pop. 1,764, elev. 655′

Murfreesboro is the seat of Pike County, which was named for Lt. Zebulon M. Pike, who explored the Southwest in the early 1800s. The area's main agricultural pursuits are cattle and poultry raising and egg production.

Murfreesboro City Hall: 204 E. Main St., P.O. Box 251, Murfreesboro, AR 71958. **Phone:** (870) 285-3732.

CRATER OF DIAMONDS STATE PARK is 2 mi. s.e. on SR 301 at 209 State Park Rd. Called the only diamond-producing site in the world open to the public, the park allows visitors to keep any precious and semiprecious stones they find. More than 70,000 diamonds have been uncovered in this ancient volcanic crater since 1906, including the 16.37-carat Amarillo Starlight. The visitor center displays another find, the 1.1-carat cut Strawn-Wagner Diamond—one of the most perfect diamonds ever certified. The Diamond Springs Water Playground is open in the summer. *See Recreation Chart and the AAA South Central CampBook.*

Though not necessary, trowels are helpful in digging for stones. Rental equipment is available at the Diamond Discovery Center, which offers an instructional video and identification of finds. **Hours:** Park open daily 8-8, Memorial Day weekend-Labor Day; 8-5, rest of year. Water playground open daily noon-6, Memorial Day weekend-third weekend in Aug. Sat.-Sun. and Labor Day, fourth weekend in Aug.-Labor Day. Park closed Jan. 1, Thanksgiving and Dec. 25.

Cost: Park $7; $4 (ages 6-12). Water playground $5.50; $3.75 (0-41 inches tall); free (ages 0-2, limited to three children per paying adult). Ages 0-10 must be with an adult age 18+. **Phone:** (870) 285-3113.

KA-DO-HA INDIAN VILLAGE is 1.5 mi. n.w. of SR 27 to 1010 Caddo Dr. This excavated location of a Mound Builder village was populated about 1,000 years ago by Kadohadocho Indians. The site includes a trading post and a museum displaying tools, pottery, weapons and jewelry. Self-guiding tours and arrowhead hunting are available. **Hours:** Daily 9-6, Memorial Day weekend-Labor Day; 9-5, rest of year. Closed Thanksgiving and Dec. 25. **Cost:** $4; $2 (ages 6-13). **Phone:** (870) 285-3736.

NORTH LITTLE ROCK (C-3)

pop. 60,433, elev. 280′

If one man could be said to have created a city, William C. Faucette created North Little Rock. After he lost the 1903 mayoral election in Little Rock, Faucette and his lawyer friends introduced a bill in the Arkansas General Assembly making the section of Little Rock north of the Arkansas River a separate city. Faucette's bill was passed in 1917, making him a new mayor in a new city.

North Little Rock Visitors Bureau: 1 Eldor Johnson Dr. in Burns Park, P.O. Box 5511, North Little Rock, AR 72119. **Phone:** (501) 758-1424 or (800) 643-4690.

Shopping areas: McCain Mall, McCain Boulevard and US 67, counts Dillard's and Sears among its stores.

ARKANSAS INLAND MARITIME MUSEUM is at 100 Riverfront Park Dr. Guided tours of the USS *Razorback* take visitors to all areas of this Balao-class submarine, which served during World War II and the Vietnam War. The sub was later sold to the Turkish Navy and rechristened the *Murat Reis.*

Tours require a moderate level of physical activity that includes climbing up and down ladders; comfortable walking shoes are advised. Not recommended for children under 6. **Time:** Allow 30 minutes minimum. **Hours:** Wed.-Fri. 10-6, Sat. 10-7, Sun. 1-6, May 15-Labor Day; Fri.-Sat. 10-6, Sun. 1-6, rest of year. Closed major holidays. **Cost:** $6; $4 (ages 6-12, ages 62+ and military with ID). **Phone:** (501) 371-8320.

ARKANSAS QUEEN departs from the North Shore Maritime Center at 100 Riverfront Park Dr. The 3-deck sternwheeler with two climate-controlled decks and a topside observation deck offers a narrated 1.5-hour sightseeing cruise along the Arkansas River; lunch is available for an additional fee. Dinner and gospel music cruises also are available.

Hours: Sightseeing cruise departs Sat. at noon. Dinner cruise departs Fri.-Sat. at 7. Gospel music cruise departs some Mon. at 6:30. Boarding begins 30 minutes before departure. Phone ahead to confirm schedule. **Cost:** Sightseeing cruise with lunch $23.75; $17.75 (ages 3-12). Sightseeing cruise $14.50; $8 (ages 3-12). Dinner cruise $38. Rates may vary; phone ahead to confirm. Reservations are recommended. **Phone:** (501) 372-5777.

BURNS PARK is at jct. I-40 and SR 176 exit 150. The 1,575-acre park offers extensive recreational facilities, including soccer and rugby fields, basketball and bocce courts, fitness trails, disk golf, miniature golf, 18-hole golf courses, a waterslide and a playground. The indoor tennis complex has handball, racquetball and volleyball courts. A visitor center contains information about the park and attractions in North Little Rock and Arkansas. *See Recreation Chart and the AAA South Central CampBook.*

Hours: Park open daily 6 a.m.-midnight. Visitor center open daily 8:30-4:30. Closed major holidays. **Cost:** Free. Fees for activities. During Holiday Lights Display in Dec. $5 per private vehicle. **Phone:** (501) 791-8537, (501) 758-1424 for the visitor center, or (800) 643-4690 out of Ark.

THE OLD MILL AT T.R. PUGH MEMORIAL PARK is off Fairway Ave. at 3800 Lakeshore Dr. This picturesque replica of an 1830s gristmill appeared in the opening scene of "Gone With the

Wind." It is believed to be the last surviving structure used in the film. Mexican sculptor Dionicio Rodríguez formed wet cement by hand to achieve the look of natural wood. *Faux bois* sculptures in the surrounding park include trees, benches, mushrooms and an ornate "timber" bridge, all crafted from concrete. **Hours:** Daily 8 a.m.-10 p.m., Apr.-Oct.; 8-7, rest of year. **Cost:** Free. **Phone:** (501) 758-1424 or (800) 643-4690.

WILD RIVER COUNTRY is off I-40 exit 148, then .5 mi. w. to 6810 Crystal Hill Rd. This theme park offers water slides, a wave pool and other water-related amusements. A children's play area and facilities for volleyball and basketball also are provided. Lockers are available. **Hours:** Mon.-Sat. 10-8, Sun. noon-8, Memorial Day weekend-Labor Day. **Cost:** $29.99; $19.99 (0-48 inches tall); free (ages 0-2 and 60+). After 3 p.m. $19.99. **Phone:** (501) 753-8600.

OUACHITA NATIONAL FOREST

Elevations in the forest range from 360 ft. on the Fourche-LaFave River to 2,681 ft. at Rich Tower. Refer to AAA maps for additional elevation information.

In west-central Arkansas and southeastern Oklahoma, the 1,613,120-acre Ouachita National Forest is known for its mountain scenery, recreational opportunities and varied wildlife. The Ouachita Mountains run east and west, rather than north and south as do most American ranges. The novaculite found in this area is highly valued for making Arkansas whetstones, used for sharpening blade tools.

Talimena Scenic Drive provides 54 miles of mountain views along SRs 88 and 1 from near Mena to near Talihina, Okla. The Ouachita National Recreation Trail is a 186-mile east-west route through the mountains from SR 9 near Little Rock to Talimena State Park in Oklahoma. A nature center and three hiking trails are available at Kerr Arboretum and Nature Center, 19 miles south of Heavener, Okla. The Jessieville Visitor Center is open daily 9-5, March to October, weekdays 8-4:30 the rest of the year. The center is 18 miles north of Hot Springs in Jessieville and features the 1.5-mile Friendship Trail, a paved woodland loop.

Developed facilities are available at Lake Sylvia, south of Perryville off SR 9; Little Pines Recreation Area, 12 miles west of Waldron on SR 248; Shady Lake, 25 miles southeast of Mena; Cedar Lake, 10 miles south of Heavener, Okla., off US 270; Charlton Recreation Area near, 20 miles west of Hot Springs; Albert Pike Recreation Area, 6 miles north of Langley off SR 84; and Mill Creek, 5 miles east of "Y" City on US 270.

The forest contains six wilderness areas: Caney Creek, 14,460 acres 25 miles southeast of Mena; Black Fork Mountain, 12,151 acres shared with Oklahoma, 18 miles northwest of Mena; Poteau Mountain, 10,884 acres 35 miles south of Fort Smith; Flatside, 10,105 acres 16 miles southwest of Perryville; Dry Creek, 6,310 acres 12 miles southwest of Booneville; and Upper Kiamichi River, 9,371 acres 25 miles east of Talihina, Okla.

Park admission is free. Information about additional recreation areas within the forest and about camping fees can be obtained from the Forest Supervisor's Office, Ouachita National Forest, 100 Reserve St., P.O. Box 1270, Hot Springs, AR 71902; phone (501) 321-5202. *See Recreation Chart and the AAA South Central CampBook.*

OZARK NATIONAL FOREST

Elevations in the forest range from 420 ft. near the town of New Blaine to 2,753 ft. at Mount Magazine. Refer to AAA maps for additional elevation information.

In the Ozark Highlands and Boston Mountains of northwestern Arkansas, the four principal divisions of the Ozark National Forest total more than a million acres. Recreational activities such as hiking, camping, canoeing, horseback riding, hunting, fishing, mountain bicycle riding, swimming and picnicking can be enjoyed in the rugged beauty of the forest.

Blanchard Springs Caverns Recreation Area, off SR 14 north of Mountain View, features a large spring that gushes 1,200 gallons of water per minute; nearby are Blanchard Springs Caverns *(see Mountain View p. 52)*.

Alum Cove Natural Bridge Recreation Area, north of Deer on FR 1206, preserves a 130-foot-long natural arch. Cove Lake, a 160-acre mountain lake southeast of Paris on SR 309 near Mount Magazine offers camping, picnicking, swimming, fishing and boating. The 150-mile-long Ozark Highland Trail affords opportunities for hiking and nature study.

Information about the forest's many other recreation areas is available from the Forest Supervisor's Office, Ozark National Forest, 605 W. Main St., P.O. Box 1008, Russellville, AR 72801; phone (479) 968-2354. *See Recreation Chart and the AAA South Central CampBook.*

PARKIN (C-6) pop. 1,602, elev. 210'

PARKIN ARCHEOLOGICAL STATE PARK is n. at jct. US 64 and SR 184 to 60 SR 184N. Ongoing excavations indicate this 17-acre farming village was occupied 1000-1550 A.D. during the Mississippi Period. Many scholars believe it was the Casqui Indian village visited by Hernando de Soto in the summer of 1541 and recorded in his journals. A large ceremonial mound has been preserved along the St. Francis River. A 12-minute DVD presentation is offered.

Self-guiding tours are available. **Time:** Allow 1 hour minimum. **Hours:** Mon.-Sat. 8-5, Sun. 1-5, Apr.-Oct.; Tues.-Sat. and Mon. holidays 8-5, Sun 1-5, rest of year. Closed Jan. 1, Thanksgiving and Dec. 24-25. **Cost:** $3; $2 (ages 6-12); $10 (family). **Phone:** (870) 755-2500.

PEA RIDGE NATIONAL MILITARY PARK (A-1)

On US 62 about 9 mi. n.e. of Rogers, in northwest Arkansas, the 4,300-acre park was the site of the Battle of Pea Ridge, also known to the Confederacy as the Battle of Elkhorn Tavern. A reconstruction of the tavern is on the original site. Largely as a result of this battle, fought March 7-8, 1862, Union forces succeeded in securing the state of Missouri. A 7-mile self-guiding driving tour through the park provides insight into the battle. A small portion of the "Trail of Tears" also is within the park.

Park open daily 8-5, driving tour until 4:30; closed Jan. 1, Thanksgiving and Dec. 25. Admission $5 (per private vehicle). Phone (479) 451-8122.

PEA RIDGE NATIONAL MILITARY PARK VISITOR CENTER is 10 mi. n.e. of Rogers via scenic US 62. Museum exhibits and a 28-minute movie, "Thunder in the Ozarks," provide background on the battle. A driving tour of the battlefield begins at the center and travels to 10 stops, including Elkhorn Tavern, with markers and audio descriptions of key points. **Hours:** Center open daily 8-5, Apr.-Oct.; 9-4, rest of year. Closed Jan. 1, Thanksgiving and Dec. 25. **Cost:** Free with park admission. **Phone:** (479) 451-8122, ext. 227.

PINE BLUFF (D-4) pop. 55,085, elev. 215′

The second oldest city in the state, Pine Bluff was founded in 1819 as a trading post by Joseph Bonne, who dealt with the Quapaw Indians. Some of the houses on W. Barraque Street date from the Civil War period.

Alliance/Greater Pine Bluff Chamber of Commerce: 510 S. Main St., P.O. Box 5069, Pine Bluff, AR 71611. **Phone:** (870) 535-0110.

ARKANSAS RAILROAD MUSEUM is at 1720 Port Rd. Old repair shops of the Cotton Belt Railway house a steam locomotive and 14 vintage railroad cars, as well as such railroad memorabilia as photographs and train parts. **Hours:** Mon.-Sat. 9-2. Closed major holidays. **Cost:** Donations. **Phone:** (870) 535-8819.

DELTA RIVERS NATURE CENTER is at 1400 Black Dog Rd. Located within the Pine Bluff Regional Park on 130 acres of woodlands, this center features exhibits that depict the natural history of Arkansas' Delta region. Nature trails provide viewing opportunities of the area's vegetation and wildlife. A 20,000-gallon freshwater outdoor aquarium contains native fish species, snakes, turtles and alligators. Interactive displays also are offered.

Hours: Tues.-Sat. 8:30-4:30 (also Fri.-Sat. 4:30-7:30, Memorial Day-Labor Day), Sun. 1-5. Fish feeding time at the aquarium is Tues.-Fri. at 11, Sat.-Sun. at 3. Closed Jan. 1 and Dec. 24-25. **Cost:** Free. **Phone:** (870) 534-0011.

JEFFERSON COUNTY HISTORICAL MUSEUM is at 201 E. 4th St. Displays in the Union Station train depot chronicle historical events that shaped the county's development. **Hours:** Mon.-Fri. 9-4, Sat. 10-2. Closed major holidays. **Cost:** Free. **Phone:** (870) 541-5402.

SOUTHEAST ARKANSAS ARTS AND SCIENCE CENTER is at 701 S. Main St. Permanent and changing exhibits include paintings, sculpture and other works by local and international artists. **Hours:** Mon.-Fri. 10-5, Sat. 1-4. Closed major holidays. **Cost:** Free. **Phone:** (870) 536-3375.

POCAHONTAS (A-5) pop. 6,518, elev. 300′

Pocahontas, a historic river port town, overlooks the once traffic-laden Black River. The Old Randolph County Courthouse, an 1872 brick Victorian structure, is in the town square; a 4-foot meteorite that fell nearby in 1859 rests across the street on the lawn of the current courthouse. Boating and fishing for bream, crappie and bass are popular along the river.

Randolph County Chamber of Commerce: 107 E. Everett St., Pocahontas, AR 72455. **Phone:** (870) 892-3956.

OLD DAVIDSONVILLE STATE PARK is 2 mi. w. on US 62, then 9 mi. s.w. on SR 166 on the Black River. This site preserves the oldest post office, courthouse and land office in the state, built 1817-22. *See Recreation Chart and the AAA South Central CampBook.* **Hours:** Office open Sun.-Thurs. 8-5, Fri.-Sat. 8-8, Memorial Day weekend-July 4; daily 8-5, July 5-Nov. 30 and Mar. 1-Fri. before Memorial Day; Mon.-Fri. 8-5, Sat.-Sun. 8-noon, rest of year. Closed Jan. 1, Thanksgiving and Dec. 25. **Cost:** Free. **Phone:** (870) 892-4708.

POWHATAN (B-4) pop. 50, elev. 290′

POWHATAN HISTORIC STATE PARK is at 4414 SR 25. The park's centerpiece is a restored 1888 two-story brick courthouse containing official Lawrence County records dating from 1813. Exhibits depict the history of Powhatan. An 1873 restored limestone jail, which contains two original cells, is one of the restored buildings on the grounds. Tours include the courthouse, jail, restored residences, businesses and the 1854 Powhatan Academy.

Note: Entry into the historic buildings is by guided tour only; town site is self-guiding. **Hours:** Tues.-Sat. 8-3, Sun. 1-3. **Cost:** Town site admission free. Guided tours $5; $2.50 (ages 6-12); $12 (family). **Phone:** (870) 878-0032.

PRAIRIE GROVE (B-1) pop. 2,540, elev. 174′

PRAIRIE GROVE BATTLEFIELD STATE PARK is e. on US 62. Marking the site of a Civil War battle fought on Dec. 7, 1862, the 838-acre park contains a 55-foot monument, 19th-century houses and buildings, a museum and a walking trail. Interpretive programs include living-history presentations. In even-numbered years the battle is re-created. A 55-minute

CD provides directions for a self-guiding tour, descriptions and recollections of participants and their families.

Hours: Park open daily 8-dusk. Museum open daily 8-5; closed Jan. 1, Thanksgiving, Dec. 24 (noon-5) and Dec. 25. **Cost:** Park free. Museum $3; $2 (ages 6-12); $10 (family). CD $4. **Phone:** (479) 846-2990.

ROGERS (A-1) pop. 38,829, elev. 1,384'

The first train steamed into the settlement now known as Rogers in 1881, 22 years after the Butterfield Overland Mail established a way station in town. Spanish and French pioneers once walked this territory, as did American Indians forced westward on the "Trail of Tears" and Civil War soldiers. Nearby recreation areas offer outdoor activities.

The historic War Eagle Mill, 11045 War Eagle Rd., is a reconstruction of an 1873 mill that burned down in 1924. This still working gristmill—the fourth mill built on this site along the War Eagle River, features an 18-foot undershot waterwheel made of cypress. The War Eagle Mill Arts and Crafts Fair is held here in October.

Rogers Chamber of Commerce: 317 W. Walnut St., Rogers, AR 72756. **Phone:** (479) 636-1240.

HOBBS STATE PARK-CONSERVATION AREA is 10 mi. e. at 21392 SR 12E. The 11,764-acre park along the southern shores of Beaver Lake is part of the large-scale power and flood control project in the White River Basin. The terrain offers plateaus, ridges, valleys, a forest and streams and harbors abundant wildlife. Its waters offer large- and small-mouth bass, crappie, bream, channel catfish and northern pike. The visitor center features interactive exhibits, a cave diorama, a wildlife viewing area and an orientation film. *See Recreation Chart and the AAA South Central CampBook.*

Campsites are primitive and at the end of a 4-mile hike. **Hours:** Park open daily 24 hours. Trails open daily 7 a.m.-1 hour after dusk. Firing range open Tues.-Sun. 8-7, during DST; 8-5, rest of year. Visitor center daily 8-5. **Phone:** (479) 789-5000.

THE ROGERS DAISY AIRGUN MUSEUM is at 202 W. Walnut St. The history of air guns and especially Daisy brand air guns is told through exhibits of the guns and their allied advertisements, packaging and promotional premiums. **Time:** Allow 30 minutes minimum. **Hours:** Mon.-Sat. 10-5. Closed major holidays. **Cost:** $2; free (ages 0-16). **Phone:** (479) 986-6873.

ROGERS HISTORICAL MUSEUM is at 322 S. 2nd St. This museum provides permanent and changing historical exhibits, including the 1895 Hawkins House, furnished in the Victorian period. Storefront replicas of a bank, barber shop and store make up First Street. The Attic is a hands-on display for children. In nearby Frisco Park the museum's Frisco caboose is open May through October. **Time:** Allow 1 hour minimum. **Hours:** Tues.-Sat. 10-4. Closed major holidays. **Cost:** Free. **Phone:** (479) 621-1154.

WAR EAGLE CAVERN is 17 mi. e. on SR 12 to 21494 Cavern Dr. Set in the Ozark mountains on the shores of Beaver Lake, the cavern once sheltered American Indians. Guided 1-hour tours reveal stalactites, stalagmites, fossils and an underground stream; a nature trail is on the grounds. The cave also is home to 100,000 Arkansas brown and grey bats. A cave maze challenges participants to find their way out. Aboveground activities include gemstone panning and the "Lost in the Woods Maze."

Cave temperature is 58 degrees F. **Time:** Allow 1 hour minimum. **Hours:** Tours Mon.-Sat. 9:30-5, Sun. noon-5, mid-Mar. through Oct. 31; Sat.-Sun. noon-5, Nov. Last tour begins 30 minutes before closing. **Cost:** Fee $11.50; $6.75 (ages 4-11). **Phone:** (479) 789-2909.

ST. CHARLES (D-5) pop. 261, elev. 200'

During the Civil War battle of June 17, 1862, a cannonball was shot through a porthole of the federal ironclad *Mound City* on the White River at St. Charles. Called by some historians the most destructive single shot of the war, it hit a steam pipe and killed nearly 100 soldiers.

WHITE RIVER NATIONAL WILDLIFE REFUGE is off SR 1 along the White River. The refuge consists of 160,000 acres of actively managed land, largely bottomland hardwood forest, with 90 miles of river and 356 lakes. This is a wintering area for large numbers of ducks and Canada geese. The visitor center offers natural history exhibits, films and a wildlife diorama depicting habitats and animals found at the refuge. Camping, hunting and fishing are available by permit. **Hours:** Refuge open daily 24 hours. Visitor center open Mon.-Fri. 8-4, Sat. 9-5, Sun. 1-5. Closed major holidays. **Cost:** Free. **Phone:** (870) 282-8200.

ST. FRANCIS NATIONAL FOREST (D-6)

Elevations in the forest range from 150 ft. on the Mississippi River to 320 ft. at Crowley's Ridge. Refer to AAA maps for additional elevation information.

In east-central Arkansas, St. Francis National Forest covers 20,977 acres at the south end of a 200-mile-long ridge that rises above the surrounding flat farmlands. The forest offers picnicking, camping, fishing, boating, swimming and hiking.

Developed recreation areas are at 625-acre Bear Creek Lake, 8 miles south of Marianna on SR 44, and at 420-acre Storm Creek Lake, 6 miles north of West Helena on SR 44. For additional information contact the Forest Supervisor, St. Francis National Forest, Box 2675, SR 44, Marianna, AR 72360; phone (870) 295-5278. *See Recreation Chart and the AAA South Central CampBook.*

SALESVILLE (A-3) pop. 437, elev. 772′

NORFORK DAM AND LAKE is at 1414 SR 177S. Part of a power and flood control project in the White River Basin, the area comprises a major recreation center offering camping, swimming and other water activities. Trout fishing is popular in the area; a federal trout hatchery just below the dam is open for self-guiding tours. *See Recreation Chart and the AAA South Central CampBook.* **Hours:** Daily 7:30-3:30. **Cost:** Free. **Phone:** (870) 425-2700 for general information, or (870) 499-5255 for the hatchery.

SCOTT (D-4) pop. 94, elev. 249′

PLANTATION AGRICULTURE MUSEUM is at jct. US 165 and SR 161. Exhibits in this 1912 general store trace the state's cotton planting heritage and plantation life from statehood in 1836 through World War II, when farm mechanization became the agricultural standard. **Time:** Allow 1 hour minimum. **Hours:** Tues.-Sat. and Mon. holidays 8-5, Sun. 1-5. Closed Jan. 1, Thanksgiving and Dec. 24-25. **Cost:** $3; $2 (ages 6-12); $10 (family). **Phone:** (501) 961-1409.

TOLTEC MOUNDS ARCHEOLOGICAL STATE PARK is 4 mi. s.e. off US 165. The park preserves the remains of prehistoric earthworks called the Toltec Mounds. Once believed to be the work of Toltec Indians from Mexico, these large mounds were probably constructed by an early American group of the Plum Bayou culture. Built A.D. 650-1050, the mounds were abandoned by 1400. Some of the 18 mounds were foundations for temples and houses, while others were burial sites.

Self-guiding tours are offered along a .7-mile trail emphasizing site preservation and research. **Hours:** Park and visitor center open Mon.-Sat. 8-5, Sun. noon-5. Closed Jan. 1, Thanksgiving and Dec. 24-25. **Cost:** $3; $2 (ages 6-12); $10 (family). **Phone:** (501) 961-9442.

SHERIDAN (D-3) pop. 3,872, elev. 228′

GRANT COUNTY MUSEUM is off SR 46 at 521 Shackleford Rd. Pioneer, American Indian and Civil War artifacts pertain to the county's history. Also featured are log buildings, including a cabin built about 1850. A history research library is available. **Hours:** Tues.-Sat. 9-4. Closed major holidays. **Cost:** $3; $1 (ages 6-18); free (Grant County residents). **Phone:** (870) 942-4496.

SMACKOVER (F-3) pop. 2,005, elev. 120′

French explorers described this heavily wooded area as *sumac couvert,* meaning "covered with sumac." The Anglicized version became Smackover. The name would become famous in 1922 with the discovery of the Smackover oil field, one of the country's largest petroleum reservoirs. The town's population swelled from 90 to 25,000 in months. Though production declined in the 1930s, oil continues to be a mainstay of the local economy.

ARKANSAS MUSEUM OF NATURAL RESOURCES is on the SR 7 bypass. Indoor and outdoor exhibits illustrate drilling methods and production techniques at this museum, which chronicles the history and development of the oil and brine industry and its impact on the area. Films and displays describe the 1920s oil boom. **Hours:** Mon.-Sat. and holidays 8-5, Sun. 1-5. Closed Jan. 1, Thanksgiving and Dec. 25. **Cost:** Free. **Phone:** (870) 725-2877.

SPRINGDALE (A-1) pop. 45,798, elev. 1,329′

ARKANSAS AND MISSOURI RAILROAD departs from the depot at 306 E. Emma Ave. Travelers ride in comfort aboard restored late 19th- and early 20th-century passenger cars on an 8-hour, 134-mile round-trip train ride through the scenic Boston Mountains to Van Buren. The full-day ride includes a 2.5-hour stopover. Friday and Saturday round-trips from Van Buren to Winslow, and Sunday round-trips from Fort Smith to Winslow also are offered. *See also Van Buren p. 58.*

Hours: Springdale-to-Van Buren trips depart Fri.-Sat. at 8, Apr.-Sept.; Wed. and Fri.-Sat. at 8, Oct.-Dec. **Cost:** Springdale-to-Van Buren fare (Apr.-Sept.) $45-$75; $41-$69 (ages 65+); $22-$37 (ages 4-12). Springdale-to-Van Buren fare (Oct.-Dec.) $60-$90; $54-$82 (ages 65+); $30-$40 (ages 4-12). Phone to confirm schedule and fares. Reservations are recommended. **Phone:** (479) 751-8600 or (800) 687-8600.

SHILOH MUSEUM OF OZARK HISTORY is at 118 W. Johnson Ave. This 2-acre regional history museum consists of various displays that focus on those who shaped Ozark history—the past residents of the area. Seven historic buildings, including a log cabin outhouse, an oak barn and the Searcy House, also are on site. Free guided tours of the Searcy House are available. Changing exhibits are offered year-round. **Time:** Allow 30 minutes minimum. **Hours:** Mon.-Sat. 10-5. Closed Jan. 1, Thanksgiving and Dec. 24-25. **Cost:** Donations. **Phone:** (479) 750-8165.

STUTTGART (D-4) pop. 9,745, elev. 228′

Surrounding Stuttgart is the rice-producing section of the Grand Prairie region, also known as one of the finest fishing areas in the country. The rice fields and the many lakes and reservoirs in the area offer excellent feeding and resting places for waterfowl.

Stuttgart hosts the Wings Over the Prairie Festival, featuring the World Championship Duck Calling Contest, in November.

Stuttgart Chamber of Commerce: 507 S. Main St., Stuttgart, AR 72160. **Phone:** (870) 673-1602.

MUSEUM OF THE ARKANSAS GRAND PRAIRIE is just n. of the city park at 921 E. 4th St. The museum contains reproductions of an 1880 homestead and an 1890 village as well as a two-thirds scale model of an 1869 church, a 1914 schoolhouse and replicas of a fire station and a newspaper office. Included are exhibits about prairie farming, wildlife, duck hunting and toys.

A videotape shows rice, soybean and fish farming; a mini-theater videotape traces the history of local crop dusting. **Time:** Allow 1 hour minimum. **Hours:** Tues.-Fri. 8-4, Sat. 10-4. Closed major holidays. **Cost:** Donations. **Phone:** (870) 673-7001.

TEXARKANA (E-1) pop. 26,448, elev. 290′

The Arkansas-Texas state line runs approximately through the center of the dual municipality of Texarkana, which has a combined population of about 61,000.

For hundreds of years before European settlement in the area, the Great Southwest Trail, the major route between the American Indian villages of the Mississippi Valley and the West and Southwest, crossed the area around what is now Texarkana. The Grand Caddoes, hospitable to explorers and settlers, farmed in the vicinity and maintained six villages along the banks of the Red River.

Shortly after 1840 a permanent settlement was established at Lost Prairie, 15 miles east of Texarkana. A number of mounds and other traces of former American Indian civilizations remain within a 30-mile radius of the town.

During the 1850s the Cairo and Fulton Railroad served portions of Arkansas and by 1874 had crossed the Red River into Texas, establishing direct rail service to St. Louis. The Texas and Pacific Railroad had laid track to the Arkansas boundary, and the place where the two lines met became a town—Texarkana.

The state line runs through the middle of the Texarkana Post Office and Courthouse, said to be the only federal building situated in two states. Built in 1932 of pink granite from Texas and limestone from Arkansas, the post office has two separate zip codes. Residents on both sides of the border enjoy the Perot Theatre, 221 Main St., a restored 1924 facility that presents a variety of Broadway shows.

Texarkana Chamber of Commerce: 819 State Line Ave., Texarkana, TX 75501. **Phone:** (903) 792-7191 or (877) 275-5289.

ACE OF CLUBS HOUSE MUSEUM is at 420 Pine St. This 22-sided house was built in 1885 reputedly from the winnings of a poker game. The Italianate Victorian-style building has three octagonal wings and one rectangular wing and features original furniture. A 15-minute videotape presentation is followed by a 1-hour guided tour. High heels and photography are not permitted. **Time:** Allow 1 hour, 30 minutes minimum. **Hours:** Tues.-Sat. 10-4. Last tour begins 1 hour before closing. Closed major holidays. **Cost:** $6; $5 (ages 60+); $4 (students with ID). **Phone:** (903) 793-4831.

DISCOVERY PLACE CHILDREN'S MUSEUM is at the corner of Pine St. and State Line Ave. at 215 Pine St. Educational and entertaining hands-on exhibits focus on science and history. A theater, a science lab and a 12-foot sound wall sculpture enhance the learning environment. **Time:** Allow 1 hour minimum. **Hours:** Tues.-Sat. 10-4. Closed major holidays. **Cost:** $4.50; free (ages 0-4). **Phone:** (903) 793-4831.

MUSEUM OF REGIONAL HISTORY is 4 blks. s. of US 59/67/71/82 at 219 N. State Line Ave. Housed in an 1879 brick building, this museum traces the region's history from the early Caddo Indians through 20th-century citizens, including early industry, post World War II and the civil rights movement. In addition to the Native American Gallery, the Scott Joplin Gallery is dedicated to the composer's early life and career in Texarkana. **Hours:** Tues.-Sat. 10-4. Closed major holidays. **Cost:** $5; $4 (ages 60+); $3.50 (students with ID and children ages 6+). **Phone:** (903) 793-4831.

VAN BUREN (B-1) pop. 18,986, elev. 406′

Settled in 1818, Van Buren is one of the oldest settlements in western Arkansas. It was a steamboat landing, a stage stop for the Butterfield Line from St. Louis to California, a main artery for commerce and the border between the Cherokee and Choctaw tribes.

A 10-block downtown area has been restored to its late 19th-century appearance, complete with old-fashioned lamps and period storefronts. Included in the restoration project are the Albert Pike Schoolhouse, Crawford County Courthouse, Mount Olive Church, Fairview Cemetery and the waterfront.

Van Buren Visitor Center: Old Frisco Depot at 813 Main St., P.O. Box 1518, Van Buren, AR 72957. **Phone:** (479) 474-6164 or (800) 332-5889.

Self-guiding tours: The Van Buren Walking Tour features 52 stops. A brochure featuring a map of the path and descriptions of the stops is available from the visitor center.

ARKANSAS AND MISSOURI RAILROAD departs from 813 Main in the Old Frisco Depot. A 70-mile round-trip train ride travels through the Boston Mountains. The 2.5-hour ride in restored early late 19th- and early 20th-century passenger cars takes passengers over three trestles, through the Winslow tunnel and offers scenic views of the mountains. An 80-mile, 3-hour trip from Fort Smith to Winslow departs the Old Frisco Depot at 100 Garrison. *See also Springdale p. 57.*

Hours: Round trips to Winslow depart Fri.-Sat. at 11, Apr.-Sept.; Wed. and Fri.-Sat. at 11, Oct.-Dec. Round trips from Fort Smith to Winslow Sat. at 11, Jan.-Mar. **Cost:** Van Buren-to-Winslow fare (Apr.-Sept.) $30-$62; $27-$57 (ages 65+); $15-$26 (ages 4-12). Van Buren-to-Winslow fare (Oct.-Dec.) $40-$72; $36-$66 (ages 65+); $20-$31 (ages 4-12). Fort Smith to Winslow fare $40-$62; $36-$56 (ages 65+); $20-$31 (ages 4-12). Phone to confirm schedules and fares. Reservations are recommended. **Phone:** (479) 751-8600 or (800) 687-8600.

WALCOTT (B-5) elev. 340′

CROWLEY'S RIDGE STATE PARK is at 2092 SR 168. The 270-acre park is in a hardwood forest atop Crowley's Ridge, a rare geological formation extending for some 200 miles from southern Missouri to eastern Arkansas. Composed of deposits of wind-blown silt, or loess, the ridge is believed to be unique in the Western Hemisphere; another exists in Siberia. A gravesite monument to Benjamin Crowley honors the first settler in the area and a soldier in the War of 1812. *See also Forrest L. Wood Crowley's Ridge Nature Center p. 48, Recreation Chart and the AAA South Central CampBook.*

Hours: Park open daily 8 a.m.-10 p.m. Visitor center open daily 8-5 (also Fri.-Sat. 5-8, Memorial Day weekend-July 4). Closed Jan. 1 and Dec. 25. **Cost:** Free. **Phone:** (870) 573-6751.

WASHINGTON (E-1) pop. 148, elev. 375′

Founded in 1825, Washington was a crossroads for travelers in every direction during the 1800s. The Southwest Trail, the earliest road across Arkansas, ran from Missouri through Little Rock and Washington to Fulton, near the Texas border. From 1831 to 1833 more than 3,000 Choctaw Indians, forcibly evicted from Mississippi, passed through Washington on their way to Oklahoma.

Texas frontiersman Sam Houston planned the Texas Revolution of 1835-36 in a Washington tavern in 1834. During the Civil War the town became the Confederate state capital after Little Rock fell to Union forces. In 1875 and again in 1883 fires destroyed much of the business district, and Washington's glory began to fade. In 1938 Hope replaced Washington as Hempstead county seat.

OLD WASHINGTON HISTORIC STATE PARK is at jct. US 278 and SR 195 at 100 S.W. Morrison. This restored village showcases 19th-century buildings and typical lifestyles of southwest Arkansas. More than 30 structures include the 1857 Augustus M. Crouch House and the 1874 Hempstead County Courthouse, which serves as the park visitor center. Various buildings are open for tours, depending on the day's interpretive theme, and docents in period costume greet visitors at each site. Christmas and Candlelight on the first Saturday in December is a highlight. Period decorations and 3,000 luminaria deck the village for this holiday event, which features strolling minstrels and carolers, candlelight tours of the buildings, surrey rides and free refreshments.

Note: Some 150 people live in Old Washington in private residences; not all buildings are open to the public. **Time:** Allow 2 hours minimum. **Hours:** Park open daily 8-5. Structures open for guided tours daily 9-noon and 1-5 (also 5-8 the first and second Sat. in Dec. for Christmas and Candlelight). Tickets must be purchased from the visitor center. Closed Jan. 1, Thanksgiving and Dec. 25. **Cost:** $8; $4 (ages 6-12). First and second Sat. in Dec. $10; $5 (ages 6-12). **Phone:** (870) 983-2684.

1836 Hempstead County Courthouse is in Old Washington Historic State Park at 409 Franklin St. Washington's schoolhouse from 1875-1914, the building first served as a courthouse and then the seat of Confederate government in Arkansas when Federal troops occupied Little Rock 1863-65.

Blacksmith Shop is in Old Washington Historic State Park at 600 Conway. This reconstruction of a frontier blacksmith shop commemorates the place where James Black reputedly made the first of what came to be known as Bowie knives. Bowie, who lived in Texas, liked Black's design and bought from him.

Block-Catts House is in Old Washington Historic State Park on the n.e. corner of Jay and Conway sts. Abraham Block built this two-story, frame, Federal-style building in 1832 and reared his 12 children in it.

B.W. Edwards Weapons Museum is in Old Washington Historic State Park at 201 Franklin St. More than 700 firearms, knives and swords are displayed in a 1925 bank.

Crouch House is on the corner of Carroll and Morrison sts. in Old Washington Historic State Park. This Greek Revival home was constructed by Augustus Crouch in 1856. Moved to its present site and restored, the house has been set aside for the study of architecture. Displays of tools and building methods reflect the period.

Print Museum is on n.w. corner of Izard and Franklin sts. in Old Washington Historic State Park. This 1915 building once was the town's post office and a bank. The printing and telegraph equipment now displayed dates from the early 1800s. Tour guides relate the history and operation of the apparatus. **Time:** Allow 30 minutes minimum.

Purdom House is in Old Washington Historic State Park at 202 S.W. Morrison. The restored 1850 house was the residence of Dr. James A.L. Purdom until his death in 1866. Period medical artifacts are displayed.

Royston House is in Old Washington Historic State Park at 105 S.W. Water St. Restored and furnished in period with some original artifacts, the house dates from 1845. It was the home of Gen. Grandison D. Royston, who served in two of the state's constitutional conventions and in the Confederate Congress.

Royston Log Cabin is on n.w. corner Jay and Conway sts. in Old Washington Historic State Park. This 1832 log cabin has furnishings and items commonly used in the early and mid-1800s. A section of the siding has been removed from the back porch to show the construction of the cabin.

Sanders Farmstead is in Old Washington Historic State Park at 105 S.W. Carroll. The Greek Revival structure is restored and furnished in period. Dating from 1849, this was the home of Simon T. Sanders, county clerk for 30 years.

The Tavern Inn is in Old Washington Historic State Park at 4954 SR 278 N. Containing many period pieces, the inn re-creates the atmosphere of 18th-century taverns that served such travelers as Davy Crockett and Jim Bowie, as well as troops en route to the Mexican War.

Trimble House is on the n.e. corner of Southwest Tr./SR 195 and Washington St. in Old Washington Historic State Park. Built in 1847 as the home of Probate Court Judge John D. Trimble, the house interprets the lives of four generations of the Trimble family, the only family to occupy the dwelling.

WEST FORK (B-1) pop. 2,042, elev. 1,339'

DEVIL'S DEN STATE PARK is 17 mi. s.w. on SR 170. The park encompasses 2,000 acres in a rugged, scenic valley of the Ozark Mountains. The park contains Devil's Den Cave and the Devil's Ice Box, where the temperature never rises above 60 degrees Fahrenheit. A videotape presentation is available at the visitor center at the intersection of SRs 170 and 74. Interpretive programs also are offered. *See Recreation Chart and the AAA South Central CampBook.*

Hours: Park open daily 8-dusk. Visitor center open daily 8-5 (also Fri.-Sat. 5-8, Memorial Day weekend-Labor Day). **Cost:** Free. **Phone:** (479) 761-3325.

WILSON (B-6) pop. 939, elev. 559'

The town of Wilson owes its success to the prosperity of Robert E. Lee Wilson. An orphan at 15, Wilson was a small-scale farmer who invested his savings wisely in the 1890s and turned a 2,100-acre swamp into one of the largest cotton plantations in the world. The cotton-growing R.E. Lee Wilson Co. and other Wilson-owned businesses became the cornerstone of the town's economy.

HAMPSON ARCHAEOLOGICAL MUSEUM STATE PARK is .2 mi. n. on US 61 at 2 Lake Dr. The museum displays American Indian artifacts unearthed from the Nodena site on the Mississippi River. A farming-based civilization occupied the 15-acre palisaded village from about 1350 to 1600. **Hours:** Tues.-Sat. and Mon. holidays 8-5, Sun. 1-5. Closed Jan. 1, Thanksgiving and Dec. 24-25. **Cost:** $2.75; $1.75 (ages 6-12); $9 (family). **Phone:** (870) 655-8622.

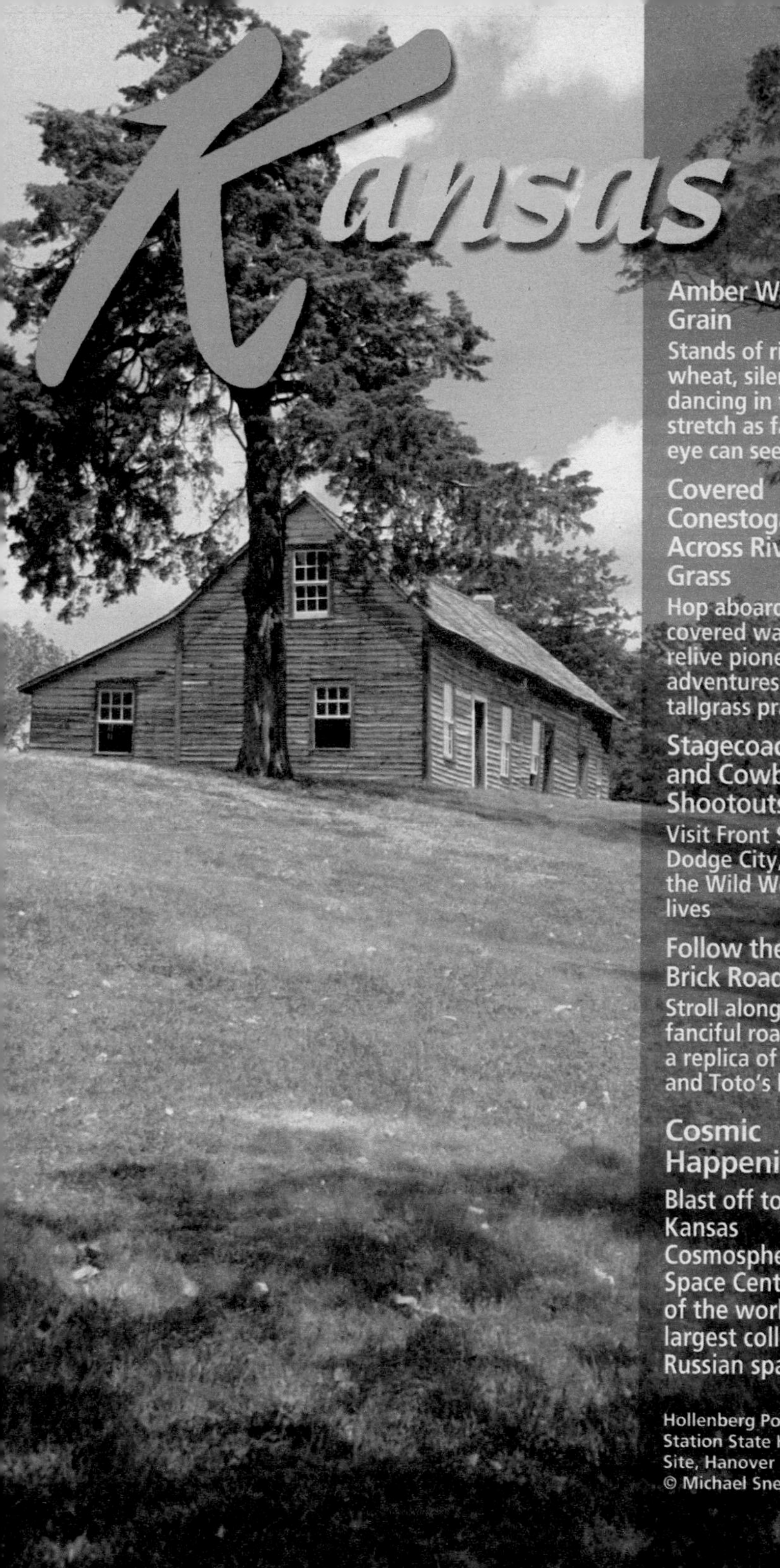

Kansas

Amber Waves of Grain

Stands of rippling wheat, silently dancing in the wind, stretch as far as the eye can see

Covered Conestogas Sail Across Rivers of Grass

Hop aboard a covered wagon and relive pioneering adventures on the tallgrass prairie

Stagecoach Rides and Cowboy Shootouts

Visit Front Street in Dodge City, where the Wild West still lives

Follow the Yellow Brick Road

Stroll along the fanciful road to visit a replica of Dorothy and Toto's house

Cosmic Happenings

Blast off to the Kansas Cosmosphere and Space Center, home of the world's largest collection of Russian space suits

Hollenberg Pony Express Station State Historic Site, Hanover

Front Street, Dodge City / © SuperStock

The Sunflower State. The Jayhawker State. The Wheat State. Midway, U.S.A.

All are fitting nicknames for Kansas, a state where the history is rich and the landscape surprisingly varied.

However, a strong argument could be made for The Pioneer State as an apropos moniker. Indeed, the state has seen its fair share of visionaries and has been the site of enough famous firsts.

Atchison native Amelia Earhart was the first woman to fly solo across the Atlantic. Frank E. Petersen of Topeka was the first African-American brigadier general in the Marine Corps. Argonian Susan Madora Salter was the first female mayor in the United States.

Kansas was the first state to ratify the amendment that allowed African-Americans the right to vote. A pair of brothers borrowed $600 to open the first Pizza Hut restaurant. And Independence was the hometown of Miss Able, the first monkey in space.

Kansas entrepreneurs invented the autopilot, the helicopter and the O'Henry candy bar. And native Walter P. Chrysler founded a cornerstone of the American automobile industry: the Chrysler Corporation.

Constant winds stir much more than fields of grain and flowers. They blow in ideas, visions and dreams.

A cyclone rips through the Kansas prairie, flinging the house in which Dorothy and her dog are held captive into "...the midst of a country of marvelous beauty. There were lovely patches of greensward all about, with stately trees bearing rich and luscious fruits. Banks of gorgeous flowers were on every hand, and birds with rare and brilliant plumage sang and fluttered in the trees and bushes."

But author L. Frank Baum needn't have tossed "The Wonderful Wizard of Oz" lead character and supporting canine out of the Jayhawker State to have found a land of similar splendor.

He could have plopped the plucky pair in any number of places in the state and have been able to continue with an interesting story.

Scenario one: The house falls amid the intricate rock formations in the Smoky Hill River Valley, southeast of Oakley. Toto barks fearfully upon encountering the menacing centerpiece of the Chalk Pyramids—Cobra Rock—which rises from the ground to resemble a snake under the spell of its charmer. Meanwhile, Dorothy, upon catching a glimpse of Castle Rock, imagines herself in the role of another fairy tale heroine, Rapunzel.

Scenario two: The house lands in the sprawling fields of the Konza Prairie, south of Manhattan in the Flint Hills. Dorothy opens the front door to find herself face to face with an apprehensive American bison, the state animal. And Toto gets lost in the swaying tall grasses.

Scenario three: The house ends up near Elk Falls. Dorothy takes Toto for a stroll across the Iron Truss Bridge, where she pauses to view the graceful cascades that tumble over rock formations in a canyon on the Elk River.

More Than Just Flatlands

Kansas is all of this and more.

Fields of sunflowers stretch heavenward, their vivid yellow blooms jumping out of a subtle background of azure blue sky. Stalks of wheat bend to and fro as the wind blows fickle over the plains. Ruts of wagon wheels give evidence of a westward migration that rumbled across the Santa Fe Trail.

You can explore sand dunes and irregular hills in the lowlands of the Arkansas River; rugged canyons and rocky bluffs around the lake at Lake Scott State Park, north of Scott City; and salt mines and marshland near Wellington and McPherson.

Kansas Historical Timeline

1804 Exploring the Louisiana Purchase territory, Meriwether Lewis and William Clark camp along the Missouri River.

Edgar Samuel Paxson
Getty Images

1854 The Kansas-Nebraska Act is passed, and the Kansas Territory opens for settlement.

1862 The Homestead Act offers individuals federal land for a small filing fee and the promise to live on and improve the land for 5 years.

1899 In Medicine Lodge, prohibitionist Carry Nation begins her crusade against the consumption of liquor.

The state boasts maple forests; the rolling Smoky Hills; Cimarron National Grasslands in its southwesternmost corner; and scores of fence posts cut from rock due to a short supply of timber.

The posts aren't the only rock oddities. Unexplained geological wonders that spring up throughout Kansas give you the chance to let your imagination run wild.

Many of the Mushroom Rocks, near Kanopolis Lake in Ellsworth County, resemble the giant fungus on which Alice found the contemplative, smoking caterpillar in "Alice in Wonderland."

Elephant Rock, near Oberlin, suggests the hulking presence of a pachyderm.

At Rock City, near Minneapolis, the deposits of sandstone boulders—some measuring nearly 30 feet in diameter—are similar enough in shape to cow chips that you might suspect gargantuan cattle once roamed the plains.

A Cast of Characters

Scenic wonders aren't all that make Kansas exceptional. The simple fact that it once was illegal to serve ice cream on cherry pie here certainly sets the state apart. But you wouldn't want to overlook the colorful characters who have left volumes of legend and lore.

During its Wild West days, Kansas embraced a population in an epic struggle of good vs. evil. Peace officers James "Wild Bill" Hickok, Wyatt Earp and William "Bat" Masterson fought valiantly in towns such as Abilene, Dodge City and Wichita to curb the lawless elements—gunslingers, swindlers, brothel keepers and the like.

Meanwhile, outlaws set out to pillage and destroy. Of the three brothers in the notorious Dalton Gang, only Emmett survived a botched bank robbery in Coffeyville; Bob and Grat were shot dead. And Jesse James had a hand in a Lawrence raid that left more than 200 citizens dead and $1.5 million in damages.

Long documented in the annals of mystery is the fate of Atchison native Amelia Earhart, the intrepid aviator whose disappearance during an attempt to fly around the world endures as a puzzle unsolved.

The history and geography of Kansas can appeal to almost anyone. Even Dorothy, after her exotic adventures along the Yellow Brick Road and in the Emerald City, was eager to return to her aunt and uncle back home.

For indeed, there is no place like Kansas.

1917
The demands of World War I bring an agriculture boom to Kansas.

1953
Dwight D. Eisenhower, who grew up in Abilene, enters the White House.

1954
The Supreme Court decision in Brown vs. The Topeka Board of Education opens the door for school desegregation nationwide.

AP Photo John Duricka

1978
Nancy Landon Kassebaum becomes the first Kansas woman elected to the U.S. Senate.

1993
Floods damage or destroy nearly one-fifth of the state's farmland.

AP Photo Beth A. Keiser

1996
Native son Senator Bob Dole unsuccessfully runs for president.

2003
Kansas becomes the first state to switch its statues displayed in the U.S. Capitol when it replaces a likeness of 19th-century Gov. George W. Glick with one of Dwight D. Eisenhower.

Recreation

If you want to get out and about in Kansas, ask not for whom the wind blows; it blows for thee. You might as well put the blustery gusts to good use.

When the air is moving, grab a sailboard and go **windsurfing.** Short, choppy waves give you a rough, but thrilling, ride on Cheney Lake, west of Wichita. If you like your rides smooth and speedy, head east out of Wichita to Eldorado Lake. Not surprisingly, both lakes also are popular for **sailing.** Another top-notch windsurfing destination is Hillsdale Lake, west of Hillsdale.

If the winds are blowing the same direction as the rivers are flowing, then it's a good day to go **canoeing.** One of the most popular spots is on the Fall River; you can rent a canoe in Eureka. Other waters that beckon to the paddler include the Kansas, Arkansas, Marais des Cygnes, Smoky Hill and Blue rivers.

When the Winds Die Down

Even on the rare occasion that the winds are quiet, there are plenty of other ways to experience the great outdoors.

Swimming, boating and **water skiing** let you keep your cool while playing in the sun. Among the hottest spots are Shawnee Mission Park, northwest of Lenexa; John Redmond Reservoir, northwest of Burlington; and Lake Garnett, in Garnett. Or check out what's going on below the water's surface. Clear water makes for nice **scuba diving** in Crawford Lake, north of Farlington.

Fishing is excellent in the basin below Webster Dam, where catches of trout (during the fall and winter), bass, catfish, crappie and bluegill are common. Lovewell Reservoir, west of Lovewell, is noted for its walleye fishing. If you like a battle, drop a line in Keith Sebelius Reservoir, west of Norton, where trophy wipers—hybrids of white and striped bass—put up a ferocious fight.

Because Kansas lies along the central flyway, the lake margins attract many migrating waterfowl. Bird **hunting** is good near Great Bend at Cheyenne Bottoms, where mallards, pintails and teals nest in the marshes.

In the fall hunters find an abundance of ring-necked pheasants, bobwhites, white-tailed deer and cottontails at Wilson Lake, north of Wilson. Greater prairie chickens are found in the Flint Hills, while lesser prairie chickens inhabit southwestern counties.

Contact the Kansas Department of Wildlife and Parks for information about hunting and fishing regulations and licensing; phone (620) 672-5911.

All Ready to Ride

If you enjoy **bicycling,** the state offers loads of trails to keep you occupied. For a leisurely ride, try the Prairie Spirit Rail Trail, which runs between Ottawa and Welda. Passes are available for a nominal fee at several trail heads along the route. For a more grueling **mountain biking** adventure head to Clinton Lake, southwest of Lawrence, where the 25-mile loop teems with protruding rocks, thick vegetation and soft soil.

To experience Kansas as the pioneers did, saddle up a horse and head to Horsethief Canyon in Kanopolis State Park. The park's 26 miles of multiuse trails are ideal for **horseback riding.** A 22-mile horseback trail follows the south side of Melvern Reservoir, south of Osage City.

Three **hiking** trails wind through the woods in Toronto State Park in Toronto. To traverse the prairie, wander the 6 miles of trails through the grasses at Prairie Center State Park, near Olathe. For a breathtaking panorama, climb atop the red buttes and mesas of the Gypsum Hills in south-central Kansas and gaze upon fields of golden wheat.

Although it won't require much of an expenditure of sweat, an ascent up the state's highest point—4,039-foot Mount Sunflower, near the Colorado border in Wallace County—might provide some comic relief. At the less-than-daunting summit is a sunflower crafted of rail spikes, a rail fence and a mailbox that holds a log in which you can record your impressive feat.

As far as spectator sports go, **greyhound racing** is high on the list with many Kansans. The state is among the primary breeding centers for the sleek dogs. In late April and early October check out National Greyhound Meets.

Recreational Activities

Throughout the TourBook, you may notice a Recreational Activities heading with bulleted listings of recreation-oriented establishments listed underneath. Similar operations also may be mentioned in Destination City recreation sections. Since normal AAA inspection criteria cannot be applied, these establishments are presented only for information. Age, height and weight restrictions may apply. Reservations often are recommended and sometimes are required. Addresses and/or phone numbers are provided so visitors can contact the attraction for additional information.

Fast Facts

POPULATION: 2,688,418.

AREA: 82,264 square miles; ranks 14th.

CAPITAL: Topeka.

HIGHEST POINT: 4,039 ft., Mount Sunflower.

LOWEST POINT: 680 ft., Verdigris River.

TIME ZONE(S): Central/Mountain. DST.

TEEN DRIVING LAWS: Unless supervised, drivers under 16 are permitted to drive only to and from school or work and are not permitted to transport non-sibling passengers. Beginning at age 16, driving is not permitted 9 p.m.-5 a.m., and no more than one non-immediate family member under 18 may be a passenger. The minimum age for an unrestricted driver's license is 16 years, 6 months. For more information about Kansas driver's license regulations phone (785) 296-3963.

SEAT BELT/CHILD RESTRAINT LAWS: Seat belts are required for driver and front-seat passengers 18 and older, as well as for ages 14-17 in other seats. Children ages 8-14, more than 80 pounds and taller than 57 inches are required to be in a child restraint or seat belt; child restraints are required for under age 8, less than 80 pounds and less than 57 inches.

CELL PHONE RESTRICTIONS: The use of a wireless communication device while driving is prohibited for instruction permit as well as restricted class C and M driver's license holders.

HELMETS FOR MOTORCYCLISTS: Required for riders under 18.

RADAR DETECTORS: Permitted.

MOVE OVER LAW: Driver is required to slow down and vacate the lane nearest stopped police, fire and rescue vehicles using audible or flashing signals. Law also requires driver to move over for tow truck drivers assisting motorists.

FIREARMS LAWS: Vary by state and/or county. Contact the Kansas Attorney General's Office, Concealed Carry Handgun Unit, Memorial Hall, 2nd Floor, 120 S.W. 10th St., Topeka, KS 66612; phone (785) 291-3765.

HOLIDAYS: Jan. 1; Martin Luther King Jr. Day, Jan. (3rd Mon.); Memorial Day, May (last Mon.); July 4; Labor Day, Sept. (1st Mon.); Veterans Day, Nov. 11; Thanksgiving, Nov. (last Thurs.); Christmas, Dec. 25.

TAXES: The Kansas statewide sales tax is 5.3 percent, with local options for an additional increment up to 2 percent. Cities and counties also may levy a tax on lodgings; rates range from 1 to 5 percent.

INFORMATION CENTERS: State welcome centers are at Belle Plaine on I-35N as well as at I-70E Milepost 7 at Goodland. There are 12 community-owned welcome centers located throughout the state. Most information centers are open daily (except holidays) 8-6, May 15-Sept. 15; 9-5, rest of year.

FURTHER INFORMATION FOR VISITORS:

Kansas Department of Commerce
Travel and Tourism Development Division
1000 S.W. Jackson St., Suite 100
Topeka, KS 66612-1354
(785) 296-2009
TTY (785) 296-3487

RECREATION INFORMATION:

Kansas Department of Wildlife and Parks
512 S.E. 25th Ave.
Pratt, KS 67124-8147
(620) 672-5911

FISHING AND HUNTING REGULATIONS:

Kansas Department of Wildlife and Parks
512 S.E. 25th Ave.
Pratt, KS 67124-8147
(620) 672-5911

ROAD AND WEATHER INFORMATION: (800) 585-7623 511 inside Kansas

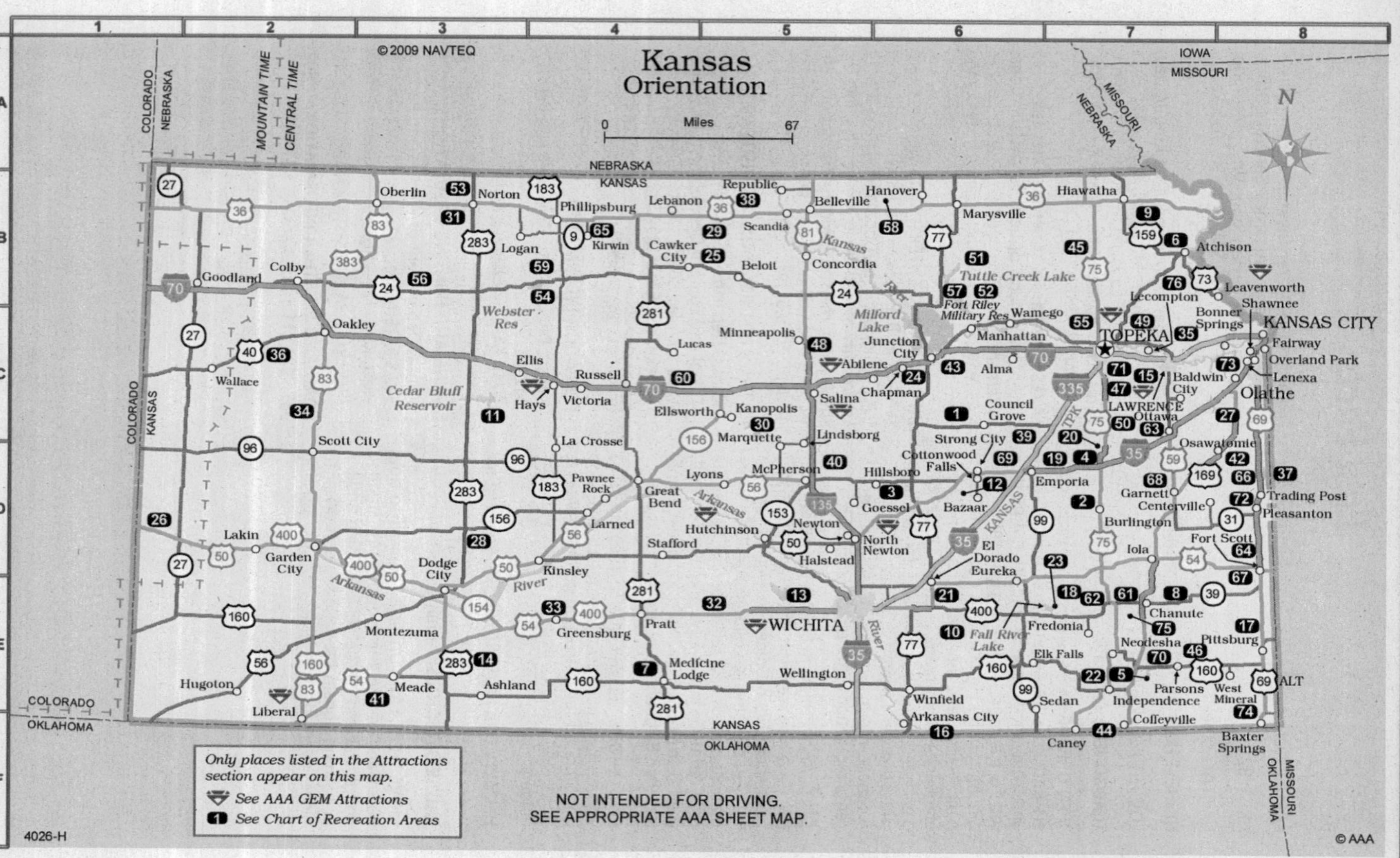
Kansas
Orientation
Miles
0
67
© 2009 NAVTEQ
KANSAS CITY
TOPEKA
WICHITA
LAWRENCE
Only places listed in the Attractions section appear on this map.
See AAA GEM Attractions
See Chart of Recreation Areas
NOT INTENDED FOR DRIVING.
SEE APPROPRIATE AAA SHEET MAP.
4026-H
© AAA

RECREATION AREAS

	MAP LOCATION	CAMPING	PICNICKING	HIKING TRAILS	BOATING	BOAT RAMP	BOAT RENTAL	FISHING	SWIMMING	PETS ON LEASH	BICYCLE TRAILS	WINTER SPORTS	VISITOR CENTER	LODGE/CABINS	FOOD SERVICE
ARMY CORPS OF ENGINEERS															
Council Grove Reservoir (C-6) 3,310 acres in Council Grove.	1	•	•	•	•	•		•	•	•			•		
John Redmond Reservoir (D-7) 9,400 acres 2 mi. n., then 1 mi. w. of Burlington off US 75. Horseback riding, hunting, water skiing.	2	•	•		•	•				•			•		
Marion Reservoir (D-6) 6,200 acres 3 mi. n.w. of Marion on the Cottonwood River off US 56. Hunting; nature trail.	3	•	•		•	•		•	•	•			•		
Melvern Lake (D-7) 18,000 acres 30 mi. e. of Emporia off SR 276. Hunting.	4	•	•	•	•	•	•	•	•	•	•		•		•
Pearson-Skubitz Big Hill Lake (E-7) 1,200 acres 4.5 mi. e. of Cherryvale off county roads. Bird watching, horseback riding.	5	•	•	•	•	•		•		•					
STATE															
Atchison State Fishing Lake (B-7) 66 acres 3.5 mi. n. and 2 mi. w. of Atchison off SR 7 at 318th St. Hunting.	6	•	•		•	•		•		•				•	
Barber State Fishing Lake (E-4) 190 acres .2 mi. n. of Medicine Lodge off US 281. Nature trail.	7	•	•		•	•		•		•					
Bourbon State Fishing Lake (E-7) 380 acres 4 mi. e. of Elsmore off US 59. Hunting.	8	•	•		•	•		•		•					
Brown State Fishing Lake (B-7) 148 acres 8 mi. s.e. of Hiawatha off US 36. Hunting.	9	•	•		•	•		•		•					
Butler State Fishing Lake (E-6) 320 acres 3 mi. n.w. of Latham off a county road. Hunting.	10	•	•		•	•		•		•					
Cedar Bluff (C-3) 900 acres 36 mi. s.w. of Hays off SR 147. Hunting.	11	•	•	•	•	•		•	•	•	•			•	•
Chase State Fishing Lake (D-6) 492 acres 2 mi. e. of Elmdale in Flint Hills. Bird watching, hunting.	12	•	•		•	•		•	•	•		•			
Cheney (E-5) 1,913 acres 20 mi. w. of Wichita via US 54 and SR 251. Hunting.	13	•	•	•	•	•		•	•	•				•	•
Clark State Fishing Lake (E-3) 1,243 acres 11 mi. s.w. of Kingsdown on SR 94. Hunting.	14	•	•		•	•		•		•					
Clinton (C-7) 1,500 acres 4 mi. w. of Lawrence off US 40. Horseback riding, hunting.	15	•	•	•	•	•	•	•	•	•	•	•	•		•
Cowley State Fishing Lake (F-6) 197 acres 13 mi. e. of Arkansas City off US 166. Hunting.	16	•	•		•	•	•	•		•					•
Crawford (E-8) 589 acres 4 mi. n. of Pittsburg off US 69.	17	•	•	•	•	•		•	•	•	•			•	
Cross Timbers (E-7) 1,075 acres 12 mi. w. of Yates Center off US 54.	18	•	•	•	•	•		•	•	•	•		•	•	
Douglas State Fishing Lake (D-7) 718 acres n.e. of Baldwin City on US 56. Hunting.	19	•	•		•	•		•		•					•
Eisenhower (C-7) 1,785 acres 4 mi. w. of Lawrence off US 40. Horseback riding, hunting.	20	•	•	•	•	•	•	•	•	•	•	•	•	•	
El Dorado (E-6) 4,000 acres 3 mi. e., then 2 mi. n. of El Dorado on US 77 off US 54. Horseback riding, hunting; nature trail.	21	•	•	•	•	•	•	•	•	•	•	•		•	
Elk City Reservoir and State Park (E-7) 857 acres 7 mi. n.w. of Independence off US 75. Hunting; nature trail.	22	•	•	•	•	•		•	•	•	•				
Fall River (D-7) 981 acres n.w. of Fall River next to Fall River Reservoir.	23	•	•	•	•	•		•	•	•	•		•	•	
Geary State Fishing Lake (C-6) 179 acres 9 mi. s. of Junction City off US 77. Hunting.	24	•	•		•	•		•		•					
Glen Elder (B-5) 1,391 acres 12 mi. w. of Beloit on US 24.	25	•	•	•	•	•	•	•	•	•	•		•	•	
Hamilton State Fishing Lake (D-1) 620 acres 3 mi. w., then 2 mi. n. of Syracuse off US 50. Bird watching, hunting.	26	•	•	•	•	•		•		•					
Hillsdale (C-8) 2,830 acres 9 mi. n.w. of Paola off US 169. Horseback riding, hunting.	27	•	•	•	•	•	•	•	•	•			•		
Hodgeman State Fishing Lake (D-3) 254 acres 2 mi. s. of Jetmore on US 283. Hunting.	28		•		•	•		•		•					
Jewell State Fishing Lake (B-5) 165 acres 10 mi. s.w. of Mankato on a county road. Hunting.	29	•	•		•	•		•		•					

RECREATION AREAS

	MAP LOCATION	CAMPING	PICNICKING	HIKING TRAILS	BOATING	BOAT RAMP	BOAT RENTAL	FISHING	SWIMMING	PETS ON LEASH	BICYCLE TRAILS	WINTER SPORTS	VISITOR CENTER	LODGE/CABINS	FOOD SERVICE
Kanopolis (C-5) 1,585 acres 12 mi. s.e. of Kanopolis off SR 141. Horseback riding.	30	●	●	●	●	●		●	●	●	●		●	●	●
Keith Sebelius Reservoir (B-3) 700 acres 3 mi. w. of Norton off US 36. Also known as Norton Reservoir.	31	●	●		●	●		●		●	●				●
Kingman State Fishing Lake (E-5) 4,622 acres 8 mi. w. of Kingman on US 54. Bird watching, hunting.	32	●	●	●	●	●		●		●					
Kiowa State Fishing Lake (E-4) 43 acres just n.w. of Greensburg on Bay St.	33		●		●	●		●		●					
Lake Scott (C-2) 925 acres 12 mi. n. of Scott City via US 83 and SR 95. Horseback riding, hunting; equestrian trails. *(See Scott City p. 102)*	34	●	●	●	●	●	●	●	●	●	●				●
Leavenworth State Fishing Lake (C-7) 341 acres 3 mi. w. and 1 mi. n. of Tonganoxie on SR 16.	35	●	●		●	●		●		●					
Logan State Fishing Lake (C-2) 271 acres 4 mi. n.w. of Russell Springs off SR 25. Hunting.	36	●	●		●	●		●		●					
Louisburg-Middle Creek State Fishing Lake (D-8) 281 acres 7 mi. s. of Louisburg on Metcalf Rd.	37	●	●		●	●		●							
Lovewell (B-5) 1,126 acres 15 mi. n.e. of Mankato off SR 14.	38	●	●	●	●	●	●	●	●	●				●	●
Lyon State Fishing Lake (C-6) 582 acres 11 mi. n.e. of Emporia on SR 170. Nature trail.	39	●	●		●	●		●		●					
McPherson State Fishing Lake (D-5) 2,245 acres 8 mi. n. of Canton off SR 86. Nature trail.	40	●	●		●	●		●		●				●	
Meade (E-3) 440 acres 12 mi. s.w. of Meade off SR 23.	41	●	●	●	●	●		●	●	●	●				
Miami State Fishing Lake (D-8) 267 acres 8 mi. e., then 5 mi. s. of Osawatomie off county roads. Hunting.	42	●	●		●	●		●		●					
Milford (C-6) 16,000 acres 4 mi. n.w. of Junction City on SR 57. Horseback riding; nature trails.	43	●	●	●	●	●	●	●	●	●	●		●	●	●
Montgomery State Fishing Lake (F-7) 408 acres 4 mi. s. of Independence via county road.	44	●	●		●	●	●	●		●					●
Nebo State Fishing Lake (B-7) 75 acres 7 mi. e., then 1 mi. s. of Holton on SR 116. Hunting.	45	●	●		●	●		●		●					
Neosho State Fishing Lake (E-7) 216 acres 7 mi. n.e. of Parsons off US 59.	46	●	●	●	●	●		●		●					
Osage State Fishing Lake (C-7) 506 acres 3 mi. s. of Carbondale off US 75.	47	●	●		●	●		●		●					
Ottawa State Fishing Lake (C-5) 711 acres 8 mi. e. of Minneapolis on SR 93. Hunting.	48	●	●	●	●	●	●	●	●	●				●	
Perry (C-7) 1,597 acres 16 mi. n.e. of Topeka off US 24. Equestrian camping, horseback riding; ATV area.	49	●	●	●	●	●	●	●	●	●	●		●	●	
Pomona Lake (C-7) 490 acres 2 mi. n.e. of Vassar on SR 268.	50	●	●	●	●	●		●	●	●		●	●		●
Pottawatomie State Fishing Lake No. 1 (B-6) 190 acres 5 mi. n. of Westmoreland on SR 99.	51	●	●	●	●	●		●		●					
Pottawatomie State Fishing Lake No. 2 (B-6) 247 acres 4 mi. n. of Manhattan off US 24.	52	●	●	●	●	●		●		●					
Prairie Dog (B-3) 1,150 acres 4 mi. w. of Norton on US 36. Historical.	53	●	●	●	●	●		●	●	●				●	
Rooks State Fishing Lake (B-4) 313 acres 5 mi. s.w. of Stockton off US 183.	54	●	●		●	●		●		●					
Shawnee State Fishing Lake (C-7) 400 acres 3 mi. n.e. of Silver Lake off US 24. Hunting.	55	●	●		●	●		●		●					
Sheridan State Fishing Lake (B-3) 335 acres 3 mi. w. of Studley off US 24.	56	●	●	●	●	●		●		●					
Tuttle Creek (B-6) 13,350 acres 5 mi. n. of Manhattan on SR 177. Equestrian camping, horseback riding, hunting.	57	●	●	●	●	●	●	●	●	●	●		●	●	●
Washington State Fishing Lake (B-6) 463 acres 10 mi. n.w. of Washington off county roads. Hunting.	58	●	●		●	●		●		●					
Webster (B-4) 880 acres 8 mi. w. of Stockton off US 24.	59	●	●	●	●	●		●	●	●				●	●
Wilson (C-4) 927 acres 10 mi. n. of Wilson via SR 232.	60	●	●	●	●	●	●	●	●	●	●		●	●	●

RECREATION AREAS

	MAP LOCATION	CAMPING	PICNICKING	HIKING TRAILS	BOATING	BOAT RAMP	BOAT RENTAL	FISHING	SWIMMING	PETS ON LEASH	BICYCLE TRAILS	WINTER SPORTS	VISITOR CENTER	LODGE/CABINS	FOOD SERVICE
Wilson State Fishing Lake (E-7) 291 acres 1.5 mi. s.e. of Buffalo on US 75.	61	•	•		•	•		•		•					
Woodson State Fishing Lake (E-7) 2,885 acres 10 mi. s.w. of Yates Center off US 54.	62	•	•	•	•	•	•	•		•					•
OTHER															
Forest Park (C-7) 50 acres off Tecumseh and N. Locust sts. at Ottawa on the Marais des Cygnes River.	63		•					•	•						•
Gunn Park (D-8) 155 acres on the w. side of Fort Scott. Paddle-boats. *(See Fort Scott p. 83)*	64	•	•					•		•					
Kirwin Reservoir (B-4) 5,000 acres 15 mi. s.e. of Phillipsburg on SR 9. Hunting.	65	•	•		•	•		•	•						
La Cygne Lake (D-8) 2,600 acres 5 mi. e. of La Cygne off US 69. Hunting.	66	•	•	•	•	•	•	•							
Lake Fort Scott (D-8) 360 acres 4 mi. s.w. of Fort Scott on Lake Rd.	67		•		•	•		•	•						
Lake Garnett (D-7) 55 acres in downtown Garnett. Golf, tennis, water skiing; race track.	68	•	•	•	•		•	•	•						
Lake Kahola (D-6) 405 acres 22 mi. n.w. of Emporia.	69	•	•		•	•		•	•	•					
Lake Parsons (E-7) 2,200 acres 4 mi. n., then 3.5 mi. w. of Parsons on a county road.	70		•	•	•	•	•	•	•			•			
Lake Shawnee (C-7) 410 acres s.e. of Topeka just outside city limits on E. 29th St.	71	•	•	•	•	•	•	•	•	•					
Marais Des Cygnes Waterfowl Refuge (D-8) 7,600 acres 7 mi. n. of Pleasanton off US 69. Hunting.	72	•	•	•				•							
Prairie Center (C-8) 300 acres .5 mi. w. of Olathe at 135th and Cedar.	73		•	•				•		•					
Riverside Park (E-8) In downtown Baxter Springs. Golf, tennis; playground.	74	•	•		•	•		•	•						
Santa Fe Park (E-7) 249 acres 2 mi. s. of Chanute on Santa Fe St.	75	•	•		•	•		•	•						
Warnock Lake (B-7) 2 mi. s.w. of Atchison.	76	•	•					•	•						

Kansas Temperature Averages Maximum/Minimum

From the records of The Weather Channel Interactive, Inc.

	JAN	FEB	MAR	APR	MAY	JUN	JUL	AUG	SEP	OCT	NOV	DEC
Concordia	36/17	43/22	54/31	64/41	74/52	85/62	91/67	88/66	80/56	68/44	51/31	40/21
Dodge City	41/19	48/24	57/31	67/41	76/52	87/62	93/67	91/66	82/57	70/44	55/30	44/22
Goodland	39/16	45/20	53/26	63/35	72/46	84/56	89/61	87/60	78/50	66/38	50/25	41/18
Topeka	37/17	44/23	55/33	66/43	75/53	85/63	89/68	88/65	80/56	69/44	53/32	41/22
Wichita	40/20	47/25	57/34	67/44	76/54	87/64	93/69	92/68	82/59	70/47	55/34	43/24

Points of Interest

ABILENE (C-5) pop. 6,543, elev. 1,155′

Though its name is of biblical origin, Abilene once was one of the unholiest and wildest towns in the West. Its reputation grew along with the city as hundreds of cowboys came to the town along the historic Chisholm Trail during the late 1800s. Nearly 3 million Texas longhorns passed through Abilene 1867-72 to be shipped east by rail. James "Wild Bill" Hickok, whose deadly accuracy with two pistols was as legendary as his icy willingness to use them, was marshal of the town in 1871.

Still, fame was not quite through with the City on the Plains; Dwight David Eisenhower, first the Supreme Allied Commander during World War II and then the 34th president of the United States, spent his boyhood years in Abilene. As president, he signed a truce to end the Korean War and passed the Federal Aid Highway Act in 1956, which created the present-day interstate highway system.

Eisenhower Park, a 57-acre tract near W. Third and Poplar sts., includes Tom Smith Stadium; a swimming pool; basketball, tennis and sand volleyball courts; picnic grounds; and landscaped gardens. Phone (785) 263-7266.

Glimpses of Abilene's past can be seen at Seelye Mansion, at 1105 N. Buckeye Ave. Great Plains Theatre, a professional regional company, presents Broadway plays June through December; phone (785) 263-4574. The city also is a major center for greyhound enthusiasts.

Abilene Convention & Visitors Bureau: 201 N.W. Second St., Abilene, KS 67410. **Phone:** (785) 263-2231 or (800) 569-5915.

Self-guiding tours: A free brochure detailing a tour past the historic houses of Abilene and Dickinson County is available from the visitors bureau and from Dickinson County Heritage Center and Museum *(see attraction listing).*

ABILENE & SMOKY VALLEY RAILROAD departs from the 1887 Rock Island Depot at 200 S. 5th St. A 10-mile train ride travels over the rolling flatlands between Abilene and Enterprise. Featured are a restored 1900s wooden dining car, an open-air gondola car, a caboose, a 1945 diesel locomotive, and a steam engine that is operated on occasion.

Time: Allow 1 hour, 30 minutes minimum. **Hours:** Departures Wed.-Sat. at 10 and 2, Sun. at 2, Memorial Day-Labor Day; Sat. at 10 and 2, Sun. at 2, May 1-day before Memorial Day and day after Labor Day-Oct. 31. Phone ahead for steam engine operation dates and to confirm schedule. **Cost:** Fare $14; $7 (ages 3-11). **Phone:** (785) 263-0118 or (888) 426-6687.

DICKINSON COUNTY HERITAGE CENTER AND MUSEUM is at 412 S. Campbell St.; the Museum of Independent Telephony *(see attraction listing)* is in the same building. Early agricultural, cow town, homemaking and industry relics illustrate pioneer life in Dickinson County. The museum also includes an outdoor area featuring an antique carousel, a blacksmith exhibit and a log cabin.

Hours: Mon.-Fri. 9-4, Sat. 10-8, Sun. 1-5, Memorial Day-Labor Day; Mon.-Fri. 9-3, Sat. 10-5, Sun. 1-5, rest of year. Closed Jan. 1-2, Thanksgiving, Sun. after Thanksgiving and Dec. 20-31. **Cost:** $4; $3 (ages 62+); $2 (ages 2-14; includes ride on carousel). Carousel $2. **Phone:** (785) 263-2681.

GEM **EISENHOWER PRESIDENTIAL LIBRARY AND MUSEUM,** 2 mi. s. of I-70 on SR 15 at S.E. Fourth St., covers 22 acres of landscaped grounds and consists of five buildings, including the visitor center, in which a 23-minute orientation film is shown. **Time:** Allow 3 hours minimum. **Hours:** Daily 9-4:45. Closed Jan. 1, Thanksgiving and Dec. 25. **Cost:** Visitor center free. **Phone:** (785) 263-6700 or (877) 746-4453.

Eisenhower Home, S.E. Fourth St., was the boyhood home of President Dwight David Eisenhower. Representative of family houses in Kansas during the late 19th century, the frame house is kept as it was in 1946. **Hours:** Daily 9-4:45. Closed Jan. 1, Thanksgiving and Dec. 25. **Cost:** Free. **Phone:** (785) 263-6700 or (877) 746-4453.

Eisenhower Museum, next to the Eisenhower Home, is constructed of Kansas limestone and contains items relating to President Dwight David Eisenhower's life and experiences from boyhood to the post-presidential years. Murals in the lobby depict events from Eisenhower's life and career. **Hours:** Daily 9-4:45. Closed Jan. 1, Thanksgiving and Dec. 25. **Cost:** $8; $6 (ages 62+ and retired military and spouse with ID); $1 (ages 8-15); free (active military with ID). **Phone:** (785) 263-6700 or (877) 746-4453.

Eisenhower Presidential Library, opposite Eisenhower Museum, houses the papers, books and historical materials accumulated by Eisenhower during his military career and his term of office. The extensive use of imported marble in the building's interior is offset by the Kansas limestone of the exterior. **Hours:** Daily 9-4:45. Closed Jan. 1, Thanksgiving and Dec. 25. **Cost:** Free. **Phone:** (785) 263-6700 or (877) 746-4453.

Place of Meditation, s. of the visitor center and w. of the library, is the final resting place of Dwight D. and Mamie Doud Eisenhower and their firstborn son, Doud Dwight Eisenhower. **Hours:** Daily 9-4:45. Closed Jan. 1, Thanksgiving and Dec. 25.

Cost: Free. **Phone:** (785) 263-6700 or (877) 46-4453.

GREYHOUND HALL OF FAME, 2 mi. s. of I-70 via SR 15 to 407 S. Buckeye Ave. (across from Eisenhower Presidential Library and Museum), has many displays about racing and greyhound dogs from ancient times to the present, including a miniature dog track display. Two resident greyhounds are on the grounds. Highlights include interactive exhibits and a 12-minute orientation film. The Hall of Fame honors legendary greyhounds from around the world as well as pioneers of the sport. **Time:** Allow 1 hour minimum. **Hours:** Daily 9-5. Closed Jan. 1, Thanksgiving and Dec. 25. **Cost:** Donations. **Phone:** (785) 263-3000.

LEBOLD MANSION is at 106 N. Vine St. The imposing Italianate five-story mansion was built in 1880 using native Kansas orange limestone. Each room has been carefully restored and is decorated to reflect different styles of the Victorian era. Guided tours, which focus on the history of the house and its owners, escort guests into public rooms, private family quarters and servants' areas.

Time: Allow 1 hour, 30 minutes minimum. **Hours:** Tues.-Sun. 10-4. Schedule may vary in winter; phone ahead. **Cost:** $10; $5 (ages 6-18). **Phone:** (785) 263-4356.

MUSEUM OF INDEPENDENT TELEPHONY is at 412 S. Campbell St., in the same building as Dickinson County Heritage Center and Museum *(see attraction listing)*. The museum relates the history of the telephone and its early independent proprietors since the original patent was issued to Alexander Graham Bell in 1876. Included are interactive exhibits of antique phones, insulators and switchboards. Half-hour guided tours are available by advance request.

Hours: Mon.-Fri. 9-4, Sat. 10-8, Sun. 1-5, Memorial Day-Labor Day; Mon.-Fri. 9-3, Sat. 10-5, Sun. 1-5, rest of year. Schedule may vary in winter; phone ahead. **Cost:** $4 (includes ride on carousel); $3 (ages 62+); $2 (ages 2-14). Carousel $2. **Phone:** (785) 263-2681.

ALMA (C-6) pop. 797, elev. 1,053'

WABAUNSEE COUNTY HISTORICAL MUSEUM, 227 Missouri St., presents exhibits relating to the county's history. A children's room, dentist's office, general store, textile shop and schoolroom reflect the early 1900s. Displays include American Indian artifacts, a World War II exhibit featuring Kansas native Gen. Lewis Walt, a 1926 Model T car, washing machines, quilts, typewriters and a 1923 Reo fire truck.

Additional exhibits are the Beecher Bible & Rifle Church display, buggies, box wagons and carriages, an 1880s McCormick Reaper, and a rifle and musket display. Genealogy information is augmented by a large photo collection. **Hours:** Tues.-Sat. 10-noon and 1-4, Sun. 1-4, Mar.-Nov.; Tues.-Wed. 10-noon and 1-4, rest of year. Closed major holidays. **Cost:** $2. **Phone:** (785) 765-2200.

ARKANSAS CITY (E-6)
pop. 11,963, elev. 1,075'

Arkansas (ar-KAN-sas) City's position, 4 miles north of the present Oklahoma border, made it a logical mustering point for one of the largest land rushes in the history of westward expansion. By the tens of thousands they lined up—eager boomers and homesteaders afoot, on horseback and with every horse-drawn conveyance possible—awaiting the gunshot that would signal the opening of the Cherokee Strip in 1893.

As the West lost its wildness, Arkansas City became what its Arkansas River site promised—a marketing and transportation center. The discovery of oil in the vicinity in the early 20th century added the refineries and other petroleum-related industries that dominated the economy through the middle part of the century.

Arkansas City Area Chamber of Commerce and Convention and Visitors Center: 106 S. Summit, P.O. Box 795, Arkansas City, KS 67005. **Phone:** (620) 442-0230 or (620) 442-0236.

CHAPLIN NATURE CENTER, 3 mi. w. via US 166, then 2 mi. n. at 27814 27th Dr., features 4 miles of nature trails that meander alongside the Arkansas River and through 230 acres of creek, prairie and forest terrain. A visitor center contains a nature library and educational displays. Events are offered throughout the year. **Time:** Allow 1 hour minimum. **Hours:** Visitor center Tues.-Sat. 9-5, Sun. 1-5, Mar. 15-June 30 and Sept. 1-Nov. 15; Tues.-Fri. 10-2, Sat. 9-5, July-Aug.; Sat. 9-5, Sun. 1-5, rest of year. Trails daily dawn-dusk. Closed major holidays. **Cost:** Donations. **Phone:** (620) 442-4133.

CHEROKEE STRIP LAND RUSH MUSEUM, 1.5 mi. s. on US 77, depicts the Sept. 16, 1893, land run in which 150,000 settlers raced to claim more than 6 million acres. An extensive collection of documents, photographs and other artifacts depicts pioneer life in the area and in the Oklahoma Territory. **Hours:** Tues.-Sat. 10-5. Closed major holidays. **Cost:** $4.50; $3.50 (ages 55+); $2 (ages 6-12). **Phone:** (620) 442-6750.

ASHLAND (E-3) pop. 975, elev. 1,950'

In 1884 a group of Kentuckians decided that a town at the junction of two major frontier trails—one from Texas to Fort Dodge, one from Santa Fe, N.M., to Sun City on the Medicine River—would prove profitable. The community took its name from Ashland, Ky., and its livelihood from supplying the countless traders, immigrants, soldiers and cowboys who plied these frontier throughways.

Its reputation for unruliness gone with the cattle drives, Ashland serves as a center of government and commerce for the surrounding Red Hills wheat farms and cattle ranches. On the east side of the courthouse at 9th and Highland streets, historic trails and other points of interest in Clark County are indicated on a 20-foot-high engraved relief map.

West of town, northeast of the intersection of US 160 and US 283, lie Big and Little basins. Both basins are sinkholes—Kansans call them sinks—created by subsidence as subterranean erosion undermined the surface stratum. Big Basin is 100 feet deep and about a mile wide. Nearby Little Basin is marked by St. Jacob's Well, a 125-foot-wide pool that never has been known to dry. It was a vital watering hole for American Indians and pioneers.

Ashland Chamber of Commerce: P.O. Box 37, Ashland, KS 67831. **Phone:** (620) 635-0427.

PIONEER-KRIER MUSEUM, w. of Main St. on US 160, displays historical items in late 19th-century room settings. Among a collection of bridle bits is one of Spanish design that is thought to have belonged to a member of Coronado's expedition. Other collections include barbed wire, fossilized bones, American Indian artifacts and musical instruments. Also featured are memorabilia from track star Wes Santee and other notable Kansans.

Time: Allow 1 hour minimum. **Hours:** Mon.-Fri. 10-noon and 1-5, Sat.-Sun. by appointment. Closed Jan. 1, Thanksgiving and Dec. 25. **Cost:** Donations. **Phone:** (620) 635-2227.

ATCHISON (B-7) pop. 10,232, elev. 798'

Independence Park, on the Atchison riverfront, marks where the Meriwether Lewis and William Clark expedition arrived on July 4, 1804. Five miles to the north lies Independence Creek, so named by Clark to commemorate the first Independence Day celebrated west of the Mississippi River.

Among the city's founders years after Lewis and Clark's travels were Benedictine monks, who established an abbey on the north bluffs, and the Benedictine Sisters, who started a convent. Atchison is known for the Atchison, Topeka & Santa Fe Railway, but before the railroad a steady stream of wagon and river traffic fed the infant town.

A marker at the Atchison courthouse commemorates a speech that Abraham Lincoln gave in 1859 and later delivered in the Cooper Union in New York City. The address brought Lincoln the recognition that resulted in his presidential nomination.

Atchison is the birthplace of Amelia Earhart, and monuments to the aviator can be seen at the downtown pedestrian mall, the International Forest of Friendship and Amelia Earhart Memorial Airport, 3 miles west. The Amelia Earhart Birthplace *(see attraction listing)* overlooks the Missouri River.

The International Forest of Friendship honors aviation and aerospace pioneers. It features trees representing the 50 states, U.S. territories and 40 foreign countries. A "moon tree" grown from a sycamore seed taken to the moon on *Apollo 14* marks a memorial dedicated to the ill-fated Apollo and Challenger crews. Memory Lane winds through the forest and offers tributes to Earhart, Charles Lindbergh, the Wright Brothers and others.

The campus of Benedictine College, on the bluff of the Missouri River, offers excellent views. Of interest near the campus are St. Benedict's Abbey, which is modeled after Benedictine monasteries of the Middle Ages, and the Abbey Chapel, which has 28 minor altars in its crypt.

Nearby Warnock Lake *(see Recreation Chart)* features swimming, fishing, camping and picnic facilities. Just 3.5 miles north and 2 miles west of town on SR 7 to 318th Street is Atchison State Fishing Lake *(see Recreation Chart and the AAA South Central CampBook)*, which also offers camping.

Atchison Convention and Visitors Bureau: 200 S. 10th St., P.O. Box 126, Atchison, KS 66002. **Phone:** (913) 367-2427 or (800) 234-1854.

AMELIA EARHART BIRTHPLACE, overlooking the Missouri River at Santa Fe and N. Terrace sts., is the house where Amelia Earhart was born in 1897 and lived until she was 12. The 1859 Victorian cottage on the bluffs of the Missouri River was owned by Earhart's grandparents. The house contains photographs, newspaper clippings and some of Earhart's belongings. **Time:** Allow 30 minutes minimum. **Hours:** Mon.-Fri. 9-4, Sat. 10-4, Sun. 1-4, Feb. 16-Dec. 14; Wed.-Sat. 10-4, Sun. 1-4, rest of year. **Cost:** $3; 50c (ages 0-12). **Phone:** (913) 367-4217.

ATCHISON COUNTY HISTORICAL SOCIETY MUSEUM is in the 1880s Santa Fe Depot at 200 S. 10th St. Displays explore local history, especially the Lewis and Clark expedition. Amelia Earhart memorabilia, railroad artifacts and a 200-piece gun collection are among the collectibles. **Tours:** Guided tours are available. **Hours:** Mon.-Sat. 9-5, Sun. noon-5, May-Oct.; Mon.-Fri. 8-5, Sat. 9-4, Sun. noon-4, rest of year. Closed Jan. 1, Easter, Thanksgiving, part of Dec. 24 and Dec. 25. **Cost:** Donations. **Phone:** (913) 367-6238.

EVAH C. CRAY HISTORICAL HOME MUSEUM, 805 N. Fifth St., was built in 1882 and resembles a Scottish castle. The restored three-story house contains 19th-century period rooms filled with antiques and memorabilia. An 18-minute videotape highlighting Atchison's historic homes and buildings is presented in the carriage house. **Time:** Allow 1 hour, 30 minutes minimum. **Hours:** Mon.-Sat. 10-4, Sun. 1-4, May-Oct. and in Dec.; Mon. and Fri.-Sat. 10-4, Sun. 1-4, Mar.-Apr.; by appointment rest of year. **Cost:** $3. **Phone:** (913) 367-3046.

BALDWIN CITY (C-7) pop. 3,400

Baldwin City, located on the Santa Fe Trail, was the scene of one of many bloody clashes between pro-slavery and anti-slavery factions in the state's territorial days. The Battle of Black Jack, which some call one of the first of the Civil War, took place nearby in 1856. John Brown and his anti-slavery troops interceded, sending the agitators home and releasing their prisoners. The 40-acre Black Jack Battlefield & Nature Park, east of Baldwin City on SR 56 in Wellsville, is home to an 1890 rmhouse and a variety of native grasses, shrubs nd trees; phone (785) 883-2106.

In the Ivan Boyd Prairie Preserve, wagon ruts arved by Conestogas that traveled west on the trail 825-75 can be seen. Serving as a more modern ath, the town's brick streets were laid in 1925-26 y master craftsman Jim Garfield Brown, an Oneida ndian.

The Maple Leaf Festival, held the third full weeknd in October, offers historical tours, a craft fair, e state's oldest quilt show as well as a pageant and arade. For further information, phone the chamber f commerce.

Douglas State Fishing Lake is nearby. *See Recreion Chart and the AAA South Central CampBook.*

aldwin City Chamber of Commerce: 720 High t., P.O. Box 501, Baldwin City, KS 66006. **Phone:** '85) 594-3200.

AKER UNIVERSITY, 618 Eighth St., is the state's dest 4-year college and has an enrollment of aproximately 900. One of its earliest donations was 100 received in 1864 from Abraham Lincoln. An ld English church was reconstructed and is open r viewing at Sixth and Fremont streets. Visitors re welcomed on the campus; tours can be arranged.

The Old Castle, on the campus at 511 Fifth St., is e oldest building in the state and now houses a useum with exhibits about early Kansas and the anta Fe Trail.

Hours: Old Castle open by appointment only. **hone:** (785) 594-6451 or (800) 873-4282.

uayle Bible Collection is in the Collins Library n the Baker University campus. Exhibits include are biblical manuscripts, clay cuneiform tablets datng from 2000 B.C., early English bibles and a leaf om a Gutenberg Bible. Also of interest is an origial 17th-century manor room. Allow 15-30 minutes inimum. **Time:** Allow 30 minutes minimum. **ours:** Fri.-Sun. 1-4. Guided tours are available by ppointment. Closed major holidays. **Cost:** Donaons. **Phone:** (785) 594-8390.

IDLAND RAILWAY is off US 56, s. on 11th St., nen w. to 1515 W. High St. Presidents William loward Taft and Theodore Roosevelt visited the 906 brick and stone Santa Fe Depot, which inludes triple-arched windows, a coal fireplace and ual gas/electric lighting systems. Built in 1867, the ne was the first railroad south of the Kansas River. 'isitors ride on restored 1900s locomotives, coaches nd cabooses as they travel through woods and armland and over a 200-foot-long bridge.

Time: Allow 2 hours minimum. **Hours:** Trains epart for Norwood Thurs. at 10:30, Sat.-Sun. and olidays at 11 and 2, last weekend in May-last veekend in Oct. Trains depart for Ottawa Junction at.-Sun. at 1 and 3:30, last weekend in May-last eekend in Oct. **Cost:** Fare to Norwood $10; $5 ages 2-11). Fare to Ottawa Junction $15; $7 (ages -11). **Phone:** (913) 721-1211, (785) 594-6982 or 800) 651-0388.

BAXTER SPRINGS BAZAAR (E-8)
pop. 4,602 elev. 843'

BAXTER SPRINGS HERITAGE CENTER AND MUSEUM is .3 mi. n. on Military Ave./US 69/US 400, just e. on E. 8th St., then just n. to 740 East Ave. The two-story facility's interpretive exhibits relate local history from the American Indian era, the late 19th century and World Wars I and II. Dioramas showcase books, clothing, letters, posters and other artifacts. An 1870s street display offers a blacksmith shop, and another interprets life in the 1930s and features a barber shop and beauty salon as well as dentist and optometrist offices.

Other displays interpret the significance of Route 66 and local mining history; many crystals, rocks and stones discovered in nearby mines are displayed.

Tours: Guided tours are available. **Time:** Allow 2 hours minimum. **Hours:** Mon.-Sat. 10-4:30, Sun. 1-4:30. Closed major holidays. **Cost:** Donations. **Phone:** (620) 856-2385.

BAZAAR (D-6) elev. 1,220'

FLINT HILLS OVERLAND WAGON TRAIN TRIPS begin at the athletic field on Neosho St., 1 blk. n. of Custer Oak Park, and offer afternoon-evening and overnight wagon train treks fashioned after those of the 1870s. The hearty pioneer meals and evening campfires are some of the highlights. Inquire about weather and refund policies.

Hours: Overnight trips depart Sat.-Sun. at 10 a.m. and return at noon the following day, June-Oct. (weather permitting). Afternoon-evening trips depart Sat. at 3, June-Oct. (weather permitting). Phone ahead to confirm schedule. **Cost:** Overnight fare $190; $180 (second paying adult in party); $150 (ages 12-21); $95 (ages 5-12); free (ages 0-4). Afternoon-evening outing $110 per person. Reservations are required. **Phone:** (316) 321-6300.

BELLEVILLE (B-5) pop. 2,239, elev. 1,550'

Located in north central Kansas, Belleville was founded in 1869 and named for early resident Anabelle Tutton. A Depression-era building boom, fueled by federal Works Project Administration (WPA) funding, resulted in many fine examples of Art Deco architecture, including the Republic County Courthouse.

A pond that formerly supplied water for Rock Island Railroad steam engines now provides yearround recreation. Rocky Pond Park offers picnicking, fishing and RV camping.

Belleville Chamber of Commerce: 1309 18th St., P.O. Box 280, Belleville, KS 66935. **Phone:** (785) 527-5524.

BOYER MUSEUM OF ANIMATED CARVINGS is at 1205 M St. The museum features the handcarved, hand-painted animated works of Kansas artist Paul Boyer. Included in the collection are mechanized creations of airplanes, cars, animals and people. Visitors can view the inner workings of the displays through glass cubes. **Tours:** Guided tours are available. **Time:** Allow 45 minutes minimum. **Hours:** Wed.-Sat. 1-5, May-Sept.; by appointment rest of year. Phone ahead to confirm schedule. **Cost:** $5; $2 (ages 6-12). **Phone:** (785) 527-5884.

HIGH BANKS HALL OF FAME AND NATIONAL MIDGET AUTO RACING MUSEUM is 1.2 mi. n. of jct. US 36 and US 81 at 1204 H St. The museum preserves racing history and features vintage race-cars, uniforms, flags, photographs and other memorabilia relating to midget auto racing. **Time:** Allow 30 minutes minimum. **Hours:** Tues.-Sun. 10-5. **Cost:** $3; $2 (ages 6-14). **Phone:** (785) 527-2526.

REPUBLIC COUNTY HISTORICAL SOCIETY MUSEUM, .75 mi. e. of US 81 at 615 28th St. (US 36), displays historical clothing, furniture and other relics from the area. On the 4-acre grounds are an 1870s log cabin, an 1872 school, an agriculture building, an 1889 round limestone smokehouse, a 1904 church and a caboose from the 1970s. **Time:** Allow 1 hour minimum. **Hours:** Mon.-Fri. 1-5, Sat. by appointment (also Sun. 1:30-4:30, Apr.-Nov.). Closed major holidays. **Cost:** $3; $1 (ages 10-16); free (ages 0-9). **Phone:** (785) 527-5971.

BELOIT (B-5) pop. 4,019, elev. 1,382′

A trading center and county seat on the Solomon River, Beloit is in the post rock country. Undeterred by the lack of trees, early farmers quarried their fence posts from Greenhorn limestone, which underlies a 200-mile-long, 10- to 40-mile-wide swath of the Smoky Hills region. The stone also was used for construction; Mitchell County Courthouse and St. John's Church are examples of post rock buildings.

A herd of about 450 buffaloes associated with the Butterfield Buffalo Ranch can be seen from the roadway 3 miles west and 2 miles north from the junction of US 24 and SR 14. For more information phone (785) 738-2717. Also of interest is the Little Red Schoolhouse on US 24N. Built in 1871, the schoolhouse has been restored to its 19th-century appearance and contains period textbooks and other historic educational materials.

Fourteen miles west of Beloit on US 24, Glen Elder Dam impounds 12,600-acre Waconda Lake. Glen Elder State Park *(see Recreation Chart and the AAA South Central CampBook)* is a center of recreational activity on the reservoir.

Beloit Area Chamber of Commerce: 123 N. Mill St., P.O. Box 582, Beloit, KS 67420. **Phone:** (785) 738-2717.

Self-guiding tours: A walking tour brochure of historic downtown is available from the chamber of commerce.

MITCHELL COUNTY HISTORICAL SOCIETY AND MUSEUM, 1 mi. s. of US 24 at 402 W. Eighth St., houses county historical memorabilia in a renovated four-story building. Displays include period rooms and collections of china, glassware, tools and clothing. Research facilities are available. **Time:** A low 1 hour minimum. **Hours:** Wed.-Fri. 10-4, Mor Tues. by appointment. Closed major holidays. **Cos** Donations. **Phone:** (785) 738-5355.

BONNER SPRINGS—

see Kansas City p. 182.

BURLINGTON (D-7) pop. 2,790, elev. 1,035′

COFFEY COUNTY HISTORICAL SOCIETY MU SEUM is 11 blks. w. of US 75 at 1101 Neosho S Highlights of the museum include a large genealog library, an impressive collection of guns and Ame can Indian arrowheads, a doll collection and a seri of rooms depicting 19th-century life. On th grounds is a restored 1896 one-room schoolhous an 1895 church and a stone gazebo. **Hours:** Mon Fri. 10-4, Sat.-Sun. 1-4. Closed major holiday **Cost:** Donations. **Phone:** (620) 364-2653 or (88 877-2653.

CANEY (F-7) pop. 2,092, elev. 770′

SAFARI ZOOLOGICAL PARK is 1.5 mi. e. of U 75 on CR 1425, following signs. Such animals as a ligators, black bears, a grizzly bear, wolves, som big cats, deer, lemurs, rabbits and primates may b seen during 1-hour guided tours of the park.

Tours: Guided tours are available. **Time:** Allo 1 hour minimum. **Hours:** Tours are offered Mon Sat. 10-3, May-July; Sat. 11-2, rest of year (weath permitting). Phone ahead to verify schedule Aug Apr. **Cost:** $10; $8 (ages 3-12 and ages 60+ **Phone:** (620) 879-2885.

CAWKER CITY (B-4) pop. 521, elev. 1,500′

Visitors can see what is said to be the world largest ball of twine in downtown Cawker City. Th ball currently contains more than 7,827,730 feet sisal twine, weighs more than 17,980 pounds and more than 40 feet in circumference. Communi members continue to add to it. The town is on th edge of Waconda Lake, where hunting and fishir are permitted in season.

CENTERVILLE (D-7) elev. 925′

ST. PHILIPPINE DUCHESNE SHRINE AND PAR is on SR 7, 8 mi. n. of jct. SR 7 and SR 52. Th shrine preserves the site of a mid-1800s Pottawa omie Indian settlement that was founded with th help of nuns and Jesuit priests. The elderly Sist Rose Philippine Duchesne particularly was devote to the cause. Several memorials, historical marke and an American Indian burial site are in the 16 acre park, as are nature trails. **Hours:** Daily dawr dusk. **Cost:** Donations. **Phone:** (913) 491-9886.

CHANUTE (E-7) pop. 9,441, elev. 930′

Basing its economy on light industries, agricu ture, limestone and oil and gas deposits, Chanute an old railroad town bearing the surname of Octa Chanute, a civil engineer for the LL&G Railwa during the early 1870s. His avocation was building and flying heavier-than-air machines. The inventor's designs were used by Orville and Wilbur Wright at Kitty Hawk, N.C.

Nearby recreation sites include Santa Fe Park *(see Recreation Chart)*, on Santa Fe Street; Wilson State Fishing Lake *(see Recreation Chart and Buffalo in the AAA South Central CampBook)*, 12 miles west via SR 39 and US 75 near Buffalo; Fall River State Park *(see Fall River in the AAA South Central CampBook)*, 23 miles west via SR 39; and Pearson-Skubitz Big Hill Lake *(see Cherryvale in the AAA South Central CampBook)*, 25 miles south via US 169.

Chanute Area Chamber of Commerce & Office of Tourism: 21 N. Lincoln Ave., P.O. Box 747, Chanute, KS 66720. **Phone:** (620) 431-3350 or (877) 431-3350.

MARTIN AND OSA JOHNSON SAFARI MUSEUM, 111 N. Lincoln Ave., presents the photographs, manuscripts, books, films and various memorabilia of Martin and Osa Johnson, early wildlife photographers and authors. Exhibits feature the couple's trips to the South Seas, Borneo and Africa 1917-36. Other features include West African masks, tribal art and a library containing a 10,000-volume natural history collection. Some of the Johnsons' films are shown by request.

Hours: Mon.-Sat. 10-5, Sun. 1-5. Closed major holidays. **Cost:** $4; $3 (ages 13-18, ages 65+ and students with ID); $2 (ages 6-12). **Phone:** (620) 431-2730.

CHAPMAN (C-6) pop. 1,241, elev. 1,115′

KANSAS AUTO RACING MUSEUM is at 1205 Manor Dr. The museum focuses on the history of motor sports in Kansas with displays of restored race cars from various eras, photographs and other memorabilia. A theater shows race film highlights, and visitors are encouraged to touch the cars. **Time:** Allow 1 hour minimum. **Hours:** Mon.-Fri. 8-5, Sat. 9-5. **Cost:** $5; $3 (ages 6-12 and 65+). **Phone:** (785) 922-6642.

COFFEYVILLE (E-7) pop. 11,021, elev. 736′

Though carefully planned, the simultaneous robbery of Coffeyville's two banks in October 1892 was not executed successfully. Because Eighth Street was being torn up where Bob, Grat and Emmett Dalton and their two confederates intended to tie their horses, they had to leave them in a parallel alley—too far for a safe getaway even under ideal circumstances.

Then, a warning of what was about to happen and a delaying ruse on the part of a bank employee gave townspeople time to arm. The running gun battle that followed left four citizens and all but one of the outlaws dead. Such was the Dalton Raid, one of the most notorious chapters in the annals of Kansas.

One of the banks involved, the Old Condon Bank at 811 Walnut St., has been restored to its original appearance. A replica of the old city jail sits in Death Alley, where the horses were left. The graves of Bob and Grat Dalton can be seen in Elmwood Cemetery, 2 blocks west of US 169.

Coffeyville once was the home of baseball pitcher Walter Johnson and of 1940 presidential candidate Wendell Willkie, who taught school in the town. A memorial to Johnson is in Walter Johnson Park.

The growth of the town is depicted in 13 murals on downtown walls, sidewalks and stores.

Coffeyville Area Chamber of Commerce: 807 Walnut St., P.O. Box 457, Coffeyville, KS 67337. **Phone:** (620) 251-2550 or (800) 626-3357.

BROWN MANSION, 1 mi. s. of jct. US 166 and US 169 on S. Walnut St., is a restored three-story mansion from the early 1900s. Built by one of Coffeyville's wealthiest men, the 16-room house is furnished in period with Tiffany glass accents and items from the United States and Europe. An information center is on the premises.

Time: Allow 1 hour minimum. **Hours:** Guided tours are given on the hour Mon.-Tues. and Thurs.-Sat. 11-4, Sun. 1-4, Mar.-Oct.; Sat. 11-4, Sun. 1-4, rest of year. Closed Easter, Thanksgiving and Dec. 25. **Cost:** $6; $3 (ages 7-17). Combination ticket with Dalton Defenders Museum $7.50; $3.50 (ages 7-17). **Phone:** (620) 251-0431.

DALTON DEFENDERS MUSEUM, 113 E. 8th St., contains items pertaining to the Coffeyville bank robberies by the Dalton Gang in 1892. Displayed are photographs, guns used in the holdup and capture, saddles, a bank safe and some of the stolen money bags. Mementos of Wendell Willkie and Walter Johnson also are exhibited.

Hours: Mon.-Sat. 10-4, Sun. 1-4. Closed Easter, Thanksgiving and Dec. 25. **Cost:** $3; $1 (ages 7-17). Combination ticket with Brown Mansion $7.50; $3.50 (ages 7-17). **Phone:** (620) 251-5944.

COLBY (B-2) pop. 5,450, elev. 3,138′

Colby is a trading and service center for the surrounding wheat- and corn-producing area.

Colby Visitors Center: 2015 S. Range Ave., Colby, KS 67701. **Phone:** (785) 460-0076.

Shopping areas: Southwind Plaza, I-70 exit 53, features artwork, Kansas products and Western memorabilia. Shops also line N. Franklin Street downtown.

NORTHWEST RESEARCH EXTENSION CENTER, w. on US 24, conducts horticultural and agricultural studies for Kansas State University. Crop research is conducted on the grounds, which also include several varieties of flower gardens. Guided tours are provided upon request during office hours. **Hours:** Grounds daily 24 hours. Office Mon.-Fri. 8-noon and 1-5; closed holidays. **Cost:** Free. **Phone:** (785) 462-7575.

PRAIRIE MUSEUM OF ART AND HISTORY, 1905 S. Franklin Ave., is a 24-acre complex that includes a restored 1930s house, a sod house, a wooden fan windmill, a country church and a one-room school. Also featured is the 1936 Cooper Barn, which houses a 7,000-square-foot exhibit documenting high plains agriculture 1870-1990.

The museum also houses the Kuska Collection, which displays some 30,000 artifacts including glass, ceramics, dolls, toys, furniture, lamps, clocks, stamps, coins and textiles. Interactive exhibits for children are offered at the Kansas Kids Corner.

Time: Allow 1 hour minimum. **Hours:** Mon.-Fri. 9-5, Sat.-Sun. 1-5, Apr.-Oct.; Tues.-Fri. 9-5, Sat.-Sun. 1-5, rest of year. Closed major holidays. **Cost:** $5; $4 (ages 65+); $2 (ages 6-16). **Phone:** (785) 460-4590.

CONCORDIA (B-5) pop. 5,714, elev. 1,363′

Concordia appeals to outdoor enthusiasts. Pheasants and quails are hunted, while the Republican River and area lakes provide good fishing. Concordia maintains five park and playground areas; free camping at Airport Park is popular with tourists traveling in recreational vehicles.

Concordia Chamber of Commerce: 606 Washington St., Concordia, KS 66901. **Phone:** (785) 243-4290.

BROWN GRAND THEATRE is 5 blks. w. of US 81 at 310 W. 6th St. Built in 1907, the theater was restored to its original state and re-opened in 1980. Once an opera house and movie theater, the building now is a community center for art displays, plays and musical performances. Half-hour guided tours featuring the history of the theater and a behind-the-scenes look at the stage are available by request. **Time:** Allow 30 minutes minimum. **Hours:** Mon.-Fri. 2-4. Guided tours are given Sat. 2-4. Closed major holidays. **Cost:** Guided tour $5. Self-guiding tour $1. **Phone:** (785) 243-2553.

CLOUD COUNTY HISTORICAL SOCIETY MUSEUM, 635 Broadway, features relics and photographs depicting area history. Of interest is a display about a local prisoner of war camp that housed German soldiers during World War II. Other exhibits contain a Steuben glass collection; a 1928 Lincoln Page airplane; a Norman Rockwell plate and calendar collection; a working, full-size windmill; an antique toy collection; 19th-century farm equipment; musical instruments; and furniture. **Time:** Allow 1 hour minimum. **Hours:** Tues.-Sat. 1-5. Closed major holidays. **Cost:** Donations. **Phone:** (785) 243-2866.

NATIONAL ORPHAN TRAIN COMPLEX is at 300 Washington St. The museum and research center tell the story of the 1854-1929 Orphan Train Movement during which more than 250,000 abandoned children were transported out of overpopulated eastern cities. The relocation, which laid the foundation for the present-day foster care system, is documented through exhibits and a video. **Time:** Allow 45 minutes minimum. **Hours:** Tues.-Fri. 9:30-noon and 1-4:30, Sat. 10-4. **Cost:** $5; $3 (ages 4-12, ages 63+ and students with ID). **Phone:** (785) 243-4471.

COTTONWOOD FALLS (D-6)
pop. 966, elev. 1,191′

Cottonwood Falls was founded as a busy agricultural and livestock center in the late 1850s. It is home to the French Renaissance-style Chase County Courthouse, built in 1873. Constructed of locally-mined limestone, the courthouse features a mansard roof, dormer windows and a cupola. Still in use, it was designed by John G. Haskell, who also designed the Kansas capitol building in Topeka. Guided tours of the courthouse are available; phone the chamber of commerce for further information.

Roniger Memorial Museum displays an extensive collection of American Indian arrowheads and other artifacts discovered during archeological excavations; phone (620) 273-6310.

Chase County Chamber of Commerce: 318 Broadway, Cottonwood Falls, KS 66845. **Phone:** (620) 273-8469 or (800) 431-6344.

COUNCIL GROVE (C-6)
pop. 2,321, elev. 1,234′

Expansive maples, elms and oaks shade the streets of Council Grove, much as they did during the meeting between Osage Indian chiefs and U.S. commissioners in the summer of 1825. From that conclave came the treaty by which the government obtained the right-of-way for the Santa Fe Trail as well as the name for this town on the Neosho River.

The remains of Council Oak, under which the agreement was signed, are enshrined at 210 E. Main St. Post Office Oak, a block farther west on Main Street, served as an unofficial post office 1825-47, when Council Grove was one of the most important stations—and the last outfitting point—on the Santa Fe Trail. Letters were left in a stone cache at its foot to be picked up by the next wagon train.

Near Post Office Oak is the "Madonna of the Trail" statue, a 16-foot-tall memorial to the courage of pioneer mothers. The statue also marks the start of the Neosho Riverwalk, a paved, landscaped walkway that begins at Main Street, crosses the Santa Fe Trail and ends a half-mile north at the Kaw Mission State Historic Site.

The massive trunk of Custer Elm is preserved 6 blocks south of Main Street on Neosho Street, near property once owned by Lt. Col. George A. Custer. This once giant tree purportedly marks the site where Custer's 7th Cavalry camped as it guarded the Santa Fe Trail. Among several remaining buildings from the town's pioneer heyday are a 19th-century jail at 502 E. Main St., the 1857 Last Chance Store at W. Main and Chautauqua streets, and the 1857 Hays House, one of the oldest continuously operated restaurants west of the Mississippi River.

The 1.25-mile Pioneer Nature Trail at Council Grove Lake, 945 Lake Rd., is part of the National

Recreation Trail and offers a glimpse of the ecosystems of the Flint Hills as well as spectacular wildflower blossoms during spring. Buffalo wallows may be seen on part of the trail's second loop. For further information, phone (620) 767-5195.

Council Grove/Morris County Chamber of Commerce and Tourism: 207 W. Main St., Council Grove, KS 66846. **Phone:** (620) 767-5413 or (800) 732-9211.

Self-guiding tours: A brochure spotting points of historic interest can be obtained from the chamber of commerce and tourism office.

KAW MISSION STATE HISTORIC SITE is at 500 N. Mission St., 5 blks. n. of US 56. Now a museum displaying mission period artifacts, the two-story stone building was erected in 1851 as a school for Kaw Indian children. Exhibits depict the history of the Kaw and the Santa Fe Trail. **Time:** Allow 30 minutes minimum. **Hours:** Wed.-Sat. 9:30-6:30. Closed major holidays. **Cost:** $3; $1 (students with ID); free (ages 0-5). **Phone:** (620) 767-5410.

DODGE CITY (D-3) pop. 26,176, elev. 2,496'

Fittingly called the "Wickedest Little City in America," Dodge City was a wide-open town during the late 1800s. Its infamous Front Street was one of the wildest on the frontier, with one well-stocked saloon for every 20 citizens. Cattlemen, buffalo hunters, soldiers, settlers, gunfighters, railroad men and mule skinners thronged the streets, to the delight and profit of the card sharks, brothel keepers and morticians.

Boot Hill Cemetery is named as such because many of its dead were buried with their boots on. Wyatt Earp and Bat Masterson were among the few able to control the city's lawless elements.

Dodge City began as a stopover on the Santa Fe Trail; wagon wheel ruts still are visible in the sod 9 miles west via US 50. By late 1872 the town was a station on the railroad. Buffalo hunting was intense in the area, and the trading of hides, meat and ultimately bones brought considerable wealth to the town. By the time the buffaloes had nearly become extinct, bellowing herds of Texas cattle had become the primary source of income, and Dodge City became one of the largest cattle markets in the country.

While Dodge City's character has changed, its purpose has not. It remains a major cattle-shipping point and serves as a supply and trade center for a large wheat-growing region.

A look at the city's early days is provided by the mural that adorns the facade of the National Beef Packing Plant, southeast of town on SR 400. It is the work of muralist Stan Herd; another of his depictions can be seen at the Bank of America at 619 N. Second Ave.

Dodge City Convention and Visitors Bureau: 400 W. Wyatt Earp Blvd., Dodge City, KS 67801. **Phone:** (620) 225-8186 or (800) 653-9378.

Self-guiding tours: More than 20 points of interest, including churches, monuments and buildings, are described in a free brochure distributed by the convention and visitors bureau. A recorded narrative to accompany the brochure can be rented for $2 or purchased for $10. A driving tour features Fort Dodge.

BOOT HILL AND FRONT STREET is on the original site of Boot Hill Cemetery. The museum contains exhibits featuring thousands of original historic items depict life in 1876 Dodge City. Visitors can see an Old West gun collection and American Indian artifacts along with buffaloes, cattle and clothing. Included in the complex are Boot Hill Cemetery, Ft. Dodge Jail, a one-room schoolhouse and an 1878 Victorian home once owned by cattle ranchers. A working general store and a saloon are along Front Street.

Food is available in summer. **Hours:** Daily 8-8, Memorial Day weekend-Labor Day; Mon.-Sat. 9-5, Sun. 1-5, rest of year. Gunfights start at noon and 7 p.m., Memorial Day weekend-Labor Day. Closed Jan. 1, Thanksgiving and Dec. 25. **Cost:** Memorial Day weekend-Labor Day $8; $7.50 (ages 7-17 and 62+); $30 (family, 2 adults and 2 or more children ages 0-16). Rest of year $7; $6.50 (ages 7-17 and 62+); $25 (family). **Phone:** (620) 227-8188.

CARNEGIE CENTER FOR THE ARTS, Second Ave. and Spruce St., is a community arts center that houses original works by local, regional and national artists. The building, completed in 1907, originally was a Carnegie library and is noted for its unusual architecture. **Time:** Allow 30 minutes minimum. **Hours:** Tues.-Fri. noon-5, Sat. 11-3, Feb.-Dec. Closed Thanksgiving and Dec. 25. **Cost:** Donations. **Phone:** (620) 225-6388.

DODGE CITY TROLLEY, 400 W. Wyatt Earp Blvd. at the convention and visitors bureau, offers 1-hour tours of Dodge City. Highlights include the original locations of Long Branch Saloon, Front Street and Fort Dodge. Passengers may not exit and re-board the trolley later. **Hours:** Trips depart daily at 9:30, 10:45, 1:30 and 3, Memorial Day to mid-Aug. **Cost:** Fare $7; $5 (ages 3-11). **Phone:** (620) 225-8186 or (800) 653-9378.

FORD HOME OF STONE AND MUSEUM, 112 E. Vine St., has 2.5-foot-thick limestone walls that have preserved the structure since 1881. Rooms are furnished in period and contain pioneer memorabilia, antique clothing and household items. Free 45-minute guided tours are offered daily. **Hours:** Mon.-Sat. 9-5, Sun. 2-4, June-Aug. **Cost:** Donations. **Phone:** (620) 227-6791.

SOLDIERS' HOME AT FORT DODGE is just s. of US 400 at 714 Sheridan St., Unit 28. The fort was a vital Army outpost from 1865, when it was established to protect the Santa Fe Trail from American Indians. Lt. Col. George A. Custer and Union generals Philip Sheridan and Winfield Hancock figured in the fort's history. Original structures were made from sod or adobe, but several 1867 buildings constructed of Kansas sandstone still are in use. A museum and library contain historical and military artifacts.

Hours: Museum and library Mon.-Tues. and Thurs.-Sat. 1-4. Closed Jan. 1, Easter, Memorial Day, Labor Day, Thanksgiving and Dec. 25. **Cost:** Free. **Phone:** (620) 227-2121.

EDGERTON—

see Kansas City p. 182.

EL DORADO (D-6) pop. 12,057, elev. 1,285′

BUTLER COUNTY HISTORY CENTER AND KANSAS OIL MUSEUM, 383 E. Central Ave., chronicles the development of the oil industry in Kansas since 1860. An orientation film about the history of oil is shown. The Glory of the Hills exhibit highlights tallgrass prairie farming and ranching. Outdoor exhibits include farm equipment, several Model-T trucks, an oil derrick, oil field buildings and equipment, a 1930s oil boom town, and a restored "shotgun" house.

Time: Allow 1 hour minimum. **Hours:** Mon.-Sat. 9-5, May-Sept.; Tues.-Fri. 9-5, Sat. noon-5, rest of year. Closed major holidays. **Cost:** $4; $3 (senior citizens); $2 (ages 6-18 and students with ID). **Phone:** (316) 321-9333.

COUTTS MEMORIAL MUSEUM OF ART, just n. of jct. US 54 and US 77 at 110 N. Main St., displays paintings, sculptures, prints and drawings by traditional, contemporary, Western and local artists. Antique furnishings and Persian rugs enhance the setting. Of particular interest is the Frederic Remington bronze collection. **Time:** Allow 1 hour minimum. **Hours:** Mon., Wed. and Fri. 1-5, Tues. and Thurs. 9-noon and 1-5, Sat. noon-4. Closed major holidays. **Cost:** Donations. **Phone:** (316) 321-1212.

ELK FALLS (E-7) pop. 112, elev. 938′

Once the site of a gristmill, the natural waterfalls for which Elk Falls was named are at the bottom of the Elk River Gorge. Pedestrians can view the waterfalls from the 1893 Iron Truss Bridge. The Prudence Crandall Historical Marker, off SR 160, is dedicated to the famed educator, emancipator and human rights activist who lived in Elk Falls from 1874 until her death in 1890; her final resting place is at Elk Hills Cemetery.

ELLIS (C-3) pop. 1,873, elev. 2,117′

ELLIS RAILROAD MUSEUM, 911 Washington St., tracks the history of the railroad in the area. Included are photographs, memorabilia, re-created stations, cars, period clothing and some 1,600 dolls. Train rides aboard a one-third scale streamliner take passengers on a 2-mile track around the museum. **Time:** Allow 1 hour minimum. **Hours:** Tues.-Sat. 10-3. Closed Easter, Thanksgiving and Dec. 25. **Cost:** Museum $3; $2 (ages 5-12). Train $3; $2 (ages 5-12). **Phone:** (785) 726-4493.

WALTER P. CHRYSLER BOYHOOD HOME AND MUSEUM is at 102 W. 10th St. The founder of Chrysler Corp. lived in this 1889 house until the age of 22. Early training as a machinist in local railroad yards helped shape his future course. The house is furnished in period and contains Chrysler memorabilia, including the industrialist's corporate desk, which was donated to the museum after his death in 1940.

Hours: Tues.-Sat. 10-4, Memorial Day-Labor Day; Tues.-Sat. 11-3, rest of year. Closed Easter, Thanksgiving and Dec. 25. **Cost:** $4; $3 (ages 63+); $2 (ages 8-15). **Phone:** (785) 726-3636.

ELLSWORTH (C-4) pop. 2,965

HODGDEN HOUSE MUSEUM COMPLEX, 104 W. South Main St., houses local memorabilia in various buildings, including the 1873 Hodgden House, a church, livery stable, rural schoolhouse, general store and a log building. A Union Pacific caboose and farm machinery also are on the grounds.

Time: Allow 1 hour minimum. **Hours:** Tues.-Sat. 9-5. Closed major holidays. **Cost:** $3; $1 (ages 6-12). Admission includes Fort Harker Museum in Kanopolis *(see attraction listing p. 89)*. **Phone:** (785) 472-3059.

EMPORIA (D-7) pop. 26,760, elev. 1,135′

Few cities are associated more widely with Kansas' journalistic tradition than Emporia, the home of William Allen White. As the outspoken editor and publisher of the *Emporia Gazette* 1895-1944, his incisive writing influenced national affairs. An essay on free speech, "To an Anxious Friend," won White a Pulitzer Prize in 1922. The William Allen White House State Historic Site, which preserves the stone Tudor-style house where he lived for 45 years, is at 927 Exchange St.; phone (620) 342-2800.

Reminders of the "Sage of Emporia" are numerous. They include the William Allen White Library at the 6,000-student Emporia State University, William Allen White Memorial Drive and a commemorative statue in Peter Pan Park. Not the least of these memorials is the *Emporia Gazette* itself, still published by his family.

In 1953 the city became the first in the nation to observe Veterans Day thanks to the forward thinking of another patriotic citizen. Because Armistice Day honored only World War I veterans, Alvin J. King proposed renaming the holiday in order to include World War II and Korean War veterans. With the endorsement of a fellow Kansan, President Dwight D. Eisenhower, Congress officially changed the name to Veterans Day one year later, and in 2003, Congress declared Emporia its founding city.

The Howe House & Welsh Farmstead, 315 E. Logan Ave., is an 1867 limestone dwelling that reflects period style. Tours may be arranged; phone (620) 342-2667. Recreational facilities are available at several sites, including Peter Pan Park, Randolph and Rural streets, and at Soden's Grove Park, which features the David Traylor Zoo of Emporia *(see attraction listing)*. White Memorial Park, at Sixth and

Merchant streets, contains park benches and street lamps in the style of the 1920s. A bust of White's son, William Lindsey White, is the main feature of the park.

Several nearby reservoirs offer fishing, boating and swimming: Lyon, Melvern, Council Grove, Pomona and John Redmond lakes *(see Recreation Chart)* all are within a 45-minute drive.

Emporia Convention and Visitors Bureau: Trusler Business Center, 719 Commercial St., Emporia, KS 66801. **Phone:** (620) 342-1600 or (800) 279-3730.

Self-guiding tours: Brochures outlining driving tours of Emporia and the Flint Hills as well as a walking tour map of downtown are available from the convention and visitors bureau.

ALL VETERANS MEMORIAL, 933 S. Commercial St., is dedicated to all U.S. war veterans, from the Civil War to Operation Iraqi Freedom and Operation Enduring Freedom. In the small, parklike setting is a World War II army tank surrounded by flags and tributes. A Huey helicopter marks the site of a Vietnam veterans' memorial. **Hours:** Daily dawn-dusk. **Cost:** Free. **Phone:** (620) 342-1600.

DAVID TRAYLOR ZOO OF EMPORIA, 75 Soden Rd. in Soden's Grove Park, displays 88 species of native and exotic birds, reptiles and mammals. Some of the exhibits can be seen on a drive-through tour. **Hours:** Walk-through area daily 10-4:30 (also Wed. and Sun. 4:30-8, Mother's Day-first Sun. in Oct.). Drive-through daily dawn-dusk. Closed Jan. 1, Thanksgiving and Dec. 25. **Cost:** Free. **Phone:** (620) 341-4365.

LYON COUNTY HISTORICAL MUSEUM, 118 E. Sixth Ave., features local and regional memorabilia, pioneer items, a log cabin furnished in period and rotating exhibits. **Hours:** Tues.-Sat. 1-5. Closed major holidays. **Cost:** Donations. **Phone:** (620) 340-6310.

NATIONAL TEACHERS HALL OF FAME, 1200 Commercial on the Emporia State University campus in Visser Hall, depicts the heritage of education in America and honors teachers who have been recognized for their commitment and dedication to teaching grades K-12. **Hours:** Mon.-Fri. 8-5, Sat. by appointment. Closed major holidays. **Cost:** Donations. **Phone:** (620) 341-5660 or (800) 968-3224.

EUREKA (D-6) pop. 2,914, elev. 1,081'

Eureka allegedly was named for the exclamation of an excited settler who discovered a spring at this site. The area is known for excellent quail, deer and turkey hunting. Recreational opportunities are available at nearby Fall River, Toronto and Woodson state parks *(see Recreation Chart and Fall River and Yates Center in the AAA South Central CampBook)*. Fall River canoe trips can be arranged April through October, and rentals are available; phone (620) 583-6481.

Eureka Area Chamber of Commerce: 309 N. Oak St., P.O. Box 563, Eureka, KS 67045. **Phone:** (620) 583-5452.

GREENWOOD COUNTY HISTORICAL SOCIETY MUSEUM, 120 W. Fourth St., has pioneer memorabilia and collections of photographs, local relics and indigenous rocks. The museum also contains a genealogical research center. The Chronicle of Greenwood County facility includes exhibits about fossils, pioneers, ranching, farming and American Indian life. **Hours:** Mon.-Fri. 10-4, Sat. by appointment. Closed major holidays. **Cost:** Donations. **Phone:** (620) 583-6682.

FAIRWAY—*see Kansas City p. 182.*

FORT RILEY (B-6)

Reached from exit 301 off I-70, Fort Riley is the home of the 1st Infantry Division. The fort was built in 1853 to protect travelers along the Santa Fe Trail. Originally established as Camp Center, the fort later was named for Gen. Bennett Riley, who led the first military escort down the Santa Fe Trail in 1829. By 1855 the fort was a cavalry post, its soldiers credited with helping open the frontier for settlement.

The 101,000-acre, 11,600-personnel military reservation includes camps Forsyth, Funston and Whitside, Marshall Army Air Field and the Custer Hill area. A large historical district offers some 270 stone buildings. The Commanding General's Mounted Color Guard stables are open daily. Tours are available. A valid driver's license or photo ID, along with vehicle registration and proof of insurance are required for entry; phone (785) 239-2737.

CUSTER HOUSE is on Sheridan Ave., Quarters 24A. Built in 1855 of native limestone, the house realistically depicts military life on the western frontier. Though Lt. Col. George A. Custer did not live in the house, it was named to honor him. A 30-minute guided tour explains about furnishings and other items. **Hours:** Mon.-Sat. 10-4, Sun. 1-4, Memorial Day-Labor Day. Last tour begins 20 minutes before closing. **Cost:** Donations. **Phone:** (785) 239-2737.

FIRST TERRITORIAL CAPITOL OF KANSAS STATE HISTORIC SITE is 3 mi. from I-70 exit 301, following signs. On the site of Pawnee, a struggling town at the edge of the Fort Riley cavalry post, the 1855 building hosted what became known as the "Bogus Legislature." Anti-slavery arguments here led to the conflict known as the "Bleeding Kansas" period of civil unrest. Restored in 1928, the capitol is now a museum furnished with period items. A self-guiding, .5-mile nature trail features native flora and fauna.

Note: Photo ID, vehicle registration and proof of insurance are required to enter the site. **Time:** Allow 1 hour minimum. **Hours:** Fri.-Sun. 1-5, Mar.-Oct.; by appointment rest of year. Trail daily dawn-dusk. Closed major holidays. **Cost:** Donations. **Phone:** (785) 784-5535, or (785) 238-1666 for tour information.

FORT RILEY 1ST INFANTRY DIVISION MUSEUM, jct. Sheridan and Custer aves. in Bldg. 207, covers the four major campaigns — World Wars I and II, Vietnam and Operation Desert Storm — in which the First Infantry Division fought. The Vietnam section offers a reconstructed jungle trail, and the World War II area features an interactive trench. **Time:** Allow 45 minutes minimum. **Hours:** Mon.-Sat. 10-4, Sun. noon-4. Closed Jan. 1, Easter, Thanksgiving and Dec. 25. **Cost:** Donations. **Phone:** (785) 239-2737.

OLD TROOPER STATUE, on the cavalry parade ground across from the Custer House on Sheridan Ave., is a memorial to the U.S. Cavalry. The statue depicts a horse nicknamed Old Bill and its soldier rider, and is based upon Frederic Remington's pen and ink sketch "Old Bill." Chief, the last cavalry horse, died in 1968 and is buried in front of the memorial.

UNITED STATES CAVALRY MUSEUM is at the jct. of Sheridan and Custer aves. in Bldg. 205. The building, which dates from 1855, originally was a hospital. The museum tells the history of the mounted horse soldier of the U.S. Cavalry 1775-1950. **Time:** Allow 1 hour minimum. **Hours:** Mon.-Sat. 9-4:30, Sun. noon-4:30. Closed Jan. 1, Easter, Thanksgiving and Dec. 25. **Cost:** Donations. **Phone:** (785) 239-2737.

FORT SCOTT (D-7) pop. 8,297, elev. 801′

Formed around a military outpost established in 1842 to keep peace along the American frontier, the town of Fort Scott survived after the fort itself was abandoned and sold in 1855. During this time, pro-slavery versus Free State conflicts were common, and Fort Scott's location 6 miles from the Missouri border made it a frequent scene of violence during the turbulent period known as "Bleeding Kansas."

During the Civil War Fort Scott was divided, with "pro-slavers" living on the east side of town and "free-staters" living on the west side. After the war, the town became a leading city of eastern Kansas and challenged Kansas City's standing as the largest rail center west of the Mississippi River.

The town's many handsome commercial buildings and elegant Victorian residences were built from the 1850s to the 1920s. Narrated "Dolly the Trolley" Tours of historic Fort Scott depart hourly from the visitor information center mid-April to early September.

Fort Scott was the boyhood home and is the final resting place of Gordon Parks, director of the popular 1970s film "Shaft."

Fort Scott Visitor Information Center: 231 E. Wall St., Fort Scott, KS 66701. **Phone:** (620) 223-3566 or (800) 245-3678.

Self-guiding tours: A free brochure detailing a historic walking tour of downtown is available from the visitor information center.

FORT SCOTT NATIONAL HISTORIC SITE covers about 17 acres on Old Fort Blvd. on the edge of downtown. Established in 1842, the fort was built on a bluff overlooking the Marmaton River. Twenty fort buildings—which include the post headquarters, officers' quarters, enlisted men's barracks, hospital, bakery, stables, guardhouse, powder magazine and quartermaster's storehouse—have been restored and furnished in period.

Exhibits explain the fort's history, including its role in westward expansion, the Bleeding Kansas era, the Civil War and in protecting the permanent American Indian frontier. **Hours:** Daily 8-5, Apr.-Sept.; 9-5, rest of year. Guided 1-hour tours are given daily at 1, June-Aug. Phone ahead for additional tour times. Closed Jan. 1, Thanksgiving and Dec. 25. **Cost:** $3; free (ages 0-15). **Phone:** (620) 223-0310.

GUNN PARK occupies 155 acres along the Marmaton River in the western part of town. Two small lakes offer fishing and paddleboats. *See Recreation Chart.* **Hours:** Daily 24 hours. **Cost:** Free. Camping $4-$8. **Phone:** (620) 223-0550.

U.S. NATIONAL CEMETERY NO. 1, E. National Ave., covers 21 acres. Established in 1862, it is one of the original 12 national cemeteries designated by President Abraham Lincoln. **Hours:** Grounds daily dawn-dusk. Office daily 8-4:30. **Cost:** Free. **Phone:** (620) 223-2840.

FREDONIA (E-7) pop. 2,600, elev. 866′

STONE HOUSE GALLERY is at 320 N. Seventh St. The gallery, housed in an 1872 building, displays changing exhibits of works by contemporary artists. In addition to monthly art exhibitions, the gallery features theatrical and dance productions as well as vocal and instrumental programs May through December. **Time:** Allow 30 minutes minimum. **Hours:** Mon.-Fri. 12:30-4:30 and by appointment. Closed major holidays. **Cost:** Donations. **Phone:** (620) 378-2052.

GARDEN CITY (D-2) pop. 28,451, elev. 2,830′

Founded in 1879, Garden City's early growth was followed by years of drought and declining population. This cycle continued until dependable irrigation systems were established at the turn of the 20th century.

The Arkansas River makes Garden City one of the state's most extensively irrigated regions; bumper crops of wheat, alfalfa and corn are produced. It also is a major cattle raising and shipping site. South of the city off US 83 a large herd of bison inhabits the nearly 4,000-acre, state-operated Sandsage Bison Range and Wildlife Area. Tours are available by reservation; phone (620) 276-9400.

Finney County Convention and Tourism Bureau: 1511 E. Fulton Terr., Garden City, KS 67846-6165. **Phone:** (620) 276-3264 or (800) 879-9803.

FINNUP PARK AND LEE RICHARDSON ZOO is s. on Bus. Rte. 83 (S. Main St.). The zoo features more than 100 species of animals from around the world, including elephants, big cats, giraffes, otters, primates, birds and bears. Local heritage is preserved at the Finney County Historical Museum. Recreational facilities include a 2.5-million-gallon swimming pool, horseshoe pits, picnic sites, basketball courts, football fields, and playgrounds.

Hours: Zoo daily 8-6:30, Apr. 1 through Labor Day; 8-4:30, rest of year. Conservation center Mon.-Fri. 8-noon and 1-5. Museum Mon.-Sat. 10-5, Sun. 1-5, Memorial Day-Labor Day; daily 1-5, rest of year. Pool daily 1-6 (also Fri.-Sun. and holidays 6-7 p.m.), Memorial Day-Labor Day. Closed Jan. 1, Thanksgiving and Dec. 25. **Cost:** Walk-through free. Drive-through $10 (day pass per private vehicle); $3 (single visit per private vehicle). **Phone:** (620) 276-1250 for the park and zoo, (620) 272-3664 for the museum, or (620) 276-1255 for the pool (seasonal).

GOESSEL (D-6) pop. 565

Goessel was founded in the late 1800s by Russian Mennonites, most of whom were wheat farmers. The town sprang up quickly with the encouragement of the Santa Fe Railroad, which sold land to the farmers at the rate of $2.37 per acre.

MENNONITE HERITAGE & AGRICULTURAL MUSEUM, 200 N. Poplar St., includes a replica of the barracks-like temporary housing built for arriving immigrants. The Turkey Red Wheat Palace displays farm implements and a 6-foot Liberty Bell made from straw and wheat kernels. The Friesen and Krause houses, Schroeder Barn, South Bloomfield and Goessel Preparatory schools, and Goessel State Bank were moved to the museum for preservation.

Time: Allow 1 hour minimum. **Hours:** Tues.-Sat. 10-5, Sun. 1-5, May-Sept.; Tues.-Sat. noon-4, Mar.-Apr. and Oct.-Nov. **Cost:** $4; $3.50 (senior citizens); $2 (ages 7-12). **Phone:** (620) 367-8200.

GOODLAND (B-2) pop. 4,948, elev. 3,687′

Chosen as the county seat in 1887, the town became known in the 1880s for its rainmaking companies. The idea came from a man who claimed to produce rain by pouring sulfuric acid on zinc to release hydrogen, which would unite with the surrounding oxygen to form water. There was no immediate reaction after Melbourne's experiment, but within a day heavy rains reportedly fell.

Earlier the town had proved equally inventive: In its war with several nearby communities for the county seat, residents employed a combination of armed force, false arrest, staged trial and theft to obtain county records. Goodland also can claim that it is the home of America's first patented helicopter.

The brick surface that remains on Main Street and some side streets was laid in 1921 by Jim Brown, an American Indian whose skill was such that he reputedly could lay up to 150 bricks a minute—as fast as five men could supply him—so accurately that no later adjustment to the bricks was necessary.

Twenty miles northeast of Goodland, a historical marker indicates where Lt. Col. George Custer discovered the bodies of the Indian scout, Lt. Lyman Kidder and the 10 cavalrymen felled in the Kidder Massacre of 1867. A map to the site is available at the Sherman County Convention and Visitors Bureau.

Today, the city serves as major retail trade center for northwest Kansas. It also is known as one of the top sunflower producers in the nation; seeds are processed here for confectionery use and for oil. Because of this distinction, Goodland was chosen as one of seven sites worldwide to display giant outdoor reproductions of Vincent van Gogh's sunflower paintings. Visible from I-70, the 80-foot-tall easel and picture is the only one of its kind in the United States.

Sherman County Convention and Visitors Bureau: 925 Main St., P.O. Box 927, Goodland, KS 67735. **Phone:** (785) 890-3515 or (888) 824-4222.

Self-guiding tours: The convention and visitors bureau offers maps for walking and driving tours that highlight historic areas.

GOODLAND HIGH PLAINS MUSEUM, 1717 Cherry St., displays a full-size, automated replica of America's first patented helicopter, built in Goodland by Purvis and Wilson in 1910. A 1902 Holsman rope-driven automobile, the Union School House, pioneer and railroad memorabilia, and prehistoric artifacts and fossils also are exhibited. Dioramas depict scenes from Goodland's history.

Time: Allow 1 hour minimum. **Hours:** Mon.-Fri. 9-5, Sat. 9-4, Sun. 1-4, June-Aug.; Mon.-Fri. 9-5, Sat. 9-4, rest of year. Closed major holidays. **Cost:** Donations. **Phone:** (785) 890-4595.

GREAT BEND (D-4) pop. 15,345, elev. 1,843′

While oil is pumped from underground reserves, wheat is harvested from the overlying fields in Great Bend, situated at the apex of the Arkansas River's sweeping arc through central Kansas.

The town was established in 1871 around the shell of Fort Zarah. It guarded the Santa Fe Trail until 1869 when diminished trail traffic and lessened American Indian threat made the post unnecessary. In 1872 the railroad arrived, bringing with it the cattle trade and all the gambling, gunplay and other amusements typical of a cattle railhead. To establish order, state law decreed that the Texas herds could move no closer than a point 30 miles west of town.

Located in Lafayette Park on the historic Santa Fe Trail is the Kansas Quilt Walk. Seven patterns of quilts reflecting the early settlement of the area are etched in the sidewalks around the park. Also noteworthy in town is the Great Bend Mural Project. A collection of outdoor murals created by local artists can be seen on area buildings. Several are located in the Main Street business area.

Fort Zarah Park, 3 miles east of town on US 56, occupies 9 acres. Thirteen miles southwest on US

56, Pawnee Rock *(see place listing p. 99)* looms above the prairie.

In a vast natural sink, 6 miles northeast via US 281 or US 156, lies Cheyenne Bottoms Wildlife Refuge. As one of the nation's largest inland marshes, it is designated as a wetland of international importance. The 41,000-acre reserve attracts great numbers of birds, including the threatened bald eagle.

Great Bend Convention and Visitors Bureau: 3007 10th St., Great Bend, KS 67530. **Phone:** (620) 792-2750 or (877) 427-9299.

BARTON COUNTY HISTORICAL SOCIETY MUSEUM AND VILLAGE, on US 281 just s. of the Arkansas River Bridge, is on the historic Santa Fe Trail and comprises 11 buildings, including a schoolhouse, church, pioneer rock house, depot, post office, blacksmith shop and four barns. The museum also has collections of dolls, vintage wedding gowns, military uniforms, unusual farm implements and antique household items. A Grand Army of the Republic display focuses on the post-Civil War period.

Time: Allow 1 hour minimum. **Hours:** Tues.-Fri. 10-5, Sat.-Sun. 1-5, mid-Apr. to mid-Nov.; Tues.-Fri. 10-5, rest of year. Additional hours available by appointment. **Cost:** $2; free (ages 0-15). **Phone:** (620) 793-5125.

BRIT SPAUGH PARK AND ZOO, at Main and 24th sts., offers a zoo, a skate park, baseball diamonds, horseshoe courts and a water park. Zoo highlights include a white Bengal tiger as well as a birds of prey show. **Hours:** Park daily 6 a.m.-midnight. Zoo daily 9-4:30. Pool daily 12:30-5:30, Memorial Day-late Aug. **Cost:** Park and zoo free. Water park $4; $3 (ages 0-17). **Phone:** (620) 793-4160 for the zoo.

SHAFER MEMORIAL ART GALLERY is 3 mi. n. on US 281, then 2 mi. e. to 245 N.E. 30th Rd. This gallery, on the Barton County Community College campus, features more than 800 watercolors, oil paintings, photographs and sculptures. Special emphasis is placed on Kansas artists, particularly the work of bronze sculptor L.E. "Gus" Shafer and painter Charles B. Rogers. The collection also contains works by John James Audubon, Marc Chagall and Pablo Picasso.

Time: Allow 30 minutes minimum. **Hours:** Mon.-Fri. 10-5, Sun. 1-4. Closed major holidays. Phone ahead to confirm schedule. **Cost:** Free. **Phone:** (620) 792-9342.

GREENSBURG (E-4) pop. 1,574, elev. 2,235'

The speed and dependability with which he drove the stagecoach between Wichita and Dodge City during the 1880s earned D.R. Green his nickname, "Cannonball." Legend has it that while riding as passenger, temperance reformer Carry Nation reached out of the coach, snatched Cannonball's cigar and hurled it onto the road. He drew rein, silently lifted the astounded lady to the roadway and left her to trudge the many remaining miles to town.

Despite Green's prowess, the day came when the Rock Island Railroad won the race against the Santa Fe Railroad, becoming the first rail line through present-day Greensburg and eliminating the need for stagecoach travel.

Greensburg Chamber of Commerce: 240 S. Main, Greensburg, KS 67054. **Phone:** (620) 723-2400.

BIG WELL, 3 blks. s. of US 54, reputedly is the largest hand-dug well in the world. It measures 32 feet in diameter, is 109 feet deep and contains 15 feet of water. It was begun in 1887 by the city and the Santa Fe Railway, which hoped to use the water for its steam-powered engines. The well was completed in 1888 and provided water for the town until 1932. Visitors descend a 105-step stairway to the bottom of the well.

Note: The well is temporarily closed to foot traffic but may be seen from a viewing canopy. Phone ahead to confirm status. **Hours:** Mon.-Sat. 9-6, Sun. 1-6, early May-Labor Day; Mon.-Sat. 10-5, Sun. 1-5, rest of year. Closed Thanksgiving and Dec. 25. **Cost:** $2; $1.50 (ages 5-12). **Phone:** (620) 723-4102.

Pallasite Meteorite is displayed in the curios shop. Consisting mainly of iron and stone and weighing more than 1,000 pounds, the meteorite was found on a nearby farm in 1949. This is one of the largest pallasites ever discovered. **Note:** The curios shop is closed indefinitely for construction. The meteorite is on display at the Sternberg Museum of Natural History, 3000 Sternberg Dr. in Hays, until construction is completed. Phone ahead for further information. **Cost:** Free. **Phone:** (620) 723-4102.

HALSTEAD (D-5) pop. 1,873, elev. 1,388'

In 1872 Bernhard Warkentin established a gristmill in Halstead—the first step in what would become one of the largest milling enterprises in the region. More important, however, was his promotion of Turkey Red wheat, the strain responsible for Kansas becoming the "Breadbasket of the Nation" *(see Newton p. 98)*. Wheat still is the foundation of Halstead's economy. The Warkentin house and barns, now a landmark, can be seen on the south bank of the Little Arkansas River.

Halstead Chamber of Commerce: P.O. Box 328, Halstead, KS 67056. **Phone:** (316) 217-4996.

KANSAS LEARNING CENTER FOR HEALTH, 505 Main St., has displays about the five senses, the various body systems, the heart, nutrition and other topics. Valeda, a talking transparent model of a woman, is the focus of a 15-minute presentation about the body's functions. Visitors learn through interactive exhibits. **Time:** Allow 1 hour minimum. **Hours:** Mon.-Fri. 10-4. Closed major holidays.

Cost: $2; $1.50 (ages 5-18 and 65+); $5 (family). **Phone:** (316) 835-2662.

HANOVER (B-6) pop. 653, elev. 1,225′

When G.H. Hollenberg closed his store in Marshall County and moved west to start a ranch near Cottonwood Creek, he knew what he was doing. The site he selected was near the Oregon Trail; the building he erected about 1857-58 served not only as his home but also as a store, tavern, stage station for the Overland Express and finally a station for the Pony Express.

The enterprise flourished, providing food, clothing, animal feed, supplies, repairs, blacksmith services and fresh horses and oxen for the passing wagon trains. The community that developed around the ranch was mainly settled by German immigrants, who named the town after Hollenberg's home in the fatherland.

Hanover Chamber of Commerce: P.O. Box 283, Hanover, KS 66945. **Phone:** (785) 337-2252.

HOLLENBERG PONY EXPRESS STATION STATE HISTORIC SITE, 4 mi. n. on SR 148, then 1 mi. e. on SR 243, is the only unaltered Pony Express station remaining in its original location. G.H. Hollenberg built the long frame structure to accommodate his home and the businesses engendered by the traffic on the Oregon Trail.

A museum contains exhibits about the history of the Oregon/California Trail and the Pony Express. A visitor center gallery depicts the evolution of transportation methods. **Hours:** Wed.-Sat. 10-5, first Wed. in Apr.-last Sat. in Oct. Closed major holidays. **Cost:** $3; $2 (ages 60+ and students with ID); free (ages 0-4). **Phone:** (785) 337-2635.

HAYS (C-3) pop. 20,013, elev. 1,997′

By the early 1860s a rising tide of travelers, settlers and railroad builders was inching across the Kansas plains. American Indians, whose lands were being usurped and whose food staple, the buffalo, was being slaughtered by the intruders, responded with increasing hostility.

For protection, Fort Fletcher was established on the banks of Big Creek on the Smoky Hill Trail. Renamed Fort Hays a year later, it became one of the era's prominent military posts. Unlike other typical frontier military outposts, however, Fort Hays had no stockade. All buildings and quarters were grouped around a parade ground.

At one time William "Buffalo Bill" Cody supplied the fort with buffalo meat. Lt. Col. George Custer's ill-fated 7th Cavalry also was encamped near the fort. By the time Fort Hays was abandoned in 1889, the town had become a thriving railroad and agricultural center.

Deeded to the state, the old military post became the site of 5,500-student Fort Hays State University and a 3,700-acre dryland agricultural research center and park, one of the largest in the world. A small buffalo herd can be seen at Frontier Park across from Fort Hays State Historic Site *(see attraction listing)*.

In summer the Hays Aquatic Park, at 4th and Main streets, provides opportunities for swimming, diving or tubing down a lazy river; phone (785) 623-2650. The Kansas Merci Boxcar Museum, 13th and Canterbury streets, features one of 49 boxcars that arrived in the United States in 1949. Filled with French food and other goods, the gifts expressed the French people's gratitude for American assistance during World War II.

Hays Convention and Visitors Bureau: 2700 Vine St., KS 67601. **Phone:** (785) 628-8202 or (800) 569-4505.

Self-guiding tours: A series of 25 markers, beginning downtown at 12th and Fort streets, designates a self-guiding walking tour. Brochures are available at the convention and visitors bureau.

ELLIS COUNTY HISTORICAL SOCIETY MUSEUM, 100 W. Seventh St., is housed in a 19th-century church building. A replica of an early schoolroom and changing exhibits of local settlers' possessions are displayed. A harness shop features saddles from a local historic ranch. **Hours:** Tues.-Fri. 10-5, Sat. 1-5, June-Aug.; Tues.-Fri. 10-5, rest of year. **Cost:** $4; $1 (ages 3-12). **Phone:** (785) 628-2624.

Volga-German Haus, on the grounds of the Ellis County Historical Society Museum, is a replica of a typical Volga-German immigrant house of the 1880s. It is filled with period furnishings. **Hours:** House tours are given by appointment; check with the museum. **Cost:** Included with museum admission. **Phone:** (785) 628-2624.

FORT HAYS STATE HISTORIC SITE, 4 mi. s. of I-70 to 1472 US 183 Alt., encompasses the restored buildings of Fort Hays, including the stone guardhouse, blockhouse and officers' quarters. Buildings contain exhibits about military and pioneer history. The visitor center features exhibits about the fort. **Time:** Allow 1 hour minimum. **Hours:** Tues.-Sat. 9-5, Sun.-Mon. 1-5. Closed major holidays. **Cost:** $3; $1 (students with ID); free (ages 0-5). **Phone:** (785) 625-6812.

GEM **STERNBERG MUSEUM OF NATURAL HISTORY,** off I-70 exit 159, 1 mi. s. on US 183, then following signs, re-creates the late Cretaceous period with dioramas of animated, life-size dinosaurs. The museum, part of Fort Hays State University, also contains one of the world's best collections of fossilized prehistoric flying reptiles and creatures from the Cretaceous sea. One particularly unusual specimen is a fish within a fish.

For children, the Discovery Room contains a giant spider model, computer work stations, live animals and hands-on activities. Changing exhibits are featured throughout the year. Guided tours are available by appointment. **Time:** Allow 2 hours minimum. **Hours:** Tues.-Sat. 9-7, Sun. 1-7. Discovery

Room hours vary; phone ahead. Closed Jan. 1, Thanksgiving and Dec. 25. **Cost:** $8; $6 (ages 60+); $5 (ages 4-12). **Phone:** (785) 628-5516 or (877) 332-1165.

STONE GALLERY, off Main St. at 107 W. Sixth St., displays the limestone, wood, clay and plaster sculptures of Pete Felten, whose public monuments can be seen throughout the state. Visitors can watch live demonstrations of the sculpting process. **Time:** Allow 30 minutes minimum. **Hours:** Mon.-Fri. 9-5. **Cost:** Free. **Phone:** (785) 625-7619.

HIAWATHA (B-7) pop. 3,417, elev. 1,085′

More than 100 varieties of maple trees, planted and cultivated by local citizens, line the streets of Hiawatha. Several city parks offer picnicking and fishing. A town clock dating from 1891 is at Seventh and Oregon streets.

Hiawatha Chamber of Commerce: 602 Oregon St., Hiawatha, KS 66434. **Phone:** (785) 742-7136.

Self-guiding tours: A brochure outlining a driving tour of late 19th-century houses is available from the chamber of commerce.

BROWN COUNTY HISTORICAL SOCIETY AND MUSEUM, in Memorial Auditorium at 611 Utah St., depicts the county's history from its settlement in 1854. A doctor's room, general store, Victorian kitchen and schoolroom are among the displays. **Time:** Allow 1 hour minimum. **Hours:** Mon.-Fri. 10-3, Sat. 10-2. Closed major holidays. **Cost:** $5; $2.50 (ages 5-12). **Phone:** (785) 742-3330.

DAVIS MEMORIAL, in Mount Hope Cemetery at the s.e. edge of town, is an unusual memorial commissioned in 1930 by John M. Davis to perpetuate the memory of his wife, Sarah. Eleven life-size statues depict Mr. and Mrs. Davis at various stages of their lives. **Time:** Allow 30 minutes minimum. **Hours:** Daily 8-dusk. **Cost:** Free. **Phone:** (785) 742-7136.

HILLSBORO (D-6) pop. 2,854, elev. 1,426′

The home of Tabor College, Hillsboro was settled mainly by German-speaking Mennonite immigrants from Russia and Poland. Arriving in the early 1870s, they are credited with bringing Turkey Red wheat to the area. Nearby recreation areas include McPherson State Fishing Lake northwest of Hillsboro and Marion Reservoir to the northeast *(see Recreation Chart and Canton and Marion in the AAA South Central CampBook)*.

Hillsboro Chamber of Commerce: 109 S. Main St., Hillsboro, KS 67063. **Phone:** (620) 947-3506.

THE MENNONITE SETTLEMENT MUSEUM is 1 mi. s. of US 56 at 501 S. Ash St. The museum celebrates the immigrant Russian and Polish Mennonites who settled in western Marion and eastern McPherson counties in the early 1870s. It includes the historic Peter Paul Loewen House, a traditional Russian Mennonite clay-brick house-barn built in 1876 in the settlement of Hoffnungsthal; the Jacob Friesen Flouring Windmill, a detailed replica of an 1876 flour mill that stood in the settlement of Gnadenau; and the 1886 one-room Kreutziger School House.

Tours: Guided tours are available. **Time:** Allow 1 hour minimum. **Hours:** Tues.-Fri. 10-noon and 1:30-4, Sat.-Sun. 2-4, Mar.-Dec. Closed major holidays. Tours depart from the Hillsboro Museums Visitor Center on the west end of the grounds. **Cost:** $3; $1 (students with ID); free (ages 0-4 with adult). **Phone:** (620) 947-3775.

THE WILLIAM F. SCHAEFFLER HOUSE MUSEUM offers guided tours departing from the Hillsboro Museums Visitor Center, 1 mi. s. of US 56 at 501 S. Ash St. The 1909 home belonged to William F. Schaeffler and his wife, Ida. They founded the Schaeffler Mercantile Co. in 1887, which by 1940 had grown into the largest department store in the county. The house contains all of its original furnishings. **Time:** Allow 15 minutes minimum. **Hours:** Tues.-Fri. 10-noon and 1:30-4, Sat.-Sun. 2-4, Mar.-Dec. Tours by appointment only. Closed major holidays. **Cost:** $3; $1 (students with ID); free (ages 0-4). **Phone:** (620) 947-3775.

HUGOTON (E-2) pop. 3,708, elev. 3,110′

STEVENS COUNTY GAS & HISTORICAL MUSEUM is at 905 S. Adams. The museum features a print shop, farm tools, American Indian artifacts and items from the early 1900s. A train depot, barber shop, church and grocery store as well as an 1887 home and a 1945 gas well are on the grounds. **Time:** Allow 30 minutes minimum. **Hours:** Mon.-Fri. 9:30-11:30 and 1-5, Sat. 2-4, June-Aug.; Mon.-Fri. 1-5, Sat. 2-4, rest of year. **Cost:** Free. **Phone:** (622) 544-8751.

HUTCHINSON (D-5) pop. 40,787, elev. 1,529′

"Salt of the Earth" has a special meaning in Hutchinson, where the mining and processing of salt has been a major industry since 1888. A bed of salt and salt/shale between 300 and 350 feet thick and some 600 feet below the surrounding wheat fields was discovered in 1887, to the consternation of drillers looking for natural gas.

Even exhausted mines are valuable; they are used by businesses, hospitals and film companies throughout the world for maximum-security storage of their records. Had the gas seekers persevered, they might have found some of the oil that now enriches the city's economy. However, it is the wheat fields themselves rather than the substances extracted from beneath them that support Hutchinson's leading industry. Other economic mainstays include agribusiness, aerospace equipment, health care, specialty vehicle manufacturing, grocery distribution and food processing.

The Fox Theatre has been restored to its 1931 art deco splendor and is open for guided tours, films and live performances; phone (620) 663-5861.

Nearly 550 acres of parks provide ample recreational opportunities. In early September the state's agricultural bounty is celebrated when Hutchinson hosts the Kansas State Fair.

Hutchinson Convention and Visitors Bureau: 117 N. Walnut St., P.O. Box 519, Hutchinson, KS 67504-0519. **Phone:** (620) 662-3391.

DILLON NATURE CENTER is at 3002 E. 30th Ave. The 10,000-square-foot visitor center houses a nature gallery featuring a diorama explaining the area's plants and animals. Other exhibits include an underground theater, aquariums and interactive displays. Three miles of mostly unpaved nature trails afford visitors an opportunity to enjoy the outdoors. **Time:** Allow 30 minutes minimum. **Hours:** Trails and grounds open Mon.-Fri. 8-dusk, Sat.-Sun. 9-dusk; closed Dec. 25. Visitor center open Mon.-Fri. 8-7, Sat. 10-5, Sun. and holidays 1-5, Apr.-Sept.; Mon.-Fri. 8-5, Sat. 10-5, Sun. and holidays 1-5, rest of year. Closed Thanksgiving and Dec. 25. **Cost:** Free. Admission is charged for programs and events. **Phone:** (620) 663-7411.

HUTCHINSON ZOO is at 6 Emerson Loop E. Among the zoo's inhabitants are eagles, ducks, foxes and deer. Visitors have the option of exploring the zoo on a miniature train. **Time:** Allow 45 minutes minimum. **Hours:** Daily 10-4:45. Closed Thanksgiving and Dec. 25. **Cost:** Zoo free. Train ride $1.50; $1 (ages 3-11). **Phone:** (620) 694-2693.

GEM SAVE **KANSAS COSMOSPHERE AND SPACE CENTER** is at 1100 N. Plum St. The facility features the Hall of Space Museum, IMAX Dome Theater, Justice Planetarium, Dr. Goddard's Lab and changing exhibitions. Highlights include an outstanding exhibit of space suits and one of the largest collections of Russian space equipment outside Moscow.

Early space exploration is detailed through exhibits about Germany's V-1 and V-2 rockets and Russia's Sputnik programs. U.S. space artifacts include the actual Apollo 13 command module, *Gemini X* and a full-scale replica of the space shuttle.

IMAX films are shown on a 44-foot screen; the planetarium presents programs about stars and space. Live shows at Dr. Goddard's Lab demonstrate the principles of rocket science.

Time: Allow 3 hours minimum. **Hours:** Mon.-Sat. 9-8, Sun. noon-8, Memorial Day-Labor Day; Mon.-Thurs. 9-5, Fri.-Sat. 9-8, Sun. noon-6, rest of year. IMAX films, planetarium and laser light shows, and Dr. Goddard's Lab demonstrations are presented daily. Closed Dec. 25. **Cost:** $15; $13 (ages 3-12 and 60+). Single venue (IMAX Dome Theater, Justice Planetarium and Dr. Goddard's Lab) $8.50; $8 (ages 3-12 and 60+). **Phone:** (620) 662-2305 or (800) 397-0330.

KANSAS UNDERGROUND SALT MUSEUM is at 3504 E. Ave. G. This tour starts with a safety video. A double-decked elevator then lowers visitors 650 feet underground into a working salt mine, where a 40-minute guided tram tour into the salt caverns is available. Visitors learn about the mining process, geology and history in the museum's gallery of exhibits and displays.

Note: The descent into the mine takes place in total darkness. For safety, children ages 0-3 are not permitted underground. Museum access is determined by elevator capacity. **Time:** Allow 1 hour, 30 minutes minimum. **Hours:** Tues.-Sat. 9-6, Sun. 1-6, May-Aug.; Tues.-Sat. 9-5, Sun. 1-5, rest of year. Last tour departs 2 hours before closing. Phone ahead to confirm schedule. **Cost:** $13.50 (ages 13+); $8.50 (ages 4-12). Reservations are recommended. **Phone:** (620) 662-1425.

RENO COUNTY MUSEUM, 100 S. Walnut St., chronicles the history of the county through five changing exhibits, with topics ranging from settlement to entertainment. Demonstrations are held throughout the year, and an interactive children's, room and a research room are featured. Outside is the 1876 Siegrist Claim House, a 1940s windmill and a jail. **Hours:** Tues.-Sat. 9-5. Closed major holidays. **Cost:** Donations. **Phone:** (620) 662-1184.

INDEPENDENCE (E-7) pop. 9,846, elev. 798'

Formerly the site of the Osage Indian Reservation, the Independence area was opened to settlement in 1870 when the Osage agreed to move to the Indian Territory in what is now Oklahoma. In 1881 natural gas was discovered and Independence grew quickly, as it did again in 1903 with the discovery of oil. Today, with its gas and oil deposits depleted, the city relies on diversified manufacturing and agriculture.

Independence was the boyhood home of Pulitzer Prize winning playwright William Inge whose Midwestern upbringing shaped such dramas as "Splendor in the Grass" and "Come Back, Little Sheba." The William Inge Collection, housed at Independence Community College, contains original manuscripts, documents and memorabilia; phone (620) 331-4100, ext. 7. Nearby Elk City Reservoir and State Park offers water sports and other recreation *(see Recreation Chart and the AAA South Central CampBook)*.

Independence Area Chamber of Commerce: 322 N. Penn, P.O. Box 386, Independence, KS 67301. **Phone:** (620) 331-1890 or (800) 882-3606.

THE INDEPENDENCE HISTORICAL MUSEUM, 123 N. 8th St., presents regional history from the 1800s to the present. Housed in a former post office built in 1911, exhibits feature American Indian culture, pioneer artifacts, Civil War military items, an 1884 schoolroom and a furnished log cabin. Guided tours are available by appointment. **Time:** Allow 1 hour minimum. **Hours:** Tues.-Sat. 10-4. Closed major holidays. **Cost:** Donations. **Phone:** (620) 331-3515.

LITTLE HOUSE ON THE PRAIRIE, 13 mi. s.w. on US 75, following signs, is a log cabin reconstructed on the site where Laura Ingalls Wilder lived 1869-71. A post office and a one-room schoolhouse are displayed. A hiking trail is available. **Hours:** Mon.-Sat. and holidays 10-5, Sun. 1-5, Mar. 15-Oct. 31. **Cost:** Donations. **Phone:** (620) 289-4238.

RIVERSIDE PARK, 1 mi. n. on US 75, then 2 blks. e. on Oak St., is a 124-acre recreational complex with a swimming pool, water park, tennis courts, a playground, miniature golf, a carousel and train ride. Band concerts are presented Tuesday evenings in summer. **Hours:** Park daily 6 a.m.-midnight. Rides operate Mon.-Sat. 6:30-9:30 p.m., Sun. 1-5:30, Memorial Day weekend-Labor Day. **Cost:** Park free. Miniature golf $1. Train ride 25c. Carousel 5c. **Phone:** (620) 332-2500.

Ralph Mitchell Zoo, on the n. side of Riverside Park, houses a variety of animals, including bears, cougars, birds, reptiles and monkeys. Peacocks roam the grounds. **Hours:** Daily 10-8, Memorial Day-Labor Day; 10-5, rest of year. **Cost:** Free. **Phone:** (620) 332-2500.

IOLA (D-7) pop. 6,302, elev. 962′

In the spring of 1855 a party of pro-slavery men founded a town about a mile and a half southwest of where Iola now stands. They named the town Cofachique in honor of an American Indian chief, and it became the seat of Allen County. Four years later, area residents decided to establish a new county seat and chose the name Iola after Iola Colborn, wife of the man who built the town's first frame house.

The town expanded rapidly after commercial quantities of natural gas were discovered in 1894, but the boom ended around 1910 after wastefulness depleted the gas deposits. Some factories remained in business, and in the early 1970s Iola saw a new wave of factory building.

Cultural events take place at Bowlus Fine Arts Center, 205 E. Madison Ave.; phone (620) 365-4765.

Iola Area Chamber of Commerce: 208 W. Madison Ave., Iola, KS 66749. **Phone:** (620) 365-5252.

ALLEN COUNTY HISTORICAL MUSEUM is at 20 S. Washington Ave. Permanent and changing exhibits describe the history and people of Allen County. The 1869 Old Jail, 203 N. Jefferson, is open for 30-minute guided tours. The jail features an 1891 steel cage block and visitors may read graffiti left by inmates. **Hours:** Tues.-Sat. 12:30-4, May-Oct.; 2-4, rest of year. Jail tours are offered Tues.-Sat. at 1:30, May-Sept. **Cost:** Donations. **Phone:** (620) 365-3051.

MAJOR GENERAL FREDERICK FUNSTON BOYHOOD HOME AND MUSEUM is at 14 S. Washington Ave. The 1860 Victorian-style house was moved to its present location, restored and furnished in period to honor Funston and his sterling military career. After enlisting in the Cuban rebel army in 1896, he won a Medal of Honor for his command of a Kansas regiment in the Philippine American War. **Time:** Allow 1 hour minimum. **Hours:** Tues.-Sat. 12:30-4, May-Oct.; 2-4, rest of year. **Cost:** Donations. **Phone:** (620) 365-3051.

JUNCTION CITY (C-6)

pop. 18,886, elev. 1,080′

Trade has been a major occupation in Junction City since its founding in 1857 at the confluence of the Smoky Hill and Republican rivers. Early commerce was conducted with travelers on the Smoky Hill Trail and with the Kansa Indians, who often came into town to buy and sell. One notable day in 1867 the wares offered by a Cheyenne war party included some newly acquired scalps.

Although feathers and war paint have since disappeared—Junction City is now a commercial center—many of the military uniforms reminiscent of the hostile 1800s endure at historic Fort Riley *(see place listing p. 82)*, which is just north.

Marking the history of Junction City and surrounding counties is Geary County Historical Society Museum, Sixth and Adams streets. Through the display of artifacts and photographs, the museum traces the progression of inhabitants since the area was settled. The Spring Valley Historic Site, US 18 and Spring Valley Road, contains a restored 1870s schoolhouse, a settler's log cabin and a barn.

Heritage Park contains the Kansas Vietnam Memorial, the 1st Infantry Division Monument, a Desert Storm Memorial and a limestone arch that commemorates participants from both sides of the Civil War. The 9-foot-tall bronze Buffalo Soldier Memorial, 18th Street and Buffalo Soldier Drive, commemorates the African-American soldiers who served in the 9th and 10th horse cavalry regiments during the Civil War.

Popular recreation sites are Milford Lake, Geary State Fishing Lake and Milford State Park. Milford Lake is the largest blue-water lake in the state. *See Recreation Chart and the AAA South Central CampBook.*

Geary County Convention and Visitors Bureau: 823 N. Washington St., Junction City, KS 66441-6846. **Phone:** (785) 238-2885 or (800) 528-2489.

MILFORD NATURE CENTER AND FISH HATCHERY, I-70 exit 295, then 5 mi. n. to SR 57 and 2 mi. w., following signs, is on Milford Reservoir. The nature center offers large dioramas depicting Kansas wildlife; live animals including snakes, turtles, birds of prey and bobcats; and hands-on displays. Hiking trails and a playground also are on the premises. Visitors may walk around the raceways at the fish hatchery. **Time:** Allow 1 hour minimum. **Hours:** Mon.-Fri. 9-4:30, Sat.-Sun. 1-5, Apr.-Sept. Tours of the fish hatchery are offered Sat.-Sun. at 1, Apr.-May. Hatchery building tour by appointment only. **Cost:** Donations. **Phone:** (785) 238-5323.

KANOPOLIS (C-5) pop. 543, elev. 1,587′

FORT HARKER MUSEUM is on SR 140. Abandoned in 1872, Fort Harker was used to protect the north central Kansas frontier from hostile American Indians. Featured are a horse-drawn ambulance, military uniforms and equipment from World Wars I and II. A train depot is on the grounds as well as junior officers' quarters.

Time: Allow 30 minutes minimum. **Hours:** Tues.-Sat. 10-5, Sun. 1-5, May-Sept.; Tues.-Fri. and Sun. 1-5, Sat. 10-5 in Apr. and Oct.; Sat. 10-5, Sun. 1-5, rest of year. Closed major holidays. **Cost:** $3; $1 (ages 6-12). Admission includes Hodgden House Museum Complex in Ellsworth *(see attraction listing p. 81)*. **Phone:** (785) 472-3059.

KANSAS CITY—

see Kansas City p. 182.

KINSLEY (D-4) pop. 1,658, elev. 2,164′

During the 1870s Kinsley shared in the boom brought by railroad expansion. The *Mercury* newspaper printed 25,000 European editions advertising the town: "Kinsley—The Cynosure Of All Eyes, The Coming Great Metropolis." But when the dust—most of which was caused by a decade of drought—had settled, an 1888 edition of the *Mercury* confessed that the boom was over as nine columns of delinquent tax notices were printed.

Today Kinsley enjoys quieter days as an agricultural center and the seat of Edwards County. The town is noted for being halfway between New York City and San Francisco—1,561 miles from either city—giving it the nickname Midway, U.S.A.

Kinsley Chamber of Commerce: 200 E. 6th St., P.O. Box 332, Kinsley, KS 67547. **Phone:** (620) 659-3642.

EDWARDS COUNTY HISTORICAL MUSEUM, jct. US 50 and US 56, features a sod house that includes an explanation of its construction, an 1884 church and blacksmith shop. The "soddy" is furnished with period items. On display are settlers' toys, quilts and clothing as well as Santa Fe Trail memorabilia, including photographs and oxen yokes. Other exhibits feature horse-drawn machinery and an early fire engine. A full-size mural on the outside of the building portrays area history.

Hours: Mon.-Sat. 9-5, Sun. 1-5, May-Sept. **Cost:** Donations. **Phone:** (620) 659-2420.

KIRWIN (B-4) pop. 229, elev. 1,695′

KIRWIN NATIONAL WILDLIFE REFUGE office is 4 mi. w. on SR 9, then 1 mi. s. on E. Xavier Rd. The refuge covers 10,778 acres surrounding Kirwin Reservoir and provides a habitat for various species of migratory waterfowl and grassland nesting birds. The 10-acre Prairie Dog Town allows visitors to view these animals from nature trails. Fishing, birdwatching and seasonal hunting are offered. Regulation information is available at refuge headquarters.

Time: Allow 3 hours minimum. **Hours:** Daily 24 hours. Office Mon.-Fri. 7:30-4. **Cost:** Free. **Phone:** (785) 543-6673.

LA CROSSE (C-4) pop. 1,376, elev. 2,068′

La Crosse, founded in 1876, is a shipping point for wheat and livestock. The town is known as the "Barbed Wire Capital of the World."

Rush County Chamber of Commerce: 905 Main St., La Crosse, KS 67548. **Phone:** (785) 222-2639.

BARBED WIRE MUSEUM, 120 W. First St., displays some 2,066 types of barbed wire, including the first 1853 patented wire, handmade barbed wire, foreign barbed wire and entanglement wire used in battle since World War I. Many related items also are displayed. **Time:** Allow 30 minutes minimum. **Hours:** Mon.-Sat. 10-4:30, Sun. 1-4:30, May 1 to mid-Sept.; by appointment rest of year. **Cost:** Donations. **Phone:** (785) 222-9900.

THE POST ROCK MUSEUM is at 202 W. First St. Post rock, a form of limestone common to this region of the state, was used extensively from the late 1870s to the mid-1930s for fence posts and in constructing bridges, houses, churches and other buildings. Displays explain how the rock was found, quarried and used. **Time:** Allow 30 minutes minimum. **Hours:** Mon.-Sat. 10-4:30, Sun. 1-4:30, May 1 to mid-Sept. **Cost:** Donations. **Phone:** (785) 222-2719.

RUSH COUNTY HISTORICAL MUSEUM, in the old Santa Fe Depot at 202 W. First St., preserves county and period history with a hodgepodge of historical relics. **Time:** Allow 30 minutes minimum. **Hours:** Mon.-Sat. 10-4:30, Sun. 1-4:30, May 1 to mid-Sept. **Cost:** Donations. **Phone:** (785) 222-2719.

LAKIN (D-2) pop. 2,316, elev. 3,002′

THE KEARNY COUNTY MUSEUM is at 111 S. Buffalo St. This complex encompasses the museum building and annex, the White House, a school house, the Santa Fe Depot, the Farm Machinery building and the Round Barn. Items include an antique printing press, and wedding dresses and kitchen appliances from the late 1800s. **Time:** Allow 30 minutes minimum. **Hours:** Tues.-Fri. 9-noon and 1-4, Sun. 1-4. **Cost:** Free. **Phone:** (620) 355-7448.

LARNED (D-4) pop. 4,236, elev. 2,002′

Midway along the Santa Fe Trail where Pawnee Creek joins the Arkansas River, the settlement of Larned emerged as the construction of the Santa Fe Railway neared Fort Larned. As the military usefulness of the fort declined, the attractiveness of the fertile agricultural lands became apparent, allowing Larned to develop into the prosperous trading center and county seat it is today.

Central States Scout Museum, 815 Broadway, displays Boy and Girl Scout memorabilia, including uniforms, awards and handbooks; phone (620) 285-6427.

Larned Area Chamber of Commerce: 502 Broadway, Larned, KS 67550. **Phone:** (620) 285-6916.

FORT LARNED NATIONAL HISTORIC SITE is 6 mi. w. via SR 156. Established in 1859 to protect mail coaches and commercial wagon trains traveling the Santa Fe Trail, the fort was an important post on the frontier until its deactivation in 1878. The site includes nine original sandstone buildings and a section of wagon-wheel rutted prairie. A visitor center has exhibits and a slide program; living-history programs are held in summer and on major holidays.

Guided tours are available by appointment. **Hours:** Daily 8:30-4:30. Closed Jan. 1, Thanksgiving and Dec. 25. **Cost:** Free. **Phone:** (620) 285-6911.

SANTA FE TRAIL CENTER MUSEUM AND LIBRARY, 2 mi. w. on SR 156, depicts the history of one of America's most important frontier pathways as well as the lifestyles of early Kansas pioneers. Permanent displays include a Wichita Indian hunting lodge, mounted buffalo, a freight wagon, period rooms, a sod house, a limestone cooling house, a one-room schoolhouse, an early African-American church and a dugout house. Changing exhibits also are presented.

Time: Allow 1 hour minimum. **Hours:** Daily 9-5, Memorial Day-Labor Day; Tues.-Sun. 9-5, rest of year. Closed Jan. 1, Thanksgiving and Dec. 25. **Cost:** $4; $2.50 (ages 12-18); $1.50 (ages 6-11). **Phone:** (620) 285-2054.

LAWRENCE (C-7) pop. 80,098, elev. 822'

Founded as an abolitionist settlement in 1854 by the New England Emigrant Aid Society, Lawrence was at the center of the controversy concerning slavery that embroiled the state prior to the Civil War. Although the anti-slavery faction won, the other side ultimately had the last word. In 1863 Confederate guerrilla William Quantrill and 400 bushwhackers swept into Lawrence and attacked the ill-prepared home guard, leaving more than 200 dead and causing $1.5 million worth of damage, thus fueling animosities and retaliations between Kansans and Missourians.

Modern day Lawrence is a vibrant smaller city with many big-city amenities. Education, transportation, agriculture and light industry provide the basis for a diverse economy. The University of Kansas and Haskell Indian Nations University, the country's only intertribal American Indian college, are focal points for education, arts and culture. Lectures, plays, films, performing arts and concerts are presented year-round at The Lied Center of Kansas; phone the box office at (785) 864-2787. The Lawrence Arts Center, 940 New Hampshire St., hosts visual art, theater and dance events; phone (785) 843-2787.

For recreational pursuits, the city has some 50 parks that offer opportunities for swimming, skateboarding, hiking, tennis, golf, camping and picnicking. Additional information and a map indicating bicycle routes and parks can be obtained at the Parks and Recreation Department, City Hall, Sixth and Massachusetts streets, and at the Lawrence Visitor Information Center, N. Second and Locust streets; phone (785) 865-4499. Clinton Lake State Park *(see Recreation Chart and the AAA South Central CampBook)* is 4 miles west of town.

Downtown Lawrence has a number of historic buildings. The Old West Lawrence Historic District, bounded by Sixth, Eighth, Tennessee and Indiana streets, contains more than 40 Victorian- and Italianate-style residences. The 1912 Liberty Hall, 642 Massachusetts St., was the first motion picture theater west of the Mississippi River.

Lawrence Convention and Visitors Bureau: 402 N. 2nd St., P.O. Box 526, Lawrence, KS 66044. **Phone:** (785) 865-4411.

Self-guiding tours: Maps for touring the city, its historic district and the University of Kansas campus are available from the convention and visitors bureau.

Shopping areas: The downtown district, running along Massachusetts Street between Sixth and 11th streets, has an eclectic mixture of locally owned shops, cafes and restaurants as well as large national chain stores.

UNIVERSITY OF KANSAS, s. of I-70 exit 202 via US 59, is on a 1,000-acre campus atop Mount Oread, which separates the valleys of the Kansas and Wakarusa rivers. A visitor center, at the corner of 15th and Iowa streets, offers maps as well as a brochure of a walking tour covering the Dole Institute of Politics museum and archives, Spencer Museum of Art, Natural History Museum, the World War II memorial campanile, and the Booth Hall of Athletics museum adjacent to the Allen Fieldhouse.

Hours: Visitor center Mon.-Fri. 8-5; closed university holidays and semester breaks. **Phone:** (785) 864-3911 for tour and general campus information.

Kenneth Spencer Research Library, 1450 Poplar Ln., contains an extensive collection of rare books, manuscripts, old maps and early photographs. Among the specialties are European books printed in the 15th through 17th centuries; books relating to Ireland and 18th-century England; the history of such sciences as botany, ornithology and zoology; and broad collections of Italian, French and English manuscripts of the 11th through 20th centuries.

Items in the Kansas Collection range from the territorial period to the present and include the University Archives, which contains information on the history of The University of Kansas.

Hours: Mon.-Fri. 9-5 (also Sat. noon-4 when school is in session). Closed major and university holidays and during semester breaks. **Cost:** Free. **Phone:** (785) 864-4334.

Robert J. Dole Institute of Politics is off I-70 exit 202, 1.7 mi. s. on Iowa St. (US 59), then w. into University of Kansas via 19th St. to 2350 Petefish Dr. The non-partisan institute contains research and archival materials related to the career of Kansas native Sen. Robert J. Dole. A museum includes interactive exhibits about his early life, military service and political accomplishments.

Memorials to the World Trade Center victims and the state's World War II veterans are included. **Time:** Allow 1 hour minimum. **Hours:** Mon.-Sat. 9-5, Sun. noon-5. Closed Jan. 1, Easter, Thanksgiving and Dec. 24-25. **Cost:** Free. **Phone:** (785) 864-4900.

GEM **Spencer Museum of Art** is at 1301 Mississippi St.; parking is available next to the university union. The museum, which contains more than 25,000 objects in its permanent collection, ranks among the finest university art museums in the country. Strengths are in Renaissance and baroque painting; American paintings and sculpture; the decorative arts of Europe, America and Asia; and graphic arts, including photographs and Japanese prints.

Permanent and changing exhibits are displayed. **Time:** Allow 1 hour minimum. **Hours:** Tues.-Sat. 10-4 (also Thurs. 4-8), Sun. noon-4. Closed major holidays. **Cost:** Free. **Phone:** (785) 864-4710.

GEM SAVE **University of Kansas Natural History Museum,** in Dyche Hall at 1345 Jayhawk Blvd., displays birds, fossils and mounted animals primarily from Kansas and the Plains states. The main floor features a panorama of North American plants and animals in natural settings and such mounted animals as Comanche, a horse that survived Lt. Col. George Custer's Last Stand. Live snakes, insects and bees comprise other exhibits. **Time:** Allow 2 hours minimum. **Hours:** Mon.-Sat. 9-5, Sun. noon-5. Closed major holidays. **Cost:** $5; $3 (children). **Phone:** (785) 864-4450.

WATKINS COMMUNITY MUSEUM OF HISTORY, 1047 Massachusetts St., is housed in a restored 1888 bank building. Displays depict area history and include a Victorian parlor, a bicentennial quilt, a 1920 electric car, a horse-drawn surrey, an 1878 playhouse and an 1850s cannon. A children's history room also is offered. Rotating exhibits feature such topics as early settlement, the Underground Railroad and Lawrence resident Dr. James Naismith, originator of the game of basketball. **Hours:** Tues.-Sat. 10-4 (also Thurs. 4-8). Closed major holidays. **Cost:** Donations. **Phone:** (785) 841-4109.

LEAVENWORTH (B-8) pop. 35,420, elev. 774'

Incorporated in 1854, Leavenworth is the oldest city in Kansas. In 1857 the firm of Russell, Majors & Waddell made the rapidly growing community the headquarters of their vast overland transportation system. In April 1860 the company's other venture, the Pony Express, used lightweight riders on fleet ponies to speed the mail from St. Joseph, Mo., to Sacramento, Calif., in as little as 9 days. Completion of the transcontinental telegraph in October 1861 rendered the service obsolete.

Leavenworth Landing Park, on the Missouri River, commemorates the city's role as "Gateway to the West." It features sculptures of a locomotive and a covered wagon as well as depictions of a railroad roundhouse and paddlewheel steamship.

Leavenworth Convention & Visitors Bureau: 518 Shawnee St., P.O. Box 44, Leavenworth, KS 66048. **Phone:** (913) 682-4113 or (800) 844-4114.

Self-guiding tours: Maps featuring area driving and walking tours are available from the convention and visitors bureau.

CARROLL MANSION is at 1128 Fifth Ave. The 16-room Victorian house, built in 1867, was expanded and embellished with fine carved woodwork in 1882. The furnishings illustrate gracious living in the 19th century. **Time:** Allow 1 hour minimum. **Hours:** Tues.-Sat. 10:30-4:30. Closed major holidays. Phone ahead to confirm schedule. **Cost:** $5; $4 (ages 60+); $3 (ages 5-12). **Phone:** (913) 682-7759.

C.W. PARKER CAROUSEL MUSEUM is .5 mi. e. on Springdale St./Spruce St. (SR 92), .4 mi. n. on S. 4th St., .2 mi. e. on Choctaw St., then just n. to 320 S. Esplanade St. across from the riverfront. The museum offers artifacts and photographs depicting the work of carnival pioneer and carousel builder C.W. Parker. Guided tours explore a workshop area at which new carousel horses are carved from wood and existing antique horses are repaired and refinished. Tours conclude with a ride on a large wooden carousel, one of three refurbished full-size carousels displayed.

Time: Allow 30 minutes minimum. **Hours:** Thurs.-Sat. 11-5, Sun. 1-5, Feb.-Dec. Closed Easter, July 4, Thanksgiving and Dec. 24-25 and 31. **Cost:** $5; $3 (ages 0-12). Carousel ride $1; $5 (6 rides). **Phone:** (913) 682-1331.

FORT LEAVENWORTH is at Seventh St. and US 73. Established in 1827 to guard the Santa Fe and Oregon trails, the fort is the oldest active Army post west of the Mississippi River. It also was an important Army headquarters during the Mexican War 1846-48.

The Santa Fe and Oregon Trail markers, the Fort Leavenworth National Cemetery and the Buffalo Soldier Monument are of interest. Maps are available for self-guiding tours in the museum. Photo ID is required for all visitors ages 17+ entering the base. **Hours:** Daily dawn-dusk. **Cost:** Free. **Phone:** (913) 684-5604.

GEM **Frontier Army Museum** is at Gibbon and Reynolds aves. opposite Bell Hall. Exhibits provide insight into the founding and development of Fort Leavenworth, the history of the frontier army and the Civil, Mexican and Indian wars. The museum includes the carriage in which Abraham Lincoln rode while visiting Leavenworth, army carriages and a full-size JN4 "Jenny" biplane.

Also displayed are examples of U.S. military dress and equipment up to World War I as well as several rare Mexican War items. Videotapes about the history of the fort are shown. **Hours:** Mon.-Fri.

9-4, Sat. 10-4. Closed major holidays. **Cost:** Donations. **Phone:** (913) 684-3767 or (913) 684-3186.

RICHARD ALLEN CULTURAL CENTER AND MUSEUM is at 412 Kiowa St. The museum highlights the roles African-Americans have played in the history of Kansas and the West with exhibits about the Buffalo Soldiers, a nickname originally applied to members of the all-black Army regiments created after the Civil War. A restored Buffalo Soldiers home features furnishings and 1920s décor.

Other exhibits include an 1860 tallow light belonging to a runaway slave, a collection of historic photos and memorabilia belonging to former Secretary of State Colin Powell. **Tours:** Guided tours are available. **Time:** Allow 1 hour minimum. **Hours:** Mon.-Sat. 10-5. Closed major holidays. **Cost:** $5; $2 (ages 0-12). **Phone:** (913) 682-8772.

LEBANON (B-4) pop. 303, elev. 760′

A stone monument 1 mile north and 1 mile west marks the historical geographical center of the 48 contiguous United States. A small park, picnic tables and a shelter house are at the site.

Lebanon City Office: 404 Main St., P.O. Box 182, Lebanon, KS 66952. **Phone:** (785) 389-1141.

LECOMPTON (B-7) pop. 608

Lecompton is on the banks of the Kaw River, in the rolling hills between Topeka and Lawrence. From its founding as Bald Eagle in 1854, until Kansas statehood was granted in 1861, this village was the territorial capital.

CONSTITUTION HALL STATE HISTORIC SITE, 319 Elmore St., is the building in which the controversial Lecompton Constitution for the admittance of Kansas into the Union as a pro-slavery state was written. The document sparked a chain of events that divided the country and eventually climaxed in the Civil War. Displays deal with significant territorial Kansas political and historical events such as the slavery debate. **Hours:** Wed.-Sat. 9-5, Sun. 1-5. Closed major holidays. **Cost:** $3; $1 (students with ID). **Phone:** (785) 887-6520.

TERRITORIAL CAPITOL-LANE MUSEUM, 640 E. Woodson St., was begun in 1855 as the territorial capitol but work was suspended in 1857 when it seemed the capital would be elsewhere. Finally completed in 1882, the building housed Lane University until 1902. Displays include pioneer and American Indian artifacts, Civil War items and an exhibit about President Dwight Eisenhower's parents, who met and married while attending Lane University. Guided 1-hour tours are available upon request. **Hours:** Wed.-Sat. 11-4, Sun. 1-5. Closed major holidays. **Cost:** Donations. **Phone:** (785) 887-6148.

LENEXA—*see Kansas City p. 183.*

LIBERAL (E-2) pop. 19,666, elev. 2,839′

Now used by the Cotton Belt Railroad, the Rock Island Railroad Bridge across the Cimarron River is one of the largest of its kind. Called "Mighty Sampson," it is 1,200 feet long and 100 feet above the riverbed. Support pylons were driven to a depth of 165 feet to resist the shifting quicksand of the river.

Liberal Convention and Tourism Bureau: 1 Yellow Brick Rd., Liberal, KS 67901. **Phone:** (620) 626-0170 or (800) 542-3725.

DOROTHY'S HOUSE/ LAND OF OZ /CORONADO MUSEUM is at 567 Yellow Brick Rd. Dorothy's House is a replica of the fictional Kansas farmhouse depicted in the 1939 motion picture, "The Wizard of Oz." A re-creation of the Yellow Brick Road leads to the Land of Oz Museum, which features exhibits about the film as well as related memorabilia. The Coronado Museum contains pictures, documents and historical items pertaining to Seward County and early Kansas.

Time: Allow 1 hour minimum. **Hours:** Guided tours are offered every 30 minutes Mon.-Sat. 9-6, Sun. 1-5, Memorial Day-Labor Day; on the hour Tues.-Sat. 9-5, Sun. 1-5, rest of year. Closed Jan. 1, Easter, Thanksgiving and Dec. 25. **Cost:** Dorothy's House and Land of Oz $5; $3.50 (ages 6-18 and 65+). Coronado Museum free. **Phone:** (620) 624-7624.

GEM **MID-AMERICA AIR MUSEUM LIBERAL, KANSAS,** 2000 W. Second St., is Kansas' largest aviation museum. Collections consist of military and civilian aircraft as well as aerospace aviation exhibits. Visitors can see World War II fighters and bombers, experimental and golden age aircraft and planes used in the Korean and Vietnam wars.

Features include the Liberal Army Airfield, Korean War exhibits, the Col. Tom A. Thomas Jr. Historic Aircraft Collection and a NASA exhibit. More than 100 aircraft are displayed, including such rare planes as the Grumman TBM Avenger, North American B-25, Rutan aircraft, Vought F4U-5N Crusader and the Douglas A-4 Skyhawk. Wind tunnel and hot air balloon exhibits are part of the Aviation Hall of Science.

Time: Allow 1 hour minimum. **Hours:** Mon.-Fri. 8-5, Sat. 10-5, Sun. 1-5. Closed Jan. 1, Thanksgiving and Dec. 25. **Cost:** $7; $5 (ages 62+); $3 (ages 6-18). **Phone:** (620) 624-5263.

LINDSBORG (C-5) pop. 3,321, elev. 1,335′

The delightful flavor of Scandinavia permeates Lindsborg, founded by a company of Swedish pioneers and farmers in 1869. Many Old World arts and crafts are practiced; studios of several Lindsborg artists feature woodcarvings, ceramics, pottery, metal craft and paintings.

Lindsborg Chamber of Commerce: 201 N. Main St., Lindsborg, KS 67456. **Phone:** (785) 227-3706 or (888) 227-2227.

BIRGER SANDZEN MEMORIAL GALLERY, at 401 N. First St. on the Bethany College campus, features the works of the Swedish-American painter and art teacher. This gallery also displays permanent and changing collections of paintings, prints, ceramics and sculptures in 10 exhibition areas. An outdoor courtyard features a fountain sculpted by the Swedish artist Carl Milles. **Hours:** Tues.-Sun. 1-5. **Cost:** Free. **Phone:** (785) 227-2220.

McPHERSON COUNTY OLD MILL MUSEUM, 5 blks. s. on Main St., then 1 blk. e., includes historic buildings, pioneer exhibits and Swedish costumes. Smoky Valley Roller Mill is one of the earliest water-powered flour mills in the state. The Swedish Pavilion, also on the grounds, originally was part of the 1904 St. Louis World's Fair. A small park and campground are on the banks of the Smoky Hill River.

Hours: Mon.-Sat. 9-5, Sun. 1-5. Closed Jan. 1, Thanksgiving and Dec. 25. **Cost:** $2; $1 (ages 6-12). **Phone:** (785) 227-3595.

RED BARN STUDIO MUSEUM is just s. on 2nd St., just w. on E. Lincoln St., then .1 mi. s. to 212 S. Main St. The museum is the former home and now restored studio of artist Lester Raymer, whose paintings, ceramics, sculptures and other creations are displayed. During guided tours, visitors learn about Raymer, who worked in the studio for nearly half a century, and the materials he used — scrap metal and wood, Masonite and recycled materials, among others — to create works of art and such objects as toys and pieces of furniture as well as the studio itself.

Time: Allow 45 minutes minimum. **Hours:** Tues.-Sun. 1-4; otherwise by appointment. **Phone:** (785) 227-2217.

LOGAN (B-3) pop. 603, elev. 1,950′

A farming and oil community on the North Fork Solomon River, Logan was established in 1872. Among the founders was a young Dane, Peter Hansen, whose son Dane became an important businessman and a friend and advisor to President Dwight Eisenhower.

DANE G. HANSEN MEMORIAL MUSEUM occupies a square block in the center of town at 110 W. Main St. Oil paintings, a collection of European and Western guns, coins and Oriental art are featured. Traveling exhibits from the Smithsonian Institution and other renowned museums also are presented. **Time:** Allow 1 hour minimum. **Hours:** Mon.-Fri. 9-noon and 1-4, Sat. 9-noon and 1-5, Sun. and holidays 1-5. Closed Jan. 1, Thanksgiving and Dec. 25. **Cost:** Free. **Phone:** (785) 689-4846.

LUCAS (C-4) pop. 436, elev. 1,493′

GARDEN OF EDEN is at Second and Kansas aves. Surrounding a 1907 stone and concrete cabin, the garden features peculiar concrete figures on the ground and perched in trees. By the time he was finished, S.P. Dinsmoor had used more than 113 tons of cement to make statues, which include biblical figures and allegorical characters expressing his social and political beliefs. Dinsmoor's body can be viewed in a glass-covered stone coffin that he built.

Tours: Guided tours are available. **Hours:** Daily 10-5, May-Oct.; daily 1-4, Mar.-Apr.; Sat.-Sun. 1-4, rest of year. **Cost:** $6; $1 (ages 6-12). **Phone:** (785) 525-6395.

GRASSROOTS ART CENTER, 213 S. Main St., displays one-of-a-kind works by self-taught Kansan folk artists. Sculptures, totems, woodcarvings, paintings, mosaics, chewing gum and other media are represented in a variety of unusual pieces, including a life-size motorcycle crafted entirely of aluminum can pull-tabs. An outdoor courtyard features limestone carvings.

Tours: Guided tours are available. **Time:** Allow 30 minutes minimum. **Hours:** Mon.-Sat. 10-5, Sun. 1-5, May-Sept.; Mon. and Thurs.-Sat. 10-4, Sun. 1-4, rest of year. Closed major holidays. **Cost:** $6; $2 (ages 6-12). **Phone:** (785) 525-6118.

LYONS (D-5) pop. 3,732, elev. 1,695′

Wheat above ground, oil and salt below—the economy of Lyons has been well-assured since the town was established as the Rice County seat in 1876. The first salt mine opened in 1890; one mine and a processing plant still operate.

In 1541 one of those who accompanied Francisco Vásquez de Coronado on his search for the treasures of Quivira was Father Juan de Padilla. Both men went back to Mexico, but a year later Padilla returned as a missionary to the American Indians. He was attacked and killed, however, and thus became the first Christian martyr in the United States. A large granite cross, 4 miles west on US 56, commemorates his work.

There also is evidence of a prehistoric culture in the area. A 150-foot-long intaglio (impression) resembling a serpent was dug into the earth by the Quivira Indians; it is 5.5 miles north on SR 14, then 5 miles east on a county road. Guided tours to the intaglio can be arranged; phone (620) 257-3941.

Lyons Chamber of Commerce: 116 East Ave. S., P.O. Box 127, Lyons, KS 67554. **Phone:** (620) 257-2842.

CORONADO-QUIVIRA MUSEUM, 105 W. Lyon St., displays items from the 16th-century Quiviran Indian culture, including such relics of European contact as chain mail. Other exhibits include items from the pioneer period, especially those relating to the nearby Santa Fe Trail. **Time:** Allow 1 hour minimum. **Hours:** Tues.-Sat. 9-5. Closed major holidays. **Cost:** $2; $1 (ages 6-12). **Phone:** (620) 257-3941.

MANHATTAN (C-6) pop. 44,831, elev. 1,019′

Most of its residents having come from northern states, Manhattan maintained a decidedly free-state stance during the "Bleeding Kansas" era. As New

England continued to send emigrants to Kansas to cement the abolitionist sympathies, organizations in the East often donated money to the settlers.

The city is nestled in the Flint Hills, so named for their bands of limestone and flint. The region, which remains largely untouched by the plow, includes the Konza Prairie. The Flint Hills are the largest remnants of tallgrass prairie on the continent; uncut or ungrazed, the native bluestem grasses can grow 8 feet high. By appointment, Kansas State University offers guided tours of the tallgrass prairie; phone (785) 587-0441. Three self-guiding trails are open dawn to dusk.

Kansas State Agricultural College, now Kansas State University, opened its doors in 1863; it was one of the first land-grant colleges in the nation. Tours of the 23,500-student campus are offered during the school year; phone (785) 532-6318.

City Park, on Poyntz Avenue between 11th and 14th streets, includes a pioneer log cabin, swimming pool, rose garden and a 30-foot statue of Johnny Kaw, a mythical Kansas wheat farmer. Tuttle Creek State Park offers 13,350 acres for sports and recreation, while Pottawatomie State Fishing Lake No. 2 offers 247 acres *(see Recreation Chart and the AAA South Central CampBook).*

Manhattan Convention and Visitors Bureau: 501 Poyntz Ave., Manhattan, KS 66502. **Phone:** (785) 776-8829 or (800) 759-0134.

Shopping areas: Manhattan Town Center Mall, at Third and Poyntz avenues, features Dillard's, JCPenney and Sears.

KANSAS STATE UNIVERSITY INSECT ZOO is .7 mi. e. on Claflin Rd., then .1 mi. n. to 1501 Denison Ave. on the university's campus. Among the zoo's exhibits are freshwater and Amazonian rain forest displays, a honeybee observatory and a leaf-cutter ant colony spread throughout the building and viewable via glass panes and tubing. Terraria house a variety of arthropods including millipedes, scorpions, tarantulas and walking sticks; visitors may interact with selected insects during guided tours.

Time: Allow 45 minutes minimum. **Hours:** Zoo open Tues.-Sat. noon-6 and by appointment. Guided tours are offered Mon. 9-5 and Tues.-Fri. 9-noon. Reservations for guided tours must be made at least 1 week in advance. **Cost:** $2; $1.50 (senior citizens). Guided tours $3. **Phone:** (785) 532-2847, or (785) 532-5891 for guided tour reservations.

MARIANNA KISTLER BEACH MUSEUM OF ART, at 14th St. and Anderson Ave. on the Kansas State University campus, houses some 6,000 pieces with special emphasis given to 20th-century Midwestern artists and photographers. The building's post-modern design is of architectural interest. **Time:** Allow 30 minutes minimum. **Hours:** Tues.-Sat. 10-5 (also Thurs. 5-8), Sun. noon-5. Closed major holidays. **Cost:** Free. **Phone:** (785) 532-7718.

RILEY COUNTY HISTORICAL MUSEUM, 2309 Claflin Rd., contains exhibits, changing displays and the Seaton Research Library. Next door is Hartford House, a restored prefabricated cabin brought to Manhattan on a steamboat in 1855. Also on the grounds is the 1870s Randolph Jail. The 1860s Goodnow House State Historic Site contains original furnishings and items belonging to Isaac Goodnow, a leader in the Free State Movement.

Note: The Goodnow House State Historic Site is closed for restoration and is scheduled to reopen in spring 2010. **Hours:** Tues.-Fri. 8:30-5, Sat.-Sun. 2-5. Library open by appointment. Closed major holidays. Phone ahead to confirm schedule. **Cost:** Donations. **Phone:** (785) 565-6490.

SUNSET ZOOLOGICAL PARK, 2333 Oak St., houses more than 330 animals. Among the 104 species are Caribbean flamingos, anteaters, tigers, red pandas and snow leopards. Exhibits include the African Forest Trail, prairie dog plains, a cheetah habitat and the Chimpanzee Habitat. Peacocks roam the grounds. **Hours:** Daily 9:30-5, Apr.-Oct.; noon-5, rest of year. **Cost:** $4; $2 (ages 3-12). **Phone:** (785) 587-2737.

MARQUETTE (C-5) pop. 542, elev. 1,388'

KANSAS MOTORCYCLE MUSEUM is at 120 N. Washington St. More than 100 motorcycles of various ages, makes and models fill this museum's two buildings. During his 6-decade-long racing career, the museum's owner won more than 600 trophies, which are on display. Visitors also will see an array of motorcycle memorabilia. **Tours:** Guided tours are available. **Time:** Allow 1 hour minimum. **Hours:** Mon.-Sat. 10-5, Sun. 1-5. **Cost:** Donations. **Phone:** (785) 546-2449.

MARYSVILLE (B-6) pop. 3,271, elev. 1,154'

Marysville, known as the "Black Squirrel City," is one of few known spots in the country in which the black squirrel lives in the wild. The squirrels first came to the city in 1912 as part of a carnival's sideshow to entertain a group of Civil War veterans. Some local youngsters released the squirrels, which scampered from their cages to freedom in the city park, where their descendants still frolic.

Marysville was settled mainly by travelers along the Oregon Trail, seven emigrant trails and the Otoe Indian and Pony Express trails. The town was named for the wife of merchant Frank Marshall, who operated a ferry across the Big Blue River. Several emigrant parties camped near the ferry crossing 1840-60.

The state's first civilian post office was established in Marysville on Nov. 11, 1854. The town also was the home of the first state bank in Kansas. Marysville and surrounding Marshall County have several national historic landmarks, including old schools, houses and churches dating from the mid-1800s (most of these buildings are not open to the public).

A Union Pacific steam locomotive, schoolhouse, sod house and an 1870 railroad depot sit in Marysville's City Park. Tile murals created by artist Rufus Seder are displayed at the Pony Express Plaza at jct. N. 7th and Center sts.

Marysville Chamber of Commerce: 101 N. 10th St., P.O. Box 16, Marysville, KS 66508. **Phone:** (785) 562-3101 or (800) 752-3965.

Self-guiding tours: Maps detailing walking and driving tours of Marysville and the surrounding area are available from the chamber of commerce.

HISTORIC COURTHOUSE is at 1207 Broadway. Built in 1891, this beautiful Romanesque structure features marble pillars and an eight-sided tower. Museum displays fill 21 rooms and include items that belonged to German and Czech settlers, baptismal fonts from early churches, farming and blacksmithing tools, a school bell from a rural school, a dentist's office and such medical equipment as an iron lung. The large courtroom has a vaulted ceiling, stained glass windows and original oak furnishings.

Tours: Guided tours are available. **Time:** Allow 1 hour minimum. **Hours:** Daily 1-4, Memorial Day weekend-Sept. 15; Mon.-Fri. 1-4, rest of year. Closed Thanksgiving and Dec. 25. **Cost:** $2; free (children). **Phone:** (785) 562-5012.

KOESTER HOUSE MUSEUM, 919 Broadway at US 77 and US 36, is a restored two-story Victorian house built by a local banker about 1874. It is furnished with elegant original pieces. A brick fence designed to prevent flooding encloses the yard. Two statues of lions flank the north gate, while two cast iron dogs guard the east gates. **Tours:** Guided tours are available. **Hours:** Mon.-Sat. 10-noon and 1-4:30, Sun. 1-4:30, Apr.-Oct.; by appointment rest of year. **Cost:** $2.50; $1 (ages 5-12). **Phone:** (785) 562-2417 or (785) 562-3101.

ORIGINAL PONY EXPRESS HOME STATION NO. 1 MUSEUM, 106 S. Eighth St., served as an 1859 headquarters for the postal riders before the introduction of the telegraph to the Western territories. The museum displays post office boxes from the state's first civilian post office, established in Marysville in 1854. **Hours:** Mon.-Sat. 10-5, Sun. noon-4, May-Oct. **Cost:** $3; $1 (ages 6-12). **Phone:** (785) 562-3825.

McPHERSON (D-5) pop. 13,770, elev. 1,490′

McPherson bears the name of Union Civil War general James Birdseye McPherson, who was killed in the Battle of Atlanta in 1864. Although Gen. McPherson never visited the Kansas city named after him, his bronze likeness has watched over the city from its perch in Memorial Park since 1917. The Santa Fe Trail, which crosses just south of McPherson, is a present-day reminder of the area's pioneer heritage.

Most early residents of McPherson were farmers lured to the area by the promise of free land. The discovery of oil in the 1920s largely shielded the local economy from the Great Depression and set the stage for an emerging industrial base.

At 100 N. Maple St. is the historically maintained 1890s McPherson County Courthouse and its 105-foot-high clock tower. The restored 1888 McPherson Opera House, 221 S. Main St., a Victorian architectural showpiece, features a 550-seat auditorium with two balconies.

McPherson Convention and Visitors Bureau: 306 N. Main St., P.O. Box 616, McPherson, KS 67460. **Phone:** (620) 241-3340 or (800) 324-8022.

Self-guiding tours: Information detailing walking and driving tours is available from the convention and visitors bureau.

MCPHERSON MUSEUM, 1130 E. Euclid St., is in a three-story 1920s house. Two floors contain fossils, American Indian artifacts, pioneer household items, meteorites, gems and minerals along with a children's learning center. Among the highlights is the first man-made diamond. For an additional fee visitors can see six N- and HO-gauge model railroads. **Time:** Allow 1 hour minimum. **Hours:** Tues.-Sat. 1-5. Closed major holidays. **Cost:** $3; $2 (ages 62+ and students with ID); $1 (ages 0-12). **Phone:** (620) 241-8464.

MEADE (E-3) pop. 1,672, elev. 2,500′

Deep artesian wells contribute to the verdancy of Meade's tree-lined streets as well as to that of surrounding farms and ranches. Meade State Park is 12 miles southwest off SR 23 *(see Recreation Chart and the AAA South Central CampBook).*

Meade Economic Development: P.O. Box 238, Meade, KS 67864. **Phone:** (620) 873-8795.

DALTON GANG HIDEOUT, ESCAPE TUNNEL AND MUSEUM, 4 blks. s. of US 54 at 502 S. Pearlette St., contains furnishings used in 1887 and an opening to a 95-foot-long tunnel leading to the barn where the gang kept their getaway horses. **Hours:** Mon.-Sat. 9-5, Sun. 1-5. Closed Jan. 1, Easter, Thanksgiving and Dec. 25. **Cost:** $4; free (ages 0-5). **Phone:** (620) 873-2731 or (800) 354-2743.

MEADE COUNTY HISTORICAL SOCIETY MUSEUM, 200 E. Carthage, offers a maze of exhibits depicting the area's history. A one-room schoolhouse, church, sod house, general store and blacksmith shop are presented. Also featured is a livery barn with a horse-drawn wicker carriage, a sheepherder's wagon and saddles. **Time:** Allow 1 hour minimum. **Hours:** Mon.-Sat. 9-5, Sun. 1-5. Closed Jan. 1, Easter, Thanksgiving and Dec. 25. **Cost:** $3; free (ages 0-5). **Phone:** (620) 873-2359.

MEDICINE LODGE (E-4)
pop. 2,193, elev. 1,468′

Because the Plains tribes believed the wooded valley of the Medicine River to be protected by the Great Spirit, they treated it accordingly, sharing the use of a small lodge where anyone could fast, pray and heal with impunity. Thus it was this spot that the Kiowa, Arapaho, Comanche, Apache and Cheyenne chose for the peace negotiations with representatives of the U.S. government in October 1867.

The list of attendees was impressive: Satanta, great chief of the Kiowa; Black Kettle of the Cheyenne; Ten Bears, the wise Comanche orator; Wolf Sleeve of the Apache; and Little Raven, the Arapaho orator. Government advisers were Gen. William Tecumseh Sherman and S.J. Crawford, governor of Kansas. Covering the event for the St. Louis *Daily Missouri Democrat* was reporter Henry M. Stanley, who, years later in Africa, would utter his query, "Dr. Livingstone, I presume?"

Not far from where it was signed, the treaty is celebrated every three years at Memorial Peace Park with an outdoor pageant re-enacting the event. Barber State Fishing Lake, offering camping, fishing and boating, also is nearby *(see Recreation Chart and the AAA South Central CampBook).*

Medicine Lodge Area Chamber of Commerce: 215 S. Iliff St., P.O. Box 274, Medicine Lodge, KS 67104-1536. **Phone:** (620) 886-3417.

CARRY A. NATION HOME is at 211 W. Fowler Ave. at Oak St. Having left her first husband, Dr. Gloyd, because of his alcoholism, Nation decided that she would become "the John Brown of Prohibition." Her first public demonstration for temperance occurred in Medicine Lodge in 1900. Ultimately her crusade took her, swinging her hatchet and bellowing song and prayer, from Kansas to national renown. Her house, furnished with personal items, now is a museum.

Time: Allow 30 minutes minimum. **Hours:** Daily 10:30-5, May-Oct.; 1-4, rest of year. Closed Jan. 1, Easter, Thanksgiving and Dec. 25. Phone ahead to confirm schedule. **Cost:** $5; $4 (ages 55+); $3 (ages 7-14). Admission includes ticket to Medicine Lodge Stockade. **Phone:** (620) 886-3553.

MEDICINE LODGE STOCKADE, in town on US 160, is a reconstruction of the original stockade built on this site in 1874 to protect the early settlers from American Indians. A log house built in 1877 has been moved to the site and furnished in period. The museum contains historical items and records. **Time:** Allow 1 hour minimum. **Hours:** Daily 10:30-5, May-Oct.; 1-4, rest of year. Closed Jan. 1, Easter, Thanksgiving and Dec. 25. Phone ahead to confirm schedule. **Cost:** $5; $4 (ages 55+); $3 (ages 7-14). Admission includes ticket to Carry A. Nation Home. **Phone:** (620) 886-3553.

MINNEAPOLIS (C-5) pop. 2,046, elev. 1,257′

Farming and stockraising in the surrounding Solomon River Valley support Minneapolis. The community's name is an arresting combination of an American Indian word for waters, *minne,* and the Greek word for city, *polis.*

Minneapolis Area Chamber of Commerce: 200 W. Second St., Minneapolis, KS 67467. **Phone:** (785) 392-3068.

Self-guiding tours: Brochures detailing four tours of the area are offered by the chamber of commerce.

ROCK CITY, 2 mi. s. on SR 106, is a group of about 200 mostly spherical or elliptical sandstone and limestone concretions. Ranging from 8 to 27 feet in diameter, they were formed underground by the precipitation of water-borne calcium carbonate in the spaces of loosely cemented sandstone. Erosion of the surface gradually uncovered the formations. **Time:** Allow 30 minutes minimum. **Hours:** Daily dawn-dusk. **Cost:** $3; 50c (ages 1-15). **Phone:** (785) 392-2092, (785) 392-2577 or (785) 488-2236.

MONTEZUMA (E-3) pop. 966, elev. 2,785′

Founded in 1912 during an intense land speculation boom, many of Montezuma's early citizens were Mennonites seeking religious freedom and fertile farmland. Wheat and grain still provide the economic mainstay, but fallow fields now yield a more unusual commodity—electricity. With some 170 windmills spread over 205 square miles just east of town, Gray County Wind Farm generates enough energy to power 33,000 homes. A good viewing area lies at the junction of US 56 and CR 17, where an information kiosk explains the operations.

STAUTH MEMORIAL MUSEUM is at 111 N. Aztec St. Displayed are clothing, crafts, decorative arts, ivory carvings, musical instruments, vases and unusual souvenirs collected by Montezuma residents Claude and Donalda Stauth during 40 years of world travel. The Fry Wildlife Collection includes exhibits relating to North American game animals and promotes education and conservation. International traveling exhibits change year-round. **Time:** Allow 30 minutes minimum. **Hours:** Tues.-Sat. 9-noon and 1-4:30, Sun. 1:30-4:30. Closed major holidays. **Cost:** Donations. **Phone:** (620) 846-2527.

NEODESHA (E-7) pop. 2,848, elev. 800′

At the confluence of the Verdigris and Fall rivers, Neodesha (Osage for "meeting of the waters") was a refining center for the area's oil fields. The town now serves as a manufacturing and agricultural center for the region.

Near the town is the grave of Little Bear, one of the great Osage chiefs. According to local legend, American Indians returning to pay homage to their chief found the grave robbed. Angered, they prepared to pillage the white settlement of Neodesha; however, one of the town's doctors pacified them by giving them a skeleton from his office—claiming it was the body of Little Bear.

Norman No. 1, jct. First and Main sts., marks the spot where the first successful commercial oil well west of the Mississippi River was drilled in 1892. The rig, now replaced with a replica, was the first to tap the rich Mid-Continental Field, which reached as far as Texas. A museum chronicles local history and features a collection of circus memorabilia donated by retired Barnum and Bailey performers hailing from Neodesha. The museum is open by appointment and the well is open daily dawn-dusk; phone (620) 325-2055.

Neodesha Chamber of Commerce: 100 S. First St., P.O. Box 266, Neodesha, KS 66757. **Phone:** (620) 325-2055.

NEWTON (D-5) pop. 17,190, elev. 1,445′

Newton's history began in 1870 when the site was chosen as a location for a new Atchison, Topeka & Santa Fe Railway terminal. Its position on the Chisholm Trail made the site a logical location. When the railroad pushed on to Dodge City and Wichita, so did Newton's wild and wicked cow town image.

As pressures against their beliefs mounted, Russian Mennonites looked to the North American prairies for a new home. Bernhard Warkentin visited central Kansas in 1872; his favorable reports elicited a wave of immigration. As a result, Newton and the surrounding area constitute the largest Mennonite settlement in the United States.

Mennonite farmers brought with them Turkey Red winter wheat seeds, which had flourished on the central European steppes. Warkentin built a gristmill at nearby Halstead *(see place listing p. 85)* and began promoting the use of this hardy new grain, which was well-suited to conditions in Kansas. His efforts at establishing hard winter wheat helped make Kansas known as the "wheat capital of the world." Warkentin's residence still stands at 211 E. First St.

Newton Convention & Visitors Bureau: 500 N. Main St., Suite 101, Newton, KS 67114. **Phone:** (316) 283-7555 or (800) 899-0455.

NORTH NEWTON (D-5) pop. 1,522, elev. 1,440′

GEM **KAUFFMAN MUSEUM** is .7 mi. s. of I-135 exit 34 at 27th and N. Main sts., across from Bethel College. The museum is on a 5-acre site that consists of woods and a re-created prairie with native grasses and wildflowers. Indoor exhibits depict the natural history of the Plains, American Indians and the culture and heritage of European Mennonites who immigrated to the Central Plains in the 1870s.

Permanent exhibits include Mennonite Immigrant Furniture, Mirror of the Martyrs and Of Land and People. Temporary exhibits often are available. Historic buildings include a late 19th-century homesteader's log cabin, a Kansas farmstead with an 1875 house and an 1886 barn.

Time: Allow 1 hour minimum. **Hours:** Tues.-Fri. 9:30-4:30, Sat.-Sun. 1:30-4:30. Closed major holidays. **Cost:** $4; $2 (ages 6-16). **Phone:** (316) 283-1612.

NORTON (B-3) pop. 3,012, elev. 2,284′

Principally an agricultural community, Norton offers a refreshing glance at national politics. The Gallery of Also Rans, in the First State Bank building at 105 W. Main St., features photographs and biographies of the nation's unsuccessful presidential candidates.

At Prairie Dog State Park, named for a large colony of prairie dogs living there, visitors can see the 1886 Hillmon School and the Adobe House, constructed in the 1890s out of mud and straw. The park is 4 miles west of town on US 36. *See Recreation Chart and the AAA South Central CampBook.*

Norton Area Chamber of Commerce: 104 S. State St., P.O. Box 97, Norton, KS 67654. **Phone:** (785) 877-2501.

OAKLEY (C-2) pop. 2,173, elev. 3,049′

At the junction of I-70, US 40 and US 83, Oakley is a busy commercial center. It gained the county seat in the same manner as many early Kansas communities, winning over Russell Springs by only three votes—hardly the plurality required by law. Although the town is not named for the cowgirl entertainer, she did perform nearby with Buffalo Bill's Wild West Show. In tribute, Annie Oakley Park, 600 E. 5th St., offers walking trails, a playground, a swimming pool and picnic facilities.

Oakley Area Chamber of Commerce: 216 Center Ave., Oakley, KS 67748. **Phone:** (785) 672-4862.

FICK FOSSIL AND HISTORY MUSEUM, 700 W. Third St., exhibits fossils, fossil folk art, rocks, minerals, local memorabilia, artwork, a glass collection from the Great Depression and antiques. Other displays include indigenous wildflowers, a sod house and photographs dating from the 1800s. **Time:** Allow 1 hour minimum. **Hours:** Mon.-Sat. 9-5, Sun. 1-5, May-Sept.; Mon.-Sat. 9-noon and 1-5, rest of year. Closed major holidays. **Cost:** Free. **Phone:** (785) 671-4839.

MONUMENT ROCKS (CHALK PYRAMIDS) are 20 mi. s. on US 83, then 4 mi. e. on a dirt road. Remnants of layer after layer of Cretaceous seabed, the wind-carved, water-eroded chalk pinnacles rise some 70 feet above the plain. This natural formation served as a landmark for pioneers and American Indians. Weathering has revealed a great variety of marine and reptilian fossils. Chalk bluffs and similar formations are characteristic of the Smoky Hill River Valley from this region east to Cedar Bluff Reservoir. No facilities are available. **Cost:** Free.

PRAIRIE DOG TOWN, off I-70 exit 70 to US 83, features animals common to western Kansas, including buffaloes, donkeys, foxes, goats, pheasants and prairie dogs. Visitors may pet and feed some animals. Animal oddities such as live 5- and 6-legged cows are on the premises. **Time:** Allow 1 hour minimum. **Hours:** Daily 9-8, Memorial Day weekend-Oct. 31. **Cost:** $6.95; $6.25 (senior citizens); $4.95 (ages 11-15); $3.95 (ages 3-10). **Phone:** (785) 672-3100.

OBERLIN (B-3) pop. 1,994, elev. 2,250′

The last American Indian raid on Kansas soil occurred in Oberlin on Sept. 29, 1878. Several days before, Chief Dull Knife and his band of Northern Cheyenne had left Indian Territory heading north in an attempt to regain their homeland in the Dakotas. On Sept. 27 they engaged a detachment of the 19th Infantry from Fort Dodge.

Two days later they raced through Decatur County, killing 19 settlers before fleeing into Nebraska with the 4th Cavalry in hot pursuit. A monument to the unfortunate settlers is in Oberlin Cemetery. Today the town is a trading center for the surrounding High Plains farming country.

Decatur County Area Chamber of Commerce: 104 S. Penn Ave., Oberlin, KS 67749. **Phone:** (785) 475-3441.

DECATUR COUNTY LAST INDIAN RAID MUSEUM, 258 S. Penn Ave., is a 14-building complex that includes a sod house, train depot, schoolhouse, land office, livery stable, an 1888 church and a 1930s gas station and grocery store. Period rooms contain pioneer and American Indian artifacts and a quilt collection. **Time:** Allow 1 hour minimum. **Hours:** Museum Tues.-Sat. 9:30-noon and 1-4, Apr.-Nov. Office only open for research Tues.-Thurs. 9:30-noon and 1-4:30, Dec.-Mar. Closed major holidays. **Cost:** $5; $3 (ages 6-12). **Phone:** (785) 475-2712.

OLATHE—*see Kansas City p. 183.*

OSAWATOMIE (C-7) pop. 4,645, elev. 853′

The word Osawatomie (Oh-suh-WAH-tuh-mee) combines the names of the two American Indian tribes who once inhabited the area, the Osage and the Pottawatomie.

As a railroad town, it was the site of pro-slavery and anti-slavery conflicts during the pre-Civil War years. In May 1856 abolitionist John Brown and a small group of followers raided neighboring houses and killed several men as a symbolic warning to the pro-slavery faction.

Several hundred pro-slavers retaliated 3 months later by killing five of Brown's men, including his son, in a raid that became known as the Battle of Osawatomie.

The Old Stone Church, at Sixth and Parker streets, was one of the state's early pioneer churches. Its first pastor was the Rev. Samuel Adair, brother-in-law to John Brown; phone (913) 755-4384.

Osawatomie Chamber of Commerce: 628 Main St., P.O. Box 63, Osawatomie, KS 66064. **Phone:** (913) 755-4114.

JOHN BROWN STATE HISTORIC SITE, 10th and Main sts., contains a statue of the abolitionist as well as the log cabin that served as his unofficial headquarters. The cabin, owned by Brown's brother-in-law, the Rev. Samuel Adair, was a station on the Underground Railroad; it contains period furniture. A stone pavilion protects the structure from the elements. The park is built on the site of the 1856 Battle of Osawatomie. A museum's exhibits interpret the conflict known as "Bleeding Kansas."

Hours: Tues.-Sat. 10-5. Closed major holidays. **Cost:** Donations. **Phone:** (913) 755-4384.

OTTAWA (C-7) pop. 11,921, elev. 910′

OLD DEPOT MUSEUM, s.w. of jct. SR 68 and US 59 at 135 W. Tecumseh St., is in a two-story limestone building that originally was a passenger depot on the Santa Fe Railroad. A model train layout depicts local railroading in 1950. Displays focus on area history; changing exhibits are presented. **Hours:** Tues.-Thurs. and Sat. 9-5, Fri. 9-7, Sun. 1-4. Closed major holidays. Phone ahead to confirm schedule. **Cost:** $3; $1 (students with ID). **Phone:** (785) 242-1250.

OVERLAND PARK—*see Kansas City p. 183.*

PARSONS (E-7) pop. 11,514

Parsons' history is closely intertwined with that of the Missouri-Kansas-Texas Railroad, also known as the KATY or MKT. It was home of the diesel shops for the line until it was sold to the Union Pacific in the 1980s.

Buildings of architectural note include the 1920s Carnegie Arts Center, formerly the town's library, and the Parsons Municipal Auditorium, which hosts concerts, theater productions and civic gatherings. The First Presbyterian Church's turrets and stained-glass windows make it a much photographed structure. Hundreds of Civil War veterans are buried at Oakwood Cemetery, known for its wartime monuments and memorials.

The Parsons Arboretum includes a visitor center, wetlands area, observation deck and an 18-hole disc golf course. Nearby, both Pearson-Skubitz Big Hill Lake and Neosho State Fishing Lake *(see Recreation Chart)* offer camping and fishing facilities.

Labette County Convention and Visitors Bureau: 1715 Corning, Parsons, KS 67357. **Phone:** (620) 421-6500 or (800) 280-6401.

PAWNEE ROCK (D-4) pop. 356, elev. 1,941′

PAWNEE ROCK STATE HISTORIC SITE, .5 mi. n. off US 56, is a sandstone citadel that was a prominent landmark for travelers on the Santa Fe Trail. American Indians are believed to have met here and used the site as a vantage point to watch for bison herds and wagon trains. Until settlers and the railroad stripped nearly 20 feet of stone from its top, mostly for use in building the Santa Fe Railroad,

Pawnee Rock rose nearly 100 feet above the plain. **Hours:** Daily dawn-dusk. **Cost:** Free. **Phone:** (785) 272-8681.

PHILLIPSBURG (B-4) pop. 2,668, elev. 1,939′

Civil War veterans were predominant among those who settled Phillipsburg in 1872 and helped to protect it during its early years. Today the town is known as a trade center and the seat of county government. The Huck Boyd Community Center is a venue for entertainment and civic events. It also houses a railroad museum and a model train layout.

Phillipsburg Area Chamber of Commerce: 270 State St., P.O. Box 326, Phillipsburg, KS 67661. **Phone:** (785) 543-2321.

FORT BISSELL, .5 blks. w. on State St./US 36 in City Park, is a reconstruction of an 1872 fort built to protect settlers from Apache Indian raids. Antiques and equipment from an early doctor's office and a barber shop are displayed. Two 1870s log houses, one of which showcases a gun collection, depict pioneer lifestyles. A furnished sod house, a one-room schoolhouse and an early general store also are on the grounds. **Hours:** Tues.-Fri. 9-4 (also Wed. 5-8), Sat. 10-4, May 1 through Labor Day; by appointment rest of year. Closed July 4. Phone ahead to confirm schedule. **Cost:** Donations. **Phone:** (785) 543-6212.

PITTSBURG (E-7) pop. 19,243, elev. 922′

Adopting and adapting the name of the Pennsylvania metropolis, Pittsburg was founded in 1876 as a mining camp. Over the years some 200 million tons of coal were excavated here. Pittsburg State University, with an enrollment of 6,500, offers educational and cultural opportunities. Nearby, several reclaimed strip pits provide swimming, fishing and other recreation.

Little Balkans Days, a festival held downtown on the Saturday before Labor Day, celebrates the community's coal-mining origins. Highlights include sports tournaments, train rides, concerts, crafts and a quilt show.

Crawford County Convention and Visitors Bureau: 117 W. Fourth St., P.O. Box 1115, Pittsburg, KS 66762. **Phone:** (620) 231-1212.

CRAWFORD COUNTY HISTORICAL MUSEUM, 651 US 69S, contains horse-drawn vehicles, vintage clothing, printing exhibits, items from deep coal-mining operations and farming implements. Also on the grounds are an 1885 schoolhouse, a 1922 Marion steam shovel and a neighborhood grocery store. **Hours:** Thurs.-Sun. 1-5. Closed major holidays. **Cost:** Donations. **Phone:** (620) 231-1440.

PLEASANTON (D-8) pop. 1,387, elev. 862′

On Oct. 25, 1864, one of the last significant Civil War battles fought west of the Mississippi River occurred along this segment of Mine Creek. Retreating southward before a pursuing Union force, about 7,000 Confederate troops established a defense on the north side of the creek.

When the vanguard of the Union force topped the rise, they faced the muzzles of thousands of pistols and rifles and eight cannons—and charged. A half-hour later the numerically superior Confederates were routed, defeated by the Union's better weapons, position and cavalry. By forcing the Confederates out of Kansas and saving Fort Scott from attack, the Battle of Mine Creek extinguished the South's hope of success in the West.

Pleasanton City Hall: 1608 Laural St., Pleasanton, KS 66075. **Phone:** (913) 352-8257.

LINN COUNTY HISTORICAL MUSEUM is 6 blks. w. of the US 69 bypass at 307 E. Park St. This museum depicts the history of early Linn County through photographs, artifacts, documents, murals, period-room settings, an old general store, a renovated 1880 depot, antique cars, a genealogy library and videotape presentations. Visitors also learn about Civil War events that occurred in the area. The museum distributes pamphlets and maps dealing with Pleasanton and all of Linn County.

Time: Allow 1 hour minimum. **Hours:** Tues. and Thurs. 9-5, Sat.-Sun. 1-5; other times by appointment. Closed Jan. 1, Thanksgiving and Dec. 25. **Cost:** Donations. **Phone:** (913) 352-8739.

MINE CREEK BATTLEFIELD STATE HISTORIC SITE is 2 mi. s. on US 69, then .5 mi. w. on SR 52. One of the last significant Civil War battles fought west of the Mississippi River occurred here in 1864. Walking trails, marked with interpretive signs, traverse the 600-acre battlefield site. A visitor center features Civil War exhibits and firsthand accounts of the battle. **Time:** Allow 1 hour minimum. **Hours:** Tues.-Sat. 10-5, first Wed. in Apr.-last Sat. in Oct. Closed major holidays. **Cost:** $3; $1 (students with ID). **Phone:** (913) 352-8890.

PRATT (E-4) pop. 6,570, elev. 1,896′

The bounty of the surrounding wheat and cattle ranches and the activity from being a shipping point on the Cotton Belt (Union Pacific) Railroad sustain Pratt.

Named for Civil War veteran Caleb Pratt, the community was established in 1884 as the railroad pushed westward. Until 1886 the community warred with neighboring Saratoga over the status of county seat. Years after Pratt's victory Saratoga citizens insisted that the Indian scare that had sent them fleeing had been fabricated so that Pratt could win a hastily called election.

During World War II the city served as a training base for crews who flew B-29 bombers. At the municipal airport the B-29 All Veterans Memorial honors these flyers and their contribution to history.

Pratt Area Chamber of Commerce: 114 N. Main St., Pratt, KS 67124. **Phone:** (620) 672-5501.

KANSAS STATE FISH HATCHERY, 2 mi. e. on US 54, then 1 mi. s. on SR 64, was one of the first to raise channel catfish. The 187-acre facility includes 87 ponds. A museum and education center feature native birds and animals in their natural habitats and aquariums with every species of fish indigenous to the state. The hatchery also is the operations office of the Kansas Department of Wildlife and Parks. **Time:** Allow 1 hour minimum. **Hours:** Mon.-Fri. 8-5. **Cost:** Donations. **Phone:** (620) 672-5911.

PRATT COUNTY HISTORICAL MUSEUM, 208 S. Ninnescah St., contains six galleries depicting aspects of local history. American Indian artifacts and items relating to area pioneers are displayed, as are period rooms from the late 1800s and sculptures woven from wheat. Old Time Main Street, a reconstructed 19th-century town, includes a general store, post office, bank, jail and icehouse. **Hours:** Mon.-Fri. 1-4, Sat.-Sun. 1-3. Closed major holidays. **Cost:** Donations. **Phone:** (620) 672-7874.

REPUBLIC (B-5) pop. 161, elev. 1,500′

PAWNEE INDIAN MUSEUM STATE HISTORIC SITE, 8 mi. n. of US 36 on SR 266, is on the site of an 1820s Pawnee Indian village. The museum building is constructed over the excavated floor of an earth lodge. Artifacts have been left exactly where they were found. Exhibits and dioramas depict Pawnee life. A nature trail is available. **Time:** Allow 1 hour minimum. **Hours:** Wed.-Sat. 9-5, Sun. 1-5. Closed major holidays. **Cost:** $3; $1 (students with ID); free (ages 0-5). **Phone:** (785) 361-2255.

RUSSELL (C-4) pop. 4,696, elev. 1,826′

Railroad station agents, section hands and military garrisons were the only inhabitants of Fossil Station until 1871, when a colony of some 60 families settled and later changed the name to Russell.

Today Russell is widely associated with former U.S. senator and 1996 presidential nominee Robert Dole, who was born here in 1923.

Architectural highlights from the city's past include the 1872 Gernon House, 818 Kansas St., and the 1879 Heym-Oliver House, 503 Kansas St. Both limestone dwellings are restored and furnished in period. Guided tours are offered by appointment; phone (785) 483-3637 or the convention and visitors bureau.

Nearby Wilson Lake offers numerous outdoor activities. *See Recreation Chart and Buffalo in the AAA South Central CampBook.*

Russell Convention & Visitors Bureau: 445 E. Wichita Ave., P.O. Box 130, Russell, KS 67665. **Phone:** (785) 483-2828 or (877) 830-3737.

DEINES CULTURAL CENTER, off I-70 at 820 N. Main St., is a three-story building housing a workshop area and two galleries containing the works of Kansas artists. The wood engravings of E. Hubert Deines are noteworthy. **Time:** Allow 30 minutes minimum. **Hours:** Tues.-Fri. 12:30-5:30, Sat.-Sun. 1-5. Closed major holidays. **Cost:** Donations. **Phone:** (785) 483-3742.

FOSSIL STATION MUSEUM, behind Russell County Court House at 331 Kansas St., is housed in a former jailhouse built in 1907. The museum depicts the history of Russell County since the 1860s and features a fossil collection and genealogy information. **Time:** Allow 1 hour minimum. **Hours:** Mon.-Fri. 11-4, Sat.-Sun. 1-4, Memorial Day-day before Labor Day. **Cost:** Donations. **Phone:** (785) 483-3637.

OIL PATCH MUSEUM, n.w. of jct. I-70 and US 281, chronicles the history of oil exploration in the area. Visitors can view drilling equipment, a walk-in storage tank and a miniature pump jack. **Time:** Allow 1 hour minimum. **Hours:** Daily 4-8, Memorial Day-Labor Day; by appointment rest of year. **Cost:** Donations. **Phone:** (785) 483-3637 or (785) 483-4796.

SALINA (C-5) pop. 45,679, elev. 1,222′

At the junction of I-70 and I-135, Salina is a major trade and distribution center for one of the greatest hard wheat belts in the world. Other agriculture as well as more than 100 diversified manufacturing firms complete the economic portrait of this city on the eastward bend of the Smoky Hill River.

Salina balances industrial growth with educational and cultural expansion. Kansas Wesleyan University and a branch of Kansas State University are important assets. The prize-winning Bicentennial Center in Kenwood Park is the scene of expositions, trade shows, concerts and sporting events.

For four days in June, the GEM Smoky Hill River Festival, held in Oakdale Park, offers art, entertainment, food, music, children's activities, and arts and crafts.

Visit Salina: 120 W. Ash St., P.O. Box 586, Salina, KS 67402-0586. **Phone:** (785) 827-9301 or (877) 725-4625.

GEM SAVE **ROLLING HILLS WILDLIFE ADVENTURE** is off I-70 exit 244, then 2 mi. s. to 625 N. Hedville Rd. Situated on 95 acres of Kansas prairie, the wildlife center features a zoo with more than 100 species of rare or endangered animals and a museum. Sheltered observation areas permit up-close viewing of animals in natural outdoor settings.

The center's collection includes such endangered species as Indian and white rhinoceroses, tigers, an orangutan and Amur leopards. An indoor reptile house features rare snakes. A children's area allows hands-on interaction with domestic animals. Narrated tram rides operate seasonally.

Time: Allow 2 hours minimum. **Hours:** Daily 8-5, Memorial Day-Labor Day; 9-5, rest of year. Closed Jan. 1 and Dec. 24-25. **Cost:** Zoo $10.95; $9.95 (ages 65+); $5.95 (ages 3-12). Museum $9.95; $8.95 (ages 65+); $4.95 (ages 3-12). Combination ticket for both zoo and museum $13.95; $12.95 (ages 65+); $7.95 (ages 3-12). Tram rides $3. Giraffe feedings $1. **Phone:** (785) 827-9488.

Rolling Hills Wildlife Adventure Museum is at 625 N. Hedville Rd. The museum leads visitors through elaborate dioramas representing seven distinct environments. Realistic robots, representing peoples from around the world, carry on a dialogue with visitors and each other about the delicate balance between man and nature. The museum also features a 360-degree, domed movie theater, an interactive children's gallery filled with hands-on displays and an area for traveling exhibits.

Time: Allow 1 hour minimum. **Hours:** Daily 8-5, Memorial Day-Labor Day; 9-5, rest of year. Closed Jan. 1 and Dec. 24-25. **Cost:** Zoo $10.95; $9.95 (ages 65+); $5.95 (ages 3-12). Museum $9.95; $8.95 (ages 65+); $4.95 (ages 3-12). Combination ticket for both zoo and museum $13.95; $12.95 (ages 65+); $7.95 (ages 3-12). Movie ticket with museum admission $2; without museum admission $3. **Phone:** (785) 827-9488.

SMOKY HILL MUSEUM is at 211 W. Iron Ave. Housed in a 1938 art deco building, the museum's collection features some 20,000 items. Exhibits include a full-size replica of a pioneer sod dugout, a general store and One Keeper's Place, where children investigate historical events. Permanent and changing exhibits are presented. **Hours:** Tues.-Fri. noon-5, Sat. 10-5, Sun. 1-5. Closed major holidays. **Cost:** Free. **Phone:** (785) 309-5776.

YESTERYEAR MUSEUM, I-70 exit 252 to 1100 W. Diamond Dr., contains a vast collection of historic items related to agricultural and rural life, including farm machinery and implements; steam engines; harvesting machinery; a one-room schoolhouse; a barber shop; a general store; a post office; a small church; and a filling station. **Time:** Allow 1 hour minimum. **Hours:** Tues.-Sat. 9-5. Closed major holidays. **Cost:** $4; free (ages 0-12). **Phone:** (785) 825-8473.

SCANDIA (B-5) pop. 436, elev. 1,450′

In the 1860s, Swedish and Norwegian immigrants left their drought-stricken homelands to start new lives in America. The town of Scandia was founded in 1868 and evolved from a settlement promoted by the Scandinavian Agricultural Society in Chicago. Scandia's founding pilgrims are recognized in a stone monument just east of the Republic River Bridge on US 36.

THE SCANDIA MUSEUM, jct. Main and Grant sts., is a tribute to the area's Norwegian and Swedish ancestors. Highlights include original artwork, a working loom, antique horse-drawn carriages, a soda fountain and family memorabilia. Wood-carved depictions of a wagon train attack and a Dodge City street scene also are presented. **Time:** Allow 1 hour minimum. **Hours:** Mon.-Sat. 1-4, Memorial Day-Labor Day; by appointment rest of year. **Cost:** Donations. **Phone:** (785) 335-2506, or (785) 335-2271 for the city library.

SCOTT CITY (C-2) pop. 3,855, elev. 2,971′

Nearby Lake Scott, part of Lake Scott State Park, is fed by underground springs that have eroded the countryside into canyons, green hills and rough terrain—a visual oasis on the flat Kansas topography. South of Scott City lies White Woman Basin, where the surface flow of White Woman Creek disappears. The stream, which rises in Colorado, completes its journey to the Arkansas River below ground.

Scott City Chamber of Commerce: 113 E. Fifth St., Scott City, KS 67871. **Phone:** (620) 872-3525.

LAKE SCOTT STATE PARK, 15 mi. n. via US 83 and SR 95, is the site of El Cuartelejo, the ruined pueblo occupied in the late 1600s by Taos and Picurie Indians who fled Spanish occupation in New Mexico. Plains Apache Indians as well as Spanish explorers and French traders camped at the pueblo. Also within the park is the Herbert and Eliza Steele Home. Their original 1888 dugout house was expanded to a four-room house using sandstone from the surrounding bluffs. *See Recreation Chart and the AAA South Central CampBook.*

Hours: Daily 24 hours. **Cost:** Apr.-Sept. $4.20 (per private vehicle). Rest of year $3.70 (per private vehicle). **Phone:** (620) 872-2061.

SEDAN (E-7) pop. 1,342, elev. 862′

Nestled in the Chautauqua Hills, Sedan once relied on oil production to sustain its economy. A yellow-brick road featuring more than 11,000 inscribed bricks runs between buildings, which were constructed from native sandstone and limestone in the late 1800s. Emmett Kelly, the clown known as Weary Willy, was born in Sedan in 1898.

Sedan Chamber of Commerce: 108 Sherman St., P.O. Box 182, Sedan, KS 67361. **Phone:** (620) 725-4033.

EMMETT KELLY MUSEUM, 204 E. Main St., displays memorabilia of this Sedan native who became a world-renowned clown. Exhibits also include a large decanter collection. **Hours:** Tues.-Fri. 10-4, Sat. 10-noon and 1-5, Apr.-Oct. **Cost:** Donations. **Phone:** (620) 725-3470.

SHAWNEE—*see Kansas City p. 184.*

STAFFORD (D-4) pop. 1,161, elev. 1,858′

QUIVIRA NATIONAL WILDLIFE REFUGE is 6 mi. n. on Main St., 6 mi. e. on 70th St., following signs, then 1 mi. n. to headquarters. The refuge covers 22,135 acres that encompass the Big and Little salt marshes, a portion of Rattlesnake Creek and several other wetlands. Bald eagles, endangered whooping cranes and various other species of migratory waterfowl find refuge here. The best seasons for wildlife viewing are spring and fall. Enjoy hiking and fishing year-round. **Time:** Allow 1 hour minimum. **Hours:** Daily dawn-dusk. **Cost:** Free. **Phone:** (620) 486-2393.

STRONG CITY (C-6) pop. 584, elev. 1,182′

At one time prairie grass blanketed a 400,000-square-mile swath of North America, stretching from the Rocky Mountains to east of the Mississippi River, and from Texas north to Saskatchewan. An 11,000-acre portion of this original grassland survives at the Tallgrass Prairie National Preserve *(see attraction listing).* Limestone just beneath the sod helped build Strong City's economy as well as countless public and private buildings throughout the west.

The annual Flint Hills Rodeo, held in early June in Strong City, is the state's oldest consecutively run professional rodeo; phone (620) 365-0451 or (620) 366-1618 for ticketing information.

TALLGRASS PRAIRIE NATIONAL PRESERVE is .75 mi. w. on US 50, then 2 mi. n. on US 177. This 10,861-acre site protects a remnant of the continent's once vast tallgrass prairie. Self-guiding tours of the 1881 Spring Hill Ranch include the restored Victorian ranch house, a massive three-story limestone barn and a one-room schoolhouse. Via bus, rangers conduct 90-minute prairie tours, which focus on natural history, the ranching legacy and ecology.

Nature trails are available, and living-history programs are offered during summer. **Hours:** Daily 9-4:30. House tours are offered on the half-hour 9:30-3:30. Bus tours depart at 11, 1 and 3, late Apr.-late Oct. Closed Jan. 1, Thanksgiving and Dec. 25. **Cost:** Free. **Phone:** (620) 273-8494.

TOPEKA (C-7) pop. 122,377, elev. 940′

Topeka was founded in 1854 when nine anti-slavery settlers met on the banks of the Kansas River, near the spot where Oregon Trail travelers made their first major river crossing on their journey to the West. The city was incorporated in 1857, and Cyrus K. Holliday, the founder of the Atchison, Topeka & Santa Fe Railway, was among the city's leaders.

When the railway began to extend its tracks westward 1854-69, Topeka defeated Tecumseh for county seat, became the state capital in 1861, survived the mayhem of the "Bleeding Kansas" era, suffered drought and withstood the fringes of the Civil War. In fact, Topeka flourished.

Almost 100 years after Topeka saw clashes between abolitionists and pro-slavery factions, it was the setting for the landmark 1954 Supreme Court ruling *Brown vs. The Topeka Board of Education,* the case that opened the door for school desegregation across the country.

Topeka hosts several annual events featuring entertainment and fun for visitors including Fiesta Mexicana Week, the Inter-tribal Pow Wow and the Huff-n-Puff Balloon Rally. For the racing enthusiast, Heartland Park offers drag racing, road course racing, and dirt track and cycling events from March through October.

Lake Shawnee, E. 29th Street and West Edge Road, and Perry State Park, 16 miles northeast, offer water sports and other outdoor recreation *(see Recreation Chart and the AAA South Central CampBook).* Heartland Park Topeka, 4 miles south on US 75, is host to national motor sports events April through October; phone (800) 437-2237.

Visit Topeka Inc.: 1275 S.W. Topeka Blvd., Topeka, KS 66612-1852. **Phone:** (785) 234-1030 or (800) 235-1030.

Shopping areas: West Ridge Mall, 1 mile south of I-70 on Wanamaker Road between 17th and 21st streets, features Dillard's, JCPenney, Macy's and Sears.

BROWN V. BOARD OF EDUCATION NATIONAL HISTORIC SITE is at 1515 S.E. Monroe St. The site commemorates the May 17, 1954, Supreme Court ruling that stated "separate educational facilities are inherently unequal," forcing desegregation of public schools in 21 states. The site consists of the Monroe Elementary School, one of the four segregated elementary schools for African-American children in Topeka, and its grounds. A visitor center contains interpretive exhibits. **Time:** Allow 1 hour minimum. **Hours:** Daily 9-5. Closed Jan. 1, Thanksgiving and Dec. 25. **Cost:** Free. **Phone:** (785) 354-4273.

COMBAT AIR MUSEUM is on J Street, hangar 602, along the flight line of Topeka Airport Forbes Field. This museum exhibits examples of aeronautical technology from all U.S. military conflicts from the early 1900s to the present, including aircraft and memorabilia. Among the more than 30 aircraft on display are an EC-121 Super Constellation, a Blue Angels F-11F Tiger, a Beech RU-8D and Meyers OTW, an F-14 Tomcat and a JN4 "Jenny" biplane. Another exhibit re-creates a German prisoner of war barracks.

Time: Allow 1 hour, 30 minutes minimum. **Hours:** Mon.-Sat. 9-4:30, Sun. noon-4:30, Mar.-Dec.; daily noon-4:30, rest of year. Last admission 1 hour before closing. Closed Jan. 1, Easter, Thanksgiving and Dec. 25. **Cost:** $6; $4 (ages 6-17 and military with ID). **Phone:** (785) 862-3303.

GAGE PARK occupies 160 acres between W. Sixth Ave. and Tenth St. on Gage Blvd. A conservatory and a miniature train are among its attractions; recreational facilities include a family aquatic center, tennis courts and a playground. Across from the Reinisch Rose Garden in the park, a restored 1908 carousel with a Wurlitzer organ is open to the public.

Hours: Park open daily 6 a.m.-11 p.m. Train and carousel operate early Apr.-Oct. 31 (weather permitting). Phone ahead to confirm schedule. **Cost:** Park free. Train $1. Carousel 75c. **Phone:** (785) 368-3838.

Reinisch Rose and Doran Rock Garden, W. Sixth Ave. and Gage Blvd. in Gage Park, covers 3 acres with many varieties of roses growing amid rock gardens and pools. The blooming season is early spring through late fall. **Hours:** Daily 6 a.m.-11 p.m. **Cost:** Free.

Topeka Zoological Park, 635 S.W. Gage Blvd., is entered from Sixth Ave. or 10th St. Beneath a dome, the Tropical Rain Forest habitat contains animals, birds and plants. Other zoo residents include nocturnal animals, lions, tigers, bears, zebras, elephants, giraffes, hippopotamuses and gorillas. A children's zoo and playground also are featured. **Hours:** Daily 9-5. Last admission is 30 minutes before closing. Closed Jan. 1 and Dec. 25. **Cost:** $5.25; $4.25 (ages 65+); $3.75 (ages 3-12). Phone ahead to confirm prices. **Phone:** (785) 368-9180.

THE GREAT OVERLAND STATION AND ALL VETERANS MEMORIAL is at 701 N. Kansas Ave. In 2004, a local preservation group completed restoration of North Topeka's neglected Union Pacific passenger depot, returning it to its 1927 splendor. The station's grand waiting room features 34-foot-high ornamented ceilings, large windows and impressive 12-foot-wide, 120-bulb chandeliers. A former storage room houses exhibits about Topeka's history and railroad heritage.

Outside the station, flags of the 50 states flank a flame-shaped sculpture, the centerpiece of the All Veterans Memorial.

Tours: Guided tours are available. **Time:** Allow 45 minutes minimum. **Hours:** Tues.-Sat. 10-4, Sun.

1-4. Last ticket sold 45 minutes before closing. Closed major holidays. **Cost:** $4; $3 (ages 62+); $2 (ages 3-12); $1 off (military with ID). **Phone:** (785) 232-5533.

GEM **KANSAS HISTORICAL SOCIETY** is at 6425 S.W. Sixth Ave. Set on 80 acres of woodlands and prairies, the complex is home to the Kansas Museum of History. The museum features exhibits relevant to Kansas history and the west such as an 1880s steam locomotive, a Southern Cheyenne teepee, a stagecoach and a Civil War section. The State Archives and Library contains genealogical information as well as a collection of historic documents, photographs and manuscripts relating Kansas history. Also on site are the Potawatomi Mission, an 1847 boarding school; and the Stach School, a 1910 one-room schoolhouse accessible by appointment.

The Nature Trail winds 2.5 miles through native grassland, along creek banks and into a wooded area. Accessible to physically impaired visitors, the East Trail portion is a .25-mile loop with interpretive signs that describe the area's natural and cultural histories. While exploring the North Trail section, visitors might see red-tailed hawks, white-tailed deer and wild turkeys.

Time: Allow 1 hour, 30 minutes minimum. **Hours:** Tues.-Sat. 9-5, Sun. 1-5. Closed major holidays. **Cost:** Museum $5; $4 (senior citizens); $3 (students with ID); free (ages 0-5). Archives and library free. **Phone:** (785) 272-8681.

Kansas Museum of History is at 6425 S.W. Sixth Ave. Exhibits at the complex detail state history from its earliest days to the present and include displays about American Indian history, forts and trails, Civil War settlement, frontier life, the arrival of the railroad, fast food, African-American history and Kansas families. In the Discovery Place children experience history firsthand by dressing in frontier costumes and visiting a Plains Indian teepee.

Time: Allow 1 hour minimum. **Hours:** Tues.-Sat. 9-5, Sun. 1-5. Discovery Place Tues.-Sat. 1-5. Closed major holidays. **Cost:** Museum $5; $4 (senior citizens); $3 (students with ID); free (ages 0-5). Discovery Place free. **Phone:** (785) 272-8681.

State Archives and Library is at 6425 S.W. Sixth Ave. Headquarters of the Kansas State Historical Society, the center offers extensive resources for genealogists and researchers of Kansas history and the West. **Time:** Allow 1 hour minimum. **Hours:** Tues.-Sat. 9-4:30. Closed major holidays. **Cost:** Free. **Phone:** (785) 272-8681, ext. 117.

OLD PRAIRIE TOWN AT WARD-MEADE HISTORIC SITE, 124 N.W. Fillmore St., offers 2.5 acres of botanical gardens surrounding the Prairie Mansion. Built about 1870, the house is furnished with period pieces and is used as a museum. Also on the grounds are a log cabin, a late 1800s schoolhouse, a church, a general store, a railroad depot, a livery stable and a drugstore.

Self-guiding and guided tours are available; building interiors can only be seen on guided tours. **Hours:** Grounds and gardens daily 8 a.m.-dusk. Drugstore and general store Mon.-Sat. 10-4, Sun. noon-4. Guided tours are offered Mon.-Fri. at 10, noon and 2, Sat.-Sun. at noon and 2. **Cost:** Self-guiding tour free. Guided tours $4.50; $4 (ages 55+); $2 (ages 6-12). **Phone:** (785) 368-3888.

GEM **STATE CAPITOL,** on Capitol Sq. between Jackson and Harrison sts. facing 10th St., contains murals by Kansas native John Steuart Curry as well as artists David H. Overmyer and Lumen Martin Winter. Other interesting works include the "Pioneer Mother" and a bronze of Abraham Lincoln by Merrill Gage.

The capitol, built in the French Renaissance style with native limestone, dates from 1866. Atop the dome is the 22-foot-high statue of Ad Astra, a Kansa Indian warrior, after whose tribe the state was named.

Hours: Mon.-Fri. 8-5. Guided 40-minute tours are given Mon.-Fri. at 9, 10, 11, 1, 2 and 3. **Cost:** Free. Tour reservations are recommended Mar.-May. **Phone:** (785) 296-3966.

TOPEKA FIRST PRESBYTERIAN CHURCH is off I-70 exit 362B, .2 mi. n.w. on 10th Ave., .2 mi. n. on S.W. Jackson St., .2 mi. n.w. on S.W. 8th Ave., then just s. to 817 S.W. Harrison St. The church is illuminated by ten Favrile glass windows designed in 1911 by artist Louis Comfort Tiffany, whose use of cobalt, copper and gold additives gives the glass its remarkably deep colors. The sanctuary houses a 1935 Möller pipe organ. Guided tours are available by appointment. **Hours:** Mon.-Fri. 7-5. **Cost:** Donations. **Phone:** (785) 233-9601.

WASHBURN UNIVERSITY, 1700 S.W. College Ave., is named for Ichabod Washburn, a New England church deacon and philanthropist who donated $25,000 to the school in 1868. His generous spirit lives on in the likeness of "Ichabod," the school mascot. Some 7,000 students are enrolled in liberal arts, business, nursing and applied studies programs. The university also is noted for its law school. **Phone:** (785) 670-1030 for campus tours.

Mulvane Art Museum, on the Washburn University campus at 17th and Jewell sts., showcases works from the mountain plains region as well as changing exhibits. Kansas and international artists are featured. **Time:** Allow 45 minutes minimum. **Hours:** Tues. 10-7, Wed.-Fri. 10-5, Sat.-Sun. 1-4. Closed major holidays and during the installation of new exhibits. Phone ahead to confirm schedule. **Cost:** Donations. **Phone:** (785) 670-1124.

TRADING POST (D-8) elev. 807'

TRADING POST MUSEUM, off US 69 near the cemetery, displays artifacts reflecting the history of the area. Represented are the American Indian period before settlement, the fur trade era, the early settlement, the Border War and the Civil War.

Hours: Tues.-Sat. 9:30-4:30, Sun. 1-5, Apr.-Nov. **Cost:** Donations. **Phone:** (913) 352-6441.

VICTORIA (C-4) pop. 1,208, elev. 1,929′

Victoria began as two separate settlements in the 1870s. North of the present town site, Volga-German immigrants founded Herzog, while just south of it was the English colony of Victoria. Local history recounts that the young Englishmen, who had brought fine cattle, sheep and horses with them, were more interested in saloons and dance halls than in raising livestock.

Within 5 years Victoria Colony had folded, unlike the settlement to the north, which had grown and prospered through the hard work of the Volga-German farmers. In 1913 the abandoned colony was absorbed, and Herzog was renamed Victoria, honoring the area's English heritage.

CATHEDRAL OF THE PLAINS, 1 mi. s. of I-70 at 900 Cathedral Ave., was erected 1908-11 mostly by hand labor. Officially named St. Fidelis Roman Catholic Church, the Romanesque cathedral is constructed of native limestone and features 141-foot spires and stained-glass windows imported from Munich, Germany. **Time:** Allow 30 minutes minimum. **Hours:** Daily dawn-dusk. **Cost:** Donations. **Phone:** (785) 735-2777.

WALLACE (C-2) pop. 67, elev. 3,310′

Founded in 1869 by the Union Pacific Railroad, Wallace soon was bursting at the seams as one of the most important shipping centers in the region. Its importance began to decline with the coming of such other railroads as the Santa Fe and the Burlington. The 1882 closing of the nearby frontier military post, Fort Wallace, cut trade even further. Several years of drought in the early 1890s convinced most of the remaining townspeople to leave, reducing Wallace to its small size.

Some of the original houses and buildings still stand. Markers and headstones in nearby Wallace Cemetery, originally Fort Wallace Cemetery, graphically describe the fates of some of the area's early settlers. A memorial honoring Custer's 7th Cavalry is at this site.

FORT WALLACE MUSEUM, .5 mi. e. on US 40 at a rest area, displays articles used by early settlers and the garrisoned troops as well as a 1907 area depot and the Pond Creek Stagecoach Station. Artifacts excavated from three counties, the old fort, and army and American Indian sites are exhibited in 45 cases. The museum also features several pieces of barbed-wire art. **Time:** Allow 30 minutes minimum. **Hours:** Mon.-Sat. 9-5, Sun. 1-5, May-Sept.; otherwise varies. **Cost:** Donations. **Phone:** (785) 891-3564.

WAMEGO (B-6) pop. 4,246

Wamego is the birthplace of Walter P. Chrysler, founder of the Chrysler Corp. Built in 1879, the Schonhoff Windmill, reputedly the only operating stone windmill in the state, can be seen in Wamego City Park. A silo featuring a mural depicting scenes of the Oregon Trail is just east of town on Oregon Trail Road.

Wamego Area Chamber of Commerce: 529 Lincoln Ave., Wamego, KS 66547. **Phone:** (785) 456-7849.

THE COLUMBIAN THEATRE, MUSEUM AND ART CENTER, 521 Lincoln Ave., features a collection of 1893 paintings from the Chicago World's Fair that depict life in late 19th-century America. A 284-seat theater offers diverse musical and dramatic performances as well as children's theater. The gallery displays regional artwork. **Time:** Allow 1 hour minimum. **Hours:** Tues.-Fri. 10-5, Sat. 10-3. Closed major holidays. **Cost:** $3. **Phone:** (785) 456-2029 or (800) 899-1893.

OLD DUTCH MILL AND WAMEGO MUSEUM COMPLEX, SR 99 s. to 4th St., then e. to Wamego City Park, features a reconstructed 1870s mill that was used as a custom grinder for feed and flour. Wamego Museum, a prairie village, displays local memorabilia. The park also contains the White Chapel School, a jail, general store, log cabin and a playground. Children's train rides can be scheduled by appointment.

Time: Allow 30 minutes minimum. **Hours:** Mon.-Sat. 10-4, Sun. 1-4, Apr.-Oct.; daily 1-4, rest of year. **Cost:** $4 (includes museum and all buildings); $3.50 (military with ID); $1 (students with ID); free (ages 0-6). **Phone:** (785) 456-2040.

SAVE **THE OZ MUSEUM** is at 511 Lincoln Ave. The museum houses one of the largest private collections of memorabilia related to the 1939 "Wizard of Oz" movie and L. Frank Baum's classic children's story. Four galleries, eight alcoves and 20 display cabinets are filled with books, toys, photographs and posters.

Time: Allow 30 minutes minimum. **Hours:** Mon.-Sat. 10-5, Sun. noon-5. Closed Easter, Thanksgiving and Dec. 25. **Cost:** $7; $4 (ages 4-12). **Phone:** (785) 458-8686.

WELLINGTON (E-5) pop. 8,647, elev. 1,189′

Located in the heart of the Kansas prairie, Wellington was named for the Duke of Wellington. The town's eight original settlers selected the present site in April 1871 because it was just north of the Indian Territory boundary line, which made it a gateway for homesteaders heading south. Wellington is the county seat for Sumner County, which calls itself "Wheat Capital of the World."

Wellington Area Chamber of Commerce: 207 S. Washington Ave., Wellington, KS 67152. **Phone:** (620) 326-7466.

CHISHOLM TRAIL MUSEUM, 502 N. Washington Ave., depicts the changing way of life in Kansas since the state was settled. While some of the displays emphasize the agricultural livelihood of the wheat belt, others depict the growth of the region resulting from the establishment of the Chisholm

Trail and the railroad. Period furniture is displayed as well as an extensive collection of dolls and local memorabilia. **Hours:** Daily 1-5, June-Oct.; Sat.-Sun. 1-5, Apr. 15-May 31 and in Nov.; by appointment rest of year. **Cost:** Donations. **Phone:** (620) 326-3820.

WEST MINERAL (E-8) pop. 243, elev. 893′

BIG BRUTUS, 6 mi. w. of SRs 7 and 102, then .5 mi. s., is the world's largest electric mining shovel. The 11-million-pound shovel, used in strip mining to remove dirt and rocks, ceased operation in 1974. Visitors can climb into the operator's seat of the 16-story machine. Both the visitor center and Big Brutus contain exhibits explaining the machine's history.

Time: Allow 1 hour minimum. **Hours:** Daily 9-7, Memorial Day-Labor Day; 9-5, Apr. 1-day before Memorial Day; 10-4, Jan.-Mar. Phone ahead to confirm schedule. **Cost:** $8; $7.50 (ages 65+); $5 (ages 6-12). **Phone:** (620) 827-6177.

WICHITA (E-5) pop. 344,284, elev. 1,397′

For 11,000 years Wichita served as a trading center and meeting place for nomadic people, but it wasn't until 1863 that the first permanent settlement of Wichita Indians was recorded. Shortly after, J.R. Mead became the first white settler when he opened a trading post and established the area as a base for the Chisholm Trail.

By 1870 Wichita, now incorporated as a city, had become a destination for cattle drives from Texas, hence the city's nickname, "Cowtown." When the cattle trade moved west to take advantage of new rail lines, Wichita fell on hard times. The city bounced back in the 1890s as commerce centered on grain began to surpass the wealth once generated by cattle.

The population of Wichita nearly doubled in 1918 after a great oil reserve was discovered nearby. In turn, the oil money allowed local entrepreneurs Lloyd Stearman, Walter Beech and Clyde Cessna to further develop Wichita's fledgling airplane industry. During World War II Wichita was the major manufacturing center for airplanes needed in the war effort, and today Wichita produces more than 40 percent of the world's general aviation aircraft.

Lake Afton Public Observatory is southwest of downtown Wichita in Goddard at 25000 W. 39th St. S. Telescopes are available and astronomy exhibits are displayed in a museum; phone (316) 978-7827.

A lively cultural life centers on the city's symphony orchestra, Music Theatre of Wichita, Wichita Grand Opera and three institutions of higher learning: Friends University, with 3,200 students; Newman University, with 2,100 students; and Wichita State University, with an enrollment of 14,500.

Recreation is as much a part of the city's life as industry and culture. Several municipal parks offer golf, swimming and other pastimes. Information can be obtained from the Park Board; phone (316) 268-4638.

The Greater Wichita Convention and Visitors Bureau: 515 S. Main St., Suite 115, Wichita, KS 67202. **Phone:** (316) 265-2800 or (800) 288-9424.

Shopping areas: Towne East Square, US 54/400 at Rock Road, features Dillard's, JCPenney, Sears and Von Maur. Towne West Square, on US 54/400 at Tracy Street, features Dillard's, JCPenney and Sears. Sheplers, 6501 W. Kellogg, specializes in western wear. The Coleman Factory Outlet Store, 239 N. St. Francis, offers outdoor gear and displays of vintage Coleman products.

Bradley Fair, Rock Road at 21st, includes Banana Republic, Chico's, Coldwater Creek, Eddie Bauer and Talbots. NewMarket Square, Maize Road at 21st, includes Old Navy and Sports Authority.

In the heart of downtown, renovated 19th-century warehouses are the setting for Old Town, which features some 100 trendy urban shops, galleries, nightclubs and restaurants.

SAVE **BOTANICA, THE WICHITA GARDENS,** 701 Amidon St., presents a diversity of native and exotic plants in 25 themed gardens on a 9.5-acre site. Gardens include the Aquatic Collection; the Xeriscape Garden; the Woodland Glade; the Teaching Garden; and the Shakespearean, rose, butterfly, woodland bird, wildflower and sensory gardens. In the Butterfly House hundreds of free-flight butterflies put on a colorful show June through September.

Tours: Guided tours are available. **Time:** Allow 1 hour minimum. **Hours:** Mon.-Sat. 9-5 (also Tues. 5-8, June-Sept.), Sun. 1-5, Apr.-Oct.; Mon.-Fri. 9-5, rest of year. Closed Jan. 1, Thanksgiving weekend and Dec. 24-25. **Cost:** $6.50; $5.50 (ages 62+); $3 (ages 5-21). Reservations are required. **Phone:** (316) 264-0448.

GEM SAVE **EXPLORATION PLACE,** at 300 N. McLean Blvd., has hands-on exhibits exploring flight, medieval life and Kansas. Changing exhibits also are featured. In Exploring Flight and Design, visitors can fly a horizontal simulator like the Wright brothers once did or design a commercial airplane.

Exploring Our Only Home allows visitors to touch a tornado and learn about indigenous creatures, including prairie dogs. Featuring a three-story stone castle, the Kids Explore area gives children the opportunity to dress as kings and queens and ride an equipony.

Digitally-produced shows are presented on a 60-foot screen in the CyberDome Theater. A playground, miniature golf course and recreation paths are offered at the outdoor Exploration Park during summer.

Time: Allow 1 hour, 30 minutes minimum. **Hours:** Tues.-Sat. 10-5 (also Thurs. 5-8), Sun.-Mon. noon-5. Closed Jan. 1, Thanksgiving and Dec. 24-25. **Cost:** $8; $7.50 (ages 65+); $6 (ages 5-15); $3 (ages 2-4). CyberDome Theater show or miniature golf game $2. **Phone:** (316) 660-0600 or (877) 904-1444.

KANSAS AFRICAN AMERICAN MUSEUM is at 601 N. Water St. Artwork, paintings and clothing reflecting African American life and culture are displayed. **Time:** Allow 30 minutes minimum. **Hours:** Mon.-Fri. 9-5, Sat. 2-6. **Cost:** Donations. **Phone:** (316) 262-7651.

KANSAS AVIATION MUSEUM, 5 mi. s. of US 54 on Oliver, then 1 mi. e. to 3350 George Washington Blvd., displays planes, aircraft engines and models. A mural of Charles A. Lindbergh's 1927 flight decorates the building's facade. **Time:** Allow 1 hour minimum. **Hours:** Mon.-Sat. 9-5, Sun. noon-5. Closed Thanksgiving and Dec. 25. **Cost:** $8; $7 (ages 60+); $6 (ages 4-12). **Phone:** (316) 683-9242.

GEM **KANSAS SPORTS HALL OF FAME** is at 238 N. Mead St. A historic boathouse contains profiles of the 190 hall of fame inductees. Galleries are dedicated to basketball, football, baseball, track and field and Olympic sports at the professional, college and high school levels. Exhibits include uniforms, photographs, equipment and a virtual sports game. Information about such famous sports personalities as Barry Sanders and Wilt Chamberlain also are featured.

Note: The hall of fame is scheduled to move to its new location at 515 S. Wichita St. in early 2010. Phone ahead to confirm the hall of fame's availability and for further information. **Time:** Allow 2 hours minimum. **Hours:** Phone ahead to confirm schedule. **Cost:** $7; $6 (ages 6-18, 65+ and military with ID); free (ages 0-5 when accompanied by an adult); $22 (family, 4 people); $18 (family, 3 people); $5 (per person in family of five or more). **Phone:** (316) 262-2038.

THE MID-AMERICA ALL-INDIAN CENTER, 650 N. Seneca St., depicts North American Indian heritage, traditions and cultures of the past and present. "Keeper of the Plains," a 44-foot-high sculpture by Blackbear Bosin, stands on the grounds. The Gallery of Nations displays tribal flags. **Time:** Allow 1 hour minimum. **Hours:** Tues.-Sat. 10-4. Closed major holidays. **Cost:** $7; $5 (ages 55+); $3 (ages 6-12). **Phone:** (316) 262-5221.

GEM SAVE **MUSEUM OF WORLD TREASURES** is at 835 E. 1st St. in Old Town. Within the museum's impressive collection of artifacts and fossils is Ivan, reputedly one of the world's most complete T. rex skeletons. The Egyptian area showcases genuine Egyptian mummies and coffins, and the Hall of Royalty depicts the grandeur of European monarchs.

The Hall of Americas presents an extensive collection of weapons and uniforms from the Revolutionary War through the Vietnam War, while the Karpeles Historic Manuscript Library features historic letters and documents. Other exhibits contain memorabilia related to the frontier era, music and composers, sports and American pop culture.

Time: Allow 2 hours minimum. **Hours:** Mon.-Sat. 10-5, Sun. noon-5. Closed Jan. 1, Easter, Thanksgiving and Dec. 25. **Cost:** $8.95; $7.95 (ages 60+); $6.95 (ages 4-12). **Phone:** (316) 263-1311.

OLD COWTOWN MUSEUM, 1865 W. Museum Blvd., consists of restorations and reproductions of more than 40 buildings dating 1865-80. Among them is the Darius Munger House, the city's first residential structure, Wichita's first jail, a general store, newspaper shop, carpenter shop, drugstore, school, a saloon and a railroad depot. Many are furnished in period. A 5-acre working farm depicts agricultural history. The Victorian Christmas Splendor is featured during the first two weeks of December. **Tours:** Guided tours are available. **Time:** Allow 1 hour minimum. **Hours:** Wed.-Sat. 9:30-4:30, Sun. noon-4:30, May-Oct.; phone ahead to verify schedule rest of year. **Cost:** $7.75; $6.50 (ages 62+); $6 (ages 12-17); $5.50 (ages 4-11). **Phone:** (316) 219-1871 or (316) 660-1864.

GEM SAVE **SEDGWICK COUNTY ZOO,** near I-235 exit 10, at 5555 Zoo Blvd., contains 247 acres with more than 2,000 animals representing 400 species. Exhibit areas include the Children's Farm; the Amphibian & Reptile Building; the Jungle, presenting tropical sights, sounds and animals; re-created habitats of Africa with elephants, baboons, giraffes and lions; and one of the largest outdoor, walk-through aviaries representing the wild regions of Australia and South America.

A close-up look at primates is offered at the Koch Orangutan and Chimpanzee Habitat. A suspension bridge takes visitors out of the village atmosphere of Nganda Island and into the Downing Gorilla Forest of Africa. An elevated boardwalk traverses the 12-acre exhibit of North America, which features native plants, bears, bison, eagles, otters and wolves. The Cessna Penguin Cove, featuring Humboldt penguins and Inca terns, reflects the coasts of Chile and Peru. The Slawson Family Tiger Trek houses Eld's deer, red pandas and tigers.

Time: Allow 3 hours minimum. **Hours:** Daily 8:30-5, Mar.-Oct.; 10-5, rest of year. **Cost:** $11; $7 (ages 62+); $6.50 (ages 4-11). **Phone:** (316) 660-9453.

ULRICH MUSEUM OF ART is e. on 17th St. to 1845 Fairmount Ave., on the Wichita State University campus. The museum showcases contemporary art, featuring more than 70 modern sculptures displayed throughout the campus. Andy Goldsworthy, Louise Nevelson, Tom Otterness, Henry Moore and Robert Indiana are among the artists represented. **Time:** Allow 1 hour minimum. **Hours:** Tues.-Fri. 11-5, Sat.-Sun. 1-5. Closed major holidays. **Cost:** Free. **Phone:** (316) 978-3664.

SAVE **WICHITA ART MUSEUM** is at 1400 W. Museum Blvd. An extensive exhibit of American art includes works by Mary Cassatt, Arthur Dove, Edward Hopper, Charles M. Russell and others. Art glass sculptures by Dale Chihuly also are featured. Changing exhibits are presented. **Time:** Allow 1 hour minimum. **Hours:** Tues.-Sat. 10-5, Sun.

noon-5. Closed major holidays. **Cost:** $5; $4 (ages 55+ and students with ID); $2 (ages 5-17); free (Sat.). **Phone:** (316) 268-4921.

WICHITA CENTER FOR THE ARTS, 9112 E. Central, is on 15 landscaped acres. The building, which has Oriental overtones, houses four galleries, an art school and a professional theater. Sculptures on the grounds give the area a parklike setting. Stage plays, family shows and special productions are scheduled year-round. **Time:** Allow 30 minutes minimum. **Hours:** Tues.-Sun. 1-5. Closed major holidays. **Cost:** Galleries free. **Phone:** (316) 634-2787.

WICHITA-SEDGWICK COUNTY HISTORICAL MUSEUM, 204 S. Main St., is in the renovated 1892 former city hall building. Area history from frontier times to the early 20th century is presented. Collections include 1890s patterned glass, fashions and children's toys. A Victorian house, a 1910 drugstore and a 1920s garage with automotive memorabilia are presented. **Hours:** Tues.-Fri. 11-4, Sat.-Sun. 1-5. Closed major holidays. **Cost:** $4; $2 (ages 6-12). **Phone:** (316) 265-9314.

WICHITA STATE UNIVERSITY is between 17th and 21st sts. Highlights of the 330-acre campus include the Corbin Education Center, designed by Frank Lloyd Wright, and a collection of more than 70 outdoor sculptures from the university's Ulrich Museum of Art *(see attraction listing)*. The student body consists of about 11,000 undergraduates and 3,000 graduate students. More than 350 fine arts performances are held on campus.

Free maps detailing the sculptures' sites are available at the museum. Campus tours are offered. **Phone:** (316) 978-3085.

Wichita State University Libraries-Special Collections and University Archives, 1845 Fairmount St., contain the university's archives, rare books and manuscripts. Collections highlight aviation, abolition, and state and local history. The library contains numerous historic Kansas photographs and maps as well as more than 400 digitized maps pertaining to the state. Changing exhibits are presented. **Hours:** Mon.-Fri. 8-5. Closed major holidays. **Cost:** Free. **Phone:** (316) 978-3590.

WINFIELD (E-6) pop. 12,206, elev. 1,127'

Local legend has it that Spanish explorer Francisco Vásquez de Coronado camped in the area during his 16th-century trek west in search of the Seven Golden Cities of Cíbola. More than 3 centuries later the land was occupied by the Osage Indians, with the first European settlers arriving during the 1860s.

Present day Winfield remembers soldiers of all wars in Memorial Park at Ninth and Fuller streets. The Vietnam War Memorial, a replica of the memorial wall in Washington, D.C., is among the monuments in the park. A directory lists the names of the 777 Kansans who lost their lives during that war.

Winfield Convention and Tourism: 123 E. 9th Ave., P.O. Box 640, Winfield, KS 67156. **Phone:** (620) 221-2421 or (877) 729-7440.

Self-guiding tours: Brochures distributed by the convention and tourism office detail driving tours highlighting the town's murals, architecture and historic homes.

THE GALLERY AT BADEN SQUARE, 1 mi. e. to 700 Gary St., displays works by local and regional artists. Changing exhibits present pottery, oil paintings, quilts and sculpture. Children's art also is displayed on occasion. **Time:** Allow 30 minutes minimum. **Hours:** Mon.-Fri. 7:30-4:30. Closed major holidays. **Cost:** Donations. **Phone:** (620) 221-2161.

Missouri
Lewis & Clark
They explored much of Missouri during their quest for the West
The Ozarks
Bubbling springs, swift rivers and deep caves adorn the rugged hillsides
Mark Twain
Take in the whitewashed fences of the river towns that were the writer's inspiration
The Arch
The tallest monument in the country symbolizes America's adventurous spirit
Trailblazing
You'll find adventure and natural beauty along Missouri's historic trails

The Gateway Arch, Jefferson National Expansion Memorial, St. Louis
© Scott T. Smith
Larry Ulrich Stock

Missouri Botanical Garden, St. Louis / Altrendo Travel / Getty Images

Missouri has always provided an open door to adventure, from the footpaths blazed by Lewis and Clark to historic Route 66. Travel one of Missouri's legendary trails to discover the state's delightful mix of frontier heritage and scenic treasures.

Your journey could begin in cosmopolitan St. Louis, wandering the cobblestone streets of Laclede's Landing. Explore the converted warehouses along the Mississippi riverfront, now filled with restaurants and clubs. A brief stroll south is rewarded with a nighttime view of the Gateway Arch.

Then, like the pioneers before you, head westward. Running beside the Missouri River is the Katy Trail, a monumental rails-to-trails conversion.

The whistles of the trains and the rumble along the tracks have been replaced by the crunch of gravel beneath your feet or your bicycle's wheels.

After you pass the striking capitol building in Jefferson City, leave the trail and follow the river's path to Independence and Kansas City. Once trailheads for the Santa Fe and Oregon trails, these cities have maintained their rich history and Western sensibilities.

And don't forget a side trip to Branson. Immerse yourself in the excitement of this vacation mecca before heading to the peaceful wooded hills of the Ozarks.

So start at the Arch, the symbol of our country's pioneering spirit, and create your own trail to adventure.

When Meriwether Lewis and William Clark returned to St. Louis with tales of their discoveries in the West, they sparked a wave of national expansion. The burgeoning towns of Independence and Kansas City became trailheads for the long and arduous journey into the unknown. But many pioneers felt they had gone far enough to find their promised land. These settlers learned what is now well known: You don't need to leave Missouri to find adventure.

Gateway to the West

Steamboats once stopped at the blossoming river towns of Hannibal and St. Charles on their way to St. Louis, the largest city west of the mighty Mississippi. These ships were loaded with supplies for settlers building the communities that would eventually shape the country. The railroad came to Kansas City, and its stockyards provided a natural cattle marketing hub for the vast Western territory.

Today, the leisurely pace of the steamboat is more suited to sightseeing excursions or gambling. The stockyards of Kansas City and the whitewashed picket fences of the river towns have given way to subdivisions and shopping malls. But The Gateway Arch, rising majestically above St. Louis' modern skyline, remains a symbol of Missouri's early role as a gateway to a new frontier.

Today's explorers can retrace the Santa Fe, Oregon and California trails, following in the footsteps of people who dared to go in search of a better life or a new beginning. They reveal many stories, from the sad steps of the Cherokees along the Trail of Tears near Cape Girardeau to the hoofbeats of the short-lived Pony Express, once headquartered in St. Joseph.

There is still more to be discovered between the rich green of the bottomland forests and the shimmering gold of the tallgrass prairie. St. Louis is a good starting point of exploration. Bicycle paths wind through Forest Park, originally the site of the 1904 St. Louis World's Fair. Today the park is home to the city's art, history and science museums as well as the Saint Louis Zoo.

While known for its jazz and barbecue, Kansas City has much more to offer. The city harbors some pretty big surprises, from the 322-foot-wide waterfall beyond the right field fence of Kauffman Stadium to the 18-foot shuttlecocks on the lawn of The Nelson-Atkins Museum of Art. The sparkling, modernistic Crown Center contrasts with the sun-warmed tiles of the Spanish-inspired Country Club Plaza.

Missouri Historical Timeline

1764 A French trading post is established at present-day St. Louis.

1804 The Lewis and Clark expedition departs from St. Charles.

Library of Congress

1811 The New Madrid earthquakes rock the Mississippi Valley.

1820 A compromise admits Missouri to the Union as a slave state while prohibiting slavery in the remaining Louisiana Territory.

Library of Congress

1835 Samuel Langhorne Clemens, better known as Mark Twain, is born in the town of Florida.

Sounds of shoppers haggling in the City Market fade with the sunlight into the smooth blues of the historic 18th and Vine District.

In the minds of many (including those who have never been there), Branson equals music theaters. But while the sheer number and variety of live entertainment offerings are indeed noteworthy, this southwestern Missouri town also lies in the heart of Ozarks country. Deep blue springs—some mere trickles, others roaring past well-worn bluffs—flow through lushly forested hills and valleys. Fishing, boating or camping in the midst of such scenery—or watching the sun set over Table Rock Lake—you might ask yourself why anyone would want to journey elsewhere.

Dreamers and Doers

The state's pioneering spirit does not just apply to those who ventured west. Missouri has been more than a gateway out; it has been a stepping stone up. Mark Twain based the adventures of Tom Sawyer and Huckleberry Finn on his own childhood in Hannibal, while Walt Disney modeled the "Main Street USA" portion of Disneyland after Marceline, his hometown.

A former slave, George Washington Carver took the knowledge that sprouted in his garden in Diamond and used it to revolutionize agriculture in the southern United States. And longtime Independence resident and former Kansas City Automobile Club employee Harry S. Truman steered our country out of World War II, paving the way for postwar prosperity.

Ragtime composer Scott Joplin, rock 'n' roller Chuck Berry, and jazz greats Duke Ellington and Miles Davis are just a few of the musical pioneers who started out in the saloons and clubs of St. Louis and Kansas City. These Missourians didn't wait for anyone to "show them": They led the way with breakthrough performances.

Missouri also has had its share of industrial visionaries. In 1860 Eberhard Anheuser, a successful St. Louis businessman, saw potential in a struggling local brewery. With the help of his son-in-law, Adolphus Busch, he tapped into the national beer market to create Anheuser-Busch Inc. (now known as Anheuser-Busch InBev), the world's largest brewer. Nebraska teenager Joyce C. Hall got off the train in Kansas City in 1910 with an idea to sell picture postcards. His mail-order business evolved into Hallmark Cards Inc., a $3.5 billion corporation. Both companies are the undisputed leaders in their respective industries.

1860 The Pony Express begins its run from St. Joseph to Sacramento.

Kean Collection Getty Images

1904 The St. Louis World's Fair attracts 20 million visitors.

Library of Congress

1945 Missouri native and former AAA sales representative Harry S. Truman becomes the 33rd U.S. president.

1966 The Gateway Arch is dedicated in St. Louis.

1993 Flooding on the Missouri and Mississippi rivers causes billions of dollars in damage across the state.

2006 Missouri, "the birthplace of the Interstate," celebrates the 50th anniversary of the Interstate Highway System.

Recreation

To experience all the adventure Missouri has to offer, you have to get out of your car. Follow scenic trails up wooded hillsides; jump in spring-fed rivers and shimmering lakes; and explore at least one of the state's more than 5,500 caves. To keep you close to the outdoor action, **campsites** at most state parks operate year-round.

Still Waters Run Deep

South-central Missouri is a water lover's paradise. Surrounded by spectacular rolling hills, Lake of the Ozarks' 54,000 acres of water beckon **boaters, water skiers**, and those who want to enjoy the area's tranquil beauty. Farther south, the crystal clear waters of Table Rock Lake offer **scuba divers** unparalleled views of an underwater forest. **Parasailing** is a leading activity at both lakes, and for those who like to skim the surface, **jet ski** rentals are available at many of the local marinas.

A laid-back afternoon of **rafting** is a wonderful way to enjoy an Ozark river. Whether out for an hour or all day, you'll never feel more relaxed. Alley Spring on the Jacks Fork River and Pulltite, Round and Big springs on the Current River are major starting points. The upper stretches of these rivers are often more challenging during spring; water levels dip in summer.

Canoeing on the Meramec River in eastern Missouri is a tranquil retreat. Meramec State Park near Sullivan features miles of picturesque riverbank scenery, bubbling springs and more than 40 caves. Paddle your way past open glades dotted with Indian paintbrush and fern-covered ravines. Canoes, rafts and inner tubes may be rented at the park, and transportation to one of several launching points is included.

Fishing is the classic pastime in Missouri. The cold water of Lake Taneycomo near Branson is a trout haven year-round. Other lakes throughout the state are teeming with small- and large-mouth bass, goggle-eye, walleye, channel cat and bluegill. Don't forget to pick up a state fishing license ($12 yearly for residents, $7 a day or $40 yearly for nonresidents, plus $7 for special "trout tags") before you start reeling them in.

The oak and hickory forests and tall prairie grass that surround all this water provide myriad **hunting** opportunities. Migrating ducks and geese rest at Swan Lake and Mingo national wildlife refuges, near Brookfield and Poplar Bluff, respectively. Quails, wild turkeys, squirrels, rabbits, raccoons and deer are plentiful throughout the state. Hunting seasons vary depending on your prey and permits are required; contact the Missouri Department of Conservation at (573) 751-4115.

Take a Walk on the Scenic Side

In 1986 the Missouri-Kansas-Texas Railroad (the "Katy") stopped running between Sedalia and St. Charles, opening the door for one of the largest rails-to-trails conversions in history. Ten years later, the Katy Trail opened to **hikers** and **bicyclists**.

The trail starts at the restored M-K-T Depot in St. Charles and runs west between towering bluffs and the curvaceous Missouri River. Trailheads with facilities are spaced about every 10 miles. While there aren't many rest stops in between, ripening mulberries beside the trail in summer may tide you over. Favorite pit stops along the 225-mile trek include the Stone Hill Winery in Hermann and the charming bistros and cafés of Rocheport, originally settled by French immigrants.

Another popular hiking route across the state is the still-evolving Ozark Trail, a series of trails that will one day form a continuous route from St. Louis to northern Arkansas. The Taum Sauk section, generally regarded as the trail's most rugged and scenic stretch, winds over sculpted ridges and mossy glades, ascends the summit of Taum Sauk Mountain (the highest in the state) and takes in Mina Sauk Falls.

For **rock climbers**, Missouri has many small craggy areas, mainly south of I-70. Johnson's Shut-Ins State Park offers some of the oldest exposed rock in the nation, a good practice area for novices. Climbing is offered from September through May; registration at park headquarters is required.

Recreational Activities

Throughout the TourBook, you may notice a Recreational Activities heading with bulleted listings of recreation-oriented establishments listed underneath. Similar operations also may be mentioned in Destination City recreation sections. Since normal AAA inspection criteria cannot be applied, these establishments are presented for information only. Age, height and weight restrictions may apply. Reservations are often recommended and sometimes required. Visitors should phone or write the attraction for additional information, and the address and phone number are provided for this purpose.

Fast Facts

POPULATION: 5,595,211.

AREA: 69,686 square miles; ranks 19th.

CAPITAL: Jefferson City.

HIGHEST POINT: 1,772 ft., Taum Sauk Mountain.

LOWEST POINT: 230 ft., St. Francis River.

TIME ZONE(S): Central. DST.

TEEN DRIVING LAWS: Driving is not permitted 1 a.m.-5 a.m. One unrelated passenger (family members exempt) under age 19 is permitted for the first six months; afterwards, no more than three passengers under age 19 are permitted. The minimum age for an unrestricted driver's license is 18. Phone (573) 751-4600 for more information about Missouri's driver's license regulations.

MINIMUM AGE FOR GAMBLING: 21.

SEAT BELT/CHILD RESTRAINT LAWS: Seat belts required for driver and front-seat passengers 16 and older. Children ages 8 until 16 and at least 57 inches and/or 80 lbs. are required to be in a child restraint or seat belt; child restraints are required for children who are under 8 years, weigh less than 80 pounds and are less than 57 inches.

CELL PHONE RESTRICTIONS: Persons under 21 are prohibited from driving while sending, reading or writing a text message.

HELMETS FOR MOTORCYCLISTS: Required for all riders.

RADAR DETECTORS: Permitted.

MOVE OVER LAW: Driver is required to slow down and vacate the lane nearest stopped police, fire and rescue vehicles using audible and flashing signals. The law also applies to recovery vehicles, such as tow trucks.

FIREARMS LAWS: Vary by state and/or county. Contact the Missouri State Highway Patrol, Attn.: Public Information, P.O. Box 568, Jefferson City, MO 65102; phone (573) 751-3313.

HOLIDAYS: Jan. 1; Martin Luther King Jr. Day, Jan. (3rd Mon.); Lincoln's Birthday, Feb. 12; Presidents Day, Feb. (3rd Mon.); Truman Day, May 8; Memorial Day, May (last Mon.); July 4; Labor Day, Sept. (1st Mon.); Columbus Day, Oct. (2nd Mon.); Veterans Day, Nov. 11; Thanksgiving; Christmas, Dec. 25.

TAXES: Missouri's statewide sales tax is 4.23 percent. Cities may impose an additional increment of up to 2.5 percent; cities not located in counties may impose up to 1.38 percent. Counties also may add increments to the sales tax. Cities may levy lodging taxes of up to 5.5 percent and up to 1.75 percent on food and beverages.

INFORMATION CENTERS: State welcome centers are 2 miles east of the Missouri-Oklahoma state line on I-44 near Joplin; in north St. Louis on Dunn Road off I-270 (Riverview exit); on I-55 at the Marston Rest Area about 40 miles north of the Missouri-Arkansas state line south of New Madrid; west of I-29, a half-mile south of junction with US 136 near Rock Port; in Hannibal, US 61N, 2 miles south of junction with US 36; in Kansas City, on the grounds of the Truman Sports Complex off I-70 at the Blue Ridge Cut-Off; and in Eagleville, I-35S, 2 miles south of Iowa state line and I-35, at mile marker 112.

The centers are open daily 8-5, Mar.-Nov.; Mon.-Sat. 8-5, rest of year. The Missouri Division of Tourism office in the Truman State Office Building, 301 W. High St., second floor, Jefferson City, provides travel information Mon.-Fri. 8-5.

FURTHER INFORMATION FOR VISITORS:

Missouri Division of Tourism
P.O. Box 1055
Jefferson City, MO 65102
(573) 751-4133
(800) 519-2300
See color ad p. 122 and on inside front cover.

RECREATION INFORMATION:

Missouri Department of Natural Resources
Division of State Parks
P.O. Box 176
Jefferson City, MO 65102
(800) 334-6946

FISHING AND HUNTING REGULATIONS:

Missouri Department of Conservation
2901 W. Truman Blvd.
Jefferson City, MO 65102
(573) 751-4115

NATIONAL FOREST INFORMATION:

Mark Twain National Forest
401 Fairgrounds Rd.
Rolla, MO 65401
(573) 364-4621
(877) 444-6777 (reservations)

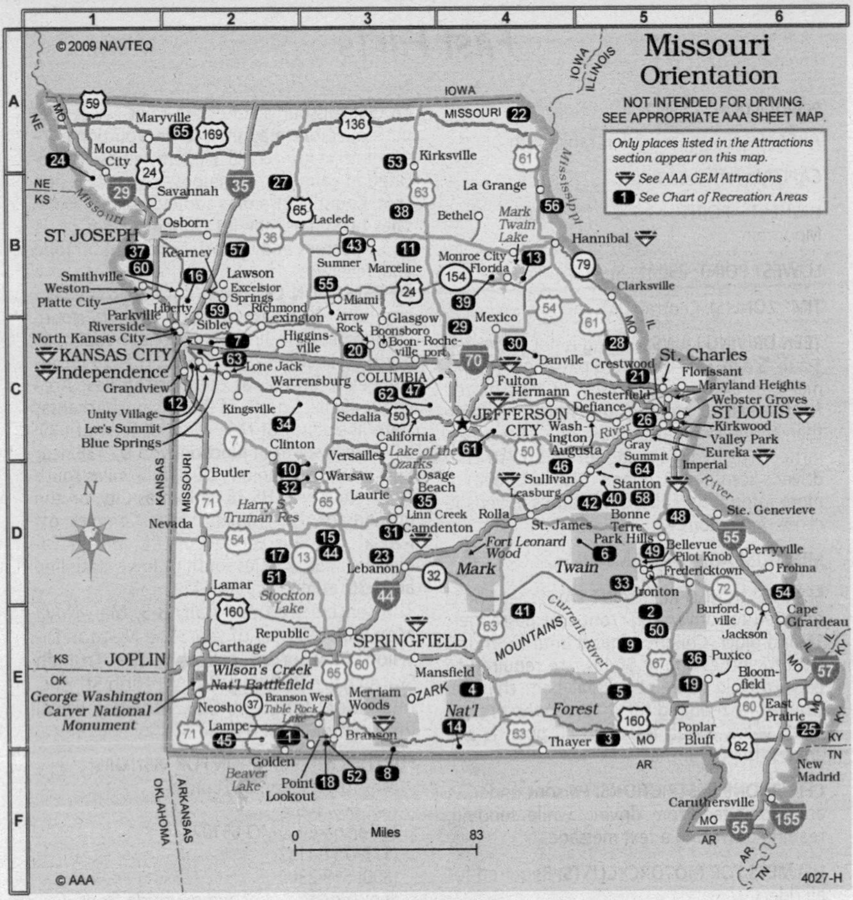

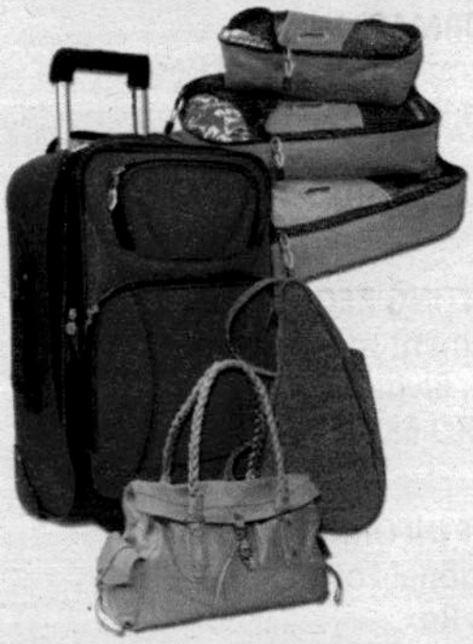

Missouri Orientation

NOT INTENDED FOR DRIVING. SEE APPROPRIATE AAA SHEET MAP.

Only places listed in the Attractions section appear on this map.

See AAA GEM Attractions

See Chart of Recreation Areas

© 2009 NAVTEQ

Miles 0 83

© AAA

4027-H

RECREATION AREAS

	MAP LOCATION	CAMPING	PICNICKING	HIKING TRAILS	BOATING	BOAT RAMP	BOAT RENTAL	FISHING	SWIMMING	PETS ON LEASH	BICYCLE TRAILS	WINTER SPORTS	VISITOR CENTER	LODGE/CABINS	FOOD SERVICE
NATIONAL FORESTS *(See place listings)*															
Mark Twain 1,500,000 acres. Southern Missouri.		●	●	●	●	●	●	●	●	●	●				
Big Bay (E-2) 680 acres 1 mi. s.e. of Shell Knob on SR 39, then 3 mi. s.e. on CR YY.	1	●	●		●	●		●	●	●					
Crane Lake (E-5) 100 acres 12 mi. s. of Ironton off SR 49 and CR E.	2		●	●	●	●		●		●	●				
Fourche Lake (E-5) 40 acres 18 mi. w. of Doniphan on US 160.	3		●	●	●	●		●		●					
Noblett Lake (E-4) 8 acres 8 mi. w. of Willow Springs on SR 76, then 1.5 mi. s. on SR 181, 3 mi. s.e. on CR AP and 1 mi. s.w. on CR 857. Horse trails.	4	●	●	●	●			●		●	●				
Pinewoods Lake (E-5) 30 acres 2 mi. w. of Ellsinore on SR 60. Electric boat motors only. Note: Swimming is permitted but not recommended; this is a managed fishery lake.	5		●	●	●	●		●	●	●	●	●			
Red Bluff (D-5) 133 acres 1 mi. e. of Davisville on CR V, then 1 mi. n. on FR 2011.	6	●	●	●				●	●	●					
NATIONAL SCENIC RIVERWAYS *(See place listings)*															
Ozark 134 miles. Southeastern Missouri. Horse trails.		●	●	●	●	●	●	●	●	●		●	●	●	●
ARMY CORPS OF ENGINEERS															
Blue Springs Lake (C-2) 720 acres .5 mi. e. of I-470 off Bowlin Rd. in Blue Springs. Marina.	7	●	●	●	●	●	●	●	●	●					
Bull Shoals Lake (F-3) 45,500 acres s.e. of Branson on the Missouri-Arkansas state line. *(See Branson p. 140)*	8	●	●	●	●	●	●	●	●	●				●	●
Clearwater Lake (E-5) 1,630 acres 7.5 mi. w. of Piedmont. Tennis; exercise trail, marina, playground.	9	●	●	●	●	●	●	●	●	●				●	●
Harry S. Truman (D-2) 55,600 acres 1.5 mi. n.w. of Warsaw on the Osage River. Horse trails, marina. *(See Warsaw p. 230)*	10	●	●	●	●	●	●	●	●	●			●	●	●
Long Branch Lake (B-3) 2,430 acres 1 mi. w. of Macon on US 36. Marina, playground.	11	●	●	●	●	●		●	●	●			●		●
Longview Lake (C-2) 930 acres 1 mi. s. of I-470 off Raytown Rd. in Kansas City. Golf; marina.	12	●	●	●	●	●	●	●	●	●	●		●		●
Mark Twain Lake (B-4) 18,600 acres 9mi. n. of Perry on CR J. Golf (nine holes); marina, playground. *(See Monroe City p. 190)*	13	●	●	●	●	●	●	●	●	●			●	●	●
Norfork Lake (E-4) 22,000 acres at Tecumseh off US 160. Marinas, playground.	14	●	●	●	●	●	●	●	●	●	●				●
Pomme de Terre (D-3) 7,800 acres 3 mi. s. of Hermitage off SR 64. Marina, playground.	15	●	●	●	●	●	●	●	●	●		●		●	●
Smithville Lake (B-2) 7,200 acres 5 mi. n. of Kansas City on SR DD, then 2 mi. e. of US 169. Golf (18 holes); horse trails, marina, playground.	16	●	●	●	●	●	●	●	●	●	●		●	●	●
Stockton (D-2) 24,900 acres 1 mi. s. of Stockton on SR 32. Horse trails, marina, playground.	17	●	●	●	●	●	●	●	●	●			●	●	●
Table Rock (F-3) 52,300 acres 5 mi. w. of Branson via SRs 76 and 165. Marina. *(See Branson p. 140)*	18	●	●	●	●	●	●	●	●	●			●	●	●
Wappapello Lake (E-5) 8,900 acres 16 mi. n.e. of Poplar Bluff via US 60 and CR T.	19	●	●	●	●	●	●	●	●	●	●		●	●	●
STATE															
Arrow Rock (C-3) 167 acres 3 blks. n. of SR 41. *(See Arrow Rock p. 122)*	20	●	●	●				●		●			●		●
Babler Memorial (C-5) 2,441 acres 20 mi. w. of St. Louis on SR 109. Tennis; horse rental, nature center.	21	●	●	●					●	●	●		●		
Battle of Athens (A-4) 401 acres 8 mi. n. of Revere off SR 81. Historic.	22	●	●	●	●	●		●		●					
Bennett Spring (D-3) 3,216 acres 12 mi. w. of Lebanon on SR 64. *(See Lebanon p. 187)*	23	●	●	●	●	●	●	●	●	●			●	●	●
Big Lake (A-1) 407 acres 11 mi. s.w. of Mound City off SR 118 on SR 111.	24	●	●		●	●		●	●	●				●	●

RECREATION AREAS

	MAP LOCATION	CAMPING	PICNICKING	HIKING TRAILS	BOATING	BOAT RAMP	BOAT RENTAL	FISHING	SWIMMING	PETS ON LEASH	BICYCLE TRAILS	WINTER SPORTS	VISITOR CENTER	LODGE/CABINS	FOOD SERVICE
Big Oak Tree (E-6) 1,028 acres 2 mi. e. of East Prairie on SR 80, then 10 mi. s. on SR 102. Electric boat motors only. *(See East Prairie p. 154)*	25		•	•	•	•		•		•			•		
Castlewood (C-5) 1,818 acres 6 mi. e. of Ballwin on Kiefer Creek Rd. off SR 100. Horse trails.	26		•	•	•	•		•		•	•				
Crowder (B-2) 1,912 acres 4 mi. w. of Trenton on SR 146. Tennis; horse trails, playground. Electric boat motors only.	27	•	•	•	•			•	•	•	•				
Cuivre River (C-5) 6,393 acres 3 mi. e. of Troy off SR 47. Horse trails. Electric boat motors only.	28	•	•	•	•	•		•	•	•			•		
Finger Lakes (C-4) 1,128 acres 10 mi. n. of Columbia on US 63. ATV and motorcycle trails. Electric boat motors only.	29	•	•		•	•		•	•	•	•				
Graham Cave (C-4) 369 acres 2 mi. w. of I-70 and SR TT. Interpretive trails, playground. *(See Danville p. 154)*	30	•	•	•	•	•		•		•			•		
Ha Ha Tonka (D-3) 3,709 acres 5 mi. s.w. of Camdenton off US 54 on CR D. Scenic; historic ruins. Boat docks are only available outside park boundaries at the Big Niangua arm of the Lake of the Ozarks.	31		•	•	•			•		•			•		
Harry S. Truman (D-2) 1,440 acres 5 mi. w. of Warsaw off SR 7 on CR UU. Marina, playground. *(See Warsaw p. 230)*	32	•	•	•	•	•	•	•	•	•					•
Johnson's Shut-Ins (D-5) 8,470 acres 8 mi. n. of Lesterville on CR N. Scenic. Pets are not permitted on Shut-Ins Trail. Note: the campground and visitor center are scheduled to be completed by April 2010.	33	•	•	•				•	•	•			•		•
Knob Noster (C-2) 3,934 acres 2 mi. s. of Knob Noster off US 50 on SR 23. Horse trails. Electric boat motors only.	34	•	•	•	•			•		•	•		•		
Lake of the Ozarks (D-3) 17,626 acres. Caverns, horse rental, marina.	35	•	•	•	•	•	•	•	•	•	•		•	•	•
Lake Wappapello (E-5) 1,854 acres 16 mi. n. of Poplar Bluff on US 67 and 9 mi. e. on SR 172. Horse trails, marina.	36	•	•	•	•	•	•	•	•	•	•			•	
Lewis and Clark (B-1) 189 acres 21 mi. s.w. of St. Joseph via US 59 and SR 45 on SR 138. Playground.	37	•	•		•	•		•	•	•					
Long Branch (B-3) 1,828 acres 2 mi. w. of Macon on US 36. Marina.	38	•	•	•	•	•		•	•	•					•
Mark Twain (B-4) 2,775 acres .5 mi. s. of Florida on SR 107. Historic. Playground.	39	•	•	•	•	•		•	•	•			•		
Meramec (D-5) 6,896 acres 4 mi. e. via SR 185. Scenic. Cavern tours; playground. *(See Sullivan p. 229)*	40	•	•	•	•	•	•	•	•	•				•	•
Montauk (E-4) 1,396 acres 21 mi. s.w. of Salem via SR 119. Historic.	41	•	•	•				•		•				•	•
Onondaga Cave (D-5) 1,317 acres 5 mi. s. on SR H. Scenic. Cavern tours; playground. *(See Leasburg p. 187)*	42	•	•	•	•	•		•	•	•			•		•
Pershing (B-3) 3,565 acres 2 mi. w. of Laclede off US 36 on SR 130. Interpretive trail, playground. Electric boat motors only.	43	•	•	•	•			•	•	•					
Pomme de Terre (D-3) 734 acres 5 mi. s. of Hermitage via SR 64. Marina.	44	•	•	•	•	•	•	•	•	•					•
Roaring River (E-2) 4,093 acres 7 mi. s. of Cassville on SR 112. Interpretive trail, playground.	45	•	•	•				•	•	•			•	•	•
Robertsville (D-4) 1,224 acres 15 mi. s.w. of Eureka off I-44.	46	•	•	•	•	•		•		•					
Rock Bridge Memorial (C-3) 2,273 acres 7 mi. s. of Columbia on SR 163. Cross-country skiing; horse trails.	47		•	•				•		•	•	•			
Saint Francois (D-5) 2,735 acres 4 mi. n. of Bonne Terre on US 67. Horse trails, playground. Motorboats not recommended.	48	•	•	•	•			•	•	•					
Saint Joe (D-5) 8,243 acres 3 mi. s. of Flat River off CR B via SR 32. ATV trails, horse trails. Electric boat motors only.	49	•	•	•	•	•		•	•	•	•				
Sam A. Baker (E-5) 5,324 acres 6 mi. n. of Patterson via SRs 34 and 143. Horse trails, nature center, playground.	50	•	•	•	•	•	•	•	•	•	•		•	•	•
Stockton (D-2) 2,176 acres 8 mi. s.e. of Stockton on SR 215. Marina.	51	•	•	•	•	•	•	•	•	•				•	•

RECREATION AREAS

	MAP LOCATION	CAMPING	PICNICKING	HIKING TRAILS	BOATING	BOAT RAMP	BOAT RENTAL	FISHING	SWIMMING	PETS ON LEASH	BICYCLE TRAILS	WINTER SPORTS	VISITOR CENTER	LODGE/CABINS	FOOD SERVICE
Table Rock (F-3) 356 acres 5 mi. w. of Branson on SR 165. Scuba diving; marina, playground. Food service in summer only. *(See Branson p. 140)*	52	•	•	•	•	•	•	•	•	•	•				•
Thousand Hills (A-3) 3,080 acres 4 mi. w. of Kirksville off SR 6 on SR 157. Marina, playground. *(See Kirksville p. 186)*	53	•	•	•	•	•	•	•	•	•	•			•	•
Trail of Tears (D-6) 3,415 acres 10 mi. n. on SR 177. Horse trails. Electric boat motors only. *(See Jackson p. 158)*	54	•	•	•	•	•		•	•	•			•		
Van Meter (B-3) 1,105 acres on SR 122 via SR 41 in Miami. Nature trails, playground. Electric boat motors only. *(See Miami p. 190)*	55	•	•	•	•			•		•			•		
Wakonda (B-4) 1,054 acres 3 mi. s. of La Grange off US 61. Playground.	56	•	•	•	•	•	•	•	•	•	•			•	
Wallace (B-2) 502 acres 6 mi. s. of Cameron on SR 121. Electric boat motors only.	57	•	•	•	•			•	•	•					
Washington (D-5) 2,148 acres 9 mi. s.w. of De Soto off SR 21. Historic. Nature center. Non-motorized boats only.	58	•	•	•	•		•	•	•	•				•	•
Watkins Woolen Mill (B-2) 1,500 acres 6 mi. n. of Excelsior Springs off SR 92 on CR RA. Historic mill tours; horse trails, interpretive trails. *(See Lawson p. 179)*	59	•	•	•	•	•		•	•	•	•		•		
Weston Bend (B-1) 1,133 acres 1 mi. s. of Weston on SR 45.	60	•	•	•				•		•	•				
OTHER															
Binder (C-4) 650 acres off US 50W in Jefferson City. Playground.	61	•	•	•	•	•		•			•				•
Cole County (C-3) 80 acres off Country Club Dr. in Jefferson City.	62		•	•				•	•						
Fleming Park (C-2) 7,809 acres e. of Kansas City on US 40 and Woods Chapel Rd. *(See Lee's Summit p. 179)*	63	•	•	•	•	•	•	•	•						•
Meramec Caverns (D-5) 110 acres 3 mi. s. of Stanton off I-44. Cavern tours. Note: Swimming is permitted but not recommended due to dangerous undertows. *(See Stanton p. 229)*	64	•	•		•	•	•	•	•	•				•	•
Mozingo Lake (A-2) 3,000 acres 3 mi. e. of Maryville on US 136. Golf. *(See Maryville p. 190)*	65	•	•	•	•	•		•	•					•	

Missouri Temperature Averages Maximum/Minimum

From the records of The Weather Channel Interactive, Inc.

	JAN	FEB	MAR	APR	MAY	JUN	JUL	AUG	SEP	OCT	NOV	DEC
Columbia	37/18	44/24	55/33	66/43	75/53	84/62	89/66	87/64	79/55	68/44	53/33	41/22
Kansas City	38/21	44/26	56/36	67/46	76/57	86/67	90/72	89/70	80/61	69/49	53/36	42/25
St. Joseph	37/16	43/22	55/32	66/42	76/54	86/63	90/67	88/64	81/55	70/43	53/32	40/21
St. Louis	38/21	45/26	55/36	66/47	77/57	86/66	91/71	88/69	81/61	69/49	54/38	42/27
Springfield	42/22	48/27	58/35	68/44	76/53	85/62	90/67	90/66	81/57	71/46	56/35	46/26

Points of Interest

ARROW ROCK (C-3) pop. 79

Arrow Rock, first settled in 1810, became an important trading center that served both farmers and westward expeditions along the Santa Fe Trail. Although the settlement was rechristened Philadelphia, it soon reverted to the name given by early explorers for the flint outcroppings in the surrounding limestone bluffs, a material that was used to make arrow points.

Artist George Caleb Bingham made his home in Arrow Rock in the early 19th century, painting scenes of frontier life on the Missouri River. Dr. John Sappington, another nearby resident, engaged in large-scale farming and the marketing of Sappington Anti-fever Pills. Two of his sons-in-law and one of his grandsons became governors of the state. The Friends of Arrow Rock offers a guided tour of Sappington's 1849 Greek Revival mansion by appointment; phone (660) 837-3231.

An 1872 Baptist church has been converted and refurbished to house the Arrow Rock Lyceum Theatre. Matinee performances are given Wed.-Thurs. and Sat.-Sun. at 2, and evening performances are at 8 p.m., June-October; phone (660) 837-3311.

ARROW ROCK STATE HISTORIC SITE is 3 blks. n. of SR 41. A town founded in 1829 is preserved at the site. Located where the Santa Fe Trail met the Missouri River, the settlement thrived, with 1,000 residents by the 1860s. The population later dwindled with the declining importance of river traffic. A visitor center has exhibits interpreting the Boone's Lick region in the early 19th century. One-hour tram tours of the grounds are conducted by the Friends of Arrow Rock for a fee *(see attraction listing)*. Picnic areas and campsites are nearby. *See Recreation Chart and the AAA South Central CampBook.*

Hours: Grounds open daily 7 a.m.-10 p.m. Visitor center open daily 10-5, June-Aug.; daily 10-4, Mar.-May and Sept.-Nov.; Fri-Sun. 10-4, rest of year. Visitor center closed Jan. 1, Thanksgiving and Dec. 25. **Cost:** Grounds and visitor center free. **Phone:** (660) 837-3330, or (660) 837-3231 for tour reservations.

Friends of Arrow Rock Guided Tours is off I-70 exit SR 41, then 13 mi. n. to the museum on Main St. within Arrow Rock State Historic Site. Tram tours visit the 1837 home of George C. Bingham and the J.P. Sites Gun Shop and Home. **Time:** Allow 1 hour minimum. **Hours:** Tours depart daily at 10, 11:30, 1:30 and 3, June-Aug.; Sat.-Sun. at 10, 11:30, 1:30 and 3, Apr.-May and Sept.-Oct. **Cost:** $5; $1.50 (ages 0-11). **Phone:** (660) 837-3231.

AUGUSTA—*see St. Louis p. 216.*

BELLEVIEW (D-5)

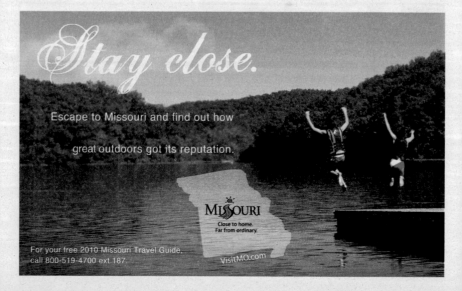

ELEPHANT ROCKS STATE PARK is s. on SR 21 to 7406 SR 21, following signs. The park's name is derived from Elephant Rock, which is 27 feet tall, 35 feet long, 17 feet wide and weighs about 680 tons. Geologists estimate the granite rock to be approximately 1.2 billion years old. The 1-mile Elephant Rocks Braille Trail, a national recreation trail, describes the park's natural features. **Hours:** Daily 8-8. **Cost:** Free. **Phone:** (573) 697-5395.

BETHEL (B-4) pop. 121

Bethel was founded in 1844 when Wilhelm Keil led settlers of German ancestry from Pennsylvania and began a communal religious colony that shared work and property but permitted private earnings. The community numbered about 650 in 1855 when Keil led part of the group west to Oregon; about 340 residents remained at Bethel. Both colonies were disbanded in 1879. More than 30 of Bethel's original buildings remain, and three houses with 1840s furnishings can be visited.

From May through October the Bethel Colony School of Arts offers classes ranging from folk arts to fine arts.

Bethel German Colony: 127 N. Main St., Bethel, MO 63434. **Phone:** (660) 284-6493.

Self-guiding tours: Walking tour brochures describing the history of Bethel and various historic houses can be picked up from the Bethel Colony Gift Shop, First and Main streets, daily 10-3, May-Nov.; phone (660) 284-6493.

BLOOMFIELD (E-6) pop. 1,952, elev. 497′

MISSOURI STATE VETERANS CEMETERY is about 3.5 n. off SR 25 from jct. US 60 at 17377 Stars and Stripes Way. A white rail fence with stone pillars encompasses this cemetery for Missouri war veterans and their spouses. A walking trail traverses the landscaped grounds, which include a lake, fountain and columbarium wall. Each burial area is sectioned off alphabetically. **Time:** Allow 30 minutes minimum. **Hours:** Daily 8 a.m.-dusk. **Cost:** Free. **Phone:** (573) 568-3871.

STARS AND STRIPES MUSEUM/LIBRARY is at 17377 Stars and Stripes Way, adjacent to the Missouri State Veterans Cemetery. It preserves the legacy of a newspaper that has bridged servicemen and women and their families through five major wars. Ten Union soldiers from Illinois, using the vacated press of *The Bloomfield Herald,* published the first issue of *The Stars and Stripes*—which they named after the American flag—on Nov. 9, 1861.

One of those original editions can be seen along with military memorabilia and displays pertaining to the many notable journalists who have served as "Stripers." **Time:** Allow 30 minutes minimum. **Hours:** Mon. and Wed.-Fri. 10-4, Sat. 10-2, Sun. 1-4. Closed Jan. 1, Easter, Thanksgiving and Dec. 25. **Cost:** Free. **Phone:** (573) 568-2055.

BLUE SPRINGS—*see Kansas City p. 176.*

BONNE TERRE (D-5) pop. 4,039

BONNE TERRE MINE TOURS is on SR 47 at Park St. and Allen St. Visitors explore the lead and silver mines that operated 1870-1962. Tours through the caverns, which are larger than the town of Bonne Terre, pass old mining tools, a flower garden, ore cars and a billion-gallon underground lake popular with scuba divers. A museum on the surface displays old mining equipment and ore samples.

Time: Allow 1 hour minimum. **Hours:** Daily 9-4, May-Sept.; Fri.-Sun. 9-4, rest of year. Last tour begins 30 minutes before closing. Boat tours are available in conjunction with walking tours Sat.-Sun. and by prior arrangement other days. Closed Dec. 25. **Cost:** Walking tour $14.50; $8.50 (ages 0-11). Combined boat/walking tour $19.50. **Phone:** (573) 358-2148 or (888) 843-3483.

BOONESBORO (C-3) elev. 820′

BOONE'S LICK STATE HISTORIC SITE is 2.1 mi. w. on SR 187 from jct. SR 87. Two salt springs, or licks, were used at the site by Daniel Boone's sons Daniel and Nathan and two partners 1806-14 to produce salt. The salt was made by heating brine in large iron pots over a furnace; 300 gallons of brine would yield 60 pounds of salt. The licks turned out 500 pounds of salt a day and required four furnaces and up to 20 workers. **Hours:** Daily dawn-dusk. **Cost:** Free. **Phone:** (660) 837-3330 or (800) 334-6946.

BOONVILLE (C-3) pop. 8,202, elev. 579′

Boonville, on the Missouri River, was an early distribution center from which wagon trains with provisions started over the old Santa Fe Trail to the Southwest. The first battle of the Civil War in Missouri was fought in Boonville on June 17, 1861, when Union troops under Gen. Nathaniel Lyon defeated state troops led by Gov. Claiborne Jackson.

Many houses and public buildings dating from the early to mid-19th century distinguish the town, which has seven historic districts. Steeped in history are such structures as the 1836 Hain House and the renovated 1848 Old Cooper County Jail. The Katy Depot Caboose Museum, located in a restored caboose, also houses the chamber of commerce.

Thespian Hall, built in 1855, is one of the oldest surviving theater buildings west of the Alleghenies. Its exterior is restored to its 1857 appearance and the interior recalls 1901. The hall is open for tours and is the site of spring and fall concerts.

Boonville Area Chamber of Commerce: 320 First St., Boonville, MO 65233. **Phone:** (660) 882-2721.

GAMBLING ESTABLISHMENTS

- **Isle of Capri** is at 100 Isle of Capri Blvd. **Hours:** Sun.-Thurs. 8 a.m.-5 a.m., Fri.-Sat. 24 hours. **Phone:** (800) 843-4753.

Branson

City Population: 6,050 **Elevation:** 722 ft.

Editor's Picks:

Shepherd of the Hills Homestead........................(see p. 136)
Silver Dollar City....................(see p. 137)
Titanic—World's Largest Museum Attraction..............(see p. 138)

Find more AAA top picks at AAA.com

Branson Landing / Branson / Lakes Area Chamber of Commerce and CVB

Branson's enormous popularity as a vacation destination is a delightfully unlikely success story. That a small southwestern Missouri town with a population of less than 10,000 would be visited by millions of people every year is unlikely enough. That it is tucked deep into the hills and hollows of the Ozarks, relatively isolated from big cities and major interstates, only makes it more unlikely. But Branson's beginnings are inextricably tied to its location, and it is the Ozark Mountains that give this little community with big appeal its own very special character.

The Ozark Plateau on which Branson sits is a nature lover's feast of rocky hillsides, rivers, lakes, streams, waterfalls, caves, grasslands and dense hardwood forests. One of the region's more intriguing geological features are the glades, often referred to as "balds" by locals, found on the south- and west-facing slopes of hills. Their typically sparse appearance is the result of prolonged sun exposure and fires—caused by lightning as well as intentional burning by American Indians and early white settlers—that kept them free of the rolling stands of oak and hickory trees that otherwise characterize the terrain.

These Ozark hills were settled by farmers who migrated to the area from the mountains of the Carolinas, Tennessee and Kentucky—themselves descendants of farmers from England, Scotland and Ireland. Staunch individualists, they were used to eking a living from small farms, but the row crops they planted on the steep hillsides quickly eroded the thin soil. By the last decades of the 19th century this region's economic history had become a series of attempts to supplement meager incomes, from lead mining, logging and harvesting mussel shells for the button industry to the production of moonshine.

The ravages of the Civil War also were devastating, particularly along the Arkansas-Missouri border. Outlaws lured by the region's inaccessibility turned it into a no man's land of violence, taking advantage of the clash between pro-slavery and antislavery advocates and ruthlessly preying on women and children while men were off fighting. In the vacuum of authority following war's end justice was virtually nonexistent. As thievery became commonplace and murder after murder went unpunished, vigilante groups organized to impose law and order—and in the process continued the reign of lawlessness.

The hillside balds became meeting spots for such gangs as the Bald Knobbers, who roamed Taney County in the 1880s meting out their own brutal brand of justice. Their tactics fell out of favor as time slowly healed the wounds resulting from the rift between Yankee and rebel, but the name ironically lives on in one of Branson's most beloved country music shows.

Getting There — *starting on p. 130*
Getting Around — *starting on p. 131*
What To See — *starting on p. 131*
What To Do — *starting on p. 139*
Where To Stay — *starting on p. 407*
Where To Dine — *starting on p. 427*
Essential Experiences — *visit AAA.com*
Editor's Event Picks — *visit AAA.com*

Founded in 1903, Branson was initially planned as an industrial center that would handle trainloads of logs, lumber and manufactured products. When incorporated on April 1, 1912, it had 1,200 residents. Shortly thereafter the idea of turning the industrial community into a tourist resort took shape. After man-made Lake Taneycomo was created in 1913 by impounding the waters of the White River, a soft drink bottling plant, a candy factory and an ice cream factory opened near the waterfront.

Long before the twinkling lights of show theaters lit up the evening sky, three humble hotels began catering to vacationers, and local businesses were encouraged to stack their lumber and bricks to present a tidier appearance. The Sammy Lane Resort—the first vacation cabins in the area—was built just upstream from downtown; they stood on stilts anchored with cables to prevent floods from washing them away.

By the 1930s Lake Taneycomo had a reputation as an inexpensive vacation spot easily accessible by car or train. Rolling green hills and the lake setting made Branson a scenic backdrop for street fairs, boat races and picnics. Following World War II the area began attracting artists and craftspeople along with returning servicemen and retirees. One local artist conceived the idea of displaying a Nativity scene on the bluff of Mount Branson, which rises above the downtown business district from the opposite shore of Lake Taneycomo. Local carpenters created the figures, some up to 28 feet tall. The annual lighting ceremonies—inaugurated in December 1949 before an awestruck crowd of thousands—started a local tradition of parades and community events that continues to this day.

Another early catalyst in the development of tourism was the 1907 publication of Harold Bell

White Water / Missouri Division of Tourism

Wright's second novel "The Shepherd of the Hills." A best-selling author of fiction, nonfiction and essays, Wright was the New York-born son of a Civil War lieutenant and a mother who encouraged his interest in art. He became a painter and later a minister in Missouri, Kansas and California.

Said to be the first American novel to sell a million copies, "The Shepherd of the Hills" told the inspirational story of a former pastor who chose to live and share his life with the citizens of rural Mutton Hollow. It offered a spiritual message based on a life lived in simplicity, and although Wright was critically maligned in his day he maintained that his intention was never to create great literature but to instead speak to ordinary citizens. Four different movies have been adapted from the novel, most notably a 1941 film starring John Wayne that made glorious use of Technicolor.

More importantly, though, the novel's Ozark Mountains setting sparked interest in Branson as a place to visit. In 1959 the play "The Shepherd of

Destination Branson

Although Branson first made a name for itself with live country music shows, tourist attractions have always been a large part of its appeal as well. Longtime favorites like Marvel Cave, the Shepherd of the Hills Homestead and Silver Dollar City are still popular today.

New attractions keep popping up, though, and one of the most impressive is the painstaking re-creation of the *Titanic* that towers above SR 76, widely known as "the Strip."

Branson/Lakes Area Chamber of Commerce & CVB

Sight and Sound Theatre, Branson. (See listing page 137)

Branson/Lakes Area Chamber of Commerce and CVB

Golfing in Branson. *(See page 141)*

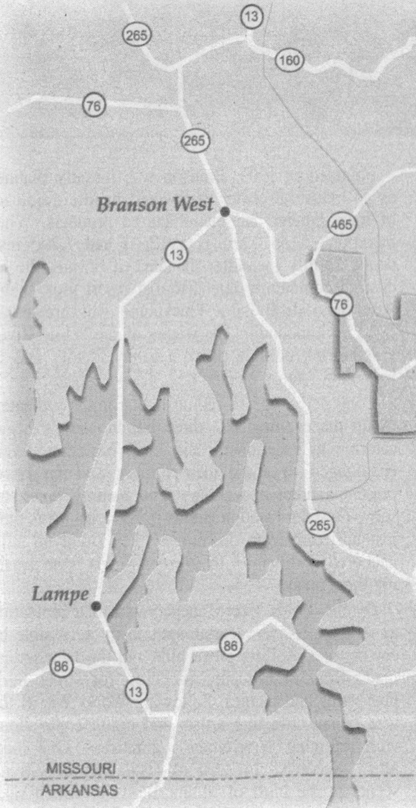

Places included in this AAA Destination City:

Titanic—World's Largest Museum Attraction, Branson. (See listing page 138)

Branson/Lakes Area Chamber of Commerce and CVB

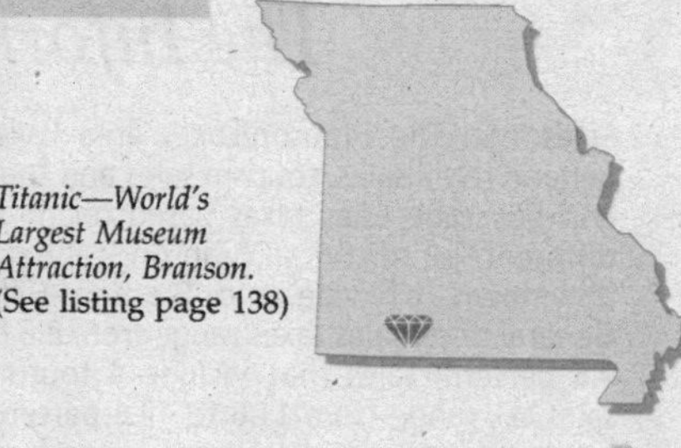

76
65
465
Merriam Woods
160
Branson
76
Point Lookout
65
MISSOURI
ARKANSAS

See Vicinity map page 132

Branson/Lakes Area Chamber of Commerce and CVB

New Americana Theatre, Branson. (See mention page 145)

The Informed Traveler

Sales Tax: The Branson/Lakes area levies general retail sales, tourism sales and food and beverage sales taxes based on three different jurisdictions: Branson Landing/downtown, citywide and Branson Hills. General retail sales taxes range from 8.6 to 9.6 percent; sales that include a tourism sales tax range from 11.6 to 12.6 percent; food and beverage sales taxes range from 8.975 to 9.975 percent.

WHOM TO CALL

Emergency: 911

Police (non-emergency): (417) 334-3300

Time and Temperature: (417) 336-5000

Hospitals: Skaggs Regional Medical Center, (417) 335-7000; CoxHealth Cox South (Springfield, MO.), (417) 269-6000; Mercy St. John's Regional Hospital (Springfield, MO.), (417) 820-2000.

WHERE TO LOOK

Newspapers

Branson is served by the *Branson Daily News,* a morning newspaper. *NBranson ETC* is a free monthly guide featuring information about area attractions, theaters, shopping and recreation. *The Shepherd of the Hills Gazette,* a free newspaper published five times a year, also has attraction, show and visitor information.

Radio

Branson radio station KRZK (106.3 FM) plays country music; KSMU (90.5 FM), affiliated with Missouri State University in Springfield, is a member of National Public Radio.

Visitor Information

Branson/Lakes Area Chamber of Commerce and CVB: P.O. Box 1897, Branson, MO 65615. **Phone:** (417) 334-4084 or (800) 214-3661. *See color ads on p. 134 & p. 143.*

TRANSPORTATION

Air Travel

Branson Airport, 1 mile south of the Hollister exit off US 65, east on Branson Creek Boulevard, then following signs to 4000 Branson Airport Blvd., is served by AirTran Airways and Sun Country Airlines and handles commercial and general aviation; phone (417) 334-7813. Springfield-Branson National Airport, 5000 W. Kearney St. in Springfield, is about 45 miles north of Branson via US 65. The drive takes 45 minutes to an hour, depending on traffic. Domestic airlines serving the airport include Allegiant Air, American, Delta and United; phone (417) 868-0500.

Several shuttle and limousine services transport passengers to and from Branson and the Springfield-Branson National Airport, including Branson Gray Line, (417) 335-4466 or (800) 237-4466; At Your Service Limousines, (417) 230-3602; and Branson Coach/Tri-Lakes Shuttle, (417) 339-4888 or (800) 841-2313. At Branson Airport, only Branson Gray Line transports passengers from the airport; the other companies may only drop off passengers.

Rental Cars

Hertz, which only operates out of Springfield-Branson National Airport, offers discounts to AAA members; phone (417) 865-1681 or (800) 654-3080. Rental cars are available at Branson Airport.

Buses

SAVE Gray Line Branson/Springfield, (800) 542-6768, provides chartered motor coach service to Branson and one-way transfers to and from Branson Airport and Springfield-Branson National Airport.

Taxis

Cab companies include Jerry's Shuttle Service & Taxi, (417) 348-1419; and Checker Cab, City Cabs and Yellow Cab, all of which can be reached at (417) 336-6769.

Public Transport

Unless you're part of a motor coach tour, getting around Branson is much easier if you have your own vehicle. One convenient alternative to driving in the historic downtown area is a free ride aboard the Discovery Trolley. The green-and-gold, hop-on and hop-off trolley makes two stops on Commercial Street near Dick's Old Time 5 & 10 and two stops at Branson Landing. Trolley maps are available at the Downtown Branson Main Street Association, 119 W. Pacific St.; phone (417) 334-1548. *See color ad p 149.*

the Hills" was first presented in the Old Mill Theater on the Shepherd of the Hills farm, perched high on a ridge just west of Dewey Bald. The farm later became a tourist attraction, the Shepherd of the Hills Homestead *(see attraction listing p. 136)*. The actors who performed opening night and in the play's early years came from the surrounding communities, and many of their children and grandchildren went on to become involved in both the play and the development of Branson's tourism industry.

Winding through the valleys and hollows of the Ozark Mountains from Branson to Eureka Springs, Ark., the White River was a natural resource waiting to be enjoyed. The harnessing of its waters to create invitingly blue Table Rock Lake for outdoor recreational use was another step in the region's development. Designed, built and operated by the U.S. Army Corps of Engineers, Table Rock Dam was completed in 1958, paving the way for fishing, boating and other activities.

In 1959 brothers Bill, Jim, Lyle and Bob Mabe set up folding chairs in Branson's City Hall and put on a show. Taking their name from the previous century's vigilante groups, they played banjo, Dobro and washtub bass, with an old washboard and the jawbone of a mule providing rhythm, and were an immediate hit with fishermen and the tourists who had begun trickling in. As their popularity grew the Mabes moved their show to an old skating rink, in the process creating Branson's first live music theater. They moved again in 1968 to the present Baldknobbers Country Music Theatre *(see p. 145)* on SR 76 (later known as Country Music Boulevard and, more recently, "the Strip"), where the "Baldknobbers Jamboree Show" continues to pack in the crowds.

The following year saw the opening of a theme park that has in some ways come to define Branson. Silver Dollar City *(see attraction listing p. 137)* rose from the site of a subterranean cavern known to the Osage Indians and first explored in 1869 by one Henry T. Blow, a St. Louis lead-mining magnate. The exploration party found no lead, but named the geological feature Marble Cave based on their belief that one of the chambers was composed of marble.

The marble turned out to be limestone, and mining efforts didn't pan out. The cave was first opened to sightseers in 1894 and eventually renamed Marvel Cave, but it wasn't until Hugo Herschend, a Chicago vacuum cleaner salesman, purchased a 99-year lease from the owners in the 1950s that its potential as a tourist attraction began to be realized. The Herschends and their two sons made their own improvements, including a tunnel and track for a train that hauled visitors 218 feet up from the cavern's depths.

Looking for ways to increase business, the family decided to build a replica of an Ozark frontier town on the lushly wooded acreage surrounding the cave, figuring it would give visitors waiting for the next tour something else to do. Silver Dollar City opened in 1960 with five shops, a church, a log cabin and a re-enactment of the feud between the Hatfields and the McCoys. Within its first year of operation Silver

Yakov Smirnoff Theatre / Branson/Lakes Area Chamber of Commerce and CVB

Dollar City was attracting four times as many visitors as the cave, which remains one of the park's attractions.

National exposure came when several episodes of "The Beverly Hillbillies"—one of the most popular television shows in the country at the time—were filmed at Silver Dollar City in 1969. Brothers Jack and Pete Herschend still own this beautifully landscaped theme park, which is known for its family-friendly atmosphere and values, a dedicated commitment to the preservation of Ozarks heritage and a working colony of artisans who create exquisitely crafted works of art.

The Presley family followed the pioneering Mabes in Branson's fledgling live music industry. Ozarks natives who first established their reputation underground—putting on shows in the caverns of southwestern Missouri—the Presleys opened the Strip's first country music theater in 1967. Forty years later, four generations of Presleys are still playing and singing the country and gospel music they grew up with at the Presleys' Country Jubilee *(see p. 145)*.

After the Missouri Pacific Railroad curtailed all passenger service on its White River line in 1960 the number of tourists coming to Branson by automobile grew even greater. To alleviate traffic congestion on winding, two-lane US 65, the highway was shortened and straightened by dynamiting through the limestone hills between Branson and Springfield. In the mid-1970s, following construction of two interchanges that routed traffic away from the congested downtown business district, a few shops and music theaters began to spring up along SR 76.

By the 1980s motels, restaurants and 16 theaters were scattered along a 3-mile stretch of the highway. The opening of the Roy Clark Celebrity Theatre in 1983 kicked off the era of big-name entertainment stars coming to town. Branson, however, remained pretty much a well-kept regional secret until the early 1990s. In 1991 the program "60 Minutes" did a feature on the town, proclaiming it "the live country music capital of the universe." The publicity catapulted Branson into its first boom period. Established names like Andy Williams, the Osmond family, Ray Stevens and Jim Stafford were soon headlining shows along SR 76, which is now commonly referred to as "the Strip."

From the beginning an emphasis was put on entertainment that was wholesome, all-American and family-friendly. And that has not wavered, even as the performance palette has broadened considerably in recent years to embrace lavish Broadway-style productions, heartthrob magicians, Vegas-inspired spectaculars, baby boomer favorites and concert appearances by rock and pop stars. The loyal Branson fan still comes for traditional country and gospel music, homespun comedy and heartfelt displays of patriotic pride—and Branson delivers on all three counts.

A second Branson boom was inaugurated in 2006, when three major attractions that are likely to bring many new visitors to town were unveiled. Foremost was the late May opening of the first phase of Branson Landing *(see p. 142)*, at $420 million the most costly and ambitious development the city has yet undertaken.

A shopping, dining and entertainment complex in the heart of the historic downtown district, Branson Landing extends for 1.5 miles along the scenic Lake Taneycomo waterfront. Its shops and restaurants appeal to everyone from kids to retirement-age vacationers, but the Landing also targets a younger, more affluent crowd with a pedestrian-oriented urban streetscape ideal for strolling and nightlife that includes a spectacular choreographed water fountain display.

A terraced, centrally located "town square" slopes down to the waterfront, providing a big open area for concerts, festivals and other entertainment events. The boardwalk that follows the lakeshore is perfect for an evening stroll, and several restaurants have outdoor seating overlooking the water. The complex also includes upscale condominiums, the Hilton Promenade boutique hotel and the Branson Convention Center, which opened in 2007. Branson Landing has even entered the local lexicon: "Meet you at the Landing!" is an oft-heard exclamation around town.

The grand opening of Titanic—World's Largest Museum Attraction *(see attraction listing on p. 138)* was presided over by none other than talk show host Regis Philbin. You can't miss the half-scale re-creation of the ocean liner that tragically sank in the Atlantic on its maiden voyage; it towers over SR 76. The museum's state-of-the-art displays set a new level for Branson attractions.

Dick Clark's American Bandstand Theater *(see p. 144)* is a showcase for the popular Legends in Concert tributes featuring live shows and concerts with celebrity impersonators. It was the first new theater to open in nearly a decade, continuing an expansion of Branson's entertainment offerings. And the big news in 2009 was the opening of the new Branson Airport, located 10 miles south of the Strip.

Branson, to a degree, sells nostalgia—a longing for a simpler time in America when people could leave their doors unlocked, every family had two parents and terrorists weren't a daily part of the evening news. But what also sets it apart is a sense of genuine friendliness, which feels neither forced nor fabricated. Visitors are made to feel welcome; you'll probably be called "darlin'" or "hon" more than a couple of times. And don't be surprised if a total stranger happens to greet you with a smile, a handshake and a warm "Welcome to the heart of the Ozarks!" Branson really is that kind of place.

Getting There

By Car

Branson receives more than 8 million visitors annually, and more than 90 percent of them drive. This can present a challenge to the existing road network, which was never meant to accommodate the number of vehicles that arrive throughout the year. More than $200 million spent on new highway construction has, however, helped lessen the bottleneck conditions that can occur in summer, the busiest season.

I-44 funnels traffic to Springfield from St. Louis and points east, and from Tulsa, Oklahoma City and points west. South from Springfield or north from Little Rock and Harrison, Ark., the main approach is via US 65, which is four lanes from Springfield south to Branson, facilitating access into town. US 65 has been widened to four lanes from Hollister, just across Lake Taneycomo from Branson, south to the Arkansas border.

More locally, the Ozark Mountain Highroad (SR 465) runs east-west for 8 miles between US 65 and SR 76 just west of the Shepherd of the Hills Homestead, offering a relaxed and less-traveled route to Table Rock Lake, the Silver Dollar City theme park and other attractions on the west side of town. North-south SR 13, which branches off SR 76, and east-west SR 86, which branches off US 65 south of Hollister, are other easy ways to get to Table Rock Lake. For a delightfully scenic day trip from Branson to popular Eureka Springs, Ark., take US 65 south to US 62, then US 62 west.

Getting Around

Street System

Historic downtown Branson, just east of US 65 via US 65 Business Route/Veterans Boulevard, forms a small, compact grid of streets running about six blocks north-south and east-west. East-west Main Street, the eastward extension of SR 76, and north-south Commercial Street are the main thoroughfares. Main Street runs into Branson Landing Boulevard, which fronts Branson Landing and beyond, Lake Taneycomo.

Branson's main drag is, of course, SR 76W, sometimes known as Country Music Boulevard and widely named simply "the Strip." The 5-mile stretch within the city limits, a two-lane highway with a center turning lane, is the heart of many Branson activities, winding past a seemingly endless procession of music theaters, attractions, shopping centers, hotels, motels and restaurants.

The other major roads are SR 248/Shepherd of the Hills Expressway, Gretna Road and Green Mountain Drive. SR 248 branches west off US 65, providing a northerly route that eventually intersects with SR 265 west of SR 76 via Shepherd of the Hills Expressway. Several popular theaters and attractions are along this stretch. Gretna Road, between SR 248 and SR 76, is lined with shopping complexes. Green Mountain Drive runs south of and parallel to SR 76.

Traffic is frequently congested along much of SR 76, particularly so before and after evening performances at the theaters, and major intersections—for example, SR 76 and Gretna Road—can become gridlocked at times. But fortunately, driving the Strip is a choice and not a necessity, thanks to three east-west "relief routes" that can be timesaving options.

Two routes are north of SR 76, and one is south. The Red Route is SR 248 from US 65 west to Shepherd of the Hills Expressway and Shepherd of the Hills Expressway west to SR 265. The Blue Route is Roark Valley Road from SR 76 to Gretna Road and Gretna Road back to SR 76. The Yellow Route is Fall Creek Road to Wildwood Drive, Wildwood Drive to Green Mountain Drive and Green Mountain Drive to SR 76.

Red, blue and yellow route signs are posted regularly along the respective roads. The Yellow Route is the most crowded of the three, so consider using the Blue or Red routes instead. Once you become familiar with these routes, however, getting around Branson is pretty much a snap. You can pick up a Time-Saver road map (created by the Branson/Lakes Area Chamber of Commerce and CVB) showing these routes as well as the location of many theaters and attractions from just about any local hotel or restaurant.

Parking

Finding a place to park in Branson is rarely a problem. Almost all of the theaters have their own large lots, and parking for most shopping centers and restaurants is plentiful. You may have to hunt for a space downtown on weekends. However, the opening of Branson Landing has made this search largely unnecessary, since the Landing's parking garage and two lots (one at each end of the complex) are within easy walking distance of downtown's shops and restaurants.

What To See

BONNIEBROOK—*see Merriam Woods p. 150.*

BRANSON AUTO MUSEUM, 1335 SR 76W, houses a collection of antique and collectible cars. Some of the vehicles are for sale while some, like Evel Knievel's Cadillac and motorcycle, are for display only. There also is a large collection of antique toys (which are for sale).

Time: Allow 1 hour minimum. **Hours:** Daily 9-7, Mar.-Dec.; 9-5, rest of year. Closing times may vary; phone ahead to confirm schedule. Closed Dec. 25. **Cost:** $13.95; $11.95 (ages 65+); $9.95 (ages 12-18); $8.95 (ages 4-11); $34.95 (family, two adults and up to four children). **Phone:** (417) 335-2600. *See color ad on p. 136.*

BRANSON'S IMAX ENTERTAINMENT COMPLEX is just e. of SR 76 at 3562 Shepherd of the Hills Expwy. This family-oriented entertainment center features several different larger-than-life IMAX adventures (including "Under the Sea" and "Ozarks Legacy & Legend") shown on a screen six stories tall and 83 feet wide. The center also has a three-screen movie theater and gift shops. The Little Opry Theatre presents live musical shows with an emphasis on traditional country and bluegrass.

Time: Allow 2 hours minimum. **Hours:** IMAX box office opens daily at 8:30 a.m.; film screenings

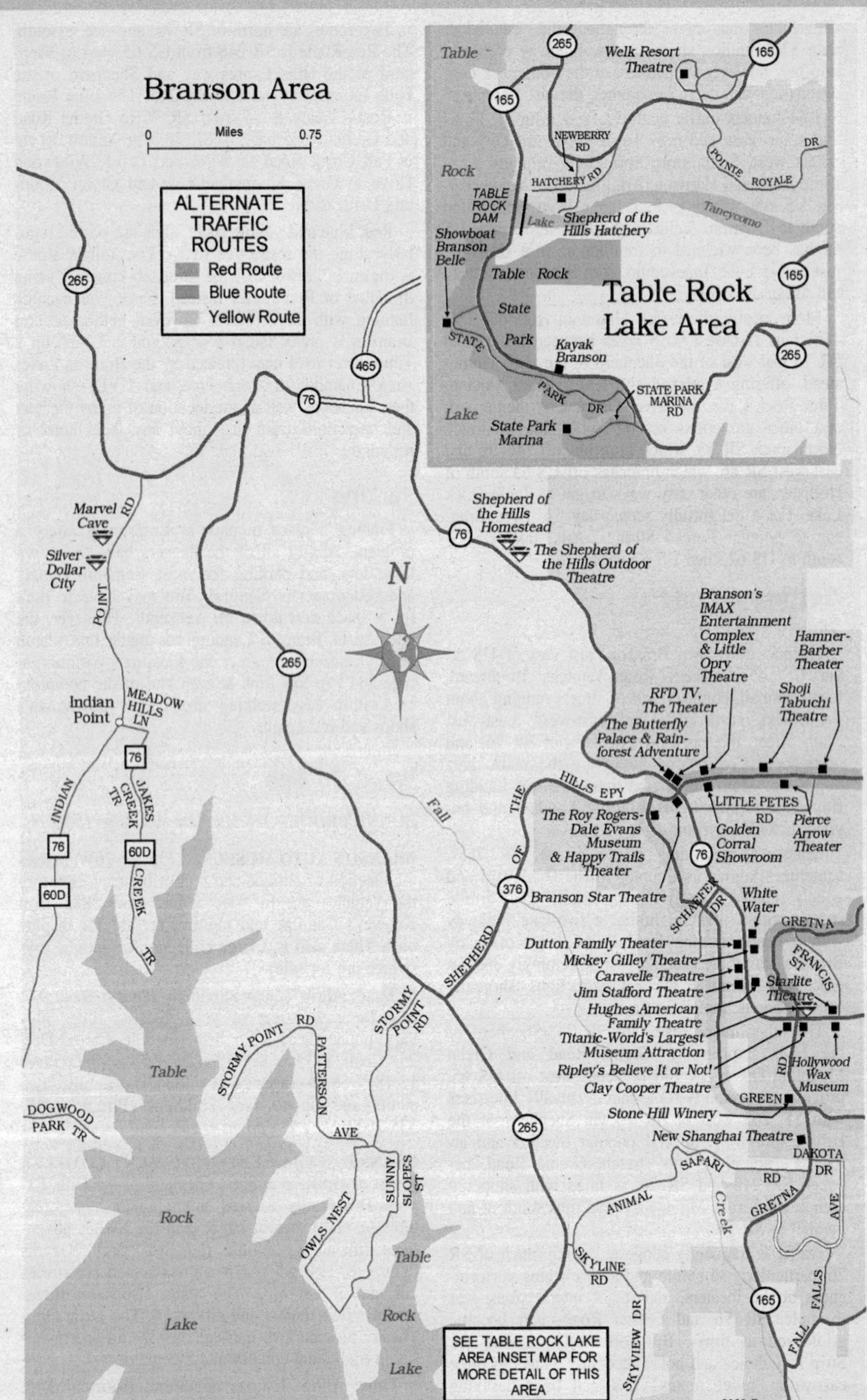

Branson Area
0 Miles 0.75
ALTERNATE TRAFFIC ROUTES
Red Route
Blue Route
Yellow Route
Table Rock Lake Area
Welk Resort Theatre
NEWBERRY RD
HATCHERY RD
POINTE ROYALE DR
TABLE ROCK DAM
Lake Taneycomo
Shepherd of the Hills Hatchery
Showboat Branson Belle
Table Rock State Park
Kayak Branson
STATE PARK DR
STATE PARK MARINA RD
State Park Marina
Table Rock Lake
Marvel Cave
Silver Dollar City
POINT RD
Indian Point
MEADOW HILLS LN
INDIAN
JAKES CREEK TR
Shepherd of the Hills Homestead
The Shepherd of the Hills Outdoor Theatre
Branson's IMAX Entertainment Complex & Little Opry Theatre
Hamner-Barber Theater
RFD TV, The Theater
Shoji Tabuchi Theatre
The Butterfly Palace & Rain-forest Adventure
SHEPHERD OF THE HILLS EPY
LITTLE PETES RD
Pierce Arrow Theater
The Roy Rogers-Dale Evans Museum & Happy Trails Theater
Golden Corral Showroom
Fall Creek
Branson Star Theatre
SCHAEFER DR
White Water
GRETNA
FRANCIS ST
Dutton Family Theater
Mickey Gilley Theatre
Caravelle Theatre
Jim Stafford Theatre
Starlite Theatre
Hughes American Family Theatre
Titanic-World's Largest Museum Attraction
Ripley's Believe It or Not!
Clay Cooper Theatre
Hollywood Wax Museum
GREEN RD
Stone Hill Winery
New Shanghai Theatre
DAKOTA DR
SAFARI RD
GRETNA AVE
ANIMAL
STORMY POINT RD
PATTERSON AVE
DOGWOOD PARK TR
OWLS NEST
SUNNY SLOPES ST
SKYLINE RD
SKYVIEW DR
FALL FALLS
Table Rock Lake
SEE TABLE ROCK LAKE AREA INSET MAP FOR MORE DETAIL OF THIS AREA
2009-D

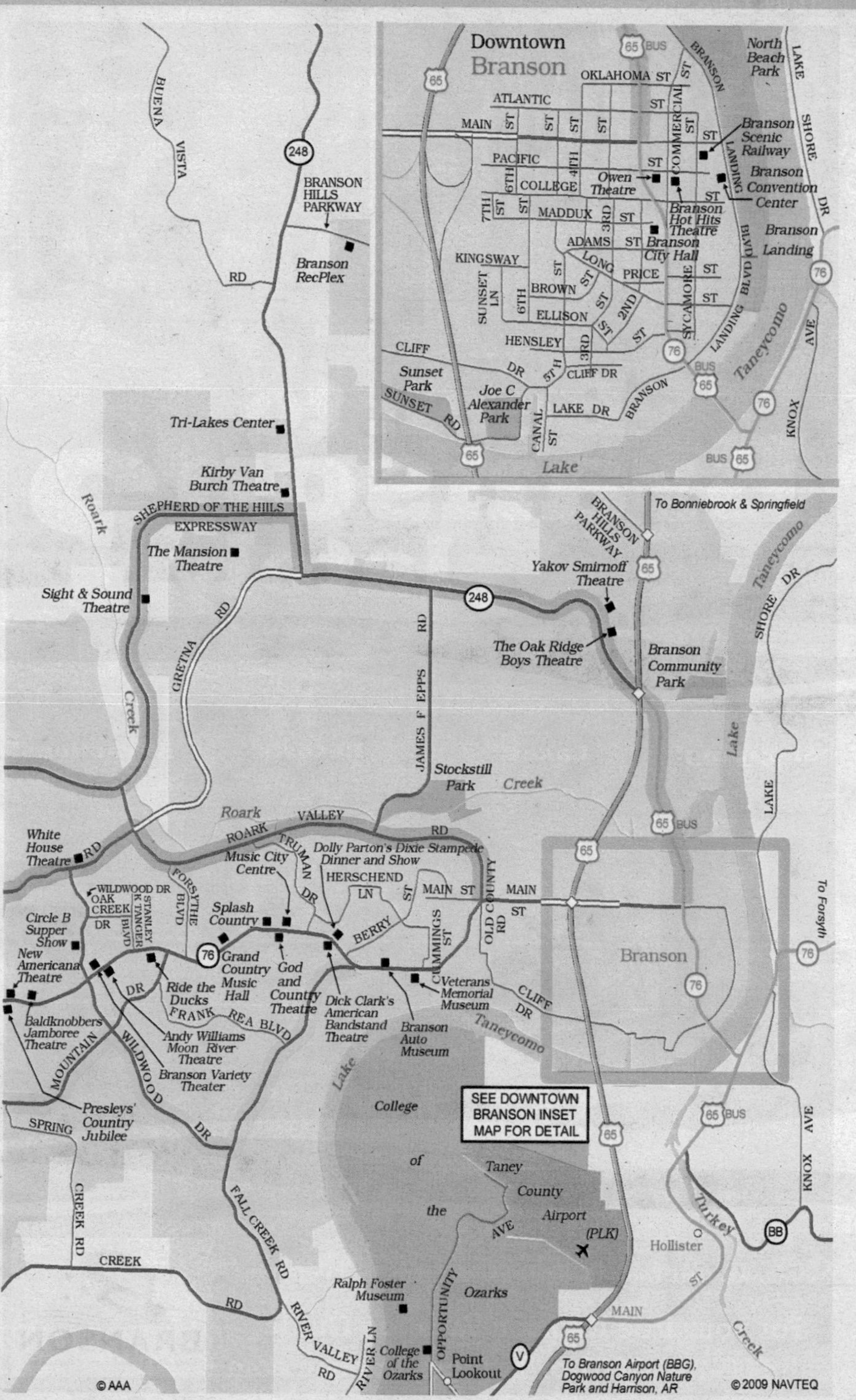
Downtown Branson
OKLAHOMA ST
ATLANTIC ST
MAIN ST
PACIFIC ST
COLLEGE ST
MADDUX ST
ADAMS ST
KINGSWAY
LONG ST
PRICE ST
BROWN ST
ELLISON ST
HENSLEY ST
CLIFF DR
LAKE DR
CANAL ST
SUNSET LN
SUNSET RD
COMMERCIAL ST
SYCAMORE ST
BRANSON LANDING BLVD
LAKE SHORE DR
KNOX AVE
North Beach Park
Branson Scenic Railway
Branson Convention Center
Branson Landing
Owen Theatre
Branson Hot Hits Theatre
Branson City Hall
Sunset Park
Joe C Alexander Park
Taneycomo
Lake
BRANSON HILLS PARKWAY
Branson RecPlex
BUENA VISTA RD
Tri-Lakes Center
Kirby Van Burch Theatre
SHEPHERD OF THE HILLS EXPRESSWAY
The Mansion Theatre
Sight & Sound Theatre
GRETNA RD
Roark Creek
JAMES F EPPS RD
To Bonniebrook & Springfield
Yakov Smirnoff Theatre
The Oak Ridge Boys Theatre
Branson Community Park
Stockstill Park
Creek
ROARK VALLEY RD
White House Theatre
Music City Centre
Dolly Parton's Dixie Stampede Dinner and Show
HERSCHEND LN
TRUMAN DR
BERRY
MAIN ST
OLD COUNTY RD
CUMMINGS ST
WILDWOOD DR
OAK CREEK DR
STANLEY BLVD
K TANGER BLVD
FORSYTHE BLVD
Circle B Supper Show
New Americana Theatre
Splash Country
Grand Country Music Hall
God and Country Theatre
Ride the Ducks
Dick Clark's American Bandstand Theatre
Branson Auto Museum
Veterans Memorial Museum
CLIFF DR
FRANK REA BLVD
Baldknobbers Jamboree Theatre
Andy Williams Moon River Theatre
Branson Variety Theater
Presleys' Country Jubilee
MOUNTAIN
WILDWOOD DR
SPRING CREEK RD
CREEK RD
Branson
To Forsyth
SEE DOWNTOWN BRANSON INSET MAP FOR DETAIL
College of the Ozarks
Taney County Airport (PLK)
OPPORTUNITY AVE
FALL CREEK RD
RIVER VALLEY RD
RIVER LN
Ralph Foster Museum
Point Lookout
Hollister
ST
MAIN
Turkey Creek
To Branson Airport (BBG), Dogwood Canyon Nature Park and Harrison, AR
© AAA
© 2009 NAVTEQ

daily 9-9. Little Opry Theatre performance times vary. Good News Gospel Hour Sun. at 9 a.m. Glen and Sue Phillips Hour Sun. at 11 a.m. Stores open daily 8:30-start of last show. **Cost:** IMAX $9.40; $5.85 (ages 4-12). Live show tickets $23. Good News Gospel Hour and the Glen and Sue Phillips Hour free. **Phone:** (417) 335-4832 or (800) 419-4832. *See color ad p. 145 and on insert.*

THE BUTTERFLY PALACE & RAINFOREST ADVENTURE is at 4106 SR 76W. This state-of-the-art complex, which also functions as a research facility, has a climate-controlled room where various tropical butterfly species flit among flowering plants. Other six-legged critters, plus a few four-legged tree frogs, reside at a small insect zoo. Visitors also can watch a 15-minute 3-D film about the life cycle of a butterfly and navigate their way through the Emerald Forest Mirror Maze (which includes a warning about bumping into the glass).

Time: Allow 2 hours minimum. **Hours:** Daily 9-5. Last ticket is sold 30 minutes before closing. Closed Thanksgiving and Dec. 25. **Cost:** $16.95; $14.95 (ages 55+); $9.95 (ages 4-12). **Phone:** (417) 332-2231.

COLLEGE OF THE OZARKS—
see Point Lookout p. 150.

DOGWOOD CANYON NATURE PARK—
see Lampe p. 150.

SAVE **DOLLY PARTON'S DIXIE STAMPEDE DINNER AND SHOW** is at 1525 SR 76W (Country Music Blvd.). Trick horseback riding, buffaloes and other live animals, singing, dancing and audience participation are all part of the entertainment at this dinner theater.

Time: Allow 2 hours minimum. **Hours:** Shows daily at 5:30 and 8 p.m., with matinees added on select days throughout the year. Phone ahead to confirm dates and show times. Closed Dec. 24-25. **Cost:** $42.99; $23.99 (ages 4-11); free (ages 0-3 on lap). **Phone:** (800) 520-5544.

HOLLYWOOD WAX MUSEUM is at 3030 SR 76W. More than 170 lifelike wax celebrities from movies, sports and television are represented, including John Wayne, Tom Cruise, Mark McGwire, Keanu Reeves and Red Skelton. There also are scenes from such popular films as the original "King Kong," "The Wizard of Oz," "Titanic," "The Matrix" and "Pirates of the Caribbean."

Time: Allow 1 hour minimum. **Hours:** Daily 8 a.m.-midnight, Mar. 15-Nov. 15; 8-6, rest of year. **Cost:** $16.95; $14.95 (ages 65+); $8.95 (ages 4-11). **Phone:** (417) 337-8277.

RALPH FOSTER MUSEUM—
see Point Lookout p. 150.

RIPLEY'S BELIEVE IT OR NOT! is at 3326 SR 76W. More than 400 odd and unusual exhibits from around the world are featured inside creatively themed galleries. Visitors can learn about the world's tallest man, see such pranks of nature as a two-headed cow and witness optical illusions. Interactive displays explore entrepreneur and anthropologist Robert Leroy Ripley's obsession with the strange and unusual.

Time: Allow 1 hour minimum. **Hours:** Daily 9:30 a.m.-11 p.m., Mar. 15-Dec. 15; 9:30-7, rest of year. Last ticket sold 1 hour before closing. **Cost:** $16.95; $15.95 (ages 55+); $8.95 (ages 4-12). **Phone:** (417) 337-5300, or (800) 998-4418, ext. 2.

THE ROY ROGERS-DALE EVANS MUSEUM & HAPPY TRAILS THEATER is at 3950 Green Mountain Dr. A larger-than-life statue of Rogers' horse Trigger rears up on its hind legs in front of the museum. Among the exhibits are TV sidekick Pat Brady's jeep "Nellybelle" and memorabilia associated with the Sons of the Pioneers, a cowboy music group formed by Rogers. Hands-on activities are available for children.

The Happy Trails Theater presents a live music show starring Roy "Dusty" Rogers Jr. Video clips of interviews with Rogers, Evans and members of their family are shown. Audio narration at each museum exhibit provides explanations of the displays in the words of the husband-and-wife motion picture and television stars.

Time: Allow 2 hours minimum. **Hours:** Museum Mon.-Sat. 9-5:30. Live shows Tues.-Sat. at 10 and 2. Closed Easter, Thanksgiving and Dec. 24-25. **Cost:** Museum $13; $6.50 (ages 13-17). Theater $27; $13.50 (ages 13-17). Combination museum and theater $38; $19 (ages 13-17). **Phone:** (417) 339-1900 or (866) 769-7643.

SHEPHERD OF THE HILLS HATCHERY is 6 mi. s.w. of downtown Branson via SRs 76W and 165, at the n. end of Table Rock Dam at 483 Hatchery Rd. Rainbow and brown trout are raised at this cold-water facility, which typically produces more than 1,100,000 catchable fish annually; it also supplies eggs and fingerlings to other trout production facilities. A visitor center features aquarium displays and exhibits that describe the trout spawning cycle and the process of fish rearing. Four hiking trails wind through wooded terrain near the Lake Taneycomo shoreline.

Hours: Visitor center open daily 9-6, Memorial Day-Labor Day; 9-5, rest of year. Guided tours Mon.-Fri. at 10, 11, 1 and 2, Memorial Day-Labor Day. Closed Jan. 1, Thanksgiving and Dec. 25. **Cost:** Free. **Phone:** (417) 334-4865.

GEM **SHEPHERD OF THE HILLS HOMESTEAD** is 2 mi. w. at 5586 SR 76W. This working homestead evokes the farm featured in Harold Bell Wright's novel "The Shepherd of the Hills." Jeep-driven guided tours take visitors past Old Matt's Cabin, home of the leading characters, which contains most of its original furnishings. Also on the site are a gristmill, sawmill, smithy, wheelwright shop and a reconstructed church similar to those in which Wright preached during his years in the Ozarks. The Backstage Tour offers a behind-the-scenes look at "The Shepherd of the Hills" outdoor show.

Stone statues of the book's characters stand on Inspiration Point, where the author lived. Inspiration Tower, standing 230 feet high, affords panoramic views of the hills and valleys surrounding the homestead. The Sons of the Pioneers perform May through October in a chuckwagon dinner show. During the Trail of Lights celebration, which takes place nightly in November and December, the homestead is decorated with more than 80 festively lighted drive-through displays.

Hours: Homestead open daily 9-5:30, late Apr. to mid-Aug.; 9-4:30, mid-Aug. to late Oct. Guided tours depart on the hour beginning at 10. Last tour begins 30 minutes before closing. Tower open daily at 9 a.m. Closing time varies from 5 to 8 p.m. (midnight when the tower is lighted for the holidays). Chuckwagon dinner show begins at 4:15. **Cost:** Homestead tour $23; $10 (ages 4-16). Inspiration Tower $10; $5 (ages 4-16). Chuckwagon dinner show $41; $20 (ages 4-16). Trail of Lights drive $10; $5 (ages 4-16). **Phone:** (417) 334-4191 or (800) 653-6288.

GEM **The Shepherd of the Hills Outdoor Theatre** is at 5586 SR 76W at Shepherd of the Hills Homestead. The story of "The Shepherd of the Hills" is dramatized in this outdoor amphitheater. Kids can participate in bullfrog races Memorial Day-Labor Day. **Hours:** Evening performances Mon.-Sat. at 8:30 p.m., late Apr. to mid-Aug.; at 7:30, mid-Aug. to late Oct. **Cost:** $39; $19 (ages 4-16). **Phone:** (417) 334-4191 or (800) 653-6288.

SIGHT & SOUND THEATRE is at 1001 Shepherd of the Hills Expwy. The 2,800-seat amphitheater presents shows with religious themes and featuring elaborate sets, exquisite costumes and animatronic and live animals. Behind-the-scenes tours explore the backstage shops used to create sets as well as the creative and technical processes that drive the performances.

Time: Allow 2 hours, 30 minutes minimum. **Hours:** Shows are offered Mon.-Sat. Showtimes vary by show and season; phone ahead for schedules. Behind-the-scenes tours are offered mid-June to mid-Dec. **Cost:** $52; $25 (ages 13-18); $16 (ages 3-12). Behind-the-scenes tour $9. **Phone:** (417) 335-7900, ext. 7141, or (800) 377-1277 Mon.-Fri. 8:30-7, Sat. 8:30-5 for reservations. *See color ad.*

GEM **SILVER DOLLAR CITY** is 5 mi. w. on SR 76W to Indian Point Rd., then about .5 mi. s. to the park entrance. This theme park combines the atmosphere of an 1880s Ozark pioneer village with 21st-century rides and thrills. The attraction celebrates its 50th anniversary in 2010 with the opening of Tom & Huck's RiverBlast, a water raft ride based on literary characters Tom Sawyer and Huck Finn. Riders armed with water soakers have to dodge water strikes from multiple targets. Other rides include the Powderkeg roller coaster, which goes from 0 to 53 mph in 2.8 seconds; the multi-looping Wildfire!; Thunderation, a runaway mine train; and the Giant Swing, which launches riders more than seven stories and nearly upside down. The Geyser Gulch children's area includes a giant tree house and a water cannon play area.

The Grand Exposition, modeled after the renowned World's Fairs and expositions held since the mid-19th century, features family-themed rides. Performances are given daily on various stages throughout the park, including music and comedy shows in the 4,000-seat Echo Hollow Amphitheater. Artisans demonstrate woodcarving, blacksmithing, leatherwork, pottery making, basket weaving and glassblowing; many of their beautiful creations are for sale. Artisans demonstrate woodcarving, blacksmithing, leatherwork, pottery making, basket weaving and glassblowing; many of their beautiful creations are for sale.

Silver Dollar City also has a well-deserved reputation for serving up some of the country's tastiest theme park food. The Culinary and Craft School offers courses on food preparation, including breads, cookies, pies and soups. Attendees can partake in hands-on demonstrations, taste samples and take home recipes compiled by the school's culinary artisans and guest chefs.

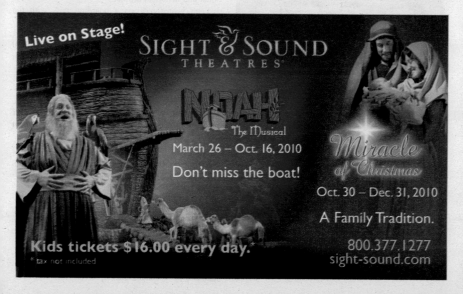

Allow a full day. **Hours:** Daily 9:30 a.m.-10 p.m., late July-early Aug.; daily 9:30-7, early June-late July (also Sat.-Sun. of Labor Day weekend); Wed.-Sun. 10-6 (also Sat. 9:30-10), mid-Sept. through Oct. 30; Thurs.-Fri. and Sun. 1-9 (also day before Thanksgiving and Dec. 23; Thanksgiving hours are 4-10), Sat. noon-9:30 (also Fri. after Thanksgiving), early Nov.-late Dec.; daily 1-9; Dec. 26-30. Days and operating hours vary Mar.-May and Aug.-Sept. Closed Dec. 24-25 and 31. Phone ahead to confirm schedule. **Cost:** (includes Marvel Cave) $53; $51 (ages 62+); $43 (ages 4-11). Culinary and Craft courses start at $12. Phone ahead to confirm rates. **Phone:** (800) 831-4386. *See color ad and on insert.*

Marvel Cave lies 500 ft. below Silver Dollar City. This wet limestone cave includes 3 miles of explored passageways and a cathedral room 400 feet long and 20 stories high. The 1-hour tour includes more than 600 stairs and is considered strenuous. A cable railway train returns visitors to the surface. Each night a 1.5-hour Lantern Light Tour (maximum 20 guests) is offered; tour guides dressed in attire representative of 1884 lead tours by lantern and share the history of the cave.

Hours: Daily 9:30 a.m.-10 p.m., late July-early Aug.; daily 9:30-7, early June-late July (also Sat.-Sun. of Labor Day weekend); Wed.-Sun. 10-6 (also Sat. 9:30-10), mid-Sept. through Oct. 30; Thurs.-Fri. and Sun. 1-9 (also day before Thanksgiving and Dec. 23; Thanksgiving hours are 4-10), Sat. noon-9:30 (also Fri. after Thanksgiving), early Nov.-late Dec.; daily 1-9, Dec. 26-30. Days and operating hours vary Mar.-May and Aug.-Sept. Cave tours depart approximately every 30 minutes. Lantern Light Tours begin 1.5 hours before closing. Closed Dec. 24-25 and 31. Phone ahead to confirm schedule.

Cost: included in Silver Dollar City admission of $53; $51 (ages 62+); $43 (ages 4-11). Lantern Light Tour $10: $5 (ages 8-11). Under age 8 are not permitted on lantern tours. Reservations are recommended for lantern tours. **Phone:** (800) 831-4386.

SPLASH COUNTRY is at Grand Country Square at 1945 SR 76W. This 40,000-square-foot indoor-outdoor water park features waterslides, a 250-foot-long lazy river, a pool with basketball hoops, and a three-level tree house with a 1,000-gallon bucket that dumps cascades of water every 8 minutes. **Hours:** Indoor park open daily 10-10. Outdoor park open daily 10-9. Outdoor park's hours may vary by season; phone ahead to verify schedule. **Cost:** $15; free (under 1). **Phone:** (417) 335-3535 or (888) 514-1088.

TALKING ROCKS CAVERN—
see Branson West p. 150.

TITANIC—WORLD'S LARGEST MUSEUM ATTRACTION is at jct. SRs 76W and 165 (Gretna Rd.). Built at half-scale to the original vessel as far back as the second smokestack, this walk-through experience focuses on the passengers and crew aboard the RMS *Titanic* when it sank after hitting an iceberg on April 14, 1912.

Highlights include a replica of the ship's Grand Staircase and a 26-foot-long scale model of the vessel's underwater bow section as seen in the 1997 blockbuster film. Among other exhibits are a regenerating "live" iceberg, re-creations of a first-class stateroom and third-class cabin, an interactive captain's bridge and gallery rooms with displays of personal and historical artifacts.

Each visitor receives a boarding pass with the name and history of a passenger who was on the ill-fated ocean liner's maiden voyage. **Time:** Allow 1 hour, 30 minutes minimum. **Hours:** Daily 9 a.m.-10 p.m., July. 1-Aug. 15; 9-9, May 17-June 30; 9-8, Sept. 3-Dec. 11. and Dec. 27-30; 9-7, Mar. 1- May 16 and Aug. 16-Sept. 2; 9-6, Dec.12- 23; 9-5, rest of year. Hours vary Dec. 24, 26 and 31. Closed Jan. 11-14 and Dec. 25. **Cost:** $19.71; $9.99 (ages 5-12). **Phone:** (417) 334-9500, or (866) 488-5079 for ticket information. *See color ad on p. 139 and on insert.*

VETERANS MEMORIAL MUSEUM is 1 mi. w. of US 65 at 1250 SR 76W. The veterans of American wars and military conflicts are honored at this museum, which has collections of uniforms and art as well as artifact exhibits. The focal point is a 70-foot-long bronze sculpture depicting 50 soldiers storming a beach. Each life-size figure represents a U.S. state and is modeled after an actual combat veteran. The names of more than 400,000 Americans killed in World War II are listed on the museum walls. Similar rolls are dedicated to casualties in Korea, Vietnam and the Persian Gulf.

Time: Allow 1 hour minimum. **Hours:** Daily 9-7, Memorial Day Weekend - Labor Day; 9-5, rest of year. Closed Dec 25. Phone ahead to confirm schedule. **Cost:** $13.50; $12.50 (veterans); $10 (ages 13-17); $5 (ages 5-12). **Phone:** (417) 336-2300.

WHITE WATER is 3.7 mi. w. on SR 76W. The water park's rides and attractions include the 500,000-gallon Surfquake wave pool; waterslides, including Ohana Falls, Bermuda Triangle and Pipeline Plunge; a Lazy River for inner tubing; the Splash Island children's play area; and RainTree Island. White Water's biggest ride is Kalani Towers, a seven-story contraption with six different slides.

Hours: Daily 10-10, July 2-10; daily 10-6 (sometimes closing time is extended until 7), May 29-July 1 and July 11-Aug. 15; Sat.-Sun. 10-6 (sometimes closing time is extended until 7), Aug. 21-Sept. 6. Phone ahead to confirm schedule. **Cost:** $36; $30 (ages 4-11); $19 (ages 62+). Phone ahead to confirm rates. **Phone:** (800) 831-4386.

RECREATIONAL ACTIVITIES

Kayaking

- **Kayak Branson**, 5403 SR 165, provides canoe and kayak rentals for Lake Taneycomo and Table Rock Lake. **Hours:** Mon.-Sat. 8-6, Sun. 10-6, mid-Mar. through Sept. 30; Mon.-Sat. 9-5, rest of year. **Phone:** (417) 336-2811.

WINERIES

- **Stone Hill Winery** is 2 blks. s. of SR 76W on SR 165. **Hours:** Tours and tastings Mon.-Sat. 8:30 a.m.-dusk, Sun. 10-6. Closed Jan. 1, Thanksgiving and Dec. 25. **Phone:** (417) 334-1897.

What To Do

Sightseeing

Boat Tours

Branson Landing Cruises depart from the Gage Marina on the Lake Taneycomo waterfront at Branson Landing. Ninety-minute sightseeing cruises (some with meals served) as well as dinner and cocktail cruises are offered on two 100-foot-long ships: the Landing Princess, which offers three open-air decks, and the Lake Queen, which has a climate-controlled lower deck and an outdoor upper deck. Reservations are required. Phone for schedules; (877) 382-6287, or (800) 979-3370 for tickets.

SHOWBOAT *BRANSON BELLE* departs from White River Landing on SR 165, 6 mi. s. of jct. SR 76W and .5 mi. s. of Table Rock Dam. This turn-of-the-20th-century-style paddle wheeler is 278 feet long and holds 700 passengers. A scenic cruise on Table Rock Lake, which lasts approximately 2.25 hours, includes lunch or dinner and a show starring a troupe of talented entertainers.

Hours: Cruises depart at noon and 4 most days (also most weekdays and Sat. at 8 p.m.), late Mar.-Dec. 31. Boarding begins 1 hour before departure. Phone ahead to confirm schedule. **Cost:** Noon lunch cruise $47; $24 (ages 4-11). Four and 8 p.m. early dinner and evening dinner cruises $55 (Sun.-Thurs.); $59 (Fri.-Sat.); $28 (ages 4-11, Sun.-Thurs.); $30 (ages 4-11, Fri.-Sat.). Fares may vary; phone ahead to confirm. Reservations are recommended. **Phone:** (417) 336-7171 or (800) 227-8587.

Bus Tours

SAVE Gray Line Branson/Springfield offers sightseeing tours of the Tri-Lakes area as well as nearby Eureka Springs, Ark.; phone (800) 542-6768.

RIDE THE DUCKS departs from 2320 SR 76W, just w. of Green Mountain Dr. (across from the Clay Cooper Theatre), as well as from the neighborhood district next to Arvest Bank in Branson Landing. The 70-minute Table Rock Lake tour aboard a restored World War II amphibious vehicle known as a duck cruises down the Strip to SR 165, heads south to Table Rock Dam and climbs off-road to the top of 1,325-foot Baird Mountain for a panoramic view of Table Rock Lake before entering the water where the Showboat *Branson Belle* is docked. The 70-minute Branson Landing tour includes historic downtown and the College of the Ozarks and then splashes into Lake Taneycomo along the Branson Landing.

Each ducks driver gives his or her own individual narration during the trip, making this a highly entertaining as well as informative Branson overview. It can get quite windy as the open-sided vehicle travels along the road; hold onto your hat.

Hours: Table Rock Lake cruises depart daily every 30 minutes 9-6, early May to mid-Aug. (also Labor Day weekend); on the hour 9-5, mid-Aug. through Oct. 31; on the hour 10-5, early Apr.-early May; on the hour 10-4, early Mar. to early Apr.; at 10, noon and 2 (also Holiday Lights at 5:30 and 6:30), Nov. 1 to mid-Dec. Branson Landing cruises depart daily every 30 minutes 10-6, Memorial Day weekend to mid-Aug. (also Labor Day weekend); on the hour 11-5, early Apr.-day before Memorial Day weekend and mid-Aug. through Oct. 31; every 1.5 hours 11-3:30, early Mar.-early Apr.; at noon, 2 and 4, Nov. 1-late Nov. Closed Easter and Thanksgiving. **Cost:** $20; $19 (ages 62+); $12 (ages 4-11); boarding passes required for ages 0-3. **Phone:** (417) 266-7600 or (877) 887-8225.

Rail Tours

BRANSON SCENIC RAILWAY departs from the depot at 206 E. Main St. Passengers enjoy a narration of the history of the area and the railroad as the 1940s and '50s rolling stock embarks on a 40-mile round trip of the scenic Ozark foothills, crossing bridges and passing through two tunnels.

Time: Allow 2 hours minimum. **Hours:** Departures Mon.-Fri. at 9, 11:30, 2 and 4:30, Sat. at 9, 11:30, 2 and 5, June-Aug. and in Oct.; Mon.-Fri. at 9, 11:30 and 2, Sat. at 9, 11:30, 2 and 5, Apr.-May, in Sept. and Nov. 1 to early Dec.; Mon.-Sat. at 9, 11:30 and 2, in Mar. Dinner train departs Sat. at 5, Apr. 1 to early Dec. Phone ahead to confirm schedule. **Cost:** $24.50; $14 (ages 3-12). **Phone:** (417) 334-6110 or (800) 287-2462.

Sports and Recreation

You could quite easily spend a week in Branson doing nothing but seeing shows, visiting attractions and going shopping. You would, however, be missing out on one of the area's most delightful assets: the great outdoors. The recreational opportunities that attracted Branson's first vacationers still abound.

Branson's location in the midst of Table Rock Lake, Bull Shoals Lake and Lake Taneycomo makes what is known as the Tri-Lakes area a terrific place for **boating, fishing** and **camping.** All kinds of activities can be enjoyed at Table Rock Lake and Dam, which was created by the U.S. Army Corps of Engineers to control floods and generate hydroelectric power. The deep-blue lake teems with bass, bluegill, crappie and catfish, making it rewarding for both novice and serious anglers. With nearly 800 miles of shoreline to explore, Table Rock *(see Recreation Chart)* also is a good location for **swimming** and **scuba diving.**

Table Rock State Park, 5272 SR 165 at the south end of Table Rock Dam, has a public marina offering easy lake access and a full range of boat rentals, including WaveRunners and fishing, pontoon and jet ski boats. Two camping areas shaded by oak and hickory trees are located along the winding shoreline, and picnic sites are scattered throughout the park. For more information phone (417) 334-4704. *See Recreation Chart.*

The Dewey Short Visitor Center has natural history exhibits and shows a fascinating 20-minute film that details the construction of Table Rock Dam. Be sure to walk the Table Rock Lakeshore Trail, which begins at the visitor center and runs south 2.2 miles to the park marina. The scenic views of the lake are heightened in the spring by flowering dogwood and redbud trees and in the fall by a display of colorful foliage. The trail is open daily dawn-dusk. The visitor center is open daily 9-5, Apr.-Oct.; phone (417) 334-4101.

Indian Point, at the south end of Indian Point Road near the entrance to Silver Dollar City, has campgrounds, a marina and a variety of lakeside resorts. The port of Kimberling City, on SR 13 south of Branson West, proclaims itself "The Bass Fishing Capital of the Ozarks." A center for boat rentals, fishing and camping, it has several waterside restaurants—including local favorite The Bearded Clam—that offer courtesy docking.

Due to their proximity to Branson, Indian Point and the area around Table Rock Dam have the region's greatest concentration of recreation facilities. But the lake spreads out far beyond the dam in a meandering series of arms and inlets, and some nature lovers prefer its western end, which has equally good fishing along with a more remote, primitive atmosphere. Cape Fair Park, in a lovely wooded setting on Table Rock's James River Arm, is a favorite with both campers and fishermen. There are prime angling spots below Virgin Bluff and across the channel from the park's boat launch ramp. For information phone (417) 538-2220.

Also administered by the U.S. Army Corps of Engineers is Bull Shoals Lake. Although it extends into southern Missouri, most of its area is in northern Arkansas. Less developed than Table Rock Lake, Bull Shoals offers many of the same activities. The 1,050-mile shoreline is indented with coves ideal for boating, fishing, swimming and water sports. This is a deep, clean lake and the water is very clear—which makes it just about unbeatable for landing crappie, bluegill, walleye and largemouth, smallmouth, white and striped bass. *See Recreation Chart.*

Hikers can trek Bull Shoals' 4-mile Wildwood Trail. The trailhead and parking area is on CR 635, which branches south off US 160 just east of Theodosia. The trail follows the lakeshore south of the Theodosia Marina. Deer outnumber people in these parts, so you're likely to spot a few.

In between these two lakes stretches 22-mile-long Lake Taneycomo. Created by the impounding of the White River, Taneycomo was a warm-water lake from 1913 until the completion of Table Rock Dam in 1958. Virtually overnight it was turned into a cold-water fishery due to the temperature of the water flowing through the dam's power generators. The Missouri Department of Conservation took advantage of this change, constructing the Shepherd of the Hills Hatchery *(see attraction listing p. 136)* at the foot of the dam.

When Table Rock Dam is generating power the water temperature drops, and for all practical purposes Taneycomo becomes a deep, cold, fast-running river. The bracing water makes it one of the best brown and rainbow trout-fishing spots in the Midwest. The lake's headwaters at the foot of Table Rock Dam offer excellent wading and fly rod fishing when power is not being generated. Only flies and hard artificial baits are permitted in this "trophy trout" area, which covers approximately 3 miles from the dam north to the mouth of Fall Creek.

Although officially a lake, serpentine Taneycomo, with its lush green banks, certainly looks more like a river. The Branson Landing Boardwalk offers a pleasant waterside stroll, and you also can walk along the shoreline via N. Lake Drive to North Beach Park, where there is a large covered pavilion and a gazebo.

Dogwood Canyon Nature Park *(see attraction listing p. 150)* has a 6-mile, round-trip paved path that is popular for **hiking** and **bicycling.** The gently sloping trail traverses wooded terrain along the canyon floor, passing waterfalls, burbling streams and stone bridges created by local stonemasons from native dolomite rock. Points of interest along the way include the Glory Hole, a 16-foot-deep, blue-green pool of water inhabited by rainbow and brown trout, and a huge sycamore tree estimated to be more than 250 years old.

Although fishing and boating still rule in the Tri-Lakes area, Branson also is gaining a reputation for **golf.** The backdrop of Ozark Mountains scenery is certainly a big part of what makes golf so appealing in Branson, in addition to the mild weather that allows practically year-round play.

Area courses include the Branson Creek Golf Club, off US 65 about 4 miles south of SR 76; the Holiday Hills Golf Club, about 3 miles east of downtown Branson via SR 76E; the LedgeStone Golf Course, just north of the junction of SR 76W and SR 265; the Pointe Royale Golf Course, on SR 165 3 miles south of SR 76W; the Thousand Hills Golf Course, on Wildwood Drive just south of SR 76W; the Murder Rock Golf and Country Club, about 4 miles south of downtown Branson via US 65 to Branson Creek Boulevard, then east to Golf Club Drive; the nine-hole, par-3 Top of the Rock Golf Course, off US 65 just north of the junction with SR 86; and the Payne Stewart Golf Course, just north of Branson Hills Parkway between SR 248 and US 65. *See color ad on p. 421 and on insert.*

Geocaching is becoming more and more popular as a family or group activity. Simply put, this is a scavenger hunt using high-tech equipment—a satellite tracking device that utilizes sophisticated global positioning technology (GPS) to determine an individual's location anywhere on Earth within a distance of approximately 6 to 20 feet. More than a dozen caches, or treasure locations, are scattered throughout the Branson/Tri-Lakes area. For additional information contact the Branson/Lakes Area Chamber of Commerce and CVB; phone (417) 334-4084 or (800) 214-3661.

If you feel like catching a **baseball** game, head up to Springfield and cheer on the Springfield Cardinals AA minor league team *(see p. 227)*. And if you need some exercise, the Branson RecPlex, half a mile east of SR 248 on Branson Hills Parkway, has a fitness center, track and basketball courts. Guest memberships are available; phone (417) 335-2368.

Shopping

Loads of people come to Branson to shop, and it's easy to see why: with a historic downtown that could almost double for Mayberry, a new waterfront shopping and dining complex at downtown's doorstep and specialty stores and centers practically everywhere you turn, the opportunities are legion.

The big news in 2006 was the opening of Branson Landing. This shopping "village," which has lovely Lake Taneycomo as a backdrop, is divided into six different districts, each with its own style of architecture. Anchors Belk Department Store and Bass Pro Shops are augmented by more than 100 additional stores and shops, including national retailers like Brookstone, Chico's, Coldwater Creek and White House/Black Market that are new to the Branson area. Eateries include both fast-food outlets and popular franchises like Famous Dave's Bar-B-Q and Joe's Crab Shack.

Branson's first Bass Pro Shops outlet isn't as large as the flagship store in Springfield but the atmosphere is similar, right down to the beautifully done nature dioramas and freshwater trout aquarium. Be sure to look up as you wander around; some of the most interesting things are above eye level. There's also a floating restaurant and a marina where boats and fishing equipment can be tested.

The town square at the center of the Landing is an open space with terraces that slope down to a waterfront boardwalk. Free concerts take place throughout the year. The square also is the site of hourly shows incorporating 186 water jet fountains and 15 cannons blasting fireballs, choreographed to special lighting and a variety of music. The dancing water display is most impressive in the evening, especially when seen from the vantage point of the boardwalk. And since Branson is famous for live performances, the Landing also features street entertainment in the form of jugglers, cloggers, clowns, magicians, musicians, singers from country and bluegrass to jazz and gospel—and even a highland piper in full Scottish regalia.

Branson Landing is a stone's throw from downtown Branson, which offers a much more down-home experience. The vintage flavor of these brick sidewalk-lined streets, adorned with Victorian-style lampposts, is maintained by the Downtown Branson Main Street Association. As a mercantile district the downtown area dates back more than a century, and strolling the streets here does seem like a step back in time.

Browsers will love Dick's Old Time 5 & 10, at 103 W. Main St. The narrow aisles of this classic "dime store" are crammed with more than 55,000 nostalgic items. You'll see more miniature figurines and key chains than you ever thought possible, but Dick's also carries practical items like kitchen dish towels and jars of homemade jam. Bee Discount, 106 W. Main St., also stocks "a little bit of everything," including gifts and souvenirs.

Branson Bill's Emporium, 110 W. Main St., has NASCAR and Coca-Cola collectibles in addition to gift items. Brier Rose, 117 E. Main St., features antiques, quilts and crocheted accessories, while the House of 1,000 Clocks, 105 S. Veterans Blvd., carries custom-made Bavarian clocks in all shapes and sizes.

Reish Shoes, 120 S. Commercial St., is downtown Branson's oldest business. Owner Joe Reish provides custom fitting, just like the good old days. For elegant girls' and women's clothing as well as home accessories and Victorian-style furnishings, wander through Rebecca's Victorian Boutique, 110 S. Commercial St., or Patricia's Victorian House, 101 W. Main St.

All sorts of specialty shopping complexes are along SR 76. If you love Christmas, by all means visit The Grand Village, 1940 SR 76, which offers a collection of clothing, craft and specialty stores and also includes no less than six Kringle's Christmas Shops, where you can search for angels, ornaments, stockings, nutcrackers, candleholders, fiber-optic Christmas trees and a host of other seasonal decorations. There also are shops specializing in art, wood crafts and handmade lace, all in an open-air setting of winding cobblestone lanes, fountains and flowers.

The Victorian Village, on Shepherd of the Hills Expressway next to the Hamner-Barber Theater, offers a variety of collectibles, including candles, gifts, jewelry, quilts and dolls, along with circus memorabilia and reproductions of paintings by inspirational artist Thomas Kinkade. About a mile west are the shops in Branson's IMAX Entertainment Complex *(see attraction listing p. 131)*, where you can grab a bite to eat at the food court while shopping for toys, jewelry, collectibles and souvenirs.

The Branson Mill Craft Village on Gretna Road is a combination specialty retail shopping center and working craft village where glass blowers, silversmiths, wood carvers, scrimshaw crafters, stained- and etched-glass makers and other artisans demonstrate their skills. You'll find everything from wind chimes, pottery, gift baskets and custom picture frames to pewter items, carved walking sticks and hand-painted gourds.

Fans of outlet shopping have three different centers to explore. The 90 stores at Factory Merchants Branson, off SR 76 on Pat Nash Drive (look for the red roofs), include Nautica, Pfaltzgraff and Reebok. The mall has two tree-shaded courtyards and an open-air food area.

The SAVE Tanger Factory Outlet Center, off SR 76 in the middle of the Strip, offers discounted bargains on men's, women's and children's clothing from retailers like Liz Claiborne, Ralph Lauren and Polo, plus shoes, housewares and fashion accessories. The Shoppes at Branson Meadows, 4562 Gretna Rd. near the Branson Mill Craft Village, has a Victorian-style look and discount retailers like Casual Male, Dress Barn, Van Heusen and Wrangler. There are other stores here as well (the House of Lloyd has gifts you won't see elsewhere in town) and a movie multiplex to keep restless kids happy.

If you don't like crowds, shop the outlet malls in January and February. The weekend following Thanksgiving, when holiday specials go on sale, is the year's busiest.

Last but certainly not least are the ubiquitous gift shops at the music theaters. Every theater has one, and some are ostentatious indeed. The Shoji Tabuchi Theatre has several separate shops in an ornate lobby filled with potted palms and Art Deco furniture, while the gift shop at the Andy Williams Moon River Theatre is notable because it is so discreet (more like a boutique).

Show DVDs and tapes, performer CDs and cassettes, and cast posters are uniformly big sellers, but you also can purchase many other keepsakes, from a Jim Stafford "cow patti" to a Baldknobbers ball cap. The most personal, of course, is an autograph, so if you happen to own an old Paul Revere & the Raiders, Righteous Brothers or Mickey Gilley album, bring it along for a personal signature—Branson's stars are very obliging of their fans.

Entertainment

For many visitors, the No. 1 reason to visit Branson is to sample the incredible variety of live entertainment. The city has long outgrown its tag "the country music capital of the universe" that was bestowed by "60 Minutes" back in the early 1990s: Today you can choose from approximately 120 different shows at more than 50 venues. And while country is still king, it is by no means the only game in town.

There's still plenty of traditional country music, of course, in shows like "Circle B Supper Show," "The Jim Owen Show" and "Keepin' It Country," as well as shows starring generation-spanning families ("Baldknobbers Jamboree Show", Presleys' Country Jubilee, the Duttons). Then there are the old reliables—familiar names like Andy Williams, Jim Stafford, Mickey Gilley and Yakov Smirnoff.

But you also can choose from shows devoted to the 1950s ("'50s at the Hop"), baby boomer favorites (Bill Medley, Paul Revere & the Raiders), tributes galore ("Legends in Concert," "The Elvis Experience starring Tony Roi"), prestidigitators (Kirby Van Burch) and flashy glitz ("Magnificent Variety," Broadway! The Star-Spangled Celebration"). The New Shanghai Circus, a world-class acrobatic extravaganza, and Sight & Sound Theatre's *(see attraction listing p. 137)* "Noah—the Musical" and "Miracle of Christmas," bring some welcome diversity to town. Sight & Sound Theatre's shows, which depict religious themes, change every few years. In short, the array of talent on any given night is truly impressive.

Performances take place year-round, with the majority occurring March through December. Top-name artists like Andy Williams, Tony Orlando, Jim Stafford, The Lennon Sisters, Mickey Gilley, The Gatlin Brothers and Pam Tillis who headline their own shows appear in Branson at least part of the year. Show schedules are subject to change; new theaters open, old theaters close and existing theaters occasionally change names. Fortunately, in Branson you're never more than a few steps away from a rack of brochures or a free newspaper, many of which publish current schedules. If you want to see a certain show at a particular time, your best bet is to call ahead.

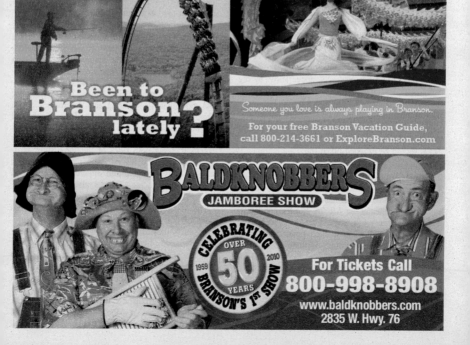

Most evening shows start at 8 p.m.; matinees usually begin at 3 p.m. There also are several popular morning shows usually beginning at 10 a.m., including the Brett Family Singers; the "Red Skelton Tribute" at Mansion America; "Smoke on the Mountain" and "A Tribute to John Denver" at the Little Opry Theatre; and the Platters. A new favorite is the Liverpool Legends, a re-creation of the Beatles. Louise Harrison, sister of "Fab Four" guitarist George Harrison, selected the group's members herself and also produces their show.

Adult ticket prices range from about $20-$50; children's ticket prices range from free to about $31. Tickets can be purchased at the theater box office or through various ticket agencies in the area. Free show guide brochures and coupon sheets, available for the taking at most area hotels, restaurants, theaters and attractions, offer a bewildering assortment of special offers; diligently collecting and sorting through these deals can end up saving you quite a bit of money. AAA members also can purchase discounted theater tickets at any AAA Missouri branch office.

Branson is a conservative town, and conservative values are emphasized. Flag-waving patriotism and pro-military sentiments are often expressed in production numbers, and evangelical Christian themes are presented at some shows. Most shows also include a merchandising spiel during intermission, encouraging customers to buy CDs, DVDs, autographed posters and sundry other memorabilia. Many of the performers generously share their time with the audience, coming out during intermission to meet fans and signing autographs in the lobby after the show.

It would literally take weeks to see every single performance in town, and few visitors have that luxury of time. The following rundown of major Branson theaters—in no particular order but collectively offering proven longevity and popularity, long-running and hot new acts, appearances by big-name stars and sheer variety—can help you make the difficult choice of who and what to see during your stay.

Note: In some theater parking lots the rear slopes sharply; visitors with limited mobility or special needs should be dropped off at the main entrance.

Recording artist and TV personality Andy Williams presides at the **Andy Williams Moon River Theatre.** Williams was the first major non-country entertainer to take up permanent residence in Branson, and his theater on SR 76 exudes good taste, with warm woodwork, sophisticated art, very comfortable seats and a koi-stocked pond (the "moon river") next to the building. Williams usually appears several months out of the year, singing his hits and performing in a variety show reminiscent of his old television shows as well as performing his much loved Christmas shows in November and December. Bill Medley of the Righteous Brothers and Paul Revere & the Raiders also perform here and offer a feast of classic '60s nuggets, from "You've Lost That Lovin' Feeling" and "Unchained Melody" to "Kicks" and "Hungry."

Mickey Gilley and his band provide slick, mainstream entertainment at the **Mickey Gilley Theatre,** on SR 76 next to the White Water theme park. Gilley, of course, gained fame after his Texas watering hole with that bucking mechanical bull, Gilley's Bar, was the setting for scenes in the 1980 film "Urban Cowboy" starring John Travolta and Debra Winger. A segment of his show reprises the movie and Gilley's cover version of Ben E. King's "Stand By Me." Jerry Lee Lewis' cousin sings other hits like "Room Full of Roses" and does some funny, seemingly ad-libbed comedy bits. The **Caravelle Theatre** across the street presents "#1 Hits of the 60s."

Another crowd-pleaser is Jim Stafford, a Branson mainstay for more than 20 years. At the **Jim Stafford Theatre** (next to the Caravelle) the man who doesn't like "Spiders and Snakes" sings, plays classical guitar and creates heartwarming comedy from everyday life. Stafford's musically accomplished son and daughter are part of the act, making this a great show for families. The theater also presents Moe Bandy performing his hits "Bandy The Rodeo Clown," "I'm Sorry For You, My Friend," "Yesterday Once More" and many more of his country classics.

More giggles await at the **Yakov Smirnoff Theatre,** where the Russian-born comic offers his philosophical insights on men and women, family and life in the United States. Juggler Slim Chance provides daring thrills and more comedy, and a troupe of Russian dancers twist, twirl and leap all over the stage. Smirnoff delivers humor from the heart, and his popular show is another family favorite. The theater is just off US 65 on SR 248.

Celebrity impersonations are always fun to see, and the stars are out in force at **Dick Clark's American Bandstand Theater,** on SR 76 across from Dolly Parton's Dixie Stampede. "Legends in Concert," live tribute shows and concerts with celebrity impersonators, began as a 2-week engagement in Las Vegas but has grown into a franchise with more than 100 rotating acts. In Branson you'll naturally see country stars like Toby Keith and Shania Twain, along with everyone from the Temptations to Tina Turner and of course, Elvis. Video screens flanking both sides of the stage show footage of the real-life legend, which can invite comparisons both favorable and unfavorable. The good news: no lip syncing. There's also a crack house band.

The **Welk Resort Theatre** on SR 165 (3 miles south of the SR 76/Gretna Road intersection presents such musical stars as The Lennon Sisters, Tony Orlando, Lee Greenwood and the Bellamy Brothers. Other artists perform concerts here as well—everyone from B.B. King to Lynyrd Skynyrd.

One of the flashiest shows in town is at the **Shoji Tabuchi Theatre** on Shepherd of the Hills Expressway (near the Branson's IMAX theater complex). Tabuchi—who has a Moe Stooge pudding bowl haircut—his wife, daughter, a troupe of dancers and a band of superbly talented professional musicians put on a show that encompasses practically every style of popular music, from swing and big band to gospel, Dixieland jazz and Broadway show tunes.

Tabuchi plays everything from "Flight of the Bumblebee" to "Over the Rainbow" on his fiddle, and the production numbers feature top-notch choreography and cool laser special effects. If nothing else, you must see this show just to experience the ladies' powder room or gentlemen's lounge; the rich wood paneling, potted palms, chandeliers, beveled glass wall tiles, onyx sinks, fresh orchids and hand-carved mahogany billiard table are all the last word in lavish.

The **New Shanghai Theatre** (on SR 165 about half a mile south of the SR 76/Gretna Road intersection) is an equally eye-popping show, but in a completely different way. Here the rather utilitarian theater is merely a backdrop for a fast-paced, colorful and thrilling procession of athletic feats.

The Acrobats of China—all from Shanghai and ranging in age from 13 to 24—display jaw-dropping strength, outrageous flexibility and amazing balance as they juggle, leap, contort and cavort across the stage. And whether balancing on precariously stacked chairs, artfully piling onto a constantly moving bicycle one by one (that's nine bodies, one bike) or performing a breathtaking aerial ballet, these gifted young people make it all look like a walk in the park. This is the kind of show where poised young women balance a dizzying number of spinning plates atop sticks simultaneously—and that's the easy part.

The Mabe family is still going strong after more than 50 years. "Branson's first show," the "Baldknobbers Jamboree Show," entertains audiences at the **Baldknobbers Country Music Theatre** *(See color ad p. 143 and on insert)* on SR 76 in the middle of the Strip. Patty, Garrett, Denton and Brandon Mabe are the latest members carrying forward the family show-business tradition, which began in 1959. The Baldknobbers show has a little bit of everything—crowd-pleasing comedy routines (courtesy of Stub Meadows, Hargus Marcel and Droopy Drawers Jr.), classic country (including a blazing "Orange Blossom Special"), hot new country hits, roof-raising gospel music and a rousing patriotic finale.

The Presley family stars in another longtime Branson favorite at the **Presleys' Country Jubilee** theater, on SR 76 across from New Americana Theatre. Four generations of this talented family appear on stage. It's a fast-paced show, with one musical number after another. There's impassioned Southern gospel singing, classic country tunes and even a bit of "new country" (i.e., current hits). Herkimer and Cecil provide the comic relief, which is downright silly. You'll laugh anyway.

Another roadhouse with a varied entertainment menu is the **Branson Variety Theater,** on SR 76 across from the Andy Williams Moon River Theatre. New York razzle-dazzle is provided by "Broadway! The Star-Spangled Celebration," with highlights from various Broadway hits performed by an energetic cast. This also is the Branson home of the international music and dance revue "Spirit of the Dance." The Twelve Irish Tenors offer perfect harmonies and Irish charm.

The Osmonds—Jay, Jimmy and Wayne—are back in Branson hosting their annual Christmas show after returning from their world tour celebrating the family's 50 years in show business.

The singing, dancing, fiddling Haygoods, seven spirited brothers and one vivacious sister who previously packed 'em in at Silver Dollar City, moved into the **New Americana Theatre,** across from Presleys' Country Jubilee at 2905 SR 76, in early 2009. The venue also hosts "Red, Hot & Blue," a costumed production show offering melodies ranging from the Big Band and jazz of the 1940s to the disco of the 1970s. The venue also hosts Tony Roi, whose Elvis tribute some say is the best in town and features the style, swagger and voice made famous by "The King." The talented Cassandré performs in "Cassandré: The Voice of an Angel."

Music City Centre, a short distance down SR 76 from Dolly Parton's Dixie Stampede, hosts a variety of national acts and performers that appear in Branson.

That's more than enough to satisfy most show fans, but Branson boasts a number of other venues. The historic **Owen Theatre** in downtown Branson has been renovated for "A Tribute To Elvis," a new show starring Joseph Hall. Hall placed in the top 10 in the 2007 "Ultimate Elvis" contest in Memphis, Tenn., and in 2008 he was in the top 10 on the NBC show "America's Got Talent."

The five talented Hughes brothers take the stage at the **Hughes American Family Theatre** on SR 76 (across from the Jim Stafford Theatre). They present both morning (featuring wives and kids) and evening (just the brothers) shows. The brothers' bond shines both vocally and during moments of good-natured banter, which recalls the brothers Smothers. The theater also features performances by SIX, the six eldest brothers from a family with ten sons. When they were young their father recognized their talent for making up songs and harmonies without instruction. They began performing a cappella and eventually landed a full-time gig.

Illusionist Kirby Van Burch, performs "How did he do that?" feats at the **Kirby Van Burch Theatre,** on SR 248 just north of Shepherd of the Hills Expressway. The props employed by the "Prince of Magic" include a real helicopter that seemingly appears out of thin air. And another family, the Duttons, display their multiple talents at the **Dutton Family Theater** on SR 76 (next to the Caravelle). With a repertoire that manages to include both Pachelbel's "Canon in D major" and the revved-up surf instrumental "Wipeout," the Duttons obviously have music in their genes.

The Oak Ridge Boys appear throughout the year at **The Oak Ridge Boys Theatre,** and entertainers like Collin Raye, Restless Heart and Debby Boone are featured seasonally. Longtime Branson entertainer Clay Cooper headlines his own show at the **Clay Cooper Theatre,** on SR 76 across from Titanic—World's Largest Museum Attraction. The **Starlite Theatre,** on SR 76 across from the Hollywood Wax Museum, presents additional live entertainment.

The **Hamner-Barber Theater** on Shepherd of the Hills Expressway (across from the **Pierce Arrow Theater**) offers two different shows: the "Hamner-Barber Variety Show," co-starring comedian and ventriloquist Jim Barber and the Hamner family's exotic illusions (which incorporate a bevy of colorful macaws and cockatoos), and champion fiddler Ricky Boen and his band, Texas Mud. *See color ad p. 139 and on insert.*

The **Sight & Sound Theatre,** 1001 Shepherd of the Hills Expwy., opened in 2008 and presents elaborate live theatrical and musical performances based on Bible stories. "Noah—The Musical" features more than 50 live and 50 animatronic animals as well as a four-story reproduction of Noah's Ark. "The Miracle of Christmas" also is presented. The theater's shows change every few years.

As if all this weren't enough to keep visitors busy, many theaters also present their own special Christmas shows during November and December, and many people come to Branson during these two months to celebrate an old-fashioned holiday season. Contact the individual theaters for details.

For a list of current theaters, see Branson Theaters on p. 147.

Special Events

For many years Branson was traditionally a summer destination, and tourist activities pretty much shut down during the winter. But these days the "season" is all year. Branson's down time (January through February) is known as Hot Winter Fun. These months mean fewer crowds and less traffic, but there's still plenty to do.

Theaters that stay open during all or part of Hot Winter Fun include the Baldknobbers Country Music Theatre, Dick Clark's American Bandstand Theater, the Hughes American Family Theatre, the Jim-Stafford Theatre and The Mansion Theatre. The Hot Winter Fun Big Show at the Jim Stafford Theatre in early February brings a slew of Branson performers together on one stage.

Ozark Mountain Spring runs from March through May and features more than 40 special events and festivals, including collector car auctions and sporting events. Kewpiesta in April is one of the planned events; it honors Ozarks artist Rose O'Neill, creator of the kewpie doll.

One of the most happening places in town is Silver Dollar City, where a bunch of fun festivals are celebrated spring through fall. World-Fest starts things off, taking place the entire month of April

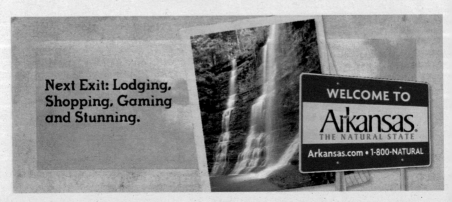

Branson Theaters

- **ANDY WILLIAMS MOON RIVER THEATRE**
  (417) 334-4500 or (800) 666-6094
- **BALDKNOBBERS COUNTRY MUSIC THEATRE**
  (417) 334-4528 or (800) 998-8908
- **BRANSON HOT HITS THEATRE**
  (417) 337-7426
- **BRANSON STAR THEATRE**
  (417) 334-7131 or (877) 733-6827
- **BRANSON VARIETY THEATER**
  (417) 334-2500 or (888) 462-7267
- **CARAVELLE THEATRE**
  (417) 334-5100
- **CIRCLE B SUPPER SHOW**
  (417) 336-3540
- **CLAY COOPER THEATRE**
  (417) 332-2529 or (888) 222-8910
- **DICK CLARK'S AMERICAN BANDSTAND THEATER**
  (417) 332-1960 or (877) 588-1957
- **DOLLY PARTON'S DIXIE STAMPEDE**
  (417) 336-3000 or (800) 520-5544
- **DUTTON FAMILY THEATER**
  (417) 332-2772 or (888) 388-8661
- **GOD AND COUNTRY THEATRE**
  (417) 334-6806
- **GOLDEN CORRAL SHOWROOM**
  (417) 336-6297
- **GRAND COUNTRY MUSIC HALL**
  (417) 335-2484
- **HAMNER-BARBER THEATER**
  (417) 334-4363 or (888) 335-2080
- **HAPPY TRAILS THEATER**
  (417) 339-1925 or (866) 769-7643
- **HUGHES AMERICAN FAMILY THEATRE**
  (417) 334-0076 or (800) 635-3688
- **JIM STAFFORD THEATRE**
  (417) 335-8080
- **KIRBY VAN BURCH THEATRE**
  (417) 337-7140
- **LITTLE OPRY THEATRE**
  (417) 335-4832
- **THE MANSION THEATRE**
  (417) 239-1333 or (866) 707-4100
- **MICKEY GILLEY THEATRE**
  (417) 334-3210 or (800) 334-1936
- **MUSIC CITY CENTRE**
  (417) 336-1600 or (877) 225-3165
- **NEW AMERICANA THEATRE**
  (417) 339-4663 or (866) 343-7469
- **NEW SHANGHAI THEATRE**
  (417) 336-8888 or (877) 212-4462
- **THE OAK RIDGE BOYS THEATRE**
  (417) 239-1333 or (866) 707-4100
- **OWEN THEATRE**
  (417) 336-2112 or (800) 358-4795
- **PIERCE ARROW THEATER**
  (417) 336-8742 or (877) 687-4241
- **PRESLEYS' COUNTRY JUBILEE**
  (417) 334-4874 or (800) 335-4874
- **RFD-TV, THE THEATRE**
  (417) 332-2282
- **THE SHEPHERD OF THE HILLS OUTDOOR THEATRE**
  (417) 334-4191 or (800) 653-6288
- **SHOJI TABUCHI THEATRE**
  (417) 334-7469
- **SHOWBOAT *BRANSON BELLE***
  (417) 336-7171 or (800) 227-8587
- **SIGHT & SOUND THEATRE**
  (417) 335-7900 or (800) 377-1277
- **SILVER DOLLAR CITY**
  (417) 336-7100 or (800) 952-6626
- **STARLITE THEATRE**
  (417) 337-9333
- **TRI-LAKES CENTER**
  (417) 336-0219
- **WELK RESORT THEATRE**
  (417) 337-7469 or (800) 505-9355
- **WHITE HOUSE THEATRE**
  (417) 335-2396 or (877) 487-2386
- **YAKOV SMIRNOFF THEATRE**
  (417) 339-2568 or (800) 942-8226

into early May. Also part of Ozark Mountain Spring, it features performers from around the globe—including Chinese acrobats, Polynesian fire dancers, Costa Rican drummers and Scottish highland dancers—showcasing their athletic skills and musical artistry at this very popular event.

Next up is the Bluegrass & BBQ, which runs from mid-May to early June. Hundreds of bluegrass performances feature both up-and-coming artists and big-name headliners. The singing and fiddling is complemented by a lip-smackin' lineup of barbecue—pit-cooking demonstrations highlight everything from Texas smoked beef brisket to St. Louis-style ribs and Memphis dry-rubbed meats, which can be doused with all kinds of different barbecue sauces.

National Kids' Fest takes place mid-June to mid-August. This festival presents special shows and exhibits ranging from extreme sports demonstrations to appearances by exotic animals to circus performances on ice. The rousing Southern Gospel Picnic brings together the rich harmonies of top-name gospel vocal groups along with another Southern tradition—an old-fashioned picnic spread featuring chicken and all the fixings plus a tempting array of desserts. This family-style music celebration runs from late August to around Sept. 10.

Artisans from around the country gather for the Festival of American Music & Crafts, held Wednesdays through Sundays from mid-September to late October. In addition to craft displays and performances by country and bluegrass musicians, the festival presents "Headin' West!", a Broadway-style musical featuring elaborate sets and special effects. Silver Dollar City wraps up the year with an Old Time Christmas in November and December.

In late September the Autumn Daze Craft Festival takes place in historic downtown Branson.

Each Nov. 5-11 Branson hosts the Veterans Homecoming celebration, which draws tens of thousands of veterans, their friends and families. The week features a variety of events, including special appearances by high-ranking military personnel, tribute shows and military reunions and concludes with a Veterans Day parade in the historic downtown.

Branson pulls out the stops for the holidays. Beginning Nov. 1 and lasting through Dec. 31, more than 5 million twinkling lights adorn the streets during the Branson Area Festival of Lights. The Branson Adoration Parade rolls through the historic downtown area in early December. This nighttime parade is a joyful expression of small-town pride and a faith-based celebration of Christmas, with lighted floats, high school marching bands, musicians and singers all ringing in the season.

The parade coincides with the lighting of the enormous Nativity Scene on Mount Branson, a tradition that goes back more than 60 years. Incorporating 40-foot-tall figures, it is lit from the first Sunday in

December through Jan. 1. Branson's music theaters also get into the spirit, presenting literally dozens of special holiday-themed productions in November and December during Ozark Mountain Christmas, and twinkling lights and themed displays decorate the streets.

The Branson Vicinity

BRANSON WEST (E-3) pop. 408, elev. 1,368'

TALKING ROCKS CAVERN is on SR 13 in Marvel Cave Park at 423 Fairy Cave Ln. Drapery helictites, musical stalactites and a 100-foot-tall formation called the Cathedral can be seen in the cave, which has approximately 140 steps to climb; concrete walks and railings are provided. A 5-minute sound and light presentation and a 400-acre nature area with walking trails also are featured.

Time: Allow 1 hour minimum. **Hours:** Daily 9:30-6, Memorial Day-Labor Day; 9:30-5, Feb. 1-day before Memorial Day and day after Labor Day-Dec. 31. **Cost:** $16.95; $8.95 (ages 4-12). **Phone:** (417) 272-3366 or (800) 600-2283.

LAMPE (E-2) elev. 1,316'

DOGWOOD CANYON NATURE PARK is s. on SR 13 to jct. SR 86, then w. about 3 mi. on SR 86 following signs to the park turnoff. Dogwood Canyon is a private refuge encompassing some 10,000 acres of Ozark wilderness. The terrain of ridges, hollows and limestone bluffs is honeycombed with caves and provides a backdrop for waterfalls, meandering streams and woodlands dominated by oaks, pines and cedars.

Activities include walking, hiking or biking along a 6-mile round-trip paved trail, trout fishing and horseback riding. A 2-hour wildlife tram tour winds along the canyon floor before crossing the Arkansas border to encounter herds of Texas longhorn cattle, American bison and elk that live in the park.

Note: Fees are likely to increase in 2010; phone ahead to confirm rates. All recreational activities are subject to weather conditions and availability. **Time:** Allow 2 hours minimum. **Hours:** Park open daily 8:30-5, May 22-Sept. 7; Tues.-Sat 8:30-5, Sun.-Mon. 9-5, Sept. 8-Oct. 31; Tues.-Sat 8:30-5, Sun.-Mon 11:30-5, Apr. 4-May 21 (weather permitting). Most activities offered Mar.-Nov. (horseback riding not available Sun.-Mon.) Phone for seasonal hours in Mar. and Nov. Closed Jan. 1 and Dec. 25. **Cost:** Fees for individual activities vary. Wildlife tram tour $25.95; $11.95 (ages 3-11). One-day Adventure Pass combining various activities $39.95; $24.95 (ages 3-11). **Phone:** (417) 779-5983.

MERRIAM WOODS (E-3) pop. 1,142

BONNIEBROOK is e. off US 65 via Rose O'Neill Rd. This three-story house was the favorite retreat of Rose O'Neill, novelist, artist and creator of the kewpie doll. Her restored home contains family furnishings as well as period items. A museum of O'Neill's works includes books, photographs, illustrations and original dolls. Walkways meander through the wooded grounds past flower gardens and brooks.

Time: Allow 1 hour minimum. **Hours:** Guided tours are given Tues.-Sat. 9-4, Apr. 1-Dec. 1. Last tour begins 1 hour before closing. Closed major holidays. **Cost:** $7; free (ages 0-12). **Phone:** (417) 561-1509 or (800) 539-7437.

POINT LOOKOUT (F-2) elev. 928'

COLLEGE OF THE OZARKS is off US 65 Bus. Rte. exit. This liberal arts college is maintained largely by students as one way of defraying the cost of education. Highlights include The College of the Ozarks Greenhouses, containing a collection of more than 7,000 plants; the neo-Gothic Williams Memorial Chapel, which has impressive stained-glass windows; and the Ralph Foster Museum *(see attraction listing)*. Also on the grounds is Edwards Mill, a water-powered mill that produces whole-grain meal. Weaving and basket making may be observed at the mill.

The Keeter Center, at the entrance to the campus, houses a lodge and Dobyns Dining Room. It features architectural details created almost entirely by students, who also prepare and serve the food. **Phone:** (417) 334-6411.

RALPH FOSTER MUSEUM is off Opportunity Ave. on the College of the Ozarks campus. Named after local radio pioneer and avid hunter, angler and conservationist Ralph Foster, the displays at this museum cover Ozarks history and life. Collections include coins, stamps, timepieces, dolls, musical instruments, American Indian artifacts and an extensive display of weapons that features gold-plated handguns, flintlocks and a gun that once belonged to Pancho Villa.

Other highlights include beautiful ornate saddles, Western gear, wildlife displays (polar bears, deer and waterfowl), antique cameos and the vintage vehicle that took the Clampett family to California in the popular 1960s TV series "The Beverly Hillbillies." The Discovery Room has interactive exhibits for kids. **Time:** Allow 2 hours minimum. **Hours:** Mon.-Sat. 9-4:30, Feb.-Dec. Closed Thanksgiving and Christmas week. **Cost:** $6; $5 (ages 62+); free (ages 0-18). **Phone:** (417) 334-6411.

This ends listings for the Branson Vicinity.
The following page resumes the alphabetical listings of cities in Missouri.

BRANSON WEST—*see Branson p. 150.*

BURFORDVILLE (E-5)

BOLLINGER MILL STATE HISTORIC SITE is .5 mi. e. of SR 34. This turbine-powered mill was first built in 1799 and reconstructed twice during the 19th century. One of only four covered bridges in Missouri is on the grounds. **Hours:** Tours of the four-story mill are given by request Mon.-Sat. 10-4, Sun. noon-4, Mar.-Nov.; Tues.-Sat. 10-4, rest of year. Closed major holidays. Phone ahead to confirm schedule. **Cost:** Tour $2.50; $1.50 (ages 6-12). **Phone:** (573) 243-4591 or (800) 334-6946.

BUTLER (D-2) pop. 4,209, elev. 850′

BATES COUNTY MUSEUM is on Elks Dr., just off Mill St. and old US 71. Eight themed rooms trace the county's history from early pioneer days through the 1970s. Exhibits feature Osage Indian artifacts, items associated with the 1821 Harmony Mission, Civil War and World War II memorabilia and a Bates County timeline. **Time:** Allow 1 hour minimum. **Hours:** Tues.-Sat. 10-4, May-Oct. Closed July 4 and Labor Day. **Cost:** $3; $2.50 (ages 65+); $1 (students with ID). **Phone:** (660) 679-0134.

CALIFORNIA (C-3) pop. 4,005, elev. 889′

BURGER'S SMOKEHOUSE, 3 mi. s. on SR 87, offers a videotape presentation detailing the country ham curing process. The visitor center features a two-and-one-half-story diorama depicting an Ozark landscape during various seasons. **Hours:** Mon.-Fri. 8-4. **Cost:** Free. **Phone:** (573) 796-3134.

CAMDENTON (D-3) pop. 2,779, elev. 1,000′

Camdenton, the seat of Camden County, is in south-central Missouri. Osage and Delaware Indians inhabited this area prior to the onset of white settlement in the 1820s. Houseboat rentals are popular along nearby Lake of the Ozarks.

Camdenton Area Chamber of Commerce: 739 W. US 54, P.O. Box 1375, Camdenton, MO 65020. **Phone:** (573) 346-2227 or (800) 769-1004.

GEM **BRIDAL CAVE** is 2 mi. n. on SR 5, then 1.5 mi. w. on Lake Rd. 5-88. Guided 1-hour tours follow concrete walks through the cave, which maintains a constant temperature of 60 F and is known for its massive onyx formations and colorful mineral deposits. The stalactite-adorned Bridal Chapel is a popular site for weddings. On the grounds are a visitor center and a boat dock. Visitors may spot such wildlife as the bald eagle, deer, turkeys and red foxes along a half-mile outdoor walking trail offering sweeping views of Thunder Mountain's rock bluffs.

Hours: Daily 9-6, Memorial Day weekend-Aug. 1; 9-4, rest of year. Closed Jan. 1, Thanksgiving and Dec. 24-25. **Cost:** $15; $7 (ages 5-12). **Phone:** (573) 346-2676.

CAPE GIRARDEAU (E-6)

pop. 35,349, elev. 350′

Named after Jean Baptiste Girardot, who established a trading post here in 1733, Cape Girardeau was settled by Spanish immigrants drawn to the area by Spain's offer of inexpensive, tax-exempt land. Flourishing river trade characterized the town before the Civil War. Cape Girardeau experienced an industrial resurgence in the 1880s with the establishment of new railroad lines.

A look at area heritage and culture is available at the Cape River Heritage Museum, 538 Independence St.; phone (573) 334-0405. The city contains many scenic parks. Court House Park overlooks the Mississippi River, while Capaha Park boasts notable rose gardens. A scenic portion of I-55 runs 57 miles north from Cape Girardeau to St. Mary.

Cape Girardeau Convention and Visitors Bureau: 400 Broadway, Suite 100, Cape Girardeau, MO 63701. **Phone:** (573) 335-1631 or (800) 777-0068.

Self-guiding tours: A pamphlet outlining a walking tour of historic downtown Cape Girardeau is available from the convention and visitors bureau.

CAPE ROCK is 2 mi. n.e. via SR 177 and E. Cape Rock Dr. Views of the Mississippi River are particularly scenic from this bluff, said to be the site of Jean Baptiste Girardot's 1733 trading post. Nothing remains of the original settlement.

ROSEMARY BERKEL AND HARRY L. CRISP II SOUTHEAST MISSOURI REGIONAL MUSEUM is at 518 S. Fountain St. in the Holland School of Visual and Performing Arts on the River Campus of Southeast Missouri State University. The collections represent regional archeology, fine art and history. Of special interest is the museum's extensive collection of prehistoric American Indian artifacts, including ceramic conch shell effigies, stone tools, and cups and bowls. Kachina dolls, blankets, baskets and examples of decorative beadwork can be seen. An interactive Lewis and Clark exhibit, a life-size diorama of an American Indian hut, exhibits about native wildlife, and a small art museum with changing exhibits also are included.

Time: Allow 1 hour minimum. **Hours:** Tues.-Fri. 10-5, Sat.-Sun. 1-4, mid-Aug. to mid-May; Tues.-Fri. 10-4, Sat.-Sun. 1-4, rest of year. Closed school holidays. **Cost:** Donations. **Phone:** (573) 651-2260, or (573) 651-2301 for tour reservations.

CARTHAGE (E-1) pop. 12,668, elev. 1,008′

Virtually destroyed during the Civil War, Carthage was subsequently rebuilt largely with marble quarried from the surrounding area. The city's historic square contains several Victorian houses built with the local stone, which also was used in the construction of the Missouri State Capitol in Jefferson City.

Another marble building is the castle-like Jasper County Courthouse, 302 S. Main St., which bristles with turrets and a tall clock spire. Inside, the mural "Forged in Fire" by Lowell Davis depicts the history of Carthage from the time of its first settlers, the Osage Indians, through the Civil War to the present.

Myra Belle Shirley—later to become Belle Starr, infamous Confederate spy and outlaw—was in her teens when the war forced her family to move from the area. Other residents were Annie Baxter, the first woman in the United States to hold elected office; ragtime musician and composer James Scott; and zoologist and lecturer Marlin Perkins, who is honored with a bronze statue in Central Park.

During the Civil War the Battle of Carthage was fought July 5, 1861. Different stages of the battle are shown by markers that begin on Civil War Road, at the baseline 8 miles north of town, and extend to Carter Park on River Street in Carthage. The Battle of Carthage State Historic Site on Chestnut Street provides an interpretive shelter that depicts the history of the battle. For further information about the battle markers contact the convention and visitors bureau.

The Powers Museum at 1617 W. Oak St. recounts the history of Carthage and the surrounding region during the late 19th and early 20th centuries. Art-Central at 1110 E. 13th St. displays the works of local artists; phone (417) 358-4404.

Carthage Convention and Visitors Bureau: 402 S. Garrison Ave., Carthage, MO 64836. **Phone:** (417) 359-8181 or (866) 357-8687.

Self-guiding tours: A historical drive about 4 miles long is defined by green street markers posted throughout the business and residential districts, both of which are distinguished by Victorian architecture.

PRECIOUS MOMENTS CHAPEL AND GARDENS is at 4105 Chapel Rd. The chapel was conceived and designed by artist Samuel J. Butcher, who in the 1970s began drawing teardrop-eyed children called "Precious Moments" to convey messages to family and friends. He further developed his signature style by depicting biblical events, which are reflected in 30 stained-glass windows and 84 murals covering the chapel's walls and ceiling. The east gallery displays a large collection of porcelain figurines and some of Butcher's early artistic work. The grounds are adorned with flower gardens, fountains and statues of inspirational figures.

Time: Allow 1 hour minimum. **Hours:** Chapel and visitor center open daily 9-5. Twenty-minute guided tours of the chapel depart daily on the hour 9-4. Closed Jan. 1, Easter, Thanksgiving and Dec. 25. **Cost:** Free. **Phone:** (800) 543-7975.

CARUTHERSVILLE (F-5) pop. 6,760

GAMBLING ESTABLISHMENTS

- **Lady Luck Casino** is at 777 E. 3rd St. **Hours:** Sun.-Thurs. 7 a.m.-3 a.m., Fri.-Sat. 24 hours. **Phone:** (573) 333-1000.

CARVER NATIONAL MONUMENT—

see George Washington Carver National Monument p. 155.

CHESTERFIELD—*see St. Louis p. 217.*

CLARKSVILLE (B-5) pop. 490, elev. 456'

Founded in 1817, Clarksville offers the first opportunity north of St. Louis to view the Mississippi River—up close—at River Front Park, which runs along the riverbank at the junction of Howard and First streets. The park offers walking paths with scenic views; steps lead right down to the river. Lock and Dam #24 is at the north end of the park and features interpretive panels about the lock, dam and river.

The town boasts a number of artisans who can be seen working their creativity in their downtown shops. From mid-December through late February, bald eagles winter in Clarksville.

Clarksville City Hall: 111 Howard St., Clarksville, MO 63336. **Phone:** (573) 242-3336.

CLINTON (C-2) pop. 9,311

HENRY COUNTY MUSEUM AND CULTURAL ARTS CENTER is at 203 W. Franklin Ave. A reconstructed 1800s village includes storefronts and replicas of a drugstore, a soda fountain, a pharmacy, a doctor's office with a collection of medical tools and devices, a barber shop, a schoolhouse, a general store and a blacksmith shop. A log cabin also is displayed across the street from the museum. **Time:** Allow 1 hour minimum. **Hours:** Mon.-Sat. 10-4, Apr.-Dec. Closed major holidays. **Cost:** $3; free (ages 0-11). **Phone:** (660) 885-8414.

COLUMBIA (C-3) pop. 84,531, elev. 738'

Columbia began in 1819 as Smithton; it was renamed and made the seat of Boone County in 1821. After Boone's Lick Trail was rerouted south through Columbia, the town became a prosperous outfitting station for westbound emigrants, some of whom chose to remain.

Columbia's residents responded to the competition to secure the appointment for a state university with the fervor of a political campaign. As a result of door-to-door canvassing and torchlight parades, a subscription of $117,000 was raised by 900 patrons, some of whom sold their houses and farms to meet their pledges. The University of Missouri *(see attraction listing)*, the first public university west of the Mississippi River, opened its doors in 1839.

MU is Missouri's national flagship university, with more than 280 degree programs and the largest library collection in the state. Its school of journalism, founded in 1908, is distinguished as the world's first. As one of only six universities in the country with medicine, veterinary medicine and law on one campus, MU also plays a significant role in professional education.

"Mizzou" is a member of the Big 12 Conference and features the state's only Division 1-A athletic program. For sports event schedules and ticket information phone (800) 228-7297.

Columbia College and Stephens College confirm Columbia's identity as a college town, though the insurance industry and medical services reinforce its economic base. The Davis Art and Curved Entrance galleries at Stephens College mount exhibits throughout the year; phone (573) 442-2211.

The 8.2-mile M-K-T Trail connects downtown Columbia to the Katy Trail, a rails-to-trails conversion that crosses the state. At the Stadium Boulevard trailhead is the Martin Luther King Jr. Memorial Garden. Trail maps are available from the convention and visitors bureau.

Columbia Convention & Visitors Bureau: 300 S. Providence Rd., Columbia, MO 65203. **Phone:** (573) 875-1231 or (800) 652-0987.

Self-guiding tours: Brochures outlining a driving tour of publicly accessible art are offered by the convention and visitors bureau.

MASONIC MUSEUM AND LIBRARY is off US 63 exit Prathersville Rd. (4 mi. n. from jct. I-70 and US 63), then .3 mi. n. to 6033 Masonic Dr. The museum's five themed galleries—Pathmakers and Patriots, Living Well, Generosity, Leadership and a space for rotating exhibits—present the memorabilia of and impart the significant contributions made by such famous Masons as explorers William Clark and Meriwether Lewis; President Harry S. Truman, who once served as Grand Master of Missouri Masons; and Laura Ingalls Wilder, a member of the Order of the Eastern Star, an organization for relatives of Masons.

Displayed are a medallion from Truman's Masonic collared apron, his gavel and pieces donated by local Masons. Exhibits outline the history of Eastern Star and Masonic chapters across the country.

Time: Allow 30 minutes minimum. **Hours:** Mon.-Fri. 9-4:30. Closed major holidays. **Cost:** Free. **Phone:** (573) 814-4663 or (800) 434-9804.

SHELTER INSURANCE GARDENS is off I-70 exit 124, s. on Stadium Blvd., then e. to 1817 W. Broadway St., behind the insurance company's headquarters. Tucked behind stone and wrought-iron gates at the home office complex of Shelter Insurance Companies are 5 acres planted with more than 300 varieties of native trees and shrubs, along with a number of annuals and perennials. Rose, shade, rock, conifer and desert gardens as well as a garden for the blind are all tagged for identification.

The site is also graced by a gazebo, a waterfall, sundial, pools and a memorial to Vietnam veterans. A free summer concert series is presented Sunday evenings, June through July. **Time:** Allow 30 minutes minimum. **Hours:** Daily dawn-dusk. Closed Dec. 25. **Cost:** Free. **Phone:** (573) 445-8441.

UNIVERSITY OF MISSOURI–COLUMBIA is on Eighth St., 3 blks. s. of Broadway St. "Mizzou," the oldest state university west of the Mississippi, has 30,000 students and 17,000 faculty and staff members. The 1,358-acre campus features a number of historic buildings. Six Ionic columns on Francis Quadrangle are all that remains of Academic Hall, destroyed by fire in 1892. Thomas Jefferson's original tombstone is on the quadrangle. With more than 5,000 trees and 650 varieties of plants, the MU grounds have been officially designated as a botanic garden.

The Geology Building has more than 100,000 fossil and rock specimens, many displayed in its ground and first floor corridors. A collection of mounted waterfowl is exhibited in the corridors of Lefevre Hall on University Avenue. On Friday visitors can watch the mid-morning feeding of reptiles in Room 202 of Stewart Hall.

Hours: Campus walking tours are given Mon.-Fri. at 10, 11 and 1:30 during the school year; Mon.-Fri. at 10 and 1, mid-May to mid-Aug., unless otherwise arranged. Two weeks' advance notice is recommended. **Cost:** Free. **Phone:** (573) 882-6333, (573) 884-7279 for Stewart Hall, or (800) 856-2181 for the Office of Visitor Relations.

George Caleb Bingham Gallery is on the University of Missouri–Columbia campus in the Fine Arts Building at 125A Hitt St. Changing exhibits of artwork by faculty and students as well as artists of national and international stature are mounted. **Hours:** Mon.-Fri. 8-5, mid-Aug. to mid-May; 7:30-4, rest of year. Closed campus holidays and between semesters. **Cost:** Free. **Phone:** (573) 882-3555.

Museum of Anthropology is on the University of Missouri–Columbia campus in room 100 in Swallow Hall. Exhibits related to the anthropological history of man are displayed on a rotating basis. **Time:** Allow 30 minutes minimum. **Hours:** Mon.-Fri. 9-4. Closed major holidays. **Cost:** Free. **Phone:** (573) 882-3573.

Museum of Art and Archaeology is on the University of Missouri–Columbia campus in Pickard Hall at jct. Ninth St. and University Ave. The museum contains a collection of ancient Egyptian, Greek and Roman art; American artworks; and European paintings, drawings, prints and sculpture from the 15th century to the present. Other exhibits feature Asian, African and pre-Columbian art. The Cast Gallery displays plaster casts of Greek and Roman sculptures. **Hours:** Tues.-Fri. 9-4, Sat.-Sun. noon-4. Closed major holidays. **Cost:** Free. **Phone:** (573) 882-3591.

State Historical Society of Missouri is on the University of Missouri–Columbia campus on the ground floor of the Ellis Library in Lowry Mall, at jct. Ninth St. and Conley Ave. Missouri newspapers, books and publications about state history and genealogy are part of an extensive collection that includes political cartoons and paintings by John J. Audubon, Thomas Hart Benton, George Caleb Bingham, Karl Bodmer and contemporary Missouri artists. Tours are given by appointment. **Hours:** Mon.-Fri. 8-4:45, Sat. 8-3:30. Gallery Tues.-Sat. 9-3:15. **Cost:** Free. **Phone:** (573) 882-7083.

WALTERS-BOONE COUNTY HISTORICAL MUSEUM is 3 mi. s. of jct. I-70/SR 63 at 3801 Ponderosa St. (Historic Ashland Pike). The history of the area is presented through historical photographs, artifacts, living-history displays and rotating exhibits. Also in the museum is the Genealogical Society of Central Missouri Library. Adjoining the museum is the Montminy Gallery, which houses the works of local artists and professors Tracy and Pierre Montminy.

A collection of photographic plates and negatives produced by Boone County photographers from the late 1800s to the 1950s also is included. **Time:** Allow 1 hour minimum. **Hours:** Wed.-Sun. 12:30-4:30, Apr.-Oct.; Wed. and Fri.-Sun. 12:30-4:30, rest of year. **Cost:** Free. **Phone:** (573) 443-8936.

CRESTWOOD—*see St. Louis p. 217.*

DANVILLE (C-4) elev. 814′

GRAHAM CAVE STATE PARK .3 mi. w. on SR 161 then 2.1 mi. n.w. to 217 SR TT. Archeological profiles of the sandstone cave at the 369-acre park indicate it was occupied by American Indians about 8000 B.C. Interpretive signage inside the cave's entrance document some of what was discovered and highlight its hidden and unique treasures. Bicycling, hiking and walking trails are on the grounds. *See Recreation Chart and the AAA South Central CampBook.* **Hours:** Daily 24 hours. **Cost:** Free. **Phone:** (573) 564-3476 or (800) 334-6946.

DEFIANCE—*see St. Louis p. 218.*

EAST PRAIRIE (E-6) pop. 3,227

BIG OAK TREE STATE PARK is 2 mi. e. on SR 80, then 10 mi. s. on SR 102. A 1.2-mile boardwalk winds through forests of virgin bottomland hardwoods, enabling visitors to see small wildlife. The trees are notable for their size and provide a habitat for more than 140 species of birds. A free booklet interprets the 10 stations along the trail. *See Recreation Chart.* **Hours:** Daily 6 a.m.-dusk. **Cost:** Free. **Phone:** (573) 649-3149 or (800) 334-6946.

EUREKA—*see St. Louis p. 218.*

EXCELSIOR SPRINGS—

see Kansas City p. 176.

FLORIDA (B-4) pop. 9

John Clemens moved from Tennessee to the new village of Florida in 1835, where he became a partner in an in-law's store and set up a law practice. His son, Samuel Langhorne Clemens, was born here and later, as Mark Twain, created some of America's early classic literature. Four years after Twain's birth the family moved to Hannibal, which served as the model for St. Petersburg, the fictional home of Huckleberry Finn and Tom Sawyer.

MARK TWAIN BIRTHPLACE AND MUSEUM STATE HISTORIC SITE is .5 mi. s. on SR 107 to 37352 Shrine Rd. in Mark Twain State Park *(see Recreation Chart and the AAA South Central CampBook).* The birthplace of Samuel Clemens is preserved within a steel, glass and stone building. The museum exhibits a handwritten manuscript of "The Adventures of Tom Sawyer" and memorabilia associated with Twain's life and times.

A reading room is available. **Time:** Allow 1 hour minimum. **Hours:** Daily 10-5, Apr. 2-Oct. 31; Wed.-Sun. 10-5, rest of year. Closed Jan. 1, Thanksgiving and Dec. 25. **Cost:** $2.50; $1.50 (ages 6-12). **Phone:** (573) 565-3449 or (800) 334-6946.

FLORISSANT—*see St. Louis p. 218.*

FORT LEONARD WOOD (D-4)

Fort Leonard Wood, in the Ozark foothills 2 miles south of I-44 from the Fort Wood exit, is a major U.S. Army training center and headquarters of the Army Engineer School. Established in 1940, the fort is named for the general who helped organize the 1st U.S. Cavalry, The Rough Riders.

Pulaski County Tourism Bureau and Visitor Center: 137 St. Robert Blvd., St. Robert, MO 65584. **Phone:** (573) 336-6355 or (877) 858-8687.

MAHAFFEY MUSEUM COMPLEX is at 495 S. Dakota Ave. The complex contains four museums: The U.S. Army Chemical Corps Museum, the U.S. Army Engineer Museum, the U.S. Army Military Police Corps Museum and the Fort Leonard Wood Museum. Walk-through dioramas and artifacts from each corps are featured. The Fort Leonard Wood Museum is a group of World War II-era buildings with items portraying daily military life at the fort. **Time:** Allow 1 hour minimum. **Hours:** Mon.-Fri. 8-4, Sat. 10-4. **Cost:** Free. **Phone:** (573) 596-0780.

FREDERICKTOWN (D-5)
pop. 3,928, elev. 741′

SILVER MINES RECREATION AREA is 3 mi. s. of SR 72 on SR D to FR 2510, on the St. Francis River in Mark Twain National Forest. At the dam site the river flows between two sheer walls of granite, the remains of the stone dam. The riverbed is strewn with huge boulders. A hiking trail leads to an old silver mine. Camping is permitted mid-March to late October. **Hours:** Daily 24 hours. **Cost:** Free. A fee is charged for camping. **Parking:** $2. **Phone:** (573) 783-7225.

FROHNA (D-6) pop. 192

Frohna was one of several settlements founded in 1839 by a group of 700 German Saxon Lutherans. Eight years later these immigrants founded the Lutheran Church-Missouri Synod. Off CR C on Saxon Memorial Drive is the Saxon Lutheran Memorial, which includes a visitor center, a log parish schoolhouse and an early log and frame house built by one of the original settlers.

FULTON (C-4) pop. 12,128, elev. 813′

Fulton, named for steamboat inventor Robert Fulton, also was the birthplace of musician, poet, novelist and reviewer Henry Bellamann, who published three books of poetry and seven novels over more than 2 decades. Bellamann's best-known novel was "Kings Row"; the 1942 film adaptation of life in a small Midwestern town at the turn of the 20th century starred Ann Sheridan and Ronald Reagan. It was filmed on location, and downtown Fulton's brick-paved streets and historic architecture have been carefully preserved in the years since.

Kingdom of Callaway Chamber of Commerce: 409 Court St., Fulton, MO 65251. **Phone:** (573) 642-3055 or (800) 257-3554.

AUTO WORLD MUSEUM is just off US 54 jct. (exit CR HH) to 200 Peacock Dr., following signs. Approximately 85 vehicles are displayed, arranged against backdrops of enlarged photos—such as a drive-in movie theater showing a John Wayne film—to provide historical context. Background information includes production details and history on now-obsolete makers like REO and Nash. Among the rare cars are examples from the 1920s and '30s, along with more recognizable icons (a '57 T-Bird, a '66 Mustang, a VW bug). The collection also includes vintage fire trucks.

Time: Allow 1 hour minimum. **Hours:** Daily 9-5, Apr.-Dec. Closed Thanksgiving. **Cost:** $8; $7 (ages 60+ and military with ID); $5 (ages 6-12). **Phone:** (573) 642-2080.

GEM **NATIONAL WINSTON CHURCHILL MUSEUM** is at jct. Westminster Ave. and W. 7th St. The Westminster College Gymnasium was the site of Churchill's prophetic "Iron Curtain" speech on March 5, 1946. To commemorate that visit, the college acquired London's historic Church of St. Mary the Virgin, Aldermanbury, which was slated for demolition, and reassembled it on the campus as a memorial.

The church stood in London's Old City for 800 years. Destroyed by the Great Fire in 1666, it was rebuilt by Sir Christopher Wren. Three hundred years later, the tons of stone walls and columns remaining after the 1940 London blitz were shipped to Fulton. The church has been reconstructed, and the bombed-out portions have been replaced.

Part of the Berlin Wall has been relocated and erected on the grounds. A library, galleries and a museum beneath the church contain Churchill letters, photographs, volumes, manuscripts, paintings and World War II memorabilia. An audiovisual program is presented.

Time: Allow 1 hour minimum. **Hours:** Daily 10-4:30. Closed Jan. 1, Thanksgiving and Dec. 25. **Cost:** $6; $5 (ages 61+); $4 (ages 12-18 and college students with ID); $3 (ages 6-11). **Phone:** (573) 592-5369.

GEORGE WASHINGTON CARVER NATIONAL MONUMENT (E-1)

George Washington Carver National Monument is southeast of Joplin and 2.5 miles southwest of Diamond on CR V. The 210-acre park preserves the birthplace of the noted scientist. Carver developed more than 300 byproducts from the peanut and more than 100 from the sweet potato, as well as new uses for cotton, soybeans, cowpeas and other crops.

Displays in the visitor center pertain to Carver's life and work in the field of botany and his career as a teacher of scientific agriculture. The Discovery

Center gives visitors the chance to try hands-on experiments.

A self-guiding .7-mile trail winds through woods and fields Carver walked as a boy. Sites along the trail include the birthplace site, the "Boy Carver" statue by Robert Amendola and the Carver family cemetery. Allow 1 hour minimum. Daily 9-5; closed Jan. 1, Thanksgiving and Dec. 25. Free. Phone (417) 325-4151.

GLASGOW (B-3) pop. 1,263, elev. 650′

GLASGOW COMMUNITY MUSEUM is at 402 Commerce St. Housed in an 1861 church building, the museum displays many items from the church as well as other artifacts and photographs from the 1800s and early 1900s. **Time:** Allow 1 hour minimum. **Hours:** Wed.-Sun. 2-5, May 15-Oct. 15. **Cost:** Donations. **Phone:** (660) 338-2377.

GOLDEN (F-2)

GOLDEN PIONEER MUSEUM is at SR 86 and CR J at the northern edge of town. Don't let the faded yellow metal exterior fool you; this museum contains an extensive and impressive collection of artifacts. Neatly displayed in glass cases are pre-Columbian, Aztec and Oaxacan black pottery, razor-sharp obsidian knives, axes, arrowheads, miniature clay figures and beautiful pieces of quartz (including a cluster that weighs more than 1,250 lbs.). Other objects are giant mastodon teeth and bones, pocket watches in mint condition, antique Kewpie dolls and a coin collection featuring the first U.S. silver dollar and some 3-cent nickels. One highlight is a beautiful turquoise carving, said to be the world's largest.

Historical exhibits pay tribute to the Indians who died during the 1837 Trail of Tears forced westward migration. The museum also has plenty of 20th-century Americana—Elvis displays, a huge collection of 1960s lunch boxes, baseball cards, and hundreds of antique glass plates and pitchers in vivid colors. **Time:** Allow 2 hours minimum. **Hours:** Tues.-Sat. 10:30-4:30, Apr.-Aug.; Thurs.-Sat. 10:30-4:30, Sept.-Oct. **Cost:** Free. **Phone:** (417) 271-3300.

GRANDVIEW—*see Kansas City p. 176.*

GRAY SUMMIT (C-5) pop. 2,640, elev. 632′

PURINA FARMS is 2 blks. n. on SR 100 to CR MM, then 1 mi. n. The complex offers a variety of educational displays along with a hands-on experience with pets and farm animals. Young visitors can romp in the hayloft, learn how many people equal the weight of one hog and attend a multimedia presentation about man's relationships with domestic animals.

Hours: Tues.-Sun. 9:30-3, Memorial Day-Labor Day; Wed.-Fri. 9:30-1, Sat.-Sun. 9:30-3, mid-Mar. through day before Memorial Day and day after Labor Day to mid-Nov. **Cost:** Free. Reservations are required. **Phone:** (314) 982-3232.

SHAW NATURE RESERVE is at jct. SR 100 and I-44. The reserve protects some 2,500 acres of natural Ozark landscape and offers 14 miles of hiking trails through such habitats as a floodplain forest, oak-hickory woods, glades, bluffs, a tall-grass prairie, savannah and wetlands. The People and the Land exhibit in the 1879 Joseph H. Manor House deals with environmental and conservation themes. The 5-acre Whitmire Wildflower Garden displays flowers native to Missouri and the eastern United States, accented by native grasses, shrubs and trees. A descriptive brochure is available at the visitor center, which also offers seasonal displays and interpretive programs.

Hours: Reserve open daily 7 a.m.-dusk. Visitor center Mon.-Fri. 8-4:30, Sat.-Sun. 9-5. Closed major holidays. **Cost:** $3; $2 (ages 65+); free (ages 0-12). **Phone:** (636) 451-3512.

HANNIBAL (B-5) pop. 17,757, elev. 470′

Samuel Clemens (Mark Twain) lived in Hannibal as a boy and later used the town as the setting for incidents in "The Adventures of Huckleberry Finn" and "The Adventures of Tom Sawyer." Another Hannibal resident was Margaret Tobin, who, after being encouraged by Clemens to tap the wealth in the Rocky Mountains, went West and became adored by Denver society. She married and later was dubbed the Unsinkable Molly Brown after rowing passengers to safety from the sinking *Titanic*.

The Garth Woodside Mansion, on Warren Barrett Drive, was the 20-room home of Col. John H. Garth, a close friend of Clemens. The 1871 Victorian mansion contains a three-story flying staircase—one with no visible means of support—ornate woodwork and hand-carved mantels of Italian marble. Much of the furniture, wall hangings, draperies and carpets belonged to the Garths. In December the mansion is adorned with Victorian holiday decorations; phone (573) 221-2789.

Already imbued with a distinctly American character through its association with Mark Twain, Hannibal also is the southern migration destination for bald eagles that live on the high Mississippi River bluffs. Many of the majestic birds can be seen at the dam at Saverton, about 9 miles south of Hannibal on SR 79.

Hannibal is at the northern end of the scenic portion of SR 79 that runs 86 miles south to St. Peters, following the Mississippi River much of the way. Tom Sawyer look-alikes descend upon Hannibal yearly to compete in the fence-painting contest during National Tom Sawyer Days, held the week of July 4.

Hannibal Convention & Visitors Bureau: 505 N. 3rd St., Hannibal, MO 63401. **Phone:** (573) 221-2477.

"ADVENTURES OF TOM SAWYER" DIORAMAS is at 323 N. Main St. Sixteen hand-carved miniature figures depict scenes from the novel. **Time:** Allow 30 minutes minimum. **Hours:** Daily 10-5. Closed Dec. 25. **Cost:** $3.50; $2.50 (ages 55+); $1.50 (ages

0-12); $15 (family, 10 or more). **Phone:** (573) 221-3525.

HANNIBAL COMPANY TROLLEY RIDE departs from 227 N. Main St. Trolley tours go to the Mark Twain Cave, Sawyer's Creek, Rockcliffe Mansion, Molly Brown's Birthplace, the Welshman Home, the *Mark Twain* Riverboat and the Mississippi River. **Hours:** Trips depart daily every 1.5 hours 9-5, mid-Apr. through Oct. 31. **Cost:** $9.75; $9.25 (ages 55+); $4.50 (ages 5-12). **Phone:** (573) 221-1161.

GEM **MARK TWAIN BOYHOOD HOME AND MUSEUM** is at 208 Hill St. The complex consists of several historic buildings and museums related to Hannibal's most famous resident. The home where Samuel Clemens lived between the ages of 7 and 18 was built by his father, John Marshall Clemens, in 1843. The restored two-story frame house is decorated with period furnishings and also contains interpretive displays, including photographs, first editions of Twain's books, original manuscripts and the desk where he wrote "The Adventures of Tom Sawyer." A 10-minute video presentation about his life is shown in the annex behind the home and museum.

The Becky Thatcher House is the home of Laura Hawkins, a childhood friend of Twain's who was the inspiration for his Thatcher character. The Huckleberry Finn House is a reconstruction of Tom Blankenship's house, Twain's inspiration for Huck Finn. Pilaster House, an old drugstore, was the home of Dr. Orville Grant, a close Clemens family friend. The family moved into Dr. Grant's house after losing their own home.

The Mark Twain Museum, 2 blocks south on Main Street, features 16 Norman Rockwell oil paintings that were used as illustrations in special editions of "The Adventures of Tom Sawyer" and "The Adventures of Huckleberry Finn"; sketches for the paintings were done by Rockwell in Hannibal 1935-36. Interactive displays depict scenes from Twain's life and writings. Visitors can also visit an interpretive center and the J.M. Clemens Justice of the Peace Office on Hill Street (originally located on Bird Street).

Note: The Becky Thatcher House is closed for renovations with the intention to reopen in 2011, but phone ahead for updates. **Time:** Allow 1 hour minimum. **Hours:** Daily 9-6, June-Aug.; Mon.-Sat. 9-5, Sun. noon-5, rest of year. Closed Jan. 1, Easter, Thanksgiving and Dec. 25. **Cost:** (includes all museum buildings) $9; $7.50 (ages 60+); $4 (ages 6-12). **Phone:** (573) 221-9010.

MARK TWAIN CAVE is 2 mi. s.e. on SR 79 to 300 Cave Hollow Rd. Samuel Clemens immortalized this underground labyrinth in "The Adventures of Tom Sawyer" as the cave in which Tom and Becky Thatcher were lost. The cave has dry, lighted passageways and a constant temperature of 52 F.

Hours: Guided 1-hour tours depart as needed daily 9-8, Memorial Day-Aug. 20 (also Labor Day weekend); 9-6, Apr. 1-day before Memorial Day and Aug. 21-Oct. 31; 10-4, rest of year. Closed Thanksgiving and Dec. 25. **Cost:** $15; $8 (ages 5-12). Combination ticket with Cameron Cave $26; $16 (ages 5-12). **Phone:** (573) 221-1656.

Cameron Cave is 2 mi. s.e. on SR 79, at Mark Twain Cave. Visitors carry lanterns during the 90-minute tour of this cave, which has been left in a nearly natural state. **Hours:** Tours depart from the Mark Twain Cave visitor center daily at 10, noon, 1:30 and 3, Memorial Day-Labor Day; by appointment day after Labor Day-Oct. 31. **Cost:** $16; $9 (ages 5-12). Combination ticket with Mark Twain Cave $26; $16 (ages 5-12). **Phone:** (573) 221-1656.

***MARK TWAIN* RIVERBOAT** docks at the foot of Center St. This triple-deck riverboat offers narrated sightseeing cruises on the Mississippi River. A 2-hour Dixieland band dinner cruise also is available. **Hours:** One-hour trips depart daily at 11, 1:30 and 4, Memorial Day-Labor Day; otherwise varies Apr.-May and Sept.-Oct. **Cost:** $14; $11 (ages 5-12). **Phone:** (573) 221-3222.

RIVERVIEW PARK occupies 465 acres on the bluffs of the Mississippi River. A statue of Samuel Clemens overlooks the river at Inspiration Point. **Hours:** Daily 6 a.m.-10 p.m. **Cost:** Free. **Phone:** (573) 221-0154.

ROCKCLIFFE MANSION is at 1000 Bird St. Considered one of the finest river estates in the country, the 30-room 1898 mansion has been restored to preserve its Art Nouveau decor. **Hours:** Daily 9-4, Memorial Day-Labor Day; Tues.-Sun. 10-3, rest of year. Closed Jan. 1, Easter, Thanksgiving and Dec. 24-25. **Cost:** $12.50; $7.50 (ages 6-12 and 65+). **Phone:** (573) 221-4140.

TOM AND HUCK MONUMENT is at the foot of Cardiff Hill. In Twain's writings the hill was called Holliday Hill, the rendezvous of Tom Sawyer and his playmates. Life-size figures of Tom Sawyer and Huck Finn, sculpted in 1926, stand on the spot.

TWAINLAND EXPRESS SIGHTSEEING TOURS departs from 400 N. 3rd St. Narrated 1-hour excursions travel through historic Hannibal. **Hours:** Tours are offered daily 10-2:30, June-Aug.; Sat.-Sun. 10-2:30 in May and Sept.-Oct. **Cost:** $9.75; $9.25 (ages 55+); $5 (ages 5-16). **Phone:** (573) 221-5593 or (800) 786-5193.

HERMANN (C-4) pop. 2,674, elev. 515'

Dissatisfied with life in Philadelphia and intent on preserving their culture, German immigrants moved to Hermann in 1836. Except during Prohibition, Hermann has been a winemaking town. Along with wineries, local industries include metalworking, plastics and shoe factories.

A legacy of fine craftsmanship is remembered at the Deutsche Schule, held in the German School of Arts and Crafts at 4th and Schiller streets, where such artisans as a basket maker, leather craftsman, potter, quilter and weaver can be seen at work. Other craft shops as well as a number of antique shops are located in town. Traditional German festivals are held in May and October.

The Deutschheim State Historic Site, 109 W. 2nd St., includes the Pommer-Gentner House and the Strehly House, both fine examples of Hermann's German heritage. Tours are available daily; phone (573) 486-2200.

Hermann Area Chamber of Commerce: 312 Market St., Hermann, MO 65041. **Phone:** (573) 486-2313 or (800) 932-8687.

HISTORIC HERMANN MUSEUM is at 312 Schiller St. at jct. 4th St. The museum, in the 1871 German School Building, has displays about steamboats and river history and exhibits late 19th-century furniture, early Hermann memorabilia and a piece of the Berlin wall. **Time:** Allow 30 minutes minimum. **Hours:** Tues.-Sat. 10-4, Sun. noon-4, Apr.-Oct. **Cost:** $3; $1 (ages 6-12). **Phone:** (573) 486-2017.

WINERIES

- **Hermannhof Winery** is at 330 E. 1st St., 2.5 blks. e. of the Mississippi River Bridge on SR 100. **Hours:** Mon.-Sat. 10-5, Sun. 11-5. Closed major holidays. **Phone:** (573) 486-5959 or (800) 393-0100.
- **Stone Hill Winery** is at 1110 Stone Hill Hwy., .2 mi. s.w. of jct. SRs 19 and 100. **Hours:** Mon.-Sat. 8:30-dusk, Sun. 10-6. Closed Jan. 1, Thanksgiving and Dec. 25. **Phone:** (573) 486-2221 or (800) 909-9463.

HIGGINSVILLE (C-2) pop. 4,682, elev. 835′

CONFEDERATE MEMORIAL STATE HISTORIC SITE is 1 mi. n.w. at jct. SRs 13 and 20. This 108-acre park contains a cemetery and monuments commemorating Confederate dead. A fishing lake is on the grounds. **Hours:** Mon.-Sat. 9-4, Sun. noon-5. **Cost:** Free. **Phone:** (660) 584-2853 or (800) 334-6946.

DID YOU KNOW

There are more theater seats in Branson than there are on Broadway in New York City.

IMPERIAL (D-5) pop. 4,373

MASTODON STATE HISTORIC SITE is off I-55 exit 186 at 1050 Charles J. Becker Dr. The Kimmswick Bone Bed, an area rich in Pleistocene fossils and bones, is preserved at the 425-acre site. Discovered in the early 19th century, this fossil bed yielded more than 60 mastodon skeletons, one of which is displayed at the site's museum. The visitor center recounts the history of the bone bed through a slide show and relics found on the site. Several trails cross the park.

Hours: Grounds open daily 8-dusk. Visitor center Mon.-Sat. 9-4:30, Sun. noon-4:30, Mar.-Nov.; Mon. and Thurs.-Sat. 11-4, Sun. noon-4, rest of year. Closed Jan. 1, Easter, Thanksgiving and Dec. 25. **Cost:** $2.50; free (ages 0-14). **Phone:** (636) 464-2976 or (800) 334-6946.

INDEPENDENCE—*see Kansas City p. 176.*

IRONTON (D-5) pop. 1,471, elev. 920′

Ironton, in the picturesque Arcadia Valley of the Ozark Mountain region, was once the headquarters of Gen. Ulysses S. Grant. St. Paul's Episcopal Church, 106 N. Knob St., epitomizes 1871 neo-Gothic architecture in Missouri. Lake Killarney is 3.5 miles east of town on SR 72; to the southwest is Taum Sauk Mountain.

JACKSON (D-5) pop. 11,947, elev. 463′

TRAIL OF TEARS STATE PARK is at 429 Moccasin Springs Rd. The 3,415-acre park contains a portion of the Trail of Tears, the route used by the Cherokees on their forced march to Oklahoma. This tract consists of wooded hills and valleys and high bluffs overlooking the Mississippi River. Deer, turkeys, hawks and foxes live year-round in the park; bald eagles come for the winter. *See Recreation Chart and the AAA South Central CampBook.* **Phone:** (573) 290-5268 or (800) 334-6946.

JEFFERSON CITY (C-4) pop. 39,636

The first building denoting Missouri's capital city, completed in 1826, was destroyed by fire in 1837; a new one begun the same year burned after it was struck by lightning in 1911. The present structure was built in 1918. The Governor's Residence was built in 1871 on the site of the original Capitol. Guided tours of the residence are given Tues. and Thurs. 10-noon and 1-3. To arrange a tour contact the governor's office; phone (573) 751-4141.

Jefferson Landing State Historic Site, on the river at the end of Jefferson Street, preserves three buildings that were the center of Jefferson City's 19th-century river trade: The 1839 Lohman Building, the 1854 Christopher Maus House and the 1855 Union Hotel. A visitor center in the Lohman Building offers a small museum and an audiovisual presentation about the history of the landing and Jefferson City.

Also of interest is the Safety Education Center and Law Enforcement Museum at the Missouri State Highway Patrol, 1510 E. Elm St. Exhibits include law enforcement antiques and five completely equipped patrol cars dating from 1931 to the present. Phone (573) 526-6149 Mon.-Fri. 8-5.

Stretching more than 200 miles from St. Charles to beyond Sedalia, Katy Trail State Park follows the former route of the Missouri-Kansas-Texas Railroad. Running parallel to the Missouri River, the trail takes hikers and bicyclists through open fields, forests and wetlands and past towering bluffs, and winds through such historic towns as Augusta, Boonville, Columbia, Defiance, Franklin and Marthasville as well as St. Charles and Jefferson City. For further information contact the Department of Natural Resources, P.O. Box 176, Jefferson City, MO 65102-0176; phone (573) 751-2479 or (800) 334-6946.

Jefferson City Convention & Visitors Bureau: 100 E. High St., P.O. Box 2227, Jefferson City, MO 65101. **Phone:** (573) 632-2820 or (800) 769-4183.

Self-guiding tours: Visitor guides and maps describing Jefferson City's historic attractions are available at the Jefferson City Convention & Visitors Bureau Mon.-Fri. 8-5.

GEM **MISSOURI STATE CAPITOL** is at 201 W. Capitol Ave. Built of Carthage stone, the building contains paintings by Thomas Hart Benton, Frank Brangwyn, N.C. Wyeth and other artists who have captured the state's legends, history and landscapes. The State Museum has exhibits interpreting Missouri's natural and cultural heritage on display in the History and Resources halls. **Hours:** Daily 8-5. Tours are given Mon.-Sat. on the hour 9-11 and 1-4, Sun. at 10, 11, 2 and 3. Closed Jan. 1, Easter, Thanksgiving and Dec. 25. **Cost:** Free. **Phone:** (573) 751-4127.

MISSOURI VETERINARY MUSEUM is at 2500 Country Club Dr. The museum contains more than 2,500 items and medical instruments relating to the veterinary profession—some extremely rare and many more than 100 years old. Videotapes about pet care and diseases can be viewed. **Time:** Allow 30 minutes minimum. **Hours:** Mon.-Fri. 9-4. **Cost:** Donations. **Phone:** (573) 636-8737.

RUNGE CONSERVATION NATURE CENTER is .5 mi. n. of jct. US 50 and US 63 on SR 179. Exhibits and nature trails depict varied Missouri habitats, including wetlands, rivers, farms, prairies, glades, forests and caves. A 2,400-gallon aquarium holds indigenous fish. **Time:** Allow 1 hour minimum. **Hours:** Mon.-Sat. 8-5, Sun. noon-5. Closed Jan. 1, Thanksgiving and Dec. 25. **Cost:** Free. **Phone:** (573) 526-5544.

JOPLIN (E-1) pop. 45,504, elev. 1,002′

Following the Civil War, mining companies that had established smelters along the Joplin Creek Valley engaged in fierce rivalry, splitting the town into two factions controlled by competing companies. The valley endured a reign of terror until the state general assembly came to the rescue in 1873 and reincorporated the two towns as the city of Joplin.

Once peace was established in Joplin, the railroad arrived and stimulated development of the zinc industry. Small plots produced great fortunes in zinc, which soon overtook lead production. Joplin's boom stabilized as smelters moved to new deposits outside town, and the more sedate industry of buying and selling ore developed. A railroad center by 1900, the city consequently attracted a number of industrial and wholesale companies.

Joplin is the home of Missouri Southern State College, which offers tours of its 310-acre campus. Noteworthy is a 2,500-piece collection of art reference material, focused on English architecture and furniture of the 16th and 17th centuries, in the Post Memorial Art Reference Library at 300 Main St.; phone (417) 782-7678.

Joplin Convention & Visitors Bureau: 602 S. Main St., Joplin, MO 64801. **Phone:** (417) 625-4789 or (800) 657-2534.

JOPLIN MUNICIPAL BUILDING is at 303 E. Third St. The last mural by Thomas Hart Benton, "Joplin at the Turn of the Century," graces the lobby. **Hours:** Mon.-Fri. 8-5. **Cost:** Free. **Phone:** (417) 624-0820.

JOPLIN MUSEUM COMPLEX is in Schifferdecker Park at Seventh St. and Schifferdecker Ave. The history of Joplin and its mining past are the focus of two museums. **Hours:** Tues.-Sat. 10-5 (also Tues. 5-7), Sun. 2-5. Closed holidays. **Cost:** $2; free (ages 0-4 and on Tues.); $5 (family). **Phone:** (417) 623-1180.

Dorothea Hoover Historical Museum, on the Schifferdecker Park grounds, is part of the Joplin Museum Complex and features a miniature animated circus, antique dolls, an 18th-century tavern, photographs and other displays recalling the Joplin of the 1870s. **Hours:** Tues.-Sat. 10-5 (also Tues. 5-7), Sun. 2-5. Closed holidays. **Cost:** (includes Tri-State Mineral Museum) $2; free (ages 0-4 and on Tues.); $5 (family). **Phone:** (417) 623-1180.

Tri-State Mineral Museum, on the Schifferdecker Park grounds, is part of the Joplin Museum Complex and displays local minerals and scale models of lead-mining apparatus. Antique mining equipment also is exhibited. **Hours:** Tues.-Sat. 10-5 (also Tues. 5-7), Sun. 2-5. Closed holidays. **Cost:** (includes Dorothea Hoover Historical Museum) $2; free (ages 0-4 and on Tues.); $5 (family). **Phone:** (417) 623-1180.

Kansas City

City Population: 441,545 **Elevation:** 1,005 ft.

Editor's Picks:

Arabia Steamboat Museum.......*(see p. 167)*

Harry S. Truman Library and Museum ....*(see p. 178)*

The Nelson-Atkins Museum of Art ....*(see p. 168)*

"I'm goin' to Kansas City, Kansas City here I come." So goes the 1950s hit with the hard to forget melody. Ditto for Kansas City – once you've sniffed its barbecue-scented air, felt the cool spray of a fountain and tapped your feet to its unique style of homegrown jazz, you'll never forget the experience, and you'll find yourself singing the city's praises.

From "Possumtrot" to the "Paris of the Plains," Kansas City has known a variety of names reflecting its history. In 1821, fur trader François Chouteau established a trading post near the Missouri River and called it "Chouteau's Town." Kansas City's prime location at the confluence of the Missouri and Kansas rivers as well as at the starting point of the Santa Fe and Oregon trails was instrumental to the area's growth.

Nicknames "Kawsmouth," "Possumtrot," and "Westport Landing" came into usage at various times during the 1800s when Kansas City was the final stop for travelers during the great westward migration, including those heading to California during the Gold Rush.

During the heyday of jazz in the 1920s and '30s, Kansas City was heralded as "The Paris of the Plains" due to its numerous jazz clubs and gambling halls and local government's bold disregard of Prohibition. "The Heart of America," a nickname still used today, refers primarily to the city's proximity to the geographic center of the United States.

By the late 1800s, the name "Kansas City" started to take a firm hold; it became official in 1850. Though the city by any other name would smell as sweet, the name Kansas City reflects both the city's modern, urban nature and its beginnings as the home of the American Indian Kansa tribe. Today, modern-day monikers "The City of Fountains" and "Barbecue Capital of the World" describe different aspects of this Midwestern city.

"The Scout", Penn Valley Park

Downtown Kansas City has been transformed with a $4.5 billion revitalization; visitors may be surprised to see that it has grown into a flourishing metropolis. Downtown's newest pride and glory is the Power & Light District, an entertainment complex spanning 8 city blocks. Opened with great fanfare in 2008, the area is brimming with hip restaurants, live music venues, dance clubs, and free rock and country music concerts in the summer.

Just footsteps away from the Power & Light District you'll find the Sprint Center, a sparkling wedding-band shaped entertainment and sports venue which opened in 2007. Glance at its mirror-like glass façade and you'll see a reflection of Kansas City's past and present in turn-of-the-20th-century red brick buildings juxtaposing gleaming stick-straight skyscrapers.

Due to downtown's renaissance, it is now the most popular entertainment choice in Kansas City; typically drawing millions of annual visitors. Kansas City's current music scene jumps, jives and wails, but its musical history goes way back to the 1920s and '30s, when blues-influenced Kansas City jazz was at its height of popularity. During this period, jazz aficionados had the pleasure of seeing musicians such as Count Basie, Charlie "Bird" Parker and Lester Young perform live.

Getting There — *starting on p. 165*

Getting Around — *starting on p. 165*

What To See — *starting on p. 166*

What To Do — *starting on p. 170*

Where To Stay — *starting on p. 464*

Where To Dine — *starting on p. 473*

Known as one of the cradles of jazz due to its heavily influential style, Kansas City also lays claim to the fact that the jam session was born here. After playing at the clubs, musicians couldn't put their instruments down and jammed together long into the night. Kansas City's fluid, spontaneous style of jazz eventually gave birth to an improvisational style called bebop; Kansas City native and saxophonist Parker was instrumental in this transition.

Besides its legendary contributions to jazz, Kansas City's cultural scene comprises a mix of art and history museums, theater, ballet, opera and an annual Shakespeare festival. Culture vultures will feel right at home in the city's high-caliber museums.

For a relaxing experience, there are plenty of serene green spaces where you can enjoy the fresh air and Mother Nature. Just footsteps away from shopping mecca Country Club Plaza, Loose Memorial Park is the ideal place to partake in a take-out meal from one of the Plaza's trendy restaurants and just, well, hang loose. The park is one of the city's most stunning, with a plush carpet of emerald grass, shade trees, a lake, picnic areas, tennis courts, jogging paths and a beautiful rose garden in-the-round surrounding a fountain.

In search of more fountains? You've come to the right place. Kansas City's collection of more than 200 fountains is interspersed throughout the city, earning Kansas City yet another nickname: "The City of Fountains." In fact, there are more fountains here than in almost any other city in the world; only Rome is thought to have more.

Originally built to provide water for the many horses that populated the city around the late 1800s, the fountains are now appreciated for their beauty and come in many shapes and sizes. At Kauffman Stadium, a 322-foot-wide fountain complete with a waterfall provides a show for spectators before games and between innings. Near Country Club Plaza in Mill Creek Park is the J.C. Nichols Fountain, named for the man who built the plaza. Eighty feet in diameter, this dramatic fountain features four 10-foot-high rearing horses, dolphins, cherubs and nine arching streams of water.

Fiesta Hispana / Missouri Division of Tourism

Of course, man cannot live by water alone. While driving around Kansas City, roll down your car window and breathe in – chances are you'll inhale the mouthwatering fragrance of barbecue sauce that permeates the air. Follow your nose to any of the plethora of barbecue restaurants; locals brag that Kansas City has more per capita than any city in the country. That's easy to believe: Just take a whiff of that barbecue-scented air and you'll see why so many call Kansas City the "Barbecue Capital of the World."

It's plain to see that Kansas City has outgrown its reputation as a cultural backwoods, blossoming into

Destination Kansas City

Kansas City wears its progress well. Once a river-bend trading post, the city evolved into a sizable commercial center that nevertheless has kept its small-town appeal intact.

Museums and historic districts celebrate varied cultural influences. And a racing roller coaster fills the bill for plain old-fashioned fun.

Missouri Division of Tourism

National World War I Museum at Liberty Memorial, Kansas City. (See listing page 168)

Missouri Division of Tourism

Vaile Mansion, Independence. (See listing page 179)

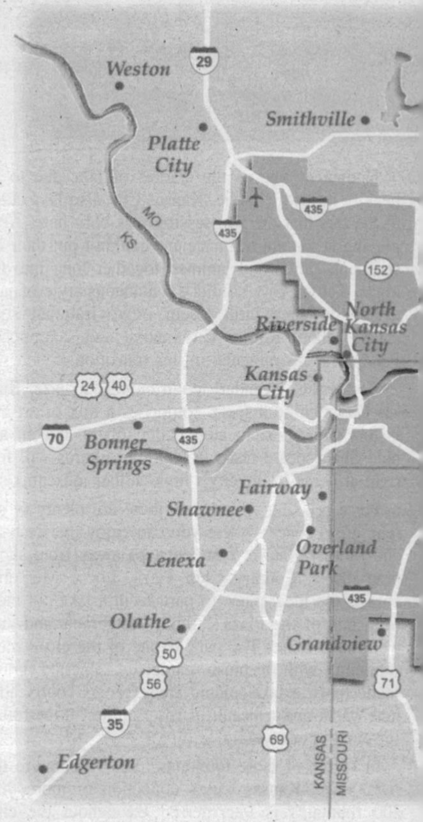

Places included in this AAA Destination City:

Missouri Division of Tourism

Harry S. Truman Library and Museum, Independence.
(See listing page 178)

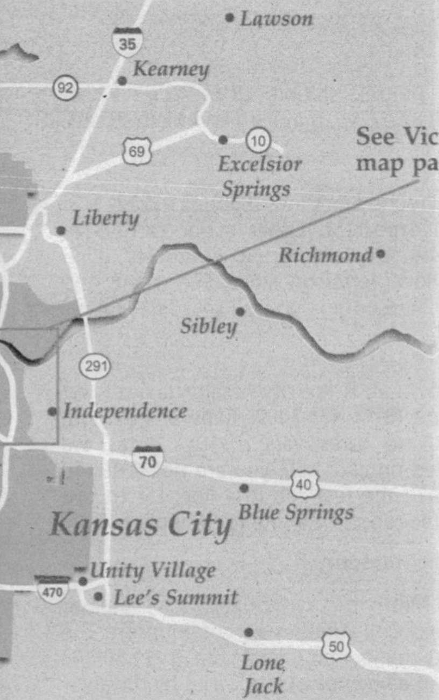

Kansas City Convention & Visitors Association

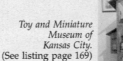

Renaissance Festival of Kansas City, Bonner Springs, Kan.
(See mention page 182)

Kansas City Convention & Visitors Association

Toy and Miniature Museum of Kansas City.
(See listing page 169)

The Informed Traveler

Sales Tax: The sales tax rate in the city of Kansas City is 7.55 percent. The city's lodging tax is 11.98 percent and there is a rental car tax of $4 per day.

WHOM TO CALL

Emergency: 911

Police (non-emergency): (816) 234-5000

Time: (913) 831-4141

Temperature: (816) 540-6021

Hospitals: Research Medical Center, (816) 276-4000; St. Joseph Medical Center, (816) 942-4400; Saint Luke's Hospital, (816) 932-2000; Saint Luke's Northland Hospital, (816) 891-6000; Truman Medical Center Hospital Hill, (816) 404-1000.

WHERE TO LOOK

Newspapers

The major daily newspaper in Kansas City is the *Kansas City Star.*

Radio

Kansas City radio station KCMO (810 AM) is an all news/weather station; KCUR (89.3 FM) is a member of National Public Radio.

Visitor Information

Kansas City Convention & Visitors Association: 1100 Main St., Suite 2200, Kansas City, MO 64105. **Phone:** (816) 221-5242, or (800) 767-7700 Mon.-Fri. 8:30-5.

Located in The City Center Square Building, the association distributes free brochures Mon.-Fri. 8:30-5; closed Jan. 1, Memorial Day, July 4, Labor Day, Thanksgiving, day after Thanksgiving and Dec. 25.

Missouri Welcome Center: 4010 Blue Ridge Cut-Off, Kansas City, MO 64133. **Phone:** (816) 889-3330.

The center is off I-70 exit 9 and Blue Ridge Cut-Off at the Harry S. Truman Sports Complex. It is open daily 8-5, Apr.-Oct.; Mon.-Sat. 8-5, rest of year.

TRANSPORTATION

Air Travel

Kansas City International Airport (KCI) is 17 miles northwest of downtown. Taxi fare into the city is about $50. Many larger hotels offer airport limousine service.

Rental Cars

Hertz, at the airport, offers discounts to AAA members; phone (816) 243-5765 or (800) 654-3080.

Rail Service

The Amtrak station, (816) 421-3622 or (800) 872-7245, is at 23rd and Main streets.

Buses

Greyhound Lines Inc., (800) 231-2222, is at 1101 Troost St. Other major carriers to Kansas City are Great Southern, Illini-Swallow, Jefferson Lines, Sunnyland and Gulf Transport.

Taxis

Yellow Cab is the city's major taxi service; phone (816) 471-5000. Cabs are deregulated, so fares vary widely. Rates are posted on each cab; you are not required to take the first cab in a line. Up to five people can share a ride for a single fare.

Public Transport

The Metro bus system serves all Greater Kansas City counties except Johnson. The exact-change fare minimum is $1.50 ($3 for an all-day pass) and varies by distance. For more details and for route information regarding construction, phone (816) 221-0660.

an energetic metropolis that attracts millions of visitors each year. Come and discover the city's special blend of smokin' barbecue, red-hot jazz, pulsating nightclubs, inspiring art collections, idyllic outdoor experiences and Midwestern charm and see what the buzz is all about.

Getting There

By Car

From the north, Kansas City is approached by two major controlled-access highways, I-35 and I-29, which merge into I-29/35, or US 71, and cross the Missouri River before leading into the downtown area via 13th Street. Running into Kansas City, Kan., from the south, I-35 provides direct controlled access to downtown via Washington Avenue and 12th Street.

On the Missouri side the fastest southern approach is via US 71, which connects with the I-435 bypass. The bypass circles the city and can be taken north to I-70. Beginning in St. Louis, I-70 bisects the state and enters Kansas City via the 13th Street exit. I-70 also is the controlled-access route from the west to downtown.

Getting Around

Street System

The Greater Kansas City area follows a basic grid pattern, slightly complicated by the Kansas and Missouri rivers. North Kansas City and Kansas City, Mo., are separated by the Missouri River, from which cross streets are numbered in ascending order well into the suburbs. The reference point for the east-west block designation in downtown Kansas City, Mo., is Main Street. Conversely, numbered streets in Kansas City, Kan., run on a north-south axis, paralleling the abrupt S-curve of the Missouri River.

State Line Road separates the Missouri and Kansas sides of the city. The street systems of both are peculiar to their own states, although several streets continue across the border unchanged. The main east-west artery over the Kansas River connecting the twin cities is I-70, which leads into US 24/40, the main route through downtown Kansas City, Kan.

I-70 also intersects other major thoroughfares that travel through and around town. The Southwest Trafficway provides rapid access into the central part of Kansas City, Mo.

Generally downtown speed limits are 25 mph or as posted. Right turns on red are permitted unless otherwise posted. Avoid rush hours, from about 6:30 to 8:30 a.m. and 3:30 to 6 p.m.

Parking

On-street parking is controlled by meters, but finding an empty space in the right spot can be difficult. Numerous commercial lots and garages are concentrated around Central and Grand avenues, between 9th and 14th streets, and at the southern edge of town. Rates average 90c per half-hour, with a maximum of $5.

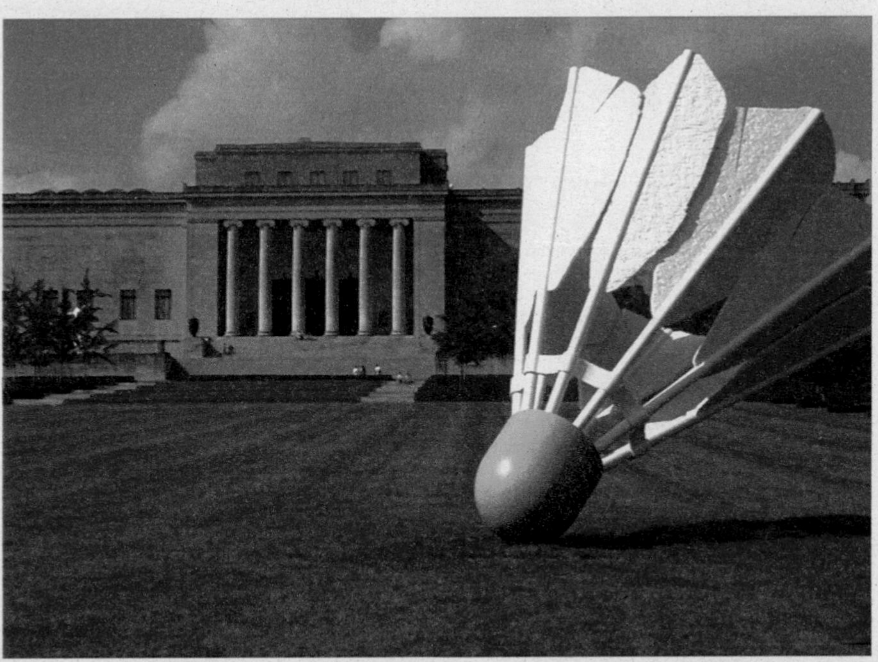

The Nelson-Atkins Museum of Art / Missouri Division of Tourism

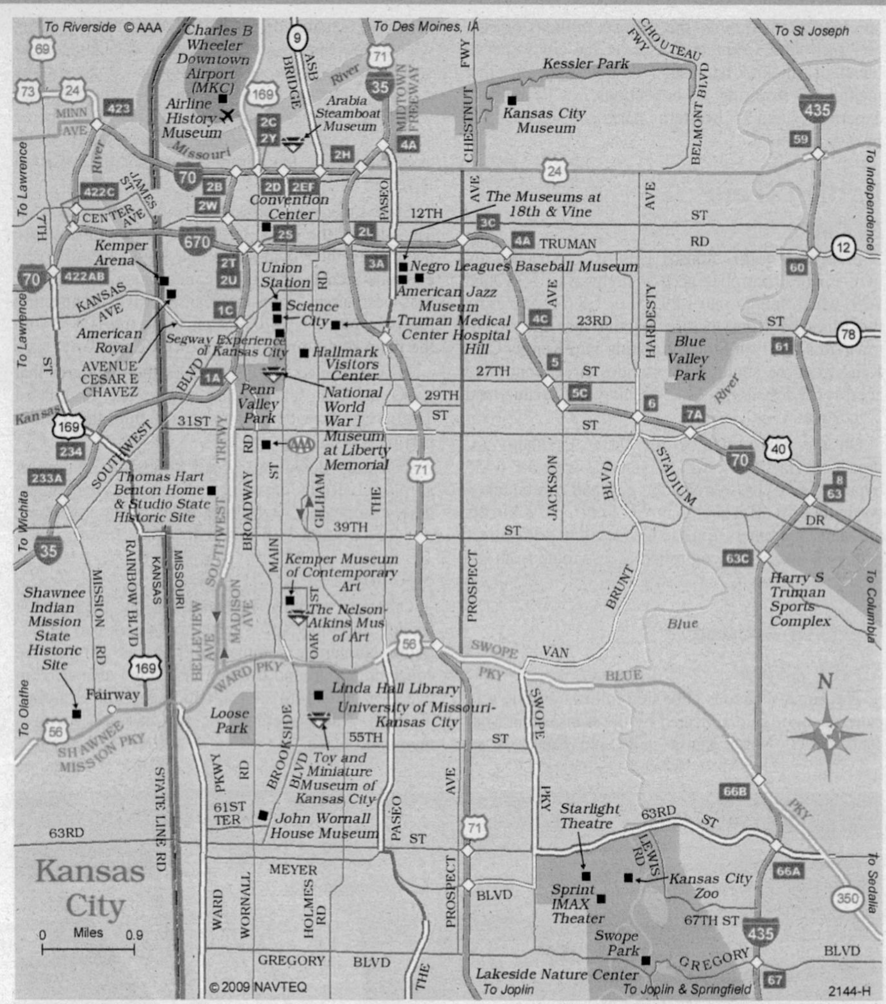

Parking also is available for $9 around the Truman Sports Complex and for $6-$15 at Kemper Arena. Several major downtown hotels are connected to the Kansas City Convention Center by an underground concourse.

What To See

AIRLINE HISTORY MUSEUM is at 201 N.W. Lou Holland Dr. The museum is housed inside the 40,000-square-foot Hangar 9, which once held aviation operations for major airlines. Of particular interest is a 1959 Lockheed Super Constellation, or "Connie," which is easily recognized by its triple tail and tip tanks on the wings. Other highlights are artifacts, photographs, uniforms and navigation instruments.

Tours: Guided tours are available. **Time:** Allow 1 hour minimum. **Hours:** Mon.-Sat. 10-4, Sun. noon-4. Last tour begins 1 hour before closing. Closed Jan. 1, Memorial Day, Thanksgiving and Dec. 25. **Cost:** $8; $7 (ages 65+ and military with ID); $4 (ages 6-12). **Phone:** (816) 421-3401 or (800) 513-9484.

AMERICAN ROYAL is 1 mi. w. from jct. 12th St. and Broadway, then .5 mi. s. on Genesee St. to 1701 American Royal Ct., following signs for Kemper Arena. American Royal began in 1899 at the Kansas City Stockyards as the nation's first purebred cattle show. From September through November, such events as livestock and horse shows, rodeos, barbecue contests and parades are held. A museum offers interactive displays relating to the agriculture and livestock industries, livestock judging and western lifestyle. Show clothing and memorabilia as well as a film detailing Kansas City history may be seen.

Food is available during events. **Time:** Allow 1 hour minimum. **Hours:** Mon.-Fri. 8:30-5, Sat.-Sun.

Leagues Baseball Museum $10; $5 (ages 4-11). **Phone:** (816) 474-8463.

Negro Leagues Baseball Museum, 1616 E. 18th St., is part of The Museums at 18th and Vine complex and recounts the formation and history of the Negro Baseball League prior to 1945, the year Jackie Robinson was signed by the Brooklyn Dodgers. Displays include pennants, autographed baseballs, photographs, biographies and an 8-minute videotape about the league narrated by former CNN anchorman Bernard Shaw.

Time: Allow 30 minutes minimum. **Hours:** Tues.-Sat. 9-6, Sun. noon-6. Closed holidays. **Cost:** $8; $3 (ages 4-11). Combination ticket with the American Jazz Museum $10; $5 (ages 4-11). **Phone:** (816) 221-1920 or (888) 221-6526.

GEM **NATIONAL WORLD WAR I MUSEUM AT LIBERTY MEMORIAL,** just s. of downtown at Pershing and Main sts. at 100 W. 26th St., is dedicated to collecting, preserving and interpreting the history of and artifacts associated with the first World War. The educational, thought-provoking displays and interactive exhibits include everything from posters, photographs, uniforms, archival films and vintage audio broadcasts to airplanes, artillery, weaponry, cannons, caissons, a 1917 model Harley-Davidson army motorcycle and a simulated World War I trench.

Chronological displays and firsthand accounts from diaries trace the history of the war from its beginning to the armistice of Nov. 11, 1918. A 217-foot-tall memorial tower has a frieze on one wall; visitors can take an elevator to an open-air observation deck at the top for panoramic views of downtown Kansas City. Several fountains grace the landscaped grounds.

Time: Allow 2 hours minimum. **Hours:** Tues.-Sun. and some Mon. holidays (including Memorial Day and Labor Day) 10-5. Closed Jan. 1, Thanksgiving and Dec. 25. **Cost:** (includes museum and tower) $12; $10 (ages 65+ and students with ID); $6 (ages 6-17); free (active and retired military with ID). **Phone:** (816) 784-1918.

GEM **THE NELSON-ATKINS MUSEUM OF ART** is 4.5 mi. s. on US 56 at 45th and Oak sts. With more than 33,000 art objects, the museum is recognized as having one of the country's finest encyclopedic art collections. Asian, American and European paintings and modern sculpture are among the prominent permanent exhibits. Ancient Egyptian, Etruscan, Greek and Roman pieces, as well as an extensive collection of English ceramics, also are displayed. Works by modern artists are featured in the 17-acre Kansas City Sculpture Park, said to hold the country's largest collection of monumental bronzes by English sculptor Henry Moore.

The 165,000-square-foot Bloch Building opened in 2007 and houses the museum's collection of African, contemporary and featured exhibitions, a reference library and a sculpture court. It also contains a premier photography collection of more than 7,000 works, including the impressive Hallmark Photography Collection featuring works from the beginning of photography to the present. Nearly all the key American photographers are represented. A surrounding reflecting pool highlights the building's north entrance. More than 6,000 square feet of new exhibition space dedicated to American Indian objects as fine art opened fall 2009.

Hours: Wed.-Fri. 10-4 (also Thurs.-Fri. 4-9), Sat. 10-5, Sun. noon-5. Guided tours depart Wed. at 1:30, Thurs.-Fri. at 1:30 and 7, Sat. at 11 and 1:30, Sun. at 1:30 and 3. Closed Jan. 1, July 4, Thanksgiving and Dec. 24-25. **Cost:** Free. **Parking:** Garage $5. **Phone:** (816) 751-1278.

OCEANS OF FUN—*see Worlds of Fun p. 170.*

PENN VALLEY PARK is at 31st and Main sts. Designer George E. Kessler transformed the 176-acre Penn Valley site from a slum area known as Vinegar Hill into this attractive retreat, the prototype for the city's park system. The park contains the American Indian memorial "The Scout," the statue "Pioneer Mother," a lake and scenic drives. **Hours:** Daily dawn-dusk. **Cost:** Free. **Phone:** (816) 784-5030.

SWOPE PARK is s.e. of downtown at jct. Meyer Blvd. and Swope Pkwy. This 1,772-acre park contains golf courses, tennis courts, picnic grounds and a swimming pool. A lagoon offers fishing, boating and ice-skating. During the summer, musicals and popular entertainers are presented nightly in the outdoor Starlight Theatre.

The park's Lakeside Nature Center houses native Missouri wildlife, has educational displays and offers nature trails. The center's staff rehabilitates injured wildlife. **Hours:** Park open daily 24 hours. Lakeside Nature Center open Tues.-Sat. 9-5, Sun. noon-4. **Cost:** Free. **Phone:** (816) 513-8960, or (816) 333-9481 for the Starlight Theatre.

Kansas City Zoo is in Swope Park at 6800 Zoo Dr. This 202-acre zoo exhibits animals in the Tropics, an indoor rain forest; Australian Outback; Asian Tiger Trail; Discovery Barn; and a 100-acre African Plains exhibit with a 4-acre chimp area. Polar bears will arrive in 2010. An endangered species carousel, train, tram, paddleboat and camel rides are available seasonally for an additional fee.

Allow a full day. **Hours:** Daily 9:30-4. Closed Jan. 1, Thanksgiving and Dec. 25. **Cost:** Wed.-Mon. $10.50; $9.50 (ages 55+); $7 (ages 3-11). Admission on Tues. $8; $7 (ages 55+); $6 (ages 3-11). **Phone:** (816) 513-5800.

THOMAS HART BENTON HOME & STUDIO STATE HISTORIC SITE is at 3616 Belleview Ave. Missouri's noted 20th-century artist lived here from 1939 until his death in 1975. The Victorian-style home and carriage house studio contain many of Benton's belongings. **Time:** Allow 30 minutes minimum. **Hours:** Mon. and Wed.-Sat. 10-4, Sun. noon-5, Apr. 15-Oct. 31; Mon. and Thurs.-Sat. 10-4, Sun. 11-4, rest of year. Closed Jan. 1, Thanksgiving by appointment. Phone ahead for event schedule. Closed major holidays. **Cost:** Museum $3; $2.50 (ages 55+); $2 (ages 3-12). Event tickets $12-$70. **Phone:** (816) 221-9800.

GEM *ARABIA* **STEAMBOAT MUSEUM** is at 400 Grand Ave. in the River Market area. The *Arabia* sank in the Missouri River in 1856 with a 200-ton cargo. This museum displays a vast collection of frontier supplies and personal belongings recovered from the steamboat in 1989, including clothing and shoes, medicines, guns, bottled fruits and vegetables, jewelry and perfume. The 6-ton stern and a paddlewheel are preserved with a full-size reproduction of the main deck. Guided tours include a theater presentation describing the excavation effort, and visitors may view a working preservation lab.

Time: Allow 1 hour, 30 minutes minimum. **Hours:** Mon.-Sat. 10-5:30, Sun. noon-5. Tours depart every 30 minutes. Last admission is 1 hour, 30 minutes before closing. Closed Jan. 1, Easter, Thanksgiving and Dec. 24-25. **Cost:** $12.50; $11.50 (ages 60+); $4.75 (ages 4-12). **Phone:** (816) 471-1856.

HALLMARK VISITORS CENTER is on 25th St. off Pershing in the Crown Center Complex. Twelve major exhibits relate the Hallmark story and the steps involved in the production of Hallmark products. Some exhibits feature Hallmark employees at work. **Hours:** Tues.-Fri. 9-5, Sat. 9:30-4:30. Closed early to mid-Jan., Thanksgiving and Dec. 25. **Cost:** Free. **Phone:** (816) 274-5672 or (816) 274-3613.

HARLEY-DAVIDSON ASSEMBLY PLANT AND VISITORS CENTER is at 11401 N. Congress. This is one of two Harley-Davidson motorcycle final assembly plants in the United States. The tour includes a videotape presentation and a chance to see the actual production line where the Dyna, Sportster and V-Rod models and the V-Rod's Revolution Powertrain motor are assembled. Audio headsets and safety glasses are provided.

Note: Tour participants must wear completely enclosed shoes. Cameras are permitted in the tour center but not on the plant tour. **Time:** Allow 1 hour, 30 minutes minimum. **Hours:** Center open Mon.-Fri. 9-3. One-hour guided tours are given Mon.-Fri. 9-1:30. Closed holidays and during model change and year-end maintenance periods. **Cost:** Free. Ages 0-11 are not permitted on the plant tour. Reservations are recommended for parties of 10 or more. **Phone:** (816) 270-8488 or (877) 883-1450.

JOHN WORNALL HOUSE MUSEUM is at jct. 61st Terr. and Wornall Rd. This restored 1858 Greek Revival plantation house is furnished in period. A formal herb garden is on the grounds. **Hours:** Tues.-Sat. 10-4, Sun. 1-4. Closed major holidays. **Cost:** $6; $5 (ages 5-12 and 60+). **Phone:** (816) 444-1858.

KANSAS CITY MUSEUM is at 3218 Gladstone Blvd., adjacent to Cliff Drive Scenic Byway and Kessler Park. The museum is housed in Corinthian Hall, a 50-room mansion built in 1910 by industrialist Robert A. Long and named for the six Corinthian columns at its entrance. The 50-seat StoryTarium theater, in what was formerly the museum's planetarium, presents documentaries, films, lectures and other history programming. The Long Family and Corinthian Hall outdoor exhibit offers vibrantly colored panels detailing the history of the Long family and the 3-acre estate and also presents a collection of vintage Kansas City postcards.

Note: Corinthian Hall and the Natural History Hall are undergoing a restoration which may last until at least 2012; both are currently closed. StoryTarium and the visitor center, on the north side of the estate, remain open. **Time:** Allow 1 hour minimum. **Hours:** Tues.-Sat. 9:30-4:30, Sun. noon-4:30. StoryTarium shows take place upon request. Closed Thanksgiving and Dec. 24-25. **Cost:** Free (during restoration period). **Phone:** (816) 483-8300.

KEMPER MUSEUM OF CONTEMPORARY ART is just e. of 45th and Main sts. at 4420 Warwick Blvd. Georgia O'Keeffe, Robert Mapplethorpe and William Wegman are among the artists represented in a permanent collection of diverse, modern works. **Time:** Allow 1 hour minimum. **Hours:** Tues.-Sat. 10-4 (also Fri.-Sat. 4-9), Sun. 11-5. Closed major holidays. **Cost:** Free. **Phone:** (816) 561-3737 or (816) 753-5784.

LINDA HALL LIBRARY adjoins the University of Missouri-Kansas City campus on Rockhill Rd. Devoted exclusively to science and technology, it is a repository for all American, British and Canadian atomic energy publications and other technical journals, some dating from the 17th century. An enormous ornamental Russian bowl of carved malachite graces the main floor. **Hours:** Mon.-Fri. 9-5 (also Mon. 5-8:30), Sat. 10-4, Sept.-July; Mon.-Fri. 9-5 (also Mon. 5-8:30), rest of year. **Cost:** Free. **Phone:** (816) 363-4600 or (800) 662-1545.

THE MUSEUMS AT 18TH AND VINE are .3 mi. s. off I-70 Paseo exit, then e. to 1616 E. 18th St. This complex, in the heart of one of the country's most celebrated jazz and blues districts, encompasses the American Jazz Museum and the Negro Leagues Baseball Museum. The Horace M. Peterson III Visitor Center offers a brief videotape celebrating the African-American community that thrived at 18th and Vine for more than 40 years.

Hours: Museums and visitor center open Tues.-Sat. 9-6, Sun. noon-6. Closed major holidays. **Cost:** Visitor center free. Each museum $8; $3 (ages 4-11). Combination ticket for both museums $10; $5 (ages 4-11). **Phone:** (816) 474-8463.

American Jazz Museum, 1616 E. 18th St., is part of The Museums at 18th and Vine complex and recalls jazz greats Louis Armstrong, Duke Ellington, Ella Fitzgerald, Charlie Parker and others through listening stations, photographs, videos and memorabilia. **Time:** Allow 1 hour minimum. **Hours:** Tues.-Sat. 9-6, Sun. noon-6. Closed holidays. **Cost:** $8; $3 (ages 4-11). Combination ticket with the Negro

Dec. 25. **Cost:** $2.50; $1.50 (ages 6-12). **ne:** (816) 931-5722 or (800) 334-6946.

GEM **TOY AND MINIATURE MUSEUM OF KANSAS CITY** is at 5235 Oak St. This museum on the campus of University of souri-Kansas City brings out the child in every- with thousands of well-loved toys and minia- s dating from the Victorian era through the 20th tury.

Each of the museum's 38 rooms is devoted to a ticular type of toy: The collection includes teddy rs; toy soldiers; board games; Victorian dolls; ive American and Asian miniatures; dollhouses; iron cars, trains and airplanes; and dolls from ry corner of the world. The Marble Gallery con- s more than 1 million miniature glass orbs; sts can play a game of marbles or watch them go und a floor-to-ceiling maze.

More than 100 dollhouses are furnished with an- ue and fine-scale miniatures made by master ftsmen. Notable pieces include a miniature rep- a of the Palace of Versailles; exquisite lacquer xes from Russia painted with fairy tale scenes; orgiana, a 26-inch-tall English doll circa 1750; wn glass vases no bigger than a thumbnail; and niature working musical instruments.

Throughout the year, the museum holds special ents including storytelling, scavenger hunts, fam- days, holiday events and craft workshops as well temporary toy exhibits. **Time:** Allow 1 hour nimum. **Hours:** Wed.-Sat. 10-4, Sun. 1-4. Last mission is 45 minutes before closing. Closed ma- holidays and the first 2 weeks of Sept. **Cost:** $6; (senior citizens and students with ID); $4 (ages 12). Ages 0-15 must be accompanied by an adult. **one:** (816) 333-2055.

NION STATION is at 30 W. Pershing Rd. More an 79,000 trains passed through this terminal at its peak in 1917, and half of all GIs deployed in World War II traveled under its great clock. Restored in 1999, the station is now home to Science City *(see attraction listing)*; KC Rail Experience, a railroad exhibit; theaters and restaurants. The Grand Hall features 95-foot ceilings with ornate plaster ornaments. The Theater District includes the five-story Extreme Screen, live performances on City Stage, and a planetarium.

Hours: Union Station open daily 6 a.m.-midnight for train arrivals and departures. Attractions open Tues.-Sat. 9:30-5:30, Sun. noon-5:30. Phone for performance schedules. **Cost:** Union Station building free. "One-way ticket" (includes planetarium, KC Rail Experience or Extreme Screen) $7; "Express ticket" (includes Science City and planetarium) $9.50; "Round-trip ticket" (includes Science City, planetarium and Extreme Screen) $14.50; "First-class ticket" (includes KC Rail Experience, Science City, planetarium and Extreme Screen) $19.50; free (ages 0-2). **Phone:** (816) 460-2020.

Science City is in Union Station at 30 W. Pershing Rd. An exhibit center, animal and nature center, a crime lab and a bicycle suspended 30 feet above ground are among the more than 50 hands-on interactive areas where visitors can learn while having fun.

Hours: Tues.-Sat. 9:30-5:30, Sun. noon-5:30. Closed Thanksgiving and Dec. 24-25 and 31. **Cost:** Union Station building free. "One-way ticket" (includes planetarium KC Rail Experience or Extreme Screen) at Union Station $7; "Express ticket" (includes Science City and planetarium) $9.50; "Round-trip ticket" (includes Science City, planetarium and Extreme Screen at Union Station) $14.50; "First-class ticket" (includes Science City and planetarium as well as Extreme Screen and KC Rail Experience at Union Station) $19.50; free (ages 0-2). **Phone:** (816) 460-2020.

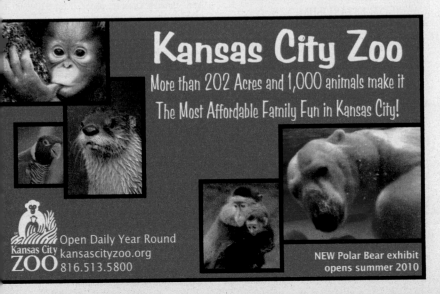

WORLDS OF FUN is off I-435 exit 54 (Parvin Rd.) at 4545 Worlds of Fun Ave. This 235-acre entertainment complex combines an amusement park and a tropical water park. Worlds of Fun offers 175 acres of rides, shows and attractions in five internationally themed areas. Featured are MAMBA, one of the tallest, longest and fastest coasters in the world; Timber Wolf, a world-class wooden coaster; ThunderHawk, a tumble and spin ride; and The Prowler, a wooden coaster reaching 51 mph. Camp Snoopy is a 1-acre playland with Peanuts-themed rides and characters.

Hours: Park opens daily at 10, mid-May to late Aug. and Labor Day weekend; Sat.-Sun. at 10, early Apr. to mid-May and day after Labor Day weekend-late Oct. Closing times vary. **Cost:** $40.99; $18.99 (ages 3+, ages 62+ and under 48 inches tall). Twilight rate $25.99 (Sat. 6 p.m.-midnight); $22.99 (Fri. after 6 p.m. and Sun. after 3 p.m.). Combination ticket with Oceans of Fun $54.99; $30.99 (ages 3+, ages 62+ and under 48 inches tall). Phone ahead to confirm rates. **Parking:** $10 per single-space vehicle. **Phone:** (816) 454-4545.

Oceans of Fun is off I-435 exit 54 (Parvin Rd.) at 4545 Worlds of Fun Ave. This 60-acre tropical-themed water park features the Surf City Wave Pool, a million-gallon pool with 4-foot waves; Hurricane Falls, an eight-story-high family raft ride; and a variety of other waterslides. Special areas of the park are designed specifically for children and for adults.

Hours: Water park opens daily at 10, Memorial Day weekend-late Aug. and Labor Day weekend. Closing time varies. **Cost:** $28.99; $15.99 (ages 3+, ages 62+ and under 48 inches tall); $17.99 (after 3 p.m.). Combination ticket with Worlds of Fun $54.99; $30.99 (ages 3+, ages 62+ and under 48 inches tall). **Parking:** $10 per single-space vehicle. **Phone:** (816) 454-4545.

GAMBLING ESTABLISHMENTS

- **Ameristar Casino** is at 3200 N. Ameristar Dr. **Hours:** Sun.-Thurs 8 a.m.-5 a.m., Fri.-Sat. 24 hours. **Phone:** (816) 414-7000 or (866) 667-3386.
- **Isle of Capri Casino** is at 1800 E. Front St. **Hours:** Sun.-Thurs. 8 a.m.-5 a.m., Fri.-Sat. 24 hours. **Phone:** (816) 855-7777 or (800) 843-4753.

What To Do

Sightseeing

Driving Tours

"Day Tours from Kansas City," a 40-page booklet detailing eight trips within a day's drive, is available to AAA/CAA members free at any AAA service office in Missouri. *See AAA Offices.*

Segway Tours

SEGWAY EXPERIENCE OF KANSAS CITY is in the center of the Grand Hall inside of Union Station at 30 W. Pershing Rd. Using Segways—self-balancing, two-wheeled personal transportation devices that respond to the rider's slightest movements—visitors coast by and learn about the architectural history and significance of such landmarks and sites as Liberty Memorial and Washington Square Park. Tours of Union Station, the country's second largest train station, focus on its hidden treasures and the features it retains from its heyday in the early 1900s. One- and 2-hour, as well as 90-minute, tours to the Kansas City Zoo also are offered.

Time: Allow 30 minutes minimum. **Hours:** Tours are offered Tues.-Sat. 10-5 (also Fri.-Sat. 5-5:30), Sun. noon-5, Apr.-Jan. Phone ahead to verify tour availability and schedule. Closed Jan. 1, Easter, Thanksgiving and Dec. 25. **Cost:** $20-$90. Reservations are required. **Phone:** (816) 531-0600.

Sports and Recreation

Major league all the way, Kansas City offers a wide range of professional sports. Following their teams with a passionate involvement, Kansas City fans pile into the 118,000-seat Harry S. Truman Sports Complex, with its outstanding stadiums for **baseball** and **football.**

The Kansas City Royals draw a loyal baseball following April through September to Kauffman Stadium, which has received a $250 million renovation that began in October 2007. The facility claims Major League Baseball's largest replay system. Phone (816) 921-8000. Football is a passion for the die-hard fans of the National Football League's Kansas City Chiefs, who play to capacity crowds in Arrowhead Stadium, phone (816) 920-9400. Renovations bringing many enhancements to the stadium are scheduled to be completed prior to the 2010 season. The Big Eight Conference games draw devoted fans from the universities of Missouri and Kansas.

College **basketball** is popular during the winter months. Major league **soccer's** Kansas City Wizards place their spell over fans at Arrowhead Stadium April through October; phone (816) 920-9300 for schedule and ticket information.

Kansas City's 302 public parks provide opportunities for a variety of recreational pursuits, including **boating, hiking** and **picnicking.** Three parks in particular are known for their natural beauty and developed facilities: Loose Memorial Park, 51st Street and Wornall Road; Swope Park *(see attraction listing p. 168)*, Meyer Boulevard and Swope Parkway; and Fleming Park *(see Recreation Chart and attraction listing p. 179)*, at US 40 and Woods Chapel Road in Lee's Summit and Blue Springs, in eastern Jackson County.

Opportunities for **golf** are available in Swope Park, which has two of the oldest and most difficult 18-hole courses in the city. The Minor Park Golf Center, Red Bridge and Holmes roads, is a challenging course. Considered by some to be the city's best course, River Oaks is just south of the Kansas City limits at 14204 St. Andrews Dr. in Grandview.

Courses outside Kansas City, Mo., include Chapel Ridge Golf Club, SR 291 and Woods Chapel Road in Lee's Summit; Rockwood Golf Course, 2400 S. Maywood Ave. in Independence; and Shamrock Hills, S. SR 291 in Lee's Summit.

Courses outside Kansas City, Kan., include Overland Park Golf Club, 12501 Quivira Rd. in Overland Park; St. Andrews Golf Club, 11099 W. 135th St. in Overland Park; and Tomahawk Hills, 17501 Midland Dr. in Shawnee.

More than 200 public **tennis** courts are within the Kansas City metropolitan area. Most are free and available on a first-come, first-served basis. The Parks and Recreation Department, (816) 513-7500, will supply locations. Swope Park has courts at the picnic area north of the Starlight Theatre.

The following parks have at least four courts: Concourse, at Anderson and Bellefontaine; King Square, at Swope Parkway and Woodland; Loose Memorial Park, at 52nd Terrace and Summit; Mill Creek Park, at 47th Street and J.C. Nichols Parkway; and Plaza, at 47th and Main streets.

Bicycling is popular on the trails in Swope Park; bicycles can be rented at Shelter House One at the park entrance.

In the winter Kansas City's parks draw visitors for **cross-country skiing.** The lagoon in Loose Memorial Park is a favorite **ice-skating** pond, as is the Ice Terrace, the outdoor ice skating rink at Crown Center, 2450 Grand Ave.

Kansas Speedway at I-70 and I-435 draws **motorsports** fans for NASCAR Sprint Cup Series, Nationwide Series and additional racing events; phone (913) 328-7223. **Horse racing** and **dog racing** are offered seasonally at Woodlands, 99th Street and Leavenworth Road off I-435 in Kansas City, Kan.; phone (913) 299-9797.

Note: Policies concerning admittance of children to pari-mutuel betting facilities vary. Phone for information.

Shopping

Kansas City may not be the first place that springs to mind when you're looking for a vacation spot with prime shopping, but visit its various shopping districts and you just may uncover the city's best-kept secret. From its days as a trading post outfitting settlers heading west, to today's upscale plazas and artsy emporiums outfitting customers in *au courant* styles from designers like Burberry and Prada, Kansas City has a long-held tradition of satisfying the needs and desires of residents and travelers through its retail establishments.

The model for today's outdoor shopping villages, Country Club Plaza (47th Street and J.C. Nichols Parkway) is the jewel in the crown of Kansas City's shopping experiences. Built by J.C. Nichols, a wealthy developer with vision, the plaza opened in 1923 and was the nation's first suburban shopping complex designed intentionally for those with automobiles. Doubting townspeople dubbed the plaza Nichol's Folly because it was built in a swampy area used for pig farming, but the plaza was a success from the start.

More than 80 years later, Country Club Plaza draws squeals of delight from shopaholics, who discover a bounty of world-famous designer shops such as Betsey Johnson, Coach and Tiffany & Co.; trendsetting brands like Anthropologie, BCBGMAXAZRIA and J.Crew; traditional clothiers including Ann Taylor, Brooks Brothers and Talbots; and local boutiques among the plaza's collection of 150 shops. Well-known chain restaurants, local bistros and the 1928 Palace at the Plaza Theater round out the mix.

Not your run-of-the-mill outdoor shopping center, Country Club Plaza was designed with Seville, Spain in mind and has the feel of an open-air European marketplace. Its breathtaking architecture has a Spanish and Moorish influence, as evidenced by the 12 towers looming over the terracotta rooftops; the most notable is a 130-foot-tall reproduction of Spain's Giralda Tower. More than 40 fountains and statues imported from Europe fill the plaza; intricate mosaic murals made of Spanish tile adorn storefronts; and terracotta planters, window boxes and street medians overflow with lush, colorful plants.

A trip to the plaza is not complete without a stop at Kansas City's own Halls department store. Hallmark Cards founder Joyce C. Hall built the first Halls in 1913; this location opened in 1965. This dignified *grand dame* of Kansas City retail takes up an entire block with 3 stories of men's and women's couture and designer fashions, shoes and accessories from such designers as Kate Spade, Manolo Blahnick and Prada.

You'll also discover home décor including crystal, silver and china; a Hallmark card shop; and decadent Christopher Elbow chocolates at Halls. Even if you have Gucci taste and a Gap pocketbook, come in and window shop. Friendly salespeople are eager to talk about the latest fashions–quite the opposite of what you might expect at an upscale store.

Special events are held year-round at the plaza. During a free concert series from May through September, reggae, rock, R&B and bluegrass music fills the air on Thursday, Saturday and Sunday evenings. To celebrate the holiday season, the plaza presents the Plaza Lighting Ceremony. Held every Thanksgiving night since 1925, the highly anticipated event draws thousands as the switch is thrown and 80 miles of sparkling lights outline shops and restaurants in a kaleidoscope of colors.

Throughout the year, explore the plaza via a horse-drawn carriage; from April through November, experience a bit of Venice on a romantic gondola ride on adjacent Brush Creek.

In contrast to the European style of Country Club Plaza, the Crown Center (2450 Grand Blvd.) opened in 1973 and is contemporary in design. Adjacent to the headquarters of Hallmark Cards in the heart of downtown, the center is anchored by Halls department store. About 30 shops on 3 levels purvey jewelry, toys, gifts, and clothing, while an assortment of restaurants runs the gamut from fast food to fine dining.

At the Crayola Store and Café, kids will be thrilled to find every Crayola product imaginable. The impeccably dressed youngster will delight in the selection at the Kid Oh! department in Halls, which features child-size versions of Juicy Couture, Lacoste and Ugg.

Many of the shops and restaurants have kid appeal, but there are plenty of choices for grown-ups. Pick up fancy collars and bowls for your pets as well as home accents at Gatos Cat Boutique and Playful Paws. Stop in at mall faves Bath & Body Works, Victoria's Secret and Waldenbooks or seek out the unusual at eclectic specialty shops hawking items such as autographed posters, holiday decorations, Russian dolls, cooking gear and electric trains.

For another type of shopping experience, try Westport Square (between Westport Road and Pennsylvania Avenue). Westport's turn-of-the-20th-century red brick buildings are occupied by shops, cafés, pubs and entertainment venues that attract a young, edgy crowd. Perhaps one of the most popular shops is StreetSide Records (4128 Broadway St.), a cool indie record store with 2 floors of used and new records, CDs and DVDs. It's easy to find StreetSide; just look for a retro building that looks like it was a diner in a previous life, topped with a neon sign.

Marked by a sign that reads "David R. Spivey—Maps Books & Fine Art," Spivey's (825 Westport Rd.) is almost as rare a find as some of the antique books that fill its 5 floors. Climb narrow, creaky stairs to see the massive collection of rare and antique books, maps, fine art, prints and first editions. Don't be surprised if you find letters autographed by Harry Truman or a first edition of Mark Twain's "Life on the Mississippi." Housed in a red brick building built in 1910, the shop is on a street that was part of the Santa Fe Trail.

Enter Pryde's Olde Westport (115 Westport Rd.) and within minutes you'll be handed a mug of coffee or tea to sip while you shop. This divine emporium overflows with charm as well as everything you need for your kitchen (except the kitchen sink). Fiesta Ware, gourmet foods, knife blocks, teapots, bakeware, potato peelers, nutmeg graters—if you can use it in the kitchen, Pryde's has it. Shop here on Friday or Saturday and buy a scrumptious made-from-scratch fruit or cream pie at the store's bakery, The Upper Crust.

Other shops worth checking out in Westport Square are Re-Runs, a vintage clothing store (4126 Pennsylvania Ave.); Lomavista Hardware (311 Westport Rd.), which sells an unlikely combination of hardware and skateboarding gear; Bon Bon Atelier (314 Westport Rd.), offering cute home décor, gifts, jewelry and fashions for the modern girl; and Central American Textile Company (4120 Pennsylvania Ave.), where you'll find hand-loomed textiles made in Guatemala.

For a true Main Street-style shopping experience, explore Brookside's shopping district (on 63rd Street between Wornall and Main streets). Serving locals since 1920, Brookside presents cafés and shops under blue and red-striped awnings including the New Dime Store (314 W. 63rd St.), an old-fashioned five-and-dime complete with creaky wood floors; Stuff (316 W. 63rd St.), an artsy bazaar offering affordable art in the forms of jewelry, home goods and other stuff; ShopGirls (6245 Brookside Plaza), a funky fashion boutique; and Brookside Barkery and Bath (118 W. 63rd St.), purveyor of pet-pampering products.

Scenesters and trendsetters flock to the Crossroads Art District, a downtown area comprising 1 square mile centered around 20th Street and Baltimore Avenue. Among its art galleries and boutiques are Retro Inferno (1500 Grand Ave.), a wonderland of fabulous midcentury furnishings and collectibles housed in a groovy 1960s-era building; Black Bamboo (1815 Wyandotte St.), offering Asian antiques and modern home furnishings; Bob Jones Shoes (1914 Grand Blvd.), a Kansas City institution with more than 100,000 pairs of shoes in stock; and Birdie's (124 W. 18th St.), specializing in lacy lingerie.

On the prowl for antiques? Seven blocks west of Country Club Plaza lies the 45th & State Line Antique, Art & Design Center, a quaint enclave of more than a dozen shops clustered on the 1700 and 1800 blocks of 45th Street, just steps away from the Kansas/Missouri state line. The center's respected merchants deal in such treasures as American, Asian and European fine art, furnishings and architectural salvage.

Thirteen miles north of downtown, Zona Rosa (8640 N. Dixson Ave.) is a little out of the way but worth the trip if you like the old-fashioned feel of Main Street shopping combined with nationally known mall stores. Outdoor spaces with fountains and park benches allow for a relaxing experience. More than 60 shops include Aéropostale, Chico's, Express, Dick's Sporting Goods, Dillard's, Gap, Kay Jewelers and Sephora. Choose from more than a dozen restaurants to satisfy your appetite.

Other Kansas City shopping malls that will meet or exceed your desire for shopping convenience are Independence Center, I-70 and SR 291 in Independence; The Legends at Village West, 1843 Village West Parkway in Kansas City, Kan.; Metcalf South Shopping Center, 9635 Metcalf Ave. in Overland Park, Kan.; Oak Park Mall, 11461 W. 95th St. in Overland Park, Kan.; Town Center Plaza, 5000 W. 119th Street in Leawood, Kan.; and Ward Parkway, 8600 Ward Pkwy.

Nightlife

Kansas City is well-known for its jazz scene—that's a given. But there's also some good rockin' to be found, and not just at midnight. Kansas City is not the sleepy Midwestern town it's rumored to be, but you may be quite sleepy after you've hit the city's top nightspots. The joints are jumping into the wee hours of the morning, but get an early start, because there's a lot of ground to cover.

One of the city's premier entertainment districts (and its newest) is downtown's **Kansas City Power & Light District** (bordered by Grand Boulevard and Baltimore Street, and 12th Street and Truman Road). The "P & L," as it's locally known, made its debut in 2008 and comprises bars, nightclubs, shops and restaurants in an eight-block area. The hub of the P & L is **The Live Block**, where music-loving crowds gather in a covered outdoor courtyard to hear national rock and country acts perform for free in the summer.

More than a dozen nightclubs surround the Live Block, which has an open liquor permit and heaters for cooler nights. The Power & Light District is also a great place to hang out for some wining and dining pre- and post-show at the Sprint Center.

Within walking distance of the P & L, the **Sprint Center** (1407 Grand Blvd.) has brought the biggest names in entertainment to Kansas City since its opening in 2007: Dave Matthews Band, Miley Cyrus, Bruce Springsteen and Trans-Siberian Orchestra are just a few who have played for audiences of about 18,000 adoring fans. Music lovers revel in the quantity and quality of live shows, but sports aficionados also fill the arena for ice hockey and college and pro basketball games.

Variety is the name of the game at the Power & Light District with an assortment of dance clubs, rock and country joints, sports bars, live music venues and laid-back pubs. Trip the light fantastic in one of its high-energy dance clubs. **Shark Bar** (1340 Grand Blvd.) and **Mosaic Lounge** (1331 Walnut St.) entertain a crowd of mostly twenty-somethings with thumping deejayed music and crowded dance floors, but there the comparison ends. Mosaic has a swanky ultra lounge vibe with comfy seating and a balcony where you can ooh and aah at the glimmering lights of downtown Kansas City. Shark Bar's beachy décor and retro 1970s surf music is summed up in its motto: "retro surf...retro dance...retro cool."

Are you ready to rock?! Things can get a little rowdy at **Angel's Rock Bar** (1323 Walnut St.), where you'll find good rockin' for a few hours before and after midnight. Order some suds, a mixed drink or fine champagne at the 130-foot-long bar and get your groove on to live or deejayed rock-and-roll tunes from the 1970s to the present.

Or is country music more your style? Put on your best cowboy boots and sashay on into **PBR Big Sky** (111 E. 13th St.) where they play both kinds of music: country and western. Make the acquaintance of Norman, the mechanical bull, but be careful: He can be a bit ornery.

If you're the pub-going type, the P & L has several choices that are sure to intoxicate. The traditional warm walnut wood décor at the following pubs welcomes whistle-whetters with the widest selections of international brews in town (there's also whiskey or wine if you want it). Keep your thirst at bay at the **Flying Saucer Draught Emporium** (101 E. 13th St.), **McFadden's Sports Saloon** (1330 Grand Blvd.); and **Raglan Road Irish Pub** (170 E. 14th St.). Boisterous barkeeps and frosty-mug-hoisting patrons contribute to the homey neighborhood bar atmosphere.

Local and national acts in a variety of genres take the stage at the P & L's **Midland by AMC** theater (1228 Main St.), which can hold up to 3,000 spectators. In 2009, ticketholders applauded comedian David Sedaris, dance troupe Celtic Thunder and musical artists including Rob Thomas, Leonard Cohen and Widespread Panic. Thirsty concertgoers can grab a cold one at the Midland's in-house bar **The Indie on Main** before and after shows; those in the bar before a show are allowed to enter the venue first.

Before the Power & Light District was even a glimmer in the city's eye, the most happening spot for hipsters was the **Westport District** (Westport Road and Pennsylvania Avenue). With its diverse assortment of restaurants, bars and boutiques ensconced in 100-year-old brick buildings, today Westport attracts locals who have been coming here for years as well as out-of-towners looking for a friendly neighborhood joint.

Kelly's Westport Inn (500 Westport Rd.), housed in what may be the city's oldest building (circa 1850), is one of the most popular pubs in this neck of the woods. Sports memorabilia hangs on the walls and neon beer signs glow in this unpretentious watering hole that long ago was home to a general store operated by Daniel Boone's grandson. Years later, singer Bono of the band U2 stopped by for a pint and gave it his seal of approval. Throw your extra quarters in the jukebox, toss back a few, and stay awhile.

The Beaumont Club (4050 Pennsylvania Ave.) has a split personality; on some nights it's a country bar and on other nights you'll see live indie, rock or country bands, but any night of the week it's a local favorite. Take your turn at one of a half-dozen pool tables or the mechanical bull. A large dance floor is perfect for line-dancing or for concertgoers to stand on.

Revisit the 1970s at **The Foundry at McCoy's** (424 Westport Rd.). Paneled walls, beaded room dividers, bean bag chairs, Pac Man and even the font on the sign outside will remind you of your aunt's basement circa 1975, except your aunt probably didn't have 140 varieties of beer to choose from on a menu with 15 categories of suds ranging from lager to pale ales. Don't feel left out if you're not a connoisseur of the poor man's champagne; The Foundry supplements its menu with fine wine and martinis named after supermodels.

Don't let the plain name of **Harry's Bar & Tables** (501 Westport Rd.) fool you. This contemporary cigar and martini bar is a chic hangout that also serves up delicious steak and seafood; the kitchen doesn't close until 2 a.m. so you can satisfy those midnight munchies. More than 50 brands of scotch and 30 types of cigars are also on the menu.

Finally, pay a visit to the **recordBar** (1020 Westport Rd.) and catch live performances by indie bands with creative names like The Caves, High Diving Ponies and Pet the Dog. You can also eat to the beat here. Pizzas come in two sizes: 45 rpm and LP, and sandwiches have names like I Melt With You and the Hip To Be Square burger.

The beat goes on at the **18th & Vine Jazz District**, which is home to some smokin' nightclubs. If you love *le jazz hot*, this is your territory. Rated among the top jazz venues on the planet by Downbeat magazine, by day **The Blue Room** (1600 E. 18th St.) is a part of the American Jazz Museum *(see attraction listing p. 167)* with memorabilia tucked under glass-topped tables, but at night the jazz is so hot it burns.

After midnight, swing by the **Mutual Musicians Foundation** (1823 Highland Ave.) where jazzmen and bluesmen burn the midnight oil during intense jam sessions that don't end until 6 in the morning. Keep in mind that the Foundation also serves alcoholic beverages until 6 a.m.

Although the 18th & Vine District is home to some amazing jazz joints, there are some legendary clubs in other parts of town. The red walls can barely contain the red-hot jazz performed nightly by quartets and solo chanteuses at **Jardine's Restaurant & Jazz Club** (4536 Main St.), near Country Club Plaza. At the **Phoenix Jazz Club** (302 W. 8th St.), live performances are standard fare every night except Sunday; the cozy brick-walled club attracts a crowd of sophisticated ladies and gentlemen.

Some may argue that hanging out in the fresh evening air under a star-filled sky may be the best way to see live concerts and Broadway shows. If that's true, the **Starlight Theatre** fills the bill. This venerable performing arts organization has been open since 1950; the 2009 concert season saw such musical performers as Stevie Wonder, No Doubt, Tori Amos and Lyle Lovett. The theater also presents five Broadway shows per year. In 2009, the lineup included productions of "Chicago," "Legally Blonde The Musical" and "Anything Goes."

It's almost a requirement for big cities to have a monthly art walk and Kansas City is no exception. First Friday happens at the **Crossroads Art District** (20th Street and Baltimore Avenue) about 1 mile south from the Power & Light District. Kick off your evening with a stroll through art galleries and boutiques from 7-9 p.m. and grab a meal or a glass of wine at the district's casually elegant bistros and lounges. Street performers and live music add to the fun street-party atmosphere.

Performing Arts

Kansas City has a rich cultural heritage. The Lyric Opera of Kansas City performs at the Lyric Theater, 11th and Central streets; for information or tickets to its three fall and two spring presentations phone (816) 471-7344. The Kansas City Ballet mounts productions of "The Nutcracker" at the Midland Theater in December, and the Lyric Theater presents performances of the Kansas City Symphony October through May. Phone (816) 931-2232 for ballet schedule information, or (816) 471-0400 for symphony information and tickets.

A tremendous reconstruction effort has turned the once-dilapidated 1912 Gem Theater, 1615 E. 18th St. in the 18th and Vine Historic District, into a center for multicultural arts, entertainment and education programming. Phone (816) 474-6262 (Gem Theater) or (816) 474-8463 (American Jazz Museum, part of the district) for information about upcoming performances and exhibitions.

The University of Missouri-Kansas City's Conservatory of Music, 4949 Cherry St., draws patrons from within as well as outside the university. Concert series also are sponsored by the Harrington Arts Program at William Jewell College.

The university-based equity company of the Kansas City Repertory Theater stages classic and modern productions in the on-campus Spencer Theater September through June; phone (816) 235-2700. Musical comedy productions, light opera and concerts of all types are on the bill at Swope Park's Starlight Theatre, the nation's second largest outdoor amphitheater. Top stars perform during the mid-June through September season; phone (816) 333-9481.

In late June or early July a work by the Bard of Avon is presented in Southmoreland Park during the Heart of America Shakespeare Festival; phone (816) 531-7728. The Theatre League brings the national touring companies of Broadway musicals to the Music Hall, 301 W. 13th St.; phone (816) 421-7500.

The Folly Theater, W. 12th and Central streets, is a restored turn-of-the-20th-century burlesque house that now presents a variety of entertainment, from children's theater to jazz concerts; phone (816) 842-5500. The Gorilla Theatre, 517 E. 18th St., stages original and avant-garde works as well as classic dramas; phone (816) 510-3372. The Martin City Melodrama and Vaudeville Co., (913) 642-7576, presents performances Thursday through Sunday evenings at 9635 Metcalf Ave. in Overland Park, Kan. The New Theatre Restaurant at 9229 Foster St. in Overland Park, (913) 649-7469, offers evening performances Tuesday through Sunday, and matinees on Sundays.

Other area theaters include the American Heartland Theatre on the third level of the Crown Center, (816) 842-9999; Capitol Federal Park at Sandstone, 633 N. 130th St. in Bonner Springs, Kan., (913) 721-3400; Comedy City at 817 Westport Rd., (816)

842-2744; Coterie Theatre on the Crown Center's first level, (816) 474-6552; the Quality Hill Playhouse at 303 W. 10th St., (816) 421-1700; Theatre for Young America at 30 W. Pershing Rd., (816) 460-2083; and the Unicorn Theatre at 3820 Main St., (816) 531-7529.

The events section of the *Kansas City Star* carries current information about the city's performing arts offerings.

Special Events

As winter begins to wane, things heat up in Kansas City with the Home, Flower, Lawn and Garden Show in mid-March and the National Association of Intercollegiate Athletics (NAIA) National Track and Field Competition during late March.

Also in March is the St. Patrick's Day parade, which threads through downtown. The 3-hour parade launches festivities that continue throughout the city well into the night. Around mid-March is the NAIA Basketball Tournament, which includes some of the best men's and women's college basketball teams in the country.

Fiesta in the Heartland is held in early May at the Crown Center, 2450 Grand Blvd. The event celebrates and commemorates *Cinco de Mayo*, the anniversary of the Mexican forces' triumph at the Battle of Puebla on May 5, 1862, in Mexico. The victory allowed members of the Mexican government—including president Benito Juárez—to escape capture by the French and eventually free Mexico from French control.

The Crown Center also sponsors free outdoor Summer on the Square activities, including the Kansas City Symphony's Radio Day in May, the Trinity Hospital Hill Run in June and the Noon Tunes on the Square entertainment series on Fridays in July.

Over the July 4th weekend the city pays tribute to its Western roots with the 2-day Jaycee's Pro Rodeo held at Benjamin Ranch, off I-435 at the E. 87th Street exit; phone (816) 761-5055.

In July Kansas City celebrates its musical heritage with the Kansas City Blues and Jazz Festival, recalling the days when 12th and Vine streets were the hangout of celebrated African-American jazz musicians in the 1920s and '30s. The festival's events are held at Liberty Memorial in Penn Valley Park.

The third full weekend of August brings the Ethnic Enrichment Festival to Swope Park, where the world's cultures are celebrated with live music and dance performances, craft exhibitions and a tempting lineup of food booths. Events include Scottish Highland games and the colorful pageantry of the Parade of Nations.

Penn Valley Park is filled with national and regional entertainers during the Spirit Festival, held Labor Day weekend; phone (816) 513-7500. Also in September, Kansas City's Hispanic community commemorates Mexico's independence from Spain with the Fiesta Hispana; phone (816) 452-4712.

Thanksgiving evening marks the Plaza Lighting Ceremony, which illuminates Country Club Plaza's fanciful towers with miles of tiny, colored lightbulbs; phone (816) 753-0100. The display lasts until January 1. The day after Thanksgiving, a nearly 100-foot Christmas tree is illuminated during a ceremony at Crown Center Square. The Mayor's Christmas Tree, decorated with more than 900 red and gold ornaments and white lights, stands as the symbol of a citywide charity drive to help people in need during the holidays.

Sports and cultural events occur all year; for details, contact the Kansas City Convention & Visitors Association.

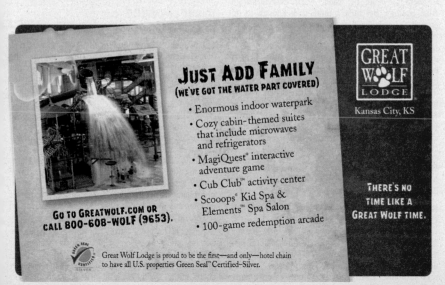

The Kansas City Vicinity

BLUE SPRINGS (C-1) pop. 48,080, elev. 962′

Drawn to the cool, deep springs of the Little Blue River, settlers heading westward in the 1800s made Blue Springs one of their final stopping points before leaving civilized territory. Named after the river, today the town is a hive of outdoor activity that revolves around the town's lakes, parks and golf courses.

Normally a quiet town that stays out of the spotlight, Blue Springs became more well-known in 2008, the year that resident David Cook took first place in the seventh season of television's "American Idol." In spite of that fact, Blue Springs doesn't have a reputation for being the place to go for nightlife.

Hidden Valley Park, 6500 N.W. Valley View Rd., plays host to the annual Blue Springs Barbecue Blaze-Off, a not-to-be-missed local tradition held the first Friday and Saturday after Labor Day. The 2-day event promises good old-fashioned American fun with barbecue cooking competitions, children's activities and live entertainment.

More than a dozen city parks feature sports courts and fields, jogging trails, picnic facilities and playgrounds. You can sled down the town's largest hill after the snow begins to fall at Keystone Park, 2214 S.W. Keystone Dr. Let canine family members run loose at Dog Park, 1049 N.E. 20th St., a 2.7-acre off-leash area for dogs of all sizes at Gregory O. Grounds Park. Skateboarders will find thrills at the skate park at 14-acre Burrus Old Mill Park, 112 N.W. Woods Chapel Rd., which is also the original site of Blue Springs.

There may not be water, water *everywhere* in Blue Springs, but there's more than enough to go around at Lake Jacomo and Blue Springs Lake, both in Fleming Park *(see Recreation Chart)*. Smooth sailing lies ahead at 970-acre Lake Jacomo for pontoon boaters, windsurfers and sailors alike, in part because horsepower is limited to no more than 40 hp for pontoon boats and sailboats, and no more than 25 hp for other types of boats. There are no horsepower limits at 720-acre Blue Springs Lake, where visitors enjoy the more exhilarating power boating, water skiing, tubing and jet skiing. There's also good fishing to be had at both lakes. Phone (816) 228-0137 for more park information.

Blue Springs Chamber of Commerce: 1000 Main St., Blue Springs, MO 64015. **Phone:** (816) 229-8558.

BURR OAK WOODS CONSERVATION NATURE CENTER is 1.2 mi. n. of jct. I-70 and SR 7 exit 20 to 1401 N.W. Park Rd. Nature trails traverse the 1,071-acre nature center, which features natural history exhibits that include a 3,000-gallon aquarium and a wildlife viewing area. **Time:** Allow 30 minutes minimum. **Hours:** Conservation area open daily 8-8, early Apr.-late Oct.; 8-5, rest of year. Center open Mon.-Sat. 8-5, Sun. noon-5; closed Jan. 1, Thanksgiving, day after Thanksgiving and Dec. 24-25. **Cost:** Free. **Phone:** (816) 228-3766.

FLEMING PARK—
see Lee's Summit p. 179

EXCELSIOR SPRINGS (B-2) pop. 10,847, elev. 939′

Saline, soda, calcium and iron manganese mineral waters have made Excelsior Springs a well-known spa. The Hall of Waters, operated by the city, has bath facilities for men and women as well as a Hall of Springs, where the waters are dispensed for drinking and for bottling at a plant.

Excelsior Springs Chamber of Commerce: 461 S. Thompson Ave., Excelsior Springs, MO 64024. **Phone:** (816) 630-6161.

GRANDVIEW (C-1) pop. 24,881, elev. 1,070′

HARRY S. TRUMAN FARM HOME is off US 71, then .7 mi. w. to 12301 Blue Ridge Blvd. Part of the Harry S. Truman National Historic Site *(see attraction listing p. 178)*, this 1894 farmstead was the home of Harry Truman's grandparents. Truman lived and worked on the farm 1906-17. The house is filled with photographs of Truman family members. Several outbuildings also are on the grounds.

Time: Allow 30 minutes minimum. **Hours:** Tours are given on the half-hour Fri.-Sun. 9:30-4, Memorial Day weekend-Labor Day weekend. **Cost:** $4; free (ages 0-16). **Phone:** (816) 254-2720.

INDEPENDENCE (C-1) pop. 113,288, elev. 1,012′

Upon his return following the end of his presidency, Harry S. Truman called Independence "the greatest town in the United States" and "the center of things for me." Truman thought the world of his hometown, and a day spent in the town's center, Independence Square, will help newcomers understand why.

Independence Square is where you'll find the office and courtroom where Truman started his political career as a county judge, and Clinton's Soda Fountain, 100 W. Maple Ave., where young Harry had his first job as a store clerk, doing everything from sweeping the floors to dispensing flavored phosphates. Sit at the fountain's 100-year-old marble counter and slurp a cherry phosphate or feast on an ice cream sundae in Harry's honor.

Take a leisurely stroll through Independence Square, much like Harry did every day during his retirement, and you'll happen upon delightful one-of-a-kind clothing boutiques, cafés and specialty shops selling trendy clothing, gifts and antiques.

If you're a Civil War buff, check out the Blue & Gray Book Shoppe, 106 E. Walnut St., whose inventory includes history books and antique area maps focusing on the War Between the States; phone (816) 252-9099. For refurbished vintage furnishings and home accessories, Luticia Clementine's, 206 N. Liberty Street, is the place to go; the store also stocks almost everything you need to outfit your baby, including frilly dresses, books and toys; phone (816) 836-3822.

A town with such rich history is bound to have some ghosts; every Friday in October, potential ghost busters take a ride in a covered wagon around Independence Square in an effort to find them. Led by paranormal experts, the 45-minute tour stops at the 1859 Jail, Marshal's Home and Museum *(see attraction listing)*. Tours are given at 7, 8, 9 and 10 p.m.; phone (816) 461-0065 for reservations.

During the holiday season, Independence Square turns into a winter wonderland. On the first 3-day weekend in November, townspeople gather for the annual tree lighting ceremony. Holiday lights are strung on red brick buildings, and chestnuts really are roasted on an open fire. Listen to carolers singing and sleigh bells ringing on a sleigh ride through the square.

While Independence is well-known for its Truman-related historic sites, it is also where the Santa Fe Trail originated in 1821 and the Oregon and California trails originated in the 1840s, earning the city the nickname "Queen City of the Trails." The moniker still holds true today as walkers, runners and cyclists stride and ride along the Little Blue Trace Trail, which runs north for 11 scenic miles along the Blue River. The trail is accessible from the Hartman Heritage Center, I-70 and Little Blue River Road; for information phone (816) 503-4800.

Independence Department of Tourism: 111 E. Maple St., Independence, MO 64050. **Phone:** (816) 325-7111 or (800) 748-7323.

Self-guiding tours: The Missouri Mormon Walking Trail, which begins at Walnut and River streets across from the Community of Christ Auditorium, is a 1-mile trail with 14 plaques commemorating early Mormon sites. The Truman Walking Trail, beginning at the Harry S Truman National Historic Site ticket office at Main Street and Truman Road, meanders 2.7 miles through the Truman neighborhood, with 44 plaques embedded in sidewalks along the way.

1859 JAIL, MARSHAL'S HOME & MUSEUM is at 217 N. Main St. This restored Civil War-era jail held such notorious characters as Frank James, William Quantrill and the Youngers. Also in the complex are the marshal's house, a local history museum and a one-room schoolhouse.

Time: Allow 30 minutes minimum. **Hours:** Mon.-Sat. 10-4, Sun. 1-4, Apr.-Oct. and day after Thanksgiving-Dec. 30. Closed Dec. 23-25. **Cost:** $5; $4.50 (ages 55+); $2 (ages 6-16). Combination ticket with Bingham-Waggoner Estate, National Frontier Trails Museum and Vaile Mansion (available Apr.-Oct.) $16. Combination ticket with Bingham-Waggoner Estate and Vaile Mansion $12. **Phone:** (816) 252-1892.

BINGHAM-WAGGONER ESTATE is at 313 W. Pacific St. The 22-room mansion was the 1864-70 home of Missouri artist George Caleb Bingham and his wife. Having seen two Civil War battles nearby, Bingham painted his controversial work "Order Number Eleven" to protest the infamous 1863 directive that drove thousands of border residents from their property if they did not swear allegiance to the Union. The Waggoner family purchased the 19-acre estate in 1879 and resided in it until 1976. The house was extensively remodeled in the 1890s and has been restored to that period.

Tours: Guided tours are available. **Time:** Allow 1 hour minimum. **Hours:** Mon.-Sat. 10-4, Sun. 1-4, Apr.-Oct. and day after Thanksgiving-Dec. 30. Closed Dec. 23-25. **Cost:** $5; $4.50 (senior citizens); $2 (ages 6-16). Combination ticket with 1859 Jail, Marshal's Home & Museum; National Frontier Trails Museum; and Vaile Mansion (available Apr.-Oct.) $16. Combination ticket with 1859 Jail, Marshal's Home & Museum and Vaile Mansion $12. **Phone:** (816) 325-7111 or (816) 461-3491.

COMMUNITY OF CHRIST WORLD HEADQUARTERS is at River and Walnut sts. Formerly known as the Reorganized Church of Jesus Christ of Latter Day Saints, the organization's headquarters features a 6,334-pipe organ in the auditorium's main conference chamber. A museum is in the 1994 temple across the street. The temple's ceiling resembles a cross section of the shell of a chambered nautilus.

Hours: Guided tours are given every half-hour Mon.-Sat. 9-11:30 and 1:30-4:30, Sun. 1-5. Recitals are given daily at 3, June-Aug.; Sun. at 3, rest of year. Closed Jan. 1, Easter, Thanksgiving and Dec. 24-25. **Cost:** Free. **Phone:** (816) 833-1000, ext. 3030.

Children's Peace Pavilion is at 1001 W. Walnut St. at the Community of Christ World Headquarters. Hands-on activities and exhibits are designed to teach children the museum's four concepts of peace: "Peace for Me" explains how to deal with one's feelings; "Peace for Us" places emphasis on the importance of relationships; "Peace for Everyone" is geared toward understanding the diversity of the human race; and "Peace for the Planet" encourages taking care of the Earth. A rain forest display includes a cave for children to explore. **Time:** Allow 1 hour minimum. **Hours:** Tues.-Sat. 9:30-4. Closed Jan. 1, Thanksgiving and Dec. 25. **Cost:** Free. **Phone:** (816) 521-3033.

HARRY S. TRUMAN COURTROOM AND OFFICE is in the Jackson County Courthouse on Independence Sq. The 25-minute multimedia feature "The Man from Independence" focuses on the 33rd president's youth and retirement years in Independence. The 30-minute sound and light show, shown by request, is presented in the restored courtroom Truman used while serving as a county judge. A tour of his adjoining office is included. **Time:** Allow 30 minutes minimum. **Hours:** Mon.-Fri. 10-3:30. **Cost:** $2; $1 (ages 6-15). **Phone:** (816) 252-7454.

GEM **HARRY S. TRUMAN LIBRARY AND MUSEUM** is on the n.e. edge of US 24 at Delaware St. The focal point of the museum, an exhibit about the Missouri native's presidential years, features a film tracing Truman's life from childhood to his swearing in as the 33rd president of the United States. In addition, audiovisual presentations dealing with difficult decisions Truman was faced with during his presidency are shown in two theaters. Exhibits and objects of artistic and historic interest examine such topics as the challenges faced in the post-World War II years, the beginning of the Cold War and the status of the nation as Truman left office in 1952.

Also displayed are a replica of Truman's oval office in the White House with the original "The Buck Stops Here" sign, the table on which the United Nations charter was signed and exhibits about the history of the presidency. President and Mrs. Truman's graves are in the courtyard.

Time: Allow 2 hours minimum. **Hours:** Mon.-Sat. 9-5 (also Thurs. 5-9, May-Sept.), Sun. noon-5. Closed Jan. 1, Thanksgiving and Dec. 25. **Cost:** $8; $7 (ages 65+); $3 (ages 6-15). **Phone:** (816) 268-8200 or (800) 833-1225.

HARRY S TRUMAN NATIONAL HISTORIC SITE is on Delaware St. off Truman Rd.; a visitor center is at 223 N. Main St. This is the house in which President and Mrs. Truman, when not in Washington, D.C., lived from their marriage in 1919 until their deaths. The Victorian home is crowded with their furnishings and other possessions. The visitor center offers a short audiovisual program.

Note: The house will close sometime in 2010 for renovations; during this time tours will not be available, but the visitor center will remain open. Alternative programming may be offered; phone ahead for additional details. The visitor center distributes tickets on a first-come, first-served basis beginning at 8:30 a.m. for each day's tours; visitors must sign for their own ticket in person. There are no reservations; tours may sell out. Parking at the historic site is limited.

Hours: Guided house tours daily every 15-30 minutes as needed 9-5, Memorial Day-Labor Day; Tues.-Sun. 9-5, rest of year. Each tour is limited to eight people. Center open daily 8:30-5. Closed Jan. 1, Thanksgiving and Dec. 25. **Cost:** $4; free (ages 0-15). **Phone:** (816) 254-9929.

MORMON VISITORS' CENTER is at 937 W. Walnut St. Exhibits, artifacts and works of art chronicle religious leader Joseph Smith Jr.'s pilgrimage from Ohio to Independence and the role of Mormon followers in the early history of Independence. **Tours:** Guided tours are available. **Hours:** Daily 9-9. **Cost:** Free. **Phone:** (816) 836-3466.

NATIONAL FRONTIER TRAILS MUSEUM is at 318 W. Pacific Ave. The museum researches, interprets and preserves the history of the pioneers and the Santa Fe, Oregon and California trails, all of which began at or near Independence. Covered wagon rides are offered seasonally (weather permitting).

Hours: Mon.-Sat. 9-4:30, Sun. 12:30-4:30. Closed Jan. 1, Thanksgiving and Dec. 24-25. **Cost:** $5; $4.50 (ages 62+); $3 (ages 6-12). Museum and wagon ride $12; $9 (ages 6-12). Combination ticket with 1859 Jail, Marshal's Home & Museum; Vaile Mansion; and Bingham-Waggoner Estate (available Apr.-Oct. only) $16. **Phone:** (816) 325-7575.

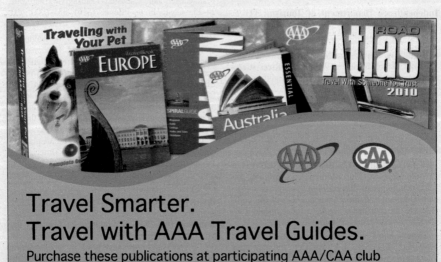

PUPPETRY ARTS INSTITUTE is at 11025 E. Winner Rd. in Englewood Plaza. The institute has a museum featuring puppets and puppet-related items. Hazelle and Woody Rollins, the owners of one of the country's most renowned puppet and marionette factories, have the remaining inventory from their factories displayed here. Guests also can create their own puppets. **Time:** Allow 1 hour minimum. **Hours:** Tues.-Sat. 10-5. Closed Jan. 1, Thanksgiving and Dec. 25. **Cost:** $3; $1.50 (ages 0-15). **Phone:** (816) 833-9777.

VAILE MANSION is at 1500 N. Liberty St. The 30-room home of local entrepreneur and mail contractor Harvey Merrick Vaile was hailed by Kansas City newspaper reporters as "the most princely house and the most comfortable home in the entire West" during its construction in the early 1880s. The restored mansion is furnished in period.

Tours: Guided tours are available. **Time:** Allow 1 hour minimum. **Hours:** Mon.-Sat. 10-4, Sun. 1-4, Apr.-Oct. **Cost:** $5; $4.50 (senior citizens); $2 (ages 6-16). Combination ticket with 1859 Jail, Marshal's Home & Museum; Bingham-Waggoner Estate; and National Frontier Trails Museum (available Apr.-Oct.) $16. Combination ticket with 1859 Jail, Marshal's Home & Museum and Bingham-Waggoner Estate $12. **Phone:** (816) 325-7111 or (816) 325-7430.

KEARNEY (B-2) pop. 5,472, elev. 829'

JESSE JAMES MUSEUM is about 1.5 mi. e. on SR 92, then 1.5 mi. n. to 21216 Jesse James Farm Rd., following signs. This historic site was the birthplace and home of Jesse James, who grew up in the house with his brother Frank. The 1822 house has been restored with period furnishings; guides relate facts and stories about the outlaws. **Hours:** Daily 9-4, May-Sept.; Mon.-Sat. 9-4, Sun. noon-4, rest of year. Closed Jan. 1, Thanksgiving and Dec. 25. **Cost:** $7.50; $6.50 (ages 62+); $4 (ages 8-15). **Phone:** (816) 736-8500.

LAWSON (B-2) pop. 2,336, elev. 1,066'

WATKINS WOOLEN MILL STATE PARK AND STATE HISTORIC SITE is off I-35 exit SR 92, 7 mi. e. to CR RA, then 1.5 mi. n. to the park entrance. This 1861 woolen mill no longer operates but is still equipped with spinners, twisters and looms. The site includes a gristmill, house and other outbuildings, as well as a museum and visitor center. *See Recreation Chart.*

Time: Allow 1 hour minimum. **Hours:** Mon.-Fri. 8-5, Sat. 9-5, Sun. 10-5, Apr.-Oct.; Mon.-Fri. 8-4:30, Sat. 9-4:30, Sun. 10-4:30, rest of year. Closed Jan. 1, Thanksgiving and Dec. 25. **Cost:** $2.50; $1.50 (ages 6-12). **Phone:** (816) 580-3387 or (800) 334-6946.

LEE'S SUMMIT (C-2) pop. 70,700, elev. 1,037'

FLEMING PARK is at US 40 and Woods Chapel Rd. Recreational activities include hiking, boating and fishing. The 100-acre native hoofed animal enclosure houses bison, elk and whitetail deer. Missouri Town 1855 *(see attraction listing)* also is on the park grounds. *See Recreation Chart.* **Hours:** Daily 6 a.m.-dusk. Closed Jan. 1 and Dec. 25. **Cost:** Park free. **Phone:** (816) 503-4800.

Missouri Town 1855 is within Fleming Park. This collection of original mid-19th-century structures, which depict a typical Midwestern antebellum community, were relocated to the site from a number of locations. Living-history interpreters explain and portray the daily routines of village residents. Old-fashioned events are held year-round. **Time:** Allow 1 hour minimum. **Hours:** Tues.-Sun. 9-4:30, Mar. 1-Nov. 15; Sat.-Sun. 9-4:30, rest of year. Closed Jan. 1 and Dec. 25. **Cost:** $5; $3 (ages 5-13 and 62+). **Phone:** (816) 524-8770.

LIBERTY (C-2) pop. 26,232, elev. 852'

Liberty Area Chamber of Commerce: 9 S. Leonard St., Liberty, MO 64068. **Phone:** (816) 781-5200.

Self-guiding tours: Dozens of downtown sites marked with "Guide by Cell" cell phone icons are part of nine audio tours exploring local history. To hear narration about any site on the routes, dial (816) 295-3110, enter the extension noted on the sign (1-83), and then press the # key. The narration service is free, but be aware that you will accrue minutes on your cell phone for the call. Brochures with a map are available at the chamber of commerce. The tours cover the downtown business district; the Dougherty, Jewell and Lightburne historic residential districts; William Jewell College; Clay County Historical Museum; and sites related to African American history, early resident Alexander Doniphan, and outlaw Jesse James.

Shopping areas: Downtown Liberty features nearly 3 dozen boutiques, including book, clothing, home décor and jewelry stores. Several of the shops are at Corbin Mill, a restored 1889 flour mill at 131 S. Water St. The Historic Downtown Liberty Farmers Market is held on Liberty Square—bordered by Kansas Avenue and Franklin, Main, and Water streets—Sat. 7-noon, May through October.

CLAY COUNTY MUSEUM AND HISTORICAL SOCIETY is at 14 N. Main St. A restored 19th-century drugstore displays patent medicines, pioneer farm tools and other artifacts of 19th-century life in Missouri. The second-floor dining room and parlor are furnished to reflect the style of the 1880s. **Time:** Allow 30 minutes minimum. **Hours:** Mon.-Sat. 1-4, Feb.-Dec. Closed major holidays. **Cost:** $2; $ 1 (ages 0-12). **Phone:** (816) 792-1849.

HISTORIC LIBERTY JAIL is at 216 N. Main St. This is a restored version—in cutaway form—of the 1833 jail in which Mormon prophet Joseph Smith was confined for 4 months beginning in 1838, and where he is said to have received several revelations concerning doctrines of the Mormon Church. **Time:**

Allow 30 minutes minimum. **Hours:** Daily 9-9. **Cost:** Free. **Phone:** (816) 781-3188.

JESSE JAMES BANK MUSEUM is at 103 N. Water St. on Liberty Square. The nation's first bank robbery carried out during daylight hours was at this site, committed by the James gang Feb. 13, 1866. The 1858 building houses Jesse James memorabilia, period furnishings and antebellum-era banking displays. **Tours:** Guided tours are available. **Time:** Allow 30 minutes minimum. **Hours:** Mon.-Sat. 10-4. **Cost:** $5.50; $5 (ages 62+); $3.50 (ages 8-15). **Phone:** (816) 736-8510.

THE WILLIAM JEWELL COLLEGE LIBRARY is on Jewell St. between Kansas and Mississippi aves. The collection includes Elizabethan and Puritan literature, archival records of Missouri history, 16th-century Anabaptist pamphlets and original illustrations by children's author Lois Lenski. **Time:** Allow 30 minutes minimum. **Hours:** Mon.-Fri. 8-4 (also Fri. 4-5), with extended hours during school terms. **Cost:** Free. **Phone:** (816) 415-7609, or (816) 781-7700, ext. 5468.

LONE JACK (C-2) pop. 528

The Battle of Lone Jack, one of the bloodiest Civil War battles in Missouri, occurred Aug. 16, 1862. Five days earlier Confederate troops had captured Independence and its Union garrison. Joined by reinforcements a few days later, the Confederates moved to Lone Jack, where they clashed with Union troops in hand-to-hand combat for 5 hours until the Union troops retreated.

LONE JACK CIVIL WAR MUSEUM is at jct. SR 150 and US 50. Local Civil War activity is depicted through exhibits, dioramas and an electronic map. Soldiers' Cemetery and a remnant of hedgerows that figured in the battle can be seen. **Hours:** Wed.-Sat. 10-4, Sun. 1-4, Apr.-Oct.; Sat. 10-4, Sun. 1-4, rest of year. Closed Jan. 1, Easter, Thanksgiving and Dec. 25. Phone ahead to confirm schedule. **Cost:** $3; $ (ages 6-12). **Phone:** (816) 697-8833 or (816) 805-1815.

NORTH KANSAS CITY (C-1) pop. 4,714

GAMBLING ESTABLISHMENTS

- **Harrah's North Kansas City** is at 1 Riverboat Dr. **Hours:** Sun.-Thurs. 8 a.m.-5 a.m., Fri.-Sat. 24 hours. **Phone:** (816) 472-7777 or (800) 427-7247.

PLATTE CITY (B-1) pop. 3,866, elev. 850'

When Missouri became part of the Union in 1821, the northwestern corner of the state was still part of the Indian Territory. It was not until the Platte Purchase of 1836 that this area was bought from the Iowa, Sac and Fox Indians.

Platte County-KCI Area Convention and Visitors Bureau: 11724 N.W. Plaza Cir., Suite 200, Kansas City, MO 64153. **Phone:** (816) 270-3979 or (888) 875-2883.

BEN FERREL PLATTE COUNTY MUSEUM is at Third and Ferrel sts. This restored 1882 Victorian house is furnished in period. The museum contains historical items pertaining to the county and surrounding areas. County records and genealogical histories are contained in the archives and library. **Time:** Allow 30 minutes minimum. **Hours:** Thurs.-Sat. noon-4, Apr.-Oct. **Cost:** $3; $1 (ages 5-18). **Phone:** (816) 431-5121.

RICHMOND (B-2) pop. 6,116, elev. 823'

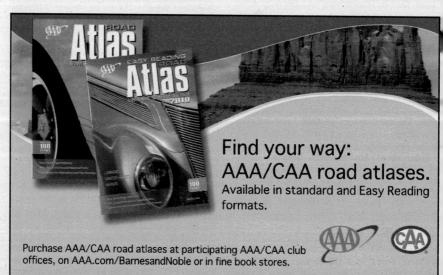

RAY COUNTY HISTORICAL SOCIETY AND MUSEUM, 901 W. Royle St., is housed in a 54-room 1910 building. Thirty-nine of the rooms display historical items, including quilts, military exhibits, taxidermy displays and vintage clothing. The building also contains rooms set up as a late 19th-century schoolroom and a doctor's office. The basement contains jail cells, wildlife displays and a reproduced barn with antique tools and machines. A library offers resources about local history, including genealogy.

Tours: Guided tours are available. **Time:** Allow 1 hour minimum. **Hours:** Wed.-Sat. 10-4. Closed Thanksgiving and Dec. 25. **Cost:** Donations. **Phone:** (816) 776-2305.

RIVERSIDE (B-1) pop. 2,979, elev. 440'

GAMBLING ESTABLISHMENTS

- ***Argosy* Casino** is e. of jct. I-635 and US 9 on US 9, following signs. **Hours:** Gaming sessions depart Mon.-Thurs. every 2 hours 8 a.m.-5 a.m., Fri.-Sun. 24 hrs. **Phone:** (816) 746-3100 or (800) 270-7711. *See color ad on p. 491.*

SIBLEY (B-2) pop. 347

FORT OSAGE is at US 24 and CR BB (Sibley Rd.). The fort is a restoration of the first U.S. outpost in the Louisiana Purchase Territory. The 1808 factory—originally an American Indian trading house—contains original furnishings from the early 1800s. A museum illustrates the trading post's operation, the role of the fort and the lifestyle of the Osage Indian tribe. A 19th-century blacksmith shop and a trade shop with typical early 1800s goods are featured.

Hours: Tues.-Sun. 9-4:30. Closed Jan. 1, May 8 (Truman Day) and Dec. 25. **Cost:** $7; $4 (ages 5-13); $3 (ages 62+). **Phone:** (816) 650-3278, or (816) 503-4860, ext. 1260.

SMITHVILLE (B-1) pop. 5,514

THE JERRY L. LITTON VISITOR CENTER is at 16311 N. CR DD, at the end of Smithville Lake *(see Recreation Chart)*. Named for the late Missouri congressman, the center highlights his life and has displays and audiovisual presentations about the Smithville Lake area and the history of water management and control by the Army Corps of Engineers. **Time:** Allow 1 hour minimum. **Hours:** Daily 8-4, Memorial Day-Labor Day; Mon.-Fri. 8-4, rest of year. **Cost:** Free. **Phone:** (816) 532-0174.

UNITY VILLAGE (C-1) pop. 140, elev. 950'

UNITY VILLAGE is at jct. SR 350 and Colbern Rd. The world headquarters of the Unity School of Christianity features historic Mediterranean-style buildings set amid 1,400 acres of woodlands, lakes, fountains and formal rose gardens. A library contains a collection of metaphysical material as well as archives. The Unity Village Chapel is open to visitors. **Time:** Allow 1 hour, 30 minutes minimum. **Hours:** Village Mon.-Thurs. 7-5, Fri.-Sun. 8-2. Chapel services Sun. at 10:30. **Cost:** Free. **Phone:** (816) 524-3550.

WESTON (B-1) pop. 1,631, elev. 775'

The pride of Weston is its more than 100 antebellum houses and buildings, similar in appearance to the Classical Revival and Federal-style houses of early 19th-century Virginia and Kentucky.

Founded along the Missouri River, Weston was visited by Meriwether Lewis and William Clark in 1804. Although the Missouri changed its course in the early 20th century, leaving docks perched along a dry riverbed, the town's Main Street tobacco warehouses are still kept full. Tobacco is grown locally and sold at auctions held from mid-November to February.

RECREATIONAL ACTIVITIES

Skiing

- **Snow Creek Ski Area**, 5 mi. n.w. on SR 45 at 1 Snow Creek Dr. **Hours:** Mon.-Fri. noon-9, Sat. and holidays 9-9, Sun. 9-8, mid-Dec. to mid-Mar. (also 4-9 p.m. Dec. 25 and Fri.-Sat. 10 p.m.-3 a.m., Jan. 1 to mid-Mar.). Closed Dec. 25. **Phone:** (816) 640-2200.

Nearby Kansas

BONNER SPRINGS pop. 6,768, elev. 795′

Most of the year Bonner Springs, just west of the Kansas City metropolitan area, concentrates on light industry and the marketing of agricultural products. On weekends from late August to mid-October, however, the town exhibits a touch of 16th-century Europe when the popular Renaissance Festival of Kansas City is held. From May through September Capitol Federal Park at Sandstone offers outdoor concerts featuring major rock, hip-hop and country artists; phone (913) 721-3400.

Bonner Springs-Edwardsville Area Chamber of Commerce: 111 Oak St., Suite C, Bonner Springs, KS 66012. **Phone:** (913) 422-5044.

NATIONAL AGRICULTURAL CENTER AND HALL OF FAME is 1 mi. n.e. off I-70 at 630 N. 126th St. (Hall of Fame Dr.). The center is devoted to achievements in the field of agriculture. Three display buildings house a diverse collection of past, present and future machinery and implements. A small steam train operates on weekends in summer. **Hours:** Tues.-Sat. 9-5, Sun. 1-5. Closed major holidays. **Cost:** $7; $6 (ages 62+); $3 (ages 5-16). **Phone:** (913) 721-1075.

WYANDOTTE COUNTY MUSEUM is at 631 N. 126th St. in Wyandotte County Park. The museum contains artifacts depicting the area's heritage. Aspects of county history portrayed range from emigrant American Indian tribes to the arrival of Europeans and the development of local industry. **Hours:** Mon.-Fri. 9-4, Sat. 9-noon. Closed holidays. **Cost:** Free. **Phone:** (913) 721-1078.

EDGERTON pop. 1,440, elev. 835′

LANESFIELD SCHOOL HISTORIC SITE is at jct. 187th St. and Dillie Rd. Built in 1869, the Lanesfield School is a one-room schoolhouse in which grades 1-8 were taught by a single teacher until its consolidation by the school district in 1963. A costumed teacher leads a tour of the building and conducts a lesson students received circa 1904. Allow 30 minutes minimum. **Hours:** Tues.-Sun. 1-5; closed major holidays. **Cost:** Free. **Phone:** (913) 893-6645.

FAIRWAY

SHAWNEE INDIAN MISSION STATE HISTORIC SITE is n. of US 56 at jct. Mission Rd. and W. 53rd St. A manual labor training school was established here in 1839 on Shawnee land—although its doors were open to 23 different tribes—and operated until 1862. The orientation video "Crossroads of Culture" recounts the mission's history and its role in westward expansion as well as such divisive eras as "Bleeding Kansas," when the Kansas territory became a battleground between pro-slavery and anti-slavery factions, and the Civil War.

The East, West and North buildings are the three remaining structures of the original 16 that once stood on the site's more than 2,000 acres. The East Building has two floors of exhibits that bring the mission's stories to life; the West Building is closed to the public due to extensive, ongoing restoration work.

Allow 30 minutes minimum. **Hours:** Tues.-Sat. 9-5. Closed state holidays. **Cost:** Admission $3; $2 (ages 61+ and students grades K-college); free (ages 0-5 and active military with ID). **Phone:** (913) 262-0867.

KANSAS CITY pop. 146,866, elev. 763′

The town of Wyandotte, established in 1858, was located in what is now the downtown area of present-day Kansas City. By the 1870s, railroads and stockyards were contributing to robust growth. Four municipalities—Armourdale, Armstrong, Kansas City and Wyandotte—consolidated in 1886 to form what today is the Kansas portion of the greater Kansas City metropolitan area.

Among those who migrated to Kansas looking for a better life in the latter part of the 19th century were African Americans known as Exodusters. Free blacks who could read, were economically able to buy property and whose self-esteem had been bolstered by military service in the Civil War, they pursued dreams of owning land and escaping the oppressive segregationist policies of Southern states, a legacy that remained despite the civil rights gains introduced by Reconstruction.

Their de facto leader was Benjamin "Pap" Singleton, who was born a slave in Tennessee, escaped to freedom in Detroit and returned to his native state after emancipation. An admirer of abolitionist John Brown's crusade against slavery in Kansas, he chose the state as a destination for the creation of organized African-American "colonies."

Singleton recruited impoverished blacks from throughout the South. Under his leadership, several Exoduster communities took shape in Wyandotte County beginning in the early 1870s, including Hoggstown, Mississippi Town, Quindaro and Rattlebone Hollow, all later incorporated into Kansas City. Quindaro—today a neighborhood on the city's northern edge—was founded by freed African Americans and abolitionists; it was a stop on the Underground Railroad and remained a thriving town until the early 20th century.

Although the organized movement to Kansas later became an unplanned rush (so much so that in 1880 Singleton was called before a U.S. Senate committee to explain the "alarming exodus" of blacks from the South), many who remained were indeed able to better their lives. But Singleton, dismayed with the racial prejudice he continued to encounter, eventually abandoned his efforts to establish African-American colonies in the United States.

These days you can find an exodus of racing fans heading to Kansas City. Grand National and NASCAR events rev up the crowds at Lakeside Speedway, 1 mile west of I-435 exit 18 at 5615 Wolcott Dr., on Friday nights from April through September; phone (913) 299-2040. At the Woodlands Race Track, 99th Street and Leavenworth Road, Thoroughbred racing takes place November to mid-August, and greyhound racing occurs mid-August through October; phone (913) 299-9797.

Note: Policies concerning admittance of children to pari-mutuel betting facilities vary. Phone for information.

KANSAS SPEEDWAY is off I-70 exit 410 (110th St.) at jct. I-435/I-70. The 1,200-acre complex plays host to NASCAR and Indy races twice a year on its tri-oval track. The Fan Walk, accessed by separate admission on race days, is an interactive area in the infield. Guests have access to a working garage as well as to Autograph Alley, where fans can mingle with drivers. Track tours depart from the guard booth at Speedway Blvd. and Michigan Dr.

Hours: NASCAR Craftsman Truck Series, ARCA RE/MAX Series and IRL IndyCar Series racing roars over July 4 weekend, while NASCAR Sprint Cup Series and Nationwide Series racing takes place the last weekend in Sept. Walk-up tours Thurs. at 4, May.-Sept. **Cost:** Tours $10; $5 (ages 0-12). Race tickets are sold in annual packages. **Phone:** (913) 328-3375 for tour information, or (866) 460-7223 for race information and tickets.

LENEXA pop. 40,238, elev. 1,052′

Na-Nex-Se, the wife of a Shawnee Indian chief, lent her name to the Kansas City suburb of Lenexa in 1869. The community attracted German, Swiss and Belgian farmers by the early 1900s, and in the 1930s was known for its prolific spinach crops.

Shawnee Mission Park, on Renner Boulevard, has one of the largest lakes in the area and offers archery, fishing, hiking trails, horseback riding, sailboats and canoes, swimming, tennis, water skiing and windsurfing. The outdoor Theater in the Park presents plays and musicals.

Lenexa Convention & Visitors Bureau: 11180 Lackman Rd., Lenexa, KS 66219. **Phone:** (913) 888-1414 or (800) 950-7867.

LEGLER BARN MUSEUM is in 53-acre Sar-Ko-Par Trails Park at 14907 W. 87th St. Pkwy. The limestone Legler barn was built on the Santa Fe Trail in 1864 by Swiss immigrant Adam Legler. Moved to its present site and restored, the barn houses pioneer relics and a prairie schooner. A restored 1912 railroad depot and a Northern Pacific caboose are nearby. Allow 30 minutes minimum. **Hours:** Tues.-Fri. 10-4, Sat.-Sun. 1-4; closed holidays. **Cost:** Donations. **Phone:** (913) 492-0038.

OLATHE pop. 92,962, elev. 1,023′

In 1856 Dr. John T. Barton, appointed physician to the Shawnee Indians, staked a claim to land to which the Shawnees were giving up tribal title and named the land after the Shawnee word for beautiful, *Olathe.* Shortly after Olathe was established, it replaced the settlement of Shawnee as the county seat.

After Kansas was admitted to the Union as a free state in 1861, the town became an easy target for Confederate guerilla commander William Quantrill and his raiders, who invaded and destroyed much of the settlement. Once the Civil War ended, however, Olathe began to rebuild. The rich farmland and a railroad brought new settlers to the area.

Olathe Area Chamber of Commerce: 18001 W. 106th St., Suite 160, Olathe, KS 66061. **Phone:** (913) 764-1050.

MAHAFFIE STAGECOACH STOP AND FARM HISTORIC SITE is w. of jct. I-35 and SR 150, at 1100 Kansas City Rd. In 1857 Indiana farmer J.B. Mahaffie arrived in Olathe with his wife and five children to purchase land for farming; by 1865 he reputedly had the largest farm and livestock herd in Olathe township. From 1865 to 1869 Mahaffie's farmstead was used as a stagecoach stop, and the basement of the house served as a dining room for travelers. Visitors can see the wood peg barn, stone icehouse and house that Mahaffie built as well as interact with costumed interpreters depicting life in the 1860s. The Heritage Center is a visitor center housing a small museum with a timeline and a Mahaffie family biography.

Time: Allow 1 hour minimum. **Hours:** Mahaffie House Wed.-Sat. 10-4, Sun. noon-4, May-Oct.; Sat. 10-4, Sun. noon-4, in Apr. and Nov. Heritage center Wed.-Sat. 10-4, Sun. noon-4, all year. Closed major holidays. Hours may vary seasonally; phone ahead to confirm schedule, including for stagecoach rides. **Cost:** Admission Wed.-Thurs. $5; $3 (ages 5-11). Admission (includes stagecoach ride) Fri.-Sun. $6; $4 (ages 5-11). Phone ahead to confirm rates. **Phone:** (913) 971-5111.

OVERLAND PARK pop. 149,080

One of the largest cities in the state, Overland Park is the leading business and commercial center for the Johnson County portion of the Kansas City metropolitan area.

Overland Park Convention & Visitors Bureau: 9001 W. 110th, Suite 100, Overland Park, KS 66210. **Phone:** (913) 491-0123 or (800) 262-7275.

DEANNA ROSE CHILDREN'S FARMSTEAD is .7 mi. w. on US 150 (135th St.) from US 69, then .2 mi. s. to 13800 Switzer Rd. at jct. 138th St. The 12-acre farmstead is home to more than 200 animals, including horses, rabbits, sheep, chickens, ducks and goats that children can pet and feed. A barn, silo, fishing pond, nature trail, playground, bank building with artifacts, a re-created one-room 1900 schoolhouse, an American Indian encampment, and flower and vegetable gardens are on the grounds.

A birds of prey exhibit features an eagle, an owl and a hawk. At the dairy barn children can pet the

cows and, with help from a life-size model of a Holstein dairy cow named Rosie, learn how they are milked. Pony and horse-drawn wagon rides, mining and goat bottle feeding also are offered.

Note: Ben's Bank is scheduled to open Apr. 1, 2010. Picnicking is only permitted outside of the park. **Hours:** Grounds open daily 9-5, Apr.-Oct. (also Tues. and Thurs. 5-8, Memorial Day-Labor Day). Wagon rides Mon.-Fri. 9-3, Sat. 9-4. Pony rides, fishing, mining and goat bottle feeding Mon.-Sat. 10-5, Sun. 11-5. **Cost:** Site free. Mining $4 or $6. Wagon ride $3; free (under 1). Fishing or pony ride $3. Goat bottle feeding $1. All-activity combination ticket $10. Children must be at least 3 years old for a pony ride. **Phone:** (913) 897-2360.

OVERLAND PARK ARBORETUM AND BOTANICAL GARDENS is .5 mi. w. of US 69 at jct. 179th St. and Antioch Rd. Multiple gardens and ecosystems cover 300 acres. The Erikson Water Garden features bird and butterfly plants and ornamental grasses. Marder Woodland Garden has regional flora, wood and stone arbors, and a koi pond. The willow trees and annuals in the Monet Garden are similar to their namesake gardens in France.

A children's garden as well as an environmental education and visitor center are available. **Time:** Allow 1 hour minimum. **Hours:** Daily 8-7:30, mid-Apr. to late Sept.; 8-5, rest of year. Closed Dec. 25. **Cost:** Free. **Phone:** (913) 685-3604.

SHAWNEE pop. 47,996

Behind its modern-day suburban facade—the city is on the southwest edge of the Kansas City metropolitan area—Shawnee is part of a recorded history that dates back to 1724.

In subsequent years the settlement, first called Gum Springs, saw the opening of the Santa Fe Trail, the arrival of the Shawnee Indians from the East, the establishment of the Shawnee Mission and finally a raid by Civil War guerrilla William Quantrill. Shawnee was the largest town in the territory until it lost the title of county seat to Olathe in 1858.

Shawnee Convention & Visitors Bureau: 15100 W. 67th St., Suite 202, Shawnee, KS 66217-9344. **Phone:** (913) 631-6545 or (888) 550-7282.

THE 1950s ALL-ELECTRIC HOUSE is off I-435 exit 6A, 1.5 mi. e. on Shawnee Mission Pkwy., then n. to 6305 Lackman Rd. The house was built in 1954 by Kansas City Power and Light as a showcase of modern electric innovations. Pink laminate kitchen counter tops, a remote controlled coffee maker and push-button lights are featured.

The bathroom has traditional lighting, along with a germ-killing light and a tanning lamp. Allow 30 minutes minimum. **Hours:** Guided tours are given every half-hour Tues.-Sun. 1-4; closed major holidays. Last tour departs 30 minutes before closing. **Cost:** Admission $2; $1 (ages 0-12). **Phone:** (913) 715-2550.

JOHNSON COUNTY MUSEUM OF HISTORY is off I-435 exit 6A, 1.5 mi. e. on Shawnee Mission Pkwy., then n. to 6305 Lackman Rd. The Seeking the Good Life exhibit has more than 500 artifacts and explores three time periods in Johnson County. These eras are 1820-1880: Settling the Land; 1880-1945: Building the Suburbs; and 1945-present: Developing an Edge City. Interactive displays also highlight the county's history.

A research library also is available. Allow 30 minutes minimum. **Hours:** Tues.-Sat. 10-4:30, Sun. 1-4:30; closed major holidays. **Cost:** Free. **Phone:** (913) 715-2550.

OLD SHAWNEE TOWN is at the jct. of 57th and Cody sts. Two log cabins, a jail, home, barn, smokehouse and schoolhouse are original 1800s structures relocated from around the area. Reproductions include a bank, general store, undertaker/cabinet shop and sod house. All are furnished with antiques. **Hours:** Tues.-Sat. 10-4:30. **Cost:** Admission $1; 50c (ages 6-12). **Phone:** (913) 248-2360.

WONDERSCOPE CHILDREN'S MUSEUM is off I-35 exit 229 (Johnson Dr.), then w. 1.4 mi. to 5700 King. Hands-on activities encourage learning about art, communications, ecology, health, nature, science and space. **Time:** Allow 1 hour minimum. **Hours:** Tues.-Sat. 10-5, Sun. noon-5 (also Mon. 10-5, Mar.-Aug.). Closed major holidays. **Cost:** Admission $7; $6 (ages 64+); $4 (ages 1-2). **Phone:** (913) 287-8888 or (913) 268-4176.

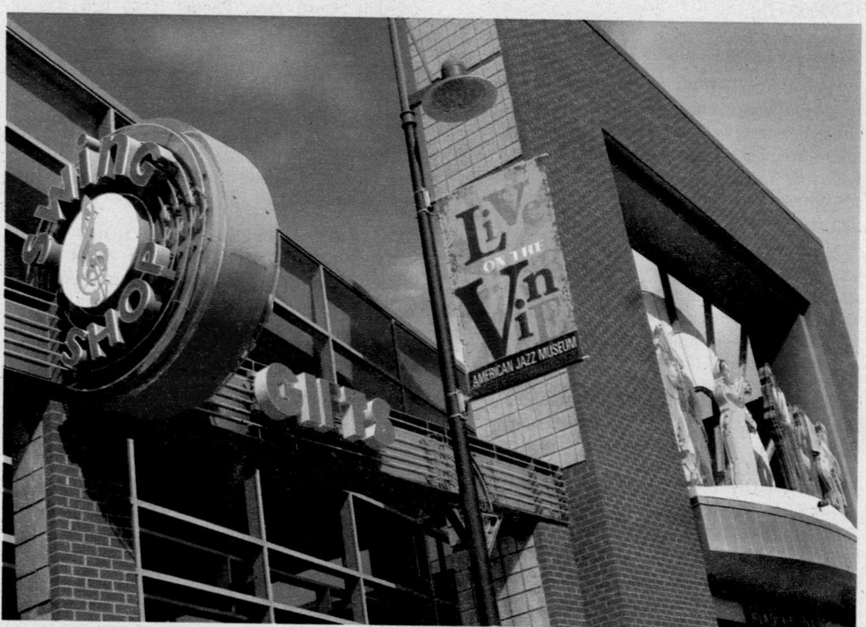

American Jazz Museum / © Don Smetzer / Alamy

This ends listings for the Kansas City Vicinity.
The following page resumes the alphabetical listings of cities in Missouri.

KEARNEY—*see Kansas City p. 179.*

KINGSVILLE (C-2) pop. 257, elev. 904′

POWELL GARDENS is at 1609 N.W. US 50, just e. of jct. SR W. Visitors may walk or take a trolley to the Perennial Garden, featuring more than 500 varieties of plants; the Rock and Waterfall Garden; the Wildlife Meadow; and the Majorie Powell Allen Chapel. A 1-mile nature trail also traverses the 835-acre park. Horticultural displays are located in the Visitor Education Center.

Time: Allow 1 hour minimum. **Hours:** Daily 9-6, Apr.-Oct.; 9-5, rest of year. Closed Jan. 1, Thanksgiving and Dec. 25. **Cost:** Apr.-Oct. $9.50; $8.50 (ages 60+); $4 (ages 5-12). Admission Nov.-Mar. $7; $6 (ages 60+); $3 (ages 5-12). **Phone:** (816) 697-2600.

KIRKSVILLE (A-3) pop. 16,988, elev. 965′

Founded in 1841 as the seat of Adair County, Kirksville was named for Jesse Kirk, who exchanged a turkey dinner for the right to name the town after himself. Truman State University and the Kirksville College of Osteopathic Medicine have transformed this former farming community into an important educational center.

The area's rural character still can be enjoyed in such nearby areas as Big Creek and Sugar Creek state forests and at the larger Thousand Hills State Park *(see Recreation Chart and the AAA South Central CampBook)*. Thousand Hills offers a petroglyph and the recreational facilities of Forest Lake.

Kirksville Area Chamber of Commerce: 304 S. Franklin, Kirksville, MO 63501-3581. **Phone:** (660) 665-3766.

STILL NATIONAL OSTEOPATHIC MUSEUM is 1 mi. w. of US 63 in the Tinning Education Center of A.T. Still University at 800 W. Jefferson St. This museum traces the roots of osteopathic medicine beginning with its founder, Dr. Andrew Taylor Still, and his establishment of the first osteopathic medical school in 1892. His medical approach was based on the belief that the keys to healing lie within the body itself. Today 10,000 students study his techniques in 20 schools.

The museum's collections of photographs, documents and artifacts span more than 120 years. Included are 1800s surgical tools, osteopathic treatment equipment and a dissected human nervous system. Within Heritage Hall are Still's birthplace cabin, relocated from Virginia, and a one-room schoolhouse where the first lectures about osteopathy were held. **Time:** Allow 1 hour minimum. **Hours:** Mon.-Fri. 8-5 (also Thurs. 5-7), Sat. noon-4. Closed major holidays. Phone ahead to confirm schedule. **Cost:** Free. **Phone:** (660) 626-2359 or (866) 626-2878.

KIRKWOOD—*see St. Louis p. 219.*

LACLEDE (B-3) pop. 415, elev. 784′

The 1868 Locust Creek Covered Bridge, 3 miles west off US 36, is one of only four covered bridges in Missouri.

GEN. JOHN J. PERSHING BOYHOOD HOME STATE HISTORIC SITE is 3 blks. e. of SR 5. This shrine to the leader of America's forces in World War I houses antique furnishings and personal effects. Also on the grounds is the one-room Prairie Mound School, where Pershing once taught. **Hours:** Mon.-Sat. 10-4, Sun. noon-6, mid-Apr. to mid-Oct.; Mon.-Sat. 10-4, Sun. noon-5, rest of year. Closed Jan. 1, Easter, Thanksgiving and Dec. 25. **Cost:** $2.50; $1.50 (ages 6-12). **Phone:** (660) 963-2525 or (800) 334-6946.

LA GRANGE (B-4) pop. 1,000

La Grange was named for the country home of the Marquis de Lafayette. Founder William Wright recorded the town plat a few years after the French general visited the United States in 1825. An early steamboat landing, the city was incorporated by the Missouri legislature in 1853, the same year St. Louis, Kansas City and St. Joseph were granted charters.

GAMBLING ESTABLISHMENTS

- **Terrible's Mark Twain Casino** is at 104 Pierce St. **Hours:** Sun.-Thurs. 8 a.m.-2 a.m., Fri.-Sat. 8 a.m.-4 a.m. **Phone:** (573) 655-4770 or (866) 454-5825.

LAKE OF THE OZARKS (C-3)

The Bagnell Dam was built on the Osage River in 1931 to form Lake of the Ozarks, Missouri's largest inland body of water and the largest man-made lake in the world at the time of its creation. Fishing, boating and swimming are popular pastimes on the 54,000-acre reservoir, which offers 1,150 miles of

---

DID YOU KNOW

The Kansas City Monarchs were the first baseball team to light the ball field for night games.

shoreline—more than the length of the California coast.

Osage Indians once hunted in the woods surrounding the lake, and it is said they left directions by bending and tying oak saplings. Hundreds of years later, examples of these strangely bent "thong trees" can still be seen.

The Community Bridge, completed in 1998, links the east and west sides of the lake. The toll bridge runs from Lake Ozark to Shawnee Bend.

The following towns on the Lake of the Ozarks are listed separately under their individual names: Camdenton, Linn Creek, Osage Beach and Warsaw *(see place listings)*.

Lake of the Ozarks Convention & Visitor Bureau: 5815 US 54, Osage Beach, MO 65065. **Phone:** (573) 348-1599 or (800) 386-5253. *See color ad.*

LAMAR (D-2) pop. 4,452, elev. 940′

HARRY S. TRUMAN BIRTHPLACE STATE HISTORIC SITE is at 1009 Truman St., near jct. US 71 and US 160. This six-room house, in which President Truman was born and lived the first year of his life, contains many of the original furnishings. **Time:** Allow 30 minutes minimum. **Hours:** Mon.-Sat. 10-4, Sun. noon-4. Closed Jan. 1, Easter, Thanksgiving and Dec. 25. **Cost:** Free. **Phone:** (417) 682-2279 or (800) 334-6946.

LAMPE—*see Branson p. 150.*

LAURIE (D-3) pop. 663, elev. 965′

NATIONAL SHRINE OF MARY, MOTHER OF THE CHURCH is 1 mi. n. on SR 5. A 14-foot stainless steel sculpture of the Virgin Mary stands in a terraced amphitheater, surrounded by landscaped fountains and pools. The Mother's Wall displays memorials engraved in black granite. An Avenue of Flags represents the home countries of visitors. **Hours:** Daily 24 hours; lights are turned off after 11 p.m. Mass is offered Sat. at 8:30 p.m., Sun. at 8:30 a.m., Memorial Day-Labor Day. **Cost:** Donations. **Phone:** (573) 374-6279.

LAWSON—*see Kansas City p. 179.*

LEASBURG (D-4) pop. 323, elev. 1,019′

GEM **ONONDAGA CAVE STATE PARK** is 5 mi. s. on SR H to 7556 SR H. One of the largest lighted caves in Missouri, Onondaga features formations ranging from lacy patterns to massive pieces of onyx. The temperature is always 57 F. Concrete walks wind through the interior. *See Recreation Chart and the AAA South Central CampBook.* **Tours:** Guided tours are available. **Time:** Allow 1 hour minimum. **Hours:** Daily 9-5, Mar.-Oct. **Cost:** $10; $8 (ages 65+); $5 (ages 6-12). **Phone:** (573) 245-6576 or (800) 334-6946.

LEBANON (D-3) pop. 12,155, elev. 1,265′

Originally named after the Wyota Indians, Lebanon was later renamed after Lebanon, Tenn. In the late 1800s residents discovered that the city's water contained magnetic properties. People flocked to the Gasconade Hotel to bathe in water that was said to contain healing qualities.

Bennett Spring State Park is located 12 miles west on SR 64. The 3,100-acre park offers nature programs and guided tours; phone (417) 532-4338 or (800) 334-6946. *See Recreation Chart.*

Jigsaw puzzles galore can be found at Nancy Ballhagen's Puzzles, about 5 miles east of Lebanon off I-44 exit 135 at 25211 Garden Crest Rd. More than 3,200 different puzzles, ranging from 100 to 18,000 pieces, are in stock. Visitors also can observe the "cutting room" where hand-cut wooden puzzles are created; phone (417) 286-3837.

Lebanon Area Chamber of Commerce: 186 N. Adams, Lebanon, MO 65536. **Phone:** (417) 588-3256.

LEE'S SUMMIT—*see Kansas City p. 179.*

LEXINGTON (B-2) pop. 4,453, elev. 698'

Lexington was founded in 1822 by settlers from Lexington, Ky. The location they chose on a bluff overlooking the Missouri River helped the city develop into a booming river port by the mid-19th century. In the 1830s and '40s Lexington was a terminus for overland trade; from here, pack mules and ox teams departed for such southwestern destinations as Santa Fe, N.M.

Lexington held strategic importance during the Civil War. The pro-South sentiment felt by many residents was reinforced when Union troops seized nearly $1 million from the Farmers' Bank of Lexington in early September 1861. On Sept. 20, the 3-day Battle of Lexington ended in a victory for the Confederates under Maj. Gen. Sterling Price. Lodged in the east column of the courthouse is a cannonball fired during the battle.

Masonic College, the headquarters of Col. James Mulligan's Union troops, has the added distinction of being the first college sponsored by the Masons. A scale model of the college occupies its original site, now in Central College Park.

During the school year the public may attend the formal dress parade of the nationally acclaimed Wentworth Military Academy Band, which performs Sun. at 2 in the large field house or on the parade grounds. The academy campus, founded in 1880, can be toured; phone (660) 259-2221.

Lexington Area Chamber of Commerce: 1029 Franklin Ave., Lexington, MO 64067. **Phone:** (660) 259-3082.

Self-guiding tours: Walking and driving tours encompass many sites in Lexington, including the Madonna of the Trail statue, antebellum houses, old churches and the Pony Express site. Brochures outlining these routes can be obtained at the Lexington Historical Museum *(see attraction listing)* or at the tourism center of the chamber of commerce.

BATTLE OF LEXINGTON STATE HISTORIC SITE, 1101 Delaware St., is the site of the Civil War conflict called the Battle of the Hemp Bales, which was so named for the bales the Confederate soldiers used as movable breastworks. Original earthworks and trenches are visible, and the historic Anderson House *(see attraction listing)* can be toured. *See Recreation Chart.*

Time: Allow 1 hour minimum. **Hours:** Tues.-Sat. (also holiday Mon.) 9-5, Sun. 10-6, Mar.-Oct.; Wed.-Sat. (also holiday Mon.) 9-5, Sun. 10-5, rest of year. Closed Jan. 1, Thanksgiving and Dec. 25. **Cost:** Free. **Phone:** (660) 259-4654 or (800) 334-6946.

Anderson House overlooks the battlefield within Battle of Lexington State Historic Site, which is at 1101 Delaware St. Soldiers engaged in skirmishes around the house, which served as a field hospital and changed from Union to Confederate hands several times. The house is preserved and furnished in period; a museum contains war items.

Hours: Guided 45-minute tours are offered on the hour Tues.-Sat. 10-4, Sun. noon-5, Apr.-July; Wed.-Sat 10-4, Sun. noon-5, Aug.-Oct. and in Mar.; by appointment rest of year. Closed Thanksgiving and Dec. 25. **Cost:** $2.50; $1.50 (ages 6-12). **Phone:** (660) 259-4654 or (800) 334-6946.

LEXINGTON HISTORICAL MUSEUM is at 112 S. 13th St. The former 1846 Cumberland Presbyterian Church contains photographs of historic Lexington and exhibits focusing on Lexington's Civil War battle and Pony Express station. **Hours:** Mon.-Fri. 1-4:30, Sat. 10-4, Sun. 1-4, June-Oct. **Cost:** $2; $1 (ages 0-12). **Phone:** (660) 259-6313.

LIBERTY—*see Kansas City p. 179.*

LINN CREEK (D-3) pop. 280, elev. 686'

SAVE **BIG SURF** is at 954 SR Y at jct. US 54. This 22-acre landscaped water park offers waves, white-water rapids, flumes and a lazy river ride. **Hours:** Daily 10-7, late June to mid-Aug.; daily 11-6, mid-Aug. through Labor Day; Mon.-Fri. 11-6, Sat. 10-7, Memorial Day weekend-late June. **Cost:** $25; $20 (ages 4-10); $11 (ages 60+); reduced rates after 3. Next-day admission (with paid receipt from the previous day) $12.50; $10 (ages 4-10). **Phone:** (573) 346-6111.

OZARK CAVERNS 6.6 mi. e. on SR A off US 54, .7 mi. n. on McCubbins Dr. then .7 mi. n.e. to 823 Ozark Caverns Rd., within Lake of the Ozarks State Park *(see Recreation Chart)*. Half-mile tours lasting 1 hour guide visitors past the caverns' geological formations, which include helictites, soda straws and stalagmites as well as the Angel Showers, a continuous shower of water which seems to emanate from the rock ceiling. The caverns are home to several bat and salamander species and a variety of invertebrates.

A visitor center presents displays about the caverns and also offers booklets outlining a 1-mile outdoor interpretive trail. Quarter-mile tours for children and 90-minute tours for adults are offered in summer. **Time:** Allow 1 hour minimum. **Hours:** Tours depart daily at 11, 12:30, 2 and 4, June 1-Aug. 15; daily at 12:30 and 2, Aug. 16-31; Sat.-Sun. at 11, 1 and 3, Apr. 16-May 31 and Sept. 1-Oct. 14. Phone ahead to confirm schedule. **Cost:** $6; $5 (ages 13-18); $4 (ages 6-12). Phone ahead to confirm rates. **Phone:** (573) 346-2500, or (800) 334-6946 for summer tour information.

LONE JACK—*see Kansas City p. 180.*

MANSFIELD (E-3) pop. 1,349, elev. 1,488'

In 1894 Laura Ingalls Wilder, her husband and small daughter moved from the prairies of the Dakota Territory to Mansfield, where they purchased a small farm on which the couple lived the rest of their lives. It was on this farm that Laura wrote the "Little House" books, favorites of children and the basis of a popular television series.

LAURA INGALLS WILDER-ROSE WILDER LANE HOME AND MUSEUM is 1 mi. e. of town square on CR A. The 1894 house contains Wilder's furniture and decorative items as they were during her occupancy. A museum contains articles about the "Little House" books, family pictures, clothing and other memorabilia associated with Wilder and her daughter, Rose Wilder Lane, also a distinguished author.

Hours: Mon.-Sat. and holidays 9-5, Sun. 12:30-5, Mar. 1 to mid-Nov. Closed Easter. **Cost:** $8; $6 (ages 65+); $4 (ages 6-17). **Phone:** (417) 924-3626 or (877) 924-7126.

MARCELINE (B-3) pop. 2,558, elev. 863'

Marceline, 3 miles south of US 36 on CR 5, was the boyhood home of beloved film producer, animator, theme park innovator and philanthropist Walter Elias Disney. Disney was born in Chicago, but the family moved to a farm near Marceline when Walt was five, and he later recalled those formative years as the best of his life. When Disney was developing his first theme park in California he had the fictitious Main Street modeled after his hometown; today the two-story brick buildings and cast-iron street lamps along Main Street USA (formerly Kansas Avenue) are reminiscent of the idealized American streetscape Disney incorporated into his parks.

Reminders of one of the 20th century's most influential individuals are scattered throughout town. E.P. Ripley Park is named after Santa Fe Railroad president E.P. Ripley. Disney—whose fondness for trains began as a child in Marceline, where he put his ear to the tracks to listen for their approach—named the first train to operate at Disneyland for Ripley. An original Santa Fe steam locomotive stands in the park, along with a gazebo built in 1898.

Walt's Barn, on the site of the Disney family farm, is a reconstruction of the barn Disney and his younger sister Ruth used to play in; today visitors are encouraged to sign their names and add a message to the walls of "Walt's Happy Place." Also on the site is the Dreaming Tree, a large cottonwood under which the young Disney spent time observing nature (a practice he referred to as "belly botany").

The Uptown Theatre, 104. N. Main St. USA, has hosted two Disney film premieres—"The Great Locomotive Chase" and "The Spirit of Mickey." The Walt Disney Post Office, 120 E. Ritchie Ave., a branch of the U.S. Post Office officially renamed in 2004, is the only federal building named after Disney.

Disney often returned to Marceline not only for personal renewal but to soak up the pastoral setting, which he incorporated into many of his films. Walt Disney's Hometown Toonfest, held in mid-September, brings internationally known cartoonists and animators to town. The festivities include a parade down Main Street USA, a Princess Tea Party for children, an apple pie-eating contest, art and craft booths and speaker presentations at the Uptown Theatre.

Marceline Area Chamber of Commerce: 209 N. Main St. USA, Marceline, MO 64658. **Phone:** (660) 376-2332.

WALT DISNEY HOMETOWN MUSEUM is downtown at 120 E. Santa Fe St. in the restored Santa Fe Railroad Depot. Exhibits focus on the Disney family's years in Marceline, Walt Disney's childhood and the family members, friends and associates who supported him in his creative pursuits. Memorabilia on display includes family letters and personal belongings, Mickey Mouse dolls and a Midget Autopia car, donated by Disney and his brother Roy, that was part of an amusement park ride at Disneyland.

Time: Allow 1 hour minimum. **Hours:** Tues.-Sat. 10-4, Sun. 1-4, Apr.-Oct. **Cost:** $5; $2.50 (ages 6-10). **Phone:** (660) 376-3343.

MARK TWAIN NATIONAL FOREST

Elevations in the forest range from 230 ft. at the boothell drainage ditches to 1,772 ft. on Taum Sauk Mountain.

In southern and central Missouri, Mark Twain National Forest encompasses 1.5 million acres in 29 counties. Scenic drives, hunting, camping, fishing, canoeing and hiking are among the many activities available in nine wilderness areas. Pinewoods Lake Recreation Area near Ellsinore features a 1.5-mile trail around the lake. A more challenging 5-mile national recreation trail skirts 99-acre Crane Lake, approximately 12 miles south of Ironton off SR 49 and CR E.

Big Bay Recreation Area, southeast of Shell Knob on SR 39, offers swimming, boating and fishing. Swimming in the Huzzah River is available at Red Bluff Recreation Area, east of Davisville on CR V. Activities at Noblett Lake Recreation Area, west of Willow Springs, include hiking, boating, camping and picnicking. Also within the forest is 49-acre Fourche Lake, about 18 miles west of Doniphan on SR 142, then 1 mile south on SR 160.

Skyline Scenic Drive, a 4-mile automobile loop, is 2 miles south of Van Buren on SR 103 and features views of the Ozark countryside. The 8-mile Sugar Camp Scenic Drive, off SR 112 near Cassville, also offers a drive through the Ozarks. Near I-70 is the 35-mile Cedar Creek Trail System. Glade Top Trail Scenic Drive, southeast of Springfield near SR 125, offers 23 miles through open glades.

Information about the forest's many national recreation areas can be obtained from the Forest Supervisor, 401 Fairgrounds Rd., Rolla, MO 65401; phone (573) 364-4621. *See Recreation Chart and the AAA South Central CampBook.*

MARYLAND HEIGHTS—*See St. Louis p. 219.*

MARYVILLE (A-1) pop. 10,581, elev. 1,034′

Maryville is named for Mary Graham, the first woman of European descent to settle in the village. She and her husband Amos built the first house in Maryville in 1844.

Mozingo Lake, 3 miles east on US 136, offers fishing, boating and hiking trails as well as camping and picnic areas. *See Recreation Chart.*

Maryville Chamber of Commerce: 423 N. Market St., Maryville, MO 64468. **Phone:** (660) 582-8643.

Self-guiding tours: The Nodaway County Historical Society publishes a driving tour of more than 30 historic buildings and 20 houses in Maryville. Brochures are available from the chamber of commerce.

NODAWAY COUNTY HISTORICAL SOCIETY MUSEUM is at 110 N. Walnut St. Asian artifacts, horse racing memorabilia, a collection of military uniforms and an interactive children's area are offered. A restored 1883 schoolhouse is on the grounds. **Time:** Allow 1 hour minimum. **Hours:** Tues.-Fri. 1-4, Mar.-Nov. Closed major holidays. **Cost:** Donations. **Phone:** (660) 582-8176.

MERRIAM WOODS—*see Branson p. 150.*

MEXICO (C-4) pop. 11,320, elev. 818′

Many Mexico residents share a love of championship horses. Located near the Salt River in Missouri's upland prairie region and established in 1837, early Mexico was encircled by racetracks. These tracks were the scene of Saturday afternoon events well attended by the locals. The trotting and pacing races at Mexico's fair in 1908 were purportedly the first in the nation to offer purses of as much as $1,500.

In the early 20th century Mexico was the center of one of the world's most important fireclay manufacturing areas. The refractories and brick factories here once held a virtual monopoly on the production of many types of fireclay products.

Rated by the Department of the Army and the Department of Education as one of the nation's top military schools, the Missouri Military Academy is the home of the Fusiliers, a national champion drill team. The public is invited to watch the battalion march in review on Sundays at 1:40 from September through May. Campus tours are available daily during the same months; phone (573) 581-1776 or (888) 564-6662.

Mexico Area Chamber of Commerce: 100 W. Jackson, Mexico, MO 65265. **Phone:** (573) 581-2765 or (800) 581-2765.

AUDRAIN COUNTY HISTORICAL SOCIETY AND AMERICAN SADDLE HORSE MUSEUM is at 501 S. Muldrow St. Gen. Ulysses S. Grant visited the 1857 Graceland house during the early days of the Civil War. The house's second owner, Colby T. Quisenberry, brought the first saddle horses into Audrain County from Kentucky. Rooms are furnished in period. The museum traces the role played by Audrain County in the development of the saddle horse.

Included are a parlor and a bedroom that has original Currier and Ives prints. Old wedding dresses and a large doll collection also are displayed. A country schoolhouse also is on the grounds. **Hours:** Tues.-Sat. 10-4, Sun. 1-4, Feb.-Dec. Closed major holidays. **Cost:** $5; $3 (ages 0-12). **Phone:** (573) 581-3910.

MIAMI (B-3) pop. 160, elev. 781′

VAN METER STATE PARK .9 mi. n. on SR 122 from jct. CR 427. The 1,100-acre park grounds preserve burial sites, ceremonial mounds, a hand-dug earthwork and other remnants of an Indian village mapped by French explorers in 1673. Exhibits and a large mural at the cultural center interpret this and other ancient and Indian cultures—some of which date from 10,000 B.C.—to inhabit the area. An 18-acre lake, hiking trails and a natural area also are on the premises. *See Recreation Chart and the AAA South Central CampBook.*

Hours: Park open daily 8 a.m.-dusk. Visitor center open Mon.-Sat. 10-4, Sun. 1-5. Phone ahead to confirm schedule. **Cost:** Free. **Phone:** (660) 886-7537 or (800) 334-6946.

MONROE CITY (B-4) pop. 2,588, elev. 745′

CLARENCE CANNON DAM AND MARK TWAIN LAKE is at 20642 SR J. The 285-mile shoreline of this 18,600-acre site provides 12 recreation areas with facilities for a variety of activities, including boating, fishing, swimming, camping, hiking and hunting *(see Recreation Chart)*. Summer campfire programs about the natural and cultural history of the area are presented at two amphitheaters.

M.W. Boudreaux Memorial Visitor Center is being rebuilt and is scheduled to reopen summer 2010. **Hours:** Office open Mon.-Fri. 7-4 (also Sat. 8-4, Apr. 1-Labor Day). Schedules for recreation areas vary; phone for information. **Cost:** Free. **Phone:** (573) 735-4097.

MOUND CITY (A-1) pop. 1,193, elev. 877′

SQUAW CREEK NATIONAL WILDLIFE REFUGE is s. on CR E to US 159, then .5 mi. w. Some 268 species of birds—including up to half a million waterfowl during migrations—inhabit the 7,200-acre refuge on the east edge of the Missouri River flood plain. Nearly 200 bald eagles winter in the refuge, which has hiking trails, observation towers, a wayside exhibit and a 10-mile auto tour route. Information leaflets are available at the office headquarters.

Hours: Refuge open daily dawn-dusk (weather permitting). Headquarters open Mon.-Fri. 7:30-4. Closed major holidays. **Cost:** Free. **Phone:** (660) 442-3187 or TTY (800) 877-8339.

NEOSHO (E-2) pop. 10,505, elev. 1,019′

Neosho was named for the Osage word describing the clear water of a large spring near the center of town. The community was the boyhood home of artist Thomas Hart Benton, whose bold caricature-like paintings and murals portrayed the nation's ideas of life west of the Mississippi River in the early 1800s.

Neosho Area Chamber of Commerce: 216 W. Spring St., Neosho, MO 64850. **Phone:** (417) 451-1925.

NATIONAL FISH HATCHERY is at 520 E. Park St. Lake Taneycomo and military reservations are stocked with rainbow trout by the hatchery, which also produces millions of 3-inch rainbow trout for transfer to federal hatcheries in Arkansas. **Hours:** Mon.-Fri. 8-4:30. **Cost:** Free. **Phone:** (417) 451-0554.

NEVADA (D-1) pop. 8,607, elev. 862′

In the 1850s Nevada found itself in the middle of the violent border warfare between proponents of slavery and abolitionists in the Kansas Territory. The situation worsened after the outbreak of the Civil War, when Kansas gangs called Jayhawkers ravaged the Missouri border counties between Nevada and Kansas City.

In response to the attacks, Confederate partisans banded together to fight behind Union lines. Considered outlaws by Unionists and heroes by border residents, the guerrilla fighters were called Bushwhackers, and Nevada was deemed the Bushwhacker Capital for its strategic position during the conflict. Bushwhackers from Nevada included Frank James and James A. "Dick" Liddil, another James gang member.

Nevada-Vernon County Chamber of Commerce: 225 W. Austin, Suite 200, Nevada, MO 64772. **Phone:** (417) 667-5300.

BUSHWHACKER MUSEUM entrance is at 212 W. Walnut St. This museum chronicles the history of Vernon County and displays artifacts from the Bushwhacker Jail, the county jail for a century (1860-1960). Also displayed are furnished rooms from the historic Hornback House as well as Civil War memorabilia relating to the Bushwhackers.

The jail is located in the same block as the museum; guided tours are available. **Time:** Allow 1 hour minimum. **Hours:** Tues.-Sat. 10-4, May-Oct.; by appointment rest of year. **Cost:** $5; $2 (ages 12-17); $1 (ages 0-11). **Phone:** (417) 667-9602.

NEW MADRID (F-6) pop. 3,334, elev. 225′

New Madrid is at the tip of New Madrid Bend, an almost 360-degree curve at one of the widest points on the Mississippi River. In 1811 the river city's growth halted when its terrain was reshaped by one of the strongest earthquakes felt in North America. This was followed by a series of quakes and tremors that occurred regularly for almost 2 years.

By the time of the Civil War, New Madrid occupied a position offering control of the Mississippi River. On March 13, 1862, after a day of heavy fighting, Brig. Gen. John Pope and his Union troops forced Confederate commodore George Hollins and his men to withdraw.

The New Madrid Observation Deck at the end of Main Street offers a good view of New Madrid Bend.

New Madrid Chamber of Commerce: 537B Mott St., New Madrid, MO 63869. **Phone:** (573) 748-5300.

HIGGERSON SCHOOL HISTORIC SITE is at jct. Main and Motts sts. The interior of this one-room schoolhouse is preserved as it was in 1948, when the white clapboard building accommodated one teacher and 32 students in eight grades. **Hours:** Wed.-Sat. 10-4, Memorial Day-Labor Day; by appointment rest of year. **Cost:** $2; $1.50 (ages 56+); $1 (ages 6-12). **Phone:** (573) 748-5716.

HUNTER-DAWSON STATE HISTORIC SITE is at 312 Dawson Rd., just e. of Main St. Built in Greek Revival and Italianate styles, this restored 15-room house is furnished as it might have looked in the mid-19th century. **Tours:** Guided tours are available. **Hours:** Mon.-Sat. 10-4, Sun. noon-4. Closed Jan. 1, Easter, Thanksgiving and Dec. 25. **Cost:** $2.50; $1.50 (ages 6-12). **Phone:** (573) 748-5340 or (800) 334-6946.

NEW MADRID HISTORICAL MUSEUM is at jct. Main and Water sts. Exhibits at the museum reflect the region's rich history, from Mississippian Indian culture to the early 20th century. Rooms are devoted to the 1811-12 earthquakes and the riverbend community's Civil War history. A collection of antique quilts also is displayed. **Time:** Allow 1 hour minimum. **Hours:** Mon.-Sat. 9-5, Sun. noon-5, Memorial Day-Labor Day; Mon.-Sat. 9-4, Sun. noon-4, rest of year. **Cost:** $2.50; $2 (ages 56+); $1.50 (ages 0-11). **Phone:** (573) 748-5944.

NORTH KANSAS CITY—

see Kansas City p. 180.

OSAGE BEACH (D-3) pop. 3,662

Osage Beach's location on Lake of the Ozarks makes it a popular vacation site. Music and comedy shows take place at the Main Street Music Hall, on Main Street at Blair's Landing.

Lake Area Chamber of Commerce: 1 Willmore Ln., Lake Ozark, MO 65049. **Phone:** (573) 348-2730.

OSBORN (B-2) pop. 455, elev. 1,035′

SHATTO MILK CO. is at 9406 N. CR 33, 8 mi. n. of jct. CR 116. This working dairy farm offers guided tours of its operations. Visitors can milk a cow and pet calves. **Hours:** Mon.-Fri. 9-6, Sat. 8-4, Sun. 9-4. Guided tours are given Tues.-Sat. at 10:30. Closed Jan. 1, Thanksgiving and Dec. 25. **Cost:** Farm free. Guided tour $5. Reservations are required for tours. **Phone:** (816) 930-3862.

OZARKS AND OZARK NATIONAL SCENIC RIVERWAYS

Stretching across southern Missouri, the Ozark Mountains rise from the Ozark Plateau. One of the oldest mountain ranges in North America, the eroded tableland extends from west of the Mississippi River in northern Arkansas to southern Missouri and northeast Oklahoma, ending in southern Illinois. The hardwood forests that blanket the Ozarks conceal approximately 4,000 caves, giving Missouri its reputation as the cave state.

Immortalized for their exceptional beauty in Harold Bell Wright's novel "The Shepherd of the Hills," the Ozarks are rich in folklore and tradition. The mountains were settled after the Civil War by Scottish mountaineers and homesteaders from Kentucky, Virginia, the Carolinas and Tennessee.

In the isolation of the hills and hollows, indigent farmers tended their moonshine stills and produced from their fiddles the first strains of what came to be known as country music.

The Ozark National Scenic Riverways embrace portions of the Current and Jacks Fork rivers. Land along both sides of the rivers is protected. Forests, with many varieties of trees, shrubs and wildflowers, cover three-fourths of the riverways. Wildlife is abundant; hunting is permitted in season.

The riverways area is noted for its many springs—more than 60 in all. Big Spring, south of Van Buren on US 60 and then 4 miles east on SR 103, is one of the nation's largest springs. Flowing from a collapsed cave, it emits an average of 286 million gallons of water a day. A two-story historic roller mill, 6 miles west of Eminence via SR 106, is preserved at Alley Spring, one of the riverways' largest springs.

Flashlight tours of Round Spring Cavern near Round Spring are offered by park interpreters during the summer. Recreational facilities in the park include camping and picnic areas. Several outfitters offer float trips on the Current and Jacks Fork rivers.

For information about seasonal interpretive programs, craft demonstrations and other activities, visit park headquarters in Van Buren, on the Current River, or write Ozark National Scenic Riverways, P.O. Box 490, Van Buren, MO 63965; phone (573) 323-4236. *See Recreation Chart and the AAA South Central CampBook.*

Towns in the Ozarks region listed in this book under their own descriptions are Branson, Defiance, Hermann, Hogan, Ironton, Jefferson City, New Madrid, Osage Beach, Rolla, St. James and Warsaw *(see place listings).*

PARK HILLS (D-5) pop. 7,861

MISSOURI MINES STATE HISTORIC SITE is off US 67, 1.8 mi. w. on SR 32, then .9 mi. s. on Park Hills Rd. This 25-acre site encompasses the original buildings of a former lead mine that operated 1906-72. A museum features mining equipment and geology exhibits as well as an extensive mineral collection. A short videotape presentation provides an introduction to the lead mining process.

Time: Allow 1 hour, 30 minutes minimum. **Hours:** Tours of the site are given Mon.-Sat. 10-4, Sun. noon-6, Apr.-Nov.; Fri.-Sat. 10-4, Sun. noon-5, rest of year. Closed Jan. 1, Easter, Thanksgiving and Dec. 25. **Cost:** Fee $2.50; $1.50 (ages 6-12). **Phone:** (573) 431-6226 or (800) 334-6946.

PERRYVILLE (D-6) pop. 7,667

The Kings Highway, which the Spanish extended from New Madrid to St. Louis in 1789, once ran through the present site of Perryville. The rolling barrens of Perry County were named for the geographically similar small plains areas of southwestern Kentucky.

Perryville Chamber of Commerce: 2 W. St. Maries St., Perryville, MO 63775. **Phone:** (573) 547-6062.

NATIONAL SHRINE OF OUR LADY OF THE MIRACULOUS MEDAL is 1.5 mi. n. on W. St. Joseph St., then .2 mi. w. on CR T. The walls and ceilings of St. Mary's of the Barrens Church and the shrine depict religious scenes and the history of the Vincentian order. On the grounds is the Marian Grotto.

Hours: Church, shrine and grounds open daily dawn-dusk. Visitor center Mon.-Fri. 9-4:30, Sat.-Sun. noon-4. Tours of the church and shrine are given Mon.-Fri. at 10 and 1, Sat.-Sun. at 1 and 3. Tours are not offered on holidays, holy days and the first weekend of Aug. **Cost:** Free. **Phone:** (573) 547-8344 or (573) 547-8343.

PILOT KNOB (D-5) pop. 697, elev. 961′

FORT DAVIDSON STATE HISTORIC SITE is at jct. SRs 21 and 221. A Union post on this site was defended by 1,450 men under Brig. Gen. Thomas Ewing Jr. when it was attacked Sept. 26-27, 1864, by Maj. Gen. Sterling Price and 12,000 Confederate troops. The siege on the earthen fort cost Price more than 1,000 men and ended his march on St. Louis.

A visitor center features exhibits and a diorama of the Battle of Pilot Knob. Only an earthwork remains of the fort. **Hours:** Visitor center open daily 10-4, Mar.-Nov.; Tues.-Sun. 10-4, rest of year. **Cost:** Free. **Phone:** (573) 546-3454 or (800) 334-6946.

PLATTE CITY—*see Kansas City p. 180.*

POINT LOOKOUT—*see Branson p. 150.*

POPLAR BLUFF (E-5) pop. 16,651, elev. 344′

After the formation of Butler County a site was needed to serve as county seat. The low poplar-covered bluffs lining the Black River were chosen, and in 1850 Poplar Bluff was founded. Poplar Bluff grew slowly until 1873, when the Iron Mountain Railroad spurred commerce and the development of the lumber industry.

When the supply of timber became depleted in the early 20th century, residents turned to farming and the storing and shipping of farm products. Railroads and highways helped make Poplar Bluff a wholesale and retail center for southeastern Missouri and northeastern Arkansas.

Greater Poplar Bluff Area Chamber of Commerce: 1111 W. Pine St., Poplar Bluff, MO 63901. **Phone:** (573) 785-7761.

THE MARGARET HARWELL ART MUSEUM is at 421 N. Main St. It presents traveling exhibits in addition to monthly changing displays from a permanent collection of works by contemporary Missouri artists, executed in a wide range of media. **Time:** Allow 30 minutes minimum. **Hours:** Tues.-Fri. noon-4, Sat.-Sun. 1-4. Museum may close when exhibits are being changed. Closed major holidays. **Cost:** Free. **Phone:** (573) 686-8002.

PUXICO (E-6) pop. 1,145, elev. 370′

MINGO NATIONAL WILDLIFE REFUGE is 1 mi. n. on SR 51. This 21,676-acre region of swampy bottomlands and wooded uplands is a haven for wintering and migrating waterfowl and other species. Fishing and limited hunting are allowed in season. Write Refuge Manager, Mingo National Wildlife Refuge, 24279 SR 51, Puxico, MO 63960.

Time: Allow 1 hour minimum. **Hours:** Visitor center open Mon.-Fri. 8-4, Sat. 9-4, Sun. noon-4, Mar.-June and Sept.-Nov.; Mon.-Fri. 8-4, rest of year. Closed major holidays. **Cost:** $3 per private vehicle. **Phone:** (573) 222-3589.

REPUBLIC (E-2) pop. 8,438

WILSON'S CREEK NATIONAL BATTLEFIELD MUSEUM is 10 mi. s.w. via SR 60, .7 mi. s.e. on Republic Rd., then 7 mi. s. on CR ZZ. The museum features a collection of Civil War memorabilia from west of the Mississippi River, including flags, photographs, uniforms, weapons and other artifacts. *(See Wilson's Creek National Battlefield p. 230).* **Time:** Allow 30 minutes minimum. **Hours:** Daily 9-noon and 1-4, Apr.-Nov. **Cost:** $5; free (ages 0-15); $10 (per private vehicle). **Phone:** (417) 732-1224.

RICHMOND—*see Kansas City p. 180.*

RIVERSIDE—*see Kansas City p. 181.*

ROCHEPORT (C-3) pop. 208, elev. 614′

Explorers Meriwether Lewis and William Clark passed through the territory around present-day Rocheport in June 1804. Founded in 1825, the town prospered due to a strategic location on the Missouri River that facilitated steamboat and ferry transportation. The Civil War subjected Rocheport to raids by both Confederate and Union troops; despite strong Southern sympathies, the town also was an important location for the activities of the Underground Railroad.

Further growth came in the 1880s and '90s when the Missouri-Kansas-Texas Railroad was built through town. Today the rail line forms the Katy Trail, which spans 225 miles across north-central Missouri from St. Charles west to Clinton. Most of the trail closely follows the Missouri River, which is lined at intervals with towering bluffs, and winds through some of the state's prettiest scenery. Ideal for walking, hiking and bicycling, the section of the trail near Rocheport (at the north end of town) also has the rail line's only tunnel, built in 1893. At the trailhead (mile marker 178.3) day users can take advantage of a public parking area and restrooms inside a reconstructed depot. Bicycles can be rented at the Trailside Café & Bike Shop, 700 First St.

Downtown Rocheport still retains its small-town tranquility, with antique and specialty shops, restaurants and bed-and-breakfasts lining a compact five-block area. The little Friends of Rocheport Museum at First and Moniteau streets documents the town's early history through photographs, books, tools and period clothing. Mighty Mo Canoe Rentals, 205 Central St., offers guided paddle trips on the Missouri River on Saturday afternoons from mid-May through the end of October; phone (573) 698-3903.

ROLLA (D-4) pop. 16,347, elev. 1,095′

Rolla was founded in 1855 when a group of railroad contractors built an office and a few warehouses near the farm of John Webber. The prospect of the railroad attracted 600 people within the following 6 months, and in 1857 a search for a town name began.

Webber, who had farmed in the area, wanted to call the town Hardscrabble. A railroad official wanted to call it Phelps Center. The suggestion of a nostalgic North Carolinian who wanted to call it Raleigh was finally approved, but the new name was spelled as the Southerner had pronounced it.

Rolla is the home of the Mid-Continent Mapping Center, National Mapping Division, US Geological Survey. The center, 1400 Independence Rd., offers tours; phone (573) 308-3500.

St. Patrick, the patron saint of engineers, is honored every March by students attending the University of Missouri at Rolla (UMR), who are dubbed knights in the Order of St. Patrick. Other festivities include a parade, a beard competition and painting Main Street a shade of green.

On the UMR campus near US 63 and State Street is UMR-Stonehenge, a partial replica of the ancient megaliths in England. The stone circle has apertures that allow the date to be told by the position of the sun's rays and permit the viewing of the North Star, features not present in the original construction. The replica is an official triangulation point in the National Geodetic Survey's North American Triangulation Network.

Rolla Area Chamber of Commerce: 1311 Kingshighway, Rolla, MO 65401. **Phone:** (573) 364-3577 or (888) 809-3817.

ED CLARK MUSEUM OF MISSOURI GEOLOGY is on Fairground Rd. in Buehler Park, .5 mi. e. of I-44 exit 184 at the Missouri Department of Natural Resources, Division of Geology and Land Survey. The museum displays minerals and fossils found in the state. **Time:** Allow 30 minutes minimum. **Hours:** Mon.-Fri. 8-5. **Cost:** Free. **Phone:** (573) 368-2100.

ST. CHARLES—*see St. Louis p. 219.*

STE. GENEVIEVE (D-6) pop. 4,476, elev. 397′

The first permanent settlement in Missouri, founded between 1725 and 1750, Ste. Genevieve is in the region that was once part of Upper Louisiana. French traditions are still evident in the festivals and the residential architecture of a town that once rivaled St. Louis in size and importance.

Great River Road Welcome Center: 66 S. Main St., Ste. Genevieve, MO 63670. **Phone:** (573) 883-7097 or (800) 373-7007.

Self-guiding tours: Information about self-guiding walking tours is available from the welcome center daily 9-4.

BOLDUC HOUSE is at 123 S. Main St. The home of Louis Bolduc, a wealthy merchant, planter and miner, is one of the few surviving examples of 18th-century French Colonial Mississippi Valley architecture. The restored 1785 house and grounds include the sill and stone foundation, massive trussed roof, 18th-century garden, enclosing *galerie* and stockade fence. The parlor, dining room and bedroom contain period French Canadian furnishings.

Time: Allow 30 minutes minimum. **Hours:** Mon.-Sat. 10-4, Sun. 11-5, Apr. 1-Nov. 1. Closed Easter. **Cost:** (includes Bolduc-LeMeilleur House) $5; $2 (students through high school with ID). **Phone:** (573) 883-3105.

BOLDUC-LEMEILLEUR HOUSE is at jct. Main and Market sts. at 121 S. Main St. This restored 1820 house is an example of combined French and American architectural influences. **Time:** Allow 30 minutes minimum. **Hours:** Mon.-Sat. 10-5, Sun. 11-5, Apr. 1-Nov. 1. Closed Easter. **Cost:** (includes Bolduc House) $5; $2 (students through high school with ID). **Phone:** (573) 883-3105.

CHURCH OF STE. GENEVIEVE is on DuBourg Pl. near Merchant St. Although the congregation was established in 1759, the present church was not built until 1876. A religious painting dating from 1663 hangs inside. **Hours:** Daily 8-4. **Cost:** Free. **Phone:** (573) 883-2731.

FELIX VALLÉ HOUSE STATE HISTORIC SITE is at Second and Merchant sts. In contrast to the vertical log houses erected by French and Spanish colonists, this 1818 house was constructed from stone in the American Federal style. Its two entrances let the building serve as both home and office for its owners. The house is furnished in period. **Hours:** Mon.-Sat. 10-4, Sun. noon-5. Closed Mon.-Tues. (Dec.-Feb.), Jan. 1, Easter, Thanksgiving and Dec. 25. **Cost:** $2.50; $1.50 (ages 6-12). **Phone:** (573) 883-7102 or (800) 334-6946.

The Amoureux House is .25 mi. s. on Main St. to 327 St. Mary's Rd., within Felix Vallé State Historic Site. This 1792 French Colonial vertical log home is one of three in the United States built using only vertical logs for its foundation. An exhibit room with information about the community's architectural history and a diorama room with a model of Ste. Genevieve circa 1832 are highlights.

Tours: Guided tours are available. **Time:** Allow 30 minutes minimum. **Hours:** Daily 10-4, June-Aug.; Sat. 10-4, Sun. noon-5, Apr.-May and Sept.-Oct. **Cost:** $1.50; 75c (ages 6-12). **Phone:** (573) 883-7102 or (800) 334-6946.

LA MAISON GUIBOURD-VALLÉ is at 1 N. Fourth St. Built in the French style by Spanish soldiers in 1784, the house was bought in 1799 by Jacques Jean René Guibourd, a French settler. The restored residence is of vertical log construction and has elegant 18th- and 19th-century French furnishings. Hand-hewn oak beams secured by wooden pegs and a Norman truss form the large attic. A garden enclosed by a brick wall contains a variety of flowering plants and trees.

Costumed guides conduct tours. **Time:** Allow 30 minutes minimum. **Hours:** Tours are given Tues.-Fri. and Sun. noon-5, Sat. 10-5, Apr. 1-first weekend in Dec. **Cost:** $4; $3.50 (ages 60+); $2 (grades K-12). **Phone:** (573) 883-7544.

STE. GENEVIEVE MUSEUM is at jct. Merchant and Third sts. Displays include American Indian relics, Civil War items, old coins, rare documents and birds mounted by John James Audubon during his residence in Ste. Genevieve. **Hours:** Mon.-Sat. 10-4, Sun. noon-4, Apr.-Oct.; daily noon-4, rest of year. Closed Jan. 1, Easter, July 4, Thanksgiving and Dec. 24-25 and 31. **Cost:** $2; 50c (students). **Phone:** (573) 883-3461.

ST. JAMES (D-4) pop. 3,704, elev. 1,087′

MARAMEC SPRING PARK is 6 mi. s. on SR 68, then 2 mi. s. on SR 8. The site of the first successful ironworks west of the Mississippi River, the park contains the Ozark Agriculture Museum, the Maramec Museum and the Maramec Nature Center. Picnicking, hiking and trout fishing facilities are available March through October. **Hours:** Daily dawn-dusk. **Cost:** Park entrance $4 (per private vehicle). **Phone:** (573) 265-7387.

Maramec Museum, 21880 Maramec Dr. within Maramec Spring Park, imparts the operation of the Maramec Iron Works 1826-76. A video presentation depicts the formation of Maramec Spring's cave and the Salem Cave and the Southern cavefish inhabitants. Other exhibits include a rain model as well as cultural and natural displays. Remains of the original facility are on the grounds. **Hours:** Daily 11-5, June-Aug.; Mon.-Fri. 10-3, Sat.-Sun. noon-4, in May; Wed.-Fri. 10-3, Sat.-Sun. noon-4 in Apr. and Sept.-Oct. **Cost:** Free. **Phone:** (573) 265-7124.

ST. JOSEPH (B-1) pop. 73,990, elev. 823′

St. Joseph was founded in 1826 by Joseph Robidoux, who established a fur trading post in the Blacksnake Hills. The mass migrations following the discovery of gold in California in 1848 and Colorado in 1858 transformed the frontier town into a major wagon train staging area and supply depot. In 1859 Robidoux drove the last spike on the Hannibal and St. Joseph Railroad, which made St. Joseph the westernmost railroad terminal.

The Pony Express launched its famous mail service on Apr. 3, 1860, from St. Joseph to Sacramento, Calif. Riders traveled the 10-day route twice a week.

Notorious outlaw Jesse James lived quietly with his family in St. Joseph, where he was known as the mild-mannered, respected Mr. Howard. He was killed in 1882 by fellow gang member Bob Ford, whose brother Charles claimed the $10,000 reward.

The Buchanan County Courthouse, 411 Jules St., originally was constructed at Fifth and Felix streets in 1873. During the Centennial Exhibition of 1876, the classical Renaissance building was called one of the most outstanding buildings in the country. Its exterior is lighted at night; the interior houses county offices.

St. Joseph Convention and Visitors Bureau: 109 S. 4th St., P.O. Box 445, St. Joseph, MO 64501. **Phone:** (816) 233-6688 or (800) 785-0360. *See color ad p. 197*

THE ALBRECHT-KEMPER MUSEUM OF ART is 2 mi. w. of I-29 at 2818 Frederick Ave. Housed in the 1935 former Albrecht Mansion, the museum displays American art from the 18th century to the present as well as special exhibits. **Hours:** Tues.-Fri. 10-4, Sat.-Sun. 1-4. Closed major holidays. **Cost:** $5; $2 (ages 65+); $1 (ages 7-17 and students with ID). **Phone:** (816) 233-7003.

DOLL MUSEUM is at 1115 S. 12th St. Old dolls in original handmade clothes are displayed. Among the changing exhibits are miniature dishes, toys, buggies and a Missouri farmhouse complete in every detail. **Hours:** Wed.-Sat. 11:30-4:30, June-Sept.; Sat.-Sun. 11:30-4:30, in Oct. **Cost:** $2.50; $2 (ages 62+); $1 (ages 6-16). **Phone:** (816) 233-1420.

THE GLORE PSYCHIATRIC MUSEUM is at 3406 Frederick Ave. It surveys the portrayal and treatment of mental illness over the years, including exhibits of antique ward furniture and such primitive early equipment as lobotomy instruments, a hydrotub, a tranquilizing chair, a restraint cage and wet sheet packs. The museum also recounts the history of a facility once known as "State Lunatic Asylum No. 2."

Time: Allow 1 hour minimum. **Hours:** Mon.-Sat. 10-5, Sun. 1-5. Closed major holidays. **Cost:** (includes The Black Archives of St. Joseph and the St. Joseph Museum) $5; $4 (ages 62+); $2 (ages 7-18). **Phone:** (816) 232-8471 or (800) 530-8866.

The Black Archives of St. Joseph, 3406 Frederick Ave. on The Glore Psychiatric Museum grounds, has exhibits depicting the history and cultural heritage of the African-American community in St. Joseph. **Hours:** Mon.-Sat. 10-5, Sun. 1-5. Closed major holidays. **Cost:** (includes The Glore Psychiatric Museum and the St. Joseph Museum) $5; $4 (ages 62+); $2 (ages 7-18). **Phone:** (816) 232-8471.

St. Joseph Museum, 3406 Frederick Ave. on The Glore Psychiatric Museum grounds, contains displays of Native American clothing, pottery, weapons and jewelry as well as exhibits chronicling the travels of explorers Meriwether Lewis and William Clark, Civil War history and St. Joseph's role in the nation's westward expansion. **Hours:** Mon.-Sat. 10-5, Sun. 1-5. Closed major holidays. **Cost:** (includes The Glore Psychiatric Museum and The Black Archives of St. Joseph) $5; $4 (ages 62+); $2 (ages 7-18). **Phone:** (816) 232-8471.

JESSE JAMES HOME is at 12th and Penn sts. on the grounds of the Patee House Museum *(see attraction listing)*. The outlaw's residence was the scene of his death at the hands of members of his gang. A bullet hole in the wall was made April 3, 1882, when James was killed. The restored house is furnished with original and period pieces. Tape recordings explain the significance of events that occurred in each room.

Hours: Mon.-Sat. 10-5, Sun. 1-5, Apr.-Oct.; Sat. 10-5, Sun. 1-5, rest of year. Mon.-Fri. hours may be offered Nov.-Mar. depending on volunteer availability and weather; phone ahead to verify schedule. **Cost:** $3; $2 (ages 60+); $1.50 (students with ID). **Phone:** (816) 232-8206.

KRUG PARK is at the n. end of the city on St. Joseph Ave. Visitors can view American bison, Texas longhorn cattle, burros, deer, ducks and geese at the park, which encompasses a natural bowl that forms an open-air amphitheater with a seating capacity of 20,000. A 26-mile scenic parkway system and a 9.5-mile greenbelt extend from Krug Park to Hyde Park. **Hours:** Daily 6 a.m.-midnight. **Cost:** Free. **Phone:** (816) 271-5500.

NATIONAL MILITARY HERITAGE MUSEUM is w. off I-29 at 701 Messanie St. Exhibits pay homage to the five branches of the U.S. military. War artillery, personal effects of soldiers, a model of the battleship USS *Missouri*, a diorama depicting two landing ship tanks (LSTs) at Iwo Jima and a collection of military vehicles are displayed. There also is a replica of the Vietnam Veterans Memorial wall in Washington, D.C. **Time:** Allow 1 hour minimum. **Hours:** Mon.-Fri. 9-5, Sat. 9-noon. Closed major holidays. **Cost:** $3; $1 (ages 6-13). **Phone:** (816) 233-4321.

PATEE HOUSE MUSEUM is at 12th and Penn sts. One of the finest hotels west of the Mississippi when it opened in 1858, it also was the headquarters of the Pony Express. The museum contains re-created Hannibal and St. Joseph Railroad and Pony Express offices, a wood-burning locomotive and mail car from the 1860s era, a street with models of St. Joseph buildings from the early 1900s, a vintage carousel known as "The Wild Thing," and antique transportation and communications collections.

Hours: Mon.-Sat. 10-5, Sun. 1-5, Apr.-Oct.; Sat. 10-5, Sun. 1-5, rest of year. Mon.-Fri. hours may be offered Nov.-Mar. depending on volunteer availability and weather; phone ahead to verify schedule. **Cost:** $5; $4 (ages 60+); $3 (ages 6-17). Carousel ride $1.50. **Phone:** (816) 232-8206.

PONY EXPRESS NATIONAL MEMORIAL is at 914 Penn St. This was the original site of the business venture that developed from the War Department's demand for speedy communications with California. Riders routinely made the 1,966-mile trip between St. Joseph and Sacramento, Calif., in 10 days. The museum houses exhibits about the creation, operation and demise of the Pony Express. **Hours:** Mon.-Sat. 9-5, Sun. 1-5. Closed Jan. 1, Thanksgiving and Dec. 24-25 and 31. **Cost:** $4; $3 (ages 60+); $2 (ages 7-18). **Phone:** (816) 279-5059.

ROBIDOUX ROW MUSEUM is at Third and Poulin sts. City founder Joseph Robidoux built this row of seven connected houses 1840-50 as temporary housing for newly arrived settlers. Four restored units remain of the building, including Robidoux's personal quarters, furnished with his possessions and period pieces, and a wintering room for westward bound pioneer families. The western section of the building, home to the St. Joseph Historical Society and Historical Society Library, contains items that belonged to Robidoux as well as period and more recent furnishings.

Hours: Tues.-Fri. 10-4, Sat.-Sun. 1-4, May-Sept.; Tues.-Sat. 1-4, Feb.-Apr. and Oct.-Dec. Closed major holidays. **Cost:** $2.50; $2 (ages 62+); $1 (ages 6-18). **Phone:** (816) 232-5861.

THE WYETH-TOOTLE MANSION is at 11th and Charles sts. Overlooking the Missouri River, this 1879 Gothic sandstone mansion was designed with a north side turret to create a resemblance to European castles. It is one of many turn-of-the-20th-century residences in the city. The first floor is furnished in period and displays photographs of the home taken in the early 1900s, while exhibits on the upper floors impart local history.

Tours: Guided tours are available. **Time:** Allow 30 minutes minimum. **Hours:** Fri.-Sat. 10-4, Sun. 1-4. Closed major holidays. **Cost:** $3; $1.50 (ages 7-18). **Phone:** (816) 232-8471 or (800) 530-8866.

GAMBLING ESTABLISHMENTS

- **Terrible's St. Jo Frontier Casino** is at 777 Winners Cir. **Hours:** Sun.-Thurs. 8 a.m.-2 a.m., Fri.-Sat. 8 a.m.-4 a.m. **Phone:** (816) 279-5514 or (800) 888-2946.

St. Louis

City Population: 348,189 **Elevation:** 585 ft.

Editor's Picks:

The Gateway Arch.................. *(see p. 209)*

Saint Louis Science Center .... *(see p. 208)*

Saint Louis Zoo...................... *(see p. 208)*

Find more AAA top picks at AAA.com

What do Judy Garland, Nelly, Joe Garagiola, Pierre Laclede and Provel have in common? The movie star, the rapper, the baseball player, the French fur trader and the cheese all have a St. Louis connection.

The city on the banks of the mighty Mississippi got its start way back in 1764, when Laclede was commissioned by a prominent New Orleans merchant to establish a trading post at the mouth of the Mississippi and Missouri rivers. The marshy site made it unsuitable as a place to build a town, and after more scouting Laclede chose a location high on a bluff 18 miles to the south. With a surrounding area rich in natural resources and the river providing an easily navigable link to New Orleans, this was a new settlement that seemed destined for success.

And prosper it did. After being governed by Spain and France the town was acquired by President Thomas Jefferson in 1803 as part of the Louisiana Purchase. Lewis and Clark set off from nearby St. Charles the following year on their great westward journey to the Pacific Ocean. The arrival of the *Zebulon M. Pike* in 1817 inaugurated the steamboat era. Late 19th-century prosperity resulted in the creation of Forest Park, an elegant greensward that is the crown jewel of the city's many parks. Anheuser-Busch, the nation's largest brewing company, opened its first brewery in St. Louis.

The Louisiana Purchase Exposition—more popularly known as the 1904 World's Fair—celebrated the centennial of the Louisiana Purchase and put the city in the world spotlight. (This is the Judy Garland connection; in the great American film musical "Meet Me in St. Louis" Garland plays a 17-year-old whose family is leaving St. Louis for New York and will therefore miss the extravaganza.)

The Gateway Arch / © Blakeway Worldwide Panoramic Images

The fair introduced and thus popularized food items that have gone on to achieve who-hasn't-had-one status, among them the hot dog and the waffle-style ice cream cone. And from this beginning comes the city's reputation for distinctive regional specialties. We're not talking about restaurants; there are plenty of those, and more than a few that are truly excellent (Tony's and Giovanni's on the Hill, to name just two). St. Louis is known for a couple of things that are really popular here and pretty hard to find elsewhere.

Provel? This mild and creamy processed blend of Swiss, provolone and cheddar cheeses is the defining ingredient in St. Louis-style pizza, which is characterized by a very thin, crackery crust, a sweet tomato sauce and finely chopped toppings, and is cut into squares or rectangles rather than pie-shaped slices. Locals love Provel; novices can try a pie with a blend of Provel and mozzarella, but any St. Louis pizza parlor will go "all mozz" if you just ask.

Another specialty is toasted ravioli. The Sicilian concoction of square-shaped pasta dough encasing a filling of meat or cheese is given a twist by being breaded and deep fried. In St. Louis "toasted rav"

Getting There — *starting on p. 203*

Getting Around — *starting on p. 204*

What To See — *starting on p. 205*

What To Do — *starting on p. 211*

Where To Stay — *starting on p. 538*

Where To Dine — *starting on p. 544*

Essential Experiences — *visit AAA.com*

Editor's Event Picks — *visit AAA.com*

most often has a ground beef filling and a sprinkling of "parm" (Parmesan cheese) on top and is served with a side of marinara sauce. You'll find it on practically every menu in town, and many joints claim theirs is the best.

All things Italian, in fact, can be found on the Hill, one of St. Louis' best-known neighborhoods. Here even the fire hydrants are painted the colors of the Italian flag, little "shotgun" houses with immaculate yards line residential streets and men play bocce (BOH-chee) ball, a game with a fleeting similarity to bowling, at the St. Louis Bocce Club. In addition to primo Italian groceries, bakeries and restaurants like Rigazzi's (infamous for beer served in a fishbowl), the Hill is noted for two baseball giants—Yogi Berra and Joe Garagiola—who grew up on Elizabeth Avenue; the local block has been dubbed Hall of Fame Place.

You can't have a discussion of St. Louis taste treats without mentioning Ted Drewes. When warm weather arrives all thoughts turn to the frozen custard stand (there are two locations, one on Chippewa Street/Old Route 66 and another on Grand Boulevard) that whips up malts, shakes, sundaes and cones for legions of loyal customers. Whether it's a concrete—milkshakes so thick they refuse to budge even when the cup is turned upside down—a Crater Copernicus (devil's food cake topped with custard, hot fudge and whipped cream) or a Terramizzou (chocolate ice cream and pistachios), a stop at Ted Drewes is as much a rite of summer as a Cardinals game.

St. Louis has an architectural as well as a culinary legacy. A number of imposing turn-of-the-20th-century brick and stone mansions still stand all over the city; take a spin down Lindell Boulevard where it runs along the northern edge of Forest Park and prepare to be impressed. You'll also see streets in the Central West End that have private gated entrances and big, immaculately maintained old houses shaded by huge oaks. Urban elegance personified, this neighborhood of trendy boutiques, trendy restaurants and sidewalk cafés isn't exactly the Left Bank, but it does feel rather Parisian. And for sheer spectacle it's hard to top the Cathedral Basilica of St. Louis. This massive Romanesque building, capped with a beautiful green-tiled dome, has an even more breathtaking interior filled with mosaic work that architect George D. Barrett wanted to be "almost barbaric in the grandeur of its color."

Soulard / Missouri Division of Tourism

Any city closing in on 250 years of existence is bound to exhibit a juxtaposition of old and new, and one of the most intriguing examples here is along the downtown riverfront. Standing at the foot of Ashley Street is the Ashley Street Power House, designated a city landmark in 1971. It opened just in time for the World's Fair and still operates; more than 100 businesses buy steam power from the

Destination St. Louis

St. Louis is filled with history. Once the major gateway for pioneers on westward trails, it's also home to the Old Courthouse, where the infamous Dred Scott trial took place.

St. Louis' waterfront was once crowded with cargo, but now casinos like the swank Lumière Place are bringing people back to downtown.

Saint Louis Science Center.
(See listing page 208)

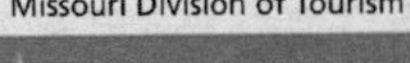

Missouri Division of Tourism

Union Station, St. Louis.
(See mention page 213)

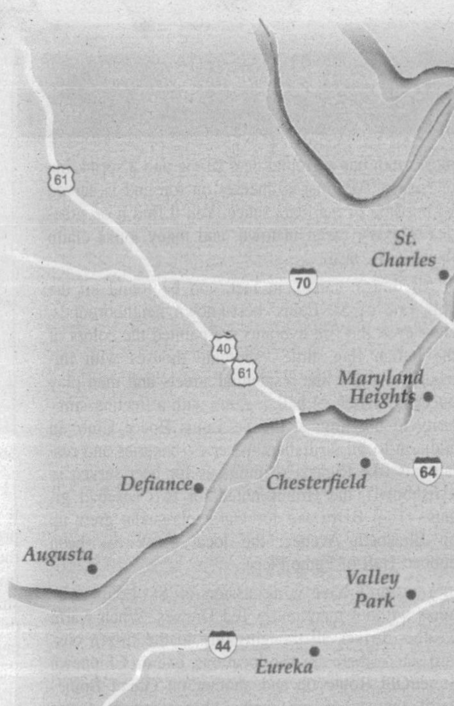

Places included in this AAA Destination City:

Saint Louis Zoo.
(See listing page 208)

Missouri Division of Tourism

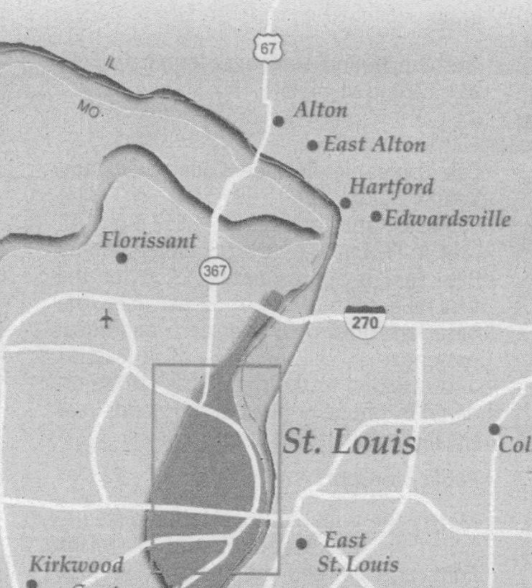

See Vicinity map
page 204

Missouri Division of Tourism

Missouri Botanical Garden, St. Louis.
(See listing page 210)

Missouri Department of Natural Resources

Scott Joplin House State Historic Site, St. Louis.
(See listing page 211)

The Informed Traveler

Sales Tax: The sales tax rate in the city of St. Louis is 7.74 percent. The city's lodging tax is 14.9 percent and there is a rental car tax of 7.82 percent.

WHOM TO CALL

Emergency: 911

Police (non-emergency): (314) 444-5555

Time and Temperature: (636) 441-8467 or (314) 321-2222

Hospitals: Barnes-Jewish Hospital, (314) 747-3000; Forest Park Community Hospital, (314) 768-3000; Missouri Baptist Medical Center (Town and Country, Mo.), (314) 996-5000; Saint Louis University Hospital, (314) 577-8000; St. Anthony's Medical Center, (314) 525-1000; St. John's Mercy Medical Center (Creve Coeur, Mo.), (314) 251-6000.

WHERE TO LOOK

Newspapers

St. Louis is served by the *Post-Dispatch,* a morning newspaper.

Radio

St. Louis radio station KMOX (1120 AM) is an all-news/weather station; KWMU (90.7 FM) is a member of National Public Radio.

Visitor Information

Missouri Welcome Center: 650 Dunn Rd., St. Louis, MO 63138. **Phone:** (314) 869-7100 daily 8-5.

St. Louis Convention and Visitors Commission: 701 Convention Plaza, Suite 300, St. Louis, MO 63101. **Phone:** (314) 421-1023, or (800) 916-0092 for general information.

The building also houses the St. Louis Visitors Center; phone (314) 342-5160 for brochures and guides.

TRANSPORTATION

Air Travel

Lambert-St. Louis International Airport is on I-70 in the northwestern section of the metropolitan area. Taxi fare from the airport is usually about $37. The area's light-rail system, MetroLink, originates at the airport and culminates at Scott Air Force Base in Shiloh, Ill. Trains run daily; schedule varies. Tickets or passes may be purchased; fares vary.

Rental Cars

Hertz offers discounts to AAA members; phone (314) 426-7555 or (800) 654-3080.

Rail Service

The Amtrak terminal, (800) 872-7245, is at 550 S. 16th St.

Buses

The Greyhound Lines Inc. terminal, (800) 231-2222, is at 1450 N. 13th St.

Taxis

Cab companies include County Cab and Yellow Cab, (314) 991-5300 or (314) 993-8294; and Laclede, (314) 652-3456. All cabs in St. Louis are on the meter system. Base fare is approximately $3.50 for the first mile, with a rate of $2 per mile. The base fare goes up $1 for each additional passenger. A fuel surcharge of at least $1 also is added to the fare. Taxis can be ordered by phone or hired at cab stands near the large downtown hotels.

Public Transport

Metro, the public transportation system—which includes MetroBus, the MetroLink light-rail train and the Metro Call-A-Ride para-transit van service—routes passengers throughout the St. Louis metropolitan region. The basic bus fare is $2; $1 (ages 5-12, 65+ and customers with disabilities). Exact cash fare is required. A MetroLink one-ride ticket is $2.25; $1.10 (ages 5-12, 65+ and customers with disabilities). Various transfers and multiday passes also are available.

For route information, current fares and hours of system operation contact MetroTransit Information Mon.-Fri. 7-7; phone (314) 231-2345, or (618) 271-2345 in Illinois.

plant. Brick with terra cotta trim, the squat building stands in stark contrast to its most prominent neighbor, Lumière Place—and not because this glitzy casino/hotel complex is more architecturally compelling.

Rising from the riverfront amid another group of old brick buildings—the historic district of Laclede's Landing—Lumière Place is the latest salvo in an ongoing effort to re-establish downtown as a place to live as well as a place to go for some nighttime fun. Existing structures were torn down to make way for Lumière's construction, part of the challenge the city faces in revitalizing the fabric of history without destroying what made it vital in the first place.

And while we're on the subject of legacies, add music to buildings and food. In addition to Nelly, the greater St. Louis area has produced such luminaries as Chuck Berry (at 83 years young, the "father of rock 'n roll" still makes local appearances) and Miles Davis. Their brass stars are imbedded in the sidewalk on Delmar Boulevard, along with other cultural contributors who collectively make up the St. Louis Walk of Fame. The street runs through the Delmar Loop, a hopping entertainment district of restaurants and nightspots where you can check out the local musical talent.

Finally, let's not forget two things that immediately say "St. Louis." Soaring 630 feet into the air, the Gateway Arch is the symbolic starting point for the arduous trek across the American West undertaken by untold numbers of 19th-century pioneers. Finnish architect Eero Saarinen's ingeniously simple stainless steel structure is cool looking whether you're up close or catching a glimpse of it from a distance, and taking the tram to the observation room at the top for views of the city is a necessary sightseeing pilgrimage.

The city's much beloved baseball team (winner of 10 World Series championships, a National League record) has been around since the early 1890s, when it was called the St. Louis Browns. In August 2009 the St. Louis Cardinals won their 10,000th game, becoming only the fourth major league franchise to achieve this milestone. Watching the Cards play at Busch Stadium (preferably with a pretzel in one hand and a foot-long brat in the other) is a summertime ritual like no other. Oh, and good luck getting a seat when arch rivals the Chicago Cubs come to town.

Getting There

By Car

As befits the Gateway to the West, a network of major interstate highways flows into St. Louis, bringing goods and people from all points of the compass. From the east come I-55, I-64, I-70 and US 40; all these highways converge at the Poplar Street Bridge to pour into the downtown area and through the western suburbs as I-64/US 40 (the Daniel Boone Expressway).

I-55 approaches from the south and I-44 from the southwest; I-70 enters from the northwest to combine in the downtown area with I-55. A bypass route

Missouri Botanical Garden / Missouri Division of Tourism

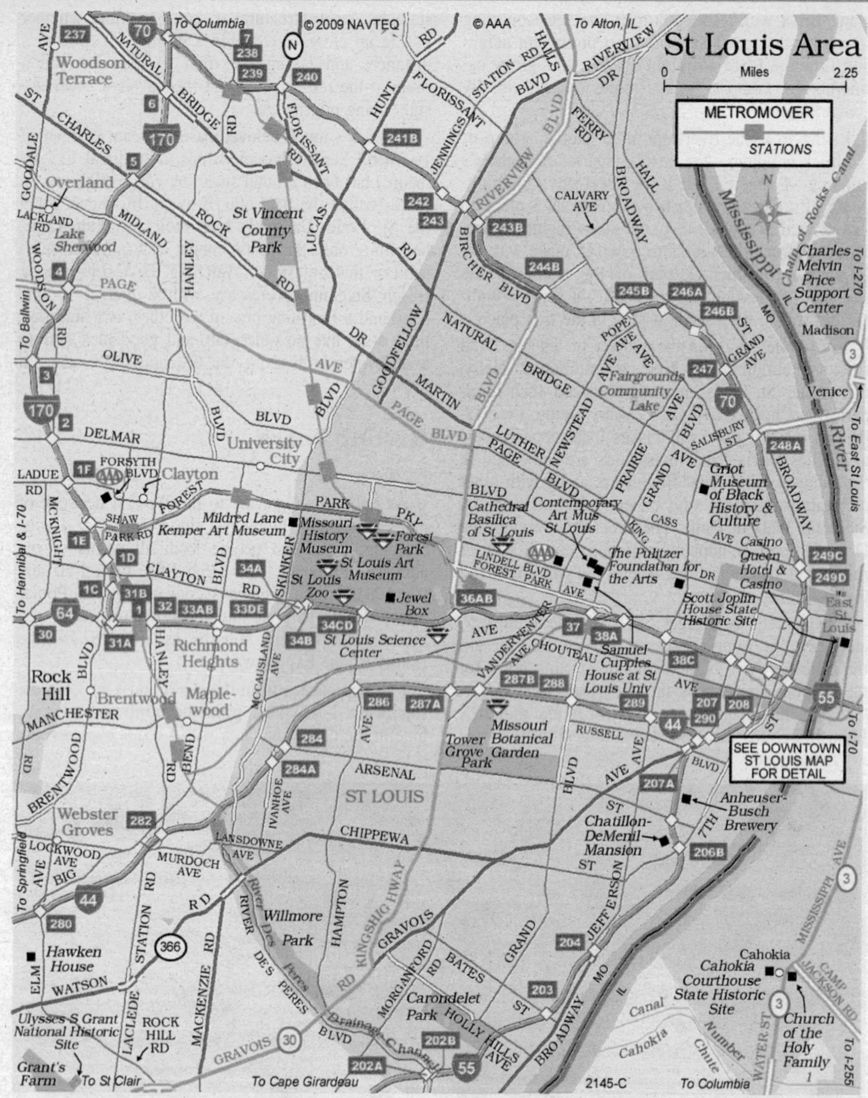

is formed by I-270, with connections to I-70, I-64, I-55, I-44 and I-170. I-270 becomes I-255 southeast of the city before connecting with I-64 and I-70 to the east in Illinois.

Note: I-64/US 40 within the greater St. Louis area has undergone major rebuilding. The newly reconstructed main lanes of I-64/US 40 are open, but construction on some of the smaller overpasses will continue through July 31, 2010. Motorists should plan to use alternate routes and allow extra time in these areas. The Missouri Department of Transportation Information Line has additional details; phone (314) 524-9191.

Getting Around

Street System

Streets in downtown St. Louis follow a basic grid pattern complicated by a system of one-way streets. Numbered streets run parallel to the Mississippi River; numbers begin at the river and run westward. The north-south dividing line is Market Street.

After a complete stop, a right turn on red is permitted unless otherwise posted. Driving during rush hours, generally from 7 to 9 a.m. and 4 to 6 p.m., should be avoided.

Parking

On-street parking is controlled by meter, but your chance of finding a space where and when you want

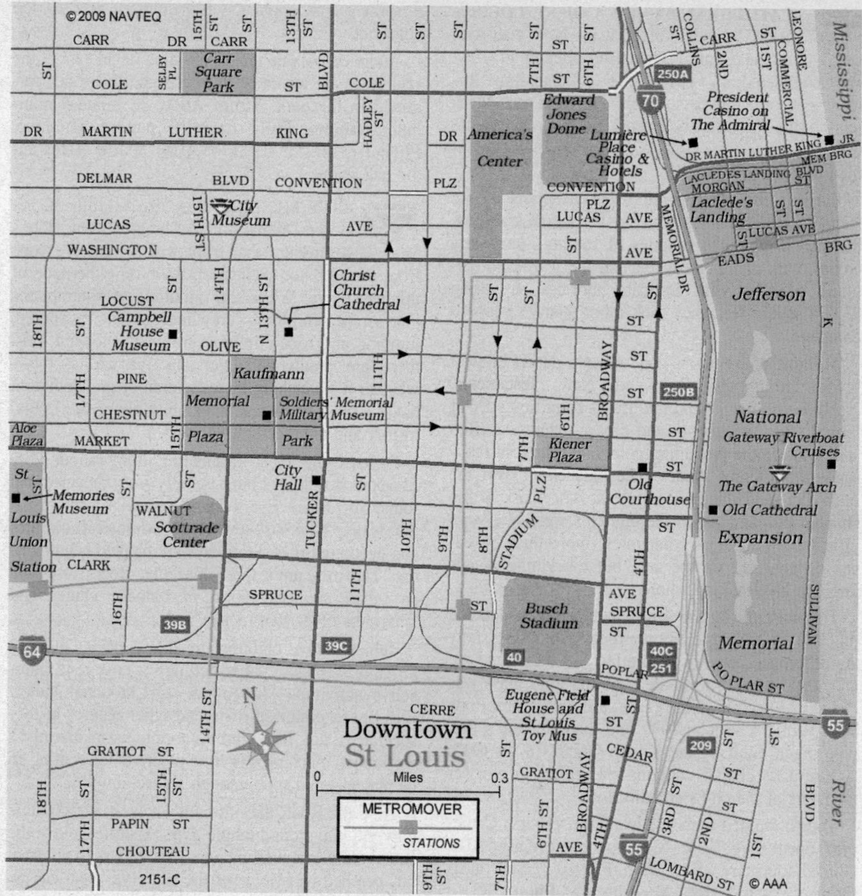

one is slight. Many commercial lots and garages are in the downtown business core and around Memorial Plaza; several multilevel garages are in the vicinity of Busch Stadium as well. Rates average $2 per hour for the first 5 hours, $4 for 6 to 13 hours, and $8 for 14 to 24 hours. For stadium events, day or night, the charge is $5-$20.

Rates for the parking garage at the Gateway Arch are $6 for the first 9 hours and 75c for each additional half-hour. Additional parking, which costs from $3 to $5 per day, can be found at private lots on the landing.

What To See

ALOE PLAZA faces Market St. between 18th and 20th sts. The 14 bronze figures comprising the "Meeting of the Waters" fountain by Swedish sculptor Carl Milles symbolize the meeting of the Mississippi and Missouri rivers.

AMERICAN KENNEL CLUB MUSEUM OF THE DOG is at 1721 S. Mason Rd., 2 mi. s. of I-64 in Queeny Park. It displays permanent and changing exhibits of fine art, artifacts and literature devoted to dogs. More than 150 informational and instructional videotapes can be viewed in the museum's theater. **Hours:** Museum open Tues.-Sat. 10-4, Sun. 1-5. Library open by appointment only. Closed major holidays. **Cost:** $5; $2.50 (ages 60+); $1 (ages 5-14). **Phone:** (314) 821-3647.

CAMPBELL HOUSE MUSEUM is downtown at 15th and Locust sts., between the YMCA building and the St. Louis Public Library. This painstakingly restored former residence epitomizes late 19th-century Victorian opulence. Built in 1851, it was the home of fur trader and entrepreneur Robert Campbell and his family 1854-1938. Carriages, furnishings, paintings, clothing, letters and a set of interior photographs taken in the mid-1880s are among the hundreds of original Campbell possessions on display. A Victorian-style gazebo stands in the garden.

Parking is available on both 15th and Locust streets. **Tours:** Guided tours are available. **Time:** Allow 30 minutes minimum. **Hours:** Wed.-Sat. 10-4, Sun. noon-4. Closed major holidays. **Cost:** $6; $4 (ages 0-12). **Phone:** (314) 421-0325.

CATHEDRAL BASILICA OF ST. LOUIS is at 4431 Lindell Blvd. at jct. Newstead Ave. in the Central West End. Begun in 1907 and completed in 1914, this commanding Romanesque structure is a prominent St. Louis landmark with its ornately decorated exterior granite walls, massive twin towers and distinctive green-tiled dome.

Entering through the imposing oak doors is like stepping back in time. True to Byzantine tradition, the interior layout is a series of soaring domes and arches, with every square inch of the walls and columns adorned with intricate mosaics. Covering 83,000 square feet, they took more than 75 years to complete.

Millions of pieces of glass tessera depict biblical scenes from the Old and New Testaments, archdiocesan events and the life of King Louis IX of France, the cathedral's—and city's—namesake. Red and gold are the prevailing colors, executed in thousands of different shades. The baldachino over the main altar and the Italian-style mosaic work in the chapels and arcades on the church's west side were installed by different companies (more than 20 artists collaborated on the art), but everything blends into one breathtaking whole.

The museum on the lower level offers a detailed timeline of the installation process. Exhibits show the difference between Byzantine and Italian mosaic styles and explain how the stunning gold glass was created. Also on display are artifacts from Pope John Paul II's visit in 1997 and the cathedral's first pipe organ, built by the Kilgen Organ Co. in 1915. A mortuary chapel contains the crypts of former members of the city's archdiocese.

Tours: Guided tours are available. **Hours:** Cathedral open daily 7-5. Museum open daily 10-4. Guided tours are given Mon.-Fri. 10-3, Sun. at 1. **Cost:** Cathedral free. Museum $2. **Phone:** (314) 373-8200, or (314) 373-8242 to schedule a tour.

CHATILLON-DeMENIL MANSION is at 3352 DeMenil Pl. This three-story Greek Revival mansion was built around 1848. Many of the elegant furnishings and wallpapers came from France. **Time:** Allow 1 hour minimum. **Hours:** Tues.-Sat. 10-3, mid-Feb. through Dec. 31. **Cost:** $5; $2 (ages 0-11). **Phone:** (314) 771-5828.

CHRIST CHURCH CATHEDRAL is at 1210 Locust St. at jct. 13th St. One of the first Protestant churches west of the Mississippi River, this Episcopal cathedral contains noteworthy reredos—ornamental screens behind altars—carved by Harry Hems of Exeter, England. An attractive garden is on the 13th Street side of the cathedral. **Hours:** Mon.-Fri. 9-4. **Cost:** Free. **Phone:** (314) 231-3454.

CITYGARDEN occupies the two blocks between 8th and 10th sts. and Chestnut and Market sts. The garden's landscaping includes flowers, shrubs and small trees, and interspersed throughout the grounds are 23 sculpture installations, many of which are whimsical or abstract in form. Three fountains, including a spray plaza popular with children, add to the character.

Audio cell phone tours providing details about the sculptures are available. Barbecue grills are not permitted in the park. **Time:** Allow 30 minutes minimum. **Hours:** Daily dawn-10 p.m. **Cost:** Free. **Phone:** (314) 289-5300, or (314) 802-9571 for audio cell phone tour.

CITY MUSEUM is at 701 N. 15th St. between Delmar and Washington aves. Here's a museum that truly will delight everyone from 8 to 80, not to mention those on either side of this age range. While the multitude of contraptions that invite climbing, crawling, sliding, stepping, jumping and rope climbing are geared toward kids, there are plenty of diversions for adults, too—whether it's watching their children or grandchildren have a blast or perusing exhibits about St. Louis' history and architectural heritage.

Perhaps the most fascinating thing about City Museum is that it is built entirely from recycled and found materials. Everywhere you look—the floor, the walls, columns—there are whimsical mosaics and decorated tiles. Stairways are painted bright colors. The museum's three mazelike floors resemble an urban phantasmagoria of tunnels, chutes and labyrinths of twisted metal.

Tables allow children to draw, paint, practice kirigami (Japanese paper cutting) or engage in interactive activities. The rooms with mounted butterflies, insects, stuffed owls and other natural history specimens are like stumbling into a taxidermist's workroom. A piano sits in another room, waiting to be played—and soon enough someone will.

Atop the Roof, the museum's newest attraction, is a hybrid playground/jungle gym 11 stories above the street. Here are such incongruous sights as a school bus perched halfway over the edge (yes, you can go inside it), a climbing cage that looks like an airborne Slinky, a pond crisscrossed with stepping stones, a giant praying mantis and Big Eli, a working Ferris wheel. You also get a 360-degree view of downtown St. Louis.

The World Aquarium features interactive touch tanks where children can pet sharks and stingrays, pick up a turtle or touch a starfish. Aquatic-themed displays and play spaces are filled with giant seashell columns and spraying jets of water. City Museum also has such oddities as the "world's largest pencil," equivalent to 1,900 regular No. 2 pencils and tipped with a 250-pound rubber eraser that really works. A troupe of magicians, clowns and acrobats from "everydaycircus" provide additional entertainment.

Time: Allow 2 hours minimum. **Hours:** Museum open Mon.-Fri. 9-5 (also Fri. 5 p.m.-1 a.m.), Sat. 9 a.m.-1 a.m., Sun. 11-5, Mar. 1-Labor Day; Wed.-Fri. 9-5 (also Fri. 5 p.m.-1 a.m.), Sat. 9 a.m.-1 a.m., Sun. 11-5, rest of year. World Aquarium open Mon.-Fri. 9-5 (also Fri. 5-11), Sat. 9 a.m.-11 p.m., Sun. 11-5, Mar. 1-Labor Day; Wed.-Fri. 9-5 (also Fri. 5-11), Sat. 9 a.m.-11 p.m., Sun. 11-5, rest of year. Atop the

Roof open Mon.-Fri. 9-5 (also Fri. 5 p.m.-1 a.m.), Sat. 9 a.m.-1 a.m., Sun. 11-5, mid-Mar.-Labor Day; Wed.-Fri. 9-5 (also Fri. 5 p.m.-1 a.m.), Sat. 9 a.m.-1 a.m., Sun. 11-5, day after Labor Day-Oct. 31. Phone ahead to confirm Atop the Roof season opening and closing dates. Closed Easter, Thanksgiving and Dec. 25.

Cost: $12; $10 (Fri.-Sat. after 5); free (ages 0-2). World Aquarium (available only with City Museum admission) $6; free (ages 0-2). Atop the Roof (available only with City Museum admission) $5; free (ages 0-2). **Parking:** $5 (per vehicle). Additional pay lots and metered street parking available. **Phone:** (314) 231-2489.

CONTEMPORARY ART MUSEUM ST. LOUIS is at 3750 Washington Blvd. The museum features art exhibitions by leading contemporary artists as well as performances, lectures and special events. **Hours:** Wed.-Sat. 10-5, Sun. 11-4. **Cost:** $5; $3 (ages 66+); free (students with ID and Wed. and Sat.). **Phone:** (314) 535-4660.

The Pulitzer Foundation for the Arts is at 3716 Washington Blvd. between Grand Blvd. and Spring Ave., on the east side of the Contemporary Art Museum St. Louis. The acclaimed building was designed by architect Tadao Ando. Paintings, sculptural installations, minimalist lead and steel sculptures and other works of art on display allow visitors to focus on their individual experience and interpretation. Among the regularly scheduled events are symphony concerts, films and poetry readings.

Time: Allow 45 minutes minimum. **Hours:** Wed. noon-5 (also first Sun. of the month), Sat. 10-5. Closed Jan. 1, July 4, Thanksgiving and Dec. 25. **Cost:** Free. **Phone:** (314) 754-1850.

EUGENE FIELD HOUSE AND ST. LOUIS TOY MUSEUM is at 634 S. Broadway. Antique and collectible toys are displayed at the birthplace and childhood home of children's poet Eugene Field, whose poems included "Little Boy Blue" and "Wynken, Blynken and Nod." The 1845 house was owned by Eugene's father, Roswell Martin Field, the attorney who represented Dred Scott in his 1853 lawsuit for freedom.

Time: Allow 1 hour minimum. **Hours:** Wed.-Sat. 10-4, Sun. noon-4, Mar.-Dec. Last admission 30 minutes before closing. Closed major holidays. **Cost:** $5; $1 (ages 0-11). **Phone:** (314) 421-4689.

FOREST PARK is bounded by Lindell, Skinker and Kingshighway blvds. and Oakland Ave. Officially opened to the public on June 24, 1876, Forest Park is one of the country's largest urban parks. Beloved by St. Louisans, the park is not only a popular spot for picnicking, jogging and bicycling but also is home to the city's major cultural institutions.

Covering 1,293 acres, Forest Park is located next to the West End residential section in the heart of downtown St. Louis. In addition to the following listed attractions, the park contains the Steinburg Memorial Skating Rink, which offers facilities for ice- and roller skating, and the 27-hole Probstein Community Golf Course. **Hours:** Daily 6 a.m.-10 p.m. **Cost:** Free. **Phone:** (314) 289-5300.

Jewel Box is at 5600 Clayton Ave. at jct. Wells and McKinley drs., within Forest Park. This Art Deco-style, glass-walled conservatory displays a permanent collection of tropical trees, foliage plants and flowers. Seasonal floral shows take place at Easter, Mother's Day and the Christmas holidays. **Time:** Allow 30 minutes minimum. **Hours:** Mon.-Sat. 9-4 (also Sat. 4-11), Sun. 9-2. **Cost:** $1; free (Mon.-Tues. 9-noon). **Phone:** (314) 531-0080.

Missouri History Museum is at jct. Lindell Blvd. and DeBaliviere Ave. in Forest Park; the museum may be entered from both the Jefferson Memorial Building and Emerson Center. The museum's interactive galleries include Seeking St. Louis, which takes a look at the lives of St. Louis citizens from the city's earliest days to the present; Lindbergh, an in-depth exploration of the aviator's famed transatlantic flight; and The 1904 World's Fair, a peek into America's future as envisioned from the standpoint of the 20th century's early years.

Visitors can also discover St. Louis traditions like breweries and baseball and learn about musicians Scott Joplin and Miles Davis. Lectures, concerts and special programs are presented regularly. **Time:** Allow 1 hour minimum. **Hours:** Daily 10-6 (also Tues. 6-8 p.m.), Memorial Day-Labor Day; 10-5 (also Tues. 5-8), rest of year. Closed Thanksgiving and Dec. 25. **Cost:** Free. A fee may be charged for special exhibits. **Phone:** (314) 746-4599. *See color ad p. 207.*

St. Louis Art Museum sits atop Art Hill at 1 Fine Arts Dr., within Forest Park. Built to house the Palace of Fine Arts pavilion at the 1904 World's Fair, this Beaux Arts-style building was designed by famed architect Cass Gilbert. Guarded by the heroic statue of Apotheosis of St. Louis, the museum's collection features more than 30,000 works of art covering nearly every culture and time period, including Oceanic art, pre-Columbian art, ancient Chinese bronzes, and European and American art of the late 19th- and 20th centuries. There is a special emphasis on 20th-century German art.

The museum also presents changing exhibitions of major touring shows and offers a resource center, library, lectures, films, classes and special events. **Time:** Allow 1 hour minimum. **Hours:** Tues.-Sun. 10-5 (also Fri. 5-9). Docent-led tours are conducted Tues.-Fri. at 10:30, Sat.-Sun. at 1:30. Closed Thanksgiving and Dec. 25. **Cost:** Free. Admission is charged for special exhibitions. **Phone:** (314) 721-0072 or TTY (314) 721-4807.

Saint Louis Science Center is at 5050 Oakland Ave. in Forest Park. The center encourages hands-on exploration of such diverse topics as aviation, cosmology, ecology, engineering, medicine and space science. Visitors can program a robot, use a radar gun to clock the speed of traffic passing under a glass bridge above I-64, conduct an experiment in the Life Science Lab and build a replica of the Gateway Arch.

The Discovery Room features imaginative science activities for ages 2-8. Nature, wildlife and adventure films from around the world are shown daily on the four-story OMNIMAX Theater. The James S. McDonnell Planetarium features a space station experience and a high-tech view of 9,000 stars in the night sky.

Time: Allow 4 hours minimum. **Hours:** Mon.-Sat. 9:30-5:30, Sun. 10:30-5:30, Memorial Day-Labor Day; Mon.-Sat. 9:30-4:30, Sun. 11:30-4:30, rest of year. Phone for OMNIMAX show times. Closed Dec. 25. **Cost:** Exhibits gallery free. OMNIMAX Theater $8; $7 (ages 0-17 and 60+). Discovery Room $3. Tickets should be purchased early in the day. Advance tickets are available. **Parking:** $8. **Phone:** (314) 289-4400 or (800) 456-7572.

Saint Louis Zoo is at 1 Government Dr. in Forest Park. About 18,000 animals representing more than 700 species from around the world reside in scenic, natural settings. Among the zoo's highlights is the lushly landscaped Fragile Forest, an outdoor compound home to separate habitats for chimpanzees, orangutans and western lowland gorillas. At Red Rocks, such big cats as lions and tigers coexist peacefully with zebras, giraffes and antelope in natural settings.

Grab your pith helmet for a trek to River's Edge, a 10-acre habitat inhabited by Asian elephants, cheetahs, giant anteaters and viewing areas that provide an opportunity to observe hippos underwater. The Monsanto Insectarium has 100 species of insects and a walk-through butterfly dome. Penguin & Puffin Coast offers a close-up look at these birds, while the Bear Pits are home to black, Andean and grizzly bears.

Young visitors to the Children's Zoo can touch animals and play at the playground. The Conservation Carousel features 64 hand-carved wooden animals, each one representing a protected or endangered species. The 1.5-mile Zooline, a miniature railroad, tours the zoo grounds. Sea lion shows take place during summer.

Time: Allow 2 hours minimum. **Hours:** Daily 9-5. Train rides are offered daily 9:30-5. Sea lion shows presented daily at 11, 1 and 3, in summer. Summer hours may vary; phone ahead. Closed Jan. 1 and Dec. 25. **Cost:** Free. Train $5; free (ages 0-1). Children's Zoo $4; free (ages 0-1 and the first hour the zoo is open). Sea lion show $3; free (ages 0-1). Carousel $3; free (the first hour the zoo is open). An all-day pass is available for $10. **Parking:** $11. **Phone:** (314) 781-0900 or (800) 966-8877.

GRANT'S FARM is on Gravois Rd. at jct. Grant Rd. Ulysses S. Grant built a cabin here in 1856 on land he once farmed. On the 281-acre tract, operated by Anheuser-Busch, are a Clydesdale stable, miniature zoo, animal feeding area and wildlife park. Clydesdales and Dalmatians are featured in a special arena presentation, and there are elephant and bird shows.

Time: Allow 1 hour, 30 minutes minimum. **Hours:** The farm is open and tram tours are offered Tues.-Fri. 9-3:30, Sat. 9-4, Sun. 9:30-4, mid-May to early Sept.; Wed.-Fri. 9-3, Sat.-Sun. 9-3:30, early Apr. to mid-May; Wed.-Fri. 9:30-2:30, Sat.-Sun. 9:30-3:30, early Sept.-early Nov. **Cost:** Free. **Parking:** $11. **Phone:** (314) 843-1700.

GRIOT MUSEUM OF BLACK HISTORY AND CULTURE is at 2505 St. Louis Ave. The museum depicts the lives and contributions of African Americans in the United States from the earliest days of slavery through the 20th century. Life-size wax figures of notable African Americans with a Missouri onnection include Dred Scott, Dr. George Washington Carver and Miles Davis. A collection of historical items includes artifacts, documents and a scale model of a slave ship.

Note: Cameras and recording devices are not permitted. **Time:** Allow 1 hour minimum. **Hours:** Tues.-Sat. 10-5. Closed Dec. 24-Jan. 1. **Cost:** $5; $4 (ages 13-17); $3.50 (ages 65+); $2.50 (ages 0-12). **Phone:** (314) 241-7057.

HOLOCAUST MUSEUM AND LEARNING CENTER is at 12 Millstone Campus Dr. in the Kopolow Building. The museum offers a chronological history of the Holocaust. Exhibits revisit personal accounts and memories of survivors who later came to St. Louis. Jewish life in prewar Europe, the rise of Nazism, and events that occurred during the 1933-45 Holocaust and following World War II are depicted through artifacts, audiovisual presentations, photographs and text panels.

Time: Allow 1 hour minimum. **Hours:** Mon.-Thurs. 9:30-4, Fri. 9:30-3, Sun. 10-4. Closed Jan. 1, Thanksgiving, Dec. 25 and all major Jewish holidays. Advance reservations are necessary for guided tours. **Cost:** Free. **Phone:** (314) 432-0020 or (314) 442-3711.

JEFFERSON BARRACKS HISTORIC PARK is at Gt. Grant Rd. and Kingston, about 10 mi. s. via the I-55 S. Broadway exit. The park's visitor center is at 345 North Rd. Established in 1826, the site was a supply post for troops in the West. A museum in the 1857 powder magazine depicts the history of the barracks, and the Ordnance Building presents changing exhibits. The laborers' house and 1851 stable have been restored. An overlook provides a view of the Mississippi River. More than 70,000 servicemen are buried in the park, one of the largest national cemeteries in the country.

Time: Allow 1 hour minimum. **Hours:** Daily dawn to half-hour before dusk. House and museum open Wed.-Sun. noon-4, Feb. 1 to mid-Dec. Closed Thanksgiving. **Cost:** Free. **Phone:** (314) 544-5714.

JEFFERSON NATIONAL EXPANSION MEMORIAL is on the riverfront at Market St. This 91-acre national park, which covers the site of the original St. Louis settlement, was established in 1935 to commemorate the westward expansion of the United States during the 19th century. The site includes The Gateway Arch, Museum of Westward Expansion, and Old Courthouse *(see attraction listings)*. **Hours:** Park daily 6 a.m.-11 p.m. Hours vary for individual sites. **Cost:** Park, museum and courthouse free. Admission is charged at the arch. **Phone:** (314) 655-1700 or TTY (800) 735-2966.

GEM **The Gateway Arch** is at Memorial Dr. and Market St. within Jefferson National Expansion Memorial park. Soaring sculpture, symbolic gateway to the West, American's tallest monument, tourist trap—the Arch is all of these things. Standing 630 feet above the site of French fur trader Pierre Laclede's 18th-century trading post, this inverted catenary curve (the same shape that a free-hanging chain takes when held at both ends) commemorates what was for thousands of 19th-century pioneers the beginning of a long and arduous westward trek.

Designed by Finnish architect Eero Saarinen, this gleaming stainless steel icon is ingenious in its simplicity, despite taking 2 years and 8 months to build (it opened to the public in 1967). The span of the two legs at ground level is the same as the height. Construction of the Arch required specially designed equipment; each leg needed to align precisely, and the margin of error for the failure of either one to do so was 1/64 of an inch.

The Journey to the Top tram ride takes you on a trip through history en route to the small observation room at the top of the Arch. Instead of a standard elevator, passengers step aboard a unique tram system with egg-shaped compartments, each compartment containing five seats. The observation room has narrow windows with views of downtown St. Louis and the Mississippi; visibility is best on clear days.

The round-trip takes about an hour. Timed tickets are issued every 10 minutes throughout the day. Two movie theaters in the underground complex beneath the Arch show three different 45-minute films: one about the monument's construction, one depicting the travels of Meriwether Lewis and William Clark and one on the settlement of the American West.

Note: The pod-like tram compartments have low, sloping ceilings and cramped quarters; for those who are claustrophobic the 4-minute ride up might be a challenging experience. Pets on a leash are permitted on the grounds except Fridays and Saturdays July through August. **Hours:** Ticket center open daily 8 a.m.-10 p.m., Memorial Day-Labor Day; 9-6, rest of year. Last tram departs 50 minutes before closing. Closed Jan. 1, Thanksgiving and Dec. 25. **Cost:** Tram ride $10; $5 (ages 3-15). Individual movie admission $7; $2.50 (ages 3-15). Combination tickets $14; $7.50 (ages 3-15). **Phone:** (314) 655-1700 or (877) 982-1410.

Museum of Westward Expansion is on Market St. at Riverfront beneath The Gateway Arch at Jefferson National Expansion Memorial. An extensive collection of artifacts is presented, including exhibits related to the Lewis and Clark expedition. Exhibits depict the social and cultural history of territories west of the Mississippi River and are presented in concentric semicircles representing interactive timelines. **Hours:** Daily 8 a.m.-10 p.m., Memorial Day-Labor Day; 9-6, rest of year. Closed Jan. 1, Thanksgiving and Dec. 25. **Cost:** Free. **Phone:** (314) 655-1700.

Old Courthouse is at 11 N. Fourth St. at Jefferson National Expansion Memorial. Completed in 1862, the courthouse was the site of the Dred Scott slavery trial. Galleries and dioramas depict St. Louis from its French and Spanish occupations through the westward expansion years to the present. **Hours:**

Daily 8-4:30. Closed Jan. 1, Thanksgiving and Dec. 25. **Cost:** Free. **Phone:** (314) 655-1700.

LACLEDE'S LANDING is on the riverfront between the Eads and Martin Luther King bridges. The renovated turn-of-the-20th-century buildings and cobblestone streets of this nine-block historic district—the site of the city's original settlement—are filled with bars, nightclubs, restaurants and offices.

The Eads Bridge, at the foot of Washington Avenue, was built in 1894. It was the first major railroad bridge across the Mississippi and the first to utilize steel truss construction. This mighty structure carries pedestrian, bicycle, motor vehicle and light rail traffic across the river, offering an unparalleled view of the Gateway Arch en route.

A self-guiding walking tour brochure is available from the Laclede's Landing Merchant's Association, 718 N. Third St., daily 9:30-4:30. **Phone:** (314) 241-5875.

LAUMEIER SCULPTURE PARK is s. of I-44 via the Lindbergh Blvd. exit at 12580 W. Rott Rd. The 116-acre park displays contemporary sculpture. Works by such celebrated artists as Vito Acconci, Alice Aycock, Mary Miss, Dennis Oppenheim and Robert Stackhouse grace the expansive lawns, which are surrounded by trees and a natural woodland with hiking trails. A museum houses changing exhibitions of contemporary artwork. Concerts are presented during the summer.

Time: Allow 1 hour minimum. **Hours:** Park open daily 8 a.m.-dusk. Museum Tues.-Fri. 10-5, Sat.-Sun. noon-5. **Cost:** Free. **Phone:** (314) 821-1209 for summer concert schedules.

GEM **THE MAGIC HOUSE—ST. LOUIS CHILDREN'S MUSEUM** is at 516 S. Kirkwood Rd. The museum's hands-on learning experiences allow children to experiment, build creativity and develop problem solving skills. Families can explore communications, mathematics and science concepts through a variety of activities. Exhibits let kids become immersed in a giant bubble, star in their own TV newscast, lift themselves up with a pulley, and play with silhouettes and shadows.

Other areas include a three-story slide; an open-air plant science exhibit; a water playground; a three-story Jack and the Beanstalk climbing structure; Poet Tree Hall; Kids' Construction Zone; Can You Solve the Mystery?; Math Path; and Star-Spangled Center, which includes a replica of the Oval Office. The electrically charged ball that makes visitors' hair stand on end is always a favorite.

Fitness Center offers creative ways for visitors to test their balance, endurance and strength. For Baby and Me is a discovery area for children under 2, and A Little Bit of Magic is a special play area for children ages 1-6. A beautifully landscaped park features an outdoor play garden and a maze with a nutrition theme.

Time: Allow 2 hours minimum. **Hours:** Mon.-Sat. 9:30-5:30 (also Fri. 5:30-9), Sun. 11-5:30, Memorial Day-Labor Day; Tues.-Fri. noon-5:30 (also Fri. 5:30-9), Sat. 9:30-5:30, Sun. 11-5:30, rest of year. A Little Bit of Magic play area open Tues.-Fri. at 10:30 during the school year. Closed Jan. 1, Easter, Thanksgiving and Dec. 25. **Cost:** $8.50; free (under 1). **Phone:** (314) 822-8900.

MEMORIAL PLAZA is on Market St. between 12th and 15th sts. Developed 1923-60, the plaza honors St. Louis' war dead. On the northern edge is the Soldiers' Memorial and Museum. The plaza is flanked by municipal buildings, including City Hall, modeled after the Hotel DeVille in Paris.

MEMORIES MUSEUM, 1820 Market St. in Union Station, is a small museum containing exhibits about the history of the railways. A collection of model trains and artifacts, including railway dishes and uniforms, can be seen. An exhibit about Union Station features a brief film about the building. **Time:** Allow 30 minutes minimum. **Hours:** Mon.-Sat. 10-9, Sun. 10-6. **Cost:** Free. **Parking:** A parking rate is charged by the hour in the Union Station lot. **Phone:** (314) 421-6655.

MILDRED LANE KEMPER ART MUSEUM is near the corner of Skinker and Forsyth blvds. at One Brookings Dr., on the Danforth Campus at Washington University. This architecturally impressive building holds an equally impressive collection of 19th-, 20th- and 21st-century art and sculpture. Highlights include paintings by Willem de Kooning, Thomas Eakins, Marsden Hartley, Henri Matisse, Joan Miró and Pablo Picasso. Computers, video and digital installations are among the various technologies incorporated into the museum's multimedia works. Cutting-edge special exhibitions are presented regularly.

The Newman Money Museum, on the building's lower level, outlines the history of money and displays rare coins and currency.

Time: Allow 45 minutes minimum. **Hours:** Wed.-Mon. 11-6 (also Fri. 6-8 p.m.). Museums closed Jan. 1, Martin Luther King Jr. Day, Memorial Day, July 4, Labor Day, Thanksgiving, day after Thanksgiving and Dec. 25. Museums close at 3 p.m. on Dec. 24 and 31. **Cost:** Free. **Phone:** (314) 935-4523 for the Kemper Art Museum, or (314) 935-9595 for the Newman Money Museum.

GEM SAVE **MISSOURI BOTANICAL GARDEN** (MOBOT) is at 4344 Shaw Blvd., just s. of I-44 exit 287B near the jct. of Vandeventer and Kingshighway. St. Louisans affectionately refer to it as "Shaw's Garden"—a tribute to the British-born businessman who sold cutlery out of a rented room in St. Louis at age 18, subsequently made a fortune in hardware, retired at 40, traveled the world, found inspiration in Europe's great botanical gardens and opened one of his own in his adopted city.

MOBOT, which celebrated its sesquicentennial in 2009, offers 79 acres of outdoor display gardens and several indoor conservatories featuring tropical and non-native plants. Historic buildings include the Spink Pavilion, housing a collection of porcelain birds and flowers, and the Tower Grove House, Shaw's country home. This mid-19th century residence is restored and furnished in period style.

Highlights? There are many, starting with the Climatron, a geodesic dome with a lovely assortment of tropical trees, plants and flowers that luxuriate in the damp, climate-controlled environment. The Schoenberg Temperate House displays medicinal and other plants from regions of the world with a Mediterranean climate. The Linnean House—named for famed botanist Carl Linnaeus—was originally used as a greenhouse to overwinter palms, tree ferns, citrus trees and other cold-sensitive plants; today it houses mostly camellias. They begin blooming in mid-December and reach their peak in mid- to late February, providing a display of floriferous beauty for winter-weary visitors.

MOBOT's Japanese Garden is the perfect place for a leisurely stroll. In front of the floral clock that showcases seasonal flower arrangements is a reflecting pool featuring a trio of angel musicians (bronze sculptures by Swedish artist Carl Milles). Floating in the pool are "Walla Wallas," whimsical glass sculptures by another renowned artist, Dale Chihuly (and don't miss Chihuly's Blue Chandelier hanging in the Ridgway Visitor Center).

Seasonal trams provide a 25-minute narrated tour of the grounds. **Hours:** Grounds and facilities open daily 9-5 (also Wed. 5-8, Memorial Day-Labor Day); closed Dec. 25. Tower Grove House open Tues.-Sat. 10-4, Sun. 1-4, Mar.-Dec.; closed Thanksgiving and Dec. 25. Tram tours Mon.-Fri. 10-4, Sat.-Sun. 9:30-4, Apr.-Oct. Guided walking tours depart daily at 10, Memorial Day-Labor Day; at 1, rest of year. **Cost:** (includes Tower Grove House) $8; free (ages 0-12). Tram tours $3; free (ages 0-2 on lap). **Phone:** (314) 577-9400 or (800) 642-8842. [11]

Doris I. Schnuck Children's Garden: A Missouri Adventure, 4344 Shaw Blvd. at Missouri Botanical Garden, offers an interactive play space with rope swings and bridges, a man-made cave, a tree house and a re-created 19th-century town square complete with a jail, general store, village hall and riverboat. Children also can play in the splash area. **Time:** Allow 1 hour minimum. **Hours:** Daily 9-5, Apr.-Oct. **Cost:** $3 (ages 3-12); free (adults with botanical garden admission).

OLD CATHEDRAL is at jct. Memorial and Walnut sts. The first church in St. Louis, a Catholic cathedral, was constructed on the site in 1770. This restored structure was dedicated in 1834 and remains in daily use. A museum contains artifacts and vestments relating to the beginning of the church. **Hours:** Cathedral open daily 6:30-2:30. Museum open 10-2:30; museum schedule varies, so phone for days open. **Cost:** Free. **Phone:** (314) 231-3250.

SAMUEL CUPPLES HOUSE AT ST. LOUIS UNIVERSITY is on John E. Connelly Mall between Grand Blvd. and Spring Ave. This 42-room Romanesque mansion, complete with 22 fireplaces, was built in 1888 at a cost of $500,000. The exterior boasts gargoyles and ornamental stonework; the interior features Tiffany windows, intricate wood paneling, and displays of fine and decorative arts dating 1400-1920. The Turshin Fine Arts Glass Collection of American and European Art Glass is displayed on the third floor.

American Sign Language guided tours are available by appointment. **Hours:** Tues.-Sat. 11-4, Feb.-Dec. Closed major holidays. **Cost:** Self-guiding tour free. Guided tour $5; free (students with ID). **Phone:** (314) 977-3575 or (314) 977-3570.

SCOTT JOPLIN HOUSE STATE HISTORIC SITE is at 2658A Delmar Blvd. The restored home of this great ragtime composer contains pictures and artifacts of the restoration process as well as narrations and articles about Joplin's life and work. **Time:** Allow 1 hour minimum. **Hours:** Mon.-Sat. 10-4, Sun. noon-4, Apr.-Oct.; Tues.-Sat. 10-4, rest of year. Closed Jan. 1, Easter, Thanksgiving and Dec. 25. **Cost:** $2.50; $1.50 (ages 6-12). **Phone:** (314) 340-5790 or (800) 334-6946.

SHAW NATURE RESERVE—
see Gray Summit p. 156.

SIX FLAGS ST. LOUIS—
see Eureka p. 218.

SOLDIERS' MEMORIAL MILITARY MUSEUM is at 1315 Chestnut St. In the central breezeway is a black granite cenotaph bearing the names of 1,075 St. Louis soldiers who died in World War I. Museum exhibits include firearms and other weapons, photographs, medals, uniforms, souvenirs, banners and memorabilia pertaining to St. Louis' military history since 1800.

Across the street are memorials to those who died in World War II, Korea and Vietnam. **Time:** Allow 1 hour minimum. **Hours:** Mon.-Fri. 9-4:30, Sat.-Sun. 10-3. Closed Jan. 1, Thanksgiving and Dec. 25. **Cost:** Free. **Phone:** (314) 622-4550.

GAMBLING ESTABLISHMENTS

- **Lumière Place Casino & Hotels** is at 999 N. 2nd St. **Hours:** Mon.-Thurs. 8 a.m.-5 a.m., Fri.-Sun. 24 hours. **Phone:** (314) 881-7777 or (877) 450-7711.
- **President Casino on *The Admiral*** is off I-70 6th St. exit, following signs. **Hours:** Sun.-Thurs. 8 a.m.-4 a.m., Fri.-Sat. 24 hours. **Phone:** (314) 622-3000 or (800) 772-3647.

What To Do

Sightseeing

Boat Tours

GATEWAY RIVERBOAT CRUISES depart from the base of the Gateway Arch. Narrated 1-hour trips on the Mississippi River are offered aboard replicas of

19th-century steamboats. Dinner and holiday cruises also are available; phone for schedule and reservations. **Hours:** Sightseeing trips depart daily at 10:30, noon, 1:30, 3 and 4:30, Memorial Day-Labor Day (weather permitting). **Cost:** $14; $8 (ages 3-15). **Phone:** (314) 621-4040 or (877) 982-1410.

Bus Tours

SAVE Gray Line, 312 W. Morris, East St. Louis, Ill., provides lecture bus tours about the city's history and major points of interest. Tours lasting 4 hours, 30 minutes and 5 hours, 30 minutes are available. Five-and-a-half-hour tour $46; $23 (ages 2-14). Four-and-a-half-hour tour $43; $21.50 (ages 2-14). For information and reservations phone (314) 241-1224.

Carriage Tours

The St. Louis Carriage Co., 1000 Cerre St., offers 15-minute, half-hour and 1-hour horse-drawn carriage tours nightly (weather permitting) of the downtown area. Carriages are available in front of such locations as The Old Spaghetti Factory at Laclede's Landing and the Adam's Mark Hotel on Chestnut Street; pickups from downtown hotels and restaurants also are offered. Phone (314) 621-3334 for a complete list of pickup locations.

Driving Tours

"Day Tours from St. Louis," a 44-page booklet detailing 10 trips within a day's drive, and a St. Louis points of interest map are available to AAA/CAA members free at any AAA service office in the St. Louis area. *See AAA Offices.*

Helicopter Tours

Fostaire Helicopter Tours covers various sections of St. Louis, focusing on major industries, waterways and other points of interest; phone (314) 421-5440.

Industrial Tours

ANHEUSER-BUSCH BREWERY is at jct. Lynch and 12th sts. Guided 2-hour complimentary tours provide an overview of the facility and include the Clydesdale stables, Beechwood Lagering Cellar, historic brew house and the Bevo packaging building. The tour concludes in the hospitality room with samples, soda and snacks. The Beermaster tour is a behind-the-scenes tour featuring all the stops on the complimentary tour as well as the brew kettle floor and hop room in the brew house; a full packaging line in the packaging building; the tack room in the stables; and the finishing cellar, where guests 21 or older may sample from the finishing tank. Gifts are also provided on this tour.

Note: Closed-toe shoes are required on the Beermaster tour, and access to behind-the-scenes areas may vary based on production schedule. Both tours involve outside walking and six flights of escalators.

Hours: Complimentary tours offered Mon.-Sat. 9-5, Sun. 11:30-5, June-Aug.; Mon.-Sat. 9-4, Sun. 11:30-4, in May; Mon.-Sat. 10-4, Sun. 11:30-4, rest of year. Beermaster tour (maximum 10 guests per tour) departs Mon.-Sat. at 10, 12:30 and 3, Sun. at 12:30, 1:45 and 3. Closed some holidays. **Cost:** Complimentary tour free. Beermaster tour $25; $10 (ages 13-20). Under 18 must be with an adult on overview tour. Advance reservations (recommended several weeks in advance) are required for Beermaster tour, and ages 0-12 are not permitted. **Phone:** (314) 577-2626.

Walking Tours

The city's historical background can be explored in Laclede's Landing, which offers a self-guiding tour of the early settlement of St. Louis *(see attraction listing p. 210)*.

The St. Louis Walk of Fame preserves the city's historical and cultural legacy by honoring the accomplishments of individuals with St. Louis connections. A brass star is engraved with the person's name, and an accompanying bronze plaque provides a brief biographical summary. More than 100 sets of stars and plaques are embedded into the sidewalks of the University City Loop, an area of little shops and cafés along Delmar Boulevard in University City, just outside the St. Louis city limits. Among the veritable who's who of famous honorees are Maya Angelou, Josephine Baker, Chuck Berry, William Burroughs, Miles Davis, Redd Foxx, Joe Garagiola, John Goodman, Ulysses S. Grant, Charles Lindbergh, Agnes Moorehead, Nelly, Marlin Perkins, Joseph Pulitzer, Tina Turner and Shelley Winters.

Sports and Recreation

The 2010 season marks the 119th year of Major League **Baseball**'s St. Louis Cardinals as a franchise and also their fourth year at Busch Stadium, which opened in 2006. The Cardinals won the World Series—their first title in 24 years—on the home field against the Detroit Tigers during the stadium's inaugural season.

The design of the ballpark offers wide concourses, elevators and escalators between levels and excellent spectator sightlines, as well as dramatic views of downtown and the Gateway Arch. For schedule and ticket information phone (314) 345-9600.

Minor league baseball fun is offered by the Frontier League Western Division's River City Rascals at the Ozzie Smith Sports Complex in O'Fallon, about 35 miles west of downtown St. Louis; phone (636) 240-2287.

The National **Football** League's St. Louis Rams play at the Edward Jones Dome at America's Center; phone (314) 982-7267. The arena football season runs from March through June for the Show-Me Believers at St. Charles Family Arena; phone (636) 896-4200.

The St. Louis Blues of the National **Hockey** League take to the ice October through April at the Scottrade Center, 14th and Clark streets; phone (314) 622-2500. The St. Charles Family Arena is the home of the River City Rage, a professional indoor football team; phone (636) 896-4200. The St. Louis Aces, (314) 647-2237, play team **tennis** in July at Dwight Davis Tennis Center in Forest Park.

Gateway International Raceway in nearby Madison, Ill., offers marquee **motorsports** events, including NHRA National, Indy Car Championship, stock and sports car events; phone (618) 482-2400.

Fairmont Park in nearby Collinsville, Ill., offers **Thoroughbred racing** April through September; phone (618) 345-4300.

Note: Policies concerning admittance of children to pari-mutuel betting facilities vary. Phone for information.

There are many **golf** courses throughout the area, including a public course at Ruth Park, 8211 Groby Rd., and three public courses at Forest Park.

Horseback riding is one of many recreational activities available at A.P. Greensfelder Park, north of I-44 on Allenton Road in nearby Pacific. The Wayne C. Kennedy Recreation Complex, on Wells Road, and Edgar M. Queeny Park, between Mason and Weidmann roads, offer **ice-skating** and tennis. The complex also offers **swimming.** Ice-skating and **roller skating** are popular at the Steinberg Memorial Skating Rink in Forest Park.

Shopping

Our No. 1 tip for a rewarding St. Louis shopping experience: zero in on the neighborhoods. This is a spread-out city of many separate communities, each with its own distinct character. Here's a quick rundown that can help you plan your shopping strategy.

The Central West End, just north and east of Forest Park, was created in the flush of expansion and prosperity that followed the 1904 World's Fair. Today it's one of the city's most pleasant shopping destinations, a neighborhood of stately turn-of-the-20th-century homes, ornate lampposts, streets lined with giant oaks and lots of sidewalk cafés for people watching when the weather's nice.

Euclid Avenue is thick with specialty shops, pubs and restaurants. Browse for home furnishings at Rothschild Antiques (398 N. Euclid) and fashion-forward women's wear at Mezzanine Wearables (389 N. Euclid), then peruse the selection at cozy Left Bank Books (399 N. Euclid). Wander through the once-abandoned auto repair warehouse now occupied by Bowood Farms (4605 Olive St.), a combination garden center, greenhouse and café that's a lush respite from the concrete jungle.

Another trendy district is the Delmar Loop (the name comes from the streetcar turnaround, or loop, that used to run through the area). The six or so blocks of Delmar Boulevard between Kingsland and Hamilton avenues form the heart of the Loop. It's a shopping, dining and nightlife destination with a lively street life courtesy of neighboring Washington University.

Eclectic is the keyword here. Vintage Vinyl (6610 Delmar) has a discriminating collection of CDs, LPs, T-shirts and posters. Next door is Sunshine Daydream, an all-purpose head shop (incense, candles, more T-shirts). Headz n Threadz (6662C Delmar) specializes in headwear, including every sports team cap under the sun. Star Clipper (6392 Delmar) carries domestic, imported and manga comics, graphic novels and pop culture memorabilia. Check out Fifi's (6172 Delmar) for punk and alternative clothing. Browse art galleries like the Componere Gallery of Art and Fashion (6509 Delmar) and Faces in the Loop (6265 Delmar). For handcrafted jewelry, locally made art and Mexican Day of the Dead dolls, go to Phoenix Rising (6331 Delmar).

The Hill, south of Manchester Avenue between Hampton Avenue and Kingshighway, is an old, established residential neighborhood with a gaggle of great Italian restaurants and specialty food markets. The shelves at J. Viviano & Sons (5139 Shaw Ave.) are loaded with jars of black olive paste, cans of anchovy-stuffed olives, bags of lupine beans, almond confetti candy and blocks of Reggiano parmesan ("the crown jewel of cheeses"). Girasole Gifts & Imports (2103 Marconi Ave.) sells ceramics, jewelry, handbags and gift items; a miniature replica of the Italian Immigrants statue (which stands across the street in front of St. Ambrose Catholic Church) is an appropriate Hill souvenir.

South Grand is one of the city's more ethnically diverse neighborhoods, and that's reflected in the shops and restaurants that line the eight-block stretch of S. Grand Boulevard between Crittenden Street and McDonald Avenue. Poke around for vintage pieces at Grand Habitat Antiques (3206 S. Grand), shop for Indian spices, Japanese eggplants and green tea ice cream at Jay International Food Co. (3172 S. Grand) or contemplate a tattoo or piercing from one of the friendly folks at Cheap TRX (3211 S. Grand).

South of downtown is Cherokee Antique Row, centered along Cherokee Street between Nebraska Avenue and DeMenil Place. In addition to antique stores and art galleries this city neighborhood has some interesting specialty shops. One of the best is Retro 101 (2303 Cherokee St.), a treasure trove of vintage stuff (think "mod" '60s furniture, funky costume jewelry and kitschy bar accessories). There's more nostalgic browsing at HearthBeats Vintage Kitchen Wares (2001 Cherokee St.), which is loaded with the likes of cut glass iced tea pitchers, oval casserole dishes and ceramic cookie jars that are cute as all get-out.

You can't miss Union Station, the hulking, red-roofed, turreted former train terminal that stands downtown on Market Street (between 18th and 20th streets). The last train pulled out on Oct. 31, 1978, but after being spruced up the station reopened as a complex housing shops, restaurants and entertainment venues. Stop by the SAVE Hard Rock Cafe for a look at memorabilia like a custom-built Peavey bass played by former Van Halen member Michael Anthony, then scope out their line of T-shirts, pins and gifts.

Baseball fans will want to stop by Cardinals Clubhouse, where the merch runs from jerseys to dugout jackets to caps. You'll find steins, coasters, glassware and Clydesdale collectibles at the Bud Shop, while Fat Sassy's stocks gifts like angels, ornaments and teddy bears.

Laclede's Landing is a complex of eateries, bars and a couple of shops housed in brick buildings that were once warehouses. Pick up a Cardinals pennant or Route 66 memento at St. Louis Souvenirs (707 N. 1st St.). Novelties, masks, red clown noses and magic supplies are what you'll find at the circus-themed Gibbol's Novelties & Costumes (811 N. 2nd St.).

The city has a couple of worthy destination malls. Upscale Plaza Frontenac, just south of I-64/40 at the intersection of Clayton Road and Lindbergh Boulevard, caters to well-to-do St. Louisans with the only Saks Fifth Avenue and Neiman Marcus stores in town, along with trendy retailers like Tiffany & Co. and Louis Vuitton. The atmosphere here is elegant throughout; even the seating areas and restrooms are smartly stylish.

West County Center, at I-270 and Manchester Road in Des Peres, is a major mall anchored by JCPenney, Macy's and Nordstrom. Among the more than 150 other retailers are familiar names like Abercrombie & Fitch, Brooks Brothers and The North Face. Anchors at the Saint Louis Galleria, I-64 and S. Brentwood Boulevard, are Dillard's and Macy's, with Nordstrom due in 2011. Shoppers can choose from some 165 additional stores and boutiques.

Westport Plaza, in a mixed-use office complex just off I-270 and Page Avenue in the western burbs, is more a place to relax after shopping since it has pick-me-ups like Starbucks and the St. Louis Bread Co., a variety of casual and higher-end restaurants, happy hour hangouts and pubs with live music.

Bargain hunters head for St. Louis Mills, SR 370 and St. Louis Mills Boulevard. With more than 175 outlets—everything from American Eagle Outfitters to diamond sellers Zales, plus outlet faves like Dress Barn, Forever 21, Levi Strauss, Tommy Hilfiger and Reebok—there's something for everyone. Refuel with a Haagen-Dazs cone or a Wetzel's pretzel, just two of this mall's *many* eateries.

Missouri farmers supply St. Louis farmers markets, and one of the best reasons to visit is for the cornucopia of locally grown fruits and veggies. The markets are also good places to pick up locally produced cheese, eggs, honey and baked goods. Shoppers in the know arrive early to snap up seasonal goodies like berries and heirloom tomatoes. And of course it's fun to just wander around soaking up the sights and smells.

The granddaddy of them all is the Soulard Farmers Market (south of downtown at the corner of 7th and Carroll streets), which has been in business in one form or another since 1779. If you're a first timer go on Saturday morning, when this big, bustling market is at its busiest and best. Shaped like a giant "H," it has stall after stall of produce—fat melons, baskets of grapes, just-picked zucchini—as well as butchers, bakers and vendors selling everything from balsamic black bean dip to aromatic soaps. It's open Wed.-Fri. 8-5, Sat. 6-5, year-round. Hint: Street parking is not plentiful and also metered, and regulations are strictly enforced; park in the free lot across 7th Street from the market.

Much smaller but equally appealing is the Kirkwood Farmers Market in downtown Kirkwood (150 E. Argonne Dr. at Taylor Avenue). Fresh, locally grown produce varies by season; in summer look for ripe peaches grown in Missouri's "boot heel," and ask about the recipe for turning them into a scrumptious peach pie. Tropical Moose ("Tro Mo" to its loyal customers) is a popular snow cone stand that sells the icy treats in more than 50 different flavors. The market is open daily from early April to late September, but Saturday mornings offer the best selection. In October it morphs into a pumpkin patch, stays open longer hours (daily 9-8) and has lots of activities for kids.

The Clayton Farmers Market also promotes local growers and emphasizes organic and seasonal fruits and vegetables. Food Network-inspired cooks come here for unusual produce like Asian squash and bell peppers in rainbow colors. It fills the west parking lot of Straub's Market (8282 Forsyth Blvd.) Saturdays 8:30-noon, late May to late October.

And if your sweet tooth demands satisfaction, do as many longtime residents do and head for Lubeley's Bakery (7815 Watson Rd. in South St. Louis). Family-owned Lubeley's has been in business for more than 70 years, turning out St. Louis specialties like the super-sweet gooey butter cake, German treats like stollen and custom-made, multi-tiered wedding cakes. A fresh-out-of-the-oven caramel pecan roll and coffee to go is as good a way as any to start your day.

Smaller-scale shopping with a healthy dollop of historic charm prevails in nearby St. Charles. If you're into antiques, crafts, gifts and collectibles, put St. Charles' Main Street at the top of your day-trip list. *See place listing p. 219.*

Nightlife

If you hit the neighborhoods during the day to go shopping, you'll hit them again when it comes time to party the night away. St. Louis music clubs and evening entertainment options tend to be concentrated in certain areas, and one of the most happening spots is the Loop.

Begin an evening on the town with drinks at the Rooftop Terrace, eight stories above Delmar Boulevard at the top of the boutique-style Moonrise Hotel. A hip, dressy thirty-something crowd lounges on fancy white couches or mingles at the patio under a revolving gray moon, snacking on marinated olives while nursing a glass of wine or one of the premium beers. A bonus is the view of the downtown skyline and the Arch in the distance, a nice backdrop for a sunset or later when the lights of the Delmar strip twinkle below.

Another place to kick off an evening is Cielo Bar, on the eighth floor of the Four Seasons Hotel St.

Louis (adjacent to Lumière Place Casino). The setting is swank—elegant flower arrangements, a roaring fire on freezing winter days, and an outdoor patio with canopy beds and a great view of the Arch that's perfect for people watching on warm summer evenings. The atmosphere helps take the sting out of pricey but tasty drinks like the vodka pear mojito.

Casinos have been instrumental in revitalizing St. Louis' downtown riverfront area, and leading the way is Lumière Place (999 N. 2nd St.). It ain't Vegas, but there's plenty of flash here for a fun night out. The main floor has a variety of game tables, some 2,000 slots showing off the latest video technology and a room for dedicated poker players. Hardcore gamblers will gripe that free drinks aren't provided while you're spending your hard-earned cash. On the plus side, Lumière has the only Peet's Coffee & Tea outlet in St. Louis. Nonsmokers take note: The smell of smoke hangs pretty heavily in the air.

You also can hit Lumière Place for dinner. Burger Bar is crowded, noisy and has a real buzz about it, as pretty people perched on bar stools scarf down custom-built burgers put together from high-end ingredients like Kobe beef, lobster and foie gras. SLeeK is a very stylish steakhouse with semi-private dining areas, subdued lighting and slick contemporary design. Prices edge toward the stratospheric, but if you hit it big in the casino a splurge here might be a just reward.

The vibe is similar at Harrah's St. Louis (777 Casino Center Dr. in Maryland Heights). The casino floor has plenty of game tables, slots and video poker machines. iBAR features stand-up blackjack tables, a full-service bar and a showgirl-style dance revue on Thursday, Friday and Saturday nights. Local bands and the occasional name artist play at the VooDoo lounge on weekends. Among the dining options here is Charlie Gitto's From the Hill, a branch of the celebrated Italian restaurant *on* the Hill.

For live music, the Loop is tops. Rock and blues bands jam it up in the Duck Room at Blueberry Hill (6504 Delmar Blvd.). St. Louis native and rock 'n roll legend Chuck Berry still makes an occasional appearance. Just about everybody, be they pop, rock, indie, acoustic or metal, plays The Pageant (6161 Delmar Blvd.). Patrons can chill out at the venue's Halo Bar before and/or after the main show. The Halo Bar also has live performances and DJ sets most nights, and there's no cover.

Local scenesters congregate at Pin-Up Bowl (6191 Delmar Blvd.), a lounge where the bartenders whip up killer martinis and specialty cocktails in outlandish colors. The kitschy decor includes a display case full of vintage bowling paraphernalia. There are 12 lanes here as well, but if you're serious about the game this is not the place to work on your delivery.

Two downtown watering holes are especially popular for live music. BB's Jazz, Blues & Soups (700 S. Broadway) brings top jazz and blues musicians to town. Memorabilia adorns the walls of this old brick building, which has done time as a boarding house, reception hall, millinery shop, transient hotel and house of ill repute. Within spitting distance of BB's is Beale on Broadway (701 S. Broadway). Down-home blues is the music of choice here, with dashes of R&B, old-school soul and roots rock.

Off Broadway (3509 Lemp Ave. in the Cherokee-Lemp Historic District) is basically a dive bar, but it's also one of the best spots in the city for live music. Acts run to folk, alt country, blues and rock, plus the occasional tribute show (Jerry Garcia, Gram Parsons and the like). This is also a good place to catch up-and-coming local bands. Another plus: The smoking area is outside.

Seeing a movie is still a relatively cheap date, and there are options besides the multiplex. The Moolah Theatre & Lounge (3821 Lindell Blvd. near the St. Louis University campus) is housed in a renovated, Moorish-style brick building that was once the Moolah Temple, a meeting place for the Shriners. The screen is huge, and the theater has a beautiful ceiling dome. If you want to hang out afterward there's a full bar and a pool table. Arrive early to snag one of the comfy leather sofas that make up the front rows.

The Tivoli (6350 Delmar Blvd. in the Loop) dates from the era of grand old movie palaces, and like many others it suffered a long period of decline, even closing briefly in the 1990s before being restored to its former glory and reopened. Display cases are filled with movie memorabilia, vintage posters line the walls and yes, there's an orchestra pit and a plush burgundy curtain. Three screens show a mix of first-run films and arthouse fare. The six screens at the Plaza Frontenac Cinema (in the Plaza Frontenac mall at Clayton Road and Lindbergh Boulevard) feature independent and foreign films, and some locals swear the concession stand has the best popcorn in town.

In the mood to laugh? The Funny Bone (614 Westport Plaza, just off I-270 and Page Avenue) presents national touring comedians and has open-mic nights when local stand-up comics take the stage. The 7:30 p.m. Saturday show is non-smoking. Reservations are recommended; phone (314) 469-6692. Quirky productions and an intimate setting make The Playhouse (635 Westport Plaza Dr.) a good choice for live theater.

And finally, is there a better way to spend a summer evening in St. Louis than attending a Cardinals game at Busch Stadium? The downtown ballpark, a stone's throw from the Arch, is invariably filled with diehard Cards fans cheering on their team. So grab a dog and a couple of bags of peanuts and take a seat under the stars. Evening home games usually start at 7:15 p.m. Single game tickets can be purchased at the 8th Street ticket windows, located just north of Gate 3, Mon.-Fri. from 9 a.m. until 2 hours after game time; to charge by phone call (314) 345-9000.

Note: *RFT* (Riverfront Times), a free newsweekly available all over town, has arts and entertainment listings.

Performing Arts

The St. Louis Symphony, founded in 1880 and one of the oldest symphony orchestras in the nation, performs in Powell Symphony Hall, 718 N. Grand Blvd., from mid-September to mid-May and presents several free outdoor concerts during the summer. The symphony also presents Kinder Koncerts, geared to ages 5 through 8, and Young People's Concerts for ages 9 and up; phone (314) 534-1700 for ticket and schedule information. The acoustically renowned Sheldon Concert Hall, 3648 Washington Blvd., presents a variety of concerts; phone (314) 533-9900.

The Muny in Forest Park is a 11,000-seat outdoor amphitheater featuring 7 weeks of Broadway-style musical theater during the summer. About 1,500 free seats at the top of the house are available on a first-come, first-served basis beginning at 7 p.m.; phone (314) 534-1111. Broadway hits also are performed at the restored 1929 Fox Theatre, 527 N. Grand Blvd. A twin to the Detroit Fox Theatre, the Fox also presents concerts and headlining entertainers in a lavish setting; phone (314) 534-1678.

The Verizon Wireless Amphitheater is a 20,000-seat venue offering concerts April through September; phone (314) 298-9944.

The Repertory Theatre of St. Louis, 130 Edgar Rd., is the home of St. Louis' regional equity theater as well as the Opera Theatre of St. Louis and Webster University's Conservatory of Theatre Arts; phone (314) 968-4925.

Dance St. Louis regularly gives performances September through April at the Fox Theatre; phone (314) 534-5000. Dance, music and drama are presented at the Edison Theatre on the campus of Washington University; phone (314) 935-6543. Stages St. Louis offers musical theater productions June through October at the Robert G. Reim Theatre at Kirkwood Civic Center; phone (314) 821-2407. The Touhill Performing Arts Center on the campus of the University of Missouri-St. Louis offers concerts, opera, comedy and dance year round; phone (314) 516-4949. Chaifetz Arena, on the campus of St. Louis University, is a multipurpose arena featuring concerts, family shows and sporting events; phone (314) 977-5000.

The St. Louis Black Repertory Company offers theater and dance presentations January through June in the Grandel Theatre, 3610 Grandel Sq.; phone (314) 534-3807. Also in the Grandel, the Off-Broadway On Grand Cabaret features Broadway cabaret performers September through December; phone (314) 534-1111.

Special Events

St. Louis warms up to spring with the Storytelling Festival in late April and early May, when both professionals and amateurs celebrate America's tale-telling traditions. Portrayals of William Shakespeare works occur during the Shakespeare Festival of St. Louis, held at Forest Park from late May to mid-June. The free outdoor performances include dance, music and a plot synopsis. Phone (314) 531-9800 for performance schedule.

Fourth of July festivities send sparks flying during Fair St. Louis, held near the Gateway Arch and along the St. Louis riverfront. The celebration attracts thousands with big-name entertainment, a family fun village and fireworks. For further information and to verify performance schedule phone (314) 434-3434.

Several events close out the summer, beginning in early September with the Japanese Festival, held at the Missouri Botanical Garden. The Forest Park Balloon Rally is held in mid-September.

Also in September is Bevo Day, an ethnic-themed festival of music, entertainment, arts and crafts, folk dancing and food and drink. The Christmas holiday season kicks off in late November during Winter Wonderland in Tilles County Park, which features thousands of twinkling lights. The St. Louis Convention and Visitors Commission can provide information; phone (314) 421-1023.

The St. Louis Vicinity

AUGUSTA (C-5) pop. 218, elev. 561'

When one thinks of American wine-producing states, California, Oregon and New York immediately come to mind. But Missouri? *Ja,* absolutely. After all, it's known for scenic river valleys, rich farmland and bucolic countryside; a winery seems to perfectly complete this pocket description.

The right combination of climate and terrain is necessary to successfully establish vineyards that will produce fine wine, and the east-central part of the state has both. The Missouri River Valley is an area characterized by hilly bluffs, thin soil and long, hot, sunny summers—all required conditions for growing grapes. Little-known fact: Missouri wines won eight gold medals at the 1873 Vienna World's Fair.

German immigrants pouring into Missouri during the mid-19th century discovered that the valley was reminiscent of the Rhine River Valley back home, both in the lay of the land and the availability of river transportation. Augusta, founded in 1836 by a follower of Daniel Boone, acquired a distinct German character while prospering as a farming community and trading center.

In the 1870s the Missouri River changed its course, eliminating the need for the town's boat landing but leaving behind hundreds of acres of fertile river bottom. Today Augusta is one of the towns along the Missouri Weinstrasse, or Wine Road (US

94) as well as a designated access point on the Katy Trail, the rails-to-trails conversion that stretches across north-central Missouri.

A nice fall day is perfect for an Augusta jaunt. It's a 45-minute drive from St. Louis (take I-70 west to exit 228, then continue southwest on US 94). Once the highway narrows to two lanes you're in the country, passing through rural scenery that's bursting with new growth in spring, a thick, lush green in summer and vibrant with fall color. In spots the winding road tunnels through over-arching clumps of trees; in other places the countryside opens up and farmland takes over. In late summer the landscape is dominated by bountiful fields of corn and soybeans.

"Downtown" (reached via Church Road or Jackson Street off US 94) is delightfully compact, just a handful of streets with a backdrop of hills. A couple of shops are along Locust Street. Browse The Uptown Store for handcrafted items created by local artisans. Stone Ledge Antiques has furniture and home accessories. Have lunch on the patio at Café Bella (5505 Locust St.), which also is open on weekends for dinner. This is a favorite stop for people biking the nearby Katy Trail. It's open every day but Tuesday and sometimes closes early on slow weekdays; phone (636) 482-4334 to confirm.

If you're visiting on a Sunday, though, you might want to save your appetite for dinner served at the American Legion Hall (corner of Church Road and Hackmann Street). Whether it's fried chicken or pork steaks served with German-style potato salad, this food is going to fill you up. There's usually live music as well. Dinner is on the first Sunday of the month February through May and the fourth Sunday of the month June through November; for more details phone (636) 228-4546.

Several wineries are just outside of town, including the Montelle Winery, about 1.5 miles east of Augusta just off US 94 (watch for the signed turnoff). It doesn't offer tours, but there's still a very good reason to stop here: Perched atop Osage Ridge, the facilities and estate vineyards are situated 400 feet above the Missouri Valley. A shaded outdoor terrace offers magnificent views that are a lovely backdrop for a leisurely wine and cheese repast. For non-wine drinkers, the café in the tasting room has Starbucks coffee. Live music takes place most weekends. The tasting room is open Mon.-Thurs. 10-5:30, Fri. 10-9, Sat. 10-10, Sun. 11-6, May-Sept.; Mon.-Fri. 10-5:30, Sat. 10-6, Sun. 11-6, rest of year. Phone (888) 595-9463.

Greater Augusta Chamber of Commerce: P.O. Box 31, Augusta, MO 63332. **Phone:** (636) 228-4005.

WINERIES

- **Mount Pleasant Winery** is at 5634 High St. at jct. Washington St. **Hours:** Grounds daily 11-5 (also Sat.-Sun. 5-6). Guided 30-minute tours are given Sat.-Sun. at 1 and 3, Apr.-Oct. Closed Jan. 1, Thanksgiving and Dec. 25. **Phone:** (636) 482-9463.

CHESTERFIELD (C-5) pop. 46,802

FAUST COUNTY PARK is off I-64 exit 19B, then 1.3 mi. n.e. on Clarkson Rd./Olive Blvd. (Olive Street Rd.) to 15185 Olive Blvd. A popular spot for picnicking, the 200-acre public park features the preserved home of Missouri's second governor as well as Faust Historical Village, a re-created 19th-century town. The 1920s-era St. Louis Carousel, with some 60 hand-carved animals, is open to the public.

Hours: Park open daily 7 a.m.-30 minutes after dusk. Carousel Tues.-Sun. 10-4, Feb.-Dec. **Cost:** Free. Carousel $1; free (ages 0-1 with paid adult). Ages 0-4 must ride the carousel with an adult. **Phone:** (314) 615-8328, or (314) 615-8383 for the carousel.

SAVE **Sophia M. Sachs Butterfly House** is off I-64 exit 19B, then 1.3 mi. n.e. on Clarkson Rd./Olive Blvd. (Olive Street Rd.) to 15193 Olive Blvd., within Faust County Park. Hundreds of tropical butterflies representing more than 60 species fly freely within this 8,000-square-foot glass conservatory. A short film details their life cycle, and a chrysalis exhibit showcases metamorphosis.

During March Morpho Mania, a monthlong event held each March, more than 1,500 morpho butterflies can be seen flying throughout the tropical conservatory. These bright blue butterflies are raised in Costa Rica, and information about their native environment is shared. **Time:** Allow 1 hour minimum. **Hours:** Daily 9-5, Memorial Day-Labor Day; Tues.-Sun. 9-4, rest of year. Last ticket is sold 30 minutes before closing. Closed Jan. 1, Thanksgiving and Dec. 25. **Cost:** $6; $4.50 (ages 65+); $4 (ages 4-12). **Phone:** (636) 530-0076.

CRESTWOOD (C-5) pop. 11,863, elev. 621'

SAPPINGTON HOUSE MUSEUM COMPLEX, 1015 S. Sappington Rd., was built in 1808. This two-story brick house is a fine example of Federal architecture. Guides conduct tours of the dwelling and provide information about its period furnishings. It also houses the Library of Americana, which features a large collection of books about decorative arts and national and local history.

Time: Allow 1 hour minimum. **Hours:** Wed.-Fri. 11-2, Sat. by appointment, Feb.-Dec. Last tour begins 30 minutes before closing. Closed Good Friday, July 4, day before Thanksgiving, Thanksgiving, Fri.-Sat. after Thanksgiving, Dec. 24-31, and the Sat. before Mon. holidays. **Cost:** $3; $1 (ages 6-12). **Phone:** (314) 822-8171.

ULYSSES S. GRANT NATIONAL HISTORIC SITE is off SR 30 (Gravois Rd.) at 7400 Grant Rd., adjacent to Grant's Farm. The 9.65-acre site, also known as White Haven, once was a plantation owned by the family of Julia Dent, wife of Ulysses S. Grant.

The grounds include five historic buildings: a two-story residence shared by Grant and his wife 1854-59, a barn, a chicken house, an icehouse and a summer kitchen. Inside the barn is an interpretive museum displaying exhibits about the Grant family and the residence. The adjacent visitor center offers a 16-minute introductory film.

Time: Allow 1 hour minimum. **Hours:** Daily 9-5. Interpretive residence tours depart every 30 minutes 9:30-4. Closed Jan. 1, Thanksgiving and Dec. 25. **Cost:** Free. **Phone:** (314) 842-3298, ext. 245.

DEFIANCE (C-5) elev. 469'

Daniel Boone, 69 years old and heavily in debt, settled here in 1799 with his wife and some of their children. Defective titles had caused the loss of his land in Kentucky; good reports from one of his sons as well as promises of land grants and honors from the Spanish brought him to Defiance.

Boone received a grant of 845 acres and served 1800-04 as the *syndic* (judge) of the Femme Osage District, a position that gave him control of all civil and military matters. The great explorer died in Defiance a number of years after being forced to sell his land to satisfy his creditors in Kentucky.

Defiance serves as an access point to the Katy Trail, known for its scenery and historic legacy. The trail, which runs almost parallel to the Missouri River, is enjoyed by hikers and bicyclists alike.

DANIEL BOONE HOME is 5 mi. w. on CR F. The frontiersman supervised construction of this four-story, Georgian-style structure, which took 7 years to build, and lived in it until his death in 1820. The house contains many Boone family belongings. Other 19th-century structures on the grounds, including a chapel and schoolhouse, have been restored. Candlelight Christmas Tours are offered the first two Friday and Saturday nights in December.

Hours: Guided 1-hour tours of the Boone home and 2-hour tours including the village are offered daily 9-6, mid-Mar. to early Nov.; 9-5, rest of year. Last tour begins 1 hour before closing. Closed Jan. 1, Easter, Thanksgiving and Dec. 24-25. **Cost:** Home tour $7; $6 (ages 55+); $4 (ages 4-11). Home and village tour $12; $10 (ages 55+); $6 (ages 4-11). Rates and hours may vary; phone ahead. **Phone:** (636) 798-2005.

EUREKA (C-6) pop. 7,676, elev. 465'

Eureka began as a railroad construction camp in 1853. The triumphant name was chosen by a surveyor upon discovering a route through the valley that would eliminate the difficult cutting and grading required by the original route. After the railroad was finished, a town was laid out, and the name remained.

Eureka Chamber of Commerce: 208 N. Central, Suite D, Eureka, MO 63025. **Phone:** (636) 938-6062.

Note: The facility is scheduled to move into a new location in Feb. 2010; phone ahead for new address.

BLACK MADONNA SHRINE AND GROTTOS is s. on SR 109 to CR FF, w. on CR FF to CR F, then s. on CR F to St. Joseph's Hill Rd., following signs. This site was chosen in 1938 by Franciscan brother Bronislaus for a tribute to the Virgin Mary and to the Black Madonna shrine in his native Poland. He worked for 22 years to complete a cedar chapel and seven grottos of Missouri barite embedded with costume jewelry, rocks and seashells. The chapel later burned and was replaced by an open-air shrine.

A picnic pavilion is available. **Hours:** Daily 9-7, May-Sept.; 9-6 in Apr. and Oct.; 9-4, rest of year. **Cost:** Donations. **Phone:** (636) 938-5361.

GEM SAVE **SIX FLAGS ST. LOUIS,** off I-44 at 4900 Six Flags Rd., has more than 100 rides, shows and attractions. The park's lineup of roller coasters includes Evel Knievel, an eight-story-tall wooden coaster named after the legendary daredevil; The Boss; Mr. Freeze; Batman: The Ride; Screamin' Eagle; Ninja; Tony Hawk's Big Spin; and the River King Mine Train.

Just for kids, Bugs Bunny National Park includes eight rides, a tree house play structure and an interactive fountain. Visitors also can experience the Thunder River white-water raft ride; Colossus, an 18-story Ferris wheel; Scooby-Doo! Ghostblasters—The Mystery of the Scary Swamp, an interactive dark ride; and Xcalibur's spinning wheel.

For water thrills, Hurricane Harbor, a 12-acre Caribbean-themed water park, features rides such as a wave pool, a lazy river, a five-story family-themed tree house, speed and tube slides, and Tornado—a thrill ride shaped like a funnel through which four-person rafts spin as they drop 132 feet to the pool below.

Hours: Park open daily, late May to mid-Aug.; Sat.-Sun., Apr. 1-late May and mid-Aug. to late Oct. Hurricane Harbor open daily, Memorial Day-Labor Day. Phone ahead to confirm schedule. **Cost:** (Includes Hurricane Harbor) $34.99; $29.99 (children under 48 inches tall); free (ages 0-2). AAA members save on select services and merchandise. See guest relations for details. **Parking:** $15. **Phone:** (636) 938-4800.

FLORISSANT (C-5) pop. 50,497

In Florissant you'll find houses typical of those built by the French settlers who settled the *fleurissant,* or "flowering," valley in 1786. The Taille de Noyer House, 1 Taille de Noyer Dr., is reached via a driveway on the McCluer High School campus at 1896 S. Florissant Rd. It is believed to be one of the oldest residences in St. Louis County. Prior to a series of expansions and renovations, the 23-room mansion was a simple cabin first used as a fur-trading post in 1790.

Old St. Ferdinand's Shrine, at St. Francois and St. Charles streets, is the oldest Catholic church between the Mississippi River and the Rockies. It is an excellent example of the Federal architectural style applied to a brick building. A convent and historical museum containing religious accouterments adjoin the 1820 church.

Greater North County Chamber of Commerce: 420 W. Washington St., Florissant, MO 63031. **Phone:** (314) 831-3500.

Self-guiding tours: A brochure describing a walking tour of Florissant is available from the chamber of commerce.

KIRKWOOD (C-6) pop. 27,324

MUSEUM OF TRANSPORTATION is w. off the I-270 Dougherty Ferry Rd. exit at 3015 Barrett Station Rd. Trains, automobiles, buses, streetcars, horse-drawn vehicles, aircraft and boats represent 150 years of American history. In addition to more than 70 locomotives, the collection includes Bobby Darin's 1964 dream car, which cost more than $93,000 and took 7 years to build.

Creation Station is a separate hands-on educational area where young children can explore different modes of transportation. The various play stations utilize puzzles, puppets, arts and crafts and other learning tools.

Time: Allow 1 hour, 30 minutes minimum. **Hours:** Mon.-Sat. 9-5, Sun. 11-5, May 1-Labor Day; Tues.-Sat. and Mon. holidays 9-4, Sun. 11-4, rest of year. Creation Station boarding times Mon.-Fri. at 9:15, 10:30 and 11:45, May 1-Labor Day; Tues.-Fri. at 9:15, 10:30 and 11:45, rest of year. Closed Jan. 1, Thanksgiving and Dec. 25. **Cost:** Museum $6; $4 (ages 5-12, ages 65+ and active military with ID); free (teachers with ID). Creation Station additional $1.50; free (under 1). **Phone:** (314) 615-8668.

POWDER VALLEY CONSERVATION CENTER is off I-44 exit 277B, .5 mi. s. on US 61, .5 mi. w. on Watson Rd., .6 mi. n. on Geyer Rd., then 1.2 mi. w. to 1715 Cragwold Rd. Exhibits include a "tree factory" that explains trees' basic structure and physiology, an active beehive and a 3,000-gallon aquarium. Three miles of paved nature trails wind through 112 acres of forest. **Time:** Allow 2 hours minimum. **Hours:** Trails open daily 8-8, early Apr.-late Oct.; 8-6, rest of year. Office daily 8-5. Closed Jan. 1, Thanksgiving and Dec. 25. **Cost:** Free. **Phone:** (314) 301-1500.

MARYLAND HEIGHTS (C-5) pop. 25,756

GAMBLING ESTABLISHMENTS

- **Harrah's Hotel & Casino** is at 777 Casino Center Dr. **Hours:** Sun.-Thurs. 9 a.m.-5 a.m., Fri.-Sat. 24 hours. **Phone:** (314) 770-8100.

ST. CHARLES (C-5) pop. 60,321, elev. 467'

Founded by French Canadians in 1769, St. Charles was first known as *Les Petites Cotes*—"the little hills"—a reference to the low bluffs that form a picturesque backdrop along the Missouri River. Present-day Missouri was then part of a vast territory under Spanish rule, although many of those who came to the region to start a new life were French nationals. But also among the arrivals was an American pioneer and soon-to-be folk hero named Daniel Boone; he and much of his extended family settled in nearby Defiance.

In 1804 Upper Louisiana was formally transferred from France to the United States, and the district of San Carlos was renamed St. Charles. That same year Meriwether Lewis arrived from St. Louis to meet up with William Clark, and the two men, along with several boats and an expedition party, left the relative comforts of civilization to embark on a great journey of discovery that would lead them all the way to the Pacific Ocean.

Take a walk around the grounds of the Lewis & Clark Boat House and Nature Center *(see attraction listing)* and you'll spot a couple of pawpaw trees. This small tree, which flourishes in the lower Missouri River Valley, produces a large, yellowish-brown, edible fruit that bears a resemblance to another edible yellow fruit, hence the pawpaw's local name—Missouri banana. On the return trip the Lewis and Clark expedition party had depleted most of their rations and ended up subsisting largely on pawpaw fruit.

Missouri was admitted to the Union on Aug. 10, 1821, and St. Charles became the state's first capital. It also was an early center for education west of the Mississippi; the Academy of the Sacred Heart was established in 1818 by Rose Philippine Duchesne, who was canonized in 1988.

This is a city that actively preserves its past, and a festival is one way to expose yourself to a little history while having a good old time. Lewis and Clark Heritage Days, held in mid-May at Frontier Park, commemorates the arrival in St. Charles of Clark and the Corps of Discovery, where the explorer met up with Lewis. A large encampment along the Missouri River is the site for demonstrations of frontier skills, period craft displays and a rousing Fife and Drum Corps muster.

In mid-August the entire city celebrates Fete des Petites Cotes, or the Festival of the Little Hills. The 19th century is revisited at this major summertime event, which offers craft demonstrations, food and musical entertainment courtesy of the St. Charles Municipal Band and popular local outfits like the bluegrass-playin' Salty Dawg Band.

Pay tribute to yesteryear at the Lewis & Clark Statue in Frontier Park (off Riverside Drive at the foot of Perry Street). Dedicated in 2003, it depicts the intrepid explorers and their dog, Seaman. Also in the park is the Katy Depot; St. Charles is the starting point of the Katy Trail, the former railroad line turned scenic bike trail that stretches west to Clinton.

Switch gears from the past to the present and stop by the Foundry Art Centre, 520 N. Main St. This gallery has studios where you can chat with local artists about their work. The center also contains several rooms with rotating exhibits of high-quality art; phone (636) 255-0270.

The St. Charles Trolley is an easy way to get from Main Street to other nearby attractions. There are nine designated stops, and you can also flag down a driver to get on or off on the spot. All it takes to board is a wooden nickel (available at Main Street shops displaying a "free trolley token" sign). The green-and-red cars run Tues.-Sat. 10-5, Sun. noon-5, Apr. 1 through the last Sunday in December.

Greater St. Charles Convention and Visitors Bureau: 230 S. Main St., St. Charles, MO 63301. **Phone:** (636) 946-7776 or (800) 366-2427. *See color ad p. 219.*

Shopping areas: If you're a fan of gift and specialty shops—all quaint with a capital "Q" and conveniently located along one street for easy browsing—you're in luck: Main Street in St. Charles has perfected this particular shopping experience.

The street, part of the St. Charles Historic District, parallels the Missouri River. Shady, brick-paved sidewalks are lined with barrel planters and hanging flower baskets. Just when you're thinking about cooling your heels for a minute an inviting bench seems to appear; the gazebo near the convention and visitors bureau (where there also are public restrooms) is a particularly pretty spot.

Many of the shops are in handsomely restored old brick and wood-frame buildings. Even if you're on a mission to find that certain something, take time to check out Silks & Treasures (319 S. Main St.) for gifts and home accessories, The Enchanted Attic (304 S. Main St.) for funky jewelry, wind chimes, crystals and such, and Cobblestone (803 S. Main St.) for Colonial-style furniture, period lighting fixtures, historical prints and other Americana.

The boutique Ooh La La (340 S. Main St.) has women's and children's clothing. Patches Quilt & Button Shoppe (337 S. Main St.) sells quilting fabric and supplies as well as the finished, handmade product. Look for children's books and tomes about local history at Main Street Books (307 S. Main St.).

Have lunch in the cozy dining room at the Mother-in-Law House Restaurant (500 S. Main St.), or sit on the leafy patio if the weather's nice. Picasso's (101 N. Main St.) is a coffee house with a relaxed air and a good selection of coffee and espresso drinks.

Of course Main Street isn't the only shopping game in town. Outdoor enthusiasts not on the hunt for tea cozies and collectible dolls head to Bass Pro Shops Sportsman's Warehouse, 1365 S. 5th St. It's a sprawling place with every conceivable type of recreational gear, plus wildlife exhibits, an indoor waterfall and a game fish aquarium.

FIRST MISSOURI STATE CAPITOL STATE HISTORIC SITE is at 200-216 S. Main St. on the riverfront. These adjoining Federal-style brick buildings were the seat of government 1821-26. The first state General Assembly met upstairs while the building's owners lived and operated a general store on the first floor. Gov. Alexander McNair's office and a committee room were off the legislative chambers.

Several rooms in the 1820 complex have been restored and decorated with period furnishings. An interpretive center offers exhibits and a slide show.

Time: Allow 1 hour minimum. **Hours:** Guided tours are given Mon.-Sat. on the hour 9-4, Sun. 11-5, Apr.-Dec.; Tues.-Sat. on the hour 9-4, Jan.-Mar. (also Sun. 11-5, in Mar.). Last tour begins 1 hour before closing. Closed Jan. 1, Easter, Thanksgiving and Dec. 25. **Cost:** $2.50; $1.50 (ages 6-12). **Phone:** (636) 940-3322 or (800) 334-6946.

LEWIS & CLARK BOAT HOUSE AND NATURE CENTER is at 1050 Riverside Dr. Exhibits relating to the Lewis and Clark expedition and the Missouri River ecosystem are featured. Dioramas, artifacts and sound effects help re-create Lewis and Clark's early 19th-century explorations. Replicas of the three boats used in the expedition are featured on the lower level. The nature center has waterfalls and plant and animal displays.

Time: Allow 30 minutes minimum. **Hours:** Mon.-Sat. 10-5, Sun. noon-5. Closed Jan. 1, Easter, Thanksgiving and Dec. 25. **Cost:** $4; $2 (ages 0-16). **Phone:** (636) 947-3199.

GAMBLING ESTABLISHMENTS

- **Ameristar St. Charles Casino, Resort & Spa** is off I-70 5th St. exit, following signs s. to One Ameristar Blvd. on the riverfront. **Hours:** Daily 8 a.m.-4 a.m. **Phone:** (636) 940-4300, (636) 949-7777 or (866) 667-3386.

VALLEY PARK (C-6) pop. 6,518

LONE ELK PARK is w. of SR 141, off N. Outer Rd. The 546-acre landscaped park contains small herds of elk, deer and bison. A lake attracts Canada geese and mallard ducks, while the wooded grounds are home to native wildlife. Animals roam freely through a portion of the park that is set aside as a drive-through area. Nature trails and picnic facilities are available. **Hours:** Daily 8-dusk. **Cost:** Free. **Phone:** (314) 615-7275.

WORLD BIRD SANCTUARY is w. of SR 141 off N. Outer Rd., across from Lone Elk Park. Located on 130 acres, the facility houses a variety of birds and reptiles. More than 250 injured or ill raptors are rehabilitated here each year. There are nature trails and displays featuring birds in their natural habitats. Naturalists are on hand to answer questions.

Time: Allow 1 hour minimum. **Hours:** Sanctuary open daily 8-5. Visitor center open daily 10-4, Memorial Day-Labor Day; 11-3, rest of year. Closed Thanksgiving and Dec. 25. **Cost:** Free. **Phone:** (636) 861-3225.

WEBSTER GROVES (C-6) pop. 23,230

A parcel of 6,002 acres, once known as "Dry Ridge," was granted to Gregoire Sarpy in 1802 by the last Spanish lieutenant governor of the Louisiana Territory. The land was developed in the late 19th century as an affluent St. Louis suburb. Webster Groves was incorporated in 1896, combining five settlements along the Pacific Railroad line.

HAWKEN HOUSE is off I-44 exit 280 (Elm Ave.), 1 mi. s. to Old Watson Rd., then .3 mi. w. to 1155 S. Rock Hill Rd. This Federal-style brick house was the residence of Christopher Hawken of the Hawken Rifle family. Built in 1857 with slave labor, the eight-room home was relocated from its original location in 1970 and is furnished with Victorian antiques.

Tours: Guided tours are available. **Time:** Allow 1 hour minimum. **Hours:** Tues. and Thurs. 11-3:30, Sun. 1-3:30, Mar.-Dec. Last tour departs 30 minutes before closing. Closed major holidays. **Cost:** $4; $2 (ages 6-12). **Phone:** (314) 968-1857.

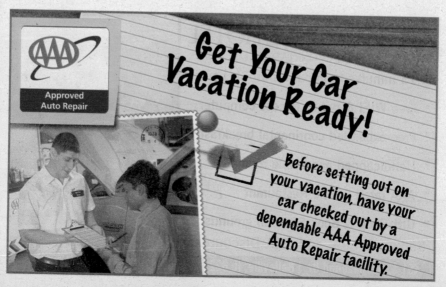

Nearby Illinois

ALTON pop. 30,496, elev. 450′

Just north of the confluence of the Mississippi and Missouri rivers, Alton was founded in the early 19th century. Col. Rufus Easton obtained the land and named the town for his son. The Eagle Packet line of boats, once built in Alton, contributed to local river traffic on the Mississippi. Riverfront Park offers a vantage point for viewing the river.

The issue of slavery found volatile expression in Alton when abolitionist editor Elijah Lovejoy was killed by a proslavery mob in 1837. The Alton Cemetery on Monument Avenue contains Lovejoy's tomb and a monument in his honor. In 1858 the last Lincoln-Douglas debate took place in town. The city's history and river heritage are among themes addressed at the Alton Museum of History and Art, 2809 College Ave.; phone (618) 462-2763.

Perhaps Alton's most renowned native son was Robert Pershing Wadlow; at 8 feet, 11.1 inches he remains the world's tallest known person. A life-size statue of Wadlow can be seen on the campus of Southern Illinois University Dental School. Near the intersection of Broadway and William are the remnants of Alton Prison, where more than 1,300 Confederate soldiers died of various diseases. A portion of the cellblock wall remains.

Alton's Victorian, Federal and GreekRevival 19th-century houses draw attention, particularly in autumn when the trees cloaking the surrounding bluffs are ablaze with fall foliage colors. The Great River Road, which runs north along the Mississippi River, has a bicycle path offering views of the river and bluffs.

Alton Regional Convention and Visitor Bureau Visitors Center: 200 Piasa St., Alton, IL 62002. **Phone:** (618) 465-6676 or (800) 258-6645.

Shopping areas: Alton's antique district, in a three-block area between George and State streets, contains more than 40 shops housed in buildings dating from the 1800s.

GAMBLING ESTABLISHMENTS

- **Argosy Casino, Alton** is on the riverfront at 219 Piasa St. **Hours:** Daily 8 a.m.-6 a.m. **Phone:** (800) 711-4263.

BELLEVILLE pop. 41,410, elev. 500′

Founded in 1814, Belleville was named by its early French settlers. The discovery of coal in 1828 attracted many German miners. The town retains much of the Teutonic influence in language, song, festivals and architecture. Manufacturers produce a variety of goods, and area coal mines yield more than 3 million tons a year. Scott Air Force Base is nearby.

Belleville Tourism Bureau: 216 E. A St., Belleville, IL 62220. **Phone:** (618) 233-6769 or (800) 677-9255.

NATIONAL SHRINE OF OUR LADY OF THE SNOWS is w. on SR 15, just e. of I-255. A 200-acre religious center under direction of the Missionary Oblates of Mary Immaculate, the shrine includes a 2,400-seat amphitheater, a replica of the Lourdes Grotto, prayer gardens and chapels. From mid-November to early January the holiday season is celebrated with Way of Lights, a special event offering Nativity displays, puppet shows and outdoor light displays. **Hours:** Open daily 8-8. **Cost:** Donations. **Phone:** (618) 397-6700 or (800) 682-2879. *See color ad p. 222.*

ST. CLAIR HISTORICAL SOCIETY is at 701 E. Washington St. This 1866 Victorian adaptation of a Greek Revival house is furnished in period. The house features changing displays of vintage clothing, toys, quilts and other household items. A historical research library also is on the premises. **Tours:** Guided tours are available. **Hours:** Open Mon.-Fri. 10-2. Closed major holidays. **Cost:** $2; $1 (ages 6-12). **Phone:** (618) 234-0600.

WILLIAM & FLORENCE SCHMIDT ART CENTER is on Southwestern Illinois College's Belleville campus at 2500 Carlyle Ave. The center's modern exterior houses changing exhibitions of photographs, paintings and lithographs by regional artists as well as samplings from its 400-piece permanent collection. Outdoors, visitors will find several sculptures in a variety of materials strategically place within the immaculately landscaped gardens, which feature colorful flower beds, container gardens and rock beds.

Time: Allow 1 hour minimum. **Hours:** Tues.-Sat. 11-5 (also Thurs. 5-8). Summer hours may vary; phone ahead to confirm. Closed major holidays. **Cost:** Free. **Phone:** (618) 222-5278, or (866) 942-7942 in St. Louis area and Illinois.

CAHOKIA pop. 16,391, elev. 401'

Cahokia was founded in 1699 by three missionaries from Québec. Its location along three rivers made it a center of commerce for the region by the mid-1700s. At the end of the French and Indian War in 1763, when this area was ceded to Great Britain, many citizens uneasy about the possibility of a British occupation moved across the Mississippi River and were instrumental in helping found St. Louis.

With the onset of the American Revolution, George Rogers Clark and his troops from Virginia occupied Cahokia, recruited a militia and organized a campaign against British forces at Vincennes, Ind. The settlement remained a British outpost until 1778. The first election for chief magistrates in Illinois was held in Cahokia, which helped establish a sense of peace and order in a territory otherwise characterized by lawlessness.

The Jarrot Mansion, 124 E. First St., was completed in 1810 and is one of the oldest brick buildings in the mid-Mississippi River Valley. **Note:** The mansion currently is closed for renovations but is open to the public during special events in February and September; phone (618) 332-1782.

Cahokia Area Chamber of Commerce: 103 Main St., Cahokia, IL 62206. **Phone:** (618) 332-4258.

CAHOKIA COURTHOUSE STATE HISTORIC SITE is off I-55/70, just w. of jct. SRs 3 and 157. Built in 1737 as a French residence, the structure was used as a courthouse until 1814. The first U.S. court sessions and elections in the state were held in this building. The visitor center has interactive exhibits that trace the French influence in 18th-century Illinois. **Hours:** Tues.-Sat. 9-5. Closed Jan. 1, Thanksgiving and Dec. 25. **Cost:** Free. **Phone:** (618) 332-1782.

CHURCH OF THE HOLY FAMILY is 4 mi. s. of I-55/70 at jct. SRs 3 and 157. Said to be the oldest church in Illinois, the 1699 stone and wood building has been in continuous use under French, British and American rule. **Time:** Allow 30 minutes minimum. **Hours:** Daily 10-3, June-Aug.; by appointment rest of year. **Cost:** Donations. **Phone:** (618) 337-4548.

COLLINSVILLE pop. 24,707

Horseradishes, log cabins and coal all are a part of Collinsville's heritage, which began when the town's first inhabitant built a log cabin overlooking the Mississippi basin in 1810. The city's name changed from Downing Station to Collinsville in 1825, and it soon became a bustling coal town. Today the area around Collinsville produces most of the world's supply of horseradishes.

Tourism Bureau of Southwestern Illinois: 10950 Lincoln Tr., Fairview Heights, IL 62208. **Phone:** (618) 397-1488 or (800) 442-1488.

GEM **CAHOKIA MOUNDS STATE HISTORIC SITE** is off I-255 exit 24 (Collinsville Rd.), then w. 1.5 mi. This 2,200-acre site preserves 65 Indian tribal mounds. Monks Mound, the site's centerpiece, covers more than 14 acres at its base and is 100 feet tall. Evidence of a once-flourishing Mississippian civilization—the center of an enormous trade empire distinguished by social and political activity—spans the years A.D. 900-1500. At its peak the site is said to have supported an estimated 20,000 inhabitants.

An interpretive center houses exhibits about the people who once lived in the region; a 15-minute film documenting the history of Cahokia; and a life-size, re-created Indian village. One-hour guided tours and hiking trails are available, as are self-guiding audiotape tours and a 17-minute video tour of the grounds.

Hours: Grounds daily 8 a.m.-dusk. Interpretive center daily 9-5, May-Oct.; Tues.-Sun. 9-5, rest of year. Guided tours are given Mon.-Sat. at 10:30 and 2:30, Sun. at 12:30 and 2:30, June-Aug.; Sat.-Sun. at 2:30, Apr.-May and Sept.-Oct. Closed Jan. 1, Election Day, Nov. 11, Thanksgiving and Dec. 25. Phone ahead to confirm schedule. **Cost:** $4; $2 (ages 0-12). **Phone:** (618) 346-5160.

EAST ALTON pop. 6,830

NATIONAL GREAT RIVERS MUSEUM is at #2 Lock and Dam Way. Next to the Mississippi River, the museum houses interactive exhibits that describe the river's natural history and its commercial importance. Visitors can view a room-size model of river bluffs that highlights area wildlife and an aquarium that is home to Mississippi River fish species.

The Pilot House simulator enables visitors to experience what it is like to steer barges through a lock. **Time:** Allow 1 hour minimum. **Hours:** Daily 9-5. Closed Jan. 1, Thanksgiving and Dec. 25. **Cost:** Free. **Phone:** (877) 462-6979.

Melvin Price Locks and Dam is at #1 Lock and Dam Way, at the National Great Rivers Museum. Part of the Upper Mississippi's flood control and navigation system, the Melvin Price Locks and Dam features two locks through which billions of dollars of goods pass each year.

Guided tours of the locks and dam depart from the adjacent museum, where visitors also can see a film about the project. Nearby Esplanade Park has bird-watching platforms from which bald eagles can often be seen. **Hours:** Tours are given daily (weather permitting) at 10, 1 and 3. **Cost:** Free. **Phone:** (877) 462-6979.

EAST ST. LOUIS pop. 31,542, elev. 418'

On the Mississippi River opposite St. Louis, East St. Louis was colonized by the French, who built a mission a few miles south at the village of Cahokia in 1699. Capt. James Piggott helped promote permanent settlement of the region when he established a ferry in 1795. Lots in Illinoistown, a village near the ferry, were auctioned off.

River traffic and trade, westward expansion and the development of the area's natural resource, coal, hastened expansion of the site. The coal was pulled by horses over wooden rails along the riverbanks; some note that this means of transporting the mineral constituted claim to the first railroad in the state, and today the East St. Louis area is a railroad center.

The Gateway Geyser, on Front Street at Trendley Avenue, is one of the world's highest fountains, reaching 627 feet. Surrounded by four smaller plumes, the fountain is centered directly across from the Gateway Arch.

Fairmount Park Race Track, in Fairmount City at Collinsville Road and I-255, offers Thoroughbred racing; phone (314) 436-1516 for schedule information.

Note: Policies concerning admittance of children to pari-mutuel betting facilities vary. Phone for information.

GAMBLING ESTABLISHMENTS

- **Casino Queen Hotel & Casino** is directly across from the Gateway Arch at 200 S. Front St. **Hours:** Daily 9 a.m.-6:30 a.m. **Phone:** (618) 874-5000 or (800) 777-0777.

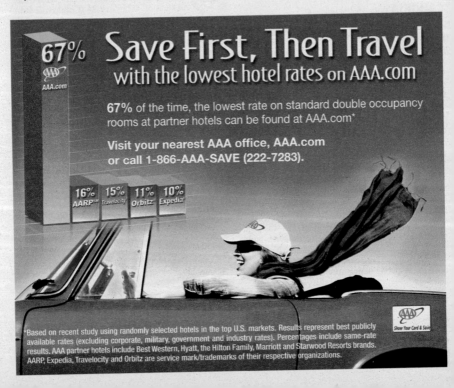

EDWARDSVILLE pop. 21,491, elev. 433′

Edwardsville has two historic areas that provide a glimpse of its past: the St. Louis Street Historic District and the LeClaire Historic District. Southern Illinois University at Edwardsville encompasses a picturesque 2,600-acre campus.

Edwardsville-Glen Carbon Chamber of Commerce: 200 University Park Dr., Suite 260, Edwardsville, IL 62025. **Phone:** (618) 656-7600.

MADISON COUNTY HISTORICAL MUSEUM AND ARCHIVAL LIBRARY is at 715 N. Main St. Housed in a restored Federal-style residence built in 1836, the museum contains period furnishings, American Indian and pioneer artifacts, antiques and a variety of changing seasonal exhibits that include quilts, needlework and historic costumes. A history and genealogy reference library is adjacent to the museum. **Time:** Allow 1 hour minimum. **Hours:** Wed.-Fri. 9-4, Sun. 1-4. Closed major holidays. **Cost:** Donations. **Phone:** (618) 656-7562.

HARTFORD pop. 1,545, elev. 430′

LEWIS & CLARK STATE HISTORIC SITE is at One Lewis & Clark Tr. near jct. SR 3 and New Poag Rd. At the confluence of the Mississippi and Missouri rivers, the site commemorates Camp River Dubois, the Lewis and Clark Expedition's 1803-04 winter encampment. Costumed guides show visitors around a full-scale log reconstruction of the camp.

The interpretive center features a 55-foot-long replica of a keelboat. A 15-minute film details the preparations Lewis and Clark made here for their journey west. **Time:** Allow 1 hour minimum. **Hours:** Daily 9-5, Memorial Day-Labor Day; Wed.-Sun. 9-5, rest of year. **Cost:** Donations. **Phone:** (618) 251-5811.

Daniel Boone Home, Defiance / Missouri Division of Tourism

This ends listings for the St. Louis Vicinity.
The following page resumes the alphabetical listings of cities in Missouri.

SAVANNAH (B-2) pop. 4,762, elev. 1,115′

ANDREW COUNTY MUSEUM AND HISTORICAL SOCIETY is at 202 E. Duncan Dr. at jct. US 71 Bus. Rte. Exhibits depict the history of Andrew County. Featured are kewpie and French doll collections, antique cars and an old general store. **Time:** Allow 1 hour minimum. **Hours:** Tues.-Sat. 10-4. Closed major holidays. **Cost:** Free. **Phone:** (816) 324-4720.

SEDALIA (C-3) pop. 20,339, elev. 909′

Gen. George R. Smith bought 1,000 acres along the Pacific Railroad right of way for $13 per acre in 1857. He called the town he platted Sedville in honor of his daughter Sarah, whom he affectionately referred to as Sed. Three years later Smith filed a larger plat that included Sedville, naming the new town Sedalia.

In June residents honor one of the best-known composers of ragtime music with the Scott Joplin Ragtime Festival. The products of Missouri's fields and factories are the centerpiece of the State Fair, held in August.

A trailhead leading to Katy Trail State Park, one of the nation's foremost rails-to-trails conversions, is just east of town.

Sedalia Area Chamber of Commerce: 600 E. Third St., Sedalia, MO 65301-4499. **Phone:** (660) 826-2222 or (800) 827-5295.

Self-guiding tours: Walking tour brochures of the downtown historic district are available from the chamber of commerce.

BOTHWELL LODGE STATE HISTORIC SITE is 6 mi. n. on US 65 at 19349 Bothwell State Park Rd. The country retreat of lawyer and businessman John Homer Bothwell was built in four sections 1897-1928. The building is furnished much the way Bothwell left it when he died in 1929. A nature trail and picnic facilities are available. **Time:** Allow 1 hour minimum. **Hours:** Guided tours are offered on the hour Mon.-Sat. 10-4, Sun. 11-4. **Cost:** $2.50; $1.50 (ages 6-12). **Phone:** (660) 827-0510 or (800) 334-6946.

DAUM MUSEUM OF CONTEMPORARY ART is at 3201 W. 16th St. on the campus of State Fair Community College. Nine galleries house both permanent and changing exhibits focusing on late 20th- and early 21st-century art. The building's sleekly modern architecture—including a three-story glass atrium wall—mirrors the works on display. **Time:** Allow 30 minutes minimum. **Hours:** Tues.-Fri. 11-5, Sat.-Sun. 1-5. Closed major holidays. **Cost:** Free. **Phone:** (660) 530-5888.

KATY DEPOT HISTORIC SITE is at 600 E. Third St., 1.6 mi. e. of US 65. The Katy Depot is a reminder of the industry and prosperity that the railroad brought to Sedalia as well as rural central Missouri. The re-created buildings on the site, including a ticket office, lunch room, dining room and women's waiting room, contain original furniture and flooring. In the women's waiting room, speaking mannequins activated by motion sensors portray two people who worked at and traveled through the depot. Several railroad-themed works of art are on the grounds.

Reservations for guided tours are required at least 2 weeks in advance. **Time:** Allow 1 hour minimum. **Hours:** Mon.-Fri. 9-5, Sat. 10-3, Apr.-Dec.; Mon.-Fri. 9-5, rest of year. Guided tours are offered 9:30-3. Closed major holidays. **Cost:** Free. Guided tours $1. **Phone:** (660) 826-2222.

SIBLEY—*see Kansas City p. 181.*

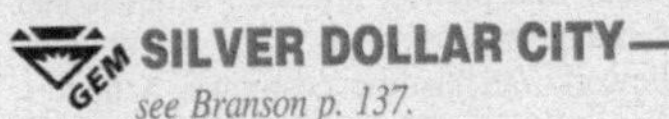

SILVER DOLLAR CITY—*see Branson p. 137.*

SMITHVILLE—*see Kansas City p. 181.*

SPRINGFIELD (E-3) pop. 151,580, elev. 1,292′

The future location of Springfield was designated by John Polk Campbell in 1829 when he carved his initials into an ash tree near the site of four springs. Strategically located at the junction of two important roads, the town flourished during the heavy westward migration of the 1850s. This key location also made the town a target during the Civil War in a battle that took place at what is now Wilson's Creek National Battlefield *(see place listing p. 230)*.

Union spy/scout James Butler Hickok, better known as Wild Bill Hickok, stayed in Springfield after the war. Achieving fame as a gunfighter, Hickok made national news in 1865 when he returned fire and killed Dave Tutt in the public square; he was later acquitted for this act.

Westward migration continued to affect Springfield. In 1926 plans for the first paved transcontinental highway in the United States were made. Stretching from the Great Lakes to the Pacific Coast, Route 66 earned the nickname Main Street USA. Traces of the old route are visible along Kearney, Glenstone, College and St. Louis streets.

The past also is evident in the historic houses and buildings along Walnut Street and in the Midtown district. Christ Episcopal Church, 601 E. Walnut St., is said to be the oldest church building in the city. Built in 1870, it features stained-glass windows and ecclesiastical Gothic architecture.

In addition to sightseeing, Springfield offers fishing, boating and picnicking at Fellows, McDaniel and Springfield lakes. Table Rock and Bull Shoals reservoirs also are nearby.

The Frisco Highline Trail, Missouri's second-longest rail trail, connects Springfield and Bolivar along the path of a former railroad line once traveled by Harry S. Truman as a precursor to his famous "Whistle Stop Campaign" in 1948. The 36-mile-long bicycling trail winds through the scenic forest and pasture lands of La Petite Gemme Prairie Natural Area, crossing over 16 trestles along the way (horseback riding is permitted between Willard and Walnut Grove). Trailheads are located in Springfield, Willard, Walnut Grove, Wishart and Bolivar. For more information contact Ozark Greenways, P.O. Box 50733, Springfield, MO 65805; phone (417) 864-2015.

The Springfield Cardinals AA minor league team is a big regional draw during baseball season. Games are played at John Q. Hammons Field, 955 E. Trafficway; phone (417) 863-2143.

Springfield Convention and Visitors Bureau Tourist Information Center: 3315 E. Battlefield Rd., Springfield, MO 65804. **Phone:** (417) 881-5300 or (800) 678-8767. *See color ad below & p. 149.*

Self-guiding tours: For pamphlets about attractions and driving tours of historic downtown Springfield contact the tourist information center.

Shopping Areas: Antique and craft shops abound in Springfield. Ozark Treasures, 1832 S. Campbell St., features more than 100 dealers. The Commercial Street Historical District offers antiques, collectibles and vintage clothing. Contemporary shopping can be found at Battlefield Mall, Battlefield Road and Glenstone Avenue; the more than 170 stores include Dillard's, JCPenney, Macy's and Sears.

Bass Pro Shops Outdoor World, 1935 S. Campbell St., caters to outdoor enthusiasts with a 140,000-gallon game fish aquarium and waterfall, wildlife exhibits and sporting demonstrations.

DICKERSON PARK ZOO is off I-44 exit 77, then 1 blk. n. to Norton Rd., following signs to 3043 N. Fort Ave. The zoo features more than 500 animals from a variety of bird and mammal species. Tigers and primates live in the Tropical Asia habitat, while gray wolves and mountain lions are among the animals that can be seen at the Missouri Habitats exhibit.

Time: Allow 2 hours minimum. **Hours:** Daily 9-5, Apr.-Sept.; 10-4, rest of year (weather permitting). Closed Jan. 1, Thanksgiving and Dec. 25. **Cost:** $7; $5 (ages 3-12 and 60+). Train rides $2; free (ages 0-1). **Phone:** (417) 864-1800.

DISCOVERY CENTER is off I-44 exit 80A, 3 mi. s. on Glenstone Ave., then 1.5 mi. w. to 438 E. St. Louis St. Interactive displays include a child-size "town" where visitors can write for a newspaper, anchor a news broadcast, withdraw play money at the bank or shop at the market. Other exhibits explore archeology, energy and anatomy.

Time: Allow 1 hour minimum. **Hours:** Tues.-Fri. 9-5 (also Fri. 5-8), Sat. 10-5, Sun. 1-5. Closed Jan. 1, Easter, Thanksgiving and Dec. 25. **Cost:** $9; $8 (ages 60+); $7 (ages 3-15). Rates for special exhibits may be higher; phone ahead. **Phone:** (417) 862-9910.

GEM **FANTASTIC CAVERNS** is 1.5 mi. n. of jct. I-44 and SR 13, then 3 mi. w. on Fantastic Caverns Rd. No walking is necessary on a 1-mile, Jeep-drawn tram tour through one of Missouri's largest caves. Fantastic Caverns has a varied history, beginning with its exploration by 12 women in 1867. As a speakeasy in the 1920s the cave was outfitted with a dance floor, gambling tables and a bar. It also served as a meeting place in the 1930s and as a country music theater in the 1960s and early 1970s. The temperature in the natural limestone cave is a constant 60 F.

Time: Allow 1 hour minimum. **Hours:** Daily 8-dusk. Closed Thanksgiving and Dec. 24-25. **Cost:** $21.50; $13.50 (ages 6-12); free (ages 0-5 with paid adult). **Phone:** (417) 833-2010.

THE HISTORY MUSEUM is at 830 Boonville Ave. Permanent collections on the third floor of the 1894 City Hall Building include regional books and documents and more than 20,000 photographs relating the history of Springfield. Changing exhibits about Ozark and Springfield history also are presented. **Hours:** Tues.-Sat. 10:30-4:30. Closed major holidays. **Cost:** $3; $2.50 (senior citizens and students with ID); $1 (ages 6-12). **Phone:** (417) 864-1976.

JAPANESE STROLL GARDEN is w. on Battlefield St. to 2400 S. Scenic in Nathanael Greene Park. A tea house and moon bridge are centerpieces of this landscaped 7.5-acre garden, which features bonsai trees and three small lakes with feeding stations for fish and ducks. **Time:** Allow 1 hour minimum. **Hours:** Thurs.-Mon. 9-7:30, Apr.-Oct. **Cost:** $3; free (ages 0-12). **Phone:** (417) 864-1049.

MISSOURI SPORTS HALL OF FAME is at 3861 E. Stan Musial Dr. (US 60). Displays of sports memorabilia evoke the memory of legendary Missouri teams and players. Interactive opportunities include a broadcast booth and a pitching cage where visitors stand behind home plate as major league pitches come in at 100-plus miles per hour. **Hours:** Mon.-Sat. 10-4, Sun. noon-4. **Cost:** $5; $4 (senior citizens); $3 (ages 6-15); $14 (family). **Phone:** (417) 889-3100 or (800) 498-5678.

SPRINGFIELD ART MUSEUM is at 1111 E. Brookside Dr. in Phelps Grove Park. The museum houses nearly 9,000 art objects, including paintings and sculptures from the 19th-, 20th- and 21st centuries. Changing exhibits of works by regionally and nationally known artists are featured. **Time:** Allow 30 minutes minimum. **Hours:** Tues.-Sat. 9-5 (also Thurs. 5-8), Sun. 1-5. Closed major holidays. **Cost:** Free. **Phone:** (417) 837-5700.

SPRINGFIELD CONSERVATION NATURE CENTER is off US 65 exit US 60W, then .7 mi. following signs to 4600 Chrisman Ave. Among 80 acres of forest, fields and creeks along Lake Springfield, the visitor center has natural history exhibits and offers hunting and fishing permits. Along the nearly 3 miles of trails visitors can spot deer, raccoons, turtles and other wildlife.

Time: Allow 1 hour minimum. **Hours:** Grounds open daily 8 a.m.-9 p.m., Mar.-Oct.; 8-6, rest of year. Visitor center open daily 8-5. Closed Jan. 1, Thanksgiving and Dec. 25. **Cost:** Free. **Phone:** (417) 888-4237.

SPRINGFIELD LITTLE THEATRE AT THE LANDERS is at 311 E. Walnut Ave. The baroque Renaissance/Napoleon architecture of this 1909 theater has been carefully preserved and restored. Once the venue for John Philip Sousa and Lillian Russell, the theater offers performances by the Springfield Little Theater troupe, as well as regional ballet and opera companies. Self-guiding tours are available. **Hours:** Mon.-Fri. 11-5, Sept.-June; 11-4, rest of year. **Cost:** Free. **Phone:** (417) 869-3869, or (417) 869-1334 for tickets.

SPRINGFIELD NATIONAL CEMETERY is at 1702 E. Seminole St. The 18-acre site contains graves of Union and Confederate soldiers as well as veterans from all wars. Five Medal of Honor recipients are buried here; their headstones are engraved in gold. **Hours:** Cemetery open daily dawn-dusk. Office open Mon.-Fri. 8-4:30. Closed Jan. 1 and Dec. 25. **Cost:** Free. **Phone:** (417) 881-9499.

GEM **WONDERS OF WILDLIFE MUSEUM & AQUARIUM** is at 500 W. Sunshine St., next to Bass Pro Shops Outdoor World. The museum stresses the importance of conserving natural resources and honors the nation's hunting and fishing heritage. Interactive exhibits with computer simulators, 160 species of live animals and aquariums totaling 700,000 gallons of water depict man's relationship with his surroundings.

The habitats of North America are explored, beginning with Walk in the Woods, where visitors progress through an Ozark woods along a suspended walkway while being serenaded by geese, doves and quails. Galleries on the lower level feature a viewing window providing underwater perspectives of freshwater pond inhabitants. The 225,000-gallon tank in the Out to Sea Gallery has a ceiling-high window separating visitors from various marine creatures.

CLOSURE INFORMATION: The site is closed until mid- to late 2010 due to an expansion and renovation project. Hours of operation and admission may vary upon reopening; phone ahead. **Time:** Allow 1 hour minimum. **Hours:** Daily 9-6. Last admission 1 hour before closing. **Cost:** $10.95; $9.95 (ages 66+, military and students with ID); $6.50 (ages 4-11). **Phone:** (417) 890-9453 or (888) 521-9497.

STANTON (D-5) elev. 871'

Stanton was named after a successful area businessman, Peter Stanton, who owned and operated a powder mill in the area during the 1850s. Stanton is on the scenic portion of I-44 that runs 171 miles west from Gray Summit to Lebanon.

JESSE JAMES MUSEUM is at I-44 exit 230. This museum explores the theory that Jesse James was not killed in 1882 but lived until the age of 103 under an assumed identity. Wax figures of James, his brother Frank, the James gang's cook and J. Frank Dalton, the man who claimed to be Jesse James, help tell the story. Antiques from the late 1800s, many of James' personal belongings and affidavits that testify to the story's authenticity are displayed. **Hours:** Daily 9-6, June-Aug.; Sat.-Sun. 9-5, Apr.-May and Sept.-Oct. **Cost:** $6; $2.50 (ages 5-11). **Phone:** (573) 927-5233.

MERAMEC CAVERNS is off I-44 exit 230, then 3 mi. s. on CR W. Discovered in 1716, the caverns accommodated powder kilns and leaching vats for Union forces during the Civil War.

In 1864 the outlaw band of Confederate William Quantrill's irregulars, of which Jesse James was a member, seized the gunpowder mill. James was so impressed with the cave that he and his gang later used it as a hideout. This colorful history suitably came to a close when a man avowed to be Jesse James held an outlaw reunion in the cave on James' 102nd birthday in 1949.

The caverns feature five floors of colorful mineral formations. At the entrance are a mineral and crystal collection and an ultraviolet rock display. Guided tours take visitors along a mile of lighted concrete walkways; the cave maintains a constant temperature of 60 F. *See Recreation Chart.* **Hours:** Tours depart daily every 25 minutes 8:30-7:30, July 1-Labor Day; 9-7, May-June; 9-5, rest of year. Closed Thanksgiving and Dec. 25. **Cost:** $18; $9 (ages 5-11). **Phone:** (573) 468-3166 or (800) 676-6105.

SULLIVAN (D-4) pop. 6,351, elev. 970'

MERAMEC STATE PARK is at 115 Meramec Park Dr. This 6,896-acre park on the Meramec River includes several springs and more than 40 caves. *See Recreation Chart and the AAA South Central CampBook.*

Hours: Grounds open daily 7 a.m.-10 p.m., Apr.-Oct.; 7 a.m.-9 p.m., rest of year. Visitor center daily 9-4:30, Apr.-Oct.; daily 8-3:30, Nov.-Dec. and in Mar.; Thurs.-Mon. 8-3:30, rest of year. Fisher Cave tours are given daily at 9:30, 11:30, 1 and 3, June-Aug.; Thurs.-Mon. at 1 and 3, Apr.-May and Sept.-Oct. **Cost:** Grounds free. Tours $6; $5 (ages 13-19); $4 (ages 6-12). **Phone:** (573) 468-6072 or (800) 334-6946.

SUMNER (B-3) pop. 142, elev. 682'

SWAN LAKE NATIONAL WILDLIFE REFUGE is 22 mi. s.w. via US 36 and SR 139; the main entrance is 1 mi. s. of Sumner on CR A at 16194 Swan Lake Ave. The wintering grounds for one of the largest concentrations of Canada geese in North America, this 10,795-acre refuge also attracts more than 100 bald eagles each winter. Waterfowl concentrations are highest in March, April, October and November. A visitor center features videotapes, exhibits and mounted wildlife. "Maxie," a 40-foot-high statue of a Canada goose, stands on the grounds.

The refuge also has a .7-mile, self-guiding Habitat Trail and an observation tower. Fishing is permitted. **Hours:** Refuge open daily dawn-dusk, Mar. 1-Oct. 15. Visitor center and office open Mon.-Fri. 8-4:30; closed major holidays. Habitat Trail and observation tower open all year. **Cost:** Free. **Phone:** (660) 856-3323 or TTY (800) 735-2966.

THAYER (E-4) pop. 2,201

GRAND GULF STATE PARK is about 6 mi. w. on CR W. The 130-foot deep chasm was left when nearly three-quarters of a mile of cavern roof collapsed. Sometimes referred to as the Little Grand Canyon, the 322-acre park includes overlooks, hiking trails and picnic areas. **Hours:** Daily 7 a.m.-dusk. **Cost:** Free. **Phone:** (417) 264-7600 or (800) 334-6946.

UNITY VILLAGE—*see Kansas City p. 181.*

VALLEY PARK—*see St. Louis p. 221.*

VERSAILLES (C-3) pop. 2,565, elev. 1,010'

Named after the city in France, Versailles came into being in 1834 when two pioneers donated 36 blocks of land on the condition that it be developed as a settlement. The new town soon became the Morgan County seat. Versailles was a regular stop on the stagecoach line between Jeffersonville and Springfield, and the Martin Hotel, which now houses the Morgan County Historical Museum *(see attraction listing)*, was its most welcoming sight, especially for weary passengers.

Versailles Area Chamber of Commerce: 109 N. Monroe, P.O. Box 256, Versailles, MO 65084. **Phone:** (573) 378-4401.

JACOB'S CAVE is 6 mi. s. on SR 5, then e. on CR TT, following signs. One of Missouri's largest caves, Jacob's Cave is known for its depth illusion, reflective pools and ceiling spongework. Along with prehistoric bones and evidence of six ice ages, the cave is said to contain the world's largest geode. **Tours:** Guided tours are available. **Time:** Allow 1 hour minimum. **Hours:** Daily 9-5, Memorial Day-Labor Day; 9-4, rest of year. **Cost:** $12; $6 (ages 5-12). **Phone:** (573) 378-4374.

MORGAN COUNTY HISTORICAL MUSEUM is at 120 N. Monroe St. Occupying the 1853 Martin Hotel, this 28-room museum includes a chapel, children's room, hotel room, doctor's office, tool room, beauty shop, schoolroom and barber shop. Some furnishings are original. **Time:** Allow 1 hour minimum. **Hours:** Daily 9-4, May 1-Oct. 15; by appointment rest of year. Closed Thanksgiving and Dec. 25. **Cost:** $3; $1 (ages 6-12). **Phone:** (573) 378-5530 to verify schedule.

WARRENSBURG (C-2) pop. 16,340

Warrensburg was named for Martin Warren, a blacksmith whose shop along a busy Osage Indian trail was a gathering place for frontier farmers. The town gained fame in 1870 as the site of the "Old Drum" trial, in which Leonidas Hornsby was accused of shooting a hunting dog owned by his brother-in-law, Charles Burden. In his appeal to the jury, Senator G.G. Vest coined the term "man's best friend" to describe the noble dog Drum.

Warrensburg is the home of Central Missouri State University, the third-largest state school in Missouri with an enrollment of 11,500 students.

Greater Warrensburg Area Chamber of Commerce and Visitors Center: 100 S. Holden St., Warrensburg, MO 64093. **Phone:** (877) 653-3786.

THE OLD COURTHOUSE is at 302 N. Main St. Site of the "Old Drum" trial, the restored 1838 courthouse includes period furnishings. A monument to the legendary hunting dog stands on the grounds. Tours include the courthouse, a 1913 one-room schoolhouse and the Mary Miller Smiser Heritage Library, which houses artifacts and records dating to the 1860s. **Time:** Allow 30 minutes minimum. **Hours:** Mon.-Fri. 1-4. Closed major holidays. **Cost:** $3. **Phone:** (660) 747-6480.

WARSAW (D-3) pop. 2,070, elev. 708'

Warsaw is a vacation center at the head of Lake of the Ozarks. Parts of the Butterfield Overland Trail, an early stagecoach route, can be hiked within town and the immediate environs. Harry S. Truman State Park *(see Recreation Chart and the AAA South Central CampBook)* offers developed recreational facilities on the Truman Dam's reservoir, formed by the Osage River.

Warsaw Chamber of Commerce: 818 E. Main St., Warsaw, MO 65355. **Phone:** (660) 438-5922 or (800) 927-7294.

BENTON COUNTY MUSEUM is at 700 Benton St. Exhibits include items from the early 1800s to 1935 as well as mounted native wildlife. **Time:** Allow 1 hour minimum. **Hours:** Tues.-Sun. 1-5, Memorial Day-Labor Day. **Cost:** Donations. **Phone:** (660) 438-6707.

HARRY S. TRUMAN DAM VISITOR CENTER is 1.5 mi. n. on US 65 to the Truman Dam exit, then 1 mi. w. following signs to Kaysinger Bluff, overlooking the dam. The center has a 23-minute audiovisual presentation about the Ozark Mountains, a photography exhibit documenting the area, a fossil display, a slide presentation about the dam project, a viewing area with telescopes and a self-guiding nature trail. *See Recreation Chart (Army Corps of Engineers listing).* **Time:** Allow 1 hour minimum. **Hours:** Daily 9-5, Mar.-Oct. **Cost:** Free. **Phone:** (660) 438-2216.

WASHINGTON (C-4) pop. 13,243

Calling itself the corncob pipe capital of the world, Washington was first settled in 1839. Many original buildings along the riverfront and downtown areas have been restored and house restaurants, specialty shops and bed and breakfast inns.

The Fort Charrette Trading Post and Village Museum, 2 miles east off Old Hwy. 100 at 966 Charrette Ln., depicts a mid- to late 1700s trading post and village and features re-created buildings decorated with antique period furnishings; the landscaped grounds are adorned with period fences as well as flower and herb gardens. Explorers Meriwether Lewis and William Clark visited the site on their way west in 1804. Among the artifact collection is the only known surviving cannon fired by or for the expedition; St. Charles had fired this one to welcome the explorers upon their arrival. Also on display is a two-wheeled oxen-pulled cart, which was used to transport pelts and supplies to and from the river. An expansive view of the Missouri River, situated 200 feet below, is considered one of the best in the state. Guided tours are available by appointment; phone (636) 239-4202.

Washington Area Chamber of Commerce: 323 W. Main St., Washington, MO 63090. **Phone:** (636) 239-2715 or (888) 792-7466.

Self-guiding tours: Guided and self-guiding walking tour information for the historic area is available from the chamber of commerce.

WEBSTER GROVES—*see St. Louis p. 221.*

WESTON—*see Kansas City p. 181.*

WILSON'S CREEK NATIONAL BATTLEFIELD (E-2)

Ten miles southwest of Springfield in the town of Republic, the battlefield is off I-44 exit 70 (CR MM), south on CR MM to US 60, south .5 mile on CR M from US 60 to CR ZZ, then 1.5 miles south on CR ZZ to FM 182 (Elm Street).

The battle of Wilson's Creek took place Aug. 10, 1861. Brig. Gen. Nathaniel Lyon, who commanded the Union forces, was the first Union general to die in battle during the Civil War. A 5-mile, self-guiding automobile tour passes eight wayside exhibits and 12 displays. A .6-mile hiking trail leads to Bloody Hill, the major battle site. The Ray House and Ray Springhouse have been restored to their 1861 appearance. Living-history programs are presented regularly on weekends Memorial Day through Labor Day.

A visitor center features a film, battle map and museum. For more information write Superintendent, Wilson's Creek National Battlefield, 6424 W. Farm Rd. 182, Republic, MO 65738-0403. Allow 2 hours minimum. Park open daily 8 a.m.-9 p.m., Memorial Day-Labor Day; 8-7, Apr. 1-day before Memorial Day and day after Labor Day-Oct. 24; 8-5, rest of year. Visitor center daily 8-5. Museum daily 9-noon and 1-4, Apr.-Nov. Closed Jan. 1, Thanksgiving and Dec. 25. Admission $5 (per private vehicle with one adult); maximum charge $10 (per private vehicle with more than one adult); free (ages 0-15). Phone (417) 732-2662.

Cowboys

Step back in time to the Old West at the National Cowboy & Western Heritage Museum

Indians

Festivals, museums and memorials highlight the proud heritage of Oklahoma's tribes

Great Plains

Playful breezes send tall grass waving into a brilliant blue horizon

America's Main Street

You can still get your kicks on Route 66

Blue Waters and Black Gold

Oklahoma, home to drilling rigs and grand lakes, proves oil and water do mix

Washita Battlefield National Historic Site, Cheyenne
© Tom Bean

Turner Falls Park, near Davis / © Jack Milchanowski / age fotostock

Whether dispossessed American Indians moving in, destitute Dust Bowl farmers moving on or cattle-driving cowboys passing through, the comings and goings of diverse groups of people helped mold the character of Oklahoma. Highway-loving travelers can just take it all in, discovering that the state's position at the nation's crossroads makes it difficult to categorize.

Is it a Southern state? The southeastern corner, with its pine-covered hills and distinctly Southern sensibility, is often called "Little Dixie." On the other hand, undulating acres of wheat and grain elevators thrusting to the sky give northern Oklahoma a Midwestern feel.

Yet the loudest singer in a chorus of voices is that of the great American West. Rodeos from one end of the state to the other both test and show off skills that have been vital to cowboys since the days of the Chisholm Trail. Powwows celebrate and preserve American Indian heritage including the tales of ancestors driven west along the "Trail of Tears." Today more than 30 tribes are headquartered in Oklahoma.

Although most likely somewhat biased, cowboy humorist Will Rogers was not far from the truth when he described his native state as the heart of America's existence.

Before the creation of America's interstate system made driving cross-country a simple matter of zipping between points A and B—before the pleasure of savoring local flavor was sacrificed in the name of progress and expediency—there was Route 66. Affectionately called "The Main Street of America," this 2,400-mile-long ribbon of pavement connected Chicago and Los Angeles on a meandering path through the heart of the nation.

Nowhere is this historic road better preserved than in Oklahoma. Small towns awaiting their first traffic light, neon-lit truck stop cafes, old-fashioned filling stations and vintage motels advertising "air-cooled rooms" still line the remaining stretches of the great highway here. That Route 66 survives in Oklahoma is only appropriate: It was State Highway Commissioner Cyrus Avery who helped plan the route and served as its biggest booster in the 1920s.

Since then US 66, as it was officially labeled, has become intimately connected with the history and character of the state. John Steinbeck dubbed it the "Mother Road" in his opus "The Grapes of Wrath," a novel which dramatized the very real plight of thousands of Depression-era "Okies" who fled the Dust Bowl for California's fertile valleys.

Cowboys and Indians

Route 66 enters the state's northeast corner, an area where the river-laced Ozark foothills meet the prairies, at the town of Quapaw. Here the route intersects with a much older and sadder byway: the "Trail of Tears." Beginning in 1830, native peoples of the southeastern United States were forced to move to the newly created Indian Territory that would later become Oklahoma. The trail takes its name from one infamous march resulting in the death of a quarter of the exiles due to exposure, hunger and fatigue.

Today Oklahoma has one of the largest American Indian populations in the country. Numerous tribal museums, along with powwows such as the Red Earth Festival held in Oklahoma City, acquaint visitors with the history and ways of life of the 37 tribes represented in the state. Many place names reflect Oklahoma's American Indian heritage.

Near El Reno Route 66 encounters the Chisholm Trail, a historic passage inseparably tied to cowboy legend roughly paralleling

Oklahoma Historical Timeline

Moundbuilders inhabit eastern Oklahoma.
A.D. 500-1300

Spanish explorer Francisco Vasquez de Coronado ventures through the area searching for a city of gold.
1541

1817-40
The federal government relocates the Five Civilized Tribes—the Cherokee, Chickasaw, Choctaw, Creek and Seminole—from their homes in the southeastern United States to Oklahoma.

Texas ranchers move their cattle along the Chisholm Trail through Oklahoma to reach the railroads in Kansas.
1866-89

©Legends Archive

1879
Humorist Will Rogers is born in Oologah.

odern US 81. In the late 19th century, thouands of Texas cattlemen drove their herds long the trail to railheads in Kansas for shipent to Eastern markets. Those paid to move e cattle north were called cowboys, and they ame to symbolize the rough, rugged, often omanticized image of life in the American Vest.

You'll find the legacy of this cowboy lifetyle in business offices throughout Oklahoma City and Tulsa, where Stetson hats and glossy eather boots compete with the requisite briefases and cell phones. And Oklahoma City elebrates the state's cattle-driving past with e National Cowboy & Western Heritage Museum, dedicated to the men and women who pioneered the West.

"The Highway That's the Best"

In 1952, Route 66 was renamed the Will Rogers Memorial Highway after Oklahoma's owboy humorist and favorite son. It passes hrough Claremore, where the Will Rogers Memorial Museum overflows with the entertainer's personal items and memorabilia. Claremore also was home to Lynn Riggs, the laywright who penned "Green Grow the Lilacs," upon which the classic musical "Oklahoma!" was based.

Route 66 connects Oklahoma's two biggest cities as well. In Tulsa the highway winds within sight of the Art Deco skyscrapers built during the city's oil boom years. Once known as "The Oil Capital of the World," the city has preserved many of its 1920s and '30s architectural gems.

West of Tulsa, Route 66 rolls through farmland and quaint towns on its way to Oklahoma City, the state capital. Literally built in a day, "OKC"—as it is called locally—materialized on the prairie April 22, 1889, during the most famous in a series of land rushes. Continuing west, remnants of 66 pass through the dry, high plains of western Oklahoma to Texola, near the Texas border.

Those who make the 400-mile trip from Quapaw to Texola on Steinbeck's "Mother Road" will not proceed quickly and may have a hard time finding it in some places—newer, wider I-40 and I-44 bypass Route 66's course through the state and several sections are closed and choked with weeds. Certainly the interstates are faster and more convenient. But by journey's end, those hardy travelers who get their kicks on Route 66 will have enjoyed a thick slice of Americana and in so doing experienced an essential part of Oklahoma.

The first commercial oil well in Oklahoma Territory is drilled in Bartlesville.
1897

Oklahoma celebrates 100 years of statehood.
2007

Hulton Archive/Getty Images

Oklahoman Wiley Post makes the first successful solo flight around the world.
1933

1889
The unassigned prairie land of the Oklahoma Territory opens for settlement.

1933-39
Years of plowing and sustained drought dry up the Great Plains region; as farmland becomes useless, hundreds of thousands of people are forced to leave their homes.

Oklahoma City National Memorial Foundation

2000
A memorial and museum are dedicated to the 168 people killed in the 1995 bombing of the Alfred P. Murrah Federal Building.

Recreation

A dry Western state evoking images of the Dust Bowl shouldn't have as much water as Oklahoma does. Though the state is naturally blessed with a multitude of rivers, the more than 200 lakes seen today are all products of human ingenuity. Dams built to control flooding have as a fringe benefit created rambling reservoirs, many of which seem purposely designed for outdoor fun. And if you're looking for flat, you'll find it in Oklahoma, but you'll also find rolling foothills and small, ancient mountain ranges in the south and east.

Dust Bowl No More

With all the water splashing behind dams in Oklahoma, **swimming** is popular. At Turner Falls Park near Davis, Honey Creek cascades down a 77-foot waterfall into a lovely natural pool. Swimmers also flock to Arcadia Lake near Edmond and to lakes Ellsworth and Lawtonka near Lawton, both fed by streams from the Wichita Mountains.

Built to control flooding on the Red River, Denison Dam impounds the vast reservoir of Lake Texoma on the Texas-Oklahoma border. The lake's serpentine shoreline is sprinkled with countless secluded coves perfect for **boating,** and numerous charter companies make getting out on the water easy. **Sailing** is particularly enjoyable here, and the swimming, **fishing, water skiing** and **wind surfing** are superb. Lake Thunderbird, near Norman, also is known for its ideal sailing and wind surfing conditions.

Lake Altus-Lugert, near Altus in Quartz Mountain State Park, is great for boating. A 3,600-acre public **hunting** area on the lake's northern shore supports large numbers of quails, turkeys and waterfowl, among other wildlife. In the Ozark foothills, the clear blue water of Grand Lake O' the Cherokees draws boaters and, in the fall, migrating white pelicans. The area around the lake is tailor-made for outdoor recreation; seven of Oklahoma's 51 state parks are scattered along its shores.

Oklahoma's lakes also support a variety of fish, giving anglers a reason to smile. Lakes Hugo, Sardis, Eufaula, John Wells and Clayton, all in the southeast, offer some of the best bass and bluegill catches. The crystal waters of Broken Bow Reservoir teem with trout; Lone Chimney Lake, in central Oklahoma, is home to bass, catfish and crappie. Surrounded by Foss State Park and the Washita National Wildlife Refuge, Foss Lake is a great spot to find walleye, bass and crappie.

Plainly More than Just Plains

While Oklahoma may be "...where the wind comes sweeping down the plain," the landscape varies markedly. Little Sahara State Park, a popular **camping** getaway, takes its name from the sand dunes reaching heights up to 40 feet along the Cimarron River. Rock hounds can dig for rare hourglass selenite crystals in a sea of salt at Great Salt Plains State Park. Lake Hudson boasts myriad bluffs and coves along more than 200 miles of shoreline, so finding an ideal spot to pitch your tent is easy.

In the western panhandle, **hiking** through the rugged landscape of canyons and mesas is a treat for the eyes. Equally rewarding is Boiling Springs State Park, named for the cool springs that bubble up through the sands of the North Canadian River. Colorful gypsum formations distinguish Alabaster Caverns State Park; natural springs, old-growth forests and venerable hills characterize the Arbuckle Mountains.

The Wichita Mountains in Oklahoma's southwestern corner offer lakes, streams, canyons and grasslands that attract hikers and **mountain bikers.** Be careful, though; once inside the Wichita Mountains National Wildlife Refuge, you might encounter the bison, longhorn cattle, antelopes and elk that have the run of the place. It's wise to let the animals have the right of way. A 3.5-mile paved road inside the refuge leads to one of Oklahoma's highest summits: 2,463-foot Mount Scott.

Oklahoma has more horses per person than any other state, and many recreation areas cater to **horseback riders.** McGee Creek and Lake Murray state parks offer a variety of trails. Visitors can rent horses for the day in Robbers Cave State Park, which once served as a hideout for such notorious outlaws as Jesse James and Belle Starr.

Recreational Activities

Throughout the TourBook, you may notice a Recreational Activities heading with bulleted listings of recreation-oriented establishments listed underneath. Similar operations also may be mentioned in Destination City recreation sections. Since normal AAA inspection criteria cannot be applied, these establishments are presented only for information. Age, height and weight restrictions may apply. Reservations often are recommended and sometimes are required. Addresses and/or phone numbers are provided so visitors can contact the attraction for additional information.

Fast Facts

POPULATION: 3,450,654.

AREA: 69,919 square miles; ranks 18th.

CAPITAL: Oklahoma City.

HIGHEST POINT: 4,973 ft., Black Mesa.

LOWEST POINT: 287 ft., Little River.

TIME ZONE(S): Central. DST.

TEEN DRIVING LAWS: Teens are not allowed to transport more than one passenger, with the exception of parents, guardians and licensed drivers over 21. Driving is not permitted 10 p.m.-5 a.m., unless the teen is going to school, work or church. The minimum age for an unrestricted license is 16 years, 6 months (with driver's education courses); 17 years, 6 months (without). Phone (405) 425-2424 for more information about Oklahoma's driver's license regulations.

SEAT BELT/CHILD RESTRAINT LAWS: Seat belts required for driver and front seat passengers 13 and older. Children ages 6-12 are required to be in a seat belt; child restraints required for under 6.

HELMETS FOR MOTORCYCLISTS: Required for riders under 18.

RADAR DETECTORS: Permitted.

MOVE OVER LAW: Driver is required to slow down and vacate the lane nearest stopped police, fire and rescue vehicles using audible or flashing signals. The law also applies to recovery vehicles, such as tow trucks.

FIREARMS LAWS: Vary by state and/or county. Contact the Oklahoma State Bureau of Investigation, 6600 N. Harvey, Oklahoma City, OK 73116; phone (405) 848-6724.

HOLIDAYS: Jan. 1; Martin Luther King Jr. Day, Jan. (3rd Mon.); Washington's Birthday, Feb. (3rd Mon.); Memorial Day, May (last Mon.); July 4; Labor Day, Sept. (1st Mon.); Veterans Day, Nov. 11; Thanksgiving, Nov. (4th Thurs.) and following Fri.; Christmas, Dec. 25.

TAXES: Oklahoma's statewide sales tax is 4.5 percent, with local options for additional increments to be levied by cities and counties. A Tourism Promotion Tax of 0.1 percent is levied on lodgings, restaurants, tour vehicles and amusement admissions.

INFORMATION CENTERS: State welcome centers are near the Oklahoma-Kansas line at I-35 exit 222 in Blackwell; east of Miami at I-44/Will Rogers Turnpike exit 313; at I-44 exit 238 east of Tulsa; near the Oklahoma-Arkansas border at I-40 exit 311 at Sallisaw; near the Oklahoma-Texas border on US 69/75 at Colbert; at the Oklahoma-Texas border on I-35 exit 5 at Thackerville; east of the Oklahoma-Texas border near Erick at I-40 exit 11; on US 412/Cherokee Turnpike just west of the Oklahoma-Arkansas border and east of Flint; north of the Oklahoma-Texas border at I-44 exit 20 near Walters; at I-40 exit 157 at Midwest City; at I-35 exit 137 (N.E. 122nd Street) in Oklahoma City; and in the Oklahoma Capitol Building at N.E. 23rd Street and Lincoln Boulevard in Oklahoma City.

With the exception of the center in the Oklahoma Capitol Building, which is open Mon.-Fri. 8-4:30 year-round, state information centers are open daily 8:30-5, with longer hours in summer; closed Thanksgiving and Dec. 25.

FURTHER INFORMATION FOR VISITORS:

Oklahoma Tourism & Recreation Department
120 N. Robinson, 6th floor
Oklahoma City, OK 73152-2002
(405) 230-8400
(800) 652-6552 out of Okla.

FISHING AND HUNTING REGULATIONS:

Oklahoma Department of Wildlife Conservation
P.O. Box 53465
Oklahoma City, OK 73152
(405) 521-3721 (fishing)
(405) 521-3852 (hunting)

NATIONAL FOREST INFORMATION:

U.S. Forest Service
Southern Regional Office
1720 Peachtree St., Suite 700
Atlanta, GA 30309
(404) 347-4243
(877) 444-6777 (reservations)

STATE PARK LODGE AND CABIN RESERVATIONS: For reservations for lodge or cabin accommodations phone (405) 230-8420 or (800) 654-8240.

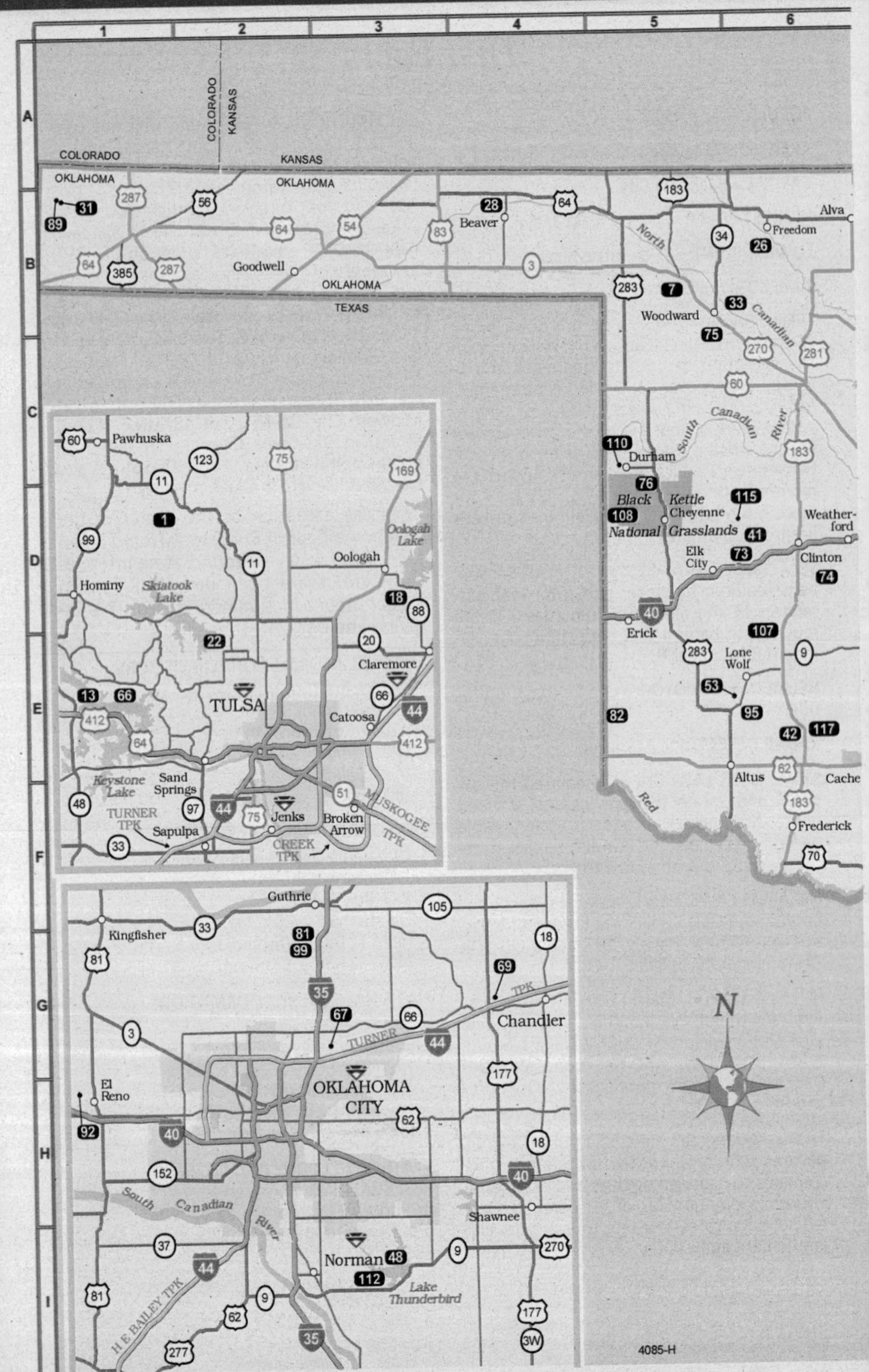
COLORADO
KANSAS
OKLAHOMA
TEXAS
Beaver
Goodwell
Alva
Freedom
Woodward
North Canadian
Durham
South Canadian River
Black Kettle National Grasslands
Cheyenne
Weatherford
Elk City
Clinton
Erick
Lone Wolf
Altus
Cache
Red
Frederick
Pawhuska
Oologah
Oologah Lake
Hominy
Skiatook Lake
Claremore
TULSA
Catoosa
Keystone Lake
Sand Springs
TURNER TPK
Sapulpa
Jenks
Broken Arrow
MUSKOGEE TPK
CREEK TPK
Guthrie
Kingfisher
Chandler
TURNER TPK
El Reno
OKLAHOMA CITY
Shawnee
South Canadian River
Norman
Lake Thunderbird
H E BAILEY TPK
N
4085-H

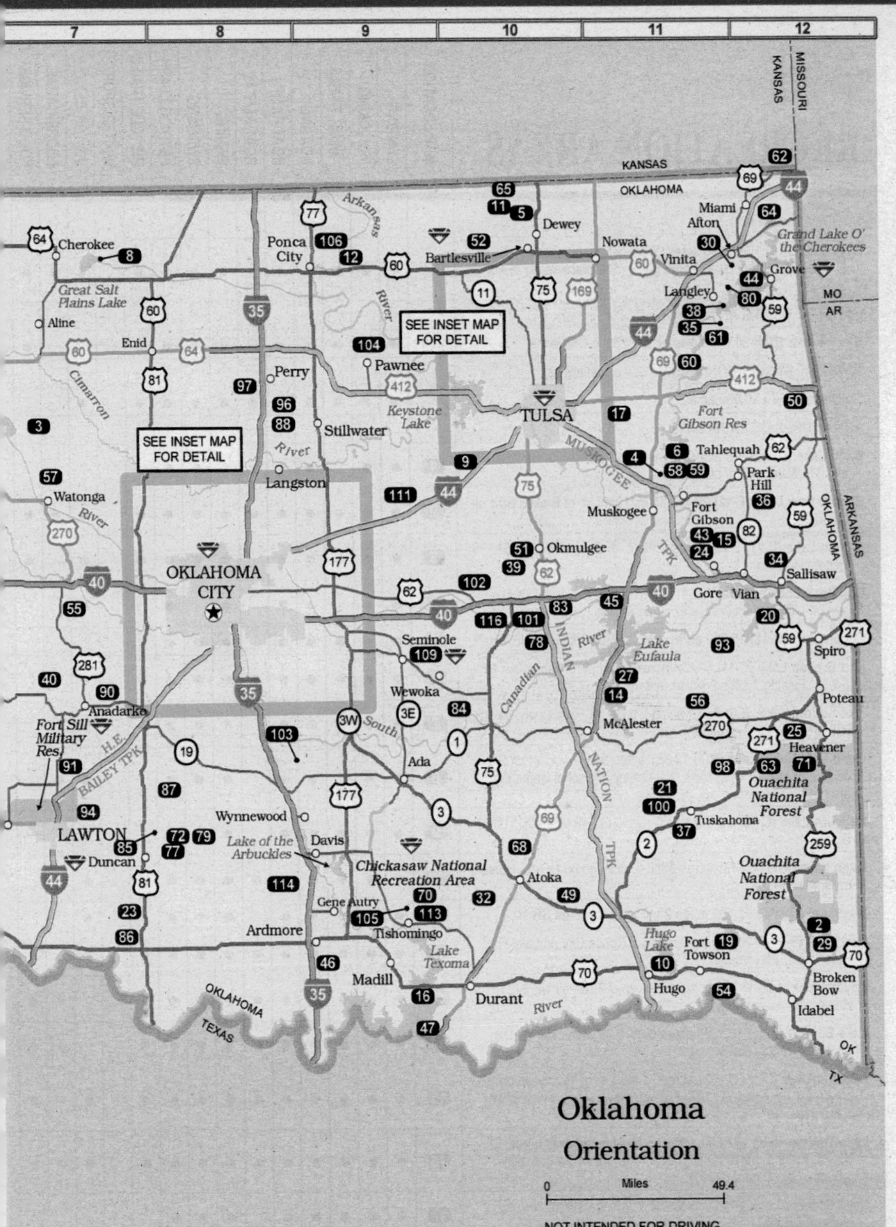
KANSAS
OKLAHOMA
MISSOURI
Cherokee
Great Salt Plains Lake
Aline
Enid
Cimarron
Ponca City
Arkansas
River
Perry
Stillwater
Langston
Watonga
SEE INSET MAP FOR DETAIL
Pawnee
Keystone Lake
Bartlesville
Dewey
Nowata
Vinita
Miami
Afton
Grand Lake O' the Cherokees
Grove
MO
AR
Langley
TULSA
Fort Gibson Res
Tahlequah
Park Hill
Fort Gibson
Muskogee
MUSKOGEE TPK
Okmulgee
OKLAHOMA CITY
Seminole
Wewoka
Ada
Canadian
South
Gore
Vian
Sallisaw
Spiro
Poteau
Lake Eufaula
INDIAN NATION TPK
McAlester
Heavener
Ouachita National Forest
Tuskahoma
Anadarko
Fort Sill Military Res
H.E. BAILEY TPK
LAWTON
Duncan
Wynnewood
Lake of the Arbuckles
Davis
Chickasaw National Recreation Area
Gene Autry
Tishomingo
Ardmore
Lake Texoma
Madill
Durant
Atoka
Hugo Lake
Fort Towson
Hugo
Broken Bow
Idabel
OKLAHOMA
TEXAS
OK
TX
ARKANSAS
Oklahoma
Orientation
0 Miles 49.4
NOT INTENDED FOR DRIVING.
SEE APPROPRIATE AAA SHEET MAP.
Only places listed in the Attractions section appear on this map.
See AAA GEM Attractions
See Chart of Recreation Areas
© 2009 NAVTEQ
© AAA

RECREATION AREAS

	MAP LOCATION	CAMPING	PICNICKING	HIKING TRAILS	BOATING	BOAT RAMP	BOAT RENTAL	FISHING	SWIMMING	PETS ON LEASH	BICYCLE TRAILS	WINTER SPORTS	VISITOR CENTER	LODGE/CABINS	FOOD SERVICE
NATIONAL FORESTS															
Ouachita (E-12) 1,613,120 acres. West-central Arkansas and southeastern Oklahoma. Horse trails. *(See place listing in Ark. p. 54)*		●	●	●	●	●		●	●	●	●		●	●	●
NATIONAL GRASSLANDS															
Black Kettle (D-5) 30,710 acres off SR 283 in Cheyenne.		●	●	●	●	●		●	●	●	●				●
NATIONAL RECREATION AREAS *(See place listings)*															
Chickasaw (F-9) 10,000 acres.		●	●	●	●	●	●	●	●	●	●		●		
ARMY CORPS OF ENGINEERS															
Birch Lake (D-1) 3,278 acres 17 mi. s.e. of Pawhuska via SRs 99 and 11. Water skiing; playground.	1	●	●		●	●		●	●	●					
Broken Bow Lake (F-12) 28,113 acres 12 mi. n. of Broken Bow off US 259.	2	●	●	●	●	●	●	●	●	●	●		●	●	●
Canton Lake (C-7) 18,901 acres 2 mi. n. of Canton on SR 58A. Recreation areas.	3	●	●	●	●	●		●	●	●	●		●		●
Chouteau Lock and Dam (C-11) 7,151 acres 7 mi. n. of Muskogee on US 69, then 3 mi. s.e. on an access road. Playground.	4	●	●		●	●		●		●			●		
Copan Lake (B-10) 15,952 acres 2 mi. s.w. of Copan off US 75.	5	●	●	●	●	●		●	●	●					
Fort Gibson Lake (C-11) 52,654 acres 15 mi. w. of Tahlequah off SR 51. Fishing, hunting; horse rental.	6	●	●	●	●	●	●	●	●	●	●			●	
Fort Supply Lake (B-5) 8,039 acres 2 mi. s. of Fort Supply via US 270 and SR 3. Playground.	7	●	●		●	●		●	●	●			●		
Great Salt Plains Lake (B-7) 12,537 acres 3 mi. n. of Jet on SR 38. Water skiing; horse trails, playground. Personal watercraft are not recommended.	8	●	●		●	●		●	●	●			●	●	
Heyburn Lake (C-10) 6,344 acres 4 mi. w. of Kellyville off 151st St. S.	9	●	●	●	●	●		●	●	●			●		
Hugo Lake (F-11) 37,425 acres 8 mi. e. of Hugo on US 70. Horse trails, playground.	10	●	●	●	●	●	●	●	●	●	●		●		
Hulah Lake (B-10) 21,505 acres 2 mi. w. of Hulah on SR 10.	11	●	●		●	●		●	●	●			●		
Kaw Lake (B-9) 49,963 acres 9 mi. e. of Ponca City on Lake Rd. Horse trails, playground.	12	●	●	●	●	●	●	●	●	●	●				●
Keystone Lake (E-1) 714 acres 16 mi. w. of Tulsa off US 64. Horse trails, playground.	13	●	●	●	●	●	●	●	●	●				●	●
Lake Eufaula (E-11) 102,200 acres 6 mi. n. of McAlester on US 69. Horse rental, playground.	14	●	●	●	●	●	●	●	●	●	●			●	●
Lake Tenkiller (D-11) 30,524 acres 21 mi. s.e. of Muskogee on SR 10, then 7 mi. e. on SR 10A. Fishing; playground, recreational complex.	15	●	●	●	●	●	●	●	●	●	●		●		●
Lake Texoma (G-9) 202,300 acres on Oklahoma-Texas border off US 75. Fishing; horse rental, horse trails, miniature golf, playground. *(See Durant p. 251)*	16	●	●	●	●	●	●	●	●	●	●		●	●	●
Newt Graham Lock and Dam (C-11) 3,787 acres 8 mi. s.w. of Inola on CR 420.	17	●	●	●	●	●		●	●	●					
Oologah Lake (D-3) 50,150 acres 8 mi. n. of Claremore via SR 88. Sailing.	18	●	●	●	●	●	●	●	●	●			●		
Pine Creek Lake (F-11) 26,179 acres 10 mi. n. of Valliant on Pine Creek Rd. Water skiing; playground.	19	●	●	●	●	●		●	●	●			●		
Robert S. Kerr Lock, Dam and Reservoir (D-12) 56,720 acres 9 mi. s. of Sallisaw off US 59. Playground.	20	●	●	●	●	●		●	●	●					
Sardis Lake (E-11) 21,564 acres 3 mi. n. of Clayton off SR 2.	21	●	●	●	●	●		●	●	●					
Skiatook Lake (E-2) 18,911 acres 5 mi. w. of Skiatook off SR 20. Water skiing.	22	●	●	●	●	●		●	●	●			●		

RECREATION AREAS

	MAP LOCATION	CAMPING	PICNICKING	HIKING TRAILS	BOATING	BOAT RAMP	BOAT RENTAL	FISHING	SWIMMING	PETS ON LEASH	BICYCLE TRAILS	WINTER SPORTS	VISITOR CENTER	LODGE/CABINS	FOOD SERVICE
Waurika Lake (F-7) 21,500 acres 6 mi. n.w. of Waurika off SR 5.	23	●	●	●	●	●	●	●	●	●			●	●	
Webbers Falls Lock and Dam (D-11) 15,953 acres 3 mi. n.w. of Gore off SR 10.	24	●	●	●	●	●		●	●	●			●		
Wister Lake (E-12) 39,170 acres 6 mi. s.w. of Poteau on US 270. Miniature golf, nature center, swimming beach, volleyball court.	25	●	●	●	●	●		●	●	●			●	●	●
STATE															
Alabaster Caverns (B-6) 200 acres 6 mi. s. of Freedom on SR 50, then .5 mi. e. on SR 50A. Scenic. Cave tours, playground. *(See Freedom p. 254)*	26	●	●	●						●			●		
Arrowhead (E-11) 2,459 acres 15 mi. n. of McAlester off US 69. Golf, tennis, water skiing; airstrip, horse trails, marina, miniature golf, playground.	27	●	●	●	●	●	●	●	●	●	●			●	●
Beaver Dunes (B-4) 520 acres 1 mi. n. of Beaver on US 270. Golf; dune buggy and motorcycle courses, playground.	28	●	●	●				●		●					
Beavers Bend (F-12) 3,522 acres 10 mi. n.e. of Broken Bow on US 259A. Tennis, water skiing; horse rental, museum, nature center, playground.	29	●	●	●	●	●	●	●	●	●			●	●	●
Bernice (B-11) 88 acres .5 mi. e. of Bernice off SR 85A. RV camping only. Playground.	30	●	●	●	●	●		●	●	●					
Black Mesa (B-1) 349 acres 27 mi. n.w. of Boise City off CR 325. Playground.	31	●	●	●				●							
Boggy Depot (F-10) 630 acres 11 mi. w. of Atoka on SR 7, then 4 mi. s. Playground.	32	●	●	●				●		●			●		
Boiling Springs (B-6) 820 acres 6 mi. n.e. of Woodward on SR 34C. Golf; playground, swimming pool.	33	●	●	●				●	●	●				●	
Brushy Lake (D-12) 90 acres 8 mi. n. of Sallisaw on US 64. Playground.	34	●	●	●	●	●		●	●	●					
Cherokee (B-11) 43 acres e. of Langley on SR 20. Golf (nine holes), scuba diving, water skiing; playground.	35	●	●		●	●		●	●	●					
Cherokee Landing (C-12) 146 acres about 12 mi. s. of Tahlequah off SR 82. Playground, swimming beach.	36	●	●		●	●		●	●	●					
Clayton Lake (F-11) 510 acres 30 mi. n.e. of Antlers on US 271. Fishing; ATV trails, playground.	37	●	●	●	●	●	●	●	●	●	●			●	
Disney/Little Blue (B-11) 32 acres e. of Disney on SR 28.	38	●	●		●	●		●	●	●					
Dripping Springs (D-10) 420 acres 6 mi. w. of Okmulgee on SR 56.	39	●	●	●	●	●		●	●	●	●				
Fort Cobb (E-7) 1,872 acres 5 mi. n.w. of Fort Cobb off SR 9. Golf, water skiing; jet ski rental, marina, playground.	40	●	●		●	●	●	●	●	●			●	●	●
Foss (D-6) 1,749 acres 15 mi. n.w. of Clinton via SRs 73 and 44. Horseback riding, water skiing; playground.	41	●	●	●	●	●	●	●	●	●	●				●
Great Plains (E-6) 487 acres 6 mi. n. of Snyder on US 183. Mountain climbing, water skiing; playground.	42	●	●	●	●	●		●	●	●	●				●
Greenleaf (D-11) 565 acres 3 mi. s. of Braggs on SR 10A. Bicycle rental, children's fishing pond, marina, miniature golf, nature center, playground, ropes course, swimming pool. Personal watercraft not permitted.	43	●	●	●	●	●	●	●	●	●	●		●	●	●
Honey Creek (B-12) 30 acres 2 mi. s.w. of Grove on SR 10. Water skiing; playground.	44	●	●		●	●		●	●	●					
Lake Eufaula (D-11) 2,853 acres 14 mi. s.w. of Checotah via I-40 and SR 150. Golf, tennis, water skiing; airstrip, horse rental, marina, playground.	45	●	●	●	●	●	●	●	●	●	●		●		●
Lake Murray (F-9) 12,496 acres 6 mi. s.e. of Ardmore off US 77. Golf (nine holes), tennis, water skiing; airstrip, horse rental, marina, nature center, playground.	46	●	●	●	●	●	●	●	●	●	●		●	●	●

RECREATION AREAS

	MAP LOCATION	CAMPING	PICNICKING	HIKING TRAILS	BOATING	BOAT RAMP	BOAT RENTAL	FISHING	SWIMMING	PETS ON LEASH	BICYCLE TRAILS	WINTER SPORTS	VISITOR CENTER	LODGE/CABINS	FOOD SERVICE
Lake Texoma (G-9) 1,882 acres 5 mi. e. of Kingston on US 70. Golf (18 holes), tennis; horseback riding trails, horse rental.	47	•	•	•	•	•	•	•	•	•	•			•	•
Lake Thunderbird (I-3) 1,834 acres 13 mi. e. of Norman on SR 9. Archery, water skiing; horse rental, horse trails, playground.	48	•	•	•	•	•	•	•	•	•	•				•
McGee Creek (F-10) 15,100 acres 18 mi. s.e. of Atoka off US 69. Water skiing; horse trails, playground.	49	•	•	•	•	•		•	•	•	•			•	
Natural Falls (C-12) 120 acres 3 mi. w. of West Siloam Springs off US 412. Playground.	50	•	•	•				•	•	•					
Okmulgee Lake (D-10) 535 acres 5 mi. w. of Okmulgee on SR 56. Water skiing; playground.	51	•	•	•	•	•		•	•	•	•		•		
Osage Hills (B-10) 1,199 acres 11 mi. w. of Bartlesville off US 60. Playground, swimming pool.	52	•	•	•	•	•	•	•	•	•	•			•	
Quartz Mountain (E-5) 4,284 acres 10 mi. s. of Lone Wolf on SR 44, then 1.5 mi. n. on SR 44A. Golf, tennis, water skiing; ATV trails, playground, swimming pool, train ride.	53	•	•	•	•	•	•	•	•	•	•		•	•	•
Raymond Gary (G-11) 64 acres 16 mi. e. of Hugo on US 70. Playground.	54	•	•		•	•	•	•	•	•				•	
Red Rock Canyon (D-7) 310 acres s. of Hinton on SR 8. Scenic. Rappelling; playground, swimming pool.	55	•	•	•				•	•	•					•
Robbers Cave (E-11) 8,246 acres 4 mi. n. of Wilburton on SR 2. Historic. Horse trails, miniature golf, playground, swimming pool.	56	•	•	•	•	•	•	•	•	•	•			•	•
Roman Nose (C-7) 515 acres 8 mi. n.w. of Watonga via SRs 8 and 8A. Golf, tennis; playground, swimming pool.	57	•	•	•	•	•	•	•	•	•	•		•	•	•
Sequoyah Bay (C-11) 303 acres 5 mi. s. of Wagoner on SR 16, then 5 mi. e. on Grey Oaks Rd. Playground.	58	•	•	•	•	•	•	•	•	•				•	•
Sequoyah/Western Hills (C-11) 2,876 acres 6 mi. e. of Wagoner on SR 51. Golf, tennis, water skiing; horse rental, marina.	59	•	•	•	•	•	•	•	•	•	•		•	•	•
Snowdale (C-11) 15 acres 2 mi. w. of Salina on SR 20. Playground.	60	•	•	•	•	•		•	•	•					
Spavinaw (B-11) 35 acres in Spavinaw on SR 20. Playgrounds.	61	•	•	•	•			•	•	•					
Spring River Canoe Trails (A-12) 35 acres 3 mi. n. of Quapaw off I-44. Primitive camping only.	62	•	•	•	•	•		•		•					
Talimena (E-12) 20 acres 6 mi. n. of Talihina on US 271. Playground.	63	•	•	•						•	•				
Twin Bridges (B-12) 63 acres 6 mi. n.e. of Fairland on US 60. Playground.	64	•	•	•	•	•		•		•				•	
Wah-Sha-She (A-10) 266 acres 4 mi. w. of Hulah on SR 10. Water skiing; playground.	65	•	•	•	•	•		•	•	•					
Walnut Creek (E-1) 1,429 acres 15 mi. w. of Tulsa via SR 51 on the n. side of Keystone Reservoir. Water skiing; horse trails, playground.	66	•	•	•	•	•		•	•	•	•			•	
OTHER															
Arcadia Lake (G-3) 5,078 acres 1.5 mi. w. of Arcadia on US 66. Fishing; horse trails, playground.	67	•	•	•	•	•		•	•	•	•		•		
Atoka Reservoir (F-10) 6,000 acres 3 mi. n.e. of Atoka on US 69. Water skiing; playgrounds.	68	•	•		•	•		•	•						
Bell Cow Lake (G-4) 1,079 acres about 3 mi. n. of Chandler on SR 18. Horse trails.	69	•	•	•	•	•		•	•	•	•				
Blue River Public Hunting and Fishing Area (F-9) 3 mi. n.e. of Tishomingo on SR 99. Canoeing, hunting, kayaking.	70	•	•					•	•	•	•	•			
Cedar Lake (E-12) 90 acres 10 mi. s. of Heavener on US 270, 3 mi. w. on Holson Valley Rd., then 1 mi. n. on FR 269. Horse rental, horse trails.	71	•	•	•	•	•		•	•	•	•				

RECREATION AREAS

Recreation Area	MAP LOCATION	CAMPING	PICNICKING	HIKING TRAILS	BOATING	BOAT RAMP	BOAT RENTAL	FISHING	SWIMMING	PETS ON LEASH	BICYCLE TRAILS	WINTER SPORTS	VISITOR CENTER	LODGE/CABINS	FOOD SERVICE
Clear Creek Lake (F-8) 560 acres 13 mi. n.e. of Duncan. Hunting; playground.	72	●	●		●	●		●	●	●					●
Clinton Lake (D-6) 355 acres 14 mi. w. of Clinton on I-40.	73		●		●	●		●		●					
Crowder Lake University Park (D-6) 22 acres 8 mi. s. of Weatherford on SR 54. Canoeing; rappelling tower, rock climbing wall, ropes course.	74	●	●	●	●	●		●	●	●	●				
Crystal Beach Park (C-5) 20 acres on the s.e. edge of Woodward. Golf (18 holes), tennis; miniature golf, playgrounds, pool with water slide.	75		●	●				●	●	●					●
Dead Indian Lake (D-5) 80 acres 10 mi. n. of Cheyenne on US 283. Hunting; playground.	76	●	●	●	●	●		●	●	●					
Duncan Lake (F-8) 400 acres 9 mi. n.e. of Duncan on Plato Rd., then .5 mi. s. on Duncan Lake Rd.	77	●	●		●	●		●	●	●					●
Dustin City Lake (D-10) 25 acres 1.5 mi. e. of Dustin off E1200 Rd.	78	●	●		●			●							
Fuqua Lake (F-8) 1,500 acres 21 mi. n.e. of Duncan off SR 29, then 1 mi. s. Hunting.	79	●	●		●	●		●	●	●					●
Grand Lake O' The Cherokees (B-12) 59,200 acres off I-44 at Vinita or Afton. Fishing, sailing; ATV trails, horse trails, playground, swimming pool.	80	●	●	●	●	●	●	●	●	●	●		●	●	●
Guthrie Lake (G-2) 230 acres 4 mi. s. of Guthrie on US 77, then 1 mi. w.	81	●	●		●	●	●	●		●					
Hall Lake (E-5) 50 acres 13 mi. n. of Hollis off SR 30.	82	●	●		●	●		●	●	●					
Henryetta City Lake (D-10) 616 acres 4 mi. e. of Henryetta on New Lake Rd. Water skiing.	83	●	●		●	●		●	●			●			
Holdenville City Lake (E-10) 550 acres 3 mi. s. of Holdenville off SR 48. Water skiing.	84	●	●		●	●		●		●					●
Humphreys Lake (F-7) 882 acres 8 mi. n.e. of Duncan off SR 29. Hunting.	85	●	●		●	●		●		●					
Jap Beaver Lake (F-7) 213 acres 4.5 mi. n.w. of Waurika off SR 5.	86		●	●	●	●		●		●					
J.W. Taylor Lake (E-8) 227 acres 7 mi. n. of Marlow on US 81, then 2 mi. e. Playground.	87	●	●		●	●		●		●					
Lake Carl Blackwell (C-8) 3,300 acres 8 mi. w. of Stillwater on SR 51. Sailing; horse trails.	88	●	●	●	●	●	●	●	●	●				●	
Lake Carl Etling (B-1) 260 acres 26 mi. n.w. of Boise City on SR 325.	89	●	●		●	●		●		●					
Lake Chickasha (E-7) 1,900 acres 15 mi. n.w. of Chickasha via US 62. Fishing, water skiing; playground.	90	●	●		●	●		●	●	●					
Lake Ellsworth (E-7) 5,600 acres 14 mi. n.e. of Lawton via I-44.	91	●	●		●	●		●	●	●					●
Lake El Reno (H-1) 175 acres at El Reno.	92	●	●	●	●	●		●	●	●	●				
Lake John Wells (D-11) 160 acres 1 mi. e. of Stigler on SR 9, then 1 mi. s. Water skiing.	93	●	●		●	●		●	●	●					
Lake Lawtonka (E-7) 1,900 acres 10 mi. n.w. of Lawton via I-44, SR 49 and SR 58. Water skiing.	94	●	●	●	●	●		●	●	●					●
Lake Lugert-Altus (E-6) 17 mi. n. of Altus via US 283.	95	●	●	●	●	●		●	●	●			●	●	●
Lake McMurtry (C-8) 6 mi. n. of Stillwater on US 177. Fishing.	96	●	●	●	●	●		●	●	●	●				
Lake Perry (C-8) 614 acres 1.5 mi. s.w. of Perry on Perry Lake Rd. Water skiing; playground.	97	●	●		●	●		●	●	●					
Lake Talihina (E-11) 56 acres 3 mi. n.w. of Talihina off SR 63A.	98	●	●	●				●		●	●				
Liberty Lake (G-2) 250 acres 5 mi. s. of Guthrie on US 77, then 2 mi. w.	99	●	●	●	●	●		●	●	●					●
Nanih Waiya Lake (E-11) 349 acres 1.5 mi. n.w. of Tuskahoma off US 271.	100	●	●	●	●	●		●		●					

RECREATION AREAS

	MAP LOCATION	CAMPING	PICNICKING	HIKING TRAILS	BOATING	BOAT RAMP	BOAT RENTAL	FISHING	SWIMMING	PETS ON LEASH	BICYCLE TRAILS	WINTER SPORTS	VISITOR CENTER	LODGE/CABINS	FOOD SERVICE
Nichols Park Lake (D-10) 600 acres 2 mi. s. of Henryetta off Indian Nation Tpke.	101	●	●		●	●		●	●	●					
Okemah Lake (D-10) 730 acres 6 mi. n. of Okemah. Hunting; playground.	102	●	●		●	●		●	●	●				●	●
Pauls Valley Lake (E-8) 750 acres 3 mi. e. of Pauls Valley off SR 19. Playground.	103	●	●		●	●		●		●					
Pawnee City Lake (B-9) 257 acres 1 mi. n. of Pawnee on SR 18. Golf, tennis, water skiing; swimming pool.	104	●	●		●	●		●	●	●					
Pennington Creek (F-9) in Tishomingo on the 300 block of South Capitol St.	105	●	●					●	●	●					
Ponca City Lake (B-9) 900 acres 3 mi. n. of Ponca City via SR 11. Archery, disc golf, golf, water skiing; swimming pool.	106	●	●	●	●	●		●		●			●	●	●
Rocky Lake (E-6) 1,205 acres .5 mi. w. and 1 mi. n. of Rocky via US 183. Playground.	107	●	●		●	●		●		●					
Skip-out Lake (D-5) 60 acres 10 mi. w. of Cheyenne on SR 47. Hunting.	108	●	●		●	●		●	●						
Sportsman Lake (D-9) 350 acres 3 mi. e. of Seminole on US 270, then 2 mi. n. and 1.5 mi. e. on county roads. Horse trails, playground.	109	●	●	●	●	●		●	●	●	●				
Spring Creek Lake (C-5) 50 acres 21 mi. n.w. of Cheyenne on US 283, then 6 mi. w. on a gravel road. Playground.	110	●	●	●	●	●		●	●	●					
Stroud Lake (C-9) 17,600 acres 3 mi. n. of Stroud off SR 99, then 3 mi. e. Water skiing; horse trails.	111	●	●		●	●		●	●						
Thunderbird Lake (I-3) 15,000 acres 12 mi. e. of Norman on SR 9. Golf, hunting; playground.	112	●	●	●	●	●	●	●	●	●	●				●
Tishomingo National Wildlife Refuge (F-9) 16,464 acres 3 mi. s. of Tishomingo via an access road off SR 78. *(See Tishomingo p. 277)*	113	●	●	●	●			●		●	●				
Turner Falls (F-8) 1,500 acres 5.2 mi. s. of Davis on US 77. Playground. *(See Davis p. 250)*	114	●	●	●				●	●	●	●			●	●
Washita National Wildlife Refuge (D-6) 8,000 acres 11 mi. w. of Clinton on SR 73, 9 mi. n. on SR 44, 4 mi. w. on SR 33, then .5 mi. n.w. on a county road.	115	●	●	●	●			●		●	●		●		
Weleetka City Lake (D-10) 30 acres 1 mi. w. of Weleetka.	116	●	●		●	●		●		●					●
Wichita Mountains National Wildlife Refuge (E-6) 59,020 acres 3 mi. n. of Cache on SR 115. *(See Cache p. 248)*	117	●	●	●	●			●		●			●		

Oklahoma Temperature Averages Maximum/Minimum

From the records of The Weather Channel Interactive, Inc.

	JAN	FEB	MAR	APR	MAY	JUN	JUL	AUG	SEP	OCT	NOV	DEC
Oklahoma City	47/26	54/31	63/39	71/48	79/58	87/66	93/71	92/70	84/62	73/51	60/38	50/29
Tulsa	47/26	53/31	62/40	72/50	80/59	88/68	94/73	93/71	84/63	74/51	60/39	50/30

Points of Interest

ADA (E-9) pop. 15,691, elev. 1,010′

Ada is the seat of Pontotoc County, an area known for oil and gas production as well as cattle raising. Byrd's Mill Spring, south on Cradduck Road following signs to Fittstown, is a popular picnicking site. Opportunities for water skiing and boating are available at Konawa Lake.

Wintersmith Park, on E. 18th Street, has walking trails, a small zoo, a miniature golf course, children's rides, horseshoe pits and a swimming pool. The park contains a restored one-room schoolhouse built in 1907; it is furnished with such items as a potbellied stove and desks that have inkwells.

Former Oklahoma Governor and U.S. Senator Robert S. Kerr was born in Ada. The Robert S. Kerr Home and Museum in Poteau *(see attraction listing p. 275)* features area history exhibits and a reproduction of his Washington, D.C., office.

Ada Area Chamber of Commerce: 209 W. Main St., P.O. Box 248, Ada, OK 74821. **Phone:** (580) 332-2506.

AFTON (B-11) pop. 1,118, elev. 784′

NATIONAL ROD & CUSTOM CAR HALL OF FAME MUSEUM is 5.3 mi. s.w. on US 60/69, 2 mi. s.e. on SR 85, then 5 mi. e. to 55251 E. SR 85A. Well-known custom car designer and builder Darryl Starbird established this museum to display classic hot rods and custom cars and to honor the imagination and craftsmanship of the men who created them. More than 50 of these exotic, one-of-a-kind cars are exhibited, about half designed by Starbird himself.

Photos and memorabilia related to these vehicles also can be seen. **Time:** Allow 45 minutes minimum. **Hours:** Wed.-Sun. 11-5, Mar.-Oct. Closed major holidays. **Cost:** $7; $4 (ages 8-12). **Phone:** (918) 257-4234.

ALINE (B-7) pop. 214, elev. 1,281′

SOD HOUSE is on SR 8, 5.5 mi. n. of US 412. Marshal McCully made the Cherokee Outlet run of 1893, staking his claim south of Aline. He built his two-room sod home with a half acre of thick buffalo grass sod and used alkali clay to plaster the inside walls. It was completed in 1894 and a wood floor was added in 1895. The museum encloses the original sod house, along with displays of artifacts, photographs and a root cellar.

An additional building has horse-drawn equipment and period farm implements. **Time:** Allow 30 minutes minimum. **Hours:** Tues.-Sat. 9-5. Closed major holidays. **Cost:** Free. **Phone:** (580) 463-2441.

ALTUS (F-6) pop. 21,447, elev. 1,388′

Altus is the center of a thriving agricultural region, the result of the 70,000-acre Lugert-Altus irrigation district. Farms produce alfalfa seed, cattle, cotton and wheat. Altus Air Force Base is another major employer. Run by the 97th Air Mobility Wing, the base serves as the Air Force's primary training facility for pilots and flight engineers who handle jumbo jet transports.

For an area that depends on irrigation to prosper, it is ironic that the city's beginnings were marked by a disastrous flood in 1891. Having fled to higher ground, settlers banded together and formed a community to help endure any further hardships the plains might bestow upon them. Altus was the town's chosen name because, according to one of the settlers, it meant "high ground."

Altus Chamber of Commerce: 301 W. Commerce St., P.O. Box 518, Altus, OK 73522. **Phone:** (580) 482-0210.

MUSEUM OF THE WESTERN PRAIRIE, 1100 Memorial Dr., depicts the history of Oklahoma's western prairie country from nomadic American Indian inhabitance to urban and agricultural communities. A reconstructed half-dugout (a pioneer house that was built partially underground) is featured. A reference library contains many first-edition publications about the area.

Note: The museum is closed for maintenance and construction with a tentative reopening date of spring 2010. **Time:** Allow 1 hour minimum. **Hours:** Tues.-Sat. 9-5. Closed major holidays. Phone ahead to confirm schedule. **Cost:** Donations. **Phone:** (580) 482-1044.

ALVA (B-6) pop. 5,288, elev. 1,332′

Alva is a business center for the surrounding ranching and farming region. The town was named after Santa Fe Railroad lawyer Alva Adams, who later was elected governor of Colorado. As one of four land-office towns for the opening of the Cherokee Outlet in 1893, Alva was an integral part of the settlement of more than 6 million acres, including what later became Woods County.

Alva is home to Northwestern Oklahoma State University, known for its programs in teaching, business, pre-law and pre-medicine.

The city began a mural project in the late 1990s, adding one or two new artistic creations each year, most concentrated around the downtown square. Many of the murals portray historical or cultural aspects of Alva, including depictions of the 1893 Cherokee Strip land run, threshing, a wheat harvest and a one-room county school.

Alva Area Chamber of Commerce: 502 Oklahoma Blvd., Alva, OK 73717. **Phone:** (580) 327-1647.

CHEROKEE STRIP MUSEUM, 901 14th St., contains artifacts from the Cherokee Strip region. Museum displays include medical and dental equipment, Western and American Indian art, farm tools, guns and military items. Period rooms include a chapel, a general store, a barbershop and portions of a 19th-century pioneer house. A one-room schoolhouse exhibits 19th-century relics. **Time:** Allow 1 hour minimum. **Hours:** Tues.-Sun. 2-5. Closed major holidays. **Cost:** Donations. **Phone:** (580) 327-2030.

ANADARKO (E-7) pop. 6,645, elev. 1,164′

The area in and around Anadarko traditionally served as hunting grounds for three major American Indian tribes. The town was founded in 1901 by white settlers claiming land used by the Kiowa, Comanche and Wichita reservations. Farming and stock raising were the major livelihoods until oil was discovered in 1920 and drilling ensued. Agriculture and oil remain the leading industries.

Local American Indian tribes include the Apache, Caddo, Delaware, Fort Sill Apache, Kiowa and Wichita. A Bureau of Indian Affairs office is in Anadarko, servicing western Oklahoma and Horton, Kan. Representative of regional American Indian heritage are the striking murals by Kiowa artists in the Federal Building at 120 S. First St.

Colorful sandstone canyons and lakes skirt US 281, which travels 16 miles north of Anadarko to Binger. From Binger a scenic portion of SR 37/152 runs 20 miles east to Minco, where US 81 begins a scenic course through the Canadian River Valley to El Reno at I-40. The Wichita Mountains are southwest of the city.

Anadarko Chamber of Commerce: 516 W. Kentucky Ave., P.O. Box 366, Anadarko, OK 73005. **Phone:** (405) 247-6651.

ANADARKO HERITAGE MUSEUM, 311 E. Main St. in the former Rock Island Depot, contains pioneer and American Indian artifacts, an American Indian doll collection, American Indian photographs and paintings, a doctor's office and a railroad ticket office. **Time:** Allow 30 minutes minimum. **Hours:** Tues.-Fri. 10-5, Sat.-Sun. 1-5. Closed major holidays. **Cost:** Donations. **Phone:** (405) 247-3240.

SAVE **INDIAN CITY USA CULTURAL CENTER,** 2.5 mi. s. on SR 8, is a re-creation of the once-common Plains Indian villages. Tepees, grass houses, earth lodges and mud huts depict dwellings of the Apache, Caddo, Comanche, Kiowa, Navajo, Pawnee, Pueblo and Wichita tribes. A museum displays items of the Southern Plains Indians. Guided tours feature tribal dances.

Time: Allow 1 hour, 30 minutes minimum. **Hours:** Daily 10-5. Guided tours are conducted on the hour. Last tour begins 1 hour before closing. **Cost:** $5 (includes museum); $3 (ages 0-11). **Phone:** (405) 247-2063 or (800) 433-5661.

NATIONAL HALL OF FAME FOR FAMOUS AMERICAN INDIANS, at the e. edge of town on US 62, is a 10-acre tract that preserves the legacies of 42 well-known American Indians in statuary. Bronze busts of each honoree line a .75-mile walkway in an outdoor garden. **Time:** Allow 1 hour minimum. **Hours:** Visitor center open Mon.-Sat. 9-5, Sun. 1-5. Closed Jan. 1, Thanksgiving and Dec. 25. **Cost:** Free. **Phone:** (405) 247-5555.

SOUTHERN PLAINS INDIAN MUSEUM, 715 E. Central Blvd. at SR 8, is operated by the Indian Arts and Crafts Board of the U.S. Department of the Interior. The center emphasizes Southern Plains Indian history and culture through permanent exhibits. Displays include beadwork, featherwork, metalwork, carvings, skin sewing and hide paintings; changing exhibits showcase contemporary American Indian art. **Time:** Allow 1 hour minimum. **Hours:** Tues.-Sat. 9-5. Closed Jan. 1, Thanksgiving and Dec. 25. **Cost:** Free. **Phone:** (405) 247-6221.

ARDMORE (F-8) pop. 23,711, elev. 868′

Ardmore was the site of a track-side tent city, which Santa Fe Railroad officials selected as a permanent townsite in 1887. Named after one official's hometown in Pennsylvania, the land was part of the Roff Brothers' 700 Ranch. The Roffs were the first homeowners in Ardmore. A replica of the ranch house was moved from Fair Park to the Carter County Historical Museum. Ranching is still an important industry, along with oil drilling and refining and tire manufacturing.

Art exhibits and music, dance and theater performances are offered at the Charles B. Goddard Center for the Visual and Performing Arts, First Avenue and D Street S.W., and at The Brass Ring Performing Arts Center, 120 A St. N.E. Two miles east of Ardmore on SR 199, the Samuel Roberts Noble Foundation specializes in medical and agricultural research.

Four municipal lakes—Ardmore City Lake, Lake Jean Neustadt, Mountain Lake and Rock Creek Reservoir—offer fishing, boating and picnicking opportunities. Southeast of the city, Lake Murray State Park *(see Recreation Chart)*, Oklahoma's largest state park, offers extensive recreational facilities. The Arbuckle Mountains, about 20 miles north of Ardmore, provide another popular recreation area. Ardmore Regional Park has walking and biking trails, a large family picnic area and a softball complex.

Ardmore Chamber of Commerce: 410 W. Main St., P.O. Box 1585, Ardmore, OK 73402. **Phone:** (580) 223-7765.

Self-guiding tours: A brochure describing two tours—a self-guiding walking tour of downtown Ardmore's historic sites as well as a driving tour covering sites throughout the city—is available at both the chamber of commerce and at city hall, 23 S. Washington.

An MP3 player is provided for use with the 26-page Historic Downtown Walking Tour booklet. The booklet is available for $12 at the Ardmore Main Street Authority, 9 A St. S.W.

ELIZA CRUCE HALL DOLL COLLECTION MUSEUM, in the Ardmore Public Library at 320 E St. N.W., contains more than 300 dolls, including rare carved wood "court dolls" that belonged to Marie Antoinette, 1830s English peddler dolls, "fashion dolls" produced by dressmakers around 1860 and ethnic dolls from all over the world. Also displayed are miniature tea sets. **Time:** Allow 30 minutes minimum. **Hours:** Mon.-Thurs. 10-8, Fri. 10-6, Sat.-Sun. 1-5. Closed major holidays. **Cost:** Free. **Phone:** (580) 223-8290.

GREATER SOUTHWEST HISTORICAL MUSEUM is at 35 Sunset Dr. The museum's main hall features an original 1895 log cabin along with reproductions of a courtroom, law office, school, general store, post office, barbershop, blacksmith shop and doctor's office. One wing exhibits military memorabilia from the American Revolution through Desert Storm. Another wing houses carriages, cameras and a working model of an oil field. **Hours:** Tues.-Sat. 10-5. Closed major holidays. **Cost:** Free. **Phone:** (580) 226-3857.

TUCKER TOWER NATURE CENTER is 7 mi. s. on SR 77S in Lake Murray State Park. Tucker Tower was designed to be a governor's retreat. Instead, this 1933 medieval-style fortress loomed over Lake Murray unfinished and unused until the early 1950s, when it was converted to a museum. Displays include part of one of the largest meteorites of its type ever discovered as well as fossils, wildlife exhibits and other artifacts.

Time: Allow 30 minutes minimum. **Hours:** Daily 9-7, Memorial Day-Labor Day; Wed.-Sun. 9-5, Feb. 1-day before Memorial Day and day after Labor Day-Nov. 30; Sat.-Sun. 9-5, rest of year. Phone ahead to confirm schedule. **Cost:** Free. **Phone:** (580) 223-2109.

ATOKA (F-10) pop. 2,988, elev. 583'

CONFEDERATE MEMORIAL MUSEUM AND CEMETERY is at 258 N. US 69. The museum houses exhibits of domestic furnishings from the early to mid-1900s, a school house display and medical instruments. Civil War-era weapons and uniforms are displayed along with memorabilia about hometown celebrities Reba McEntire and world champion bull rider Lane Frost. The cemetery was used when measles swept through a Confederate camp, killing many soldiers. **Time:** Allow 1 hour minimum. **Hours:** Museum Mon.-Fri. 9-4. Cemetery daily 24 hours. Closed major holidays. **Cost:** Free. **Phone:** (580) 889-7192.

BARTLESVILLE (B-9) pop. 34,748, elev. 695'

A replica of the first oil well of commercial importance drilled in Oklahoma is in Johnstone Park, which adjoins the Bartlesville city limits. The original well, Nellie Johnstone No. 1, has been reproduced as a memorial to oilmen.

Bartlesville Area Convention and Visitors Bureau: 201 S.W. Keeler Ave., P.O. Box 2366, Bartlesville, OK 74005. **Phone:** (918) 336-8708 or (800) 364-8708.

BARTLESVILLE AREA HISTORY MUSEUM is at 401 S. Johnstone Ave., on the fifth floor of the City Center Building. The museum, in a 1913 former hotel, documents the history and growth of Bartlesville and the surrounding territory. Area American Indian tribes, pioneers and the area's oil and mineral story are all portrayed through artifacts, photographs and displays. A theater shows a 15-minute film about Bartlesville's history. **Time:** Allow 30 minutes minimum. **Hours:** Tues-Sat. 10-4. Closed major holidays. **Cost:** Free. **Phone:** (918) 338-4290.

FRANK PHILLIPS HOME is at 1107 S.E. Cherokee Ave. The neoclassic mansion is the restored home of Frank Phillips, founder of Phillips Petroleum Co. Built 1908-09, the three-level house is noted for its collection of decorative arts. It is furnished with the family's original belongings, which have been placed in the home according to 1930 photographs; highlights include Philippine mahogany, handcrafted ceilings and Waterford crystal chandeliers. A permanent exhibit—Frank and Jane Phillips, Oklahoma Oil Pioneers—is in the garage.

Time: Allow 1 hour minimum. **Hours:** Tours Wed.-Sat. 10-5, second Sun. of the month 1-5. Last tour begins 1 hour before closing. Closed major holidays. **Cost:** Donations. **Phone:** (918) 336-2491.

PHILLIPS PETROLEUM COMPANY MUSEUM is downtown at 410 Keeler Ave. The history and development of the Phillips Petroleum Co. beginning with its Bartlesville roots is traced through exhibits that recall the company's pioneering attitude, its growth into a large corporation, how its oil and gas products reach consumers and how the Phillips brand became well-known worldwide. **Hours:** Mon.-Sat. 10-4. Closed major holidays. **Cost:** Free. **Phone:** (918) 661-8687.

PRICE TOWER ARTS CENTER is at 510 Dewey Ave. Housed in a 19-story Frank Lloyd Wright-designed skyscraper completed in 1956, the arts center features a permanent collection dedicated to art, architecture and design as well as temporary exhibitions. A guided tour examines the top three floors, including the restored 1956 Wright interiors of H.C. Price Co.'s executive office and corporate apartment. A short film provides background about Wright and the tower.

Time: Allow 1 hour minimum. **Hours:** Arts center Tues.-Sat. 10-5, Sun. noon-5. Tours are given Tues.-Thurs. at 11 and 2, Fri.-Sat. at 11, noon, 1 and 2, Sun. at 2. Tour times may vary; phone ahead. Closed Jan. 1, Thanksgiving and Dec. 25. **Cost:** $4; $3 (ages 65+); free (ages 0-16). Guided tour $10; $8 (ages 65+); $5 (ages 0-16 and students with ID).

Reservations for tours are strongly recommended. **Phone:** (918) 336-4949.

GEM SAVE **WOOLAROC RANCH, MUSEUM AND WILDLIFE PRESERVE** is 12 mi. s.w. on SR 123. Covering 3,600 acres of rugged timberland, oilman Frank Phillips' Woolaroc Ranch depicts the culture and legacy of the American West.

Woolaroc (the name comes from the *woo*ds, *la*kes and *roc*ks that are part of the Osage Hills area) was designed as a retreat for Phillips, a place where he could get back to nature. What began as a small cabin became an elaborate log lodge with eight bedrooms. Completed in 1927, the house is decorated in a rustic lodge style.

The museum is highlighted by works by Frederic Remington, Charles M. Russell and other Western artists; artifacts from 40 American Indian tribes that lived in Oklahoma; a collection of Colt firearms; and exhibits of Western gear.

More than 700 animals, including buffalo, elk, deer and water buffalo, can often be seen on a driving tour through the animal preserve. Phillips wanted the preserve to retain the feel of the West as he recalled it prior to the turn of the 20th century. Nature trails allow visitors to explore the grounds, and a petting barn is available in summer. A multimedia show is presented in the Heritage Center.

Time: Allow 3 hours minimum. **Hours:** Tues.-Sun. 10-5, Memorial Day-Labor Day; Wed.-Sun. 10-5, rest of year. Petting barn open June-Aug. Closed Thanksgiving and Dec. 25. **Cost:** $8; $6 (ages 65+); free (ages 0-11). **Phone:** (918) 336-0307 or (888) 966-5276.

BEAVER (B-4) pop. 1,570

Beaver resides along the banks of the Beaver River and thus received its name. A statue of the town mascot, a giant buck-toothed "Big Beaver," greets visitors. Beaver Dunes State Park *(see Recreation Chart)*, just north on US 270, offers nature trails and more than 120 acres of sand dunes suitable for motorcycle riding.

Beaver County Chamber of Commerce: 22 W. 2nd St., Box 878, Beaver, OK 73932. **Phone:** (580) 625-4726.

JONES AND PLUMMER TRAIL MUSEUM, s. on US 270 at the Beaver County Fairgrounds, commemorates a trail named for a cattle company and built by fur traders to haul buffalo hides. Displays chronicle the trail's history; exhibits include period handicrafts, clothing, implements and tools, prehistoric fossils, American Indian relics, a ranch buggy and a windmill. There also is a rural schoolhouse. **Time:** Allow 30 minutes minimum. **Hours:** Tues. and Thurs.-Sat. 1-5. Closed Jan. 1, July 4, Thanksgiving and Dec. 25. **Cost:** Donations. **Phone:** (580) 625-4439.

BROKEN ARROW—*see Tulsa p. 287.*

BROKEN BOW (G-12) pop. 4,230

Broken Bow lies in the heart of Oklahoma's timberland region and is the southern terminus of a scenic section of US 259 that runs 62 miles north to the town of Page. Shortleaf and loblolly pine fuel the area's lumber industry, and Oklahoma's state flower, mistletoe, is abundant. Rainbow and brownie trout are stocked biweekly at a fishery that extends from the Broken Bow Dam to the US 70 bridge.

Broken Bow Chamber of Commerce: 113 W. Martin Luther King Dr., Broken Bow, OK 74728. **Phone:** (580) 584-3393 or (800) 528-7337.

FOREST HERITAGE CENTER, 7 mi. n. in Beavers Bend State Park *(see Recreation Chart)*, focuses on the relationship between man and forest from prehistoric times to the present. Exhibits include trees; petrified logs and tools; forest industry artifacts; 14 dioramas painted by Harry Rossoll, creator of Smokey Bear; wooden sculptures; and carvings.

The seven-sided museum is built around an open courtyard filled with native trees, shrubs and wildflowers. Several hiking and nature trails are nearby. Historic forestry photos and wood art exhibits also are on the premises. **Hours:** Daily 8-5. **Cost:** Donations. **Phone:** (580) 494-6497.

CACHE (F-6) pop. 2,371, elev. 1,271′

WICHITA MOUNTAINS NATIONAL WILDLIFE REFUGE visitor center is 3 mi. n. on SR 115 at jct. SR 49; the refuge headquarters is w. of the visitor center. The 59,020-acre refuge protects buffaloes, longhorn cattle, elk, deer and turkeys. The strangely eroded, often vividly colored mountains form one of the nation's oldest ranges. The Charons Garden Wilderness Area preserves rugged portions of these mountains.

A paved road leads to Mount Scott's summit, and a scenic stretch of SR 49 passes through the refuge. The visitor center has exhibits, an audio driving tour and a video presentation. Fishing, camping, picnicking and boating are permitted in designated areas. More than 15 miles of hiking trails wind through scrub oak forests, boulder-strewn mountains and prairie grasslands. Phone for information about interpretive programs and guided tours. *See Recreation Chart.*

Hours: Refuge open daily 24 hours. Visitor center daily 8-6, mid-Mar. to mid-Nov.; 8-4:30, rest of year. Phone ahead to confirm visitor center hours. The refuge headquarters offers visitor information Mon.-Fri. 8-4:30. Closed major holidays. **Cost:** Free. **Phone:** (580) 429-3222.

CATOOSA—*see Tulsa p. 287.*

CHANDLER (G-4) pop. 2,842, elev. 942′

ROUTE 66 INTERPRETIVE CENTER is at 400 E. SR 66 at jct. Mickey Clarkson Ave. Housed in the city's National Guard Armory, built by the Works Progress Administration (WPA) 1936-37, the center is unusual in that it features beds representing motels along the historic road from which visitors can watch videos about Route 66.

Seats from a Model A, a World War II Jeep and a '65 Mustang offer vantage points from which to watch clips from each vehicle's respective era. Billboards reminiscent of those that lined Route 66 also provide a link to the past. **Time:** Allow 30 minutes minimum. **Hours:** Daily 10-5, Easter-Labor Day; Tues.-Sat. 10-5, rest of year. **Cost:** $5; $4 (students with ID and senior citizens). **Phone:** (405) 258-1300.

CHEROKEE (B-7) pop. 1,630, elev. 1,175'

Cherokee is in one of the richest farming areas in the state; major products include wheat, alfalfa and livestock. The fertile lands also yield oil and natural gas from the extensive reserves of the Anadarko Basin.

Cherokee Main Street Chamber of Commerce: 121 E. Main St., Cherokee, OK 73728. **Phone:** (580) 596-3575, ext. 122.

SALT PLAINS NATIONAL WILDLIFE REFUGE is off SR 38, 2 mi. s. of jct. SRs 11 and 38. The 32,000-acre refuge encompasses the Great Salt Plains. The area, once valued for its thin covering of salt, draws visitors who dig for selenite crystals on the salt flats. Visitors are allowed to dig in areas designated with orange "Dig Area" signs only.

The dam on the Salt Fork of the Arkansas River has transformed much of the area into the Great Salt Plains Lake. The salt flats, among the largest in the Midwest, are west of the lake. Migratory birds, beavers, coyotes and deer are residents.

The Eagle Roost Nature Trail at refuge headquarters is a self-guiding walk through habitats that shelter various species living in the refuge. Visitors also can take a 2.5-mile automobile tour route near the nature trail. Just east of the refuge is Great Salt Plains Lake State Park *(see Recreation Chart)*.

Note: Visitors must remain in areas designated for public use; driving on the salt flats is prohibited. Allow 2 hours minimum for the nature trail and 4 hours minimum for the crystal area. **Hours:** Refuge open to vehicle traffic daily dawn-dusk. Headquarters open Mon.-Fri. 7:30-4, Sat. 10-5, Sun. 1-5, Apr. 1-Oct. 15; Mon.-Fri. 7:30-4, rest of year. The selenite crystal digging area is open daily dawn-dusk, Apr. 1-Oct. 15. **Cost:** Free. **Phone:** (580) 626-4794.

CHEYENNE (D-5) pop. 778

Cheyenne was site of the 1868 Battle of the Washita, in which Lt. Col. George A. Custer initiated an attack upon Chief Black Kettle and his people. This was the first attack in a campaign to quell uprisings by the Cheyenne and Arapaho, who felt the government had broken promises made at the 1867 peace treaty signing in Medicine Lodge, Kan. *(see place listing p. 96)*. Also in Cheyenne is Black Kettle National Grassland *(see Recreation Chart)*.

Cheyenne Chamber of Commerce: 101 S. L.L. Males Ave., P.O. Box 57, Cheyenne, OK 73628. **Phone:** (580) 497-3318.

WASHITA BATTLEFIELD NATIONAL HISTORIC SITE, 2 mi. w. on SR 47A, is the site of Lt. Col. George A. Custer's 1868 charge against the sleeping Cheyenne village of Chief Black Kettle, the first attack in an attempt to halt rebellious acts by the Cheyenne and Arapaho. The Indians believed the federal government was not living up to promises included in an 1867 peace treaty. Custer's attack set the stage for his defeat 8 years later at Little Big Horn.

The visitor center, .9 mile west on SR 47A, also serves as the headquarters for Black Kettle National Grassland. The center has panoramic views of the Washita River Valley and features exhibits and a 27-minute film, Destiny at Dawn: Loss and Victory on the Washita, detailing the events leading to Custer's charge.

Park ranger talks and tours begin at an overlook pavilion at the battlefield site on SR 47A; the overlook also is the beginning of a 1.5-mile self-guiding loop trail.

Hours: Historic site daily dawn-dusk. Visitor center daily 8-5. Ranger programs Sat.-Sun. at 9, 10, 11, 2, 3 and 4, Memorial Day-Labor Day; otherwise by request or appointment when staff is available. Closed Thanksgiving and Dec. 25. **Cost:** Free. **Phone:** (580) 497-2742.

GEM CHICKASAW NATIONAL RECREATION AREA (F-9)

Near Sulphur on US 177 and SR 7, the Chickasaw National Recreation Area encompasses 10,000 acres in south-central Oklahoma. Woods and streams with small waterfalls characterize this region, which is known for its mineral waters. Springs within the area have been classified as sulphur, freshwater and bromide.

A small herd of buffalo in a natural setting recalls the vast herds that once roamed the territory. Campfire talks, children's programs and nature walks are summer features. Arbuckle Dam impounds the Lake of the Arbuckles at the confluence of Buckhorn, Guy Sandy and Rock creeks.

Various recreational facilities are offered at specified sites, including six campgrounds. There are several picnic areas, and other facilities are in nearby Sulphur. The 2,350-acre Lake of the Arbuckles offers swimming and boating; a safety inspection for boats is available at launch ramps. A state license is required for fishing; hunting is permitted in season.

The recreation area is split into two districts: The Lake District includes Lake of the Arbuckles, and the Platt District includes Travertine Nature Center and 67-acre Veteran's Lake. Pets are permitted but must be restricted at all times; they are not allowed in swimming areas.

For more information contact the Superintendent, Chickasaw National Recreation Area, 1008 W. 2nd St., Sulphur, OK 73086; phone (580) 622-3161. *See*

Recreation Chart and the AAA South Central CampBook.

TRAVERTINE NATURE CENTER is 2 mi. from the Chickasaw National Recreation Area headquarters at jct. US 177 and Broadway Rd. Straddling Travertine Creek, the interpretive center exhibits live animals and reptiles native to the surrounding woods, plains and streams. Rangers sometimes carry a live snake for visitors to handle; slides, movies and demonstrations provide further insight into man's relationship with nature.

Hours: Nature center daily 9-5:30, Memorial Day-Labor Day; 8-4:30, rest of year. Ranger programs Fri.-Sun. at 3, Memorial Day-Labor Day; Sat.-Sun. at 3, rest of year. Phone ahead to confirm ranger program schedule. Closed Jan. 1, Thanksgiving and Dec. 25. **Cost:** Free. **Phone:** (580) 622-3165.

CLAREMORE—*see Tulsa p. 287.*

CLINTON (D-6) pop. 8,833, elev. 1,564′

Clinton is a major shipping center for the area's cotton, wheat and cattle industries. Recreational opportunities are offered at the Washita River. Foss State Park *(see Recreation Chart)* covers 1,749 acres northwest of town, and the Clinton Dam creates a 700-acre lake along the city limits. The nearby 8,000-acre Washita National Wildlife Refuge offers opportunities for wildlife observation and limited hunting and fishing *(see Recreation Chart)*.

Clinton Chamber of Commerce: 101 S. 4th St., Frisco Center, Clinton, OK 73601. **Phone:** (580) 323-2222.

SAVE **OKLAHOMA ROUTE 66 MUSEUM** is off I-40 exit 65; take I-40 Bus. Rte. w. to 2229 W. Gary Blvd. The museum tells the story of Route 66 and the history of transportation, reflecting American life from the 1920s through the 1970s. Notable are the World's Largest Curio Cabinet, vintage automobiles and a replica of a roadside diner.

Time: Allow 30 minutes minimum. **Hours:** Mon.-Sat. 9-7, Sun. 1-6, May-Aug.; Mon.-Sat. 9-5, Sun. 1-5, Feb.-Apr. and Sept.-Nov.; Tues.-Sat. 9-5, rest of year. Closed holidays and first week in Jan. **Cost:** $3; $2.50 (ages 65+); $1 (ages 6-18). **Phone:** (580) 323-7866.

DAVIS (F-9) pop. 2,610

Near Davis in the Arbuckle Mountains is 1,500-acre Turner Falls Park, 5.25 miles south on US 77. The scenic park has a 77-foot waterfall that has created several natural swimming pools. The park also features streams and ponds cutting through rock and hills, camp sites, cabins, caves (too small to enter) and hiking trails. Phone (580) 369-2988 for additional information. *See Recreation Chart.*

Davis Chamber of Commerce: 100 E. Main St., P.O. Box 5, Davis, OK 73030. **Phone:** (580) 369-2402.

ARBUCKLE WILDERNESS, on the access road of I-35 exit 51 (Turner Falls), is a 400-acre wildlife park in the Arbuckle Mountains. A 6.5-mile scenic drive winds through the park where nearly 1,000 exotic animals roam freely. Visitors are permitted to feed the animals from their car, but only with food purchased at the gate. A walk-through zoo, playground, entertainment, bumper boats, cookouts, go-carts and safari bus are featured.

Hours: Sun.-Thurs. 9-6, Fri.-Sat. 9-7, mid-Mar. through Labor Day; daily 9-5, rest of year. Schedule may vary in winter (weather permitting). **Cost:** $14.99; $13.99 (ages 55+); $12.99 (ages 4-11). **Phone:** (580) 369-3383 or (800) 738-7275.

DEWEY (B-10) pop. 3,179

Dewey, named for Adm. George Dewey, was founded by pioneer J.H. Bartles, who also founded Bartlesville. Bartles brought new meaning to the term "traveling salesman" when he decided to move his store from Bartlesville to Dewey because of the railroad stop. After building a road between the two towns, Bartles loaded his store onto large log rollers and hitched it up to a team of oxen. During the 5 months it took to move and resettle the structure, the store remained open for business.

By previous arrangement, tours are available of Prairie Song, a re-created 1800s prairie village 5.5

miles east on Durham Road. The village features a bank, chapel, general store, homestead cabin, log schoolhouse, railroad station and saloon; phone (918) 534-2662.

DEWEY HOTEL MUSEUM, 2 blks. w. of US 75 at 801 N. Delaware St., was completed in 1900 as one of the first buildings in town. Topped by three cupolas, the three-story Victorian structure has been restored and is furnished with turn-of-the-20th-century antiques. Many of the guests who gambled in the hotel's third-story tower room became giants in Oklahoma's oil industry. **Hours:** Mon.-Sat. 10-4, Sun. 1-4, Apr.-Nov. Closed major holidays. **Cost:** $2.50; $1.50 (students with ID); free (ages 0-12 with adult). **Phone:** (918) 534-0215.

TOM MIX MUSEUM, 2 blks. w. of US 75 at 721 N. Delaware St., exhibits memorabilia about the Western movie star. Originally a rodeo performer in the 101 Ranch's Wild West Show, Tom Mix won fame and fortune during Hollywood's silent film era. His elaborate costumes, guns, saddles, hats and other items are displayed, and his films are shown regularly. **Hours:** Tues.-Sat. 10-4:30, Sun. 1-4:30, Mar.-Dec.; Sat. 10-4:30, Sun. 1-4:30, in Feb. (weather permitting). Closed major holidays. **Cost:** $2:50; $1 (children). **Phone:** (918) 534-1555.

DUNCAN (F-7) pop. 22,505

GEM SAVE **CHISHOLM TRAIL HERITAGE CENTER** is at 1000 Chisholm Trail Pkwy. The history of the Chisholm Trail—the route used to move large herds of cattle between Texas ranches and Kansas railroads—is recounted through paintings, sculptures, a miniature 245-foot Chisholm Trail walkway, a museum and a theater that simulates a 19th-century cattle drive. Interactive displays allow visitors to make trail drive decisions and practice some cowpoke skills. A life-size bronze statue depicting a cattle drive is a museum highlight.

The Garis Gallery of the American West houses a rotating collection of bronzes, drawings and paintings depicting frontier- and trail-era life created by national and local artists, including Frederic Remington and Charles M. Russell. A self-guided audio tour and electronic interactive devices provide details about the artists and works on display.

Time: Allow 1 hour minimum. **Hours:** Mon.-Sat. 10-5, Sun. 1-5. Closed Jan. 1, Easter, Thanksgiving and Dec. 25. **Cost:** $6; $5 (ages 55+); $4 (ages 5-17 and military with ID); $17 (family, two adults and four children); free (military in uniform). **Phone:** (580) 252-6692.

STEPHENS COUNTY HISTORICAL MUSEUM is off Beech Ave. in Fuqua Park. Housed in the former National Guard Armory, the museum depicts life in rural Oklahoma at the end of the 19th century. Mannequins dressed in period costumes re-create frontier scenes in a blacksmith shop, a log cabin, a pioneer kitchen and other early settings. Gems, antique toys and a Plains Indian exhibit are among other displays. **Tours:** Guided tours are available. **Time:** Allow 30 minutes minimum. **Hours:** Tues. and Thurs.-Sat. 1-5. Closed major holidays. **Cost:** Donations. **Phone:** (580) 252-0717.

DURANT (G-10) pop. 13,549, elev. 643′

The capital of the Choctaw Nation was moved to Durant after Oklahoma became a state in 1907. The Choctaw Nation Tribal Headquarters is at the intersection of 16th and Locust.

An unusual statue stands on the front lawn of the Durant City Hall. Known as the World's Largest Peanut, the monument is a tribute to Bryan County peanut growers and processors.

Durant Area Chamber of Commerce: 215 N. 4th Ave., Durant, OK 74701. **Phone:** (580) 924-0848.

LAKE TEXOMA RECREATION AREA lies along the Oklahoma-Texas border. The 89,000-acre Lake Texoma was created in 1944 with the construction of Denison Dam for flood control along the Red River. The 202,300-acre recreation area offers boating, camping, golf, hiking and swimming. *See Recreation Chart.*

Hours: Daily 6 a.m.-10 p.m., Apr.-Sept. Phone ahead to confirm schedule. **Cost:** Boat ramp fee $3. Beach fee $4 (per private vehicle) or $1 per person; free (ages 0-11). **Phone:** (903) 465-4990, (903) 465-1491 for lake level and temperature information, or (877) 444-6777 for campground reservations.

THREE VALLEY MUSEUM is at 401 W. Main St. Housed in a former machine shop, the museum features exhibits about the history of southeastern Oklahoma. The Native American Gallery portrays the cultures of various local tribes including the Caddo, Wichita, Chickasaw and Choctaw. The Transportation room contains antique vehicles, and Small Town, Circa 1900-1930 is filled with historic items donated from area businesses. **Tours:** Guided tours are available. **Hours:** Mon.-Fri. 1-5. Closed major holidays. **Cost:** Donations. **Phone:** (580) 920-1907.

DURHAM (C-5) elev. 465′

METCALFE MUSEUM is 1.3 mi. s. on SR 30, 4 mi. e. on SR 33, then 3 mi. s., following signs. "Sagebrush Artist" Augusta Corson Metcalfe's family homestead contains many pieces of her artwork, which depict the Washita Valley's beauty and the struggles of the pioneers who settled there from the late 19th through the mid-20th century.

Also featured are two nature trails, a pioneer house with period furnishings, a saloon with advertisements from that era and buildings with displays and memorabilia. **Time:** Allow 30 minutes minimum. **Hours:** Tues.-Sat. 10-5 or by appointment, Mar.-Nov. **Cost:** Donations. **Phone:** (580) 655-4467.

ELK CITY (D-5) pop. 10,510, elev. 1,912′

In the late 1800s Elk City was a rest stop for cattlemen driving herds along the Great Western Trail from Texas to Kansas. Oil was discovered in 1947, and the "black gold" flowed until reserves were depleted in the late 1960s. Interests then turned to deep gas exploration in Elk City and the surrounding Anadarko Basin. The town is on historic Route 66.

The quarter horse, which is notable as both a racehorse and the cowboy's mount of choice, is raised in and around Elk City. The breed almost disappeared with the cowboy era but was reintroduced in the 1940s.

Elk City Chamber of Commerce: 1016 E. Airport Industrial Blvd., P.O. Box 972, Elk City, OK 73648. **Phone:** (580) 225-0207 or (800) 280-0207.

ELK CITY OLD TOWN MUSEUM COMPLEX, across from the park at jct. Pioneer Rd. and US 66, is a continuous restoration project that re-creates an early Western town. A museum in a late 19th-century Victorian frame house contains detailed period furnishings. Upstairs is the Beutler Brothers Rodeo Hall. The complex also features the Farm and Ranch Museum, the Transportation Museum, the National Route 66 Museum, an American Indian tepee, a pioneer doctor's office, the Pioneer Memorial Chapel, a railroad station, a schoolhouse, a Victorian gazebo and a wagon yard.

Hours: Mon.-Sat. 9-7, Sun. 1-5, Memorial Day-Labor Day; Mon.-Sat. 9-5, Sun. 2-5, rest of year. Closed major holidays. **Cost:** $5 (includes all museums and other sites within the complex); $4 (ages 6-16 and senior citizens). **Phone:** (580) 225-6266.

National Route 66 Museum, at the Elk City Old Town Museum Complex, takes visitors on a trip through the famous route's history with photographs, old signs and vintage automobiles. **Hours:** Mon.-Sat. 9-7, Sun. 1-5, Memorial Day-Labor Day; Mon.-Sat. 9-5, Sun. 2-5, rest of year. Closed major holidays. **Cost:** $3. Combination ticket with Elk City Old Town Museum Complex $5; $4 (ages 6-16 and senior citizens). **Phone:** (580) 225-6266.

EL RENO—*see Oklahoma City p. 270.*

ENID (B-7) pop. 47,045, elev. 1,246′

Although some sources hold that the town's name came from Alfred, Lord Tennyson's "Idylls of the King," more colorful stories credit the naming of Enid to cattle drovers who turned the "Dine" sign on the cook's tent upside down.

In an effort to encourage the Rock Island Railroad to stop at Enid rather than its rival North Enid, an unknown party sawed through the supports on a railroad trestle southeast of town. While attempting to pass through Enid on its usual route, the train fell into a gully, thereby making its first official "stop" at Enid. Enid later was included on the route.

Greater Enid Chamber of Commerce: 210 Kenwood Blvd., P.O. Box 907, Enid, OK 73702. **Phone:** (580) 237-2494 or (888) 229-2443.

Shopping areas: More than 50 specialty stores as well as anchor stores Dillard's, JCPenney and Sears comprise Oakwood Mall, at W. Owen K. Garriott and S. Oakwood roads.

CHEROKEE STRIP REGIONAL HERITAGE CENTER, 507 S. 4th St., exhibits American Indian and pioneer artifacts depicting the settlement of the area from 1893 to the present. On the museum grounds is the Humphrey Heritage Village, which includes four historic buildings: a one-room schoolhouse, a church, a Victorian house and the original Enid land office. The museum also has a learning center that features video presentations.

Note: The center, formerly the Museum of the Cherokee Strip, is closed while an expansion is under way; reopening is planned for summer 2010. Phone ahead to confirm status. A satellite location is available at Oakwood Mall, 4125 W. Owen K. Garriott Rd., until the center reopens. **Time:** Allow 1 hour minimum. **Hours:** Mon.-Fri. 9-5, Sat. 10-6. Closed major holidays. **Cost:** Phone ahead to confirm admission. **Phone:** (580) 237-1907.

MR. & MRS. DAN MIDGLEY MUSEUM is 1 blk. s. of jct. US 412 and US 81 at 1001 Sequoyah Dr. The museum is in a 1947 house constructed with more than 30 kinds of rock excavated by Dan and Libbie Midgley. Displays include family artifacts of these prosperous farmers who were among the state's earliest landowners.

Antique dishes, furniture and farm tools; a fireplace made of petrified wood and fossil stones; a trophy room with hunted animals; and a fluorescent rock collection are shown. **Time:** Allow 1 hour minimum. **Hours:** Wed.-Fri. 1-4:30, Sat. 2-4:30. Closed major holidays. **Cost:** Donations. **Phone:** (580) 234-7265.

RAILROAD MUSEUM OF OKLAHOMA, 702 N. Washington, has a collection of train cars and objects that were used on local trains. China and silver services, steam engine bells, line maps and postcards are among the memorabilia on display; train buffs can peruse a library of railroading books. A room is devoted to model railroads. Rail excursions are offered twice annually. **Hours:** Tues.-Fri. 1-4, Sat. 10-1, Sun. 2-5. Closed major holidays. **Cost:** Donations. **Phone:** (580) 233-3051.

ERICK (E-5) pop. 1,023, elev. 2,064′

ROGER MILLER MUSEUM is at jct. Roger Miller Blvd. and Sheb Wooley Ave. Artifacts and memorabilia related to songwriter and entertainer Roger Miller, who grew up on a farm outside Erick, are displayed. Miller is known for his 1960s Grammy-winning hits "Dang Me" and "King of the Road."

The museum's collection includes clothing, handwritten lyrics, instruments, music, photographs and videos. The motorcycle Miller was riding when he met Elvis Presley is a highlight. **Time:** Allow 30 minutes minimum. **Hours:** Wed.-Sat. 10-5, Sun. 1-5, Mon.-Tues. by appointment only. Closed major holidays. **Cost:** $3; $2 (ages 12-17 and 62+). **Phone:** (580) 526-3833.

FORT GIBSON (D-11) pop. 4,054, elev. 534'

Fort Gibson is a rural community near the site of a fort that was established in 1824 as part of a network of garrisons built to maintain peace along the frontier and to quell conflicts with the Osage Indians. The fort also served as a communication and supply center for fur traders and explorers of the Southwest. It was occupied by Union troops during the Civil War and abandoned in 1890.

About a mile from Fort Gibson Historic Site is Fort Gibson National Cemetery, established in 1868. Among the graves in the officers' circle are those of two women: Sam Houston's Cherokee wife, Talihina, and a young woman from Massachusetts named Vivia. Legend states that Vivia disguised herself as a soldier and followed her former lover to Fort Gibson, where she killed him in retaliation for rejecting her. The American Indians were blamed for his death, and Vivia's gender was not discovered until she died.

Fort Gibson Chamber of Commerce: 112 N. Lee St., P.O. Box 730, Fort Gibson, OK 74434. **Phone:** (918) 478-4780.

SAVE **FORT GIBSON HISTORIC SITE** is n. of US 62 on SR 80, following signs. The fort was occupied by the U.S. Army 1824-90. Reconstructed in 1936, the site includes a visitor center, walking trails and a museum that houses military relics found in the area. The barracks, stockade and 13 original buildings can be seen.

Time: Allow 1 hour minimum. **Hours:** Tues.-Sat. 10-5, Apr.-Oct.; Thurs.-Sun. 10-5, rest of year. Closed Thanksgiving and Dec. 25. **Cost:** $3; $2.50 (ages 65+); $1 (ages 6-18). **Phone:** (918) 478-4088.

FORT SILL (E-7)

GEM **FORT SILL NATIONAL HISTORIC LANDMARK AND MUSEUM** is at 437 Quanah Rd.; the interpretive center is in Building 435. The fort, which consists of 50 buildings from the original 19th-century military outpost, retains its frontier atmosphere. It was established in 1869 by Gen. Philip Sheridan to control the Southern Plains tribes and, at the same time, protect their lands from encroachment.

Since the fort has been in continuous use since the Indian Wars period, it is virtually unchanged. The site remains an active Army post, with many of the original family living quarters still being used for that purpose.

The fort interprets early cavalry and infantry history (including Col. George Custer's 7th Cavalry and the famous 10th Cavalry Buffalo Soldiers); the Apache, Comanche and Kiowa tribes; the settlement of early Oklahoma; and the history of the area's early military and law enforcement divisions.

Among the graves in seven American Indian cemeteries are those of Geronimo and Quanah Parker, the last chief of the Comanches. Visitors can see barracks restored to resemble those used by cavalry soldiers in 1875 and the stone Quartermaster Corral, which has been returned to its original appearance. The Post Guardhouse has exhibits focusing on the early law enforcement mission of the Army and the Indian police. The Warrior's Journey gallery addresses the American Indian collections in the museum.

Living history presentations, which take place on a regular basis, include such activities as the firing of Civil War-era muzzle-loading cannons, Indian baseball and programs about the Army's Buffalo Soldiers.

Note: Photo ID is required. **Time:** Allow 1 hour, 30 minutes minimum. **Hours:** Tues.-Sat. 8:30-5; closed Jan. 1-2, Thanksgiving and Dec. 25-26. Cemeteries daily dawn-dusk. **Cost:** Free. **Phone:** (580) 442-5123.

Artillery Park, just s. on Corral Rd. near Fort Sill National Historic Landmark and Museum, is an outdoor museum containing more than 100 large-scale artillery weapons and other associated items. Included are "Atomic Annie," a 280-millimeter cannon that fired the first atomic artillery round; captured artillery from the Iraq wars; and U.S. Army missiles and rockets that date from 1944 to the present, including a display about Desert Storm artillery.

Note: Artillery Park is in the process of relocating to a site across the road from its current location. Phone ahead for information. **Time:** Allow 30 minutes minimum. **Hours:** Tues.-Sat. 8:30-5; closed Jan. 1-2, Thanksgiving and Dec. 25-26. **Cost:** Free. **Phone:** (580) 442-5123.

FORT TOWSON (F-11) pop. 611

The town of Fort Towson sprang up as a center of pioneer and American Indian trade after the nearby military fort was established in 1824.

DID YOU KNOW

Oklahoma has more man-made lakes than any other state.

FORT TOWSON HISTORIC SITE is 1 mi. e. on US 70, then .7 mi. n. at sign. The ruins of Fort Towson, built as an outpost to maintain peace and regulate trade between area settlers and American Indians, are preserved at this site. A sutler's store—an establishment owned by a peddler who followed an army unit selling items to soldiers—has been reconstructed, and a museum contains items excavated from the site. **Time:** Allow 30 minutes minimum. **Hours:** Tues.-Sat. 9-5, Sun. 1-5. Closed major holidays. **Cost:** Free. **Phone:** (580) 873-2634.

FREDERICK (F-6) pop. 4,637, elev. 1,306′

Frederick was created in 1902 when the towns of Gosnell and Hazel merged to take advantage of the Blackwell, Enid & Southwestern Railroad, which began construction in Texas in 1901 and was completed in the Frederick area in 1903. More than a century later the economic focus of the agriculture-based community is its production of cattle, cotton and wheat.

In 1905 President Theodore Roosevelt visited Frederick to meet Jack Abernathy, a wolf hunter whose hunting skills earned him the nickname "Catch 'em Alive" Abernathy. Upon learning of Abernathy's hunting skills, the president went on a wolf hunt with Abernathy. The two men forged a close friendship lasting until Roosevelt's death in 1919.

In 1910 Abernathy's sons, 10-year-old Louis "Bud" and 6-year-old Temple, traveled alone on horseback from Frederick to Washington, D.C., to meet President William Howard Taft. They proceeded north to New York City to meet Roosevelt upon his return from an African safari; afterwards, the children drove 2,500 miles home to Frederick in a Brush automobile. A restored Brush car, similar to the one driven by the boys, is displayed at the Pioneer Heritage Townsite Center *(see attraction listing)*.

Frederick Chamber of Commerce and Industry: 100 S. Main St., Frederick, OK 73542. **Phone:** (580) 335-2126.

HACKBERRY FLAT WILDLIFE MANAGEMENT AREA is 1 mi. s. on US 183 from jct. SR 5, 3 mi. e. on Airport Rd., then 4 mi. s. on an access road, following signs. Visitors may observe more than 200 bird species frequenting the 7,120-acre area's wetland habitats. Regional shorebirds, wading birds and such raptors as peregrine and prairie falcons and ferruginous and rough-legged hawks have been identified at the area. Quail, waterfowl, bobcats and coyotes are among other wildlife that may be seen.

Note: Chiggers and ticks may be in the area's high grasses; bug spray and protective clothing are recommended. **Hours:** Wildlife area open daily 24 hours. Visitor center open second Sat. of the month 9-2. Phone ahead to confirm visitor center hours. **Cost:** Free. **Phone:** (580) 335-5262.

PIONEER HERITAGE TOWNSITE CENTER, 201 N. 9th St., is an outdoor village containing both original and replica buildings from 1920s southwestern Oklahoma. Such structures as a church, schoolhouse, supply store and train depot are furnished in period. Demonstrations explain the area's industrial history of cotton farming and railroad transportation.

An interactive exhibit showcases a restored Brush automobile similar to the one driven by Louis "Bud" and Temple Abernathy during their journey from New York City to Frederick in 1910. **Time:** Allow 45 minutes minimum. **Hours:** Mon.-Fri. 9-3, Sat.-Sun. by appointment. **Cost:** Free. **Phone:** (580) 335-5844.

FREEDOM (B-6) pop. 271

Situated on the Cimarron River, Freedom is known for a granite monument, Cimarron Cowboy, that depicts a wrangler from the early days of the town's settlement. The monument is in a park at the intersection of Eagle Pass and Main. A mural titled "Posting the Colors" also is visible from Main Street.

Freedom Chamber of Commerce: 1085 Main St., P.O. Box 125, Freedom, OK 73842. **Phone:** (580) 621-3276.

ALABASTER CAVERNS STATE PARK is 6 mi. s. on SR 50, then .5 mi. e. on SR 50A. The 200-acre park surrounds a large gypsum cave, which can be seen on a .75-mile guided tour. The cave contains selenite and alabaster formations. Various species of bats are found within the caverns. The park also has nature trails, camping, a horseshoe pit and a volleyball court. *See Recreation Chart.*

A light jacket and comfortable shoes are recommended for cave tours. **Time:** Allow 1 hour minimum. **Hours:** Park open daily 24 hours. Guided cave tours conducted daily 9-5, Memorial Day weekend-Labor Day weekend; 9-4, rest of year. Closed Thanksgiving and Dec. 25. **Cost:** Park free. Cavern tour $8; $6 (ages 62+); $5 (ages 6-12). **Phone:** (580) 621-3381.

FREEDOM MUSEUM is 2 blks. e. off SR 50 on Main St. Early Oklahoma memorabilia includes antiques, clothing and one of the largest barbed wire collections in the country, containing more than 700 different types of wire. Of special note is the display of prehistoric fossils recovered from archeological digs northwest of Freedom. **Hours:** Tues.-Fri. 10-3, May 1-Jan. 2 or by appointment. Closed major holidays. **Cost:** Donations. **Phone:** (580) 621-3533.

GENE AUTRY (F-9) pop. 99, elev. 729′

GENE AUTRY OKLAHOMA MUSEUM, 47 Prairie St., has memorabilia about film and TV star Gene Autry, who once owned a ranch adjacent to the town, and other Western stars. The museum shares the legacy of the singing cowboys of the "B" Western movies of the 1930s, '40s and '50s. **Time:** Allow 1 hour minimum. **Hours:** Mon.-Sat. 10-4. Closed major holidays. **Cost:** Donations. **Phone:** (580) 294-3047.

GOODWELL (B-2) pop. 1,192, elev. 3,286′

Goodwell is within Oklahoma's panhandle, the 34-mile-wide and 168-mile-long strip of land that lies between the borders of Kansas and Texas. Before this area became part of the Oklahoma Territory in 1890 it was known as "No Man's Land" because it was unclaimed.

The Rock Island Railroad line helped to establish the town around 1903. Common sense came into play in the naming of Goodwell. During the construction of the railroad, workers were impressed with the soft water they found in a newly drilled well.

NO MAN'S LAND HISTORICAL MUSEUM, on Sewell St. on the campus of Panhandle State University, contains pioneer and American Indian artifacts depicting the development of Oklahoma's "No Man's Land" that later became the heart of the Dust Bowl. There also are alabaster carvings, dinosaur footprints, geological exhibits and mounted animals. **Time:** Allow 1 hour minimum. **Hours:** Tues.-Sat. 10-4, June-Aug.; Tues.-Fri. 10-noon and 1-3, Sat. 10-4, rest of year. Closed major holidays. **Cost:** Free. **Phone:** (580) 349-2670.

GORE (D-11) pop. 850

Gore was the stopping point for Cherokee Indians as they migrated west in 1828. They established a council ground and in 1829 welcomed Sam Houston—who later married a Cherokee—into their tribe. The settlement remained the capital of what became the Cherokee Nation West until the Eastern Cherokees, who were forced to join their Western counterparts via the "Trail of Tears," gained control of the nation and relocated the capital to Tahlequah in 1843.

Gore Chamber of Commerce: 1009 N. Main St., P.O. Box 943, Gore, OK 74435. **Phone:** (918) 489-2534.

CHEROKEE COURTHOUSE (TAHLONTEESKEE), 2.5 mi. e. on US 64/SR 10, is the restored courthouse and council house of the Cherokee Nation West. The tribe named its headquarters Tahlonteeskee after the chief who founded the Western Cherokee Nation. The buildings contain drawings depicting significant events in the tribe's history, along with American Indian artifacts, tools and photographs. **Hours:** Mon.-Sat. 9-5, Sun. 1-5, other times by appointment. Closed Thanksgiving and Dec. 25. **Cost:** Free. **Phone:** (918) 489-5663.

GROVE (B-12) pop. 5,131

GEM **HAR-BER VILLAGE,** 3.5 mi. w. on Har-Ber Rd., is on the shores of Grand Lake O' the Cherokees. Created by Harvey and Bernice Jones, the founders of Jones Truck Lines, this reconstructed 19th-century village encompasses more than 100 log cabin buildings as well as collections of glassware, dolls, china, furniture and farm machinery. Other exhibits include primitives (American Indian pottery or artifacts made before the advent of a spoken language) and arctic animals.

Included among the buildings are a bank, a beauty shop, a courthouse, a dentist's office, a drug store, a jewelry store, a one-room schoolhouse, a post office and stills. A visitor center contains a pictorial history exhibit of the area. An ecology center and an herb garden also are on the grounds.

Time: Allow 3 hours minimum. **Hours:** Mon.-Sat. 9-6, Sun. 12:30-6, Mar. 1-Oct. 14; Mon.-Sat. 9-5, Sun. 12:30-5, Oct. 15-Nov. 15. Last admission is 1 hour before closing. **Cost:** $3.50; $2.50 (ages 62+); free (ages 0-13). **Phone:** (918) 786-3488, or (918) 786-6446 for the visitor center.

LENDONWOOD GARDENS is 1 mi. e. of US 59 at 1308 W. 13th St. (Har-Ber Rd.). The garden features five areas, several with an Oriental theme. The Zen Garden has bonsai plants; the Oriental Garden contains a pond and rhododendrons; and the Japanese pond area has conifers, Japanese maples and a tea house. The American Backyard with drought-resistant plants and the English Terrace Garden with dwarf hostas complement the other areas.

The bronze "Angel of Hope" statue, in a quiet setting, commemorates lost loved ones, especially children. **Time:** Allow 30 minutes minimum. **Hours:** Daily dawn-dusk. **Cost:** Donations. **Phone:** (918) 786-2938.

GUTHRIE—*see Oklahoma City p. 270.*

HEAVENER (E-12) pop. 3,201

At the base of 1,200-foot-high Poteau Mountain in the Ouachita Range, Heavener was carved out of land known to the Choctaws as the "Prairie of the Tall Grass." It was named for Joe Heavener, a local merchant and owner of the original townsite. The town lies along a scenic section of US 59/270 that runs 26 miles between Poteau and Page.

Heavener Chamber of Commerce: 501 W. 1st St., Heavener, OK 74937. **Phone:** (918) 653-4303.

HEAVENER-RUNESTONE STATE PARK, 3 mi. n.e. off US 59/270 on CR E1460, following signs, contains a 12-foot-high, 10-foot-wide stone with runic alphabet carvings believed to have been made by Viking explorers about 750. The stone can be reached via a 100-yard trail. An interpretive center, community building, amphitheater, picnic area and a playground also are available. **Time:** Allow 1 hour minimum. **Hours:** Park open daily 8-dusk. Interpretive center open Wed.-Mon. 8-5. **Cost:** Free. **Phone:** (918) 653-2241.

PETER CONSER HOME, 5 mi. s. on US 59, then 3 mi. w., is the restored house of the leader of the Choctaw Nation. Peter Conser also was a wealthy merchant and captain of the Choctaw Lighthorse, an early law enforcement group. Antiques and photographs are displayed. **Hours:** Wed.-Sat. 10-5, Sun. 1-5. Closed major holidays. **Cost:** Donations. **Phone:** (918) 653-2493.

HOMINY—*see Tulsa p. 287.*

HUGO (G-11) pop. 5,536, elev. 550′

Once known as Circus City, USA, Hugo constitutes the winter headquarters of the five-ring Carson & Barnes and the Kelly-Miller Bros. circuses. Monuments to circus performers can be found in a section of the Mount Olivet Cemetery. Hugo also is home to the 13,500-acre Hugo Lake *(see Recreation Chart)*, where bass and crappie are plentiful.

Hugo Chamber of Commerce: 200 S. Broadway, Hugo, OK 74743. **Phone:** (580) 326-7511.

HUGO FRISCO DEPOT MUSEUM is downtown in the 300 block of N. B St. Built in 1914 on the main line from Dallas to St. Louis, the Frisco Depot houses American Indian artifacts, antiques, a miniature train exhibit and railroad memorabilia. **Hours:** Tues.-Sat. 10-4. **Cost:** Donations. **Phone:** (580) 326-6630.

IDABEL (G-12) pop. 6,952, elev. 489′

MUSEUM OF THE RED RIVER is at 812 E. Lincoln Rd. The museum, whose collections include works from around the world, specializes in prehistoric to contemporary North, Central and South American Indian art. Archeological findings from the Caddoan Indians, who lived in the area about 900-1700, as well as historic items of the Choctaw Indians, who were relocated into the region in the 1830s, are displayed.

A gallery features a complete cast skeleton of an Acrocanthosaurus atokensis, a meat-eating dinosaur that once roamed the area. **Time:** Allow 1 hour minimum. **Hours:** Tues.-Sat. 10-5, Sun. 1-5. Closed Jan. 1, July 4, Thanksgiving and Dec. 25. **Cost:** Free. **Phone:** (580) 286-3616.

JENKS—*see Tulsa p. 287.*

KINGFISHER (G-1) pop. 4,380, elev. 1,051′

Nicknamed "The Buckle of the Wheat Belt," Kingfisher is among the largest wheat markets in the world. The town was founded during the land run of 1889 and was named after a cattleman called King Fisher, who operated a stagecoach station and line. The Chisholm Trail passed through the area.

Kingfisher Chamber of Commerce: 123 W. Miles, Kingfisher, OK 73750. **Phone:** (405) 375-4445.

CHISHOLM TRAIL MUSEUM AND GOVERNOR SEAY MANSION are 5 blks. w. of US 81 at 605 Zellers Ave. The museum has pioneer and American Indian articles as well as a timeline describing the history of the Chisholm Trail. The mansion, across the street at 11th and Overstreet, was built in 1892 and is restored and furnished in period.

A late 1890s village located behind the museum features two log cabins, a bank, a schoolhouse and a church. Allow 1 hour minimum for the museum, 30 minutes for the mansion. **Hours:** Tues.-Sat. 10-5. Closed major holidays. **Cost:** Donations. **Phone:** (405) 375-5176.

LANGLEY (B-11) pop. 669, elev. 760′

PENSACOLA DAM, .5 mi. e. of jct. SRs 28 and 82, impounds 66-mile-long Grand Lake O' The Cherokees, spanning the river between Disney and Langley; the length of the dam and spillways is 6,565 feet. One-hour guided tours of the dam, completed in 1940, begin at the west side of the dam. **Hours:** Power plant tours daily 9:30-4, Memorial Day weekend-Labor Day. **Cost:** Free. **Phone:** (918) 782-9594.

LANGSTON—*see Oklahoma City p. 271.*

LAWTON (F-7) pop. 92,757, elev. 1,111′

On the morning of Aug. 6, 1901, Lawton was merely a tumbleweed connection on a vast American Indian reservation. By evening it had blossomed into a town of 10,000, the last of the Oklahoma cities to spring up overnight. Lawton was created by a land lottery, in which successful bidders without the cash for immediate payment were allowed 30 minutes in which to get the money before the lot was put up for sale again.

Lawton Chamber of Commerce and Industry: 629 S.W. C Ave., Suite A, P.O. Box 1376, Lawton, OK 73502. **Phone:** (580) 355-3541 or (800) 872-4540.

Shopping areas: Central Mall, just off I-44 on C Avenue, has Dillard's, JCPenney and Sears as its anchor stores.

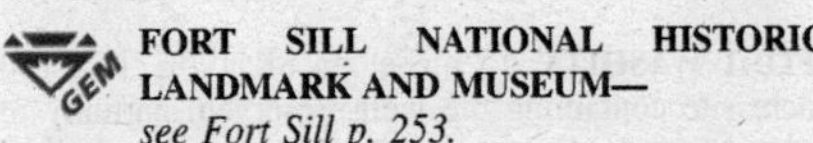

FORT SILL NATIONAL HISTORIC LANDMARK AND MUSEUM— *see Fort Sill p. 253.*

THE HISTORIC MATTIE BEAL HOME is at 1008 S.W. 5th St. at jct. Summit Ave. The house was built 1907-09 for Mattie Beal, a young Kansan who won a 160-acre plot in the 1901 Oklahoma land lottery. The 14-room house was, for many years, one of the finest in Lawton.

A philanthropist, Ms. Beal donated land for parks, a church and a school. She also subdivided her property into affordable lots for new settlers. The house has been restored to the 1923 time period. Highlights include the original grand staircase, curved front door, the second floor ballroom, stained glass windows and an Italian marble mantle.

Hours: Thurs.-Sun. noon-3, Feb.-Dec. Closed Thanksgiving and Dec. 25. **Cost:** $4; $3 (ages 60+); $2 (students grades K-12). **Phone:** (580) 678-3156.

MUSEUM OF THE GREAT PLAINS, in Elmer Thomas Park at 601 Ferris Ave., interprets the relationship between man and the plains environment. Exhibits depict the fur trade and cattle industries, the life of the frontier soldier and technological development on the plains. Replicas of a fur-trading fort and a train depot with a locomotive are displayed as well as a collection of farm machinery. Living-history programs are presented Tuesday through Saturday in the fort's trading post.

Time: Allow 1 hour minimum. **Hours:** Mon.-Sat. 10-5, Sun. 1-5. Closed Jan. 1, Thanksgiving and Dec. 25. **Cost:** $6; $5 (ages 60+); $2.50 (ages 7-11). **Phone:** (580) 581-3460.

LONE WOLF (E-6) pop. 500, elev. 1,554′

QUARTZ MOUNTAIN STATE RESORT PARK NATURE CENTER, 10 mi. s. on SR 44, then 1.5 mi. n. on SR 44A, features exhibits about local cultural history, geology, fauna and flora. Ten nature trails are on the grounds; an interpretive trail takes hikers .2 mile along a wooded stream. Another trail, .5 mile in length, climbs 1,500 feet to a mountain summit. A hands-on children's area as well as provisions for boating, camping and picnicking are available. *See Recreation Chart.* **Hours:** Park open daily 24 hours. Nature center open Wed.-Sun. 8-4. **Cost:** Free. **Phone:** (580) 563-2238.

MADILL (F-9) pop. 3,410

Originally supported by surrounding farms and ranches, Madill's economic base changed dramatically in 1945 when Denison Dam was built. The dam flooded the agricultural land and created Lake Texoma *(see Recreation Chart)*, one of Oklahoma's most popular resort areas. To capitalize on its new lakeside location, the town became a recreation center.

Marshall County Chamber of Commerce: 400 W. Overton St., P.O. Box 542, Madill, OK 73446. **Phone:** (580) 795-2431.

FORT WASHITA, 15 mi. e. on SR 199E, is a 150-acre site containing the well-preserved, partially restored remains of an American Indian fort built in 1842. The Chickasaws and Choctaws used the fort for protection from the Plains Indians, as did pioneers traveling westward. It was last occupied by the Confederate Army during the Civil War. **Time:** Allow 1 hour minimum. **Hours:** Mon.-Sat. 9-4:30, Sun. 1-4:30. Closed major holidays. **Cost:** Donations. **Phone:** (580) 924-6502.

McALESTER (E-11) pop. 17,783, elev. 734′

McAlester began as a tent store owned by J.J. McAlester at the crossroads of the old California Trail and the Texas Road. He later discovered and mined coal in the area.

Because McAlester had married a Choctaw Indian, which made him a member of the Choctaw Nation, the American Indians claimed rights to his newly found wealth. When McAlester protested, the tribal court ruled in his favor; however, the Choctaw chief sentenced him to death in spite of this decision. McAlester made a dramatic escape and later served the state as lieutenant governor.

McAlester Scottish Rite Temple, 2nd and Adams streets, has an auditorium with Egyptian decor. Guided tours are available by reservation; phone (918) 423-6360.

Six miles north is Lake Eufaula *(see Recreation Chart)*. The Eufaula Dam's powerhouse, off SR 71, is open for tours by appointment; phone (918) 484-5439.

McAlester Area Chamber of Commerce and Agriculture: 345 E. Adams, P.O. Box 759, McAlester, OK 74502. **Phone:** (918) 423-2550.

PIONEER COAL MINER MEMORIAL, at 3rd and Chadick sts. in Chadick Park, pays tribute to the thousands of coal miners who worked in the area's mines. The memorial is comprised of a bronze, life-size statue of a miner as well as the Wall of Memories, which contains the names of more than 1,700 miners who died in the profession. **Time:** Allow 30 minutes minimum. **Hours:** Daily dawn-dusk. **Cost:** Free.

MIAMI (B-11) pop. 13,704, elev. 798′

COLEMAN THEATRE BEAUTIFUL, 103 N. Main St., is a restored 1929 vaudeville movie theater. Guided tours offer visitors a chance to see its mahogany staircases, crystal chandeliers, stained-glass panels and original Wurlitzer pipe organ. Theater performances are given on a regular basis. **Time:** Allow 1 hour minimum. **Hours:** Tues.-Fri. 10-4, Sat. 10-2. Closed Dec. 25. **Cost:** Donations. **Phone:** (918) 540-2425.

MUSKOGEE (D-11) pop. 38,310, elev. 601′

The town takes its name from the Muscogee tribe of the Creek Nation who moved to Oklahoma in the 1830s. Muskogee also was the home of notable Oklahoma historians Grant and Carolyn Foreman, who wrote a number of books about the Five Civilized Tribes. The couple's residence, the Thomas-Foreman Historic Home at 1419 W. Okmulgee, contains their original furniture and is open Friday and Saturday; phone (918) 686-6624.

Honor Heights Park, at 40th Street and Park Boulevard, is a 132-acre park with extensive plantings of azaleas, roses and irises surrounding lakes, lily ponds and picnic grounds.

Muskogee Convention and Tourism: 310 W. Broadway, Muskogee, OK 74401. **Phone:** (918) 682-2401.

Shopping areas: Arrowhead Mall, 501 N. Main, has Dillard's, JCPenney and Sears as its anchor stores.

ATALOA LODGE MUSEUM, on the Bacone College campus, displays more than 20,000 American Indian artifacts collected from tribes throughout the country. **Hours:** Wed.-Sat. 8:30-5:30, Sun. 1-5. **Cost:** Donations. **Phone:** (918) 781-7283.

SAVE **FIVE CIVILIZED TRIBES MUSEUM,** Agency Hill on Honor Heights Dr., is in the 1875 Union Indian Agency building. Displays and artifacts depict the history and culture of the Cherokee, Chickasaw, Choctaw, Creek and Seminole Indians.

An art gallery and a library also are on the premises. **Time:** Allow 1 hour minimum. **Hours:** Mon.-Fri. 10-5, Sat. 10-2. Closed Jan. 1, Thanksgiving and Dec. 25. **Cost:** $3; $2 (ages 65+); $1.50 (students with ID); free (ages 0-5). **Phone:** (918) 683-1701.

OKLAHOMA MUSIC HALL OF FAME & MUSEUM is at 401 S. 3rd St. The hall of fame and museum, in the renovated former Frisco freight depot, honors Oklahoma's music history and legacy. The state's musicians, including Gene Autry, Roy Clark, Woody Guthrie, Merle Haggard, Toby Keith, Roger Miller, Patti Page and Carrie Underwood have contributed much to the roots of American music.

Plaques with biographical information link the artist with Oklahoma, and a touch screen allows visitors to access videos of the inducted performers. **Time:** Allow 30 minutes minimum. **Hours:** Tues.-Sat. 10-5. Closed major holidays. **Cost:** $3; $2 (ages 1-12 and 62+). **Phone:** (918) 687-0800.

USS *BATFISH* WAR MEMORIAL PARK MUSEUM, Port of Muskogee exit off the Muskogee Tpke. at 3500 Batfish Rd., offers self-guiding tours of the USS *Batfish,* a World War II submarine that sank three enemy submarines and 11 other enemy vessels during battle. Tours include the torpedo room and crew cabins. The museum also contains monuments to other submarines lost during the war and a Walk of Honor that honors all veterans.

Hours: Wed.-Sat. 10-6, Sun. 1-6, Mar. 15-Oct. 15 (weather permitting); Thurs.-Sat. 10-5, Sun. 1-5, rest of year. Closed major holidays. **Cost:** $6; $4 (ages 62+); $3 (ages 7-13). Cash only. **Phone:** (918) 682-6294.

NORMAN—*see Oklahoma City p. 271.*

NOWATA (B-11) pop. 3,971

Nowata received its name from a Delaware Indian word, *no-we-ata,* meaning "welcome." The Delaware tribe, called Lenape in their native language, migrated to the Cherokee Nation in 1866, following an agreement set forth by the Cherokee. The pact allowed the newcomers to reside within the Cherokee Nation yet retain their independence as Delaware Indians.

Nowata Chamber of Commerce: 126 S. Maple St., P.O. Box 202, Nowata, OK 74048. **Phone:** (918) 273-2301.

NOWATA COUNTY HISTORICAL SOCIETY MUSEUM, 121 S. Pine St., contains an extensive collection of local memorabilia. Twenty-one rooms display American Indian and cowboy artifacts, period clothing, oil drilling and agricultural equipment, military items, dolls, antique furniture and early household utensils. **Hours:** Tues.-Sat. 1-4. Closed major holidays. **Cost:** Donations. **Phone:** (918) 273-1191.

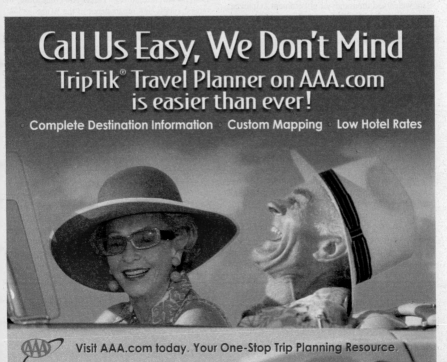

Oklahoma City

City Population: 506,132 **Elevation:** 1,201 ft.

Editor's Picks:

National Cowboy & Western Heritage Museum................*(see p. 266)*
Oklahoma City National Memorial & Museum............*(see p. 267)*
Science Museum Oklahoma.......*(see p. 267)*

Jeremy Woodhouse / Getty Images

Born in an afternoon, built over a field of black gold, and redesigned by architect I.M. Pei, Oklahoma City has a history with few plateaus. Between noon and sundown on April 22, 1889, the unassigned prairie lands of the Oklahoma Territory were opened for settlement, and 10,000 land claims surrounding a Santa Fe Railroad station site were made in one afternoon. Oklahoma City literally blossomed overnight.

Established as state capital in 1910, Oklahoma City welcomed thousands of government employees, whose arrival swelled its population to the largest in the state. Manufacturing concerns were established along with the development of natural resources. As it did with many cities, World War I boosted the economy.

On Dec. 4, 1928, what would become a major force in Oklahoma City's economic future surfaced: The first oil well within the city limits struck a gusher. It changed not only the economy but the scenery. Oil derricks sprouted throughout town, adding a familiar silhouette to the city's rapidly changing skyline.

The most renowned strike was the Mary Sudik, which blew in 1930 and lasted for 11 days, spreading oil as far as 15 miles. Producing wells still are found on the Capitol grounds, and more than 2,000 wells are either within or adjacent to the city limits. The pool on which Oklahoma City rests is considered among the richest ever developed in the United States.

Along with the discovery of oil, drilling equipment and petroleum refining industries flourished. World War II and the postwar years contributed to this economic growth through the establishment of Douglas Aircraft Co. and Tinker Air Force Base, the largest supply and repair depot in the world.

Aviation remains a major industry, with the FAA Aeronautical Center and the Civil Aeromedical Institute making their home at Will Rogers World Airport. "OKC," as the city is affectionately called by its residents, also is the state's leading wholesale and distribution point and ranks among the eight primary livestock markets in the country. More than 855 manufacturing concerns are in operation.

The Oklahoma National Stockyards, 2501 Exchange Ave., was founded in 1910 and is said to be the world's largest cattle market. Visitors can watch the cattle auctions on Monday and Tuesday; phone (405) 235-8675 for information.

Among Oklahoma City's main public buildings is the Civic Center, which covers six blocks in the heart of downtown. It includes the city hall, county building, police department and Civic Center Music Hall, which seats 3,200. Also a focus in the downtown area is Cox Business Services Convention Center, Broadway and Sheridan. The center includes an arena with a seating capacity of more than

Getting There — *starting on p. 261*
Getting Around — *starting on p. 264*
What To See — *starting on p. 264*
What To Do — *starting on p. 268*
Where To Stay — *starting on p. 613*
Where To Dine — *starting on p. 622*

15,000, an exhibition arena and a number of meeting rooms. The nearby Myriad Gardens holds such seasonal events as the Spring Festival of the Arts and Fourth of July activities.

To complement the city's successful commercial growth, Oklahoma City's leaders recommended a new look for downtown. In 1964 well-known urban architect I.M. Pei created a master redevelopment plan. Inspired by Copenhagen's Tivoli Gardens, the rejuvenated area includes lakes, water concourses, landscaped hills, an amphitheater and a striking glass and steel botanical bridge containing a greenhouse with exotic plants.

Another innovative addition was the Metro Concourse System of tunnels and skywalks, which connects major hotels, office buildings, conference areas, restaurants and retail establishments within the downtown area.

Despite a sleek and sophisticated appearance, Oklahoma City has not forgotten its pervasive Western and American Indian heritage. It sprang from Indian Territory, and the 39 American Indian tribes still represented in the state hold regular tribal activities in and around the city. Their artwork decorates building interiors and is displayed in local galleries and museums.

The skills of horses and cowboys are revered at many rodeos and horse shows as well as at the National Cowboy & Western Heritage Museum *(see attraction listing p. 266)*. Cowboys still practice their trade at horse and cattle ranches in the surrounding region, and Western wear has withstood the capricious trends of fashion. Heritage has proven a stabilizing influence in a rapidly changing environment.

Bricktown / © Gibson Stock Photography

Getting There

By Car

Transcontinental I-40 is the primary east-west route through the area; it traverses the heart of the city, offering easy interchanges with main streets and other through routes. I-44, a shorter east-west corridor, angles in from the northeast and the southwest, skirting the western side of the city and offering frequent interchanges.

Except for its path through the city, I-44 is a toll highway throughout most of Oklahoma; its various segments are known as the Will Rogers Turnpike, Turner Turnpike and H.E. Bailey Turnpike. Other east-west routes serving the area mainly accommodate local traffic and include US 62, US 270 and old US 66, which parallels I-44 from the northeast and I-40 from the west.

I-35 bisects both the nation and Oklahoma City, bringing travelers from Lake Superior to the north and from the Mexican border to the south. It courses

Destination Oklahoma City

In Oklahoma City visitors can find re-created buildings, cowboy and rodeo museums, and other reminders of early days. But don't take it for a one-horse town.

Although the city's sleek skyscrapers and extensive metro system show that OKC lies firmly in the present, its residents take great pride in its grand, colorful past.

© Witold Skrypczak SuperStock

Henry Overholser Mansion, Oklahoma City.
(See listing page 266)

Oklahoma City CVB

National Cowboy & Western Heritage Museum, Oklahoma City.
(See listing page 266)

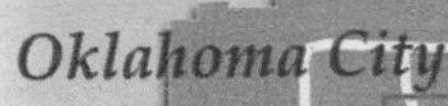

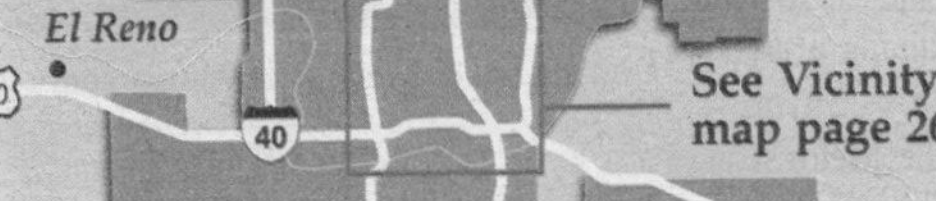

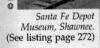

© Mike Booth / Alamy

Santa Fe Depot Museum, Shawnee.
(See listing page 272)

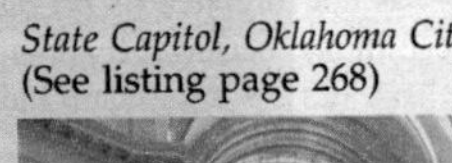

State Capitol, Oklahoma City.
(See listing page 268)

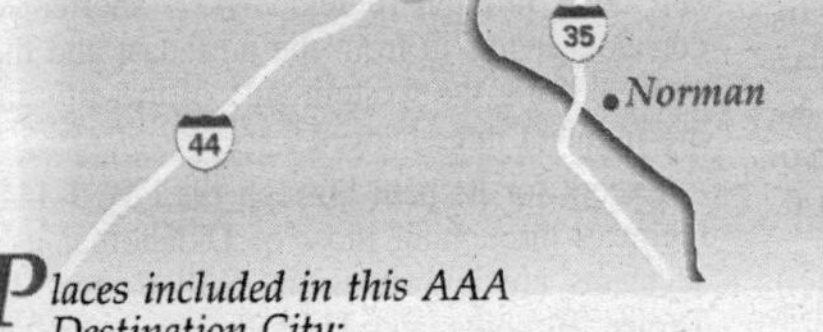

Oklahoma City CVB

Places included in this AAA Destination City:

The Informed Traveler

Sales Tax: Oklahoma City levies a sales tax of 8.38 percent, a lodging tax of 13.87 percent and a rental car tax of 14.37 percent.

WHOM TO CALL

Emergency: 911

Police (non-emergency): (405) 297-1000

Fire: (405) 297-3439

Time and Temperature: (405) 599-1234

Hospitals: Deaconess Hospital, (405) 946-5581; Integris Baptist Medical Center, (405) 949-3011; Integris Southwest Medical Center, (405) 636-7000; Mercy Health Center, (405) 755-1515; Oklahoma University Medical Center, (405) 271-4700; St. Anthony Hospital, (405) 272-7000.

WHERE TO LOOK

Newspapers

The city's major newspaper, the *Daily Oklahoman,* is distributed in the morning.

Radio

Oklahoma City radio station KTOK (1000 AM) is a news station; KCSC (90.1 FM) is a member of National Public Radio.

Visitor Information

Oklahoma City Convention and Tourism Bureau: 189 W. Sheridan, Oklahoma City, OK 73102. **Phone:** (405) 297-8912 or (800) 225-5652.

Visitors guides, maps and brochures are available Mon.-Fri. 8:30-5.

Greater Oklahoma City Chamber of Commerce: 123 Park Ave., Oklahoma City, OK 73102. **Phone:** (405) 297-8900.

The chamber dispenses visitor information Mon.-Fri. 8:30-5.

TRANSPORTATION

Air Travel

Will Rogers World Airport is 10 miles southwest of downtown. Airport parking is $4-$23 per day. Cabs averages 20-30 minutes to the downtown area; the average cost is $20. Airport vans depart frequently and provide shuttle service between the airport and downtown for $17 per person.

Rental Cars

Several rental car agencies serve the Oklahoma City area both downtown and at the airport. Hertz, (405) 681-2341 or (800) 654-3080, offers discounts to AAA members.

Rail Service

Amtrak's Heartland Flyer provides daily train service between Oklahoma City and Fort Worth, Texas. The station is at 100 South E.K. Gaylord Blvd. For schedule and ticket information phone (800) 872-7245.

Buses

Greyhound Lines Inc., Jefferson Lines, MK & O Lines and Oklahoma Transportation Co. are the major bus lines that serve the city. They all operate out of the same terminal at 427 W. Sheridan Ave.; for schedule information phone (405) 235-6425.

Taxis

Cab companies include A1 Taxi Service, (405) 321-3111; Town Taxi, (405) 366-8999; and Yellow Cab, (405) 232-6161. Taxis are metered and charge $2-$3 per call and an additional $1.80-$2.25 per mile. There is a $1 charge for each additional passenger ages 6+.

Public Transport

METRO Transit operates buses, trolleys and boats throughout the metropolitan area. The main terminal is at 300 S.W. 7th St. Bus fare is $1.25; 60c (ages 6-17). Transfers are free.

Oklahoma Spirit Trolleys travel through the downtown area (the Red and Blue lines) and the I-40/Meridian corridor (the Orange line). The trolleys resemble traditional American streetcars. Red and Blue line fare is 25c; 10c (ages 6-17, ages 60+ and the physically impaired). The Orange line is $1; 50c (ages 6-17, ages 60+ and the physically impaired). A 1-day pass is $2; a 3-day pass is $3. Exact change is required. For schedule and route information for buses and trolleys phone (405) 235-7433.

Oklahoma River Cruises offers boat transportation on a 7-mile stretch of the Oklahoma River linking the downtown area with a concentration of lodgings along Meridian Avenue. The boats can be boarded for the 1.25-hour trip at the Regatta Park landing, 725 S. Lincoln Blvd. south of downtown, or the Meridian landing, near S.W. 15th Street and Meridian Avenue. One-way fare for the trips, which operate April through December, is $9; $8 (ages 60+ and the physically disabled Sat.-Sun.); $6 (ages 6-12); $4.50 (ages 60+ and the physically disabled Mon.-Fri.). Round-trip fare is $12; $11 (ages 60+ and the physically disabled Sat.-Sun.); $8 (ages 6-12); $6 (ages 60+ and the physically disabled Mon.-Fri.). Fares include same-day use of the trolley system. For schedule information phone (405) 702-7755.

along the city's east side with frequent interchanges. US 77 closely parallels I-35 and serves mostly local traffic. Also of importance is SR 3, which provides access to Will Rogers and Wiley Post airports as it skirts the city's west side.

I-240 (the Southwest Expressway) combines with I-44 and I-35 to form a loop around Oklahoma City, providing a bypass of the downtown area.

Getting Around

Street System

Except for the area around the Capitol and state office buildings, Oklahoma City is laid out in a grid pattern with streets either running north-south or east-west. The numbered streets run east-west both north and south of Main Street; named north-south streets intersect them. East-west address numbers start at Grand Avenue, and north-south numbers begin at Broadway.

Unless otherwise posted, the speed limit on most streets is 25 to 30 mph. Rush hour traffic, 7:30-9 a.m. and 4-6 p.m., should be avoided.

Parking

Ample parking is available downtown. There are many commercial garages, and most hotels provide parking for guests. Rates are $1-$2 per hour, or $7 per day.

What To See

45TH INFANTRY DIVISION MUSEUM, .7 mi. w. off I-35 at 2145 N.E. 36th St., traces Oklahoma's military history from 1541 to the present. Exhibited are items from Adolf Hitler's Munich office, uniforms, firearms and what is said to be the world's largest collection of Bill Mauldin's "Willie and Joe" cartoons. More than 60 military vehicles, aircraft and artillery are outdoors.

A military weapons collection illustrates the development of American military arms from the American Revolution to the Persian Gulf War. **Time:** Allow 1 hour minimum. **Hours:** Museum Tues.-Fri. 9-4:15, Sat. 10-4:15, Sun. 1-4:15. Outdoor military park closes 45 minutes after museum. Closed Jan. 1 and Dec. 25. **Cost:** Donations. **Phone:** (405) 424-5313.

99s MUSEUM OF WOMEN PILOTS is at 4300 Amelia Earhart Rd. at the entrance to Will Rogers World Airport. The 99s were founded in 1929 by a group of female pilots that included Amelia Earhart. Displays trace the history of women in aviation and include exhibits about Earhart, the 1929 Women's Air Derby, World War II, air racing and the space program. The group is named for the number of women who formed the group's original membership.

Time: Allow 1 hour minimum. **Hours:** Mon.-Fri. 9-4, Sat. 10-4. Closed major holidays. **Cost:** $5; $4 (ages 60+); $3 (students grades K-12). **Phone:** (405) 685-9990.

FRONTIER CITY, 12 mi. n. off I-35 exit 136 (Hefner Rd.) on the I-35N service road, is both a re-created 1880s Oklahoma town and an amusement

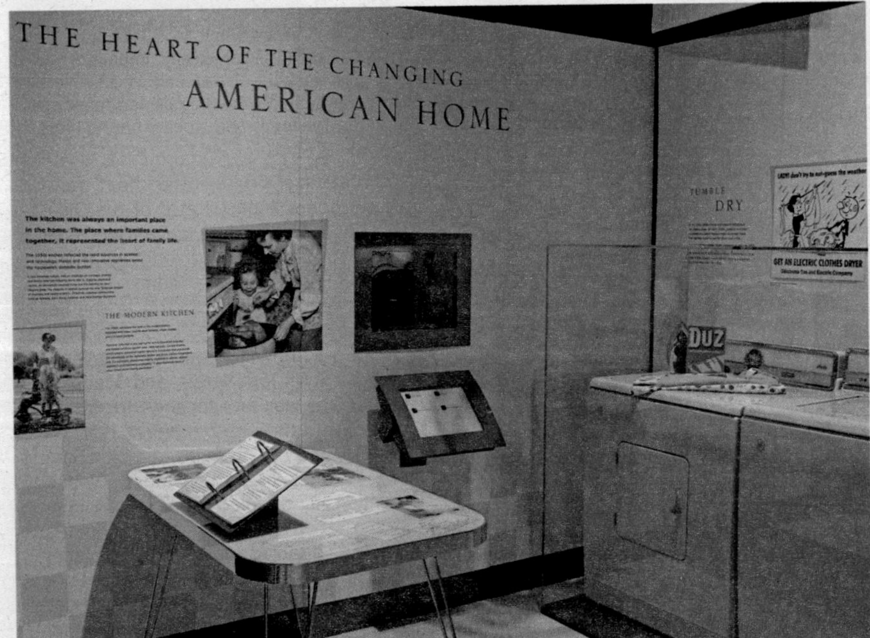

Oklahoma History Center / © Richard Cummins / Photolibrary

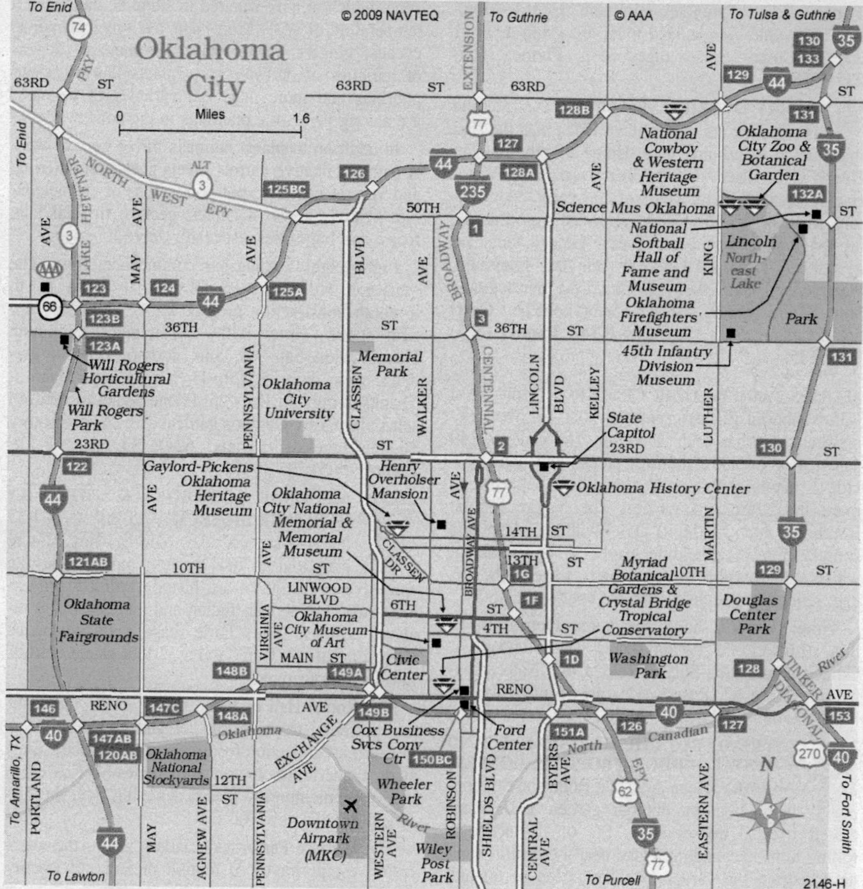

park. Featured are the vertical thrill ride Eruption and roller coasters, which include Steel Lasso, Diamond Back, Silver Bullet and Wildcat. Gunfights, live shows and musical reviews are staged daily.

Time: Allow 1 hour minimum. **Hours:** Mon.-Fri. 10:30-9, Sat. 10:30 a.m.-11 p.m., Sun. noon-9, Memorial Day to mid-Aug.; Fri. 6-11 p.m., Sat. noon-11, Sun. noon-10, in Oct.; Sat. 10:30-8, Sun. noon-7, late Mar.-day before Memorial Day; Sat.-Sun. noon-8, mid-Aug. through Sept. 30. Phone ahead to confirm schedule. **Cost:** $34.99; $19.99 (under 48" tall, senior citizens and the physically impaired); free (ages 0-2). **Parking:** $7. **Phone:** (405) 478-2140 or (405) 478-2412.

GEM **GAYLORD-PICKENS OKLAHOMA HERITAGE MUSEUM** is at jct. N.W. 13th St. and Shartel Ave. at 1400 Classen Dr. The museum's Oklahoma Through Its People gallery includes five interactive exhibits focusing on the state's heritage and its effect on the achievements and contributions of revered Oklahomans. The ONEOK Tell Your Story exhibit allows visitors to recount experiences and memories of their own heritage and keep a recording as a memento of their visit. Built in 1927, the building was formerly home to the Mid-Continent Life Insurance Co.; a tour of the company's president's office as furnished in the 1920s is offered.

The museum also houses the Oklahoma Hall of Fame, which honors the accomplishments of more than 600 individuals inducted since 1928, including Gene Autry, Reba McEntire, Mickey Mantle, Will Rogers and Jim Thorpe.

Time: Allow 1 hour minimum. **Hours:** Tues.-Fri. 9-5, Sat. 10-5. Closed Jan. 1, Thanksgiving and Dec. 25. **Cost:** $7; $5 (ages 6-17 and 62+). **Phone:** (405) 235-4458 or (888) 501-2059.

HARN HOMESTEAD & 1889ERS MUSEUM is at 1721 N. Lincoln Blvd. near N.E. 16th St. The property was the former estate of William Fremont Harn, a land agent responsible for investigating claim disputes arising from the land run of 1889. The 10-acre homestead includes a modified 1904 Victorian-style farmhouse, outbuildings, historic gardens and the city's first two-story structure.

A replica of the original cedar barn contains a rare indoor windmill that protrudes from the roof.

Time: Allow 30 minutes minimum. **Hours:** Mon.-Fri. 10-4. One-hour guided tours are given at 11, 1 and 3. **Cost:** $5; $4 (ages 65+). **Phone:** (405) 235-4058.

SAVE **HENRY OVERHOLSER MANSION,** 15th and N. Hudson sts. in Heritage Hills, was the first mansion in Oklahoma City. Home of city founder Henry Overholser, the building exemplifies Victorian residential architecture of the early 20th century. Most of the furnishings, imported from Europe, are original to the house. **Tours:** Guided tours are available. **Time:** Allow 30 minutes minimum. **Hours:** Wed.-Sat. 10-3, Feb.-Dec. Last tour begins 1 hour before closing. Closed major holidays. **Cost:** $5; $3 (ages 55+); $1 (ages 6-18). **Phone:** (405) 525-5325.

MARTIN PARK NATURE CENTER is 11 mi. w. of I-35 Memorial Rd. exit; enter at 5000 W. Memorial between Meridian and McArthur. The center's 140 acres of woodlands, prairies, creeks and pond provide a natural habitat for armadillos, beavers and more than 200 bird species. The Nature Exhibit Building contains exhibits about wildlife, plants and conservation. Self-guiding nature trails, some of which are accessible to wheelchairs, traverse the refuge; guided nature hikes also are conducted.

Time: Allow 2 hours minimum. **Hours:** Wed.-Sun. 9-6; closed holidays and Dec. 24-Jan. 1. Guided nature hike Sun. at 2:30. **Cost:** Nature center free. Hike $2. Reservations are required for the hike. **Phone:** (405) 755-0676.

GEM SAVE **MYRIAD BOTANICAL GARDENS AND CRYSTAL BRIDGE TROPICAL CONSERVATORY,** Reno Ave. and Robinson St., contains both an outdoor garden and an enclosed tropical conservatory. Set on 17 acres of rolling hills surrounding a lake near the central business district, the garden was the vision of oil and gas magnate Dean A. McGee, CEO of Kerr-McGee Corp. Architect I.M. Pei was commissioned to create McGee's dream.

The result is a stunning, serene landscape that includes a lake with huge koi and goldfish, winding paths, fountains, hundreds of trees and an assortment of colorful plantings that bloom from winter through fall. Sculptures add to the enchanting scene, and a bridge across the lake provides views of the city's skyline. Among the flowers that blossom at differing times during the year are pansies, wisteria, daylilies, peonies, daffodils, tulips, chrysanthemums and black-eyed Susans.

The 224-foot-long, seven-story-high conservatory is a cylinder 70 feet in diameter made of more than 3,000 translucent acrylic panels. You know you're in a tropical environment as soon as you enter and the warm, humid air envelops you.

The conservatory is divided into two areas: the Tropical Rain Forest Zone (known as the Wet Mountain) and the Dry Tropical Zone (Dry Mountain). The lush wet zone is where you'll find a 35-foot waterfall and a skywalk across the center of the conservatory that offers panoramic views. The dry zone, which is only watered in summer, can reach a temperature of 95 F. More than 100 types of palms, cycads, gingers, funnel-shaped bromeliads, dozens of varieties of orchids, spiny plants known as euphorbias and more than 100 varieties of begonias are among the exotic plantings in the conservatory.

In addition to plants, animals thrive here as well. A pair of talkative parrots greets guests on entering, and visitors can also spot populations of chameleon-like lizards known as anoles; geckos; tropical fish; frogs; and butterflies, especially zebra longwings.

Lightweight clothing is recommended. **Note:** The attraction will close in May 2010 for a 6- to 8-month construction project. Phone ahead to confirm status. **Time:** Allow 30 minutes minimum. **Hours:** Mon.-Sat. 9-6, Sun. noon-6. Outdoor gardens open daily 6 a.m.-11 p.m. Closed Jan. 1, Thanksgiving and Dec. 25. Phone ahead to confirm schedule. **Cost:** Outdoor gardens free. Conservatory $6; $5 (ages 13-18 and 62+); $3 (ages 4-12). **Phone:** (405) 297-3995.

GEM SAVE **NATIONAL COWBOY & WESTERN HERITAGE MUSEUM** is .5 mi. w. of I-35 via I-44 at 1700 N.E. 63rd St. This 32-acre memorial to our Western pioneers has an extensive collection of art, historic artifacts and exhibits about American Indian and pioneer life in realistic settings. James Earle Fraser's 18-foot statue "The End of the Trail" and a 33-foot statue of Buffalo Bill are featured.

The Rodeo Hall of Fame has legendary performers' portraits, trophies, saddles and memorabilia. A Western art collection features works by Albert Bierstadt, Frederic Remington and Charles M. Russell as well as contemporary pieces depicting both the historical and the new West.

The Western Performers Gallery shows the idealized West portrayed in motion pictures. Prosperity Junction replicates a circa 1900 western cattle town at dusk with full-size structures, including a saloon, school and church.

Time: Allow 2 hours minimum. **Hours:** Daily 9-5. Closed Jan. 1, Thanksgiving and Dec. 25. **Cost:** $10; $8.50 (ages 62+ and students with ID); $4.50 (ages 6-12). **Phone:** (405) 478-2250.

NATIONAL SOFTBALL HALL OF FAME AND MUSEUM, off I-35 at 2801 N.E. 50th St., presents the history and honors the greats of this popular amateur sport. **Time:** Allow 30 minutes minimum. **Hours:** Mon.-Fri. 9-4, Sat. 10-4, Sun. 1-4, Memorial Day-Labor Day; Mon.-Fri. 9-4, rest of year. Closed Jan. 1, Thanksgiving and Dec. 25. **Cost:** $6; $3 (ages 0-14). **Phone:** (405) 424-5266 ext. 0.

OKLAHOMA CITY MUSEUM OF ART is at 415 Couch Dr. The three-level structure offers visitors a collection of American and European art, including a comprehensive group of glass sculptures by Dale Chihuly, and also hosts special exhibitions drawn from throughout the world.

Galleries feature portraits, landscapes, modern art, photography, sculpture, abstract art and decorative and fine arts. A repertoire cinema presents international, independent and classic films.

Audio tours are available. **Time:** Allow 1 hour, 30 minutes minimum. **Hours:** Museum Tues.-Sat. 10-5 (also Thurs. 5-9), Sun. noon-5. Films are shown Thurs.-Sun.; phone ahead for schedule. Closed Jan. 1, July 4, Thanksgiving and Dec. 25. **Cost:** Museum $12; $10 (ages 62+ and students with ID). Films $8; $6 (ages 62+ and students with ID). **Phone:** (405) 236-3100 or (800) 579-9278.

GEM **OKLAHOMA CITY NATIONAL MEMORIAL & MUSEUM,** bordered by Robinson and Harvey aves. and 4th and 6th sts., was built in remembrance of the victims, survivors and rescuers of the Alfred P. Murrah Federal Building bombing on Apr. 19, 1995. Twin gates, marking the east and west entrances to the memorial, represent 9:01 and 9:03, the minutes before and after the tragedy.

Each of the 168 lives lost is represented by a chair made of bronze, stone and glass. The plot used for the field of chairs is the same size and configuration as the blueprint of the destroyed building. The memorial also has a reflecting pool; a special area for children; and the Survivor Tree, a 60-year-old American elm that miraculously withstood the blast. **Hours:** Daily 24 hours. Rangers are on-site 9-5:30. **Cost:** Free. **Phone:** (405) 235-3313 or (888) 542-4673.

GEM **Memorial Museum** is at 620 N. Harvey Ave., on the Oklahoma City National Memorial site. In the former Journal Record Building that withstood the bombing of the Murrah Federal Building, the museum's galleries serve as a timeline of that event, beginning with the morning of Apr. 19, 1995. From the first exhibit depicting everyday morning activities in Oklahoma City through the last exhibit about hope for the future, the museum examines various aspects of that act of terrorism.

Audiotape from a hearing being conducted across the street provides the sounds of the explosion and the resulting panic and confusion. Media coverage of the event is shown, as the story moves from rescue and recovery to investigation and capture. Stories told by survivors, family members and rescuers provide personal remembrances of the tragedy. The Gallery of Honor is a tribute to the 168 lives lost.

Time: Allow 2 hours minimum. **Hours:** Mon.-Sat. 9-6, Sun. 1-6. Last admission 1 hour before closing. Closed Jan. 1, Thanksgiving and Dec. 24-25. **Cost:** $10; $8 (ages 62+); $6 (ages 6-17 and college students with ID). **Phone:** (405) 235-3313 or (888) 542-4673.

GEM **OKLAHOMA CITY ZOO & BOTANICAL GARDEN,** at Martin Luther King Ave. and Remington Pl., is home to more than 2,100 animals, including 50 endangered or threatened species. Great EscApe features gorillas, orangutans and chimpanzees in a rain forest environment. Cat Forest/Lion Overlook is a naturalistic habitat for large and small wild cats. The 8-acre Oklahoma Trails exhibit is home to more than 800 animals native to Oklahoma, including grizzly and black bears, mountain lions, river otters, bobcats and bison.

The Fins and Feathers Show, within the marine life attraction Aquaticus, features sea lions Midge and Moe and a group of their bird friends performing in 15- to 20-minute shows. Rides are available on the Endangered Species Carousel, Centennial Choo Choo and the Safari Tram for additional fees.

Time: Allow 2 hours minimum. **Hours:** Zoo daily 9-5. Aquaticus performances Wed.-Fri. at 10 and noon, Sat. at 10, noon and 2, Sun. at noon and 2 (weather permitting). Closed Jan. 1, Thanksgiving and Dec. 25. **Cost:** $7; $4 (ages 3-11 and 65+). Aquaticus shows $2; $1 (ages 3-11). **Phone:** (405) 424-3344.

OKLAHOMA FIREFIGHTERS' MUSEUM, 2716 N.E. 50th St., contains a collection of antique fire apparatuses, tools and machinery used since 1736. Highlights of the collection include an early 20th-century "Metropolitan" steamer and a reconstruction of the first fire station in Oklahoma. **Hours:** Mon.-Sat. 9-4:30, Sun. 1-4:30. Closed major holidays. **Cost:** $5; $4 (ages 55+); $2 (ages 6-12). **Phone:** (405) 424-3440.

GEM **OKLAHOMA HISTORY CENTER,** 2401 N. Laird Ave., showcases the state's history with its thousands of artifacts and more than 200 interactive exhibits in five galleries. Topics include aviation, commerce, culture, geology, heritage and transportation. Major exhibits depict the history of American Indian tribes living in the state and settler life during the Oklahoma land runs.

Outdoor sculptures, four oil derricks and the .25-mile Red River Journey, which replicates the river valley and its plant life, adorn the grounds. Extensive archives and research materials, including genealogy records and newspapers, are available.

Time: Allow 2 hours minimum. **Hours:** Mon.-Sat. 10-5. Closed Jan. 1, Thanksgiving and Dec. 25. **Cost:** $5; $4 (ages 62+); $3 (students with ID); free (ages 0-5); $15 (family, up to six people). **Phone:** (405) 522-5248.

GEM **SCIENCE MUSEUM OKLAHOMA** is at jct. N.E. 52nd St. and Martin Luther King Ave. This science center, a Smithsonian affiliate, features more than 350 interactive exhibits; thousands of space, aviation and cultural artifacts; a planetarium; two halls of fame; and the Dome Theater.

Science Live! is a daily, live entertainment performance that engages the audience in scientific fun. A Segway course lets visitors ride one of these vehicles and navigate an obstacle course. Gadget Trees is a gigantic tree house with one of the longest spiral slides in the country. Destination Space looks at the challenges of manned space exploration, while Tinkering Garage lets visitors be creative and build imaginative structures. The Dome Theater's 70-foot screen and sound system immerse IMAX moviegoers in a larger-than-life movie experience.

The Oklahoma Aviation and Space Hall of Fame honors Oklahoma natives who have made significant contributions to flight, and the International Gymnastics Hall of Fame recognizes champions of one of the world's oldest sports through portraits, videos, medals, apparatuses and sculptures.

Time: Allow 2 hours minimum. **Hours:** Mon.-Fri. 9-5, Sat. 9-6, Sun. 11-6. Closed Thanksgiving and Dec. 24-25. **Cost:** $10.95 (includes all permanent exhibits, Science Live!, planetarium and museums); $8.95 (ages 3-12 and 65+). Dome Theater only $8.45; $6.95 (ages 3-12 and 65+). Combination rate with Dome Theater $14.95; $11.95 (ages 3-12 and 65+). An additional fee may be charged for traveling exhibits. **Phone:** (405) 602-6664.

Red Earth Museum, in Science Museum Oklahoma at 2100 N.E. 52nd St., examines American Indian cultures and lifestyles through displays of artifacts and art dating from prehistory. Highlights include totem poles and an extensive collection of cradleboards representing the craftsmanship of Indian tribes from throughout the United States. **Hours:** Mon.-Fri. 9-5, Sat. 9-6, Sun. 11-6. Closed Thanksgiving and Dec. 24-25. **Cost:** Included with fee for Science Museum Oklahoma. **Phone:** (405) 427-5228.

STATE CAPITOL, 2300 Lincoln Blvd., is an adaptation of classical Greek and Roman architecture. On the grounds is the Capitol Site No. 1 oil well, originally nicknamed Petunia No. 1 because drilling began in November 1941 in the middle of a flower bed. The building is the only Capitol in the world with an oil well beneath it.

At the south entrance is "Statue of a Cowboy," by Constance Warren. A bronze statue of an American Indian caps the dome. **Time:** Allow 1 hour minimum. **Hours:** Mon.-Fri. 7-7, Sat.-Sun. and holidays 9-4. Guided tours of the building are offered on the hour Mon.-Fri. 9-11 and 1-3. **Cost:** Free. **Phone:** (405) 521-3356.

WHITE WATER BAY, 5 mi. w. off I-40 exit 145 (Meridian Ave.) at 3908 W. Reno, is a 20-acre water park with more than 30 water rides, including a giant wave pool, waterslides, body flumes, inner tube courses and activity pools as well as a children's playland.

Time: Allow 1 hour minimum. **Hours:** Mon.-Thurs. 10:30-7, Fri.-Sun. 10:30-8, Memorial Day-early Aug.; Sat.-Sun. 10:30-6, mid-May through day before Memorial Day and mid-Aug. through Labor Day. Schedule varies early Aug. to mid-Aug.; phone ahead. **Cost:** $25.99; $21.99 (under 48 inches tall and senior citizens); free (ages 0-2). **Parking:** $5. **Phone:** (405) 478-2140.

WILL ROGERS HORTICULTURAL GARDENS is just w. off I-44 exit 123A at 3400 N.W. 36th St. Within the gardens are the Ed Lycan Conservatory, where visitors can enjoy a large cacti and succulent collection; the arboretum, planted mostly with trees native to Oklahoma, such as oaks, junipers, crab apples, crape myrtles and redbuds; a 2-acre rose garden; irises, daylilies and peonies; and a bust of the state's favorite son on the north side of the lake.

The azaleas are impressive when they bloom in the spring. **Time:** Allow 30 minutes minimum. **Hours:** Daily 7-7, Apr.-Oct.; 7-4, rest of year. **Cost:** Free. **Phone:** (405) 943-0827.

What To Do

Sports and Recreation

Oklahoma City's parks offer the setting for almost any activity. **Tennis, swimming** and **picnicking** facilities are plentiful at Will Rogers Park, 36th Street and N. Portland. **Boating** and **fishing** are popular at lakes Hefner, Draper and Overholser. Lake Hefner is particularly known for its good **sailing. Water skiing** can be enjoyed at Draper Lake.

Additionally, **jogging** trails are available at Earlywine Park, S.W. 119th and May; Lake Hefner, N. Grand Boulevard between May and Portland; and Memorial Park, 34th and Classen. The Oklahoma City Parks and Recreation Department offers information about all of their facilities; phone (405) 297-2211.

Golf courses are readily available. Public links include nine-hole courses such as Brookside Golf Course, 9016 S. Shields Blvd.; Lakeside Golf Course, 3400 N. Eastern Ave.; and The Links Golf & Athletic Club, 700 N.E. 122nd St. For 18-hole courses offerings include Earlywine Golf Course, 11600 S. Portland Ave; Lake Hefner Golf Course, 4491 S. Lake Hefner Dr.; Lincoln Park Golf Course, 4001 N.E. Grand Blvd.; and Trosper Golf Club, 2301 S.E. 29th St.

Spectator sports also are favorite pastimes. The RedHawks, the Triple A **baseball** farm team of the Texas Rangers, draw fans every spring to AT&T Bricktown Ballpark, 2 S. Mickey Mantle Dr.; phone (405) 218-1000. Fall welcomes college **football** as the University of Oklahoma's Sooners, members of the Big Twelve conference, begin their season at Owen Field in Norman; phone (405) 325-2424 or (800) 456-4668.

Basketball rounds out the sports year. The National Basketball Association's newest team, the Oklahoma City Thunder—formerly the Seattle SuperSonics—plays at Ford Center, 100 W. Reno Ave. The team is in action from late October to mid-April; phone (405) 602-8700. Oklahoma City University's Stars play at Freede Center, N.W. 27th and Florida streets; phone (405) 208-4667. The Sooners from the University of Oklahoma compete at Lloyd Noble Center in Norman; phone (405) 325-2424.

State Fair Speedway at 444 Land Rush is the scene of **automobile racing** on Friday nights from late March to mid-September; phone (405) 948-6796. The city also plays host to a number of **rodeos** and **horse shows** throughout the year *(see Special Events)*. The Remington Park pari-mutuel racetrack at US 35 and US 44 offers quarter horse and Thoroughbred **horse racing**; phone (405) 424-1000.

Note: Policies concerning admittance of children to pari-mutuel betting facilities vary. Phone for information.

Shopping

Whether you are looking for Western wear or the latest in high fashion, you can find it in Oklahoma City's department stores and specialty shops.

Establishments that sell cowboy hats, boots and belts are Cattlemen's Western Wear, 1312 S. Agnew Ave.; Langston's Western Wear, 2224 Exchange Ave.; Sheplers Western Wear, 812 S. Meridian; and Tener's, 4320 W. Reno. Other characteristic Oklahoma City purchases are American Indian art and jewelry.

Several enclosed malls are convenient for one-stop shopping. To the north is the posh 50 Penn Place, N.W. 50th and Pennsylvania Avenue, noted for its exclusive shops. Across the street is Penn Square Mall, one of the largest malls in the area, where Dillard's, JCPenney and Macy's are the anchor stores. Also north of the city is Quail Springs, Memorial Road at Pennsylvania Avenue, with anchors Dillard's, JCPenney, Macy's and Sears.

Shops, nightclubs and restaurants crowd the historic commercial area known as Bricktown, named for its many turn-of-the-20th-century red brick warehouses. A canal lined with eateries offering outdoor seating winds through Bricktown and links downtown OKC with parks and the Oklahoma River.

Performing Arts

Oklahoma City offers a diverse palette of cultural entertainment. Ballet Oklahoma, (405) 848-8637, stages elaborate productions at the Civic Center Music Hall, 201 N. Walker Ave. The music hall also is the home of the Oklahoma City Philharmonic, (405) 232-7575, which performs both classical and pop music. Their seasons run concurrently from September through May. The Chamber Music Series of Oklahoma City, (405) 974-2415, complements the symphony's season with its concerts at Christ the King Church, 8005 Dorset Dr., from October to early April.

Oklahoma City University's music school also contributes to the performing arts scene with six musical performances and vocal and instrumental performances scheduled throughout the year; phone (405) 208-5345 or (800) 633-7242. The Canterbury Choral Society, (405) 232-7464, performs October through May at the Civic Center Music Hall.

In summer the great outdoors provides a showcase for pop and rock concerts at the amphitheaters at Frontier City and the Oklahoma City Zoo & Botanical Garden. Plenty of guitar playin', banjo pickin' and foot stompin' goes on at Del City's Oklahoma Country-Western Museum and Hall of Fame, 3925 S.E. 29th St., during Blue Grass Music Society performances on the second Saturday of each month from September through May. Country music is the theme Saturday nights at the Oklahoma Opry, 404 W. Commerce; phone (405) 632-8322.

Oklahoma City's theater scene offers several choices. The productions of the Black Liberated Arts Center focus on African American culture and are held at various locations throughout the city; phone (405) 524-3800. A professional summer stock company, the Lyric Theatre, performs musicals from June through August at the Civic Center Music Hall; for ticket information phone (405) 297-2264.

Locals show their talent in a six-play season of musicals and dramas at the Jewel Box Theatre, 3700 N. Walker; phone (405) 521-1786.

Special Events

Home of the National Cowboy & Western Heritage Museum, Oklahoma City also pays tribute to the cowboy's trusted companion, the horse. Several national and international horse shows and at least 20 state and regional competitions are held throughout the year. The major shows take place at the State Fairgrounds Arena at 10th and N. May.

The Grand National Morgan Horse Show is held in October. The World Championship Quarter Horse Show is in mid-November. The season ends in December with the Barrel Racing Futurity and the National Reining Futurity. In a similar Western vein, the GEM Chuck Wagon Gathering and Children's Cowboy Festival, held in late May, is a family event featuring chuck wagon cooks from across the country as well as entertainment.

With a large American Indian population, Oklahoma is rich with American Indian culture and tradition. One such tradition is the powwow, when tribe members in full costume gather for days filled with traditional competitions, dance, music and food. These powwows take place throughout the summer, and many are held in Oklahoma City.

One of the largest powwows is the Red Earth Festival; representatives from more than 100 tribes gather during the first weekend in June to celebrate and share their heritage. For more information about this and other events contact the Oklahoma City Convention and Visitors Bureau; phone (405) 297-8912.

The city celebrates the visual and performing arts during April and September art festivals held in area parks; the events feature singers and musicians performing throughout the day as well as artists displaying their works. The activity is enhanced by food stands serving international cuisines. One such show, An Affair of the Heart, takes place in February and October and includes 1,000 art and craft exhibitors.

In September the Oklahoma State Fair transforms the 435-acre State Fairgrounds into a lively happening. One of the largest state fairs in the country, the 11-day event features ice shows, car races, livestock and cooking contests and a rodeo. Closing out the year, the GEM Garden Lights celebration, held the day after Thanksgiving through the end of the year at Myriad Botanical Gardens and Crystal Bridge Tropical Conservatory, glows with thousands of twinkling lights among the trees and trails.

The Oklahoma City Vicinity

EL RENO (H-1) pop. 16,212, elev. 1,360'

El Reno was established in June 1889 when the Rock Island Railroad picked a site on the south bank of the North Canadian River for a depot. Angry citizens of nearby Reno City decided they did not want to be left out of any future railroad riches. They packed their belongings and loaded their houses, stores and even a hotel onto log rollers, forded the river and resettled in the new town of El Reno.

The Heritage Express Trolley transports riders Wednesday through Sunday from Heritage Park through the downtown area. A scenic portion of US 81 runs 12 miles south from El Reno through the Canadian River Valley to Minco.

El Reno Chamber of Commerce: 206 N. Bickford, El Reno, OK 73036. **Phone:** (405) 262-1188.

CANADIAN COUNTY HISTORICAL MUSEUM, 300 S. Grand, is housed in the 1906 Rock Island Depot and features American Indian objects, vintage clothing, toys and model trains as well as the depot's original ticket office, a doctor's office and an old fashioned kitchen.

Relocated historic buildings on the museum grounds include a 1910 school house, an 1892 hotel, a 1918 Red Cross canteen, a 19th-century jail, a Mennonite church and a restored caboose. Trolley rides are offered. **Time:** Allow 30 minutes minimum. **Hours:** Wed.-Sat. 10-5, Sun. 1-5. Closed Jan. 1, July 4, Thanksgiving and Dec. 25. **Cost:** Donations. Trolley rides $3; $1.50 (ages 0-11 and 65+). **Phone:** (405) 262-5121.

HISTORIC FORT RENO, 7107 W. Cheyenne, began as a military camp in 1874 at the Darlington Indian Agency. A year later a permanent military reservation was established as a base for U.S. cavalry and infantry units. The fort also served as a frontier post, an army remount station 1908-47 and as a POW camp for captured German soldiers during World War II.

Visitors may walk through its chapel and cemetery. A visitor center features historic photographs and other memorabilia. **Hours:** Mon.-Fri. 10-5, Sat.-Sun. 10-4. Closed Jan. 1 and Dec. 25. **Cost:** Donations. **Phone:** (405) 262-3987.

GUTHRIE (F-2) pop. 9,925, elev. 961'

As the focal point of the 1889 Oklahoma land rush, Guthrie became a tent city of 15,000 residents by nightfall on April 22, 1889, the day the Unassigned Lands of Oklahoma were officially opened for settlement. Oklahoma was admitted to the Union in 1907, and Guthrie became the first capital of the state. At some point in their lives, Lon Chaney, Tom Mix, Carry Nation and Will Rogers all lived in Guthrie.

Ninety percent of Guthrie's original buildings remain intact; the city has one of the largest districts on the National Register of Historic Places. French architect Joseph Foucart designed most of the town's eclectic Victorian structures.

The Pollard Theater, a renovated early 20th-century opera house at 120 W. Harrison, presents productions performed by Guthrie's resident theater company. Houses dating from Guthrie's territorial and early statehood days line E. Harrison, Oklahoma, Cleveland, Noble and Warner streets. Trolley tours of the historic district depart from the intersection of 2nd and Harrison; phone (405) 282-6000.

Guthrie Convention and Visitors Bureau: 212 W. Oklahoma, P.O. Box 995, Guthrie, OK 73044. **Phone:** (405) 282-1947 or (800) 299-1889.

OKLAHOMA SPORTS MUSEUM is at 315 W. Oklahoma Ave. The museum houses a collection of memorabilia honoring athletes, coaches and sports teams with connections to Oklahoma. Sports celebrities and champions highlighted include Troy Aikman, Mickey Mantle, Shannon Miller and Jim Thorpe. **Time:** Allow 1 hour minimum. **Hours:** Tues.-Sat. 10-4. Closed major holidays. **Cost:** $5; $3 (ages 60+); $1 (children); $10 (family). **Phone:** (405) 260-1342.

OKLAHOMA TERRITORIAL MUSEUM, 406 E. Oklahoma Ave., contains exhibits and artifacts pertaining to life in territorial Oklahoma and the land run of 1889. The Carnegie Library, part of the complex, was built 1902-03 and was the site of the inaugurations of the last territorial governor and the first state governor. **Time:** Allow 1 hour minimum. **Hours:** Tues.-Sat. 9-5. Closed major holidays. **Cost:** Donations. **Phone:** (405) 282-1889.

SCOTTISH RITE MASONIC TEMPLE, 900 E. Oklahoma Ave., sits on the site originally intended for the state capitol building. The temple bought the land for $1, and a promise to administer "certain improvements," after the state capital relocated to Oklahoma City. These improvements totaled more than $3 million and have created the Gothic, Egyptian, Victorian, Italian and American Indian embellishments found within this Greek Revival building.

Time: Allow 1 hour minimum. **Hours:** Tours are given Mon.-Fri. at 10 and 2; closed holidays and during Masonic functions. **Cost:** Fee $5; free (students with ID and children). Students and children must be accompanied by an adult. **Phone:** (405) 282-1281.

STATE CAPITAL PUBLISHING MUSEUM, 301 W. Harrison St., is in a restored 1902 Victorian commercial structure that was the home of the first newspaper published in the Oklahoma Territory. High ceilings, ornate gilt radiators and intricate grillwork and woodwork distinguish the building.

The museum contains documents and equipment relating to the history of territorial newspaper publishing and printing in the state.

Note: The museum is temporarily closed due to budget cuts; phone for more information. **Time:** Allow 30 minutes minimum. **Hours:** Thurs.-Sat. 9-5. Closed major holidays. Phone ahead to confirm schedule. **Cost:** Donations. **Phone:** (405) 282-1889.

LANGSTON (C-8) pop. 1,670, elev. 955′

MELVIN B. TOLSON BLACK HERITAGE CENTER is on the first floor of Sanford Hall on the campus of Langston University. Named in honor of award-winning poet Melvin B. Tolson, an English and drama professor at the historically black institution 1947-65, the center is a repository of materials relating to the black experience, including books, videos and periodicals in addition to collections of African and African-American arts and crafts.

In addition to his academic achievements, Tolson also served four terms as mayor of Langston and as poet laureate of Liberia. **Time:** Allow 30 minutes minimum. **Hours:** Mon.-Fri. 8-5 (also Thurs. 5-8), mid-Aug. to late May; Mon.-Fri. 8-5, rest of year. Closed major holidays. **Cost:** Free. **Phone:** (405) 466-3346.

NORMAN (I-2) pop. 95,694, elev. 1,168′

Shortly after its 1889 beginnings and with a population of 500, Norman boasted four churches, two newspapers and 29 businesses. A year later the University of Oklahoma was established.

The Norman and Cleveland County Historical Museum, 508 N. Peters Ave., is in a 1900 Queen Anne-style house once owned by William S. Moore, a Norman businessman. Tours of the house are available; phone (405) 321-0156.

Recreational opportunities in the Norman vicinity are available at Lake Thunderbird State Park, 13 miles east on SR 9. *See Recreation Chart.*

Norman Convention and Visitors Bureau: 223 E. Main St., Norman, OK 73069. **Phone:** (405) 366-8095 or (800) 767-7260.

Shopping areas: Dillard's, JCPenney and Sears are the anchor stores at Sooner Mall, 3301 W. Main St.

LITTLE RIVER ZOO is at 3405 S.E. 120th Ave. More than 400 animals, including rescued wildlife, make their home at this 55-acre refuge. A guided tour includes a petting zoo and kangaroo enclosure where visitors can hand-feed animals. **Time:** Allow 1 hour minimum. **Hours:** Daily 10-5. **Cost:** $8; $6 (ages 55+); $5 (ages 3-11). **Phone:** (405) 366-7229.

GEM **UNIVERSITY OF OKLAHOMA,** off I-35 Lindsey St. exit, is a national research university with more than 30,000 students and 1,700 faculty members. The 3,000-acre campus houses 13 colleges; seven medical and health-related colleges are at sites in Tulsa and Oklahoma City. The university is a national leader in meteorology and energy-related disciplines. Tours can be arranged at the visitor center in Jacobson Hall, 550 Parrington Oval.

Time: Allow 2 hours minimum. **Hours:** Tours are available Mon.-Fri. at 9 and 2, Sat. at 9:30. Closed holidays and holiday weekends. **Cost:** Free. **Phone:** (405) 325-2151 or (800) 234-6868.

Fred Jones Jr. Museum of Art, 555 Elm Ave. on the University of Oklahoma campus, includes French Impressionism works, American Indian art and contemporary American pieces from its permanent collection as well as rotating exhibitions throughout the year. Special events are held weekly.

Time: Allow 1 hour, 30 minutes minimum. **Hours:** Tues.-Fri. 10-5 (also Fri. 5-9), Sun. 1-5. Closed major holidays. **Cost:** $5; $4 (ages 65+); $3 (ages 6-17); free (Tues.). **Phone:** (405) 325-3272.

SAVE **Sam Noble Oklahoma Museum of Natural History,** 2401 Chautauqua Ave. on the University of Oklahoma campus, offers a look back 300 million years at the state's natural history. Visitors can experience hands-on science activities, view dinosaur skeletons and walk through realistic dioramas that depict outdoor settings. Also displayed are artifacts from worldwide civilizations.

Time: Allow 1 hour, 30 minutes minimum. **Hours:** Mon.-Sat. 10-5, Sun. 1-5. Closed Jan. 1, Thanksgiving and Dec. 25. **Cost:** $5; $4 (ages 65+

and military with ID); $3 (ages 6-17); free (first Mon. of the month). **Phone:** (405) 325-4712.

W.B. Bizzell Memorial Library, 401 W. Brooks on the University of Oklahoma campus, has more than 4 million volumes. There are five special collections: the History of Science Collection, with books by Charles Darwin, Galileo and others; the Western History Collection, which includes historical photographs, books and manuscripts; the Bass Business History Collection; the Carl Albert Congressional Archives, which contain congressional papers; and the Nichols Bible Collection.

Allow 30 minutes minimum. **Hours:** Library open Mon.-Sat. at 7:30, Sun. at noon; closing times vary. Closed major holidays. Phone ahead to confirm schedule. **Cost:** Free. **Phone:** (405) 325-4142.

SHAWNEE (H-4) pop. 28,692, elev. 1,043'

Shawnee was settled in a matter of minutes after the American Indian Territory of which it was a part was opened to pioneer settlement. Emerging as a bustling railroad town, Shawnee made a bid to become the capital of Oklahoma in 1910 but lost the honor to Oklahoma City. The town's fortunes turned, however, with the discovery of oil in 1926. Since then Shawnee's industry has diversified to include the manufacture of electronic equipment, aircraft parts, clothing and hair dryers.

Shawnee Convention and Visitors Bureau: 131 N. Bell, P.O. Box 1613, Shawnee, OK 74802. **Phone:** (405) 275-9780 or (888) 404-9633.

MABEE-GERRER MUSEUM OF ART is at 1900 W. MacArthur St. on the campus of St. Gregory's University. The museum, which has collections of Renaissance art and antiquities, also sponsors changing contemporary exhibits. African, Greek, American Indian and 19th-century American and European art is displayed at various times throughout the year.

Time: Allow 1 hour, 30 minutes minimum. **Hours:** Tues.-Sat. 10-5, Sun. 1-4. Closed major holidays. **Cost:** $5; $4 (ages 65+); $3 (ages 6-16 and students with ID). **Phone:** (405) 878-5300.

SANTA FE DEPOT MUSEUM, 614 E. Main St., is in a building that was once the town's train depot. The museum chronicles Shawnee's history with antique automobiles, dolls, furniture, clothing, tools and a pump organ. Also on the grounds is the first house built in Shawnee. **Time:** Allow 1 hour minimum. **Hours:** Tues.-Fri. 10-4, Sat.-Sun. 2-4. Closed major holidays. **Cost:** $2; $1 (students with ID). **Phone:** (405) 275-8412.

Oklahoma City National Memorial & Museum / © Michael Snell / Alamy

This ends listings for the Oklahoma City Vicinity.
The following page resumes the alphabetical listings of cities in Oklahoma.

OKMULGEE (D-10) pop. 13,022, elev. 678′

Okmulgee, a Creek word meaning "bubbling water," was capital of the Muscogee Creek Nation a half century before Oklahoma became a state, and it remains the capital.

Dripping Springs State Park, 6 miles west of town on SR 56 to 16830 Dripping Springs Rd., offers camping, swimming, fishing and boating; phone (918) 756-5971. *See Recreation Chart.*

Okmulgee Tourism Development: 112 N. Morton, Okmulgee, OK 74447. **Phone:** (918) 758-1015.

CREEK COUNCIL HOUSE MUSEUM, 106 W. 6th St., dates from 1878 and was the seat of tribal government until statehood. The museum contains Muscogee Creek Indian craftwork and historical documents and artifacts. **Time:** Allow 1 hour minimum. **Hours:** Tues.-Sat. 10-4:30. Closed Jan. 1, Thanksgiving and Dec. 25. **Cost:** Donations. **Phone:** (918) 756-2324.

OOLOGAH—*see Tulsa p. 288.*

OUACHITA NATIONAL FOREST—

see place listing in Arkansas p. 54.

PARK HILL (C-12) pop. 3,936, elev. 740′

CHEROKEE HERITAGE CENTER, 21192 S. Keeler Dr., is at the site of the first Cherokee Female Seminary; three columns remain after fire destroyed the building in 1887. The center, operated by the Cherokee National Historical Society, includes three sites in addition to an archives and genealogy center that maintain historical records.

Hours: Mon.-Sat. 10-5, Sun. 1-5, Feb.-Dec. Closed Easter, Thanksgiving and Dec. 24-25. **Cost:** $8.50 (includes Adams Corner Rural Village, Cherokee National Museum and Tsa-La-Gi Ancient Village); $7.50 (ages 55+ and college students with ID); $5 (ages 5-18). **Phone:** (918) 456-6007 or (888) 999-6007.

Adams Corner Rural Village, entered through the Cherokee Heritage Center, is a detailed reconstruction of a small crossroads community dating 1875-90, the final years of the Old Cherokee Nation. A working general store is stocked with old-fashioned items as well as candy and snacks. Demonstrations include quilting, woodworking and fingerweaving (a means of weaving items without using a loom). A farm features animals typical of this period.

Hours: Mon.-Sat. 10-5, Sun. 1-5, Feb.-Dec. Closed Easter, Thanksgiving and Dec. 24-25. **Cost:** $8.50 (includes Cherokee National Museum and Tsa-La-Gi Ancient Village); $7.50 (ages 55+ and college students with ID); $5 (ages 5-18). **Phone:** (918) 456-6007 or (888) 999-6007.

Cherokee National Museum, 21192 S. Keeler Dr., uses multimedia exhibits, displays, artifacts and artwork to depict the history of the Cherokees from the white man's arrival in North America to the present. A highlight is the Trail of Tears exhibit.

Time: Allow 1 hour minimum. **Hours:** Mon.-Sat. 10-5, Sun. 1-5, Feb.-Dec. Closed Easter, Thanksgiving and Dec. 24-25. **Cost:** $8.50 (includes Adams Corner Rural Village and Tsa-La-Gi Ancient Village); $7.50 (ages 55+ and college students with ID); $5 (ages 5-18). **Phone:** (918) 456-6007 or (888) 999-6007.

Tsa-La-Gi Ancient Village, 21192 S. Keeler Dr., is a re-creation of a 16th-century Cherokee settlement. Such skills as basket weaving, flint knapping and pottery making are demonstrated regularly.

Allow 1 hour minimum for guided tour. **Hours:** Mon.-Sat. 10-5, Sun. 1-5, Feb.-Dec. Closed Easter, Thanksgiving and Dec. 24-25. **Cost:** $8.50 (includes Adams Corner Rural Village and Cherokee National Museum); $7.50 (ages 55+ and college students with ID); $5 (ages 5-18). **Phone:** (918) 456-6007 or (888) 999-6007.

MURRELL HOME, 19479 E. Murrell Home Rd., is the restored 1845 residence of George M. Murrell, who married the niece of Cherokee Prinicipal Chief John Ross. Although looted during the Civil War, the house is the only remaining antebellum plantation home in Oklahoma. It is furnished with some original pieces. A .7-mile nature trail accommodates wheelchairs. **Hours:** Tues.-Sat. 10-5, Sun. 1-5, Mar.-Oct.; Wed.-Sat. 10-5, Sun. 1-5, rest of year. Closed major holidays. **Cost:** Donations. **Phone:** (918) 456-2751.

PAWHUSKA—*see Tulsa p. 288.*

PAWNEE (C-9) pop. 2,230, elev. 822′

More than 30 years before Oklahoma became a state, the town's original settlers were aided by the Pawnee Indians, a peaceful tribe who inhabited the area for many years. A man who taught among the Pawnees, Gordon W. Lillie, alias Pawnee Bill, also was one of the leaders of the Oklahoma "boomers," a group that pushed for the opening of the territory to settlement in 1889.

Pawnee Bill is best known, however, as a showman who traveled through Europe and America with wife May Manning, performing and preserving scenes from a dying way of life—that of the Wild West cowboys.

Besides the Pawnees, four other tribes remain: the Kaws, the Otoes, the Poncas and the Tonkawas. The Pawnee Indian Agency, American Indian schools and a hospital serve the area.

Pawnee Community Chamber of Commerce: 613 Harrison St., Pawnee, OK 74058. **Phone:** (918) 762-2108.

PAWNEE BILL RANCH SITE, .5 mi. w. on US 64 at Blue Hawk Peak, consists of Pawnee Bill's original mansion and several ranch buildings with displays of artifacts, furniture, clothing, weapons and art objects. A museum and visitor center house his personal effects. Buffaloes, longhorn cattle and horses roam the area. Fishing opportunities are available. **Time:** Allow 2 hours minimum. **Hours:**

Tues.-Sat. 10-5, Sun.-Mon. 1-4, Apr.-Oct.; Wed.-Sat. 10-5, Sun. 1-4, rest of year. Closed major holidays. **Cost:** Donations. **Phone:** (918) 762-2513.

PERRY (C-8) pop. 5,230, elev. 989′

Born as a tent city of 25,000 on Sept. 16, 1893, Perry was first known for its large population of sooners, gamblers and ruffians and its 14 saloons. Federal marshals soon brought order, however, and energies turned to farming and building businesses and industries.

Perry Chamber of Commerce: 300 6th St., P.O. Box 426, Perry, OK 73077. **Phone:** (580) 336-4684.

CHEROKEE STRIP MUSEUM is .5 mi. e. off I-35 Fir Ave. exit. The museum, which depicts pioneer life on the Cherokee Strip *(see Ponca City)*, has a furnished one-room school built in 1895, a tepee, a barn with early farm machinery and sod busting implements. A living-history program is conducted in the schoolhouse during the school year.

Exhibits feature a general store, the office of the seventh governor of Oklahoma and early physician's and dentist's offices. **Time:** Allow 1 hour minimum. **Hours:** Tues.-Fri. 9-5, Sat. 10-4; closed holidays and the first 2 weeks in Jan. **Cost:** Donations. **Phone:** (580) 336-2405.

PONCA CITY (B-8) pop. 25,919, elev. 1,003′

Ponca City was created in true Oklahoma fashion during the land runs of the late 1800s. On Sept. 16, 1893, homesteaders lined up for a race to claim one of the 160-acre lots in the area surrounding what would soon be Ponca City. Certificates for lots in the business section were sold for $2 each.

Ponca City was built in the midst of the Cherokee Strip, a narrow section of land 50 miles wide that had been reserved for the American Indians as buffalo hunting grounds. President Grover Cleveland instead opened the land to settlement. When oil was discovered in 1910, E.W. Marland, who later became governor of Oklahoma, established Marland Oil, thereby propelling Ponca City into the age of industrialization.

Ponca City Tourism: 420 E. Grand Ave., Ponca City, OK 74601. **Phone:** (580) 763-8092.

CONOCO MUSEUM is at 501 W. South Ave. Exhibits such as A Proud Heritage, Ponca City Proud, Getting to the Future First, Setting the Pace and Marketing Conoco present the story of the oil company and its Ponca City history. Classic commercials, a visible gravity-fed gas pump and a film presentation can be seen. **Tours:** Guided tours are available. **Time:** Allow 30 minutes minimum. **Hours:** Mon.-Sat. 10-5, Sun. 1-5. Closed major holidays. **Cost:** Free. **Phone:** (580) 765-8687.

MARLAND ESTATE MANSION, 901 Monument Rd., was the second home of E.W. Marland, pioneer oilman and 10th governor of Oklahoma. Built in the late 1920s and modeled after the Florentine estates of the Italian Renaissance, the 55-room mansion includes a museum with petroleum exhibits and memorabilia relating to Marland.

Time: Allow 1 hour minimum. **Hours:** Mon.-Sat. 10-5, Sun. 1-5. Guided tours are available Mon.-Fri. at 1:30, Sat.-Sun. at 1:30 and 3. Closed Jan. 1, Easter, Thanksgiving and Dec. 25. **Cost:** $7; $5 (ages 12-17 and 65+); $4 (ages 6-11). **Phone:** (580) 767-0420 or (800) 422-8340.

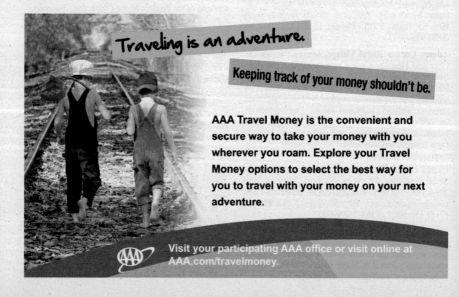

Bryant Baker Studio, on the grounds of the Marland Estate Mansion, is a replica of the artist's New York studio. Baker, known for his bronze sculpture "The Pioneer Woman," which stands in Ponca City, was the winner of a competition sponsored by E.W. Marland to create a memorial to the courageous women who helped settle this country. The studio contains a collection of plaster and bronze busts created by the sculptor.

MARLAND'S GRAND HOME, 1000 E. Grand Ave., is the 1916 home of E.W. Marland, millionaire oilman and 10th governor of Oklahoma. The building includes three museums. **Time:** Allow 1 hour minimum. **Hours:** Tues.-Sat. 10-5. Closed major holidays. **Cost:** $3 (includes 101 Ranch Room, D.A.R. Memorial Museum and Indian Museum); $1 (ages 0-16). **Phone:** (580) 767-0427.

101 Ranch Room, 1000 E. Grand Ave., contains memorabilia from the Miller Brothers 101 Ranch, where E.W. Marland discovered his first oil well. During the early 1900s the ranch spread across four counties and stretched 101,000 miles. Displays include saddles, ropes and photographs from the 101 Ranch Real Wild West Show, which toured the world from 1908 until the Great Depression in 1929.

Hours: Tues.-Sat. 10-5. Closed major holidays. **Cost:** $3 (includes Marland's Grand Home, D.A.R. Memorial Museum and Indian Museum); $1 (ages 0-16). **Phone:** (580) 767-0427.

D.A.R. Memorial Museum, 1000 E. Grand Ave., displays historical books, documents, furnishings and clothing collected by the Daughters of the American Revolution. Of interest is a 13-star U.S. flag taken from a Revolutionary War battlefield. **Hours:** Tues.-Sat. 10-5. Closed major holidays. **Cost:** $3 (includes Marland's Grand Home, 101 Ranch Room and Indian Museum); $1 (ages 0-16). **Phone:** (580) 767-0427.

Indian Museum, 1000 E. Grand Ave., features artifacts and artwork from more than 30 tribes with special emphasis on local groups such as the Kaw, Osage, Otoe, Ponca, and Tonkawa. Costumes, moccasins, belts and headbands showcase examples of intricate beadwork. **Hours:** Tues.-Sat. 10-5. Closed major holidays. **Cost:** $3 (includes Marland's Grand Home, 101 Ranch Room and D.A.R. Memorial Museum); $1 (ages 0-16). **Phone:** (580) 767-0427.

SAVE **PIONEER WOMAN STATUE AND MUSEUM,** 701 Monument Rd., is a tribute to the women who settled new territory with their families. Exhibits showcase tools, clothing, furniture and personal items that belonged to pioneers; inaugural gowns of Oklahoma's first ladies also are displayed. A 17-foot-tall bronze statue, commissioned by oilman and 10th governor of Oklahoma E.W. Marland, depicts a pioneer woman and her son. **Time:** Allow 1 hour minimum. **Hours:** Tues.-Sat. 9-5, Mon. 10-9. Closed major holidays. **Cost:** $3; $2.50 (ages 66+); $1 (ages 6-18). **Phone:** (580) 765-6108.

STANDING BEAR PARK AND MUSEUM is at jct. US 60, 77 and 177. A 22-foot statue of Ponca chief Standing Bear is the focal point of the 63-acre park, which also includes a pond; a walking trail through native grasses and wildflowers; a memorial grove; a 60-foot-diameter viewing court with boulders representing the six area tribes; and the museum, which features displays about the tribes. **Time:** Allow 30 minutes minimum. **Hours:** Mon.-Fri. 9-5, Sat. 10-2. **Cost:** Free. **Phone:** (580) 762-1514.

POTEAU (E-12) pop. 7,939

Poteau, situated on the banks of the Poteau River, is almost entirely surrounded by mountains. The Winding Stair and Kiamichi mountains are on the southwest horizon, while the Poteau Range dominates the view to the south. Cavanal, said to be the world's highest hill, provides a splendid view of Sugar Loaf Mountain.

The town is an outfitting center for recreation in nearby Ouachita National Forest *(see place listing in Arkansas p. 54)*. Wister Lake *(see Recreation Chart)* also is in the area. A scenic stretch of US 59/270 extends 25 miles south to the US 259 intersection before the town of Page.

Poteau Chamber of Commerce: 201 S. Broadway, Poteau, OK 74953. **Phone:** (918) 647-9178.

ROBERT S. KERR HOME AND MUSEUM is 6 mi. s.w. via US 59, following signs. This former home of U.S. Senator Robert S. Kerr is now a bed-and-breakfast and conference center. An adjacent museum has area history exhibits—including rune stones believed to have been carved by Viking explorers; artifacts from the Spiro Indian mound, built 700-1350; Choctaw Nation documents and memorabilia; pioneer items, such as unusual types of barbed wire; and a reproduction of the senator's Washington, D.C., office.

Time: Allow 1 hour minimum. **Hours:** Museum Sun.-Fri. 1-5, Sat. 10-5. The home can be toured by appointment. Closed major holidays. **Cost:** Donations. **Phone:** (918) 647-8221.

SALLISAW (D-12) pop. 7,989, elev. 533′

Sallisaw, surrounded by agricultural land in the northeastern section of the state, is home to Blue Ribbon Downs, the state's first pari-mutuel racetrack. Two miles west of Sallisaw at I-40 and US 64, the track features Thoroughbred, paint, Appaloosa and quarter horse racing Friday through Sunday, August through November.

Note: Policies concerning admittance of children to pari-mutuel betting facilities vary. Phone for information.

Dwight Mission, about 9 miles northwest, operated as a mission school for the Cherokee for more than a century after its founding in 1828. The town's name is derived from a French word meaning "salt provisions."

Sallisaw Chamber of Commerce: 301 E. Cherokee Ave., P.O. Box 251, Sallisaw, OK 74955. **Phone:** (918) 775-2558.

FOURTEEN FLAGS MUSEUM, jct. US 59/64 at 400 E. Cherokee St., has exhibits that depict the lifestyles of early settlers. A general store, a Union Pacific caboose and several log cabins furnished with homestead artifacts are included. **Hours:** Daily 8-4. Phone ahead to confirm schedule. **Cost:** Free. **Phone:** (918) 775-2558 for the chamber of commerce.

SEQUOYAH'S HOME SITE is 3 mi. n. on US 59, then 7 mi. e. on SR 101. The 1829 log cabin, one of the state's oldest, was Sequoyah's home before and after the "Trail of Tears" march and contains farm implements he made. The interpretive center describes the Cherokee Nation's history and the Cherokee language syllabus Sequoyah invented. The simplicity of his system enabled the Cherokee to teach and publish within a few years.

Though he never learned English, Sequoyah developed an alphabet using modified letters from English, Greek and Hebrew to represent the sounds in the Cherokee language. It was hoped that a written language would preserve the Cherokee culture. The redwoods of the West were named in his honor. **Hours:** Tues.-Fri. 9-5, Sat.-Sun. 2-5. Closed major holidays. **Cost:** Free. **Phone:** (918) 775-2413.

SAND SPRINGS—*see Tulsa p. 288.*

SAPULPA—*see Tulsa p. 289.*

SEMINOLE (D-9) pop. 6,899

Named after the Seminole Indians who previously settled the site, the town reached its peak in 1926 when a large oil pool was tapped. Thousands rushed to the site, and the Seminole post office is reported to have received mail for more than 100,000 people.

Seminole Chamber of Commerce: 326 E. Evans, P.O. Box 1190, Seminole, OK 74868. **Phone:** (405) 382-3640.

GEM SAVE **JASMINE MORAN CHILDREN'S MUSEUM** is 1 mi. w. of jct. SR 9/US 377 at 1714 W. Wrangler Blvd. (SR 9W). This hands-on museum is in the form of a child-size town complete with street signs. A courthouse, grocery store, fire station, hospital, television studio and other settings are incorporated into a community just for children.

Exhibits are designed to stimulate the imagination. A child can assume various roles in a community by donning a grocer's apron, dentist's jacket or firefighter's uniform. Other highlights include model trains and airplanes, a doll house with more than 1,000 pieces of furniture, an aquarium, a soap bubble factory, a room of mirrors and computer displays.

A 1936 fire truck, 1921 Model T and 1927 caboose can be explored. Children can enter a soundproof room, use a wheelchair or experiment with braille. **Time:** Allow 1 hour minimum. **Hours:** Tues.-Sat. 10-5, Sun. 1-5; closed major holidays and 2 weeks following Labor Day. **Cost:** $8; $7 (ages 60+); free (ages 0-2 with parent). **Phone:** (405) 382-0950.

SHAWNEE—*see Oklahoma City p. 272.*

SPIRO (D-12) pop. 2,227

Spiro was spawned by the Kansas City Southern Railway in 1895. It adopted most of the citizens of nearby Scullyville, the capital of the Choctaw Indian Agency's northern district and a booming trading post that was decimated by Union troops during the Civil War. All that remains of Scullyville, east on US 271, are the ruins of an American Indian agency building and a church.

Spiro Area Chamber of Commerce: 210 S. Main St., Spiro, OK 74953. **Phone:** (918) 962-3816.

SPIRO MOUNDS ARCHEOLOGICAL CENTER is 3 mi. e. on SR 9, then 4.2 mi. n. Oklahoma's only archeological park, comprising 150 acres, has 12 American Indian mounds built 600-1450. The interpretive center displays artifacts and grave goods—valuables buried with the deceased—and explains the symbolism of American Indian artwork and ceremonies.

A trail leads to the mounds and the Spiro Culture House, a reproduction of a type of American Indian dwelling used circa 1000. **Time:** Allow 2 hours minimum. **Hours:** Wed.-Sat. 9-5, Sun. noon-5. Closed state holidays. **Cost:** Free. **Phone:** (918) 962-2062.

STILLWATER (C-9) pop. 39,065, elev. 870′

On April 22, 1889, the town of Stillwater was born with a population of 300. A year later the Oklahoma Agricultural and Mechanical College, now Oklahoma State University, was founded, and Stillwater became one of the Southwest's major educational centers. The city also is known as a center for agribusiness, medical services and industry. Experimental farms can be seen along highways leading into town.

Stillwater is the home of the National Wrestling Hall of Fame, 405 W. Hall of Fame Ave., (405) 377-5243, and the Sheerar Cultural and Heritage Center Museum, 702 S. Duncan St., (405) 377-0359.

Stillwater Convention and Visitors Bureau: 409 S. Main St., Stillwater, OK 74074. **Phone:** (405) 743-3697 or (800) 991-6717.

GARDINER ART GALLERY IN THE BARTLETT CENTER FOR STUDIO ARTS is on the Oklahoma State University campus. Once a women's residence hall, the Georgian-style building has been renovated to provide studio space for artists and a setting for their work. In addition, the gallery sponsors touring art exhibitions and houses a permanent collection of works in wood, bronze and print media. **Hours:** Mon.-Fri. 8-5. During special events, the museum may be open only Sat.-Sun.; phone ahead. Closed major holidays. **Cost:** Free. **Phone:** (405) 744-6016.

OKLAHOMA MUSEUM OF HIGHER EDUCATION is between Hester and Knoblock sts. n. of University Ave. on the campus of Oklahoma State University. Housed in the 1894 Old Central building, the first permanent building on the university's campus, the museum has exhibits depicting the history of the university and of higher education throughout Oklahoma. Traveling exhibits cover a variety of subjects. **Tours:** Guided tours are available. **Hours:** Wed.-Fri. 9-11 and noon-5, Sat. 10-4. Closed major holidays. Phone ahead to confirm schedule. **Cost:** Donations. **Phone:** (405) 744-6799.

TAHLEQUAH (C-11) pop. 14,458, elev. 861′

In a region of lakes within the foothills of the Ozark Mountains, Tahlequah has been the capital of the Cherokee Indian Nation since 1839. Old Cherokee government buildings still standing are the 1844 Supreme Court Building, the 1867 Cherokee Capitol Building and the 1844 Cherokee National Prison.

Designated a scenic highway, SR 10 winds 30 miles northeast from Tahlequah, intersecting with US 412 and US 59 in the town of Kansas. Two miles north of the junction of US 62 and SR 10, Elephant Rock Nature Park offers 120 acres with nature and hiking trails and access to the Illinois River for fishing and swimming.

Tahlequah Area Chamber of Commerce and Tourism Council: 123 E. Delaware St., Tahlequah, OK 74464-2817. **Phone:** (918) 456-3742 or (800) 456-4860.

Self-guiding tours: City maps, announcements of community activities and brochures outlining self-guiding tours of Tahlequah's historic sites are available at the chamber of commerce.

CHEROKEE HERITAGE CENTER—*see Park Hill p. 273.*

MURRELL HOME—*see Park Hill p. 273.*

TISHOMINGO (F-9) pop. 3,162

Historically significant as the capital of the Chickasaw Nation, Tishomingo is on Lake Texoma. After serving as the last Chickasaw capitol, the granite Victorian Gothic building at N. Fisher and W. 8th streets housed the Johnston County Courthouse 1907-89. Guided tours of the building are available. The restored 1902 Indian Territory Bank of the Chickasaw Nation, a block from Court House Square, houses the Johnston County Museum of History.

Johnston County Chamber of Commerce: 106 W. Main, Tishomingo, OK 73460. **Phone:** (580) 371-2175.

CHICKASAW COUNCIL HOUSE is on Court House Sq. The museum contains the restored first council house of the Chickasaw Nation as well as photographs and artifacts depicting the history of the Chickasaw tribe before their migration from Mississippi and Alabama to Oklahoma 1838-40. **Time:** Allow 1 hour minimum. **Hours:** Mon.-Fri. 9-6, Sat. 10-4. Closed major holidays. **Cost:** Free. **Phone:** (580) 371-3351.

TISHOMINGO NATIONAL WILDLIFE REFUGE is 3 mi. s. on Refuge Rd.; its headquarters is e. off SR 78. The refuge covers 16,464 acres on the Upper Washita arm of Lake Texoma. It lies in the central flyway and functions primarily as a migratory waterfowl refuge.

Eagles, hawks, ducks, geese and pelicans are among the migratory birds found in the refuge; deer, bobcats and beavers also are residents. Limited fishing and hunting are permitted in designated sections. *See Recreation Chart.* **Time:** Allow 1 hour minimum. **Hours:** Refuge open daily dawn-dusk. Headquarters open Mon.-Fri. 7:30-4. **Cost:** Free. **Phone:** (580) 371-2402.

Tulsa

City Population: 393,049 **Elevation:** 689 ft.

Editor's Picks:

Gilcrease Museum..................*(see p. 282)*

Philbrook Museum of Art........ *(see p. 283)*

Tulsa Zoo and Living Museum... *(see p. 284)*

© Don Sibley / Tulsa Metro Chamber of Commerce

As Oklahoma's second largest city, Tulsa is the product of an unlikely mixture of oil and water; the development of these two liquid resources spurred the city's rapid economic growth and made Tulsa into the vibrant, bustling community it is today.

Tulsa's beginnings date to 1836 when a band of displaced Creek Indians from Alabama built a council fire under a sturdy oak tree, ending a long, harsh journey over the "Trail of Tears." The name Tulsa is derived from the Creek word "Tullahassee" or "Talahassee," meaning "old town."

While early settlers were attracted to the lush banks of the Arkansas River, the area remained largely undeveloped until a trading post opened in 1846, signaling the beginning of organized commerce in the area. Tulsa became the official name of the town with the creation of the first post office in 1879.

The arrival of the St. Louis-San Francisco Railway provided further impetus for growth. Farmers, ranchers and traders were attracted to the area's increasingly stable system of transportation. One of the first organized groups, a union Sunday school, held class in a tent belonging to a railroad carpenter. By the time Tulsa was incorporated on Jan. 8, 1898, cattle shipping had become the principal industry.

On June 25, 1901, the pace of the town's development quickened. Drillers operating a rig known as Sue Bland #1 struck black gold, creating the state's first commercially important oil well. Eager prospectors swarmed into the area, repeating the frenzy of the land rushes a few years earlier. A second major strike tapped into the large reserves at the Ida Glenn farm in 1905. Oil prices began to climb after pipelines were established to the Gulf of Mexico.

As oil fortunes were literally being made overnight, enterprising Tulsans began an aggressive campaign to attract oilmen to establish themselves in the community. The result was a building boom that also created hotels, office buildings, paved roads, bridges and more railroad links.

Train trips organized by civic leaders to promote Tulsa were common at the turn of the 20th century, and humorist Will Rogers was known to accompany these early business boosters. Their vision helped to elevate Tulsa from a dusty cow town in American Indian Territory to a dynamic urban center with a vigorous economy.

Development of wat er resources has enabled Tulsa to boast the largest number of man-made lakes in the nation. Barge traffic between the Tulsa Port of Catoosa and New Orleans qualifies Tulsa as a major inland harbor. This 445-mile navigation system links Oklahoma with domestic ports in the surrounding five-state area through a complex system of dams, lakes, reservoirs and locks.

While at one time everyone in Tulsa seemed to be involved in some way with the oil business, the city now has a more diversified economy. Although more than 1,000 area firms are still associated with the petroleum business, current industries include aviation, computer technology, financial services, health care, manufacturing and mining. Among the fastest growing are aerospace engineering and telecommunications.

Getting There — *starting on p. 279*

Getting Around — *starting on p. 279*

What To See — *starting on p. 282*

What To Do — *starting on p. 285*

Where To Stay — *starting on p. 649*

Where To Dine — *starting on p. 658*

The area earns its nickname "Green Country" from an abundance of parks and gardens that enhance the city's urban appearance. Many acres of parkland have been preserved despite Tulsa's numerous industries. River Parks, the scene of more than 25 festivals, includes a lake with a floating stage as well as a lengthy trail system on the east and west banks of the Arkansas River.

In Tulsa—a young city mindful of its roots—recreation, cultural arts and industry all come together to form a pleasant setting with a promising future.

Utica Square / © Don Sibley
Tulsa Metro Chamber of Commerce

Getting There

By Car

Several major highways lead to and from Tulsa. One of the most important is I-44, which approaches the city from the northeast as the Will Rogers Turnpike and from the southwest as the Turner Turnpike. Although I-44 bypasses the downtown area, the city's center is accessible from I-44 by way of numerous interchanges. Martin Luther King Jr. Memorial Expressway (I-244/US 412) is a major access route from I-44 to the heart of Tulsa.

US 75 leads into downtown Tulsa from both the north and the south; the southern segment is known as the Okmulgee Expressway, which becomes the Indian Nation Turnpike farther south.

US 64/412 approaches the city from the west as the Cimarron Turnpike, but becomes the Keystone Expressway before entering the city limits. The Muskogee Turnpike is a major access highway from the southeast. Converging with SR 51, it enters Tulsa as the Broken Arrow Expressway.

East of the city, the Mingo Valley Expressway (US 169) approaches from the north; it is connected to downtown via I-244. Historic Route 66, which at one time carried traffic from Chicago to Southern California, passes through downtown as 11th Street.

Getting Around

Street System

The east-west dividing line is Main Street, while Admiral Boulevard is the city's north-south bisector. Numbered streets run east and west beginning 1 block south of Admiral, unless otherwise designated. A right turn on red is permitted after a complete stop, unless otherwise posted.

Parking

Ample parking is available downtown. There are many commercial garages and lots, and most hotels provide free parking for guests. Rates in the commercial garages are $1 per half-hour or $1-$10 per day.

Destination Tulsa

Although Tulsa was developed with help from the unlikely mixture of natural resources oil and water, its many lakes, parks and attractions blend nicely to create a beautiful city.

Museums, an amusement park, botanical gardens and a zoo offer Tulsa's visitors an appealing combination of flora, fauna and fun.

Oklahoma Tourism

Will Rogers Memorial Museum, Claremore. (See listing page 287)

Philbrook Museum of Art, Tulsa. (See listing page 283)

© John Elk III
Lonely Planet Images

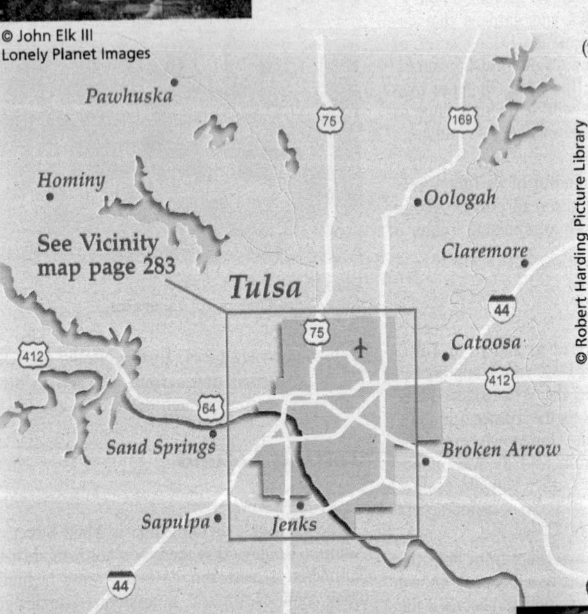

Boston Avenue United Methodist Church, Tulsa. (See listing page 282)

© Robert Harding Picture Library
SuperStock

Tulsa Zoo and Living Museum. (See listing page 284)

© Tulsa Zoo and Living Museum

Places included in this AAA Destination City:

The Informed Traveler

Sales Tax: The Tulsa area has a sales tax of 8.52 percent, a lodging tax of 13.52 percent and a rental car tax of 14.51 percent.

WHOM TO CALL

Emergency: 911

Police (non-emergency): (918) 596-9222

Fire: (918) 596-9444

Time and Temperature: (918) 477-1000

Hospitals: Hillcrest Medical Center, (918) 579-1000; Oklahoma State University Medical Center, (918) 587-2561; Saint Francis Hospital, (918) 494-2200; St. John Medical Center, (918) 744-2345; SouthCrest Hospital, (918) 294-4000.

WHERE TO LOOK

Newspapers

Tulsa World, the city's daily newspaper, is distributed in the morning.

Radio

Tulsa radio station KRMG (740 AM) is a news station. KWGS (89.5 FM) is a member of National Public Radio.

Visitor Information

Tulsa Metro Chamber of Commerce: Williams Center Tower II, Suite 150, 2 W. 2nd St., Tulsa, OK 74103. **Phone:** (918) 585-1201 or (800) 558-3311.

Maps and visitor information are available Mon.-Fri. 8-5.

TRANSPORTATION

Air Travel

With service to most major cities in the United States, Tulsa International Airport is just northeast of downtown and is easily accessible by way of I-244 or US 169. Airport on-site parking costs range from $10-$18 per day. Taxi fare to downtown Tulsa is approximately $24 one way.

Rental Cars

Hertz, (800) 654-3080, offers discounts to AAA members. For listings of other agencies check the telephone directory.

Buses

Greyhound Lines Inc. and Jefferson Lines are the major bus lines serving the city. Both operate out of the terminal at 317 S. Detroit Ave.; phone (918) 584-4428 for schedule information.

Taxis

Cab companies include American Shuttle Service, (918) 744-1111; Checker Cab, (918) 838-7999; Executive Cab Co., (918) 747-8481; and Yellow Checker Cab, (918) 582-6161. Taxis are metered and charge $1.50-$2 plus $1.50-$2 for each mile. There is a $2 charge for each additional passenger.

Public Transport

Tulsa Transit operates buses throughout the metropolitan area and includes stops at attractions and shopping centers. The main terminal is at 319 S. Denver Ave. between Peoria and Utica avenues; phone (918) 582-2100 for schedules and information.

What To See

BIG SPLASH WATER PARK, 4707 E. 21st St., is a water theme park featuring the Motion Ocean wave pool, a water roller coaster, a seven-story waterslide, two speed slides, a lazy river, a kiddie pool for toddlers and a sand volleyball court. **Time:** Allow 4 hours minimum. **Hours:** Mon.-Thurs. 10-6, Fri.-Sat. 10-8, Sun. noon-6, Memorial Day-Labor Day. **Cost:** $22.95; $18.95 (under 48 inches tall); $15.95 (Sun.); $12.95 (Fri.-Sat. after 4 p.m.); free (ages 0-3). **Phone:** (918) 749-7385.

BOSTON AVENUE UNITED METHODIST CHURCH, 1301 S. Boston Ave., is an interesting example of modern skyscraper architecture applied to a large church. Completed in 1929, the building is noted for its Art Deco design. Guided tours are available by appointment. **Time:** Allow 1 hour minimum. **Hours:** Mon.-Fri. 8:30-4:45. **Cost:** Free. **Phone:** (918) 583-5181.

GEM SAVE **GILCREASE MUSEUM** is off US 64/SR 51 at 1400 N. Gilcrease Museum Rd. The museum is known for its comprehensive collection of art of the American West, including works by Albert Bierstadt, Thomas Moran, Frederic Remington and Charles Russell.

Paintings, drawings, prints and sculpture by more than 400 artists from the 18th century to the present are included in the museum's collection. Artists include John James Audubon, John Singleton Copley, Winslow Homer, John Singer Sargent, James McNeill Whistler and N.C. Wyeth. A collection of American Indian art and artifacts, along with historical manuscripts, documents and maps also is featured. Anthropological and archeological collections feature artifacts from North, Central and South American cultures.

Time: Allow 3 hours minimum. **Hours:** Tues.-Sun. 10-5. Guided tours are given at 2. Closed Dec. 25. **Cost:** $8; $6 (ages 62+ and military with ID); $5 (college students with ID); free (ages 0-18 and first Tues. of the month). An additional fee may be charged for special exhibitions. **Phone:** (918) 596-2700, or (918) 596-2787 for information about special exhibitions and fees.

The Gardens at Gilcrease Museum, on the museum grounds at 1400 N. Gilcrease Museum Rd., comprises 23 acres of thematic formal gardens, including Victorian, Colonial, pre-Columbian and pioneer styles. Paved walking trails allow for exploration, and guided tours are available. **Hours:** Daily dawn-11 p.m. Garden tours are given Sat. at 1, May-June and Sept.-Oct. Closed Dec. 25. **Cost:** Donations. **Phone:** (918) 596-2700.

OKLAHOMA JAZZ HALL OF FAME is at E. 1st St. and S. Boston Ave. Exhibits containing photos, musical instruments, albums, clothing and other memorabilia help illustrate the stories of the state's jazz, blues and gospel greats. Concerts and special events are held periodically. **Time:** Allow 30 minutes minimum. **Hours:** Mon.-Fri. 9-5, Sat. by appointment. Closed major holidays. **Cost:** Free. **Phone:** (918) 281-8600.

Totem Pole Park, near Claremore / © Richard Cummins / Alamy

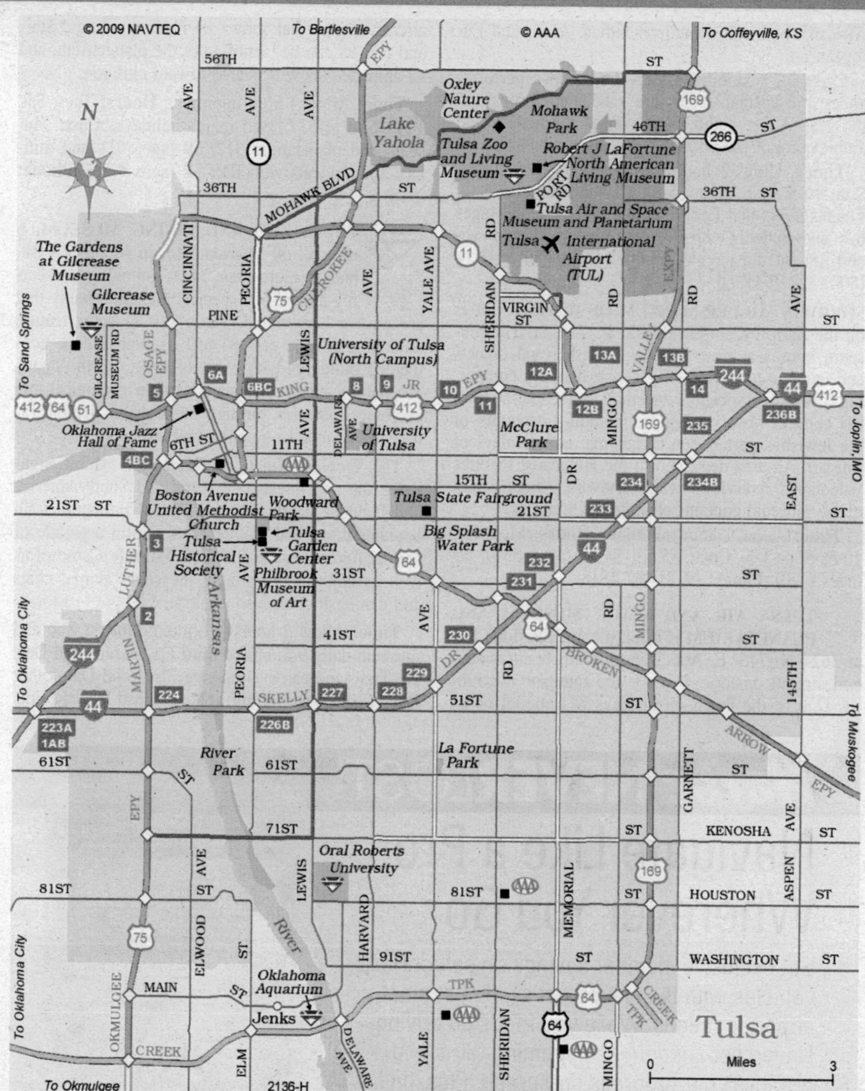

ORAL ROBERTS UNIVERSITY, 7777 S. Lewis Ave., has a 200-foot glass and steel prayer tower, a seven-story diamond-shaped library and graduate center complex, a sports center, symphony hall, chapel, carillon and television production studio. The Prayer Tower Visitor Center offers views of the campus from its observation deck as well as a 20-minute multimedia presentation about the university and a 36-minute presentation about the life of Oral Roberts. Campus tours are available.

Time: Allow 3 hours minimum. **Hours:** Visitor center Mon.-Sat. noon-5; closed Jan. 1, Thanksgiving and Dec. 24-25 and 31. **Cost:** Free. **Phone:** (918) 495-6807 for campus tour times.

OXLEY NATURE CENTER, in Mohawk Park at 6700 Mohawk Blvd., comprises 800 acres of natural vegetation and walking trails. A visitor center has displays describing unusual local birds and a beehive with a see-through panel and entrance tube. **Hours:** Park open daily 7 a.m.-9 p.m. Nature center daily 8-5. Visitor center Mon.-Sat. 10-4:30, Sun. noon-4:30. **Cost:** Free. **Phone:** (918) 669-6644.

PHILBROOK MUSEUM OF ART is at 2727 S. Rockford Rd., 1 blk. e. of Peoria Ave. at 27th Pl. This elaborate Italian Renaissance-style villa set on 23 acres of formal and informal gardens was the palatial home of oilman Waite Phillips and his wife Genevieve. Built in the late 1920s, it now houses permanent collections of

African, American, American Indian, Asian and European art.

Changing exhibitions, lectures, films, performances and special events are scheduled throughout the year. A free audio tour covering the history and architecture of the villa and gardens is available.

Time: Allow 2 hours minimum. **Hours:** Tues.-Sun. 10-5 (also Thurs. 5-8). Closed Jan. 1, July 4, Thanksgiving and Dec. 25. **Cost:** $7.50; $5.50 (ages 62+ and students with ID); free (ages 0-18 and second Sat. of the month). **Phone:** (918) 749-7941 or (800) 324-7941.

SHERWIN MILLER MUSEUM OF JEWISH ART is on the Zarrow Campus at 2021 E. 71st St. The museum houses ancient artifacts; Jewish ritual objects and items used in rites of passage; displays comparing a range of societies and their influence on Jewish culture; history exhibits, including accounts of the Jewish experience in Oklahoma; and displays of fine art. An area dedicated to the Holocaust features videotaped interviews with survivors. Another part of the museum contains changing exhibitions.

Time: Allow 1 hour minimum. **Hours:** Mon.-Fri. 10-5, Sun. 1-5. **Cost:** $5.50; $4.50 (ages 55+); $3 (ages 6-20). **Phone:** (918) 492-1818.

SAVE **TULSA AIR AND SPACE MUSEUM AND PLANETARIUM** is 6 mi. n.e. off Sheridan Rd. at 3624 N. 74th E. Ave. The museum features several aircraft, historic displays and interactive exhibits. One of the hands-on displays is a model of an aircraft engine that shows its inner workings. Stars and planets can be identified at the planetarium, and an animated show is geared toward children.

Time: Allow 1 hour minimum. **Hours:** Tues.-Sat. 10-5, Sun. 1-5. Closed major holidays. **Cost:** Museum and planetarium $12; $9 (ages 62+ and military and students with ID); $7 (ages 4-12). **Phone:** (918) 834-9900.

GEM SAVE **TULSA ZOO AND LIVING MUSEUM,** 6 mi. n.e. off Sheridan Rd. in Mohawk Park, houses more than 2,800 animals representing almost 500 species, including many that are rare or endangered. The zoo's 84 acres feature outdoor exhibit areas as well as nine indoor eco-themed buildings with exhibits about North American natural history. Displays explain geological and ecological features through audiovisual demonstrations, live animals, graphics and artifacts.

The Tropical American Rainforest exhibit highlights the rain forests of Central and South America and includes nearly 500 animals. A miniature train operates daily, and children can ride in a parade of animal figures on the ARVEST Wildlife Carousel as well as enjoy a playground. Seasonal animal chats and demonstrations also are available.

Time: Allow 2 hours minimum. **Hours:** Zoo and museum daily 9-5; closed third Fri. in June and Dec. 25. Train and carousel operate Memorial Day-Labor Day (weather permitting); phone ahead for schedule.

Cost: $8; $6 (ages 65+); $4 (ages 3-11). Round-trip train ride $2; $1 (one-way). Carousel $1. Parking $2. **Phone:** (918) 669-6600.

WOODWARD PARK, 21st St. and Peoria Ave., is a 34-acre city park containing the Tulsa Garden Center and the Tulsa Historical Society & History Museum in addition to other areas of horticultural interest, including rock gardens, an herb garden, a conservatory and more than 15,000 azaleas. **Hours:** Daily 7 a.m.-dusk. **Cost:** Free. **Phone:** (918) 746-5133.

Tulsa Garden Center, 1.5 mi. s. of SR 51 at 2435 S. Peoria Ave. in Woodward Park, is the former 1919 home of wealthy oilman David Travis. Included on the grounds are the Linnaeus Teaching Garden, a demonstration space for home gardeners; the Tulsa Rose Garden, created by the Works Progress Administration (WPA) 1934-35, with more than 250 varieties of roses on five terraced levels enhanced by stone walls and fountains; and the 3-acre Tulsa Arboretum.

Hours: Mon.-Fri. 8:30-4; closed Jan. 1, Memorial Day, July 4, Labor Day, Thanksgiving and Dec. 24-31. Linnaeus Teaching Garden Tues.-Fri. 9-4, Sat. 9-5 (also Sun. 1-4, Mother's Day-day before Labor Day). Docent tours are given by appointment. **Cost:** Donations. **Phone:** (918) 746-5125.

Tulsa Historical Society & History Museum, 2445 S. Peoria Ave. in Woodward Park, is in the renovated 1919 mansion built for Tulsa oil producer Samuel Travis. The Revival-style house has eight galleries dedicated to changing exhibits about the area's history.

The Vintage Gardens, on the grounds, have paved walkways; outdoor statues, including the Five Moons, life-size depictions of American Indian ballerinas from Oklahoma; and cornerstones and other architectural elements from former Tulsa buildings. **Time:** Allow 30 minutes minimum. **Hours:** Tues.-Sat. 10-4. Closed major holidays. **Cost:** Donations. **Phone:** (918) 712-9484.

What To Do

Sightseeing

Walking Tours

Tulsa's historical business district mirrors the wealth of the oil industry through its opulent Art Deco architecture. Some of the finest examples of zigzag skyscrapers, the streamline style of the 1930s and the classical style popular during the Great Depression are displayed.

Visitors may choose to explore the area on foot; between 2nd and 6th streets and Cincinnati and Cheyenne streets there are approximately 40 Art Deco sites. The Tulsa Union Depot, built in 1931, is on 1st Street; the Philtower, known as the "Queen of the Tulsa skyline," can be found on 5th Street near Boston Street; the Mincks-Adams Hotel, with its terra cotta facade, is at 4th and Cheyenne streets; and the National Bank of Tulsa, containing a lavish lobby, is at 320 S. Boston St.

The Tulsa Metro Chamber of Commerce has maps detailing a walking tour of the Art Deco District; phone (918) 585-1201 or (800) 558-3311.

Sports and Recreation

With hundreds of miles of lakeshore within a 2-hour drive of their city, Tulsans enjoy a variety of water sports. **Fishing, boating** and **water skiing** are popular on any one of the 48 lakes in the Tulsa vicinity including Birch, Eufaula, Fort Gibson, Fountainhead, Greenleaf, Keystone, Skiatook and Tenkiller. Provisions for **swimming** and **picnicking** are plentiful.

Hikers have their choice of trails at nearby Chandler Park and Heyburn, Okmulgee and Oologah lakes, to name a few. A recreation area on one of the largest bodies of water in Oklahoma, Grand Lake o' the Cherokees, is home to 36 holes of year-round **golf**. LaFortune Park in southern Tulsa has a popular three-mile **jogging** track around two 18-hole golf courses and a public swimming pool.

City and county parks are numerous. Among them is Mohawk Park on 36th Street N., one of the largest municipal parks in the nation. Near downtown, the River Parks system offers miles of jogging, walking and **bicycling** trails along the banks of the Arkansas River. Many area parks feature lighted **softball** diamonds.

The Tulsa Drillers, the Double A farm team of **baseball**'s Colorado Rockies, plays in ONEOK Field in downtown's Greenwood district; phone (918) 744-5901 for schedule information. **Ice hockey** fans flock to the BOK Center to watch the Tulsa Oilers; phone (918) 632-7825.

At the college level the University of Tulsa Golden Hurricanes and the Oral Roberts University Golden Eagles both field competitive baseball and **basketball** teams. Fans of **football** find plenty of gridiron action every fall at the University of Tulsa's Skelly Stadium; phone (918) 631-4688.

Those who enjoy the thrill of "playing the ponies" can visit Fair Meadows at Expo Square for pari-mutuel Thoroughbred and quarter **horse racing** at various dates during the year; phone (918) 743-7223.

Note: Policies concerning admittance of children to pari-mutuel betting facilities vary. Phone for information.

Shopping

From small, exclusive boutiques to large, bargain-packed malls, Tulsa's shopping centers provide visitors with a wide range of choices. With more than one million square feet of retail floor space, Woodland Hills Mall, 71st Street and Memorial Drive, is said to be the largest in the state. The mall comprises more than 165 stores including Dillard's, JCPenney, Macy's and Sears.

Utica Square, 21st Street S. and Utica Avenue, caters to upscale tastes and also serves as the backdrop for live performances in summer. Centered about a rustic, restored barn at 51st Street S. and Sheridan Avenue, The Farm offers a variety of boutiques in a setting that is reminiscent of a village square.

Among the retailers at Tulsa Promenade, 41st Street and S. Yale Avenue, are Dillard's, JCPenney and Macy's.

Performing Arts

Early Tulsa settlers included cultured people who brought their appreciation of music with them, thus sowing the seeds for future growth of the arts.

The Tulsa Opera presents a season of internationally renowned productions. The Performing Arts Center (PAC), E. 2nd Street and Cincinnati Avenue in downtown Tulsa, was built with a combination of public and private funds. It serves as the hub of the arts entertainment community in the city. For ticket information phone (918) 596-7111. In addition, Tulsa Ballet performs in Chapman Music Hall at the Tulsa Performing Arts Center; for ticket information phone (918) 749-6006.

The Tulsa Spotlighters present "The Drunkard," a 19th-century melodrama that has been in regular production since 1953. The play, which encourages audience participation, is followed by "The Olio," an old-fashioned variety show. The landmark Spotlight Theatre, 1381 Riverside Dr., serves as the play's venue; phone (918) 587-5030.

Special Events

Several events keep Tulsans in touch with their heritage. The Tulsa Indian Art Festival is held in February at Expo Square with more than 35 American Indian tribes participating from across the country. The city celebrates the arts in mid-May with the Tulsa International Mayfest, held in the Main Mall downtown. The Juneteenth Festival in mid-June highlights African-American music traditions with jazz, blues and gospel performances.

The Pinto World Championship Horse Show in June features more than 750 colorful horses and 1,300 riders; the event is held at Expo Square. Following the departure of the pintos, Expo Square is also the site of the Palomino Horse Breeders of America World Championship Horse Show, held in July.

More than 600 exhibitors display arts, crafts, antiques and collectibles during An Affair of the Heart, held in mid-July and mid-November at Expo Square.

The Inter-Tribal Indian Club of Tulsa Powwow of Champions held in mid-August attracts dancers from throughout the United States to participate in contests and other cultural activities. Also in August, Jazz Fest showcases nationally known jazz performers.

The Oklahoma Scottish Games and Gathering is held in mid-September at River Parks West, 2105 S. Jackson Ave. The festival includes a Scottish athletic competition for both men and women plus Scottish entertainment. Tents are set up by Scottish clans, food vendors and various Celtic merchants.

The Brush Creek Bazaar held in early October features more than 100 arts and crafts exhibitors, music, performing and visual arts and youth activities.

The Tulsa State Fair is held at Expo Square in the fall. Fall also brings Oktoberfest, with Austrian and German folk bands, European food, arts and crafts, folk dancers and a children's entertainment tent. The American Bicycle Association Grand Nationals motocross competition draws bicyclists from the U.S. and foreign countries to Expo Square in November.

The Tulsa Vicinity

BROKEN ARROW (F-2)

pop. 74,859, elev. 755′

BLUE BELL CREAMERIES TOUR is at 8201 E. SR 51, just. s. of jct. 81st St. Guided tours and a video presentation explain how the creamery makes its Blue Bell ice cream products. Tour guides trace the production process from the delivery of the dry goods, through the machinery that makes the ice cream and the packaging of the finished product. An overlook provides a view of the work area. An ice cream sample is available at the completion of the tour.

Time: Allow 45 minutes minimum. **Hours:** Guided tours are given Mon.-Fri. 9-2 by appointment. Closed major holidays. **Cost:** $2; $1 (ages 6-18 and 55+). **Phone:** (918) 258-5100, or (800) 365-0325, ext. 450.

CATOOSA (E-3) pop. 5,449, elev. 605′

ARKANSAS RIVER HISTORICAL SOCIETY MUSEUM is at 5350 Cimarron Rd., at the Tulsa Port of Catoosa. The museum contains photographs and artifacts relating to the development of the McClellan-Kerr Arkansas River Navigation System.

A videotape explains the system's history. Visitors can see a working scale model of a boat traveling through a lock and can also see and walk on the deck of the towboat *Charley Border*. **Time:** Allow 30 minutes minimum. **Hours:** Mon.-Fri. 8-4:30. Closed major holidays. **Cost:** Donations. **Phone:** (918) 266-2291.

CLAREMORE (E-3) pop. 15,873, elev. 608′

Claremore was the home of Lynn Riggs, author of "Green Grow the Lilacs," the play that inspired the musical "Oklahoma!" Northeast of town on SR 28A near Foyil stands what is said to be the world's largest totem pole. Carved of stone and concrete, this 90-foot by 18-foot monument to the American Indian is the center of Totem Pole Park. The park also has a museum and picnic area.

Claremore Area Chamber of Commerce: 419 W. Will Rogers Blvd., Claremore, OK 74017. **Phone:** (918) 341-2818.

GEM **J.M. DAVIS ARMS & HISTORICAL MUSEUM,** 333 N. Lynn Riggs Blvd. (US 66), houses a diverse collection of firearms, swords and knives; Western, Civil War-era and American Indian artifacts; music boxes and musical instruments; steins; political buttons; statues; and World War I posters. More than 50,000 items are on display. A library provides reference works.

The area's Western heritage is remembered through displays of saddles, Stetsons, cattle brands and lariats as well as American Indian pottery and arrowheads.

Antique musical instruments such as Victrolas and banjos are displayed as are 1,200 German beer steins and more than 600 World War I posters. A group of statuary art by late 19th-century sculptor John Rogers depicts vignettes of everyday life. **Hours:** Mon.-Sat. 8:30-5, Sun. 10-5. Closed Thanksgiving and Dec. 25. **Cost:** Donations. **Phone:** (918) 341-5707.

GEM **WILL ROGERS MEMORIAL MUSEUM,** 1720 W. Will Rogers Blvd., is a ranch-style museum overlooking Claremore on the site where Will Rogers planned to build a home. In the foyer is a well-known bronze sculpture of Rogers by Jo Davidson. Among personal items exhibited are an international saddle collection, miniature saddles, riding whips and ropes.

Dioramas highlight Rogers' life and stints as a rodeo performer, vaudeville sensation, columnist, author and star of some 70 films. Documentaries and several of Will Rogers' movies are shown continuously; a hands-on children's area specializes in American Indian life. A library and archives are included; the Rogers' family tomb is in a sunken garden. **Time:** Allow 1 hour minimum. **Hours:** Daily 8-5. **Cost:** Donations. **Phone:** (918) 341-0719 or (800) 324-9455.

HOMINY (D-1) pop. 2,584, elev. 282′

Hominy lies in the center of the former Osage Indian Reservation, composed of different bands of Osage Indians who were relocated from Kansas in 1872. Early residents named the town after the Osage chief Ho Mo I, meaning "night walker."

A series of 40 murals that depict American Indian folklore can be seen on the sides of buildings throughout Hominy. Nearby recreational facilities include Skiatook and Keystone lakes *(see Recreation Chart).*

Hominy Chamber of Commerce: 300 W. Main St., P.O. Box 99, Hominy, OK 74035. **Phone:** (918) 885-4939.

FRED DRUMMOND HOME, 305 N. Price, reflects the lifestyle of Fred and Addie Drummond, who built one of the most successful trading and ranching operations in the area. The Victorian three-story house, completed in 1905, has been painstakingly restored as it appeared in the early 20th century and contains most of its original furnishings. **Time:** Allow 30 minutes minimum. **Hours:** Wed.-Sat. 9-5, Sun. 1-5. Last tour begins 30 minutes before closing. Closed major holidays. **Cost:** Donations. **Phone:** (918) 885-2374.

JENKS (F-2) pop. 9,557

What do a river, a railroad, oil, farming, antiques and an aquarium have in common? They all played a major role in the evolution of Jenks, a vibrant community on the Arkansas River just southwest of Tulsa.

Although its location on the river was advantageous, it was the Midland Valley Railroad that put Jenks on the map. The town was established in 1905 as a weigh station for the railroad. It wasn't long, however, before oil was discovered nearby, and Jenks became the site of "tank farms" to store the black gold.

The oil fields eventually played out, and farming became the area's economic mainstay; cotton, vegetables, dairy cattle and livestock production were prominent players.

Two more recent developments, though, are responsible for luring visitors to the city. The early 20th-century brick buildings on Main Street began to be filled with antique stores, adding to downtown's turn-of-the-century, country-style charm. The town claims that more than 600 dealers have treasures to sell in what has come to be known as the Antique Capital of Oklahoma.

The second development, the decision to build the Oklahoma Aquarium *(see attraction listing)* in Jenks, though, was a major coup. The attraction, on the west bank of the Arkansas River, draws close to a half-million visitors to the city each year.

If you want to do some shopping, grab a bite or just plain relax after your aquarium visit, head to Riverwalk Crossing, a trendy entertainment district overlooking the river. You might even be able to catch some live music at the outdoor amphitheater.

GEM SAVE **OKLAHOMA AQUARIUM** is at 300 Aquarium Dr. Home to more than 4,000 animals from around the world, the aquarium is divided into galleries that include the Shark Adventure, where visitors can walk through a clear acrylic tunnel surrounded by 500,000 gallons of water and schools of sharks. Marvels & Mysteries of the Deep houses seahorses, moon jellies, octopuses, lobsters and shrimp. Other unusual sea creatures can be found in the Bio-Diversity gallery, which includes crabs, jellies, sea stars, sea squirts and sponges.

The Adaptation gallery illustrates how animals have adapted to their habitats. A variety of coastal environments are re-created in the Oceans gallery, which also features touch tanks. Visitors can watch divers feed colorful fish at the Coral Reef exhibit, and a museum houses an extensive collection of antique fishing tackle.

Time: Allow 2 hours minimum. **Hours:** Daily 10-6 (also Tues. 6-9 p.m.). Last admission 1 hour before closing. Closed Dec. 25. **Cost:** $13.95; $11.95 (ages 63+ and military with ID); $9.95 (ages 3-12). **Phone:** (918) 296-3474.

OOLOGAH (D-3) pop. 883, elev. 657′

WILL ROGERS BIRTHPLACE RANCH is 1.5 mi. n. of SR 88 on CR 411. The 1870 home is on a hill overlooking Oologah Lake and is furnished with family memorabilia and period antiques. Longhorn cattle roam the ranch. Historic videotapes are shown continuously. **Hours:** Daily 8-5. **Cost:** Donations. **Phone:** (918) 275-4201 or (800) 324-9455.

PAWHUSKA (C-1) pop. 3,629, elev. 847′

Pawhuska is capital of the Osage Nation, the wealthiest American Indian tribe in America. The town was named after Pahuiska, chief of the Osage Tribe at the beginning of the 19th century. Pawhuska was later the home of the first Boy Scout troop in America, organized by Rev. John Mitchell in May 1909.

The architectural diversity of Pawhuska's downtown historic district stems from the prosperity that came with the oil strike on Osage land in 1921. Buildings of note include the 1887 Gothic-style Immaculate Conception Catholic Church; the Constantine Theatre and the 1894 City Hall, originally the Osage Agency house.

Pawhuska Chamber of Commerce: 210 W. Main St., Pawhuska, OK 74056. **Phone:** (918) 287-1208.

OSAGE COUNTY HISTORICAL SOCIETY MUSEUM, 700 N. Lynn Ave., displays relics of the Old West, the oil industry and the nation's first Boy Scout troop in addition to American Indian artifacts. **Hours:** Mon.-Sat. 9-5. Closed Thanksgiving and Dec. 25. **Cost:** Donations. **Phone:** (918) 287-9119.

OSAGE TRIBAL MUSEUM, 819 Grandview Ave., exhibits American Indian regalia and arts and crafts. **Hours:** Tues.-Sat. 8:30-5. Closed major holidays. **Cost:** Free. **Phone:** (918) 287-5441.

TALLGRASS PRAIRIE PRESERVE, 18 mi. n. on Kihekah, following signs to preserve headquarters, is a 39,000-acre open range that supports more than 750 species of plants in addition to bison, prairie chickens, bob-white quails, wild turkeys, squirrels and rabbits. The preserve's managers hope to re-create a functioning tallgrass prairie ecosystem at the site. Visitors can take a driving tour along the preserve's gravel roads. **Hours:** Daily dawn-dusk. **Cost:** Free. **Phone:** (918) 287-4803.

SAND SPRINGS (F-1) pop. 17,451

West of downtown Tulsa, Sand Springs is nestled in the steep and wooded hills overlooking the Arkansas River, providing a setting often used as a backdrop in movies. Boating and sailing are available at Keystone Lake *(see Recreation Chart)*.

Sand Springs Area Chamber of Commerce: 121 N. Main St., Sand Springs, OK 74063. **Phone:** (918) 245-3221.

SAVE **DISCOVERYLAND!,** 5 mi. s.w. on 41st St., presents the Rogers and Hammerstein play "Oklahoma!" in a 1,500-seat outdoor amphitheater under the stars. Horses and wagons, as well as a real surrey with the fringe on top, are highlights of the production. A barbecue dinner precedes the shows at an additional cost. Free pony rides for children are available before the show.

Inquire about weather policies. **Time:** Allow 2 hours, 30 minutes minimum. **Hours:** Performances Mon.-Sat. at 7:30 p.m., early June to mid-Aug. Barbecue dinner 6-7:30. **Cost:** $19.95; free (ages 0-10). Barbecue dinner is an additional $10.95; $6.95 (ages 0-10). Reservations are recommended. **Phone:** (918) 245-6552 for tickets.

SAPULPA (F-1) pop. 19,166

The town of Sapulpa was named for Sepulcher, a Creek Indian whose unlikely name evolved over time, thanks to misspellings and mispronunciations, into "Sapuipa." He established a trading post one mile south of the present city around 1850, and in 1886 the Atlantic & Pacific Railroad extended its line from Red Fork to this area and called it Sapulpa Station.

After the 1905 Glen Pool oil discovery 8 miles to the southeast, Sapulpa grew into a city that served the oil industry. The town then developed into an agricultural shipping center and now is supported by glass plants, a pottery factory and several small pipe and steel manufacturing plants.

Frankoma Pottery, 9549 Frankoma Rd., is one of the few potteries in the country that uses local clay to produce its products. The company, which has made handcrafted earthenware pottery since 1933, offers tours of its plant; phone (918) 224-5511.

Sapulpa Area Chamber of Commerce: 101 E. Dewey, Sapulpa, OK 74066. **Phone:** (918) 224-0170.

SAPULPA HISTORICAL SOCIETY MUSEUM is at 100 E. Lee St. Local history is featured on guided tours through the museum exhibits, which showcase Creek and Yuchi Indians, the Glen Pool Oil Field and the Frisco Railroad. Late 19th- and early 20th-century appliances depict advances in technology. A fully restored 1922 Waite Phillips filling station is located across the street from the museum. **Time:** Allow 2 hours minimum. **Hours:** Mon.-Tues. and Thurs. 10-3, Wed. 10-noon and 1-3. Closed major holidays. **Cost:** Donations. **Phone:** (918) 224-4871.

Discoveryland!, Sand Springs / © Christian Heeb

This ends listings for the Tulsa Vicinity.
The following page resumes the alphabetical listings of cities in Oklahoma.

TUSKAHOMA (E-11) elev. 582′

Selected by the Choctaw Nation as its capital in 1883, Tuskahoma remained the seat of Choctaw government until after Oklahoma became a state in 1907. The town's name comes from *tushka homma*, which means "red warriors."

CHOCTAW NATION MUSEUM is off US 271N, following signs, in the former capitol building of the Choctaw Nation. The three-story, red-brick structure was completed in 1884 and houses exhibits of pottery, clothing, arrowheads and photographs illustrating the way of life of the Choctaw people. **Time:** Allow 30 minutes minimum. **Hours:** Mon.-Sat. 8-4:30. Closed major holidays. **Cost:** Free. **Phone:** (918) 569-4465.

VIAN (D-11) pop. 1,362, elev. 550′

SEQUOYAH NATIONAL WILDLIFE REFUGE, off I-40 exit 297, then 3 mi. s. following signs, was established in 1970 to provide a habitat for waterfowl and other migratory birds. The majority of the 20,800-acre refuge is comprised of bottomland and is home to mallards, snow geese, hawks, bobwhite quails and various reptiles. A 6-mile automobile tour winds throughout the refuge, where photograph blinds and observation towers are present. **Hours:** Automobile tour daily dawn-dusk. Refuge headquarters open Mon.-Fri. 7:30-4. **Cost:** Free. **Phone:** (918) 773-5251.

VINITA (B-11) pop. 6,472

Vinita was named by a Cherokee Indian, Col. Elias C. Boudinot, after sculptress Vinnie Ream, whose most renowned work is the pensive statue of Abraham Lincoln at the U.S. Capitol. Boudinot fell in love with the young artist while she was in Washington, D.C., on a commission to create the statue. The first woman to be granted such a federal art commission, Ream's sculpture was unveiled in 1871, the same year Vinita was founded.

Since the days of the longhorn cattle drives from Texas, ranching has been an important industry in Vinita. Early cattlemen, however, would hardly recognize the Brangus, which is a hardy combination of purebred Brahman and Aberdeen-Angus cattle. The breed was created by Raymond Pope, a rancher who lived in the area.

The Eastern Trails Museum, inside the Vinita Public Library at 215 W. Illinois St., outlines Oklahoma history through displays of regional American Indian and pioneer artifacts and memorabilia from World Wars I and II; phone (918) 256-2115.

Vinita is an access point for the recreational opportunities on the western shore of Grand Lake O' the Cherokees, created in 1941 with the completion of the Pensacola Dam on the Grand River. *See Recreation Chart.*

Vinita Area Chamber of Commerce: 125 S. Scraper, PSO Building, P.O. Box 882, Vinita, OK 74301. **Phone:** (918) 256-7133.

WATONGA (C-7) pop. 4,658, elev. 1,552′

Founded in 1892, Watonga was named for the Arapaho chief Watonga, or Black Coyote. The town now is a major manufacturer of cheese. Recreational activities abound at nearby Roman Nose State Park *(see Recreation Chart)*.

Watonga Chamber of Commerce: SR 8, P.O. Box 537, Watonga, OK 73772-0357. **Phone:** (580) 623-5452.

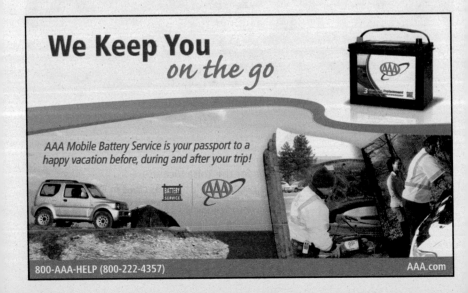

T.B. FERGUSON HOME is at 519 N. Weigle Ave. The white frame Victorian house was built in 1901 for Thompson Benton Ferguson, the sixth territorial governor of Oklahoma. Prior to serving as governor, Ferguson was the founder and publisher of the *Watonga Republican,* which is still in existence. The home has been restored and is decorated in period. **Time:** Allow 30 minutes minimum. **Hours:** Wed.-Fri. 1-5, Sat. 9-5. Closed major holidays. Phone ahead to confirm schedule. **Cost:** Donations. **Phone:** (580) 623-5069.

WEATHERFORD (D-6)

pop. 9,859, elev. 1,647′

On the afternoon of April 18, 1892, Oklahoma began its third land run; throngs of men and women gathered at the border of Cheyenne and Arapaho country, waiting for a chance at land ownership. The next morning they rose early, arriving by wagon and on foot to establish the town of Weatherford.

Once a stop on historic Route 66, Weatherford is home to Southwestern Oklahoma State University, known for its school of pharmacy.

Weatherford Area Chamber of Commerce: 522 W. Rainey, Room 224, P.O. Box 857, Weatherford, OK 73096. **Phone:** (580) 772-7744 or (800) 725-7744.

STAFFORD AIR & SPACE MUSEUM, 3000 Logan Rd. at the Stafford Airport, is a tribute to the Weatherford native's military and aeronautical career. On display are space suits worn by Stafford during four of his space missions as well as aircraft models, a Gemini capsule seat, Apollo-Soyuz docking collar and photographs from the Apollo 10 mission. Visitors can view such aircraft as an F-16, MiG 21 and a T-38 in addition to a replica of the *Wright Flyer* and *Spirit of St. Louis.*

Hours: Mon.-Sat. 9-5, Sun. 1-5. Closed Jan. 1, Easter, Memorial Day, July 4, Labor Day, Thanksgiving and Dec. 25. **Cost:** $5; $2 (ages 6-18 and students with ID). **Phone:** (580) 772-5871.

WEWOKA (E-9) pop. 3,562

The end of the Seminole Indians' "Trail of Tears" journey from Florida, Wewoka became the capital of the Seminole Nation in 1866. Homesteaders appeared at the beginning of the 20th century with the arrival of the Rock Island Railroad. The town became one of the state's leading oil producers overnight with the discovery of the rich Greater Seminole Field in 1926.

The sudden swell in population caused freighting problems for the railroad and stocking problems for local merchants, who were forced to explain to customers that their goods were lost in the "Wewoka Switch." This excuse was used so often that the phrase "caught in a Wewoka Switch" became a popular way of saying that one was caught between a rock and a hard place.

Wewoka Chamber of Commerce: 101 W. Park, Wewoka, OK 74884. **Phone:** (405) 257-5485.

SEMINOLE NATION MUSEUM is downtown at 524 S. Wewoka Ave., 1 blk. e. of SR 56. Dioramas, artifacts, crafts, paintings and other exhibits depict the history of the Seminoles and aspects of their culture. Other displays pertain to pioneers and the Oklahoma oil boom. There also is an art gallery. **Time:** Allow 1 hour minimum. **Hours:** Mon.-Sat. 10-5, Feb.-Dec. Closed major holidays. **Cost:** Donations. **Phone:** (405) 257-5580.

WOODWARD (B-5) pop. 11,853, elev. 1,893′

As were many Oklahoma towns, Woodward was created in a single day. Between noon and sunset on Sept. 16, 1893, when the Cherokee Outlet was opened for homesteading, Woodward became a trade and banking center. It also was on the Western Cattle Trail, which ran from Texas to Dodge City, Kan. The city is a marketing center for a wheat-growing and cattle-raising region.

Woodward Chamber of Commerce: 1006 Oklahoma Ave., P.O. Box 1026, Woodward, OK 73802. **Phone:** (580) 256-7411 or (800) 364-5352.

PLAINS INDIANS AND PIONEERS MUSEUM, 2009 Williams Ave., contains historical material pertaining to northwestern Oklahoma. A homesteader's cabin with an attached stable, displays about the area's American Indians and a portrayal of local agricultural development 1880-1950 are among the exhibits presented. **Time:** Allow 1 hour minimum. **Hours:** Tues.-Sat. 10-5. Closed major holidays. **Cost:** Donations. **Phone:** (580) 256-6136.

SOUTHERN PLAINS RANGE RESEARCH STATION, 2000 18th St., is one of the largest agricultural experiment stations in the country. At the 920-acre field station, research is conducted about farming and ranching techniques. A self-guiding tree tour is available. **Time:** Allow 1 hour minimum. **Hours:** Mon.-Fri. 7:30-4. **Cost:** Free. **Phone:** (580) 256-7449.

WYNNEWOOD (E-8) pop. 2,367, elev. 896′

G.W. EXOTIC ANIMAL PARK is off I-35 exit 64, then 1 blk. e. following signs. This 16-acre sanctuary shelters hundreds of exotic animals, most of which were rescued from cruelty and neglect. Among the animals that visitors can see are bears, bobcats, camels, lions, monkeys and tigers as well as domesticated animals. Plaques for each animal recount the often miserable circumstances in which they were found along with their physical condition at the time.

Time: Allow 1 hour minimum. **Hours:** Daily 8-7, early Apr.-late Oct.; 10-5, rest of year. **Cost:** $10; $8 (ages 3-12 and 65+). **Phone:** (405) 665-5197.

America on the Move is made possible by generous support from General Motors Corporation, AAA, State Farm Companies Foundation, The History Channel, United States Congress, U.S. Department of Transportation, Exxon Mobil, American Public Transportation Association, American Road & Transportation Builders Association, Association of American Railroads, National Asphalt Pavement Association, The UPS Foundation.

Ships' Registry: The Bahamas
©Disney C8001303
AAA
CAA

Arkansas

The Old Mill at T.R. Pugh Memorial Park, North Little Rock © Dennis Flaherty / Jaynes Gallery / Danita Delimont Stock Photography

ALMA pop. 4,160

COMFORT INN & SUITES Book at AAA.com Phone: (479)632-4141

Hotel
$59-$95 All Year

Address: 439 Hwy 71 N 72921 **Location:** I-40, exit 13, just n. **Facility:** 62 one-bedroom standard units, some with whirlpools. 2 stories (no elevator), interior/exterior corridors. *Bath:* combo or shower only. **Parking:** on-site. **Amenities:** voice mail, irons, hair dryers. **Leisure Activities:** whirlpool, limited exercise equipment. **Guest Services:** coin laundry, wireless Internet. **Business Services:** meeting rooms, business center. ASK / SOME UNITS FEE

ALTUS pop. 817

WHERE TO DINE

WIEDERKEHR WEINKELLER RESTAURANT Phone: 479/468-3551

German
$7-$29

The wine cellar of this national historic landmark dates to 1880, which is when J. Wiederkehr built it. Alpine decor enhances the intimate, candlelit atmosphere. Homemade quiche Lorraine is one outstanding example of the Swiss cuisine. Casual dress. **Bar:** Full bar. **Reservations:** suggested. **Hours:** 11 am-3 & 5-9 pm, Sun 11 am-9 pm. Closed major holidays. **Address:** SR 186 72821 **Location:** I-40, exit 41, 4.5 mi s. **Parking:** on-site. **Historic**

ARKADELPHIA pop. 10,912

BEST WESTERN-CONTINENTAL INN Book great rates at AAA.com Phone: (870)246-5592

Hotel
$69-$99 3/1-9/30
$65-$79 10/1-2/28

Address: 136 Valley St 71923 **Location:** I-30, exit 78, just e. **Facility:** 56 one-bedroom standard units. 2 stories (no elevator), exterior corridors. *Bath:* combo or shower only. **Parking:** on-site. **Amenities:** voice mail, irons, hair dryers. **Pool(s):** outdoor. **Leisure Activities:** playground. **Guest Services:** valet and coin laundry, wireless Internet. **Business Services:** PC. **Free Special Amenities: expanded continental breakfast and high-speed Internet.**

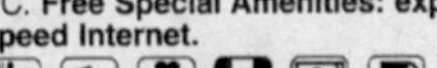
/ SOME UNITS FEE

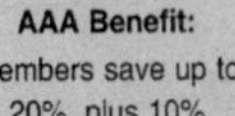

AAA Benefit:
Members save up to 20%, plus 10% bonus points with rewards program.

HAMPTON INN Book great rates at AAA.com Phone: 870/403-0800

Hotel
Rates not provided

Address: 108 Malvern Rd 71923 **Location:** I-30, exit 78, just ne. **Facility:** 58 one-bedroom standard units, some with whirlpools. 3 stories, interior corridors. *Bath:* combo or shower only. **Parking:** on-site. **Amenities:** high-speed Internet, voice mail, irons, hair dryers. **Pool(s):** heated indoor. **Leisure Activities:** whirlpool, exercise room. **Guest Services:** valet and coin laundry, wireless Internet. **Business Services:** meeting rooms, business center. CALL / SOME UNITS

AAA Benefit:
Members save up to 10% everyday!

WHERE TO DINE

FISH NET FAMILY RESTAURANT Menu on AAA.com Phone: 870/246-7885

Seafood
$6-$13

The restaurant features casual, relaxed dining amid rustic, nautical decor. The specialty is farm-raised catfish, but guests will also find a good selection of steak, chicken and other fresh seafood entrees. The service is friendly and attentive. Casual dress. **Reservations:** suggested. **Hours:** 4 pm-9 pm, Sun 11 am-8 pm; hours vary off season. Closed: 12/25; also Mon. **Address:** 5000 Valley St 71923 **Location:** I-30, exit 78, 2 mi nw on SR 7. **Parking:** on-site.

BATESVILLE pop. 9,445

BEST WESTERN SCENIC MOTOR INN Book great rates at AAA.com Phone: (870)698-1855

Motel
$64-$72 All Year

Address: 773 Batesville Blvd 72501 **Location:** 1.5 mi s on US 167. **Facility:** 38 one-bedroom standard units. 2 stories (no elevator), exterior corridors. **Parking:** on-site. **Amenities:** high-speed Internet, voice mail, irons, hair dryers. **Pool(s):** outdoor. **Guest Services:** valet laundry, wireless Internet. **Free Special Amenities: local telephone calls and high-speed Internet.** / SOME UNITS

AAA Benefit:
Members save up to 20%, plus 10% bonus points with rewards program.

COMFORT SUITES *Book at AAA.com* **Phone:** (870)698-1900

Hotel
$89-$109 All Year

Address: 1227 N St. Louis St 72501 **Location:** 1 mi n on US 167. **Facility:** Smoke free premises. 66 one-bedroom standard units, some with whirlpools. 3 stories, interior corridors. *Bath:* combo or shower only. **Parking:** on-site. **Amenities:** high-speed Internet, voice mail, safes (fee), irons, hair dryers. **Pool(s):** heated indoor. **Leisure Activities:** whirlpool, exercise room. **Guest Services:** valet and coin laundry, wireless Internet. **Business Services:** meeting rooms, business center.

ASK

HOLIDAY INN EXPRESS *Book at AAA.com* **Phone:** (870)698-2700

Hotel
$108-$208 10/1-2/28
$104-$208 3/1-9/30

Address: 1130 White Dr 72501 **Location:** 1 mi n on US 167. **Facility:** 65 one-bedroom standard units, some with whirlpools. 3 stories, interior corridors. *Bath:* combo or shower only. **Parking:** on-site. **Terms:** cancellation fee imposed. **Amenities:** high-speed Internet, dual phone lines, voice mail, irons, hair dryers. **Pool(s):** heated indoor. **Leisure Activities:** whirlpool, exercise room. **Guest Services:** valet and coin laundry, wireless Internet. **Business Services:** business center.

ASK CALL / SOME UNITS

RAMADA INN OF BATESVILLE *Book at AAA.com* **Phone:** (870)698-1800

Hotel
$85-$165 All Year

Address: 1325 N St. Louis St 72501 **Location:** 1 mi n on US 167. **Facility:** 122 units. 121 one-bedroom standard units, some with whirlpools. 1 one-bedroom suite with whirlpool. 2 stories (no elevator), exterior corridors. **Parking:** on-site. **Terms:** cancellation fee imposed. **Amenities:** voice mail, irons, hair dryers. **Pool(s):** outdoor. **Leisure Activities:** whirlpool. **Guest Services:** valet and coin laundry, wireless Internet. **Business Services:** meeting rooms, PC.

ASK / SOME UNITS FEE

SUPER 8-BATESVILLE *Book at AAA.com* **Phone:** (870)793-5888

Motel
$59-$75 All Year

Address: 1287 N St. Louis St 72501 **Location:** 1 mi n on US 167. **Facility:** 49 one-bedroom standard units. 2 stories (no elevator), interior corridors. **Parking:** on-site. **Amenities:** safes, hair dryers. **Guest Services:** valet laundry, wireless Internet.

ASK / SOME UNITS FEE

— WHERE TO DINE —

COLTON'S STEAKHOUSE & GRILL **Phone:** 870/793-7427

Steak
$5-$24

A bucket of peanuts on the table, an upbeat Old-West atmosphere and a good selection of steak, chicken and ribs await guests at the casual steakhouse. Casual dress. **Bar:** Full bar. **Hours:** 11 am-10 pm, Fri & Sat-11 pm. Closed: 11/25, 12/25. **Address:** 5 Eagle Mountain Dr 72501 **Location:** 0.4 mi s of jct E Harrison St. **Parking:** on-site.

BELLA VISTA pop. 16,582

The following lodging was either not evaluated or did not meet AAA rating requirements but is listed for your information only.

VACATION RENTALS BELLA VISTA VILLAGE **Phone:** 479/855-1111

fyi

Not evaluated. **Address:** 430 Town Center 72714 **Location:** Jct US 71 and SR 340. Facilities, services, and decor characterize a mid-scale property.

BENTON pop. 21,906

BEST WESTERN INN BENTON *Book great rates at AAA.com* **Phone:** (501)778-9695

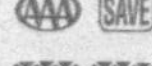

Hotel
$65-$70 All Year

Address: 17036 I-30 72019 **Location:** I-30, exit 117, just w. **Facility:** 65 one-bedroom standard units, some with whirlpools. 2 stories (no elevator), exterior corridors. **Parking:** on-site. **Amenities:** high-speed Internet, irons, hair dryers. **Pool(s):** outdoor. **Guest Services:** coin laundry, wireless Internet. **Free Special Amenities: full breakfast and high-speed Internet.**

/ SOME UNITS FEE

AAA Benefit:
Members save up to 20%, plus 10% bonus points with rewards program.

— WHERE TO DINE —

COLTON'S STEAKHOUSE & GRILL **Phone:** 501/778-6100

Steak
$5-$24

A bucket of peanuts on the table, an upbeat Old-West atmosphere and a good selection of steak, chicken and ribs await guests at the casual steakhouse. Casual dress. **Hours:** 11 am-10 pm, Fri & Sat-11 pm. Closed: 11/25, 12/25. **Address:** 1925 Landers Dr 72015 **Location:** Just w of jct Congo Rd. **Parking:** on-site.

DIXIE CAFE **Phone:** 501/315-6200

Regional American
$7-$11

Southern-style home cooking-chicken-fried steak, meat loaf, pork chops, turnip greens, mashed potatoes and fresh veggies-appeals to families who visit the restaurant's classic "Norman Rockwell" atmosphere. Casual dress. **Hours:** 11 am-10 pm. Closed: 11/25, 12/25. **Address:** 17306 I-30 72015 **Location:** I-30, exit 25. **Parking:** on-site.

The following restaurant has not been evaluated by AAA but is listed for your information only.

WENG'S CHINA BUFFET

Phone: 501/776-0888

fyi Not evaluated. Set up for both lunch and dinner, the buffet lines up a wide variety of favorite dishes. **Address:** 17332 Hwy I-30 72015 **Location:** I-30, exit 118, just s on west service road.

BENTONVILLE pop. 19,730

BEST WESTERN CASTLEROCK INN & SUITES Book great rates at AAA.com **Phone:** (479)845-7707

Hotel
$59-$89 All Year

Address: 501 SE Walton Blvd 72712 **Location:** I-540, exit 85, 1.2 mi w. **Facility:** 89 one-bedroom standard units. 3 stories, interior corridors. *Bath:* combo or shower only. **Parking:** on-site. **Amenities:** high-speed Internet, irons, hair dryers. **Pool(s):** heated indoor. **Leisure Activities:** whirlpool, exercise room. **Guest Services:** coin laundry, wireless Internet. **Business Services:** meeting rooms, PC. **Free Special Amenities: continental breakfast and high-speed Internet.**

CALL / SOME UNITS

AAA Benefit: Members save up to 20%, plus 10% bonus points with rewards program.

CLARION HOTEL & CONVENTION CENTER Book at AAA.com **Phone:** (479)464-4600

Hotel
$84-$119 All Year

Address: 211 SE Walton Blvd 72712 **Location:** I-540, exit 85, 1.2 mi w. **Facility:** Smoke free premises. 105 units. 99 one-bedroom standard units, some with whirlpools. 6 one-bedroom suites. 3 stories, interior/exterior corridors. *Bath:* combo or shower only. **Parking:** on-site. **Amenities:** video games (fee), high-speed Internet, dual phone lines, voice mail, irons, hair dryers. **Pool(s):** heated indoor. **Leisure Activities:** exercise room. **Guest Services:** valet and coin laundry, wireless Internet. **Business Services:** conference facilities, business center.

ASK CALL / SOME UNITS FEE

COMFORT SUITES BENTONVILLE/ROGERS Book great rates at AAA.com **Phone:** 479/254-9099

Hotel
Rates not provided

Address: 2011 SE Walton Blvd 72712 **Location:** I-540, exit 85, just w. **Facility:** Smoke free premises. 115 one-bedroom standard units. 4 stories, interior corridors. *Bath:* combo or shower only. **Parking:** on-site. **Amenities:** high-speed Internet, voice mail, irons, hair dryers. **Pool(s):** heated indoor. **Leisure Activities:** whirlpool, exercise room. **Guest Services:** valet and coin laundry, wireless Internet. **Business Services:** meeting rooms, business center. **Free Special Amenities: continental breakfast and high-speed Internet.** / SOME UNITS FEE

COURTYARD BY MARRIOTT Book great rates at AAA.com **Phone:** (479)273-3333

Hotel
$143-$175 All Year

Address: 1001 McClain Rd 72712 **Location:** US 71, exit 88, just e. Located in Beau Terre Office Park. **Facility:** Smoke free premises. 90 units. 87 one-bedroom standard units, some with whirlpools. 3 one-bedroom suites. 3 stories, interior corridors. *Bath:* combo or shower only. **Parking:** on-site. **Terms:** cancellation fee imposed. **Amenities:** dual phone lines, voice mail, irons, hair dryers. **Pool(s):** heated indoor. **Leisure Activities:** whirlpool, exercise room. **Guest Services:** valet and coin laundry, area transportation, wireless Internet. **Business Services:** meeting rooms, business center.

CALL

COURTYARD Marriott

AAA Benefit: Members save a minimum 5% off the best available rate.

DOUBLETREE GUEST SUITES BENTONVILLE Book great rates at AAA.com **Phone:** (479)845-7770

Hotel
$99-$199 All Year

Address: 301 SE Walton Blvd 72712 **Location:** I-540, exit 85, 1.1 mi w. **Facility:** 140 one-bedroom suites. 5 stories, interior corridors. *Bath:* combo or shower only. **Parking:** on-site. **Terms:** 1-7 night minimum stay, cancellation fee imposed. **Amenities:** video games (fee), high-speed Internet, dual phone lines, voice mail, irons, hair dryers. **Pool(s):** heated indoor. **Leisure Activities:** whirlpool, exercise room. **Guest Services:** valet and coin laundry, wireless Internet. **Business Services:** meeting rooms, business center.

CALL / SOME UNITS

AAA Benefit: Members save 5% or more everyday!

HILTON GARDEN INN Book great rates at AAA.com **Phone:** (479)464-7300

Hotel
$59-$189 All Year

Address: 2204 SE Walton Blvd 72712 **Location:** I-540, exit 85, just w. **Facility:** 133 one-bedroom standard units. 3 stories, interior corridors. *Bath:* combo or shower only. **Parking:** on-site. **Terms:** 1-7 night minimum stay, cancellation fee imposed. **Amenities:** video games (fee), high-speed Internet, dual phone lines, voice mail, irons, hair dryers. **Pool(s):** heated indoor. **Leisure Activities:** whirlpool, exercise room. **Guest Services:** valet and coin laundry, wireless Internet. **Business Services:** meeting rooms, business center.

/ SOME UNITS

AAA Benefit: Members save 5% or more everyday!

HOLIDAY INN EXPRESS Book at AAA.com

Hotel

$65-$139 All Year

Phone: (479)271-2222

Address: 2205 SE Walton Blvd 72712 **Location:** I-540, exit 85, just w. **Facility:** Smoke free premises. 84 one-bedroom standard units, some with whirlpools. 4 stories, interior corridors. *Bath:* combo or shower only. **Parking:** on-site. **Amenities:** high-speed Internet, dual phone lines, voice mail, irons, hair dryers. **Leisure Activities:** exercise room. **Guest Services:** valet and coin laundry, wireless Internet. **Business Services:** meeting rooms, business center.

ASK / SOME UNITS

LA QUINTA INN & SUITES Book at AAA.com

Hotel

$55-$139 All Year

Phone: (479)271-7555

Address: 1001 SE Walton Blvd 72712 **Location:** I-540, exit 85, 0.7 mi w. **Facility:** 107 units. 95 one-bedroom standard units. 12 one-bedroom suites, some with efficiencies. 3 stories, interior corridors. *Bath:* combo or shower only. **Parking:** on-site. **Amenities:** video library (fee), DVD players, voice mail, irons, hair dryers. **Pool(s):** heated indoor. **Leisure Activities:** whirlpool, exercise room. **Guest Services:** valet and coin laundry, wireless Internet. **Business Services:** meeting rooms, business center. ASK CALL / SOME UNITS

MICROTEL INN & SUITES BENTONVILLE Book at AAA.com

Hotel

$55-$65 All Year

Phone: (479)271-6699

Address: 911 SE Walton Blvd 72712 **Location:** I-540, exit 85, 0.8 mi w. **Facility:** 78 one-bedroom standard units. 3 stories, interior corridors. **Parking:** on-site. **Amenities:** high-speed Internet, voice mail, irons, hair dryers. **Leisure Activities:** exercise room. **Guest Services:** wireless Internet. **Business Services:** meeting rooms. / SOME UNITS FEE

SLEEP INN Book at AAA.com

Hotel

$69-$89 All Year

Phone: (479)464-4400

Address: 215 SE Walton Blvd 72712 **Location:** I-540, exit 85, 1.2 mi w. **Facility:** 103 one-bedroom standard units. 2 stories, interior corridors. *Bath:* combo or shower only. **Parking:** on-site. **Terms:** 4 day cancellation notice-fee imposed. **Amenities:** high-speed Internet, voice mail, irons, hair dryers. **Pool(s):** heated outdoor. **Guest Services:** valet and coin laundry, wireless Internet. **Business Services:** PC. ASK / SOME UNITS FEE

SPRINGHILL SUITES BY MARRIOTT Book great rates at AAA.com

Hotel

$116-$142 All Year

Phone: (479)464-4777

Address: 2304 SE Walton Blvd 72712 **Location:** I-540, exit 85, just w. **Facility:** Smoke free premises. 67 one-bedroom standard units. 3 stories, interior corridors. *Bath:* combo or shower only. **Parking:** on-site. **Terms:** cancellation fee imposed. **Amenities:** high-speed Internet, dual phone lines, voice mail, irons, hair dryers. **Pool(s):** heated indoor. **Leisure Activities:** whirlpool, exercise room. **Guest Services:** valet and coin laundry, wireless Internet. **Business Services:** meeting rooms, business center.

AAA Benefit:
Members save a minimum 5% off the best available rate.

TOWNEPLACE SUITES BY MARRIOTT BENTONVILLE/ROGERS Book great rates at AAA.com

Extended Stay Hotel

$121-$147 All Year

Phone: (479)621-0202

Address: 3100 SE 14th St 72712 **Location:** I-540, exit 86, just e. **Facility:** Smoke free premises. 78 units. 65 one-bedroom standard units with kitchens. 9 one- and 4 two-bedroom suites, some with efficiencies or kitchens. 4 stories, interior corridors. *Bath:* combo or shower only. **Parking:** on-site. **Terms:** cancellation fee imposed. **Amenities:** video library, DVD players, high-speed Internet, dual phone lines, voice mail, irons, hair dryers. **Pool(s):** heated indoor. **Leisure Activities:** exercise room. **Guest Services:** valet and coin laundry, wireless Internet. **Business Services:** meeting rooms, business center.

CALL / SOME UNITS FEE

AAA Benefit:
Members save a minimum 5% off the best available rate.

WINGATE BY WYNDHAM Book at AAA.com

Hotel

Rates not provided

Phone: 479/418-5400

Address: 7400 SW Old Farm Blvd 72712 **Location:** 7.4 mi w of jct Walton and SW Regional Airport blvds. **Facility:** 102 one-bedroom standard units. 4 stories, interior corridors. *Bath:* combo or shower only. **Parking:** on-site. **Amenities:** high-speed Internet, voice mail, safes, irons, hair dryers. **Pool(s):** heated indoor. **Leisure Activities:** whirlpool, exercise room. **Guest Services:** coin laundry, wireless Internet. **Business Services:** meeting rooms, business center.

CALL / SOME UNITS FEE

WHERE TO DINE

RIVER GRILLE

American

$6-$38

Phone: 479/271-4141

Service is sophisticated and the cuisine of excellent quality at this classy grill. Creative presentation marks the wonderful creme brulee. Dressy casual. **Bar:** Full bar. **Reservations:** suggested. **Hours:** 11 am-2:30 & 4:30-9:30 pm, Sat from 5 pm. Closed major holidays; also Sun. **Address:** 1003 McClain Rd 72712 **Location:** I-540, exit 88, just e. **Parking:** on-site.

BERRYVILLE pop. 4,433

FAIRWAY MOTOR INN — **Phone:** 870/423-3395

Motel
$70-$75 3/1-11/15
$50-$65 11/16-2/28

Address: 577 Hwy 62 W 72616 **Location:** On US 62, 2.5 mi w. Located in a rural area. **Facility:** 21 one-bedroom standard units. 2 stories (no elevator), exterior corridors. **Parking:** on-site. **Pool(s):** outdoor. **Leisure Activities:** basketball, horseshoes. **Guest Services:** wireless Internet. **Free Special Amenities: local telephone calls and high-speed Internet.** / SOME UNITS

BLYTHEVILLE pop. 18,272

BEST WESTERN BLYTHEVILLE INN *Book great rates at AAA.com* — **Phone:** (870)762-5200

Motel
$72-$79 3/1-9/1
$63-$69 9/2-2/28

Address: 1101 Kari Ln 72315 **Location:** I-55, exit 63, just nw. **Facility:** 40 one-bedroom standard units, some with whirlpools. 2 stories (no elevator), exterior corridors. **Parking:** on-site. **Terms:** cancellation fee imposed. **Amenities:** high-speed Internet, irons, hair dryers. **Pool(s):** outdoor. **Leisure Activities:** exercise room. **Guest Services:** coin laundry, wireless Internet. **Business Services:** PC. **Free Special Amenities: full breakfast and high-speed Internet.** / SOME UNITS

AAA Benefit:
Members save up to 20%, plus 10% bonus points with rewards program.

HAMPTON INN *Book great rates at AAA.com* — **Phone:** 870/763-5220

Hotel
Rates not provided

Address: 301 N Frontage Rd 72315 **Location:** I-55, exit 67, just nw. **Facility:** 87 one-bedroom standard units. 2 stories, exterior corridors. **Parking:** on-site. **Amenities:** video games (fee), voice mail, irons, hair dryers. **Pool(s):** outdoor. **Guest Services:** valet laundry, wireless Internet. **Business Services:** PC.

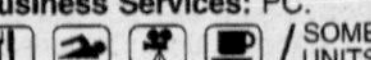  

AAA Benefit:
Members save up to 10% everyday!

HOLIDAY INN *Book at AAA.com* — **Phone:** (870)763-5800

Hotel
$90-$104 All Year

Address: 1121 E Main St 72315 **Location:** I-55, exit 67, just w. **Facility:** 152 units. 149 one-bedroom standard units. 3 one-bedroom suites. 2 stories (no elevator), interior/exterior corridors. **Parking:** on-site. **Amenities:** video games (fee), dual phone lines, voice mail, irons, hair dryers. **Pool(s):** outdoor, heated indoor. **Leisure Activities:** whirlpool, exercise room. **Guest Services:** valet and coin laundry, wireless Internet. **Business Services:** conference facilities, business center.

ASK / SOME UNITS FEE

QUALITY INN *Book at AAA.com* — **Phone:** (870)763-7081

Hotel
$72-$78 All Year

Address: 1520 E Main St 72315 **Location:** I-55, exit 67, just w. **Facility:** 105 one-bedroom standard units. 2 stories (no elevator), exterior corridors. **Parking:** on-site. **Amenities:** irons, hair dryers. **Pool(s):** outdoor. **Guest Services:** valet laundry, wireless Internet. **Business Services:** meeting rooms, PC. ASK / SOME UNITS FEE

WHERE TO DINE

OLYMPIA — **Phone:** 870/838-1204

Steak
$6-$18

A selection of steak, seafood and pasta dishes is served in a comfortable atmosphere. Casual dress. **Bar:** Full bar. **Hours:** 11 am-9:30 pm, Fri & Sat-10:30 pm. Closed: 5/31, 7/4. **Address:** I-55 & SR 18 72315 **Location:** I-55, exit 67, just w. **Parking:** on-site.

BRINKLEY pop. 3,940

BAYMONT INN & SUITES *Book at AAA.com* — **Phone:** (870)734-4300

Hotel
$65-$75 All Year

Address: 1815 N Main St 72021 **Location:** I-40, exit 216, just n. **Facility:** 60 one-bedroom standard units, some with whirlpools. 2 stories (no elevator), interior corridors. *Bath:* combo or shower only. **Parking:** on-site. **Amenities:** safes, irons, hair dryers. **Pool(s):** heated indoor. **Leisure Activities:** exercise room. **Guest Services:** coin laundry, wireless Internet.

ASK / SOME UNITS

BRYANT pop. 9,764

AMERICAS BEST VALUE INN Book at AAA.com Phone: (501)653-7800

Motel
$55-$90 All Year

Address: 407 W Commerce St 72022 **Location:** I-30, exit 123, just sw. **Facility:** 32 one-bedroom standard units, some with whirlpools. 2 stories (no elevator), exterior corridors. **Parking:** on-site, winter plug-ins. **Amenities:** voice mail, hair dryers. **Guest Services:** wireless Internet.

ASK / SOME UNITS FEE

COMFORT INN & SUITES Book great rates at AAA.com Phone: (501)653-4000

AAA SAVE
Hotel
$60-$90 All Year

Address: 209 W Commerce St 72022 **Location:** I-30, exit 123, just w. **Facility:** 78 units. 73 one-bedroom standard units, some with whirlpools. 5 one-bedroom suites. 3 stories, interior corridors. *Bath:* combo or shower only. **Parking:** on-site. **Amenities:** high-speed Internet, dual phone lines, voice mail, safes (fee), irons, hair dryers. **Pool(s):** heated indoor. **Leisure Activities:** putting green, exercise room, basketball. **Guest Services:** coin laundry, wireless Internet. **Business Services:** meeting rooms, business center. **Free Special Amenities: full breakfast and high-speed Internet.**

/ SOME UNITS

HAMPTON INN Book great rates at AAA.com Phone: (501)847-3200

Hotel
$89-$119 All Year

Address: 307 Office Park Dr 72022 **Location:** I-30, exit 123, just w. **Facility:** 76 one-bedroom standard units. 4 stories, interior corridors. *Bath:* combo or shower only. **Parking:** on-site. **Terms:** 1-7 night minimum stay, cancellation fee imposed. **Amenities:** video games (fee), high-speed Internet, voice mail, irons, hair dryers. **Pool(s):** heated outdoor. **Leisure Activities:** exercise room. **Guest Services:** valet and coin laundry, wireless Internet. **Business Services:** meeting rooms, business center.

CALL / SOME UNITS

HOLIDAY INN EXPRESS Book great rates at AAA.com Phone: (501)847-0900

AAA SAVE
Hotel
$79-$109 All Year

Address: 2915 Main St 72022 **Location:** I-30, exit 123, just n on west service road. **Facility:** 64 one-bedroom standard units, some with whirlpools. 2 stories, interior corridors. *Bath:* combo or shower only. **Parking:** on-site. **Amenities:** high-speed Internet, voice mail, irons, hair dryers. **Pool(s):** outdoor. **Guest Services:** valet and coin laundry, wireless Internet. **Business Services:** meeting rooms. **Free Special Amenities: expanded continental breakfast and high-speed Internet.**

CALL / SOME UNITS

HOMETOWN HOTEL.COM Book great rates at AAA.com Phone: (501)653-0123

AAA SAVE
Hotel
$64-$84 All Year

Address: 2921 Main St 72022 **Location:** I-30, exit 123, just nw. **Facility:** Smoke free premises. 46 one-bedroom standard units. 3 stories, interior/exterior corridors. *Bath:* combo or shower only. **Parking:** on-site. **Terms:** 7 day cancellation notice. **Amenities:** high-speed Internet, voice mail, irons, hair dryers. **Guest Services:** valet laundry, wireless Internet. **Business Services:** PC. **Free Special Amenities: expanded continental breakfast and high-speed Internet.**

CALL

SUPER 8 Book at AAA.com Phone: (501)847-7888

Motel
$50-$75 All Year

Address: 201 Dell Dr 72022 **Location:** I-30, exit 123, just e. **Facility:** 33 one-bedroom standard units, some with whirlpools. 2 stories (no elevator), exterior corridors. **Parking:** on-site. **Amenities:** irons, hair dryers. **Guest Services:** wireless Internet.

ASK / SOME UNITS FEE

VISTA INN & SUITES Book great rates at AAA.com Phone: (501)847-7120

AAA SAVE
Hotel
$65-$96 All Year

Address: 210 Office Park Dr 72022 **Location:** I-30, exit 123, just w. **Facility:** 33 one-bedroom standard units, some with whirlpools. 2 stories (no elevator), exterior corridors. **Parking:** on-site. **Terms:** 7 day cancellation notice-fee imposed. **Amenities:** high-speed Internet, irons, hair dryers. *Some:* DVD players. **Pool(s):** outdoor. **Leisure Activities:** exercise room. **Guest Services:** coin laundry, wireless Internet. **Business Services:** PC.

/ SOME UNITS FEE

WHERE TO DINE

TA MOLLY'S Phone: 501/653-2600

Mexican
$6-$11

Hearty portions of Mexican cuisine are served promptly in the inviting dining room. Casual dress. **Hours:** 11 am-9 pm, Fri & Sat-10 pm. Closed: 11/25, 12/25. **Address:** 206 W Commerce St 72022 **Location:** I-30, exit 123, just w. **Parking:** on-site.

CABOT pop. 15,261

WHERE TO DINE

DIXIE CAFE Phone: 501/843-1700

Regional American
$7-$11

Southern-style home cooking-chicken-fried steak, meat loaf, pork chops, turnip greens, mashed potatoes and fresh veggies-appeals to families who visit the restaurant's classic "Norman Rockwell" atmosphere. Casual dress. **Hours:** 11 am-10 pm. Closed: 11/25, 12/25. **Address:** 302 S Rockwood Dr 72023 **Location:** Just sw of jct Main St. **Parking:** on-site.

CAMDEN pop. 13,154

COMFORT INN *Book at AAA.com* **Phone:** 870/836-9000

Hotel
Rates not provided

Address: 1 Ridgecrest Dr 71701 **Location:** Just w of jct US 79 and 278. **Facility:** 69 one-bedroom standard units, some with whirlpools. 3 stories, interior corridors. *Bath:* combo or shower only. **Parking:** on-site. **Amenities:** high-speed Internet, dual phone lines, voice mail, safes (fee), irons, hair dryers. **Pool(s):** heated indoor. **Leisure Activities:** putting green, exercise room, sports court. **Guest Services:** valet and coin laundry, wireless Internet. **Business Services:** meeting rooms, PC.

CALL / SOME UNITS FEE

HOLIDAY INN EXPRESS *Book at AAA.com* **Phone:** 870/836-8100

Hotel
Rates not provided

Address: 1450 US Hwy 278 W 71701 **Location:** 1 mi w of jct US 79 and 278. **Facility:** 64 one-bedroom standard units, some with whirlpools. 2 stories, interior corridors. *Bath:* combo or shower only. **Parking:** on-site. **Amenities:** high-speed Internet, dual phone lines, voice mail, irons, hair dryers. **Pool(s):** outdoor. **Guest Services:** valet and coin laundry, wireless Internet. **Business Services:** meeting rooms, business center. CALL / SOME UNITS

CLARKSVILLE pop. 7,719

BEST WESTERN SHERWOOD INN *Book great rates at AAA.com* **Phone:** (479)754-7900

Hotel
$53-$79 All Year

Address: 1207 S Rogers Ave 72830 **Location:** I-40, exit 58, just n. **Facility:** 53 units. 52 one-bedroom standard units. 1 two-bedroom suite with kitchen. 2 stories (no elevator), exterior corridors. **Parking:** on-site. **Amenities:** high-speed Internet, irons, hair dryers. **Pool(s):** outdoor. **Leisure Activities:** whirlpool. **Guest Services:** coin laundry, wireless Internet. **Business Services:** PC. **Free Special Amenities: continental breakfast and high-speed Internet.**

/ SOME UNITS

AAA Benefit:
Members save up to 20%, plus 10% bonus points with rewards program.

HAMPTON INN CLARKSVILLE *Book great rates at AAA.com* **Phone:** (479)754-4444

Hotel
$78-$88 All Year

Address: 2630 W Clark Rd 72830 **Location:** I-40, exit 55, just n. **Facility:** 62 one-bedroom standard units, some with whirlpools. 2 stories, interior corridors. *Bath:* combo or shower only. **Parking:** on-site. **Terms:** 1-7 night minimum stay, cancellation fee imposed. **Amenities:** voice mail, irons, hair dryers. **Pool(s):** heated indoor. **Leisure Activities:** whirlpool. **Guest Services:** coin laundry, wireless Internet. **Business Services:** meeting rooms, business center. **Free Special Amenities: expanded continental breakfast and local telephone calls.**

CALL / SOME UNITS

AAA Benefit:
Members save up to 10% everyday!

QUALITY INN & SUITES *Book at AAA.com* **Phone:** (479)754-3000

Hotel
$75-$125 All Year

Address: 1167 S Rogers Ave 72830 **Location:** I-40, exit 58, just n. **Facility:** 51 one-bedroom standard units, some with whirlpools. 2-3 stories (no elevator), exterior corridors. **Parking:** on-site. **Amenities:** high-speed Internet, irons, hair dryers. **Pool(s):** outdoor. **Guest Services:** coin laundry, wireless Internet. **Business Services:** business center.

ASK / SOME UNITS

CLINTON pop. 2,283

BEST WESTERN HILLSIDE INN *Book great rates at AAA.com* **Phone:** (501)745-4700

Hotel
$66-$120 All Year

Address: 1025 Hwy 65 B 72031 **Location:** Just w of jct US 62. **Facility:** 36 one-bedroom standard units. 2 stories (no elevator), exterior corridors. **Parking:** on-site. **Amenities:** high-speed Internet, irons, hair dryers. **Pool(s):** outdoor. **Guest Services:** wireless Internet. **Business Services:** PC.

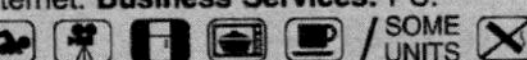

AAA Benefit:
Members save up to 20%, plus 10% bonus points with rewards program.

FREE local telephone calls and high-speed Internet

CONWAY pop. 43,167

BEST WESTERN CONWAY

Book great rates at AAA.com

Phone: (501)329-9855

Hotel
$70-$75 All Year

Address: 816 E Oak St 72032 **Location:** I-40, exit 127, just n. **Facility:** 70 units. 68 one-bedroom standard units. 2 one-bedroom suites. 2 stories (no elevator), exterior corridors. *Bath:* combo or shower only. **Parking:** on-site. **Amenities:** irons, hair dryers. *Some:* high-speed Internet. **Pool(s):** outdoor. **Guest Services:** valet and coin laundry, wireless Internet. **Business Services:** meeting rooms, PC. **Free Special Amenities: local telephone calls and high-speed Internet.**

/ SOME UNITS

AAA Benefit:
Members save up to 20%, plus 10% bonus points with rewards program.

CANDLEWOOD SUITES

Book at AAA.com

Phone: (501)329-8551

Extended Stay Hotel
$89-$149 All Year

Address: 2360 Sanders St 72033 **Location:** I-40, exit 125, just se. **Facility:** 65 units. 61 one-bedroom standard units with efficiencies. 4 one-bedroom suites with efficiencies. 3 stories, interior corridors. *Bath:* combo or shower only. **Parking:** on-site. **Amenities:** DVD players, high-speed Internet, voice mail, irons, hair dryers. **Leisure Activities:** exercise room. **Guest Services:** valet and coin laundry, wireless Internet. **Business Services:** business center.

ASK / SOME UNITS FEE

COMFORT SUITES

Book great rates at AAA.com

Phone: (501)329-8548

Hotel
$89-$129 3/1-10/31
$89-$119 11/1-2/28

Address: 705 Museum Rd 72032 **Location:** I-40, exit 127, just ne. **Facility:** Smoke free premises. 72 one-bedroom standard units, some with whirlpools. 3 stories, interior corridors. *Bath:* combo or shower only. **Parking:** on-site. **Terms:** cancellation fee imposed. **Amenities:** high-speed Internet, voice mail, safes, irons, hair dryers. **Pool(s):** heated indoor. **Leisure Activities:** exercise room. **Guest Services:** valet and coin laundry, wireless Internet. **Business Services:** meeting rooms, business center. **Free Special Amenities: expanded continental breakfast and high-speed Internet.**

CALL

COUNTRY INN & SUITES BY CARLSON

Book great rates at AAA.com

Phone: (501)932-0500

Hotel
$85-$159 All Year

Address: 750 Amity Rd 72032 **Location:** I-40, exit 127, just ne. **Facility:** Smoke free premises. 67 units. 40 one-bedroom standard units, some with whirlpools. 27 one-bedroom suites. 4 stories, interior corridors. *Bath:* combo or shower only. **Parking:** on-site. **Terms:** cancellation fee imposed. **Amenities:** high-speed Internet, voice mail, irons. **Pool(s):** heated indoor. **Leisure Activities:** whirlpool, exercise room. **Guest Services:** coin laundry, wireless Internet. **Business Services:** meeting rooms, business center. **Free Special Amenities: full breakfast and high-speed Internet.**

CALL

HAMPTON INN

Book great rates at AAA.com

Phone: (501)329-8999

Hotel
$99-$101 All Year

Address: 810 Museum Rd 72032 **Location:** I-40, exit 127, just n. **Facility:** 75 one-bedroom standard units, some with whirlpools. 3 stories, interior corridors. *Bath:* combo or shower only. **Parking:** on-site. **Terms:** 1-7 night minimum stay, cancellation fee imposed. **Amenities:** voice mail, irons, hair dryers. **Pool(s):** outdoor. **Leisure Activities:** exercise room. **Guest Services:** valet and coin laundry, wireless Internet. **Business Services:** meeting rooms, PC.

/ SOME UNITS

AAA Benefit:
Members save up to 10% everyday!

HILTON GARDEN INN

Book great rates at AAA.com

Phone: (501)329-1444

Hotel
$89-$179 All Year

Address: 805 Amity Rd 72032 **Location:** I-40, exit 127, just n. **Facility:** 103 one-bedroom standard units. 4 stories, interior corridors. *Bath:* combo or shower only. **Parking:** on-site. **Terms:** 1-7 night minimum stay, cancellation fee imposed. **Amenities:** high-speed Internet, voice mail, irons, hair dryers. **Pool(s):** heated indoor. **Leisure Activities:** whirlpool, exercise room. **Guest Services:** valet and coin laundry, wireless Internet. **Business Services:** meeting rooms, business center.

CALL / SOME UNITS

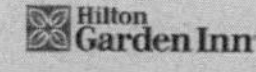

AAA Benefit:
Members save 5% or more everyday!

HOLIDAY INN EXPRESS HOTEL & SUITES

Book great rates at AAA.com

Phone: (501)450-9112

Hotel
$89-$149 All Year

Address: 2370 Sanders St 72033 **Location:** I-40, exit 125, just s. **Facility:** 69 one-bedroom standard units, some with whirlpools. 3 stories, interior corridors. *Bath:* combo or shower only. **Parking:** on-site. **Amenities:** high-speed Internet, dual phone lines, voice mail, irons, hair dryers. **Pool(s):** heated indoor. **Leisure Activities:** exercise room. **Guest Services:** valet and coin laundry, wireless Internet. **Business Services:** meeting rooms, business center. **Free Special Amenities: expanded continental breakfast and high-speed Internet.** / SOME UNITS

QUALITY INN Book great rates at AAA.com **Phone:** 501/329-0300

Hotel
Rates not provided

Address: 150 Hwy 65 N 72033 **Location:** I-40, exit 125, just n. **Facility:** 60 one-bedroom standard units, some with efficiencies (no utensils) and/or whirlpools. 2 stories (no elevator), exterior corridors. **Parking:** on-site. **Amenities:** dual phone lines, voice mail, irons, hair dryers. **Pool(s):** outdoor. **Guest Services:** valet laundry, wireless Internet.
/ SOME UNITS FEE

SUPER 8-CONWAY Book at AAA.com **Phone:** (501)505-8880

Hotel
$66-$109 All Year

Address: 2430 Sanders St 72032 **Location:** I-40, exit 125, just se. **Facility:** 64 one-bedroom standard units, some with whirlpools. 2 stories (no elevator), interior corridors. *Bath:* combo or shower only. **Parking:** on-site. **Amenities:** hair dryers. **Pool(s):** heated indoor. **Guest Services:** valet and coin laundry, wireless Internet. ASK / SOME UNITS

WHERE TO DINE

CHINA TOWN RESTAURANT **Phone:** 501/450-9090

Chinese
$5-$10

The food is hot, tasty and all-you-can-eat when you dine on the buffet at China Town, which features Mandarin and Cantonese dishes. The popular luncheon buffet is served Monday-Friday 11 am-2 pm and Sunday 11:30 am-3:30 pm and includes veggies and dessert. Casual dress. **Hours:** 11 am-9:30 pm, Fri & Sat-10 pm, Sun-9 pm. Closed: 11/25, 12/25. **Address:** 201 Hwy 65 N, Suite 60 72032 **Location:** I-40, exit 125, just n; in Conway Towne Center. **Parking:** on-site.

COLTON'S STEAKHOUSE & GRILL **Phone:** 501/329-6454

Steak
$5-$24

A bucket of peanuts on the table, an upbeat Old-West atmosphere and a good selection of steak, chicken and ribs await guests at the casual steakhouse. Casual dress. **Bar:** Full bar. **Hours:** 11 am-10 pm. Closed: 11/25, 12/25. **Address:** 120 E Oak 72032 **Location:** I-40, exit 127, just s. **Parking:** on-site.

DIXIE CAFE **Phone:** 501/327-4777

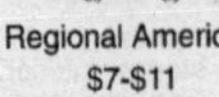

Regional American
$7-$11

Southern-style home cooking-chicken-fried steak, meat loaf, pork chops, turnip greens, mashed potatoes and fresh veggies-appeals to families who visit the restaurant's classic "Norman Rockwell" atmosphere. Casual dress. **Hours:** 11 am-10 pm. Closed: 11/25, 12/25. **Address:** 1101 Fendley Dr 72032 **Location:** I-40, exit 125, 0.5 mi s. **Parking:** on-site.

MARKETPLACE GRILL **Phone:** 501/336-0011

American
$8-$23

The restaurant is big on menu variety, incorporating freshly made pasta, pizzas, dressings and sauces. Steaks, Cajun dishes and seafood also are served in the spacious, inviting dining room. Casual dress. **Hours:** 11 am-9 pm, Fri & Sat-10 pm. Closed: 1/1, 11/25, 12/25. **Address:** 600 Skyline Dr 72032 **Location:** I-40, exit 125, just nw. **Parking:** on-site.

EL DORADO pop. 21,530

COUNTRY INN & SUITES BY CARLSON Book at AAA.com **Phone:** 870/881-0455

Hotel
Rates not provided

Address: 2413 W Hillsboro St 71730 **Location:** Just e of jct US 82 and 82B. **Facility:** 71 units. 59 one-bedroom standard units. 12 one-bedroom suites, some with whirlpools. 3 stories, interior corridors. *Bath:* combo or shower only. **Parking:** on-site. **Amenities:** high-speed Internet, voice mail, irons, hair dryers. **Pool(s):** heated indoor. **Leisure Activities:** whirlpool, exercise room. **Guest Services:** valet and coin laundry, wireless Internet. **Business Services:** meeting rooms, business center.
/ SOME UNITS

HAMPTON INN Book great rates at AAA.com **Phone:** (870)862-1800

Hotel
$90-$99 All Year

Address: 2312 Junction City Rd 71730 **Location:** Just e of jct US 167 and 82B. **Facility:** 69 one-bedroom standard units, some with whirlpools. 3 stories, interior corridors. *Bath:* combo or shower only. **Parking:** on-site. **Terms:** 1-7 night minimum stay, cancellation fee imposed. **Amenities:** video games (fee), high-speed Internet, dual phone lines, voice mail, irons, hair dryers. **Pool(s):** outdoor. **Leisure Activities:** whirlpool, exercise room. **Guest Services:** valet and coin laundry, wireless Internet. **Business Services:** meeting rooms, PC.

AAA Benefit:
Members save up to 10% everyday!

LA QUINTA INN EL DORADO Book at AAA.com **Phone:** (870)863-6677

Hotel
$55-$100 All Year

Address: 2303 Junction City Rd 71730 **Location:** Just e of jct US 167 and 82B. **Facility:** 70 one-bedroom standard units. 2 stories (no elevator), interior/exterior corridors. *Bath:* combo or shower only. **Parking:** on-site. **Amenities:** high-speed Internet, voice mail, irons, hair dryers. **Pool(s):** outdoor. **Leisure Activities:** exercise room. **Guest Services:** coin laundry, wireless Internet. **Business Services:** meeting rooms, PC. ASK / SOME UNITS

EUREKA SPRINGS pop. 2,278

1886 CRESCENT HOTEL & SPA Book great rates at AAA.com **Phone:** (479)253-9766

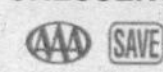

Historic Hotel
$169-$219 3/1-12/15
$179-$194 12/16-2/28

Address: 75 Prospect Ave 72632 **Location:** 1.3 mi n of jct SR 23 on US 62B Historic Loop. **Facility:** Circa 1886 and known as the "Grand Old Lady of the Ozarks"; the lobby and rooms have been restored to their original style of decor. Smoke free premises. 72 units. 64 one-bedroom standard units. 7 one- and 1 two-bedroom suites, some with whirlpools. 5 stories, interior corridors. **Parking:** on-site. **Terms:** 2 night minimum stay - seasonal and/or weekends, 3 day cancellation notice-fee imposed. **Amenities:** irons, hair dryers. *Some:* high-speed Internet. **Dining:** 2 restaurants. **Pool(s):** outdoor. **Leisure Activities:** hiking trails, spa. *Fee:* country club privileges, Victorian wedding court. **Guest Services:** area transportation, wireless Internet. **Business Services:** meeting rooms. **Free Special Amenities: local telephone calls and high-speed Internet.**

FEE / SOME UNITS FEE

1905 BASIN PARK HOTEL Book great rates at AAA.com **Phone:** (479)253-7837

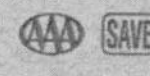

Historic Hotel
$112-$149 3/1-12/15
$89-$109 12/16-2/28

Address: 12 Spring St 72632 **Location:** 0.7 mi n of jct US 62 via SR 23 N; downtown. **Facility:** Built in 1905, some units still have the original furnishings. Smoke free premises. 61 units. 47 one-bedroom standard units, some with whirlpools. 14 one-bedroom suites, some with whirlpools. 7 stories, interior corridors. *Bath:* combo or shower only. **Parking:** on-site (fee) and valet. **Terms:** 2 night minimum stay - seasonal and/or weekends, 3 day cancellation notice-fee imposed. **Amenities:** irons, hair dryers. *Some:* high-speed Internet. **Dining:** The Balcony Bar & Restaurant, see separate listing, entertainment. **Leisure Activities:** whirlpool, sun deck, spa. *Fee:* country club privileges. **Guest Services:** area transportation, wireless Internet. **Business Services:** conference facilities.

/ SOME UNITS FEE

FREE local telephone calls and high-speed Internet

ANGEL AT ROSE HALL **Phone:** (479)253-5405

Bed & Breakfast
$135-$219 All Year

Address: 46 Hillside Ave 72632 **Location:** 1.2 mi n on SR 23, just sw. **Facility:** The house features antique Victorian decor and five units with gas fireplaces. The breakfast room has several tables that seat 2 to 4 each. Smoke free premises. 5 one-bedroom standard units with whirlpools. 2 stories (no elevator), interior corridors. **Parking:** on-site. **Terms:** 2 night minimum stay - weekends, age restrictions may apply, 28 day cancellation notice-fee imposed. **Amenities:** video library, DVD players, CD players, voice mail, hair dryers. **Leisure Activities:** gazebo, patio. *Fee:* country club privileges. **Guest Services:** wireless Internet.

ARSENIC & OLD LACE B&B **Phone:** (479)253-5454

Bed & Breakfast
$139-$279 All Year

Address: 60 Hillside Ave 72632 **Location:** 1.2 mi n on SR 23, just sw; downtown. Located in a residential area. **Facility:** Victorian antiques and stained-glass windows embellish the parlor of the B&B, and the rooms—each with a gas fireplace—vary in theme. 5 one-bedroom standard units with whirlpools. 3 stories (no elevator), interior/exterior corridors. **Parking:** on-site. **Terms:** 2 night minimum stay - weekends, age restrictions may apply, 15 day cancellation notice-fee imposed. **Amenities:** video library, DVD players, CD players, irons, hair dryers. **Guest Services:** wireless Internet.

ASK / SOME UNITS FEE

BAVARIAN INN **Phone:** 479/253-8128

Hotel
$70-$130 10/1-11/25
$68-$128 3/1-9/30

Address: 325 W Van Buren St 72632 **Location:** 1 mi w of jct US 62 and SR 23. **Facility:** 21 one-bedroom standard units with whirlpools. 3 stories (no elevator), exterior corridors. **Parking:** on-site. **Terms:** open 3/1-11/25, office hours 8 am-9 pm, 3 day cancellation notice. **Amenities:** irons, hair dryers. *Some:* dual phone lines. **Dining:** restaurant, see separate listing. **Pool(s):** outdoor. **Guest Services:** wireless Internet.

/ SOME UNITS FEE

BEST WESTERN-EUREKA INN Book great rates at AAA.com **Phone:** (479)253-9551

Hotel
$60-$120 3/1-11/13
$60-$90 11/14-2/28

Address: 101 E Van Buren St 72632 **Location:** Just w of jct US 62 and SR 23 N. **Facility:** Smoke free premises. 85 one-bedroom standard units, some with whirlpools. 2 stories (no elevator), interior/exterior corridors. **Parking:** on-site. **Amenities:** irons, hair dryers. *Some:* high-speed Internet. **Dining:** The Gazebo Restaurant, see separate listing. **Pool(s):** heated outdoor. **Leisure Activities:** sauna, whirlpool, exercise room. *Fee:* golf privileges. **Guest Services:** wireless Internet. **Business Services:** meeting rooms, PC. **Free Special Amenities: room upgrade (subject to availability with advance reservations).**

/ SOME UNITS FEE FEE

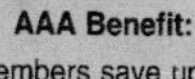

AAA Benefit:
Members save up to 20%, plus 10% bonus points with rewards program.

BEST WESTERN INN OF THE OZARKS *Book great rates at AAA.com* **Phone:** (479)253-9768

Hotel
$70-$200 3/1-11/27
$60-$170 11/28-2/28

Address: 207 W Van Buren St 72632 **Location:** 0.5 mi w of jct US 62 and SR 23. **Facility:** 122 units. 118 one-bedroom standard units, some with whirlpools. 4 one-bedroom suites. 2 stories (no elevator), exterior corridors. *Bath:* combo or shower only. **Parking:** on-site. **Terms:** 3 day cancellation notice. **Amenities:** voice mail, irons, hair dryers. *Some:* high-speed Internet. **Dining:** Myrtie Mae's, see separate listing. **Pool(s):** heated outdoor. **Leisure Activities:** whirlpool, miniature golf, lighted tennis court, table tennis, pavilion, playground, shuffleboard. *Fee:* game room. **Guest Services:** coin laundry, wireless Internet. **Business Services:** conference facilities, PC. *(See color ad below)*

AAA Benefit: Members save up to 20%, plus 10% bonus points with rewards program.

 / SOME UNITS FEE  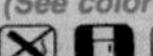 

FREE local telephone calls and high-speed Internet

BRACKENRIDGE LODGE **Phone:** 479/253-6803

Motel
$49-$149 3/1-11/30
$42-$129 12/1-2/28

Address: 352 W Van Buren St 72632 **Location:** 1 mi w of jct US 62 and SR 23. **Facility:** 12 units. 10 one-bedroom standard units, some with whirlpools. 2 cabins. 1 story, exterior corridors. *Bath:* combo or tub only. **Parking:** on-site. **Terms:** 2 night minimum stay - weekends, 7 day cancellation notice-fee imposed. **Amenities:** video library (fee). *Some:* CD players, irons, hair dryers. **Pool(s):** heated outdoor. **Guest Services:** wireless Internet.

ASK / SOME UNITS FEE

COLONIAL INN *Book great rates at AAA.com* **Phone:** (479)253-7300

Hotel
$48-$150 3/1-12/10

Address: 154 Huntsville Rd 72632 **Location:** Just s of jct US 62 and SR 23. **Facility:** 29 units. 28 one- and 1 two-bedroom standard units, some with kitchens and/or whirlpools. 2 stories (no elevator), interior/exterior corridors. **Parking:** on-site. **Terms:** open 3/1-12/10, 2-3 night minimum stay - seasonal and/or weekends, 3 day cancellation notice-fee imposed. **Pool(s):** heated outdoor. **Guest Services:** area transportation-trolley stop, wireless Internet. **Free Special Amenities: continental breakfast and high-speed Internet.** / SOME UNITS FEE

▼ See AAA listing above ▼

DAYS INN Book at AAA.com

Phone: (479)253-8863

Motel

$54-$179 3/1-11/28 & 2/10-2/28

Address: 120 W Van Buren St 72632 **Location:** Just w of jct US 62 and SR 23. **Facility:** 24 one-bedroom standard units, some with whirlpools. 2 stories (no elevator), exterior corridors. **Parking:** on-site. **Terms:** open 3/1-11/28 & 2/10-2/28, 3 day cancellation notice-fee imposed. **Amenities:** irons, hair dryers. **Pool(s):** heated outdoor. **Leisure Activities:** basketball. **Guest Services:** wireless Internet.

ASK / SOME UNITS FEE

HEARTSTONE INN & COTTAGES Book great rates at AAA.com

Phone: (479)253-8916

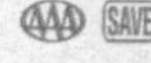

Historic Bed & Breakfast

$100-$175 All Year

Address: 35 Kings Hwy 72632 **Location:** On US 62B Historic Loop, just n of jct US 62; downtown. Located in a residential area. **Facility:** Cozy rooms and charming decorations are inviting characteristics found at the restored Victorian home, located on the historic loop. Smoke free premises. 11 units. 9 one-bedroom standard units, some with whirlpools. 2 cottages. 2 stories (no elevator), interior/exterior corridors. **Parking:** on-site. **Terms:** 2-3 night minimum stay - seasonal and/or weekends, age restrictions may apply, 10 day cancellation notice-fee imposed. **Amenities:** video library, DVD players, irons, hair dryers. **Leisure Activities:** golf club & pool privileges. **Guest Services:** wireless Internet. **Free Special Amenities: full breakfast and high-speed Internet.** / SOME UNITS

INN AT ROSE HALL

Phone: (479)253-8035

Bed & Breakfast

$129-$189 All Year

Address: 56 Hillside Ave 72632 **Location:** 1.2 mi n on SR 23, just sw. **Facility:** The Inn at Rose Hall has a scenic hillside view near historic downtown; Victorian-themed rooms feature fireplaces and whirlpool tubs. Smoke free premises. 5 one-bedroom standard units with whirlpools. 2 stories (no elevator), interior corridors. *Bath:* combo or tub only. **Parking:** on-site. **Terms:** 2 night minimum stay - weekends, age restrictions may apply, 14 day cancellation notice-fee imposed. **Amenities:** video library, irons, hair dryers. *Some:* DVD players, CD players. **Guest Services:** wireless Internet. **Free Special Amenities: full breakfast and high-speed Internet.**

QUALITY INN & SUITES Book great rates at AAA.com

Phone: (479)253-5040

Hotel

$70-$150 All Year

Address: 3010 E Van Buren St 72632 **Location:** 0.8 mi e of jct US 62 and SR 23. **Facility:** Smoke free premises. 81 units. 79 one-bedroom standard units. 2 one-bedroom suites with whirlpools. 2 stories, interior/exterior corridors. *Bath:* combo or shower only. **Parking:** on-site. **Amenities:** high-speed Internet, voice mail, irons, hair dryers. **Pool(s):** heated indoor. **Leisure Activities:** whirlpool. *Fee:* arcade games. **Guest Services:** coin laundry, wireless Internet. **Business Services:** meeting rooms, PC. **Free Special Amenities: full breakfast and high-speed Internet.**

/ SOME UNITS

RED BUD VALLEY RESORT — **Phone:** 479/253-9028

Vacation Rental Cabin
Rates not provided

Address: 369 CR 340 72632 **Location:** 0.8 mi s of jct US 62 on CR 302 (Rockhouse Rd). Located in a quiet area. **Facility:** Log cabins, ranging from family to luxury style, are nestled in a serene mountain locale with outstanding views. 16 cabins. 2 stories (no elevator), exterior corridors. *Bath:* combo or shower only. **Parking:** on-site. **Amenities:** video library, DVD players, hair dryers. *Some:* CD players, irons. **Leisure Activities:** paddleboats, fishing, hiking trails, playground. **Business Services:** meeting rooms.

WHERE TO DINE

AUTUMN BREEZE RESTAURANT — **Phone:** 479/253-7734

American
$10-$40

On the restaurant's eclectic menu are such specialties as coconut beer-battered shrimp, prime rib, rack of lamb, chicken cordon bleu and a fabulous chocolate soufflé for dessert. Dressy casual. **Bar:** Beer & wine. **Hours:** Open 3/2-12/31; 5 pm-9 pm. Closed: 11/25, 12/25; also Sun. **Address:** 190 Huntsville Rd 72632 **Location:** 0.4 mi s of jct US 62 and SR 23. **Parking:** on-site.

THE BALCONY BAR & RESTAURANT — **Phone:** 479/253-7837

American
$6-$19

Diners can enjoy varied sandwiches and other American dishes while keeping an eye on the shops and street activity from balcony seats. Casual dress. **Bar:** Full bar. **Hours:** Open 3/1-1/31 & 2/14-2/28; 11 am-10 pm, Sat-11 pm, Sun-9 pm. Closed: 12/25. **Address:** 12 Spring St 72632 **Location:** 0.7 mi n of jct US 62 via SR 23 N; downtown; in 1905 Basin Park Hotel. **Parking:** street.

BAVARIAN INN RESTAURANT — **Phone:** 479/253-7741

German
$12-$19

German and Czech foods are prepared to please guests' tastes. The dining room reflects the style of a Swiss chateau. Casual dress. **Bar:** Full bar. **Hours:** Open 3/5-11/30; 5 pm-9 pm, Sat from 4:30 pm. Closed: 11/25. **Address:** 325 W Van Buren St 72632 **Location:** 1 mi w of jct US 62 and SR 23; in Bavarian Inn. **Parking:** on-site.

DEVITOS — **Phone:** 479/253-6807

Italian
$7-$24

The fresh, grilled trout with lemon and butter sauce is superb at DeVitos. It's the specialty; the family raises trout on their own farm. Diners will also find well-prepared, traditional Italian dishes, all to be enjoyed in a warm, intimate atmosphere. Casual dress. **Bar:** Full bar. **Hours:** Open 3/1-12/31 & 2/14-2/28; 11 am-2 & 5-9 pm. Closed: 11/25, 12/25; also Wed. **Address:** 5 Center St 72632 **Location:** Center. **Parking:** street.

ERMILIO'S — **Phone:** 479/253-8806

Italian
$9-$24

Set in a restored Victorian home, the restaurant provides a warm, friendly atmosphere that's suitable for family dining. Among examples of Italian "home cooking" are such specialties as homemade eggplant parmesan, Italian sausage, meatball lasagna and marinated filet mignon. Casual dress. **Bar:** Full bar. **Reservations:** not accepted. **Hours:** Open 3/16-2/28; 5 pm-9 pm; call for hours in winter. Closed: 11/25, 12/25. **Address:** 26 White St 72632 **Location:** 2.8 mi nw on US 62B Historic Loop. **Parking:** on-site.

THE GAZEBO RESTAURANT — **Phone:** 479/253-9551

Regional American
$6-$9

A good selection of sandwich items, soup and salads are served in a dining room with a gazebo as its centerpiece. A salad bar is an option for lunch, and breakfast is always a popular time. Casual dress. **Reservations:** accepted. **Hours:** Open 3/1-12/31; 7 am-10:30 pm. **Address:** 101 E Van Buren St 72632 **Location:** Just w of jct US 62 and SR 23 N; in Best Western-Eureka Inn. **Parking:** on-site.

LOCAL FLAVOR CAFE — **Phone:** 479/253-9522

American
$6-$20

The cheerful atmosphere provides a good view of street activity and outdoor dining is available, weather permitting. The creamy tomato soup is delicious, as is the brie plate with homemade bread and fresh fruit. Casual dress. **Bar:** Beer & wine. **Hours:** 11 am-9 pm, Sun 8 am-2 & 5-9 pm; to 3 pm, Wed-Sat to 9 pm, Sun 8 am-2 & 5-9 pm off season. Closed: 11/25, 12/24, 12/25. **Address:** 73 S Main St 72632 **Location:** 0.5 mi n of jct US 62 and SR 63; in historic downtown. **Parking:** street.

MYRTIE MAE'S — *Menu on AAA.com* — **Phone:** 479/253-9768

AAA

Regional American
$6-$19

This locally popular restaurant features country-style cooking such as fried chicken and possum pie (chocolate cream cheese). Myrtie Mae's has a Victorian decor, a casual, family-type atmosphere, and friendly, attentive service. Casual dress. **Bar:** Full bar. **Reservations:** accepted. **Hours:** 7 am-8:30 pm, Fri & Sat-9 pm. **Address:** 207 W Van Buren St 72632 **Location:** 0.5 mi w of jct US 62 and SR 23; in Best Western Inn of the Ozarks. **Parking:** on-site. *(See color ad p 308)*

ROGUE'S MANOR AT SWEET SPRING — **Phone:** 479/253-4911

American
$14-$40

The restaurant occupies a restored Victorian home in the downtown area on the historic loop. Next to one of the famous town springs, the house is listed on the National Register of Historic Places. The kitchen prepares such hearty selections as ostrich steak. Casual dress. **Bar:** Full bar. **Reservations:** suggested. **Hours:** 5 pm-9 pm. Closed: Mon & Tues. **Address:** 124 Spring St 72632 **Location:** 0.5 mi n on US 62B Historic Loop; in historic district. **Parking:** street.

SPARKY'S — **Phone:** 479/253-6001

American
$4-$26

Locals frequent this spot for hanging out in comfort and enjoying casual sandwiches or juicy steak. Casual dress. **Bar:** Full bar. **Reservations:** not accepted. **Hours:** Open 4/1-2/28; 11 am-9 pm. Closed: 12/24, 12/25; also 10/31 & Sun. **Address:** 147 E Van Buren St 72632 **Location:** Just e of jct US 62 and SR 23. **Parking:** on-site.

FAYETTEVILLE pop. 58,047

BEST WESTERN WINDSOR SUITES *Book great rates at AAA.com* **Phone:** (479)587-1400

Hotel
$72-$81 All Year

Address: 1122 S Futrall Dr 72701 **Location:** I-540, exit 62, just se. **Facility:** 68 units. 66 one-bedroom standard units, some with whirlpools. 2 one-bedroom suites with whirlpools. 2 stories (no elevator), exterior corridors. *Bath:* combo or shower only. **Parking:** on-site. **Amenities:** high-speed Internet, voice mail, irons, hair dryers. **Pool(s):** heated indoor. **Leisure Activities:** exercise room. **Guest Services:** coin laundry, wireless Internet. **Business Services:** business center. **Free Special Amenities: continental breakfast and high-speed Internet.**
/ SOME UNITS FEE

AAA Benefit:
Members save up to 20%, plus 10% bonus points with rewards program.

COMFORT INN *Book at AAA.com* **Phone:** (479)695-2121

Hotel
$80-$150 All Year

Address: 735 Shiloh Dr 72704 **Location:** I-540, exit 62, just w. **Facility:** 60 one-bedroom standard units, some with whirlpools. 2 stories, interior corridors. *Bath:* combo or shower only. **Parking:** on-site. **Amenities:** high-speed Internet, voice mail, irons, hair dryers. *Fee:* video games, safes. **Pool(s):** outdoor. **Leisure Activities:** exercise room. **Guest Services:** valet and coin laundry, wireless Internet. **Business Services:** PC. / SOME UNITS

COUNTRY INN & SUITES BY CARLSON *Book at AAA.com* **Phone:** (479)571-5177

Hotel
$90-$179 All Year

Address: 1234 Steamboat Dr 72704 **Location:** I-540, exit 64, just nw. **Facility:** 65 units. 53 one-bedroom standard units, some with whirlpools. 12 one-bedroom suites, some with kitchens (no utensils). 3 stories, interior corridors. *Bath:* combo or shower only. **Parking:** on-site. **Terms:** cancellation fee imposed. **Amenities:** high-speed Internet, voice mail, irons, hair dryers. **Pool(s):** heated indoor. **Leisure Activities:** whirlpool, exercise room. **Guest Services:** valet and coin laundry, wireless Internet. **Business Services:** meeting rooms, business center.
ASK / SOME UNITS

COURTYARD BY MARRIOTT *Book great rates at AAA.com* **Phone:** (479)571-4900

Hotel
$134-$164 All Year

Address: 600 E Van Asche Dr 72703 **Location:** Just e of jct Mall Ave. **Facility:** Smoke free premises. 114 units. 110 one-bedroom standard units. 4 one-bedroom suites. 4 stories, interior corridors. *Bath:* combo or shower only. **Parking:** on-site. **Terms:** cancellation fee imposed. **Amenities:** high-speed Internet, dual phone lines, voice mail, irons, hair dryers. **Pool(s):** heated indoor. **Leisure Activities:** whirlpool, exercise room. **Guest Services:** valet and coin laundry, wireless Internet. **Business Services:** meeting rooms, business center.
CALL

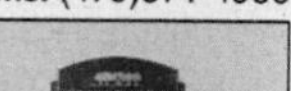

AAA Benefit:
Members save a minimum 5% off the best available rate.

FAIRFIELD INN BY MARRIOTT *Book great rates at AAA.com* **Phone:** (479)587-8600

Hotel
$80-$98 All Year

Address: 720 Millsap Rd 72703 **Location:** I-540, exit 67, 1.6 mi e, then just s on US 71B. **Facility:** Smoke free premises. 61 one-bedroom standard units. 3 stories, interior corridors. *Bath:* combo or shower only. **Parking:** on-site. **Terms:** cancellation fee imposed. **Amenities:** irons, hair dryers. **Pool(s):** heated indoor. **Leisure Activities:** whirlpool. **Guest Services:** valet laundry, wireless Internet. **Business Services:** PC.
/ SOME UNITS

AAA Benefit:
Members save a minimum 5% off the best available rate.

HAMPTON INN *Book great rates at AAA.com* **Phone:** (479)587-8300

Hotel
$99-$199 All Year

Address: 915 Krupa Dr 72704 **Location:** I-540, exit 62, just w. **Facility:** 95 units. 87 one-bedroom standard units. 8 one-bedroom suites, some with whirlpools. 4 stories, interior corridors. *Bath:* combo or shower only. **Parking:** on-site. **Terms:** 1-7 night minimum stay, cancellation fee imposed. **Amenities:** high-speed Internet, voice mail, irons, hair dryers. **Pool(s):** heated indoor. **Leisure Activities:** sauna, whirlpool, exercise room. **Guest Services:** valet and coin laundry, wireless Internet. **Business Services:** meeting rooms, business center.
CALL / SOME UNITS

AAA Benefit:
Members save up to 10% everyday!

HOLIDAY INN EXPRESS HOTEL & SUITES-UNIVERSITY OF ARKANSAS AREA *Book at AAA.com* **Phone:** (479)444-6006

Hotel
$95-$299 All Year

Address: 1251 N Shiloh Dr 72704 **Location:** I-540, exit 64, just nw. **Facility:** 110 units. 79 one-bedroom standard units. 31 one-bedroom suites. 5 stories, interior corridors. *Bath:* combo or shower only. **Parking:** on-site. **Terms:** cancellation fee imposed. **Amenities:** high-speed Internet, voice mail, irons, hair dryers. **Leisure Activities:** exercise room. **Guest Services:** valet laundry, wireless Internet. **Business Services:** meeting rooms, business center. ASK / SOME UNITS

HOMEWOOD SUITES BY HILTON *Book great rates at AAA.com* **Phone:** (479)442-3000

Extended Stay Hotel
$64-$189 All Year

Address: 1305 N Palak Dr 72704 **Location:** I-540, exit 64, just nw. **Facility:** 96 units. 32 one-bedroom standard units with efficiencies. 60 one- and 4 two-bedroom suites with efficiencies. 4 stories, interior corridors. *Bath:* combo or shower only. **Parking:** on-site. **Terms:** 1-7 night minimum stay, cancellation fee imposed. **Amenities:** DVD players, high-speed Internet, voice mail, irons, hair dryers. **Pool(s):** heated indoor. **Leisure Activities:** whirlpool, exercise room, basketball. **Guest Services:** valet and coin laundry, wireless Internet. **Business Services:** meeting rooms, business center.

CALL / SOME UNITS

AAA Benefit:
Members save 5% or more everyday!

PRATT PLACE INN **Phone:** (479)966-4441

Country Inn
$225-$595 All Year

Address: 2231 W Markham Rd 72701 **Location:** Just w of jct N Cross Ave. **Facility:** An elegant inn with many upscale touches, the hotel offers many rooms with a private veranda, fireplace and large, walk-in shower with body jets. Smoke free premises. 7 one-bedroom standard units, some with whirlpools. 3 stories, interior corridors. *Bath:* combo or shower only. **Parking:** on-site. **Terms:** 7 day cancellation notice-fee imposed. **Amenities:** DVD players, high-speed Internet, voice mail, safes, irons, hair dryers. **Leisure Activities:** spa. **Guest Services:** wireless Internet. **Business Services:** meeting rooms, fax. **Free Special Amenities: expanded continental breakfast and early check-in/late check-out.**

SLEEP INN BY CHOICE HOTELS *Book at AAA.com* **Phone:** (479)587-8700

Hotel
$60-$100 All Year

Address: 728 Millsap Rd 72703 **Location:** I-540, exit 67, 1.6 mi e, then just s on US 71B. **Facility:** 61 one-bedroom standard units. 3 stories, interior corridors. *Bath:* combo or shower only. **Parking:** on-site. **Amenities:** irons, hair dryers. **Guest Services:** valet laundry, wireless Internet.

ASK / SOME UNITS FEE

WHERE TO DINE

A Q CHICKEN HOUSE **Phone:** 479/443-7555

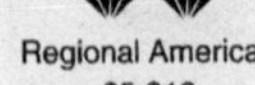

Regional American
$5-$13

Best known for its fried chicken meals, the restaurant has been popular since 1947 and boasts service to more than a million guests per year. The home-cooked chicken dishes come pan-fried, grilled, roasted or barbecued. Families love the inviting atmosphere, and the food is a good value. Country cozy decor features walls adorned with etched tin pictures and country artifacts and booth and table seating. A uniformed service staff is casual and friendly, offering attentive service. Casual dress. **Bar:** Beer & wine. **Hours:** 11 am-9 pm, Fri & Sat-9:30 pm. **Address:** 1925 N College Ave 72703 **Location:** I-540, exit 67, 1.6 mi e, then 2.4 mi s on US 71B. **Parking:** on-site.

COLTON'S STEAKHOUSE & GRILL **Phone:** 479/973-0876

Steak
$5-$24

A bucket of peanuts on the table, an upbeat Old-West atmosphere and a good selection of steak, chicken and ribs await guests at the casual steakhouse. Casual dress. **Bar:** Full bar. **Hours:** 11 am-10 pm, Fri & Sat-11 pm. Closed: 11/25, 12/25. **Address:** 642 E Millsap Rd 72703 **Location:** I-540, exit 67, 1.6 mi e, just s on US 71B, then just w. **Parking:** on-site.

DIXIE CAFE **Phone:** 479/444-6660

Regional American
$7-$11

Southern-style home cooking-chicken-fried steak, meat loaf, pork chops, turnip greens, mashed potatoes and fresh veggies-appeals to families who visit the restaurant's classic "Norman Rockwell" atmosphere. Casual dress. **Hours:** 11 am-10 pm. Closed: 11/25, 12/25. **Address:** 3875 N Shiloh Dr 72703 **Location:** I-540, exit 67, 1.6 mi, then just n on College Ave. **Parking:** on-site.

ELLA'S RESTAURANT **Phone:** 479/582-1400

French
$7-$35

A prime spot for business lunches, social occasions and romantic dinners, Ella's abounds with ageless sophistication and elegance. Variety characterizes a menu that lists not only pizza, sandwiches and salads but also the popular seared Maine scallops, foie gras, duck breast and beef tenderloin. Casual dress. **Bar:** Full bar. **Hours:** 7-10 am, 11-2 & 5-10 pm, Sat 7 am-11 & 5-10 pm, Sun 6 am-10 & 11-2 pm. Closed: 1/1, 11/25, 12/25. **Address:** 465 N Arkansas Ave 72701 **Location:** Jct Maple and N Arkansas Ave. **Parking:** on-site.

MADAME WU'S CHINESE RESTAURANT **Phone:** 479/251-1818

Chinese
$5-$15

Set off a busy crossroads, this restaurant specializes in Chinese country cooking, with menu offerings from gan shao shrimp and crispy squid to Long Island duckling and various appetizers and soups. Offering trendy decor with Oriental undertones, the dining room features painted walls with chair rails and glass-topped tables with a cherry finish and Oriental-style chairs. Uniformed servers are gracious while providing timely delivery and removal of plates as well as attentive follow-up. Casual dress. **Hours:** 11 am-2:30 & 5-9 pm, Fri-10 pm, Sat 5 pm-10 pm. Closed: 7/4, 11/25, 12/25. **Address:** 1818 N Crossover Rd 72701 **Location:** On SR 265; jct SR 45; in Crossroads Village. **Parking:** on-site.

UNCLE GAYLORD'S RESTAURANT & BAR **Phone:** 479/444-0605

American
$8-$25

The specialty is Italian pizza at the family-friendly restaurant, which fosters a relaxed atmosphere. **Bar:** Full bar. **Hours:** 8 am-1:30 & 5-close, Sun-1:30 pm; Saturday & Sunday brunch. Closed: 11/25, 12/25; also Mon. **Address:** 315 W Mountain St 72701 **Location:** Just w of jct US 71B; downtown. **Parking:** on-site.

FORDYCE pop. 4,799

DAYS INN Book at AAA.com

Phone: (870)352-2400

Hotel

$72-$105 All Year

Address: 2500 W 4th St 71742 **Location:** US 79/167, 1 mi w. **Facility:** 47 one-bedroom standard units, some with whirlpools. 2 stories (no elevator), interior/exterior corridors. **Parking:** on-site. **Amenities:** high-speed Internet, irons, hair dryers. *Some:* DVD players, CD players. **Pool(s):** outdoor. **Leisure Activities:** exercise room. **Guest Services:** coin laundry, wireless Internet. **Business Services:** PC. / SOME UNITS FEE

WHERE TO DINE

KLAPPENBACH BAKERY

Phone: 870/352-7771

Deli

$6

Although Klappenbach is perhaps best known for its large mail-order bakery business, it also does right by those who stop in for a made-to-order delicatessen sandwich and indulgent sweet treat for lunch. Casual dress. **Hours:** 6 am-5 pm, Sat-3 pm. Closed major holidays; also Sun & Mon. **Address:** 108 W 4th St 71742 **Location:** Center. **Parking:** on-site.

FORREST CITY pop. 14,774

BEST WESTERN COLONY INN Book great rates at AAA.com

Phone: 870/633-0870

Hotel

Rates not provided

Address: 2333 N Washington St 72335 **Location:** I-40, exit 241A, just s. **Facility:** 104 one-bedroom standard units. 2 stories (no elevator), exterior corridors. **Parking:** on-site. **Amenities:** voice mail, irons, hair dryers. *Some:* high-speed Internet. **Pool(s):** outdoor. **Guest Services:** coin laundry, wireless Internet. **Business Services:** PC. **Free Special Amenities: local telephone calls and high-speed Internet.**

AAA Benefit: Members save up to 20%, plus 10% bonus points with rewards program.

HAMPTON INN Book great rates at AAA.com

Phone: (870)630-9000

Hotel

$110-$122 All Year

Address: 300 Holiday Dr 72335 **Location:** I-40, exit 241B, just n. **Facility:** Smoke free premises. 70 one-bedroom standard units, some with whirlpools. 2 stories, interior corridors. *Bath:* combo or shower only. **Parking:** on-site. **Terms:** 1-7 night minimum stay, cancellation fee imposed. **Amenities:** high-speed Internet, voice mail, irons, hair dryers. **Pool(s):** outdoor. **Leisure Activities:** exercise room. **Guest Services:** valet laundry, wireless Internet. **Business Services:** meeting rooms, business center.

AAA Benefit: Members save up to 10% everyday!

HOLIDAY INN Book at AAA.com

Phone: (870)633-6300

Hotel

$70-$100 All Year

Address: 200 Holiday Dr 72335 **Location:** I-40, exit 241B, just n. **Facility:** 79 one-bedroom standard units. 2 stories (no elevator), exterior corridors. **Parking:** on-site. **Amenities:** high-speed Internet, voice mail, safes, irons, hair dryers. **Pool(s):** outdoor. **Leisure Activities:** playground, exercise room. **Guest Services:** valet and coin laundry, wireless Internet. **Business Services:** meeting rooms, business center. ASK / SOME UNITS

FORT SMITH pop. 80,268

ASPEN HOTEL & SUITES Book at AAA.com

Phone: 479/452-9000

Hotel

Rates not provided

Address: 2900 S 68th St 72903 **Location:** I-540, exit 8B (Rogers Ave), just e. **Facility:** Smoke free premises. 57 one-bedroom standard units, some with whirlpools. 2 stories, interior corridors. **Parking:** on-site. **Amenities:** voice mail, irons, hair dryers. **Pool(s):** outdoor. **Leisure Activities:** limited exercise equipment. **Guest Services:** valet and coin laundry, wireless Internet. **Business Services:** meeting rooms, PC. / SOME UNITS

BAYMONT INN & SUITES FORT SMITH Book at AAA.com

Phone: 479/484-5770

Hotel

Rates not provided

Address: 2123 Burnham Rd 72903 **Location:** I-540, exit 8A (Rogers Ave), just w. **Facility:** 99 units. 97 one-bedroom standard units, some with kitchens. 2 one-bedroom suites. 3 stories, interior corridors. **Parking:** on-site. **Amenities:** video games (fee), voice mail, irons, hair dryers. **Pool(s):** outdoor. **Leisure Activities:** exercise room. **Guest Services:** valet laundry, wireless Internet. / SOME UNITS

BELAND MANOR BED & BREAKFAST

Phone: (479)782-3300

Bed & Breakfast

$109-$185 All Year

Address: 1320 S Albert Pike 72903 **Location:** I-540, exit 8A (Rogers Ave), 1.3 mi w. **Facility:** This traditional, Colonial-style home boasts large guest rooms. Smoke free premises. 7 one-bedroom standard units, some with whirlpools. 2 stories (no elevator), interior corridors. *Bath:* combo or shower only. **Parking:** on-site. **Terms:** age restrictions may apply, 5 day cancellation notice. **Amenities:** video library, voice mail, hair dryers. *Some:* DVD players, CD players. **Leisure Activities:** limited exercise equipment. **Guest Services:** wireless Internet. **Business Services:** meeting rooms, PC.

COMFORT INN Book at AAA.com Phone: (479)484-0227

Hotel
$80-$110 All Year

Address: 2120 Burnham Rd 72903 **Location:** I-540, exit 8A (Rogers Ave), just w. **Facility:** 89 one-bedroom standard units, some with whirlpools. 2 stories (no elevator), interior corridors. *Bath:* combo or shower only. **Parking:** on-site. **Amenities:** voice mail, safes (fee), irons, hair dryers. **Pool(s):** heated indoor. **Leisure Activities:** whirlpool, exercise room. **Guest Services:** valet and coin laundry, wireless Internet. **Business Services:** PC.

ASK / SOME UNITS

COURTYARD BY MARRIOTT DOWNTOWN FORT SMITH Book great rates at AAA.com Phone: (479)783-2100

AAA SAVE

Hotel
$125-$153 All Year

Address: 900 Rogers Ave 72901 **Location:** Just s of US 64 (Garrison Ave); downtown. **Facility:** Smoke free premises. 138 units. 132 one-bedroom standard units, some with whirlpools. 6 one-bedroom suites. 4 stories, interior corridors. *Bath:* combo or shower only. **Parking:** on-site. **Terms:** cancellation fee imposed. **Amenities:** high-speed Internet, voice mail, irons, hair dryers. **Pool(s):** heated indoor. **Leisure Activities:** whirlpool, exercise room. **Guest Services:** valet and coin laundry, wireless Internet. **Business Services:** meeting rooms, business center. **Free Special Amenities: newspaper.**

CALL / SOME UNITS FEE

COURTYARD Marriott

AAA Benefit:
Members save a minimum 5% off the best available rate.

GUESTHOUSE INN Book great rates at AAA.com Phone: (479)646-5100

AAA SAVE

Hotel
$59-$72 All Year

Address: 3600 Grinnell Ave 72908 **Location:** I-540, exit 12, 0.5 mi se. **Facility:** 61 one-bedroom standard units. 2 stories (no elevator), interior corridors. **Parking:** on-site. **Amenities:** irons, hair dryers. *Some:* high-speed Internet. **Pool(s):** outdoor. **Leisure Activities:** limited exercise equipment. **Guest Services:** coin laundry, wireless Internet. **Business Services:** PC. **Free Special Amenities: expanded continental breakfast and high-speed Internet.**

/ SOME UNITS FEE

HAMPTON INN Book great rates at AAA.com Phone: (479)452-2000

Hotel
$99-$139 All Year

Address: 6201-C Rogers Ave 72903 **Location:** I-540, exit 8B (Rogers Ave), just e. **Facility:** 178 units. 160 one-bedroom standard units, some with whirlpools. 18 one-bedroom suites. 4 stories, interior corridors. *Bath:* combo or shower only. **Parking:** on-site. **Terms:** 1-7 night minimum stay, cancellation fee imposed. **Amenities:** high-speed Internet, dual phone lines, voice mail, irons, hair dryers. **Pool(s):** heated indoor. **Leisure Activities:** whirlpool, exercise room, sports court. **Guest Services:** valet and coin laundry, wireless Internet. **Business Services:** meeting rooms, business center.

/ SOME UNITS

AAA Benefit:
Members save up to 10% everyday!

HOLIDAY INN CITY CENTER FORT SMITH Book great rates at AAA.com Phone: 479/783-1000

AAA SAVE

Hotel
Rates not provided

Address: 700 Rogers Ave 72901 **Location:** Just s of US 64 (Garrison Ave); downtown. **Facility:** 255 units. 248 one-bedroom standard units. 7 one-bedroom suites, some with whirlpools. 9 stories, interior corridors. *Bath:* combo or shower only. **Parking:** on-site and valet. **Terms:** check-in 4 pm. **Amenities:** voice mail, irons, hair dryers. **Pool(s):** heated indoor. **Leisure Activities:** sauna, whirlpool, exercise room. **Guest Services:** valet laundry, airport transportation-Fort Smith Regional Airport, area transportation, wireless Internet. **Business Services:** conference facilities, business center.

CALL / SOME UNITS FEE

HOLIDAY INN EXPRESS Book at AAA.com Phone: 479/452-7500

Hotel
Rates not provided

Address: 6813 Phoenix Ave 72903 **Location:** I-540, exit 8A (Rogers Ave), 0.6 mi e, then 0.5 mi s. **Facility:** 63 units. 60 one-bedroom standard units, some with whirlpools. 3 one-bedroom suites, some with whirlpools. 3 stories, interior corridors. *Bath:* combo or shower only. **Parking:** on-site. **Amenities:** high-speed Internet, voice mail, irons, hair dryers. **Pool(s):** heated indoor. **Leisure Activities:** whirlpool, exercise room. **Guest Services:** valet and coin laundry, wireless Internet. **Business Services:** meeting rooms, business center.

/ SOME UNITS FEE

HOMEWOOD SUITES BY HILTON FORT SMITH Book great rates at AAA.com Phone: (479)452-7100

Extended Stay Hotel
$89-$139 All Year

Address: 7300 Phoenix Ave 72903 **Location:** I-540, exit 8A (Rogers Ave), 1.1 mi e, just s. **Facility:** 88 units. 35 one-bedroom standard units with efficiencies. 50 one- and 3 two-bedroom suites with efficiencies, some with whirlpools. 4 stories, interior corridors. *Bath:* combo or shower only. **Parking:** on-site. **Terms:** check-in 4 pm, 1-7 night minimum stay, cancellation fee imposed. **Amenities:** video library, DVD players, high-speed Internet, voice mail, irons, hair dryers. **Pool(s):** heated outdoor. **Leisure Activities:** exercise room, sports court. **Guest Services:** valet and coin laundry, wireless Internet. **Business Services:** meeting rooms, business center.

CALL / SOME UNITS

AAA Benefit:
Members save 5% or more everyday!

RESIDENCE INN BY MARRIOTT *Book great rates at AAA.com*

Phone: (479)478-8300

Extended Stay Hotel
$116-$142 All Year

Address: 3005 S 74th St 72903 **Location:** I-540, exit 8A (Rogers Ave), 0.8 mi e. **Facility:** Smoke free premises. 78 units. 27 one-bedroom standard units with efficiencies. 39 one- and 12 two-bedroom suites, some with efficiencies or kitchens. 3 stories, interior corridors. *Bath:* combo or shower only. **Parking:** on-site. **Terms:** cancellation fee imposed. **Amenities:** high-speed Internet, dual phone lines, voice mail, irons, hair dryers. **Pool(s):** heated outdoor. **Leisure Activities:** whirlpool, exercise room, sports court. **Guest Services:** valet and coin laundry, wireless Internet. **Business Services:** meeting rooms, PC.

/ SOME UNITS FEE

AAA Benefit: Members save a minimum 5% off the best available rate.

— WHERE TO DINE —

ART'S BBQ & GRILL

Phone: 479/452-2550

Barbecue
$4-$13

Patrons shouldn't let the modest exterior and decor affect their enjoyment of the vast choice of tasty barbecue and side dishes on order here. Casual dress. **Bar:** Beer & wine. **Hours:** 11 am-9 pm, Sun-7 pm. **Address:** 4620 Rogers Ave 72903 **Location:** I-540, exit 8A (Rogers Ave), 1 mi w. **Parking:** on-site.

CALICO COUNTY RESTAURANT

Phone: 479/452-3299

Regional American
$5-$14

You'll be served hearty portions of good, home-style meals at Calico County. This country-style restaurant delivers corn bread, yeast rolls and hot cinnamon rolls with each meal. Service is attentive and cheerful, and the decor is nostalgic. Casual dress. **Bar:** Beer & wine. **Hours:** 6:30 am-9 pm, Fri & Sat-10 pm, Sun 7 am-9 pm. Closed: 11/25, 12/25. **Address:** 2401 S 56th St 72903 **Location:** I-540, exit 8A (Rogers Ave), 0.3 mi w on SR 22, then just s. **Parking:** on-site.

CATFISH COVE

Phone: 479/646-8835

Regional American
$9-$15

This 29-year-old restaurant has the "best of the best" fried catfish filets, say local newspaper readers. They also offer a buffet, fresh seafood, barbecue ribs, steak and homemade cobbler in a relaxed, rustic-style atmosphere with a hint of the 1880s. Casual dress. **Hours:** 11 am-2 & 4:30-9 pm, Fri & Sat-9:30 pm, Sun 11 am-8:30 pm. Closed major holidays; also Mon. **Address:** 1615 Phoenix Ave 72901 **Location:** I-540, exit 10, 1.5 mi sw. **Parking:** on-site.

LIN'S GARDEN CHINESE RESTAURANT

Phone: 479/484-5090

Chinese
$4-$10

Lin's Garden spreads out a large selection of common Chinese dishes—including preparations of pork, chicken and beef, as well as rice, lo mein, soups and desserts—on its popular buffet. Casual dress. **Hours:** 11 am-10 pm, Fri & Sat-10:30 pm. Closed: 11/25, 12/25. **Address:** 7308 Rogers Ave 72903 **Location:** I-540, exit 8B (Rogers Ave), 0.7 mi e. **Parking:** on-site.

MARIA'S MEXICAN RESTAURANT

Phone: 479/452-2328

Mexican
$4-$12

Fajitas, chiles rellenos and steak ranchero are all favorite choices here, but the menu lists plenty of other traditional Mexican choices, which are served in hearty portions with modest prices. Casual dress. **Hours:** 11 am-10 pm. Closed: 11/25, 12/25. **Address:** 8640 Rogers Ave 72903 **Location:** I-540, exit 8B (Rogers Ave), 1.6 mi e. **Parking:** on-site.

MARKETPLACE GRILL

Phone: 479/424-1310

American
$8-$23

The eatery has a large, inviting dining room, and the menu includes a variety of dishes. Many ingredients are made in-house and offer enhanced quality. Casual dress. **Hours:** 11 am-8:30 pm, Fri & Sat-9:30 pm. Closed: 11/25, 12/25. **Address:** 8302 Phoenix Ave 72903 **Location:** I-540, exit 8B (Rogers Ave), 1.5 mi e, then just s. **Parking:** on-site.

THE RED BARN STEAK HOUSE

Phone: 479/783-4075

Steak
$9-$30

You might be amused at the prospect of dining in a restored old barn at a table situated in a converted horse stall. But you're sure to enjoy the Red Barn dining experience. It features a quaint setting, flavorful steaks and shrimp, and attentive service. Casual dress. **Bar:** Full bar. **Reservations:** suggested. **Hours:** 5 pm-9 pm, Fri & Sat-10 pm. Closed: major holidays, 12/24; also Sun & Mon. **Address:** 3716 Newlon Rd 72904 **Location:** 4 mi n on US 71B, 1 mi w, follow signs. **Parking:** on-site.

TALIANO'S RESTAURANT

Phone: 479/785-2292

Italian
$13-$35

Taliano's features homemade, handmade pasta and sauce, and lasagna is one of their fine specialties. The restaurant, located in a Victorian home built in 1887, is listed on the National Register of Historic Places. Guests should expect casual dining in a relaxed atmosphere. Casual dress. **Bar:** Beer & wine. **Reservations:** accepted. **Hours:** 5 pm-9:45 pm. Closed major holidays; also Sun. **Address:** 201 N 14th St 72901 **Location:** Just e of US 64 N and 71B; jct N 14th and North B sts. **Parking:** on-site. **Historic**

VARSITY SPORTS GRILL

Phone: 479/494-7173

American
$6-$16

A sports theme is reflected throughout this upbeat, lively restaurant. Patrons can enjoy appetizers and sandwiches while they shoot pool or can settle down for a more complete dinner, such as rib-eye steak or blackened chicken Alfredo. Casual dress. **Bar:** Full bar. **Hours:** 11 am-10 pm, Fri & Sat-11 pm. Closed: 11/25, 12/25. **Address:** 318 Garrison Ave 72901 **Location:** Center of downtown. **Parking:** on-site.

GENTRY pop. 2,165

APPLE CREST INN BED & BREAKFAST — **Phone:** (479)736-8201

Bed & Breakfast
$89-$180 All Year

Address: 12758 S Hwy 59 72734 **Location:** On SR 59, 1 mi s. **Facility:** Located in the midst of the Ozark Mountains, this B&B features guest rooms decorated with Victorian furnishings and collectibles from around the world. Smoke free premises. 6 one-bedroom standard units, some with whirlpools. 3 stories (no elevator), interior corridors. **Parking:** on-site. **Terms:** check-in 4 pm, 14 day cancellation notice-fee imposed. **Amenities:** video library. **Guest Services:** wireless Internet. **Business Services:** PC. ASK / SOME UNITS

GREENBRIER pop. 3,042

HILLTOP INN & SUITES — **Phone:** 501/679-5100

Hotel
$80-$85 All Year

Address: 124 N Broadview St 72058 **Location:** Just n of town. **Facility:** 50 one-bedroom standard units, some with whirlpools. 2 stories (no elevator), interior/exterior corridors. **Parking:** on-site. **Amenities:** high-speed Internet, hair dryers. *Some:* DVD players, irons. **Pool(s):** outdoor. **Guest Services:** coin laundry, wireless Internet. **Business Services:** business center.
ASK / SOME UNITS

HARDY pop. 578

BEST WESTERN VILLAGE INN — *Book great rates at AAA.com* — **Phone:** (870)856-2176

AAA SAVE
Motel
$63-$90 All Year

Address: 3587 Hwy 62/412 72542 **Location:** 2 mi sw on US 62/412. **Facility:** 41 one-bedroom standard units. 2 stories (no elevator), exterior corridors. **Parking:** on-site. **Amenities:** irons, hair dryers. *Some:* high-speed Internet. **Pool(s):** outdoor. **Guest Services:** wireless Internet. **Business Services:** PC. **Free Special Amenities: preferred room (subject to availability with advance reservations) and high-speed Internet.** / SOME UNITS

AAA Benefit:
Members save up to 20%, plus 10% bonus points with rewards program.

HARRISON pop. 12,152

HAMPTON INN — *Book great rates at AAA.com* — **Phone:** (870)365-0505

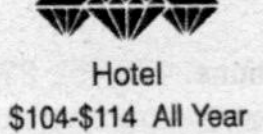

Hotel
$104-$114 All Year

Address: 121 Hwy 43 E 72601 **Location:** Just e from jct US 62/65/412 and SR 43. **Facility:** 63 one-bedroom standard units. 3 stories, interior corridors. *Bath:* combo or shower only. **Parking:** on-site. **Terms:** 1-7 night minimum stay, cancellation fee imposed. **Amenities:** high-speed Internet, voice mail, irons, hair dryers. **Pool(s):** heated indoor. **Leisure Activities:** whirlpool, exercise room. **Guest Services:** coin laundry, wireless Internet. **Business Services:** meeting rooms, business center.

AAA Benefit:
Members save up to 10% everyday!

HOLIDAY INN EXPRESS HOTEL & SUITES — *Book at AAA.com* — **Phone:** (870)741-3636

Hotel
$89-$125 All Year

Address: 117 Hwy 43 E 72601 **Location:** Just e of jct US 62/65/412 and SR 43. **Facility:** 90 one-bedroom standard units, some with whirlpools. 4 stories, interior corridors. *Bath:* combo or shower only. **Parking:** on-site. **Amenities:** high-speed Internet, dual phone lines, voice mail, irons, hair dryers. **Pool(s):** heated indoor. **Leisure Activities:** sauna, whirlpool. *Fee:* game room. **Guest Services:** coin laundry, wireless Internet. **Business Services:** meeting rooms.
ASK / SOME UNITS FEE

QUALITY INN — *Book at AAA.com* — **Phone:** 870/741-7676

Hotel
Rates not provided

Address: 1210 Hwy 62/65 N 72601 **Location:** 1 mi n on US 62/65/412. Located in a commercial area. **Facility:** 93 units. 89 one-bedroom standard units. 4 one-bedroom suites, some with whirlpools. 2 stories (no elevator), interior/exterior corridors. *Bath:* combo or shower only. **Parking:** on-site. **Amenities:** high-speed Internet, irons, hair dryers. **Pool(s):** heated outdoor. **Guest Services:** coin laundry, wireless Internet. **Business Services:** conference facilities.
/ SOME UNITS FEE

— WHERE TO DINE —

COLTON'S STEAKHOUSE & GRILL — **Phone:** 870/741-1834

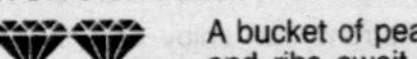

Steak
$5-$24

A bucket of peanuts on the table, an upbeat Old-West atmosphere and a good selection of steak, chicken and ribs await guests at the casual steakhouse. Casual dress. **Hours:** 11 am-10 pm, Fri & Sat-11 pm. Closed: 11/25, 12/25. **Address:** 820 Hwy 62/65 N 72601 **Location:** Just s of jct US 62/65/412 and SR 43. **Parking:** on-site.

DIAMOND HEAD RESTAURANT

Phone: 870/743-8888

Chinese
$6-$8

Guests can select from a variety of traditional dishes or from some steak or seafood choices. Casual dress. **Hours:** 11 am-9 pm. Closed: 11/25, 12/25; also Mon. **Address:** 1408 Hwy 62/65 N 72601 **Location:** On US 62, 2 mi n. **Parking:** on-site.

DIXIE CAFE

Phone: 870/365-0900

Regional American
$7-$11

Southern-style home cooking-chicken-fried steak, meat loaf, pork chops, turnip greens, mashed potatoes and fresh veggies-appeals to families who visit the restaurant's classic "Norman Rockwell" atmosphere. Casual dress. **Hours:** 11 am-10 pm. Closed: 11/25, 12/25. **Address:** 1212 Hwy 62/65 N 72601 **Location:** Center. **Parking:** on-site.

The following restaurant has not been evaluated by AAA but is listed for your information only.

NEIGHBORS MILL BAKERY & CAFE

Phone: 870/741-6455

fyi

Not evaluated. Freshly prepared dinners are served by a friendly staff. Bakery items can be ordered for takeout. **Address:** 1012 Hwy 65 72601 **Location:** 1.6 mi n on US 62/65/412.

HELENA pop. 6,323

EDWARDIAN INN

Phone: 870/338-9155

Historic Bed & Breakfast
Rates not provided

Address: 317 Biscoe St 72342 **Location:** 2 mi se on US 49B. **Facility:** This historic inn, a 1904 Colonial Revival, features elegant antiques and period pieces. Quarter-sawn oak woodwork is found throughout. Smoke free premises. 12 one-bedroom standard units. 3 stories (no elevator), interior corridors. **Parking:** on-site. **Amenities:** *Some:* DVD players. **Guest Services:** wireless Internet. **Business Services:** meeting rooms.

HOPE pop. 10,616

BEST WESTERN OF HOPE *Book great rates at AAA.com*

Phone: (870)777-9222

AAA SAVE

Hotel
$86-$105 All Year

Address: 1800 Holiday Dr 71801 **Location:** I-30, exit 30, just nw. **Facility:** 74 one-bedroom standard units. 2 stories (no elevator), exterior corridors. *Bath:* combo or shower only. **Parking:** on-site. **Amenities:** high-speed Internet, voice mail, irons, hair dryers. **Pool(s):** outdoor. **Guest Services:** coin laundry, airport transportation-Hope Airport, wireless Internet. **Business Services:** meeting rooms, PC. **Free Special Amenities: full breakfast and preferred room (subject to availability with advance reservations).**

/ SOME UNITS FEE

AAA Benefit:
Members save up to 20%, plus 10% bonus points with rewards program.

HOT SPRINGS pop. 35,750

BAYMONT ON THE LAKE *Book at AAA.com*

Phone: 501/520-5522

Hotel
Rates not provided

Address: 5321 Central Ave 71913 **Location:** 4 mi s of jct US 270 and SR 7. **Facility:** 84 one-bedroom standard units, some with whirlpools. 4 stories, interior corridors. *Bath:* combo or shower only. **Parking:** on-site. **Amenities:** video games (fee), dual phone lines, voice mail, irons, hair dryers. **Pool(s):** outdoor. **Leisure Activities:** exercise room. **Guest Services:** valet and coin laundry, wireless Internet. **Business Services:** meeting rooms, business center.

CALL / SOME UNITS

BEST WESTERN WINNER'S CIRCLE *Book great rates at AAA.com* **Phone:** (501)624-2531

Hotel
$75-$130 All Year

Address: 2520 Central Ave 71901 **Location:** 1.3 mi n of jct US 270 and SR 7. Located across from Oaklawn Park. **Facility:** 120 one-bedroom standard units. 2 stories (no elevator), exterior corridors. **Parking:** on-site. **Amenities:** high-speed Internet, safes, irons, hair dryers. **Pool(s):** outdoor. **Guest Services:** coin laundry, wireless Internet. **Business Services:** PC. **Free Special Amenities: expanded continental breakfast and preferred room (subject to availability with advance reservations).**

AAA Benefit:
Members save up to 20%, plus 10% bonus points with rewards program.

CLARION RESORT *Book at AAA.com* **Phone:** (501)525-1391

Hotel
$85-$165 All Year

Address: 4813 Central Ave 71913 **Location:** 5.5 mi s of jct US 270 and SR 7. **Facility:** 149 units. 147 one-bedroom standard units, some with whirlpools. 2 one-bedroom suites. 7 stories, interior corridors. *Bath:* combo or shower only. **Parking:** on-site. **Terms:** check-in 4 pm, 2 night minimum stay - seasonal and/or weekends. **Amenities:** high-speed Internet, voice mail, irons, hair dryers. *Fee:* video games, safes. **Pool(s):** outdoor. **Leisure Activities:** boat dock, fishing, playground, horseshoes, volleyball. *Fee:* boats. **Guest Services:** valet and coin laundry, wireless Internet. **Business Services:** conference facilities, PC (fee).

ASK FEE / SOME UNITS FEE

COMFORT INN & SUITES *Book at AAA.com* **Phone:** (501)623-1700

Hotel
$99-$109 All Year

Address: 3627 Central Ave 71913 **Location:** Just n of jct US 270. **Facility:** Smoke free premises. 83 one-bedroom standard units, some with whirlpools. 3 stories, interior corridors. *Bath:* combo or shower only. **Parking:** on-site. **Amenities:** high-speed Internet, dual phone lines, voice mail, safes, irons, hair dryers. **Pool(s):** heated indoor. **Guest Services:** valet and coin laundry, wireless Internet. **Business Services:** meeting rooms, PC. ASK FEE / SOME UNITS

EMBASSY SUITES HOT SPRINGS-HOTEL & SPA *Book great rates at AAA.com* **Phone:** (501)624-9200

Hotel
$109-$259 All Year

Address: 400 Convention Blvd 71901 **Location:** Just w of jct US 70. **Facility:** 246 one-bedroom suites, some with whirlpools. 9 stories, interior corridors. *Bath:* combo or shower only. **Parking:** on-site and valet. **Terms:** 1-7 night minimum stay, cancellation fee imposed. **Amenities:** dual phone lines, voice mail, safes, irons, hair dryers. *Fee:* video games, high-speed Internet. **Dining:** Bistro 400, see separate listing. **Pool(s):** heated indoor. **Leisure Activities:** whirlpool, exercise room, spa. **Guest Services:** valet and coin laundry, wireless Internet. **Business Services:** conference facilities, business center. **Free Special Amenities: full breakfast and newspaper.**

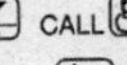 CALL 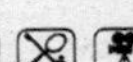  

/ SOME UNITS FEE

AAA Benefit:
Members save 5% or more everyday!

HAMPTON INN *Book great rates at AAA.com* **Phone:** (501)525-7000

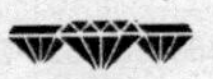

Hotel
$109-$130 All Year

Address: 151 Temperance Hill Rd 71913 **Location:** 1 mi s of jct US 270 and SR 7. Located across from Hot Springs Mall. **Facility:** 82 one-bedroom standard units, some with whirlpools. 4 stories, interior corridors. *Bath:* combo or shower only. **Parking:** on-site. **Terms:** 1-7 night minimum stay, cancellation fee imposed. **Amenities:** voice mail, irons, hair dryers. **Pool(s):** outdoor. **Guest Services:** valet laundry, wireless Internet. **Business Services:** meeting rooms.

AAA Benefit:
Members save up to 10% everyday!

STAYBRIDGE SUITES *Book great rates at AAA.com* **Phone:** (501)525-6500

Extended Stay Hotel
$89-$199 All Year

Address: 103 Lookout Cir 71913 **Location:** 3.5 mi s of jct US 270 and SR 7. **Facility:** 85 units. 40 one-bedroom standard units with efficiencies. 37 one- and 8 two-bedroom suites with efficiencies. 4 stories, interior corridors. *Bath:* combo or shower only. **Parking:** on-site. **Amenities:** DVD players, high-speed Internet, voice mail, irons, hair dryers. **Pool(s):** heated indoor. **Leisure Activities:** whirlpool, exercise room. **Guest Services:** valet and coin laundry, wireless Internet. **Business Services:** meeting rooms, business center. *(See color ad p 319)*

CALL / SOME UNITS FEE

FREE expanded continental breakfast and high-speed Internet

TourBookMark

Lodging Listing Symbols

Member Values

[AAA] or [CAA] or [SAVE] offers members a rate guarantee and up to two special amenities as part of their Official Appointment partnership with AAA.

- [ASK] May offer discount
- [fyi] Informational listing only
- [ECO] Certified by eco-certification organizations

Member Services

- Airport transportation
- Pets allowed (call property for restrictions and fees)
- Restaurant on premises
- Restaurant off premises (walking distance)
- 24-hour room service
- Full bar
- Child care
- Accessibility features (call property for available services and amenities)

Leisure Activities

- Full-service casino
- Pool
- Health club on premises
- Health club off premises (walking distance)
- Recreational activities

In-Room Amenities

- Designated non-smoking rooms
- Movies
- Refrigerator
- Microwave
- Coffee maker
- No air conditioning
- No TV
- No cable TV
- No telephones

Safety Features

(Mexico and Caribbean only)

- [S] Sprinklers
- [D] Smoke detectors

Call property for detailed information about fees & restrictions relating to the lodging listing symbols.

CHOICE HOTELS INTERNATIONAL®

Book today at choicehotels.com or 800.228.1222

We'll see you there.

CHOICE HOTELS INTERNATIONAL®

SUPER 8 *Book at AAA.com*

Phone: (501)525-0188

Hotel

$69-$89 All Year

Address: 4726 Central Ave 71913 **Location:** 5 mi s of jct US 270. **Facility:** 63 one-bedroom standard units. 3 stories, interior corridors. **Parking:** on-site. **Terms:** cancellation fee imposed. **Amenities:** high-speed Internet, irons, hair dryers. **Pool(s):** outdoor. **Leisure Activities:** whirlpool. **Guest Services:** wireless Internet. ASK / SOME UNITS

The following lodging was either not evaluated or did not meet AAA rating requirements but is listed for your information only.

EMERALD ISLE RESORT

Phone: 501/525-3696

fyi

Not evaluated. **Address:** 5371 Central Ave 71913 **Location:** 6 mi s of jct US 270 and SR 7. Facilities, services, and decor characterize a mid-scale property.

WHERE TO DINE

ANGEL'S ITALIAN RESTAURANT

Phone: 501/609-9323

Italian

$9-$17

In what originally was a bank in the early 1900s, the restaurant exudes character. The dining room affords a street view of downtown. Handmade pizzas are a favorite, but other dishes offer equal flavor and quality. Casual dress. **Bar:** Full bar. **Hours:** 11:30 am-9 pm. Closed: 1/1, 11/25, 12/25; also Sun. **Address:** 600 Central Ave 71901 **Location:** 0.6 mi n of jct US 70 and SR 7. **Parking:** street.

BACK PORCH GRILL

Phone: 501/525-0885

Steak

$10-$38

Diners will find an open grill in the center of the dining room, from which they can watch their steaks cooking from start to finish. Seafood and pasta dishes look as good as they taste. Casual dress. **Bar:** Full bar. **Reservations:** suggested. **Hours:** 4 pm-10 pm. Closed: 11/25, 12/25; also Sun. **Address:** 4810 Central Ave 71913 **Location:** 5.5 mi s of jct US 270 and SR 7. **Parking:** on-site.

BELLE ARTI RISTORANTE

Phone: 501/624-7474

Italian

$12-$35

An Old World setting of high ceilings and arched doorways sets the stage for excellent cuisine of pasta, steaks and seafood. The filet, with green peppercorns and a creamy cognac sauce, is superb. Casual dress. **Bar:** Full bar. **Reservations:** required, weekends. **Hours:** 11:30 am-4 & 5-10:30 pm. Closed: 12/25. **Address:** 719 Central Ave 71901 **Location:** Just s of jct Central Ave and Spring St; downtown. **Parking:** street.

BISTRO 400

Phone: 501/321-4421

American

$9-$33

The upscale yet comfortable setting is enhanced by a good selection of familiar dishes. Casual dress. **Bar:** Full bar. **Reservations:** accepted. **Hours:** 11 am-2 & 5-10 pm. **Address:** 400 Convention Blvd 71901 **Location:** Just w of jct US 70; in Embassy Suites Hot Springs. **Parking:** on-site and valet.

BRICK HOUSE GRILL

Phone: 501/321-2926

Steak

$5-$21

Steak and seafood selections are popular for dinner, while lunch centers primarily on sandwiches and lighter fare. The atmosphere is casual and inviting. Casual dress. **Bar:** Full bar. **Hours:** 11 am-9 pm, Sun from 5 pm. Closed major holidays. **Address:** 801 Central Ave 71901 **Location:** Just n of jct US 70 and SR 7; in Spencer's Corner. **Parking:** on-site.

▼ *See AAA listing p 318* ▼

COLTON'S STEAKHOUSE & GRILL **Phone:** 501/623-2110

Steak
$5-$24

A bucket of peanuts on the table, an upbeat Old-West atmosphere and a good selection of steak, chicken and ribs await guests at the casual steakhouse. Casual dress. **Bar:** Full bar. **Hours:** 11 am-10 pm, Fri & Sat-11 pm. Closed: 11/25, 12/25. **Address:** 120 Crawford 71913 **Location:** 0.9 mi n of jct US 270 and SR 7. **Parking:** on-site.

DIXIE CAFE **Phone:** 501/624-2100

Regional American
$7-$11

Southern-style home cooking-chicken-fried steak, meat loaf, pork chops, turnip greens, mashed potatoes and fresh veggies-appeals to families who visit the restaurant's classic "Norman Rockwell" atmosphere. Casual dress. **Bar:** Beer & wine. **Hours:** 11 am-10 pm. Closed: 11/25, 12/25. **Address:** 3623 Central Ave 71913 **Location:** Just n of jct US 270 and SR 7. **Parking:** on-site.

HOT SPRINGS BRAU HAUS **Phone:** 501/624-7866

German
$8-$13

German food served in tantalizing combinations dominates the menu. Patrons are all but certain to find their favorites in the re-created brau haus. Casual dress. **Bar:** Full bar. **Reservations:** not accepted. **Hours:** 3 pm-10 pm, Fri & Sat-11 pm. Closed major holidays; also Mon. **Address:** 801 Central Ave 71901 **Location:** Just n of jct US 70 and SR 7; in Spencer's Corner. **Parking:** on-site.

LA HACIENDA **Phone:** 501/525-8203

Traditional Mexican
$4-$16

Diners seeking very good food reminiscent of Mexican food served much farther west will agree that La Hacienda is the place to stop for lunch or dinner. The service is friendly and efficient, and the portions are quite large. Casual dress. **Bar:** Full bar. **Hours:** 11 am-10 pm, Sun 11 am-2 & 5-10 pm. Closed major holidays. **Address:** 3836 Central Ave 71913 **Location:** SR 7, 1.5 mi s of Oaklawn Race Track. **Parking:** on-site.

NEW CHINA **Phone:** 501/525-8868

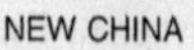

Chinese
$6-$8

The daily buffet lines up a large selection of choices at New China, a local favorite. Casual dress. **Hours:** 11 am-9:30 pm, Fri & Sat-10 pm. Closed: 11/25. **Address:** 4510 Central Ave 71913 **Location:** 1.4 mi s of jct US 270 and SR 7. **Parking:** on-site.

HOT SPRINGS VILLAGE pop. 8,397

The following lodging was either not evaluated or did not meet AAA rating requirements but is listed for your information only.

LOS LAGOS **Phone:** 501/915-9062

fyi

Not evaluated. **Address:** 1 Los Lagos Dr 71909. Facilities, services, and decor characterize a mid-scale property.

JACKSONVILLE pop. 29,916

BEST WESTERN INN *Book great rates at AAA.com* **Phone:** (501)982-8181

Hotel
$80-$90 All Year

Address: 1600 John Harden Dr 72076 **Location:** US 67/167, exit 10B southbound; exit 11 northbound. **Facility:** 67 one-bedroom standard units, some with whirlpools. 2 stories (no elevator), exterior corridors. **Parking:** on-site. **Amenities:** irons, hair dryers. *Some:* high-speed Internet. **Pool(s):** outdoor. **Leisure Activities:** exercise room. **Guest Services:** coin laundry, wireless Internet. **Business Services:** meeting rooms, PC. **Free Special Amenities: full breakfast and high-speed Internet.**

AAA Benefit:
Members save up to 20%, plus 10% bonus points with rewards program.

COMFORT INN *Book at AAA.com* **Phone:** (501)985-4400

Hotel
$80-$110 All Year

Address: 1500 John Harden Dr 72076 **Location:** US 67/167, exit 10B southbound; exit 11 northbound. **Facility:** Smoke free premises. 59 one-bedroom standard units, some with whirlpools. 2 stories (no elevator), interior corridors. *Bath:* combo or shower only. **Parking:** on-site. **Terms:** 4 day cancellation notice. **Amenities:** high-speed Internet, voice mail, irons, hair dryers. **Pool(s):** outdoor. **Leisure Activities:** exercise room. **Guest Services:** coin laundry, wireless Internet. **Business Services:** business center.

SUPER 8 *Book at AAA.com* **Phone:** (501)982-9219

Hotel
$60-$125 All Year

Address: 1850 John Harden Dr 72076 **Location:** US 67/167, exit 10B southbound; exit 11 northbound. **Facility:** 58 one-bedroom standard units, some with whirlpools. 2 stories (no elevator), exterior corridors. **Parking:** on-site. **Amenities:** high-speed Internet, irons, hair dryers. **Pool(s):** heated indoor. **Leisure Activities:** whirlpool, exercise room. **Guest Services:** coin laundry, wireless Internet. **Business Services:** meeting rooms, PC.

JOHNSON pop. 2,319

INN AT THE MILL Book at AAA.com
Hotel
Rates not provided

Phone: 479/443-1800

Address: 3906 Greathouse Springs Rd 72741 **Location:** I-540, exit 69, just e. **Facility:** 46 units. 44 one-bedroom standard units, some with whirlpools. 2 one-bedroom suites with whirlpools. 2 stories (no elevator), interior corridors. **Parking:** on-site. **Amenities:** DVD players, voice mail, safes, irons, hair dryers. *Some:* high-speed Internet. **Dining:** James At The Mill, see separate listing. **Guest Services:** valet laundry, wireless Internet. **Business Services:** meeting rooms, PC. / SOME UNITS

WHERE TO DINE

JAMES AT THE MILL
American
$8-$36

Phone: 479/443-1400

Ozark Plateau cuisine is the claim to fame at the sophisticated restaurant, where entrees are presented with style and panache. Both the food and service are superb, so dining expectations will be more than met. The interesting setting incorporates beautiful outdoor enhancements. Dressy casual. **Bar:** Full bar. **Reservations:** suggested. **Hours:** 5:30 pm-10 pm. Closed: 1/1, 11/25, 12/25; also Sun. **Address:** 3906 Greathouse Springs Rd 72741 **Location:** I-540, exit 69, just e; in Inn at the Mill. **Parking:** on-site.

JONESBORO pop. 55,515

COMFORT INN & SUITES Book at AAA.com
Hotel
$65-$78 All Year

Phone: (870)972-9000

Address: 2911 Gilmore Dr 72401 **Location:** US 63, exit Stadium Blvd/Caraway Rd, just n. **Facility:** 108 units. 63 one-bedroom standard units, some with whirlpools. 45 one-bedroom suites, some with whirlpools. 5 stories, interior corridors. **Parking:** on-site. **Terms:** cancellation fee imposed. **Amenities:** dual phone lines, voice mail, irons, hair dryers. **Pool(s):** outdoor. **Leisure Activities:** exercise room. **Guest Services:** valet laundry, wireless Internet. **Business Services:** meeting rooms, business center. ASK / SOME UNITS FEE

HAMPTON INN *Book great rates at AAA.com* **Phone:** (870)974-9500

Hotel

$77-$144 All Year

Address: 2900 Phillips Dr 72401 **Location:** US 63, exit Stadium Blvd/Caraway Rd, just n. **Facility:** 62 one-bedroom standard units, some with whirlpools. 3 stories, interior corridors. *Bath:* combo or shower only. **Parking:** on-site. **Terms:** 1-7 night minimum stay, cancellation fee imposed. **Amenities:** high-speed Internet, voice mail, irons, hair dryers. **Pool(s):** outdoor. **Leisure Activities:** exercise room. **Guest Services:** valet and coin laundry, wireless Internet. **Business Services:** business center. / SOME UNITS

AAA Benefit:

Members save up to 10% everyday!

HILTON GARDEN INN JONESBORO *Book great rates at AAA.com* **Phone:** 870/931-7727

fyi

Hotel

$107-$135 All Year

Too new to rate, opening scheduled for September 2009. **Address:** 2840 S Caraway Rd 72401. **Amenities:** 120 units, coffeemakers, microwaves, refrigerators. **Terms:** 1-7 night minimum stay, cancellation fee imposed.

Hilton Garden Inn **AAA Benefit:**

Members save 5% or more everyday!

HOLIDAY INN EXPRESS *Book at AAA.com* **Phone:** (870)932-5554

Hotel

$85-$125 All Year

Address: 2407 Phillips Dr 72401 **Location:** US 63, exit Stadium Blvd/Caraway Rd, just n. **Facility:** Smoke free premises. 102 one-bedroom standard units. 4 stories, interior corridors. *Bath:* combo or shower only. **Parking:** on-site. **Amenities:** dual phone lines, voice mail, irons, hair dryers. **Pool(s):** heated outdoor. **Leisure Activities:** exercise room. **Guest Services:** valet and coin laundry, wireless Internet. **Business Services:** meeting rooms, business center.

ASK / SOME UNITS FEE

HOLIDAY INN OF JONESBORO *Book at AAA.com* **Phone:** (870)935-2030

Hotel

$72-$99 All Year

Address: 3006 S Caraway Rd 72401 **Location:** US 63, exit Stadium Blvd/Caraway Rd, just n. **Facility:** 179 one-bedroom standard units, some with whirlpools. 2 stories (no elevator), interior/exterior corridors. *Bath:* combo or shower only. **Parking:** on-site. **Terms:** cancellation fee imposed. **Amenities:** voice mail, irons, hair dryers. **Pool(s):** heated indoor. **Leisure Activities:** whirlpool, exercise room. **Guest Services:** valet and coin laundry, area transportation, wireless Internet. **Business Services:** conference facilities, business center.

ASK / SOME UNITS FEE

WEST WASHINGTON GUEST HOUSE **Phone:** 870/935-9300

Bed & Breakfast

Rates not provided

Address: 534 W Washington 72401 **Location:** Just w of jct Main St; downtown. **Facility:** This older home has all the modern amenities and conveniences, but mixed with the charm of yesteryear. Smoke free premises. 12 units. 11 one-bedroom standard units. 1 one-bedroom suite with whirlpool. 3 stories (no elevator), interior corridors. **Parking:** on-site. **Guest Services:** wireless Internet.

WHERE TO DINE

COLTON'S STEAKHOUSE & GRILL **Phone:** 870/802-4000

Steak

$5-$24

A bucket of peanuts on the table, an upbeat Old-West atmosphere and a good selection of steak, chicken and ribs await guests at the casual steakhouse. Casual dress. **Bar:** Full bar. **Reservations:** not accepted. **Hours:** 11 am-10 pm, Fri & Sat-11 pm. Closed: 11/25, 12/25. **Address:** 2309 E Parker Rd 72401 **Location:** US 63, exit Stadium Blvd/Caraway Rd, just s. **Parking:** on-site.

DIXIE CAFE **Phone:** 870/932-9400

Regional American

$7-$11

Southern-style home cooking-chicken-fried steak, meat loaf, pork chops, turnip greens, mashed potatoes and fresh veggies-appeals to families who visit the restaurant's classic "Norman Rockwell" atmosphere. Casual dress. **Hours:** 11 am-10 pm. Closed: 11/25, 12/25. **Address:** 2406 S Caraway Rd 72401 **Location:** US 63, exit Stadium Blvd/Caraway Rd, 0.5 mi n. **Parking:** on-site.

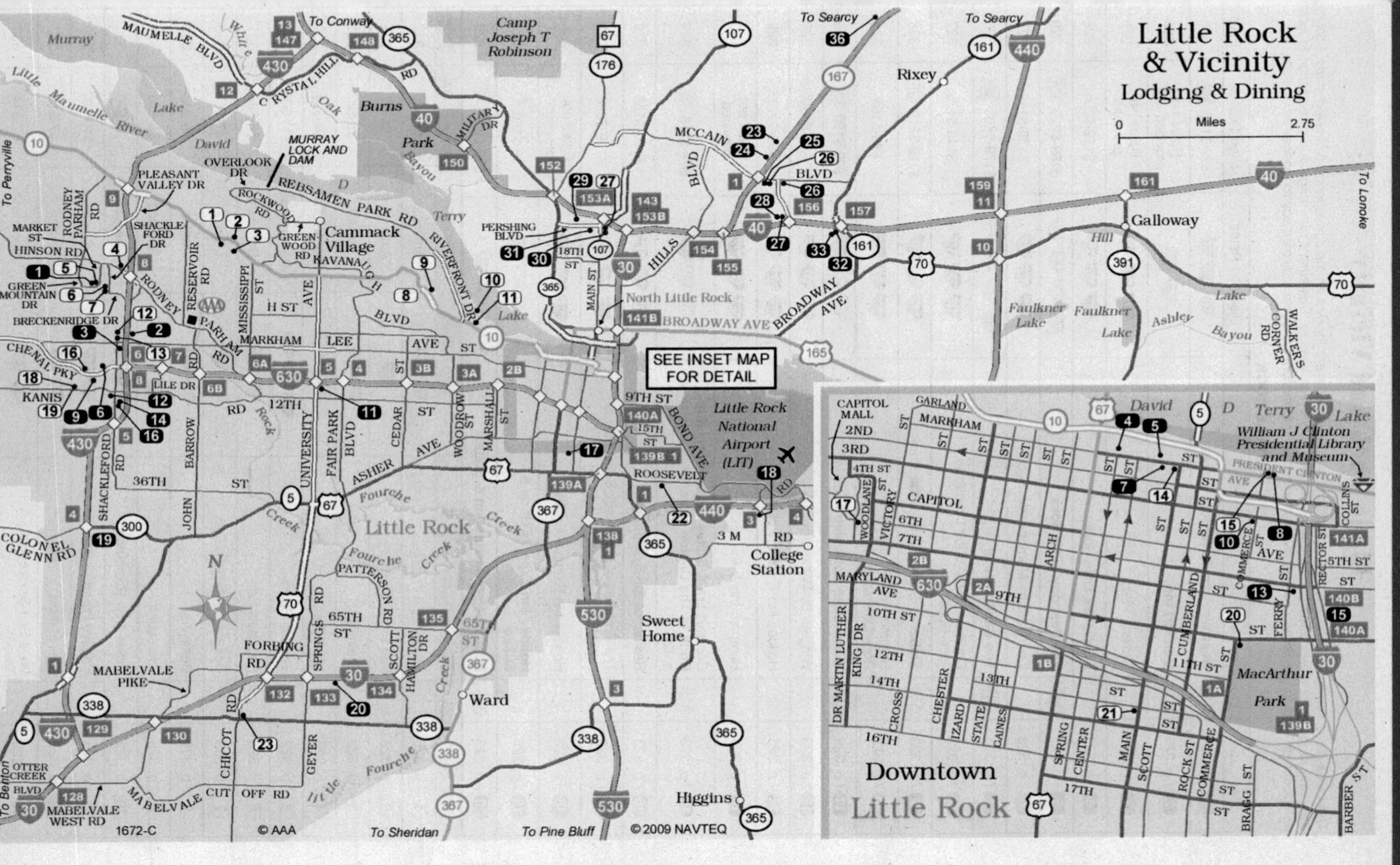
Little Rock
& Vicinity
Lodging & Dining
Miles
0
2.75
SEE INSET MAP FOR DETAIL
Little Rock National Airport (LIT)
North Little Rock
Cammack Village
Little Rock
Sweet Home
College Station
Galloway
Rixey
Ward
Higgins
Camp Joseph T Robinson
William J Clinton Presidential Library and Museum
MacArthur Park
Downtown
Little Rock
© 2009 NAVTEQ
© AAA
1672-C

Little Rock and Vicinity

This index helps you "spot" where approved lodgings and restaurants are located on the corresponding detailed maps. Lodgin daily rate range is for comparison only and show the property's high season. Restaurant rate range is a combination of lunc and/or dinner. Turn to the listing page for more detailed rate information and consult display ads for special promotions.

LITTLE ROCK

Map Page	OA	Lodgings	Diamond Rated	High Season	Page
1 / p. 323	AAA	**Best Western Governors Suites**	◆◆◆	$99-$149 SAVE	326
2 / p. 323	AAA	**Comfort Inn**	◆◆	Rates not provided SAVE	326
3 / p. 323		Crowne Plaza	◆◆◆	Rates not provided	328
4 / p. 323		Doubletree Little Rock	◆◆◆	$129-$204	328
5 / p. 323	AAA	**The Peabody Little Rock**	◆◆◆◆	$159-$229 SAVE	329
6 / p. 323		Courtyard by Marriott-Little Rock	◆◆◆	$139-$149	327
7 / p. 323	AAA	**The Capital Hotel**	◆◆◆◆	$179-$800 SAVE	326
8 / p. 323		Courtyard by Marriott Downtown Little Rock	◆◆◆	$143-$175	327
9 / p. 323	AAA	**Embassy Suites Hotel Little Rock**	◆◆◆	$119-$219 SAVE	328
10 / p. 323		Hampton Inn & Suites/Little Rock-Downtown	◆◆◆	$89-$159	328
11 / p. 323	AAA	**Hilton Little Rock Metro Center**	◆◆◆	$99-$199 SAVE	329
12 / p. 323		Wingate By Wyndham	◆◆◆	$90-$139	329
13 / p. 323		Holiday Inn Presidential	◆◆◆	$99-$119	329
14 / p. 323		Hampton Inn & Suites	◆◆◆	Rates not provided	328
15 / p. 323	AAA	**Comfort Inn & Suites, Downtown Little Rock @ The Clinton Library** - see color ad p 327	◆◆◆	$79-$119 SAVE	327
16 / p. 323		Residence Inn by Marriott	◆◆◆	$130-$158	329
17 / p. 323		The Empress of Little Rock Small Luxury Hotel & Bed & Breakfast	◆◆◆	$139-$299	328
18 / p. 323		Holiday Inn Express Airport	◆◆◆	Rates not provided	329
19 / p. 323	AAA	**Holiday Inn Express Hotel & Suites**	◆◆◆	$109-$159 SAVE	329
20 / p. 323	AAA	**Best Western Luxury Inn & Suites**	◆◆	$80-$90 SAVE	326

Map Page	OA	Restaurants	Diamond Rated	Cuisine	Meal Range	Page
1 / p. 323		Trio's	◆◆	American	$7-$28	332
2 / p. 323		The Purple Cow	◆	American	$4-$7	331
3 / p. 323		Graffiti's	◆◆	Italian	$5-$23	331
4 / p. 323		1620 Restaurant	◆◆◆	Continental	$9-$24	330
5 / p. 323		Vesuvio Bistro	◆◆◆	Mediterranean	$14-$30	332
6 / p. 323		Gaucho's Grill	◆◆	Brazilian	$6-$22	331
7 / p. 323		Cozymel's Mexican Grill	◆◆	Mexican	$7-$17	330
8 / p. 323		Bene Vita	◆◆	Italian	$6-$25	330
9 / p. 323		Loca Luna	◆◆	Seafood	$6-$25	331
10 / p. 323		Brave New Restaurant	◆◆◆	American	$9-$30	330
11 / p. 323		Cajun's Wharf	◆◆	Cajun	$16-$37	330
12 / p. 323		Star of India	◆◆	Indian	$7-$12	332
13 / p. 323		West End Smokehouse & Tavern	◆◆	American	$7-$14	332

Map Page	OA	Restaurants (cont'd)	Diamond Rated	Cuisine	Meal Range	Page
14 / p. 323	AAA	**Ashley's at The Capital**	◆◆◆◆	Continental	$13-$49	330
15 / p. 323		Sonny Williams' Steak Room	◆◆◆	Steak	$28-$59	331
16 / p. 323		The Purple Cow	◆	American	$4-$7	331
17 / p. 323		Capriccio	◆◆◆	Italian	$9-$36	330
18 / p. 323	AAA	**The Faded Rose**	◆◆	Creole	$4-$20	331
19 / p. 323		Fu Lin	◆◆	Chinese	$4-$17	331
20 / p. 323		Best Impressions	◆◆◆	American	$8-$11	330
21 / p. 323		Juanita's Mexican Cafe & Cantina	◆◆	Mexican	$6-$14	331
22 / p. 323		Homer's Restaurant	◆	American	$3-$6	331
23 / p. 323		Dong Hai China Buffet	◆	Chinese	$4-$10	331

NORTH LITTLE ROCK

Map Page	OA	Lodgings	Diamond Rated	High Season	Page
23 / p. 323		Hampton Inn-North Little Rock/McCain	◆◆◆	$99-$139	335
24 / p. 323		La Quinta Inn & Suites	◆◆	$69-$95	336
25 / p. 323		La Quinta Inn	◆◆	$55-$79	336
26 / p. 323		Holiday Inn Express Hotel & Suites	◆◆◆	Rates not provided	335
27 / p. 323		Fairfield Inn by Marriott	◆◆	$113-$138	335
28 / p. 323		Residence Inn by Marriott-North	◆◆◆	$135-$165	336
29 / p. 323		Hampton Inn	◆◆◆	Rates not provided	335
30 / p. 323		Country Inn & Suites By Carlson	◆◆◆	Rates not provided	335
31 / p. 323		Holiday Inn-North	◆◆◆	$90-$99	336
32 / p. 323	AAA	**Red Roof Inn**	◆◆	$68-$85 SAVE	336
33 / p. 323		Comfort Inn	◆◆	Rates not provided	335

Map Page	OA	Restaurants	Diamond Rated	Cuisine	Meal Range	Page
26 / p. 323		Las Palmas	◆◆	Mexican	$6-$11	336
27 / p. 323		Royal Buffet	◆◆	Chinese	$5-$7	336

SHERWOOD

Map Page	OA	Lodging	Diamond Rated	High Season	Page
36 / p. 323	AAA	**Best Western Sherwood Inn & Suites**	◆◆◆	$60-$89 SAVE	343

LITTLE ROCK pop. 183,133 (See map and index starting on p. 323)—See also NORTH LITTLE ROCK.

AIRPORT TRAVELODGE Book at AAA.com **Phone:** (501)490-2200

Hotel
$60-$69 All Year

Address: 7615 Fluid Dr 72206 **Location:** I-440, exit 5, just n. **Facility:** 39 one-bedroom standard units. 2 stories (no elevator), exterior corridors. **Parking:** on-site. **Amenities:** hair dryers. **Guest Services:** wireless Internet. ASK / SOME UNITS FEE

BEST WESTERN GOVERNORS SUITES Book great rates at AAA.com **Phone:** (501)224-8051 **1**

Hotel
$99-$149 All Year

Address: 1501 Merrill Dr 72211 **Location:** I-430, exit 8, 0.5 mi w, then just s. **Facility:** Smoke free premises. 49 units. 44 one-bedroom standard units, some with whirlpools. 5 one-bedroom suites. 3 stories, interior corridors. **Parking:** on-site. **Terms:** cancellation fee imposed. **Amenities:** video library, high-speed Internet, irons, hair dryers. *Some:* DVD players. **Dining:** Vesuvio Bistro, see separate listing. **Pool(s):** outdoor. **Guest Services:** valet and coin laundry, wireless Internet. **Business Services:** meeting rooms, business center.

FREE full breakfast and early check-in/late check-out

BEST WESTERN LUXURY INN & SUITES Book great rates at AAA.com **Phone:** (501)562-4448 **20**

Hotel
$80-$90 All Year

Address: 8219 I-30 72209 **Location:** I-30, exit 133, just se on E Service Rd. **Facility:** 38 one-bedroom standard units. 2 stories (no elevator), exterior corridors. **Parking:** on-site. **Amenities:** high-speed Internet, irons, hair dryers. **Pool(s):** outdoor. **Guest Services:** wireless Internet. **Business Services:** PC. **Free Special Amenities: expanded continental breakfast and high-speed Internet.** / SOME UNITS FEE

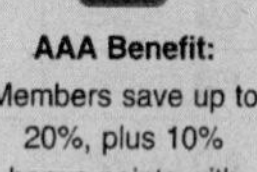

AAA Benefit:
Members save up to 20%, plus 10% bonus points with rewards program.

THE CAPITAL HOTEL Book great rates at AAA.com **Phone:** (501)374-7474 **7**

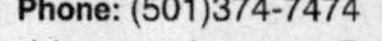

Historic Hotel
$179-$800 All Year

Address: 111 W Markham St 72201 **Location:** At Markham and Louisiana sts; downtown. **Facility:** A Greco-Roman marbled lobby and original stained-glass ceiling reflects the property's 19th-century style and charm. Smoke free premises. 94 units. 90 one-bedroom standard units. 4 one-bedroom suites. 4 stories, interior corridors. **Parking:** valet. **Amenities:** high-speed Internet, dual phone lines, voice mail, safes, irons, hair dryers. *Some:* DVD players, CD players. **Dining:** 2 restaurants, also, Ashley's at The Capital, see separate listing, entertainment. **Guest Services:** valet laundry, wireless Internet. **Business Services:** meeting rooms, business center. **Free Special Amenities: newspaper and high-speed Internet.** 24 / SOME UNITS

COMFORT INN Book great rates at AAA.com **Phone:** 501/227-0120 **2**

Hotel
Rates not provided

Address: 300 Markham Center Dr 72205 **Location:** I-430, exit 6, just e on Markham St, then just n. **Facility:** 70 one-bedroom standard units, some with whirlpools. 3 stories, interior corridors. *Bath:* combo or shower only. **Parking:** on-site. **Amenities:** irons, hair dryers. **Leisure Activities:** exercise room. **Guest Services:** wireless Internet. **Business Services:** PC.

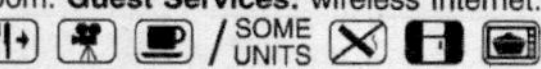

(See map and index starting on p. 323)

COMFORT INN & SUITES, DOWNTOWN LITTLE ROCK @ THE CLINTON LIBRARY *Book great rates at AAA.com* **Phone:** (501)687-7700 15

Hotel
$79-$119 All Year

Address: 707 I-30 72202 **Location:** I-30, exit 140A, just e. **Facility:** Smoke free premises. 150 one-bedroom standard units. 9 stories, interior corridors. *Bath:* combo or shower only. **Parking:** on-site. **Terms:** cancellation fee imposed. **Amenities:** high-speed Internet, dual phone lines, voice mail, irons, hair dryers. *Fee:* video games, safes. **Pool(s):** outdoor. **Leisure Activities:** exercise room. **Guest Services:** valet and coin laundry, airport transportation-Adams Field Airport, area transportation-within 3 mi, wireless Internet. **Business Services:** conference facilities, business center. *(See color ad below)*

/ SOME UNITS FEE

FREE expanded continental breakfast and high-speed Internet

COURTYARD BY MARRIOTT DOWNTOWN LITTLE ROCK *Book great rates at AAA.com* **Phone:** (501)975-9800 8

Hotel
$143-$175 All Year

Address: 521 President Clinton Ave 72201 **Location:** I-30, exit 141A. **Facility:** Smoke free premises. 120 one-bedroom standard units, some with whirlpools. 6 stories, interior corridors. *Bath:* combo or shower only. **Parking:** on-site (fee). **Terms:** cancellation fee imposed. **Amenities:** high-speed Internet, voice mail, irons, hair dryers. **Pool(s):** heated indoor. **Leisure Activities:** whirlpool, exercise room. **Guest Services:** valet and coin laundry, wireless Internet. **Business Services:** meeting rooms, business center.

AAA Benefit:
Members save a minimum 5% off the best available rate.

COURTYARD BY MARRIOTT-LITTLE ROCK *Book great rates at AAA.com* **Phone:** (501)227-6000 6

Hotel
$139-$149 All Year

Address: 10900 Financial Center Pkwy 72211 **Location:** Jct I-430 and 630, exit Shackleford Rd. **Facility:** Smoke free premises. 149 units. 137 one-bedroom standard units. 12 one-bedroom suites. 3 stories, interior corridors. *Bath:* combo or shower only. **Parking:** on-site. **Terms:** cancellation fee imposed. **Amenities:** high-speed Internet, voice mail, irons, hair dryers. **Pool(s):** heated outdoor. **Leisure Activities:** whirlpool, exercise room. **Guest Services:** valet and coin laundry, wireless Internet. **Business Services:** meeting rooms, business center.

ECO CALL / SOME UNITS

AAA Benefit:
Members save a minimum 5% off the best available rate.

▼ See AAA listing above ▼

(See map and index starting on p. 323)

CROWNE PLAZA — *Book at AAA.com* — **Phone:** 501/223-3000 — 3

Hotel
Rates not provided

Address: 201 S Shackleford Rd 72211 **Location:** Jct I-430 and 630. **Facility:** Smoke free premises. 244 units. 237 one-bedroom standard units, some with whirlpools. 7 one-bedroom suites. 5 stories, interior/exterior corridors. **Parking:** on-site. **Amenities:** video games (fee), CD players, high-speed Internet, dual phone lines, irons, hair dryers. **Pool(s):** heated indoor/outdoor. **Leisure Activities:** exercise room. **Guest Services:** valet and coin laundry, wireless Internet. **Business Services:** conference facilities, business center. / SOME UNITS

DOUBLETREE LITTLE ROCK — *Book great rates at AAA.com* — **Phone:** (501)372-4371 — 4

Hotel
$129-$204 All Year

Address: 424 W Markham St 72201 **Location:** Downtown. **Facility:** 288 units. 276 one-bedroom standard units. 12 one-bedroom suites, some with whirlpools. 14 stories, interior corridors. *Bath:* combo or shower only. **Parking:** on-site. **Terms:** 1-7 night minimum stay, cancellation fee imposed. **Amenities:** dual phone lines, voice mail, irons, hair dryers. **Pool(s):** outdoor. **Leisure Activities:** exercise room. **Guest Services:** valet laundry, area transportation, wireless Internet. **Business Services:** conference facilities, business center.
/ SOME UNITS

DOUBLETREE® HOTELS·SUITES·RESORTS·CLUBS
AAA Benefit:
Members save 5% or more everyday!

EMBASSY SUITES HOTEL LITTLE ROCK — *Book great rates at AAA.com* — **Phone:** (501)312-9000 — 9

AAA SAVE
Hotel
$119-$219 All Year

Address: 11301 Financial Centre Pkwy 72211 **Location:** Jct I-430 and 630, just w. **Facility:** 251 one-bedroom suites, some with whirlpools. 9 stories, interior corridors. *Bath:* combo or shower only. **Parking:** on-site. **Terms:** 1-7 night minimum stay, cancellation fee imposed. **Amenities:** high-speed Internet (fee), dual phone lines, voice mail, irons, hair dryers. **Pool(s):** heated indoor. **Leisure Activities:** sauna, whirlpool, exercise room. **Guest Services:** valet and coin laundry, wireless Internet. **Business Services:** conference facilities, business center. **Free Special Amenities: full breakfast and newspaper.**
CALL
/ SOME UNITS FEE

EMBASSY SUITES HOTELS®
AAA Benefit:
Members save 5% or more everyday!

THE EMPRESS OF LITTLE ROCK SMALL LUXURY HOTEL & BED & BREAKFAST — *Book at AAA.com* — **Phone:** (501)374-7966 — 17

Historic Bed & Breakfast
$139-$299 All Year

Address: 2120 S Louisiana St 72206 **Location:** I-630, exit 1B, 0.6 mi s. **Facility:** Elegant furnishings fill this 1888 Victorian property. Smoke free premises. 9 one-bedroom standard units, some with whirlpools. 2-3 stories (no elevator), interior corridors. *Bath:* combo or shower only. **Parking:** on-site. **Terms:** office hours 8 am-6 pm, age restrictions may apply, 7 day cancellation notice-fee imposed. **Amenities:** video library, DVD players, CD players, irons, hair dryers. **Guest Services:** valet laundry, wireless Internet. **Business Services:** meeting rooms. ASK FEE

HAMPTON INN & SUITES — *Book great rates at AAA.com* — **Phone:** 501/537-3000 — 14

Hotel
Rates not provided

Address: 1301 S Shackleford Rd 72211 **Location:** I-430, exit 5, just n. **Facility:** Smoke free premises. 126 units. 92 one-bedroom standard units. 34 one-bedroom suites. 5 stories, interior corridors. *Bath:* combo or shower only. **Parking:** on-site. **Amenities:** video games (fee), high-speed Internet, dual phone lines, voice mail, irons, hair dryers. **Pool(s):** heated indoor. **Leisure Activities:** whirlpool, exercise room. **Guest Services:** valet and coin laundry, wireless Internet. **Business Services:** meeting rooms, business center. CALL / SOME UNITS

Hampton Inn & Suites
AAA Benefit:
Members save up to 10% everyday!

HAMPTON INN & SUITES/LITTLE ROCK-DOWNTOWN — *Book great rates at AAA.com* — **Phone:** (501)244-0600 — 10

Hotel
$89-$159 All Year

Address: 320 Commerce St 72201 **Location:** Just s of jct 3rd St. **Facility:** Smoke free premises. 119 one-bedroom standard units. 8 stories, interior corridors. **Parking:** on-site (fee). **Terms:** 1-7 night minimum stay, cancellation fee imposed. **Amenities:** high-speed Internet, dual phone lines, voice mail, irons, hair dryers. **Pool(s):** outdoor. **Leisure Activities:** exercise room. **Guest Services:** valet and coin laundry, wireless Internet. **Business Services:** meeting rooms, business center.
CALL

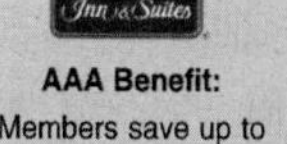

AAA Benefit:
Members save up to 10% everyday!

See map and index starting on p. 323)

HILTON LITTLE ROCK METRO CENTER *Book great rates at AAA.com* **Phone:** (501)664-5020 **11**

Hotel
$99-$199 All Year

Address: 925 S University Ave 72204 **Location:** I-630, exit 5 (University Ave), just s. **Facility:** Smoke free premises. 263 one-bedroom standard units, some with whirlpools. 3 stories, interior corridors. *Bath:* combo or shower only. **Parking:** on-site. **Terms:** 1-7 night minimum stay, cancellation fee imposed. **Amenities:** video games (fee), high-speed Internet, dual phone lines, voice mail, irons, hair dryers. **Pool(s):** outdoor. **Leisure Activities:** adjacent to golf course, exercise room. **Guest Services:** valet and coin laundry, wireless Internet. **Business Services:** conference facilities, business center. CALL / SOME UNITS FEE

Hilton
AAA Benefit: Members save 5% or more everyday!

HOLIDAY INN EXPRESS AIRPORT *Book at AAA.com* **Phone:** 501/490-4000 **18**

Hotel
Rates not provided

Address: 3121 Bankhead Dr 72206 **Location:** I-440, exit 3, just s. **Facility:** 190 one-bedroom standard units. 2 stories, interior/exterior corridors. **Parking:** on-site. **Amenities:** high-speed Internet, voice mail, irons, hair dryers. **Pool(s):** heated indoor. **Leisure Activities:** exercise room. *Fee:* game room. **Guest Services:** valet and coin laundry, wireless Internet. **Business Services:** meeting rooms, business center. / SOME UNITS

HOLIDAY INN EXPRESS HOTEL & SUITES *Book great rates at AAA.com* **Phone:** (501)224-2600 **19**

Hotel
$109-$159 All Year

Address: 4900 Talley Rd 72204 **Location:** I-430, exit 4, just e. **Facility:** 85 units. 83 one-bedroom standard units. 2 one-bedroom suites with whirlpools. 3 stories, interior corridors. *Bath:* combo or shower only. **Parking:** on-site. **Terms:** cancellation fee imposed. **Amenities:** high-speed Internet, voice mail, irons, hair dryers. **Pool(s):** heated indoor. **Leisure Activities:** whirlpool, exercise room. **Guest Services:** coin laundry, wireless Internet. **Business Services:** meeting rooms, business center. **Free Special Amenities: expanded continental breakfast and high-speed Internet.** CALL / SOME UNITS

HOLIDAY INN PRESIDENTIAL *Book at AAA.com* **Phone:** (501)375-2100 **13**

Hotel
$99-$119 All Year

Address: 600 I-30 72202 **Location:** I-30, exit 140B, just w. **Facility:** Smoke free premises. 150 units. 146 one-bedroom standard units, some with whirlpools. 4 one-bedroom suites. 8 stories, interior corridors. *Bath:* combo or shower only. **Parking:** on-site. **Amenities:** dual phone lines, voice mail, irons, hair dryers. **Pool(s):** outdoor. **Leisure Activities:** exercise room. **Guest Services:** valet and coin laundry, area transportation, wireless Internet. **Business Services:** conference facilities, business center. ASK CALL / SOME UNITS

THE PEABODY LITTLE ROCK *Book great rates at AAA.com* **Phone:** (501)906-4000 **5**

Hotel
$159-$229 All Year

Address: 3 Statehouse Plaza 72201 **Location:** Downtown. **Facility:** Ducks patrol the waters of an indoor fountain at this upscale hotel, where displays of fine art add a sophisticated ambience to common areas. Smoke free premises. 418 units. 396 one-bedroom standard units. 20 one-, 1 two- and 1 three-bedroom suites, some with whirlpools. 20 stories, interior corridors. *Bath:* combo or shower only. **Parking:** on-site (fee) and valet. **Terms:** cancellation fee imposed. **Amenities:** high-speed Internet, dual phone lines, voice mail, irons, hair dryers. **Dining:** Capriccio, see separate listing. **Leisure Activities:** saunas, exercise room. **Guest Services:** valet laundry, airport transportation-Little Rock Regional Airport, wireless Internet. **Business Services:** conference facilities, business center. **Free Special Amenities: newspaper and high-speed Internet.** Affiliated with A Preferred Hotel. / SOME UNITS

RESIDENCE INN BY MARRIOTT *Book great rates at AAA.com* **Phone:** (501)312-0200 **16**

Extended Stay Hotel
$130-$158 All Year

Address: 1401 S Shackleford Rd 72211 **Location:** I-430, exit 5, just n. **Facility:** Smoke free premises. 96 units. 24 one-bedroom standard units with efficiencies. 56 one- and 16 two-bedroom suites, some with efficiencies or kitchens. 3-4 stories, interior corridors. *Bath:* combo or shower only. **Parking:** on-site. **Terms:** cancellation fee imposed. **Amenities:** high-speed Internet, dual phone lines, voice mail, irons, hair dryers. **Pool(s):** outdoor. **Leisure Activities:** whirlpool, exercise room, sports court. **Guest Services:** valet and coin laundry, wireless Internet. **Business Services:** PC. / SOME UNITS FEE

AAA Benefit: Members save a minimum 5% off the best available rate.

TOWNEPLACE SUITES - LITTLE ROCK *Book great rates at AAA.com* **Phone:** 501/225-6700

fyi
Extended Stay Hotel
$107-$131 All Year

Too new to rate, opening scheduled for September 2009. **Address:** 12 Crossings Ct 72205 **Location:** I-430, exit 5, 0.5 mi se. **Amenities:** 114 units, coffeemakers, microwaves, refrigerators. **Terms:** cancellation fee imposed.

AAA Benefit: Members save a minimum 5% off the best available rate.

WINGATE BY WYNDHAM *Book at AAA.com* **Phone:** (501)227-6800 **12**

Hotel
$90-$139 All Year

Address: 1212 S Shackleford Rd 72211 **Location:** I-430, exit 5, just n. **Facility:** 93 units. 87 one-bedroom standard units. 6 one-bedroom suites with whirlpools. 4 stories, interior corridors. *Bath:* combo or shower only. **Parking:** on-site. **Amenities:** video games (fee), high-speed Internet, dual phone lines, voice mail, safes, irons, hair dryers. **Pool(s):** heated outdoor. **Leisure Activities:** whirlpool, exercise room. **Guest Services:** valet laundry, wireless Internet. **Business Services:** meeting rooms, business center. ASK CALL / SOME UNITS

(See map and index starting on p. 323)

WHERE TO DINE

1620 RESTAURANT **Phone:** 501/221-1620 4

Continental
$9-$24

This out-of-the-way restaurant has an elegant atmosphere and quiet setting. The eclectic menu selection are contemporary Continental and very good; they include steak, seafood, chops and pasta. Guests wi have a large selection of wines from which to choose. Casual dress. **Bar:** Full ba **Reservations:** suggested. **Hours:** 5:30 pm-9 pm, Fri & Sat-10 pm. Closed major holidays; also Sur **Address:** 1620 Market St 72212 **Location:** I-430, exit 8, 0.6 mi w on Rodney Parham Rd, then 0.3 mi s **Parking:** on-site.

ASHLEY'S AT THE CAPITAL **Phone:** 501/370-7011 14

Continental
$13-$49

A three-course prix fixe menu is offered at dinner while lunch focuses on an express menu or two- an three-course prix fixe selections. With several choices, everyone should find something to their liking. Som menu items change seasonally but fresh seafood, prime steaks and pasta are always available. Dress casual. **Bar:** Full bar. **Reservations:** required. **Hours:** 6:30-10 am, 11-2 & 5:30-10 pm, Sun 6:30 am-10 & 11-2 pm. **Address:** 111 W Markham St 72201 **Location:** At Markham and Louisiana sts; downtown; in Th Capital Hotel. **Parking:** valet.

BENE VITA **Phone:** 501/666-8482 8

Italian
$6-$25

Locals love this popular spot for its good variety of well-prepared Italian fare. Casual dress. **Bar:** Full ba **Reservations:** not accepted. **Hours:** 11 am-1:30 & 5-9 pm, Fri & Sat-10 pm. Closed: 11/25, 12/25 **Address:** 3701 Old Cantrell Rd 72202 **Location:** I-30, exit 141A (Cantrell Rd/SR 10), 3.2 mi w. **Parking** on-site.

BEST IMPRESSIONS **Phone:** 501/907-5946 20

American
$8-$11

Light-colored decor and large windows are a nice match for the attractive dishes and offerings. Dress casual. **Bar:** Full bar. **Reservations:** suggested. **Hours:** 11 am-2 pm. Closed: 11/25, 12/25; also Mon **Address:** 501 E 9th St 72202 **Location:** I-30, exit 140A, just w; in Arkansas Arts Center. **Parking:** on-site.

BRAVE NEW RESTAURANT **Phone:** 501/663-2677 10

American
$9-$30

The out-of-the-way restaurant's creative entrees include great preparations of fresh seafood. Waits are common due to this place's popularity. Dressy casual. **Bar:** Full bar. **Reservations:** suggested. **Hours:** 11 am-2 & 5-10 pm, Sat from 5 pm. Closed: 11/25, 12/25; also Sun. **Address:** 2300 Cottondale Ln, Suite 105 72202 **Location:** Just n of jct Cottondale Ln. **Parking:** on-site.

CAJUN'S WHARF **Phone:** 501/375-5351 11

Cajun
$16-$37

Appointed in wharf decor, the rustic restaurant specializes in seafood but also prepares steaks and othe dishes. Casual dress. **Bar:** Full bar. **Hours:** 5 pm-10 pm, Fri & Sat-11 pm. Closed: 11/25, 12/25; also Sun **Address:** 2400 Cantrell Rd 72202 **Location:** I-30, exit 141A (Cantrell Rd/SR 10), 2.2 mi w. **Parking** on-site.

CAPRICCIO **Phone:** 501/399-8000 17

Italian
$9-$36

Preparations of fine Italian cuisine tempt diners who come to unwind in an upscale, comfortable setting Semi-formal attire. **Bar:** Full bar. **Reservations:** suggested. **Hours:** 6:30-10:30 am, 11-2 & 5-10 pm **Address:** 3 Statehouse Plaza 72201 **Location:** Downtown; in The Peabody Little Rock. **Parking:** valet.

COZYMEL'S MEXICAN GRILL **Phone:** 501/954-7100 7

Mexican
$7-$17

A clear favorite at this lively, bright spot is the signature pork rostisada with sauteed vegetables, rice and black beans. Casual dress. **Bar:** Full bar. **Hours:** 11 am-10 pm, Fri & Sat-11 pm. Closed: 11/25, 12/25. **Address:** 10 Shackleford Dr 72211 **Location:** Jct I-430 and 630, 0.5 mi n. **Parking:** on-site.

DIXIE CAFE **Phone:** 501/568-6444

Regional American
$7-$11

Southern-style home cooking-chicken-fried steak, meat loaf, pork chops, turnip greens, mashed potatoes and fresh veggies-appeals to families who visit the restaurant's classic "Norman Rockwell" atmosphere Casual dress. **Hours:** 11 am-10 pm. Closed: 11/25, 12/25. **Address:** 10011 I-30 72209 **Location:** I-30, exit 16. **Parking:** on-site.

DIXIE CAFE **Phone:** 501/224-3728

Regional American
$7-$11

Southern-style home cooking-chicken-fried steak, meat loaf, pork chops, turnip greens, mashed potatoes and fresh veggies-appeals to families who visit the restaurant's classic "Norman Rockwell" atmosphere. Casual dress. **Hours:** 11 am-10 pm. Closed: 11/25, 12/25. **Address:** 10700 N Rodney Parham Rd 72212 **Location:** I-430, exit 8 (Rodney Parham Rd), just nw; in Pleasant Valley Shopping Center. **Parking:** on-site.

DIXIE CAFE **Phone:** 501/663-9336

Regional American
$7-$11

Southern-style home cooking-chicken-fried steak, meat loaf, pork chops, turnip greens, mashed potatoes and fresh veggies-appeals to families who visit the restaurant's classic "Norman Rockwell" atmosphere. Casual dress. **Hours:** 11 am-10 pm. Closed: 11/25, 12/25. **Address:** 1301 Rebsamen Park Rd 72202 **Location:** I-30, exit 141A (Cantrell Rd/SR 10), 3 mi w. **Parking:** on-site.

(See map and index starting on p. 323)

DONG HAI CHINA BUFFET

Phone: 501/568-5588 (23)

Chinese
$4-$10

Szechuan, Hunan and Cantonese dishes make up the menu, as well as the buffet. Friendly servers navigate the comfortable dining room. Casual dress. **Hours:** 11 am-9 pm, Fri & Sat-10 pm. Closed: 11/25. **Address:** 1001 Mabelvale Plaza 72209 **Location:** I-30, exit 130, just se. **Parking:** on-site.

THE FADED ROSE

Phone: 501/224-3377 (18)

Creole
$4-$20

New Orleans decor lends to the sometimes boisterous atmosphere. Specialties include blackened beef tenderloin topped with sauteed crawfish tails, trout garnished with crab meat and other Creole dishes. Casual dress. **Bar:** Full bar. **Hours:** 11 am-10 pm, Thurs-Sat to 11 pm, Sun noon-9:30 pm. Closed: 11/25, 12/25. **Address:** 400 N Bowman Rd 72211 **Location:** I-430, exit Shackleford Rd, 0.8 mi w on Markham St, then just n. **Parking:** on-site.

FU LIN

Phone: 501/225-8989 (19)

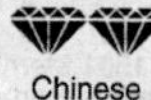

Chinese
$4-$17

Fu Lin's is very popular with local residents. It has a wide selection of dishes served in a relaxed, casual, contemporary atmosphere; Sunday buffet is also available. The Hunan shrimp, moo goo gai pan and egg fu yong are superb choices. Casual dress. **Bar:** Full bar. **Hours:** 11 am-10 pm, Fri & Sat-11 pm, Sun-9 pm. Closed: 11/25. **Address:** 200 N Bowman Rd 72211 **Location:** I-430, exit Shackleford Rd, 0.8 mi w on Markham St, then just n. **Parking:** on-site.

GAUCHO'S GRILL

Phone: 501/954-8787 (6)

Brazilian
$6-$22

This churrascaria is known for its beef, pork, chicken and shrimp, but patrons also can try fish and pasta dishes. Casual dress. **Bar:** Full bar. **Hours:** 11 am-2 & 5-9:30 pm. Closed: 11/25, 12/25. **Address:** 11 Shackleford Dr 72211 **Location:** Jct I-430 and 630, 0.5 mi n. **Parking:** on-site.

GRAFFITI'S

Phone: 501/224-9079 (3)

Italian
$5-$23

Graffiti's is a quaint, little eatery that provides a good dining experience. The restaurant has a colorful and contemporary setting and offers traditional steak, seafood dishes and several "lite bites" low calorie dishes, as well as prompt and attentive service by its knowledgeable staff. Casual dress. **Bar:** Full bar. **Hours:** 5 pm-9 pm, Fri & Sat-9:30 pm. Closed major holidays; also Sun. **Address:** 7811 Cantrell Rd 72227 **Location:** I-430, exit 9 (Cantrell Rd), 2 mi e. **Parking:** on-site.

HOMER'S RESTAURANT

Phone: 501/374-1400 (22)

American
$3-$6

Don't let the humble exterior deceive, because good home-style dinners, sandwiches and desserts await inside. Casual dress. **Hours:** 7 am-2 pm. Closed major holidays; also Sat & Sun. **Address:** 2001 E Roosevelt Rd 72206 **Location:** I-440, exit 3, 0.3 mi n, then 1.5 mi w. **Parking:** on-site.

JUANITA'S MEXICAN CAFE & CANTINA

Phone: 501/372-1228 (21)

Mexican
$6-$14

Juanita's is a very popular restaurant that offers a fun and lively atmosphere and decor. Nightly specials include rib-eye and grilled salmon, the San Antonio dinner, and a good selection of tacos and enchiladas. Generous portions and friendly service. Casual dress. Entertainment. **Bar:** Full bar. **Reservations:** accepted. **Hours:** 11 am-2 & 5-9 pm, Fri-10 pm, Sat 11 am-10 pm. Closed major holidays; also Sun. **Address:** 1300 Main St 72202 **Location:** I-630, exit 1A, just s. **Parking:** on-site.

LOCA LUNA

Phone: 501/663-4666 (9)

Seafood
$6-$25

Wood-fired brick oven pizzas, steak, seafood and chops are a few of the choices served in a lively, vibrant atmosphere. Casual dress. **Bar:** Full bar. **Reservations:** not accepted. **Hours:** 11 am-2 & 5:30-9 pm, Fri-10 pm, Sat 5:30 pm-10 pm, Sun 11 am-2:30 & 5:30-9 pm; Sunday brunch. Closed: 11/25, 12/25. **Address:** 3519 Old Cantrell Rd 72202 **Location:** I-30, exit 141A (Cantrell Rd/SR 10), 3.3 mi nw. **Parking:** on-site.

THE PURPLE COW

Phone: 501/224-4433 (16)

American
$4-$7

The '50s-style diner is complete with a soda fountain bar and jukebox. The menu consists of favorites from the era, such as well-prepared sandwiches, soups and ice cream concoctions. Casual dress. **Bar:** Beer only. **Hours:** 11 am-9 pm, Fri & Sat-10 pm, Sun 10 am-9 pm. Closed: 1/1, 11/25, 12/25. **Address:** 11602 Chenal Pkwy 72212 **Location:** 0.6 mi w of jct I-430 and 630. **Parking:** on-site.

THE PURPLE COW

Phone: 501/221-3555 (2)

American
$4-$7

Families and children love the restaurant's imaginative retro decor and jukebox music from a 1950s soda-fountain diner. The varied menu of tasty sandwiches, homemade soups and entree salads lends to the relaxed theme and environment. Upbeat servers are friendly and prompt. Casual dress. **Bar:** Full bar. **Hours:** 11 am-9 pm, Fri & Sat-10 pm. Closed: 1/1, 11/25, 12/25. **Address:** 8026 Cantrell Rd 72207 **Location:** I-430, exit 9 (Cantrell Rd), 1.8 mi e. **Parking:** on-site.

SHORTY SMALL'S

Phone: 501/224-3344

American
$7-$19

Focusing on ribs, fried catfish, sandwiches and cheesecake, this restaurant is popular with the locals. The rustic and nostalgic atmosphere is family-oriented, and the feel is casual, hectic and sometimes noisy. Casual dress. **Bar:** Full bar. **Hours:** 11 am-10 pm. Closed: 12/25. **Address:** 11100 Rodney Parham Rd 72212 **Location:** I-430, exit 8, 0.4 mi w. **Parking:** on-site.

SONNY WILLIAMS' STEAK ROOM

Phone: 501/324-2999 (15)

Steak
$28-$59

In the city's Market District, the upscale restaurant serves dishes noteworthy for both their taste and visual appeal. Casual dress. **Bar:** Full bar. **Hours:** 5 pm-11 pm. Closed: 11/25, 12/25; also Sun. **Address:** 500 President Clinton Ave 72201 **Location:** Jct St. Vincent Plaza. **Parking:** on-site (fee) and valet.

(See map and index starting on p. 323)

STAR OF INDIA — **Phone:** 501/227-9900 (12)

Indian
$7-$12

The quiet restaurant's blend of outstanding service and magnificent food results in a truly delightful dining experience. The house specialty is lamb with spinach. Stop by at lunchtime for the appealing buffet. Casual dress. **Bar:** Beer & wine. **Reservations:** not accepted. **Hours:** 11 am-3 & 5-10 pm. Closed: 11/25, 12/25. **Address:** 301 N Shackleford Rd 72211 **Location:** Just n of jct Markham St; in West Chase Plaza Shopping Center. **Parking:** on-site.

TRIO'S — **Phone:** 501/221-3330 (1)

American
$7-$28

Representative of French, Italian and American dishes are shrimp enchiladas, sea bass and Madagascar beef tenderloin. Casual dress. **Bar:** Full bar. **Reservations:** accepted. **Hours:** 11 am-2:30 & 5:30-9:30 pm. Closed major holidays; also Sun. **Address:** 8201 Cantrell Rd, Suite 100 72227 **Location:** I-430, exit 9 (Cantrell Rd), 1.7 mi e. **Parking:** on-site.

VESUVIO BISTRO — **Phone:** 501/225-0500 (5)

Mediterranean
$14-$30

Well-prepared dishes with Sicilian influences are served in this cozy, fine dining establishment. A nice selection of wines and superb desserts help round out the evening. Dressy casual. **Bar:** Full bar. **Reservations:** suggested. **Hours:** 5 pm-10 pm. Closed major holidays; also Sun. **Address:** 1501 Merrill Dr #B 72211 **Location:** I-430, exit 8, 0.5 mi w, then just s; in Best Western Governors Suites. **Parking:** on-site.

WEST END SMOKEHOUSE & TAVERN — **Phone:** 501/224-7665 (13)

American
$7-$14

Many patrons visit the lively restaurant and bar simply for the variety of appetizers, but it also offers plenty of more substantial choices, including burgers, barbecue and salads. Casual dress. **Bar:** Full bar. **Reservations:** not accepted. **Hours:** 3 pm-1 am, Fri-Sun from 11 am. Closed: 11/25, 12/25. **Address:** 215 N Shackleford Rd 72211 **Location:** Jct I-430 and 630, 0.5 mi n. **Parking:** on-site.

LONOKE pop. 4,287

DAYS INN *Book great rates at AAA.com* — **Phone:** (501)676-5138

AAA SAVE
Hotel
$60-$75 All Year

Address: 105 Dee Dee Ln 72086 **Location:** I-40, exit 175, just n. **Facility:** 61 one-bedroom standard units, some with whirlpools. 2 stories (no elevator), exterior corridors. *Bath:* combo or shower only. **Parking:** on-site. **Amenities:** irons, hair dryers. **Pool(s):** outdoor. **Guest Services:** coin laundry, wireless Internet. **Business Services:** PC. **Free Special Amenities: expanded continental breakfast and high-speed Internet.** / SOME UNITS FEE

HOLIDAY INN EXPRESS HOTEL & SUITES *Book great rates at AAA.com* — **Phone:** (501)676-7800

AAA SAVE
Hotel
$104-$151 All Year

Address: 104 Dee Dee Ln 72086 **Location:** I-40, exit 175, just n. **Facility:** 62 units. 59 one-bedroom standard units. 3 one-bedroom suites. 3 stories, interior corridors. *Bath:* combo or shower only. **Parking:** on-site. **Amenities:** high-speed Internet, voice mail, irons, hair dryers. **Pool(s):** heated indoor. **Leisure Activities:** exercise room. *Fee:* game room. **Guest Services:** valet and coin laundry, wireless Internet. **Business Services:** meeting rooms, business center. **Free Special Amenities: expanded continental breakfast and high-speed Internet.**
CALL / SOME UNITS FEE

SUPER 8 *Book great rates at AAA.com* — **Phone:** (501)676-8880

AAA SAVE
Hotel
$70-$80 All Year

Address: 102 Dee Dee Ln 72086 **Location:** I-40, exit 175, just n. **Facility:** 46 one-bedroom standard units, some with whirlpools. 2 stories (no elevator), interior corridors. **Parking:** on-site. **Amenities:** irons, hair dryers. **Pool(s):** heated indoor. **Guest Services:** wireless Internet. **Free Special Amenities: expanded continental breakfast and high-speed Internet.**
/ SOME UNITS FEE

MAGNOLIA pop. 10,858

HOLIDAY INN EXPRESS HOTEL & SUITES *Book at AAA.com* — **Phone:** (870)234-5161

Hotel
$109-$135 All Year

Address: 1604 E Main St 71753 **Location:** Just w of jct US 82, 79 and 82B. **Facility:** 56 one-bedroom standard units, some with whirlpools. 3 stories, interior corridors. *Bath:* combo or shower only. **Parking:** on-site. **Terms:** cancellation fee imposed. **Amenities:** high-speed Internet, voice mail, irons, hair dryers. **Pool(s):** heated indoor. **Leisure Activities:** exercise room. **Guest Services:** valet and coin laundry, wireless Internet. **Business Services:** meeting rooms, business center.
ASK CALL / SOME UNITS

—— WHERE TO DINE ——

CHEN & CHEN — **Phone:** 870/234-3100

Chinese
$5-$8

The menu comprises a wide variety of dishes, but most local patrons choose the buffet offerings for lunch and dinner. Casual dress. **Hours:** 11 am-10 pm, Fri & Sat-11 pm. Closed: 11/25, 12/25. **Address:** 309 N Fredrick St 71753 **Location:** 0.6 mi w of jct US 79 and 82B. **Parking:** on-site.

MALVERN pop. 9,021

COMFORT INN *Book at AAA.com* **Phone:** 501/467-3300

Hotel

Rates not provided

Address: 2320 Leopard Ln 72104 **Location:** I-30, exit 98A, just e. **Facility:** 51 one-bedroom standard units, some with whirlpools. 3 stories, interior corridors. *Bath:* combo or shower only. **Parking:** on-site. **Amenities:** high-speed Internet, voice mail, irons, hair dryers. **Pool(s):** outdoor. **Guest Services:** coin laundry, wireless Internet. / SOME UNITS

MARION pop. 8,901

BEST WESTERN-REGENCY MOTOR INN *Book great rates at AAA.com* **Phone:** (870)739-3278

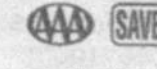

Hotel

$60-$66 All Year

Address: 3635 I-55 72364 **Location:** I-55, exit 10, just nw. **Facility:** 60 one-bedroom standard units. 2 stories (no elevator), exterior corridors. **Parking:** on-site, winter plug-ins. **Amenities:** irons, hair dryers. **Pool(s):** outdoor. **Guest Services:** coin laundry, wireless Internet. **Business Services:** PC. **Free Special Amenities: expanded continental breakfast and high-speed Internet.** / SOME UNITS

AAA Benefit:
Members save up to 20%, plus 10% bonus points with rewards program.

MCGEHEE pop. 4,570

BEST WESTERN MCGEHEE *Book great rates at AAA.com* **Phone:** (870)222-3564

Motel

$71-$74 All Year

Address: 1202 Hwy 65 N 71654 **Location:** Center. **Facility:** 27 one-bedroom standard units. 1 story, exterior corridors. *Bath:* combo or shower only. **Parking:** on-site. **Amenities:** high-speed Internet, irons, hair dryers. **Pool(s):** outdoor. **Guest Services:** wireless Internet. **Business Services:** PC. **Free Special Amenities: local telephone calls and high-speed Internet.** / SOME UNITS FEE

AAA Benefit:
Members save up to 20%, plus 10% bonus points with rewards program.

MONTICELLO pop. 9,146

DAYS INN *Book at AAA.com* **Phone:** (870)367-1881

Hotel

$68-$82 All Year

Address: 317 Hwy 425 N 71655 **Location:** Just n of jct US 278. **Facility:** 55 one-bedroom standard units, some with whirlpools. 2 stories (no elevator), exterior corridors. *Bath:* combo or shower only. **Parking:** on-site. **Terms:** cancellation fee imposed. **Amenities:** irons, hair dryers. **Pool(s):** outdoor. **Guest Services:** coin laundry, wireless Internet.

ASK / SOME UNITS

MOUNTAIN HOME pop. 11,012

COMFORT INN *Book great rates at AAA.com* **Phone:** (870)424-9000

Hotel

$70-$165 All Year

Address: 1031 Highland Cir 72653 **Location:** 1.5 mi e on US 62B. **Facility:** 80 units. 78 one-bedroom standard units, some with whirlpools. 2 one-bedroom suites with whirlpools. 2 stories (no elevator), interior/exterior corridors. *Bath:* combo or shower only. **Parking:** on-site. **Amenities:** high-speed Internet, irons, hair dryers. **Pool(s):** outdoor. **Leisure Activities:** exercise room. **Guest Services:** valet and coin laundry, wireless Internet. **Business Services:** meeting rooms, PC. **Free Special Amenities: expanded continental breakfast and high-speed Internet.**

CALL / SOME UNITS FEE

DAYS INN *Book at AAA.com* **Phone:** (870)425-1010

Hotel

$69-$77 All Year

Address: 1746 E Hwy 62B 72653 **Location:** On US 62B, 2.3 mi e. **Facility:** 53 one-bedroom standard units, some with whirlpools. 2 stories (no elevator), interior corridors. *Bath:* combo or shower only. **Parking:** on-site. **Amenities:** high-speed Internet, irons, hair dryers. *Some:* safes. **Pool(s):** outdoor. **Leisure Activities:** whirlpool. **Guest Services:** valet laundry, wireless Internet. **Business Services:** PC.

ASK CALL / SOME UNITS FEE

HAMPTON INN

Phone: 870/425-0344

Hotel
$95-$105 All Year

Address: 955 Coley Dr 72653 **Location:** 1.4 mi e on US 62B. **Facility:** Smoke free premises. 51 one-bedroom standard units. 3 stories, interior corridors. *Bath:* combo or shower only. **Parking:** on-site. **Terms:** 1-7 night minimum stay, cancellation fee imposed. **Amenities:** high-speed Internet, voice mail, irons, hair dryers. **Pool(s):** heated indoor. **Leisure Activities:** whirlpool, exercise room. **Guest Services:** valet and coin laundry, wireless Internet. **Business Services:** meeting rooms, business center.

AAA Benefit: Members save up to 10% everyday!

HOLIDAY INN EXPRESS *Book at AAA.com*

Phone: (870)425-6200

Hotel
$95-$115 All Year

Address: 1005 Coley Dr 72653 **Location:** 1.4 mi e on US 62B. **Facility:** 61 one-bedroom standard units. 3 stories, interior corridors. *Bath:* combo or shower only. **Parking:** on-site. **Amenities:** voice mail, irons, hair dryers. **Pool(s):** outdoor. **Leisure Activities:** whirlpool, exercise room. **Guest Services:** valet laundry, wireless Internet. **Business Services:** meeting rooms, business center.
ASK CALL / SOME UNITS FEE

SUPER 8-MOUNTAIN HOME *Book at AAA.com*

Phone: (870)424-5600

Motel
$65 All Year

Address: 865 Hwy 62 E 72653 **Location:** On US 62B, 1.3 mi e. **Facility:** 40 one-bedroom standard units. 2 stories (no elevator), interior corridors. **Parking:** on-site. **Terms:** cancellation fee imposed. **Amenities:** hair dryers. **Guest Services:** wireless Internet.
ASK / SOME UNITS FEE

TEAL POINT RESORT

Phone: 870/492-5145

Cottage
$99-$419 5/22-11/30
$75-$399 3/1-5/21

Address: 715 Teal Point Rd 72653-7151 **Location:** 7 mi e on US 62, 0.6 mi n on CR 406, follow signs. **Facility:** One- to four-bedroom housekeeping cottages. 22 units. 5 one-bedroom standard units with kitchens, some with whirlpools. 7 houses and 10 cottages. 1 story, exterior corridors. *Bath:* combo or shower only. **Parking:** on-site. **Terms:** open 3/1-11/30, check-out 9 am, 3-7 night minimum stay - seasonal and/or weekends, 45 day cancellation notice-fee imposed. **Pool(s):** outdoor. **Leisure Activities:** rental boats, marina, fishing, lawn games, recreation room, playground. *Fee:* bass, pontoon & ski boats, game room. **Guest Services:** coin laundry, wireless Internet. **Business Services:** meeting rooms. / SOME UNITS FEE

WHERE TO DINE

FRED'S FISH HOUSE

Phone: 870/492-5958

American
$6-$20

Catfish filets and homemade hush puppies are the specialties at this no-frills spot, which offers a large variety of seafood, steak, chicken, soups and appetizers. Located in a rural spot, the restaurant evokes a casual, comfortable setting. Families, visitors and fishermen alike can enjoy the lake view from the outdoor patio. Casual dress. **Bar:** Beer & wine. **Hours:** 11 am-8 pm, Fri & Sat-9 pm, Sun noon-7 pm; seasonal hours may vary. Closed: 11/25, 12/25. **Address:** Hwy 62 E 72653 **Location:** 4 mi w of jct US 62 business route. **Parking:** on-site.

SALSAS MEXICAN RESTAURANT

Phone: 870/425-4292

Mexican
$4-$9

Traditional Mexican dishes are served in a brightly colored, festive dining room. Tacos, burritos and enchiladas are some of the favorites. Casual dress. **Bar:** Full bar. **Hours:** 11 am-9:30 pm, Fri & Sat-10:30 pm. Closed: 11/25, 12/25. **Address:** 953 Hwy 62 E 72653 **Location:** On US 62B, 1.4 mi e. **Parking:** on-site.

The following restaurant has not been evaluated by AAA but is listed for your information only.

DINO'S ITALIAN CUISINE

Phone: 870/492-5080

fyi

Not evaluated. For some years, locals have visited the favored spot when they crave classic Italian cuisine. **Address:** 4628 Hwy 62 E 72653

MOUNTAIN VIEW pop. 2,876

BEST WESTERN FIDDLERS INN *Book great rates at AAA.com*

Phone: (870)269-2828

Motel
$60-$111 All Year

Address: 601 Sylomore Ave 72560 **Location:** 1 mi n on SR 5, 9 and 14. **Facility:** 48 units. 46 one-bedroom standard units. 2 one-bedroom suites with whirlpools. 2 stories (no elevator), exterior corridors. **Parking:** on-site. **Terms:** 7 day cancellation notice. **Amenities:** irons, hair dryers. *Some:* high-speed Internet. **Pool(s):** heated outdoor. **Guest Services:** wireless Internet. **Free Special Amenities: continental breakfast and high-speed Internet.** / SOME UNITS FEE

AAA Benefit: Members save up to 20%, plus 10% bonus points with rewards program.

THE INN AT MOUNTAIN VIEW Phone: 870/269-4200

Bed & Breakfast
$89-$145 3/1-12/21 & 2/1-2/28

Address: 307 W Washington St 72560 **Location:** Center. **Facility:** Charming restored historic home circa 1886. Smoke free premises. 11 units. 6 one-bedroom standard units. 5 one-bedroom suites. 2 stories (no elevator), interior corridors. *Bath:* combo or shower only. **Parking:** on-site. **Terms:** open 3/1-12/21 & 2/1-2/28, 2 night minimum stay - seasonal and/or weekends, cancellation fee imposed. **Business Services:** meeting rooms. / SOME UNITS

OZARK FOLK CENTER CABINS AT DRY CREEK Phone: 870/269-3871

Hotel
$72 All Year

Address: 1032 Park Ave 72560 **Location:** 0.8 mi w of jct SR 5, 9 and 14. Located in a secluded area. **Facility:** Smoke free premises. 60 one-bedroom standard units. 1 story, exterior corridors. *Bath:* combo or shower only. **Parking:** on-site. **Terms:** 2 night minimum stay - seasonal and/or weekends, cancellation fee imposed. **Amenities:** irons, hair dryers. **Pool(s):** outdoor. **Guest Services:** wireless Internet. **Business Services:** conference facilities.

NORTH LITTLE ROCK pop. 60,433 (See map and index starting on p. 323)—See also LITTLE ROCK.

COMFORT INN *Book at AAA.com* Phone: 501/955-9453 33

Hotel
Rates not provided

Address: 5710 Pritchard Dr 72117 **Location:** I-40, exit 157, just s. **Facility:** 48 one-bedroom standard units, some with whirlpools. 2 stories (no elevator), interior corridors. *Bath:* combo or shower only. **Parking:** on-site, winter plug-ins. **Amenities:** high-speed Internet, irons, hair dryers. *Some:* dual phone lines. **Pool(s):** outdoor. **Leisure Activities:** exercise room. **Guest Services:** coin laundry, wireless Internet. **Business Services:** meeting rooms, business center.
/ SOME UNITS FEE

COUNTRY INN & SUITES BY CARLSON *Book at AAA.com* Phone: 501/758-2002 30

Hotel
Rates not provided

Address: 110 E Pershing Blvd 72114 **Location:** I-40, exit 153A, just se. **Facility:** Smoke free premises. 55 units. 43 one-bedroom standard units, some with whirlpools. 12 one-bedroom suites. 3 stories, interior corridors. *Bath:* combo or shower only. **Parking:** on-site. **Amenities:** voice mail, irons, hair dryers. **Pool(s):** outdoor. **Guest Services:** valet and coin laundry, wireless Internet. **Business Services:** meeting rooms, PC.

FAIRFIELD INN BY MARRIOTT *Book great rates at AAA.com* Phone: (501)945-9777 27

Hotel
$113-$138 All Year

Address: 4120 Healthcare Dr N 72117 **Location:** I-40, exit 156, just nw. **Facility:** Smoke free premises. 86 one-bedroom standard units. 4 stories, interior corridors. *Bath:* combo or shower only. **Parking:** on-site. **Terms:** cancellation fee imposed. **Amenities:** voice mail, irons, hair dryers. **Pool(s):** heated indoor. **Leisure Activities:** whirlpool. **Guest Services:** valet laundry, wireless Internet. **Business Services:** PC.

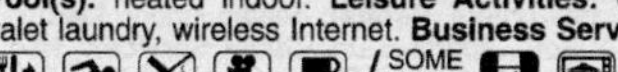

FAIRFIELD Marriott
AAA Benefit:
Members save a minimum 5% off the best available rate.

HAMPTON INN *Book great rates at AAA.com* Phone: 501/771-2090 29

Hotel
Rates not provided

Address: 500 W 29th St 72114 **Location:** I-40, exit 152. **Facility:** 123 one-bedroom standard units. 4 stories, interior corridors. **Parking:** on-site. **Amenities:** video games (fee), voice mail, irons, hair dryers. **Pool(s):** outdoor. **Leisure Activities:** exercise room. **Guest Services:** valet laundry, wireless Internet. **Business Services:** meeting rooms, PC.
/ SOME UNITS

AAA Benefit:
Members save up to 10% everyday!

HAMPTON INN-NORTH LITTLE ROCK/MCCAIN *Book great rates at AAA.com* Phone: (501)753-8660 23

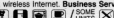

Hotel
$99-$139 All Year

Address: 4801 W Commercial Dr 72116 **Location:** US 67/167, exit 1B (McCain Blvd), just n on west service road. **Facility:** Smoke free premises. 62 units. 59 one-bedroom standard units. 3 one-bedroom suites with whirlpools. 3 stories, interior corridors. *Bath:* combo or shower only. **Parking:** on-site. **Terms:** 1-7 night minimum stay, cancellation fee imposed. **Amenities:** high-speed Internet, voice mail, irons, hair dryers. **Pool(s):** outdoor. **Leisure Activities:** exercise room. **Guest Services:** valet and coin laundry, wireless Internet. **Business Services:** meeting rooms, business center.
/ SOME UNITS

AAA Benefit:
Members save up to 10% everyday!

HOLIDAY INN EXPRESS HOTEL & SUITES *Book at AAA.com* Phone: 501/945-4800 26

Hotel
Rates not provided

Address: 4306 E McCain Blvd 72117 **Location:** US 67/167, exit 1A, just e. **Facility:** 70 one-bedroom standard units. 3 stories, interior corridors. *Bath:* combo or shower only. **Parking:** on-site. **Amenities:** high-speed Internet, dual phone lines, voice mail, irons, hair dryers. **Pool(s):** heated indoor. **Leisure Activities:** limited exercise equipment. **Guest Services:** valet and coin laundry, wireless Internet. **Business Services:** meeting rooms, business center.

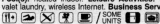

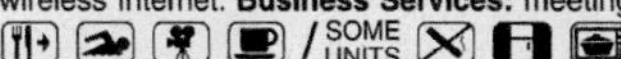

(See map and index starting on p. 323)

HOLIDAY INN-NORTH Book at AAA.com Phone: (501)758-1851 31

Hotel
$90-$99 All Year

Address: 120 W Pershing Blvd 72114 **Location:** I-40, exit 152 westbound; exit 153A eastbound. **Facility:** 143 one-bedroom standard units. 4 stories, interior corridors. **Parking:** on-site. **Amenities:** voice mail, irons, hair dryers. **Pool(s):** outdoor. **Leisure Activities:** exercise room. **Guest Services:** valet and coin laundry, wireless Internet. **Business Services:** meeting rooms, business center. ASK / SOME UNITS FEE

LA QUINTA INN Book at AAA.com Phone: (501)758-8888 25

Hotel
$55-$79 All Year

Address: 4100 E McCain Blvd 72117 **Location:** Jct US 67/167, exit 1A northbound; exit 1 southbound. **Facility:** 120 one-bedroom standard units. 2 stories (no elevator), exterior corridors. **Parking:** on-site. **Amenities:** video games (fee), voice mail, irons, hair dryers. *Some:* high-speed Internet. **Pool(s):** outdoor. **Guest Services:** coin laundry, wireless Internet. **Business Services:** meeting rooms, PC. ASK / SOME UNITS

LA QUINTA INN & SUITES Book at AAA.com Phone: (501)945-0808 24

Hotel
$69-$95 All Year

Address: 4311 Warden Rd 72116 **Location:** US 67/167, exit 1B northbound; exit 1 southbound. **Facility:** 99 units. 96 one-bedroom standard units. 3 one-bedroom suites. 3 stories, interior corridors. *Bath:* combo or shower only. **Parking:** on-site. **Amenities:** video games (fee), voice mail, irons, hair dryers. *Some:* high-speed Internet. **Pool(s):** outdoor. **Leisure Activities:** exercise room. **Guest Services:** coin laundry, wireless Internet. **Business Services:** PC. ASK / SOME UNITS

RED ROOF INN Book great rates at AAA.com Phone: (501)945-0080 32

AAA SAVE
Hotel
$68-$85 All Year

Address: 5711 Pritchard Dr 72117 **Location:** I-40, exit 157, just s. **Facility:** 52 one-bedroom standard units. 2 stories (no elevator), interior corridors. *Bath:* combo or shower only. **Parking:** on-site. **Terms:** cancellation fee imposed. **Amenities:** *Some:* high-speed Internet. **Pool(s):** outdoor. **Guest Services:** coin laundry, airport transportation-Little Rock National Airport, wireless Internet. **Free Special Amenities: expanded continental breakfast and high-speed Internet.** / SOME UNITS

RESIDENCE INN BY MARRIOTT-NORTH Book great rates at AAA.com Phone: (501)945-7777 28

Extended Stay Hotel
$135-$165 All Year

Address: 4110 Healthcare Dr 72117 **Location:** I-40, exit 156. **Facility:** Smoke free premises. 96 units. 36 one-bedroom standard units with efficiencies. 44 one- and 16 two-bedroom suites, some with efficiencies or kitchens. 4 stories, interior corridors. *Bath:* combo or shower only. **Parking:** on-site. **Terms:** cancellation fee imposed. **Amenities:** dual phone lines, voice mail, irons, hair dryers. **Pool(s):** heated indoor. **Leisure Activities:** whirlpool, exercise room, sports court. **Guest Services:** valet and coin laundry, wireless Internet. **Business Services:** meeting rooms, PC. / SOME UNITS FEE

The following lodging was either not evaluated or did not meet AAA rating requirements but is listed for your information only.

HILTON GARDEN INN NORTH LITTLE ROCK **Phone:** 501/945-7444

fyi

Not evaluated. **Address:** 4100 Glover Ln 72117. Facilities, services, and decor characterize a mid-scale property.

WHERE TO DINE

DIXIE CAFE **Phone:** 501/758-4777

Regional American
$7-$11

Southern-style home cooking-chicken-fried steak, meat loaf, pork chops, turnip greens, mashed potatoes and fresh veggies-appeals to families who visit the restaurant's classic "Norman Rockwell" atmosphere. Casual dress. **Hours:** 11 am-10 pm. Closed: 11/25, 12/25. **Address:** 2724 Lakewood Village Pl 72116 **Location:** US 67/167, exit 1. **Parking:** on-site.

LAS PALMAS **Phone:** 501/945-8010 26

Mexican
$6-$11

The locals flock to the comfortable restaurant to find well-prepared Mexican dishes. Service is friendly and efficient. Casual dress. **Bar:** Beer only. **Hours:** 11 am-9 pm, Fri & Sat-10 pm, Sun 11:30 am-9:30 pm. Closed major holidays. **Address:** 4154 E McCain Blvd 72117 **Location:** US 67/167, exit 1A, just e. **Parking:** on-site.

ROYAL BUFFET **Phone:** 501/753-8885 27

Chinese
$5-$7

A good selection of Oriental dishes is always available on the daily buffet. Casual dress. **Hours:** 11 am-10 pm. Closed: 11/25. **Address:** 109 E Pershing Blvd 72114 **Location:** I-40, exit 152, just s. **Parking:** on-site.

(See map and index starting on p. 323)

SHORTY SMALL'S

Phone: 501/753-8111

American
$7-$19

Focusing on ribs, fried catfish, sandwiches and cheesecake, this restaurant is popular with the locals. The rustic and nostalgic atmosphere is family-oriented, and the feel is casual, hectic and sometimes noisy. Casual dress. **Bar:** Full bar. **Hours:** 11 am-10 pm. Closed: 12/25. **Address:** 4317 Warden Rd 72216 **Location:** US 67/167, exit 1 southbound; exit 1B northbound. **Parking:** on-site.

PARAGOULD pop. 22,017

BEST WESTERN RUSTIC INN *Book great rates at AAA.com*

Phone: 870/239-2161

Hotel
Rates not provided

Address: 3009 Linwood Dr 72450 **Location:** 2.3 mi s of jct US 412 and 49. **Facility:** 41 one-bedroom standard units, some with whirlpools. 2 stories (no elevator), interior/exterior corridors. **Parking:** on-site. **Amenities:** high-speed Internet, irons, hair dryers. **Pool(s):** outdoor. **Guest Services:** wireless Internet. **Business Services:** PC. **Free Special Amenities: local telephone calls and high-speed Internet.**

/ SOME UNITS

AAA Benefit:
Members save up to 20%, plus 10% bonus points with rewards program.

WHERE TO DINE

DIXIE CAFE

Phone: 870/239-2000

Regional American
$7-$11

Southern-style home cooking-chicken-fried steak, meat loaf, pork chops, turnip greens, mashed potatoes and fresh veggies-appeals to families who visit the restaurant's classic "Norman Rockwell" atmosphere. Casual dress. **Hours:** 11 am-10 pm. Closed: 11/25, 12/25. **Address:** 2904 W Kings Hwy 72450 **Location:** 1.2 mi w of jct US 49. **Parking:** on-site.

PINE BLUFF pop. 55,085

BEST WESTERN PRESIDENTIAL HOTEL *Book great rates at AAA.com*

Phone: (870)535-6300

Hotel
$70-$140 All Year

Address: 3104 Market St 71601 **Location:** I-530, exit 46, just n. **Facility:** 58 one-bedroom standard units, some with whirlpools. 3 stories, interior corridors. *Bath:* combo or shower only. **Parking:** on-site. **Amenities:** high-speed Internet, voice mail, irons, hair dryers. **Pool(s):** outdoor. **Leisure Activities:** exercise room. **Guest Services:** coin laundry, wireless Internet. **Business Services:** business center. **Free Special Amenities: continental breakfast and high-speed Internet.**

/ SOME UNITS FEE

AAA Benefit:
Members save up to 20%, plus 10% bonus points with rewards program.

COMFORT INN *Book at AAA.com*

Phone: (870)535-5300

Hotel
$55-$99 All Year

Address: 2809 Pines Mall Dr 71601 **Location:** I-530, exit 46, just n. Located across from Pines Mall. **Facility:** 50 one-bedroom standard units, some with whirlpools. 2 stories (no elevator), interior corridors. *Bath:* combo or shower only. **Parking:** on-site. **Amenities:** high-speed Internet, irons, hair dryers. **Pool(s):** outdoor. **Guest Services:** valet and coin laundry, wireless Internet. **Business Services:** PC. ASK / SOME UNITS FEE

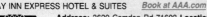

DAYS INN & SUITES *Book at AAA.com*

Phone: (870)534-1800

Hotel
$64-$69 All Year

Address: 406 N Blake St 71601 **Location:** Just n of jct US 65B and 79B. **Facility:** 51 one-bedroom standard units, some with efficiencies (no utensils) and/or whirlpools. 2 stories (no elevator), exterior corridors. *Bath:* combo or shower only. **Parking:** on-site. **Terms:** cancellation fee imposed. **Amenities:** high-speed Internet, voice mail, irons, hair dryers. **Pool(s):** outdoor. **Guest Services:** coin laundry, wireless Internet. **Business Services:** meeting rooms, PC.

ASK / SOME UNITS FEE

HOLIDAY INN EXPRESS HOTEL & SUITES *Book at AAA.com*

Phone: (870)879-3800

Hotel
$94-$104 All Year

Address: 3620 Camden Rd 71603 **Location:** I-530, exit 39, just sw. **Facility:** Smoke free premises. 67 one-bedroom standard units, some with whirlpools. 3 stories, interior corridors. *Bath:* combo or shower only. **Parking:** on-site. **Terms:** cancellation fee imposed. **Amenities:** high-speed Internet, dual phone lines, voice mail, irons, hair dryers. **Pool(s):** outdoor. **Guest Services:** valet and coin laundry, wireless Internet. **Business Services:** meeting rooms, business center.

ASK CALL FEE / SOME UNITS FEE

The following lodging was either not evaluated or did not meet AAA rating requirements but is listed for your information only.

HAMPTON INN & SUITES PINE BLUFF — **Phone:** 870/850-7488

fyi

Not evaluated. **Address:** 511 Mallard Loop 71603. Facilities, services, and decor characterize a mid-scale property.

AAA Benefit: Members save up to 10% everyday!

WHERE TO DINE

COLONIAL STEAKHOUSE — **Phone:** 870/536-3488

Steak
$17-$30

The steakhouse offers a good selection of steaks, which are prepared to the diner's liking. Casual dress. **Bar:** Full bar. **Hours:** 5 pm-9 pm. Closed: 11/25, 12/25; also Sun & Mon. **Address:** 111 W 8th Ave 71601 **Location:** Just w of jct Main St. **Parking:** on-site.

POCAHONTAS pop. 6,518

DAYS INN & SUITES — Book at AAA.com — **Phone:** 870/892-9500

Hotel
Rates not provided

Address: 2805 Hwy 67 S 72455 **Location:** 1.7 mi s. **Facility:** 58 one-bedroom standard units, some with whirlpools. 3 stories, interior corridors. *Bath:* combo or shower only. **Parking:** on-site. **Amenities:** irons, hair dryers. **Pool(s):** heated indoor. **Leisure Activities:** whirlpool, exercise room. **Guest Services:** coin laundry, wireless Internet. **Business Services:** meeting rooms, PC.

/ SOME UNITS FEE

ROGERS pop. 38,829

ALOFT ROGERS-BENTONVILLE — Book great rates at AAA.com — **Phone:** 479/268-6799

AAA SAVE
Hotel
Rates not provided

Address: 1103 S 52nd St 72758 **Location:** I-540, exit 83, just nw. **Facility:** Smoke free premises. 130 one-bedroom standard units. 6 stories, interior corridors. *Bath:* shower only. **Parking:** on-site. **Amenities:** high-speed Internet, voice mail, safes, irons, hair dryers. **Pool(s):** heated outdoor. **Leisure Activities:** exercise room. **Guest Services:** valet and coin laundry, wireless Internet. **Business Services:** meeting rooms, business center. **Free Special Amenities: local telephone calls and high-speed Internet.**

/ SOME UNITS

aloft — A VISION OF W HOTELS

AAA Benefit: Enjoy the new twist, get up to 15% off Starwood Preferred Guest® bonuses.

CANDLEWOOD SUITES — Book at AAA.com — **Phone:** (479)636-2783

Extended Stay Hotel
$103-$132 All Year

Address: 4601 W Rozell St 72757 **Location:** I-540, exit 85, 0.5 mi n on 46th St. **Facility:** 130 units. 118 one-bedroom standard units with efficiencies. 12 one-bedroom suites with efficiencies. 4 stories, interior corridors. *Bath:* combo or shower only. **Parking:** on-site. **Amenities:** video library, DVD players, high-speed Internet, dual phone lines, voice mail, irons, hair dryers. **Pool(s):** heated indoor. **Leisure Activities:** exercise room. **Guest Services:** valet and coin laundry, wireless Internet. **Business Services:** meeting rooms, business center.

ASK / SOME UNITS FEE

COUNTRY INN & SUITES BY CARLSON — Book great rates at AAA.com — **Phone:** (479)633-0055

AAA SAVE
Hotel
$59-$159 All Year

Address: 4304 W Walnut St 72756 **Location:** I-540, exit 85, just e. **Facility:** Smoke free premises. 110 units. 77 one-bedroom standard units, some with whirlpools. 33 one-bedroom suites. 4 stories, interior corridors. *Bath:* combo or shower only. **Parking:** on-site. **Terms:** cancellation fee imposed. **Amenities:** voice mail, irons, hair dryers. *Some:* DVD players. **Pool(s):** heated indoor. **Leisure Activities:** whirlpool, exercise room. **Guest Services:** valet and coin laundry, wireless Internet. **Business Services:** meeting rooms, business center.

/ SOME UNITS

EMBASSY SUITES NORTHWEST ARKANSAS — Book great rates at AAA.com — **Phone:** (479)254-8400

AAA SAVE
Hotel
$109-$259 All Year

Address: 3303 Pinnacle Hills Pkwy 72758 **Location:** I-540, exit 83, just w, then 0.6 mi s. **Facility:** 400 one-bedroom suites, some with whirlpools. 9 stories, interior corridors. *Bath:* combo or shower only. **Parking:** on-site and valet. **Terms:** 1-7 night minimum stay, cancellation fee imposed. **Amenities:** dual phone lines, voice mail, safes, irons, hair dryers. *Fee:* video games, high-speed Internet. **Pool(s):** heated indoor. **Leisure Activities:** sauna, whirlpool, exercise room, spa. **Guest Services:** valet and coin laundry, area transportation-within 5 mi, wireless Internet. **Business Services:** conference facilities, business center. **Free Special Amenities: full breakfast and newspaper.**

/ SOME UNITS FEE

EMBASSY SUITES HOTELS

AAA Benefit: Members save 5% or more everyday!

FAIRFIELD INN & SUITES BY MARRIOTT *Book great rates at AAA.com* **Phone:** (479)936-5900

Hotel
$121-$147 All Year

Address: 4611 W Rozell St 72756 **Location:** I-540, exit 85, 0.5 mi n on 46th St. **Facility:** Smoke free premises. 99 one-bedroom standard units, some with whirlpools. 3 stories, interior corridors. *Bath:* combo or shower only. **Parking:** on-site. **Terms:** cancellation fee imposed. **Amenities:** high-speed Internet, dual phone lines, voice mail, irons, hair dryers. *Some:* CD players. **Pool(s):** heated indoor. **Leisure Activities:** whirlpool, exercise room. **Guest Services:** valet and coin laundry, wireless Internet. **Business Services:** meeting rooms, business center.

CALL / SOME UNITS

AAA Benefit:
Members save a minimum 5% off the best available rate.

HAMPTON INN-BENTONVILLE ROGERS *Book great rates at AAA.com* **Phone:** (479)986-0500

Hotel
$69-$139 All Year

Address: 4501 W Walnut St 72756 **Location:** I-540, exit 85, just e. **Facility:** 122 one-bedroom standard units, some with whirlpools. 4 stories, interior corridors. *Bath:* combo or shower only. **Parking:** on-site. **Terms:** 1-7 night minimum stay, cancellation fee imposed. **Amenities:** video games (fee), dual phone lines, voice mail, irons, hair dryers. **Pool(s):** heated indoor. **Leisure Activities:** whirlpool, exercise room. **Guest Services:** valet and coin laundry, wireless Internet. **Business Services:** business center. **Free Special Amenities: expanded continental breakfast and high-speed Internet.**

CALL / SOME UNITS

AAA Benefit:
Members save up to 10% everyday!

HOMEWOOD SUITES BY HILTON *Book great rates at AAA.com* **Phone:** (479)636-5656

Extended Stay Hotel
$79-$149 All Year

Address: 4302 W Walnut St 72756 **Location:** I-540, exit 85, just e. **Facility:** 126 units. 44 one-bedroom standard units with efficiencies. 79 one- and 3 two-bedroom suites with efficiencies. 4 stories, interior corridors. *Bath:* combo or shower only. **Parking:** on-site. **Terms:** 1-7 night minimum stay, cancellation fee imposed. **Amenities:** video library, DVD players, voice mail, irons, hair dryers. **Pool(s):** heated indoor. **Leisure Activities:** whirlpool, exercise room. **Guest Services:** valet and coin laundry, wireless Internet. **Business Services:** meeting rooms, business center. CALL / SOME UNITS

HOMEWOOD SUITES Hilton

AAA Benefit:
Members save 5% or more everyday!

HYATT PLACE ROGERS/BENTONVILLE Book great rates at AAA.com **Phone:** (479)633-8555

Hotel

$69-$189 All Year

Address: 4610 W Walnut St 72756 **Location:** I-540, exit 85, just e. **Facility:** Smoke free premises. 103 one-bedroom standard units. 5 stories, interior corridors. *Bath:* combo or shower only. **Parking:** on-site. **Terms:** cancellation fee imposed. **Amenities:** high-speed Internet, dual phone lines, voice mail, irons, hair dryers. **Pool(s):** heated outdoor. **Leisure Activities:** exercise room. **Guest Services:** valet laundry, wireless Internet. **Business Services:** meeting rooms, business center. **Free Special Amenities: continental breakfast and high-speed Internet.**

HYATT PLACE

AAA Benefit: Ask for the AAA rate and save 10%.

MAINSTAY SUITES Book at AAA.com **Phone:** (479)636-3232

Extended Stay Hotel

$74-$109 All Year

Address: 301 S 45th St 72758 **Location:** I-540, exit 85, just se. **Facility:** Smoke free premises. 96 units. 53 one-bedroom standard units with efficiencies. 40 one- and 3 two-bedroom suites with efficiencies. 4 stories, interior corridors. *Bath:* combo or shower only. **Parking:** on-site. **Amenities:** video library, DVD players, high-speed Internet, voice mail, irons, hair dryers. **Pool(s):** heated outdoor. **Leisure Activities:** exercise room. **Guest Services:** valet and coin laundry, wireless Internet. **Business Services:** meeting rooms, business center.

ASK CALL

MICROTEL INN & SUITES Book at AAA.com **Phone:** (479)636-5551

Hotel

$59-$89 3/1-11/30

$49-$69 12/1-2/28

Address: 909 S 8th St 72756 **Location:** 0.5 mi s of jct Walnut St. **Facility:** Smoke free premises. 51 one-bedroom standard units. 3 stories, interior corridors. **Parking:** on-site. **Amenities:** high-speed Internet, voice mail, irons, hair dryers. **Guest Services:** coin laundry, wireless Internet.

ASK / SOME UNITS

RESIDENCE INN BY MARRIOTT Book great rates at AAA.com **Phone:** (479)636-5900

Extended Stay Hotel

$139-$169 All Year

Address: 4611 W Locust St 72756 **Location:** I-540, exit 85, 0.4 mi n on 46th St. **Facility:** Smoke free premises. 88 units. 28 one-bedroom standard units, some with efficiencies or kitchens. 44 one- and 16 two-bedroom suites, some with efficiencies or kitchens. 4 stories, interior corridors. *Bath:* combo or shower only. **Parking:** on-site. **Terms:** cancellation fee imposed. **Amenities:** video library (fee), DVD players, high-speed Internet, voice mail, irons, hair dryers. **Pool(s):** heated indoor. **Leisure Activities:** whirlpool, exercise room, sports court. **Guest Services:** valet and coin laundry, wireless Internet. **Business Services:** meeting rooms, PC.

CALL / SOME UNITS FEE

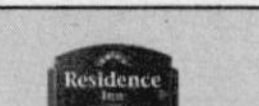

AAA Benefit: Members save a minimum 5% off the best available rate.

WHERE TO DINE

ABUELO'S THE FLAVOR OF MEXICO **Phone:** 479/621-0428

Mexican

$7-$17

In addition to a large selection of Mexican dishes, diners will find a 14-ounce rib-eye and beef tenderloin medallions on the menu. Casual dress. **Bar:** Full bar. **Hours:** 11 am-10 pm, Fri & Sat-11 pm. Closed: 11/25, 12/25. **Address:** 4005 W Walnut St 72756 **Location:** I-540, exit 85, just e. **Parking:** on-site.

COLTON'S STEAKHOUSE & GRILL **Phone:** 479/636-3336

Steak

$5-$24

A bucket of peanuts on the table, an upbeat Old-West atmosphere and a good selection of steak, chicken and ribs await guests at the casual steakhouse. Casual dress. **Bar:** Full bar. **Reservations:** not accepted. **Hours:** 11 am-10 pm, Fri & Sat-11 pm. Closed: 11/25, 12/25. **Address:** 4700 W Locust 72756 **Location:** I-540, exit 85, 0.4 mi n on 46th St. **Parking:** on-site.

DIXIE CAFE **Phone:** 479/631-8700

Regional American

$7-$11

Southern-style home cooking-chicken-fried steak, meat loaf, pork chops, turnip greens, mashed potatoes and fresh veggies-appeals to families who visit the restaurant's classic "Norman Rockwell" atmosphere. Casual dress. **Hours:** 11 am-10 pm. Closed: 11/25, 12/25. **Address:** 4600 W Rozell St 72756 **Location:** I-540, exit 85, 0.5 mi n on 46th St. **Parking:** on-site.

RIB CRIB BBQ AND GRILL **Phone:** 479/631-2742

Barbecue

$6-$14

Most guests need extra napkins to tackle the ribs, brisket, ham, pork and chicken selections. The menu also lists sandwiches and wraps, along with tempting sides and large desserts. The decor is decidedly Western. Casual dress. **Bar:** Beer only. **Hours:** 11 am-10 pm. Closed: 11/25, 12/25. **Address:** 3604 Walnut St 72756 **Location:** I-540, exit 85, 0.7 mi e. **Parking:** on-site.

RUSSELLVILLE pop. 23,682

BEST WESTERN INN

Book great rates at AAA.com

Phone: (479)967-1000

Hotel

$65-$84 All Year

Address: 2326 N Arkansas Ave 72802 **Location:** I-40, exit 81, just s. **Facility:** 99 one-bedroom standard units, some with whirlpools. 2 stories (no elevator), exterior corridors. **Parking:** on-site. **Terms:** 30 day cancellation notice. **Amenities:** irons, hair dryers. *Some:* high-speed Internet. **Pool(s):** outdoor. **Leisure Activities:** whirlpool, limited exercise equipment. **Guest Services:** valet and coin laundry, wireless Internet. **Business Services:** meeting rooms, PC. **Free Special Amenities: local telephone calls and high-speed Internet.**

/ SOME UNITS

AAA Benefit:

Members save up to 20%, plus 10% bonus points with rewards program.

FAIRFIELD INN & SUITES BY MARRIOTT

Book great rates at AAA.com

Phone: (479)967-9030

Hotel

$89-$94 All Year

Address: 120 E Harrell Dr 72802 **Location:** I-40, exit 81, just se. **Facility:** Smoke free premises. 73 units. 70 one-bedroom standard units, some with whirlpools. 3 one-bedroom suites. 3 stories, interior corridors. *Bath:* combo or shower only. **Parking:** on-site. **Terms:** cancellation fee imposed. **Amenities:** dual phone lines, voice mail, irons, hair dryers. *Some:* CD players. **Pool(s):** heated indoor. **Leisure Activities:** whirlpool, exercise room. **Guest Services:** valet and coin laundry, wireless Internet. **Business Services:** meeting rooms, business center.

CALL

AAA Benefit:

Members save a minimum 5% off the best available rate.

HAMPTON INN RUSSELLVILLE

Book great rates at AAA.com

Phone: (479)858-7199

Hotel

$85-$105 All Year

Address: 2304 N Arkansas Ave 72802 **Location:** I-40, exit 81, just s. **Facility:** 83 one-bedroom standard units, some with whirlpools. 2 stories, interior corridors. *Bath:* combo or shower only. **Parking:** on-site. **Terms:** check-in 4 pm, 1-7 night minimum stay, cancellation fee imposed. **Amenities:** voice mail, irons, hair dryers. **Pool(s):** heated indoor. **Leisure Activities:** whirlpool, exercise room. **Guest Services:** valet and coin laundry, wireless Internet. **Business Services:** meeting rooms, business center.

CALL / SOME UNITS

AAA Benefit:

Members save up to 10% everyday!

HOLIDAY INN

Book at AAA.com

Phone: (479)968-4300

Hotel

$75-$79 All Year

Address: 2407 N Arkansas Ave 72801 **Location:** I-40, exit 81, just s. **Facility:** 144 units. 142 one-bedroom standard units. 2 one-bedroom suites. 2 stories (no elevator), exterior corridors. **Parking:** on-site. **Amenities:** irons, hair dryers. **Dining:** Cagle's Mill, see separate listing. **Pool(s):** outdoor. **Leisure Activities:** exercise room. **Guest Services:** valet and coin laundry, wireless Internet. **Business Services:** meeting rooms, business center.

ASK / SOME UNITS FEE

QUALITY INN

Book at AAA.com

Phone: (479)967-7500

Hotel

$65-$90 All Year

Address: 3019 E Parkway Dr 72802 **Location:** I-40, exit 84, just s. **Facility:** 60 one-bedroom standard units, some with whirlpools. 2 stories (no elevator), exterior corridors. **Parking:** on-site. **Amenities:** high-speed Internet, irons, hair dryers. **Pool(s):** outdoor. **Guest Services:** wireless Internet.

ASK / SOME UNITS FEE

WHERE TO DINE

CAGLE'S MILL

Phone: 479/968-4300

Regional American

$7-$20

Prime rib and opossum pie are the specialties at Cagle's Mill, which has an upscale, rustic decor and a warm and hospitable atmosphere. The lunch buffet is very good with several salad varieties. Be certain to leave room for the wonderful desserts. Casual dress. **Hours:** 6-10:30 am, 11-1:30 & 4:30-9 pm, Sat & Sun 7 am-10:30 & 4:30-9 pm. **Address:** 2407 N Arkansas Ave 72801 **Location:** I-40, exit 81, just s; in Holiday Inn. **Parking:** on-site.

COLTON'S STEAKHOUSE & GRILL

Phone: 479/880-2333

Steak

$5-$24

A bucket of peanuts on the table, an upbeat Old-West atmosphere and a good selection of steak, chicken and ribs await guests at the casual steakhouse. Casual dress. **Hours:** 11 am-10 pm, Fri & Sat-11 pm. Closed: 11/25, 12/25. **Address:** 2320 N Arkansas Ave 72801 **Location:** I-40, exit 81, just s. **Parking:** on-site.

DIXIE CAFE

Phone: 479/968-4800

Regional American

$7-$11

Southern-style home cooking-chicken-fried steak, meat loaf, pork chops, turnip greens, mashed potatoes and fresh veggies-appeals to families who visit the restaurant's classic "Norman Rockwell" atmosphere. Casual dress. **Hours:** 11 am-10 pm. Closed: 11/25, 12/25. **Address:** 105 E Harrell 72801 **Location:** I-40, exit 81, just se. **Parking:** on-site.

ITALIAN GARDENS CAFE Phone: 479/967-1707

Italian
$5-$12

Community residents in the mood for Italian food come to the Italian Gardens Cafe. Traditional dishes are served in hearty portions. Casual dress. **Hours:** 11 am-2 & 5-9 pm. Closed major holidays; also Sun & Mon. **Address:** 319 W Main St 72801 **Location:** Center. **Parking:** on-site.

MADAME WU'S HUNAN CHINESE RESTAURANT Phone: 479/968-4569

Chinese
$5-$13

You'll have an extensive menu to choose from here. Try the sauteed beef with mushrooms and veggies, crispy sesame chicken or tasty Hunan shrimp. Madame Wu's has a casually elegant decor. Casual dress. **Reservations:** accepted. **Hours:** 11 am-2:30 & 4:30-9:30 pm, Fri-10 pm, Sat 4:30 pm-10 pm. Closed major holidays. **Address:** 914 S Arkansas Ave 72801 **Location:** I-40, exit 81, 2.7 mi s on US 7. **Parking:** on-site.

SEARCY pop. 18,928

BEST WESTERN SEARCY *Book great rates at AAA.com* **Phone:** 501/279-9191

Hotel
Rates not provided

Address: 501 Willow St 72143 **Location:** US 67/167, exit 46, just w, then just n. **Facility:** 71 one-bedroom standard units, some with whirlpools. 3 stories, interior corridors. *Bath:* combo or shower only. **Parking:** on-site. **Amenities:** high-speed Internet, dual phone lines, voice mail, safes, irons, hair dryers. **Pool(s):** heated indoor. **Leisure Activities:** exercise room. **Guest Services:** valet and coin laundry, wireless Internet. **Business Services:** meeting rooms, business center. **Free Special Amenities: local telephone calls and high-speed Internet.**

/ SOME UNITS

AAA Benefit:
Members save up to 20%, plus 10% bonus points with rewards program.

RODEWAY INN & SUITES *Book great rates at AAA.com* **Phone:** (501)279-1200

Hotel
$70-$100 All Year

Address: 120 N Rand Dr 72143 **Location:** US 67/167, exit 46, just w. **Facility:** 40 one-bedroom standard units, some with whirlpools. 2 stories (no elevator), exterior corridors. **Parking:** on-site. **Terms:** cancellation fee imposed. **Amenities:** high-speed Internet, irons, hair dryers. *Some:* DVD players. **Pool(s):** outdoor. **Guest Services:** coin laundry, wireless Internet. **Business Services:** PC. **Free Special Amenities: expanded continental breakfast and high-speed Internet.**

/ SOME UNITS

SUPER 8-SEARCY *Book great rates at AAA.com* **Phone:** (501)268-8988

Hotel
$70-$100 All Year

Address: 1200 Truman Baker Dr 72143 **Location:** US 67/167, exit 45, just ne. **Facility:** 49 one-bedroom standard units, some with whirlpools. 2 stories, interior corridors. **Parking:** on-site. **Amenities:** high-speed Internet, irons, hair dryers. *Some:* DVD players. **Pool(s):** heated indoor. **Leisure Activities:** exercise room. **Guest Services:** complimentary laundry, wireless Internet. **Business Services:** PC. **Free Special Amenities: full breakfast and high-speed Internet.**

/ SOME UNITS

The following lodging was either not evaluated or did not meet AAA rating requirements but is listed for your information only.

HOLIDAY INN EXPRESS & SUITES SEARCY Phone: 501/279-9991

fyi

Not evaluated. **Address:** 3660 Ferren Tr 72143 **Location:** US 67/167, exit 46. Facilities, services, and decor characterize a mid-scale property.

WHERE TO DINE

COLTON'S STEAKHOUSE & GRILL Phone: 501/268-5777

Steak
$5-$24

A bucket of peanuts on the table, an upbeat Old-West atmosphere and a good selection of steak, chicken and ribs await guests at the casual steakhouse. Casual dress. **Bar:** Full bar. **Hours:** 11 am-10 pm. Closed: 11/25, 12/25. **Address:** 3002 E Race Ave 72143 **Location:** US 67, exit 46, 0.5 mi w. **Parking:** on-site.

DIXIE CAFE Phone: 501/278-5200

Regional American
$7-$11

Southern-style home cooking-chicken-fried steak, meat loaf, pork chops, turnip greens, mashed potatoes and fresh veggies-appeals to families who visit the restaurant's classic "Norman Rockwell" atmosphere. Casual dress. **Hours:** 11 am-10 pm. Closed: 11/25, 12/25. **Address:** 205 S Poplar St 72143 **Location:** US 67, exit 46, just sw. **Parking:** on-site.

SHERWOOD pop. 21,511 (See map and index starting on p. 323)

BEST WESTERN SHERWOOD INN & SUITES *Book great rates at AAA.com* **Phone:** (501)835-7556 36

Hotel
$60-$89 All Year

Address: 7533 Warden Rd 72120 **Location:** US 67/167, exit 5, 0.6 mi s on W Service Rd. **Facility:** 60 one-bedroom standard units, some with whirlpools. 2 stories (no elevator), interior corridors. *Bath:* combo or shower only. **Parking:** on-site. **Amenities:** high-speed Internet, irons, hair dryers. **Pool(s):** outdoor. **Leisure Activities:** exercise room. **Guest Services:** coin laundry, wireless Internet. **Business Services:** business center. **Free Special Amenities: local telephone calls and high-speed Internet.**

/ SOME UNITS

AAA Benefit:
Members save up to 20%, plus 10% bonus points with rewards program.

SILOAM SPRINGS pop. 10,843

HAMPTON INN SILOAM SPRINGS *Book great rates at AAA.com* **Phone:** (479)215-1000

Hotel
$99-$159 All Year

Address: 2171 Ravenwood Plaza 72761 **Location:** Just n of jct US 412. **Facility:** Smoke free premises. 66 one-bedroom standard units. 3 stories, interior corridors. *Bath:* combo or shower only. **Parking:** on-site. **Terms:** 1-7 night minimum stay, cancellation fee imposed. **Amenities:** high-speed Internet, voice mail, irons, hair dryers. **Pool(s):** heated indoor. **Leisure Activities:** exercise room. **Guest Services:** valet and coin laundry, wireless Internet. **Business Services:** meeting rooms, business center. **Free Special Amenities: expanded continental breakfast and high-speed Internet.**

CALL / SOME UNITS

AAA Benefit:
Members save up to 10% everyday!

SUPER 8 *Book at AAA.com* **Phone:** (479)524-8898

Motel
$63-$80 All Year

Address: 1800 Hwy 412 W 72761 **Location:** Center. **Facility:** 30 one-bedroom standard units. 1 story, exterior corridors. *Bath:* combo or shower only. **Parking:** on-site. **Terms:** cancellation fee imposed. **Amenities:** irons, hair dryers. **Pool(s):** outdoor. **Guest Services:** coin laundry, wireless Internet. ASK / SOME UNITS FEE

SPRINGDALE pop. 45,798

COMFORT SUITES *Book great rates at AAA.com* **Phone:** (479)725-1777

Hotel
$70-$109 All Year

Address: 1099 Rieff St 72762 **Location:** I-540, exit 72, just w. **Facility:** Smoke free premises. 69 one-bedroom standard units, some with whirlpools. 3 stories, interior corridors. *Bath:* combo or shower only. **Parking:** on-site. **Amenities:** high-speed Internet, dual phone lines, voice mail, irons, hair dryers. **Pool(s):** heated indoor. **Leisure Activities:** whirlpool, exercise room. **Guest Services:** valet and coin laundry, wireless Internet. **Business Services:** meeting rooms, business center. **Free Special Amenities: expanded continental breakfast and high-speed Internet.**

HAMPTON INN & SUITES *Book great rates at AAA.com* **Phone:** (479)756-3500

Hotel
$79-$149 All Year

Address: 1700 S 48th St 72762 **Location:** I-540, exit 72, just e. **Facility:** 102 units. 67 one-bedroom standard units. 35 one-bedroom suites with efficiencies. 3 stories, interior corridors. *Bath:* combo or shower only. **Parking:** on-site. **Terms:** 1-7 night minimum stay, cancellation fee imposed. **Amenities:** video games (fee), high-speed Internet, voice mail, irons, hair dryers. *Some:* dual phone lines. **Pool(s):** heated outdoor. **Leisure Activities:** exercise room. **Guest Services:** valet and coin laundry, wireless Internet. **Business Services:** meeting rooms, PC. **Free Special Amenities: continental breakfast and newspaper.**

CALL / SOME UNITS

AAA Benefit:
Members save up to 10% everyday!

HOLIDAY INN NORTHWEST AR HOTEL & CONVENTION CENTER *Book at AAA.com* **Phone:** (479)751-8300

Hotel
$89-$159 All Year

Address: 1500 S 48th St 72762 **Location:** I-540, exit 72, just e. **Facility:** 206 units. 184 one-bedroom standard units. 22 one-bedroom suites, some with whirlpools. 8 stories, interior corridors. *Bath:* combo or shower only. **Parking:** on-site. **Amenities:** video games (fee), high-speed Internet, voice mail, irons, hair dryers. **Pool(s):** heated indoor. **Leisure Activities:** sauna, whirlpool, exercise room. **Guest Services:** valet and coin laundry, wireless Internet. **Business Services:** conference facilities, business center. ASK / SOME UNITS FEE

LA QUINTA INN & SUITES *Book at AAA.com* **Phone:** 479/751-2626

Hotel
Rates not provided

Address: 1300 S 48th St 72764 **Location:** I-540, exit 72, just e. **Facility:** 100 units. 96 one-bedroom standard units. 4 one-bedroom suites. 4 stories, interior corridors. *Bath:* combo or shower only. **Parking:** on-site. **Amenities:** video games (fee), voice mail, irons, hair dryers. **Pool(s):** heated indoor. **Leisure Activities:** whirlpool, exercise room. **Guest Services:** valet and coin laundry, wireless Internet. **Business Services:** meeting rooms.

CALL / SOME UNITS

RESIDENCE INN BY MARRIOTT *Book great rates at AAA.com* **Phone:** (479)872-9100

Extended Stay Hotel
$125-$153 All Year

Address: 1740 S 48th St 72762 **Location:** I-540, exit 72, just e to 48th St, then just s. **Facility:** Smoke free premises. 72 units. 33 one-bedroom standard units, some with efficiencies or kitchens. 27 one- and 12 two-bedroom suites, some with efficiencies or kitchens. 3 stories, interior corridors. *Bath:* combo or shower only. **Parking:** on-site. **Terms:** cancellation fee imposed. **Amenities:** high-speed Internet, dual phone lines, voice mail, irons, hair dryers. **Pool(s):** heated indoor. **Leisure Activities:** whirlpool, putting green, exercise room, sports court. **Guest Services:** valet and coin laundry, wireless Internet. **Business Services:** meeting rooms, PC.

/ SOME UNITS FEE

AAA Benefit: Members save a minimum 5% off the best available rate.

SLEEP INN & SUITES *Book at AAA.com* **Phone:** (479)756-5800

Hotel
$89-$199 All Year

Address: 1056 Rieff St 72762 **Location:** I-540, exit 72, just e. **Facility:** 72 one-bedroom standard units, some with whirlpools. 4 stories, interior corridors. *Bath:* combo or shower only. **Parking:** on-site. **Amenities:** high-speed Internet, voice mail, irons, hair dryers. *Some:* DVD players (fee). **Pool(s):** heated indoor. **Leisure Activities:** sauna, exercise room. **Guest Services:** valet and coin laundry, wireless Internet. **Business Services:** meeting rooms, business center.

ASK / SOME UNITS

WHERE TO DINE

A Q CHICKEN HOUSE **Phone:** 479/751-4633

Regional American
$5-$8

This restaurant has been popular with local residents since 1947. Its pan-fried chicken is the house specialty, but they offer a good variety of other tasty dishes served in plentiful portions. The servers are cordial and attentive. Casual dress. **Bar:** Beer & wine. **Hours:** 11 am-8:30 pm, Fri & Sat-9 pm, Sun-8 pm. Closed: 11/25, 12/24, 12/25. **Address:** 1207 N Thompson 72765 **Location:** I-540, exit 72, 2.6 mi e on US 412, then 1.4 mi n on US 71B. **Parking:** on-site.

MARKETPLACE GRILL **Phone:** 479/750-5200

American
$9-$24

The restaurant is big on menu variety, incorporating freshly made pasta, pizzas, dressings and sauces. Steaks, Cajun dishes and seafood also are served in the spacious, inviting dining room. Casual dress. **Hours:** 11 am-9:30 pm, Fri & Sat-10:30 pm. Closed: 1/1, 11/25, 12/25. **Address:** 1636 S 48th St 72762 **Location:** I-540, exit 72, just se. **Parking:** on-site.

SUNSET GRILL **Phone:** 479/872-9594

American
$6-$8

Guests are offered a choice of traditional home-cooked meals, which are served in good-size portions. Casual dress. **Hours:** 6 am-2 pm, Fri also 5 pm-8 pm, Sat & Sun 7 am-2 pm. Closed: 1/1, 4/4, 12/25; also Mon & week of Thanksgiving. **Address:** 3418 W Sunset Ave, Suite A 72762 **Location:** I-540, exit 72, 1 mi e. **Parking:** on-site.

STAR CITY pop. 2,471

STAR CITY INN & SUITES *Book at AAA.com* **Phone:** (870)628-6883

Hotel
$57-$95 All Year

Address: 1308 N Lincoln St 71667 **Location:** Just n on US 425. **Facility:** 46 one-bedroom standard units. 2 stories (no elevator), interior corridors. **Parking:** on-site. **Amenities:** high-speed Internet, hair dryers. **Pool(s):** outdoor. **Guest Services:** coin laundry. **Business Services:** meeting rooms.

ASK / SOME UNITS FEE

STUTTGART pop. 9,745

DAYS INN & SUITES *Book great rates at AAA.com* **Phone:** (870)673-3616

SAVE

Hotel
$77-$150 All Year

Address: 708 W Michigan St 72160 **Location:** Just w on US 63/79. **Facility:** 39 one-bedroom standard units. 2 stories (no elevator), exterior corridors. **Parking:** on-site. **Amenities:** high-speed Internet, dual phone lines, irons, hair dryers. *Some:* safes. **Pool(s):** outdoor. **Leisure Activities:** exercise room. **Guest Services:** valet and coin laundry, wireless Internet. **Business Services:** business center. **Free Special Amenities: continental breakfast and high-speed Internet.**

/ SOME UNITS FEE

TEXARKANA pop. 26,448

BEST WESTERN TEXARKANA INN & SUITES *Book great rates at AAA.com* **Phone:** (870)774-1534

SAVE

Hotel
$92-$109 All Year

Address: 5219 Cross Roads Pkwy 71854 **Location:** I-30, exit 228B, just ne on service road. **Facility:** Smoke free premises. 76 one-bedroom standard units. 3 stories, interior corridors. *Bath:* combo or shower only. **Parking:** on-site. **Amenities:** high-speed Internet, dual phone lines, voice mail, irons, hair dryers. **Pool(s):** outdoor. **Leisure Activities:** exercise room. **Guest Services:** valet and coin laundry, area transportation-within 5 mi, wireless Internet. **Business Services:** PC. **Free Special Amenities: full breakfast and high-speed Internet.**

CALL

AAA Benefit: Members save up to 20%, plus 10% bonus points with rewards program.

CLARION HOTEL LA CROSSE HOTEL Book great rates at AAA.com **Phone:** (870)774-3521

Hotel
$109 All Year

Address: 5100 N State Line Ave 71854 **Location:** I-30, exit 223B, just n. **Facility:** 204 units. 203 one-bedroom standard units. 1 two-bedroom suite with kitchen (no utensils). 4 stories, interior corridors. *Bath:* combo or shower only. **Parking:** on-site. **Amenities:** high-speed Internet, voice mail, irons, hair dryers. **Pool(s):** heated indoor. **Leisure Activities:** whirlpool, indoor recreation area, exercise room. *Fee:* game room. **Guest Services:** valet and coin laundry, airport transportation-Texarkana Municipal Airport, area transportation-within 5 mi, wireless Internet. **Business Services:** meeting rooms, PC. **Free Special Amenities: early check-in/late check-out and high-speed Internet.**
/ SOME UNITS FEE

LA QUINTA INN & SUITES Book at AAA.com **Phone:** (870)773-1000

Hotel
$79-$99 All Year

Address: 5102 N State Line Ave 71854 **Location:** I-30, exit 223B, just n. **Facility:** 101 units. 98 one-bedroom standard units. 3 one-bedroom suites. 4 stories, interior corridors. **Parking:** on-site. **Amenities:** video games (fee), voice mail, irons, hair dryers. *Some:* high-speed Internet. **Pool(s):** outdoor. **Leisure Activities:** exercise room. **Guest Services:** valet and coin laundry, wireless Internet. ASK / SOME UNITS

WHERE TO DINE

CATTLEMANS STEAKHOUSE **Phone:** 870/774-4481

Steak
$10-$25

This restaurant features the traditional steak dishes with basic presentation and preparation methods, but they also serve a nice variety of chicken and fried, broiled or blackened seafood. You'll find the service friendly and attentive. Casual dress. **Bar:** Full bar. **Reservations:** accepted. **Hours:** 5:30 pm-9:30 pm, Fri & Sat-10 pm. Closed major holidays; also Sun. **Address:** 4018 State Line Ave 72632 **Location:** I-30, exit 223A, 0.5 mi s. **Parking:** on-site.

LA CARRETA MEXICAN CAFE **Phone:** 870/774-0075

Tex-Mex
$8-$15

A large selection of traditional dishes is served in a festive, open dining room. Casual dress. **Bar:** Full bar. **Hours:** 11 am-10 pm, Fri & Sat-11 pm. Closed: 11/25, 12/25. **Address:** 3908 State Line Ave 71854 **Location:** I-30, exit 223A, 0.5 mi se. **Parking:** on-site.

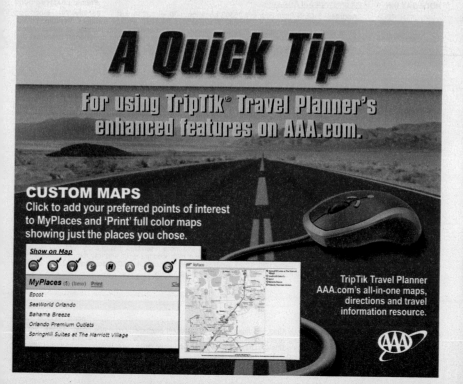

TEXARKANA, TX

COMFORT SUITES — Book at AAA.com — **Phone:** 903/223-0951

Hotel
Rates not provided

Address: 215 Richill Dr 75503 **Location:** I-30, exit 220B. **Facility:** Smoke free premises. 70 units. 68 one- and 2 two-bedroom standard units. 3 stories, interior corridors. *Bath:* combo or shower only. **Parking:** on-site. **Amenities:** high-speed Internet, dual phone lines, voice mail, safes (fee), irons, hair dryers. **Pool(s):** heated indoor. **Leisure Activities:** putting green, exercise room. **Guest Services:** valet and coin laundry, wireless Internet. **Business Services:** meeting rooms, PC, fax (fee).

CALL

HAMPTON INN & SUITES — Book great rates at AAA.com — **Phone:** 903/832-3499

Hotel
Rates not provided

Address: 4601 Cowhorn Creek Rd 75503 **Location:** I-30, exit 220B, 0.4 mi w, on south service road. **Facility:** 81 one-bedroom standard units. 4 stories, interior corridors. *Bath:* combo or shower only. **Parking:** on-site. **Amenities:** video games (fee), high-speed Internet, voice mail, irons, hair dryers. **Pool(s):** heated indoor. **Leisure Activities:** exercise room. **Guest Services:** valet and coin laundry, wireless Internet. **Business Services:** meeting rooms, PC, fax (fee).

CALL / SOME UNITS

AAA Benefit:
Members save up to 10% everyday!

LA QUINTA INN — Book at AAA.com — **Phone:** (903)794-1900

Hotel
$65-$109 All Year

Address: 5201 State Line Ave 75503 **Location:** I-30, exit 223A, sw of jct US 59 and 71. **Facility:** 130 units. 128 one-bedroom standard units. 2 one-bedroom suites. 2 stories (no elevator), exterior corridors. **Parking:** on-site. **Amenities:** video games (fee), voice mail, irons, hair dryers. **Pool(s):** outdoor. **Guest Services:** wireless Internet. **Business Services:** fax (fee).

ASK / SOME UNITS

RAMADA INN — Book at AAA.com — **Phone:** 903/792-3366

Hotel
Rates not provided

Address: 5401 N State Line Ave 75503 **Location:** I-30, exit 223B, 0.3 mi n on US 71. **Facility:** 120 one-bedroom standard units, some with whirlpools. 3 stories, interior corridors. **Parking:** on-site. **Amenities:** high-speed Internet, dual phone lines, irons, hair dryers. **Pool(s):** outdoor. **Leisure Activities:** whirlpool. **Guest Services:** valet and coin laundry, area transportation, wireless Internet. **Business Services:** PC, fax. / SOME UNITS FEE

RODEWAY INN — Book great rates at AAA.com — **Phone:** (903)792-6688

Hotel
$63-$73 All Year

Address: 5105 N State Line Ave 75503 **Location:** I-30, exit 223A, just sw. **Facility:** 74 one-bedroom standard units, some with whirlpools. 2 stories (no elevator), exterior corridors. **Parking:** on-site. **Amenities:** irons, hair dryers. **Pool(s):** outdoor. **Guest Services:** coin laundry, wireless Internet. **Business Services:** PC, fax (fee). **Free Special Amenities: expanded continental breakfast and high-speed Internet.** / SOME UNITS FEE

WHERE TO DINE

BRYCE'S CAFETERIA — **Phone:** 903/792-1611

American
$9-$14

Classic American favorites are offered at the traditional cafeteria, a great place for diners who are looking for generous portions of hearty comfort food. The self-service spot is near the mall and offers a view of the surrounding area. Casual dress. **Hours:** 11 am-2 & 5-8 pm, Sat & Sun 11 am-8 pm. Closed: 1/1, 12/25. **Address:** 2021 Mall Dr 75503 **Location:** I-30, exit 222 (Summerhill Rd), just s to Mall Dr, then just w. **Parking:** on-site.

DIXIE DINER #2 — **Phone:** 903/223-0841

American
$9-$16

People in the Texarkana area rely on the small chain of restaurants for down-home family favorites. Beef, chicken, pork, fish and vegetable dishes all are made in house. A slice of homemade pie is the perfect finish to a meal. Casual dress. **Hours:** 10:30 am-9 pm. Closed: 11/25, 12/25. **Address:** 4115 N King Hwy, Suite 120 75503 **Location:** I-30, exit 218, just n. **Parking:** on-site.

GRANDY'S RESTAURANT — **Phone:** 903/832-5206

American
$4-$7

Fried chicken and country-fried steak are menu standbys at the restaurant, a regional franchise. The decor is a step up from that of most quick-serve eateries and more resembles that of a conventional restaurant. Some elements of increased service include additional rolls, iced tea refills and tray removal. Casual dress. **Hours:** 6 am-9 pm. Closed: 11/25, 12/25. **Address:** 3225 Kennedy Ln 75503 **Location:** I-30, exit 220B, just se on Richmond Rd to Kennedy Ln, then just e. **Parking:** on-site.

TONTITOWN pop. 942

WHERE TO DINE

MARY MAESTRI'S — **Phone:** 479/361-2536

Italian
$12-$30

An area institution since 1923, the fine dining establishment prepares homemade Italian cuisine. Set on a busy highway, the one-level building has very pleasant roadside appeal. Inside, the foyer boasts photographs of various political figures and celebrities who have dined here. Wearing semi-formal attire, the staff is very attentive and happy to answer questions and address guests' needs in a timely manner. Dressy casual. **Bar:** Full bar. **Hours:** 5:30 pm-9:30 pm. Closed major holidays. **Address:** 956 E Henri De Tonti Blvd 72770 **Location:** On US 412 at SR 112. **Parking:** on-site.

TRUMANN pop. 6,889

DAYS INN & SUITES — Book at AAA.com — **Phone:** 870/483-8383

Hotel
Rates not provided

Address: 400 Commerce Dr 72472 **Location:** US 63, exit 29, just e. **Facility:** 54 one-bedroom standard units. 2 stories, interior/exterior corridors. *Bath:* combo or shower only. **Parking:** on-site. **Amenities:** high-speed Internet, voice mail, irons, hair dryers. **Pool(s):** outdoor. **Leisure Activities:** exercise room. **Guest Services:** coin laundry, wireless Internet. **Business Services:** meeting rooms, PC. / SOME UNITS FEE

VAN BUREN pop. 18,986

BEST WESTERN VAN BUREN INN — Book great rates at AAA.com — **Phone:** (479)474-8100

AAA SAVE
Hotel
$75-$83 All Year

Address: 1903 N 6th St 72956 **Location:** I-40, exit 5, just n. **Facility:** 58 one-bedroom standard units. 2 stories (no elevator), exterior corridors. *Bath:* combo or shower only. **Parking:** on-site. **Amenities:** high-speed Internet, voice mail, irons, hair dryers. **Pool(s):** outdoor. **Guest Services:** valet laundry, wireless Internet. **Business Services:** meeting rooms. **Free Special Amenities: full breakfast and newspaper.**
/ SOME UNITS FEE

AAA Benefit: Members save up to 20%, plus 10% bonus points with rewards program.

HAMPTON INN — Book great rates at AAA.com — **Phone:** (479)471-7447

Hotel
$90-$119 All Year

Address: 1916 N 6th St 72956 **Location:** I-40, exit 5, just ne. **Facility:** 64 one-bedroom standard units, some with whirlpools. 3 stories, interior corridors. *Bath:* combo or shower only. **Parking:** on-site. **Terms:** 1-7 night minimum stay, cancellation fee imposed. **Amenities:** high-speed Internet, voice mail, irons, hair dryers. **Pool(s):** heated indoor. **Leisure Activities:** exercise room. **Guest Services:** valet and coin laundry, wireless Internet. **Business Services:** meeting rooms, PC.
CALL / SOME UNITS

AAA Benefit: Members save up to 10% everyday!

SLEEP INN & SUITES — Book at AAA.com — **Phone:** (479)262-6776

Hotel
$67-$77 All Year

Address: 1633 N 12th Ct 72956 **Location:** 0.6 mi e of jct SR 59. **Facility:** Smoke free premises. 58 one-bedroom standard units, some with whirlpools. 3 stories, interior corridors. *Bath:* combo or shower only. **Parking:** on-site. **Amenities:** high-speed Internet, voice mail, irons, hair dryers. **Pool(s):** heated indoor. **Leisure Activities:** exercise room. **Guest Services:** coin laundry, wireless Internet. **Business Services:** meeting rooms, business center.
ASK CALL / SOME UNITS FEE

— WHERE TO DINE —

EL LORITO **Phone:** 479/410-2463

Mexican
$6-$8

Ample portions of a nice variety of dishes contribute to the restaurant's popularity with the locals. Casual dress. **Bar:** Beer only. **Hours:** 11 am-9 pm. Closed: 11/25, 12/25. **Address:** 511 Broadway St 72956 **Location:** Just w of jct Main St. **Parking:** on-site.

WEST HELENA pop. 8,689

BEST WESTERN INN *Book great rates at AAA.com* **Phone:** (870)572-2592

Hotel
$69-$96 All Year

Address: 1053 Hwy 49 W 72390 **Location:** US 49, 3 mi w. **Facility:** 63 one-bedroom standard units, some with whirlpools. 2 stories (no elevator), exterior corridors. **Parking:** on-site. **Amenities:** voice mail, irons, hair dryers. *Some:* high-speed Internet. **Pool(s):** outdoor. **Leisure Activities:** exercise room. **Guest Services:** coin laundry, wireless Internet. **Business Services:** PC. **Free Special Amenities: full breakfast and high-speed Internet.** / SOME UNITS

AAA Benefit:
Members save up to 20%, plus 10% bonus points with rewards program.

WEST MEMPHIS pop. 27,666

BEST WESTERN WEST MEMPHIS INN *Book great rates at AAA.com* **Phone:** (870)735-7185

Hotel
$75-$105 All Year

Address: 3401 Service Loop Rd 72301 **Location:** I-55, exit 4, just nw. **Facility:** 39 one-bedroom standard units. 2 stories (no elevator), interior corridors. **Parking:** on-site. **Terms:** 7 day cancellation notice. **Amenities:** irons, hair dryers. **Pool(s):** outdoor. **Guest Services:** wireless Internet. **Free Special Amenities: continental breakfast and high-speed Internet.** / SOME UNITS

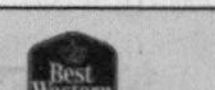

AAA Benefit:
Members save up to 20%, plus 10% bonus points with rewards program.

RAMADA INN *Book at AAA.com* **Phone:** (870)732-1102

Hotel
$69-$139 All Year

Address: 2003 S Service Rd 72301 **Location:** I-40, exit 279A. **Facility:** 76 one-bedroom standard units. 2 stories (no elevator), interior corridors. **Parking:** on-site. **Amenities:** dual phone lines, voice mail, irons, hair dryers. **Pool(s):** outdoor. **Leisure Activities:** exercise room. **Guest Services:** valet and coin laundry, wireless Internet. **Business Services:** meeting rooms, PC.
ASK / SOME UNITS

— WHERE TO DINE —

MARGARITA'S MEXICAN RESTAURANT & CANTINA **Phone:** 870/702-7314

Mexican
$5-$14

Varied well-prepared dishes are served promptly in the quaint but festive restaurant. Casual dress. **Bar:** Beer & wine. **Reservations:** not accepted. **Hours:** 11 am-10 pm. Closed: 11/25, 12/25. **Address:** 1100 1/2 Ingram Blvd 72301 **Location:** I-40, exit 279A, just s. **Parking:** on-site.

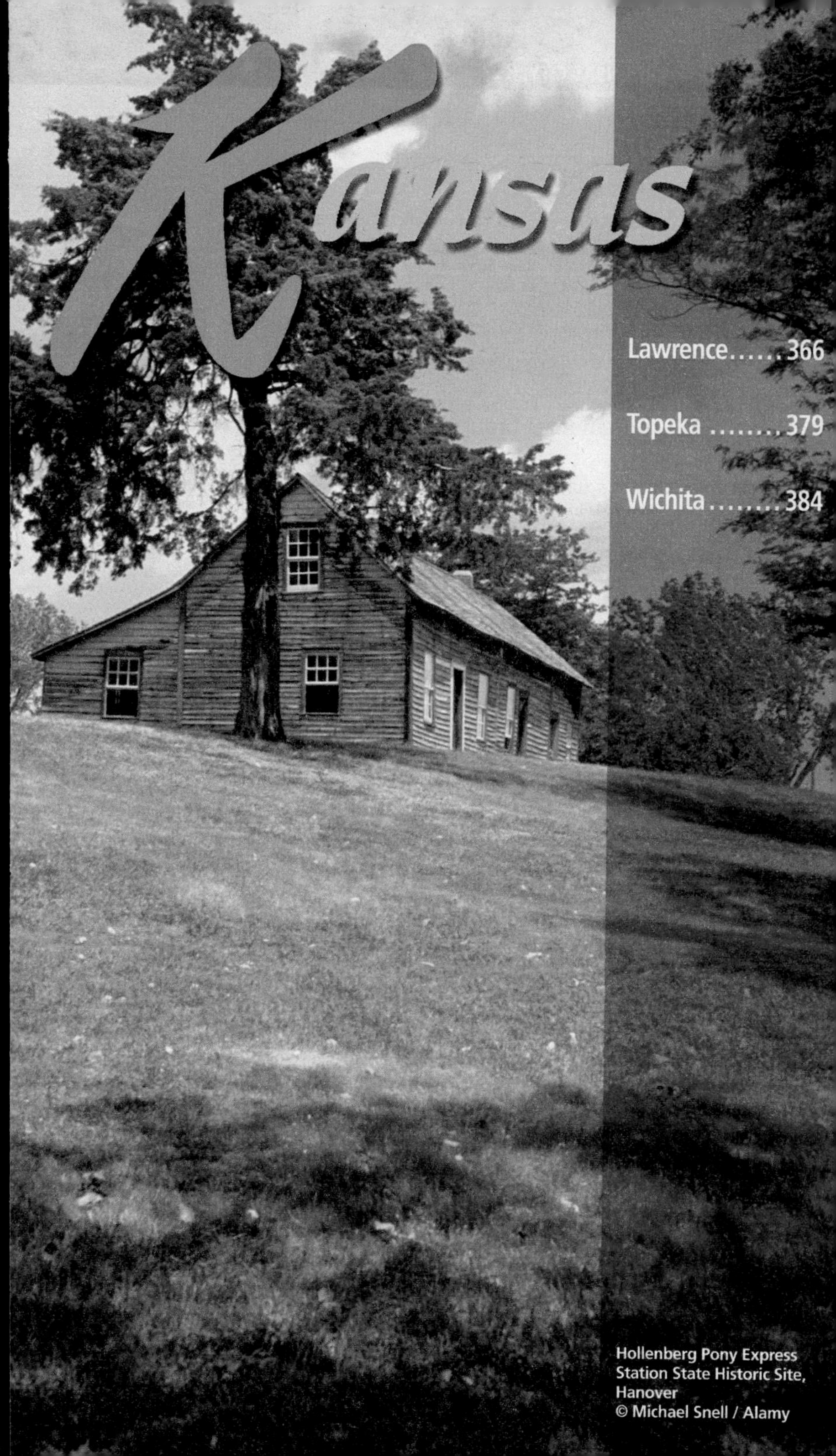

Kansas

Hollenberg Pony Express Station State Historic Site, Hanover

ABILENE pop. 6,543

DIAMOND MOTEL Book great rates at AAA.com **Phone:** (785)263-2360

Motel
$40-$75 All Year

Address: 1407 NW 3rd St 67410 **Location:** I-70, exit 275, 1.3 mi s, then 1 mi w. **Facility:** 29 one-bedroom standard units. 1 story, exterior corridors. **Parking:** on-site. **Amenities:** hair dryers. **Guest Services:** wireless Internet. **Business Services:** PC.

/ SOME UNITS

FREE continental breakfast and high-speed Internet

HOLIDAY INN EXPRESS HOTEL & SUITES Book at AAA.com **Phone:** (785)263-4049

Hotel
$94-$104 All Year

Address: 110 E Lafayette Ave 67410 **Location:** I-70, exit 275, just n. **Facility:** 61 one-bedroom standard units, some with whirlpools. 2 stories, interior corridors. *Bath:* combo or shower only. **Parking:** on-site. **Amenities:** high-speed Internet, dual phone lines, voice mail, irons, hair dryers. **Pool(s):** heated indoor. **Leisure Activities:** sauna, whirlpool, exercise room. **Guest Services:** valet and coin laundry, wireless Internet. **Business Services:** meeting rooms, PC.

ASK CALL / SOME UNITS FEE

SUPER 8 Book at AAA.com **Phone:** (785)263-4545

Hotel
$63-$82 All Year

Address: 2207 N Buckeye 67410 **Location:** I-70, exit 275, just s. **Facility:** 61 one-bedroom standard units. 3 stories (no elevator), interior corridors. **Parking:** on-site. **Terms:** 5 day cancellation notice. **Guest Services:** wireless Internet. **Business Services:** PC.

ASK CALL / SOME UNITS FEE

— WHERE TO DINE —

BROOKVILLE HOTEL **Phone:** 785/263-2244

American
$14

The historic Brookville Hotel, in the center of town, was built in 1870. The restaurant has been family-owned and operated since 1915. The unique dining experience offers ample portions of the excellent family-style fried chicken. Knowledgeable service. Casual dress. **Bar:** Full bar. **Reservations:** suggested. **Hours:** 5 pm-7:30 pm, Sat 11:30 am-2 & 4:30-7:30 pm, Sun 11:30 am-2 & 5-7 pm; hours may vary 11/1-3/31. Closed major holidays; also Mon & Tues. **Address:** 105 E Lafayette Ave 67410 **Location:** I-70, exit 275, just n, then just e. **Parking:** on-site. **Historic**

THE KIRBY HOUSE **Phone:** 785/263-7336

American
$7-$23

Located in a restored Victorian home built in 1885 by local banker Thomas Kirby, the restaurant offers a menu with many delicate offerings of steak, seafood, pasta, chicken and pork. The desserts are delicious. A full coffee bar is available. Casual dress. **Bar:** Full bar. **Reservations:** suggested. **Hours:** 11 am-2 & 5-8 pm. Closed: 1/1, 12/25; also Sun. **Address:** 205 NE 3rd St 67410 **Location:** I-70, exit 275, 1.3 mi s, then just e. **Parking:** street. CALL

ANDOVER pop. 6,698

ANDOVER EXPRESS INN **Phone:** 316/733-8881

Motel
$57-$63 All Year

Address: 222 W US Hwy 54 67002 **Location:** 2.2 mi e of jct SR 96. **Facility:** 38 one-bedroom standard units. 2 stories (no elevator), exterior corridors. **Parking:** on-site. **Terms:** cancellation fee imposed. **Pool(s):** outdoor. **Guest Services:** coin laundry, wireless Internet. **Business Services:** meeting rooms, PC. **Free Special Amenities: continental breakfast and high-speed Internet.**

/ SOME UNITS FEE

ARKANSAS CITY pop. 11,963

— WHERE TO DINE —

SIRLOIN STOCKADE **Phone:** 620/442-0000

Regional Steak
$6-$9

The steakhouse lines up buffet items, including pizza, tacos, soups, salads and desserts, providing both excellent variety and a good value. Rotating theme nights might allow for the sampling of sushi, barbecue and seafood. The buffet also may serve to complement a quality steak. Rolls are baked several times daily. Casual dress. **Reservations:** not accepted. **Hours:** 11 am-9 pm. Closed: 11/25, 12/25. **Address:** 2825 N Summit St 67005 **Location:** On US 77, just n of jct W Bryant and E Windsor rds. **Parking:** on-site.

ATCHISON pop. 10,232

AMERICINN LODGE & SUITES OF ATCHISON *Book at AAA.com* **Phone:** (913)367-4000

Hotel
$74-$85 All Year

Address: 500 US 73 66002 **Location:** Just s at US 59 and 73. **Facility:** 45 units. 42 one-bedroom standard units, some with whirlpools. 3 one-bedroom suites with whirlpools. 2 stories (no elevator), interior corridors. *Bath:* combo or shower only. **Parking:** on-site. **Terms:** cancellation fee imposed. **Amenities:** high-speed Internet, irons, hair dryers. **Pool(s):** heated indoor. **Leisure Activities:** sauna, whirlpool. **Guest Services:** coin laundry. **Business Services:** meeting rooms, PC.
ASK CALL / SOME UNITS FEE

SUPER 8 *Book at AAA.com* **Phone:** (913)367-7666

Hotel
$70-$160 All Year

Address: 509 S 9th St 66002 **Location:** Just s of jct US 59, on US 73. **Facility:** 45 one-bedroom standard units. 3 stories (no elevator), interior corridors. **Parking:** on-site. **Terms:** 7 day cancellation notice. **Amenities:** hair dryers. *Some:* irons. **Guest Services:** coin laundry, wireless Internet.
/ SOME UNITS

WHERE TO DINE

HOOF & HORN STEAKHOUSE AT THE RIVER HOUSE RESTAURANT **Phone:** 913/367-1010

American
$5-$22

Patrons can appreciate good river views from the renovated, old-style dining room, which has many large windows and a patio. The menu lists traditional and contemporary haute cuisine. This place is popular with the local community. Some favorites include steaks, the veggie sandwich and spinach salad. Casual dress. **Bar:** Full bar. **Reservations:** accepted. **Hours:** 4 pm-9 pm, Fri & Sat-10 pm. Closed major holidays; also Sun & Mon. **Address:** 101 Commercial St 66002 **Location:** Just e of downtown; on Missouri River. **Parking:** on-site.

BAXTER SPRINGS pop. 4,602

BAXTER INN-4-LESS **Phone:** (620)856-2106

Hotel
$43-$70 All Year

Address: 2451 Military Ave 66713 **Location:** On US 69 alternate route, 1 mi s of jct US 166. **Facility:** 32 one-bedroom standard units. 2 stories (no elevator), interior corridors. **Parking:** on-site. **Guest Services:** wireless Internet. ASK / SOME UNITS FEE

BELLEVILLE pop. 2,239

AMERICAS BEST VALUE INN *Book great rates at AAA.com* **Phone:** (785)527-2231

Motel
$49-$54 All Year

Address: 1616 Hwy 36 66935 **Location:** Jct US 81 and 36; northwest corner; just up hill. **Facility:** 40 units. 38 one- and 1 two-bedroom standard units. 1 one-bedroom suite. 1 story, exterior corridors. **Parking:** on-site. **Terms:** office hours 7 am-10 pm. **Amenities:** irons, hair dryers. *Some:* DVD players, high-speed Internet. **Pool(s):** outdoor. **Leisure Activities:** whirlpool. **Guest Services:** coin laundry, wireless Internet. **Business Services:** PC. **Free Special Amenities: continental breakfast and room upgrade (subject to availability with advance reservations).**
/ SOME UNITS

SUPER 8 *Book at AAA.com* **Phone:** 785/527-2112

Hotel
Rates not provided

Address: 1410 28th St 66935 **Location:** On US 36, 0.5 mi e of jct US 81. **Facility:** 35 one-bedroom standard units, some with whirlpools. 2 stories (no elevator), interior corridors. **Parking:** on-site, winter plug-ins. **Terms:** office hours 6 am-11 pm. **Amenities:** hair dryers. **Leisure Activities:** whirlpool. **Guest Services:** coin laundry, wireless Internet.
/ SOME UNITS FEE

BELOIT pop. 4,019

SUPER 8 *Book at AAA.com* **Phone:** (785)738-4300

Hotel
$54-$99 All Year

Address: 3018 W Hwy 24 67420 **Location:** Just e of jct SR 14. **Facility:** 40 one-bedroom standard units. 2 stories (no elevator), interior/exterior corridors. *Bath:* combo or shower only. **Parking:** on-site, winter plug-ins. **Terms:** 3 night minimum stay - seasonal and/or weekends, 3 day cancellation notice. **Amenities:** irons, hair dryers. *Some:* DVD players. **Guest Services:** coin laundry, wireless Internet. **Business Services:** meeting rooms, PC.
ASK CALL / SOME UNITS FEE

BONNER SPRINGS—See Nearby MO City Of Kansas City p. 492.

BURLINGTON pop. 2,790

COUNTRY HAVEN INN **Phone:** (620)364-8260

Hotel
$65-$75 All Year

Address: 207 Cross St 66839 **Location:** Just e of US 75; 1 mi n of center. **Facility:** 24 one-bedroom standard units. 2 stories (no elevator), interior corridors. **Parking:** on-site, winter plug-ins. **Amenities:** voice mail, hair dryers. **Guest Services:** wireless Internet. **Business Services:** meeting rooms, PC. ASK CALL / SOME UNITS FEE

CHANUTE pop. 9,441

CHANUTE SAFARI INN Book at AAA.com Phone: (620)431-9460

Motel
$40-$50 All Year

Address: 3428 S Santa Fe 66720 **Location:** US 169, exit 35th St, 1.5 mi e. **Facility:** 41 one-bedroom standard units. 1 story, exterior corridors. **Parking:** on-site, winter plug-ins. **Terms:** office hours 7 am-11 pm, cancellation fee imposed. **Amenities:** *Some:* irons, hair dryers. **Pool(s):** outdoor. **Guest Services:** coin laundry, wireless Internet. ASK / SOME UNITS FEE

GUEST HOUSE MOTOR INN Phone: 620/431-0600

Motel
$40-$50 All Year

Address: 1814 S Santa Fe 66720 **Location:** US 169, exit 35th St, 2.5 mi ne. **Facility:** 29 one-bedroom standard units. 2 stories (no elevator), exterior corridors. **Parking:** on-site. **Terms:** cancellation fee imposed. **Amenities:** *Some:* irons. **Pool(s):** outdoor. **Guest Services:** wireless Internet. ASK / SOME UNITS FEE

TIOGA SUITES HOTEL Book at AAA.com Phone: (620)431-3343

Hotel
$59-$99 All Year

Address: 12 E Main St 66720 **Location:** Center. **Facility:** 33 units. 31 one-bedroom standard units. 2 one-bedroom suites. 6 stories, interior corridors. *Bath:* combo or shower only. **Parking:** on-site and street. **Terms:** office hours 8 am-midnight. **Amenities:** DVD players, voice mail, irons, hair dryers. **Leisure Activities:** massage. **Guest Services:** coin laundry, wireless Internet. **Business Services:** meeting rooms, business center. ASK / SOME UNITS

CLAY CENTER pop. 4,564

CEDAR COURT MOTEL Phone: 785/632-2148

Motel
$49-$75 All Year

Address: 905 Crawford St 67432 **Location:** On US 24, just e of jct SR 15. **Facility:** 54 one-bedroom standard units, some with whirlpools. 1-2 stories (no elevator), exterior corridors. *Bath:* combo or shower only. **Parking:** on-site. **Amenities:** *Some:* dual phone lines, irons, hair dryers. **Dining:** El Puerto Mexican Restaurant, see separate listing. **Pool(s):** outdoor. **Guest Services:** wireless Internet. ASK CALL M / SOME UNITS FEE

WHERE TO DINE

EL PUERTO MEXICAN RESTAURANT Phone: 785/632-5112

Mexican
$4-$12

The menu at this spot offers a good variety of filling entree items, including some that are quite spicy. The fajitas are a good choice. Service is fast. Casual dress. **Reservations:** accepted. **Hours:** 11 am-9 pm, Fri-10 pm, Sat-9:30 pm, Sun-2:30 pm. Closed major holidays. **Address:** 901 Crawford St 67432 **Location:** On US 24, just e of jct SR 15; next to Cedar Court Motel. **Parking:** on-site.

COFFEYVILLE pop. 11,021

WHERE TO DINE

SIRLOIN STOCKADE Phone: 620/251-8156

Regional Steak
$6-$9

The steakhouse lines up buffet items, including pizza, tacos, soups, salads and desserts, providing both excellent variety and a good value. Rotating theme nights might allow for the sampling of sushi, barbecue and seafood. The buffet also may serve to complement a quality steak. Rolls are baked several times daily. Casual dress. **Reservations:** not accepted. **Hours:** 6 am-9 pm. Closed: 11/25, 12/25. **Address:** 104 W 11th St 67337 **Location:** On US 169 and 166; center. **Parking:** on-site.

COLBY pop. 5,450

COMFORT INN

Book at AAA.com

Phone: (785)462-3833

Hotel

$84-$130 All Year

Address: 2225 S Range Ave 67701 **Location:** I-70, exit 53 (SR 25), just s. **Facility:** 77 units. 71 one-bedroom standard units. 6 one-bedroom suites. 2 stories (no elevator), interior corridors. *Bath:* combo or shower only. **Parking:** on-site, winter plug-ins. **Amenities:** voice mail, safes (fee), irons, hair dryers. *Some:* high-speed Internet, dual phone lines. **Dining:** City Limits Bar & Grill, see separate listing. **Pool(s):** heated indoor. **Leisure Activities:** whirlpool, exercise room. **Guest Services:** coin laundry, wireless Internet. **Business Services:** conference facilities, PC.

ASK CALL / SOME UNITS FEE

CROWN INN

Phone: 785/462-3943

Motel

$55-$80 All Year

Address: 2320 S Range Ave 67701 **Location:** I-70, exit 53 (SR 25), just s. Adjacent to Southwind Plaza. **Facility:** 29 one-bedroom standard units. 1 story, exterior corridors. **Parking:** on-site, winter plug-ins. **Terms:** office hours 6:50 am-midnight, cancellation fee imposed. **Amenities:** irons, hair dryers. *Some:* high-speed Internet. **Guest Services:** wireless Internet. **Business Services:** PC. **Free Special Amenities: continental breakfast and high-speed Internet.**

/ SOME UNITS

DAYS INN

Book great rates at AAA.com

Phone: (785)462-8691

Hotel

$75-$90 All Year

Address: 1925 S Range Ave 67701 **Location:** I-70, exit 53 (SR 25), 0.3 mi n. **Facility:** 45 one-bedroom standard units. 2 stories (no elevator), interior corridors. **Parking:** on-site. **Terms:** cancellation fee imposed. **Amenities:** irons, hair dryers. **Pool(s):** heated indoor. **Leisure Activities:** whirlpool. **Guest Services:** wireless Internet. **Free Special Amenities: expanded continental breakfast and high-speed Internet.** / SOME UNITS

HOLIDAY INN EXPRESS HOTEL & SUITES

Book great rates at AAA.com

Phone: (785)462-8787

Hotel

$95-$155 All Year

Address: 645 W Willow St 67701 **Location:** I-70, exit 53 (SR 25), just ne. **Facility:** 72 units. 69 one-bedroom standard units. 3 one-bedroom suites, some with whirlpools. 3 stories, interior corridors. *Bath:* combo or shower only. **Parking:** on-site. **Amenities:** high-speed Internet, dual phone lines, voice mail, irons, hair dryers. **Pool(s):** heated indoor. **Leisure Activities:** sauna, exercise room. **Guest Services:** coin laundry, wireless Internet. **Business Services:** meeting rooms, PC. **Free Special Amenities: expanded continental breakfast and high-speed Internet.**

CALL / SOME UNITS

MOTEL 6 #4245

Book great rates at AAA.com

Phone: (785)462-8201

Hotel

$40-$70 3/1-9/30

$40-$66 10/1-2/28

Address: 1985 S Range Ave 67701 **Location:** I-70, exit 53 (SR 25), just n. **Facility:** 46 one-bedroom standard units. 2 stories (no elevator), interior/exterior corridors. **Parking:** on-site, winter plug-ins. **Guest Services:** coin laundry, wireless Internet. **Business Services:** PC. **Free Special Amenities: local telephone calls and high-speed Internet.** / SOME UNITS

SUPER 8

Book great rates at AAA.com

Phone: (785)462-8248

Hotel

$65-$75 All Year

Address: 1040 Zelfer Ave 67701 **Location:** I-70, exit 53 (SR 25), 0.3 mi n, then just w. **Facility:** 62 one-bedroom standard units, some with whirlpools. 2 stories (no elevator), interior corridors. **Parking:** on-site, winter plug-ins. **Amenities:** hair dryers. **Leisure Activities:** whirlpool. **Guest Services:** coin laundry, wireless Internet. **Free Special Amenities: expanded continental breakfast and high-speed Internet.** / SOME UNITS

WHERE TO DINE

CITY LIMITS BAR & GRILL

Phone: 785/462-6565

American

$10-$25

This casual bar and grill prepares USDA Choice steaks, grilled salmon, shrimp, chicken-fried steak and lighter fare along the lines of sandwiches. The all-you-can-eat salad bar lines up fresh vegetables and fixings. Do browse the dessert menu, which lists made-in-house treats, some of which are unexpected. Casual dress. **Bar:** Full bar. **Reservations:** accepted. **Hours:** 5 pm-10 pm. Closed major holidays; also Sun. **Address:** 2227 S Range Rd 67701 **Location:** I-70, exit 53 (SR 25), just s; in Comfort Inn. **Parking:** on-site. CALL

MONTANA MIKE'S

Phone: 785/462-7178

Steak

$7-$20

This steakhouse offers a dining experience for the whole family. A rustic look with Western appointments characterizes the dining room. Although it's hard to go wrong with a hearty steak of USDA Choice aged beef, guests also can try smoked, fire-grilled chicken breast, chicken-fried steak, baby back ribs and other selections. Casual dress. **Bar:** Full bar. **Reservations:** not accepted. **Hours:** 11 am-9 pm, Fri & Sat-10 pm; seasonal hours vary. Closed: 11/25, 12/25; also Mon. **Address:** 1855 S Range Rd 67701 **Location:** I-70, exit 53 (SR 25), 0.3 mi n, then just e. **Parking:** on-site. CALL

COLUMBUS pop. 3,396

MAPLE UNCOMMON Book at AAA.com **Phone:** (620)429-3130

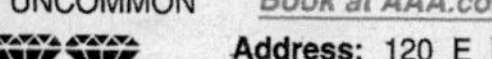

Boutique Hotel
$84-$135 All Year

Address: 120 E Maple St 66725 **Location:** Just e of square; downtown. **Facility:** Individually decorated rooms. Smoke free premises. 7 units. 6 one- and 1 two-bedroom standard units. 2 stories (no elevator), interior corridors. **Parking:** street. **Terms:** 3 day cancellation notice-fee imposed. **Guest Services:** complimentary and valet laundry, area transportation, wireless Internet. **Business Services:** meeting rooms. ASK

CONCORDIA pop. 5,714

HOLIDAY INN EXPRESS HOTEL & SUITES Book at AAA.com **Phone:** 785/243-2700

Hotel
Rates not provided

Address: 2175 Lincoln St 66901 **Location:** On US 81, 1.5 mi s of center. **Facility:** Smoke free premises. 61 one-bedroom standard units, some with whirlpools. 3 stories, interior corridors. *Bath:* combo or shower only. **Parking:** on-site, winter plug-ins. **Amenities:** high-speed Internet, voice mail, irons, hair dryers. **Pool(s):** heated indoor. **Leisure Activities:** whirlpool, exercise room. **Guest Services:** complimentary laundry, wireless Internet. **Business Services:** meeting rooms, business center. CALL / SOME UNITS

SUPER 8-CONCORDIA Book at AAA.com **Phone:** (785)243-4200

Hotel
$60-$65 All Year

Address: 1320 Lincoln St 66901 **Location:** On US 81, 1 mi s of center. **Facility:** 44 one-bedroom standard units. 2 stories (no elevator), interior/exterior corridors. **Parking:** on-site, winter plug-ins. **Amenities:** hair dryers. *Some:* irons. **Guest Services:** wireless Internet. **Business Services:** PC. ASK / SOME UNITS FEE

WHERE TO DINE

EL PUERTO **Phone:** 785/243-6165

Mexican
$5-$12

This modest and casual downtown Mexican eatery turns out well-prepared fajitas, tacos and special offerings of shrimp salad, beef steak ranchero and many combination plates. Casual dress. **Reservations:** not accepted. **Hours:** 11 am-9 pm, Fri & Sat-10 pm, Sun-3 pm. Closed major holidays. **Address:** 217 W 6th St 66901 **Location:** Just w of US 81; downtown. **Parking:** street.

COTTONWOOD FALLS pop. 966

GRAND CENTRAL HOTEL **Phone:** (620)273-6763

AAA SAVE

Historic Country Inn
$160-$190 All Year

Address: 215 Broadway 66845 **Location:** Just w of US 177; center of downtown. **Facility:** The hotel, built in 1884 and renovated in 1995, features rich Western flair, oversize guest rooms and large spa-style showers. Smoke free premises. 10 one-bedroom standard units. 2 stories (no elevator), interior corridors. *Bath:* shower only. **Parking:** on-site, winter plug-ins. **Terms:** cancellation fee imposed. **Amenities:** high-speed Internet, hair dryers. *Some:* DVD players. **Dining:** Grand Central Grill, see separate listing. **Leisure Activities:** recreation programs. **Guest Services:** valet laundry, wireless Internet. **Business Services:** meeting rooms, fax. **Free Special Amenities: expanded continental breakfast.** / SOME UNITS

WHERE TO DINE

GRAND CENTRAL GRILL Menu on AAA.com **Phone:** 620/273-6763

AAA

American
$6-$28

This restaurant features Sterling Silver USDA choice steaks. The menu also offers unique entrees, such as fettuccini portabella, open range kabobs, eggplant parmesan and desserts that are prepared in-house. Save room for the grand creme brulee—you won't be disappointed. Casual dress. **Bar:** Full bar. **Reservations:** suggested. **Hours:** 11 am-9 pm. Closed: 1/1, 11/25, 12/25; also Sun. **Address:** 215 Broadway 66845 **Location:** Just w of US 177; center of downtown; in Grand Central Hotel. **Parking:** on-site.

COUNCIL GROVE pop. 2,321

THE COTTAGE HOUSE HOTEL & MOTEL **Phone:** (620)767-6828

AAA SAVE

Historic Hotel
$55-$175 3/1-12/1
$50-$165 12/2-2/28

Address: 25 N Neosho 66846 **Location:** Just n of Main St; downtown. **Facility:** Modern comforts in nostalgic surroundings. Some modest motel units. Individually decorated, charming inn rooms. 40 one-bedroom standard units. 1-2 stories (no elevator), interior/exterior corridors. *Bath:* combo or shower only. **Parking:** on-site, winter plug-ins. **Terms:** age restrictions may apply, 7 day cancellation notice-fee imposed. **Amenities:** video library. *Some:* DVD players, irons, hair dryers. **Leisure Activities:** sauna, whirlpool. **Guest Services:** wireless Internet. **Business Services:** meeting rooms. **Free Special Amenities: expanded continental breakfast and local telephone calls.** FEE / SOME UNITS FEE

WHERE TO DINE

HAYS HOUSE 1857 RESTAURANT **Phone:** 620/767-5911

American
$5-$27

Listed on the National Register of Historic Places, this restaurant offers a wide variety of homestyle foods as well as beef that's aged on the premises. Aromatic breads and desserts also are prepared in house. Casual dress. **Bar:** Full bar. **Reservations:** suggested, for dinner Sat. **Hours:** 11 am-8 pm, Fri-9 pm, Sat 6 am-9 pm, Sun 6 am-8 pm; hours vary in winter. Closed: 12/25. **Address:** 112 W Main St 66846 **Location:** On US 56; downtown. **Parking:** on-site. **Historic**

DERBY pop. 17,807

The following lodging was either not evaluated or did not meet AAA rating requirements but is listed for your information only.

HAMPTON INN DERBY

Phone: 316/425-7900

fyi

Not evaluated. **Address:** 1701 Cambridge St 67037. Facilities, services, and decor characterize a mid-scale property.

AAA Benefit: Members save up to 10% everyday!

WHERE TO DINE

RIB CRIB BBQ AND GRILL

Phone: 316/788-9902

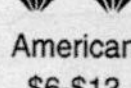

American
$6-$13

Most guests need extra napkins to tackle the ribs, brisket, ham, pork and chicken selections. The menu also lists sandwiches and wraps, along with tempting sides and large desserts. The decor is decidedly Western. Casual dress. **Bar:** Beer only. **Hours:** 11 am-10 pm. Closed major holidays. **Address:** 1440 N Rock Rd 67037 **Location:** At jct Meadowlark. **Parking:** on-site.

DODGE CITY pop. 26,176

BEST WESTERN COUNTRY INN & SUITES *Book great rates at AAA.com*

Phone: (620)225-7378

Hotel
$100-$120 All Year

Address: 506 N 14th Ave 67801 **Location:** Just n of jct US 50 business route (Wyatt Earp Blvd). **Facility:** Smoke free premises. 66 units. 64 one-bedroom standard units, some with whirlpools. 2 one-bedroom suites. 3 stories, interior/exterior corridors. *Bath:* combo or shower only. **Parking:** on-site. **Amenities:** high-speed Internet, voice mail, irons, hair dryers. *Some:* DVD players. **Pool(s):** heated indoor. **Leisure Activities:** whirlpool, exercise room. **Guest Services:** valet and coin laundry, wireless Internet. **Business Services:** meeting rooms, business center. **Free Special Amenities: full breakfast and high-speed Internet.**

CALL / SOME UNITS FEE

AAA Benefit: Members save up to 20%, plus 10% bonus points with rewards program.

COMFORT INN *Book at AAA.com*

Phone: 620/338-8700

Hotel
Rates not provided

Address: 2000 W Wyatt Earp Blvd 67801 **Location:** 1.3 mi w on US 50 business route. **Facility:** 54 one-bedroom standard units. 2 stories (no elevator), interior corridors. **Parking:** on-site. **Amenities:** high-speed Internet, voice mail, irons, hair dryers. **Pool(s):** heated indoor. **Leisure Activities:** whirlpool, exercise room. **Guest Services:** valet laundry, wireless Internet. **Business Services:** PC. / SOME UNITS

HOLIDAY INN EXPRESS *Book at AAA.com*

Phone: 620/227-5000

Hotel
Rates not provided

Address: 2320 W Wyatt Earp Blvd 67801 **Location:** 1.4 mi w on US 50 business route. **Facility:** 63 units. 60 one-bedroom standard units, some with whirlpools. 3 one-bedroom suites with whirlpools. 2 stories, interior corridors. *Bath:* combo or shower only. **Parking:** on-site. **Amenities:** high-speed Internet, voice mail, irons, hair dryers. **Pool(s):** heated indoor. **Leisure Activities:** whirlpool, exercise room. **Guest Services:** valet and coin laundry, wireless Internet. **Business Services:** meeting rooms, business center. / SOME UNITS FEE

LA QUINTA INN & SUITES *Book at AAA.com*

Phone: (620)225-7373

Hotel
$89-$139 All Year

Address: 2400 W Wyatt Earp Blvd 67801 **Location:** 1.4 mi w on US 50 business route. **Facility:** 77 units. 71 one-bedroom standard units. 6 one-bedroom suites with whirlpools. 4 stories, interior corridors. *Bath:* combo or shower only. **Parking:** on-site. **Amenities:** high-speed Internet, voice mail, irons, hair dryers. **Pool(s):** heated indoor. **Leisure Activities:** whirlpool, exercise room. **Guest Services:** valet and coin laundry, wireless Internet. **Business Services:** meeting rooms, business center. CALL / SOME UNITS FEE

SUPER 8 *Book at AAA.com*

Phone: 620/225-3924

Hotel
Rates not provided

Address: 1708 W Wyatt Earp Blvd 67801 **Location:** 1.2 mi w on US 50 business route. **Facility:** 63 one-bedroom standard units. 3 stories (no elevator), interior corridors. **Parking:** on-site, winter plug-ins. **Amenities:** irons, hair dryers. **Pool(s):** outdoor. **Guest Services:** wireless Internet.

/ SOME UNITS FEE

WHERE TO DINE

EL CHARRO RESTAURANT

Phone: 620/225-0371

Traditional Mexican
$5-$15

This restaurant features large portions of traditional and Tex-Mex offerings, with even a few 'north of the border selections' available. The staff is helpful and the Southwestern style decor is fun. Casual dress. **Bar:** Beer only. **Reservations:** accepted. **Hours:** 11 am-9 pm, Fri & Sat-10 pm. Closed major holidays; also Sun. **Address:** 1209 W Wyatt Earp Blvd 67801 **Location:** 0.7 mi w on US 50 business route. **Parking:** on-site.

KING'S BUFFET

Phone: 620/338-8618

Chinese
$5-$9

Although the selections on the lunch and dinner buffets are ample, guests have the option of ordering from a large selection of menu entrees. Casual dress. **Hours:** 11 am-10 pm, Fri & Sat-10:30 pm, Sun 11:30 am-10 pm. **Address:** 1005 W Wyatt Earp Blvd 67801 **Location:** Center. **Parking:** on-site.

MONTANA MIKE'S

Phone: 620/408-9551

Steak
$7-$20

This steakhouse offers a dining experience for the whole family. A rustic look with Western appointments characterizes the dining room. Although it's hard to go wrong with a hearty steak of USDA Choice aged beef, guests also can try smoked, fire-grilled chicken breast, chicken-fried steak, baby back ribs and other selections. Casual dress. **Bar:** Full bar. **Hours:** 11 am-9 pm, Fri & Sat-10 pm. Closed: 11/25, 12/25. **Address:** 700 W Wyatt Earp Blvd 67801 **Location:** Center. **Parking:** on-site.

EL DORADO pop. 12,057

BEST WESTERN RED COACH INN *Book great rates at AAA.com*

Phone: (316)321-6900

Hotel
$65-$120 All Year

Address: 2525 W Central Ave 67042 **Location:** I-35, exit 71, 0.5 mi e. **Facility:** 73 one-bedroom standard units, some with whirlpools. 2 stories (no elevator), exterior corridors. **Parking:** on-site. **Amenities:** irons, hair dryers. **Pool(s):** heated indoor. **Leisure Activities:** sauna, whirlpool, limited exercise equipment. **Guest Services:** wireless Internet. **Business Services:** meeting rooms, PC. **Free Special Amenities: local telephone calls and high-speed Internet.**

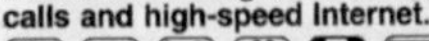

AAA Benefit:
Members save up to 20%, plus 10% bonus points with rewards program.

SUPER 8-EL DORADO *Book at AAA.com*

Phone: (316)321-4888

Motel
$45-$95 All Year

Address: 2530 W Central Ave 67042 **Location:** I-35, exit 71, 0.5 mi e. **Facility:** 49 one-bedroom standard units. 2 stories (no elevator), interior corridors. **Parking:** on-site, winter plug-ins. **Amenities:** safes (fee), irons, hair dryers. **Guest Services:** wireless Internet.

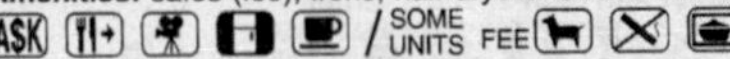

WHERE TO DINE

OKLAHOMA BOY'S BBQ

Phone: 316/452-5535

Barbecue
$6-$13

This unassuming restaurant is located at the north end of a strip mall. Don't let the counter service and paper plates distract you from quality barbecue dishes served with a choice of sauces. Casual dress. **Bar:** Beer only. **Reservations:** not accepted. **Hours:** 11 am-8 pm, Sun-7:30 pm. Closed: 4/4, 11/25, 12/25. **Address:** 626 N Main St 67042 **Location:** 0.4 mi n of Central Ave. **Parking:** on-site.

ELLIS pop. 1,873

— WHERE TO DINE —

ARTHUR'S PIZZA & MEXICAN FOODS

Phone: 785/726-4683

Pizza
$5-$15

The downtown eatery prepares a combination of Mexican food and pizza in a contemporary setting. Dine-in, take-out and delivery service are available. The food is tasty and well-prepared. Casual dress. **Bar:** Beer only. **Reservations:** not accepted. **Hours:** 11 am-8:30 pm, Fri & Sat-9 pm. Closed major holidays; also Wed. **Address:** 103 W 9th St 67637 **Location:** I-70, exit 145, 0.6 mi s; corner of Washington and W 9th sts; downtown. **Parking:** street.

ELLSWORTH pop. 2,965

AMERICAS BEST VALUE INN — Book great rates at AAA.com

Phone: 785/472-3116

SAVE

Hotel
Rates not provided

Address: 1414 Foster Rd 67439 **Location:** Jct SR 140 and 156. **Facility:** 36 units. 35 one-bedroom standard units. 1 one-bedroom suite with whirlpool. 1 story, exterior corridors. *Bath:* combo or shower only. **Parking:** on-site, winter plug-ins. **Amenities:** irons, hair dryers. *Some:* high-speed Internet, dual phone lines. **Pool(s):** heated indoor. **Leisure Activities:** whirlpool. **Guest Services:** coin laundry, wireless Internet. **Business Services:** meeting rooms, PC. **Free Special Amenities: continental breakfast and high-speed Internet.**

CALL / SOME UNITS

EMPORIA pop. 26,760

BEST WESTERN HOSPITALITY HOUSE — Book great rates at AAA.com

Phone: (620)342-7587

SAVE

Hotel
$70-$90 All Year

Address: 3021 W Hwy 50 66801 **Location:** I-35, exit 127, just e. **Facility:** Smoke free premises. 56 units. 53 one-bedroom standard units. 3 one-bedroom suites, some with whirlpools. 1 story, interior/exterior corridors. **Parking:** on-site. **Amenities:** irons, hair dryers. **Pool(s):** heated indoor. **Leisure Activities:** whirlpool. **Guest Services:** valet laundry, wireless Internet. **Business Services:** meeting rooms. **Free Special Amenities: preferred room (subject to availability with advance reservations) and high-speed Internet.**

/ SOME UNITS

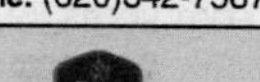

AAA Benefit:
Members save up to 20%, plus 10% bonus points with rewards program.

CANDLEWOOD SUITES — Book at AAA.com

Phone: (620)343-7756

Extended Stay Hotel
$79-$129 All Year

Address: 2602 Candlewood Dr 66801 **Location:** I-35, exit 128 (Industrial St), just n, then just e. **Facility:** Smoke free premises. 60 units. 56 one-bedroom standard units with efficiencies. 4 one-bedroom suites with efficiencies. 3 stories, interior corridors. *Bath:* combo or shower only. **Parking:** on-site, winter plug-ins. **Amenities:** video library, DVD players, CD players, high-speed Internet, dual phone lines, voice mail, irons, hair dryers. **Leisure Activities:** exercise room. **Guest Services:** complimentary and valet laundry, wireless Internet. **Business Services:** meeting rooms, business center. ASK / SOME UNITS FEE

COMFORT INN — Book at AAA.com

Phone: 620/342-9700

Hotel
Rates not provided

Address: 2836 W 18th Ave 66801 **Location:** I-35, exit 128 (Industrial St), just nw. **Facility:** 44 one-bedroom standard units, some with whirlpools. 2 stories (no elevator), interior corridors. *Bath:* combo or shower only. **Parking:** on-site. **Amenities:** high-speed Internet, irons, hair dryers. **Pool(s):** heated indoor. **Leisure Activities:** exercise room. **Guest Services:** valet and coin laundry, wireless Internet. **Business Services:** PC. / SOME UNITS FEE

FAIRFIELD INN BY MARRIOTT — Book great rates at AAA.com

Phone: (620)342-4445

Hotel
$71-$87 All Year

Address: 2930 Eaglecrest Dr 66801 **Location:** I-35, exit 128 (Industrial St), just nw. **Facility:** Smoke free premises. 57 one-bedroom standard units. 3 stories, interior corridors. *Bath:* combo or shower only. **Parking:** on-site, winter plug-ins. **Terms:** cancellation fee imposed. **Amenities:** irons, hair dryers. **Pool(s):** heated indoor. **Leisure Activities:** whirlpool. **Guest Services:** wireless Internet. **Business Services:** PC.

/ SOME UNITS

AAA Benefit:
Members save a minimum 5% off the best available rate.

HOLIDAY INN EXPRESS HOTEL & SUITES — Book at AAA.com

Phone: 620/341-9393

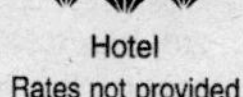

Hotel
Rates not provided

Address: 2921 W 18th Ave 66801 **Location:** I-35, exit 128 (Industrial St), just nw. **Facility:** Smoke free premises. 58 units. 56 one-bedroom standard units, some with whirlpools. 2 one-bedroom suites with whirlpools. 3 stories, interior corridors. *Bath:* combo or shower only. **Parking:** on-site, winter plug-ins. **Amenities:** dual phone lines, voice mail, irons, hair dryers. **Pool(s):** heated indoor. **Leisure Activities:** whirlpool, limited exercise equipment. **Guest Services:** coin laundry, wireless Internet. **Business Services:** meeting rooms, PC.

SUPER 8

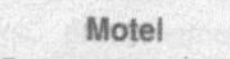

Motel
Rates not provided

Phone: 620/342-7567

Address: 2913 W Hwy 50 66801 **Location:** I-35, exit 127, 0.8 mi e. **Facility:** Smoke free premises. 45 one-bedroom standard units. 2 stories (no elevator), interior corridors. *Bath:* combo or shower only. **Parking:** on-site, winter plug-ins. **Amenities:** safes (fee). **Guest Services:** coin laundry, wireless Internet. **Free Special Amenities: continental breakfast and high-speed Internet.**

/ SOME UNITS FEE

— WHERE TO DINE —

MONTANA MIKE'S

Steak
$7-$20

Phone: 620/343-7481

This steakhouse offers a dining experience for the whole family. A rustic look with Western appointments characterizes the dining room. Although it's hard to go wrong with a hearty steak of USDA Choice aged beef, guests also can try smoked, fire-grilled chicken breast, chicken-fried steak, baby back ribs and other selections. Casual dress. **Bar:** Full bar. **Hours:** 11 am-9 pm, Fri & Sat-10 pm. Closed: 11/25, 12/25; also Mon. **Address:** 3010 Eaglecrest Dr 66801 **Location:** I-35, exit 128 (Industrial St), just nw. **Parking:** on-site.

FORT SCOTT pop. 8,297

THE COURTLAND HOTEL & AVEDA DAY SPA

Historic Bed & Breakfast
$59-$129 All Year

Phone: 620/223-0098

Address: 121 E 1st St 66701 **Location:** Just w of US 69; downtown. **Facility:** Smaller guest rooms in restored 1906 hotel. Smoke free premises. 15 one-bedroom standard units. 2 stories (no elevator), interior corridors. *Bath:* combo or shower only. **Parking:** on-site. **Terms:** 14 day cancellation notice-fee imposed. **Amenities:** irons, hair dryers. *Some:* DVD players. **Leisure Activities:** limited exercise equipment. *Fee:* massage. **Guest Services:** valet laundry, wireless Internet. **Business Services:** meeting rooms. ASK / SOME UNITS

FORT SCOTT INN

Hotel
Rates not provided

Phone: 620/223-0100

Address: 101 State St 66701 **Location:** On US 69 Bypass, exit US 54 southbound; exit 3rd St northbound. **Facility:** 77 one-bedroom standard units. 2 stories (no elevator), interior/exterior corridors. **Parking:** on-site. **Amenities:** dual phone lines, voice mail, irons, hair dryers. *Some:* high-speed Internet. **Pool(s):** outdoor. **Leisure Activities:** sauna, whirlpool, exercise room. **Guest Services:** coin laundry, wireless Internet. **Business Services:** meeting rooms, PC.

/ SOME UNITS FEE

LYONS' TWIN MANSIONS BED & BREAKFAST AND SPA

Historic Bed & Breakfast
Rates not provided

Phone: 620/223-3644

Address: 742 S National Ave 66701 **Location:** Jct US 69 and 54 E, 0.3 mi w on Wall St, then 0.6 mi s. **Facility:** The residence is a well-appointed 1876 mansion. Three guest units are located in the guest house in the rear. Smoke free premises. 8 units. 7 one-bedroom standard units, some with whirlpools. 1 two-bedroom suite with whirlpool. 3 stories (no elevator), interior corridors. *Bath:* combo or shower only. **Parking:** on-site. **Amenities:** DVD players, CD players, irons, hair dryers. *Some:* high-speed Internet. **Leisure Activities:** whirlpool. *Fee:* massage. **Guest Services:** valet laundry, wireless Internet. **Business Services:** meeting rooms. FEE

— WHERE TO DINE —

EL CHARRO

Mexican
$4-$16

Phone: 620/223-9944

The restaurant's decor says "Mexico," while its extensive menu centers on traditional favorites, such as chimichangas, fajitas, vegetarian dishes and combination plates. Service is fast and efficient. Casual dress. **Bar:** Full bar. **Reservations:** not accepted. **Hours:** 11 am-9 pm, Fri & Sat-10:30 pm, Sun-8 pm. Closed major holidays. **Address:** 22 S Main St 66701 **Location:** Downtown. **Parking:** street.

GARDEN CITY pop. 28,451

AMERICINN LODGE & SUITES OF GARDEN CITY *Book at AAA.com*

Hotel
$89-$165 All Year

Phone: (620)272-9860

Address: 3020 E Kansas Ave 67846 **Location:** Jct US 50, 83 and SR 156. **Facility:** Smoke free premises. 72 units. 71 one-bedroom standard units, some with whirlpools. 1 one-bedroom suite with whirlpool. 3 stories, interior corridors. *Bath:* combo or shower only. **Parking:** on-site, winter plug-ins. **Amenities:** high-speed Internet, voice mail, irons, hair dryers. **Pool(s):** heated indoor. **Leisure Activities:** whirlpool, exercise room. **Guest Services:** valet and coin laundry. **Business Services:** meeting rooms, PC. ASK / SOME UNITS FEE

BEST WESTERN RED BARON HOTEL *Book great rates at AAA.com*

Hotel
$76-$80 All Year

Phone: (620)275-4164

Address: 2205 E Hwy 50 67846 **Location:** 2.3 mi e on US 50 business route, at US 83 Bypass. **Facility:** 68 one-bedroom standard units. 2 stories (no elevator), exterior corridors. *Bath:* combo or shower only. **Parking:** on-site, winter plug-ins. **Amenities:** high-speed Internet, irons, hair dryers. **Pool(s):** heated outdoor. **Leisure Activities:** playground. **Guest Services:** valet and coin laundry, wireless Internet. **Business Services:** business center. **Free Special Amenities: expanded continental breakfast and high-speed Internet.**

/ SOME UNITS FEE

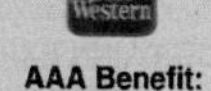

AAA Benefit:
Members save up to 20%, plus 10% bonus points with rewards program.

CLARION INN & CONFERENCE CENTER *Book great rates at AAA.com* **Phone:** (620)275-7471

Hotel
$85-$120 All Year

Address: 1911 E Kansas Ave 67846 **Location:** 0.5 mi w of US 50 and 83 Bypass, on SR 156. **Facility:** Smoke free premises. 109 one-bedroom standard units, some with whirlpools. 2 stories, interior corridors. *Bath:* combo or shower only. **Parking:** on-site, winter plug-ins. **Amenities:** voice mail, irons, hair dryers. **Pool(s):** heated indoor. **Leisure Activities:** whirlpool, exercise room. **Guest Services:** valet laundry, airport transportation-Garden City Regional Airport, area transportation-within 5 mi, wireless Internet. **Business Services:** conference facilities, business center. **Free Special Amenities: full breakfast and local telephone calls.**

/ SOME UNITS FEE

COMFORT INN *Book great rates at AAA.com* **Phone:** 620/275-5800

Hotel
Rates not provided

Address: 2608 E Kansas Ave 67846 **Location:** Jct US 50, 83 and SR 156. **Facility:** Smoke free premises. 62 one-bedroom standard units, some with whirlpools. 3 stories, interior corridors. *Bath:* combo or shower only. **Parking:** on-site. **Amenities:** high-speed Internet, voice mail, irons, hair dryers. **Pool(s):** heated indoor. **Leisure Activities:** whirlpool, steamroom, limited exercise equipment. **Guest Services:** valet and coin laundry, wireless Internet. **Business Services:** meeting rooms, business center. **Free Special Amenities: full breakfast and high-speed Internet.**

/ SOME UNITS FEE

HAMPTON INN *Book great rates at AAA.com* **Phone:** (620)272-0454

Hotel
$90-$120 All Year

Address: 2505 E Crestway Dr 67846 **Location:** US 50/83/400, exit SR 156, just sw. **Facility:** Smoke free premises. 83 one-bedroom standard units, some with whirlpools. 4 stories, interior corridors. *Bath:* combo or shower only. **Parking:** on-site. **Terms:** 1-7 night minimum stay, cancellation fee imposed. **Amenities:** high-speed Internet, voice mail, irons, hair dryers. **Pool(s):** heated indoor. **Leisure Activities:** whirlpool, exercise room. **Guest Services:** valet laundry, wireless Internet. **Business Services:** meeting rooms. CALL

AAA Benefit:
Members save up to 10% everyday!

HOLIDAY INN EXPRESS HOTEL & SUITES *Book at AAA.com* **Phone:** 620/275-5900

Hotel
Rates not provided

Address: 2502 E Kansas Ave 67846 **Location:** Jct US 50, 83 and SR 156. **Facility:** Smoke free premises. 69 units. 68 one-bedroom standard units. 1 one-bedroom suite with whirlpool. 3 stories, interior corridors. *Bath:* combo or shower only. **Parking:** on-site, winter plug-ins. **Terms:** check-in 4 pm. **Amenities:** high-speed Internet, dual phone lines, voice mail, irons, hair dryers. **Pool(s):** heated indoor. **Leisure Activities:** whirlpool, exercise room. **Guest Services:** valet and coin laundry, wireless Internet. **Business Services:** meeting rooms, business center.

/ SOME UNITS FEE

WHEAT LANDS RODEWAY INN *Book great rates at AAA.com* **Phone:** (620)276-2387

Hotel
$57-$81 All Year

Address: 1311 E Fulton St 67846 **Location:** 1 mi e on US 50 business route. **Facility:** 107 one-bedroom standard units, some with whirlpools. 2 stories (no elevator), exterior corridors. **Parking:** on-site, winter plug-ins. **Terms:** 5 day cancellation notice. **Amenities:** high-speed Internet, irons, hair dryers. **Pool(s):** outdoor. **Leisure Activities:** exercise room. **Guest Services:** valet and coin laundry, wireless Internet. **Business Services:** meeting rooms, PC.

/ SOME UNITS

WHERE TO DINE

WHEAT LANDS RESTAURANT & LOUNGE **Phone:** 620/276-2768

American
$6-$18

The Wheat Lands Restaurant offers nicely prepared steaks, a well-stocked fresh salad bar and blueberry pie made in-house. They also serve a lunch buffet every day except Saturday. The atmosphere is casual, and service is prompt and attentive. Casual dress. **Bar:** Full bar. **Reservations:** accepted. **Hours:** 6:30 am-2 pm, Sun from 7:30 am. Closed: 12/25. **Address:** 1408 E Fulton 67846 **Location:** 1 mi e on US 50 business route; in Rodeway Inn. **Parking:** on-site.

GARDNER—See Nearby MO City Of Kansas City p. 492.

GARNETT pop. 3,368

GARNETT INN SUITES & RV PARK **Phone:** (785)448-6800

Hotel
$60-$78 All Year

Address: 109 Prairie Plaza Pkwy 66032 **Location:** On US 169, 1.6 mi n of jct US 59. **Facility:** 24 units. 23 one-bedroom standard units, some with whirlpools. 1 one-bedroom suite with whirlpool. 2 stories (no elevator), interior corridors. **Parking:** on-site. **Terms:** office hours 6 am-11 pm. **Amenities:** high-speed Internet, voice mail, hair dryers. **Leisure Activities:** hiking trails, limited exercise equipment. **Guest Services:** coin laundry, wireless Internet. **Business Services:** meeting rooms, PC. ASK CALL / SOME UNITS FEE

GODDARD pop. 2,037

EXPRESS INN **Phone:** (316)794-3366

Motel
$56-$65 All Year

Address: 19941 W Kellogg Dr 67052 **Location:** Just se of jct US 54/400 and 199th St. **Facility:** 35 one-bedroom standard units. 2 stories (no elevator), exterior corridors. **Parking:** on-site, winter plug-ins. **Amenities:** voice mail. **Guest Services:** coin laundry, wireless Internet. **Business Services:** PC. **Free Special Amenities: continental breakfast and high-speed Internet.**

/ SOME UNITS FEE

GOODLAND pop. 4,948

COMFORT INN   Book at AAA.com   **Phone:** (785)899-7181

Hotel
$89-$120 All Year

Address: 2519 Enterprise Rd 67735 **Location:** I-70, exit 17 (SR 27), just n. **Facility:** 49 one-bedroom standard units, some with whirlpools. 2 stories (no elevator), interior corridors. *Bath:* combo or shower only. **Parking:** on-site, winter plug-ins. **Terms:** cancellation fee imposed. **Amenities:** voice mail, irons, hair dryers. **Pool(s):** heated indoor. **Leisure Activities:** whirlpool, exercise room. **Guest Services:** coin laundry, wireless Internet.

ASK CALL / SOME UNITS FEE

HOLIDAY INN EXPRESS HOTEL & SUITES   Book great rates at AAA.com   **Phone:** (785)890-9060

Hotel
$105-$135 5/1-2/28
$96-$129 3/1-4/30

Address: 2631 Enterprise Rd 67735 **Location:** I-70, exit 17 (SR 27), just s. **Facility:** Smoke free premises. 73 units. 62 one-bedroom standard units. 11 one-bedroom suites, some with whirlpools. 3 stories, interior corridors. *Bath:* combo or shower only. **Parking:** on-site. **Amenities:** high-speed Internet, voice mail, irons, hair dryers. **Pool(s):** heated indoor. **Leisure Activities:** whirlpool, exercise room. **Guest Services:** coin laundry, wireless Internet. **Business Services:** meeting rooms, business center. **Free Special Amenities: full breakfast and high-speed Internet.**

CALL / SOME UNITS

SUPER 8   Book at AAA.com   **Phone:** (785)890-7566

Hotel
$66-$78 All Year

Address: 2520 Commerce Rd 67735 **Location:** I-70, exit 17 (SR 27), just n. **Facility:** 47 one-bedroom standard units. 2 stories (no elevator), exterior corridors. **Parking:** on-site, winter plug-ins. **Amenities:** irons, hair dryers. *Some:* high-speed Internet. **Guest Services:** wireless Internet.

ASK / SOME UNITS FEE

GREAT BEND pop. 15,345

BEST WESTERN ANGUS INN   Book great rates at AAA.com   **Phone:** (620)792-3541

Hotel
$68-$78 All Year

Address: 2920 10th St 67530 **Location:** 0.8 mi w on US 56 and SR 96/156. **Facility:** 90 one-bedroom standard units, some with whirlpools. 2 stories (no elevator), interior/exterior corridors. **Parking:** on-site, winter plug-ins. **Amenities:** video library, DVD players, high-speed Internet, voice mail, irons, hair dryers. **Pool(s):** heated indoor. **Leisure Activities:** sauna, whirlpool, exercise room. *Fee:* game room. **Guest Services:** valet and coin laundry, airport transportation-Great Bend Municipal Airport, wireless Internet. **Business Services:** meeting rooms, PC. **Free Special Amenities: local telephone calls and high-speed Internet.**

/ SOME UNITS FEE

AAA Benefit:
Members save up to 20%, plus 10% bonus points with rewards program.

HIGHLAND HOTEL & CONVENTION CENTER   Book great rates at AAA.com   **Phone:** (620)792-2431

Hotel
$64-$85 All Year

Address: 3017 W 10th St 67530 **Location:** 1 mi w on US 56 and SR 96/156. **Facility:** 172 one-bedroom standard units. 2 stories (no elevator), interior/exterior corridors. *Bath:* combo or shower only. **Parking:** on-site. **Terms:** check-in 4 pm. **Amenities:** *Some:* high-speed Internet. **Pool(s):** heated indoor. **Leisure Activities:** sauna, whirlpool, miniature golf, exercise room. **Guest Services:** valet and coin laundry, airport transportation-Great Bend Municipal Airport, wireless Internet. **Business Services:** meeting rooms, PC. **Free Special Amenities: local telephone calls and high-speed Internet.**

/ SOME UNITS FEE

WHERE TO DINE

KIOWA KITCHEN   **Phone:** 620/793-9855

Mexican
$3-$9

The restaurant is a favorite among locals in the mood for Mexican food. The menu incorporates a good variety. Casual dress. **Bar:** Beer only. **Hours:** 11 am-9 pm, Sun-3 pm. Closed major holidays; also Mon-Wed. **Address:** 214 E Barton County Rd A 67530 **Location:** 2 mi e on US 56. **Parking:** on-site.

MONTANA MIKE'S   **Phone:** 620/792-5930

Steak
$7-$20

This steakhouse offers a dining experience for the whole family. A rustic look with Western appointments characterizes the dining room. Although it's hard to go wrong with a hearty steak of USDA Choice aged beef, guests also can try smoked, fire-grilled chicken breast, chicken-fried steak, baby back ribs and other selections. Casual dress. **Bar:** Full bar. **Hours:** 5 pm-9 pm, Fri & Sat-10 pm. Closed: 11/25, 12/25. **Address:** 906 McKinley St 67530 **Location:** Just s of jct US 56. **Parking:** on-site.

HAYS pop. 20,013

AMERICAS BEST VALUE INN VAGABOND   Book at AAA.com   **Phone:** (785)625-2511

Motel
$65-$163 3/1-10/15
$60-$161 10/16-2/28

Address: 2524 Vine St 67601 **Location:** I-70, exit 159 (US 183), 1 mi s. **Facility:** 92 units. 88 one- and 2 two-bedroom standard units. 2 one-bedroom suites with whirlpools. 1-2 stories (no elevator), exterior corridors. *Bath:* combo or shower only. **Parking:** on-site. **Amenities:** irons, hair dryers. **Pool(s):** outdoor. **Leisure Activities:** whirlpools, exercise room. **Guest Services:** valet and coin laundry, wireless Internet. **Business Services:** PC.

ASK / SOME UNITS

BAYMONT INN & SUITES *Book at AAA.com* **Phone:** (785)625-8103

Hotel

$69-$74 All Year

Address: 3801 N Vine St 67601 **Location:** I-70, exit 159 (US 183), just sw. **Facility:** 107 one-bedroom standard units, some with whirlpools. 2 stories (no elevator), interior/exterior corridors. *Bath:* combo or shower only. **Parking:** on-site, winter plug-ins. **Terms:** check-in 4 pm, cancellation fee imposed. **Amenities:** video games (fee), voice mail, irons, hair dryers. **Leisure Activities:** exercise room. **Guest Services:** valet and coin laundry, wireless Internet. **Business Services:** meeting rooms, PC.

ASK / SOME UNITS

BEST WESTERN BUTTERFIELD INN *Book great rates at AAA.com* **Phone:** (785)621-4337

AAA SAVE

Hotel

$110-$140 All Year

Address: 1010 E 41st St 67601 **Location:** I-70, exit 159 (US 183), just n, then just e. **Facility:** Smoke free premises. 71 one-bedroom standard units. 3 stories, interior corridors. *Bath:* combo or shower only. **Parking:** on-site. **Amenities:** high-speed Internet, voice mail, irons, hair dryers. **Pool(s):** heated indoor. **Leisure Activities:** whirlpool, exercise room. **Guest Services:** valet and coin laundry, wireless Internet. **Business Services:** meeting rooms, business center. **Free Special Amenities: expanded continental breakfast and high-speed Internet.**

CALL

AAA Benefit:

Members save up to 20%, plus 10% bonus points with rewards program.

COMFORT INN & SUITES *Book at AAA.com* **Phone:** (785)625-9322

Hotel

$65-$120 All Year

Address: 1001 E 41st St 67601 **Location:** I-70, exit 159 (US 183), just n. **Facility:** Smoke free premises. 55 one-bedroom standard units. 3 stories, interior corridors. *Bath:* combo or shower only. **Parking:** on-site, winter plug-ins. **Terms:** cancellation fee imposed. **Amenities:** irons, hair dryers. **Pool(s):** heated indoor. **Leisure Activities:** whirlpool, exercise room. **Guest Services:** valet laundry, wireless Internet. **Business Services:** PC.

ASK CALL / SOME UNITS

FAIRFIELD INN HAYS *Book great rates at AAA.com* **Phone:** (785)625-3344

Hotel

$99-$109 All Year

Address: 377 Mopar Dr 67601 **Location:** I-70, exit 159 (US 183), just nw on north service road. **Facility:** Smoke free premises. 62 one-bedroom standard units, some with whirlpools. 3 stories, interior corridors. *Bath:* combo or shower only. **Parking:** on-site, winter plug-ins. **Terms:** cancellation fee imposed. **Amenities:** high-speed Internet, irons, hair dryers. **Pool(s):** heated indoor. **Leisure Activities:** whirlpool, exercise room. **Guest Services:** valet laundry, wireless Internet. **Business Services:** PC.

CALL / SOME UNITS

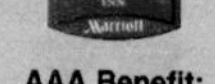

AAA Benefit:

Members save a minimum 5% off the best available rate.

HAMPTON INN *Book great rates at AAA.com* **Phone:** (785)621-4444

Hotel

$99-$120 All Year

Address: 4002 General Hays Rd 67601 **Location:** I-70, exit 159 (US 183), just n, then e. **Facility:** 80 one-bedroom standard units, some with whirlpools. 4 stories, interior corridors. *Bath:* combo or shower only. **Parking:** on-site. **Terms:** 1-7 night minimum stay, cancellation fee imposed. **Amenities:** video games (fee), high-speed Internet, voice mail, irons, hair dryers. **Pool(s):** heated indoor. **Leisure Activities:** whirlpool, exercise room. **Guest Services:** valet and coin laundry, wireless Internet. **Business Services:** meeting rooms, business center.

CALL / SOME UNITS

AAA Benefit:

Members save up to 10% everyday!

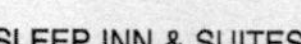

SLEEP INN & SUITES *Book at AAA.com* **Phone:** (785)625-2700

Hotel

$65-$100 All Year

Address: 1011 E 41st St 67601 **Location:** I-70, exit 159 (US 183), just n. **Facility:** Smoke free premises. 55 one-bedroom standard units. 4 stories, interior corridors. *Bath:* combo or shower only. **Parking:** on-site, winter plug-ins. **Terms:** cancellation fee imposed. **Amenities:** voice mail, irons, hair dryers. **Pool(s):** heated indoor. **Leisure Activities:** whirlpool, exercise room. **Guest Services:** valet and coin laundry, wireless Internet. **Business Services:** PC.

ASK CALL / SOME UNITS

WHERE TO DINE

GELLA'S DINER & LB. BREWING CO. **Phone:** 785/621-2739

American

$9-$23

This new microbrewery and restaurant focuses on American fare, including some interesting choices. In addition to appetizers and salads, the menu lists grilled Atlantic salmon, rainbow trout, certified Angus steaks, chicken dishes, smoked pork chops, Salisbury steak and even specialty sandwiches. For those who care to indulge, this place also features award-winning microbrews. Casual dress. **Bar:** Full bar. **Reservations:** not accepted. **Hours:** 11 am-10 pm, Thurs-Sat to 11 pm. Closed major holidays. **Address:** 117 E 11th St 67601 **Location:** Just e of Main St; downtown. **Parking:** street. CALL

GUTIERREZ MEXICAN RESTAURANT **Phone:** 785/625-4402

Traditional Mexican

$8-$14

Serving Kansans since 1984, the local favorite prepares traditional entrees, including fajitas, burritos, chimichangas and burritos. Dessert selections are interesting and appetizing. An espresso cafe opens daily at 7 am. Casual dress. **Bar:** Full bar. **Reservations:** accepted. **Hours:** 11 am-9 pm, Fri & Sat-10 pm. Closed: 4/4, 11/25, 12/25. **Address:** 1106 E 27th St 67601 **Location:** I-70, exit 159 (US 183), 1 mi s, then just e. **Parking:** on-site.

MONTANA MIKE'S — Phone: 785/628-8786

Steak
$7-$20

This steakhouse offers a dining experience for the whole family. A rustic look with Western appointments characterizes the dining room. Although it's hard to go wrong with a hearty steak of USDA Choice aged beef, guests also can try smoked, fire-grilled chicken breast, chicken-fried steak, baby back ribs and other selections. Casual dress. **Bar:** Full bar. **Reservations:** not accepted. **Hours:** 11 am-9 pm, Fri & Sat-10 pm; seasonal hours vary. Closed: 11/25, 12/25; also Mon. **Address:** 3216 Vine St 67601 **Location:** I-70, exit 159 (US 183), 0.4 mi s. **Parking:** on-site. CALL

ROOFTOPS RESTAURANT & LOUNGE — Phone: 785/628-8631

Steak
$6-$22

Rooftops Restaurant is locally owned and well known for its excellent city views. The dining room is tastefully decorated and the service staff is professional and friendly. The cuisine is flavorful, including the baked halibut Italiano and USDA Choice steak. The chicken dijonaise is a favorite and prime rib is offered on Wednesday, Friday and Saturday. Casual dress. **Bar:** Full bar. **Reservations:** suggested. **Hours:** 11 am-2 & 5-10 pm, Sat 5 pm-11 pm. Closed major holidays; also Sun. **Address:** 1200 Main St 67601 **Location:** Downtown; in Emprise Bank Building, 6th Floor. **Parking:** on-site.

HERINGTON pop. 2,563

HERINGTON INN & SUITES — Phone: (785)258-3300

Hotel
$65-$86 All Year

Address: 565 Hwy 77 67449 **Location:** US 77, just w. **Facility:** 27 units. 26 one-bedroom standard units. 1 one-bedroom suite with whirlpool. 2 stories (no elevator), interior corridors. **Parking:** on-site. **Terms:** office hours 6 am-10 pm. **Amenities:** high-speed Internet, voice mail, hair dryers. **Leisure Activities:** exercise room. **Business Services:** PC.

ASK CALL / SOME UNITS

HESSTON pop. 3,509

AMERICINN LODGE & SUITES OF HESSTON — Book at AAA.com — Phone: (620)327-2053

Hotel
$80-$150 All Year

Address: 2 Leonard Ct 67062 **Location:** I-135, exit 40, just e. **Facility:** 42 one-bedroom standard units, some with whirlpools. 2 stories, interior corridors. *Bath:* combo or shower only. **Parking:** on-site. **Amenities:** high-speed Internet, hair dryers. *Some:* irons. **Pool(s):** heated indoor. **Leisure Activities:** whirlpool. **Guest Services:** coin laundry, wireless Internet. **Business Services:** meeting rooms, PC.

ASK / SOME UNITS FEE

HILLSBORO pop. 2,854

COUNTRY HAVEN INN — Phone: (620)947-2929

Hotel
$64-$75 All Year

Address: 804 Western Heights 67063 **Location:** On US 56; center. **Facility:** 24 one-bedroom standard units, some with whirlpools. 2 stories (no elevator), interior corridors. **Parking:** on-site, winter plug-ins. **Amenities:** voice mail. **Guest Services:** wireless Internet.

ASK / SOME UNITS FEE

HOLTON pop. 3,353

SUPER 8 — Book at AAA.com — Phone: (785)364-1988

Hotel
$70-$170 All Year

Address: 300 S Arizona Ave 66436 **Location:** On US 75, just s of jct US 75 and SR 116. **Facility:** 36 one-bedroom standard units, some with whirlpools. 2 stories (no elevator), interior corridors. *Bath:* combo or shower only. **Parking:** on-site. **Terms:** 7 day cancellation notice. **Amenities:** irons, hair dryers. *Some:* DVD players, CD players. **Guest Services:** coin laundry, wireless Internet.

CALL / SOME UNITS

HUTCHINSON pop. 40,787

COMFORT INN — Book at AAA.com — Phone: 620/663-7822

Hotel
Rates not provided

Address: 1621 Super Plaza 67501 **Location:** Just w of jct SR 61 and N 17th Ave. Located in a commercial area. **Facility:** 63 one-bedroom standard units, some with kitchens and/or whirlpools. 3 stories (no elevator), interior corridors. *Bath:* combo or shower only. **Parking:** on-site. **Amenities:** irons, hair dryers. **Pool(s):** outdoor. **Guest Services:** valet laundry, wireless Internet. **Business Services:** PC.

/ SOME UNITS FEE

DAYS INN — Book at AAA.com — Phone: 620/665-3700

Hotel
Rates not provided

Address: 1420 N Lorraine St 67501 **Location:** Just nw of jct SR 61 and N 11th Ave. **Facility:** 65 one-bedroom standard units. 3 stories, interior corridors. *Bath:* combo or shower only. **Parking:** on-site. **Amenities:** high-speed Internet, irons, hair dryers. **Leisure Activities:** exercise room. **Guest Services:** wireless Internet.

/ SOME UNITS FEE

HAMPTON INN *Book great rates at AAA.com* **Phone:** (620)665-9800

Hotel
$90-$160 All Year

Address: 1401 1/2 E 11th St 67501 **Location:** Just se of jct SR 61. **Facility:** 69 one-bedroom standard units, some with whirlpools. 3 stories, interior corridors. *Bath:* combo or shower only. **Parking:** on-site. **Terms:** 1-7 night minimum stay, cancellation fee imposed. **Amenities:** high-speed Internet, voice mail, irons, hair dryers. **Pool(s):** heated indoor. **Leisure Activities:** whirlpool, exercise room. **Guest Services:** valet laundry, wireless Internet. **Business Services:** meeting rooms, PC.

/ SOME UNITS

AAA Benefit:
Members save up to 10% everyday!

HOLIDAY INN EXPRESS HOTEL & SUITES *Book at AAA.com* **Phone:** (620)669-5200

Hotel
$105-$165 All Year

Address: 1601 Super Plaza 67501 **Location:** Just w of jct SR 61 and N 17th Ave. **Facility:** 69 units. 62 one-bedroom standard units. 7 one-bedroom suites, some with whirlpools. 3 stories, interior corridors. *Bath:* combo or shower only. **Parking:** on-site, winter plug-ins. **Terms:** cancellation fee imposed. **Amenities:** dual phone lines, voice mail, irons, hair dryers. **Pool(s):** heated indoor. **Leisure Activities:** whirlpool, exercise room. **Guest Services:** valet and coin laundry, wireless Internet. **Business Services:** meeting rooms, business center.

A$K CALL / SOME UNITS

WHERE TO DINE

AIRPORT STEAK HOUSE **Phone:** 620/662-4281

Steak
$9-$20

While this restaurant specializes in nicely prepared steaks, seafood and other dishes are also available. Casual dress. **Bar:** Full bar. **Reservations:** accepted. **Hours:** 11 am-9 pm, Fri & Sat-10 pm. Closed: 12/25. **Address:** 1100 Airport Rd 67501 **Location:** Just e of jct 11th Ave. **Parking:** on-site.

ANCHOR INN **Phone:** 620/669-0311

Mexican
$3-$7

The Anchor Inn is a locally popular restaurant operated by the owner/family's third generation. The family serves traditional Mexican dishes and a few burger selections in hearty, satisfying portions. The older building was recently restored. Casual dress. **Bar:** Full bar. **Hours:** 11 am-2 & 5-9 pm. Closed major holidays; also Sun. **Address:** 128 S Main St 67501 **Location:** Center. **Parking:** street.

MONTANA MIKE'S **Phone:** 620/669-6886

Steak
$7-$20

This steakhouse offers a dining experience for the whole family. A rustic look with Western appointments characterizes the dining room. Although it's hard to go wrong with a hearty steak of USDA Choice aged beef, guests also can try smoked, fire-grilled chicken breast, chicken-fried steak, baby back ribs and other selections. Casual dress. **Bar:** Full bar. **Hours:** 11 am-9 pm, Fri & Sat-10 pm. Closed: 11/25, 12/25. **Address:** 925 E 30th St 67502 **Location:** 0.5 mi w of SR 61. **Parking:** on-site.

ROY'S HICKORY PIT BBQ **Phone:** 620/663-7421

Barbecue
$5-$8

First-timers shouldn't let the outside of this place fool them. Inside is an array of well-prepared barbecue dishes. Locals flock here, as the parking lot tells. Casual dress. **Reservations:** not accepted. **Hours:** 11 am-3 pm. Closed major holidays; also Sun & Mon. **Address:** 1018 W 5th Ave 67501 **Location:** 1 mi w of jct Main St. **Parking:** on-site.

SIRLOIN STOCKADE **Phone:** 620/663-5951

Regional Steak
$6-$9

The steakhouse lines up buffet items, including pizza, tacos, soups, salads and desserts, providing both excellent variety and a good value. Rotating theme nights might allow for the sampling of sushi, barbecue and seafood. The buffet also may serve to complement a quality steak. Rolls are baked several times daily. Casual dress. **Reservations:** not accepted. **Hours:** 11 am-9 pm. Closed: 11/25, 12/25. **Address:** 1526 E 17th Ave 67502 **Location:** Just w of jct SR 61. **Parking:** on-site.

INDEPENDENCE pop. 9,846

APPLETREE INN *Book at AAA.com* **Phone:** (620)331-5500

Hotel
$99-$145 All Year

Address: 201 N 8th St 67301 **Location:** At 8th and Laurel sts. **Facility:** 64 one-bedroom standard units, some with whirlpools. 2 stories, interior/exterior corridors. *Bath:* combo or shower only. **Parking:** on-site, winter plug-ins. **Amenities:** voice mail, irons, hair dryers. *Some:* DVD players. **Pool(s):** heated indoor. **Leisure Activities:** whirlpools. **Guest Services:** valet laundry, wireless Internet. **Business Services:** business center.

/ SOME UNITS

MICROTEL INN & SUITES *Book great rates at AAA.com* **Phone:** (620)331-0088

AAA SAVE

Hotel
$73-$80 All Year

Address: 2917 W Main St 67301 **Location:** 1.2 mi e of jct US 75 and 160. **Facility:** 69 one-bedroom standard units. 3 stories, interior corridors. *Bath:* combo or shower only. **Parking:** on-site, winter plug-ins. **Terms:** 7 day cancellation notice. **Amenities:** high-speed Internet, irons, hair dryers. **Guest Services:** valet laundry, wireless Internet. **Free Special Amenities: continental breakfast and high-speed Internet.**

CALL / SOME UNITS FEE

SUPER 8 *Book at AAA.com* **Phone:** (620)331-8288

Hotel
$61-$76 All Year

Address: 2800 W Main St 67301 **Location:** 1.3 mi e of jct US 160 and 75. **Facility:** 51 one-bedroom standard units. 2 stories (no elevator), interior corridors. **Parking:** on-site, winter plug-ins. **Amenities:** high-speed Internet, hair dryers. **Pool(s):** outdoor. **Guest Services:** coin laundry, wireless Internet.

A$K / SOME UNITS FEE

— WHERE TO DINE —

EL PUEBLITO — **Phone:** 620/331-5860

Mexican
$5-$9

A favorite of area residents, the restaurant serves a variety of freshly prepared Mexican dishes. Casual dress. **Hours:** 11 am-9 pm. Closed major holidays. **Address:** 1721 N Penn Ave 67301 **Location:** 1 mi n on US 75. **Parking:** on-site.

UNCLE JACK'S RESTAURANT & BAR — **Phone:** 620/331-5225

American
$5-$25

A New York City-inspired setting greets you in this downtown dining room along with traditional dishes with a trendy twist. Try the buffalo breaded shrimp for an appetizer, then have a juicy, KC strip steak cooked to perfection. Casual dress. **Bar:** Full bar. **Reservations:** accepted. **Hours:** 11 am-9 pm, Fri & Sat-10 pm. Closed major holidays; also Sun. **Address:** 104 N Penn Ave 67301 **Location:** Center. **Parking:** on-site.

IOLA pop. 6,302

BEST WESTERN INN — *Book great rates at AAA.com* — **Phone:** (620)365-5161

Motel
$62-$69 All Year

Address: 1315 N State St 66749 **Location:** Jct US 54 and 169, 1.5 mi w on US 54, then 0.8 mi n. **Facility:** 58 one-bedroom standard units. 1 story, exterior corridors. *Bath:* combo or shower only. **Parking:** on-site. **Amenities:** high-speed Internet, voice mail, irons, hair dryers. **Pool(s):** heated outdoor. **Guest Services:** coin laundry, wireless Internet. **Business Services:** meeting rooms, PC. **Free Special Amenities: continental breakfast and high-speed Internet.**

AAA Benefit:
Members save up to 20%, plus 10% bonus points with rewards program.

SUPER 8 IOLA — *Book at AAA.com* — **Phone:** 620/365-3030

Hotel
Rates not provided

Address: 200 Bills Way 66749 **Location:** Jct US 54 and 169. **Facility:** 49 one-bedroom standard units, some with whirlpools. 2 stories, interior corridors. **Parking:** on-site. **Amenities:** high-speed Internet, voice mail, irons, hair dryers. **Pool(s):** heated indoor. **Leisure Activities:** whirlpool, limited exercise equipment. **Guest Services:** coin laundry, wireless Internet. **Business Services:** meeting rooms, PC. CALL / SOME UNITS FEE

— WHERE TO DINE —

EL CHARRO — **Phone:** 620/365-7771

Mexican
$4-$16

The eatery offers a wide variety of authentic Mexican cuisine. Take note: Some dishes are quite spicy. Service is fast. Casual dress. **Bar:** Beer only. **Reservations:** not accepted. **Hours:** 11 am-9 pm, Fri & Sat-10 pm, Sun-8 pm. Closed major holidays. **Address:** 19 W Madison Ave 66749 **Location:** Downtown. **Parking:** street.

JUNCTION CITY pop. 18,886

BEST WESTERN J.C. INN — *Book great rates at AAA.com* — **Phone:** (785)210-1212

Hotel
$85-$100 All Year

Address: 604 E Chestnut St 66441 **Location:** I-70, exit 298, just w. **Facility:** 45 one-bedroom standard units, some with whirlpools. 2 stories (no elevator), interior corridors. *Bath:* combo or shower only. **Parking:** on-site. **Terms:** cancellation fee imposed. **Amenities:** high-speed Internet, irons, hair dryers. **Pool(s):** heated indoor. **Leisure Activities:** exercise room. **Guest Services:** coin laundry, wireless Internet. **Business Services:** PC. **Free Special Amenities: expanded continental breakfast and local telephone calls.**

CALL / SOME UNITS FEE

AAA Benefit:
Members save up to 20%, plus 10% bonus points with rewards program.

CANDLEWOOD SUITES — *Book at AAA.com* — **Phone:** (785)238-1454

Extended Stay Hotel
$80-$179 All Year

Address: 100 S Hammons Dr 66441 **Location:** I-70, exit 298, just w. **Facility:** 83 units. 75 one-bedroom standard units with efficiencies. 8 one-bedroom suites with efficiencies. 3 stories, interior corridors. *Bath:* combo or shower only. **Parking:** on-site. **Terms:** cancellation fee imposed. **Amenities:** DVD players, high-speed Internet, dual phone lines, voice mail, irons, hair dryers. **Leisure Activities:** exercise room, sports court. **Guest Services:** complimentary laundry. **Business Services:** business center. ASK CALL / SOME UNITS FEE

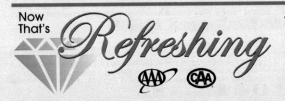

COURTYARD BY MARRIOTT JUNCTION CITY Book great rates at AAA.com

Phone: (785)210-1500

Hotel

$89-$109 All Year

Address: 310 Hammons Dr 66441 **Location:** I-70, exit 298, just w. **Facility:** Smoke free premises. 119 units. 113 one-bedroom standard units. 6 one-bedroom suites. 3 stories, interior corridors. *Bath:* combo or shower only. **Parking:** on-site. **Terms:** cancellation fee imposed. **Amenities:** high-speed Internet, dual phone lines, voice mail, irons, hair dryers. **Pool(s):** heated indoor. **Leisure Activities:** whirlpool, exercise room. **Guest Services:** coin laundry, wireless Internet. **Business Services:** conference facilities, business center.

CALL / SOME UNITS FEE

COURTYARD Marriott

AAA Benefit: Members save a minimum 5% off the best available rate.

HOLIDAY INN EXPRESS Book at AAA.com

Phone: (785)762-4200

Hotel

$99-$150 All Year

Address: 120 N East St 66441 **Location:** I-70, exit 298, just nw. **Facility:** 60 one-bedroom standard units, some with whirlpools. 2 stories, interior corridors. *Bath:* combo or shower only. **Parking:** on-site. **Amenities:** high-speed Internet, dual phone lines, voice mail, irons, hair dryers. **Pool(s):** heated indoor. **Leisure Activities:** whirlpool, exercise room. **Guest Services:** coin laundry, wireless Internet. **Business Services:** meeting rooms, PC.

ASK CALL / SOME UNITS FEE

HOWARD JOHNSON INN Book at AAA.com

Phone: (785)238-7887

Hotel

$55-$105 All Year

Address: 1214 S Washington St 66441 **Location:** I-70, exit 296, just n. **Facility:** 45 one-bedroom standard units. 2 stories (no elevator), interior corridors. *Bath:* combo or shower only. **Parking:** on-site. **Amenities:** irons, hair dryers. **Pool(s):** heated indoor. **Leisure Activities:** whirlpool. **Guest Services:** wireless Internet. **Business Services:** PC. ASK / SOME UNITS

WHERE TO DINE

PEKING CHINESE RESTAURANT

Phone: 785/238-2336

Chinese

$5-$12

The Peking Chinese Restaurant has friendly service and a varied selection of dishes, including Mongolian beef and a crab rangoon appetizer. The atmosphere is casual and family-style, with Oriental decor, and the staff is personable and pleasant. Casual dress. **Reservations:** not accepted. **Hours:** 11 am-2 & 4-9:30 pm, Sat from 11:30 am. Closed: 7/4, 11/25, 12/25; also Mon. **Address:** 836 S Washington St 66441 **Location:** I-70, exit 296, just n. **Parking:** on-site.

SIRLOIN STOCKADE

Phone: 785/238-1817

Regional Steak

$6-$9

The steakhouse lines up buffet items, including pizza, tacos, soups, salads and desserts, providing both excellent variety and a good value. Rotating theme nights might allow for the sampling of sushi, barbecue and seafood. The buffet also may serve to complement a quality steak. Rolls are baked several times daily. Casual dress. **Reservations:** not accepted. **Hours:** 11 am-9 pm. Closed: 11/25, 12/25. **Address:** 426 Golden Belt Blvd 66441 **Location:** I-70, exit 296. **Parking:** on-site.

KANSAS CITY—See Nearby MO City Of Kansas City p. 492.

LANSING pop. 9,199

ECONO LODGE Book at AAA.com

Phone: (913)727-2777

Hotel

$50-$70 All Year

Address: 504 N Main 66043 **Location:** I-70, exit 224 (Leavenworth), 10 mi n on US 73 and SR 7. **Facility:** 37 one-bedroom standard units. 2 stories (no elevator), interior corridors. **Parking:** on-site. **Terms:** check-in 4 pm. **Amenities:** high-speed Internet. **Guest Services:** valet laundry, wireless Internet. ASK / SOME UNITS FEE

HOLIDAY INN EXPRESS HOTEL & SUITES Book at AAA.com

Phone: (913)250-1000

Hotel

$99-$279 All Year

Address: 120 Express Dr 66043 **Location:** I-70, exit 224 (Leavenworth), 10 mi n on US 73 and SR 7. **Facility:** 67 units. 52 one-bedroom standard units. 15 one-bedroom suites. 3 stories, interior corridors. *Bath:* combo or shower only. **Parking:** on-site. **Terms:** cancellation fee imposed. **Amenities:** dual phone lines, voice mail, irons, hair dryers. *Some:* high-speed Internet. **Pool(s):** heated indoor. **Leisure Activities:** whirlpool, exercise room. **Guest Services:** valet and coin laundry, wireless Internet. **Business Services:** meeting rooms, PC.

ASK CALL / SOME UNITS

LARNED pop. 4,236

BEST WESTERN TOWNSMAN INN Book great rates at AAA.com

Phone: (620)285-3114

AAA SAVE

Hotel

$56-$66 All Year

Address: 123 E 14th St 67550 **Location:** Jct US 56 and SR 156. **Facility:** 43 one-bedroom standard units. 1 story, exterior corridors. *Bath:* combo or shower only. **Parking:** on-site, winter plug-ins. **Amenities:** irons, hair dryers. *Some:* high-speed Internet. **Pool(s):** outdoor. **Guest Services:** wireless Internet. **Business Services:** PC. **Free Special Amenities: continental breakfast and high-speed Internet.**

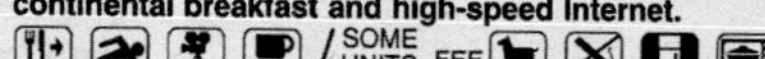

AAA Benefit: Members save up to 20%, plus 10% bonus points with rewards program.

LAWRENCE pop. 80,098

AMERICAS BEST VALUE INN Book at AAA.com **Phone:** 785/842-5721

Hotel
Rates not provided

Address: 515 McDonald Dr 66049 **Location:** I-70, exit 202, 0.8 mi s, then just w. **Facility:** 49 one-bedroom standard units. 3 stories (no elevator), interior corridors. **Parking:** on-site, winter plug-ins. **Amenities:** safes (fee). **Guest Services:** valet and coin laundry, wireless Internet.

/ SOME UNITS FEE

BAYMONT INN & SUITES Book great rates at AAA.com **Phone:** (785)838-4242

AAA SAVE
Hotel
$60-$155 All Year

Address: 740 Iowa St 66044 **Location:** I-70, exit 202, 1 mi s on US 59. **Facility:** 68 one-bedroom standard units, some with whirlpools. 3 stories, interior corridors. *Bath:* combo or shower only. **Parking:** on-site. **Amenities:** high-speed Internet, irons, hair dryers. **Pool(s):** heated indoor. **Leisure Activities:** whirlpool, exercise room. **Guest Services:** coin laundry, wireless Internet. **Business Services:** PC. **Free Special Amenities: continental breakfast and high-speed Internet.**

CALL / SOME UNITS

BEST WESTERN LAWRENCE Book great rates at AAA.com **Phone:** (785)843-9100

AAA SAVE
Hotel
$90-$120 All Year

Address: 2309 Iowa St 66046 **Location:** On US 59; jct SR 10. Adjacent to Kansas University. **Facility:** 100 units. 98 one- and 2 two-bedroom standard units, some with whirlpools. 2-3 stories, interior/exterior corridors. *Bath:* combo or shower only. **Parking:** on-site. **Terms:** cancellation fee imposed. **Amenities:** voice mail, irons, hair dryers. **Pool(s):** heated indoor. **Leisure Activities:** whirlpool, limited exercise equipment. **Guest Services:** coin laundry, wireless Internet. **Business Services:** meeting rooms, PC. **Free Special Amenities: expanded continental breakfast and high-speed Internet.**

CALL / SOME UNITS FEE

AAA Benefit:
Members save up to 20%, plus 10% bonus points with rewards program.

CIRCLE S RANCH & COUNTRY INN **Phone:** 785/843-4124

Resort Hotel
Rates not provided

Address: 3325 Circle S Ln 66044 **Location:** I-70, exit 204, 2.6 mi n on US 59, 5.6 mi n on CR 1045, then 2 mi e on 35th St (gravel road). Located in a rural area. **Facility:** Surrounded by scenic views of woods, open range and rolling hills, the ranch is a good spot from which to view buffalo, cows and peacocks. Smoke free premises. 12 one-bedroom standard units, some with whirlpools. 3 stories (no elevator), interior corridors. *Bath:* combo or shower only. **Parking:** on-site. **Terms:** check-in 4 pm. **Amenities:** CD players, hair dryers. *Some:* irons. **Leisure Activities:** whirlpool, fishing, hiking trails. *Fee:* massage. **Guest Services:** wireless Internet. **Business Services:** meeting rooms.

ECONO LODGE Book at AAA.com **Phone:** (785)842-7030

Hotel
$49-$199 All Year

Address: 2222 W 6th St 66049 **Location:** I-70, exit 202, 1 mi s. **Facility:** 110 one-bedroom standard units, some with whirlpools. 3 stories (no elevator), interior corridors. **Parking:** on-site. **Amenities:** voice mail, irons, hair dryers. **Pool(s):** outdoor. **Leisure Activities:** exercise room. *Fee:* massage. **Guest Services:** valet and coin laundry, wireless Internet. **Business Services:** meeting rooms, PC. ASK / SOME UNITS FEE

ELDRIDGE HOTEL Book great rates at AAA.com **Phone:** (785)749-5011

AAA SAVE
Historic Hotel
$145-$300 All Year

Address: 701 Massachusetts St 66044 **Location:** I-70, exit 204, 1.5 mi s to downtown, on 3rd St. **Facility:** Modern comforts in restored landmark. Many rooms are 2-room suites. Smoke free premises. 56 units. 5 one-bedroom standard units. 51 one-bedroom suites. 5 stories, interior corridors. *Bath:* combo or shower only. **Parking:** valet. **Terms:** check-in 4 pm, cancellation fee imposed. **Amenities:** voice mail, irons, hair dryers. **Dining:** Ten Restaurant, see separate listing. **Leisure Activities:** limited exercise equipment. **Guest Services:** valet laundry, wireless Internet. **Business Services:** meeting rooms, PC. **Free Special Amenities: early check-in/late check-out and high-speed Internet.** / SOME UNITS

HAMPTON INN *Book great rates at AAA.com* **Phone:** (785)841-4994

Hotel
$99-$139 All Year

Address: 2300 W 6th St 66049 **Location:** I-70, exit 202, 0.8 mi s, then just w. **Facility:** 89 one-bedroom standard units, some with whirlpools. 3 stories, interior corridors. *Bath:* combo or shower only. **Parking:** on-site. **Terms:** 1-7 night minimum stay, cancellation fee imposed. **Amenities:** voice mail, irons, hair dryers. **Pool(s):** heated indoor. **Leisure Activities:** whirlpool, exercise room. **Guest Services:** wireless Internet. **Business Services:** meeting rooms, PC.
CALL / SOME UNITS

AAA Benefit:
Members save up to 10% everyday!

HOLIDAY INN *Book great rates at AAA.com* **Phone:** (785)841-7077

Hotel
$99-$119 All Year

Address: 200 McDonald Dr 66044 **Location:** I-70, exit 202, 0.5 mi s on US 59. **Facility:** Smoke free premises. 192 units. 191 one-bedroom standard units. 1 one-bedroom suite with whirlpool. 4 stories, interior corridors. *Bath:* combo or shower only. **Parking:** on-site. **Terms:** check-in 4 pm, cancellation fee imposed. **Amenities:** voice mail, irons, hair dryers. **Pool(s):** heated indoor. **Leisure Activities:** whirlpool, miniature golf, pool table, recreation atrium, exercise room. *Fee:* game room. **Guest Services:** valet and coin laundry, wireless Internet. **Business Services:** conference facilities, PC.
/ SOME UNITS FEE

HOLIDAY INN EXPRESS HOTEL & SUITES *Book great rates at AAA.com* **Phone:** (785)749-7555

Hotel
$89-$174 All Year

Address: 3411 SW Iowa St 66046 **Location:** I-70, exit 197 (SR 10), 8.4 mi e to US 59, then just n. **Facility:** Smoke free premises. 78 units. 74 one-bedroom standard units, some with whirlpools. 4 one-bedroom suites. 3 stories, interior corridors. *Bath:* combo or shower only. **Parking:** on-site. **Amenities:** high-speed Internet, dual phone lines, voice mail, safes, irons, hair dryers. **Pool(s):** heated indoor. **Leisure Activities:** whirlpool, bicycles, hiking trails, exercise room. **Guest Services:** coin laundry, wireless Internet. **Business Services:** meeting rooms, business center.
CALL / SOME UNITS FEE

QUALITY INN *Book at AAA.com* **Phone:** (785)842-5100

Motel
$69-$169 All Year

Address: 801 Iowa St 66049 **Location:** I-70, exit 202, 1 mi s on US 59. **Facility:** 67 one-bedroom standard units, some with whirlpools. 3 stories (no elevator), interior/exterior corridors. *Bath:* combo or shower only. **Parking:** on-site. **Terms:** cancellation fee imposed. **Amenities:** safes (fee), irons, hair dryers. **Pool(s):** outdoor. **Leisure Activities:** exercise room. **Guest Services:** valet and coin laundry, wireless Internet. **Business Services:** meeting rooms, PC.
ASK / SOME UNITS FEE

WHERE TO DINE

JADE MONGOLIAN BARBEQUE **Phone:** 785/865-5233

Chinese
$6-$15

Guests can either sample from the large buffet and salad bar or order from the menu. Entrees are prepared to the diner's preference after selections are made from the raw food bar. Choices are plentiful. Casual dress. **Bar:** Full bar. **Reservations:** not accepted. **Hours:** 11 am-10 pm, Fri & Sat-10:30 pm. Closed major holidays. **Address:** 1511 W 23rd St 66049 **Location:** On SR 10 (23rd St), 0.5 mi e of US 59. **Parking:** on-site.

MONTANA MIKE'S **Phone:** 785/749-3005

Steak
$7-$20

This steakhouse offers a dining experience for the whole family. A rustic look with Western appointments characterizes the dining room. Although it's hard to go wrong with a hearty steak of USDA Choice aged beef, guests also can try smoked, fire-grilled chicken breast, chicken-fried steak, baby back ribs and other selections. Casual dress. **Bar:** Full bar. **Reservations:** accepted. **Hours:** 11 am-9 pm, Fri & Sat-10 pm. Closed: 11/25, 12/25; also Mon. **Address:** 1015 Iowa St 66044 **Location:** I-70, exit 202, 1.3 mi s on US 59. **Parking:** on-site.

PACHAMAMA'S **Phone:** 785/841-0990

Continental
$6-$31

Guests will find international cuisine at Pachamama's, where the menu changes monthly and its wine selection is varied. Its upscale decor features a subtle rain forest decor, open, airy spaces and an outstanding view of Alvamar Golf Course. Dining on a private patio is an option. Dressy casual. **Bar:** Full bar. **Reservations:** required. **Hours:** 11 am-2 & 5-9:30 pm, Fri & Sat-10 pm. Closed major holidays; also Sun & Mon. **Address:** 800 New Hampshire St 66044 **Location:** I-70, exit 204, 1 mi s; downtown. **Parking:** on-site. CALL

PANDA & PLUM GARDEN **Phone:** 785/843-4312

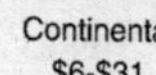

Chinese
$5-$13

Close to many stores, the restaurant employs fast, friendly servers. Patrons can relax in the cozy dining room and browse an extensive menu or choose the buffet, which lines up a small variety of good selections. Casual dress. **Bar:** Full bar. **Reservations:** not accepted. **Hours:** 11:30 am-9:30 pm, Fri & Sat-10 pm, Sun-9 pm. **Address:** 1500 W 6th St 66044 **Location:** I-70, exit 202, 1 mi s, then 0.5 mi e. **Parking:** on-site.

TELLER'S RESTAURANT AND BAR **Phone:** 785/843-4111

Italian
$7-$29

A historic character permeates the building, which in the late 1800s functioned as a bank. Beautiful, custom-made art adorns the two-story walls. With an award-winning wine selection, this elegant restaurant serves a variety of Italian and American specialties that are sure to leave a lasting impression. Casual dress. **Bar:** Full bar. **Reservations:** accepted. **Hours:** 11 am-10 pm, Fri & Sat-11 pm, Sun 9 am-2 & 3-10 pm. Closed: 7/4, 12/25. **Address:** 746 Massachusetts St 66044 **Location:** I-70, exit 204, 1.5 mi s; downtown. **Parking:** on-site. CALL

TEN RESTAURANT **Phone:** 785/749-5011

American
$5-$22

Located in a historic hotel, this restaurant has been lovingly restored to the grandeur of the Civil War era. The restaurant features a good variety of well-prepared entrees including steaks, grilled salmon, pork loin with raspberry maple glaze, and tortellini pasta. Casual dress. **Bar:** Full bar. **Reservations:** accepted. **Hours:** 7 am-10 pm, Fri & Sat-11 pm. **Address:** 701 Massachusetts St 66044 **Location:** I-70, exit 204, 1.5 mi s to downtown, on 3rd St; in Eldridge Hotel. **Parking:** on-site. **Historic**

LEAWOOD—See Nearby MO City Of Kansas City p. 494.

LENEXA—See Nearby MO City Of Kansas City p. 495.

LIBERAL pop. 19,666

AMERICAS BEST VALUE INN *Book great rates at AAA.com* **Phone:** (620)624-6203

Motel
$54-$64 All Year

Address: 564 E Pancake Blvd 67901 **Location:** 0.8 w of jct US 54 and 83. **Facility:** 30 one-bedroom standard units. 1 story, exterior corridors. **Parking:** on-site, winter plug-ins. **Terms:** 2 night minimum stay - seasonal and/or weekends, cancellation fee imposed. **Amenities:** hair dryers. **Guest Services:** coin laundry, wireless Internet. **Free Special Amenities: continental breakfast and high-speed Internet.** / SOME UNITS FEE

BLUEBIRD INN BED & BREAKFAST **Phone:** 620/624-0720

Bed & Breakfast
$88-$110 All Year

Address: 221 W 6th St 67901 **Location:** Just w of jct US 83 business route (Kansas Ave). **Facility:** One-story stone house on well-maintained and landscaped corner lot. Wood deck at the rear of property is open air with several chairs for guest enjoyment. This is a non-smoking residence; however, smoking is permitted outdoors. The property is frequented by casual travelers, as well as business persons. Smoke free premises. 4 one-bedroom standard units, some with whirlpools. 1 story, interior corridors. *Bath:* combo or shower only. **Parking:** on-site. **Terms:** check-in 4 pm, cancellation fee imposed. **Amenities:** video library, DVD players, high-speed Internet, hair dryers.
ASK / SOME UNITS

HOLIDAY INN EXPRESS HOTEL & SUITES *Book at AAA.com* **Phone:** (620)624-9700

Hotel
$97-$152 All Year

Address: 1550 N Lincoln Ave 67901 **Location:** 1.5 mi n on US 83 business route. **Facility:** Smoke free premises. 67 units. 61 one-bedroom standard units, some with whirlpools. 6 one-bedroom suites. 3 stories, interior corridors. *Bath:* combo or shower only. **Parking:** on-site. **Amenities:** dual phone lines, voice mail, irons, hair dryers. *Some:* high-speed Internet. **Pool(s):** heated indoor. **Leisure Activities:** whirlpool, exercise room. **Guest Services:** valet and coin laundry, wireless Internet. **Business Services:** meeting rooms, business center.
ASK / SOME UNITS

▼ See AAA listing p 369 ▼

LIBERAL INN **Phone:** (620)624-7254

Hotel
$65-$79 All Year

Address: 603 E Pancake Blvd 67901 **Location:** 0.5 mi w of jct US 54 and 83. **Facility:** 124 units. 120 one-bedroom standard units. 4 one-bedroom suites. 2 stories (no elevator), interior corridors. **Parking:** on-site. **Amenities:** *Some:* DVD players, irons. **Dining:** Branding Iron Restaurant, see separate listing. **Pool(s):** heated indoor. **Leisure Activities:** whirlpool. **Guest Services:** valet and coin laundry, airport transportation-Liberal Municipal Airport, wireless Internet. **Business Services:** meeting rooms, PC. *(See color ad p 368)*
/ SOME UNITS

FREE preferred room (subject to availability with advance reservations) and high-speed Internet

WHERE TO DINE

BRANDING IRON RESTAURANT **Phone:** 620/624-7254

American
$5-$18

You'll appreciate the generous portions of delicious steak, catfish and barbecue ribs at the Branding Iron. The warm, casual atmosphere, home-cooked foods and friendly, attentive service make this a popular restaurant with just about everyone. Casual dress. **Bar:** Full bar. **Hours:** 6 am-10:30 pm, Sun 7 am-10 pm. Closed: 11/25, 12/25. **Address:** 603 E Pancake Blvd 67901 **Location:** 0.5 mi w of jct US 54 and 83; in Liberal Inn. **Parking:** on-site. *(See color ad p 368)*

CATTLEMANS CAFE II **Phone:** 620/626-5553

American
$5-$10

Locals flock to the restaurant for good home cooking and generous portions. Casual dress. **Hours:** 10:30 am-10:30 pm. Closed: 11/25, 12/25. **Address:** 744 E Pancake Blvd 67901 **Location:** Jct US 54 and 83, just w. **Parking:** on-site.

LA HACIENDA **Phone:** 620/626-7319

Mexican
$8-$17

A favorite among locals, the restaurant specializes in Mexican fare. For those who enjoy seafood prepared in the Mexican tradition, the choices are plentiful. Casual dress. **Bar:** Full bar. **Hours:** 11 am-3 & 5-9 pm, Fri & Sat-10 pm, Sun-8 pm. Closed major holidays. **Address:** 339 E Pancake Blvd 67901 **Location:** US 54, just e of jct US 83. **Parking:** on-site.

TASTE OF CHINA **Phone:** 620/626-7388

Chinese
$6-$9

The buffet, which lines up a good array of quality food, is a favorite among many local residents. Casual dress. **Hours:** 11 am-10:30 pm. Closed: 11/25. **Address:** 741 E Pancake Blvd 67901 **Location:** Just w of jct US 54 and 83. **Parking:** on-site.

LINDSBORG pop. 3,321

VIKING MOTEL **Phone:** 785/227-3336

Motel
Rates not provided

Address: 446 Harrison St 67456 **Location:** I-135, exit 78, 4 mi sw. Located within easy access to Bethany College. **Facility:** 24 one-bedroom standard units. 2 stories (no elevator), exterior corridors. **Parking:** on-site. **Pool(s):** outdoor. **Leisure Activities:** horseshoes. **Guest Services:** wireless Internet. / SOME UNITS

LYONS pop. 3,732

CELEBRATION CENTRE INN & SUITES **Phone:** (620)680-6022

Motel
$65-$100 All Year

Address: 1108 E Hwy 56 67554 **Location:** 2 mi e of jct SR 14 and US 56. **Facility:** 30 units. 29 one-bedroom standard units, some with whirlpools. 1 one-bedroom suite with whirlpool. 2 stories, interior corridors. **Parking:** on-site, winter plug-ins. **Terms:** office hours 6 am-11 pm. **Amenities:** high-speed Internet, voice mail, hair dryers. *Some:* DVD players. **Leisure Activities:** limited exercise equipment. **Guest Services:** coin laundry, wireless Internet. **Business Services:** business center.
ASK / SOME UNITS FEE

LYONS INN *Book great rates at AAA.com* **Phone:** (620)257-5185

Motel
$59-$76 All Year

Address: 817 W Main St 67554 **Location:** 0.8 mi w on SR 96 and US 56. **Facility:** 28 one-bedroom standard units. 2 stories (no elevator), interior corridors. *Bath:* combo or shower only. **Parking:** on-site, winter plug-ins. **Guest Services:** wireless Internet. **Free Special Amenities: expanded continental breakfast and high-speed Internet.** / SOME UNITS

MANHATTAN pop. 44,831

BEST WESTERN MANHATTAN INN

Book great rates at AAA.com — **Phone:** 785/537-8300

Hotel

Rates not provided

Address: 601 E Poyntz Ave 66502 **Location:** SR 177, 0.4 mi e on US 24 (Frontage Rd). **Facility:** Smoke free premises. 45 one-bedroom standard units, some with whirlpools. 2 stories (no elevator), interior corridors. *Bath:* combo or shower only. **Parking:** on-site. **Amenities:** high-speed Internet, voice mail, irons, hair dryers. **Pool(s):** heated indoor. **Leisure Activities:** limited exercise equipment. **Guest Services:** coin laundry, wireless Internet. **Business Services:** PC. **Free Special Amenities: expanded continental breakfast and high-speed Internet.**

CALL / SOME UNITS FEE

AAA Benefit: Members save up to 20%, plus 10% bonus points with rewards program.

CLARION HOTEL

Book great rates at AAA.com — **Phone:** (785)539-5311

Hotel

$80-$139 9/3-2/28
$70-$129 3/1-9/2

Address: 530 Richards Dr 66502 **Location:** On SR 18 (Ft. Riley Blvd), 0.3 mi e of jct SR 113. **Facility:** Smoke free premises. 197 units. 196 one-bedroom standard units. 1 one-bedroom suite. 3 stories, interior/exterior corridors. *Bath:* combo or shower only. **Parking:** on-site. **Terms:** check-in 4 pm. **Amenities:** video games (fee), voice mail, irons, hair dryers. **Dining:** 2 restaurants. **Pool(s):** heated indoor. **Leisure Activities:** sauna, whirlpool, miniature golf, indoor recreation area, exercise room. *Fee:* game room. **Guest Services:** valet and coin laundry, airport transportation-Manhattan Municipal Airport, wireless Internet. **Business Services:** conference facilities, business center. **Free Special Amenities: high-speed Internet.**

/ SOME UNITS FEE

FAIRFIELD INN BY MARRIOTT

Book great rates at AAA.com — **Phone:** (785)539-2400

Hotel

$103-$125 All Year

Address: 300 Colorado St 66502 **Location:** Just w of jct SR 177 and 18 (Ft. Riley Blvd). **Facility:** Smoke free premises. 98 one-bedroom standard units. 3 stories, interior corridors. *Bath:* combo or shower only. **Parking:** on-site. **Terms:** cancellation fee imposed. **Amenities:** dual phone lines, voice mail, irons, hair dryers. **Pool(s):** heated indoor. **Leisure Activities:** whirlpool, exercise room. **Guest Services:** valet laundry, wireless Internet. **Business Services:** meeting rooms, PC.

CALL

AAA Benefit: Members save a minimum 5% off the best available rate.

HAMPTON INN

Book great rates at AAA.com — **Phone:** (785)539-5000

Hotel

$95-$195 All Year

Address: 501 E Poyntz Ave 66502 **Location:** SR 177, 0.3 mi e on US 24 (Frontage Rd). **Facility:** Smoke free premises. 72 units. 71 one-bedroom standard units. 1 one-bedroom suite. 3 stories, interior corridors. *Bath:* combo or shower only. **Parking:** on-site. **Terms:** check-in 4 pm, 1-7 night minimum stay, cancellation fee imposed. **Amenities:** dual phone lines, voice mail, irons, hair dryers. *Some:* high-speed Internet. **Pool(s):** heated indoor. **Leisure Activities:** whirlpool, exercise room. **Guest Services:** valet and coin laundry, wireless Internet. **Business Services:** meeting rooms, PC.

CALL / SOME UNITS

AAA Benefit: Members save up to 10% everyday!

HOLIDAY INN AT THE CAMPUS

Book at AAA.com — **Phone:** (785)539-7531

Hotel

$119-$199 9/1-2/28
$99-$169 3/1-8/31

Address: 1641 Anderson Ave 66502 **Location:** 1 mi n of SR 18 (Ft. Riley Blvd). Opposite Kansas State University. **Facility:** Smoke free premises. 113 one-bedroom standard units, some with whirlpools. 6 stories, interior corridors. **Parking:** on-site. **Terms:** cancellation fee imposed. **Amenities:** dual phone lines, voice mail, irons, hair dryers. **Pool(s):** outdoor. **Leisure Activities:** exercise room. **Guest Services:** valet and coin laundry, wireless Internet. **Business Services:** conference facilities, business center.

ASK / SOME UNITS FEE

MANHATTAN SUPER 8

Book at AAA.com — **Phone:** (785)537-8468

Hotel

$65-$125 All Year

Address: 200 Tuttle Creek Blvd 66502 **Location:** Jct US 24 (Frontage Rd) and SR 177. Located across the street from a major mall. **Facility:** Smoke free premises. 85 one-bedroom standard units. 3 stories (no elevator), interior corridors. **Parking:** on-site. **Amenities:** safes (fee), hair dryers. *Some:* irons. **Leisure Activities:** exercise room. **Guest Services:** coin laundry, wireless Internet. **Business Services:** meeting rooms, PC.

ASK / SOME UNITS FEE

MOTEL 6 - 152

Book at AAA.com — **Phone:** (785)537-1022

Motel

$51-$61 5/22-2/28
$45-$55 3/1-5/21

Address: 510 Tuttle Creek Blvd 66502 **Location:** 0.3 mi ne on US 24 (Frontage Rd) and SR 177. **Facility:** 87 one-bedroom standard units. 2 stories (no elevator), exterior corridors. *Bath:* shower only. **Parking:** on-site. **Pool(s):** heated outdoor. **Guest Services:** coin laundry.

CALL / SOME UNITS

QUALITY INN *Book at AAA.com* **Phone:** (785)770-8000

Hotel
$70-$170 All Year

Address: 150 E Poyntz Ave 66502 **Location:** Jct US 24 (Frontage Rd) and SR 177. Railroad tracks behind hotel. **Facility:** Smoke free premises. 65 one-bedroom standard units, some with whirlpools. 3 stories, interior corridors. *Bath:* combo or shower only. **Parking:** on-site. **Terms:** cancellation fee imposed. **Amenities:** voice mail, irons, hair dryers. **Pool(s):** heated indoor. **Leisure Activities:** whirlpool, limited exercise equipment. **Guest Services:** wireless Internet.

ASK CALL &M / SOME UNITS

WHERE TO DINE

BAMBOO BUFFET **Phone:** 785/539-8299

Chinese
$6-$8

In the evenings, snow crab is included in the large selection on the buffets for a small extra charge. The menu lists an excellent variety of entrees. Casual dress. **Reservations:** not accepted. **Hours:** 11 am-9:30 pm, Fri & Sat-10 pm. Closed: 11/25, 12/25. **Address:** 2304 Stagg Hill Rd 66502 **Location:** 0.3 mi e on SR 18 (Ft. Riley Blvd) from jct SR 113, just s. **Parking:** on-site.

HARRY'S UPTOWN **Phone:** 785/537-1300

Continental
$9-$37

Enjoy casual fine dining set in the comfortable atmosphere of a historic building at Harry's Uptown. They serve a good variety of creatively prepared chicken, beef and fresh seafood dishes. The server staff is friendly and attentive to your needs. Casual dress. **Bar:** Full bar. **Reservations:** suggested. **Hours:** 11 am-2 & 5-9 pm, Fri-10 pm, Sat 5 pm-10 pm. Closed: 1/1, 11/25, 12/25; also Sun. **Address:** 418 Poyntz Ave 66502 **Location:** Downtown. **Parking:** street. **Historic**

KITES GRILLE AND BAR **Phone:** 785/537-7500

American
$7-$14

Serving a wide variety of items, this sports bar and grill has something for everyone. Guests can take a seat at the center island bar and tune into one of the many wall-mounted, flat-panel TVs broadcasting sports events or check out all the K State memorabilia adorning the walls. This spot offers a dare to try and eat the three-pound cheeseburger, and the cookie bake—a warm chocolate chip cookie baked in a dish, then topped with a scoop of ice cream and chocolate sauce—comes highly recommended. Casual dress. **Bar:** Full bar. **Reservations:** accepted. **Hours:** 11 am-11 pm. Closed: 4/4, 12/25. **Address:** 8200 South Port Dr, Suite 111 66502 **Location:** 1.5 mi e on US 24 (E Poyntz Ave). **Parking:** on-site. CALL &M

KITES GRILLE AND BAR **Phone:** 785/776-4300

American
$7-$14

Serving a wide variety of items, this sports bar and grill has something for everyone. Guests can take a seat at the center island bar and tune into one of the many wall-mounted, flat-panel TVs broadcasting sports events or check out all the K State memorabilia adorning the walls. This spot offers a dare to try and eat the three-pound cheeseburger, and the cookie bake—a warm chocolate chip cookie baked in a dish, then topped with a scoop of ice cream and chocolate sauce—comes highly recommended. Casual dress. **Bar:** Full bar. **Reservations:** accepted. **Hours:** 11 am-11 pm. **Address:** 615 N 12th St 66502 **Location:** 1 mi w of US 24 (Tuttle Creek Blvd); in Aggieville area. **Parking:** on-site. CALL &M

LITTLE APPLE BREWING COMPANY **Phone:** 785/539-5500

American
$5-$29

Known locally for certified Angus steak and award-winning microbrew, Little Apple has a casual atmosphere with a Western flair. They feature a good selection, fresh ingredients and ample portions of burgers, sandwiches, steaks and Mexican dishes. Casual dress. **Bar:** Full bar. **Reservations:** accepted. **Hours:** 11 am-10 pm, Fri & Sat-11 pm, Sun-9:30 pm. Closed major holidays. **Address:** 1110 Westloop Shopping Center 66502 **Location:** Off SR 113 (Seth Child Rd); in Westloop Shopping Center. **Parking:** on-site.

SIRLOIN STOCKADE **Phone:** 785/776-0516

Regional Steak
$6-$9

The steakhouse lines up buffet items, including pizza, tacos, soups, salads and desserts, providing both excellent variety and a good value. Rotating theme nights might allow for the sampling of sushi, barbecue and seafood. The buffet also may serve to complement a quality steak. Rolls are baked several times daily. Casual dress. **Reservations:** not accepted. **Hours:** 11 am-9 pm, Fri-9:30 pm, Sat 8 am-9:30 pm, Sun 8 am-9 pm. Closed: 11/25, 12/25. **Address:** 325 E Poyntz Ave 66502 **Location:** Center. **Parking:** on-site.

WHISKEY CREEK WOOD FIRE GRILL **Phone:** 785/776-7300

American
$9-$22

Guests can watch as their steak is cooked over a wood-burning fire and throw peanut shells on the floor at this fun, casual steakhouse. The menu's wide variety includes chicken, pasta and barbecue dishes. A rustic theme evokes the wild, wild West. Casual dress. **Bar:** Full bar. **Reservations:** not accepted. **Hours:** 11 am-10 pm, Fri & Sat-11 pm. Closed: 11/25, 12/25. **Address:** 200 Manhattan Town Center 66502 **Location:** On SR 18 (Ft. Riley Blvd), just w of jct SR 177. **Parking:** on-site.

MARYSVILLE pop. 3,271

HERITAGE INN EXPRESS **Phone:** 785/562-5588

Hotel
Rates not provided

Address: 1155 Pony Express Hwy 66508 **Location:** 2 mi e on US 36 (Pony Express Hwy). **Facility:** 41 one-bedroom standard units, some with whirlpools. 2 stories (no elevator), interior corridors. **Parking:** on-site. **Amenities:** hair dryers. **Leisure Activities:** limited exercise equipment. **Guest Services:** coin laundry, wireless Internet. **Business Services:** meeting rooms.

/ SOME UNITS FEE

MARYSVILLE SURF MOTEL **Phone:** (785)562-2354

Motel
$75-$86 3/1-10/1
$55-$70 10/2-2/28

Address: 2105 Center St 66508 **Location:** 1 mi e on US 36 (Pony Express Hwy). **Facility:** 52 one-bedroom standard units. 2 stories (no elevator), interior/exterior corridors. *Bath:* combo or shower only. **Parking:** on-site, winter plug-ins. **Terms:** 7 day cancellation notice. **Amenities:** irons, hair dryers. **Leisure Activities:** sauna, whirlpool, exercise room. **Guest Services:** coin laundry, wireless Internet. **Business Services:** PC. ASK / SOME UNITS FEE

MCPHERSON pop. 13,770

AMERICAS BEST VALUE INN *Book great rates at AAA.com* **Phone:** (620)241-8881

Hotel
$56-$95 All Year

Address: 2110 E Kansas Ave 67460 **Location:** I-135, exit 60, just w. **Facility:** 39 one-bedroom standard units. 2 stories (no elevator), interior corridors. *Bath:* combo or shower only. **Parking:** on-site. **Terms:** 3 day cancellation notice. **Amenities:** safes (fee), hair dryers. **Guest Services:** coin laundry, wireless Internet. CALL / SOME UNITS FEE

BEST WESTERN HOLIDAY MANOR MOTEL *Book great rates at AAA.com* **Phone:** (620)241-5343

Hotel
$75-$95 All Year

Address: 2211 E Kansas Ave 67460 **Location:** I-135, exit 60, just w. **Facility:** 109 one-bedroom standard units, some with whirlpools. 2 stories (no elevator), interior/exterior corridors. *Bath:* combo or shower only. **Parking:** on-site, winter plug-ins. **Amenities:** high-speed Internet, voice mail, irons, hair dryers. **Pool(s):** outdoor, heated indoor. **Leisure Activities:** whirlpool, exercise room. **Guest Services:** valet laundry, wireless Internet. **Business Services:** conference facilities, PC. **Free Special Amenities: continental breakfast and high-speed Internet.** / SOME UNITS

Best Western
AAA Benefit:
Members save up to 20%, plus 10% bonus points with rewards program.

HOLIDAY INN EXPRESS **Phone:** 620/241-5566

Hotel
Rates not provided

Address: 2302 E Kansas Ave 67460 **Location:** I-135, exit 60, just w. **Facility:** Smoke free premises. 76 one-bedroom standard units. 3 stories, interior corridors. *Bath:* combo or shower only. **Parking:** on-site. **Amenities:** high-speed Internet, voice mail, irons, hair dryers. **Pool(s):** heated indoor. **Leisure Activities:** whirlpool, exercise room. **Guest Services:** coin laundry, wireless Internet. **Business Services:** meeting rooms, PC. **Free Special Amenities: expanded continental breakfast and high-speed Internet.** CALL

—— WHERE TO DINE ——

LA FIESTA **Phone:** 620/245-0033

Mexican
$6-$14

Locals head to this festive eatery, especially in the early evening, to nosh on traditional, flavorful Mexican cuisine. House specialties are offered nightly but patrons shouldn't overlook the many popular options on the menu, such as burritos, chalupas, tacos, enchiladas and fajitas. Casual dress. **Bar:** Full bar. **Reservations:** not accepted. **Hours:** 11 am-9 pm, Fri & Sat-10 pm. Closed major holidays. **Address:** 2090 E Kansas Ave 67460 **Location:** I-135, exit 60, just w. **Parking:** on-site.

MEADE pop. 1,672

DALTON'S BEDPOST MOTEL **Phone:** 620/873-2131

Motel
$60-$64 11/1-2/28
$54 3/1-10/31

Address: 519 E Carthage St 67864 **Location:** On US 54. **Facility:** 12 one-bedroom standard units. 1 story, exterior corridors. *Bath:* shower only. **Parking:** on-site, winter plug-ins. **Guest Services:** wireless Internet. **Free Special Amenities: continental breakfast and high-speed Internet.** / SOME UNITS

MERRIAM—See Nearby MO City Of Kansas City p. 496.

MORAN pop. 562

HEDGE APPLE ACRES BED & BREAKFAST **Phone:** (620)237-4646

Bed & Breakfast
$85-$95 All Year

Address: 4430 US Hwy 54 66755 **Location:** Jct US 54 and 59, 2.1 mi e. Located in a quiet area. **Facility:** Smoke free premises. 4 one-bedroom standard units, some with whirlpools. 2 stories (no elevator), interior corridors. *Bath:* combo or shower only. **Parking:** on-site. **Terms:** 14 day cancellation notice-fee imposed. **Leisure Activities:** fishing, hiking trails. **Guest Services:** wireless Internet. ASK

NEWTON pop. 17,190

BEST WESTERN RED COACH INN *Book great rates at AAA.com*

Phone: (316)283-9120

Hotel
$80-$100 All Year

Address: 1301 E 1st St 67114 **Location:** I-135, exit 31, just w. **Facility:** Smoke free premises. 81 one-bedroom standard units, some with whirlpools. 2 stories (no elevator), interior/exterior corridors. **Parking:** on-site, winter plug-ins. **Amenities:** irons, hair dryers. **Pool(s):** heated indoor. **Leisure Activities:** whirlpool, limited exercise equipment. *Fee:* game room. **Guest Services:** coin laundry, wireless Internet. **Business Services:** meeting rooms. **Free Special Amenities: local telephone calls and high-speed Internet.**

/ SOME UNITS FEE

AAA Benefit: Members save up to 20%, plus 10% bonus points with rewards program.

OBERLIN pop. 1,994

LANDMARK INN

Phone: 785/475-2340

Historic Country Inn
$79-$129 All Year

Address: 189 S Penn Ave 67749 **Location:** Corner of Penn Ave and Hall St; downtown. **Facility:** The inn — located in a restored bank building, circa 1886 — features both antique and replicated antique furnishings and a friendly staff. Smoke free premises. 7 units. 6 one-bedroom standard units, some with whirlpools. 1 one-bedroom suite. 2-3 stories (no elevator), interior/exterior corridors. *Bath:* combo or shower only. **Parking:** street. **Terms:** office hours 6 am-midnight, cancellation fee imposed. **Amenities:** video library, voice mail. **Dining:** Teller Room Restaurant, see separate listing. **Leisure Activities:** sauna, limited exercise equipment. **Guest Services:** coin laundry, wireless Internet.

ASK CALL

—— WHERE TO DINE ——

TELLER ROOM RESTAURANT

Phone: 785/475-2340

American
$7-$18

In a restored circa 1886 bank building, the restaurant treats patrons to a distinctive experience. The dining room has vintage wall coverings, cherry woodwork and reproduction gas lights. The daily changing menu lists a little something for everyone. Save room for one of the scrumptious desserts, all of which are prepared in house. Casual dress. **Reservations:** suggested. **Hours:** 11:30 am-1:30 pm, Thurs-Sat also 6 pm-8 pm. Closed: 4/4, 11/25, 12/25; also Sun. **Address:** 189 S Penn Ave 67749 **Location:** Corner of Penn Ave and Hall St; downtown; in LandMark Inn. **Parking:** street. CALL

OLATHE—See Nearby MO City Of Kansas City p. 497.

OTTAWA pop. 11,921

BEST WESTERN OTTAWA INN *Book great rates at AAA.com*

Phone: (785)242-2224

Hotel
$80-$130 All Year

Address: 212 E 23rd St 66067 **Location:** I-35, exit 183 (US 59). **Facility:** 52 one-bedroom standard units. 2 stories (no elevator), interior/exterior corridors. **Parking:** on-site. **Amenities:** voice mail, irons, hair dryers. *Some:* high-speed Internet. **Pool(s):** heated indoor. **Leisure Activities:** whirlpool. **Guest Services:** valet and coin laundry, wireless Internet. **Business Services:** PC. **Free Special Amenities: expanded continental breakfast and high-speed Internet.**

CALL / SOME UNITS FEE

AAA Benefit: Members save up to 20%, plus 10% bonus points with rewards program.

COMFORT INN *Book at AAA.com*

Phone: (785)242-9898

Hotel
$90-$170 All Year

Address: 2335 S Oak St 66067 **Location:** I-35, exit 183 (US 59), just ne. **Facility:** 60 one-bedroom standard units, some with whirlpools. 3 stories, interior corridors. *Bath:* combo or shower only. **Parking:** on-site, winter plug-ins. **Amenities:** high-speed Internet, voice mail, irons, hair dryers. *Fee:* video games, safes. **Pool(s):** heated indoor. **Leisure Activities:** whirlpool, exercise room. **Guest Services:** valet laundry, wireless Internet. **Business Services:** PC.

ASK CALL / SOME UNITS

ECONO LODGE *Book great rates at AAA.com*

Phone: (785)242-3400

Hotel
$55-$70 All Year

Address: 2331 S Cedar Rd 66067 **Location:** I-35, exit 183 (US 59). **Facility:** 56 one-bedroom standard units. 2 stories (no elevator), interior corridors. **Parking:** on-site, winter plug-ins. **Amenities:** irons, hair dryers. **Pool(s):** outdoor. **Guest Services:** wireless Internet. **Business Services:** PC. **Free Special Amenities: expanded continental breakfast and high-speed Internet.**

/ SOME UNITS FEE

—— WHERE TO DINE ——

SIRLOIN STOCKADE

Phone: 785/242-4329

Regional Steak
$6-$9

The steakhouse lines up buffet items, including pizza, tacos, soups, salads and desserts, providing both excellent variety and a good value. Rotating theme nights might allow for the sampling of sushi, barbecue and seafood. The buffet also may serve to complement a quality steak. Rolls are baked several times daily. Casual dress. **Reservations:** not accepted. **Hours:** 11 am-9 pm. Closed: 11/25, 12/25. **Address:** 2230 S Princeton St 66067 **Location:** I-35, exit 183 (US 59), just n. **Parking:** on-site.

OVERLAND PARK—See Nearby MO City Of Kansas City p. 499.

PAOLA pop. 5,011

PAOLA INN AND SUITES Book at AAA.com **Phone:** (913)294-3700

Hotel
$95-$98 All Year

Address: 1600 E Hedge Lane Ct 66071 **Location:** US 169, exit 127 (Baptiste Dr), just w. **Facility:** Smoke free premises. 39 units. 35 one-bedroom standard units, some with whirlpools. 4 one-bedroom suites. 3 stories, interior corridors. *Bath:* combo or shower only. **Parking:** on-site. **Amenities:** high-speed Internet, voice mail, irons, hair dryers. **Pool(s):** outdoor. **Leisure Activities:** whirlpool, exercise room. **Guest Services:** coin laundry, wireless Internet. **Business Services:** PC.

ASK CALL / SOME UNITS FEE

PARK CITY pop. 5,814 (See map and index starting on p. 384)

BEST WESTERN HOTEL & SUITES Book great rates at AAA.com **Phone:** (316)832-9387 38

Hotel
$70-$100 All Year

Address: 915 E 53rd St N 67219 **Location:** I-135, exit 13, just w. **Facility:** 149 units. 146 one-bedroom standard units, some with whirlpools. 3 one-bedroom suites with whirlpools. 2 stories (no elevator), interior/exterior corridors. *Bath:* combo or shower only. **Parking:** on-site. **Terms:** cancellation fee imposed. **Amenities:** high-speed Internet, voice mail, irons, hair dryers. **Pool(s):** heated indoor. **Leisure Activities:** whirlpool, putting green, indoor recreation area, exercise room, shuffleboard. *Fee:* game room. **Guest Services:** valet and coin laundry, wireless Internet. **Business Services:** conference facilities, PC. **Free Special Amenities: full breakfast and high-speed Internet.**

/ SOME UNITS FEE

AAA Benefit:
Members save up to 20%, plus 10% bonus points with rewards program.

COMFORT INN NORTH Book at AAA.com **Phone:** (316)744-7711 35

Hotel
$89-$110 All Year

Address: 990 Connolly Ct 67219 **Location:** I-135, exit 14, just ne. **Facility:** Smoke free premises. 61 one-bedroom standard units, some with kitchens (no utensils) and/or whirlpools. 2 stories (no elevator), interior corridors. *Bath:* combo or shower only. **Parking:** on-site. **Amenities:** high-speed Internet, safes (fee), irons, hair dryers. **Pool(s):** heated indoor. **Leisure Activities:** limited exercise equipment. **Guest Services:** coin laundry, wireless Internet.

ASK / SOME UNITS

PARK CITY EXPRESS INN & SUITES Book great rates at AAA.com **Phone:** (316)927-3900 37

Hotel
$63-$80 All Year

Address: 792 Beaumont St 67219 **Location:** I-135, exit 14, just sw. **Facility:** 54 units. 53 one-bedroom standard units. 1 one-bedroom suite. 3 stories, interior corridors. *Bath:* combo or shower only. **Parking:** on-site. **Terms:** cancellation fee imposed. **Amenities:** DVD players, irons, hair dryers. **Pool(s):** outdoor. **Leisure Activities:** whirlpool, exercise room. **Guest Services:** coin laundry, wireless Internet. **Business Services:** business center. **Free Special Amenities: expanded continental breakfast and high-speed Internet.** / SOME UNITS FEE

SUPER 8-WICHITA NORTH/PARK CITY Book at AAA.com **Phone:** (316)744-2071 36

Motel
$45-$70 All Year

Address: 6075 Air Cap Dr 67219 **Location:** I-135, exit 14, just sw. **Facility:** 59 one-bedroom standard units. 2 stories (no elevator), interior corridors. **Parking:** on-site, winter plug-ins. **Amenities:** safes (fee), hair dryers. **Guest Services:** coin laundry, wireless Internet.

ASK / SOME UNITS FEE

PARSONS pop. 11,514

BEST WESTERN PARSONS INN Book great rates at AAA.com **Phone:** (620)423-0303

Hotel
$70-$125 All Year

Address: 101 E Main St 67357 **Location:** 1.5 mi e. **Facility:** 41 one-bedroom standard units, some with whirlpools. 2 stories (no elevator), interior corridors. *Bath:* combo or shower only. **Parking:** on-site. **Terms:** 3 day cancellation notice. **Amenities:** irons, hair dryers. *Some:* high-speed Internet. **Pool(s):** heated indoor. **Leisure Activities:** exercise room. **Guest Services:** coin laundry, wireless Internet. **Business Services:** meeting rooms, PC. **Free Special Amenities: continental breakfast and high-speed Internet.** / SOME UNITS FEE

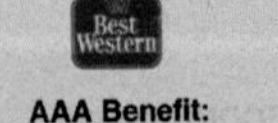

AAA Benefit:
Members save up to 20%, plus 10% bonus points with rewards program.

SLEEP INN & SUITES Book great rates at AAA.com **Phone:** (620)421-6126

Hotel
$70-$82 All Year

Address: 1807 Harding Dr 67357 **Location:** Just sw of jct US 59 and 400. **Facility:** Smoke free premises. 50 one-bedroom standard units, some with whirlpools. 2 stories, interior corridors. *Bath:* combo or shower only. **Parking:** on-site. **Terms:** cancellation fee imposed. **Amenities:** high-speed Internet, voice mail, safes, hair dryers. **Pool(s):** heated indoor. **Leisure Activities:** whirlpool, exercise room. **Guest Services:** coin laundry, wireless Internet. **Business Services:** PC. **Free Special Amenities: full breakfast and high-speed Internet.**

CALL / SOME UNITS FEE

WHERE TO DINE

SIRLOIN STOCKADE — **Phone:** 620/421-0022

Regional Steak
$6-$9

The steakhouse lines up buffet items, including pizza, tacos, soups, salads and desserts, providing both excellent variety and a good value. Rotating theme nights might allow for the sampling of sushi, barbecue and seafood. The buffet also may serve to complement a quality steak. Rolls are baked several times daily. Casual dress. **Reservations:** not accepted. **Hours:** 11 am-9 pm. Closed: 11/25, 12/25. **Address:** 1000 W Main St 67357 **Location:** Just e of jct US 59 and 400. **Parking:** on-site.

PHILLIPSBURG pop. 2,668

COTTONWOOD INN — **Phone:** (785)543-2125

Motel
$65-$99 All Year

Address: 1200 State St 67661 **Location:** 1 mi e on US 36/183. **Facility:** 40 one-bedroom standard units, some with whirlpools. 2 stories (no elevator), exterior corridors. *Bath:* combo or shower only. **Parking:** on-site, winter plug-ins. **Terms:** office hours 6 am-11 pm, 7 day cancellation notice-fee imposed. **Pool(s):** heated outdoor. **Leisure Activities:** exercise room. **Guest Services:** wireless Internet. **Business Services:** meeting rooms. ASK / SOME UNITS

PITTSBURG pop. 19,243

COMFORT INN & SUITES — Book at AAA.com — **Phone:** (620)231-8800

Hotel
$115-$190 All Year

Address: 4009 Parkview Dr 66762 **Location:** 2 mi n on US 69 from jct SR 126. **Facility:** Smoke free premises. 70 one-bedroom standard units, some with whirlpools. 3 stories, interior corridors. *Bath:* combo or shower only. **Parking:** on-site. **Terms:** 7 day cancellation notice-fee imposed. **Amenities:** voice mail, safes (fee), irons, hair dryers. **Pool(s):** heated indoor. **Leisure Activities:** whirlpool, hiking trails, exercise room. **Guest Services:** valet and coin laundry, wireless Internet. **Business Services:** PC. ASK CALL / SOME UNITS

HOLIDAY INN EXPRESS & SUITES — Book at AAA.com — **Phone:** 620/231-1177

Hotel
Rates not provided

Address: 4011 Parkview Dr 66762 **Location:** 2 mi n on US 69 from jct SR 126. **Facility:** Smoke free premises. 72 one-bedroom standard units, some with whirlpools. 3 stories, interior corridors. *Bath:* combo or shower only. **Parking:** on-site. **Amenities:** high-speed Internet, voice mail, irons, hair dryers. **Pool(s):** heated outdoor. **Leisure Activities:** whirlpool, exercise room. **Guest Services:** valet and coin laundry, wireless Internet. **Business Services:** meeting rooms, business center. CALL

LAMPLIGHTER INN & SUITES — Book great rates at AAA.com — **Phone:** (620)231-8700

AAA SAVE
Hotel
$79-$129 All Year

Address: 4020 Parkview Dr 66762 **Location:** 2.3 mi n on US 69 from jct SR 126. **Facility:** 100 units. 99 one-bedroom standard units. 1 one-bedroom suite. 2 stories (no elevator), interior/exterior corridors. *Bath:* combo or shower only. **Parking:** on-site. **Amenities:** DVD players, voice mail, irons, hair dryers. *Some:* high-speed Internet. **Pool(s):** outdoor. **Leisure Activities:** whirlpool, table tennis, exercise room, gazebo, grill. **Guest Services:** wireless Internet. **Business Services:** meeting rooms, PC. **Free Special Amenities: expanded continental breakfast and high-speed Internet.** CALL / SOME UNITS

SUPER 8 — Book at AAA.com — **Phone:** (620)232-1881

Hotel
$53-$69 All Year

Address: 3108 N Broadway Ave 66762 **Location:** 2.1 mi n on US 69 from jct SR 126. **Facility:** 64 one-bedroom standard units. 3 stories (no elevator), interior corridors. **Parking:** on-site. **Amenities:** safes (fee), hair dryers. *Some:* irons. **Guest Services:** wireless Internet. ASK / SOME UNITS FEE

WHERE TO DINE

CHICKEN ANNIE'S ORIGINAL — **Phone:** 620/231-9460

American
$5-$10

You'll enjoy the home-style cooking and casual dining of Chicken Annie's, where the featured dish is, of course, chicken, which is nicely seasoned and perfectly cooked. The German potato salad, German coleslaw and onion rings are also tasty and fresh. Casual dress. **Bar:** Full bar. **Reservations:** accepted. **Hours:** 4 pm-8:30 pm, Sat-9 pm, Sun 11 am-8 pm. Closed: 11/25, 12/24, 12/25; also Mon. **Address:** 1143 E 600th Ave 66762 **Location:** 5 mi n on US 69 from SR 126, 3.5 mi e on rural road, follow signs. **Parking:** on-site.

CHICKEN MARY'S — **Phone:** 620/231-9510

American
$5-$12

Chicken Mary's specializes in—what else?—chicken, but it's prepared with a very old, German, family recipe and has great flavor. Chicken dominates the basic menu of mostly homemade selections. It has a casual atmosphere and simple decor. Casual dress. **Bar:** Beer only. **Reservations:** accepted. **Hours:** 4 pm-8:30 pm, Sat-9 pm, Sun 11 am-8 pm. Closed major holidays; also Mon. **Address:** 1133 E 600th Ave 66762 **Location:** 5 mi n on US 69, 3.5 mi e on rural road, follow signs. **Parking:** on-site.

EL CHARRO — **Phone:** 620/232-5763

Mexican
$4-$16

The eatery offers a wide variety of authentic Mexican cuisine and fast service. Be careful; they mean it when they say some dishes are spicy. Casual dress. **Bar:** Full bar. **Reservations:** accepted. **Hours:** 11 am-9 pm, Fri & Sat-10 pm, Sun-8 pm. Closed major holidays. **Address:** 3102 N Broadway Ave 66762 **Location:** 2 mi n on US 69 from jct SR 126. **Parking:** on-site.

JIM'S STEAKHOUSE & LOUNGE **Phone:** 620/231-5770

American
$6-$25

Most menu items are homemade at Jim's, which is very popular with local residents and has been in business for 60 years. Its casual, family-style atmosphere is comfortable, lighthearted, quiet and pleasant plus the server staff is very nice. Casual dress. **Bar:** Full bar. **Reservations:** accepted, except weekends. **Hours:** 4:30 pm-10 pm. Closed major holidays; also Sun. **Address:** 1912 N Broadway Ave 66762 **Location:** 2 mi n of jct US 69 and SR 126, on US 69. **Parking:** on-site.

PRAIRIE VILLAGE—See Nearby MO City Of Kansas City p. 504.

PRATT pop. 6,570

COMFORT SUITES **Phone:** 620/672-9999

Hotel
$120-$160 All Year

Address: 704 Allison Ln 67124 **Location:** Just n of jct US 54 and SR 81. **Facility:** Smoke free premises. 67 one-bedroom standard units. 3 stories, interior corridors. *Bath:* combo or shower only. **Parking:** on-site. **Amenities:** high-speed Internet, voice mail, irons, hair dryers. **Pool(s):** heated indoor. **Leisure Activities:** whirlpool, exercise room. **Guest Services:** complimentary laundry, wireless Internet. **Business Services:** meeting rooms, business center.

ASK / SOME UNITS FEE

EVERGREEN INN & RV PARK **Phone:** 620/672-6431

Motel
$59-$100 All Year

Address: 20001 W US Hwy 54 67124 **Location:** 3 mi w. **Facility:** 17 one-bedroom standard units. 1 story, exterior corridors. *Bath:* combo or shower only. **Parking:** on-site, winter plug-ins. **Pool(s):** heated outdoor. **Guest Services:** coin laundry, wireless Internet.

ASK / SOME UNITS FEE

REGENCY INN & SUITES **Phone:** 620/672-9433

Hotel
$78 All Year

Address: 1401 W US Hwy 54 67124 **Location:** 2 mi w. **Facility:** 67 one-bedroom standard units. 2 stories (no elevator), interior corridors. *Bath:* combo or shower only. **Parking:** on-site, winter plug-ins. **Amenities:** voice mail, irons, hair dryers. **Pool(s):** heated indoor. **Leisure Activities:** limited exercise equipment. **Guest Services:** valet laundry, wireless Internet. **Business Services:** meeting rooms, business center. ASK / SOME UNITS

WHERE TO DINE

RICK'S **Phone:** 620/672-3681

American
$5-$16

This locally popular restaurant features a home-style cuisine and a casual atmosphere that's great for birthday celebrations and special occasions. The standard cafe fare offers seafood, beef dishes, pasta and sandwiches. Casual dress. **Hours:** 6 am-8:30 pm. Closed major holidays. **Address:** 20005 W US Hwy 54 67124 **Location:** 3 mi w. **Parking:** on-site.

RUSSELL pop. 4,696

AMERICINN LODGE & SUITES OF RUSSELL *Book at AAA.com* **Phone:** (785)483-4200

Hotel
$75-$125 All Year

Address: 1430 S Fossil St 67665 **Location:** I-70, exit 184 (US 281), just n. **Facility:** 54 units. 45 one-bedroom standard units, some with whirlpools. 9 one-bedroom suites, some with whirlpools. 3 stories, interior corridors. *Bath:* combo or shower only. **Parking:** on-site. **Terms:** cancellation fee imposed. **Amenities:** high-speed Internet, dual phone lines, voice mail, irons, hair dryers. *Some:* DVD players, CD players. **Pool(s):** heated indoor. **Leisure Activities:** sauna, whirlpool, exercise room. **Guest Services:** coin laundry, wireless Internet. **Business Services:** conference facilities, business center.

ASK CALL / SOME UNITS FEE

DAYS INN *Book at AAA.com* **Phone:** 785/483-6660

Motel
Rates not provided

Address: 1225 S Fossil St 67665 **Location:** I-70, exit 184 (US 281), just n. **Facility:** 48 one-bedroom standard units. 2 stories (no elevator), exterior corridors. **Parking:** on-site, winter plug-ins. **Amenities:** hair dryers. **Pool(s):** outdoor. **Guest Services:** wireless Internet. **Business Services:** PC. / SOME UNITS FEE

WHERE TO DINE

MERIDY'S **Phone:** 785/483-4300

American
$6-$27

This local favorite is known for its down-home cooking and friendly, casual atmosphere. The restaurant proudly serves breakfast, lunch and dinner and features freshly cut steaks and a daily buffet. Casual dress. **Bar:** Full bar. **Reservations:** accepted. **Hours:** 6 am-10 pm, Sun 7 am-8 pm. Closed: 11/25, 12/25. **Address:** 1220 S Fossil St 67665 **Location:** I-70, exit 184 (US 281), just n. **Parking:** on-site.

SALINA pop. 45,679

AMERICA'S BEST INN *Book great rates at AAA.com* **Phone:** (785)825-2500

AAA SAVE

Hotel
$62-$79 3/1-9/15
$56-$73 9/16-2/28

Address: 429 W Diamond Dr 67401 **Location:** I-70, exit 252, just n. **Facility:** 35 units. 34 one-bedroom standard units. 1 one-bedroom suite. 2 stories (no elevator), interior corridors. **Parking:** on-site. **Guest Services:** coin laundry, wireless Internet. **Business Services:** PC. **Free Special Amenities: continental breakfast and high-speed Internet.**

CALL / SOME UNITS FEE

BAYMONT INN & SUITES 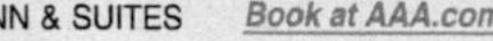 Book at AAA.com Phone: 785/493-9800

Hotel
Rates not provided

Address: 745 W Schilling Rd 67401 **Location:** I-135, exit 89 (Schilling Rd), just w. **Facility:** 53 one-bedroom standard units, some with whirlpools. 2 stories, interior corridors. *Bath:* combo or shower only. **Parking:** on-site. **Amenities:** high-speed Internet, voice mail, irons, hair dryers. **Pool(s):** heated indoor. **Leisure Activities:** whirlpool, waterslide, limited exercise equipment. **Guest Services:** valet and coin laundry, wireless Internet. **Business Services:** PC.
CALL / SOME UNITS FEE

BEST WESTERN HEART OF AMERICA INN Book great rates at AAA.com **Phone:** (785)827-9315

Hotel
$78-$95 All Year

Address: 632 Westport Blvd 67401 **Location:** I-135, exit 92, just e. **Facility:** 99 one-bedroom standard units. 2 stories (no elevator), interior/exterior corridors. *Bath:* combo or shower only. **Parking:** on-site. **Terms:** cancellation fee imposed. **Amenities:** voice mail, irons, hair dryers. **Pool(s):** heated indoor. **Leisure Activities:** whirlpool. **Guest Services:** wireless Internet. **Business Services:** conference facilities, PC. **Free Special Amenities: continental breakfast and preferred room (subject to availability with advance reservations).**
/ SOME UNITS FEE

AAA Benefit:
Members save up to 20%, plus 10% bonus points with rewards program.

BEST WESTERN MID-AMERICA INN Book great rates at AAA.com **Phone:** (785)827-0356

Motel
$88-$92 All Year

Address: 1846 N 9th St 67401 **Location:** I-70, exit 252, just s. **Facility:** 108 one-bedroom standard units. 2 stories (no elevator), exterior corridors. *Bath:* combo or shower only. **Parking:** on-site, winter plug-ins. **Terms:** 30 day cancellation notice-fee imposed. **Amenities:** irons, hair dryers. **Pool(s):** outdoor, heated indoor. **Leisure Activities:** whirlpool. **Guest Services:** wireless Internet. **Business Services:** meeting rooms, PC. **Free Special Amenities: local telephone calls and high-speed Internet.**
CALL / SOME UNITS

AAA Benefit:
Members save up to 20%, plus 10% bonus points with rewards program.

CANDLEWOOD SUITES Book at AAA.com **Phone:** (785)823-6939

Extended Stay Hotel
$55-$109 All Year

Address: 2650 Planet Ave 67401 **Location:** I-135, exit 89 (Schilling Rd), just e to S 9th St, 0.5 mi n to Belmont, then just w. **Facility:** 69 one-bedroom standard units with efficiencies. 3 stories, interior corridors. *Bath:* combo or shower only. **Parking:** on-site. **Terms:** cancellation fee imposed. **Amenities:** video library, DVD players, CD players, dual phone lines, voice mail, irons, hair dryers. **Leisure Activities:** exercise room. **Guest Services:** complimentary and valet laundry, wireless Internet. **Business Services:** meeting rooms, business center.
ASK CALL / SOME UNITS FEE

COMFORT INN Book at AAA.com **Phone:** 785/826-1711

Hotel
Rates not provided

Address: 1820 W Crawford St 67401 **Location:** I-135, exit 92, just e. **Facility:** 60 one-bedroom standard units. 2 stories (no elevator), interior corridors. **Parking:** on-site. **Amenities:** safes (fee), irons, hair dryers. **Pool(s):** heated indoor. **Leisure Activities:** whirlpool. **Guest Services:** valet laundry, wireless Internet.
CALL / SOME UNITS FEE

COUNTRY INN & SUITES BY CARLSON Book great rates at AAA.com **Phone:** (785)827-1271

Hotel
$105-$175 All Year

Address: 2760 S 9th St 67401 **Location:** I-135, exit 89 (Schilling Rd), just e, then 0.3 mi n. **Facility:** 72 units. 40 one-bedroom standard units, some with whirlpools. 32 one-bedroom suites. 3 stories, interior corridors. *Bath:* combo or shower only. **Parking:** on-site. **Amenities:** dual phone lines, voice mail, irons, hair dryers. **Pool(s):** heated indoor. **Leisure Activities:** whirlpool, exercise room. **Guest Services:** valet and coin laundry, wireless Internet. **Business Services:** meeting rooms, PC. **Free Special Amenities: expanded continental breakfast and early check-in/late check-out.**
CALL / SOME UNITS

COURTYARD BY MARRIOTT Book great rates at AAA.com **Phone:** (785)309-1300

Hotel
$112-$136 All Year

Address: 3020 Riffel Dr 67401 **Location:** I-135, exit 89 (Schilling Rd), just e. **Facility:** Smoke free premises. 80 units. 77 one-bedroom standard units, some with whirlpools. 3 one-bedroom suites. 3 stories, interior corridors. *Bath:* combo or shower only. **Parking:** on-site. **Terms:** cancellation fee imposed. **Amenities:** high-speed Internet, voice mail, irons, hair dryers. **Pool(s):** heated indoor. **Leisure Activities:** whirlpool, exercise room. **Guest Services:** valet and coin laundry, wireless Internet. **Business Services:** meeting rooms, PC.

AAA Benefit:
Members save a minimum 5% off the best available rate.

DAYS INN Book at AAA.com **Phone:** (785)823-9791

Hotel
$55-$129 All Year

Address: 407 W Diamond Dr 67401 **Location:** I-70, exit 252, just n. **Facility:** 45 one-bedroom standard units. 2 stories (no elevator), interior corridors. **Parking:** on-site. **Terms:** cancellation fee imposed. **Amenities:** hair dryers. **Pool(s):** heated indoor. **Leisure Activities:** whirlpool. **Guest Services:** wireless Internet.
ASK / SOME UNITS FEE

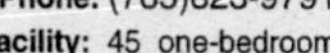

FAIRFIELD INN *Book great rates at AAA.com* **Phone:** (785)823-6900

Hotel
$80-$98 All Year

Address: 1740 W Crawford St 67401 **Location:** I-135, exit 92, 0.3 mi e. **Facility:** Smoke free premises. 63 one-bedroom standard units. 3 stories, interior corridors. *Bath:* combo or shower only. **Parking:** on-site. **Terms:** cancellation fee imposed. **Amenities:** irons, hair dryers. **Pool(s):** heated indoor. **Leisure Activities:** whirlpool. **Guest Services:** valet laundry, wireless Internet. **Business Services:** PC.

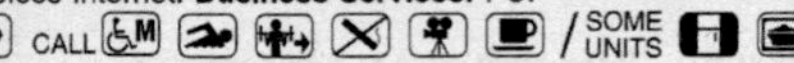

AAA Benefit:
Members save a minimum 5% off the best available rate.

HAMPTON INN *Book great rates at AAA.com* **Phone:** (785)823-9800

Hotel
$99-$115 All Year

Address: 401 W Schilling Rd 67401 **Location:** I-135, exit 89 (Schilling Rd), just e. **Facility:** 68 one-bedroom standard units. 3 stories, interior corridors. *Bath:* combo or shower only. **Parking:** on-site. **Terms:** 1-7 night minimum stay, cancellation fee imposed. **Amenities:** voice mail, irons, hair dryers. **Pool(s):** heated indoor. **Leisure Activities:** whirlpool, exercise room. **Guest Services:** valet and coin laundry, wireless Internet. **Business Services:** PC. CALL / SOME UNITS

AAA Benefit:
Members save up to 10% everyday!

HOLIDAY INN EXPRESS HOTEL & SUITES *Book at AAA.com* **Phone:** (785)827-9000

Hotel
$85-$149 All Year

Address: 201 E Diamond Dr 67401 **Location:** I-70, exit 252, just ne. **Facility:** Smoke free premises. 93 units. 91 one-bedroom standard units, some with whirlpools. 2 one-bedroom suites with whirlpools. 3 stories, interior corridors. *Bath:* combo or shower only. **Parking:** on-site. **Amenities:** voice mail, irons, hair dryers. *Some:* dual phone lines. **Pool(s):** heated indoor. **Leisure Activities:** exercise room. **Guest Services:** valet and coin laundry, wireless Internet. **Business Services:** meeting rooms, PC.

QUALITY INN & SUITES *Book great rates at AAA.com* **Phone:** 785/825-2111

Hotel
Rates not provided

Address: 2110 W Crawford St 67401 **Location:** I-135, exit 92, just w. **Facility:** 106 units. 95 one-bedroom standard units. 11 one-bedroom suites, some with whirlpools. 2 stories (no elevator), interior corridors. *Bath:* combo or shower only. **Parking:** on-site. **Amenities:** irons, hair dryers. **Pool(s):** heated indoor. **Leisure Activities:** whirlpool, putting green, 2 lighted tennis courts, indoor recreation area, billiards, table tennis, basketball, shuffleboard, volleyball. *Fee:* game room. **Guest Services:** valet and coin laundry, wireless Internet. **Business Services:** conference facilities, PC. **Free Special Amenities: expanded continental breakfast and high-speed Internet.**

CALL / SOME UNITS FEE

SUPER 8 I-70 *Book great rates at AAA.com* **Phone:** 785/823-8808

Hotel
Rates not provided

Address: 120 E Diamond Dr 67401 **Location:** I-70, exit 252, just ne. **Facility:** 49 one-bedroom standard units. 2 stories (no elevator), interior corridors. *Bath:* combo or shower only. **Parking:** on-site, winter plug-ins. **Amenities:** hair dryers. *Some:* irons. **Pool(s):** heated indoor. **Leisure Activities:** whirlpool. **Guest Services:** coin laundry, wireless Internet. **Business Services:** PC. **Free Special Amenities: continental breakfast and high-speed Internet.**

CALL / SOME UNITS FEE

WHERE TO DINE

DAIMARU STEAK HOUSE **Phone:** 785/820-5500

Japanese
$6-$20

Examples of the many lunch and dinner combinations include lobster and top sirloin or rib-eye and shrimp. Children's selections are available. Sake is worth a try. Casual dress. **Bar:** Beer & wine. **Reservations:** accepted. **Hours:** 11 am-2:30 & 4:30-10 pm, Fri-10:30 pm, Sat noon-10:30 pm, Sun noon-9 pm. Closed: 11/25. **Address:** 1601 W Crawford St 67401 **Location:** I-135, exit 92, 0.5 mi e. **Parking:** on-site.

HONG KONG BUFFET **Phone:** 785/820-8683

Chinese
$9-$12

An all-you-can-eat buffet is offered at lunch and dinner along with a long list of dishes on the menu; no MSG and low salt in all cuisine. Casual dress. **Reservations:** not accepted. **Hours:** 11 am-9:30 pm, Fri & Sat-10 pm, Sun-9 pm. Closed: 11/25. **Address:** 2445 S 9th St 67401 **Location:** I-135, exit 89, just e to 9th St, then 0.5 mi n. **Parking:** on-site.

MARTINELLI'S LITTLE ITALY **Phone:** 785/826-9190

Italian
$6-$22

Snug booths line several cozy dining rooms at this popular spot. The list of appetizers and desserts will impress thanks to their creativity and presentations. A wide variety of Italian cuisine includes a very good selection of pastas. Casual dress. **Bar:** Full bar. **Reservations:** accepted, suggested weekends. **Hours:** 11 am-10 pm, Sun-9 pm. Closed major holidays. **Address:** 158 S Santa Fe 67401 **Location:** On northwest corner of Walnut and Santa Fe; downtown. **Parking:** street.

RUSSELL'S RESTAURANT **Phone:** 785/825-5733

American
$7-$18

Russell's casual diner features an extensive, wholesome menu that's appealing to locals and travelers alike. You might try the chicken-fried steak, catfish, or the choice aged Kansas City strip, but be sure to save room for the homemade pies. Casual dress. **Reservations:** accepted. **Hours:** 24 hours. **Address:** 649 Westport Blvd 67401 **Location:** I-135, exit 92, just ne. **Parking:** on-site.

TUCSON'S STEAKHOUSE SALOON **Phone:** 785/820-9595

Southwestern
$9-$23

A popular spot with the locals, this eatery features well-cooked steaks and sides. Most menu items are inspired by the southwest, including Southwest egg rolls, steaks and Cajun pastas. Homemade bread served with all entrées is a fantastic addition. Light and fun atmosphere welcomes all patrons. Casual dress. **Bar:** Full bar. **Reservations:** accepted. **Hours:** 4 pm-10 pm, Fri & Sat 11 am-11 pm, Sun 11 am-10 pm. Closed: 11/25, 12/25. **Address:** 2750 S 9th St 67401 **Location:** I-135, exit 89 (Schilling Rd), just e, then 0.3 mi n. **Parking:** on-site.

SCOTT CITY pop. 3,855

BEST WESTERN EL-QUARTELEJO INN & SUITES *Book great rates at AAA.com* **Phone:** (620)872-7373

Hotel
$100 All Year

Address: 1610 S Main St 67871 **Location:** 1 mi s of jct US 83 and 96. **Facility:** Smoke free premises. 50 one-bedroom standard units. 2 stories, interior corridors. *Bath:* combo or shower only. **Parking:** on-site. **Amenities:** high-speed Internet, irons, hair dryers. **Pool(s):** heated indoor. **Leisure Activities:** whirlpool, exercise room. **Guest Services:** coin laundry, wireless Internet. **Business Services:** business center. **Free Special Amenities: full breakfast and high-speed Internet.**

CALL

AAA Benefit:
Members save up to 20%, plus 10% bonus points with rewards program.

SHARON SPRINGS pop. 835

OAK TREE INN *Book at AAA.com* **Phone:** 785/852-4664

Hotel
Rates not provided

Address: 801 N Hwy 27 67758 **Location:** Jct US 40 and SR 27. **Facility:** Smoke free premises. 50 one-bedroom standard units. 2 stories (no elevator), interior/exterior corridors. *Bath:* combo or shower only. **Parking:** on-site, winter plug-ins. **Amenities:** *Some:* irons, hair dryers. **Leisure Activities:** exercise room. **Guest Services:** coin laundry, wireless Internet. **Business Services:** meeting rooms.

CALL / SOME UNITS

SHAWNEE—See Nearby MO City Of Kansas City p. 504.

TOPEKA pop. 122,377

BAYMONT INN & SUITES *Book at AAA.com* **Phone:** (785)273-0003

Hotel
$75-$120 All Year

Address: 1401 SW Ashworth Pl 66604 **Location:** I-470, exit 1 (Wanamaker Rd), just ne; I-70, exit 356A (Wanamaker Rd), 1 mi s. **Facility:** 62 one-bedroom standard units. 2 stories (no elevator), exterior corridors. *Bath:* combo or shower only. **Parking:** on-site. **Amenities:** voice mail, irons, hair dryers. **Pool(s):** outdoor. **Leisure Activities:** whirlpool, exercise room. **Guest Services:** valet laundry, wireless Internet. **Business Services:** PC.

ASK CALL / SOME UNITS

BEST WESTERN TOPEKA INN & SUITES *Book great rates at AAA.com* **Phone:** (785)228-2223

Hotel
$75-$100 All Year

Address: 700 SW Fairlawn Rd 66606 **Location:** I-70, exit 357A, just ne. **Facility:** 45 one-bedroom standard units, some with whirlpools. 2 stories (no elevator), interior corridors. **Parking:** on-site. **Amenities:** high-speed Internet, irons, hair dryers. **Pool(s):** heated indoor. **Leisure Activities:** whirlpool, exercise room. **Guest Services:** valet laundry, wireless Internet. **Business Services:** PC. **Free Special Amenities: continental breakfast and high-speed Internet.**

/ SOME UNITS FEE

AAA Benefit:
Members save up to 20%, plus 10% bonus points with rewards program.

CAPITOL PLAZA HOTEL *Book at AAA.com* **Phone:** (785)431-7200

Hotel
$79-$149 All Year

Address: 1717 SW Topeka Blvd 66612 **Location:** I-70, exit SE 8th Ave, 1.6 mi s; I-470, exit Topeka Blvd, 2.9 mi n. **Facility:** 224 units. 215 one-bedroom standard units. 9 one-bedroom suites, some with whirlpools. 7 stories, interior corridors. *Bath:* combo or shower only. **Parking:** on-site. **Amenities:** video games (fee), high-speed Internet, voice mail, irons, hair dryers. **Pool(s):** heated indoor. **Leisure Activities:** sauna, whirlpool, exercise room. **Guest Services:** valet and coin laundry, area transportation, wireless Internet. **Business Services:** conference facilities, business center.

ASK CALL / SOME UNITS

CLUBHOUSE INN & SUITES *Book great rates at AAA.com* **Phone:** 785/273-8888

Hotel
Rates not provided

Address: 924 SW Henderson 66615 **Location:** I-70, exit 356 (Wanamaker Rd), just sw. **Facility:** 121 units. 104 one-bedroom standard units. 17 one-bedroom suites, some with whirlpools. 2 stories (no elevator), interior corridors. *Bath:* combo or shower only. **Parking:** on-site. **Amenities:** high-speed Internet, voice mail, irons, hair dryers. **Pool(s):** heated outdoor. **Leisure Activities:** whirlpool, gazebo, grills, picnic tables. **Guest Services:** valet and coin laundry, wireless Internet. **Business Services:** meeting rooms, PC. *(See color ad below)*
/ SOME UNITS FEE

FREE full breakfast and newspaper

COMFORT INN BY CHOICE HOTELS *Book at AAA.com* **Phone:** (785)273-5365

Hotel
$70-$129 All Year

Address: 1518 SW Wanamaker Rd 66604 **Location:** I-470, exit 1 (Wanamaker Rd). **Facility:** 66 one-bedroom standard units. 2 stories (no elevator), interior corridors. **Parking:** on-site. **Amenities:** irons, hair dryers. **Pool(s):** heated indoor. **Leisure Activities:** whirlpool. **Guest Services:** wireless Internet.
ASK / SOME UNITS FEE

COUNTRY INN & SUITES BY CARLSON, TOPEKA WEST *Book at AAA.com* **Phone:** (785)478-9800

Hotel
$75-$125 All Year

Address: 6020 SW 10th St 66615 **Location:** I-70, exit 356 (Wanamaker Rd), just sw. **Facility:** 58 units. 43 one-bedroom standard units, some with whirlpools. 15 one-bedroom suites, some with whirlpools. 3 stories, interior corridors. *Bath:* combo or shower only. **Parking:** on-site. **Amenities:** high-speed Internet, voice mail, irons, hair dryers. **Pool(s):** heated indoor. **Leisure Activities:** whirlpool, exercise room. **Guest Services:** valet and coin laundry, wireless Internet.
ASK CALL / SOME UNITS FEE

COURTYARD BY MARRIOTT *Book great rates at AAA.com* **Phone:** (785)271-6165

Hotel
$108-$132 All Year

Address: 2033 SW Wanamaker Rd 66604 **Location:** I-70, exit 356 (Wanamaker Rd), 1.5 mi s. **Facility:** Smoke free premises. 90 units. 87 one-bedroom standard units. 3 one-bedroom suites. 3 stories, interior corridors. *Bath:* combo or shower only. **Parking:** on-site. **Terms:** cancellation fee imposed. **Amenities:** dual phone lines, voice mail, irons, hair dryers. *Some:* high-speed Internet. **Pool(s):** heated indoor. **Leisure Activities:** whirlpool, exercise room. **Guest Services:** valet and coin laundry, wireless Internet. **Business Services:** meeting rooms, business center.
CALL / SOME UNITS

AAA Benefit:
Members save a minimum 5% off the best available rate.

▼ See AAA listing above ▼

FAIRFIELD INN BY MARRIOTT *Book great rates at AAA.com* **Phone:** (785)273-6800

Hotel
$71-$87 All Year

Address: 1530 SW Westport Dr 66604 **Location:** I-470, exit 1 (Wanamaker Rd). **Facility:** Smoke free premises. 62 one-bedroom standard units. 3 stories, interior corridors. **Parking:** on-site. **Terms:** cancellation fee imposed. **Amenities:** irons, hair dryers. *Some:* high-speed Internet. **Pool(s):** heated indoor. **Leisure Activities:** whirlpool. **Guest Services:** valet laundry, wireless Internet. **Business Services:** PC.

/ SOME UNITS

AAA Benefit:
Members save a minimum 5% off the best available rate.

HAMPTON INN *Book great rates at AAA.com* **Phone:** 785/228-0111

Hotel
Rates not provided

Address: 1515 SW Arrowhead Rd 66604 **Location:** I-470, exit 1B, just se. **Facility:** 89 one-bedroom standard units. 4 stories, interior corridors. *Bath:* combo or shower only. **Parking:** on-site. **Amenities:** high-speed Internet, voice mail, irons, hair dryers. **Pool(s):** heated indoor. **Leisure Activities:** whirlpool, exercise room. **Guest Services:** valet and coin laundry, wireless Internet. **Business Services:** meeting rooms, business center.

CALL / SOME UNITS

AAA Benefit:
Members save up to 10% everyday!

HOLIDAY INN EXPRESS HOTEL & SUITES *Book at AAA.com* **Phone:** 785/228-9500

Hotel
Rates not provided

Address: 901 SW Robinson Ave 66606 **Location:** I-70, exit 356 (Wanamaker Rd), just se. **Facility:** 81 units. 80 one-bedroom standard units, some with whirlpools. 1 one-bedroom suite with whirlpool. 3 stories, interior corridors. *Bath:* combo or shower only. **Parking:** on-site. **Amenities:** video games (fee), CD players, high-speed Internet, dual phone lines, voice mail, irons, hair dryers. **Pool(s):** heated indoor. **Leisure Activities:** whirlpool, exercise room. *Fee:* game room. **Guest Services:** valet and coin laundry, wireless Internet. **Business Services:** meeting rooms, business center. CALL / SOME UNITS

HOLIDAY INN HOLIDOME *Book at AAA.com* **Phone:** (785)272-8040

Hotel
$99-$139 All Year

Address: 605 Fairlawn Rd 66606 **Location:** I-70, exit 357A, just sw. **Facility:** 197 units. 189 one-bedroom standard units, some with whirlpools. 8 one-bedroom suites. 2-4 stories, interior/exterior corridors. *Bath:* combo or shower only. **Parking:** on-site. **Terms:** check-in 4 pm. **Amenities:** high-speed Internet, dual phone lines, voice mail, irons, hair dryers. **Pool(s):** heated indoor. **Leisure Activities:** whirlpool, waterslide, exercise room. *Fee:* game room. **Guest Services:** valet and coin laundry, wireless Internet. **Business Services:** conference facilities, business center.

ASK / SOME UNITS

HYATT PLACE TOPEKA *Book great rates at AAA.com* **Phone:** (785)273-0066

Contemporary Hotel
$89-$199 All Year

Address: 6021 SW 6th Ave 66615 **Location:** I-70, exit 356 (Wanamaker Rd), just n. **Facility:** Smoke free premises. 126 one-bedroom standard units. 6 stories, interior corridors. *Bath:* combo or shower only. **Parking:** on-site. **Terms:** cancellation fee imposed. **Amenities:** dual phone lines, voice mail, safes, irons, hair dryers. *Some:* high-speed Internet. **Pool(s):** heated outdoor. **Leisure Activities:** exercise room. **Guest Services:** valet and coin laundry, wireless Internet. **Business Services:** meeting rooms, business center. **Free Special Amenities: continental breakfast and high-speed Internet.**

CALL

HYATT PLACE
AAA Benefit:
Ask for the AAA rate and save 10%.

RAMADA HOTEL & CONVENTION CENTER *Book at AAA.com* **Phone:** 785/234-5400

Hotel
Rates not provided

Address: 420 SE 6th Ave 66607 **Location:** I-70, exit 362B, just e. **Facility:** Smoke free premises. 256 units. 228 one-bedroom standard units, some with whirlpools. 28 one-bedroom suites, some with kitchens (no utensils) and/or whirlpools. 11 stories, interior corridors. *Bath:* combo or shower only. **Parking:** on-site. **Amenities:** voice mail, irons, hair dryers. *Some:* DVD players, CD players, high-speed Internet. **Pool(s):** outdoor, heated indoor. **Leisure Activities:** sauna, whirlpool, exercise room. *Fee:* massage, game room. **Guest Services:** valet and coin laundry, wireless Internet. **Business Services:** conference facilities, business center.

CALL / SOME UNITS

RESIDENCE INN BY MARRIOTT *Book great rates at AAA.com* **Phone:** (785)271-8903

Extended Stay Hotel
$89-$109 All Year

Address: 1620 SW Westport Dr 66604 **Location:** I-470, exit 1 (Wanamaker Rd), just se. **Facility:** Smoke free premises. 66 units. 18 one-bedroom standard units with efficiencies. 36 one- and 12 two-bedroom suites, some with efficiencies or kitchens. 3 stories, interior corridors. *Bath:* combo or shower only. **Parking:** on-site. **Terms:** cancellation fee imposed. **Amenities:** voice mail, irons, hair dryers. **Pool(s):** heated indoor. **Leisure Activities:** whirlpool, exercise room, sports court. **Guest Services:** valet and coin laundry, wireless Internet. **Business Services:** PC.

CALL / SOME UNITS FEE

AAA Benefit:
Members save a minimum 5% off the best available rate.

THE SENATE LUXURY SUITES *Book at AAA.com* **Phone:** (785)233-505

Historic Hotel
$80-$120 All Year

Address: 900 SW Tyler St 66612 **Location:** Just w of state capitol; downtown **Facility:** Contemporary rooms fill this historic hotel, built in 1928. 51 units. 18 one-bedroom standar units. 26 one- and 7 two-bedroom suites, some with whirlpools. 3 stories, interior corridors. **Parking** on-site. **Terms:** cancellation fee imposed. **Amenities:** *Some:* DVD players, high-speed Internet, ha dryers. **Leisure Activities:** whirlpool, exercise room. **Guest Services:** valet and coin laundry, wireles Internet. **Business Services:** meeting rooms, PC.

ASK / SOME UNITS

SLEEP INN & SUITES *Book at AAA.com* **Phone:** (785)228-250

Hotel
$80-$100 All Year

Address: 1024 SW Wanamaker Rd 66604 **Location:** I-70, exit 356 (Wanamaker Rd), just s **Facility:** 64 one-bedroom standard units. 3 stories, interior corridors. *Bath:* combo or shower only **Parking:** on-site. **Terms:** cancellation fee imposed. **Amenities:** high-speed Internet, voice mail, safe (fee), irons, hair dryers. **Pool(s):** heated indoor. **Leisure Activities:** whirlpool, exercise room. **Gues Services:** coin laundry, wireless Internet. **Business Services:** meeting rooms, business center.

ASK CALL / SOME UNITS FEE

SUPER 8 AT FORBES LANDING *Book great rates at AAA.com* **Phone:** (785)862-222

SAVE
Hotel
$70-$140 All Year

Address: 5922 S Topeka Blvd 66619 **Location:** I-470, exit 6, 2.2 mi s. **Facility:** 63 one-bedroon standard units, some with whirlpools. 3 stories, interior corridors. *Bath:* combo or shower only **Parking:** on-site. **Amenities:** high-speed Internet, voice mail, safes (fee), hair dryers. *Some:* irons **Pool(s):** heated indoor. **Guest Services:** coin laundry. **Business Services:** meeting rooms, PC. **Fre Special Amenities: expanded continental breakfast and high-speed Internet.**

CALL / SOME UNITS FEE

WHERE TO DINE

ANNIE'S PLACE *Menu on AAA.com* **Phone:** 785/273-084

American
$5-$16

Breads and desserts are prepared in-house at Annie's Place, where the menu offers fresh food and a goo variety. The servers are friendly and knowledgeable; the contemporary decor is simple and attractive; an the coconut cream pie tastes great! Casual dress. **Bar:** Full bar. **Reservations:** accepted. **Hours:** 11 am-9 pm. Closed major holidays. **Address:** 4014 Gage Center Dr 66604 **Location:** I-70, exit 358B (Gage St), 1.5 mi s; in Gage Shopping Center. **Parking:** on-site.

BLIND TIGER BREWERY & RESTAURANT **Phone:** 785/267-2739

American
$7-$18

Beers brewed on site and hickory-smoked meats are big features at the casual restaurant. You will have fu watching staff work the huge beer tanks, making several award-winning beers. Extensive list of entrees o menu. Relaxing and festive atmosphere in this rustic restaurant. Casual dress. **Bar:** Full bar **Reservations:** accepted. **Hours:** 11 am-11 pm, Fri & Sat-midnight. Closed: 11/25, 12/25. **Address:** 417 SW 37th St 66611 **Location:** I-470, exit 6, 0.4 mi n on Topeka Blvd, then just e. **Parking:** on-site.

BOSS HAWG'S BARBEQUE **Phone:** 785/273-730

American
$6-$21

The barbecue eatery features reasonably priced food and a relaxed atmosphere. Service is fast and friendly A good and wholesome family restaurant. Large list of entrees, including both barbecued items and others without the barbecue. Casual dress. **Bar:** Full bar. **Reservations:** accepted. **Hours:** 11 am-9 pm, Fri & Sat 10 pm. Closed: 11/25, 12/25. **Address:** 2833 SW 29th St 66614 **Location:** I-470, exit 3, 1.5 mi e; a Brookwood Shopping Center, on terrace. **Parking:** on-site. CALL

CASA AUTHENTIC MEXICAN FOOD RESTAURANT **Phone:** 785/266-450

Mexican
$5-$21

This casual restaurant turns out well-prepared Mexican favorites. Prepared fresh daily, the guacamole i excellent. Casual dress. **Bar:** Full bar. **Reservations:** accepted. **Hours:** 11 am-9 pm, Thurs-Sat to 10 pm Closed major holidays. **Address:** 3320 S Topeka Blvd 66611 **Location:** I-470, exit 6, 0.7 mi n. **Parking** on-site.

NEW CITY **Phone:** 785/271-8646

Continental
$15-$28

Lunch service is typically a limited menu ordered from a deli counter while dinner is a full, sit-down service with white cloth-covered tables. Innovative dishes are offered on the regular menu, and there's always a nightly fresh fish special. Menu highlights include the killer salad, popular at both lunch and dinner, and the expertly prepared beef tenderloin served at dinner. Different risottos are served with many of the dishes Dressy casual. **Bar:** Full bar. **Reservations:** accepted. **Hours:** 11 am-2 & 5:30-8:30 pm, Fri-9:30 pm, Sa 5:30 pm-9:30 pm. Closed major holidays; also Sun. **Address:** 4005 SW Gage Center Dr 66604 **Location:** I-70, exit 358B (Gage St), 1.5 mi s; in Gage Shopping Center. **Parking:** on-site.

PAISANO'S ITALIAN RISTORANTE **Phone:** 785/273-010

Italian
$6-$16

Paisano's has a warm and intimate atmosphere as the pleasant backdrop for serving its authentic cuisine The Marco Polo fettucini Alfredo and lasagna are good choices, as is the primavera pasta for a vegetarian dish. Good beverage selection also. Casual dress. **Bar:** Full bar. **Reservations:** accepted. **Hours:** 11 am-10 pm, Fri & Sat-11 pm. Closed: 11/25, 12/25. **Address:** 4043 SW 10th Ave 66604 **Location:** I-70, exit 358B (Gage St), 1 mi s; in Fleming Place Shopping Plaza. **Parking:** on-site.

PAT'S PIG **Phone:** 785/862-7427

Barbecue
$4-$15

If you're a drag-racing fan, you'll love this place. The walls are adorned with photos of popular drag-racing stars, all have dined here. The restaurant features authentic hickory-smoked barbecue in a relaxed atmosphere. Try the ribs served whole—wow! Casual dress. **Bar:** Beer only. **Reservations:** not accepted **Hours:** 11 am-9 pm, Fri & Sat-10 pm. Closed major holidays; also Sun. **Address:** 5900 SW Topeka Blvd 66619 **Location:** I-470, exit 6, 2 mi s. **Parking:** on-site.

TIMBERLINE STEAKHOUSE & GRILL **Phone:** 785/228-1155

American
$8-$20

The casual restaurant's menu features fresh-cut steaks, poultry, pork, ribs and seafood. Casual dress. **Bar:** Full bar. **Reservations:** not accepted. **Hours:** 4 pm-10 pm, Fri & Sat 11 am-11 pm, Sun 11 am-9 pm. Closed: 11/25, 12/25. **Address:** 1425 SW Wanamaker Rd 66615 **Location:** I-70, exit 356 (Wanamaker Rd), 0.5 mi s. **Parking:** on-site. CALL

ULYSSES pop. 5,960

SINGLE TREE INN *Book at AAA.com* **Phone:** 620/356-1500

Hotel
Rates not provided

Address: 2033 W Oklahoma St 67880 **Location:** 1.5 mi w on US 160. **Facility:** Smoke free premises. 43 one-bedroom standard units, some with whirlpools. 2 stories (no elevator), interior corridors. **Parking:** on-site, winter plug-ins. **Amenities:** irons, hair dryers. **Leisure Activities:** limited exercise equipment. **Guest Services:** coin laundry, wireless Internet. **Business Services:** meeting rooms, PC.

/ SOME UNITS FEE

UNIONTOWN pop. 288

WYATT EARP INN & HOTEL **Phone:** 620/756-4990

Hotel
$65-$200 All Year

Address: 100 5th St 66779 **Location:** On SR 3; west side of town. **Facility:** Smoke free premises. 26 units. 25 one-bedroom standard units, some with kitchens and/or whirlpools. 1 one-bedroom suite. 1 story, interior corridors. *Bath:* combo or shower only. **Parking:** on-site. **Terms:** 30 day cancellation notice. **Guest Services:** wireless Internet. **Business Services:** meeting rooms.

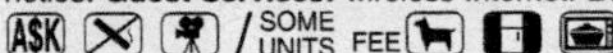

ASK / SOME UNITS FEE

WAKEENEY pop. 1,924

BEST WESTERN WAKEENEY INN & SUITES *Book great rates at AAA.com* **Phone:** (785)743-2700

AAA SAVE

Hotel
$70-$120 All Year

Address: 525 S 1st St 67672 **Location:** I-70, exit 127, just n. **Facility:** 50 one-bedroom standard units, some with efficiencies. 3 stories, interior corridors. *Bath:* combo or shower only. **Parking:** on-site, winter plug-ins. **Amenities:** irons, hair dryers. *Some:* high-speed Internet. **Pool(s):** heated indoor. **Leisure Activities:** whirlpool, exercise room. **Guest Services:** valet and coin laundry, wireless Internet. **Business Services:** PC. **Free Special Amenities: full breakfast and high-speed Internet.**

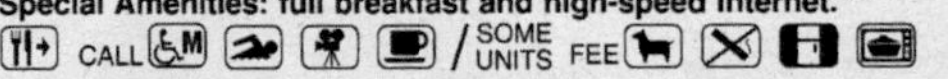

CALL / SOME UNITS FEE

AAA Benefit:
Members save up to 20%, plus 10% bonus points with rewards program.

SUPER 8 *Book at AAA.com* **Phone:** (785)743-6442

Hotel
$55-$85 All Year

Address: 709 S 13th St 67672 **Location:** I-70, exit 128, just n. **Facility:** Smoke free premises. 43 one-bedroom standard units. 2 stories (no elevator), interior corridors. *Bath:* combo or shower only. **Parking:** on-site, winter plug-ins. **Amenities:** hair dryers. **Guest Services:** coin laundry, wireless Internet.

ASK / SOME UNITS FEE

WAMEGO pop. 4,246

SIMMER MOTEL **Phone:** (785)456-2304

Motel
$46-$100 All Year

Address: 1215 Hwy 24 W 66547 **Location:** Jct SR 99, 0.5 mi w. **Facility:** 34 units. 27 one-bedroom standard units, some with whirlpools. 7 one-bedroom suites. 1 story, exterior corridors. **Parking:** on-site. **Terms:** 7 day cancellation notice. **Amenities:** voice mail. **Pool(s):** outdoor. **Leisure Activities:** playground. **Guest Services:** coin laundry, wireless Internet.

/ SOME UNITS FEE

WELLS

TRADER'S LODGE BED & BREAKFAST **Phone:** 785/488-3930

Bed & Breakfast
$70-$90 All Year

Address: 1392 210th Rd 67467 **Location:** 2 mi n; stay on blacktop. Located in a quiet rural area. **Facility:** Smoke free premises. 4 one-bedroom standard units. 2 stories (no elevator), interior corridors. *Bath:* shower only. **Parking:** on-site. **Terms:** check-in 5 pm, 7 day cancellation notice. **Amenities:** hair dryers. **Leisure Activities:** exercise room. **Guest Services:** TV in common area.

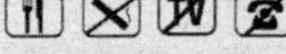

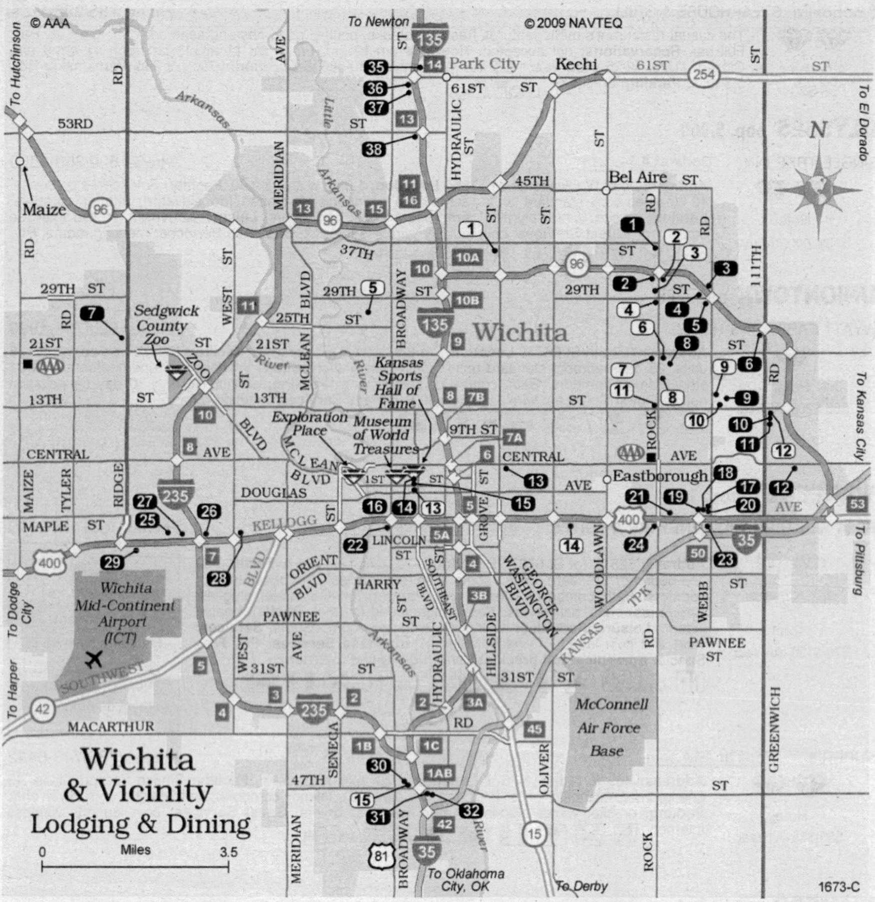

Wichita
& Vicinity
Lodging & Dining
0 Miles 3.5
© AAA
© 2009 NAVTEQ
1673-C
To Hutchinson
To Newton
To El Dorado
To Kansas City
To Pittsburg
To Oklahoma City, OK
To Derby
To Harper
To Dodge City
Park City
Kechi
Bel Aire
Maize
Wichita
Eastborough
Sedgwick County Zoo
Kansas Sports Hall of Fame
Exploration Place
Museum of World Treasures
Wichita Mid-Continent Airport (ICT)
McConnell Air Force Base
Arkansas
Little Arkansas
River
MERIDIAN AVE
BROADWAY
HYDRAULIC ST
ROCK RD
WOODLAWN
GREENWICH
WEBB
OLIVER
HILLSIDE
GROVE
SENECA
MAIZE
TYLER
RIDGE
WEST ST
MCLEAN BLVD
SOUTHEAST BLVD
GEORGE WASHINGTON BLVD
KANSAS TPK
SOUTHWEST
53RD
61ST
45TH
37TH
29TH ST
25TH ST
21ST ST
13TH ST
9TH ST
CENTRAL AVE
DOUGLAS AVE
1ST ST
KELLOGG
MAPLE ST
LINCOLN ST
ORIENT BLVD
HARRY ST
PAWNEE ST
31ST ST
MACARTHUR RD
47TH ST
111TH

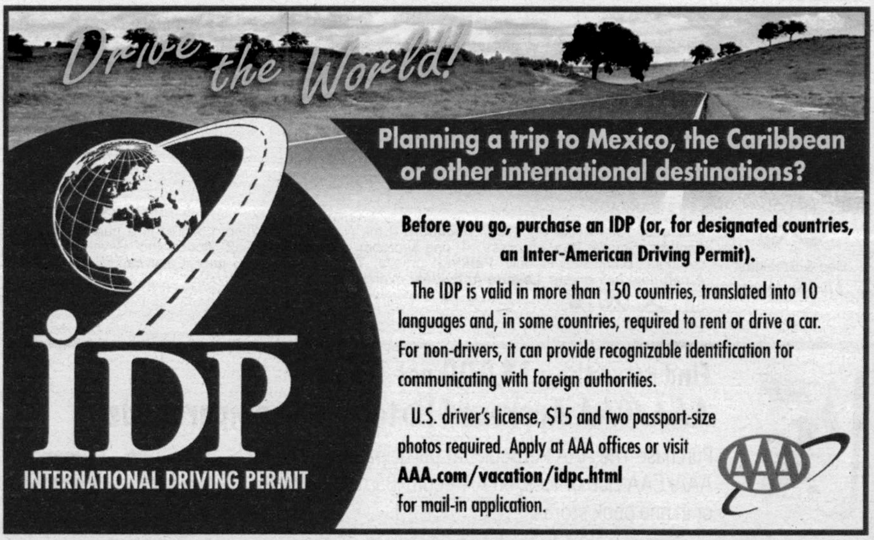

Drive the World!
Planning a trip to Mexico, the Caribbean or other international destinations?
Before you go, purchase an IDP (or, for designated countries, an Inter-American Driving Permit).
The IDP is valid in more than 150 countries, translated into 10 languages and, in some countries, required to rent or drive a car. For non-drivers, it can provide recognizable identification for communicating with foreign authorities.
U.S. driver's license, $15 and two passport-size photos required. Apply at AAA offices or visit AAA.com/vacation/idpc.html for mail-in application.
IDP
INTERNATIONAL DRIVING PERMIT
AAA

Airport Accommodations

Map Page	OA	WICHITA MID-CONTINENT	Diamond Rated	High Season	Page
29 / p. 384	AAA	**Best Western Airport Inn & Conference Center, 1 mi ne of airport**	♦♦	$91-$120 SAVE	387
26 / p. 384	AAA	**Quality Suites Airport, 1.3 mi ne of airport**	♦♦	$90-$129 SAVE	390

Wichita and Vicinity

This index helps you "spot" where approved lodgings and restaurants are located on the corresponding detailed maps. Lodging daily rate range is for comparison only and show the property's high season. Restaurant rate range is a combination of lunch and/or dinner. Turn to the listing page for more detailed rate information and consult display ads for special promotions.

WICHITA

Map Page	OA	Lodgings	Diamond Rated	High Season	Page
1 / p. 384		Wichita Inn-North	♦♦	$65-$79	391
2 / p. 384		Holiday Inn Express-North	♦♦	$102-$107	390
3 / p. 384		Candlewood Suites-Wichita Northeast	♦♦	$81-$82	387
4 / p. 384		TownePlace Suites by Marriott	♦♦	$107-$131	391
5 / p. 384		Courtyard By Marriott	♦♦♦	$125-$153	388
6 / p. 384		Hampton Inn & Suites	♦♦♦	$89-$159	389
7 / p. 384		Hawthorn Suites at Reflection Ridge	♦♦♦	$109-$139	389
8 / p. 384		Hilton Garden Inn-Wichita	♦♦♦	$139-$189	389
9 / p. 384		Homewood Suites by Hilton@The Waterfront	♦♦♦	$119-$169	390
10 / p. 384		Springhill Suites by Marriott	♦♦♦	$143-$175	391
11 / p. 384		Residence Inn by Marriott at Plazzio	♦♦♦	$143-$175	391
12 / p. 384		Cresthill Suites Hotel	♦♦	$108	388
13 / p. 384		Wesley Inn	♦♦	$91	391
14 / p. 384		Courtyard by Marriott Wichita at Old Town	♦♦♦	$161-$197	388
15 / p. 384		Hotel At Old Town	♦♦♦	$169-$399	390
16 / p. 384	AAA	**Hyatt Regency Wichita**	♦♦♦	$89-$229 SAVE	390
17 / p. 384		Fairfield Inn by Marriott	♦♦	$89-$99	388
18 / p. 384		Comfort Inn by Choice Hotels	♦♦	Rates not provided	388
19 / p. 384		Hampton Inn by Hilton	♦♦♦	$89-$149	389
20 / p. 384		Hawthorn Suites Wichita East	♦♦♦	$80-$116	389
21 / p. 384	AAA	**Wichita Inn-East**	♦♦	$54-$66 SAVE	391
22 / p. 384		Holiday Inn Hotel & Suites Convention Center	♦♦♦	$79-$109	390
23 / p. 384		Super 8-Wichita/East	♦♦	$51-$90	391
24 / p. 384	AAA	**Holiday Inn**	♦♦♦	$72-$101 SAVE	389
25 / p. 384		Candlewood Suites	♦♦	$69-$129	387
26 / p. 384	AAA	**Quality Suites Airport**	♦♦	$90-$129 SAVE	390
27 / p. 384		La Quinta Inn & Suites	♦♦♦	$89-$159	390
28 / p. 384	AAA	**Hampton Inn-West**	♦♦♦	$99-$169 SAVE	389
29 / p. 384	AAA	**Best Western Airport Inn & Conference Center**	♦♦	$91-$120 SAVE	387
30 / p. 384	AAA	**Best Western Governors Inn & Suites**	♦♦	$79-$89 SAVE	387
31 / p. 384	AAA	**Comfort Inn** - see color ad p 388	♦♦	$64-$72 SAVE	387

WICHITA (cont'd)

Map Page	OA	Lodgings (cont'd)	Diamond Rated	High Season	Page
32 / p. 384	AAA	**AmericInn of Wichita**	◆◆	$75-$94 SAVE	387

Map Page	OA	Restaurants	Diamond Rated	Cuisine	Meal Range	Page
1 / p. 384		Stroud's Restaurant Bar & Grill	◆◆	American	$8-$18	394
2 / p. 384		Chelseas Bar & Grill	◆◆	American	$7-$19	392
3 / p. 384		Jimmie's Diner	◆	American	$4-$8	392
4 / p. 384		Olive Tree Bistro	◆◆◆	Continental	$13-$37	392
5 / p. 384		Thai Tradition	◆◆	Thai	$6-$17	394
6 / p. 384		Yia Yia's Euro Bistro	◆◆◆	European	$8-$29	394
7 / p. 384		Malaysia Cafe	◆	Chinese	$4-$6	392
8 / p. 384		Red Rock Canyon Grill	◆◆	American	$12-$26	392
9 / p. 384		Chester's Chophouse & Wine Bar	◆◆◆	Steak	$6-$38	392
10 / p. 384		Abuelo's The Flavor of Mexico	◆◆◆	Mexican	$7-$17	391
11 / p. 384		Kwan Court	◆◆	Asian	$6-$22	392
12 / p. 384		BG Bolton's Sports Grill	◆◆	American	$7-$18	392
13 / p. 384		River City Brewery Co	◆◆	American	$7-$15	392
14 / p. 384		Scotch & Sirloin	◆◆◆	Steak	$6-$28	394
15 / p. 384		Hog Wild Pit Bar-B-Q	◆	Barbecue	$4-$8	392

PARK CITY

Map Page	OA	Lodgings	Diamond Rated	High Season	Page
35 / p. 384		Comfort Inn North	◆◆	$89-$110	374
36 / p. 384		Super 8-Wichita North/Park City	◆	$45-$70	374
37 / p. 384	AAA	**Park City Express Inn & Suites**	◆◆	$63-$80 SAVE	374
38 / p. 384	AAA	**Best Western Hotel & Suites**	◆◆	$70-$100 SAVE	374

WICHITA pop. 344,284 (See map and index starting on p. 384)

AMERICINN OF WICHITA *Book great rates at AAA.com* **Phone:** (316)529-4848 

Hotel
$75-$94 All Year

Address: 4848 S Laura 67216 **Location:** I-135, exit 1 A/B (47th St S), just ne. **Facility:** Smoke free premises. 52 one-bedroom standard units. 2 stories, interior corridors. *Bath:* combo or shower only. **Parking:** on-site. **Amenities:** voice mail, irons, hair dryers. **Pool(s):** heated indoor. **Leisure Activities:** whirlpool. **Guest Services:** valet laundry, wireless Internet. **Business Services:** PC.
/ SOME UNITS FEE

BEST WESTERN AIRPORT INN & CONFERENCE CENTER *Book great rates at AAA.com* **Phone:** (316)942-5600 

Hotel
$91-$120 All Year

Address: 6815 W Kellogg St 67209 **Location:** I-235, exit 7, 0.6 mi w on US 54 (S Frontage Rd). **Facility:** Smoke free premises. 129 units. 128 one-bedroom standard units, some with whirlpools. 1 one-bedroom suite with whirlpool. 2 stories, interior corridors. *Bath:* combo or shower only. **Parking:** on-site. **Amenities:** high-speed Internet, voice mail, irons, hair dryers. **Pool(s):** heated indoor. **Leisure Activities:** whirlpool, putting green, exercise room, shuffleboard. *Fee:* game room. **Guest Services:** valet and coin laundry, airport transportation-Wichita Mid-Continent Airport, area transportation-within 5 mi, wireless Internet. **Business Services:** meeting rooms, PC. **Free Special Amenities: expanded continental breakfast and high-speed Internet.**
/ SOME UNITS

AAA Benefit:
Members save up to 20%, plus 10% bonus points with rewards program.

BEST WESTERN GOVERNORS INN & SUITES *Book great rates at AAA.com* **Phone:** (316)522-0775 

Hotel
$79-$89 All Year

Address: 4742 S Emporia 67216 **Location:** I-135, exit 1 A/B (47th St S), just sw. **Facility:** 58 one-bedroom standard units, some with whirlpools. 3 stories, interior corridors. *Bath:* combo or shower only. **Parking:** on-site. **Amenities:** irons, hair dryers. *Some:* high-speed Internet. **Pool(s):** outdoor. **Leisure Activities:** limited exercise equipment. **Guest Services:** valet and coin laundry, wireless Internet. **Business Services:** meeting rooms, PC. **Free Special Amenities: continental breakfast and high-speed Internet.** / SOME UNITS FEE

AAA Benefit:
Members save up to 20%, plus 10% bonus points with rewards program.

CANDLEWOOD SUITES *Book at AAA.com* **Phone:** (316)942-0400 

Extended Stay Hotel
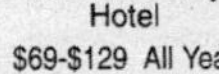
$69-$129 All Year

Address: 570 S Julia 67209 **Location:** I-235, exit 7, 0.4 mi nw on Dugan Rd. **Facility:** 81 units. 69 one-bedroom standard units with efficiencies. 12 one-bedroom suites with efficiencies. 3 stories, interior corridors. *Bath:* combo or shower only. **Parking:** on-site. **Amenities:** video library, DVD players, high-speed Internet, dual phone lines, voice mail, irons, hair dryers. **Leisure Activities:** exercise room. **Guest Services:** complimentary and valet laundry. **Business Services:** business center. ASK / SOME UNITS FEE

CANDLEWOOD SUITES-WICHITA NORTHEAST *Book at AAA.com* **Phone:** (316)634-6070 

Extended Stay Hotel
$81-$82 All Year

Address: 3141 N Webb Rd 67226 **Location:** SR 96, exit Webb Rd, just nw. **Facility:** 108 units. 107 one-bedroom standard units with kitchens. 1 one-bedroom suite with kitchen. 3 stories, interior corridors. *Bath:* combo or shower only. **Parking:** on-site. **Amenities:** video library, DVD players, high-speed Internet, voice mail, irons, hair dryers. **Leisure Activities:** exercise room. **Guest Services:** valet and coin laundry. ASK CALL / SOME UNITS FEE

COMFORT INN *Book great rates at AAA.com* **Phone:** (316)522-1800 31

Hotel
$64-$72 9/1-2/28
$59-$72 3/1-8/31

Address: 4849 S Laura 67216 **Location:** I-135, exit 1A/B (47th St S), just e. **Facility:** 114 units. 112 one-bedroom standard units. 2 one-bedroom suites. 2 stories (no elevator), interior corridors. *Bath:* combo or shower only. **Parking:** on-site. **Terms:** 7 day cancellation notice. **Amenities:** irons, hair dryers. **Pool(s):** heated outdoor. **Guest Services:** coin laundry, wireless Internet. **Business Services:** PC. **Free Special Amenities: full breakfast and high-speed Internet.**
(See color ad p 388)

(See map and index starting on p. 384)

COMFORT INN BY CHOICE HOTELS Book at AAA.com — **Phone:** 316/686-2844 — 18

Hotel
Rates not provided

Address: 9525 E Corporate Hills Dr 67207 **Location:** I-35, exit 50, just ne. **Facility:** 58 one-bedroom standard units. 3 stories, interior corridors. *Bath:* combo or shower only. **Parking:** on-site. **Amenities:** irons, hair dryers. **Pool(s):** heated indoor. **Leisure Activities:** whirlpool. **Guest Services:** valet laundry, wireless Internet. **Business Services:** PC.

/ SOME UNITS FEE

COURTYARD BY MARRIOTT Book great rates at AAA.com — **Phone:** (316)636-4600 — 5

Hotel
$125-$153 All Year

Address: 2975 N Webb Rd 67226 **Location:** SR 96, exit Webb Rd, just s. **Facility:** Smoke free premises. 90 units. 87 one-bedroom standard units, some with whirlpools. 3 one-bedroom suites. 3 stories, interior corridors. *Bath:* combo or shower only. **Parking:** on-site. **Terms:** cancellation fee imposed. **Amenities:** dual phone lines, voice mail, irons, hair dryers. **Pool(s):** heated indoor. **Leisure Activities:** whirlpool, exercise room. **Guest Services:** valet and coin laundry, wireless Internet. **Business Services:** meeting rooms, PC.

CALL / SOME UNITS

AAA Benefit: Members save a minimum 5% off the best available rate.

COURTYARD BY MARRIOTT WICHITA AT OLD TOWN Book great rates at AAA.com — **Phone:** (316)264-5300 — 14

Hotel
$161-$197 All Year

Address: 820 E 2nd St N 67202 **Location:** Just ne of jct Rock Island St. **Facility:** Smoke free premises. 128 units. 125 one-bedroom standard units. 3 one-bedroom suites. 6 stories, interior corridors. *Bath:* combo or shower only. **Parking:** on-site (fee) and valet. **Terms:** cancellation fee imposed. **Amenities:** video games (fee), high-speed Internet, dual phone lines, voice mail, irons, hair dryers. **Leisure Activities:** whirlpool, exercise room. **Guest Services:** valet and coin laundry, area transportation, wireless Internet. **Business Services:** meeting rooms, business center.

CALL / SOME UNITS

AAA Benefit: Members save a minimum 5% off the best available rate.

CRESTHILL SUITES HOTEL Book at AAA.com — **Phone:** (316)689-8000 — 12

Extended Stay Hotel
$108 All Year

Address: 12111 E Central Ave 67206 **Location:** 1.7 mi e of jct Webb Rd. **Facility:** 62 units. 36 one-bedroom standard units with kitchens. 18 one- and 8 two-bedroom suites with kitchens. 2 stories, interior corridors. *Bath:* combo or shower only. **Parking:** on-site. **Amenities:** video library, high-speed Internet, dual phone lines, voice mail, irons, hair dryers. **Pool(s):** outdoor. **Leisure Activities:** limited exercise equipment. **Guest Services:** complimentary and valet laundry, area transportation. **Business Services:** meeting rooms, business center.

ASK / SOME UNITS FEE

FAIRFIELD INN BY MARRIOTT Book great rates at AAA.com — **Phone:** (316)685-3777 — 17

Hotel
$89-$99 All Year

Address: 333 S Webb Rd 67207 **Location:** I-35, exit 50, just ne. **Facility:** Smoke free premises. 104 one-bedroom standard units. 2 stories (no elevator), interior corridors. **Parking:** on-site, winter plug-ins. **Terms:** cancellation fee imposed. **Amenities:** high-speed Internet, irons, hair dryers. **Pool(s):** heated outdoor. **Guest Services:** valet laundry, wireless Internet. **Business Services:** PC.

/ SOME UNITS

AAA Benefit: Members save a minimum 5% off the best available rate.

▼ See AAA listing p 387 ▼

See map and index starting on p. 384)

HAMPTON INN & SUITES Book great rates at AAA.com **Phone:** (316)636-5594 6

Hotel
$89-$159 All Year

Address: 2433 N Greenwich Rd 67226 **Location:** Just s of jct SR 96. **Facility:** Smoke free premises. 102 one-bedroom standard units. 4 stories, interior corridors. *Bath:* combo or shower only. **Parking:** on-site. **Terms:** 1-7 night minimum stay, cancellation fee imposed. **Amenities:** high-speed Internet, voice mail, irons, hair dryers. **Pool(s):** heated indoor. **Leisure Activities:** exercise room. **Guest Services:** valet and coin laundry, wireless Internet. **Business Services:** meeting rooms, business center.

CALL / SOME UNITS

AAA Benefit:
Members save up to 10% everyday!

HAMPTON INN BY HILTON Book great rates at AAA.com **Phone:** (316)686-3576 19

Hotel
$89-$149 All Year

Address: 9449 E Corporate Hills Dr 67207 **Location:** I-35, exit 50, just ne. **Facility:** 81 one-bedroom standard units. 3 stories, interior corridors. *Bath:* combo or shower only. **Parking:** on-site. **Terms:** 1-7 night minimum stay, cancellation fee imposed. **Amenities:** voice mail, irons, hair dryers. **Pool(s):** heated indoor. **Leisure Activities:** whirlpool. **Guest Services:** valet laundry, wireless Internet. **Business Services:** PC.

CALL / SOME UNITS

AAA Benefit:
Members save up to 10% everyday!

HAMPTON INN-WEST Book great rates at AAA.com **Phone:** (316)945-4100 28

Hotel
$99-$169 All Year

Address: 3800 W Kellogg Dr 67213 **Location:** US 54, exit West St, just e on north service road. **Facility:** 121 units. 120 one-bedroom standard units. 1 one-bedroom suite with whirlpool. 4 stories, interior corridors. *Bath:* combo or shower only. **Parking:** on-site. **Terms:** 1-7 night minimum stay, cancellation fee imposed. **Amenities:** voice mail, irons, hair dryers. *Some:* dual phone lines. **Pool(s):** outdoor. **Leisure Activities:** exercise room. **Guest Services:** valet laundry, airport transportation-Wichita Mid-Continent Airport, wireless Internet. **Business Services:** meeting rooms, business center.

/ SOME UNITS

AAA Benefit:
Members save up to 10% everyday!

HAWTHORN SUITES AT REFLECTION RIDGE Book at AAA.com **Phone:** (316)729-5700 7

Hotel
$109-$139 All Year

Address: 2405 N Ridge Rd 67205 **Location:** I-235, exit 10, 1.7 mi w on Zoo Blvd/21st St N, then just n. **Facility:** 52 one-bedroom standard units, some with whirlpools. 2 stories, interior corridors. *Bath:* combo or shower only. **Parking:** on-site. **Terms:** 3 day cancellation notice. **Amenities:** DVD players, voice mail, irons, hair dryers. **Leisure Activities:** exercise room. **Guest Services:** valet and coin laundry, wireless Internet. **Business Services:** meeting rooms, PC.

ASK / SOME UNITS FEE

HAWTHORN SUITES WICHITA EAST Book at AAA.com **Phone:** (316)686-7331 20

Extended Stay Hotel
$80-$116 All Year

Address: 411 S Webb Rd 67207 **Location:** I-35, exit 50, just ne. **Facility:** Smoke free premises. 64 one-bedroom standard units with kitchens. 2 stories (no elevator), exterior corridors. **Parking:** on-site. **Terms:** cancellation fee imposed. **Amenities:** voice mail, irons, hair dryers. *Some:* DVD players. **Pool(s):** outdoor. **Leisure Activities:** whirlpool, sports court. **Guest Services:** valet and coin laundry, wireless Internet. **Business Services:** PC.

ASK / SOME UNITS FEE

HILTON GARDEN INN-WICHITA Book great rates at AAA.com **Phone:** (316)219-4444 8

Hotel
$139-$189 All Year

Address: 2041 N Bradley Fair Pkwy 67206 **Location:** SR 96, exit Rock Rd, 1.7 mi s, just e. Located in a shopping area. **Facility:** 103 one-bedroom standard units. 3 stories, interior corridors. *Bath:* combo or shower only. **Parking:** on-site. **Terms:** 1-7 night minimum stay, cancellation fee imposed. **Amenities:** high-speed Internet, dual phone lines, voice mail, irons, hair dryers. **Pool(s):** heated indoor. **Leisure Activities:** whirlpool, exercise room. **Guest Services:** valet and coin laundry, area transportation, wireless Internet. **Business Services:** meeting rooms, business center.

CALL / SOME UNITS

Hilton Garden Inn
AAA Benefit:
Members save 5% or more everyday!

HOLIDAY INN Book great rates at AAA.com **Phone:** (316)686-7131 24

Hotel
$72-$101 All Year

Address: 549 S Rock Rd 67207 **Location:** I-35, exit 50, 0.5 mi w. **Facility:** Smoke free premises. 251 units. 238 one-bedroom standard units. 6 one- and 7 two-bedroom suites, some with whirlpools. 2-9 stories, interior/exterior corridors. *Bath:* combo or shower only. **Parking:** on-site, winter plug-ins. **Amenities:** dual phone lines, voice mail, irons, hair dryers. *Some:* high-speed Internet. **Dining:** Green Mill Restaurant & Bar, see separate listing. **Pool(s):** heated outdoor, heated indoor. **Leisure Activities:** whirlpool, exercise room. **Guest Services:** valet and coin laundry, airport transportation-Wichita Mid-Continent Airport, area transportation-within 5 mi, wireless Internet. **Business Services:** meeting rooms, business center. **Free Special Amenities: newspaper and high-speed Internet.**

/ SOME UNITS FEE

(See map and index starting on p. 384)

HOLIDAY INN EXPRESS-NORTH Book at AAA.com Phone: (316)634-3900 2

Hotel
$102-$107 All Year

Address: 7824 E 32nd St N 67226 **Location:** SR 96 E, exit Rock Rd, just sw. **Facility:** Smoke free premises. 70 one-bedroom standard units. 3 stories, interior corridors. *Bath:* combo or shower only. **Parking:** on-site. **Amenities:** dual phone lines, voice mail, irons, hair dryers. **Pool(s):** heated indoor. **Leisure Activities:** whirlpool. **Guest Services:** valet laundry, wireless Internet. **Business Services:** PC. ASK / SOME UNITS

HOLIDAY INN HOTEL & SUITES CONVENTION CENTER Book at AAA.com Phone: (316)269-2090 22

Hotel
$79-$109 All Year

Address: 221 E Kellogg St 67211 **Location:** Just sw of jct US 54/400 and Broadway. **Facility:** 150 units. 120 one-bedroom standard units. 30 one-bedroom suites. 7 stories, interior corridors. *Bath:* combo or shower only. **Parking:** on-site. **Amenities:** high-speed Internet, voice mail, irons, hair dryers. **Pool(s):** heated outdoor. **Leisure Activities:** sauna, whirlpool, exercise room. **Guest Services:** valet and coin laundry, area transportation, wireless Internet. **Business Services:** meeting rooms, business center. ASK CALL / SOME UNITS

HOMEWOOD SUITES BY HILTON@THE WATERFRONT Book great rates at AAA.com Phone: (316)260-8844 9

Extended Stay Hotel
$119-$169 All Year

Address: 1550 N Waterfront Pkwy 67206 **Location:** Just e of jct 13th and Webb rds. **Facility:** 104 units. 38 one-bedroom standard units with efficiencies. 63 one- and 3 two-bedroom suites with efficiencies, some with whirlpools. 4 stories, interior corridors. *Bath:* combo or shower only. **Parking:** on-site. **Terms:** 1-7 night minimum stay, cancellation fee imposed. **Amenities:** video library, DVD players, high-speed Internet, dual phone lines, voice mail, irons, hair dryers. **Pool(s):** heated indoor. **Leisure Activities:** whirlpool, putting green, exercise room. **Guest Services:** valet and coin laundry, area transportation, wireless Internet. **Business Services:** meeting rooms, business center. CALL / SOME UNITS FEE

HOMEWOOD SUITES Hilton
AAA Benefit:
Members save 5% or more everyday!

HOTEL AT OLD TOWN Book at AAA.com Phone: (316)267-4800 15

Extended Stay Hotel
$169-$399 All Year

Address: 830 E First St 67202 **Location:** Just nw of jct First and Mosley sts; center. **Facility:** Smoke free premises. 115 units. 103 one-bedroom standard units with efficiencies. 12 one-bedroom suites with efficiencies and whirlpools. 4 stories, interior corridors. *Bath:* combo or shower only. **Parking:** on-site. **Terms:** cancellation fee imposed. **Amenities:** video library, CD players, high-speed Internet, dual phone lines, voice mail, irons, hair dryers. **Leisure Activities:** exercise room. **Guest Services:** complimentary and valet laundry, wireless Internet. **Business Services:** conference facilities, PC. ASK CALL

HYATT REGENCY WICHITA Book great rates at AAA.com Phone: (316)293-1234 16

AAA SAVE
Hotel
$89-$229 All Year

Address: 400 W Waterman 67202 **Location:** Just w of jct Main St and Waterman; downtown. **Facility:** 303 units. 301 one-bedroom standard units. 2 one-bedroom suites. 17 stories, interior corridors. *Bath:* combo or shower only. **Parking:** on-site (fee). **Terms:** cancellation fee imposed. **Amenities:** video games (fee), dual phone lines, voice mail, irons, hair dryers. **Dining:** 2 restaurants. **Pool(s):** heated indoor. **Leisure Activities:** whirlpools, exercise room. **Guest Services:** valet laundry, airport transportation-Wichita Mid-Continent Airport, area transportation-within 2 mi, wireless Internet. **Business Services:** conference facilities, business center. **Free Special Amenities: expanded continental breakfast.** / SOME UNITS

HYATT HOTELS & RESORTS
AAA Benefit:
Ask for the AAA rate and save 10%.

LA QUINTA INN & SUITES Book at AAA.com Phone: (316)943-2181 27

Hotel
$89-$159 All Year

Address: 5500 W Kellogg Dr 67209 **Location:** I-235, exit 7, just nw. **Facility:** 140 units. 132 one-bedroom standard units. 8 one-bedroom suites. 5 stories, interior corridors. *Bath:* combo or shower only. **Parking:** on-site. **Amenities:** video games (fee), voice mail, irons, hair dryers. *Some:* high-speed Internet. **Pool(s):** heated indoor. **Leisure Activities:** whirlpool, exercise room. **Guest Services:** valet and coin laundry, wireless Internet. **Business Services:** meeting rooms, PC. ASK / SOME UNITS

QUALITY SUITES AIRPORT Book great rates at AAA.com Phone: (316)945-2600 26

AAA SAVE

Hotel
$90-$129 All Year

Address: 658 Westdale Dr 67209 **Location:** Jct I-235 and US 54. Adjacent to Towne West Square. **Facility:** 50 one-bedroom standard units. 3 stories, interior corridors. **Parking:** on-site. **Terms:** 3 day cancellation notice. **Amenities:** irons, hair dryers. **Pool(s):** outdoor. **Leisure Activities:** exercise room. **Guest Services:** valet laundry, airport transportation-Wichita Mid-Continent Airport, area transportation-within 5 mi, wireless Internet. **Business Services:** meeting rooms, PC. **Free Special Amenities: expanded continental breakfast and high-speed Internet.** / SOME UNITS FEE

See map and index starting on p. 384)

RESIDENCE INN BY MARRIOTT AT PLAZZIO *Book great rates at AAA.com* Phone: (316)682-7300 11

Extended Stay Hotel
$143-$175 All Year

Address: 1212 N Greenwich 67206 **Location:** SR 96, exit 13th St, 0.5 mi sw. **Facility:** Smoke free premises. 93 units. 54 one-bedroom standard units with kitchens. 32 one- and 7 two-bedroom suites with kitchens. 4 stories, interior corridors. *Bath:* combo or shower only. **Parking:** on-site. **Terms:** cancellation fee imposed. **Amenities:** video library (fee), high-speed Internet, voice mail, irons, hair dryers. *Some:* DVD players. **Pool(s):** heated outdoor. **Leisure Activities:** whirlpool, putting green, exercise room, sports court. **Guest Services:** valet and coin laundry, wireless Internet. **Business Services:** meeting rooms, business center.

CALL / SOME UNITS FEE

AAA Benefit:
Members save a minimum 5% off the best available rate.

SPRINGHILL SUITES BY MARRIOTT *Book great rates at AAA.com* Phone: (316)681-1800 10

Contemporary Hotel
$143-$175 All Year

Address: 1220 N Greenwich Rd 67226 **Location:** SR 96, exit 13th St, 0.5 mi sw. **Facility:** Smoke free premises. 102 one-bedroom standard units. 4 stories, interior corridors. *Bath:* combo or shower only. **Parking:** on-site. **Terms:** cancellation fee imposed. **Amenities:** high-speed Internet, voice mail, irons, hair dryers. *Some:* DVD players (fee). **Pool(s):** heated indoor. **Leisure Activities:** exercise room. **Guest Services:** coin laundry, wireless Internet. **Business Services:** meeting rooms, business center.

CALL

AAA Benefit:
Members save a minimum 5% off the best available rate.

SUPER 8-WICHITA/EAST *Book at AAA.com* Phone: (316)686-3888 23

Hotel
$51-$90 All Year

Address: 527 S Webb Rd 67207 **Location:** I-35, exit 50, just e. **Facility:** 119 one-bedroom standard units. 3 stories (no elevator), interior corridors. **Parking:** on-site. **Amenities:** safes (fee), hair dryers. **Guest Services:** coin laundry, wireless Internet. **Business Services:** meeting rooms, business center.

ASK / SOME UNITS FEE

TOWNEPLACE SUITES BY MARRIOTT *Book great rates at AAA.com* Phone: (316)631-3773 4

Extended Stay Hotel
$107-$131 All Year

Address: 9444 E 29th St N 67226 **Location:** SR 96, exit Webb Rd, just sw. **Facility:** Smoke free premises. 82 units. 69 one-bedroom standard units with efficiencies. 13 one-bedroom suites with efficiencies. 3 stories, interior corridors. *Bath:* combo or shower only. **Parking:** on-site. **Terms:** cancellation fee imposed. **Amenities:** dual phone lines, voice mail, irons, hair dryers. **Leisure Activities:** exercise room. **Guest Services:** valet and coin laundry, wireless Internet. **Business Services:** PC.

CALL / SOME UNITS FEE

AAA Benefit:
Members save a minimum 5% off the best available rate.

WESLEY INN Phone: (316)858-3343 13

Hotel
$91 All Year

Address: 3343 E Central Ave 67208 **Location:** Just e of jct Hillside St. Located across from Wesley Medical Center. **Facility:** Smoke free premises. 74 one-bedroom standard units. 4 stories, interior corridors. *Bath:* combo or shower only. **Parking:** on-site. **Amenities:** video library, voice mail, irons, hair dryers. **Guest Services:** valet and coin laundry, wireless Internet. **Business Services:** PC.

ASK FEE / SOME UNITS FEE

WICHITA INN-EAST Phone: (316)685-8291 21

Hotel
$54-$66 All Year

Address: 8220 E Kellogg Dr 67207 **Location:** I-35, exit 50, 0.4 mi w. **Facility:** 91 one-bedroom standard units. 3 stories, interior corridors. **Parking:** on-site. **Amenities:** video library, voice mail, irons, hair dryers. **Guest Services:** valet and coin laundry, wireless Internet. **Free Special Amenities: continental breakfast and high-speed Internet.** / SOME UNITS

WICHITA INN-NORTH Phone: (316)636-2022 1

Hotel
$65-$79 All Year

Address: 3741 N Rock Rd 67226 **Location:** SR 96, exit Rock Rd, just n. **Facility:** 100 one-bedroom standard units. 3 stories, interior corridors. *Bath:* combo or shower only. **Parking:** on-site. **Amenities:** video library, voice mail, irons, hair dryers. **Guest Services:** valet and coin laundry, wireless Internet. ASK FEE / SOME UNITS

— WHERE TO DINE —

ABUELO'S THE FLAVOR OF MEXICO Phone: 316/634-2230 10

Mexican
$7-$17

A little extra attention to presentation enhances the traditional Mexican dishes. Distinguishing the casual decor are some upscale touches. Casual dress. **Bar:** Full bar. **Hours:** 11 am-10 pm, Fri & Sat-11 pm. Closed: 11/25, 12/25. **Address:** 1413 N Waterfront Pkwy 67206 **Location:** 1.2 mi w of jct SR 96 and 13th St. **Parking:** on-site.

(See map and index starting on p. 384)

BG BOLTON'S SPORTS GRILL **Phone:** 316/558-8600 12

American
$7-$18

Guests can dine in the bar area or in the separate dining room of the nicely decorated sports grill, which prepares a good variety of dishes. Casual dress. **Bar:** Full bar. **Hours:** 11 am-10 pm, Fri & Sat-11 pm Closed: 11/25, 12/25. **Address:** 11423 E 13th St 67206 **Location:** Just w of jct SR 96. **Parking:** on-site.

CHELSEAS BAR & GRILL **Phone:** 316/636-1103 2

American
$7-$19

At Chelsea's you'll enjoy well-prepared entrees that include beef, chicken, seafood, duck and veal dishes as well as fresh ingredients in all courses. An open grill allows you to watch while the chef prepares your meals. Servers are prompt and friendly. Casual dress. **Bar:** Full bar. **Reservations:** accepted. **Hours:** 11 am-10 pm, Fri & Sat-11 pm, Sun 5 pm-9 pm. Closed: 1/1, 12/25. **Address:** 2949 N Rock Rd 67226 **Location:** 0.5 mi s of jct SR 96. **Parking:** on-site.

CHESTER'S CHOPHOUSE & WINE BAR **Phone:** 316/201-1300 9

Steak
$6-$38

Upscale decor and attractive dishes are common observations at the fine-dining restaurant. Dressy casual. **Bar:** Full bar. **Reservations:** suggested. **Hours:** 4:30 pm-9 pm, Fri & Sat-10 pm. Closed: 11/25, 12/25. **Address:** 1550 N Webb Rd 67206 **Location:** 1.8 mi s of jct SR 96. **Parking:** on-site.

GRANITE CITY FOOD & BREWERY **Phone:** 316/636-5050

American
$6-$20

The popular restaurant and brewery caters to travelers, business professionals, sports enthusiasts and children. The varying menu centers on American fare. Favorites include honey-rosemary filet mignon, barbecue ribs, a nice array of salads and classic sandwiches. Save room for one of the tasty, large-portioned desserts. Five to six beer varieties are brewed on the premises. Casual dress. **Bar:** Full bar. **Reservations:** not accepted. **Hours:** 11 am-midnight, Fri & Sat-1 am, Sun 10 am-10 pm. Closed: 11/25, 12/25. **Address:** 2244 N Webb Rd 67226 **Location:** Just n of E 21st St. **Parking:** on-site.

GREEN MILL RESTAURANT & BAR **Phone:** 316/687-6455

Italian
$6-$20

The eatery prepares top-notch pizzas; a good variety of appetizers, salads, sandwiches and pasta; and some steaks and seafood. Diablo wings are a great way to start the meal. Casual dress. **Bar:** Full bar. **Reservations:** accepted. **Hours:** 11 am-10 pm. Closed: 12/25. **Address:** 549 S Rock Rd 67207 **Location:** I-35, exit 50, 0.5 mi w; in Holiday Inn. **Parking:** on-site.

HOG WILD PIT BAR-B-Q **Phone:** 316/522-7636 15

Barbecue
$4-$8

Tender, flavorful barbecue is ordered via the service line. Those who don't carry out their food have a choice from plenty of seats in the good-sized dining room. Casual dress. **Hours:** 11 am-8 pm. Closed major holidays. **Address:** 662 E 47th St 67216 **Location:** I-135, exit 1B, just s. **Parking:** on-site.

JIMMIE'S DINER **Phone:** 316/636-1818 3

American
$4-$8

The diner's decor, including jukeboxes at each table, harks back to the 1950s. This place hops at breakfast time. Casual dress. **Hours:** 6 am-9 pm. Closed: 11/25, 12/25. **Address:** 3111 N Rock Rd 67226 **Location:** Just s of jct SR 96. **Parking:** on-site.

KWAN COURT **Phone:** 316/634-1828 11

Asian
$6-$22

An expansive sushi bar complements many traditional Japanese and Chinese dishes. Casual dress. **Bar:** Full bar. **Reservations:** accepted. **Hours:** 11 am-2:30 & 5-10 pm, Fri & Sat-11 pm. Closed major holidays. **Address:** 1443 N Rock Rd 67206 **Location:** Just n of jct 13th St. **Parking:** on-site.

MALAYSIA CAFE **Phone:** 316/685-8838 7

Chinese
$4-$6

Guests order at the register before grabbing a cafe table to enjoy their hearty portions of Malaysian fare. Casual dress. **Hours:** 11 am-9:30 pm, Sat & Sun from noon. Closed: 11/25, 12/25. **Address:** 7777 E 21st St, Suite 150 67206 **Location:** Just w of jct Rock Rd. **Parking:** on-site.

OLIVE TREE BISTRO **Phone:** 316/636-1100 4

Continental
$13-$37

This bistro features expertly prepared, high-quality foods and fresh ingredients served with nice presentation. The menu features a variety of dry-aged steaks but has other dishes such as lamb and lobster. Semi-formal attire. **Bar:** Full bar. **Reservations:** suggested. **Hours:** 5:30 pm-9 pm, Fri & Sat-10 pm, Sun 10:30 am-2:30 pm. Closed major holidays. **Address:** 2949 N Rock Rd 67226 **Location:** 0.5 mi s of jct SR 96. **Parking:** on-site.

RED ROCK CANYON GRILL **Phone:** 316/636-1844 8

American
$12-$26

Featuring a wood-fired rotisserie, the restaurant prepares steaks, lamb, pork chops, fresh fish and ribs. The open dining room provides a view of the show kitchen and bar, which centers the room. Casual dress. **Bar:** Full bar. **Reservations:** accepted. **Hours:** 5 pm-10 pm, Fri & Sat-11 pm, Sun 11 am-9 pm. Closed: 11/25, 12/25. **Address:** 1844 N Rock Rd 67207 **Location:** SR 96, exit Rock Rd, 2.6 mi s; in Bradley Fair Shopping Center. **Parking:** on-site.

RIVER CITY BREWERY CO **Phone:** 316/263-2739 13

American
$7-$15

The brewery's six draft microbrews paired with the eatery's innovative pizza creations and varied comfort foods. The colorful spot is in the renovated Old Town district. Casual dress. **Bar:** Full bar. **Reservations:** not accepted. **Hours:** 11 am-10 pm, Fri & Sat-11 pm. Closed: 11/25, 12/25. **Address:** 150 N Mosley St 67202 **Location:** Just se of jct First and Mosley sts. **Parking:** on-site.

(See map and index starting on p. 384)

SCOTCH & SIRLOIN Phone: 316/685-8701 (14

Steak
$6-$28

The Scotch & Sirloin features an upscale, Tudor-pub atmosphere and a cuisine offering "sterling silver beef, prime rib and gourmet cheesecake as their specialties. Business travelers and couples enjoy this restaurant. Good service. Casual dress. **Bar:** Full bar. **Reservations:** suggested. **Hours:** 11 am-3 & 5-1 pm, Sat & Sun from 5 pm. Closed major holidays. **Address:** 5325 E Kellogg St 67218 **Location:** I-35, ex 50, 2.4 mi w. **Parking:** on-site.

STROUD'S RESTAURANT BAR & GRILL Phone: 316/838-2454 (1

American
$8-$18

Enjoy home-style cooking, a casual family atmosphere and friendly service at Stroud's, which is famous fc its succulent pan-fried chicken. The menu also lists pork chops, chicken-fried steak and seafood. Th restaurant is located in a rural area. Casual dress. **Bar:** Full bar. **Hours:** 5 pm-9 pm, Fri 11 am-2 & 4-10 pm Sat 4 pm-10 pm, Sun 11 am-9 pm. Closed: 7/4, 12/25. **Address:** 3661 N Hillside St 67219 **Location:** Just of jct SR 96. **Parking:** on-site.

THAI TRADITION Phone: 316/687-1500 (5

Thai
$6-$17

Authentic and well-prepared Thai cuisine is complemented by Chinese and vegetarian selections at this family-owned restaurant. The lemon grass soup bursts with flavor with the addition of kalanga roots. Try this favorite of the locals: savory moonflower roast duck. Casual dress. **Bar:** Full bar. **Hours:** 11 am-2:30 & 5-1 pm, Fri & Sat-11 pm. Closed major holidays. **Address:** 650 N Carriage Pkwy, Suite 120 67208 **Location:** mi n of US 54, on Edgemoor, just e. **Parking:** on-site.

WHISKEY CREEK WOOD FIRE GRILL Phone: 316/265-0707

American
$9-$22

Guests can watch as their steak is cooked over a wood-burning fire and throw peanut shells on the floor a this fun, casual steakhouse. The menu's wide variety includes chicken, pasta and barbecue dishes. A rusti theme evokes the wild, wild West. Casual dress. **Bar:** Full bar. **Hours:** 11 am-10 pm, Fri & Sat-11 pm, Sun 9 pm. Closed: 11/25, 12/25. **Address:** 233 N Mosley 67202 **Location:** Just s of jct E 2nd St N. **Parking** on-site.

YIA YIA'S EURO BISTRO Phone: 316/634-1000 (6

European
$8-$29

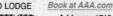

Stained-glass sconces cast a warm glow on perfectly set tables that are ideal for entertaining a group or couple out for a romantic dinner. The cuisine is European inspired with a few Southwestern twists. Try the succulent grilled beef tenderloin topped with a black pepper Gorgonzola Chianti sauce. The desserts also are delicious. Casual dress. **Bar:** Full bar. **Reservations:** accepted. **Hours:** 11 am-10 pm, Fri & Sat-11 pm Closed: 7/4, 12/25. **Address:** 8115 E 21st St N 67226 **Location:** SR 96, exit Rock Rd, 1.7 mi s. **Parking** on-site.

WINFIELD pop. 12,206

COMFORT INN Book at AAA.com Phone: (620)221-7529

Hotel
$90-$99 All Year

Address: 3800 S Pike Rd 67156 **Location:** On US 77, 1 mi s. **Facility:** 51 one-bedroom standard units, some with whirlpools. 2 stories (no elevator), interior/exterior corridors. **Parking:** on-site **Amenities:** safes, irons, hair dryers. **Pool(s):** outdoor. **Leisure Activities:** exercise room. **Guest Services:** valet and coin laundry, wireless Internet. **Business Services:** meeting rooms, PC.

ASK / SOME UNITS FEE

ECONO LODGE Book at AAA.com Phone: (620)221-9050

Motel
$60-$120 All Year

Address: 1710 Main St 67156 **Location:** 0.5 mi s of jct US 77 and 160. **Facility:** 29 one-bedroom standard units. 2 stories (no elevator), exterior corridors. **Parking:** on-site. **Amenities:** hair dryers. **Guest Services:** wireless Internet. ASK / SOME UNITS FEE

The Gateway Arch, Jefferson National Expansion Memorial, St. Louis

Missouri Orientation Map To Destinations

Major destinations are color-coded to index boxes, which display vicinity communities you will find listed within that destination's section of the book.
Cities outside major destination vicinities are listed in alphabetical order throughout the book.
Use the *Comprehensive City Index* at the back of this book to find every city's listing locations.

AVA pop. 3,021

AVA SUPER 8 *Book at AAA.com* **Phone:** (417)683-1343

Hotel
$70-$90 All Year

Address: 1711 S Jefferson St 65608 **Location:** Jct SR 5 S and 76; 1.5 mi s of SR 14. **Facility:** 40 one-bedroom standard units, some with whirlpools. 2 stories (no elevator), interior corridors. **Parking:** on-site. **Amenities:** high-speed Internet, voice mail, hair dryers. *Some:* irons. **Guest Services:** coin laundry, wireless Internet. **Business Services:** meeting rooms, PC.
ASK CALL / SOME UNITS FEE

BALLWIN—See St. Louis p. 552.

BELTON pop. 21,730

COMFORT INN - BELTON *Book at AAA.com* **Phone:** 816/322-8700

Hotel
Rates not provided

Address: 17205 S US Hwy 71 64012 **Location:** Jct US 71, just e on SR 58, then just s on E Outer Rd. **Facility:** 50 one-bedroom standard units. 2 stories (no elevator), interior corridors. *Bath:* combo or shower only. **Parking:** on-site. **Amenities:** high-speed Internet, dual phone lines, voice mail, irons, hair dryers. **Pool(s):** outdoor. **Leisure Activities:** limited exercise equipment. **Guest Services:** wireless Internet. **Business Services:** PC. / SOME UNITS

WHERE TO DINE

ODEN'S BBQ **Phone:** 816/322-3072

American
$5-$15

Families prefer this spot for casual dining in a rustic, country-style atmosphere. Included in a good offering of sandwich selections are barbecue beef, pork and chicken. Service is friendly and efficient. Casual dress. **Reservations:** not accepted. **Hours:** 11 am-9 pm, Fri & Sat-10 pm, Sun-8 pm. Closed major holidays; also Mon. **Address:** 1302 N Scott St 64012 **Location:** Jct US 71, just w on 155th St, then 0.8 mi s. **Parking:** on-site.

BERKELEY—See St. Louis p. 552.

BETHANY pop. 3,087

COMFORT INN BETHANY *Book great rates at AAA.com* **Phone:** 660/425-8006

AAA SAVE
Hotel
Rates not provided

Address: 496 S 39th St 64424 **Location:** I-35, exit 92, just nw. **Facility:** 50 one-bedroom standard units, some with whirlpools. 3 stories, interior corridors. *Bath:* combo or shower only. **Parking:** on-site. **Amenities:** irons, hair dryers. *Some:* high-speed Internet. **Pool(s):** heated indoor. **Leisure Activities:** whirlpool, exercise room. **Guest Services:** coin laundry, wireless Internet. **Business Services:** PC. **Free Special Amenities: continental breakfast and high-speed Internet.**
/ SOME UNITS FEE

FAMILY BUDGET INN *Book great rates at AAA.com* **Phone:** (660)425-7915

AAA SAVE
Motel
$45-$54 All Year

Address: 4014 Miller St 64424 **Location:** I-35, exit 92. **Facility:** 78 one-bedroom standard units. 1 story, interior corridors. *Bath:* combo or shower only. **Parking:** on-site, winter plug-ins. **Terms:** cancellation fee imposed. **Amenities:** *Some:* irons, hair dryers. **Pool(s):** outdoor. **Guest Services:** coin laundry, wireless Internet. **Business Services:** meeting rooms. **Free Special Amenities: continental breakfast and high-speed Internet.** / SOME UNITS FEE

WHERE TO DINE

TOOT-TOOT FAMILY RESTAURANT **Phone:** 660/425-7001

AAA
American
$4-$15

Most people order the buffet, which is offered for lunch and dinner and is a good value. Full menu available. The good-tasting food is appetizingly presented, the server staff is friendly and helpful, and the decor is rustic Americana. Casual dress. **Reservations:** not accepted. **Hours:** 6 am-10 pm. Closed: 12/25. **Address:** 3101 Miller St 64424 **Location:** I-35, exit 92, 0.3 mi w on US 136. **Parking:** on-site.

BEVIER pop. 723

WHERE TO DINE

THE PEAR TREE **Phone:** 660/773-6666

American
$17-$50

There's much owner pride here, and rightfully so. In an atmosphere suitable for both casual and special-occasion dining, guests nosh on exceptional onion rings in between bites of outstanding beef and seafood specialties. The luscious cheesecake is on equal footing. The rural, historic setting is worth driving the few extra miles. Casual dress. **Bar:** Full bar. **Reservations:** accepted. **Hours:** Open 3/1-12/31 & 2/1-2/28; 4:30 pm-9:30 pm. Closed: major holidays, 12/24; also Sun & Mon. **Address:** 222 N Macon St 63532 **Location:** Jct US 63 and 36, 5.4 mi w on US 36, then 1 mi s. **Parking:** street.

BLUE SPRINGS—See Kansas City p. 484.

BOLIVAR pop. 9,143

COMFORT INN BOLIVAR *Book at AAA.com* **Phone:** (417)326-6169

Hotel

$70-$80 All Year

Address: 2451 Tower Dr 65613 **Location:** SR 13, exit T, just w to N Outer Rd, then 0.5 mi w. **Facility:** 42 one-bedroom standard units, some with whirlpools. 2 stories (no elevator), interior corridors. *Bath:* combo or shower only. **Parking:** on-site. **Terms:** cancellation fee imposed. **Amenities:** high-speed Internet, voice mail, irons, hair dryers. **Leisure Activities:** exercise room. **Guest Services:** coin laundry, wireless Internet. **Business Services:** meeting rooms, business center.

ASK CALL / SOME UNITS

BOONVILLE pop. 8,202

BOONVILLE COMFORT INN *Book great rates at AAA.com* **Phone:** (660)882-5317

Hotel

$60-$150 All Year

Address: 2427 Mid America Industrial Dr 65233 **Location:** I-70, exit 101, just sw. **Facility:** 51 one-bedroom standard units. 2 stories (no elevator), interior corridors. *Bath:* combo or shower only. **Parking:** on-site. **Amenities:** safes (fee), irons, hair dryers. **Pool(s):** heated indoor. **Leisure Activities:** whirlpool. **Guest Services:** coin laundry, wireless Internet. **Free Special Amenities: expanded continental breakfast and high-speed Internet.**

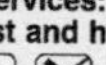

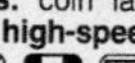

/ SOME UNITS FEE

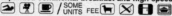

RIVERCENE MANSION BED & BREAKFAST **Phone:** 660/848-2497

Historic Bed & Breakfast

Rates not provided

Address: 127 CR 463 65274 **Location:** I-70, exit 103, 3.6 mi n to CR 463, then just e. Located in a quiet rural area. **Facility:** This charming 1869 inn offers large, antique-filled rooms, and is on the National Register of Historic Places. Smoke free premises. 9 units. 8 one- and 1 two-bedroom standard units, some with whirlpools. 3 stories (no elevator), interior corridors. *Bath:* combo or shower only. **Parking:** on-site. **Amenities:** hair dryers. **Guest Services:** wireless Internet.

/ SOME UNITS

Destination Branson

pop. 6,050

A lot of people think "shows" when they think of Branson, but there's much more to this southwestern Missouri city.

Nestled in the heart of the Ozarks, Branson offers all kinds of outdoor recreation, from boating and fishing to hiking and spelunking. Shopping is another favorite pastime, and Branson Landing is the latest place to do it. This waterfront shopping "village" also features live entertainment and a dancing fountain show.

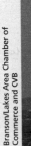

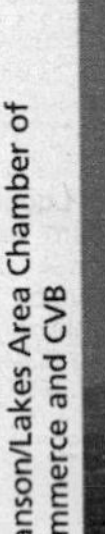

Branson/Lakes Area Chamber of Commerce and CVB

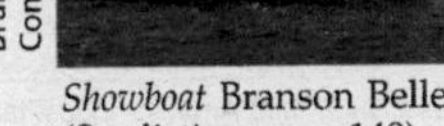

Showboat Branson Belle.
(See listing page 140)

Branson/Lakes Area Chamber of Commerce and CVB

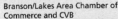

Silver Dollar City, Branson.
(See listing page 137)

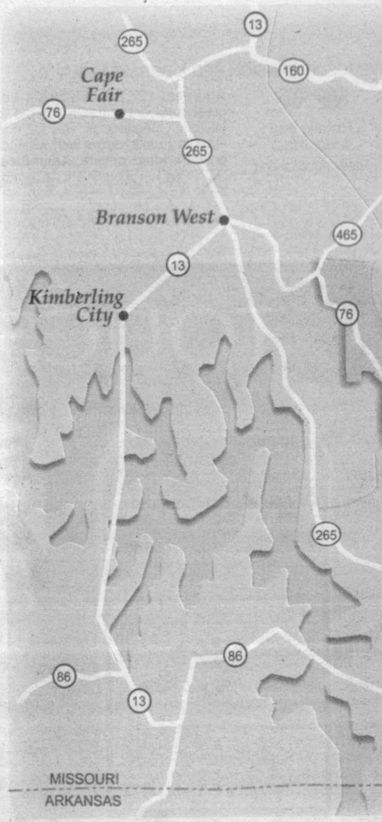

Places included in this AAA Destination City:

Branson Landing.
(See mention page 142)

Branson/Lakes Area Chamber of Commerce & CVB

65
465
76
160
76
Branson
65
Hollister
65 BUS
65
Ridgedale
MISSOURI
ARKANSAS

See Vicinity map page 402

Missouri Division of Tourism

Table Rock Lake.
(See mention page 141)

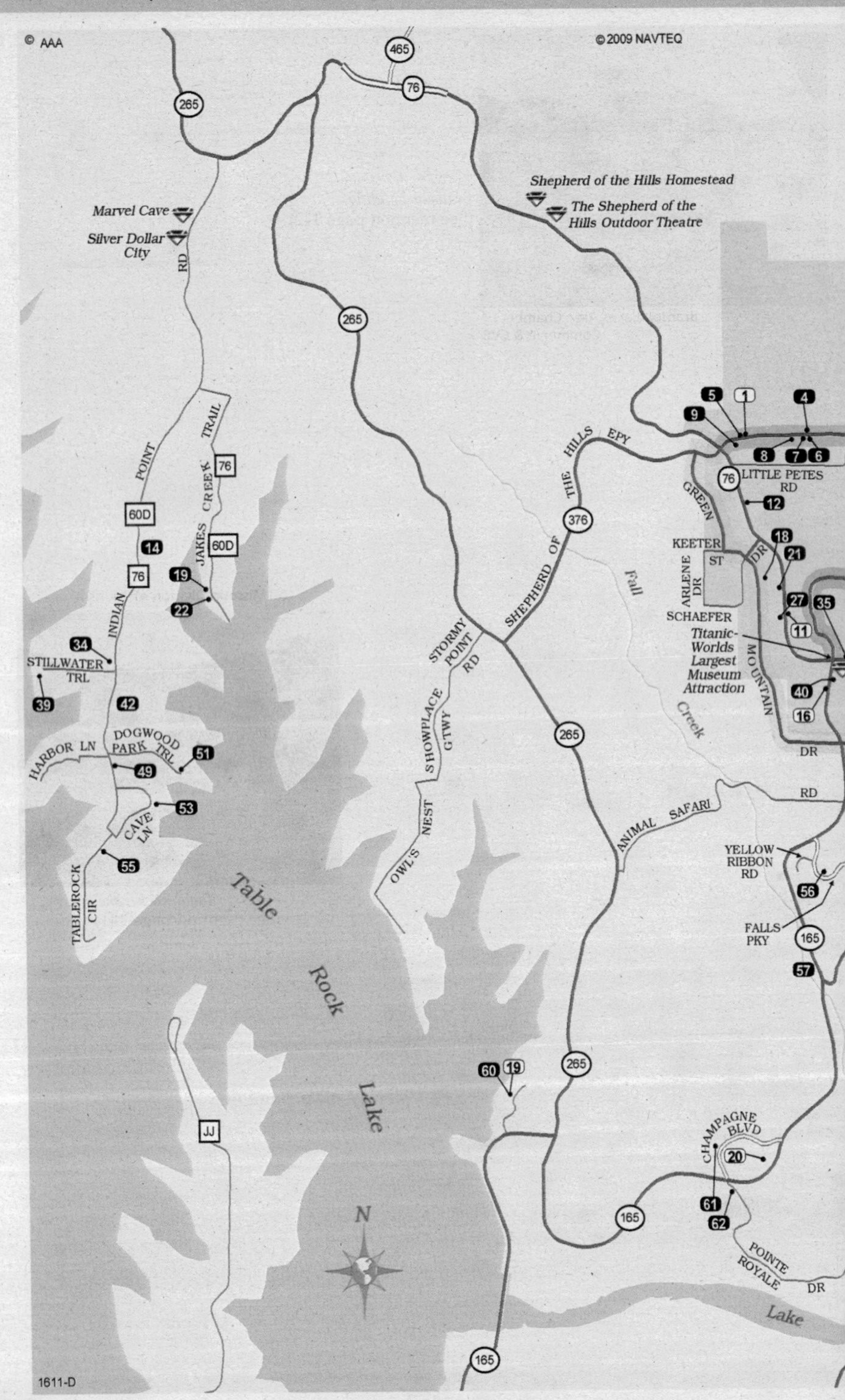
© AAA
© 2009 NAVTEQ
Marvel Cave
Silver Dollar City
Shepherd of the Hills Homestead
The Shepherd of the Hills Outdoor Theatre
Titanic-Worlds Largest Museum Attraction
Table Rock Lake
Lake
Fall Creek
INDIAN POINT RD
JAKES CREEK TRAIL
SHEPHERD OF THE HILLS EPY
STORMY POINT RD
SHOWPLACE GTWY
OWL'S NEST
ANIMAL SAFARI
LITTLE PETES RD
GREEN MOUNTAIN DR
KEETER ST
ARLENE DR
SCHAEFER
STILLWATER TRL
HARBOR LN
DOGWOOD PARK TRL
CAVE LN
TABLEROCK CIR
YELLOW RIBBON RD
FALLS PKY
CHAMPAGNE BLVD
POINTE ROYALE DR
N
1611-D

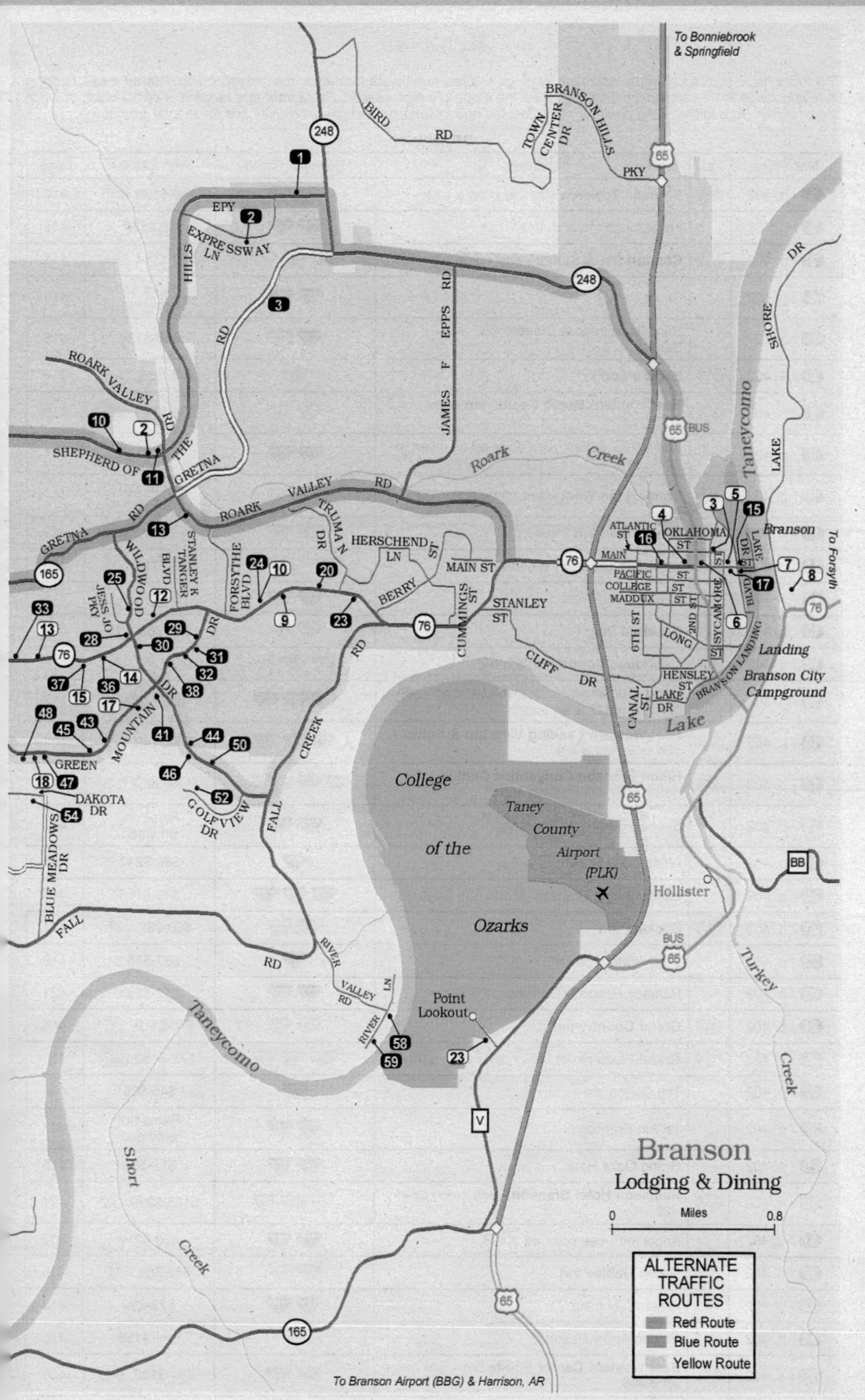
Branson
Lodging & Dining
Miles
0
0.8
ALTERNATE TRAFFIC ROUTES
Red Route
Blue Route
Yellow Route
To Bonniebrook & Springfield
To Forsyth
To Branson Airport (BBG) & Harrison, AR
College of the Ozarks
Taney County Airport (PLK)
Point Lookout
Hollister
Branson
Branson Landing
Branson City Campground
Lake Taneycomo
Roark Creek
Turkey Creek
Short Creek
Taneycomo

Branson

This index helps you "spot" where approved lodgings and restaurants are located on the corresponding detailed maps. Lodging daily rate range is for comparison only and show the property's high season. Restaurant rate range is a combination of lunch and/or dinner. Turn to the listing page for more detailed rate information and consult display ads for special promotions.

BRANSON

Map Page	OA	Lodgings	Diamond Rated	High Season	Page
1 / p. 402	AAA	**Branson Towers** - see color ad p 412	◆◆	$50-$120 SAVE	410
2 / p. 402		Foxborough Inn & Suites	◆◆	$60-$90	415
3 / p. 402	AAA	**Comfort Inn & Suites** - see color ad p 409	◆◆◆	$85-$114 SAVE	413
4 / p. 402		Cascades Inn	◆◆	Rates not provided	410
5 / p. 402		Honeysuckle Inn & Conference Center	◆◆	$60-$120	418
6 / p. 402	AAA	**Eagle's Lodge**	◆	$45-$85 SAVE	414
7 / p. 402	AAA	**Best Western Music Capital Inn** - see color ad p 409	◆◆	$64-$120 SAVE	410
8 / p. 402		Amazinn & Suites - see color ad on insert, p 428	◆◆	$60-$199	407
9 / p. 402	AAA	**Comfort Inn West** - see color ad p 409	◆◆	Rates not provided SAVE	414
10 / p. 402	AAA	**Scenic Hills Inn** - see color ad p 422	◆◆	$47-$120 SAVE	422
11 / p. 402	AAA	**Westgate Branson Woods Resort**	◆◆◆	$52-$116 SAVE	425
12 / p. 402		Hampton Inn-West	◆◆	$80-$135	417
13 / p. 402	AAA	**Rosebud Inn**	◆◆	$62-$69 SAVE	422
14 / p. 402	AAA	**Treehouse Condo Rentals Inc**	◆◆◆	$80-$259 SAVE	424
15 / p. 402		Hilton Promenade at Branson Landing - see color ad p 417 & on insert	◆◆◆	$129-$324	417
16 / p. 402	AAA	**Best Western Landing View Inn & Suites** - see color ad p 408	◆◆◆	$79-$149 SAVE	408
17 / p. 402	AAA	**Hilton Branson Convention Center** - see color ad p 417 and on insert	◆◆◆◆	$159-$259 SAVE	417
18 / p. 402		Super 8 Central of Branson	◆◆	Rates not provided	423
19 / p. 402		Artilla Cove Resort	◆	$60-$247	408
20 / p. 402		La Quinta Inn Branson (Music City Centre)	◆◆◆	$49-$105	419
21 / p. 402	AAA	**Dockers Inn**	◆◆	$50-$82 SAVE	414
22 / p. 402		Calm Waters Resort	◆	$57-$150	410
23 / p. 402		Ramada Resort & Conference Center	◆◆	$59-$109	421
24 / p. 402	AAA	**Grand Country Inn**	◆◆	$70-$119 SAVE	415
25 / p. 402	AAA	**Grand Plaza Hotel** - see color ad p 416	◆◆◆	$72-$160 SAVE	415
27 / p. 402		The Dutton Inn	◆	$45-$65	414
28 / p. 402		1st Inn Branson	◆◆	Rates not provided	407
29 / p. 402		Grand Oaks Hotel	◆◆	$79-$99	415
30 / p. 402	AAA	**Radisson Hotel Branson** - see color ad p 420	◆◆◆	$105-$239 SAVE	421
31 / p. 402		Angel Inn - see color ad p 428	◆◆	$50-$219	407
32 / p. 402	AAA	**Green Gables Inn**	◆◆	$62-$69 SAVE	416
33 / p. 402		Howard Johnson	◆◆	$72-$92	418
34 / p. 402		Golden Arrow Resort	◆	$44-$158	415
35 / p. 402	AAA	**Best Western Center Pointe Inn** - see color ad p 409	◆◆	$64-$120 SAVE	408

BRANSON (cont'd)

Map Page	OA	Lodgings (cont'd)	Diamond Rated	High Season	Page
36 / p. 402	AAA	**Clarion Hotel at the Palace**	♦♦	$75-$115 SAVE	411
37 / p. 402		Quality Inn & Suites on the Strip	♦♦	Rates not provided	420
38 / p. 402	AAA	**Branson Super 8**	♦	$55-$80 SAVE	410
39 / p. 402	AAA	**Still Waters Condominium Resort**	♦♦♦	$49-$600 SAVE	423
40 / p. 402		Fairfield Inn by Marriott	♦♦	$59-$77	414
41 / p. 402	AAA	**Comfort Inn-Thousand Hills** - see color ad p 409	♦♦	Rates not provided SAVE	413
42 / p. 402	AAA	**The Village At Indian Point** - see color ad p 425	♦♦♦	$100-$270 SAVE	424
43 / p. 402		Holiday Inn Express Green Mountain Drive - see color ad on insert	♦♦	$99-$149	418
44 / p. 402	AAA	**Econo Lodge**	♦♦	$45-$70 SAVE	414
45 / p. 402		Alpenrose Inn	♦	$55-$76	407
46 / p. 402		Thousand Hills Golf Resort - see color ad p 423	♦♦♦	$89-$229	424
47 / p. 402	AAA	**Stone Castle Hotel & Conference Center** - see color ad on insert, p 1	♦♦	$69-$119 SAVE	423
48 / p. 402		Branson's Best	♦♦	Rates not provided	410
49 / p. 402	AAA	**Eagle's View Cottages & Condos** - see color ad p 418	♦♦	$42-$235 SAVE	414
50 / p. 402		Residence Inn by Marriott	♦♦♦	$89-$139	421
51 / p. 402	AAA	**Indian Point Lodge & Condos** - see color ad p 418	♦♦	$49-$239 SAVE	418
52 / p. 402		Grand Crowne Resorts	♦♦♦	$99-$579	415
53 / p. 402	AAA	**Trail's End Resort** - see color ad p 418	♦♦	$45-$229 SAVE	424
54 / p. 402	AAA	**All American Inn & Suites**	♦♦	$79-$99 SAVE	407
55 / p. 402		Tribesman Resort	♦♦	$70-$110	424
56 / p. 402	AAA	**Lodge at the Falls**	♦♦	$59-$79 SAVE	420
57 / p. 402	AAA	**Fall Creek Inn & Suites**	♦♦	$42-$69 SAVE	415
58 / p. 402		Lazy Valley Resort	♦	$64-$220	419
59 / p. 402	AAA	**Lilleys' Landing Resort**	♦♦	$65-$250 SAVE	419
60 / p. 402	AAA	**Chateau on the Lake Resort & Spa** - see color ad p 412	♦♦♦♦	$109-$359 SAVE	411
61 / p. 402	AAA	**Welk Resort Branson** - see color ad p 426 and on insert	♦♦	$59-$139 SAVE	425
62 / p. 402	AAA	**Pointe Royale Condominium Resort** - see color ad p 419	♦♦	$99-$134 SAVE	420

Map Page	OA	Restaurants	Diamond Rated	Cuisine	Meal Range	Page
1 / p. 402		McFarlain's Family Restaurant - see color ad p 135	♦♦	American	$6-$14	429
2 / p. 402		B T Bones Steakhouse	♦♦	Steak	$8-$29	427
3 / p. 402	AAA	**Bleu Olive Mediterranean Grille & Bar**	♦♦♦	Mediterranean	$8-$26	427
4 / p. 402		Ruby Lena's Tea Room & Antiques	♦♦	American	$6-$8	430
5 / p. 402	AAA	**Rocky's Italian Restaurant**	♦♦	Italian	$7-$20	430
6 / p. 402		Farmhouse Restaurant	♦	American	$5-$10	427
7 / p. 402		Waxy O'Shea's	♦♦	Irish	$6-$16	430
8 / p. 402		Candlestick Inn Restaurant & Lounge	♦♦♦	Seafood	$24-$48	427
9 / p. 402		Outback Steak & Oyster Bar	♦♦	Steak	$6-$25	429

Map Page	OA	Restaurants (cont'd)	Diamond Rated	Cuisine	Meal Range	Page
10 / p. 402		Grand Country Buffet	◆◆	American	$7-$13	429
11 / p. 402		Gilley's Texas Cafe	◆◆	American	$7-$17	429
12 / p. 402		Wasabi Japanese Steak & Sushi	◆◆	Japanese	$7-$16	430
13 / p. 402		Charlie's Steak Ribs & Ale	◆◆	American	$5-$25	427
14 / p. 402	AAA	**Buckingham's Restaurant & Oasis Lounge**	◆◆◆	American	$15-$40	427
15 / p. 402		Sadie's Sideboard & Smokehouse	◆◆	Regional American	$5-$17	430
16 / p. 402		Uptown Cafe	◆◆	American	$5-$10	430
17 / p. 402		Pasta House	◆◆	Italian	$8-$22	429
18 / p. 402		Dockers Restaurant	◆◆	American	$7-$20	427
19 / p. 402	AAA	**Chateau Grille**	◆◆◆	American	$10-$38	427
20 / p. 402		Luigi's Pizza Kitchen South	◆	Italian	$5-$14	429

HOLLISTER

Map Page	OA	Restaurant	Diamond Rated	Cuisine	Meal Range	Page
23 / p. 402	AAA	**The Keeter Center at College of the Ozarks**	◆◆◆	American	$8-$20	432

BRANSON pop. 6,050 (See map and index starting on p. 402)

1ST INN BRANSON Book at AAA.com Phone: 417/334-7000 28

Hotel
Rates not provided

Address: 2719 W Hwy 76 65616 **Location:** 2.5 mi w of jct SR 76 (Country Music Blvd) and US 65. **Facility:** Smoke free premises. 132 units. 130 one-bedroom standard units, some with whirlpools. 2 one-bedroom suites. 3 stories, interior/exterior corridors. **Parking:** on-site. **Amenities:** voice mail, irons, hair dryers. **Pool(s):** outdoor. **Leisure Activities:** miniature golf, limited exercise equipment. **Guest Services:** coin laundry, wireless Internet.

ALL AMERICAN INN & SUITES Book great rates at AAA.com Phone: (417)334-2800 54

AAA SAVE
Hotel
$79-$99 3/1-12/31
$59-$69 1/1-2/28

Address: 3102 Falls Pkwy 65616 **Location:** Jct Green Mountain Rd and SR 165, just e to Dakota St. **Facility:** Smoke free premises. 81 units. 79 one-bedroom standard units, some with whirlpools. 2 one-bedroom suites. 2 stories, interior corridors. *Bath:* combo or shower only. **Parking:** on-site. **Amenities:** voice mail, hair dryers. **Pool(s):** outdoor. **Guest Services:** complimentary laundry, wireless Internet. **Business Services:** meeting rooms, PC. **Free Special Amenities: expanded continental breakfast and high-speed Internet.** CALL

ALPENROSE INN Phone: 417/336-4600 45

Motel
$55-$76 6/1-12/17
$45-$55 4/1-5/31

Address: 2875 Green Mountain Dr 65616 **Location:** Jct SR 76 (Country Music Blvd) and Green Blvd. **Facility:** Smoke free premises. 51 units. 50 one-bedroom standard units. 1 one-bedroom suite with kitchen. 2-3 stories (no elevator), exterior corridors. **Parking:** on-site. **Terms:** open 4/1-12/17, office hours 6:30 am-11 pm. **Amenities:** hair dryers. *Some:* DVD players, CD players, irons. **Pool(s):** outdoor. **Guest Services:** wireless Internet. **Business Services:** PC.
/ SOME UNITS

AMAZINN & SUITES Book at AAA.com Phone: (417)334-2300 8

Motel
$60-$199 11/1-12/13
$45-$189 3/4-10/31

Address: 3311 Shepherd of the Hills Expwy 65616 **Location:** Jct Gretna Rd (Blue Route), 1.1 mi e. **Facility:** 149 one-bedroom standard units, some with whirlpools. 2 stories (no elevator), exterior corridors. **Parking:** on-site. **Terms:** open 3/4-12/13, 2 night minimum stay - seasonal and/or weekends. **Amenities:** hair dryers. **Pool(s):** outdoor. **Leisure Activities:** whirlpool. **Guest Services:** coin laundry, wireless Internet. **Business Services:** meeting rooms, PC, fax (fee).
(See color ad on insert & p 428)
A$K CALL / SOME UNITS

ANGEL INN Book at AAA.com Phone: (417)334-6500 31

Hotel
$50-$219 All Year

Address: 2350 Green Mountain Dr 65616 **Location:** 1.5 mi w of jct SR 76 (Country Music Blvd) and US 65, just s. **Facility:** 113 one-bedroom standard units, some with whirlpools. 2-4 stories, exterior corridors. *Bath:* combo or shower only. **Parking:** on-site. **Amenities:** voice mail, irons, hair dryers. **Pool(s):** heated indoor. **Leisure Activities:** whirlpool. **Guest Services:** wireless Internet. **Business Services:** PC.
(See color ad p 428 and on insert)
A$K CALL / SOME UNITS

▼ See AAA listing p 423 ▼

(See map and index starting on p. 402)

ARTILLA COVE RESORT — Phone: 417/338-2346 **19**

Cabin
$60-$247 3/1-8/14
$60-$172 8/15-2/28

Address: 1123 Jakes Creek Tr 65616 **Location:** Jct SR 76 (Country Music Blvd) and 265, 1 mi s on Indian Point Rd, 1.1 mi e. Located in a quiet area. **Facility:** Smoke free premises. 10 units. 4 one-, 1 two- and 1 three-bedroom suites with kitchens. 4 cottages. 1 story, exterior corridors. *Bath:* combo or shower only. **Parking:** on-site. **Terms:** office hours 8 am-8 pm, check-out 9:30 am, 1-3 night minimum stay - seasonal, 28 day cancellation notice-fee imposed. **Amenities:** DVD players, irons. **Pool(s):** outdoor. **Leisure Activities:** rental boats, rental paddleboats, fishing, hiking trails, playground. *Fee:* boat dock. **Guest Services:** coin laundry, wireless Internet.

BEST WESTERN CENTER POINTE INN — Book great rates at AAA.com — Phone: (417)334-1894 **35**

AAA SAVE
Hotel
$64-$120 All Year

Address: 3215 W Hwy 76 65616 **Location:** On SR 76 (Country Music Blvd); jct SR 165. **Facility:** 164 units. 163 one- and 1 two-bedroom standard units, some with whirlpools. 2-4 stories, interior/exterior corridors. **Parking:** on-site. **Amenities:** voice mail, irons, hair dryers. **Pool(s):** outdoor, heated indoor. **Leisure Activities:** sauna, whirlpools, billiards, exercise room. *Fee:* game room. **Guest Services:** coin laundry, wireless Internet. **Business Services:** PC. **Free Special Amenities: local telephone calls and high-speed Internet.**

(See color ad p 409) / SOME UNITS

AAA Benefit:
Members save up to 20%, plus 10% bonus points with rewards program.

BEST WESTERN LANDING VIEW INN & SUITES — Book great rates at AAA.com — Phone: (417)334-6464 **16**

AAA SAVE
Hotel
$79-$149 All Year

Address: 403 W Main (Hwy 76) 65616 **Location:** 0.3 mi e from SR 76 (Country Music Blvd) and US 65. **Facility:** 109 units. 104 one-bedroom standard units. 5 one-bedroom suites with whirlpools. 2-4 stories (no elevator), exterior corridors. **Parking:** on-site. **Amenities:** DVD players, high-speed Internet, irons, hair dryers. **Pool(s):** heated indoor. **Leisure Activities:** sauna, whirlpool, sun deck. **Guest Services:** valet and coin laundry, wireless Internet. **Business Services:** meeting rooms, PC, fax.

(See color ad below)

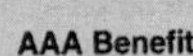

AAA Benefit:
Members save up to 20%, plus 10% bonus points with rewards program.

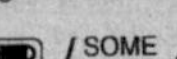
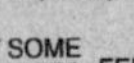

/ SOME UNITS FEE

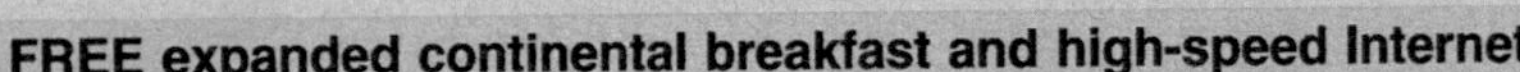

FREE expanded continental breakfast and high-speed Internet

(See map and index starting on p. 402)

BEST WESTERN MUSIC CAPITAL INN *Book great rates at AAA.com* **Phone:** (417)334-8378 7

Hotel
$64-$120 All Year

Address: 3257 Shepherd of the Hills Expwy 65616 **Location:** 0.3 mi e from jct SR 76 (Country Music Blvd). **Facility:** Smoke free premises. 93 one-bedroom standard units, some with whirlpools. 3-4 stories, interior corridors. *Bath:* combo or shower only. **Parking:** on-site. **Amenities:** voice mail, irons, hair dryers. **Pool(s):** heated indoor. **Leisure Activities:** sauna, whirlpool, exercise room. *Fee:* game room. **Guest Services:** coin laundry, wireless Internet. **Business Services:** PC. **Free Special Amenities: continental breakfast and high-speed Internet.** *(See color ad p 409)*
CALL / SOME UNITS

AAA Benefit:
Members save up to 20%, plus 10% bonus points with rewards program.

BRANSON'S BEST **Phone:** 417/336-2378 48

Hotel
Rates not provided

Address: 3150 Green Mountain Dr 65616 **Location:** 3 mi w from jct US 65 and SR 76 (Country Music Blvd), just s. Located in Thousand Hills. **Facility:** 66 units. 65 one-bedroom standard units. 1 one-bedroom suite with kitchen. 2-3 stories (no elevator), exterior corridors. **Parking:** on-site. **Terms:** open 3/1-12/15. **Amenities:** high-speed Internet, irons, hair dryers. **Pool(s):** outdoor. **Guest Services:** wireless Internet. **Business Services:** PC. / SOME UNITS

BRANSON SUPER 8 *Book great rates at AAA.com* **Phone:** (417)334-8880 38

Hotel
$55-$80 All Year

Address: 2490 Green Mountain Dr 65616 **Location:** 1.5 mi w of jct SR 76 (Country Music Blvd) and US 65, just s. **Facility:** Smoke free premises. 73 one-bedroom standard units, some with whirlpools. 2-3 stories (no elevator), interior corridors. **Parking:** on-site. **Amenities:** high-speed Internet, voice mail, hair dryers. **Pool(s):** outdoor. **Guest Services:** wireless Internet. **Business Services:** meeting rooms, PC. **Free Special Amenities: expanded continental breakfast and high-speed Internet.**
CALL / SOME UNITS

BRANSON TOWERS **Phone:** 417/336-4500 1

Hotel
$50-$120 3/1-12/15
$40-$70 12/16-2/28

Address: 236 Shepherd of the Hills Expwy 65616 **Location:** Jct US 65, 2.2 mi nw on SR 248, just w. **Facility:** 208 units. 202 one-bedroom standard units, some with whirlpools. 6 one-bedroom suites, some with whirlpools. 3 stories, interior corridors. **Parking:** on-site. **Terms:** cancellation fee imposed. **Amenities:** irons, hair dryers. **Pool(s):** heated indoor. **Leisure Activities:** whirlpool. *Fee:* air hockey, game room. **Guest Services:** coin laundry, wireless Internet. **Business Services:** meeting rooms. *(See color ad p 412)*
/ SOME UNITS

FREE expanded continental breakfast and high-speed Internet

CALM WATERS RESORT **Phone:** 417/338-8963 22

Cottage
$57-$150 3/1-12/31

Address: 1043 Jakes Creek Tr 65616 **Location:** Jct SR 76 (Country Music Blvd) and 265, 0.6 mi w, 1 mi s on Indian Point Rd, then 1 mi e. **Facility:** 16 units. 4 one-bedroom standard units with efficiencies. 2 two-bedroom suites with efficiencies. 1 house and 9 cottages. 1 story, exterior corridors. *Bath:* combo or shower only. **Parking:** on-site. **Terms:** open 3/1-12/31, office hours 8 am-10 pm, check-out 9:30 am, 3 night minimum stay, 28 day cancellation notice-fee imposed. **Pool(s):** outdoor. **Leisure Activities:** steamroom, rental boats, paddleboats, fishing. *Fee:* boat dock. **Guest Services:** coin laundry, wireless Internet. **Business Services:** fax.
/ SOME UNITS

CASCADES INN **Phone:** 417/335-8424 4

Hotel
Rates not provided

Address: 3226 Shepherd of the Hills Expwy 65616 **Location:** Jct SR 76 (Country Music Blvd), just e. **Facility:** Smoke free premises. 159 units. 157 one-bedroom standard units, some with whirlpools. 2 one-bedroom suites. 4 stories, interior corridors. *Bath:* combo or shower only. **Parking:** on-site. **Terms:** open 3/1-12/30. **Amenities:** irons, hair dryers. **Pool(s):** heated indoor. **Leisure Activities:** whirlpool, exercise room. *Fee:* massage, game room. **Guest Services:** coin laundry, wireless Internet. **Business Services:** meeting rooms. *Fee:* PC, fax. / SOME UNITS

(See map and index starting on p. 402)

CHATEAU ON THE LAKE RESORT & SPA Book great rates at AAA.com **Phone:** (417)334-1161 60

Resort Hotel

$109-$359 All Year

Address: 415 N State Hwy 265 65616 **Location:** Just n of jct SR 165 and 265. **Facility:** An exceptional property offering elegance and many unique features, including a mixture of Ozark hospitality and sophisticated service. Smoke free premises. 301 units. 244 one-bedroom standard units. 57 one-bedroom suites, some with whirlpools. 10 stories, interior corridors. *Bath:* combo or shower only. **Parking:** on-site and valet. **Terms:** check-in 4 pm, 3 day cancellation notice-fee imposed. **Amenities:** video games (fee), high-speed Internet, dual phone lines, voice mail, safes, irons, hair dryers. *Some:* DVD players, CD players. **Dining:** 3 restaurants, also, Chateau Grille, see separate listing. **Pool(s):** heated outdoor, heated indoor. **Leisure Activities:** saunas, whirlpools, rental boats, canoeing, paddleboats, fishing, 2 lighted tennis courts, recreation programs, 52-seat theater, nature trail, hiking trails, playground, exercise room, spa. *Fee:* marina, waterskiing, scuba diving, charter fishing, personal watercraft, pontoon boats. **Guest Services:** valet and coin laundry, wireless Internet. **Business Services:** conference facilities, business center. *(See color ad p 412)*

CALL / SOME UNITS FEE

FREE newspaper

CLARION HOTEL AT THE PALACE Book great rates at AAA.com **Phone:** (417)334-7666 36

Hotel

$75-$115 5/30-2/28
$85-$99 3/1-5/29

Address: 2820 W Hwy 76 65615 **Location:** SR 76 (Country Music Blvd), 3 mi w of jct US 65. **Facility:** Smoke free premises. 166 units. 164 one-bedroom standard units, some with whirlpools. 2 two-bedroom suites, some with kitchens. 5-7 stories, interior/exterior corridors. *Bath:* combo or shower only. **Parking:** on-site. **Amenities:** high-speed Internet, voice mail, safes (fee), irons, hair dryers. *Some:* DVD players, CD players. **Dining:** Buckingham's Restaurant & Oasis Lounge, see separate listing. **Pool(s):** heated outdoor, heated indoor. **Leisure Activities:** sauna, whirlpools, exercise room. *Fee:* massage. **Guest Services:** coin laundry, airport transportation-Point Lookout Airport, area transportation-within 5 mi, wireless Internet. **Business Services:** conference facilities, PC, fax. **Free Special Amenities: expanded continental breakfast and high-speed Internet.**

CALL

▼ See AAA listing p 431 ▼

▼ See AAA listing p 410 ▼

▼ See AAA listing p 411 ▼

(See map and index starting on p. 402)

COMFORT INN & SUITES Book great rates at AAA.com Phone: (417)335-4731 3

Hotel
$85-$114 6/4-2/28
$80-$109 3/1-6/3

Address: 5150 Gretna Rd 65616 **Location:** 2.9 mi n of jct SR 76 (Country Music Blvd). **Facility:** Smoke free premises. 102 units. 101 one-bedroom standard units, some with whirlpools. 1 cottage. 1-4 stories, interior/exterior corridors. *Bath:* combo or shower only. **Parking:** on-site. **Terms:** cancellation fee imposed. **Amenities:** high-speed Internet, voice mail, safes (fee), irons, hair dryers. **Pool(s):** heated indoor. **Leisure Activities:** sauna, whirlpool, billiards, picnic areas, walking trail, exercise room, horseshoes. *Fee:* game room. **Guest Services:** valet and coin laundry, wireless Internet. **Business Services:** PC. **Free Special Amenities: expanded continental breakfast and high-speed Internet.** *(See color ad p 409)*

ECO

COMFORT INN-THOUSAND HILLS Book great rates at AAA.com Phone: 417/335-4727 41

Hotel
Rates not provided

Address: 203 S Wildwood Dr 65616 **Location:** Jct US 65, 2 mi w on SR 76 (Country Music Blvd), then just s. **Facility:** Smoke free premises. 108 units. 105 one- and 3 two-bedroom standard units, some with whirlpools. 3-4 stories, interior corridors. *Bath:* combo or shower only. **Parking:** on-site. **Amenities:** high-speed Internet, voice mail, irons, hair dryers. **Pool(s):** heated indoor. **Leisure Activities:** sauna, whirlpool, billiards, exercise room. *Fee:* game room. **Guest Services:** coin laundry, wireless Internet. **Business Services:** meeting rooms, PC, fax. **Free Special Amenities: expanded continental breakfast and high-speed Internet.** *(See color ad p 409)*

ECO / SOME UNITS

(See map and index starting on p. 402)

COMFORT INN WEST Book great rates at AAA.com **Phone:** 417/334-8694 9

Hotel

Rates not provided

Address: 3601 Shepherd of the Hills Expwy 65616 **Location:** Just e of jct SR 76 (Country Music Blvd). **Facility:** Smoke free premises. 87 units. 79 one-bedroom standard units. 8 one-bedroom suites, some with whirlpools. 2-3 stories, exterior corridors. **Parking:** on-site. **Terms:** open 3/6-1/3. **Amenities:** high-speed Internet, voice mail, irons, hair dryers. **Pool(s):** heated indoor. **Leisure Activities:** whirlpool. **Guest Services:** coin laundry, wireless Internet. **Business Services:** PC. **Free Special Amenities: expanded continental breakfast and high-speed Internet.** *(See color ad p 409)*

ECO / SOME UNITS

DOCKERS INN Book great rates at AAA.com **Phone:** (417)334-3600 21

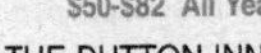

Motel

$50-$82 All Year

Address: 3060 Green Mountain Dr 65616 **Location:** SR 376, 0.7 mi e on SR 76 (Country Music Blvd), just s. **Facility:** Smoke free premises. 78 one-bedroom standard units. 3 stories (no elevator), exterior corridors. **Parking:** on-site. **Terms:** office hours 7 am-11 pm, cancellation fee imposed. **Amenities:** hair dryers. **Pool(s):** outdoor. **Guest Services:** wireless Internet. **Business Services:** meeting rooms, PC, fax. **Free Special Amenities: expanded continental breakfast and high-speed Internet.** / SOME UNITS FEE

THE DUTTON INN **Phone:** (417)334-8873 27

Hotel

$45-$65 3/1-12/14

Address: 3454 W Hwy 76 65616 **Location:** 0.7 mi e of jct SR 376, just s. **Facility:** Smoke free premises. 78 one-bedroom standard units. 2-3 stories, exterior corridors. **Parking:** on-site. **Terms:** open 3/1-12/14, office hours 6:30 am-midnight, cancellation fee imposed. **Amenities:** voice mail, hair dryers. **Guest Services:** coin laundry, wireless Internet. **Business Services:** meeting rooms, PC, fax.

ASK / SOME UNITS

EAGLE'S LODGE **Phone:** (417)336-2666 6

Hotel

$45-$85 All Year

Address: 3221 Shepherd of the Hills Expwy 65616 **Location:** 0.3 mi e of jct SR 76 (Country Music Blvd). **Facility:** 66 one-bedroom standard units. 4 stories (no elevator), exterior corridors. *Bath:* combo or shower only. **Parking:** on-site. **Terms:** office hours 7 am-11 pm. **Amenities:** hair dryers. *Some:* irons. **Pool(s):** outdoor. **Guest Services:** coin laundry, wireless Internet. **Business Services:** fax (fee). **Free Special Amenities: continental breakfast and room upgrade (subject to availability with advance reservations).** / SOME UNITS FEE

EAGLE'S VIEW COTTAGES & CONDOS Book great rates at AAA.com **Phone:** (417)338-2227 49

Resort Condominium

$42-$235 All Year

Address: 71 Dogwood Park Tr 65616 **Location:** Jct SR 265, 0.6 mi w on SR 76 (Country Music Blvd), 2.9 mi s on Indian Point Rd, then just e. **Facility:** Roadside units, some with lake view. 48 units with fireplaces; some with washer and dryer. 94 units. 44 one-bedroom standard units, some with kitchens and/or whirlpools. 15 one-, 20 two- and 1 three-bedroom suites with whirlpools, some with efficiencies or kitchens. 14 cottages. 1-3 stories (no elevator), exterior corridors. *Bath:* combo or shower only. **Parking:** on-site. **Terms:** office hours 8 am-9 pm, check-in 4 pm, 2-4 night minimum stay - seasonal and/or weekends, 21 day cancellation notice-fee imposed. **Amenities:** video library (fee), voice mail. *Some:* DVD players, irons. **Pool(s):** heated outdoor. **Leisure Activities:** whirlpools, rental boats, paddleboats, marina, scuba diving, snorkeling, fishing, pontoon and deck boats, badminton, tetherball, nature trail, playground, horseshoes, shuffleboard, volleyball. *Fee:* waterskiing, personal watercraft, game room. **Guest Services:** wireless Internet. **Business Services:** fax (fee). **Free Special Amenities: local telephone calls and high-speed Internet.** *(See color ad p 418)*

ECONO LODGE Book great rates at AAA.com **Phone:** (417)336-4849 44

Motel

$45-$70 All Year

Address: 230 S Wildwood Dr 65616 **Location:** 2 mi w on SR 76 (Country Music Blvd), just s. **Facility:** 63 units. 62 one-bedroom standard units, some with whirlpools. 1 one-bedroom suite with whirlpool. 2-3 stories (no elevator), exterior corridors. *Bath:* combo or shower only. **Parking:** on-site. **Amenities:** high-speed Internet. *Some:* irons, hair dryers. **Pool(s):** outdoor. **Leisure Activities:** whirlpool. **Guest Services:** coin laundry, wireless Internet. **Business Services:** fax (fee). **Free Special Amenities: continental breakfast and local telephone calls.**

CALL / SOME UNITS

FAIRFIELD INN BY MARRIOTT Book great rates at AAA.com **Phone:** (417)336-5665 40

Hotel

$59-$77 All Year

Address: 220 SR 165 S 65616 **Location:** US 65, 3.8 mi w on SR 76 (Country Music Blvd), just s. **Facility:** Smoke free premises. 100 one-bedroom standard units. 4 stories, interior corridors. *Bath:* combo or shower only. **Parking:** on-site. **Terms:** cancellation fee imposed. **Amenities:** high-speed Internet, irons, hair dryers. **Pool(s):** heated indoor. **Leisure Activities:** whirlpool. **Guest Services:** wireless Internet. **Business Services:** PC, fax (fee).

AAA Benefit:

Members save a minimum 5% off the best available rate.

(See map and index starting on p. 402)

FALL CREEK INN & SUITES — Phone: (417)348-1683 57

SAVE

Hotel
$42-$69 All Year

Address: 995 Hwy 165 65616 **Location:** Jct SR 76 (Country Music Blvd), 1.5 mi s on SR 165. **Facility:** 101 units. 95 one-bedroom standard units. 6 one-bedroom suites with whirlpools. 3 stories (no elevator), exterior corridors. **Parking:** on-site. **Terms:** office hours 7 am-11 pm, cancellation fee imposed. **Amenities:** *Some:* DVD players, irons, hair dryers. **Pool(s):** outdoor. **Leisure Activities:** horseshoes. **Guest Services:** coin laundry, wireless Internet. **Business Services:** fax (fee). **Free Special Amenities: continental breakfast and high-speed Internet.**

/ SOME UNITS FEE

FOXBOROUGH INN & SUITES — Phone: 417/335-4369 2

Motel
$60-$90 All Year

Address: 235 Expressway Ln 65616 **Location:** US 65, exit Shepherd of the Hills Expwy, 2.3 mi w, just sw. **Facility:** 117 units. 82 one-bedroom standard units, some with whirlpools. 35 condominiums. 3 stories (no elevator), exterior corridors. **Parking:** on-site. **Amenities:** voice mail, hair dryers. *Some:* irons. **Pool(s):** outdoor. **Leisure Activities:** exercise room, game room. **Guest Services:** coin laundry, wireless Internet. **Business Services:** meeting rooms, fax.

ASK CALL &M / SOME UNITS FEE

GOLDEN ARROW RESORT — Phone: 417/338-2245 34

Motel
$44-$158 3/1-12/15

Address: 2869 Indian Point Rd 65616 **Location:** Jct SR 76 and 265, 0.6 mi w, then 2.8 mi s. **Facility:** 21 units. 2 one-bedroom standard units. 9 one-, 8 two- and 2 three-bedroom suites, some with efficiencies or kitchens. 1 story, exterior corridors. **Parking:** on-site. **Terms:** open 3/1-12/15, 3 night minimum stay - seasonal, 21 day cancellation notice-fee imposed. **Pool(s):** outdoor. **Leisure Activities:** whirlpool, hiking trails, playground, basketball, horseshoes, shuffleboard. **Guest Services:** coin laundry. / SOME UNITS FEE

GRAND COUNTRY INN — Phone: (417)335-3535 24

SAVE

Hotel
$70-$119 All Year

Address: 1945 W 76 Country Music Blvd 65616 **Location:** Jct US 65, 1.9 mi w. Adjacent to the mall; 76 Music Hall Theater on premises. **Facility:** 319 one-bedroom standard units. 2-3 stories (no elevator), exterior corridors. *Bath:* combo or shower only. **Parking:** on-site. **Amenities:** irons, hair dryers. **Dining:** 3 restaurants. **Pool(s):** 2 outdoor, heated indoor. **Leisure Activities:** whirlpool, indoor/outdoor water park. *Fee:* miniature golf, game room. **Guest Services:** coin laundry, wireless Internet. **Business Services:** meeting rooms. **Free Special Amenities: local telephone calls and early check-in/late check-out.** / SOME UNITS

GRAND CROWNE RESORTS — *Book at AAA.com* — Phone: (417)332-8330 52

Condominium
$99-$579 All Year

Address: 300 Golf View Dr 65616 **Location:** Jct US 65, 3 mi w on SR 76 (Country Music Blvd), then 1 mi s. **Facility:** This well-maintained property is located minutes from Branson's main attractions; one- and two-bedroom units feature a fully-equipped kitchen. Registration is off site. 468 condominiums. 5 stories, exterior corridors. **Parking:** on-site. **Terms:** off-site registration, check-in 4 pm, 2-3 night minimum stay - seasonal, 5 day cancellation notice-fee imposed. **Amenities:** DVD players, voice mail, irons, hair dryers. **Pool(s):** heated indoor. **Leisure Activities:** whirlpools, playground, exercise room, basketball. **Guest Services:** complimentary and valet laundry, wireless Internet. **Business Services:** PC. ASK CALL &M / SOME UNITS

GRAND OAKS HOTEL — *Book at AAA.com* — Phone: (417)336-6423 29

Hotel
$79-$99 3/1-12/31
$69-$89 1/1-2/28

Address: 2315 Green Mountain Dr 65616 **Location:** Jct US 65, 1.5 mi w on SR 76 (Country Music Blvd), then just s. **Facility:** Smoke free premises. 201 one-bedroom standard units, some with whirlpools. 3-4 stories, interior corridors. *Bath:* combo or shower only. **Parking:** on-site. **Amenities:** irons, hair dryers. **Pool(s):** outdoor, heated indoor. **Leisure Activities:** whirlpools. *Fee:* exercise room. **Guest Services:** coin laundry, wireless Internet. **Business Services:** meeting rooms, PC. ASK CALL &M / SOME UNITS

GRAND PLAZA HOTEL — *Book great rates at AAA.com* — Phone: (417)336-6646 

SAVE

Hotel
$72-$160 All Year

Address: 245 N Wildwood Dr 65616 **Location:** 2.5 mi w of jct US 65. **Facility:** 200 one-bedroom standard units, some with whirlpools. 10 stories, interior corridors. *Bath:* combo or shower only. **Parking:** on-site. **Amenities:** high-speed Internet, voice mail, irons, hair dryers. **Pool(s):** heated indoor. **Leisure Activities:** whirlpool, exercise room. *Fee:* game room. **Guest Services:** coin laundry, wireless Internet. **Business Services:** meeting rooms, PC, fax (fee).
(See color ad p 416)

/ SOME UNITS

FREE full breakfast and high-speed Internet

(See map and index starting on p. 402)

GREEN GABLES INN — **Phone:** 417/336-3400 **32**

Hotel
$62-$69 11/1-12/19
$51-$59 3/1-10/31

Address: 2400 Green Mountain Dr 65616 **Location:** Jct US 65, 2 mi w on SR 76 (Country Music Blvd), then just s. **Facility:** 54 one-bedroom standard units. 2-3 stories (no elevator), exterior corridors. *Bath:* combo or shower only. **Parking:** on-site. **Terms:** open 3/1-12/19, office hours 6:30 am-11 pm, 2 night minimum stay - seasonal and/or weekends, cancellation fee imposed. **Amenities:** hair dryers. **Pool(s):** outdoor. **Guest Services:** wireless Internet. **Free Special Amenities: continental breakfast and high-speed Internet.** / SOME UNITS

▼ See AAA listing p 415 ▼

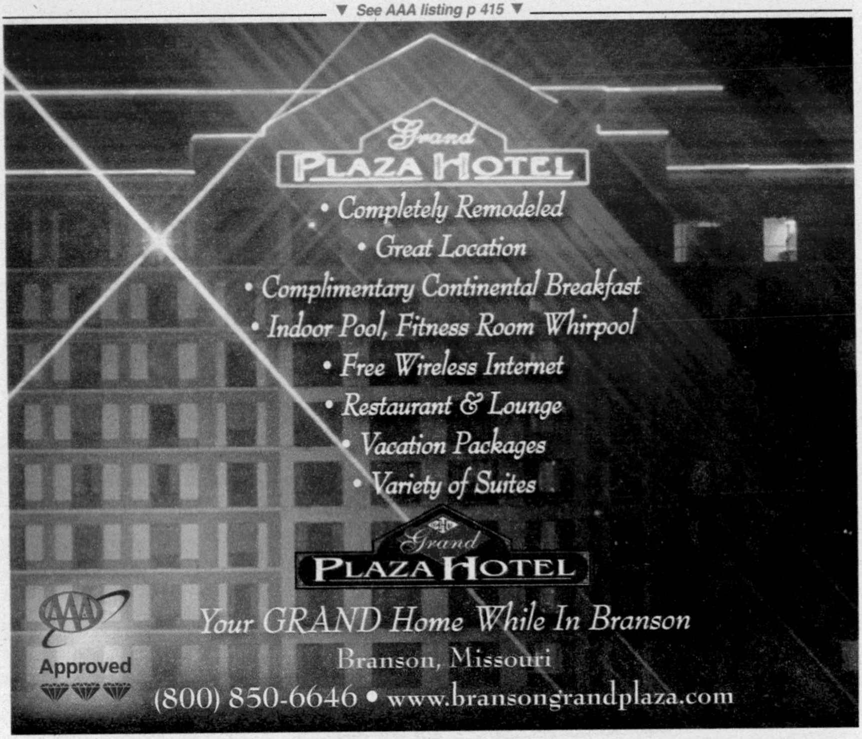

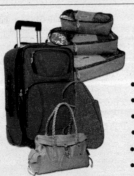

(See map and index starting on p. 402)

HAMPTON INN BRANSON HILLS PKWY Book great rates at AAA.com Phone: (417)243-7800

Hotel
$79-$169 All Year

Address: 200 Payne Stewart Dr 65616 **Location:** US 65, exit Branson Hills Pkwy, just w, then just n. **Facility:** 89 one-bedroom standard units. 4 stories, interior corridors. *Bath:* combo or shower only. **Parking:** on-site. **Terms:** check-in 4 pm, 1-7 night minimum stay, cancellation fee imposed. **Amenities:** voice mail, irons, hair dryers. **Pool(s):** heated indoor. **Leisure Activities:** exercise room. **Guest Services:** wireless Internet. **Business Services:** meeting rooms, business center.
(See color ad p 421 and on insert)

CALL / SOME UNITS FEE

AAA Benefit:
Members save up to 10% everyday!

HAMPTON INN-WEST Book great rates at AAA.com Phone: (417)337-5762 12

Hotel
$80-$135 All Year

Address: 3695 W Hwy 76 65616 **Location:** 0.3 mi s of jct SR 76 (Country Music Blvd) and Shepherd of the Hills Expwy. Located at entrance to Remington Theater. **Facility:** 109 one-bedroom standard units, some with whirlpools. 5 stories, interior corridors. *Bath:* combo or shower only. **Parking:** on-site. **Terms:** 1-7 night minimum stay, cancellation fee imposed. **Amenities:** voice mail, irons, hair dryers. **Pool(s):** heated indoor. **Leisure Activities:** whirlpool, exercise room. **Guest Services:** coin laundry, wireless Internet. **Business Services:** meeting rooms, PC.

CALL / SOME UNITS

AAA Benefit:
Members save up to 10% everyday!

HILTON BRANSON CONVENTION CENTER Book great rates at AAA.com Phone: (417)336-5400 17

AAA SAVE

Hotel
$159-$259 All Year

Address: 200 E Main St 65616 **Location:** Main St; at Branson Landing Shopping Complex. **Facility:** In an excellent location, this luxury high-rise hotel offers standard rooms, suites and condos, each with sumptuous bedding and a comfortable decor. 294 units. 250 one-bedroom standard units. 44 one-bedroom suites with efficiencies and whirlpools. 12 stories, interior corridors. *Bath:* combo or shower only. **Parking:** on-site (fee) and valet. **Terms:** check-in 4 pm, 1-7 night minimum stay, cancellation fee imposed. **Amenities:** dual phone lines, voice mail, safes, irons, hair dryers. *Fee:* video games, high-speed Internet. *Some:* CD players. **Pool(s):** heated indoor. **Leisure Activities:** whirlpool, exercise room. **Guest Services:** wireless Internet. **Business Services:** conference facilities, business center. **Free Special Amenities: newspaper.**
(See color ad below and on insert)

CALL / SOME UNITS FEE

Hilton
AAA Benefit:
Members save 5% or more everyday!

HILTON PROMENADE AT BRANSON LANDING Book great rates at AAA.com Phone: (417)336-5500 15

Hotel
$129-$324 All Year

Address: 3 Branson Landing 65616 **Location:** In Branson Landing shopping district. **Facility:** 242 units. 165 one-bedroom standard units. 77 one-bedroom suites with kitchens and whirlpools. 4 stories, interior corridors. *Bath:* combo or shower only. **Parking:** on-site (fee) and valet. **Terms:** check-in 4 pm, 1-7 night minimum stay, cancellation fee imposed. **Amenities:** dual phone lines, voice mail, irons, hair dryers. *Fee:* video games, high-speed Internet. *Some:* CD players. **Pool(s):** heated indoor. **Leisure Activities:** whirlpool, exercise room. **Guest Services:** wireless Internet. **Business Services:** meeting rooms, business center.
(See color ad below and on insert)

SOME UNITS FEE

Hilton
AAA Benefit:
Members save 5% or more everyday!

(See map and index starting on p. 402)

HOLIDAY INN EXPRESS GREEN MOUNTAIN DRIVE Book at AAA.com Phone: (417)336-2100 43

Hotel

$99-$149 3/1-11/30

$89-$139 12/1-2/28

Address: 2801 Green Mountain Dr 65616 **Location:** 2 mi w on SR 76 (Country Music Blvd), just s on Wildwood Dr, then just w. **Facility:** 120 units. 118 one-bedroom standard units, some with whirlpools. 2 one-bedroom suites with kitchens and whirlpools. 5 stories, interior corridors. *Bath:* combo or shower only. **Parking:** on-site. **Amenities:** voice mail, irons, hair dryers. **Pool(s):** outdoor. **Leisure Activities:** whirlpool. **Guest Services:** coin laundry, wireless Internet. ***(See color ad p. 419 and on insert)***

ASK / SOME UNITS

HONEYSUCKLE INN & CONFERENCE CENTER Phone: (417)335-2030 5

Hotel

$60-$120 All Year

Address: 3598 Shepherd of the Hills Expwy 65616 **Location:** Just e of jct SR 76 (Country Music Blvd). **Facility:** Smoke free premises. 210 one-bedroom standard units, some with whirlpools. 2-3 stories (no elevator), exterior corridors. *Bath:* combo or shower only. **Parking:** on-site. **Terms:** 3 day cancellation notice-fee imposed. **Amenities:** voice mail, hair dryers. **Pool(s):** outdoor, heated indoor. **Leisure Activities:** whirlpool. **Guest Services:** coin laundry, wireless Internet. **Business Services:** meeting rooms, business center. ASK CALL

HOWARD JOHNSON Book at AAA.com Phone: (417)336-5151 33

Hotel

$72-$92 3/3-12/18

Address: 3027-A W Hwy 76 65616 **Location:** On SR 76 (Country Music Blvd), 3.5 mi w of jct US 65. **Facility:** 345 units. 344 one-bedroom standard units. 1 one-bedroom suite with whirlpool. 3-4 stories, exterior corridors. **Parking:** on-site. **Terms:** open 3/3-12/18. **Amenities:** irons, hair dryers. **Pool(s):** outdoor. **Leisure Activities:** whirlpools, playground. **Guest Services:** coin laundry, wireless Internet. **Business Services:** meeting rooms, PC, fax (fee).

ASK / SOME UNITS FEE FEE

INDIAN POINT LODGE & CONDOS Book great rates at AAA.com Phone: (417)338-2250 51

Resort Condominium

$49-$239 All Year

Address: 71 Dogwood Park Tr 65616 **Location:** Jct SR 265, 0.6 mi w on SR 76 (Country Music Blvd), 2.9 mi s on Indian Point Rd, then just e. **Facility:** On lakefront with variety of appointments. All condominium units with fireplaces; some with washer and dryer. 48 units. 6 one-bedroom standard units with efficiencies. 11 one-, 26 two- and 5 three-bedroom suites, some with efficiencies, kitchens and/or whirlpools. 1-3 stories (no elevator), exterior corridors. **Parking:** on-site. **Terms:** office hours 8 am-9 pm, check-in 4 pm, 2-4 night minimum stay - seasonal and/or weekends, 21 day cancellation notice-fee imposed. **Amenities:** video library (fee), voice mail. *Some:* DVD players, irons. **Pool(s):** heated outdoor. **Leisure Activities:** whirlpools, rental boats, paddleboats, marina, scuba diving, snorkeling, fishing, badminton, tetherball, nature trail, playground, horseshoes, shuffleboard, volleyball. *Fee:* waterskiing, personal watercraft, pontoon & deck boat, game room. **Guest Services:** wireless Internet. **Business Services:** fax (fee). **Free Special Amenities: local telephone calls and high-speed Internet.** *(See color ad below)* CALL

(See map and index starting on p. 402)

LA QUINTA INN BRANSON (MUSIC CITY CENTRE) Book at AAA.com Phone: (417)332-1575 20

Hotel
$49-$105 All Year

Address: 1835 W Hwy 76 65616 **Location:** 1.6 mi w of jct US 65. **Facility:** Smoke free premises. 98 one-bedroom standard units, some with whirlpools. 2-3 stories, interior/exterior corridors. *Bath:* combo or shower only. **Parking:** on-site. **Amenities:** high-speed Internet, voice mail, irons, hair dryers. *Some:* dual phone lines. **Pool(s):** heated indoor. **Leisure Activities:** sauna, whirlpool, exercise room. **Guest Services:** coin laundry, wireless Internet. **Business Services:** meeting rooms, fax.

LAZY VALLEY RESORT Phone: 417/334-2397 58

Motel
$64-$220 All Year

Address: 285 River Ln 65616 **Location:** 1 mi w of US 65 on SR 76 (Country Music Blvd), 2.5 mi s on Fall Creek Rd to River Valley Rd. **Facility:** 17 units. 9 one- and 3 two-bedroom standard units, some with efficiencies. 4 two-bedroom suites, some with efficiencies or kitchens. 1 house. 1 story, exterior corridors. *Bath:* combo or shower only. **Parking:** on-site. **Terms:** 3 night minimum stay - seasonal, 60 day cancellation notice-fee imposed. **Amenities:** *Some:* irons. **Pool(s):** outdoor. **Leisure Activities:** fishing, basketball. *Fee:* boats, marina.

CALL / SOME UNITS FEE

LILLEYS' LANDING RESORT Phone: 417/334-6380 59

Resort Motel
$65-$250 All Year

Address: 367 River Ln 65616 **Location:** Jct US 65, 1 mi w on SR 76, 2.5 mi s on Fall Creek Rd, follow signs. **Facility:** Located in a quiet area on Upper Lake Taneycomo near many recreational activities, the motel offers a relaxed experience. In-room smoking is available Jan-Feb. Smoke free premises. 24 units. 7 one-bedroom standard units, some with efficiencies or kitchens. 3 one-, 10 two- and 4 three-bedroom suites with kitchens. 1-2 stories, exterior corridors. *Bath:* combo or shower only. **Parking:** on-site. **Terms:** 3 night minimum stay - seasonal and/or weekends, 56 day cancellation notice-fee imposed. **Amenities:** *Some:* irons. **Pool(s):** outdoor. **Leisure Activities:** rental boats, marina, fishing, pavilion overlooks lake, playground, basketball, horseshoes. **Guest Services:** coin laundry, wireless Internet. **Business Services:** meeting rooms.

/ SOME UNITS FEE

▼ See AAA listing p 420 ▼

(See map and index starting on p. 402)

LODGE AT THE FALLS Book great rates at AAA.com **Phone:** (417)336-3255 56

Hotel
$59-$79 3/1-12/31

Address: 3245 Falls Pkwy 65616 **Location:** Jct SR 76 (Country Music Blvd), 0.9 mi s on SR 165. **Facility:** 110 one-bedroom standard units. 2-3 stories (no elevator), exterior corridors. *Bath:* combo or shower only. **Parking:** on-site. **Terms:** open 3/1-12/31. **Amenities:** high-speed Internet, voice mail, safes (fee), hair dryers. **Pool(s):** outdoor. **Guest Services:** wireless Internet. **Business Services:** PC, fax (fee). **Free Special Amenities: expanded continental breakfast and high-speed Internet.**

POINTE ROYALE CONDOMINIUM RESORT Book great rates at AAA.com **Phone:** (417)334-5614 62

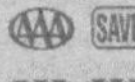

Vacation Rental Condominium
$99-$134 6/1-2/28
$99-$129 3/1-5/31

Address: 158A Pointe Royale Dr 65616 **Location:** SR 165, 2.9 mi s of jct SR 76 (Country Music Blvd). **Facility:** Offering expansive grounds and facilities, the property features individually decorated rooms; all have washer and dryers and many have fireplaces. 180 units. 45 one-, 105 two- and 30 three-bedroom suites with kitchens, some with whirlpools. 2-3 stories (no elevator), exterior corridors. **Parking:** on-site. **Terms:** office hours 7 am-midnight, check-in 4 pm, 14 day cancellation notice-fee imposed. **Amenities:** DVD players, voice mail, irons, hair dryers. **Dining:** 2 restaurants. **Pool(s):** 2 outdoor, heated indoor. **Leisure Activities:** whirlpool, fishing, 2 lighted tennis courts, pavilion, grill, hiking trails, playground, exercise room, basketball. *Fee:* golf-18 holes, massage. **Guest Services:** complimentary laundry, wireless Internet. **Business Services:** meeting rooms. *(See color ad p 419)*

/ SOME UNITS

FREE local telephone calls and preferred room (subject to availability with advance reservations)

QUALITY INN & SUITES ON THE STRIP Book at AAA.com **Phone:** 417/334-1194 37

Hotel
Rates not provided

Address: 2834 W Hwy 76 65616 **Location:** Jct US 65, 2 mi w. **Facility:** 113 units. 109 one-bedroom standard units, some with whirlpools. 2 one- and 2 two-bedroom suites. 2-4 stories, exterior corridors. **Parking:** on-site. **Amenities:** dual phone lines, irons, hair dryers. **Pool(s):** outdoor, heated indoor. **Leisure Activities:** whirlpool. **Guest Services:** coin laundry, wireless Internet. **Business Services:** meeting rooms, PC, fax. / SOME UNITS FEE

▼ See AAA listing p 421 ▼

(See map and index starting on p. 402)

RADISSON HOTEL BRANSON Book great rates at AAA.com **Phone:** (417)335-5767 30

AAA SAVE

Hotel

$105-$239 All Year

Address: 120 S Wildwood Dr 65616 **Location:** Jct US 65, 2 mi w on SR 76 (Country Music Blvd), then just s. **Facility:** 472 units. 445 one-bedroom standard units. 27 one-bedroom suites with whirlpools. 10 stories, interior corridors. *Bath:* combo or shower only. **Parking:** on-site. **Terms:** 3 day cancellation notice-fee imposed. **Amenities:** voice mail, irons, hair dryers. *Some:* high-speed Internet. **Dining:** 2 restaurants. **Pool(s):** heated indoor/outdoor. **Leisure Activities:** sauna, whirlpool, exercise room. **Guest Services:** valet laundry, wireless Internet. *Fee:* airport transportation-Branson Airport, area transportation-within 5 mi. **Business Services:** conference facilities, business center. *(See color ad p 420)*

FEE CALL / SOME UNITS FEE

FREE newspaper and high-speed Internet

RAMADA RESORT & CONFERENCE CENTER Book at AAA.com **Phone:** (417)334-1000 23

Hotel

$59-$109 3/1-12/31

Address: 1700 Hwy 76 W 65616 **Location:** Jct SR 76 (Country Music Blvd) and US 65, 1.5 mi w. **Facility:** 292 units. 288 one-bedroom standard units, some with whirlpools. 4 one-bedroom suites with kitchens and whirlpools. 2-6 stories, exterior corridors. *Bath:* combo or shower only. **Parking:** on-site. **Terms:** open 3/1-12/31, cancellation fee imposed. **Amenities:** irons, hair dryers. **Pool(s):** 2 outdoor. **Leisure Activities:** putting green, playground, exercise room, basketball, horseshoes, shuffleboard, volleyball. *Fee:* game room. **Guest Services:** coin laundry, wireless Internet. **Business Services:** meeting rooms, PC. ASK / SOME UNITS FEE

RESIDENCE INN BY MARRIOTT Book great rates at AAA.com **Phone:** (417)336-4077 50

Extended Stay Hotel

$89-$139 All Year

Address: 280 Wildwood Dr S 65616 **Location:** 2 mi w on SR 76 (Country Music Blvd), just s. **Facility:** Smoke free premises. 85 units. 21 one-bedroom standard units with efficiencies. 49 one- and 15 two-bedroom suites, some with efficiencies or kitchens. 3 stories, interior corridors. *Bath:* combo or shower only. **Parking:** on-site. **Terms:** cancellation fee imposed. **Amenities:** voice mail, irons, hair dryers. **Pool(s):** heated indoor. **Leisure Activities:** whirlpool, exercise room, sports court. **Guest Services:** coin laundry, wireless Internet. **Business Services:** PC.

CALL / SOME UNITS FEE

AAA Benefit:

Members save a minimum 5% off the best available rate.

▼ See AAA listing p 417 ▼

(See map and index starting on p. 402)

ROCK VIEW RESORT

Motel

$65-$98 3/1-9/13
$60-$92 9/14-2/28

Phone: 417/334-4678

Address: 1049 Park View Dr 65672 **Location:** Jct US 65, 4.4 mi w on SR 165, 0.3 mi s via Dale Dr, then 0.7 mi w. **Facility:** Smoke free premises. 12 units. 7 one- and 2 two-bedroom standard units with efficiencies. 3 one-bedroom suites with efficiencies. 1-2 stories (no elevator), exterior corridors. *Bath:* combo or shower only. **Parking:** on-site. **Terms:** office hours 8 am-6 pm, 3 night minimum stay - seasonal, 21 day cancellation notice-fee imposed. **Pool(s):** outdoor. **Leisure Activities:** rental boats, fishing, playground, basketball, horseshoes, volleyball. *Fee:* paddleboats, boat dock. **Guest Services:** wireless Internet. / SOME UNITS FEE

ROSEBUD INN

Hotel

$62-$69 11/1-12/19
$51-$59 3/1-10/31

Phone: 417/336-4000 13

Address: 1415 Roark Valley Rd 65616 **Location:** Jct US 65, 2 mi nw on SR 248, then 1.7 mi sw via Gretna Rd. **Facility:** Smoke free premises. 64 one-bedroom standard units. 2-3 stories, interior/exterior corridors. *Bath:* combo or shower only. **Parking:** on-site. **Terms:** open 3/1-12/19, 2 night minimum stay - seasonal and/or weekends, cancellation fee imposed. **Amenities:** hair dryers. **Pool(s):** outdoor. **Guest Services:** wireless Internet. **Free Special Amenities: expanded continental breakfast and high-speed Internet.**

SCENIC HILLS INN *Book great rates at AAA.com*

Hotel

$47-$120 3/1-12/20
$40-$99 1/28-2/28

Phone: (417)336-8855 10

Address: 2422 Shepherd of the Hills Expwy 65616 **Location:** Jct SR 76 (Country Music Blvd), 1.1 mi e. **Facility:** 66 one-bedroom standard units, some with whirlpools. 3-4 stories, interior corridors. *Bath:* combo or shower only. **Parking:** on-site. **Terms:** open 3/1-12/20 & 1/28-2/28, office hours 7 am-11 pm, 2 night minimum stay, cancellation fee imposed. **Amenities:** high-speed Internet, irons, hair dryers. **Pool(s):** outdoor. **Leisure Activities:** whirlpool. **Guest Services:** coin laundry, wireless Internet. *(See color ad below)*

/ SOME UNITS FEE

FREE expanded continental breakfast and high-speed Internet

▼ See AAA listing above ▼

2 PERSONS

2 Nights *plus* **a Show!**
ONLY $139^95! plus tx

3 Nights *plus* **3 Shows!**
ONLY $249^95! plus tx

5 Nights *plus* **9 Shows!**
ONLY $599^95! plus tx

- Free Deluxe Breakfast *(w/fresh baked cinnamon rolls!)*
- Indoor Corridors & Elevator!
- Free WI-FI!
- Handicap & Non-Smoking Rooms
- Discount Tickets Service
- Children under 16 FREE with parents!

AAA **1-888-800-5577**
www.ScenicHillsInn.com
2422 Shepherd of the Hills Expy. • Branson, MO 65616

(See map and index starting on p. 402)

STILL WATERS CONDOMINIUM RESORT Phone: (417)338-2323 39

Resort Condominium
$49-$600 3/1-12/31 & 2/11-2/28

Address: 21 Stillwater Tr 65616 **Location:** Jct SR 265, 0.6 mi w on SR 76 (Country Music Blvd), then 2 mi s on Indian Point Rd. **Facility:** This sprawling resort offers a wide variety of room types and a vast array of seasonal recreational activities, both of which center on Table Rock Lake. Lake activities and the restaurant offer limited services in the off season. Smoke free premises. 182 units. 15 one-bedroom standard units with efficiencies, some with whirlpools. 26 one-, 118 two- and 23 three-bedroom suites with kitchens and whirlpools. 1-4 stories, exterior corridors. **Parking:** on-site. **Terms:** open 3/1-12/31 & 2/11-2/28, office hours 8 am-10 pm, check-in 4 pm, 2-4 night minimum stay - seasonal and/or weekends, 14 day cancellation notice-fee imposed. **Amenities:** video library (fee), DVD players, voice mail, irons, hair dryers. **Pool(s):** 3 outdoor. **Leisure Activities:** whirlpools, waterslide, rental boats, paddleboats, kayak, personal watercraft, board games, pavilion, bicycles, hiking trails, playground, basketball, horseshoes, volleyball. *Fee:* boat dock, waterskiing, game room. **Guest Services:** coin laundry, wireless Internet. **Business Services:** fax (fee). **Free Special Amenities: high-speed Internet.**

STONE CASTLE HOTEL & CONFERENCE CENTER *Book great rates at AAA.com* Phone: (417)335-4700 

Hotel
$69-$119 All Year

Address: 3050 Green Mountain Dr 65616 **Location:** Jct SR 76 (Country Music Blvd) and US 65, 3 mi w on SR 76, 0.8 mi s. **Facility:** Smoke free premises. 299 units. 296 one- and 3 two-bedroom standard units, some with efficiencies and/or whirlpools. 3-4 stories, interior corridors. *Bath:* combo or shower only. **Parking:** on-site. **Amenities:** voice mail, irons, hair dryers. *Some:* DVD players, CD players. **Pool(s):** 2 heated indoor. **Leisure Activities:** whirlpools. *Fee:* game room. **Guest Services:** valet and coin laundry, wireless Internet. **Business Services:** meeting rooms, fax (fee). **Free Special Amenities: full breakfast and high-speed Internet.** *(See color ad p 407 and on insert)*

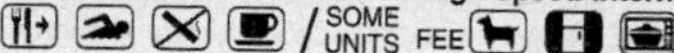

SUPER 8 CENTRAL OF BRANSON *Book at AAA.com* Phone: 417/336-3300 

Hotel
Rates not provided

Address: 3470 Keeter St 65616 **Location:** SR 76 (Country Music Blvd), just s; w of Gretna Rd (SR 165). **Facility:** 78 one-bedroom standard units. 3 stories (no elevator), exterior corridors. **Parking:** on-site. **Amenities:** irons, hair dryers. **Pool(s):** outdoor. **Guest Services:** coin laundry, wireless Internet. **Business Services:** PC. CALL / SOME UNITS FEE

▼ See AAA listing p 424 ▼

(See map and index starting on p. 402)

THOUSAND HILLS GOLF RESORT *Book great rates at AAA.com* **Phone:** (417)336-5873 46

Resort Condominium
$89-$229 All Year

Address: 245 S Wildwood Dr 65616 **Location:** Jct US 65, 3 mi w on SR 76 (Country Music Blvd), then 0.5 mi s. **Facility:** Expansive grounds and facilities are featured at this property offering individually decorated rooms, some overlooking the golf course. Registration is located off site. Smoke free premises. 335 units. 35 one-, 150 two- and 40 three-bedroom suites with whirlpools, some with efficiencies or kitchens. 110 cabins. 1-4 stories, exterior corridors. **Parking:** on-site. **Terms:** office hours 6:30 am-midnight, check-in 4 pm, 14 day cancellation notice-fee imposed. **Amenities:** DVD players, voice mail, irons, hair dryers. *Some:* CD players, high-speed Internet, safes. **Pool(s):** 7 outdoor, 2 heated indoor. **Leisure Activities:** whirlpools, lighted tennis court, exercise room, sports court, basketball, shuffleboard. *Fee:* golf-18 holes. **Guest Services:** complimentary and valet laundry, wireless Internet. **Business Services:** meeting rooms, business center. ***(See color ad p 423)***

ASK CALL

TRAIL'S END RESORT **Phone:** (417)338-2633 53

Vacation Rental Cabin
$45-$229 All Year

Address: 71 Dogwood Park Tr 65616 **Location:** Jct SR 265, 0.6 mi w on SR 76 (Country Music Blvd), 2.9 mi s on Indian Point Rd, then just e. **Facility:** Cabins and motel units in wooded area on lake. Cabin units have fireplaces. 30 units. 5 one-bedroom standard units with efficiencies. 4 one- and 3 two-bedroom suites with efficiencies. 18 cabins. 1 story, exterior corridors. *Bath:* combo or shower only. **Parking:** on-site. **Terms:** office hours 8 am-9 pm, check-in 4 pm, 2-4 night minimum stay - seasonal and/or weekends, 21 day cancellation notice-fee imposed. **Amenities:** video library (fee), voice mail. *Some:* DVD players. **Pool(s):** heated outdoor. **Leisure Activities:** whirlpool, rental boats, paddleboats, marina, scuba diving, snorkeling, fishing, badminton, tetherball, nature trail, playground, horseshoes, shuffleboard, volleyball. *Fee:* waterskiing, personal watercraft, pontoon & deck boats, game room. **Guest Services:** wireless Internet. **Business Services:** fax (fee). **Free Special Amenities: local telephone calls and high-speed Internet.** *(See color ad p 418)*

TREEHOUSE CONDO RENTALS INC *Book great rates at AAA.com* **Phone:** (417)338-5199 14

Condominium
$80-$259 All Year

Address: 129 Treehouse Ln 65616 **Location:** 0.5 mi w of jct SR 76 (Country Music Blvd) and 265, 4 mi s on Indian Point Rd, just w. **Facility:** Independently decorated and situated in a secluded area, select from fully-equipped studio units and one-, two- or three-bedroom condos. 52 units. 2 one-bedroom standard units with kitchens. 7 one-, 27 two- and 16 three-bedroom suites with kitchens, some with whirlpools. 3-4 stories, exterior corridors. *Bath:* combo or shower only. **Parking:** on-site. **Terms:** office hours 8 am-5 pm, 2-3 night minimum stay, 10 day cancellation notice-fee imposed. **Amenities:** DVD players, irons, hair dryers. **Pool(s):** outdoor. **Guest Services:** complimentary laundry, wireless Internet. **Business Services:** meeting rooms, PC. **Free Special Amenities: local telephone calls and preferred room (subject to availability with advance reservations).**

TRIBESMAN RESORT **Phone:** (417)338-2616 55

Resort Cottage
$70-$110 All Year

Address: 416 Cave Lane on Indian Point Rd 65616 **Location:** Jct SR 265, 0.6 mi w on SR 76 (Country Music Blvd), 3 mi s. **Facility:** Wooded grounds. Some contemporary condo-style units. Extensive facilities. Smoke free premises. 61 units. 14 one-, 9 two- and 1 three-bedroom suites, some with efficiencies or kitchens. 37 cottages. 1-2 stories (no elevator), exterior corridors. *Bath:* combo or shower only. **Parking:** on-site. **Terms:** office hours 8 am-9 pm, check-in 4 pm, 3-5 night minimum stay - seasonal, 21 day cancellation notice-fee imposed. **Amenities:** irons. **Pool(s):** 4 outdoor, heated indoor. **Leisure Activities:** whirlpools, rental boats, rental canoes, rental paddleboats, fishing, recreation programs in summer, hiking trails, shuffleboard. *Fee:* boat dock, game room. **Guest Services:** complimentary laundry, wireless Internet. **Business Services:** meeting rooms, PC.

THE VILLAGE AT INDIAN POINT **Phone:** (417)338-8800 42

Condominium
$100-$270 All Year

Address: 24 Village Tr 65616 **Location:** 2.5 mi s of jct SR 76 (Country Music Blvd) on Indian Point Rd. **Facility:** Nestled on lush, wooded acreage, this resort offers fully-equipped cabin-like units which are handsomely furnished. All units with stone wood-burning fireplaces. Smoke free premises. 80 condominiums. 3 stories (no elevator), exterior corridors. **Parking:** on-site. **Terms:** check-in 3:30 pm, 2 night minimum stay - seasonal, 31 day cancellation notice-fee imposed. **Amenities:** video library (fee), high-speed Internet. *Some:* DVD players, irons, hair dryers. **Pool(s):** heated indoor. **Leisure Activities:** sauna, whirlpool, boat dock, fishing, board games, tetherball, hiking trails, playground, exercise room, basketball, horseshoes. *Fee:* game room. **Guest Services:** complimentary laundry. **Business Services:** meeting rooms, fax. *(See color ad p 425)*

/ SOME UNITS FEE

FREE local telephone calls and high-speed Internet

(See map and index starting on p. 402)

WELK RESORT BRANSON Book great rates at AAA.com **Phone:** (417)336-3575 61

Hotel
$59-$139 All Year

Address: 1984 State Hwy 165 65616 **Location:** 2.9 mi s of jct SR 76 (Country Music Blvd). **Facility:** Smoke free premises. 159 one-bedroom standard units. 4 stories, interior corridors. *Bath:* combo or shower only. **Parking:** on-site. **Terms:** 3 day cancellation notice-fee imposed. **Amenities:** voice mail, irons, hair dryers. **Pool(s):** heated outdoor, heated indoor/outdoor. **Leisure Activities:** whirlpools, waterslide, water playground, miniature golf, board & outdoor games, air hockey, billiards, foosball, cards, playground, exercise room. *Fee:* game room. **Guest Services:** coin laundry, wireless Internet. **Business Services:** meeting rooms, PC. *(See color ad p 426 and on insert)*

CALL / SOME UNITS

FREE full breakfast and high-speed Internet

WESTGATE BRANSON WOODS RESORT Book great rates at AAA.com **Phone:** (417)334-2324 11

Resort Condominium
$52-$116 All Year

Address: 2201 Roark Valley Rd 65616 **Location:** US 65, exit SR 248 (Shepherd of the Hills Expwy), 3.7 mi w, just n. **Facility:** Situated in a quiet, wooded setting, the property offers a variety of rooms, including spacious log cabin-style units with attractive decor. 626 units. 201 one-bedroom standard units. 3 one-bedroom suites with kitchens. 37 cabins and 385 condominiums. 1-6 stories, exterior corridors. *Bath:* combo or shower only. **Parking:** on-site. **Terms:** check-in 4 pm, cancellation fee imposed. **Amenities:** video library (fee), voice mail, irons, hair dryers. *Some:* DVD players, CD players, safes. **Pool(s):** 2 outdoor, heated indoor. **Leisure Activities:** whirlpool, recreation programs, pavilions, grills, fire pit, RV parking, table tennis, foosball, horseback riding, playground, exercise room, basketball, shuffleboard, volleyball. **Guest Services:** coin laundry, wireless Internet. **Business Services:** meeting rooms, business center.

   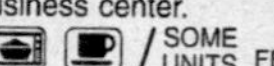  / SOME UNITS FEE

▼ See AAA listing p 424 ▼

(See map and index starting on p. 402)

The following lodgings were either not evaluated or did not meet AAA rating requirements but are listed for your information only.

CASTLE ROCK RESORT & WATERPARK **Phone:** 417/336-6000

fyi Not evaluated. **Address:** 3001 Green Mountain Dr 65616 **Location:** 2.5 mi w on SR 76 (Country Music Blvd) from US 65, 0.4 mi s. Facilities, services, and decor characterize a mid-scale property.

HORIZONS BY MARRIOTT AT BRANSON **Phone:** 417/348-3100

fyi Not evaluated. **Address:** 2929 Green Mountain Dr 65616. Facilities, services, and decor characterize a mid-scale property.

▼ See AAA listing p 425 ▼

(See map and index starting on p. 402)

SOUTHERN OAKS INN

Phone: 417/335-8108

fyi

Not evaluated. **Address:** 3295 Shepherd of the Hills 65616 **Location:** Jct SR 76 (Country Music Blvd), 0.3 mi e. Facilities, services, and decor characterize a mid-scale property.

STORMY POINT VILLAGE BY SUMMER WINDS

Phone: 417/338-0721

fyi

Not evaluated. **Location:** Jct SR 265 and 376, just n to Stormy Point Rd, then 2.3 mi w. Facilities, services, and decor characterize a mid-scale property.

WHERE TO DINE

BLEU OLIVE MEDITERRANEAN GRILLE & BAR

Phone: 417/332-2538 (3)

AAA

Mediterranean
$8-$26

Offering traditional Greek foods, everything on the menu at this modern restaurant is made in house. Popular choices range from a signature gyro to the more adventuresome moussaka. Homemade desserts are a wonderful way to top off the dining experience. Casual dress. **Bar:** Full bar. **Reservations:** accepted. **Hours:** 11 am-2:30 & 4:30-9:30 pm, Fri & Sat-10:30 pm; Easter & Mother's Day brunch. Closed major holidays; also Sun. **Address:** 204 N Commercial St 65616 **Location:** Just ne of jct US 65 and SR 76; downtown. **Parking:** street. CALL &M

B T BONES STEAKHOUSE

Phone: 417/335-2002 (2)

Steak
$8-$29

The atmosphere is casual and rustic in the spacious dining room. Steaks feature prominently on the diverse menu. This place tends to become lively at night. Dressy casual. Entertainment. **Bar:** Full bar. **Reservations:** not accepted. **Hours:** 11 am-10 pm, Fri & Sat-11 pm. Closed: 12/24, 12/25. **Address:** 2280 Shepherd of the Hills Expwy 65616 **Location:** Jct SR 76 (Country Music Blvd), 1.3 mi e. **Parking:** on-site.

BUCKINGHAM'S RESTAURANT & OASIS LOUNGE *Menu on AAA.com*

Phone: 417/337-7777 (14)

AAA

American
$15-$40

Buckingham's offers a fine-dining experience with an unusual African-safari atmosphere. Beef, wild-game meats, seafood and pasta are featured on the menu, and some meals are cooked tableside. Locals enjoy this place. Casual dress. **Bar:** Full bar. **Reservations:** suggested. **Hours:** Open 3/1-1/31; 4:30 pm-9 pm. Closed: 12/25; also Sun. **Address:** 2820 W Hwy 76 65616 **Location:** SR 76 (Country Music Blvd), 3 mi w of jct US 65; in Clarion Hotel at the Palace. **Parking:** on-site. CALL &M

CANDLESTICK INN RESTAURANT & LOUNGE

Phone: 417/334-3633 (8)

Seafood
$24-$48

Since 1962, the casually intimate restaurant has specialized in angus beef strip steaks, tenderloin and filets, as well as such fresh seafood dishes as salmon and trout. Nestled on a hilltop, the upscale dining room overlooks downtown. Dressy casual. **Bar:** Full bar. **Reservations:** suggested. **Hours:** 5 pm-9 pm, Fri & Sat-10 pm. Closed: 12/25; also Mon. **Address:** 127 Taney St 65616 **Location:** 1.5 mi e on SR 76 E, 0.3 mi w of road sign, then just s on Candlestick Rd. **Parking:** on-site.

CANTINA LAREDO

Phone: 417/334-6062

Mexican
$10-$28

The sophisticated restaurant captures patrons' attention with its offerings of authentic Mexican fare. Casual dress. **Bar:** Full bar. **Reservations:** accepted. **Hours:** 11 am-10 pm; closing hours may vary. Closed: 11/25, 12/25. **Address:** 1001 Branson Landing 65616 **Location:** Downtown. **Parking:** on-site (fee). CALL &M

CHARLIE'S STEAK RIBS & ALE

Phone: 417/334-6090 (13)

American
$5-$25

The menu centers on steaks and barbecue specialties, but daily lunch and dinner specials also are popular. A rustic theme weaves through the casual atmosphere. Nightly entertainment from Tuesday through Saturday helps contribute to a mood that can get lively in the evening hours. Casual dress. **Bar:** Full bar. **Reservations:** not accepted. **Hours:** Open 3/1-1/31; 11 am-9 pm; to 11 pm in season. Closed: 4/4, 11/25, 12/25. **Address:** 3009 W Hwy 76 65616 **Location:** 2.5 mi w of jct SR 76 (Country Music Blvd) and US 65. **Parking:** on-site.

CHATEAU GRILLE

Phone: 417/243-1777 (19)

AAA

American
$10-$38

The fine-dining establishment affords beautiful views of the lake. Service is polished and the food innovative. Dressy casual. **Bar:** Full bar. **Reservations:** suggested. **Hours:** 6:30 am-10 pm. **Address:** 415 N State Hwy 265 65616 **Location:** Just n of jct SR 165 and 265; in Chateau on the Lake Resort & Spa. **Parking:** on-site and valet.

DOCKERS RESTAURANT

Phone: 417/332-0044 (18)

American
$7-$20

When you get near this restaurant, you should have no trouble recognizing it: it's built to look like a riverboat. You'll walk across a faux dock to enter the dining room where you'll find a casual atmosphere and a bountiful buffet. Casual dress. **Reservations:** not accepted. **Hours:** Open 4/1-12/15; 7 am-9 pm; closing hours may vary off season. **Address:** 3100 Green Mountain Dr 65616 **Location:** SR 165, just e. **Parking:** on-site.

FARMHOUSE RESTAURANT

Phone: 417/334-9701 (6)

American
$5-$10

Guests are urged to try the chicken-fried steak dinner. For dessert, go for the blackberry cobbler or an apple dumpling with cinnamon sauce and cinnamon ice cream or homemade cherry pie. The list of temptations goes on and on. Casual dress. **Reservations:** not accepted. **Hours:** 7 am-8 pm; Fri & Sat-9 pm in season. Closed: 11/25, 12/25. **Address:** 119 W Main St 65616 **Location:** Just e of jct US 65 and SR 76 (Country Music Blvd); downtown. **Parking:** street. CALL &M

(See map and index starting on p. 402)

GILLEY'S TEXAS CAFE

Phone: 417/335-2755 (11)

American
$7-$17

Mickey Gilley's namesake restaurant presents a diverse menu that includes barbecue and Southwestern fare. Casual dress. **Bar:** Full bar. **Reservations:** not accepted. **Hours:** Open 3/1-12/15; 11 am-11 pm. Closed: 11/25, 12/25. **Address:** 3457 W Hwy 76 65616 **Location:** On SR 76 (Country Music Blvd), just w of jct SR 165; next to Mickey Gilley Theatre. **Parking:** on-site. CALL

GRAND COUNTRY BUFFET

Phone: 417/335-2434 (10)

American
$7-$13

Friendly country charm exudes from the cozy restaurant. Many homemade selections, including tasty sweet corn pops, line a tempting buffet. Casual dress. **Reservations:** not accepted. **Hours:** 7 am-8 pm; seasonal hours may vary. **Address:** 1945 W Hwy 76 65616 **Location:** 1.9 mi w of jct US 65; in 76 Music Hall & Grand Ladies Complex. **Parking:** on-site.

LUIGI'S PIZZA KITCHEN SOUTH

Phone: 417/334-3344 (20)

Italian
$5-$14

This casual pizzeria is in a small shopping center adjacent to the Welk Theater and Hotel. As with most pizzerias, the emphasis is on good food, prepared quickly and served promptly. Casual dress. **Reservations:** not accepted. **Hours:** 11 am-10 pm, Fri & Sat-midnight; to 9 pm 1/1-3/30. Closed: 11/25, 12/25. **Address:** 1972-P State Hwy 165 65616 **Location:** On SR 165, 2.9 mi s of jct SR 76 (Country Music Blvd); in Marketplace Center Shopping Plaza. **Parking:** on-site.

MCFARLAIN'S FAMILY RESTAURANT

Phone: 417/336-4680 (1)

American
$6-$14

The restaurant serves Ozark cookin' at its best. Fried green tomatoes, chicken pot pie and blackberry cobbler are among the favorites here. The atmosphere is lively and fun. This is the type of place where guests can bring the whole family. Casual dress. **Reservations:** not accepted. **Hours:** 7:30 am-8:15 pm, Fri & Sat-9:15 pm; to 9:15 pm, Fri & Sat-10:15 pm 6/1-9/2; 11 am 8:15 pm 12/16-3/14. Closed: 12/24. **Address:** 3562 Shepherd of the Hills Expwy 65616 **Location:** Jct SR 76 (Country Music Blvd), just e; in Imax Entertainment Complex. **Parking:** on-site. *(See color ad p 135)* CALL

OUTBACK STEAK & OYSTER BAR

Phone: 417/334-6306 (9)

Steak
$6-$25

Hearty portions of grilled steaks and seafood are served in a casually rustic, Australian atmosphere. Diners can enjoy live music and outdoor dining with a view of bungee jumping in season. Alligator tail and oysters are popular menu items. Casual dress. **Bar:** Full bar. **Reservations:** not accepted. **Hours:** 11 am-10 pm, Fri & Sat-11 pm. **Address:** 1914 W Hwy 76 65616 **Location:** US 65, 1.5 mi w; in Outback Roadhouse Motel & Suites. **Parking:** on-site.

PASTA HOUSE

Phone: 417/337-9882 (17)

Italian
$8-$22

The restaurant reflects the Old World in a contemporary and comfortable atmosphere. The menu centers on traditional favorites. Try pecan chocolate cake for dessert. Casual dress. **Bar:** Full bar. **Reservations:** accepted. **Hours:** 11 am-10 pm, Fri & Sat-11 pm; hours may vary off season. Closed: 12/25. **Address:** 2690 Green Mountain Dr 65616 **Location:** Jct US 65, 2 mi w on SR 76 (Country Music Blvd), just s; behind Grand Palace. **Parking:** on-site. CALL

(See map and index starting on p. 402)

RIB CRIB BBQ AND GRILL **Phone:** 417/337-7427

Barbecue
$6-$16

Most guests need extra napkins to tackle the ribs, brisket, ham, pork and chicken selections. The menu also lists sandwiches and wraps, along with tempting sides and large desserts. The decor is decidedly Western. Casual dress. **Bar:** Beer only. **Reservations:** not accepted. **Hours:** 11 am-10 pm. Closed: 11/25, 12/25. **Address:** 1855 W Hwy 76 65616 **Location:** 1.6 mi w of jct US 65. **Parking:** on-site. CALL

ROCKY'S ITALIAN RESTAURANT **Phone:** 417/335-4765 (5)

Italian
$7-$20

Rocky's comes highly recommended by local residents, who like its exceptional food and casual, warm atmosphere. They say the shrimp, lasagna and chicken picata are excellent choices. The building is a restored feedmill built at the turn-of-the-century. Casual dress. **Bar:** Full bar. **Reservations:** not accepted. **Hours:** 11 am-9 pm. Closed major holidays; also Sun. **Address:** 120 N Sycamore 65616 **Location:** Just n of Main St. **Parking:** on-site.

RUBY LENA'S TEA ROOM & ANTIQUES **Phone:** 417/239-2919 (4)

American
$6-$8

This quaint tea room offers a menu of homemade quiches, sandwiches and desserts. It's known for its homemade cream pies, and the coconut cream pie is legendary. Casual dress. **Reservations:** accepted. **Hours:** Open 3/1-12/19; 11 am-3 pm. Closed major holidays; also Sun & Mon. **Address:** 224 W Main St 65616 **Location:** On SR 76 (Country Music Blvd); downtown. **Parking:** on-site. CALL

SADIE'S SIDEBOARD & SMOKEHOUSE **Phone:** 417/334-3619 (15)

Regional American
$5-$17

The casual, family-oriented establishment lays out a buffet with a good variety of down-home country comfort food for breakfast, lunch and dinner. Features include barbecue, beef, pork, chicken, catfish and smoked ham. Casual dress. **Reservations:** not accepted. **Hours:** Open 3/1-12/31; 7 am-8 pm, Fri & Sat-9 pm; hours vary in winter. Closed: 12/24, 12/25. **Address:** 2830 W Hwy 76 65616 **Location:** 3.5 mi w on SR 76 (Country Music Blvd) from jct US 65. **Parking:** on-site. CALL

SHORTY SMALL'S **Phone:** 417/334-8797

American
$7-$19

Focusing on ribs, fried catfish, sandwiches and cheesecake, this restaurant is popular with the locals. The rustic and nostalgic atmosphere is family-oriented, and the feel is casual, hectic and sometimes noisy. Casual dress. **Bar:** Full bar. **Reservations:** not accepted. **Hours:** 11 am-10 pm. Closed: 12/25. **Address:** 3270 Yellow Ribbon Rd 65616 **Location:** Jct SR 76 (Country Music Blvd) and SR 165, 1 mi s; near Tony Orlando Theater. **Parking:** on-site.

UPTOWN CAFE **Phone:** 417/336-3535 (16)

American
$5-$10

The Uptown Cafe nostalgically replicates a 1950s-style Route 66 diner, complete with jukebox music, art deco ambience, and soda fountain treats. They specialize in steakburgers, meatloaf, country-fried chicken, banana splits and hot fudge sundaes. Casual dress. **Bar:** Beer & wine. **Reservations:** not accepted. **Hours:** 7 am-8 pm; to 11 pm, Fri & Sat-midnight 6/1-9/6; hours may vary. Closed: 11/25, 12/25. **Address:** 285 SR 165 65616 **Location:** Jct SR 76 (Country Music Blvd), just s. **Parking:** on-site. CALL

WASABI JAPANESE STEAK & SUSHI **Phone:** 417/336-1177 (12)

Japanese
$7-$16

Casual, friendly staff members serve tasty, traditional Japanese cuisine. Diners can choose fresh items from the sushi bar as well as great tempura and steaks. Casual dress. **Bar:** Beer & wine. **Reservations:** required. **Hours:** 11 am-10 pm, Fri & Sat-11 pm, Sun noon-9 pm. **Address:** 2005 W Hwy 76, #201 65616 **Location:** Just e off Green Mountain Rd; in Vista Plaza. **Parking:** on-site. CALL

WAXY O'SHEA'S **Phone:** 417/348-1759 (7)

Irish
$6-$16

With a fun atmosphere and some traditional dishes—like beer cheese soup and bangers and mash—this eatery brings the feel of an Irish pub to the Ozarks. Live entertainment is common here, especially on the weekends. Before 4 pm, non-smoking sections can be found. Casual dress. **Bar:** Full bar. **Reservations:** not accepted. **Hours:** 11 am-midnight. **Address:** 235 Branson Landing 65616 **Location:** Downtown; Branson Landing. **Parking:** on-site. CALL

The following restaurants have not been evaluated by AAA but are listed for your information only.

DANNA'S BAR B QUE AND BURGER SHOP **Phone:** 417/337-5527

fyi

Not evaluated. Cheerfully unadorned, the restaurant invites patrons to bring the family for burgers and BBQ, and while they're at it, a root beer float. This place epitomizes an authentic roadside burger joint. **Address:** 963 Hwy 165 65615 **Location:** 1.5 mi s of jct SR 76 (Country Music Blvd).

LUIGI'S PIZZA KITCHEN NORTH **Phone:** 417/339-4544

fyi

Not evaluated. The casual pizzeria is in a small shopping center. The emphasis is on good food, prepared quickly and served promptly. **Address:** 1447 State Hwy 248, Suite F 65616 **Location:** Jct SR 248 and James Epps Rd, just sw; in Cedar Ridge Center.

The Branson Vicinity

BRANSON WEST pop. 408

BEST WESTERN BRANSON INN & CONFERENCE CENTER *Book great rates at AAA.com*

Phone: (417)338-2141

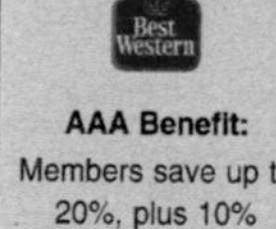

Hotel

$72-$79 All Year

Address: 8514 Hwy 76 65737 **Location:** Jct SR 265, 1.1 mi w on SR 76. **Facility:** 145 one-bedroom standard units, some with whirlpools. 3 stories, interior corridors. **Parking:** on-site. **Amenities:** irons, hair dryers. **Pool(s):** heated indoor. **Leisure Activities:** whirlpool, pool table, air hockey. *Fee:* game room. **Guest Services:** coin laundry, area transportation-Silver Dollar City, wireless Internet. **Business Services:** meeting rooms, business center. *(See color ad p 411)*

/ SOME UNITS

AAA Benefit: Members save up to 20%, plus 10% bonus points with rewards program.

FREE expanded continental breakfast and high-speed Internet

LAKEVIEW INN

Phone: 417/272-8195

Hotel

Rates not provided

Address: 10930 W State Hwy 76 65737 **Location:** 2 mi w of jct SR 76 and 265. **Facility:** 66 one-bedroom standard units. 2-3 stories (no elevator), exterior corridors. **Parking:** on-site. **Pool(s):** outdoor. **Guest Services:** coin laundry, wireless Internet. **Business Services:** meeting rooms. / SOME UNITS

SHADY ACRE MOTEL

Phone: 417/338-2316

Motel

Rates not provided

Address: 8722 State Hwy 76 65737 **Location:** Jct SR 265, 1.3 mi w. Located in a quiet area. **Facility:** 16 one-bedroom standard units, some with efficiencies. 1-2 stories (no elevator), exterior corridors. **Parking:** on-site. **Terms:** office hours 8 am-8:30 pm. **Pool(s):** outdoor. **Leisure Activities:** *Fee:* charter fishing. **Guest Services:** wireless Internet. / SOME UNITS

WHERE TO DINE

DANNA'S BAR-B-QUE & BURGER SHOP

Phone: 417/272-1945

Barbecue

$5-$15

This casual eatery prepares wonderful barbecue, including pulled pork, beef and ribs. Additionally, the large and creative burgers are a good choice. Casual dress. **Bar:** Beer only. **Reservations:** not accepted. **Hours:** 11 am-8 pm, Fri & Sat-9 pm. Closed: 11/25, 12/25; also Sun. **Address:** 15 Hope Way (SR 13) 65737 **Location:** 0.5 mi s of jct SR 13 and SR 76; next to Hope Church. **Parking:** on-site. CALL

CAPE FAIR

WHERE TO DINE

KOPPIE'S DINER **Phone:** 417/538-4312

American
$5-$10

A cheerful soda fountain theme characterizes the restaurant, which serves Chicago's Vienna Beef hot dogs, burgers, sandwiches, soup and salads. Ice cream shakes, malts and sundaes are among desserts. Fishermen's lunch boxes are available. Casual dress. **Bar:** Beer only. **Reservations:** accepted. **Hours:** 11 am-8 pm, Fri & Sat-9 pm. Closed: 12/25. **Address:** 9215 State Hwy 173 65624 **Location:** Jct SR 76 and 173. **Parking:** on-site.

HOLLISTER pop. 3,867 (See map and index starting on p. 402)

WESTGATE BRANSON LAKES AT EMERALD POINTE **Phone:** 417/334-4944

AAA SAVE

Resort Condominium
$71-$206 All Year

Address: 750 Emerald Pointe Dr 65672 **Location:** Jct US 65 and SR 265, 1 mi w to Hill Haven Rd, then 2 mi s. **Facility:** Located on the shores of Table Rock Lake, the one- and two-bedroom units offer luxury and comfort with great guest amenities. Smoke free premises. 158 units. 144 one- and 8 two-bedroom suites with kitchens, some with whirlpools. 6 condominiums. 2-4 stories, exterior corridors. **Parking:** on-site. **Terms:** check-in 4 pm, cancellation fee imposed. **Amenities:** video library (fee), DVD players, CD players, voice mail, irons, hair dryers. **Pool(s):** outdoor, heated indoor. **Leisure Activities:** whirlpool, marina, fishing, miniature golf, recreation programs, table tennis, pavilion with barbecue grills, exercise room, basketball, horseshoes, shuffleboard. **Guest Services:** complimentary laundry. **Business Services:** fax (fee).

CALL / SOME UNITS FEE

The following lodging was either not evaluated or did not meet AAA rating requirements but is listed for your information only.

THE VILLAS AT BRANSON CREEK **Phone:** 417/332-3259

fyi

Not evaluated. **Address:** 1250 Golf Club Dr 65672 **Location:** I-65, exit Maple St, 7.8 mi nw; in Murder Rock Golf Club House. Facilities, services, and decor characterize a mid-scale property.

WHERE TO DINE

THE KEETER CENTER AT COLLEGE OF THE OZARKS **Phone:** 417/239-1900 23

AAA

American
$8-$20

Friendly service is the hallmark of this restaurant, which features Ozark country cooking and a casual atmosphere where children are welcomed. The Sunday buffet is good. The College of the Ozarks owns and operates this place as a part of the work program required of all students. Casual dress. **Reservations:** suggested, Sun. **Hours:** 10:30 am-8 pm, Sun 10 am-2 pm. Closed: 12/25. **Address:** 1 Opportunity Way 65726 **Location:** Jct SR 76; 2 mi s on US 65, 0.8 mi w on CR V; at College of the Ozarks. **Parking:** on-site. CALL

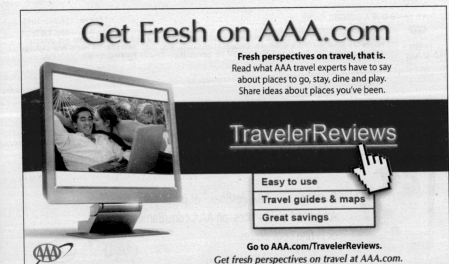

KIMBERLING CITY pop. 2,253

The following lodging was either not evaluated or did not meet AAA rating requirements but is listed for your information only.

WATERS EDGE ON TABLE ROCK LAKE CABIN AND RV RESORT

Phone: 417/739-5377

fyi Not evaluated. **Address:** 72 Marina Way 65686 **Location:** SR 13, 0.3 mi n on Kimberling Blvd, just e on Bass Ave, then just s. Facilities, services, and decor characterize an economy property.

RIDGEDALE

The following lodging was either not evaluated or did not meet AAA rating requirements but is listed for your information only.

BIG CEDAR LODGE

Phone: 417/335-2777

fyi Not evaluated. **Address:** 612 Devils Pool Rd 65739. Facilities, services, and decor characterize a mid-scale property.

This ends listings for the Branson Vicinity.
The following page resumes the alphabetical listings of cities in Missouri.

BRANSON WEST—See Branson p. 431.

BRENTWOOD—See St. Louis p. 552.

BRIDGETON—See St. Louis p. 553.

BROOKFIELD pop. 4,769

BEST WESTERN BROOKFIELD *Book great rates at AAA.com* **Phone:** (660)258-4900

Hotel
$89-$109 All Year

Address: 28622 Hwy 11 64628 **Location:** US 36, exit Business Rt 36, just se. **Facility:** 31 one-bedroom standard units, some with whirlpools. 2 stories, interior corridors. *Bath:* combo or shower only. **Parking:** on-site. **Amenities:** high-speed Internet, irons, hair dryers. **Pool(s):** outdoor. **Guest Services:** wireless Internet. **Business Services:** PC. **Free Special Amenities: expanded continental breakfast and high-speed Internet.**

CALL / SOME UNITS FEE

AAA Benefit: Members save up to 20%, plus 10% bonus points with rewards program.

CAMDENTON pop. 2,779

SLEEP INN & SUITES *Book great rates at AAA.com* **Phone:** (573)346-4501

AAA SAVE
Hotel
$100-$150 3/1-9/9
$90-$115 9/10-2/28

Address: 1390 E Hwy 54 65020 **Location:** On US 54. **Facility:** 62 units. 60 one-bedroom standard units, some with whirlpools. 2 one-bedroom suites with whirlpools. 4 stories, interior corridors. *Bath:* combo or shower only. **Parking:** on-site. **Terms:** cancellation fee imposed. **Amenities:** high-speed Internet, voice mail, safes (fee), irons, hair dryers. **Pool(s):** outdoor, heated indoor. **Leisure Activities:** whirlpool, gazebo, patio, exercise room. **Guest Services:** valet and coin laundry, wireless Internet. **Business Services:** meeting rooms, PC. **Free Special Amenities: expanded continental breakfast and high-speed Internet.** / SOME UNITS

CAMERON pop. 8,312

BEST WESTERN ACORN INN *Book great rates at AAA.com* **Phone:** (816)632-2187

AAA SAVE
Motel
$79-$95 All Year

Address: 2210 E US 36 64429 **Location:** I-35, exit 54, 0.3 mi e. **Facility:** 40 one-bedroom standard units. 1 story, exterior corridors. *Bath:* combo or shower only. **Parking:** on-site, winter plug-ins. **Amenities:** irons, hair dryers. **Pool(s):** outdoor. **Guest Services:** valet and coin laundry, airport transportation-Cameron Memorial Airport, area transportation, wireless Internet. **Business Services:** PC. **Free Special Amenities: local telephone calls and high-speed Internet.**

/ SOME UNITS

AAA Benefit: Members save up to 20%, plus 10% bonus points with rewards program.

COMFORT INN *Book at AAA.com* **Phone:** 816/632-5655

Hotel
Rates not provided

Address: 1803 Comfort Ln 64429 **Location:** I-35, exit 54, just e. **Facility:** 60 one-bedroom standard units, some with whirlpools. 2 stories, interior corridors. **Parking:** on-site. **Amenities:** safes, irons, hair dryers. **Pool(s):** heated indoor. **Leisure Activities:** sauna, whirlpool, waterslide. **Guest Services:** coin laundry, wireless Internet. **Business Services:** PC.

/ SOME UNITS

DAYS INN *Book at AAA.com* **Phone:** 816/632-6666

Hotel
Rates not provided

Address: 601 E Bryan Rd 64429 **Location:** I-35, exit 54, 0.5 mi w on US 36. **Facility:** 47 one-bedroom standard units. 2 stories (no elevator), interior corridors. *Bath:* combo or shower only. **Parking:** on-site, winter plug-ins. **Amenities:** irons, hair dryers. **Pool(s):** heated indoor. **Guest Services:** wireless Internet. **Business Services:** PC. / SOME UNITS

ECONO LODGE *Book great rates at AAA.com* **Phone:** (816)632-6571

AAA SAVE
Hotel
$60-$75 All Year

Address: 220 E Grand 64429 **Location:** I-35, exit 54, 0.5 mi w on US 36, then just s on US 69. **Facility:** 36 one-bedroom standard units. 2 stories (no elevator), exterior corridors. *Bath:* combo or shower only. **Parking:** on-site. **Amenities:** high-speed Internet. **Pool(s):** outdoor. **Free Special Amenities: continental breakfast and high-speed Internet.**

/ SOME UNITS FEE

SUPER 8 *Book at AAA.com* **Phone:** (816)632-8888

Hotel
$62-$78 All Year

Address: 1710 N Walnut St 64429 **Location:** I-35, exit 54, 0.5 mi w on US 36. **Facility:** 41 one-bedroom standard units, some with whirlpools. 2 stories (no elevator), interior corridors. **Parking:** on-site, winter plug-ins. **Amenities:** high-speed Internet, irons, hair dryers. **Pool(s):** heated indoor. **Leisure Activities:** whirlpool. **Guest Services:** wireless Internet. **Business Services:** PC.

ASK / SOME UNITS FEE

CANTON pop. 2,557

COMFORT INN CANTON *Book at AAA.com* **Phone:** 573/288-8800

Hotel
Rates not provided

Address: 1701 Oak St 63435 **Location:** US 61, exit US 61 business route/CR P, just e. **Facility:** 60 one-bedroom standard units, some with whirlpools. 3 stories, interior corridors. *Bath:* combo or shower only. **Parking:** on-site. **Amenities:** high-speed Internet, voice mail, safes (fee), irons, hair dryers. **Pool(s):** heated indoor. **Leisure Activities:** whirlpool. *Fee:* game room. **Guest Services:** coin laundry, wireless Internet. **Business Services:** meeting rooms, business center.

/ SOME UNITS FEE

CAPE FAIR—See Branson p. 432.

CAPE GIRARDEAU pop. 35,349

BELLEVUE BED AND BREAKFAST **Phone:** 573/335-3302

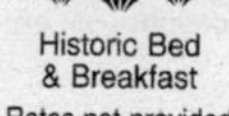

Historic Bed & Breakfast
Rates not provided

Address: 312 Bellevue St 63701 **Location:** Between Lorimier and Fountain sts. Located in a quiet residential area. **Facility:** The restored 1891 Victorian home features period decor and antiques. Theme guest rooms boast period detail. Smoke free premises. 4 one-bedroom standard units, some with whirlpools. 2 stories (no elevator), interior corridors. *Bath:* combo or shower only. **Parking:** on-site. **Terms:** check-in 4 pm. **Amenities:** video library, DVD players, CD players, hair dryers. **Guest Services:** area transportation, wireless Internet. **Business Services:** PC, fax.

DRURY LODGE-CAPE GIRARDEAU *Book at AAA.com* **Phone:** (573)334-7151

Hotel
$80-$130 All Year

Address: 104 S Vantage Dr 63701 **Location:** I-55, exit 96 (William St), just e. **Facility:** 139 one-bedroom standard units. 2 stories (no elevator), interior/exterior corridors. **Parking:** on-site. **Terms:** cancellation fee imposed. **Amenities:** high-speed Internet, voice mail, irons, hair dryers. **Dining:** Cedar Street, see separate listing. **Pool(s):** outdoor. **Leisure Activities:** exercise room. **Guest Services:** valet and coin laundry, wireless Internet. **Business Services:** conference facilities, PC.

ASK / SOME UNITS

DRURY SUITES-CAPE GIRARDEAU *Book at AAA.com* **Phone:** (573)339-9500

Hotel
$100-$150 All Year

Address: 3303 Campster Dr 63701 **Location:** I-55, exit 96 (William St), just w. Located in a commercial area. **Facility:** 87 units. 8 one-bedroom standard units. 79 one-bedroom suites, some with efficiencies. 5 stories, interior corridors. *Bath:* combo or shower only. **Parking:** on-site, winter plug-ins. **Terms:** cancellation fee imposed. **Amenities:** high-speed Internet, voice mail, irons, hair dryers. **Pool(s):** heated indoor. **Leisure Activities:** whirlpool, exercise room. **Guest Services:** valet and coin laundry, wireless Internet. **Business Services:** meeting rooms, PC.

ASK CALL / SOME UNITS

HAMPTON INN-CAPE GIRARDEAU *Book great rates at AAA.com* **Phone:** (573)651-3000

Hotel
$108-$133 All Year

Address: 103 Cape W Pkwy 63701 **Location:** I-55, exit 96 (William St), 0.3 mi sw. Located in a commercial area. **Facility:** Smoke free premises. 81 units. 79 one-bedroom standard units. 2 one-bedroom suites. 3 stories, interior corridors. *Bath:* combo or shower only. **Parking:** on-site, winter plug-ins. **Terms:** 1-7 night minimum stay, cancellation fee imposed. **Amenities:** high-speed Internet, voice mail, irons, hair dryers. **Leisure Activities:** exercise room. **Guest Services:** valet laundry, wireless Internet.

CALL / SOME UNITS

AAA Benefit:
Members save up to 10% everyday!

HOLIDAY INN EXPRESS HOTEL & SUITES *Book at AAA.com* **Phone:** (573)334-4491

Hotel
$89-$149 All Year

Address: 3253 William St 63701 **Location:** I-55, exit 96 (William St), just e. **Facility:** Smoke free premises. 102 one-bedroom standard units, some with whirlpools. 4 stories, interior corridors. *Bath:* combo or shower only. **Parking:** on-site. **Terms:** cancellation fee imposed. **Amenities:** video games (fee), high-speed Internet, dual phone lines, voice mail, irons, hair dryers. **Pool(s):** heated indoor. **Leisure Activities:** whirlpool, exercise room. *Fee:* game room. **Guest Services:** valet and coin laundry, wireless Internet. **Business Services:** meeting rooms, PC.

ASK CALL

PEAR TREE INN BY DRURY-CAPE GIRARDEAU *Book at AAA.com* **Phone:** (573)334-3000

Hotel
$70-$115 All Year

Address: 3248 William St 63701 **Location:** I-55, exit 96 (William St), just e. **Facility:** 78 one-bedroom standard units. 3 stories, interior corridors. **Parking:** on-site. **Terms:** cancellation fee imposed. **Amenities:** high-speed Internet, irons, hair dryers. **Pool(s):** outdoor. **Leisure Activities:** exercise room privileges. **Guest Services:** valet laundry, wireless Internet.

ASK / SOME UNITS

VICTORIAN INN & SUITES *Book at AAA.com* **Phone:** 573/651-4486

Hotel
Rates not provided

Address: 3265 William St 63701 **Location:** I-55, exit 96 (William St), just e. **Facility:** 133 units. 132 one-bedroom standard units, some with whirlpools. 1 one-bedroom suite with whirlpool. 2 stories (no elevator), interior/exterior corridors. *Bath:* combo or shower only. **Parking:** on-site, winter plug-ins. **Amenities:** video games (fee), high-speed Internet, dual phone lines, voice mail, irons, hair dryers. **Pool(s):** heated indoor. **Leisure Activities:** whirlpool, exercise room. *Fee:* game room. **Guest Services:** valet and coin laundry, wireless Internet. **Business Services:** meeting rooms, PC.

CALL / SOME UNITS

WHERE TO DINE

BELLA ITALIA **Phone:** 573/332-7800

Italian
$6-$19

The popular storefront restaurant treats patrons to thoughtful service and fine food, including sandwiches, calzones, salads, pasta dishes, pizza and Old World favorites. Casual dress. **Bar:** Full bar. **Reservations:** not accepted. **Hours:** 11 am-9 pm, Fri & Sat-10 pm, Sun-8 pm. Closed major holidays. **Address:** 20 N Spanish St 63701 **Location:** 2 blks w of Mississippi River; in historic downtown. **Parking:** street. **Historic**

BG'S OLDE TYME DELI & SALOON **Phone:** 573/335-8860

American
$5-$8

The popular restaurant prepares home-style dinners and smokes its barbecue pork on the premises. Among offerings are Mexican dishes, catfish and chicken and dumplings soup as well as a large selection of sandwiches. Casual dress. **Bar:** Full bar. **Reservations:** accepted. **Hours:** 11 am-10 pm, Fri & Sat-11 pm. Closed: 1/1, 11/25, 12/25. **Address:** 205 S Plaza Way 63703 **Location:** I-55, exit 96 (William St), 1.8 mi e. **Parking:** on-site.

CEDAR STREET **Phone:** 573/332-7427

American
$5-$18

Patrons can unwind in a pleasant atmosphere to sample ribs, steaks and fajitas. Flowerpot bread with flavored butters is enjoyable. Casual dress. **Bar:** Full bar. **Reservations:** accepted. **Hours:** 6 am-10 pm, Sat from 7 am, Sun 7 am-9 pm. Closed: 12/25. **Address:** 104 S Vantage Dr 63701 **Location:** I-55, exit 96 (William St), just w; in Drury Lodge-Cape Girardeau. **Parking:** on-site. CALL

MOLLIE'S CAFE & BAR **Phone:** 573/339-1661

Northern Continental
$12-$28

The restaurant features a good variety of seafood, beef and pork specialty selections that showcase the chef's unusual and creative methods. Meals are prepared with fresh ingredients and served in a Continental art nouveau dining room that can seem stark to those expecting soft textures and warm colors. Casual dress. **Bar:** Full bar. **Reservations:** suggested, weekends. **Hours:** 5 pm-10 pm, Fri & Sat-11 pm. Closed: 1/1, 11/25, 12/25; also Sun. **Address:** 11 S Spanish St 63703 **Location:** I-55, exit 96 (William St), 4.5 mi e, then just n. **Parking:** street.

CARTHAGE pop. 12,668

BEST WESTERN PRECIOUS MOMENTS HOTEL *Book great rates at AAA.com* **Phone:** (417)359-5900

Hotel
$79-$130 3/1-12/31
$72-$120 1/1-2/28

Address: 2701 Hazel St 64836 **Location:** Just e of jct US 71 and SR HH. **Facility:** 122 one-bedroom standard units, some with whirlpools. 2 stories, interior corridors. *Bath:* combo or shower only. **Parking:** on-site. **Terms:** check-in 4 pm. **Amenities:** voice mail, irons, hair dryers. **Pool(s):** heated indoor. **Leisure Activities:** exercise room. **Guest Services:** coin laundry, wireless Internet. **Business Services:** PC. **Free Special Amenities: local telephone calls and high-speed Internet.**

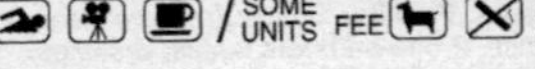

AAA Benefit: Members save up to 20%, plus 10% bonus points with rewards program.

ECONO LODGE *Book great rates at AAA.com* **Phone:** (417)358-3900

Hotel
$54-$64 All Year

Address: 1441 W Central 64836 **Location:** Just ne of jct US 71 and SR 96. **Facility:** 82 units. 81 one-bedroom standard units. 1 one-bedroom suite. 2 stories (no elevator), interior/exterior corridors. *Bath:* combo or shower only. **Parking:** on-site. **Amenities:** safes (fee), hair dryers. *Some:* irons. **Pool(s):** heated indoor. **Leisure Activities:** whirlpool. **Guest Services:** wireless Internet. **Business Services:** meeting rooms, PC. **Free Special Amenities: expanded continental breakfast and high-speed Internet.** SOME UNITS FEE

SUPER 8 *Book at AAA.com* **Phone:** 417/359-9000

Hotel
Rates not provided

Address: 416 W Fir Rd 64836 **Location:** Just e of jct US 71 and SR HH. **Facility:** 56 one-bedroom standard units. 2 stories (no elevator), interior corridors. **Parking:** on-site. **Amenities:** hair dryers. **Leisure Activities:** whirlpool. **Guest Services:** coin laundry, wireless Internet. SOME UNITS FEE

WHERE TO DINE

BAM-BOO GARDENS **Phone:** 417/358-1611

Chinese
$4-$8

Many locals enjoy the buffet offerings, but patrons can order from the menu as well. Casual dress. **Hours:** 11 am-9 pm, Fri-10 pm. Closed: 11/25, 12/25. **Address:** 102 N Garrison Ave 64836 **Location:** 1 mi e of jct US 71 and SR 96. **Parking:** on-site.

SIRLOIN STOCKADE **Phone:** 417/358-1765

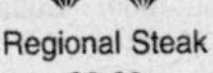

Regional Steak
$6-$9

The steakhouse lines up buffet items, including pizza, tacos, soups, salads and desserts, providing both excellent variety and a good value. Rotating theme nights might allow for the sampling of sushi, barbecue and seafood. The buffet also may serve to complement a quality steak. Rolls are baked several times daily. Casual dress. **Reservations:** not accepted. **Hours:** 11 am-9 pm. Closed: 11/25, 12/25. **Address:** 1027 W Central 64836 **Location:** 0.5 mi e of jct US 71 and SR 96. **Parking:** on-site.

CHESTERFIELD—See St. Louis p. 554.

CHILLICOTHE pop. 8,968

BEST WESTERN INN *Book great rates at AAA.com* **Phone:** (660)646-0572

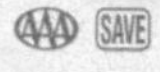

Hotel
$65-$113 All Year

Address: 1020 S Washington St 64601 **Location:** Jct US 36 and 65 (Washington St). **Facility:** Smoke free premises. 58 units. 52 one-bedroom standard units. 6 one-bedroom suites. 1-3 stories (no elevator), interior/exterior corridors. *Bath:* combo or shower only. **Parking:** on-site. **Amenities:** irons, hair dryers. **Pool(s):** outdoor. **Guest Services:** coin laundry, wireless Internet. **Business Services:** meeting rooms, PC. **Free Special Amenities: expanded continental breakfast and high-speed Internet.**

CALL / SOME UNITS FEE

AAA Benefit:
Members save up to 20%, plus 10% bonus points with rewards program.

CHILLICOTHE SUPER 8 *Book at AAA.com* **Phone:** (660)646-7888

Hotel
$55-$78 All Year

Address: 580 Old Hwy 36 E 64601 **Location:** Jct US 36 and 65 (Washington St), 0.8 mi e. **Facility:** 54 one-bedroom standard units, some with whirlpools. 2 stories (no elevator), interior corridors. **Parking:** on-site, winter plug-ins. **Terms:** cancellation fee imposed. **Amenities:** irons, hair dryers. **Guest Services:** coin laundry, wireless Internet. **Business Services:** PC.

ASK / SOME UNITS FEE

WHERE TO DINE

BEIJING CHINESE RESTAURANT **Phone:** 660/646-4112

Chinese
$5-$10

The popular spot offers a generous buffet and menu selections of favorites, as well as casual atmosphere, friendly service and a good value. Casual dress. **Bar:** Beer & wine. **Reservations:** accepted. **Hours:** 11 am-2 & 4:30-9:30 pm, Sat 11 am-2:30 & 4:30-9:30 pm, Sun 2:30 pm-9:30 pm. Closed: 11/25, 12/25. **Address:** 327 Washington St 64601 **Location:** 1 mi n on US 65 (Washington St). **Parking:** on-site.

WASHINGTON STREET FOOD & DRINK COMPANY **Phone:** 660/646-4058

American
$6-$15

The atmosphere is comfortable and relaxed. Good menu selections are topped by a better array of tempting desserts, including hand-mixed chocolate, vanilla or cherry colas and fried cheesecake. Casual dress. **Bar:** Full bar. **Reservations:** accepted. **Hours:** 11 am-10 pm, Fri & Sat-10:30 pm, Sun-9 pm. Closed major holidays. **Address:** 1100 N Washington St 64601 **Location:** 1.9 mi n on US 65 (Washington St). **Parking:** on-site.

CLAYTON—See St. Louis p. 555.

CLINTON pop. 9,311

BEST WESTERN COLONIAL MOTEL *Book great rates at AAA.com* **Phone:** (660)885-2206

Motel
$59-$69 All Year

Address: 106 S Baird St 64735 **Location:** Jct SR 7 and 13. **Facility:** 32 one-bedroom standard units. 1-2 stories (no elevator), exterior corridors. **Parking:** on-site, winter plug-ins. **Amenities:** high-speed Internet, irons, hair dryers. **Pool(s):** outdoor. **Business Services:** PC.

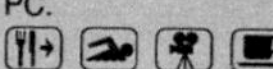

/ SOME UNITS FEE

AAA Benefit:
Members save up to 20%, plus 10% bonus points with rewards program.

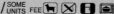

FREE expanded continental breakfast and high-speed Internet

HAMPTON INN *Book great rates at AAA.com* **Phone:** (660)885-4488

Hotel
$79-$105 All Year

Address: 900 Kansas Ave 64735 **Location:** Just s of jct SR 7 and 18. **Facility:** 65 one-bedroom standard units. 3 stories, interior corridors. *Bath:* combo or shower only. **Parking:** on-site. **Terms:** 1-7 night minimum stay, cancellation fee imposed. **Amenities:** high-speed Internet, voice mail, irons, hair dryers. **Pool(s):** heated indoor. **Leisure Activities:** exercise room. **Guest Services:** valet laundry, wireless Internet. **Business Services:** meeting rooms.

CALL   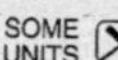 / SOME UNITS  

AAA Benefit:
Members save up to 10% everyday!

PARKFIELD INN

Hotel
$59-$120 All Year

Book at AAA.com

Phone: (660)890-6188

Address: 506 Kansas Ave 64735 **Location:** Just s of jct SR 7 and 18. **Facility:** 60 units. 59 one-bedroom standard units, some with whirlpools. 1 one-bedroom suite with whirlpool. 2 stories, interior corridors. *Bath:* combo or shower only. **Parking:** on-site, winter plug-ins. **Amenities:** irons, hair dryers. **Pool(s):** heated indoor. **Leisure Activities:** whirlpool. **Guest Services:** coin laundry, wireless Internet. **Business Services:** meeting rooms, PC. / SOME UNITS

WHERE TO DINE

PANDA GARDEN BUFFET RESTAURANT

Chinese
$5-$8

Phone: 660/885-9090

Although patrons can order from the diverse menu, choices on the popular buffet are plentiful. Casual dress. **Hours:** 11 am-9 pm, Fri & Sat-10 pm. Closed: 11/25, 12/25. **Address:** 1407 E Ohio St 64735 **Location:** Just n of jct SR 7 and 13. **Parking:** on-site.

COLUMBIA pop. 84,531

BEST WESTERN COLUMBIA INN

Hotel
$69-$105 All Year

Book great rates at AAA.com

Phone: (573)474-6161

Address: 3100 I-70 Dr SE 65201 **Location:** I-70, exit 128A, just s, then just e. **Facility:** 122 units. 121 one-bedroom standard units. 1 one-bedroom suite. 2 stories (no elevator), interior corridors. *Bath:* combo or shower only. **Parking:** on-site. **Amenities:** voice mail, irons, hair dryers. *Some:* DVD players, high-speed Internet. **Pool(s):** outdoor. **Leisure Activities:** barbecue grill, exercise room. **Guest Services:** wireless Internet. **Business Services:** conference facilities, PC. **Free Special Amenities: full breakfast and room upgrade (subject to availability with advance reservations).** *(See color ad below)*

CALL / SOME UNITS FEE

AAA Benefit: Members save up to 20%, plus 10% bonus points with rewards program.

CANDLEWOOD SUITES

Extended Stay Hotel
$89-$209 All Year

Book at AAA.com

Phone: (573)817-0525

Address: 3100 Wingate Ct 65201 **Location:** I-70, exit 128A, just s on US 63, just e on I-70 Dr SE, then just s on Keene St. **Facility:** 80 units. 58 one-bedroom standard units with efficiencies. 22 one-bedroom suites with efficiencies. 3 stories, interior corridors. *Bath:* combo or shower only. **Parking:** on-site. **Amenities:** video library, DVD players, high-speed Internet, dual phone lines, voice mail, irons, hair dryers. **Leisure Activities:** exercise room. **Guest Services:** complimentary and valet laundry, wireless Internet.

ASK CALL / SOME UNITS FEE

COMFORT SUITES

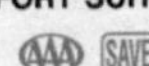

Hotel
$89-$150 All Year

Book great rates at AAA.com

Phone: (573)443-0055

Address: 1010 Business Loop 70 W 65202 **Location:** I-70, exit 125 (West Blvd), just sw. **Facility:** Smoke free premises. 85 one-bedroom standard units. 4 stories, interior corridors. *Bath:* combo or shower only. **Parking:** on-site. **Amenities:** high-speed Internet, voice mail, irons, hair dryers. **Pool(s):** heated indoor. **Leisure Activities:** exercise room. **Guest Services:** valet and coin laundry, wireless Internet. **Business Services:** meeting rooms, PC. **Free Special Amenities: full breakfast and high-speed Internet.**

CALL

▼ See AAA listing above ▼

COUNTRY INN & SUITES BY CARLSON *Book at AAA.com* **Phone:** (573)445-8585

Hotel
$89-$169 3/1-11/30
$79-$119 12/1-2/28

Address: 817 N Keene St 65201 **Location:** I-70, exit 128A, e to Keene St, just right. **Facility:** Smoke free premises. 85 units. 67 one-bedroom standard units, some with whirlpools. 18 one-bedroom suites. 3 stories, interior corridors. *Bath:* combo or shower only. **Parking:** on-site. **Terms:** 2 night minimum stay - weekends. **Amenities:** high-speed Internet, voice mail, irons, hair dryers. **Pool(s):** heated indoor. **Leisure Activities:** whirlpool, exercise room. **Guest Services:** coin laundry, wireless Internet. **Business Services:** meeting rooms, business center.

ASK CALL

COURTYARD BY MARRIOTT-COLUMBIA *Book great rates at AAA.com* **Phone:** (573)443-8000

Hotel
$116-$142 All Year

Address: 3301 LeMone Industrial Blvd 65201 **Location:** I-70, exit 128A, s on US 63 to CR AC exit, then just ne. **Facility:** Smoke free premises. 133 units. 129 one-bedroom standard units, some with whirlpools. 4 one-bedroom suites. 4 stories, interior corridors. *Bath:* combo or shower only. **Parking:** on-site. **Terms:** cancellation fee imposed. **Amenities:** video games (fee), high-speed Internet, dual phone lines, voice mail, irons, hair dryers. **Pool(s):** heated indoor. **Leisure Activities:** whirlpool, exercise room. **Guest Services:** valet and coin laundry, airport transportation-Columbia Regional Airport, wireless Internet. **Business Services:** conference facilities, business center. **Free Special Amenities: newspaper and high-speed Internet.**

CALL

AAA Benefit:
Members save a minimum 5% off the best available rate.

DRURY INN-COLUMBIA *Book at AAA.com* **Phone:** (573)445-1800

Hotel
$85-$179 All Year

Address: 1000 Knipp St 65203 **Location:** I-70, exit 124 (Stadium Blvd), just s. **Facility:** 123 units. 119 one-bedroom standard units. 4 one-bedroom suites. 5 stories, interior corridors. **Parking:** on-site. **Terms:** cancellation fee imposed. **Amenities:** high-speed Internet, dual phone lines, voice mail, irons, hair dryers. **Pool(s):** heated indoor. **Leisure Activities:** whirlpool, exercise room. **Guest Services:** valet and coin laundry, wireless Internet. **Business Services:** meeting rooms, PC.

ASK / SOME UNITS

EXTENDED STAYAMERICA-COLUMBIA-STADIUM BLVD *Book at AAA.com* **Phone:** (573)445-6800

Extended Stay Hotel
$59-$69 All Year

Address: 2000 Business Loop 70 W 65203 **Location:** I-70, exit 124 (Stadium Blvd), just ne. **Facility:** 95 one-bedroom standard units with efficiencies. 3 stories, interior corridors. *Bath:* combo or shower only. **Parking:** on-site. **Terms:** cancellation fee imposed. **Amenities:** voice mail, irons. **Guest Services:** coin laundry, wireless Internet. ASK / SOME UNITS FEE

HAMPTON INN *Book great rates at AAA.com* **Phone:** (573)886-9392

Hotel
$89-$149 All Year

Address: 3410 Clark Ln 65202 **Location:** I-70, exit 128A, just ne. **Facility:** 121 one-bedroom standard units, some with whirlpools. 5 stories, interior corridors. *Bath:* combo or shower only. **Parking:** on-site. **Terms:** 1-7 night minimum stay, cancellation fee imposed. **Amenities:** video games (fee), high-speed Internet, voice mail, irons, hair dryers. **Pool(s):** heated indoor. **Leisure Activities:** whirlpool, exercise room. **Guest Services:** valet and coin laundry, wireless Internet. **Business Services:** business center.

CALL / SOME UNITS

AAA Benefit:
Members save up to 10% everyday!

HAMPTON INN & SUITES COLUMBIA AT THE UNIVERSITY OF MISSOURI *Book great rates at AAA.com* **Phone:** (573)214-2222

Hotel
$109-$129 All Year

Address: 1225 Fellows Pl 65201 **Location:** Just sw of jct SR 740 and 763. Located near University of Missouri Stadium. **Facility:** Smoke free premises. 133 one-bedroom standard units, some with whirlpools. 4 stories, interior corridors. *Bath:* combo or shower only. **Parking:** on-site. **Terms:** check-in 4 pm, 1-7 night minimum stay, cancellation fee imposed. **Amenities:** video games (fee), high-speed Internet, voice mail, irons, hair dryers. **Pool(s):** heated indoor. **Leisure Activities:** whirlpool, exercise room. **Guest Services:** valet and coin laundry, wireless Internet. **Business Services:** conference facilities, business center.

CALL

AAA Benefit:
Members save up to 10% everyday!

HOLIDAY INN EXECUTIVE CENTER *Book great rates at AAA.com* **Phone:** 573/445-8531

Hotel

Rates not provided

Address: 2200 I-70 Dr SW 65203 **Location:** I-70, exit 124 (Stadium Blvd), just w. **Facility:** 311 units. 305 one-bedroom standard units, some with whirlpools. 2 one- and 4 two-bedroom suites, some with whirlpools. 6 stories, interior corridors. *Bath:* combo or shower only. **Parking:** on-site. **Terms:** check-in 4 pm. **Amenities:** voice mail, irons, hair dryers. *Some:* DVD players. **Dining:** 2 restaurants. **Pool(s):** heated outdoor, heated indoor. **Leisure Activities:** whirlpool, exercise room. *Fee:* massage. **Guest Services:** valet and coin laundry, airport transportation (fee)-Columbia Regional Airport, wireless Internet, personal trainer, beauty salon, shoeshine. **Business Services:** conference facilities, business center. **Free Special Amenities: local telephone calls and high-speed Internet.**

FEE CALL / SOME UNITS FEE

STONEY CREEK INN AND CONFERENCE CENTER *Book at AAA.com* **Phone:** 573/442-6400

Hotel

Rates not provided

Address: 2601 S Providence Rd 65203 **Location:** I-70, exit 126 (Providence Rd/SR 163), 3 mi s; on west outer road. **Facility:** Smoke free premises. 180 units. 177 one-bedroom standard units, some with efficiencies and/or whirlpools. 3 one-bedroom suites with efficiencies and whirlpools. 4 stories, interior corridors. *Bath:* combo or shower only. **Parking:** on-site. **Amenities:** high-speed Internet, voice mail, irons, hair dryers. *Some:* DVD players, dual phone lines. **Pool(s):** heated indoor/outdoor. **Leisure Activities:** sauna, whirlpool, exercise room. *Fee:* game room. **Guest Services:** valet and coin laundry, wireless Internet. **Business Services:** conference facilities, business center.

/ SOME UNITS

SUPER 8-CLARK LANE IN COLUMBIA *Book at AAA.com* **Phone:** (573)474-8488

Motel

$57-$104 All Year

Address: 3216 Clark Ln 65202 **Location:** I-70, exit 128A, northeast corner. **Facility:** 75 units. 71 one- and 3 two-bedroom standard units. 1 one-bedroom suite with kitchen (no utensils). 3 stories (no elevator), interior corridors. **Parking:** on-site. **Amenities:** high-speed Internet, hair dryers. *Some:* irons. **Guest Services:** wireless Internet. ASK / SOME UNITS FEE

WHERE TO DINE

ADDISON'S **Phone:** 573/256-1995

American

$7-$18

Forget table cloths, uniformed waiters or candlelight dining, Addison's is a downtown eatery which serves sophisticated dishes in a casual atmosphere. Casual dress. **Bar:** Full bar. **Reservations:** accepted, weekdays. **Hours:** 11 am-10 pm. Closed: 11/25, 12/25. **Address:** 709 Cherry St 65201 **Location:** Between 7th and 8th sts; downtown. **Parking:** street.

CHERRY STREET ARTISAN CAFE THEATRE GALLERY **Phone:** 573/817-3274

American

$5-$10

The cafe features intentionally simple but quality furnishings and decor, live music during lunch weekdays, some small-scale live theatre and poetry reading. In the off hours, it's a place to "hang out"; a little like being in a library, only you can eat, drink, and don't have to whisper, although relaxing is acceptable as well. Casual dress. Entertainment. **Bar:** Beer & wine. **Reservations:** accepted. **Hours:** 6:30 am-10 pm, Thurs & Fri-midnight, Sat 7 am-midnight, Sun noon-10 pm. Closed: 12/25; also Sun. **Address:** 111 9th St , Suite 10 65201 **Location:** At 9th and Cherry sts; in lower level of City Centre; downtown. **Parking:** street. CALL

D. ROWE'S **Phone:** 573/443-8004

American

$8-$15

Guests can expect a comfortable, relaxed Missouri sports teams-themed atmosphere. It's a great place to watch college football games and nosh on a huge appetizer, salad, sandwich, steak or pasta dish. Casual dress. **Bar:** Full bar. **Reservations:** not accepted. **Hours:** 11 am-10 pm, Fri & Sat-11 pm, Sun-9 pm. Closed major holidays; also Sun in summer. **Address:** 1005 Club Village Dr 65203 **Location:** US 63, exit Grindstone Pkwy, 3.6 mi w, then just n. **Parking:** on-site.

FELINI **Phone:** 573/256-5025

Mediterranean

$7-$15

The pleasing family-owned and operated establishment serves Mediterranean and Kosovar food, as well as calzones and pasta dishes. Casual dress. **Bar:** Beer & wine. **Reservations:** accepted. **Hours:** 11 am-2 & 5-10 pm, Sat 11 am-11 pm, Sun noon-8 pm. Closed: 7/4, 11/25, 12/25. **Address:** 700 E Broadway St 65203 **Location:** Corner of S 7th and E Broadway sts; downtown. **Parking:** street. CALL

GRAND CRU **Phone:** 573/443-2600

American

$8-$38

Innovative menu items are presented in a comfortable atmosphere. Outside patios and inside fireplaces enhance the mood during all seasons. This place provides a special occasion experience at a reasonable price. Dressy casual. **Bar:** Full bar. **Reservations:** suggested. **Hours:** 11 am-9 pm, Sat 5 pm-10 pm. Closed: 5/31, 12/24, 12/25; also Sun. **Address:** 2600 S Providence Rd 65203 **Location:** 1.2 mi s of Stadium Blvd, on east outer road. **Parking:** on-site. CALL

GREAT WALL CHINESE SUPER BUFFET *Menu on AAA.com* **Phone:** 573/446-3888

Chinese

$5-$8

This Chinese restaurant features buffet lines with more than fifty different dishes to choose from plus a Mongolian barbecue area where diners can select from a variety of raw ingredients which are then stir-fried on a domed grill while you watch. Casual dress. **Reservations:** accepted. **Hours:** 11 am-9 pm, Fri & Sat-10 pm. Closed: 11/25. **Address:** 2005 W Worley St 65203 **Location:** I-70, exit 124 (Stadium Blvd), 0.4 mi s. **Parking:** on-site.

JACK'S GOURMET RESTAURANT **Phone:** 573/449-3927

Continental

$14-$36

Particularly appropriate for special occasions, the atmosphere is just as welcoming for business meals as for romantic evenings. Wines pair with selections from the extensive menu. A pianist performs nightly. Casual dress. Entertainment. **Bar:** Full bar. **Reservations:** suggested. **Hours:** 5 pm-10 pm. Closed major holidays; also Sun. **Address:** 1903 E Business Loop I-70 65201 **Location:** Jct Old US 63, exit 128 westbound; exit 127 eastbound, 0.3 mi s on SR 763, then 0.8 mi e. **Parking:** on-site. CALL

MURRY'S

Phone: 573/442-4969

American
$5-$17

Lending to the lively and fun atmosphere are jazz-related posters, photographs and, at certain times of the week, a piano player. A favorite among locals in the know, this place is busy and popular. The menu lists a nice variety of entrees with good flavor and presentation. Servers are attentive and prompt. A jazz band plays on Saturday nights. Casual dress. **Bar:** Full bar. **Reservations:** not accepted. **Hours:** 11 am-midnight. Closed major holidays; also Sun. **Address:** 3107 Green Meadows Way 65203 **Location:** I-70, exit 126 (Providence St), 3.5 mi s, then just w; in Green Meadows Plaza. **Parking:** on-site.

THE PASTA FACTORY

Phone: 573/449-3948

Italian
$7-$12

In a late 1800s red-brick factory building, the restaurant has a New Orleans-type courtyard and lots of memorabilia. Pasta dishes are widely varied, and other choices, such as rotisserie chicken, also are offered. Favorite selections are mostaccioli con salsiccia—tubular pasta with Italian sausage—and the traditional chicken marsala. Casual dress. **Bar:** Full bar. **Reservations:** accepted. **Hours:** 11 am-10 pm, Fri & Sat-10:30 pm. Closed major holidays. **Address:** 1020 E Broadway St, Suite F 65201 **Location:** Corner of Broadway and Hitt sts; entrance from courtyard on east side of building; downtown. **Parking:** street.

TELLERS GALLERY AND BAR

Phone: 573/441-8355

American
$5-$16

Among hints of trendy sophistication are the changing gallery exhibits and menu selections that reflect the same qualities. This place is known for its wonderful salads, but many other offerings also are sure to satisfy. Casual dress. **Bar:** Full bar. **Reservations:** accepted. **Hours:** 11 am-10 pm, Fri & Sat-midnight. Closed major holidays; also Sun. **Address:** 820 E Broadway St 65201 **Location:** Corner of 9th and Broadway sts; downtown. **Parking:** street. CALL

CONCORDIA pop. 2,360

— WHERE TO DINE —

BIFFLE'S SMOKE HOUSE BAR-B-Q

Phone: 660/463-7232

Barbecue
$4-$20

Family-owned and operated for 25 years, the restaurant centers its menu on hickory-smoked meats. Casual dress. **Bar:** Beer & wine. **Reservations:** accepted. **Hours:** 11 am-10 pm, Fri & Sat-11 pm. Closed: 4/4, 11/25, 12/25; also for dinner 12/24 & 12/31. **Address:** 103 NE 2nd St 64020 **Location:** I-70, exit 58, just se. **Parking:** on-site.

CREVE COEUR—See St. Louis p. 557.

CUBA pop. 3,230

BEST WESTERN CUBA INN *Book great rates at AAA.com*

Phone: (573)885-7707

SAVE

Motel
$60-$90 All Year

Address: 246 Hwy P 65453 **Location:** I-44, exit 208 (SR 19), just n, then just e. **Facility:** 52 one-bedroom standard units, some with whirlpools. 1 story, exterior corridors. **Parking:** on-site, winter plug-ins. **Amenities:** voice mail, irons, hair dryers. *Some:* high-speed Internet. **Pool(s):** outdoor. **Guest Services:** wireless Internet. **Business Services:** PC. **Free Special Amenities: full breakfast and high-speed Internet.**

/ SOME UNITS FEE

AAA Benefit:
Members save up to 20%, plus 10% bonus points with rewards program.

SUPER 8 *Book at AAA.com*

Phone: (573)885-2087

Motel
$60-$115 All Year

Address: 28 Hwy P 65453 **Location:** I-44, exit 208 (SR 19), just n, then just w. **Facility:** 58 units. 53 one-bedroom standard units. 5 one-bedroom suites, some with whirlpools. 3 stories, interior/exterior corridors. **Parking:** on-site. **Amenities:** safes (fee), hair dryers. **Guest Services:** coin laundry, wireless Internet. **Business Services:** PC.

ASK / SOME UNITS FEE

EARTH CITY—See St. Louis p. 558.

EDMUNDSON—See St. Louis p. 558.

EUREKA—See St. Louis p. 559.

FENTON—See St. Louis p. 559.

FESTUS pop. 9,660

DRURY INN-FESTUS *Book at AAA.com*

Phone: (636)933-2400

Hotel
$80-$134 All Year

Address: 1001 Veterans Blvd 63028 **Location:** I-55, exit 175, just e. Located in a commercial area. **Facility:** 58 one-bedroom standard units. 3 stories, interior corridors. **Parking:** on-site. **Terms:** cancellation fee imposed. **Amenities:** high-speed Internet, voice mail, irons, hair dryers. **Pool(s):** outdoor. **Leisure Activities:** exercise room. **Guest Services:** valet and coin laundry, wireless Internet. **Business Services:** PC. ASK / SOME UNITS

FLORISSANT—See St. Louis p. 560.

FORISTELL—See St. Louis p. 560.

FRONTENAC—See St. Louis p. 561.

FULTON pop. 12,128

LOGANBERRY INN BED & BREAKFAST **Phone:** 573/642-9229

Bed & Breakfast
$99-$199 All Year

Address: 310 W 7th St 65251 **Location:** Jct US 54, exit CR F, 1 mi e, just n to Westminster, then just e. **Facility:** A typical Victorian painted lady, the charming B&B is just a short walk from the campus of Westminster College and has hosted many dignitaries. Smoke free premises. 5 one-bedroom standard units, some with whirlpools. 2 stories (no elevator), interior corridors. *Bath:* combo or shower only. **Parking:** on-site. **Terms:** check-in 4 pm, age restrictions may apply, 14 day cancellation notice-fee imposed. **Amenities:** video library, DVD players, CD players, hair dryers. *Some:* irons. **Leisure Activities:** whirlpool. **Guest Services:** wireless Internet. **Business Services:** fax.

ASK / SOME UNITS FEE

—— WHERE TO DINE ——

BEKS **Phone:** 573/592-7117

American
$8-$18

Part wine bar, part coffee house, Beks offers innovative food. Daily specials are highlights of the menu, and most dishes are creative takes on American favorites. Pastry desserts are homemade, and guests will find an expansive selection of beers, from imports and domestics. Located in downtown Fulton in a restored bank building, the three-story dining room sets the stage for a unique experience. Casual dress. **Bar:** Beer & wine. **Reservations:** suggested. **Hours:** 8 am-9 pm, Fri & Sat-10 pm. Closed: 4/4, 11/25, 12/25; also Sun. **Address:** 511 Court St 65251 **Location:** Between 5th and 6th sts. **Parking:** street. CALL

GRANDVIEW—See Kansas City p. 484.

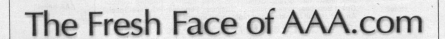

HANNIBAL pop. 17,757

QUALITY INN & SUITES *Book great rates at AAA.com* **Phone:** (573)221-4001

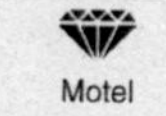

Hotel
$90-$129 3/1-11/1
$80-$119 11/2-2/28

Address: 120 Lindsey Dr 63401 **Location:** 2 mi w on US 36, exit Shinn Ln to south service road, then 0.6 mi e. **Facility:** 94 units. 77 one-bedroom standard units, some with whirlpools. 17 one-bedroom suites. 3 stories, interior corridors. *Bath:* combo or shower only. **Parking:** on-site. **Amenities:** high-speed Internet, voice mail, irons, hair dryers. **Pool(s):** heated indoor. **Leisure Activities:** whirlpool, exercise room. *Fee:* game room. **Guest Services:** coin laundry, wireless Internet. **Business Services:** meeting rooms, PC. / SOME UNITS FEE

SUPER 8 *Book at AAA.com* **Phone:** (573)221-5863

Motel
$55-$120 All Year

Address: 120 Huckleberry Heights Dr 63401 **Location:** Jct US 36, 1.5 mi s on US 61. **Facility:** 59 one-bedroom standard units. 3 stories (no elevator), interior corridors. **Parking:** on-site. **Amenities:** hair dryers. **Pool(s):** heated outdoor. **Guest Services:** wireless Internet.
ASK / SOME UNITS FEE

WHERE TO DINE

FIDDLESTICKS FOOD & SPIRITS CO **Phone:** 573/406-0493

American
$6-$19

On the west edge of the city along busy US 36, the restaurant presents a menu of steak, seafood, sandwiches, pasta and more in a crisp but casual setting. A lighter fare menu is offered after 9 pm. Casual dress. **Bar:** Full bar. **Reservations:** not accepted. **Hours:** 10:45 am-10 pm. Closed: 11/25, 12/25. **Address:** 8945 Hwy 36 63401 **Location:** 2 mi w on US 36, exit Shinn Ln to south service road, then 0.6 mi e. **Parking:** on-site.

LOGUE'S RESTAURANT **Phone:** 573/248-1854

American
$5-$10

Logue's is a family restaurant with a good menu selection of daily specials: fried chicken, spaghetti, baked turkey and burgers. The server staff is friendly, the atmosphere is casual, and prices are quite reasonable. Casual dress. **Reservations:** not accepted. **Hours:** 6 am-9 pm, Sun-8 pm. Closed major holidays. **Address:** 121 Huckleberry Heights Dr 63401 **Location:** On US 36, 1.5 mi s of jct US 36. **Parking:** on-site.

LULA BELLE'S **Phone:** 573/221-6662

American
$7-$24

Near several attractions, the restaurant serves a limited number of menu selections at lunch but a much larger number at dinner. Attentive, friendly servers complement the casual atmosphere and comfortable setting. Guests can expect an all-you-can-eat family-style menu on Sundays. Casual dress. **Bar:** Full bar. **Reservations:** accepted. **Hours:** 11 am-2 & 4-9 pm, Fri & Sat-10 pm. Closed major holidays; also Sun. **Address:** 111 Bird St 63401 **Location:** In historic district; adjacent to river. **Parking:** on-site.

MARK TWAIN DINETTE & FAMILY RESTAURANT **Phone:** 573/221-5511

American
$5-$12

There's a little something for everyone in the popular diner, established in 1942. Home-made meals are served in dining room booths or at the counter. Guests can get food to go at the old-time drive up. The eatery is in the historic area, adjacent to Mark Twain Home. Casual dress. **Reservations:** not accepted. **Hours:** 6 am-8 pm; hours vary in winter. Closed: 11/25, 12/25. **Address:** 400 N 3rd St 63401 **Location:** Jct US 36 and SR 79. **Parking:** on-site.

TJ'S SUPPER CLUB **Phone:** 573/221-5551

American
$5-$21

Specializing in delicious prime rib, TJ's is also known for its extensive menu of steak, fresh seafood, chicken, pasta and salad. Its very comfortable atmosphere is friendly and relaxed, and Mark Twain historic sites are close by. Good wine selection. Casual dress. **Bar:** Full bar. **Reservations:** accepted. **Hours:** 11 am-10 pm, Fri & Sat-11 pm; closing hours may vary. Closed major holidays. **Address:** 211 Munger Ln 63401 **Location:** Jct US 36 and 61, 0.5 mi w on US 36. **Parking:** on-site.

HARRISONVILLE pop. 8,946

HARRISONVILLE INN & SUITES *Book great rates at AAA.com* **Phone:** (816)884-3200

Motel
$55-$98 All Year

Address: 2201 Rockhaven Rd 64701 **Location:** Just n of jct US 71 and SR 291. **Facility:** 45 one-bedroom standard units, some with whirlpools. 1-2 stories (no elevator), exterior corridors. **Parking:** on-site, winter plug-ins. **Terms:** cancellation fee imposed. **Amenities:** irons, hair dryers. *Some:* high-speed Internet. **Pool(s):** outdoor. **Guest Services:** coin laundry, wireless Internet. **Free Special Amenities: continental breakfast and high-speed Internet.**
/ SOME UNITS FEE

HAYTI pop. 3,207

DRURY INN & SUITES-HAYTI CARUTHERSVILLE *Book at AAA.com* **Phone:** (573)359-2702

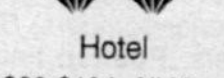

Hotel
$80-$134 All Year

Address: 1317 Hwy 84 63851 **Location:** I-55, exit 19 (US 412/SR 84), just w. **Facility:** 99 one-bedroom standard units, some with efficiencies and/or whirlpools. 3 stories, interior corridors. **Parking:** on-site, winter plug-ins. **Terms:** cancellation fee imposed. **Amenities:** dual phone lines, voice mail, irons, hair dryers. **Pool(s):** heated indoor. **Leisure Activities:** whirlpool, exercise room. **Guest Services:** coin laundry, wireless Internet. **Business Services:** meeting rooms, PC.
ASK / SOME UNITS

HAZELWOOD—See St. Louis p. 561.

HERMANN pop. 2,674

HERMANN HILL — **Phone:** 573/486-4455

Bed & Breakfast
$187-$419 3/1-12/31
$198-$345 1/1-2/28

Address: 711 Wein St 65041 **Location:** SR 19 (Market St), just w on W 6th St, just s on Washington St, then 0.3 mi w on W 10th St. **Facility:** On a bluff surrounded by a vineyard, the inn features rich common areas and spacious rooms with a fireplace and balcony; cottages also are available. Smoke free premises. 18 units. 8 one-bedroom standard units with whirlpools. 8 one- and 2 two-bedroom suites with whirlpools. 2-4 stories, interior/exterior corridors. **Parking:** on-site. **Terms:** check-in 4 pm, 2 night minimum stay, age restrictions may apply, 10 day cancellation notice-fee imposed. **Amenities:** video library, DVD players, irons, hair dryers. *Some:* CD players. **Leisure Activities:** hiking trails. **Guest Services:** area transportation, wireless Internet. / SOME UNITS

WINE VALLEY INN — **Phone:** 573/486-0706

Historic Bed & Breakfast
$107-$235 All Year

Address: 403 Market St 65041 **Location:** At Market and 4th sts. **Facility:** The historic Begemann Building offers two- and three-room suites, all with a kitchenette and dining area, in a warm and relaxed atmosphere. Smoke free premises. 12 units. 4 one-bedroom standard units. 8 one-bedroom suites, some with whirlpools. 2 stories, interior corridors. *Bath:* combo or shower only. **Parking:** on-site. **Terms:** check-in 4 pm, age restrictions may apply, 14 day cancellation notice-fee imposed. **Amenities:** video library, DVD players, CD players, high-speed Internet, hair dryers. **Guest Services:** wireless Internet. **Business Services:** meeting rooms. ASK

WHERE TO DINE

SIMON'S ON THE WATERFRONT — **Phone:** 573/486-2030

American
$5-$15

Within walking distance of shopping and several lodgings, the spacious, homey spot turns out New Orleans-inspired dishes and some barbecue, too. Also on the menu are casual burgers, fine steaks and German dishes. Strudel is a sweet meal-enders. Casual dress. **Bar:** Full bar. **Reservations:** accepted. **Hours:** 11 am-8 pm, Fri & Sat-9 pm. Closed: 9/6, 12/25; also Mon & Tues. **Address:** 4 Schiller St 65041 **Location:** 1 blk w of Amtrak station. **Parking:** street.

VINTAGE RESTAURANT AT STONE HILL WINERY — **Phone:** 573/486-3479

German
$6-$26

Casual and vintage charm highlight the cozy restaurant, which occupies a former horse barn. It's not unusual for diners to be seated in what was once a horse stall, next to the original feed trough and hay chute. Cordial, attentive servers explain preparations of traditional German cuisine. Since this place is adjacent to a winery, the wine list fittingly includes a number of local vintages. Casual dress. **Bar:** Beer & wine. **Reservations:** suggested, for dinner Sat. **Hours:** Open 3/1-12/31 & 2/1-2/28; 11 am-4:30 & 5-8:30 pm, Fri-9 pm, Sat-9:30 pm; hours may vary in winter. Closed: 11/25, 12/24, 12/25; also Wed & Thurs 3/1-4/30 & 11/1-12/31. **Address:** 1110 Stone Hill Hwy 65041 **Location:** SR 19 (Market St), just w on SR 100, follow signs; at Stone Hill Winery. **Parking:** on-site. **Historic**

HIGGINSVILLE pop. 4,682

SUPER 8-HIGGINSVILLE — *Book at AAA.com* — **Phone:** (660)584-7781

Hotel
$62-$67 All Year

Address: 6471 Oakview Ln 64037 **Location:** I-70, exit 49 (SR 13), just se. **Facility:** 43 one-bedroom standard units. 2 stories (no elevator), interior corridors. *Bath:* combo or shower only. **Parking:** on-site, winter plug-ins. **Amenities:** voice mail, irons, hair dryers. **Leisure Activities:** *Fee:* game room. **Guest Services:** coin laundry, wireless Internet. ASK / SOME UNITS FEE

HOLLISTER—See Branson p. 432.

HOLTS SUMMIT pop. 2,935

AMERICAS BEST VALUE INN-JEFFERSON CITY — *Book at AAA.com* — **Phone:** (573)896-8787

Hotel
$60-$80 All Year

Address: 150 City Plaza 65043 **Location:** Jct US 54 and CR 00, just w, then just s. **Facility:** 30 one-bedroom standard units, some with whirlpools. 2 stories (no elevator), interior corridors. **Parking:** on-site. **Terms:** cancellation fee imposed. **Amenities:** irons. *Some:* high-speed Internet. **Guest Services:** coin laundry, wireless Internet. ASK / SOME UNITS

INDEPENDENCE—See Kansas City p. 484.

JACKSON pop. 11,947

COMFORT SUITES — *Book at AAA.com* — **Phone:** (573)204-0014

Hotel
$70-$150 All Year

Address: 2904 Old Orchard Rd 63755 **Location:** I-55, exit 99, 0.5 mi e, then just n. **Facility:** Smoke free premises. 64 one-bedroom standard units, some with whirlpools. 3 stories, interior corridors. *Bath:* combo or shower only. **Parking:** on-site. **Amenities:** voice mail, irons, hair dryers. **Pool(s):** heated indoor. **Leisure Activities:** whirlpool, exercise room. **Guest Services:** valet and coin laundry, wireless Internet. **Business Services:** meeting rooms, business center.
ASK CALL / SOME UNITS FEE

DRURY INN & SUITES-JACKSON, MO *Book at AAA.com* **Phone:** (573)243-9200

Hotel
$80-$149 All Year

Address: 225 Drury Ln 63755 **Location:** I-55, exit 105 (SR 61), 0.3 mi w. Located in a rural area. **Facility:** 80 units. 50 one-bedroom standard units. 30 one-bedroom suites. 4 stories, interior corridors. *Bath:* combo or shower only. **Parking:** on-site. **Terms:** cancellation fee imposed. **Amenities:** voice mail, irons, hair dryers. **Pool(s):** heated indoor. **Leisure Activities:** whirlpool, exercise room. **Guest Services:** valet and coin laundry, wireless Internet. **Business Services:** meeting rooms, PC.

ASK CALL / SOME UNITS

WHERE TO DINE

The following restaurant has not been evaluated by AAA but is listed for your information only.

TRACTORS CLASSIC AMERICAN GRILL **Phone:** 573/243-0340

fyi Not evaluated. The eatery serves traditional American fare, including some very large burgers. **Address:** 124 S High St 63755

JAMESPORT pop. 505

WHERE TO DINE

GINGERICH DUTCH PANTRY & BAKERY **Phone:** 660/684-6212

American
$4-$15

There's no pretense here—just delicious, homemade offerings, right down to the bread and jam. Casual dress. **Reservations:** accepted. **Hours:** 10:30 am-5 pm, Thurs-3 pm, Sat 7 am-8 pm, Mon 10:30 am-8 pm; to 3 pm, Fri 10:30 am-8 pm, Sat 7 am-5 pm 12/1-3/31. Closed: 11/25, 12/25; also Sun. **Address:** 120 S Broadway 64648 **Location:** 1 mi s of jct SR 6 and 190. **Parking:** street. CALL

JANE

BOONESLICK LODGE *Book at AAA.com* **Phone:** (417)226-1888

Hotel
$64-$115 All Year

Address: 21140 US Hwy 71 64856 **Location:** Just s on US 71. **Facility:** 45 one-bedroom standard units, some with whirlpools. 2 stories (no elevator), interior corridors. *Bath:* combo or shower only. **Parking:** on-site, winter plug-ins. **Amenities:** high-speed Internet, voice mail, safes (fee), hair dryers. **Pool(s):** heated outdoor. **Leisure Activities:** whirlpool. **Guest Services:** coin laundry, wireless Internet. **Business Services:** PC. ASK / SOME UNITS FEE

JEFFERSON CITY pop. 39,636

BEST WESTERN CAPITAL INN *Book great rates at AAA.com* **Phone:** (573)635-4175

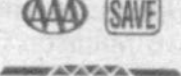

Hotel
$95 All Year

Address: 1937 Christy Dr 65101 **Location:** US 54, exit Ellis Blvd, just se. **Facility:** Smoke free premises. 75 one-bedroom standard units, some with whirlpools. 3 stories, interior corridors. *Bath:* combo or shower only. **Parking:** on-site. **Amenities:** high-speed Internet, voice mail, irons, hair dryers. **Pool(s):** heated indoor. **Leisure Activities:** whirlpool, exercise room. **Guest Services:** coin laundry, wireless Internet. **Business Services:** meeting rooms, business center. **Free Special Amenities: expanded continental breakfast and high-speed Internet.**

CALL

AAA Benefit:
Members save up to 20%, plus 10% bonus points with rewards program.

CAPITOL PLAZA HOTEL AND CONVENTION CENTER *Book at AAA.com* **Phone:** (573)635-1234

Hotel
$139 1/2-2/28
$89-$124 3/1-1/1

Address: 415 W McCarty St 65101 **Location:** On US 50 and 63 S, just e of jct US 54. **Facility:** 255 units. 214 one-bedroom standard units. 41 one-bedroom suites, some with whirlpools. 9 stories, interior corridors. *Bath:* combo or shower only. **Parking:** on-site. **Terms:** cancellation fee imposed. **Amenities:** high-speed Internet (fee), voice mail, irons, hair dryers. **Pool(s):** heated indoor. **Leisure Activities:** sauna, whirlpool, exercise room. **Guest Services:** valet laundry, area transportation, wireless Internet. **Business Services:** conference facilities, business center.

ASK CALL / SOME UNITS FEE

HOLIDAY INN EXPRESS *Book great rates at AAA.com* **Phone:** (573)634-4040

Hotel
$75-$94 All Year

Address: 1716 Jefferson St 65109 **Location:** US 54, exit Ellis Blvd. **Facility:** 70 one-bedroom standard units, some with whirlpools. 4 stories, interior corridors. *Bath:* combo or shower only. **Parking:** on-site. **Amenities:** high-speed Internet, irons, hair dryers. **Pool(s):** heated indoor. **Leisure Activities:** sauna, whirlpool, exercise room. **Guest Services:** valet laundry, wireless Internet. **Business Services:** meeting rooms. **Free Special Amenities: expanded continental breakfast and high-speed Internet.** / SOME UNITS

SUPER 8 JEFFERSON CITY *Book at AAA.com* **Phone:** (573)636-5456

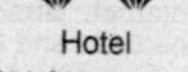

Hotel
$50-$90 All Year

Address: 1710 Jefferson St 65109 **Location:** US 54, exit Ellis Blvd, 0.3 mi nw on frontage road. **Facility:** 77 one-bedroom standard units. 3 stories (no elevator), interior corridors. **Parking:** on-site. **Amenities:** safes (fee), hair dryers. **Leisure Activities:** exercise room. **Guest Services:** valet and coin laundry, wireless Internet. **Business Services:** PC, fax.

ASK / SOME UNITS FEE

TRUMAN HOTEL & CONFERENCE CENTER *Book at AAA.com* **Phone:** 573/635-7171

Hotel
Rates not provided

Address: 1510 Jefferson St 65109 **Location:** US 54, exit Ellis Blvd, 0.5 mi nw. **Facility:** 232 units. 228 one-bedroom standard units. 4 one-bedroom suites, some with whirlpools. 2-3 stories (no elevator), interior/exterior corridors. *Bath:* combo or shower only. **Parking:** on-site. **Amenities:** voice mail, irons, hair dryers. *Some:* high-speed Internet. **Pool(s):** outdoor. **Leisure Activities:** exercise room. **Guest Services:** valet laundry, area transportation, wireless Internet. **Business Services:** conference facilities. FEE / SOME UNITS FEE

WHERE TO DINE

ALEXANDRO'S RESTAURANT **Phone:** 573/634-7740

American
$13-$35

Highly recommended by locals, the restaurant's atmosphere is suitable for both casual and special occasions. The menu offers a good number of specialty items such as seafood, steak, lamb, veal, some Greek selections and pastas. Casual dress. **Bar:** Full bar. **Reservations:** accepted. **Hours:** 5 pm-10 pm. Closed major holidays; also Sun. **Address:** 2125 Missouri Blvd 65109 **Location:** US 50, just s on Dixie Rd. **Parking:** on-site.

DAS STEIN HAUS **Phone:** 573/634-3869

German
$7-$23

Das Stein Haus features hearty portions of German, Swiss, French and American dishes in its cuisine. Meals offered include beef rouladen, veal, lamb, chicken, duckling and frog legs. Its four dining rooms have a cozy atmosphere in a German decor. Casual dress. **Bar:** Full bar. **Reservations:** suggested. **Hours:** 11 am-1 & 5-9:30 pm, Sat & Sun from 5 pm. Closed: 12/24. **Address:** 1436 Southridge Dr 65109 **Location:** US 54, exit Stadium Dr, just n, 0.5 mi w on Jefferson St, just n on Zumwalt Rd, then just e. **Parking:** on-site.

DOMENICO'S **Phone:** 573/893-5454

Italian
$5-$23

Located in a shopping plaza, Domenico's serves up traditional Italian favorites such as veal parmigiano, chicken marsala and shrimp scampi. a house specialty is steak Arcobasso, named for the family which owns and operates this comfortably upscale restaurant. Casual dress. **Bar:** Full bar. **Reservations:** accepted. **Hours:** 4 pm-10 pm. Closed major holidays; also Sun. **Address:** 3702 W Truman Blvd 65109 **Location:** 4 mi w on US 50, then 0.3 mi n; in Capitol Plaza West. **Parking:** on-site.

EL JIMADOR MEXICAN RESTAURANT **Phone:** 573/636-6228

Mexican
$4-$10

With a cheerful decor and atmosphere, this is a local recommendation offering good sized portions for a good value. Casual dress. **Bar:** Full bar. **Reservations:** accepted, Sun-Wed. **Hours:** 11 am-10 pm, Fri & Sat-10:30 pm, Sun-9 pm. Closed: 12/25. **Address:** 512 Ellis Blvd 65101 **Location:** US 54, exit Ellis Blvd, 1.4 mi e. **Parking:** on-site. CALL

MADISON'S CAFE **Phone:** 573/634-2988

Italian
$6-$24

This restaurant is popular with professional business people, who enjoy its large portions of good hot food. The restaurant features homemade pasta and other offerings served in a relaxed atmosphere. It's just down the street from the State Capitol. Casual dress. **Bar:** Full bar. **Reservations:** accepted. **Hours:** 11 am-9:30 pm, Fri-10:30 pm, Sat 4:30 pm-10:30 pm. Closed major holidays; also Sun. **Address:** 216 Madison 65101 **Location:** Between High St and E Capitol Ave; just e of capitol building. **Parking:** street.

MEL'S COUNTRY CAFE **Phone:** 573/893-9115

American
$4-$10

The cafe's name says it all. The house specialty is chicken-fried steak, but there are many other offerings, including all-day breakfast items. Homemade pie is a must for dessert. Casual dress. **Reservations:** not accepted. **Hours:** 6 am-8 pm, Sun-2 pm. Closed: 11/25, 12/24, 12/25; also Mon. **Address:** 2421 Industrial Dr 65109 **Location:** US 50, exit Dix Rd, just n, then 0.8 mi w. **Parking:** on-site.

JOPLIN pop. 45,504

BEST WESTERN OASIS INN & SUITES *Book great rates at AAA.com* **Phone:** (417)781-6776

AAA SAVE

Hotel
$79-$149 All Year

Address: 3508 S Range Line Rd 64804 **Location:** I-44, exit 8B, just nw. **Facility:** 91 units. 73 one-bedroom standard units, some with whirlpools. 18 one-bedroom suites, some with kitchens and/or whirlpools. 2 stories (no elevator), exterior corridors. **Parking:** on-site. **Amenities:** high-speed Internet, irons, hair dryers. **Pool(s):** outdoor. **Leisure Activities:** limited exercise equipment. **Guest Services:** complimentary and valet laundry, wireless Internet. **Business Services:** PC. **Free Special Amenities: expanded continental breakfast and high-speed Internet.** / SOME UNITS FEE

Best Western

AAA Benefit:
Members save up to 20%, plus 10% bonus points with rewards program.

CANDLEWOOD SUITES *Book great rates at AAA.com* **Phone:** (417)623-9595

AAA SAVE

Extended Stay Hotel
$99-$129 All Year

Address: 3512 S Range Line Rd 64804 **Location:** I-44, exit 8B, just nw. **Facility:** 83 one-bedroom standard units with efficiencies. 4 stories, interior corridors. *Bath:* combo or shower only. **Parking:** on-site. **Amenities:** video library, DVD players, high-speed Internet, voice mail, irons, hair dryers. **Leisure Activities:** exercise room. **Guest Services:** valet and coin laundry, wireless Internet. **Business Services:** meeting rooms, business center. **Free Special Amenities: local telephone calls and high-speed Internet.** CALL / SOME UNITS FEE

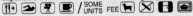

COMFORT INN & SUITES *Book at AAA.com* **Phone:** (417)627-0400

Hotel

$80-$149 3/1-8/31
$70-$119 9/1-2/28

Address: 3400 S Range Line Rd 64804 **Location:** I-44, exit 8B, just n. **Facility:** 82 one-bedroom standard units, some with whirlpools. 3 stories, interior corridors. *Bath:* combo or shower only. **Parking:** on-site. **Terms:** cancellation fee imposed. **Amenities:** high-speed Internet, irons, hair dryers. **Pool(s):** indoor. **Leisure Activities:** whirlpool, exercise room. **Guest Services:** wireless Internet. **Business Services:** PC. ASK / SOME UNITS

DRURY INN & SUITES-JOPLIN *Book at AAA.com* **Phone:** (417)781-8000

Hotel

$85-$184 All Year

Address: 3601 S Range Line Rd 64804 **Location:** I-44, exit 8B, just ne. **Facility:** 107 units. 101 one-bedroom standard units. 6 one-bedroom suites. 4 stories, interior corridors. **Parking:** on-site, winter plug-ins. **Terms:** cancellation fee imposed. **Amenities:** high-speed Internet, voice mail, irons, hair dryers. **Pool(s):** heated indoor. **Leisure Activities:** whirlpool, exercise room. **Guest Services:** valet and coin laundry, wireless Internet. **Business Services:** meeting rooms, business center.
ASK CALL / SOME UNITS

HAMPTON INN-JOPLIN *Book great rates at AAA.com* **Phone:** 417/659-9900

Hotel

Rates not provided

Address: 3107 E 36th St 64804 **Location:** I-44, exit 8B, just ne. **Facility:** Smoke free premises. 89 units. 88 one-bedroom standard units. 1 one-bedroom suite. 3 stories, interior corridors. *Bath:* combo or shower only. **Parking:** on-site. **Amenities:** high-speed Internet, voice mail, irons, hair dryers. **Pool(s):** heated outdoor. **Leisure Activities:** exercise room. **Guest Services:** valet laundry, wireless Internet. **Business Services:** PC.
CALL

AAA Benefit:
Members save up to 10% everyday!

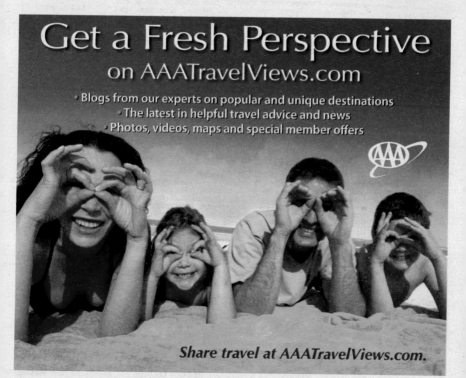

HILTON GARDEN INN Book great rates at AAA.com Phone: (417)206-3322

Hotel
$70-$139 All Year

Address: 2644 E 32nd St 64804 **Location:** I-44, exit 8B, just w of US 71 business route (Range Line Rd). **Facility:** 96 units. 88 one-bedroom standard units, some with whirlpools. 8 one-bedroom suites. 4 stories, interior corridors. *Bath:* combo or shower only. **Parking:** on-site. **Terms:** 1-7 night minimum stay, cancellation fee imposed. **Amenities:** high-speed Internet, voice mail, irons, hair dryers. **Pool(s):** heated indoor. **Leisure Activities:** whirlpool, exercise room. **Guest Services:** valet and coin laundry, wireless Internet. **Business Services:** meeting rooms, business center. CALL / SOME UNITS

LA QUINTA INN Book at AAA.com Phone: (417)781-0500

Hotel
$65-$119 All Year

Address: 3320 S Range Line Rd 64804 **Location:** I-44, exit 8B, just n. **Facility:** 161 units. 151 one-bedroom standard units, some with whirlpools. 10 one-bedroom suites. 3 stories, interior corridors. **Parking:** on-site. **Amenities:** voice mail, irons, hair dryers. *Some:* high-speed Internet. **Pool(s):** outdoor, heated indoor. **Leisure Activities:** whirlpool, exercise room. **Guest Services:** valet and coin laundry, wireless Internet. **Business Services:** meeting rooms, business center.
ASK / SOME UNITS

RESIDENCE INN BY MARRIOTT-JOPLIN Book great rates at AAA.com Phone: (417)782-0908

AAA SAVE
Extended Stay Hotel
$119-$129 All Year

Address: 3128 E Hammons Blvd 64804 **Location:** I-44, exit 8B, just ne. **Facility:** Smoke free premises. 114 units. 28 one-bedroom standard units with kitchens. 75 one- and 11 two-bedroom suites, some with efficiencies or kitchens. 4 stories, interior corridors. *Bath:* combo or shower only. **Parking:** on-site. **Terms:** cancellation fee imposed. **Amenities:** video games (fee), high-speed Internet, dual phone lines, voice mail, irons, hair dryers. **Pool(s):** heated outdoor. **Leisure Activities:** whirlpools, exercise room, sports court. **Guest Services:** valet and coin laundry, wireless Internet. **Business Services:** meeting rooms, business center. **Free Special Amenities: expanded continental breakfast and newspaper.**
CALL / SOME UNITS FEE

SLEEP INN Book great rates at AAA.com Phone: 417/782-1212

AAA SAVE
Hotel
Rates not provided

Address: 4100 Hwy 43 S 64803 **Location:** I-44, exit 4, just s. **Facility:** 61 one-bedroom standard units. 2 stories (no elevator), interior corridors. *Bath:* combo or shower only. **Parking:** on-site. **Amenities:** voice mail, irons, hair dryers. **Guest Services:** coin laundry, wireless Internet.
/ SOME UNITS FEE

TOWNEPLACE SUITES BY MARRIOTT JOPLIN Book great rates at AAA.com Phone: (417)659-8111

Extended Stay Hotel
$80-$98 All Year

Address: 4026 Arizona Ave 64804 **Location:** I-44, exit 8A, just sw. **Facility:** Smoke free premises. 73 units. 66 one-bedroom standard units. 7 one-bedroom suites. 4 stories, interior corridors. *Bath:* combo or shower only. **Parking:** on-site. **Terms:** cancellation fee imposed. **Amenities:** video library, DVD players, high-speed Internet, voice mail, irons, hair dryers. **Pool(s):** heated indoor. **Leisure Activities:** exercise room. **Guest Services:** valet and coin laundry, wireless Internet. **Business Services:** meeting rooms, business center.
CALL / SOME UNITS FEE

WHERE TO DINE

BELLA PEPPER'S ITALIAN KITCHEN Phone: 417/781-7711

Italian
$6-$13

Dimmed lighting and understated Italian-style decor contribute to a relaxing atmosphere at this eatery offering homemade Italian fare with traditional and American Italian specialties. The artichoke and spinach formaggio dip appetizer is a delicious way to start a meal. Diners can then choose from many pasta selections, each with different combinations of sauces and toppings. The dessert menu, which changes daily, offers a wide variety. Casual dress. **Reservations:** accepted. **Hours:** 11 am-9 pm. Closed major holidays; also Sun. **Address:** 2525 S Range Line Rd 64804 **Location:** I-44, exit 8B, 1.2 mi n. **Parking:** on-site.

DEL RIO BORDERTOWN CAFE Phone: 417/206-0423

Mexican
$7-$18

This large Mexican restaurant has multiple varieties of burritos and combination dinners, and its menu includes a section offering "north of the border" selections. The cafe projects a neat atmosphere, with lots of interesting decorative elements amid its lively surroundings. The sopapillas, served with a cream cheese and honey dipping sauce, are fantastic. Casual dress. **Bar:** Full bar. **Reservations:** accepted. **Hours:** 11 am-9:30 pm, Fri & Sat-10:30 pm, Sun-9 pm. Closed: 4/4, 11/25, 12/25. **Address:** 1801 Range Line Rd 64801 **Location:** I-44, exit 8B, 4 mi n on US 71. **Parking:** on-site.

GREAT WALL RESTAURANT

Phone: 417/624-3889

Chinese

$5-$8

A large buffet is set up for lunch and dinner. Mongolian barbecue is a favorite. Casual dress. **Reservations:** accepted. **Hours:** 11 am-9:30 pm, Fri & Sat-10:30 pm, Sun-9 pm. Closed: 11/25. **Address:** 2705 Range Line Rd 64804 **Location:** I-44, exit 8B, 1 mi n. **Parking:** on-site.

JIM BOB'S STEAKS & RIBS

Phone: 417/781-3300

American

$7-$24

Peanut shells litter the floor of the popular Texas-style steak house. Its casual, country-themed decor includes some stuffed, mounted wildlife. Barbecue dishes are a favorite among townsfolk. Casual dress. **Bar:** Full bar. **Reservations:** accepted. **Hours:** 11 am-10 pm. Closed: 9/6, 11/25, 12/25; also Sun. **Address:** 2040 Range Line Rd 64804 **Location:** I-44, exit 8B, 1.4 mi n on US 71. **Parking:** on-site.

PIZZA BY STOUT

Phone: 417/782-1616

Pizza

$5-$18

This locally-owned, family-operated pizza and beer establishment dates back to 1968. With fresh pizzas, sandwiches and a salad bar, the menu lists some variations, but most people will have a hard time trying to decide from among the massive number of beer selections. A wide variety of regions, flavors and types are represented in nearly 100 beers available on draft and in bottles. Casual dress. **Bar:** Beer & wine. **Reservations:** accepted. **Hours:** 11 am-10 pm, Fri & Sat-11 pm, Sun-3 pm. Closed: 1/1, 11/25, 12/25; also 12/31. **Address:** 2101 Range Line Rd 64804 **Location:** I-44, exit 8B, 1.4 mi n on US 71. **Parking:** on-site.

RIB CRIB BBQ AND GRILL

Phone: 417/206-7427

Barbecue

$6-$14

Most guests need extra napkins to tackle the ribs, brisket, ham, pork and chicken selections. The menu also lists sandwiches and wraps, along with tempting sides and large desserts. The decor is decidedly Western. Casual dress. **Bar:** Beer only. **Reservations:** not accepted. **Hours:** 11 am-10 pm. Closed: 11/25, 12/25. **Address:** 2915 E 24th St 64804 **Location:** I-44, exit 8B, 1.4 mi n. **Parking:** on-site.

WILDER'S STEAKHOUSE

Phone: 417/623-7230

Steak

$9-$36

A distinctive 1920s setting—with a large bar, towering ceilings and high-backed privacy booths—characterizes the main dining area. Steak and seafood dishes are well-prepared. Served only on Saturday, prime rib is the house favorite. Casual dress. **Bar:** Full bar. **Hours:** 5 pm-9:30 pm, Fri & Sat-10 pm. Closed major holidays; also Sun. **Address:** 1216 Main St 64801 **Location:** Center. **Parking:** on-site.

Destination Kansas City

pop. 441,545

A far cry from its trading post roots, Kansas City today is laced with skyscrapers but still long on charm.

Head outside to enjoy ice-skating, cool jazz and lip-smacking barbecue. Then come back in and wander the 85-acre corporate headquarters, retail complex and visitor center operated by greeting-card giant Hallmark.

Missouri Division of Tourism

Penn Valley Park, Kansas City.
(See mention page 168)

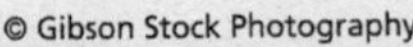

Country Club Plaza, Kansas City.
(See mention page 171)

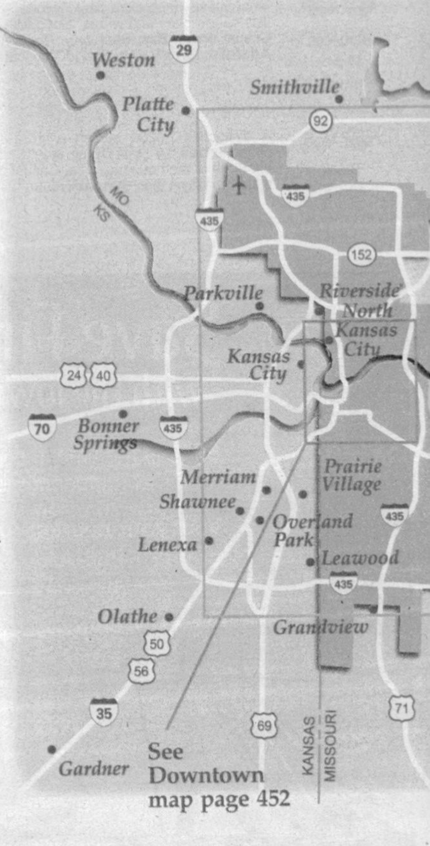

Places included in this AAA Destination City:

Kansas Speedway, Kansas City, Kan.
(See listing page 183)

See Vicinity map page 456

Cinco de Mayo Festival, Kansas City.
(See mention page 175)

Kansas City Royals.
(See mention page 170)

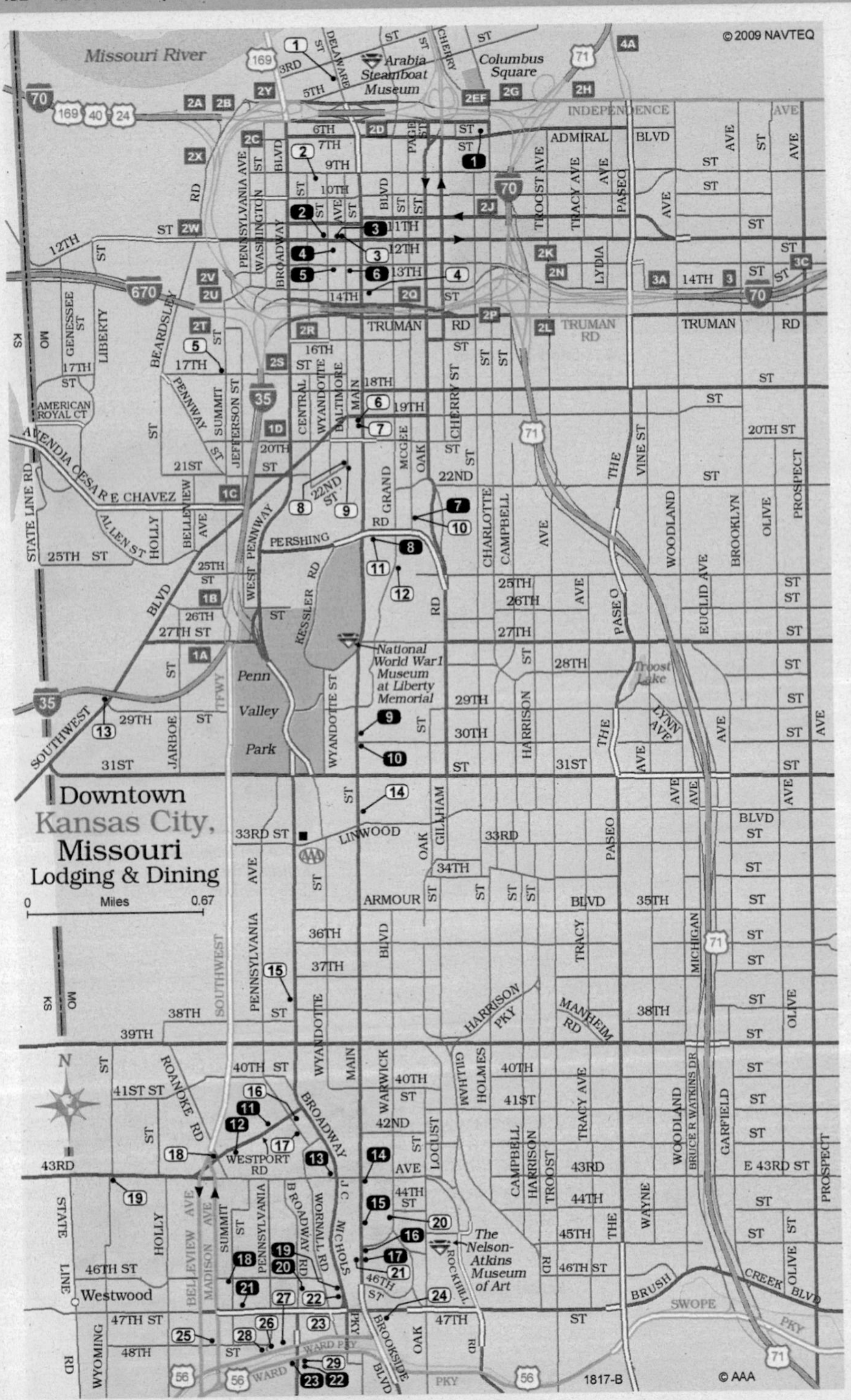
Downtown
Kansas City, Missouri
Lodging & Dining
0 Miles 0.67
© 2009 NAVTEQ
© AAA
1817-B
Missouri River
Arabia Steamboat Museum
Columbus Square
National World War I Museum at Liberty Memorial
Penn Valley Park
The Nelson-Atkins Museum of Art
Troost Lake
Westwood

Downtown Kansas City

This index helps you "spot" where approved lodgings and restaurants are located on the corresponding detailed maps. Lodging daily rate range is for comparison only and show the property's high season. Restaurant rate range is a combination of lunch and/or dinner. Turn to the listing page for more detailed rate information and consult display ads for special promotions.

DOWNTOWN KANSAS CITY

Map Page	OA	Lodgings	Diamond Rated	High Season	Page
1 / p. 452	AAA	**Comfort Inn & Suites Downtown**	◆◆	$70-$120 SAVE	464
2 / p. 452	AAA	**Marriott Kansas City Downtown**	◆◆◆	$188-$230 SAVE	468
3 / p. 452	AAA	**Hotel Phillips**	◆◆◆◆	Rates not provided SAVE	467
4 / p. 452		Holiday Inn Aladdin Downtown Kansas City	◆◆◆	$99-$199	466
5 / p. 452		Crowne Plaza Kansas City Downtown	◆◆◆	$99-$159	465
6 / p. 452	AAA	**Hilton President Kansas City** - see color ad p 466	◆◆◆◆	$119-$219 SAVE	465
7 / p. 452	AAA	**Hyatt Regency Crown Center**	◆◆◆	$89-$399 SAVE	467
8 / p. 452	AAA	**The Westin Crown Center** - see color ad p 472	◆◆◆◆	$129-$329 SAVE	471
9 / p. 452		Residence Inn by Marriott Downtown/Union Hill	◆◆◆	$143-$175	469
10 / p. 452		Fairfield Inn Kansas City/Union Hill	◆◆◆	$109-$119	465
11 / p. 452	AAA	**The Q Hotel & Spa**	◆◆◆	Rates not provided SAVE	468
12 / p. 452		Holiday Inn Express Westport	◆◆◆	Rates not provided	466
13 / p. 452		Embassy Suites Hotel Kansas City-Plaza	◆◆◆	$129-$229	465
14 / p. 452	AAA	**Best Western Seville Plaza Hotel** - see color ad p 464	◆◆◆	$83-$139 SAVE	464
15 / p. 452	AAA	**Marriott-Kansas City-Country Club Plaza**	◆◆◆	$159-$209 SAVE	468
16 / p. 452		Holiday Inn At The Plaza, Kansas City	◆◆◆	$79-$129	466
17 / p. 452		Homestead Studio Suites-Kansas City/ Country Club Plaza	◆◆	$85-$170	466
18 / p. 452		Hampton Inn & Suites-Country Club Plaza	◆◆◆	$99-$229	465
19 / p. 452		Courtyard by Marriott-Country Club Plaza	◆◆◆	$152-$186	464
20 / p. 452		Residence Inn by Marriott Kansas City Country Club Plaza	◆◆◆	$159-$169	469
21 / p. 452	AAA	**Sheraton Suites Country Club Plaza** - see color ad p 470	◆◆◆	Rates not provided SAVE	471
22 / p. 452		The Raphael Hotel	◆◆◆	Rates not provided	468
23 / p. 452	AAA	**The InterContinental Kansas City at the Plaza** - see color ad p 467	◆◆◆◆	$149-$449 SAVE	468

Map Page	OA	Restaurants	Diamond Rated	Cuisine	Meal Range	Page
1 / p. 452		Cafe Al Dente	◆◆	Italian	$6-$16	473
2 / p. 452	AAA	**Savoy Grill**	◆◆◆	Seafood	$7-$43	475
3 / p. 452		12 Baltimore	◆◆	American	$10-$18	473
4 / p. 452		Bristol Seafood Grill	◆◆◆	Seafood	$10-$39	473
5 / p. 452		Blue Bird Bistro	◆◆	American	$5-$32	473
6 / p. 452		Michael Smith	◆◆◆	American	$11-$38	475
7 / p. 452		1924 Main	◆◆◆	American	$10-$55	473

Map Page	OA	Restaurants (cont'd)	Diamond Rated	Cuisine	Meal Range	Page
8 / p. 452		Lidia's Kansas City	♦♦♦	Northern Italian	\$10-\$29	474
9 / p. 452		Fiorella's Jack Stack Barbeque - Freight House	♦♦	Barbecue	\$6-\$30	474
10 / p. 452		Peppercorn Duck Club	♦♦♦	American	\$15-\$39	475
11 / p. 452	AAA	**Benton's Steak & Chop House**	♦♦♦	American	\$25-\$38	473
12 / p. 452	AAA	**The American Restaurant at Crown Center**	♦♦♦♦	American	\$17-\$80	473
13 / p. 452		Ponak's Mexican Kitchen & Bar	♦♦	Mexican	\$4-\$10	475
14 / p. 452		Gates Bar-B-Q	♦♦	American	\$10-\$20	474
15 / p. 452		Chubby's	♦	American	\$4-\$7	474
16 / p. 452		Harry's Bar & Tables	♦♦	American	\$7-\$17	474
17 / p. 452		Californos	♦♦♦	American	\$8-\$24	473
18 / p. 452		PotPie	♦♦	American	\$7-\$23	475
19 / p. 452		Booze Fish Wine Bar	♦♦	International	\$8-\$16	473
20 / p. 452		Cafe Sebastienne	♦♦♦	American	\$8-\$27	473
21 / p. 452		Jardine's Restaurant & Jazz Club	♦♦	American	\$6-\$30	474
22 / p. 452		Figlio	♦♦	Italian	\$9-\$23	474
23 / p. 452		Starker's Restaurant	♦♦♦	New American	\$22-\$52	475
24 / p. 452		Grand Street Cafe	♦♦♦	American	\$9-\$30	474
25 / p. 452		JJ's Restaurant	♦♦♦	Continental	\$7-\$37	474
26 / p. 452		Plaza III, The Steakhouse	♦♦♦	Steak	\$12-\$52	475
27 / p. 452		Kona Grill	♦♦♦	Pacific Rim	\$9-\$30	474
28 / p. 452		re:Verse	♦♦♦	Mediterranean	\$7-\$28	475
29 / p. 452		Chaz on the Plaza	♦♦♦	Continental	\$8-\$32	474

AAA

At 60 mph, if you reach down to change the radio station you can travel the length of a football field.

Stay Focused

Keep your mind on the road.

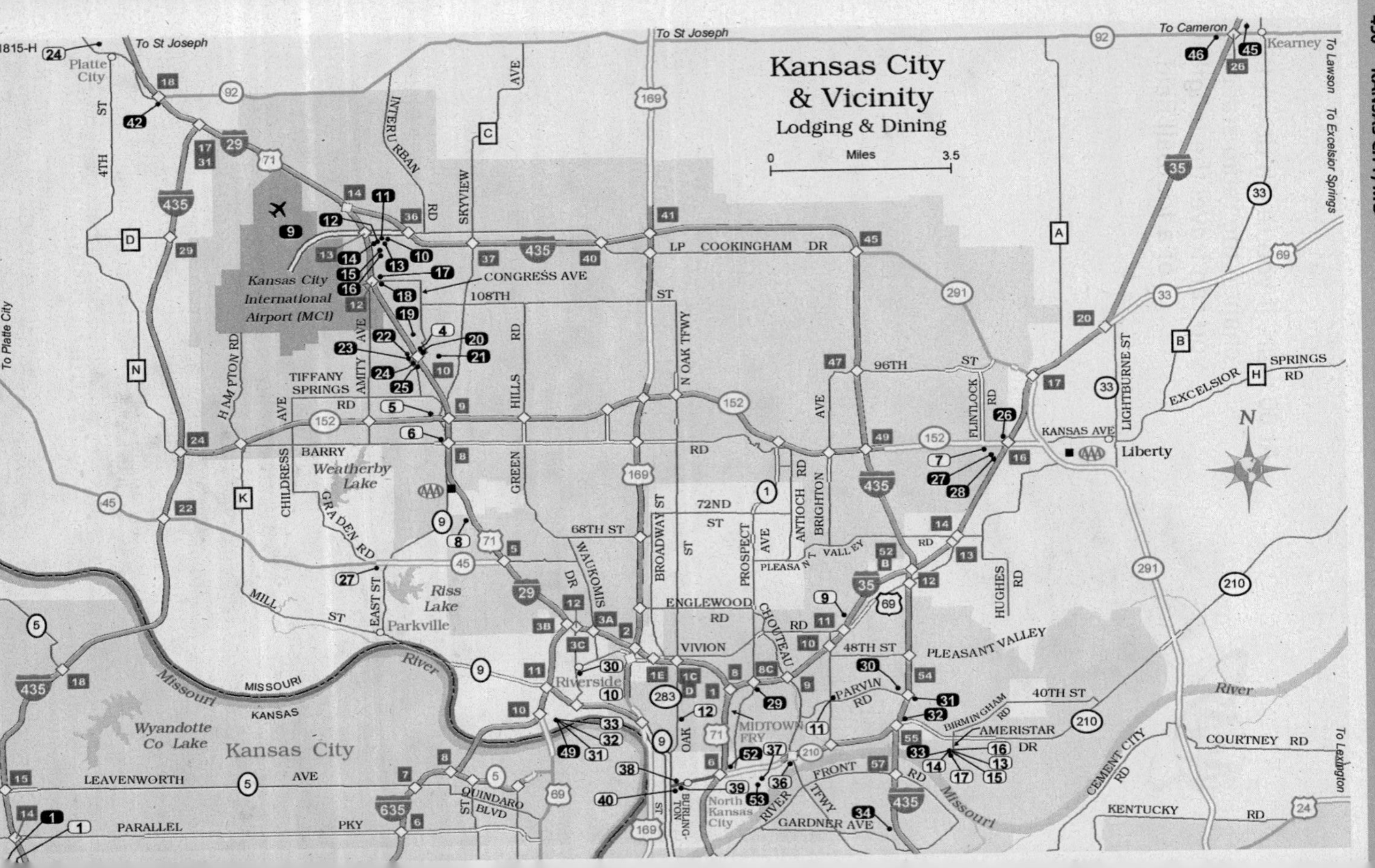
Kansas City
& Vicinity
Lodging & Dining
0
Miles
3.5
To St Joseph
To Cameron
To Lawson
To Excelsior Springs
To Lexington
To Platte City
1815-H
Platte City
Kearney
Liberty
Riverside
Parkville
North Kansas City
Kansas City
Weatherby Lake
Riss Lake
Wyandotte Co Lake
Kansas City International Airport (MCI)
Missouri
River
MISSOURI
KANSAS
4TH ST
INTERURBAN RD
SKYVIEW AVE
LP COOKINGHAM DR
CONGRESS AVE
108TH ST
N OAK TFWY
96TH ST
FLINTLOCK RD
KANSAS AVE
LIGHTBURNE ST
EXCELSIOR SPRINGS RD
HAMPTON RD
AMITY AVE
TIFFANY SPRINGS RD
CHILDRESS AVE
BARRY RD
GREEN HILLS RD
GRADEN RD
MILL ST
EAST ST
68TH ST
WAUKOMIS DR
BROADWAY ST
72ND ST
PROSPECT AVE
ANTIOCH RD
BRIGHTON AVE
PLEASANT VALLEY RD
HUGHES RD
ENGLEWOOD RD
VIVION
CHOUTEAU
48TH ST
PLEASANT VALLEY
PARVIN RD
40TH ST
BIRMINGHAM RD
AMERISTAR DR
COURTNEY RD
CEMENT CITY RD
KENTUCKY RD
MIDTOWN FRY
OAK
BURLINGTON
FRONT ST
RIVER TFWY
GARDNER AVE
LEAVENWORTH AVE
PARALLEL PKY
QUINDARO BLVD

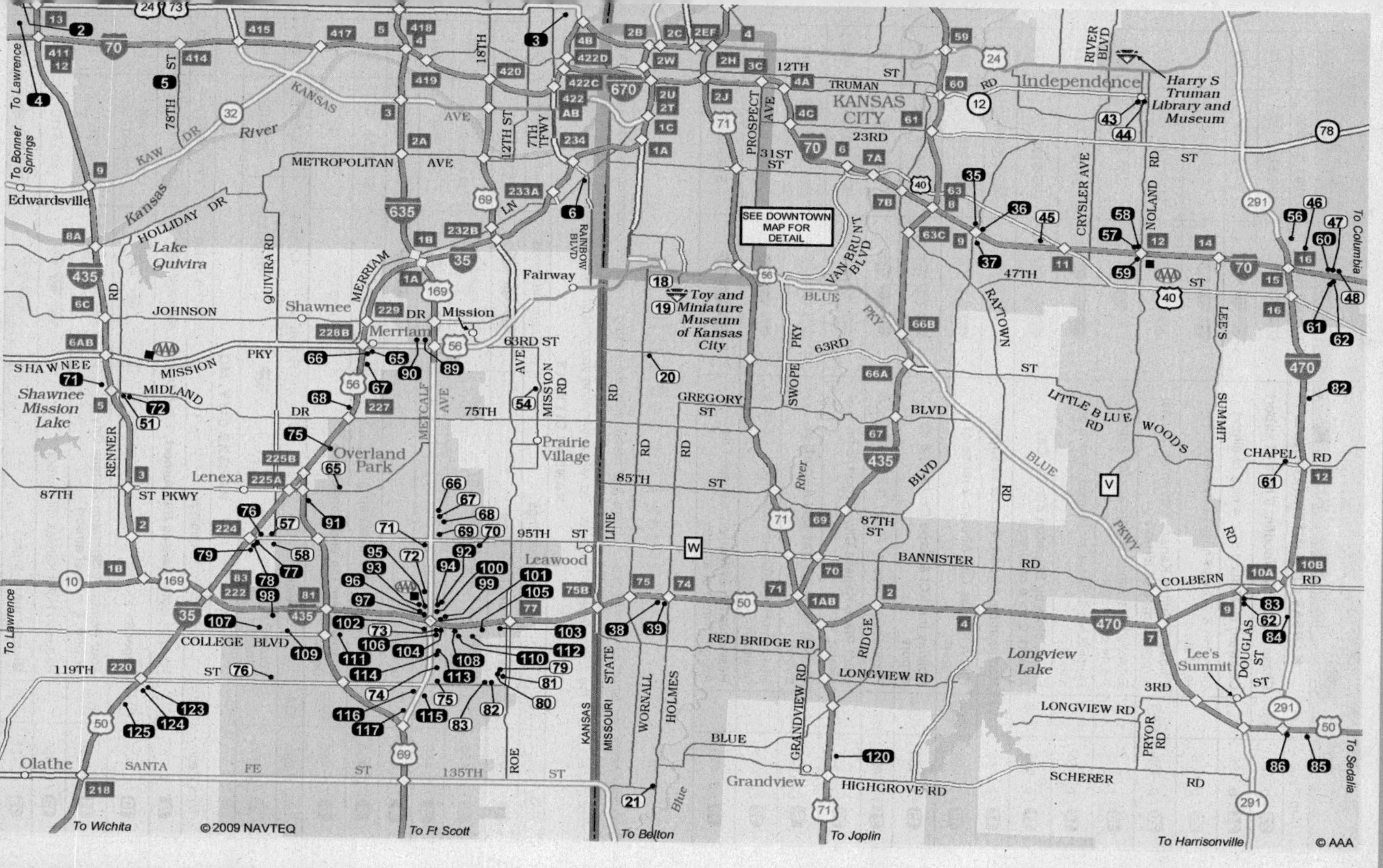

To Columbia
To Sedalia
To Harrisonville
To Joplin
To Belton
To Ft Scott
To Wichita
To Lawrence
To Bonner Springs
Harry S Truman Library and Museum
Independence
KANSAS CITY
SEE DOWNTOWN MAP FOR DETAIL
Toy and Miniature Museum of Kansas City
Lee's Summit
Longview Lake
Grandview
Leawood
Prairie Village
Overland Park
Fairway
Mission
Merriam
Shawnee
Lenexa
Olathe
Edwardsville
Lake Quivira
Shawnee Mission Lake
RAINBOW BLVD
LEE'S SUMMIT RD
NOLAND RD
RAYTOWN RD
BANNISTER RD
COLBERN RD
DOUGLAS ST
CHAPEL RD
TRUMAN RD
PROSPECT AVE
SWOPE PKY
GREGORY ST
HOLMES RD
WORNALL RD
STATE LINE RD
MISSOURI
KANSAS
METCALF AVE
ROE AVE
MISSION RD
QUIVIRA RD
RENNER RD
COLLEGE BLVD
SANTA FE ST
METROPOLITAN AVE
MERRIAM LN
© 2009 NAVTEQ
© AAA

Airport Accommodations

Map Page	OA	KANSAS CITY INTERNATIONAL	Diamond Rated	High Season	Page
23 / p. 456	AAA	**Chase Suites by Woodfin, 3 mi s of airport**	◆◆◆	$99-$159 SAVE	476
24 / p. 456		Courtyard by Marriott-KCI, 4 mi s of airport	◆◆◆	$129-$139	476
22 / p. 456		Drury Inn & Suites-Kansas City Airport, 3 mi se of airport	◆◆◆	$85-$189	476
20 / p. 456	AAA	**Embassy Suites Kansas City-International Airport, 3 mi s of airport**	◆◆◆	$119-$209 SAVE	477
16 / p. 456		Extended StayAmerica-Kansas City Airport, 1.8 mi e of airport	◆	$50-$110	477
14 / p. 456		Fairfield Inn & Suites by Marriott, 3 mi e of airport	◆◆◆	$116-$142	477
11 / p. 456	AAA	**Four Points by Sheraton Kansas City Airport, 2 mi e of airport**	◆◆◆	$55-$195 SAVE	478
17 / p. 456	AAA	**Hampton Inn Airport, 2 mi se of airport**	◆◆	$59-$169 SAVE	479
18 / p. 456	AAA	**Hilton Kansas City Airport, 2 mi se of airport**	◆◆◆	$89-$189 SAVE	479
15 / p. 456	AAA	**Holiday Inn KCI & Expo Center, 1.8 mi e of airport**	◆◆◆	$79-$139 SAVE	480
21 / p. 456		Homewood Suites by Hilton, 3 mi s of airport	◆◆◆	$89-$169	480
25 / p. 456	AAA	**Hyatt Place Kansas City Airport, 3 mi s of airport**	◆◆◆	$79-$199 SAVE	480
9 / p. 456	AAA	**Marriott Hotel-Kansas City Airport, at airport**	◆◆◆	$169-$179 SAVE	481
12 / p. 456		Radisson Hotel Kansas City Airport, 1.8 mi e of airport	◆◆◆	$90-$110	481
19 / p. 456		Residence Inn by Marriott, Kansas City Airport, 3 mi e of airport	◆◆◆	$143-$175	481

Kansas City and Vicinity

This index helps you "spot" where approved lodgings and restaurants are located on the corresponding detailed maps. Lodging daily rate range is for comparison only and show the property's high season. Restaurant rate range is a combination of lunch and/or dinner. Turn to the listing page for more detailed rate information and consult display ads for special promotions.

KANSAS CITY, KS

Map Page	OA	Lodgings	Diamond Rated	High Season	Page
1 / p. 456		Hampton Inn Village West	◆◆◆	$119-$169	493
2 / p. 456	AAA	**Great Wolf Lodge-Kansas City** - see color ad p 175	◆◆◆	Rates not provided SAVE	493
3 / p. 456		Hilton Garden Inn	◆◆◆	$59-$149	494
4 / p. 456		Chateau Avalon	◆◆◆	$139-$499	492
5 / p. 456	AAA	**Comfort Inn** - see color ad p 493	◆◆	$70-$250 SAVE	492
6 / p. 456	AAA	**Best Western Inn and Conference Center**	◆◆	$90 SAVE	492

Map Page	OA	Restaurant	Diamond Rated	Cuisine	Meal Range	Page
1 / p. 456		Yukon Base Camp Grill at Cabela's	◆	Wild Game	$5-$12	494

KANSAS CITY, MO

Map Page	OA	Lodgings	Diamond Rated	High Season	Page
9 / p. 456	AAA	**Marriott Hotel-Kansas City Airport**	◆◆◆	$169-$179 SAVE	481
10 / p. 456	AAA	**Super 8 - KCI**	◆◆	Rates not provided SAVE	481
11 / p. 456	AAA	**Four Points by Sheraton Kansas City Airport, 2 mi e of airport**	◆◆◆	$55-$195 SAVE	478
12 / p. 456		Radisson Hotel Kansas City Airport	◆◆◆	$90-$110	481
13 / p. 456	AAA	**Microtel Inn & Suites**	◆◆	$55-$65 SAVE	481

KANSAS CITY, MO (cont'd)

Map Page	OA	Lodgings (cont'd)	Diamond Rated	High Season	Page
14 / p. 456		Fairfield Inn & Suites by Marriott	◆◆◆	$116-$142	477
15 / p. 456	AAA	**Holiday Inn KCI & Expo Center**	◆◆◆	$79-$139 SAVE	480
16 / p. 456		Extended StayAmerica-Kansas City Airport	◆	$50-$110	477
17 / p. 456	AAA	**Hampton Inn Airport** - see color ad p 479	◆◆	$59-$169 SAVE	479
18 / p. 456	AAA	**Hilton Kansas City Airport**	◆◆◆	$89-$189 SAVE	479
19 / p. 456		Residence Inn by Marriott, Kansas City Airport	◆◆◆	$143-$175	481
20 / p. 456	AAA	**Embassy Suites Kansas City-International Airport**	◆◆◆	$119-$209 SAVE	477
21 / p. 456		Homewood Suites by Hilton	◆◆◆	$89-$169	480
22 / p. 456		Drury Inn & Suites-Kansas City Airport	◆◆◆	$85-$189	476
23 / p. 456	AAA	**Chase Suites by Woodfin**	◆◆◆	$99-$159 SAVE	476
24 / p. 456		Courtyard by Marriott-KCI	◆◆◆	$129-$139	476
25 / p. 456	AAA	**Hyatt Place Kansas City Airport**	◆◆◆	$79-$199 SAVE	480
26 / p. 456	AAA	**Hampton Inn-Kansas City/Liberty**	◆◆◆	$99-$149 SAVE	479
27 / p. 456		Holiday Inn Express	◆◆	$99-$109	480
28 / p. 456	AAA	**Fairfield Inn & Suites Kansas City-Liberty**	◆◆	$109-$129 SAVE	478
29 / p. 456	AAA	**Best Western Country Inn-North**	◆◆	$50-$150 SAVE	476
30 / p. 456		Fairfield Inn & Suites by Marriott Kansas City	◆◆◆	$80-$130	477
31 / p. 456	AAA	**Holiday Inn Kansas City Northeast**	◆◆◆	$79-$99 SAVE	480
32 / p. 456		Red Roof Inn-North-Worlds of Fun	◆◆	$43-$100	481
33 / p. 456	AAA	**Ameristar Hotel & Casino**	◆◆◆	$119-$549 SAVE	476
34 / p. 456		La Quinta Inn & Suites - Northeast	◆◆◆	$69-$109	481
35 / p. 456		Drury Inn & Suites-Kansas City Stadium	◆◆◆	$80-$169	477
36 / p. 456		Holiday Inn Kansas City SE - Water Park	◆◆◆	Rates not provided	480
37 / p. 456	AAA	**Holiday Inn-Sports Complex**	◆◆◆	$79-$189 SAVE	480
38 / p. 456		Courtyard by Marriott	◆◆◆	$129-$139	476
39 / p. 456		Extended StayAmerica-Kansas City South	◆	$55-$120	477

Map Page	OA	Restaurants	Diamond Rated	Cuisine	Meal Range	Page
4 / p. 456		Smoke Box Bar-B-Que	◆	Barbecue	$6-$15	483
5 / p. 456		Tomfooleries	◆◆	American	$8-$24	483
6 / p. 456		Smokehouse Bar-B-Que	◆◆	Barbecue	$7-$24	483
7 / p. 456		Corner Cafe	◆◆	American	$5-$15	482
8 / p. 456		Tasty Thai	◆◆	Thai	$8-$20	483
9 / p. 456		Stroud's North	◆◆	American	$8-$25	483
10 / p. 456		The Cafe at Briarcliff Village	◆◆	American	$9-$20	482
11 / p. 456		The Alamo	◆◆	Mexican	$5-$14	482
12 / p. 456		Cascone's Italian Restaurant	◆◆	Italian	$7-$23	482
13 / p. 456		Horizon's Buffet	◆◆	International	$12-$24	482
14 / p. 456		DeliLux	◆	Deli	$5-$8	482
15 / p. 456		Falcon Diner	◆◆	American	$7-$15	482

Map Page	OA	Restaurants (cont'd)	Diamond Rated	Cuisine	Meal Range	Page
16 / p. 456		Amerisports Brew Pub		American	$8-$20	482
17 / p. 456		Arthur Bryant's Barbeque		Barbecue	$7-$10	482
18 / p. 456		**Osteria Il Centro**		Northern Italian	$9-$18	483
19 / p. 456		Aixois		French	$6-$32	481
20 / p. 456		Carmen's Cafe		Italian	$8-$26	482
21 / p. 456		Fiorella's Jack Stack Barbecue of Martin City		Barbecue	$7-$26	482

PLATTE CITY

Map Page	OA	Lodging	Diamond Rated	High Season	Page
42 / p. 456		**Best Western Airport Inn & Suites KCI North**		$70-$95 SAVE	488

Map Page	OA	Restaurant	Diamond Rated	Cuisine	Meal Range	Page
24 / p. 456		Shields Manor Bistro		American	$20-$45	488

KEARNEY

Map Page	OA	Lodgings	Diamond Rated	High Season	Page
45 / p. 456		Kearney Super 8		$50-$180	486
46 / p. 456		Kearney Lodging		Rates not provided	486

RIVERSIDE

Map Page	OA	Lodging	Diamond Rated	High Season	Page
49 / p. 456		**Argosy Casino Hotel & Spa** - see color ad p 491		$159-$259 SAVE	490

Map Page	OA	Restaurants	Diamond Rated	Cuisine	Meal Range	Page
30 / p. 456		Corner Cafe		American	$7-$12	490
31 / p. 456		Crazy Olives		American	$6-$16	490
32 / p. 456		The Journey		Steak	$20-$40	490
33 / p. 456		Terrace Buffet		International	$11-$23	490

NORTH KANSAS CITY

Map Page	OA	Lodgings	Diamond Rated	High Season	Page
52 / p. 456		La Quinta Inn Kansas City North		$45-$149	487
53 / p. 456		Harrah's North Kansas City Casino and Hotel		Rates not provided	487

Map Page	OA	Restaurants	Diamond Rated	Cuisine	Meal Range	Page
36 / p. 456		The Range Steakhouse		Steak	$14-$38	488
37 / p. 456		The Buffet		American	$10-$22	487
38 / p. 456		Kelso's		American	$7-$17	488
39 / p. 456		Chappell's Restaurant & Sports Museum		American	$7-$21	488
40 / p. 456		Paul & Jack's Tavern		American	$6-$20	488

INDEPENDENCE

Map Page	OA	Lodgings	Diamond Rated	High Season	Page
56 / p. 456		Fairfield Inn by Marriott		$90-$120	485
57 / p. 456		**Super 8 Independence**		$50-$120 SAVE	485
58 / p. 456		**Best Western Truman Inn**		$50-$110 SAVE	484
59 / p. 456		**Quality Inn & Suites - East**		$67-$89 SAVE	485
60 / p. 456		**Hilton Garden Inn Independence**		$149-$229 SAVE	485
61 / p. 456		**Comfort Suites**		$89-$139 SAVE	484

INDEPENDENCE (cont'd)

Map Page	OA	Lodgings (cont'd)	Diamond Rated	High Season	Page
62 / p. 456	AAA	**Holiday Inn Express Hotel & Suites**	◆◆◆	Rates not provided SAVE	485

Map Page	OA	Restaurants	Diamond Rated	Cuisine	Meal Range	Page
43 / p. 456		The Rheinland Restaurant	◆◆	German	$7-$16	486
44 / p. 456		Ophelia's Restaurant & Inn	◆◆◆	American	$8-$32	486
45 / p. 456		V's Italiano Ristorante	◆◆	Italian	$7-$26	486
46 / p. 456		Smokehouse Bar-B-Que	◆◆	Barbecue	$7-$24	486
47 / p. 456		Hereford House	◆◆◆	Steak	$7-$38	485
48 / p. 456		On the Border Mexican Grill & Cantina	◆◆	Southwestern	$6-$14	485

MERRIAM, KS

Map Page	OA	Lodgings	Diamond Rated	High Season	Page
65 / p. 456		Drury Inn-Merriam/Shawnee Mission Parkway	◆◆◆	$65-$149	496
66 / p. 456		Homestead Studio Suites Hotel-Kansas City-Shawnee Mission	◆◆	$50-$110	496
67 / p. 456	AAA	**Quality Inn**	◆◆	$60-$80 SAVE	496
68 / p. 456		Hampton Inn & Suites	◆◆◆	$89-$179	496

SHAWNEE, KS

Map Page	OA	Lodgings	Diamond Rated	High Season	Page
71 / p. 456		Courtyard by Marriott	◆◆◆	$152-$186	504
72 / p. 456		Hampton Inn-Shawnee	◆◆◆	$99-$149	505

Map Page	OA	Restaurant	Diamond Rated	Cuisine	Meal Range	Page
51 / p. 456		Barley's Brewhaus	◆◆◆	American	$7-$27	505

LENEXA, KS

Map Page	OA	Lodgings	Diamond Rated	High Season	Page
75 / p. 456		Extended Stay Deluxe-Kansas City-Lenexa-87th St	◆◆	$55-$120	495
76 / p. 456		La Quinta Inn Kansas City (Lenexa)	◆◆	$49-$119	495
77 / p. 456		Crowne Plaza Lenexa - Overland Park	◆◆◆	$69-$209	495
78 / p. 456		Super 8-Lenexa	◆◆	$55-$120	495
79 / p. 456	AAA	**Comfort Inn**	◆◆	$71-$99 SAVE	495

Map Page	OA	Restaurants	Diamond Rated	Cuisine	Meal Range	Page
57 / p. 456		Shogun Sushi & Steak Restaurant	◆◆◆	Japanese	$7-$23	495
58 / p. 456		Bo Lings	◆◆	Chinese	$8-$23	495

LEE'S SUMMIT

Map Page	OA	Lodgings	Diamond Rated	High Season	Page
82 / p. 456	AAA	**Lee's Summit Holiday Inn Express**	◆◆	$74-$109 SAVE	487
83 / p. 456	AAA	**Hampton Inn**	◆◆◆	$79-$109 SAVE	487
84 / p. 456		Fairfield Inn by Marriott Lee's Summit	◆◆	$77-$94	486
85 / p. 456		Super 8	◆◆	$69-$160	487
86 / p. 456		Comfort Inn by Choice Hotels	◆◆	$63-$80	486

Map Page	OA	Restaurants	Diamond Rated	Cuisine	Meal Range	Page
61 / p. 456		O'Bryan's Irish Pub & Grille	◆◆	American	$8-$24	487
62 / p. 456		Jose Pepper's	◆◆	Southwestern	$7-$12	487

OVERLAND PARK, KS

Map Page	OA	Lodgings	Diamond Rated	High Season	Page
89 / p. 456		Ramada Overland Park-Mission	♦♦♦	$69-$149	502
90 / p. 456		Econo Lodge Inn & Suites	♦♦	$60-$90	500
91 / p. 456	AAA	**Holiday Inn Hotel & Suites**	♦♦♦	$79-$169 SAVE	501
92 / p. 456	AAA	**Hampton Inn-Kansas City/Overland Park**	♦♦♦	$69-$159 SAVE	500
93 / p. 456		Homewood Suites	♦♦♦	$99-$199	501
94 / p. 456		Embassy Suites Hotel-Overland Park	♦♦♦	$99-$189	500
95 / p. 456		Extended Stay Deluxe Kansas City-Overland Park-Metcalf	♦♦	$65-$140	500
96 / p. 456		La Quinta Inn & Suites	♦♦♦	$59-$129	502
97 / p. 456	AAA	**Comfort Inn & Suites**	♦♦♦	Rates not provided SAVE	499
98 / p. 456		Extended StayAmerica-Kansas City-Overland Park/Convention Center	♦♦	$55-$120	500
99 / p. 456		Super 8	♦♦	$55-$65	503
100 / p. 456		Wyndham Garden Hotel-Overland Park	♦♦♦	Rates not provided	503
101 / p. 456	AAA	**Red Roof Inn-Overland Park**	♦♦	$45-$100 SAVE	502
102 / p. 456	AAA	**Overland Park Marriott Hotel**	♦♦♦	$169-$179 SAVE	502
103 / p. 456	AAA	**Hyatt Place Kansas City/Overland Park/ Convention Center**	♦♦♦	$69-$199 SAVE	501
104 / p. 456		Drury Inn & Suites-Overland Park	♦♦♦	$85-$199	499
105 / p. 456		Holiday Inn Hotel & Suites Convention Center Overland Park	♦♦♦	$79-$139	501
106 / p. 456		Pear Tree Inn by Drury-Overland Park	♦♦	$60-$124	502
107 / p. 456		Candlewood Suites	♦♦♦	$59-$99	499
108 / p. 456	AAA	**Chase Suites Convention Center**	♦♦♦	$89-$209 SAVE	499
109 / p. 456	AAA	**Holtze Executive Village**	♦♦♦	$79-$219 SAVE	501
110 / p. 456	AAA	**Sheraton Overland Park Hotel at the Convention Center**	♦♦♦	Rates not provided SAVE	502
111 / p. 456		Doubletree Hotel	♦♦♦	$89-$219	499
112 / p. 456	AAA	**Hilton Garden Inn**	♦♦♦	$89-$199 SAVE	500
113 / p. 456	AAA	**Hyatt Place Kansas City/Overland Park/ Metcalf**	♦♦♦	$69-$189 SAVE	501
114 / p. 456		Courtyard by Marriott	♦♦♦	$129-$139	499
115 / p. 456		Residence Inn by Marriott	♦♦♦	$159-$179	502
116 / p. 456		SpringHill Suites By Marriott	♦♦♦	$119-$129	503
117 / p. 456		Fairfield Inn & Suites Overland Park	♦♦♦	$129-$139	500

Map Page	OA	Restaurants	Diamond Rated	Cuisine	Meal Range	Page
65 / p. 456		India Palace	♦♦	Indian	$6-$15	504
66 / p. 456		Bo Ling's	♦♦	Chinese	$6-$15	503
67 / p. 456		The Longbranch Steakhouse	♦♦	Steak	$5-$20	504
68 / p. 456		Johnny Cascone's Italian Restaurant	♦♦	Italian	$6-$24	504
69 / p. 456		China Star Buffet	♦	Chinese	$7-$9	503
70 / p. 456		Sushi Gin	♦♦	Japanese	$7-$20	504
71 / p. 456		Fiorella's Jack Stack Barbecue of Overland Park, Inc	♦♦	Barbecue	$6-$30	503

Map Page	OA	Restaurants (cont'd)	Diamond Rated	Cuisine	Meal Range	Page
72 / p. 456		Jose Peppers Border Grill & Cantina	2 diamonds	Mexican	$6-$13	504
73 / p. 456		K.C. Masterpiece Barbecue & Grill	2 diamonds	American	$6-$25	504
74 / p. 456		J. Alexander's Restaurant	3 diamonds	American	$8-$28	504
75 / p. 456		Andy's Wok	2 diamonds	Chinese	$6-$14	503
76 / p. 456		Barley's Brewhaus & Restaurant	2 diamonds	American	$8-$26	503

GRANDVIEW

Map Page	OA	Lodging	Diamond Rated	High Season	Page
120 / p. 456	AAA	**Holiday Inn Express Hotel & Suites**	3 diamonds	$80-$159 SAVE	484

OLATHE, KS

Map Page	OA	Lodgings	Diamond Rated	High Season	Page
123 / p. 456		Comfort Suites at Olathe Station	3 diamonds	$90-$130	497
124 / p. 456		Hampton Inn	3 diamonds	$109-$189	498
125 / p. 456		Fairfield Inn & Suites	3 diamonds	$116-$142	498

PARKVILLE

Map Page	OA	Restaurant	Diamond Rated	Cuisine	Meal Range	Page
27 / p. 456		Nick and Jake's	2 diamonds	American	$8-$27	488

PRAIRIE VILLAGE, KS

Map Page	OA	Restaurant	Diamond Rated	Cuisine	Meal Range	Page
54 / p. 456		Cafe Provence	2 diamonds	French	$8-$38	504

LEAWOOD, KS

Map Page	OA	Restaurants	Diamond Rated	Cuisine	Meal Range	Page
79 / p. 456		Hereford House	3 diamonds	American	$8-$25	494
80 / p. 456		Han Shin Japanese Steak House	3 diamonds	Japanese	$6-$40	494
81 / p. 456		Coyote Grill	3 diamonds	American	$7-$20	494
82 / p. 456		On The Border	2 diamonds	Mexican	$6-$14	494
83 / p. 456		The Bristol Seafood Grill	3 diamonds	Seafood	$8-$35	494

DOWNTOWN KANSAS CITY (See map and index starting on p. 452)

BEST WESTERN SEVILLE PLAZA HOTEL *Book great rates at AAA.com* **Phone:** (816)561-9600 

Hotel
$83-$139 All Year

Address: 4309 Main St 64111 **Location:** Jct 43rd St, just s. **Facility:** Smoke free premises. 77 one-bedroom standard units, some with whirlpools. 4 stories, interior corridors. **Parking:** on-site. **Amenities:** high-speed Internet, voice mail, irons, hair dryers. *Some:* CD players. **Leisure Activities:** exercise room. **Guest Services:** valet laundry, wireless Internet. **Business Services:** meeting rooms, business center. *(See color ad below)*

CALL / SOME UNITS

AAA Benefit: Members save up to 20%, plus 10% bonus points with rewards program.

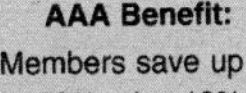

FREE continental breakfast and high-speed Internet

COMFORT INN & SUITES DOWNTOWN *Book great rates at AAA.com* **Phone:** (816)472-8808 

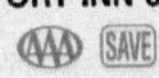

Hotel
$70-$120 All Year

Address: 770 Admiral Blvd 64106 **Location:** At Charlotte and Admiral blvds. **Facility:** 111 one-bedroom standard units, some with whirlpools. 3 stories, interior corridors. *Bath:* combo or shower only. **Parking:** on-site, winter plug-ins. **Terms:** 3 day cancellation notice. **Amenities:** safes (fee), irons, hair dryers. **Pool(s):** heated indoor. **Leisure Activities:** exercise room. **Guest Services:** valet and coin laundry, wireless Internet. **Business Services:** meeting rooms, PC. **Free Special Amenities: expanded continental breakfast and newspaper.** / SOME UNITS

COURTYARD BY MARRIOTT-COUNTRY CLUB PLAZA *Book great rates at AAA.com* **Phone:** (816)285-9755 

Historic Hotel
$152-$186 All Year

Address: 4600 J C Nichols Pkwy 64112 **Location:** Jct 47th St, just n. **Facility:** The lobby and bar area are enhanced by wood-beamed ceilings and each floor by unique, classic doors; the circular driveway is quaint and inviting. Smoke free premises. 123 one-bedroom standard units. 6 stories, interior corridors. *Bath:* combo or shower only. **Parking:** on-site. **Terms:** cancellation fee imposed. **Amenities:** video games (fee), high-speed Internet, voice mail, irons, hair dryers. **Pool(s):** heated outdoor. **Leisure Activities:** whirlpool, exercise room. **Guest Services:** complimentary and valet laundry, wireless Internet. **Business Services:** meeting rooms, business center.

AAA Benefit: Members save a minimum 5% off the best available rate.

(See map and index starting on p. 452)

CROWNE PLAZA KANSAS CITY DOWNTOWN *Book at AAA.com* **Phone:** (816)474-6664 5

Hotel
$99-$159 All Year

Address: 1301 Wyandotte St 64105 **Location:** Just s of I-70, US 24 and 40. **Facility:** Smoke free premises. 385 units. 286 one-bedroom standard units. 99 one-bedroom suites. 28 stories, interior corridors. *Bath:* combo or shower only. **Parking:** on-site (fee). **Terms:** cancellation fee imposed. **Amenities:** CD players, voice mail, irons, hair dryers. **Pool(s):** heated outdoor. **Leisure Activities:** exercise room. **Guest Services:** valet laundry, area transportation, wireless Internet. **Business Services:** conference facilities, business center.

EMBASSY SUITES HOTEL KANSAS CITY-PLAZA *Book great rates at AAA.com* **Phone:** (816)756-1720 13

Hotel
$129-$229 All Year

Address: 220 W 43rd St 64111 **Location:** At Broadway and 43rd sts; in Country Club Plaza. **Facility:** 266 one-bedroom suites. 12 stories, interior corridors. *Bath:* combo or shower only. **Parking:** on-site. **Terms:** 1-7 night minimum stay, cancellation fee imposed. **Amenities:** video games (fee), voice mail, irons, hair dryers. **Pool(s):** heated indoor. **Leisure Activities:** sauna, whirlpool, exercise room. **Guest Services:** valet and coin laundry, area transportation, wireless Internet. **Business Services:** meeting rooms, business center.

AAA Benefit:
Members save 5% or more everyday!

FAIRFIELD INN KANSAS CITY/UNION HILL *Book great rates at AAA.com* **Phone:** (816)931-5700 10

Hotel
$109-$119 All Year

Address: 3001 Main St 64108 **Location:** Jct 31st St, just n. **Facility:** Smoke free premises. 116 units. 114 one-bedroom standard units, some with whirlpools. 2 one-bedroom suites. 3-4 stories, interior corridors. *Bath:* combo or shower only. **Parking:** on-site. **Terms:** cancellation fee imposed. **Amenities:** high-speed Internet, voice mail, irons, hair dryers. **Pool(s):** heated indoor. **Leisure Activities:** whirlpool, exercise room. **Guest Services:** valet laundry, wireless Internet. **Business Services:** meeting rooms, PC.

CALL / SOME UNITS

AAA Benefit:
Members save a minimum 5% off the best available rate.

HAMPTON INN & SUITES-COUNTRY CLUB PLAZA *Book great rates at AAA.com* **Phone:** (816)448-4600 18

Hotel
$99-$229 All Year

Address: 4600 Summit St 64112 **Location:** Jct 47th St, just n; in Country Club Plaza. **Facility:** 203 units. 160 one-bedroom standard units. 43 one-bedroom suites, some with efficiencies and/or whirlpools. 9 stories, interior corridors. *Bath:* combo or shower only. **Parking:** on-site. **Terms:** check-in 4 pm, 1-7 night minimum stay, cancellation fee imposed. **Amenities:** video games (fee), dual phone lines, voice mail, irons, hair dryers. *Some:* DVD players, high-speed Internet. **Pool(s):** heated indoor. **Leisure Activities:** exercise room. **Guest Services:** valet and coin laundry, wireless Internet. **Business Services:** meeting rooms, business center.

/ SOME UNITS

AAA Benefit:
Members save up to 10% everyday!

HILTON PRESIDENT KANSAS CITY *Book great rates at AAA.com* **Phone:** (816)221-9490 6

AAA SAVE

Historic Hotel
$119-$219 All Year

Address: 1329 Baltimore Ave 64105 **Location:** Jct 14th St. **Facility:** Built in the 1920s and recently refurbished, the hotel combines old-style charm with modern elegance; Frank Sinatra performed here. Smoke free premises. 213 units. 187 one-bedroom standard units. 26 one-bedroom suites. 13 stories, interior corridors. *Bath:* combo or shower only. **Parking:** on-site (fee) and valet. **Terms:** 1-7 night minimum stay, cancellation fee imposed. **Amenities:** dual phone lines, voice mail, irons, hair dryers. *Fee:* video games, high-speed Internet. *Some:* CD players. **Dining:** 2 restaurants. **Leisure Activities:** rooftop pool privileges, exercise room. **Guest Services:** valet laundry, area transportation-within 5 mi, wireless Internet. **Business Services:** conference facilities, business center. *(See color ad p 466)*

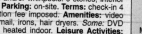

AAA Benefit:
Members save 5% or more everyday!

24 / SOME UNITS FEE

FREE local telephone calls and newspaper

(See map and index starting on p. 452)

HOLIDAY INN ALADDIN DOWNTOWN KANSAS CITY Book at AAA.com Phone: (816)421-8888 4

Boutique Hotel
$99-$199 All Year

Address: 1215 Wyandotte St 64105 **Location:** Just s of I-70, US 24 and 40. **Facility:** In a historic, circa 1920s building near the convention center, the hotel features the original marble floors and pillars in the atrium lobby. Smoke free premises. 193 units. 191 one-bedroom standard units. 2 one-bedroom suites, some with whirlpools. 16 stories, interior corridors. *Bath:* combo or shower only. **Parking:** on-site (fee) and valet. **Terms:** check-in 4 pm, cancellation fee imposed. **Amenities:** DVD players, CD players, high-speed Internet, voice mail, irons, hair dryers. **Leisure Activities:** exercise room, spa. **Guest Services:** coin laundry, wireless Internet. **Business Services:** meeting rooms, business center.
ASK / SOME UNITS

HOLIDAY INN AT THE PLAZA, KANSAS CITY Book at AAA.com Phone: (816)753-7400 16

Hotel
$79-$129 All Year

Address: One E 45th St 64111 **Location:** Jct Main St; in Country Club Plaza. **Facility:** 235 one-bedroom standard units. 5 stories, interior corridors. *Bath:* combo or shower only. **Parking:** on-site. **Terms:** cancellation fee imposed. **Amenities:** dual phone lines, voice mail, irons, hair dryers. **Pool(s):** heated outdoor. **Leisure Activities:** exercise room. **Guest Services:** valet and coin laundry, area transportation, wireless Internet. **Business Services:** conference facilities, business center.
ASK CALL / SOME UNITS FEE

HOLIDAY INN EXPRESS WESTPORT Book at AAA.com Phone: 816/931-1000 12

Hotel
Rates not provided

Address: 801 Westport Rd 64111 **Location:** Jct Main St, 0.5 mi w; in Westport Plaza area. **Facility:** Smoke free premises. 109 one-bedroom standard units. 6 stories, interior corridors. *Bath:* combo or shower only. **Parking:** on-site. **Amenities:** video games (fee), dual phone lines, voice mail, irons, hair dryers. *Some:* high-speed Internet. **Leisure Activities:** exercise room. **Guest Services:** valet laundry, wireless Internet. **Business Services:** meeting rooms, PC.
CALL / SOME UNITS FEE

HOMESTEAD STUDIO SUITES-KANSAS CITY/ COUNTRY CLUB PLAZA Book at AAA.com Phone: (816)531-2212 17

Extended Stay Hotel
$85-$170 All Year

Address: 4535 Main St 64111 **Location:** Jct 45th St, just s; just ne of Country Club Plaza. **Facility:** 101 one-bedroom standard units with efficiencies. 3 stories, interior corridors. *Bath:* combo or shower only. **Parking:** on-site. **Terms:** office hours 7 am-11 pm, cancellation fee imposed. **Amenities:** voice mail, irons. **Leisure Activities:** exercise room. **Guest Services:** valet and coin laundry, wireless Internet. ASK CALL / SOME UNITS FEE

▼ See AAA listing p 465 ▼

(See map and index starting on p. 452)

HOTEL PHILLIPS Book great rates at AAA.com **Phone:** 816/221-7000 3

Historic Hotel

Rates not provided

Address: 106 W 12th St 64105 **Location:** Jct Wyandotte St, just e. **Facility:** This restored hotel dating from 1931 is a boutique-style property featuring many original architectural elements. 217 one-bedroom standard units. 20 stories, interior corridors. *Bath:* combo or shower only. **Parking:** valet. **Amenities:** high-speed Internet (fee), dual phone lines, voice mail, irons, hair dryers. *Some:* safes. **Dining:** 12 Baltimore, see separate listing. **Leisure Activities:** exercise room. *Fee:* massage. **Guest Services:** valet laundry, wireless Internet. **Business Services:** meeting rooms, business center. **Free Special Amenities: newspaper.** Affiliated with A Preferred Hotel.

/ SOME UNITS FEE

HYATT REGENCY CROWN CENTER Book great rates at AAA.com **Phone:** (816)421-1234 

Hotel

$89-$399 All Year

Address: 2345 McGee St 64108 **Location:** In Crown Center area. **Facility:** 731 units. 704 one-bedroom standard units. 27 one-bedroom suites. 40 stories, interior corridors. *Bath:* combo or shower only. **Parking:** on-site (fee) and valet. **Terms:** cancellation fee imposed. **Amenities:** voice mail, irons, hair dryers. *Some:* CD players, high-speed Internet (fee), safes. **Dining:** 5 restaurants, also, Peppercorn Duck Club, see separate listing. **Pool(s):** heated outdoor. **Leisure Activities:** saunas, whirlpool, steamrooms, board games. **Guest Services:** valet laundry, area transportation-downtown, wireless Internet. **Business Services:** conference facilities, business center. **Free Special Amenities: preferred room (subject to availability with advance reservations).**

ECO  CALL     / SOME UNITS

HYATT HOTELS & RESORTS

AAA Benefit:

Ask for the AAA rate and save 10%.

▼ See AAA listing p 468 ▼

(See map and index starting on p. 452)

THE INTERCONTINENTAL KANSAS CITY AT THE PLAZA Book great rates at AAA.com **Phone:** (816)756-1500 23

Hotel
$149-$449 All Year

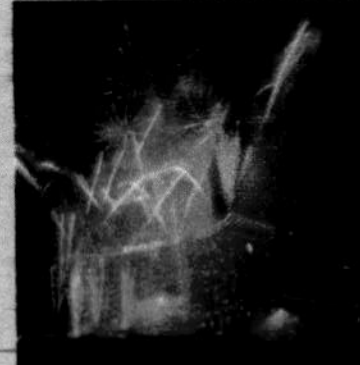

Address: 401 Ward Pkwy 64112 **Location:** Jct Wornall Rd; in Country Club Plaza. **Facility:** Located in a fashionable shopping district with upscale cafes and restaurants, this hotel offers spacious rooms and upgraded services and amenities. Smoke free premises. 366 units. 347 one-bedroom standard units. 19 one-bedroom suites. 12 stories, interior corridors. *Bath:* combo or shower only. **Parking:** on-site (fee) and valet. **Terms:** cancellation fee imposed. **Amenities:** dual phone lines, voice mail, safes, honor bars, irons, hair dryers. **Pool(s):** outdoor. **Leisure Activities:** saunas, steamrooms. **Guest Services:** valet laundry, wireless Internet. **Business Services:** conference facilities, business center. *(See color ad p 467)*

/ SOME UNITS FEE

MARRIOTT-KANSAS CITY-COUNTRY CLUB PLAZA Book great rates at AAA.com **Phone:** (816)531-3000 15

Hotel
$159-$209 All Year

Address: 4445 Main St 64111 **Location:** Jct 45th St. **Facility:** Smoke free premises. 295 units. 293 one-bedroom standard units. 2 one-bedroom suites. 19 stories, interior corridors. *Bath:* combo or shower only. **Parking:** on-site (fee) and valet. **Terms:** cancellation fee imposed. **Amenities:** dual phone lines, voice mail, irons, hair dryers. **Pool(s):** heated indoor. **Leisure Activities:** whirlpool. **Guest Services:** valet laundry, area transportation-Plaza, wireless Internet. **Business Services:** conference facilities, business center. / SOME UNITS

Marriott HOTELS & RESORTS
AAA Benefit:
Members save a minimum 5% off the best available rate.

MARRIOTT KANSAS CITY DOWNTOWN Book great rates at AAA.com **Phone:** (816)421-6800 2

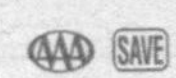

Hotel
$188-$230 All Year

Address: 200 W 12th St 64105 **Location:** Jct Wyandotte St. **Facility:** Smoke free premises. 983 units. 978 one-bedroom standard units. 5 one-bedroom suites, some with kitchens. 18-22 stories, interior corridors. *Bath:* combo or shower only. **Parking:** on-site (fee) and valet. **Terms:** cancellation fee imposed. **Amenities:** voice mail, irons, hair dryers. **Dining:** 2 restaurants. **Pool(s):** heated indoor. **Leisure Activities:** *Fee:* massage. **Guest Services:** valet laundry, wireless Internet. **Business Services:** conference facilities, business center.

ECO / SOME UNITS

Marriott HOTELS & RESORTS
AAA Benefit:
Members save a minimum 5% off the best available rate.

THE Q HOTEL & SPA Book great rates at AAA.com **Phone:** 816/931-0001 11

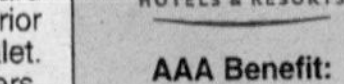

Hotel
Rates not provided

Address: 560 Westport Rd 64111 **Location:** Jct Main St, 0.4 mi w; in Westport Plaza area. **Facility:** Smoke free premises. 123 one-bedroom standard units, some with whirlpools. 4 stories, interior corridors. *Bath:* combo or shower only. **Parking:** on-site. **Amenities:** video games (fee), high-speed Internet, dual phone lines, voice mail, irons, hair dryers. **Leisure Activities:** spa. **Guest Services:** valet laundry, area transportation-within 3 mi, wireless Internet. **Business Services:** meeting rooms, business center. ECO / SOME UNITS FEE

THE RAPHAEL HOTEL Book at AAA.com **Phone:** 816/756-3800 22

Historic Hotel
Rates not provided

Address: 325 Ward Pkwy 64112 **Location:** Corner of Wornall Rd; in Country Club Plaza. **Facility:** A large circular drive with a picturesque statue greets arriving guests. Rooms feature contemporary appointments; some with a small bath. Smoke free premises. 126 units. 54 one-bedroom standard units. 72 one-bedroom suites, some with whirlpools. 9 stories, interior corridors. *Bath:* combo or shower only. **Parking:** on-site and valet. **Terms:** check-in 4 pm. **Amenities:** high-speed Internet, voice mail, safes, honor bars, irons, hair dryers. **Dining:** Chaz on the Plaza, see separate listing. **Guest Services:** valet laundry, wireless Internet. **Business Services:** business center.

CALL

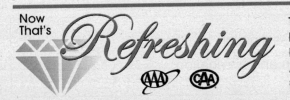

(See map and index starting on p. 452)

RESIDENCE INN BY MARRIOTT DOWNTOWN/
UNION HILL Book great rates at AAA.com

Phone: (816)561-3000 9

Extended Stay Hotel

$143-$175 All Year

Address: 2975 Main St 64108 **Location:** Jct 31st St, just n. **Facility:** Smoke free premises. 96 units. 80 one-bedroom standard units with kitchens. 16 two-bedroom suites with kitchens. 2-3 stories (no elevator), exterior corridors. *Bath:* combo or shower only. **Parking:** on-site. **Terms:** cancellation fee imposed. **Amenities:** video games (fee), voice mail, irons, hair dryers. *Some:* high-speed Internet. **Pool(s):** outdoor. **Leisure Activities:** exercise room. **Guest Services:** valet and coin laundry, area transportation, wireless Internet. **Business Services:** meeting rooms, business center.

ECO / SOME UNITS FEE

AAA Benefit: Members save a minimum 5% off the best available rate.

RESIDENCE INN BY MARRIOTT KANSAS CITY
COUNTRY CLUB PLAZA Book great rates at AAA.com

Phone: (816)753-0033 20

Extended Stay Hotel

$159-$169 All Year

Address: 4601 Broadway Blvd 64112 **Location:** Jct JC Nichols Pkwy, just w on 46th Terr; in Country Club Plaza. **Facility:** Smoke free premises. 106 units. 56 one-bedroom standard units with efficiencies. 38 one- and 12 two-bedroom suites, some with efficiencies or kitchens. 6 stories, interior corridors. *Bath:* combo or shower only. **Parking:** on-site. **Terms:** cancellation fee imposed. **Amenities:** video games (fee), high-speed Internet, dual phone lines, voice mail, irons, hair dryers. **Pool(s):** heated indoor. **Leisure Activities:** whirlpool, exercise room, sports court. **Guest Services:** valet and coin laundry, wireless Internet. **Business Services:** meeting rooms, business center.

/ SOME UNITS FEE

AAA Benefit: Members save a minimum 5% off the best available rate.

▼ See AAA listing p 471 ▼

(See map and index starting on p. 452)

SHERATON SUITES COUNTRY CLUB PLAZA Book great rates at AAA.com **Phone:** 816/931-4400 21

Hotel
Rates not provided

Address: 770 W 47th St 64112 **Location:** Jct Summit St; in Country Club Plaza. **Facility:** Smoke free premises. 257 one-bedroom suites. 18 stories, interior corridors. *Bath:* combo or shower only. **Parking:** on-site (fee) and valet. **Amenities:** dual phone lines, voice mail, irons, hair dryers. *Fee:* video games, high-speed Internet. *Some:* DVD players. **Pool(s):** heated indoor/outdoor. **Leisure Activities:** whirlpool, exercise room. **Guest Services:** valet and coin laundry, wireless Internet. **Business Services:** meeting rooms, business center. (See color ad p 470)

CALL / SOME UNITS

Sheraton HOTELS & RESORTS

AAA Benefit:
Members get up to 15% off, plus Starwood Preferred Guest® bonuses.

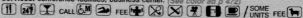

THE WESTIN CROWN CENTER Book great rates at AAA.com **Phone:** (816)474-4400 8

Hotel
$129-$329 All Year

Address: 1 E Pershing Rd 64108 **Location:** 0.5 mi s. **Facility:** Connected with Crown Center, a popular shopping area, the expansive hotel's lobby is highlighted by a large waterfall and open walkways. Smoke free premises. 729 units. 724 one-bedroom standard units. 5 one-bedroom suites. 18 stories, interior corridors. *Bath:* combo or shower only. **Parking:** on-site (fee) and valet. **Terms:** 3 day cancellation notice-fee imposed. **Amenities:** voice mail, safes, irons, hair dryers. *Fee:* video games, high-speed Internet. *Some:* DVD players, CD players, fax. **Dining:** 2 restaurants, also, Benton's Steak & Chop House, see separate listing. **Pool(s):** heated outdoor. **Leisure Activities:** sauna, whirlpool, 2 lighted tennis courts, jogging, sports court, shuffleboard. *Fee:* massage. **Guest Services:** valet laundry, wireless Internet, tanning facilities. **Business Services:** conference facilities, business center. (See color ad p 472)

 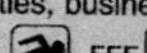  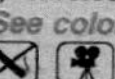  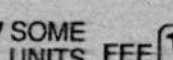 

24 CALL FEE / SOME UNITS FEE

WESTIN HOTELS & RESORTS

AAA Benefit:
Enjoy up to 15% off your next stay, plus Starwood Preferred Guest® bonuses.

▼ See AAA listing p 471 ▼

(See map and index starting on p. 452)

WHERE TO DINE

12 BALTIMORE Phone: 816/346-4410 (3)

American
$10-$18

The casual but sophisticated establishment's dining room sometimes bustles with activity from the lunch and after-work crowds. Casual dress. **Bar:** Full bar. **Reservations:** accepted. **Hours:** 6:30 am-1 am, Sun-11 pm. **Address:** 106 W 12th St 64105 **Location:** Jct Wyandotte St, just e; in Hotel Phillips. **Parking:** on-site and valet.

1924 MAIN Phone: 816/472-1924 (7)

American
$10-$55

Nestled in a restored older building, the restaurant offers a variety of innovative menu choices, including must-try panzanella salad. A large wine list and live entertainment is available. Dressy casual. **Bar:** Full bar. **Reservations:** suggested. **Hours:** 5 pm-10 pm, Fri-Sun also 11 am-2 pm. Closed: 12/25; also Mon. **Address:** 1924 Main St 64108 **Location:** Jct 19th St, just s. **Parking:** on-site.

THE AMERICAN RESTAURANT AT CROWN CENTER Phone: 816/545-8001 (12)

American
$17-$80

The recipient of several awards for the quality of its food, the restaurant presents imaginative dishes with superior flavors. Adding to the dining experience are impeccable service, a refined dining room with unusual, washed-oak accents and an impressive wine selection of nearly 1,400 bottles. The dining room offers nice views of the Crown Center area. Semi-formal attire. Entertainment. **Bar:** Full bar. **Reservations:** suggested. **Hours:** 5:30 pm-10 pm. Closed major holidays; also Sun. **Address:** 200 E 25th St, Suite 400 64108 **Location:** At 25th and Grant sts; on top floor of Halls Department Store; in Crown Center area. **Parking:** on-site and valet.

BENTON'S STEAK & CHOP HOUSE Phone: 816/474-4400 (11)

American
$25-$38

Featuring great steak, chops and seafood, Benton's offers a panoramic view from 20 stories above the city. All diners receive a small bucket of large, cold shrimp for an appetizer. The restaurant displays original artwork by Thomas Hart Benton. Weekly wine promotions. Dressy casual. **Bar:** Full bar. **Reservations:** suggested. **Hours:** 5:30 pm-10 pm, Sun 10 am-2 pm. Closed: Mon. **Address:** 1 E Pershing Rd 64108 **Location:** 0.5 mi s; in The Westin Crown Center. **Parking:** on-site and valet.

BLUE BIRD BISTRO Phone: 816/221-7559 (5)

American
$5-$32

A Blue Bird blue-plate special is offered daily for lunch. Organic beef tenderloin, bison and free-range chicken, veggie burgers, hummus and pasta are some of the offerings. Casual dress. **Bar:** Full bar. **Reservations:** accepted. **Hours:** 7 am-10 pm, Sun 10 am-2 pm. Closed major holidays. **Address:** 1700 Summit St 64108 **Location:** Jct Broadway, 0.5 mi w on 17th St. **Parking:** street.

BOOZE FISH WINE BAR Phone: 816/561-5995 (19)

International
$8-$16

The cozy, attractive bistro presents an imaginative appetizer menu, a selection of light entrees and an impressive wine list. Casual dress. **Bar:** Full bar. **Hours:** 4 pm-12:30 am, Fri-1:30 am, Sat 5 pm-1:30 pm. Closed major holidays; also Sun. **Address:** 1511 Westport Rd 64111 **Location:** In Westport Plaza. **Parking:** on-site.

BRISTOL SEAFOOD GRILL Phone: 816/448-6007 (4)

Seafood
$10-$39

All seafood items are flown in daily so expect the freshest of everything. Many menu options evolve and change but some popular choices remain year round, including king crab legs, crab cakes with just the right amount of spice and the very popular biscuits that accompany all meals. This modern restaurant is in the heart of the Power and Light District and offers a comfortable patio that's great for people-watching on nice days. Dressy casual. **Bar:** Full bar. **Reservations:** suggested. **Hours:** 11 am-10 pm, Fri & Sat-11 pm, Sun 11 am-2 & 4-9 pm. Closed: 5/31, 9/6, 12/25. **Address:** 51 E 14th St 64106 **Location:** Jct 14th and Main sts. **Parking:** valet and street. CALL &M

CAFE AL DENTE Phone: 816/472-9444 (1)

Italian
$6-$16

Popular with both tourists and locals, the cafe serves prepared-to-order selections. The pleasant location invites relaxation. Casual dress. **Bar:** Full bar. **Reservations:** not accepted. **Hours:** 11 am-10 pm. Closed major holidays; also Sun. **Address:** 412 D Delaware St 64105 **Location:** Jct 5th St; in Historic River Market. **Parking:** on-site and street. CALL &M

CAFE SEBASTIENNE Phone: 816/561-7740 (20)

American
$8-$27

Located in a contemporary art museum, the cafe has a cozy ambience for up to 48 diners. The menu offers many creative dishes including alfresco fare, and there's patio seating by the waterfall. Many lively works of art decorate the walls. Dressy casual. **Bar:** Full bar. **Reservations:** accepted. **Hours:** 11 am-2:30 pm, Fri & Sat also 5:30 pm-9:30 pm. Closed: 7/4, 11/25, 12/25; also Mon. **Address:** 4420 Warwick Blvd 64111 **Location:** Jct 45th St, just e; in Kemper Museum of Contemporary Art. **Parking:** on-site.

CALIFORNOS Phone: 816/531-7878 (17)

American
$8-$24

Loads of outdoor seating is available in season, but inside is also a treat. Fresh-minded and contemporary dishes incorporate flavors of the West Coast. Dressy casual. **Bar:** Full bar. **Reservations:** accepted. **Hours:** 11 am-3 & 5-10 pm, Fri-11 pm, Sat noon-3 & 5-11 pm. Closed major holidays; also Sun. **Address:** 4124 Pennsylvania Ave 64111 **Location:** In Westport Plaza area. **Parking:** on-site and valet.

(See map and index starting on p. 452)

CHAZ ON THE PLAZA

Phone: 816/756-3800 29

Continental
$8-$32

The weekly changing menu features selections to please a broad array of tastes. Guests can dine leisurel in any one of the cozy dining rooms. Casual dress. Entertainment. **Bar:** Full bar. **Reservations:** suggested **Hours:** 6:30-10 am, 11-3 & 5-10 pm, Sat 7 am-3 & 5-11 pm, Sun 7 am-12:30 & 5-9 pm. Closed: 1/1 **Address:** 325 Ward Pkwy 64112 **Location:** Corner of Wornall Rd; in Country Club Plaza; in The Raphae Hotel. **Parking:** on-site and valet.

CHUBBY'S

Phone: 816/931-2482 15

American
$4-$7

Although the '50s-style diner bustles, service is warm and friendly. The menu lists a large selection including breakfast items served all day. Casual dress. **Reservations:** accepted. **Hours:** 24 hours. Close major holidays. **Address:** 3756 Broadway St 64111 **Location:** Just w of 37th St. **Parking:** on-site.

FIGLIO

Phone: 816/561-0505 22

Italian
$9-$23

Pizza baked in a wood-burning oven and handmade fresh pasta are restaurant favorites. Casual dress. **Bar:** Full bar. **Reservations:** accepted. **Hours:** 11 am-10 pm, Fri & Sat-11 pm, Sun 10:30 am-9 pm. Closed 12/25. **Address:** 209 W 46th Terr 64112 **Location:** Jct JC Nichols Pkwy; in Country Club Plaza. **Parking:** on-site.

FIORELLA'S JACK STACK BARBEQUE - FREIGHT HOUSE

Phone: 816/472-7427 9

Barbecue
$6-$30

Located in a refurbished freight house, this eatery serves up some of the best barbecue in town. Menu items include burnt ends, many varieties of smoked meats, steaks and seafood. The baked beans are award winning. Casual dress. **Bar:** Full bar. **Reservations:** required. **Hours:** 11 am-10 pm, Fri & Sat-10:30 pm, Sun-9 pm. Closed: 11/25, 12/25. **Address:** 101 W 22nd St 64108 **Location:** Jct Baltimore Ave. **Parking:** on-site. CALL

GATES BAR-B-Q

Phone: 816/753-0828 14

American
$10-$20

A city original, the family restaurant was established in 1946. Service is fast, and "Hi, may I help you?" is the immediate greeting. Casual dress. **Bar:** Full bar. **Reservations:** not accepted. **Hours:** 10 am-midnight, Fri & Sat-1 am. Closed: 11/25, 12/25. **Address:** 3205 Main St 64111 **Location:** At Main and Linwood sts. **Parking:** on-site.

GRAND STREET CAFE

Phone: 816/561-8000 24

American
$9-$30

Martini Monday and nightly live jazz are draws to the glamorous dining room. Seasonal fare is prepared with flair. Casual dress. **Bar:** Full bar. **Reservations:** accepted. **Hours:** 11 am-10 pm, Fri & Sat-11 pm, Sun 10 am-9 pm. Closed: 7/4, 12/25. **Address:** 4740 Grand Ave 64112 **Location:** In Country Club Plaza. **Parking:** on-site.

HARRY'S BAR & TABLES

Phone: 816/561-3950 16

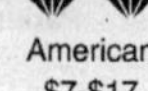

American
$7-$17

Occupying a corner location in the popular Westport area, the establishment is an elegant mix of a cigar and martini bar and restaurant. The casual dinner menu lists classic favorites with a twist. Casual dress. **Bar:** Full bar. **Reservations:** not accepted. **Hours:** 3 pm-3 am, Sat & Sun from 5 pm. **Address:** 501 Westport Rd 64111 **Location:** Jct Main St, 0.4 mi w; in Westport Plaza area. **Parking:** on-site.

JARDINE'S RESTAURANT & JAZZ CLUB

Phone: 816/561-6480 21

American
$6-$30

Wonderful navy bean soup stands out at the warm, comfortable and slightly contemporary restaurant. Live jazz every night. Casual dress. Entertainment. **Bar:** Full bar. **Reservations:** suggested, weekends. **Hours:** 4:30 pm-10 pm, Fri-midnight, Sat 5:30-midnight, Sun 6 pm-10 pm. Closed major holidays. **Address:** 4536 Main St 64111 **Location:** In Westport Plaza area. **Parking:** on-site.

JJ'S RESTAURANT

Phone: 816/561-7136 25

Continental
$7-$37

Sitting on a pleasant tree-lined street just west of the Country Club Plaza, this little restaurant is a perfect place for a quiet tete-a-tete or a leisurely business luncheon. An astounding selection of wines complements offerings from the constantly changing bistro-type menu. A knowledgeable staff will eagerly make recommendations and offer insight. Casual dress. **Bar:** Full bar. **Reservations:** suggested, weekends. **Hours:** 11 am-4 & 5-10 pm, Fri & Sat-11 pm, Sun 5 pm-10 pm. Closed major holidays; also Super Bowl Sun. **Address:** 910 W 48th St 64112 **Location:** Just w of Country Club Plaza; between Belleview Ave and Roanoke Pkwy. **Parking:** valet and street.

KONA GRILL

Phone: 816/931-5888 27

Pacific Rim
$9-$30

The eclectic menu reflects Pacific influences. In addition to noodle dishes and sushi, it lists specialties of macadamia nut chicken and lemon grass-encrusted swordfish. The dining room has a large aquarium, a private area and a sushi bar. The patio opens during warm weather. Casual dress. **Bar:** Full bar. **Reservations:** accepted. **Hours:** 11 am-11 pm. Closed: 11/25, 12/25. **Address:** 444 Ward Pkwy 64112 **Location:** Just w of Wornall Rd; in Country Club Plaza. **Parking:** on-site.

LIDIA'S KANSAS CITY

Phone: 816/221-3722 8

Northern Italian
$10-$29

An old railroad freight building is now home to the popular restaurant, which nestles in beside other trendy eateries. Beautifully redone, the interior sports contemporary design and decor blends dramatically with the original vaulted ceilings and brick walls. Homemade Italian food is prepared with flair. Dressy casual. **Bar:** Full bar. **Reservations:** suggested. **Hours:** 11 am-2 & 5-9 pm, Fri & Sat-10 pm; Saturday & Sunday brunch. Closed major holidays. **Address:** 101 W 22nd St 64108 **Location:** Jct Baltimore Ave. **Parking:** on-site.

(See map and index starting on p. 452)

MICHAEL SMITH

Phone: 816/842-2202 (6)

American
$11-$38

Michael Smith, a James Beard Award winning chef, is known for innovative, seasonally-changing recipes that erupt with unique flavors. The elegant entrees range from poultry, game, seafood and beef but of particular interest and a house favorite is the Eight Hour Pork Roast. Appetizers are creative with such delicious choices as diver sea scallops, braised rabbit and sauteed skate wing. A large wine selection is available. Semi-formal attire. **Bar:** Full bar. **Reservations:** required. **Hours:** 11:30 am-2 & 5-10 pm, Sat from 5 pm. Closed major holidays; also Sun & Mon. **Address:** 1900 Main St 64108 **Location:** Jct 19th and Main sts. **Parking:** street.

PEPPERCORN DUCK CLUB

Phone: 816/398-4845 (10)

American
$15-$39

The upscale restaurant nurtures a relaxing ambience. After feasting on the chef's specialty rotisserie duck, patrons can salivate over the fabulous chocolate dessert bar, which is laden with elaborate meal-enders. Dressy casual. **Bar:** Full bar. **Reservations:** suggested. **Hours:** 5:30 pm-9:30 pm, Fri & Sat-10 pm. Closed major holidays; also Sun-Wed. **Address:** 2345 McGee St 64108 **Location:** In Crown Center area; in Hyatt Regency Crown Center. **Parking:** on-site and valet.

PLAZA III, THE STEAKHOUSE

Phone: 816/753-0000 (26)

Steak
$12-$52

Tender, melt-in-your-mouth Kansas City steaks, prime rib, salmon, chicken, pork with sides of fresh mashed potatoes and vegetables or sauteed mushrooms in butter sauce—delicious! A variety of salads and classic appetizers and an assortment of tempting, decadent desserts all served in a sophisticated and classic atmosphere by professionally trained staff. It doesn't get any better than this. Extensive wine selection. Dressy casual. **Bar:** Full bar. **Reservations:** suggested. **Hours:** 11 am-3 & 5-10 pm, Fri & Sat-11 pm, Sun 5 pm-10 pm. Closed: 12/25. **Address:** 4749 Pennsylvania Ave 64112 **Location:** On US 56; in Country Club Plaza. **Parking:** on-site.

PONAK'S MEXICAN KITCHEN & BAR

Phone: 816/753-0775 (13)

Mexican
$4-$10

Consistently voted "Best Mexican" by area publications, this is a great place to gather with friends and family for dinner and cocktails (try the fabulous margaritas). A local staple since 1975, the establishment is popular for its fantastic food and quick, friendly service. Cooking inspirations come from Mexico's Sonora region, with popular choices including queso, burritos and enchiladas. Casual dress. **Bar:** Full bar. **Reservations:** accepted, except weekends. **Hours:** 11 am-10 pm, Fri & Sat-11 pm, Sun-9 pm. Closed: 4/4, 11/25, 12/25. **Address:** 2856 Southwest Blvd 64108 **Location:** I-35, exit 234 (7th St), 0.4 mi s to Southwest Blvd, then 0.8 mi ne. **Parking:** on-site.

POTPIE

Phone: 816/561-2702 (18)

American
$7-$23

The atmosphere is equal parts cozy, warm and comfortable. Food options, including a terrific rendition of a BLT, range from familiar to more distinctive. Casual dress. **Bar:** Full bar. **Reservations:** suggested, weekends. **Hours:** 11 am-10 pm, Fri-11 pm, Sat 5 pm-11 pm. Closed major holidays; also Sun, Mon & 1st week of Jan. **Address:** 904 Westport Rd 64111 **Location:** In Westport Plaza area. **Parking:** on-site and street.

RE:VERSE

Phone: 816/931-7811 (28)

Mediterranean
$7-$28

In the popular Plaza area, the trendy restaurant maintains and air of casual sophistication. Creativity distinguishes the menu. Dressy casual. **Bar:** Full bar. **Reservations:** suggested. **Hours:** 11 am-11 pm, Fri-midnight, Sat 9:30 am-midnight, Sun 9:30 am-11 pm. Closed: 1/1, 12/25. **Address:** 618 Ward Pkwy 64113 **Location:** At Jefferson and Ward Pkwy; in Country Club Plaza area. **Parking:** on-site (fee).

SAVOY GRILL

Phone: 816/842-3890 (2)

Seafood
$7-$43

Well-established since 1903, this restaurant specializes in fresh seafood and prime beef prepared with excellent flavors and presentations. Enhanced by dignified, professional service, the restaurant boasts a turn-of-the-century elegance and is conveniently located downtown within a short walk of several hotels. High-back booths give a feeling of coziness and intimacy. Casual dress. **Bar:** Full bar. **Reservations:** suggested. **Hours:** 11 am-11 pm, Fri & Sat-midnight, Sun 4 pm-10 pm. Closed: 12/25. **Address:** 219 W 9th St 64105 **Location:** Just s of I-70, US 24 and 40. **Parking:** on-site.

STARKER'S RESTAURANT

Phone: 816/753-3565 (23)

New American
$22-$52

International influences pepper contemporary dishes, which are complemented by an extensive wine list. Dressy casual. **Bar:** Full bar. **Reservations:** suggested. **Hours:** 11:30 am-2 & 5:30-10 pm, Sat from 5:30 pm. Closed major holidays; also Sun. **Address:** 201 W 47th St 64112 **Location:** At 47th and Wyandotte sts; in Country Club Plaza. **Parking:** street.

The following restaurants have not been evaluated by AAA but are listed for your information only.

HIBACHI, THE JAPANESE STEAK HOUSE

Phone: 816/753-0707

fyi

Not evaluated. Full teppanyaki dinners and meals prepared tableside are restaurant features. **Address:** 4745 Wyandotte St 64112 **Location:** In Country Club Plaza.

LE FOU FROG

Phone: 816/474-6060

fyi

Not evaluated. The intimate yet energetic atmosphere brims with the tastes and flavors of old coastal Marseilles. **Address:** 400 E 5th St 64108

KANSAS CITY pop. 441,545 (See map and index starting on p. 456)

AMERISTAR HOTEL & CASINO *Book great rates at AAA.com* **Phone:** (816)414-7000 33

AAA SAVE

Hotel
$119-$549 All Year

Address: 3200 N Ameristar Dr 64161 **Location:** I-435, exit 55B, 1.2 mi e on SR 210, then just s. **Facility:** Open boarding on gambling boat. Live celebrity entertainment on most weekends. Atrium has street-scape decor with painted blue skies on the ceiling. 184 units. 172 one-bedroom standard units. 12 one-bedroom suites. 11 stories, interior corridors. *Bath:* combo or shower only. **Parking:** valet. **Terms:** check-in 4 pm. **Amenities:** video games (fee), high-speed Internet, dual phone lines, voice mail, safes, honor bars, irons, hair dryers. **Dining:** 5 restaurants, also, Amerisports Brew Pub, Arthur Bryant's Barbeque, DeliLux, Falcon Diner, Great Plains Cattle Company, Horizon's Buffet, see separate listings. **Leisure Activities:** 18 movie theater screens. *Fee:* game room. **Guest Services:** valet laundry, wireless Internet. **Business Services:** conference facilities.

/ SOME UNITS

BEST WESTERN COUNTRY INN-NORTH *Book great rates at AAA.com* **Phone:** (816)459-7222 29

AAA SAVE

Motel
$50-$150 All Year

Address: 2633 NE 43rd St 64117 **Location:** I-35, exit 8C (Antioch Rd), just s on SR 1, then just e. **Facility:** 44 one-bedroom standard units. 2 stories (no elevator), exterior corridors. **Parking:** on-site. **Amenities:** irons, hair dryers. *Some:* high-speed Internet. **Pool(s):** outdoor. **Guest Services:** coin laundry, wireless Internet. **Business Services:** PC. **Free Special Amenities: continental breakfast and high-speed Internet.**

AAA Benefit:
Members save up to 20%, plus 10% bonus points with rewards program.

CHASE SUITES BY WOODFIN *Book great rates at AAA.com* **Phone:** (816)891-9009 23

AAA SAVE

Hotel
$99-$159 All Year

Address: 9900 NW Prairie View Rd 64153 **Location:** I-29, exit 10, just w, then just n. **Facility:** Smoke free premises. 112 units. 84 one-bedroom standard units with kitchens. 12 one- and 16 two-bedroom suites with kitchens. 2 stories (no elevator), exterior corridors. *Bath:* combo or shower only. **Parking:** on-site. **Terms:** cancellation fee imposed. **Amenities:** high-speed Internet, voice mail, irons, hair dryers. *Some:* CD players. **Pool(s):** heated outdoor. **Leisure Activities:** whirlpool, gazebo with grill, exercise room, sports court. **Guest Services:** valet and coin laundry, airport transportation-Kansas City International Airport, area transportation-within 5 mi, wireless Internet. **Business Services:** meeting rooms, business center. **Free Special Amenities: expanded continental breakfast and newspaper.** / SOME UNITS FEE

COURTYARD BY MARRIOTT *Book great rates at AAA.com* **Phone:** (816)941-3333 38

Hotel
$129-$139 All Year

Address: 500 E 105th St 64131 **Location:** I-435, exit 74, just s on Holmes St, then just w. **Facility:** Smoke free premises. 149 units. 138 one-bedroom standard units. 11 one-bedroom suites. 3 stories, interior corridors. *Bath:* combo or shower only. **Parking:** on-site. **Terms:** cancellation fee imposed. **Amenities:** high-speed Internet, dual phone lines, voice mail, irons, hair dryers. **Pool(s):** heated indoor. **Leisure Activities:** whirlpool, exercise room. **Guest Services:** valet and coin laundry, area transportation, wireless Internet. **Business Services:** meeting rooms, PC.

ECO CALL / SOME UNITS

AAA Benefit:
Members save a minimum 5% off the best available rate.

COURTYARD BY MARRIOTT-KCI *Book great rates at AAA.com* **Phone:** (816)891-7500 24

Hotel
$129-$139 All Year

Address: 7901 NW Tiffany Springs Pkwy 64153 **Location:** I-29, exit 10, just w. **Facility:** Smoke free premises. 149 units. 138 one-bedroom standard units. 11 one-bedroom suites. 3 stories, interior corridors. *Bath:* combo or shower only. **Parking:** on-site. **Terms:** cancellation fee imposed. **Amenities:** high-speed Internet, dual phone lines, voice mail, irons, hair dryers. **Pool(s):** heated indoor. **Leisure Activities:** whirlpool, exercise room. **Guest Services:** valet and coin laundry, area transportation, wireless Internet. **Business Services:** meeting rooms, PC.

ECO CALL / SOME UNITS

AAA Benefit:
Members save a minimum 5% off the best available rate.

DRURY INN & SUITES-KANSAS CITY AIRPORT *Book at AAA.com* **Phone:** (816)880-9700 22

Hotel
$85-$189 All Year

Address: 7900 NW Tiffany Springs Pkwy 64153-2310 **Location:** I-29, exit 10, just w. **Facility:** 122 units. 106 one-bedroom standard units. 16 one-bedroom suites. 5 stories, interior corridors. *Bath:* combo or shower only. **Parking:** on-site. **Terms:** cancellation fee imposed. **Amenities:** high-speed Internet, voice mail, irons, hair dryers. **Pool(s):** heated indoor/outdoor. **Leisure Activities:** whirlpool, exercise room. **Guest Services:** valet and coin laundry, wireless Internet. **Business Services:** meeting rooms, business center.

ASK CALL / SOME UNITS

(See map and index starting on p. 456)

DRURY INN & SUITES-KANSAS CITY STADIUM Book at AAA.com — **Phone:** (816)923-3000 35

Hotel
$80-$169 All Year

Address: 3830 Blue Ridge Cutoff 64133 **Location:** I-70, exit 9 (Blue Ridge Cutoff), just nw. Located across Truman Sports Complex and Chiefs and Royals stadiums. **Facility:** 123 units. 111 one-bedroom standard units. 12 one-bedroom suites. 5 stories, interior corridors. **Parking:** on-site. **Terms:** cancellation fee imposed. **Amenities:** high-speed Internet, voice mail, irons, hair dryers. **Pool(s):** outdoor. **Leisure Activities:** exercise room. **Guest Services:** valet and coin laundry, wireless Internet. **Business Services:** meeting rooms, business center.

ASK CALL / SOME UNITS

EMBASSY SUITES KANSAS CITY-INTERNATIONAL AIRPORT Book great rates at AAA.com — **Phone:** (816)891-7788 20

Hotel
$119-$209 All Year

Address: 7640 NW Tiffany Springs Pkwy 64153 **Location:** I-29, exit 10, just e. **Facility:** 237 one-bedroom suites, some with whirlpools. 8 stories, interior corridors. *Bath:* combo or shower only. **Parking:** on-site. **Terms:** 1-7 night minimum stay, cancellation fee imposed. **Amenities:** dual phone lines, voice mail, irons, hair dryers. *Fee:* video games, high-speed Internet. **Pool(s):** heated indoor. **Leisure Activities:** sauna, whirlpool, exercise room. **Guest Services:** valet and coin laundry, airport transportation-Kansas City International Airport, area transportation-within 2 mi, wireless Internet. **Business Services:** conference facilities, business center. **Free Special Amenities: full breakfast and newspaper.**

CALL / SOME UNITS FEE

AAA Benefit:
Members save 5% or more everyday!

EXTENDED STAYAMERICA-KANSAS CITY AIRPORT Book at AAA.com — **Phone:** (816)270-7829 16

Extended Stay Hotel
$50-$110 All Year

Address: 11712 NW Plaza Cir 64153 **Location:** I-29, exit 13, just e on CR D, just s on Ambassador Dr, then just w. **Facility:** 109 one-bedroom standard units with efficiencies. 3 stories, interior corridors. *Bath:* combo or shower only. **Parking:** on-site. **Terms:** office hours 7 am-11 pm, cancellation fee imposed. **Amenities:** high-speed Internet, voice mail, irons. *Some:* dual phone lines. **Guest Services:** coin laundry, area transportation (fee), wireless Internet.

ASK / SOME UNITS FEE

EXTENDED STAYAMERICA-KANSAS CITY SOUTH Book at AAA.com — **Phone:** (816)943-1315 39

Extended Stay Hotel
$55-$120 All Year

Address: 550 E 105th St 64131 **Location:** I-435, exit 74, just s on Holmes Rd, then just w. **Facility:** 119 one-bedroom standard units with efficiencies. 3 stories, interior corridors. *Bath:* combo or shower only. **Parking:** on-site. **Terms:** cancellation fee imposed. **Amenities:** voice mail, irons. **Guest Services:** coin laundry, wireless Internet.

ASK / SOME UNITS FEE

FAIRFIELD INN & SUITES BY MARRIOTT Book great rates at AAA.com — **Phone:** (816)464-2424 14

Hotel
$116-$142 All Year

Address: 11820 NW Plaza Cir 64153 **Location:** I-29, exit 13, just e on CR D, just s on Ambassador Dr, then just w. **Facility:** Smoke free premises. 129 one-bedroom standard units, some with whirlpools. 3 stories, interior corridors. *Bath:* combo or shower only. **Parking:** on-site, winter plug-ins. **Terms:** cancellation fee imposed. **Amenities:** high-speed Internet, voice mail, irons, hair dryers. **Pool(s):** heated indoor. **Leisure Activities:** whirlpool, exercise room. **Guest Services:** valet and coin laundry, area transportation, wireless Internet. **Business Services:** meeting rooms, PC.

CALL

AAA Benefit:
Members save a minimum 5% off the best available rate.

FAIRFIELD INN & SUITES BY MARRIOTT KANSAS CITY Book great rates at AAA.com — **Phone:** (816)452-6212 30

Hotel
$80-$130 All Year

Address: 4231 N Corrington Ave 64117 **Location:** I-435, exit 54 northbound, just w on Parvin Rd; exit southbound, 1 mi s on service road, just w on Parvin Rd, then just n. Located across from large amusement park. **Facility:** Smoke free premises. 70 one-bedroom standard units. 3 stories, interior corridors. *Bath:* combo or shower only. **Parking:** on-site. **Terms:** cancellation fee imposed. **Amenities:** voice mail, irons, hair dryers. *Some:* CD players, high-speed Internet. **Pool(s):** heated indoor. **Leisure Activities:** whirlpool. **Guest Services:** valet and coin laundry, wireless Internet. **Business Services:** PC.

CALL / SOME UNITS

AAA Benefit:
Members save a minimum 5% off the best available rate.

(See map and index starting on p. 456)

FAIRFIELD INN & SUITES KANSAS CITY-LIBERTY *Book great rates at AAA.com* **Phone:** (816)792-4000 

Hotel
$109-$129 All Year

Address: 8101 N Church Rd 64158 **Location:** I-35, exit 16 (SR 152), just w, then just s. **Facility:** Smoke free premises. 99 one-bedroom standard units. 2 stories, interior corridors. *Bath:* combo or shower only. **Parking:** on-site. **Terms:** cancellation fee imposed. **Amenities:** voice mail, irons, hair dryers. **Pool(s):** heated indoor. **Leisure Activities:** whirlpool, exercise room. **Guest Services:** valet and coin laundry, airport transportation (fee)-Kansas City International Airport, wireless Internet. **Business Services:** meeting rooms, business center. **Free Special Amenities: expanded continental breakfast and high-speed Internet.**

FEE CALL

AAA Benefit:
Members save a minimum 5% off the best available rate.

FOUR POINTS BY SHERATON KANSAS CITY AIRPORT *Book great rates at AAA.com* **Phone:** (816)464-2345 11

Hotel
$55-$195 All Year

Address: 11832 NW Plaza Cir 64153 **Location:** I-29, exit 13, e on CR D, just s on Ambassador Dr, then just w. **Facility:** Smoke free premises. 200 one-bedroom standard units, some with whirlpools. 5 stories, interior corridors. *Bath:* combo or shower only. **Parking:** on-site. **Amenities:** video games (fee), voice mail, irons, hair dryers. **Pool(s):** outdoor. **Leisure Activities:** exercise room. *Fee:* game room. **Guest Services:** valet and coin laundry, airport transportation-Kansas City International Airport, area transportation-within 5 mi, wireless Internet. **Business Services:** meeting rooms, PC. *(See color ad below)*

CALL / SOME UNITS FEE

FOUR POINTS BY SHERATON

AAA Benefit:
Members get up to 15% off, plus Starwood Preferred Guest® bonuses.

FREE newspaper and preferred room (subject to availability with advance reservations)

▼ *See AAA listing above* ▼

(See map and index starting on p. 456)

HAMPTON INN AIRPORT Book great rates at AAA.com Phone: (816)464-5454 17

Hotel
$59-$169 All Year

Address: 11212 N Newark Cir 64153 **Location:** I-29, exit 12, just ne. **Facility:** 120 one-bedroom standard units. 4 stories, interior corridors. *Bath:* combo or shower only. **Parking:** on-site. **Terms:** 1-7 night minimum stay, cancellation fee imposed. **Amenities:** video games (fee), voice mail, irons, hair dryers. **Pool(s):** outdoor. **Leisure Activities:** exercise room. **Guest Services:** valet and coin laundry, airport transportation-Kansas City International Airport, area transportation-within 2 mi, wireless Internet. **Business Services:** meeting rooms, PC. *(See color ad below)* CALL / SOME UNITS

AAA Benefit:
Members save up to 10% everyday!

FREE expanded continental breakfast and high-speed Internet

HAMPTON INN-KANSAS CITY/LIBERTY Book great rates at AAA.com Phone: (816)415-9600 

Hotel
$99-$149 All Year

Address: 8551 N Church Rd 64158 **Location:** I-35, exit 16 (SR 152), just nw. **Facility:** 122 one-bedroom standard units, some with whirlpools. 4 stories, interior corridors. *Bath:* combo or shower only. **Parking:** on-site. **Terms:** 1-7 night minimum stay, cancellation fee imposed. **Amenities:** video games (fee), high-speed Internet, dual phone lines, voice mail, irons, hair dryers. **Pool(s):** heated indoor. **Leisure Activities:** whirlpool, exercise room. **Guest Services:** valet and coin laundry, wireless Internet. **Business Services:** business center. **Free Special Amenities: expanded continental breakfast and high-speed Internet.** CALL / SOME UNITS

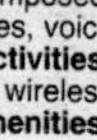

AAA Benefit:
Members save up to 10% everyday!

HILTON KANSAS CITY AIRPORT Book great rates at AAA.com Phone: (816)891-8900 

Hotel
$89-$189 All Year

Address: 8801 NW 112th St 64153 **Location:** I-29, exit 12, just se. **Facility:** 347 one-bedroom standard units. 11 stories, interior corridors. *Bath:* combo or shower only. **Parking:** on-site. **Terms:** 1-7 night minimum stay, cancellation fee imposed. **Amenities:** dual phone lines, voice mail, irons, hair dryers. *Fee:* video games, high-speed Internet. **Pool(s):** heated indoor/outdoor. **Leisure Activities:** whirlpool, 2 lighted tennis courts, exercise room, basketball. **Guest Services:** valet and coin laundry, airport transportation-Kansas City International Airport, area transportation-nearby shopping, wireless Internet. **Business Services:** conference facilities, business center.

CALL / SOME UNITS FEE

AAA Benefit:
Members save 5% or more everyday!

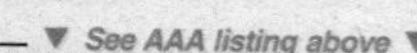

(See map and index starting on p. 456)

HOLIDAY INN EXPRESS Book at AAA.com **Phone:** (816)781-5555 **27**

Hotel
$99-$109 6/1-2/28
$89-$99 3/1-5/31

Address: 8230 N Church Rd 64158 **Location:** I-35, exit 16 (SR 152), just w to N Church Rd, then just s. **Facility:** 71 one-bedroom standard units, some with whirlpools. 3 stories, interior corridors. *Bath:* combo or shower only. **Parking:** on-site. **Amenities:** high-speed Internet, dual phone lines, voice mail, irons. **Pool(s):** heated indoor. **Leisure Activities:** exercise room. **Guest Services:** valet and coin laundry, wireless Internet. **Business Services:** business center.

ASK / SOME UNITS

HOLIDAY INN KANSAS CITY NORTHEAST Book great rates at AAA.com **Phone:** (816)455-1060 **31**

AAA SAVE
Hotel
$79-$99 All Year

Address: 7333 NE Parvin Rd 64117 **Location:** I-435, exit 54, just w. Opposite Worlds Of Fun Amusement Park. **Facility:** 165 one-bedroom standard units. 3 stories, interior corridors. *Bath:* combo or shower only. **Parking:** on-site. **Terms:** cancellation fee imposed. **Amenities:** video games (fee), dual phone lines, voice mail, irons, hair dryers. **Pool(s):** heated indoor. **Leisure Activities:** sauna, whirlpool, foosball, table tennis, exercise room. *Fee:* game room. **Guest Services:** valet and coin laundry, area transportation-within 5 mi, wireless Internet. **Business Services:** meeting rooms, PC. **Free Special Amenities: full breakfast and high-speed Internet.**

CALL / SOME UNITS FEE

HOLIDAY INN KANSAS CITY SE - WATER PARK Book at AAA.com **Phone:** 816/737-0200 **36**

Hotel
Rates not provided

Address: 9103 E 39th St 64133 **Location:** I-70, exit 9 (Blue Ridge Cutoff), just ne. Across from Truman Sports Complex and Chiefs and Royals Stadiums. **Facility:** Smoke free premises. 372 units. 364 one-bedroom standard units. 8 one-bedroom suites. 15 stories, interior corridors. *Bath:* combo or shower only. **Parking:** on-site. **Terms:** check-in 4 pm. **Amenities:** dual phone lines, voice mail, irons, hair dryers. **Pool(s):** heated outdoor, heated indoor. **Leisure Activities:** whirlpool, exercise room. **Guest Services:** valet and coin laundry, area transportation, wireless Internet. **Business Services:** conference facilities, business center. / SOME UNITS

HOLIDAY INN KCI & EXPO CENTER Book great rates at AAA.com **Phone:** (816)801-8400 **15**

AAA SAVE
Hotel
$79-$139 All Year

Address: 11728 N Ambassador Dr 64153 **Location:** I-29, exit 13, just e on CR D, then just s. Adjacent to KCI Expo Center. **Facility:** Smoke free premises. 141 units. 140 one-bedroom standard units. 1 one-bedroom suite. 6 stories, interior corridors. *Bath:* combo or shower only. **Parking:** on-site. **Amenities:** high-speed Internet, dual phone lines, voice mail, irons, hair dryers. **Pool(s):** heated indoor. **Leisure Activities:** sun deck, exercise room. **Guest Services:** valet and coin laundry, airport transportation-Kansas City International Airport, area transportation-within 5 mi, wireless Internet. **Business Services:** conference facilities, business center. **Free Special Amenities: local telephone calls and high-speed Internet.**

CALL / SOME UNITS FEE

HOLIDAY INN-SPORTS COMPLEX Book great rates at AAA.com **Phone:** (816)353-5300 **37**

AAA SAVE
Hotel
$79-$189 All Year

Address: 4011 Blue Ridge Cutoff 64133 **Location:** I-70, exit 9 (Blue Ridge Cutoff), just se. Located across from Truman Sports Complex, Chiefs and Royals stadiums. **Facility:** Smoke free premises. 168 one-bedroom standard units. 7 stories, interior corridors. *Bath:* combo or shower only. **Parking:** on-site. **Amenities:** dual phone lines, voice mail, irons, hair dryers. **Pool(s):** heated indoor. **Leisure Activities:** sauna, whirlpool, exercise room. **Guest Services:** valet and coin laundry, wireless Internet. **Business Services:** meeting rooms, PC.

CALL / SOME UNITS FEE

HOMEWOOD SUITES BY HILTON Book great rates at AAA.com **Phone:** (816)880-9880 **21**

Extended Stay Hotel
$89-$169 All Year

Address: 7312 NW Polo Dr 64153 **Location:** I-29, exit 10, just e. **Facility:** 116 units. 109 one- and 7 two-bedroom suites with efficiencies. 3 stories, interior corridors. *Bath:* combo or shower only. **Parking:** on-site. **Terms:** 1-7 night minimum stay, cancellation fee imposed. **Amenities:** video games (fee), dual phone lines, voice mail, irons, hair dryers. *Some:* high-speed Internet. **Pool(s):** heated outdoor. **Leisure Activities:** whirlpool, exercise room, sports court. **Guest Services:** valet and coin laundry, wireless Internet. **Business Services:** meeting rooms, business center.

/ SOME UNITS FEE

AAA Benefit:
Members save 5% or more everyday!

HYATT PLACE KANSAS CITY AIRPORT Book great rates at AAA.com **Phone:** (816)891-0871 **25**

AAA SAVE
Hotel
$79-$199 All Year

Address: 7600 NW 97th Terr 64153 **Location:** I-29, exit 10, just sw. **Facility:** 134 one-bedroom standard units. 6 stories, interior corridors. *Bath:* combo or shower only. **Parking:** on-site. **Terms:** cancellation fee imposed. **Amenities:** video games (fee), high-speed Internet, dual phone lines, voice mail, safes, irons, hair dryers. **Pool(s):** heated outdoor. **Leisure Activities:** exercise room. **Guest Services:** valet laundry, airport transportation-Kansas City International Airport, area transportation-within 5 mi, wireless Internet. **Business Services:** meeting rooms, business center. **Free Special Amenities: continental breakfast and high-speed Internet.** / SOME UNITS

AAA Benefit:
Ask for the AAA rate and save 10%.

(See map and index starting on p. 456)

LA QUINTA INN & SUITES - NORTHEAST Book at AAA.com Phone: (816)483-7900 34

Hotel
$69-$109 All Year

Address: 1051 N Cambridge Ave 64120 **Location:** I-435, exit 57, just w, then just s. **Facility:** 119 one-bedroom standard units. 2 stories (no elevator), interior corridors. *Bath:* combo or shower only. **Parking:** on-site. **Amenities:** voice mail, irons, hair dryers. **Pool(s):** heated outdoor. **Leisure Activities:** whirlpool, exercise room, basketball. **Guest Services:** valet and coin laundry, wireless Internet. ASK / SOME UNITS

MARRIOTT HOTEL-KANSAS CITY AIRPORT Book great rates at AAA.com Phone: (816)464-2200 9

AAA SAVE

Hotel
$169-$179 All Year

Address: 775 Brasilia Ave 64153 **Location:** I-29, exit 13, 1 mi w on Cookingham Dr, exit Bern St, just n, then just w. Located on Kansas City International Airport grounds. **Facility:** Smoke free premises. 384 units. 382 one-bedroom standard units. 2 one-bedroom suites. 6-9 stories, interior corridors. *Bath:* combo or shower only. **Parking:** on-site. **Terms:** cancellation fee imposed. **Amenities:** dual phone lines, voice mail, irons, hair dryers. *Fee:* video games, high-speed Internet. **Pool(s):** heated indoor. **Leisure Activities:** whirlpool, exercise room, volleyball. **Guest Services:** valet and coin laundry, airport transportation-Kansas City International Airport, wireless Internet. **Business Services:** conference facilities, business center.
CALL / SOME UNITS

Marriott HOTELS & RESORTS
AAA Benefit:
Members save a minimum 5% off the best available rate.

MICROTEL INN & SUITES Book great rates at AAA.com Phone: (816)270-1200 13

AAA SAVE

Hotel
$55-$65 All Year

Address: 11831 NW Plaza Cir 64153 **Location:** I-29, exit 13, just e on CR D, then just s. **Facility:** 80 one-bedroom standard units. 3 stories, interior corridors. **Parking:** on-site. **Amenities:** voice mail, irons, hair dryers. **Guest Services:** airport transportation-Kansas City International Airport, wireless Internet. **Business Services:** PC. **Free Special Amenities: local telephone calls and newspaper.**
/ SOME UNITS FEE

RADISSON HOTEL KANSAS CITY AIRPORT Book at AAA.com Phone: (816)464-2423 12

Hotel
$90-$110 All Year

Address: 11828 NW Plaza Cir 64153 **Location:** I-29, exit 13, just e on CR D, just s on Ambassador Dr, then just w. **Facility:** 138 units. 130 one-bedroom standard units. 8 one-bedroom suites. 7 stories, interior corridors. **Parking:** on-site. **Terms:** cancellation fee imposed. **Amenities:** high-speed Internet, voice mail, irons, hair dryers. **Pool(s):** heated indoor. **Leisure Activities:** whirlpool, exercise room. **Guest Services:** valet and coin laundry, area transportation, wireless Internet. **Business Services:** meeting rooms, business center.
ASK CALL / SOME UNITS FEE

RED ROOF INN-NORTH-WORLDS OF FUN Book at AAA.com Phone: (816)452-8585 32

Motel
$43-$100 All Year

Address: 3636 NE Randolph Rd 64161 **Location:** I-435, exit 55B northbound; exit 55 southbound, just e on SR 210, then just n. **Facility:** 108 one-bedroom standard units. 2 stories (no elevator), exterior corridors. *Bath:* combo or shower only. **Parking:** on-site. **Amenities:** video games (fee), voice mail. **Guest Services:** wireless Internet. ASK CALL / SOME UNITS

RESIDENCE INN BY MARRIOTT, KANSAS CITY AIRPORT Book great rates at AAA.com Phone: (816)741-2300 19

Extended Stay Hotel
$143-$175 All Year

Address: 10300 N Ambassador Dr 64153 **Location:** I-29, exit 10, just ne, then 1.5 mi. **Facility:** Smoke free premises. 152 units. 16 one-bedroom standard units with efficiencies. 114 one- and 22 two-bedroom suites with efficiencies. 4 stories, interior corridors. *Bath:* combo or shower only. **Parking:** on-site, winter plug-ins. **Terms:** check-in 4 pm, cancellation fee imposed. **Amenities:** video games (fee), high-speed Internet, voice mail, safes, irons, hair dryers. **Pool(s):** heated indoor. **Leisure Activities:** whirlpool, exercise room, sports court. **Guest Services:** valet and coin laundry, area transportation, wireless Internet. **Business Services:** meeting rooms, business center.
CALL / SOME UNITS FEE

AAA Benefit:
Members save a minimum 5% off the best available rate.

SUPER 8 - KCI Phone: 816/464-2002 10

Hotel
Rates not provided

Address: 11900 NW Plaza Cir 64153 **Location:** I-29, exit 13, just e on CR D, then just s. **Facility:** 41 one-bedroom standard units. 2 stories (no elevator), exterior corridors. **Parking:** on-site. **Amenities:** irons, hair dryers. **Guest Services:** airport transportation-Kansas City International Airport, area transportation (fee)-local shopping, wireless Internet. **Business Services:** PC. **Free Special Amenities: expanded continental breakfast and high-speed Internet.**
/ SOME UNITS FEE

WHERE TO DINE

AIXOIS Phone: 816/333-3305 19

French
$6-$32

Guests seating inside the crowded but intimate bistro or on the patio can sample roasted chicken and duck, trout in lemon butter, beef tenderloin and creme brulee. Casual dress. **Bar:** Full bar. **Reservations:** accepted. **Hours:** 11:30 am-10 pm. Closed: 1/1, 12/25; also Sun. **Address:** 251 E 55th St 64113 **Location:** S of Country Club Plaza. **Parking:** on-site. CALL

(See map and index starting on p. 456)

THE ALAMO — **Phone:** 816/452-2600 (11)

Mexican
$5-$14

Mexican and American favorites are served in an inviting dining room. Appetizers, soups, salads, burgers, sandwiches and "pieza" share menu space with traditional entrees. Casual dress. **Bar:** Full bar. **Reservations:** accepted. **Hours:** 11 am-10 pm, Fri & Sat-11 pm. Closed major holidays. **Address:** 5010 NE Parvin Rd 64117 **Location:** 1.5 mi w at N Brighton St. **Parking:** on-site.

AMERISPORTS BREW PUB — **Phone:** 816/414-7000 (16)

American
$8-$20

Sports fans can salivate over big burgers, pizza and frosty brews while keeping tabs on the action on 40 TV screens, including a 56-foot video wall. Casual dress. **Bar:** Full bar. **Reservations:** not accepted. **Hours:** 4 pm-11 pm, Fri & Sat-midnight, Sun-10 pm. **Address:** 3200 N Ameristar Dr 64161 **Location:** I-435, exit 55B, 1.2 mi e on SR 210, then just s; in Ameristar Hotel & Casino. **Parking:** on-site. CALL

ARTHUR BRYANT'S BARBEQUE — **Phone:** 816/414-7474 (17)

Barbecue
$7-$10

An offshoot of a Kansas City institution, this restaurant features slow-smoked barbecue. Casual dress. **Reservations:** not accepted. **Hours:** 11 am-10 pm, Fri & Sat-1 am. **Address:** 3200 N Ameristar Dr 64161 **Location:** I-435, exit 55B, 1.2 mi e on SR 210, then just s; in Ameristar Hotel & Casino. **Parking:** on-site. CALL

THE CAFE AT BRIARCLIFF VILLAGE — **Phone:** 816/505-2221 (10)

American
$9-$20

Located in The Shops at Briarcliff Village, this is a buzzing spot for lunches, and folks pack the popular Sunday brunch buffet. The lunch menu favors salads and sandwiches as well as lighter entree selections, while a variety of macaroons highlight the homemade dessert offerings. The dining room sports comfortable, modern decor with a light, open feeling. Casual dress. **Bar:** Full bar. **Reservations:** accepted. **Hours:** 11 am-9 pm, Fri-10 pm, Sat 8 am-10 pm, Sun 8 am-5 pm. Closed: 1/1, 7/4, 12/25. **Address:** 4125 N Mulberry Dr 64116 **Location:** I-169, exit Briarcliff Pkwy, just e. **Parking:** on-site.

CARMEN'S CAFE — **Phone:** 816/333-4048 (20)

Italian
$8-$26

Tapas, salads, chicken, veal, seafood, steak and pasta are sure to please those seeking Italian-American cuisine. Casual dress. **Bar:** Full bar. **Reservations:** not accepted. **Hours:** 11 am-10 pm, Fri-11 pm, Sat 4 pm-11 pm. Closed major holidays; also Sun. **Address:** 6307 Brookside Plaza 64113 **Location:** Just s of Country Club Plaza. **Parking:** on-site.

CASCONE'S ITALIAN RESTAURANT — **Phone:** 816/454-7977 (12)

Italian
$7-$23

You'll enjoy the great selection of delicious and well-presented pasta dishes at the locally popular Cascone's. You'll also appreciate the romantic ambience and casual decor. The serving staff is friendly, prompt and attentive. House specialties also include several selections of poultry, veal, pork, beef, and seafood. Many appetizers including calamari fritti and escargot. Dressy casual. **Bar:** Full bar. **Reservations:** suggested. **Hours:** 11 am-3 & 4-10 pm, Fri & Sat-11 pm, Sun noon-8 pm. Closed: 7/4, 11/25, 12/25. **Address:** 3737 N Oak Tfwy 64116 **Location:** 3 mi n via SR 9 and 283. **Parking:** on-site.

CORNER CAFE — **Phone:** 816/415-0050 (7)

American
$5-$15

With a bustling atmosphere and interesting decor, the eatery offers a good variety of menu selections; something for everyone. Casual dress. **Reservations:** not accepted. **Hours:** 5 am-10 pm. Closed: 11/25, 12/25. **Address:** 8301 N Flintlock Rd 64157 **Location:** I-35, exit 16, 0.3 mi nw. **Parking:** on-site. CALL

DELILUX — **Phone:** 816/414-2596 (14)

Deli
$5-$8

Ideal for a quick meal or snack, this deli features sandwiches, salads and pies. Casual dress. **Reservations:** not accepted. **Hours:** 11 am-5 am. **Address:** 3200 N Ameristar Dr 64161 **Location:** I-435, exit 55B, 1.2 mi e on SR 210, then just s; in Ameristar Hotel & Casino. **Parking:** on-site. CALL

FALCON DINER — **Phone:** 816/414-7170 (15)

American
$7-$15

The American diner's menu focuses on classic American favorites, including Kansas City strip steak. Casual dress. **Reservations:** not accepted. **Hours:** 7 am-11 pm, Fri & Sat-2 am. **Address:** 3200 N Ameristar Dr 64161 **Location:** I-435, exit 55B, 1.2 mi e on SR 210, then just s; in Ameristar Hotel & Casino. **Parking:** on-site. CALL

FIORELLA'S JACK STACK BARBECUE OF MARTIN CITY — **Phone:** 816/942-9141 (21)

Barbecue
$7-$26

Guests can savor award-winning barbecue in a cozy and rustic atmosphere with old black-and-white photographs, a fireplace and an outdoor patio. The menu lines up hickory-wood-fired meats, chicken, steaks and seafood, as well as salads and sandwiches. Casual dress. **Bar:** Full bar. **Reservations:** not accepted. **Hours:** 11 am-10 pm, Fri & Sat-10:30 pm, Sun-9 pm. Closed: 11/25, 12/25. **Address:** 13441 Holmes St 64145 **Location:** I-470, exit 74, 4 mi s to jct Holmes and 135th sts. **Parking:** on-site.

HORIZON'S BUFFET — **Phone:** 816/414-2617 (13)

International
$12-$24

Guests can wander amid stations named Chinatown, K.C. Country Bar-B-Que, Farmer's Market, Viva Mexico and Mama Mia's, but a visit here is incomplete without a stop at the Sweet Dreams dessert bar. Casual dress. **Bar:** Beer only. **Reservations:** not accepted. **Hours:** 11 am-3 & 4-9:30 pm, Fri-10:30 pm, Sat 9 am-10:30 pm, Sun 9 am-9:30 pm. **Address:** 3200 N Ameristar Dr 64161 **Location:** I-435, exit 55B, 1.2 mi e on SR 210, then just s; in Ameristar Hotel & Casino. **Parking:** on-site and valet. CALL

(See map and index starting on p. 456)

MINSKY'S PIZZA CAFE & BAR

Phone: 816/741-2737

American

$3-$16

Patrons can choose from a large selection of specialty pizzas, sandwiches, salads and pasta in a comfortably worn atmosphere. Casual dress. **Bar:** Full bar. **Reservations:** not accepted. **Hours:** 11 am-11 pm, Fri & Sat-midnight. Closed: 4/4, 11/25, 12/25. **Address:** 7007 NW Barry Rd 64153 **Location:** I-29, exit 8 (NW Barry Rd), just sw. **Parking:** on-site. CALL

OSTERIA IL CENTRO

Phone: 816/561-2369 (18)

Northern Italian

$9-$18

With its engaging music and colorful, creative decor, the trendy bistro exudes relaxed sophistication. Menu options are tempting. Although the dress code is casual, dressy casual is the norm. Casual dress. **Bar:** Full bar. **Reservations:** not accepted. **Hours:** 4 pm-10 pm, Fri & Sat-11 pm. Closed major holidays; also Sun. **Address:** 5101 Main St 64112 **Location:** Jct 51st St; in Country Club Plaza area. **Parking:** on-site.

SMOKE BOX BAR-B-QUE

Phone: 816/891-8011 (4)

Barbecue

$6-$15

This casual, family-run barbecue restaurant features large and tasty portions of beef, ham, pork and ribs. There is also a variety of sandwiches available. Casual dress. **Bar:** Beer & wine. **Reservations:** not accepted. **Hours:** 10 am-9 pm. Closed major holidays; also Sun. **Address:** 10020 N Ambassador Dr 64153 **Location:** I-29, exit 10, just ne. **Parking:** on-site.

SMOKEHOUSE BAR-B-QUE

Phone: 816/587-3337 (6)

Barbecue

$7-$24

This restaurant mixes casual and upscale elements in its decor. The menu lists a wide range of traditional hickory-smoked barbecue preparations centering on pork, turkey, sausage and chicken. Casual dress. **Bar:** Full bar. **Reservations:** accepted. **Hours:** 11 am-10 pm, Sun-9 pm. Closed: 4/4, 11/25, 12/25. **Address:** 8451 NW Prairie View Rd 64152 **Location:** I-29, exit 8, just w on Barry Rd, then just n; in Zona Rosa. **Parking:** on-site.

STROUD'S NORTH

Phone: 816/454-9600 (9)

American

$8-$25

You'll enjoy this restaurant's casual, rustic decor, tasty food, and fast, friendly service. The specialty here is fried chicken, but the catfish and steak are excellent too. The large portions of food are served family-style by a prompt and attentive server staff. Casual dress. **Bar:** Full bar. **Reservations:** not accepted. **Hours:** 5 pm-9:30 pm, Fri 11 am-10:30 pm, Sat 2 pm-10:30 pm, Sun 11 am-9:30 pm. Closed: 11/25, 12/24, 12/25. **Address:** 5410 NE Oak Ridge Rd 64119 **Location:** I-35, exit 11 (Vivion Rd) southbound to NE Oak Ridge Rd; exit N Brighton northbound, just n to Vivion Rd, then just e to NE Oak Ridge Rd, follow signs. **Parking:** on-site.

TASTY THAI

Phone: 816/584-8801 (8)

Thai

$8-$20

Food flavored with peppers, basil, lemongrass and coconut milk is prepared in generous portions. Among selections are sesame chicken, curry dishes and fragrant soups. Casual dress. **Bar:** Beer & wine. **Reservations:** not accepted. **Hours:** 11 am-9:30 pm, Fri & Sat-10 pm, Sun noon-8 pm. Closed major holidays. **Address:** 7104 NW Prairie View Rd 64151 **Location:** I-29, exit 6, just w; in shopping center. **Parking:** on-site.

TOMFOOLERIES

Phone: 816/746-8668 (5)

American

$8-$24

A lively atmosphere prevails in the eclectic and contemporary dining room. Guests' attentions are drawn to the giant plasma TV and the train circling on an overhead track. The menu blends creative cuisine and some old favorites. Casual dress. **Bar:** Full bar. **Reservations:** accepted. **Hours:** 11 am-1 am, Sun from 9:30 am. Closed: 11/25, 12/25. **Address:** 8680 NW Prairie View Rd 64153 **Location:** I-29, exit 8 (NW Barry Rd); in Zona Rosa Shopping Complex. **Parking:** on-site.

The following restaurants have not been evaluated by AAA but are listed for your information only.

ARTHUR BRYANT'S BARBEQUE

Phone: 816/231-1123

fyi

Not evaluated. This eatery is a well-established, very casual Kansas City barbecue joint featuring huge beef, ham, pork and turkey sandwiches. **Address:** 1727 Brooklyn Ave 64127 **Location:** 1.2 mi e on SR 210, then just s.

GREAT PLAINS CATTLE COMPANY

Phone: 816/414-7420

fyi

Not evaluated. The menu lists chargrilled steaks, buffalo rib-eye and, for the adventuresome, fried rattlesnake. **Address:** 3200 N Ameristar Dr 64161 **Location:** I-435, exit 55B, 1.2 mi e on SR 210, then just s; in Ameristar Hotel & Casino.

PEARL'S OYSTER BAR

Phone: 816/414-2047

fyi

Not evaluated. Raw bar items, steamers and fresh fish are served in a casual setting overlooking the casino. **Address:** 3200 N Ameristar Dr 64161 **Location:** I-435, exit 55B, 1.2 mi e on SR 210, then just s; in Ameristar Hotel & Casino.

The Kansas City Vicinity

BLUE SPRINGS pop. 48,080

HAMPTON INN BLUE SPRINGS *Book great rates at AAA.com* **Phone:** (816)220-3844

Hotel
$79-$119 All Year

Address: 900 NW South Outer Rd 64015 **Location:** I-70, exit 20 (SR 7), just s, then just w. **Facility:** 70 one-bedroom standard units, some with whirlpools. 3 stories, interior corridors. *Bath:* combo or shower only. **Parking:** on-site. **Terms:** 1-7 night minimum stay, cancellation fee imposed. **Amenities:** video games (fee), voice mail, irons, hair dryers. **Pool(s):** heated indoor. **Leisure Activities:** whirlpool. **Guest Services:** valet laundry, wireless Internet. **Business Services:** meeting rooms, PC.

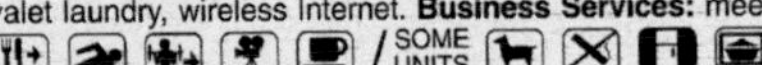

WHERE TO DINE

ZARDA BAR-B-Q **Phone:** 816/229-9999

Barbecue
$5-$11

Hickory-smoked ribs are slow-cooked over flames to be savored in the casual, comfortable atmosphere. Casual dress. **Reservations:** not accepted. **Hours:** 11 am-9 pm; Fri & Sat-10 pm in winter. Closed: 11/25, 12/25. **Address:** 214 N 7 Hwy 64014 **Location:** I-70, exit 20 (SR 7), 0.7 mi sw. **Parking:** on-site.

GRANDVIEW pop. 24,881 (See map and index starting on p. 456)

HOLIDAY INN EXPRESS HOTEL & SUITES *Book great rates at AAA.com* **Phone:** (816)268-5858 120

Hotel
$80-$159 All Year

Address: 12801 S 71 Hwy 64030 **Location:** I-71, exit Main St, on Outer Rd, east side. **Facility:** 72 one-bedroom standard units, some with whirlpools. 4 stories, interior corridors. *Bath:* combo or shower only. **Parking:** on-site. **Amenities:** high-speed Internet, voice mail, irons, hair dryers. **Pool(s):** heated indoor. **Leisure Activities:** whirlpool, exercise room. **Guest Services:** valet and coin laundry, wireless Internet. **Business Services:** meeting rooms, business center. **Free Special Amenities: full breakfast and high-speed Internet.** CALL / SOME UNITS

INDEPENDENCE pop. 113,288 (See map and index starting on p. 456)

BEST WESTERN TRUMAN INN *Book great rates at AAA.com* **Phone:** (816)254-0100 58

Motel
$50-$110 All Year

Address: 4048 S Lynn Court Dr 64055 **Location:** I-70, exit 12, just n on Noland Rd, then just w. **Facility:** 108 one-bedroom standard units. 2 stories (no elevator), exterior corridors. **Parking:** on-site. **Amenities:** irons, hair dryers. *Some:* high-speed Internet. **Pool(s):** outdoor. **Guest Services:** wireless Internet. **Business Services:** meeting rooms, PC.

/ SOME UNITS FEE

FREE expanded continental breakfast and high-speed Internet

COMFORT SUITES *Book great rates at AAA.com* **Phone:** (816)373-9880 61

Hotel
$89-$139 All Year

Address: 19751 E Valley View Pkwy 64057 **Location:** I-70, exit 17, just s on Little Blue Pkwy, then just w. **Facility:** Smoke free premises. 88 units. 86 one-bedroom standard units. 2 one-bedroom suites. 3 stories, interior corridors. *Bath:* combo or shower only. **Parking:** on-site. **Amenities:** high-speed Internet, dual phone lines, voice mail, irons, hair dryers. **Pool(s):** heated indoor. **Leisure Activities:** whirlpool, exercise room. **Guest Services:** valet and coin laundry, wireless Internet. **Business Services:** meeting rooms, PC.

CALL / SOME UNITS FEE

(See map and index starting on p. 456)

FAIRFIELD INN BY MARRIOTT Book great rates at AAA.com Phone: (816)795-1616 56

Hotel
$90-$120 All Year

Address: 18700 E 37th Terr S 64057 **Location:** I-70, exit 15B (SR 291 N), just e on 39th St, then just n on Arrowhead Ave; behind Kohl's Shopping Center. **Facility:** Smoke free premises. 63 one-bedroom standard units. 3 stories, interior corridors. *Bath:* combo or shower only. **Parking:** on-site. **Terms:** cancellation fee imposed. **Amenities:** irons, hair dryers. **Pool(s):** heated indoor. **Leisure Activities:** whirlpool. **Guest Services:** valet laundry, wireless Internet. **Business Services:** PC.

/ SOME UNITS

AAA Benefit:
Members save a minimum 5% off the best available rate.

HILTON GARDEN INN INDEPENDENCE Book great rates at AAA.com Phone: (816)350-3000 60

Hotel
$149-$229 All Year

Address: 19677 E Jackson Dr 64057 **Location:** I-70, exit 17 (Little Blue Pkwy), just n, then just w. **Facility:** 201 one-bedroom standard units. 6 stories, interior corridors. *Bath:* combo or shower only. **Parking:** on-site. **Terms:** 1-7 night minimum stay, cancellation fee imposed. **Amenities:** video games (fee), high-speed Internet, dual phone lines, voice mail, irons, hair dryers. **Pool(s):** heated indoor. **Leisure Activities:** whirlpool, exercise room. **Guest Services:** valet and coin laundry, area transportation-within 5 mi, wireless Internet. **Business Services:** conference facilities, business center. **Free Special Amenities: newspaper and high-speed Internet.**

CALL / SOME UNITS

Hilton Garden Inn

AAA Benefit:
Members save 5% or more everyday!

HOLIDAY INN EXPRESS HOTEL & SUITES Book great rates at AAA.com Phone: 816/795-8889 62

Hotel
Rates not provided

Address: 19901 E Valley View Pkwy 64057 **Location:** I-70, exit 17 (Little Blue Pkwy), just e, then w on E Valley View Pkwy (Eastland Business Park). **Facility:** 91 one-bedroom standard units. 3 stories, interior corridors. *Bath:* combo or shower only. **Parking:** on-site. **Amenities:** high-speed Internet, dual phone lines, voice mail, irons, hair dryers. **Pool(s):** heated indoor. **Leisure Activities:** whirlpool, exercise room. **Guest Services:** valet and coin laundry, wireless Internet. **Business Services:** meeting rooms, business center.

CALL / SOME UNITS FEE

QUALITY INN & SUITES - EAST Book great rates at AAA.com Phone: (816)373-8856 59

Hotel
$67-$89 All Year

Address: 4200 S Noland Rd 64055 **Location:** I-70, exit 12, just s. **Facility:** 87 one-bedroom standard units, some with whirlpools. 2 stories (no elevator), interior corridors. *Bath:* combo or shower only. **Parking:** on-site. **Amenities:** voice mail, irons, hair dryers. *Some:* safes (fee). **Leisure Activities:** table tennis. **Guest Services:** coin laundry, wireless Internet. **Business Services:** meeting rooms, PC. **Free Special Amenities: full breakfast and high-speed Internet.**

/ SOME UNITS

SUPER 8 INDEPENDENCE Book great rates at AAA.com Phone: (816)833-1888 57

Hotel
$50-$120 3/1-9/30
$40-$120 10/1-2/28

Address: 4032 S Lynn Court Dr 64055 **Location:** I-70, exit 12, just n on Noland Rd, then just w. **Facility:** 78 one-bedroom standard units, some with whirlpools. 3 stories (no elevator), interior corridors. **Parking:** on-site. **Amenities:** safes (fee), hair dryers. *Some:* irons. **Pool(s):** heated outdoor. **Guest Services:** coin laundry, wireless Internet. **Business Services:** PC.

/ SOME UNITS FEE

FREE expanded continental breakfast and high-speed Internet

WHERE TO DINE

HEREFORD HOUSE Phone: 816/795-9200 47

Steak
$7-$38

An area favorite since 1957, the eatery builds its menu on Midwestern corn-fed beef, which is aged and hand-cut. Kansas City strip and prime rib are house specialties. Guests won't go home hungry. Casual dress. **Bar:** Full bar. **Reservations:** suggested. **Hours:** 11 am-9 pm, Sat noon-11 pm. Closed: 11/25, 12/25. **Address:** 19721 E Jackson Dr 64057 **Location:** I-70, exit 17 (Little Blue Pkwy), 0.4 mi nw. **Parking:** on-site.

ON THE BORDER MEXICAN GRILL & CANTINA Phone: 816/795-6198 48

Southwestern
$6-$14

Located in a quickly growing area, the restaurant features a menu offering a good selection of your favorites, plus some contemporary twists. Casual dress. **Bar:** Full bar. **Reservations:** not accepted. **Hours:** 11 am-10 pm, Fri & Sat-11 pm. Closed: 11/25, 12/25. **Address:** 19921 E Jackson Dr 64057 **Location:** I-70, exit 17 (Little Blue Pkwy), just nw. **Parking:** on-site. CALL

(See map and index starting on p. 456)

OPHELIA'S RESTAURANT & INN **Phone:** 816/461-4525 44

American
$8-$32

The restaurant caters to patrons whose palates demand creative cuisine. The atmosphere is casual and trendy. Live light jazz adds to the ambience on Friday and Saturday nights. Wine tastings are held Fridays from 6 to 8 pm. Dressy casual. **Bar:** Full bar. **Reservations:** accepted. **Hours:** 11 am-9 pm, Fri & Sat-10 pm, Sun-2:30 pm. Closed: 1/1, 12/25. **Address:** 201 N Main St 64050 **Location:** I-435, exit 60, 4 mi e on SR 12 (Truman Rd); in Independence Square; in The Inn at Ophelia's. **Parking:** street.

THE RHEINLAND RESTAURANT **Phone:** 816/461-5383 43

German
$7-$16

Menu selections are delightful in the warm and cozy atmosphere. This spot is busy at lunchtime and on fair-weather days, but the wait is worthwhile. Casual dress. **Bar:** Beer & wine. **Reservations:** accepted. **Hours:** 11 am-9 pm, Sun & Mon-2:30 pm. Closed major holidays. **Address:** 208 N Main St 64050 **Location:** In Independence Square. **Parking:** street.

SMOKEHOUSE BAR-B-QUE **Phone:** 816/795-5555 46

Barbecue
$7-$24

The casual dining room is decorated traditionally. Patrons can nosh on tasty barbecue selections, including sandwiches and dinners of fish, ribs, chicken, beef, pork, ham, turkey and sausage. Casual dress. **Bar:** Full bar. **Reservations:** not accepted. **Hours:** 11 am-9:30 pm, Sun-9 pm. Closed: 4/4, 11/25, 12/25. **Address:** 19000 E 39th St 64057 **Location:** I-70, exit 17 (Little Blue Pkwy), 0.6 mi n, then 0.8 mi w. **Parking:** on-site. CALL

V'S ITALIANO RISTORANTE **Phone:** 816/353-1241 45

Italian
$7-$26

Family owned and operated since 1964, the restaurant serves specialties from Northern and Southern Italy in a cozy, quiet atmosphere. Casual dress. **Bar:** Full bar. **Reservations:** suggested. **Hours:** 11 am-9:30 pm, Fri-10:30 pm, Sat 11:30 am-10:30 pm, Sun 10 am-8 pm. Closed major holidays. **Address:** 10819 E Hwy 40 64055 **Location:** I-70, exit 11 (US 40), 0.3 mi n. **Parking:** on-site.

KEARNEY pop. 5,472 (See map and index starting on p. 456)

KEARNEY LODGING **Phone:** 816/628-5000 46

Hotel
Rates not provided

Address: 601 Centerville Ave 64060 **Location:** I-35, exit 26, just w. **Facility:** 40 one-bedroom standard units, some with whirlpools. 2 stories (no elevator), interior corridors. *Bath:* combo or shower only. **Parking:** on-site. **Amenities:** high-speed Internet, irons, hair dryers. **Pool(s):** heated indoor. **Leisure Activities:** whirlpool. **Guest Services:** wireless Internet. **Business Services:** meeting rooms, PC. / SOME UNITS FEE

KEARNEY SUPER 8 Book at AAA.com **Phone:** (816)628-6800 45

Hotel
$50-$180 All Year

Address: 210 Platte Clay Way 64060 **Location:** I-35, exit 26, just e on SR 92, then just n. **Facility:** 47 one-bedroom standard units, some with efficiencies and/or whirlpools. 2 stories (no elevator), interior corridors. **Parking:** on-site. **Terms:** cancellation fee imposed. **Amenities:** hair dryers. **Guest Services:** wireless Internet. **Business Services:** PC.

ASK / SOME UNITS FEE

WHERE TO DINE

OUTLAW'S BARBEQUE & SALOON **Phone:** 816/628-6500

American
$5-$13

Baby back ribs, chicken, steaks, burgers and sandwiches are just a few of the items served in the comfortable setting, which is appropriate for all occasions. Casual dress. **Bar:** Full bar. **Reservations:** not accepted. **Hours:** 11 am-9 pm, Fri & Sat-10 pm. Closed major holidays; also Sun. **Address:** 129 E Washington St 64060 **Location:** Downtown. **Parking:** street.

LEE'S SUMMIT pop. 70,700 (See map and index starting on p. 456)

COMFORT INN BY CHOICE HOTELS Book at AAA.com **Phone:** (816)524-8181 86

Hotel
$63-$80 3/1-8/31
$58-$75 9/1-2/28

Address: 607 SE Oldham Pkwy 64081 **Location:** Jct US 50 and SR 291 N. **Facility:** 52 one-bedroom standard units. 2 stories (no elevator), interior corridors. **Parking:** on-site, winter plug-ins. **Amenities:** irons, hair dryers. **Pool(s):** heated indoor. **Leisure Activities:** whirlpool. **Guest Services:** valet laundry, wireless Internet.

ASK CALL / SOME UNITS FEE

FAIRFIELD INN BY MARRIOTT LEE'S SUMMIT Book great rates at AAA.com **Phone:** (816)524-7572 84

Hotel
$77-$94 All Year

Address: 1301 NE Windsor Dr 64086 **Location:** I-470, exit 10B, 0.5 mi s on SR 291. **Facility:** Smoke free premises. 57 one-bedroom standard units. 3 stories, interior corridors. *Bath:* combo or shower only. **Parking:** on-site. **Terms:** cancellation fee imposed. **Amenities:** irons, hair dryers. **Pool(s):** heated indoor. **Leisure Activities:** whirlpool. **Guest Services:** valet laundry, wireless Internet. **Business Services:** PC.

CALL / SOME UNITS

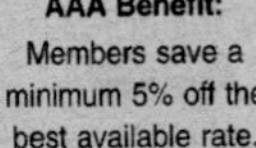

AAA Benefit:
Members save a minimum 5% off the best available rate.

(See map and index starting on p. 456)

HAMPTON INN *Book great rates at AAA.com* **Phone:** (816)347-8600 

Hotel
$79-$109 All Year

Address: 1751 NE Douglas St 64086 **Location:** I-470, exit 9, just se. **Facility:** 109 one-bedroom standard units, some with whirlpools. 3 stories, interior corridors. *Bath:* combo or shower only. **Parking:** on-site. **Terms:** 1-7 night minimum stay, cancellation fee imposed. **Amenities:** video games (fee), dual phone lines, voice mail, irons, hair dryers. **Pool(s):** heated indoor. **Leisure Activities:** whirlpool, exercise room. **Guest Services:** valet and coin laundry, wireless Internet. **Business Services:** meeting rooms, business center. **Free Special Amenities: full breakfast and high-speed Internet.**

CALL / SOME UNITS

AAA Benefit:
Members save up to 10% everyday!

LEE'S SUMMIT HOLIDAY INN EXPRESS *Book great rates at AAA.com* **Phone:** (816)795-6400 82

Hotel
$74-$109 All Year

Address: 4825 NE Lakewood Way 64064 **Location:** I-470, exit 14, just e on Bowlin Rd, then 0.4 mi s. **Facility:** 75 one-bedroom standard units, some with whirlpools. 3 stories, interior corridors. *Bath:* combo or shower only. **Parking:** on-site. **Amenities:** high-speed Internet, dual phone lines, voice mail, irons, hair dryers. **Pool(s):** heated indoor. **Leisure Activities:** whirlpool, exercise room. **Guest Services:** valet laundry, wireless Internet. **Business Services:** meeting rooms, PC.

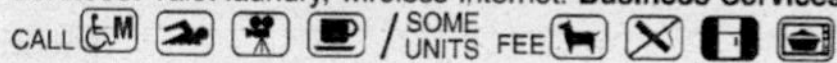

CALL / SOME UNITS FEE

SUPER 8 *Book at AAA.com* **Phone:** (816)524-8863 85

Hotel
$69-$160 3/1-11/30
$65-$150 12/1-2/28

Address: 963 SE Oldham Pkwy 64081 **Location:** Jct US 50 and SR 291 (north exit), just s on SR 291, just e on Outler Rd, then 0.5 mi on frontage road. **Facility:** 61 units. 60 one-bedroom standard units, some with whirlpools. 1 one-bedroom suite with whirlpool. 3 stories, interior corridors. *Bath:* combo or shower only. **Parking:** on-site. **Terms:** cancellation fee imposed. **Amenities:** irons, hair dryers. **Pool(s):** heated indoor. **Leisure Activities:** whirlpool, limited exercise equipment. **Guest Services:** wireless Internet. CALL / SOME UNITS

WHERE TO DINE

JOSE PEPPER'S **Phone:** 816/246-9555 62

Southwestern
$7-$12

New and traditional selections are listed on the inventive menu. Contemporary decor gives the dining room a lively feel. Casual dress. **Bar:** Full bar. **Reservations:** not accepted. **Hours:** 11 am-10 pm, Fri & Sat-11 pm. Closed: 11/25, 12/25. **Address:** 1667 NE Douglas Rd 64086 **Location:** I-470, exit 9, just se. **Parking:** on-site.

O'BRYAN'S IRISH PUB & GRILLE **Phone:** 816/373-5888 61

American
$8-$24

A plethora of plasma-screen TVs showing every match, game and bout possible cover most of the walls at this eatery. The menu has a wide selection and variety of appetizers and sandwiches. While it isn't on the menu, guests can request their sandwich on pretzel bread. It's worth remembering! Casual dress. **Bar:** Full bar. **Reservations:** not accepted. **Hours:** 11 am-1:30 am. Closed: 11/25, 12/25. **Address:** 700 NE Woods Chapel Rd 64064 **Location:** I-470, exit 12, just w. **Parking:** on-site.

NORTH KANSAS CITY pop. 4,714 (See map and index starting on p. 456)

HARRAH'S NORTH KANSAS CITY CASINO AND HOTEL *Book at AAA.com* **Phone:** 816/472-7777 53

Hotel
Rates not provided

Address: One Riverboat Dr 64116 **Location:** I-29/35, exit 6A, 1.4 mi e on SR 210, then just s on Chouteau Thrwy. **Facility:** This spacious hotel, located along the Missouri River, features full gaming options. 392 units. 323 one-bedroom standard units. 69 one-bedroom suites, some with whirlpools. 6-11 stories, interior corridors. *Bath:* combo or shower only. **Parking:** on-site. **Terms:** check-in 4 pm. **Amenities:** voice mail, irons, hair dryers. *Some:* DVD players, high-speed Internet, dual phone lines, safes. **Dining:** The Buffet, The Range Steakhouse, see separate listings. **Guest Services:** valet and coin laundry, wireless Internet. **Business Services:** conference facilities, PC.

CALL FEE / SOME UNITS

LA QUINTA INN KANSAS CITY NORTH *Book at AAA.com* **Phone:** (816)221-1200 52

Hotel
$45-$149 All Year

Address: 2214 Taney Rd 64116 **Location:** I-29/35, exit 6A, just e on SR 210, then just n. **Facility:** 96 one-bedroom standard units. 3 stories, interior corridors. **Parking:** on-site. **Amenities:** video games (fee), voice mail, irons, hair dryers. *Some:* high-speed Internet. **Guest Services:** wireless Internet.

ASK FEE / SOME UNITS

WHERE TO DINE

THE BUFFET **Phone:** 816/472-7777 37

American
$10-$22

Diners can make selections from buffet stations titled Heritage, Center Cut, KV's BBQ Pit, Wok & Roll, Tour of Italy and American. It's worth sampling some of each, provided there's some room left at the end for a visit to The Sweet Spot. Casual dress. **Reservations:** not accepted. **Hours:** 7-10:30 am, 11-3 & 4-9:30 pm, Fri & Sat-10:30 pm. **Address:** One Riverboat Dr 64116 **Location:** I-29/35, exit 6A, 1.4 mi e on SR 210, then just s on Chouteau Thrwy; in Harrah's North Kansas City Casino and Hotel. **Parking:** on-site. CALL

(See map and index starting on p. 456)

CHAPPELL'S RESTAURANT & SPORTS MUSEUM Phone: 816/421-0002 (39)

American
$7-$21

One of the country's most famous sports bars, this neighborhood establishment is filled with museum-quality memorabilia. Menu features steaks, sandwiches, lite selections, prime rib and Saturday night spiced shrimp. Casual dress. **Bar:** Full bar. **Reservations:** accepted. **Hours:** 11 am-10 pm. Closed major holidays; also Sun. **Address:** 323 Armour Rd 64116 **Location:** I-29, exit 6B, 0.7 mi w. **Parking:** street.

KELSO'S Phone: 816/221-8899 (38)

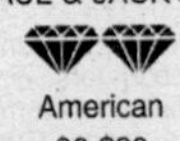

American
$7-$17

A touch of class and sophistication can be enjoyed along with great pizza at this casual eatery in the revitalized Northtown area. Casual dress. **Bar:** Full bar. **Reservations:** not accepted. **Hours:** 11 am-10 pm, Fri & Sat-midnight, Sun noon-5 pm. Closed major holidays. **Address:** 300 Armour Rd 64116 **Location:** I-29, exit 6B, 0.7 mi w. **Parking:** street.

PAUL & JACK'S TAVERN Phone: 816/221-9866 (40)

American
$6-$20

The eatery, popular with the locals, presents a small-town atmosphere with ample pub fare selections. Casual dress. **Bar:** Full bar. **Reservations:** accepted. **Hours:** 10:30 am-9:30 pm. Closed major holidays; also Sun. **Address:** 1808 Clay St 64116 **Location:** I-29, exit 6B, 1 mi sw. **Parking:** street.

THE RANGE STEAKHOUSE Phone: 816/889-7159 (36)

Steak
$14-$38

The steakhouse with a Southwestern setting features grilled-to-order steaks, prime rib, seafood and poultry entrees. Casual dress. **Bar:** Full bar. **Reservations:** accepted. **Hours:** 5 pm-10 pm, Fri & Sat-11 pm. **Address:** One Riverboat Dr 64116 **Location:** I-29/35, exit 6A, 1.4 mi e on SR 210, then just s on Chouteau Thrwy; in Harrah's North Kansas City Casino and Hotel. **Parking:** on-site. CALL

OAK GROVE (JACKSON COUNTY) pop. 5,535

ECONO LODGE *Book at AAA.com* Phone: 816/690-3681

Motel
Rates not provided

Address: 410 SE 1st St 64075 **Location:** I-70, exit 28, just s on Broadway St, just e on SE 4th St, then just n. **Facility:** 39 one-bedroom standard units. 2 stories (no elevator), exterior corridors. **Parking:** on-site. **Amenities:** hair dryers. **Guest Services:** wireless Internet.

/ SOME UNITS FEE

PARKVILLE pop. 4,059 (See map and index starting on p. 456)

WHERE TO DINE

NICK AND JAKE'S Phone: 816/584-8535 (27)

American
$8-$27

With two owners and creators, this is a two-for-one type of place. Those seeking a quiet dinner while watching the kitchen staff prepare meals in the glass-encased kitchen should ask for a seat in Jake's dining room, but those wanting to catch the big game should sit in Nick's lively bar area. With fare varying from Kobe beef burgers to innovative sandwiches and creative traditional favorites, the menu should please nearly every diner. Huge desserts are homemade. Casual dress. **Bar:** Full bar. **Reservations:** not accepted. **Hours:** 11 am-11 pm, Fri & Sat-midnight, Sun 10 am-10 pm. Closed: 11/25, 12/25. **Address:** 6325 Lewis St, Suite 110 64152 **Location:** I-29, exit 5, 2.3 mi w on Tom Watson Pkwy, then just s. **Parking:** on-site.

CALL

PLATTE CITY pop. 3,866 (See map and index starting on p. 456)

BEST WESTERN AIRPORT INN & SUITES KCI NORTH *Book great rates at AAA.com* Phone: (816)858-0200 (42)

Hotel
$70-$95 All Year

Address: 2512 NW Prairie View Rd 64079 **Location:** I-29, exit 18, just e, then just s. **Facility:** 71 units. 68 one-bedroom standard units, some with whirlpools. 3 one-bedroom suites, some with whirlpools. 3 stories, interior corridors. *Bath:* combo or shower only. **Parking:** on-site, winter plug-ins. **Terms:** cancellation fee imposed. **Amenities:** irons, hair dryers. *Some:* high-speed Internet. **Pool(s):** heated indoor. **Leisure Activities:** sauna, whirlpool, exercise room. **Guest Services:** valet and coin laundry, airport transportation-Kansas City International Airport, wireless Internet. **Business Services:** meeting rooms, PC. **Free Special Amenities: expanded continental breakfast and high-speed Internet.**

CALL

/ SOME UNITS FEE

AAA Benefit:
Members save up to 20%, plus 10% bonus points with rewards program.

WHERE TO DINE

SHIELDS MANOR BISTRO Phone: 816/858-5557 (24)

American
$20-$45

The limited but frequently changing menu centers on steak, seafood, poultry, pasta and fusion cuisine. Weekend nights are suited to romantic candlelight dinners, and patio seating is available in season. Dressy casual. **Bar:** Beer & wine. **Reservations:** required. **Hours:** 5:30 pm-close. Closed: Sun-Wed. **Address:** 121 Main St 64079 **Location:** In historic downtown. **Parking:** street.

RIVERSIDE pop. 2,979 (See map and index starting on p. 456)

ARGOSY CASINO HOTEL & SPA Book great rates at AAA.com **Phone:** (816)746-3100 

Hotel
$159-$259 12/31-2/28
$149-$239 3/1-12/30

Address: 777 NW Argosy Pkwy 64150 **Location:** I-635, exit Argosy Pkwy, just e. **Facility:** A glass-encased shower and rain showerhead add a touch of luxury; the onsite spa and attached riverboat casino offer tons of fun and relaxation. 258 units. 250 one-bedroom standard units. 8 one-bedroom suites. 9 stories, interior corridors. *Bath:* combo or shower only. **Parking:** on-site and valet. **Terms:** check-in 4 pm, cancellation fee imposed. **Amenities:** video games (fee), voice mail, safes, irons, hair dryers. **Dining:** 2 restaurants, also, Crazy Olives, The Journey, Terrace Buffet, see separate listings. **Leisure Activities:** exercise room, spa. **Guest Services:** valet laundry, wireless Internet. **Business Services:** meeting rooms, business center. *(See color ad p 491)*

/ SOME UNITS

WHERE TO DINE

CORNER CAFE **Phone:** 816/741-2570 (30)

American
$7-$12

In a convenient location, this popular eatery offers many homemade selections, giving comfort food extra points. Casual dress. **Reservations:** not accepted. **Hours:** 5 am-10 pm. Closed: 11/25, 12/25. **Address:** 4541 NW Gateway Ave 64150 **Location:** Jct SR 9, exit US 69, 1 mi n. **Parking:** on-site.

CRAZY OLIVES **Phone:** 816/746-3100 (31)

American
$6-$16

The casual, relaxed restaurant features items from sandwiches to entrees. The dining room is an open, European style-tavern with large-screen televisions. Casual dress. **Bar:** Full bar. **Reservations:** not accepted. **Hours:** 11:30 am-1 am, Fri & Sat-3 am. **Address:** 777 NW Argosy Pkwy 64150 **Location:** I-635, exit Argosy Pkwy, just e; in Argosy Casino Hotel & Spa. **Parking:** on-site. CALL

THE JOURNEY **Phone:** 816/746-3100 (32)

Steak
$20-$40

While steaks cooked over mesquite wood fires are the specialty at this eatery, seafood, poultry and pasta dishes are other tasty options. The decor in the dining room is inspired by the style of the West African coast. Casual dress. **Bar:** Full bar. **Reservations:** not accepted. **Hours:** 4 pm-10 pm, Fri & Sat-11 pm. **Address:** 777 NW Argosy Pkwy 64150 **Location:** I-635, exit Argosy Pkwy, just e; in Argosy Casino Hotel & Spa. **Parking:** on-site. CALL

TERRACE BUFFET **Phone:** 816/746-3100 (33)

International
$11-$23

An international buffet has variety of stations for both hot and cold items as well as a carved meat station. The dessert bar is an all-around favorite. Casual dress. **Bar:** Full bar. **Reservations:** not accepted. **Hours:** 7-10:30 am, 11-3 & 3:30-9:30 pm, Fri & Sat-11 pm. **Address:** 777 NW Argosy Pkwy 64150 **Location:** I-635, exit Argosy Pkwy, just e; in Argosy Casino Hotel & Spa. **Parking:** on-site. CALL

SMITHVILLE pop. 5,514

WHERE TO DINE

JUSTUS DRUGSTORE A RESTAURANT **Phone:** 816/532-2300

American
$14-$27

With a quiet, quaint atmosphere, the eatery occupies a former drugstore. Its open kitchen allows guests to watch skilled chefs prepare meals off the ever-evolving, changing menu featuring fresh ingredients from local purveyors. All items are prepared to order. Unique flavor profiles are designed specifically by the owner and head chef, who often makes table visits. A limited menu usually includes seasonal selections of a chicken dish, beef, pork and a vegetarian dish, plus nightly specials. Dressy casual. **Bar:** Full bar. **Reservations:** suggested. **Hours:** 5:30 pm-10 pm, Fri & Sat-11 pm, Sun-9 pm. Closed major holidays; also Mon. **Address:** 106 W Main St 64089 **Location:** Between Mill and Bridge sts. **Parking:** street.

WESTON pop. 1,631

WHERE TO DINE

AMERICA BOWMAN RESTAURANT **Phone:** 816/640-5235

Irish
$8-$15

Outfitted with rustic decor that recalls an old Irish pub setting, the restaurant provides a cozy and quaint dining experience. Excellent stew, soups, sandwiches, salads and appetizers are offered. A labyrinth of corridors and tunnels connects six dining rooms, including a three-level lounge and microbrewery 55 feet underground. Casual dress. **Bar:** Full bar. **Reservations:** accepted. **Hours:** 11:30 am-9 pm; call for hours on major holidays. Closed: 11/25, 12/24, 12/25. **Address:** 500 Welt St 64098 **Location:** Center. **Parking:** on-site.

Nearby Kansas

BONNER SPRINGS pop. 6,768

HOLIDAY INN EXPRESS Book at AAA.com Phone: 913/721-5300

Hotel
Rates not provided

Address: 13031 Ridge Ave 66012 **Location:** I-70, exit 224. **Facility:** 63 one-bedroom standard units, some with whirlpools. 3 stories, interior corridors. *Bath:* combo or shower only. **Parking:** on-site. **Terms:** check-in 4 pm. **Amenities:** dual phone lines, voice mail, irons, hair dryers. *Some:* CD players. **Pool(s):** heated indoor. **Leisure Activities:** whirlpool, exercise room. **Guest Services:** wireless Internet. **Business Services:** PC. CALL / SOME UNITS

GARDNER pop. 9,396

SUPER 8 Book at AAA.com Phone: (913)856-8887

Hotel
$65-$150 All Year

Address: 2001 E Santa Fe 66030 **Location:** I-35, exit 210. **Facility:** 56 one-bedroom standard units, some with whirlpools. 2 stories (no elevator), interior corridors. **Parking:** on-site. **Amenities:** safes (fee), hair dryers. **Pool(s):** outdoor. **Guest Services:** coin laundry, wireless Internet.
ASK CALL / SOME UNITS FEE

KANSAS CITY pop. 146,866 (See map and index starting on p. 456)

BEST WESTERN INN AND CONFERENCE CENTER Book great rates at AAA.com Phone: (913)677-3060 6

Hotel
$90 All Year

Address: 501 Southwest Blvd 66103 **Location:** I-35, exit 234 (7th St), 0.4 mi s to Southwest Blvd, then just w. **Facility:** 113 one-bedroom standard units, some with whirlpools. 2 stories (no elevator), interior corridors. **Parking:** on-site. **Amenities:** voice mail, irons, hair dryers. *Some:* high-speed Internet, dual phone lines. **Pool(s):** heated outdoor. **Leisure Activities:** whirlpool, exercise room. **Guest Services:** coin laundry, area transportation-within 3 mi, wireless Internet. **Business Services:** meeting rooms, PC. **Free Special Amenities: full breakfast and high-speed Internet.** / SOME UNITS FEE

AAA Benefit:
Members save up to 20%, plus 10% bonus points with rewards program.

CANDLEWOOD SUITES Book at AAA.com Phone: (913)788-9929

Extended Stay Hotel
$99-$109 6/1-2/28
$89-$99 3/1-5/31

Address: 10920 Parallel Pkwy 66109 **Location:** I-435, exit 14B, just w. **Facility:** 98 units. 68 one-bedroom standard units with efficiencies. 30 one-bedroom suites with efficiencies. 3 stories, interior corridors. *Bath:* combo or shower only. **Parking:** on-site. **Terms:** cancellation fee imposed. **Amenities:** video library, DVD players, CD players, high-speed Internet, voice mail, irons, hair dryers. **Leisure Activities:** exercise room. **Guest Services:** valet and coin laundry, wireless Internet.
ASK CALL / SOME UNITS FEE

CHATEAU AVALON Book at AAA.com Phone: (913)596-6000 4

Hotel
$139-$499 All Year

Address: 701 Village W Pkwy 66111 **Location:** I-435, exit 13B (State Ave), just w to Village W Pkwy, then 0.4 mi sw. **Facility:** Smoke free premises. 62 one-bedroom suites with whirlpools. 3 stories, interior corridors. **Parking:** on-site. **Terms:** check-in 4 pm, 3 day cancellation notice-fee imposed. **Amenities:** video library, DVD players, CD players, high-speed Internet, voice mail, hair dryers. **Leisure Activities:** *Fee:* massage. **Business Services:** meeting rooms. ASK

COMFORT INN Book great rates at AAA.com Phone: (913)299-5555 5

Hotel
$70-$250 All Year

Address: 234 N 78th St 66112 **Location:** I-70, exit 414 (78th St), just s. **Facility:** 45 one-bedroom standard units, some with whirlpools. 3 stories, interior corridors. *Bath:* combo or shower only. **Parking:** on-site. **Terms:** cancellation fee imposed. **Amenities:** irons, hair dryers. **Pool(s):** heated indoor. **Leisure Activities:** whirlpool, limited exercise equipment. **Guest Services:** wireless Internet. **Business Services:** PC.
(See color ad p 493) / SOME UNITS

FREE expanded continental breakfast and high-speed Internet

(See map and index starting on p. 456)

COUNTRY INN & SUITES BY CARLSON, KC VILLAGE WEST Book at AAA.com

Phone: (913)299-4700

Hotel
$99-$149 All Year

Address: 1805 N 110th St 66111 **Location:** I-435, exit 14B, 0.8 mi w on Parallel Pkwy, then just s. Adjacent to Kansas Speedway. **Facility:** Smoke free premises. 117 units. 67 one-bedroom standard units. 47 one- and 3 two-bedroom suites, some with efficiencies and/or whirlpools. 3 stories, interior corridors. *Bath:* combo or shower only. **Parking:** on-site. **Terms:** cancellation fee imposed. **Amenities:** high-speed Internet, voice mail, irons, hair dryers. **Pool(s):** heated indoor. **Leisure Activities:** whirlpool, exercise room. **Guest Services:** coin laundry, wireless Internet. **Business Services:** meeting rooms, business center. ASK CALL

GREAT WOLF LODGE-KANSAS CITY Book great rates at AAA.com

Phone: 913/299-7001 2

Hotel
Rates not provided

Address: 10401 Cabela Dr 66111 **Location:** I-435, exit 13B (State Ave). **Facility:** Smoke free premises. 281 units. 251 one-bedroom standard units, some with whirlpools. 30 one-bedroom suites. 4 stories, interior corridors. *Bath:* combo or shower only. **Parking:** on-site. **Terms:** check-in 4 pm. **Amenities:** video library, video games (fee), voice mail, irons, hair dryers. **Pool(s):** outdoor, heated indoor. **Leisure Activities:** whirlpools, indoor water park, exercise room, spa, game room. **Guest Services:** coin laundry, wireless Internet. **Business Services:** meeting rooms, PC. *(See color ad p 175)*

ECO

HAMPTON INN VILLAGE WEST Book great rates at AAA.com

Phone: (913)328-1400 1

Hotel
$119-$169 All Year

Address: 1400 Village W Pkwy 66111 **Location:** I-435, exit 13B (State Ave), just w. **Facility:** 76 units. 74 one-bedroom standard units. 2 one-bedroom suites, some with whirlpools. 3 stories, interior corridors. *Bath:* combo or shower only. **Parking:** on-site. **Terms:** 1-7 night minimum stay, cancellation fee imposed. **Amenities:** video games (fee), high-speed Internet, dual phone lines, voice mail, irons, hair dryers. **Pool(s):** heated indoor. **Leisure Activities:** exercise room. **Guest Services:** valet and coin laundry, wireless Internet. **Business Services:** PC.

 CALL    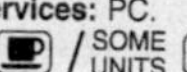 / SOME UNITS

AAA Benefit:
Members save up to 10% everyday!

▼ See AAA listing p 492 ▼

(See map and index starting on p. 456)

HILTON GARDEN INN *Book great rates at AAA.com* **Phone:** (913)342-7900 3

Hotel
$59-$149 All Year

Address: 520 Minnesota Ave 66101 **Location:** I-70, exit 423A (Minnesota Ave/5th St) eastbound, 0.5 mi n; exit Minnesota Ave westbound, just w. **Facility:** 147 units. 146 one-bedroom standard units. 1 one-bedroom suite. 6 stories, interior corridors. *Bath:* combo or shower only. **Parking:** on-site. **Terms:** 1-7 night minimum stay, cancellation fee imposed. **Amenities:** video games (fee), high-speed Internet, dual phone lines, voice mail, irons, hair dryers. **Pool(s):** heated indoor. **Leisure Activities:** whirlpool, exercise room. **Guest Services:** valet and coin laundry, wireless Internet. **Business Services:** conference facilities, business center.

AAA Benefit:
Members save 5% or more everyday!

WHERE TO DINE

JAZZ A LOUISIANA KITCHEN **Phone:** 913/328-0003

Cajun
$8-$14

Patrons can select from daily specials or from a regular menu, which includes such popular choices as chicken a la mere, beignets, crawfish and gumbo. The restaurant's open layout radiates an Easy Street vibe. Weekends typically bring out a house band to liven the atmosphere and create a real N'Orleans feel. Casual dress. **Bar:** Full bar. **Reservations:** not accepted. **Hours:** 11 am-midnight, Fri & Sat-1 am. Closed: 7/4, 11/25, 12/25. **Address:** 1859 Village West Pkwy 66111 **Location:** I-435, exit 13B (State Ave), just sw. **Parking:** on-site.

YUKON BASE CAMP GRILL AT CABELA'S **Phone:** 913/328-3173 1

Wild Game
$5-$12

This grill has multiple choices for cafeteria-style dining. The menu lists preparations of such wild game as elk, ostrich, bison, buffalo and venison. Casual dress. **Reservations:** not accepted. **Hours:** 9 am-9 pm, Sun 10 am-7 pm. Closed major holidays. **Address:** 10300 Cabela Dr 66111 **Location:** I-435, exit 13B (State Ave), just n. **Parking:** on-site.

LEAWOOD pop. 27,656 (See map and index starting on p. 456)

ALOFT LEAWOOD *Book great rates at AAA.com* **Phone:** 913/345-9430

fyi
Hotel
$89-$199 All Year

Too new to rate, opening scheduled for September 2009. **Address:** 11620 Ash St 66211 **Location:** I-435, exit 77B, 1.1 mi s, then just e; in Town Center shopping area. **Amenities:** 156 units, pets.

AAA Benefit:
Enjoy the new twist, get up to 15% off Starwood Preferred Guest® bonuses.

WHERE TO DINE

THE BRISTOL SEAFOOD GRILL **Phone:** 913/663-5777 83

Seafood
$8-$35

The restaurant has a lively atmosphere and stylish decor that includes an impressive stained-glass dome. Excellent entrees display creative preparation and presentation methods. Guests will find flavorful seafood stew, soft-shell crab and mesquite-grilled fish. Casual dress. **Bar:** Full bar. **Reservations:** suggested. **Hours:** 11 am-10 pm, Fri & Sat-11 pm, Sun 10 am-2 & 4:30-9 pm. Closed: 12/25. **Address:** 5400 W 119th St 66209 **Location:** I-435, exit 77B, 1.3 mi s on Nall Ave; northeast corner of Nall Ave and 119th St; in Town Center Plaza. **Parking:** on-site.

COYOTE GRILL **Phone:** 913/451-8888 81

American
$7-$20

Prime steak, chops and fresh seafood are examples of the restaurant's contemporary cowboy cuisine. Casual dress. **Bar:** Full bar. **Reservations:** accepted. **Hours:** 11 am-10 pm, Fri & Sat-11 pm, Sun 10 am-9 pm. Closed: 7/4, 12/25. **Address:** 4701 Town Center Dr 66211 **Location:** I-435, exit 77A (Roe Ave), 1 mi s; southwest corner of 117th St and Roe Ave. **Parking:** on-site. CALL M

HAN SHIN JAPANESE STEAK HOUSE **Phone:** 913/327-1118 80

Japanese
$6-$40

Small groups of people sit around a large, hot grill where the chef makes his magic and puts on a good show using sharp knives. Daily lunch and dinner specials are among offerings. Casual dress. **Bar:** Full bar. **Reservations:** accepted. **Hours:** 11 am-2:30 & 4:30-9:30 pm, Sat 11:30 am-11 pm, Sun noon-9:30 pm. Closed: 11/25, 12/25. **Address:** 4817 W 117th St 66211 **Location:** I-435, exit 77A (Roe Ave), 1 mi s, then just sw; in Town Center Plaza. **Parking:** on-site.

HEREFORD HOUSE **Phone:** 913/327-0800 79

American
$8-$25

A flair of elegance dresses up the rustic decor at the Hereford House. This restaurant specializes in steak and prime rib entrees as well as a variety of seafood and combination dinners. Wine bottles and Southwestern memorabilia are displayed throughout. Casual dress. **Bar:** Full bar. **Reservations:** accepted. **Hours:** 11 am-10 pm, Sat from 3 pm. Closed major holidays. **Address:** 5001 Town Center Dr 66211 **Location:** I-435, exit 77B (Nall Ave), 0.8 mi s, then 0.3 mi e on 117th St; in Town Center Plaza. **Parking:** on-site. CALL M

ON THE BORDER **Phone:** 913/327-0400 82

Mexican
$6-$14

Mesquite-grilled buffalo fajitas and a good selection of more traditional offerings such as tacos and enchiladas are featured at this locally popular restaurant. Tempting desserts of Kahlua cream pie and sopapillas are also offered. Service is superb. Casual dress. **Bar:** Full bar. **Reservations:** not accepted. **Hours:** 11 am-10 pm, Fri & Sat-11 pm. Closed: 11/25, 12/25. **Address:** 5200 W 119th St 66209 **Location:** I-435, exit 77A (Roe Ave), 1.5 mi s to 119th St, then just w. **Parking:** on-site. CALL M

LENEXA pop. 40,238 (See map and index starting on p. 456)

COMFORT INN Book great rates at AAA.com **Phone:** (913)438-6969 79

Hotel

$71-$99 All Year

Address: 12601 W 96th Terr 66215 **Location:** I-35, exit 224 (95th St), just se. **Facility:** Smoke free premises. 67 one-bedroom standard units, some with whirlpools. 3 stories, interior corridors. *Bath:* combo or shower only. **Parking:** on-site. **Amenities:** irons, hair dryers. **Pool(s):** heated indoor. **Leisure Activities:** whirlpool, exercise room. **Guest Services:** valet and coin laundry, wireless Internet. **Business Services:** PC. **Free Special Amenities: continental breakfast and high-speed Internet.** CALL

CROWNE PLAZA LENEXA - OVERLAND PARK Book at AAA.com **Phone:** (913)217-1000 77

Hotel

$69-$209 All Year

Address: 12601 W 95th St 66215 **Location:** I-35, exit 224 (95th St). **Facility:** Smoke free premises. 270 units. 264 one-bedroom standard units. 6 one-bedroom suites, some with whirlpools. 4 stories, interior corridors. *Bath:* combo or shower only. **Parking:** on-site. **Amenities:** CD players, voice mail, irons, hair dryers. **Pool(s):** heated indoor. **Leisure Activities:** whirlpool, exercise room. *Fee:* game room. **Guest Services:** valet and coin laundry, wireless Internet. **Business Services:** conference facilities, business center. ASK CALL / SOME UNITS

EXTENDED STAY DELUXE-KANSAS CITY-LENEXA-87TH ST Book at AAA.com **Phone:** (913)894-5550 75

Extended Stay Hotel

$55-$120 All Year

Address: 8015 Lenexa Dr 66215 **Location:** I-35, exit 227 (75th St), 1 mi s on east frontage road. **Facility:** Smoke free premises. 116 units. 113 one-bedroom standard units with efficiencies. 3 one-bedroom suites with efficiencies. 3 stories, exterior corridors. *Bath:* combo or shower only. **Parking:** on-site. **Terms:** cancellation fee imposed. **Amenities:** dual phone lines, voice mail, irons, hair dryers. **Pool(s):** heated outdoor. **Leisure Activities:** limited exercise equipment, basketball. **Guest Services:** valet and coin laundry, wireless Internet. **Business Services:** meeting rooms. ASK CALL / SOME UNITS FEE

LA QUINTA INN KANSAS CITY (LENEXA) **Phone:** (913)492-5500 76

Hotel

$49-$119 All Year

Address: 9461 Lenexa Dr 66215 **Location:** I-35, exit 224 (95th St), just ne; entrance left on Monrovia Rd, off 95th St. **Facility:** Smoke free premises. 107 units. 104 one-bedroom standard units. 3 one-bedroom suites. 3 stories, interior corridors. *Bath:* combo or shower only. **Parking:** on-site. **Amenities:** video games (fee), voice mail, irons, hair dryers. **Pool(s):** outdoor. **Guest Services:** coin laundry, wireless Internet. **Business Services:** PC. ASK / SOME UNITS

SUPER 8-LENEXA Book at AAA.com **Phone:** (913)888-8899 78

Hotel

$55-$120 All Year

Address: 9601 Westgate Dr 66215 **Location:** I-35, exit 224 (95th St), just se. **Facility:** 101 one-bedroom standard units. 3 stories (no elevator), interior corridors. **Parking:** on-site. **Amenities:** safes (fee), irons, hair dryers. **Guest Services:** wireless Internet. **Business Services:** PC. ASK CALL / SOME UNITS FEE

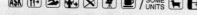

WHERE TO DINE

BO LINGS **Phone:** 913/888-6618 58

Chinese

$8-$23

The restaurant offers creative dishes — some made to order — and a very good selection of appetizers and entrees; no MSG in sauces and most dinners. Casual dress. **Bar:** Full bar. **Reservations:** not accepted. **Hours:** 11 am-9:30 pm, Fri & Sat-10:30 pm. Closed: 7/4, 11/25, 12/25. **Address:** 9576 Quivira Rd 66215 **Location:** I-435, exit 82 (Quivira Rd), 1 mi n; across from Oak Park Strip Mall. **Parking:** on-site.

SHOGUN SUSHI & STEAK RESTAURANT **Phone:** 913/438-3888 57

Japanese

$7-$23

The sushi bar lines up a good selection, including many kinds of maki rolls. Guests also can order teriyaki, tempura, sashimi, teppanyaki and combination Japanese plates. Casual dress. **Bar:** Full bar. **Reservations:** accepted. **Hours:** 11:30 am-2:30 & 5-9:30 pm, Fri-10 pm, Sat noon-10 pm, Sun 5 pm-9 pm. Closed major holidays. **Address:** 12028 W 95th St 66215 **Location:** I-35, exit 224 (95th St), just e; in Oak Park Commons. **Parking:** on-site.

MERRIAM pop. 11,008 (See map and index starting on p. 456)

DRURY INN-MERRIAM/SHAWNEE MISSION PARKWAY Book at AAA.com Phone: (913)236-9200 65

Hotel
$65-$149 All Year

Address: 9009 W Shawnee Mission Pkwy 66202 **Location:** I-35, exit 228B (Shawnee Mission Pkwy), just se. **Facility:** 111 one-bedroom standard units. 4 stories, interior corridors. **Parking:** on-site. **Terms:** cancellation fee imposed. **Amenities:** high-speed Internet, voice mail, irons, hair dryers. **Pool(s):** outdoor. **Leisure Activities:** limited exercise equipment. **Guest Services:** valet and coin laundry, wireless Internet. **Business Services:** meeting rooms, PC.

ASK CALL / SOME UNITS

HAMPTON INN & SUITES Book great rates at AAA.com Phone: (913)722-0800 68

Hotel
$89-$179 All Year

Address: 7400 W Frontage Rd 66203 **Location:** I-35, exit 227, just nw. **Facility:** 85 units. 56 one-bedroom standard units. 29 one-bedroom suites with efficiencies, some with whirlpools. 4 stories, interior corridors. *Bath:* combo or shower only. **Parking:** on-site. **Terms:** 1-7 night minimum stay, cancellation fee imposed. **Amenities:** video games (fee), dual phone lines, voice mail, irons, hair dryers. **Pool(s):** heated indoor. **Leisure Activities:** whirlpool, exercise room. **Guest Services:** valet and coin laundry, wireless Internet. **Business Services:** meeting rooms, PC.

CALL / SOME UNITS

Hampton Inn & Suites
AAA Benefit:
Members save up to 10% everyday!

HOMESTEAD STUDIO SUITES HOTEL-KANSAS CITY-SHAWNEE MISSION Book at AAA.com Phone: (913)236-6006 66

Extended Stay Hotel
$50-$110 All Year

Address: 6451 E Frontage Rd 66202 **Location:** I-35, exit 228B (Shawnee Mission Pkwy), just se. **Facility:** 141 one-bedroom standard units with efficiencies. 2 stories (no elevator), exterior corridors. *Bath:* combo or shower only. **Parking:** on-site. **Terms:** office hours 6:30 am-10 pm, cancellation fee imposed. **Amenities:** voice mail, irons. **Guest Services:** coin laundry, wireless Internet.

ASK CALL FEE / SOME UNITS FEE

QUALITY INN Book great rates at AAA.com Phone: (913)262-4448 67

AAA SAVE
Hotel
$60-$80 All Year

Address: 6601 E Frontage Rd 66202 **Location:** I-35, exit 228A, just ne. **Facility:** 127 one-bedroom standard units. 3 stories, interior/exterior corridors. *Bath:* combo or shower only. **Parking:** on-site. **Amenities:** irons, hair dryers. **Pool(s):** outdoor. **Guest Services:** valet laundry, wireless Internet. **Business Services:** meeting rooms, PC. **Free Special Amenities: continental breakfast and high-speed Internet.** CALL FEE / SOME UNITS FEE

(See map and index starting on p. 456)

FAIRFIELD INN & SUITES 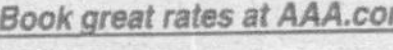 Phone: (913)768-7000 125

Hotel
$116-$142 All Year

Address: 12245 Strang Line Rd 66062 **Location:** I-35, exit 220 (119th St), just e to Strang Line Rd, then 0.7 mi s. **Facility:** Smoke free premises. 84 one-bedroom standard units. 3 stories, interior corridors. *Bath:* combo or shower only. **Parking:** on-site. **Terms:** cancellation fee imposed. **Amenities:** voice mail, irons, hair dryers. **Pool(s):** heated indoor. **Leisure Activities:** whirlpool, exercise room. **Guest Services:** valet and coin laundry, wireless Internet. **Business Services:** PC.

AAA Benefit:
Members save a minimum 5% off the best available rate.

HAMPTON INN Book great rates at AAA.com Phone: (913)393-1111 124

Hotel
$109-$189 All Year

Address: 12081 S Strang Line Rd 66062 **Location:** I-35, exit 220 (119th St), just sw. **Facility:** 115 one-bedroom standard units, some with whirlpools. 3 stories, interior corridors. *Bath:* combo or shower only. **Parking:** on-site. **Terms:** 1-7 night minimum stay, cancellation fee imposed. **Amenities:** voice mail, irons, hair dryers. *Some:* high-speed Internet. **Pool(s):** heated indoor. **Leisure Activities:** whirlpool, exercise room. **Guest Services:** valet laundry, wireless Internet. **Business Services:** meeting rooms, PC.

CALL / SOME UNITS

AAA Benefit:
Members save up to 10% everyday!

HOLIDAY INN Book at AAA.com Phone: (913)829-4000

Hotel
$84-$154 All Year

Address: 101 W 151st St 66061 **Location:** I-35, exit 215 (151st St). Adjacent to Olathe Medical Center. **Facility:** Smoke free premises. 154 units. 152 one-bedroom standard units. 2 one-bedroom suites with whirlpools. 2 stories (no elevator), interior corridors. *Bath:* combo or shower only. **Parking:** on-site. **Terms:** check-in 4 pm. **Amenities:** video games (fee), voice mail, irons, hair dryers. **Pool(s):** heated outdoor. **Leisure Activities:** whirlpool, exercise room. **Guest Services:** valet and coin laundry, area transportation, wireless Internet. **Business Services:** conference facilities, business center.

ASK / SOME UNITS FEE

LA QUINTA INN & SUITES Book great rates at AAA.com Phone: (913)254-0111

AAA SAVE

Hotel
$90-$200 All Year

Address: 20570 W 151st St 66061 **Location:** I-35, exit 215 (151st St), just w. Adjacent to mall. **Facility:** Smoke free premises. 106 units. 94 one-bedroom standard units. 12 one-bedroom suites. 3 stories, interior corridors. *Bath:* combo or shower only. **Parking:** on-site. **Amenities:** high-speed Internet, voice mail, irons, hair dryers. **Pool(s):** heated indoor. **Leisure Activities:** whirlpool, exercise room. **Guest Services:** valet and coin laundry, area transportation-within 5 mi, wireless Internet. **Business Services:** meeting rooms, business center.

CALL / SOME UNITS

FREE expanded continental breakfast and high-speed Internet

MICROTEL INN OLATHE Book at AAA.com Phone: 913/397-9455

Hotel
Rates not provided

Address: 1501 S Hamilton Cir 66061 **Location:** I-35, exit 215 (151st St); jct 151st St and CR 7 N, just nw of jct I-35. **Facility:** 67 one-bedroom standard units. 3 stories, interior corridors. *Bath:* combo or shower only. **Parking:** on-site. **Pool(s):** heated indoor. **Leisure Activities:** whirlpool. **Guest Services:** coin laundry, wireless Internet.

CALL / SOME UNITS FEE

SLEEP INN Book great rates at AAA.com Phone: (913)390-9500

AAA SAVE

Hotel
$85-$105 All Year

Address: 20662 W 151st St 66061 **Location:** I-35, exit 215 (151st St), 0.4 mi sw, follow signs. **Facility:** 77 one-bedroom standard units, some with whirlpools. 3 stories, interior corridors. *Bath:* combo or shower only. **Parking:** on-site. **Terms:** cancellation fee imposed. **Amenities:** voice mail, irons, hair dryers. *Some:* high-speed Internet. **Pool(s):** heated indoor. **Leisure Activities:** whirlpool. **Guest Services:** valet laundry, wireless Internet. **Business Services:** PC. **Free Special Amenities: continental breakfast and high-speed Internet.**

CALL / SOME UNITS FEE

WHERE TO DINE

JOE'S CRAB SHACK Phone: 913/393-2929

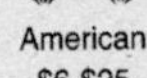

American
$6-$25

The popular seafood restaurant specializes in a year-round variety of crab: Alaskan king, Dungeness, snow and blue. Among other offerings are fresh shrimp, hearty gumbo, clam chowder and classic steaks and chicken. Casual dress. **Bar:** Full bar. **Reservations:** not accepted. **Hours:** 11 am-10 pm, Fri & Sat-11 pm. Closed: 11/25, 12/25. **Address:** 11965 S Strang Line Rd 66062 **Location:** I-35, exit 220 (119th St), just se. **Parking:** on-site.

OLATHE pop. 92,962 (See map and index starting on p. 456)

BEST WESTERN OLATHE HOTEL & SUITES Book great rates at AAA.com Phone: (913)440-9762

Hotel
$90-$150 All Year

Address: 1580 S Hamilton Cir 66061 **Location:** I-35, exit 215 (151st St), just nw. **Facility:** Smoke free premises. 67 one-bedroom standard units. 3 stories, interior corridors. *Bath:* combo or shower only. **Parking:** on-site, winter plug-ins. **Amenities:** high-speed Internet, voice mail, irons, hair dryers. *Some:* DVD players. **Pool(s):** heated indoor. **Leisure Activities:** whirlpool, exercise room. **Guest Services:** wireless Internet. **Business Services:** meeting rooms, PC. *(See color ad below)*

/ SOME UNITS FEE

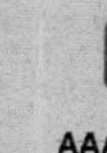

AAA Benefit:
Members save up to 20%, plus 10% bonus points with rewards program.

FREE full breakfast and high-speed Internet

CANDLEWOOD SUITES OLATHE Book at AAA.com Phone: (913)768-8888

Extended Stay Hotel
$83-$99 All Year

Address: 15490 S Rogers Rd 66062 **Location:** I-35, exit 215 (151st St), just sw. **Facility:** 85 units. 68 one-bedroom standard units with efficiencies. 17 one-bedroom suites with efficiencies. 4 stories, interior corridors. *Bath:* combo or shower only. **Parking:** on-site, winter plug-ins. **Amenities:** video library, DVD players, high-speed Internet, voice mail, irons, hair dryers. **Leisure Activities:** exercise room. **Guest Services:** complimentary and valet laundry, wireless Internet. **Business Services:** PC.

ASK CALL / SOME UNITS FEE

COMFORT SUITES AT OLATHE STATION Book at AAA.com Phone: (913)397-0100 123

Hotel
$90-$130 All Year

Address: 12070 S Strang Line Rd 66062 **Location:** I-35, exit 220 (119th St), just se. **Facility:** Smoke free premises. 87 units. 75 one-bedroom standard units, some with whirlpools. 12 one-bedroom suites, some with whirlpools. 3 stories, interior corridors. *Bath:* combo or shower only. **Parking:** on-site. **Terms:** check-in 4 pm. **Amenities:** video games, voice mail, irons, hair dryers. *Some:* dual phone lines. **Pool(s):** heated indoor. **Leisure Activities:** whirlpool, exercise room. **Guest Services:** valet and coin laundry, wireless Internet. **Business Services:** meeting rooms, PC.

ASK CALL / SOME UNITS

(See map and index starting on p. 456)

ZIO'S ITALIAN KITCHEN

Phone: 913/782-2225

Italian
$8-$17

The warm, comfortable atmosphere and Old World decor complement the menu. Meals are a good value, and so is the service. This small chain specializes in Italian cuisine, including oven-baked pizzas and pasta dishes. Guests are encouraged to get creative with their pizzas by mixing and matching from a list of 24 toppings. Particularly tempting dishes are Artichoke spinach pasta, chicken parmigiana, and Shrimp Limone. Casual dress. **Bar:** Full bar. **Reservations:** accepted. **Hours:** 11 am-10 pm, Fri & Sat-11 pm. Closed: 12/25. **Address:** 11981 S Strang Line Rd 66062 **Location:** I-35, exit 220 (119th St), just se. **Parking:** on-site.

OVERLAND PARK pop. 149,080 (See map and index starting on p. 456)

CANDLEWOOD SUITES *Book at AAA.com*

Phone: (913)469-5557 107

Extended Stay Hotel
$59-$99 All Year

Address: 11001 Oakmont St 66210 **Location:** I-435, exit 82 (Quivira Rd), 0.5 mi s, 0.3 mi w on College Ave, then just n. **Facility:** Smoke free premises. 122 units. 98 one-bedroom standard units with efficiencies. 24 one-bedroom suites with efficiencies. 3 stories, interior corridors. *Bath:* combo or shower only. **Parking:** on-site. **Terms:** office hours 7 am-11 pm. **Amenities:** video library, DVD players, CD players, high-speed Internet, dual phone lines, voice mail, irons, hair dryers. **Leisure Activities:** exercise room. **Guest Services:** complimentary and valet laundry.

ASK CALL / SOME UNITS FEE

CHASE SUITES CONVENTION CENTER *Book great rates at AAA.com*

Phone: (913)491-3333 108

AAA SAVE

Extended Stay Hotel
$89-$209 All Year

Address: 6300 W 110th St 66211 **Location:** I-435, exit 79 (Metcalf Ave/US 169), 0.3 mi s on US 169, 0.5 mi e on College Blvd to Lamar Ave, then just n. **Facility:** Smoke free premises. 112 units. 84 one-bedroom standard units with kitchens. 28 two-bedroom suites with kitchens. 2 stories (no elevator), exterior corridors. *Bath:* combo or shower only. **Parking:** on-site. **Terms:** cancellation fee imposed. **Amenities:** voice mail, irons, hair dryers. *Some:* CD players. **Pool(s):** heated outdoor. **Leisure Activities:** whirlpool, barbecue grill, sports court. **Guest Services:** valet and coin laundry, area transportation-within 5 mi, wireless Internet. **Business Services:** meeting rooms, business center. **Free Special Amenities: expanded continental breakfast and newspaper.**

/ SOME UNITS FEE

COMFORT INN & SUITES *Book great rates at AAA.com*

Phone: 913/648-7858 97

AAA SAVE

Hotel
Rates not provided

Address: 7200 W 107th St 66212 **Location:** I-435, exit 79 (Metcalf Ave/US 169), just nw. **Facility:** Smoke free premises. 82 units. 79 one-bedroom standard units, some with kitchens. 3 one-bedroom suites, some with whirlpools. 4 stories, interior corridors. *Bath:* combo or shower only. **Parking:** on-site. **Amenities:** voice mail, irons, hair dryers. **Pool(s):** outdoor. **Leisure Activities:** exercise room. **Guest Services:** valet and coin laundry, wireless Internet. **Business Services:** meeting rooms, PC. **Free Special Amenities: expanded continental breakfast and high-speed Internet.**

CALL / SOME UNITS FEE

COURTYARD BY MARRIOTT *Book great rates at AAA.com*

Phone: (913)339-9900 114

Hotel
$129-$139 All Year

Address: 11301 Metcalf Ave 66210 **Location:** I-435, exit 79 (Metcalf Ave/US 169), 0.6 mi s. **Facility:** Smoke free premises. 149 units. 137 one-bedroom standard units. 12 one-bedroom suites. 3 stories, interior corridors. *Bath:* combo or shower only. **Parking:** on-site. **Terms:** cancellation fee imposed. **Amenities:** video games (fee), high-speed Internet, voice mail, irons, hair dryers. **Pool(s):** heated indoor. **Leisure Activities:** whirlpool, exercise room. **Guest Services:** complimentary and valet laundry, wireless Internet. **Business Services:** meeting rooms, PC.

ECO CALL / SOME UNITS

DOUBLETREE HOTEL *Book great rates at AAA.com*

Phone: (913)451-6100 111

Hotel
$89-$219 All Year

Address: 10100 College Blvd 66210 **Location:** I-435, exit 81 (US 69), 0.5 mi s, then just e. **Facility:** Smoke free premises. 356 units. 334 one-bedroom standard units, some with whirlpools. 22 one-bedroom suites. 18 stories, interior corridors. *Bath:* combo or shower only. **Parking:** on-site. **Terms:** 1-7 night minimum stay, cancellation fee imposed. **Amenities:** high-speed Internet, dual phone lines, voice mail, irons, hair dryers. **Pool(s):** heated indoor. **Leisure Activities:** sauna, whirlpool, racquetball court, jogging, exercise room. **Guest Services:** valet laundry, area transportation, wireless Internet. **Business Services:** conference facilities, business center.

CALL / SOME UNITS

DRURY INN & SUITES-OVERLAND PARK *Book at AAA.com*

Phone: (913)345-1500 104

Hotel
$85-$199 All Year

Address: 10963 Metcalf Ave 66210 **Location:** I-435, exit 79 (Metcalf Ave/US 169), just se. **Facility:** Smoke free premises. 170 units. 117 one-bedroom standard units. 53 one-bedroom suites. 7 stories, interior corridors. *Bath:* combo or shower only. **Parking:** on-site. **Terms:** cancellation fee imposed. **Amenities:** high-speed Internet, dual phone lines, voice mail, irons, hair dryers. *Some:* safes. **Pool(s):** heated indoor/outdoor. **Leisure Activities:** whirlpool, exercise room. **Guest Services:** valet and coin laundry, wireless Internet. **Business Services:** meeting rooms, PC.

ASK CALL / SOME UNITS

(See map and index starting on p. 456)

ECONO LODGE INN & SUITES *Book at AAA.com* **Phone:** (913)262-9600 90

Hotel
$60-$90 All Year

Address: 7508 Shawnee Mission Pkwy 66202 **Location:** I-35, exit 228B, 0.5 mi e. **Facility:** Smoke free premises. 77 one-bedroom standard units, some with kitchens. 2 stories (no elevator), exterior corridors. **Parking:** on-site. **Terms:** cancellation fee imposed. **Amenities:** high-speed Internet, voice mail, irons, hair dryers. **Pool(s):** outdoor. **Guest Services:** coin laundry, wireless Internet. **Business Services:** meeting rooms, PC. ASK / SOME UNITS FEE

EMBASSY SUITES HOTEL-OVERLAND PARK *Book great rates at AAA.com* **Phone:** (913)649-7060 94

Hotel
$99-$189 All Year

Address: 10601 Metcalf Ave 66212 **Location:** I-435, exit 79 (Metcalf Ave/US 169), just ne. **Facility:** Smoke free premises. 199 units. 12 one-bedroom standard units. 175 one- and 12 two-bedroom suites. 7 stories, interior corridors. **Parking:** on-site. **Terms:** 1-7 night minimum stay, cancellation fee imposed. **Amenities:** video games (fee), voice mail, irons, hair dryers. **Pool(s):** heated indoor. **Leisure Activities:** whirlpool, exercise room. **Guest Services:** valet and coin laundry, area transportation, wireless Internet. **Business Services:** meeting rooms, business center. CALL

EMBASSY SUITES HOTELS®
AAA Benefit:
Members save 5% or more everyday!

EXTENDED STAYAMERICA-KANSAS CITY-OVERLAND PARK/CONVENTION CENTER *Book at AAA.com* **Phone:** (913)661-9299 98

Extended Stay Hotel
$55-$120 All Year

Address: 10750 Quivira Rd 66210 **Location:** I-435, exit 82 (Quivira Rd), just sw. **Facility:** Smoke free premises. 119 units. 117 one-bedroom standard units with efficiencies. 2 one-bedroom suites with efficiencies. 3 stories, interior corridors. *Bath:* combo or shower only. **Parking:** on-site. **Terms:** cancellation fee imposed. **Amenities:** voice mail, irons. **Guest Services:** coin laundry, wireless Internet. **Business Services:** meeting rooms. ASK CALL / SOME UNITS FEE

EXTENDED STAY DELUXE KANSAS CITY-OVERLAND PARK-METCALF *Book at AAA.com* **Phone:** (913)642-2299 95

Extended Stay Hotel
$65-$140 All Year

Address: 7201 W 106th St 66212 **Location:** I-435, exit 79 (Metcalf Ave/US 169), just nw. **Facility:** Smoke free premises. 133 units. 100 one-bedroom standard units with efficiencies. 33 one-bedroom suites, some with efficiencies or kitchens. 3 stories, interior corridors. *Bath:* combo or shower only. **Parking:** on-site. **Terms:** cancellation fee imposed. **Amenities:** DVD players, dual phone lines, voice mail, irons, hair dryers. **Leisure Activities:** exercise room. **Guest Services:** valet and coin laundry, wireless Internet. **Business Services:** meeting rooms. ASK CALL / SOME UNITS FEE

FAIRFIELD INN & SUITES OVERLAND PARK *Book great rates at AAA.com* **Phone:** (913)338-3600 117

Hotel
$129-$139 All Year

Address: 12440 Blue Valley Pkwy 66213 **Location:** I-435, exit 79 (Metcalf Ave/US 169), 1.7 mi s on, just w on 123rd St, then just s. **Facility:** Smoke free premises. 110 one-bedroom standard units. 4 stories, interior corridors. *Bath:* combo or shower only. **Parking:** on-site. **Terms:** cancellation fee imposed. **Amenities:** high-speed Internet, voice mail, irons, hair dryers. **Pool(s):** heated indoor. **Leisure Activities:** whirlpool, exercise room. **Guest Services:** valet and coin laundry, wireless Internet. **Business Services:** meeting rooms, business center. CALL / SOME UNITS

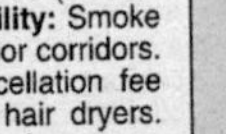

AAA Benefit:
Members save a minimum 5% off the best available rate.

HAMPTON INN-KANSAS CITY/OVERLAND PARK *Book great rates at AAA.com* **Phone:** (913)341-1551 92

AAA SAVE

Hotel
$69-$159 All Year

Address: 10591 Metcalf Frontage Rd 66212 **Location:** I-435, exit 79 (Metcalf Ave/US 169), 0.3 mi ne. **Facility:** Smoke free premises. 133 one-bedroom standard units. 5 stories, interior corridors. *Bath:* combo or shower only. **Parking:** on-site. **Terms:** 1-7 night minimum stay, cancellation fee imposed. **Amenities:** video games (fee), voice mail, irons, hair dryers. **Pool(s):** heated outdoor. **Leisure Activities:** whirlpool, exercise room. **Guest Services:** valet and coin laundry, wireless Internet. **Business Services:** meeting rooms, PC. **Free Special Amenities: expanded continental breakfast and high-speed Internet.** CALL

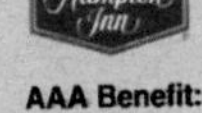

AAA Benefit:
Members save up to 10% everyday!

HILTON GARDEN INN *Book great rates at AAA.com* **Phone:** (913)345-2661 112

AAA SAVE

Hotel
$89-$199 All Year

Address: 5800 College Blvd 66211 **Location:** I-435, exit 77B (Nall Ave), just sw. **Facility:** Smoke free premises. 125 one-bedroom standard units, some with whirlpools. 4 stories, interior corridors. *Bath:* combo or shower only. **Parking:** on-site. **Terms:** 1-7 night minimum stay, cancellation fee imposed. **Amenities:** video games (fee), high-speed Internet, dual phone lines, voice mail, irons, hair dryers. **Pool(s):** heated indoor. **Leisure Activities:** whirlpool, exercise room. **Guest Services:** valet and coin laundry, wireless Internet. **Business Services:** meeting rooms, business center. CALL

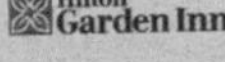

AAA Benefit:
Members save 5% or more everyday!

(See map and index starting on p. 456)

HOLIDAY INN HOTEL & SUITES

Book great rates at AAA.com

Phone: (913)888-8440 91

AAA SAVE

Hotel

$79-$169 All Year

Address: 8787 Reeder Rd 66214 **Location:** I-35, exit 225A (87th St), just se. **Facility:** Smoke free premises. 191 units. 154 one-bedroom standard units. 37 one-bedroom suites. 8 stories, interior corridors. *Bath:* combo or shower only. **Parking:** on-site. **Terms:** cancellation fee imposed. **Amenities:** dual phone lines, voice mail, irons, hair dryers. **Dining:** Green Mill Restaurant & Bar, see separate listing. **Pool(s):** heated indoor/outdoor. **Leisure Activities:** sauna, whirlpool, exercise room. *Fee:* game room. **Guest Services:** valet and coin laundry, area transportation-within 3 mi, wireless Internet. **Business Services:** conference facilities, PC. **Free Special Amenities: newspaper and high-speed Internet.** / SOME UNITS

HOLIDAY INN HOTEL & SUITES CONVENTION CENTER OVERLAND PARK

Book at AAA.com

Phone: (913)312-0900 105

Hotel

$79-$139 All Year

Address: 10920 Nall Ave 66211 **Location:** I-435, exit 77B (Nall Ave), just sw. **Facility:** Smoke free premises. 119 units. 79 one-bedroom standard units. 40 one-bedroom suites, some with whirlpools. 5 stories, interior corridors. *Bath:* combo or shower only. **Parking:** on-site. **Terms:** cancellation fee imposed. **Amenities:** high-speed Internet, dual phone lines, voice mail, irons, hair dryers. **Pool(s):** heated indoor/outdoor. **Leisure Activities:** exercise room. **Guest Services:** valet and coin laundry, area transportation, wireless Internet. **Business Services:** meeting rooms, business center. ASK CALL / SOME UNITS

HOLTZE EXECUTIVE VILLAGE

Book great rates at AAA.com

Phone: (913)344-8100 109

AAA SAVE

Hotel

$79-$219 All Year

Address: 11400 College Blvd 66210 **Location:** I-435, exit 82 (Quivira Rd), 0.5 mi s, then just e. **Facility:** Smoke free premises. 214 units. 98 one-bedroom standard units, some with whirlpools. 116 one-bedroom suites with kitchens, some with whirlpools. 3 stories, exterior corridors. *Bath:* combo or shower only. **Parking:** on-site. **Terms:** cancellation fee imposed. **Amenities:** video games (fee), high-speed Internet, voice mail, irons, hair dryers. *Some:* dual phone lines. **Pool(s):** heated outdoor. **Leisure Activities:** whirlpool, exercise room. **Guest Services:** valet and coin laundry, area transportation-within 6 mi, wireless Internet. **Business Services:** meeting rooms, PC. **Free Special Amenities: full breakfast and high-speed Internet.** CALL / SOME UNITS FEE

HOMEWOOD SUITES

Book great rates at AAA.com

Phone: (913)341-5576 93

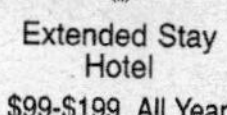

Extended Stay Hotel

$99-$199 All Year

Address: 10556 Marty Ave 66212 **Location:** I-435, exit 79 (Metcalf Ave/US 169), just nw. **Facility:** Smoke free premises. 92 units. 85 one- and 7 two-bedroom suites with efficiencies. 4 stories, interior corridors. *Bath:* combo or shower only. **Parking:** on-site. **Terms:** 1-7 night minimum stay, cancellation fee imposed. **Amenities:** voice mail, irons, hair dryers. *Fee:* video library, video games. **Pool(s):** heated outdoor. **Leisure Activities:** whirlpool, exercise room, sports court. **Guest Services:** valet and coin laundry, area transportation, wireless Internet. **Business Services:** meeting rooms, business center. CALL

AAA Benefit:

Members save 5% or more everyday!

HYATT PLACE KANSAS CITY/OVERLAND PARK/ CONVENTION CENTER

Book great rates at AAA.com

Phone: (913)491-9002 103

AAA SAVE

Contemporary Hotel

$69-$199 All Year

Address: 5001 W 110th St 66211 **Location:** I-435, exit 77B (Nall Ave), just se. **Facility:** 134 one-bedroom suites. 6 stories, interior corridors. *Bath:* combo or shower only. **Parking:** on-site. **Terms:** cancellation fee imposed. **Amenities:** video games (fee), dual phone lines, voice mail, safes, irons, hair dryers. *Some:* high-speed Internet. **Pool(s):** heated outdoor. **Leisure Activities:** exercise room. **Guest Services:** valet laundry, area transportation-within 5 mi, wireless Internet. **Business Services:** meeting rooms, business center. **Free Special Amenities: continental breakfast and high-speed Internet.** CALL / SOME UNITS

HYATT PLACE

AAA Benefit:

Ask for the AAA rate and save 10%.

HYATT PLACE KANSAS CITY/OVERLAND PARK/METCALF

Book great rates at AAA.com

Phone: (913)451-2553 113

AAA SAVE

Contemporary Hotel

$69-$189 All Year

Address: 6801 W 112th St 66211 **Location:** I-435, exit 79 (Metcalf Ave/US 169), 0.6 mi s. **Facility:** Smoke free premises. 124 one-bedroom standard units. 6 stories, interior corridors. *Bath:* combo or shower only. **Parking:** on-site. **Terms:** cancellation fee imposed. **Amenities:** video games (fee), dual phone lines, voice mail, safes, irons, hair dryers. *Some:* high-speed Internet. **Pool(s):** heated outdoor. **Leisure Activities:** exercise room. **Guest Services:** valet and coin laundry, area transportation-within 5 mi, wireless Internet. **Business Services:** meeting rooms, business center. **Free Special Amenities: continental breakfast and high-speed Internet.** CALL

AAA Benefit:

Ask for the AAA rate and save 10%.

(See map and index starting on p. 456)

LA QUINTA INN & SUITES *Book at AAA.com* **Phone:** (913)648-5555 96

Hotel
$59-$129 All Year

Address: 10610 Marty St 66212 **Location:** I-435, exit 79 (Metcalf Ave/US 169), just nw. **Facility:** Smoke free premises. 143 units. 121 one-bedroom standard units. 22 one-bedroom suites. 3 stories, interior corridors. *Bath:* combo or shower only. **Parking:** on-site. **Amenities:** voice mail, irons, hair dryers. *Some:* video games (fee). **Pool(s):** heated outdoor. **Leisure Activities:** whirlpool, exercise room. **Guest Services:** valet and coin laundry, wireless Internet. **Business Services:** meeting rooms, PC.

A$K / SOME UNITS

OVERLAND PARK MARRIOTT HOTEL *Book great rates at AAA.com* **Phone:** (913)451-8000 102

Hotel
$169-$179 All Year

Address: 10800 Metcalf Ave 66210 **Location:** I-435, exit 79 (Metcalf Ave/US 169), just sw. **Facility:** Smoke free premises. 399 units. 392 one-bedroom standard units, some with whirlpools. 7 one-bedroom suites. 11 stories, interior corridors. *Bath:* combo or shower only. **Parking:** on-site (fee) and valet. **Terms:** cancellation fee imposed. **Amenities:** dual phone lines, voice mail, safes, irons, hair dryers. *Fee:* video games, high-speed Internet. **Dining:** 2 restaurants. **Pool(s):** heated indoor/outdoor. **Leisure Activities:** whirlpool, exercise room. **Guest Services:** valet and coin laundry, area transportation-within 2 mi, wireless Internet. **Business Services:** conference facilities, business center.

Marriott HOTELS & RESORTS
AAA Benefit:
Members save a minimum 5% off the best available rate.

PEAR TREE INN BY DRURY-OVERLAND PARK *Book at AAA.com* **Phone:** (913)451-0200 106

Hotel
$60-$124 All Year

Address: 10951 Metcalf Ave 66210 **Location:** I-435, exit 79 (Metcalf Ave/US 169), just se. **Facility:** Smoke free premises. 149 one-bedroom standard units. 4 stories, interior corridors. **Parking:** on-site. **Terms:** cancellation fee imposed. **Amenities:** voice mail, irons, hair dryers. **Pool(s):** heated outdoor. **Leisure Activities:** exercise room. **Guest Services:** valet and coin laundry, wireless Internet. **Business Services:** meeting rooms, business center.

A$K CALL / SOME UNITS

RAMADA OVERLAND PARK-MISSION *Book at AAA.com* **Phone:** (913)262-3010 89

Hotel
$69-$149 All Year

Address: 7240 Shawnee Mission Pkwy 66202 **Location:** I-35, exit 228B (Shawnee Mission Pkwy), 1 mi e. **Facility:** Smoke free premises. 151 one-bedroom standard units. 2 stories (no elevator), interior/exterior corridors. *Bath:* combo or shower only. **Parking:** on-site. **Amenities:** voice mail, irons, hair dryers. **Pool(s):** heated indoor. **Leisure Activities:** sauna, whirlpool, exercise room, sports court. *Fee:* game room. **Guest Services:** valet and coin laundry, wireless Internet. **Business Services:** conference facilities, PC.

A$K CALL / SOME UNITS FEE

RED ROOF INN-OVERLAND PARK *Book great rates at AAA.com* **Phone:** (913)341-0100 101

Motel
$45-$100 All Year

Address: 6800 W 108th St 66211 **Location:** I-435, exit 79 (Metcalf Ave/US 169), just ne. **Facility:** Smoke free premises. 106 one-bedroom standard units. 2 stories (no elevator), exterior corridors. *Bath:* combo or shower only. **Parking:** on-site. **Amenities:** video games (fee), voice mail. **Guest Services:** wireless Internet. **Business Services:** meeting rooms. **Free Special Amenities:** **local telephone calls.**

CALL / SOME UNITS

RESIDENCE INN BY MARRIOTT *Book great rates at AAA.com* **Phone:** (913)491-4444 115

Extended Stay Hotel
$159-$179 All Year

Address: 12010 Blue Valley Pkwy 66213 **Location:** I-435, exit 79 (Metcalf Ave/US 169), 1.3 mi s. **Facility:** Smoke free premises. 120 units. 61 one-bedroom standard units with efficiencies. 38 one- and 21 two-bedroom suites, some with efficiencies or kitchens. 3 stories, interior corridors. *Bath:* combo or shower only. **Parking:** on-site. **Terms:** cancellation fee imposed. **Amenities:** high-speed Internet, dual phone lines, voice mail, irons, hair dryers. **Pool(s):** heated indoor. **Leisure Activities:** whirlpool, putting green, exercise room, sports court. **Guest Services:** valet and coin laundry, wireless Internet. **Business Services:** meeting rooms, PC.

CALL / SOME UNITS FEE

AAA Benefit:
Members save a minimum 5% off the best available rate.

SHERATON OVERLAND PARK HOTEL AT THE CONVENTION CENTER *Book great rates at AAA.com* **Phone:** 913/234-2100 110

Hotel
Rates not provided

Address: 6100 College Blvd 66211 **Location:** I-435, exit 79 (Metcalf Ave/US 169), just s to College Blvd, then 0.6 mi e. **Facility:** Smoke free premises. 412 units. 393 one-bedroom standard units. 19 one-bedroom suites. 20 stories, interior corridors. *Bath:* combo or shower only. **Parking:** on-site. **Amenities:** dual phone lines, voice mail, irons, hair dryers. *Fee:* video games, high-speed Internet. *Some:* safes. **Pool(s):** heated indoor. **Leisure Activities:** whirlpool, exercise room. **Guest Services:** valet laundry, wireless Internet. **Business Services:** conference facilities, business center.

CALL / SOME UNITS

Sheraton HOTELS & RESORTS
AAA Benefit:
Members get up to 15% off, plus Starwood Preferred Guest® bonuses.

(See map and index starting on p. 456)

SPRINGHILL SUITES BY MARRIOTT *Book great rates at AAA.com* **Phone:** (913)491-0010 

Hotel
$119-$129 All Year

Address: 12000 Blue Valley Pkwy 66213 **Location:** I-435, exit 79 (Metcalf Ave/US 169), 1.3 mi s. Located in a busy retail area. **Facility:** Smoke free premises. 102 one-bedroom standard units. 4 stories, interior corridors. *Bath:* combo or shower only. **Parking:** on-site. **Terms:** cancellation fee imposed. **Amenities:** high-speed Internet, dual phone lines, voice mail, irons, hair dryers. **Pool(s):** heated indoor. **Leisure Activities:** whirlpool, exercise room. **Guest Services:** valet and coin laundry, wireless Internet. **Business Services:** PC.

CALL

AAA Benefit:
Members save a minimum 5% off the best available rate.

SUPER 8 *Book at AAA.com* **Phone:** (913)341-4440 99

Hotel
$55-$65 All Year

Address: 10750 Barkley St 66211 **Location:** I-435, exit 79 (Metcalf Ave/US 169), just n to 107th St, then just e. **Facility:** Smoke free premises. 90 one-bedroom standard units. 3 stories, interior corridors. *Bath:* combo or shower only. **Parking:** on-site. **Terms:** cancellation fee imposed. **Amenities:** voice mail, hair dryers. **Pool(s):** heated outdoor. **Guest Services:** coin laundry, wireless Internet. **Business Services:** PC.

ASK CALL / SOME UNITS FEE

WYNDHAM GARDEN HOTEL-OVERLAND PARK *Book at AAA.com* **Phone:** 913/383-2550 100

Hotel
Rates not provided

Address: 7000 W 108th St 66211 **Location:** I-435, exit 79 (Metcalf Ave/US 169), just ne. **Facility:** Smoke free premises. 180 one-bedroom standard units. 2 stories (no elevator), interior corridors. *Bath:* combo or shower only. **Parking:** on-site. **Amenities:** high-speed Internet, voice mail, irons, hair dryers. **Pool(s):** heated outdoor. **Leisure Activities:** exercise room. **Guest Services:** valet and coin laundry, area transportation, wireless Internet. **Business Services:** conference facilities, PC.

CALL / SOME UNITS FEE

WHERE TO DINE

ANDY'S WOK **Phone:** 913/469-6788 75

Chinese
$6-$14

Andy's serves a good variety of Cantonese and Mandarin dishes, and the spicier, peppery dishes native to the Hunan and Szechuan provinces are well-prepared and nicely presented. Business people frequently dine here for lunch. Comfortable ambience. Casual dress. **Bar:** Full bar. **Reservations:** accepted. **Hours:** 11 am-9:30 pm, Fri & Sat-10:30 pm. **Address:** 6357 W 119th St 66209 **Location:** I-435, exit 79 (Metcalf Ave/US 169), 2 mi s, then just e. **Parking:** on-site.

BARLEY'S BREWHAUS & RESTAURANT **Phone:** 913/663-4099 76

American
$8-$26

Guests can select from 99 varieties of beer to complement aged Kansas City strip steak and sausage, which is cut in house, as well as barbecue back ribs, tasty Hawaiian chicken and many creative sandwiches. Soups, dressings and sauces are made from scratch. Casual dress. **Bar:** Full bar. **Reservations:** accepted, Sat-Thurs. **Hours:** 11 am-10 pm, Fri & Sat-11 pm. **Address:** 11924 W 119th St 66213 **Location:** I-435, exit 82 (Quivira Rd), 1 mi s. **Parking:** on-site.

BO LING'S **Phone:** 913/341-1718 66

Chinese
$6-$15

This is a locally popular establishment offering good selections served in a light and airy atmosphere. The Beijing duck, dim sum and cream caramel custard are very good. The dinner menu is extensive and offers large portions with good presentation. Casual dress. **Bar:** Full bar. **Reservations:** not accepted. **Hours:** 11 am-9:30 pm, Fri & Sat-10:30 pm. Closed: 7/4, 11/25, 12/25. **Address:** 9055 Metcalf Ave 66212 **Location:** I-435, exit 79 (Metcalf Ave/US 169), 2 mi n; in Gateway 2000 Plaza Shopping Center. **Parking:** on-site.

CHINA STAR BUFFET **Phone:** 913/381-8882 69

Chinese
$7-$9

Several buffet tables are set up with an ample variety of entrees, appetizers and salads. The dining room is large, modern and well-illuminated. The pleasant owner/manager seats guests and makes them feel welcomed. Casual dress. **Reservations:** not accepted. **Hours:** 11 am-9:30 pm, Fri & Sat-10:30 pm. Closed: 11/25. **Address:** 9421 Metcalf Ave 66212 **Location:** I-435, exit 79 (Metcalf Ave/US 169), 1 mi n. **Parking:** on-site.

FIORELLA'S JACK STACK BARBECUE OF OVERLAND PARK, INC **Phone:** 913/385-7427 71

Barbecue
$6-$30

The popular, comfortable eatery has a big Hereford mural on the wall and lots of wooden pig sculptures. While hickory-smoked meats and sides are the big draw, diners also can get steaks and seafood. Casual dress. **Bar:** Full bar. **Reservations:** accepted. **Hours:** 11 am-10 pm, Fri & Sat-10:30 pm, Sun-9 pm. Closed: 11/25, 12/25. **Address:** 9520 Metcalf Ave 66212 **Location:** I-435, exit 79 (Metcalf Ave/US 169), 1 mi n to 95th St. **Parking:** on-site. CALL

GREEN MILL RESTAURANT & BAR **Phone:** 913/888-8440

American
$8-$16

The eatery prepares top-notch pizzas; a good variety of appetizers, salads, sandwiches and pasta; and some steaks and seafood. Diablo wings are a great way to start the meal. Casual dress. **Bar:** Full bar. **Reservations:** not accepted. **Hours:** 6:30 am-2 & 5-11 pm, Fri-midnight, Sat 7 am-2 & 5-midnight, Sun 7 am-2 & 5-10 pm. Closed: 12/25. **Address:** 8787 Reeder Rd 66214 **Location:** I-35, exit 225A (87th St), just se; in Holiday Inn Hotel & Suites. **Parking:** on-site.

(See map and index starting on p. 456)

INDIA PALACE **Phone:** 913/381-1680 (65)

Indian
$6-$15

This restaurant has spicy fare from an enticing menu that is generous in portions and taste. If you're uninitiated, try the lunch buffet before launching into unknown territory. They offer 11 different breads and fiery, well-prepared curries. Casual dress. **Bar:** Beer & wine. **Reservations:** accepted. **Hours:** 11:30 am-2:15 & 5-9:30 pm, Sat & Sun 11:30 am-2:30 & 5-10 pm. Closed: 7/4, 11/25, 12/25; also Tues. **Address:** 9918 W 87th St 66212 **Location:** I-35, exit 225A (87th St), 1 mi e. **Parking:** on-site.

J. ALEXANDER'S RESTAURANT **Phone:** 913/469-1995 (74)

American
$8-$28

The busy and casual restaurant prepares classic fare—including steak, grilled fish and prime rib—in the open kitchen. The dessert menu is excellent. Casual dress. **Bar:** Full bar. **Reservations:** not accepted. **Hours:** 11 am-10 pm, Fri & Sat-11 pm. Closed: 11/25, 12/25. **Address:** 11471 Metcalf Ave 66212 **Location:** I-435, exit 79 (Metcalf Ave/US 169), 1 mi s. **Parking:** on-site.

JOHNNY CASCONE'S ITALIAN RESTAURANT **Phone:** 913/381-6837 (68)

Italian
$6-$24

Johnny Cascone's features beef and seafood selections in addition to a large selection of pasta dishes. The baked lasagna, pasta with fresh asparagus, and chicken spidinni are especially good. You'll appreciate the casual and relaxed ambience. Casual dress. **Bar:** Full bar. **Reservations:** accepted. **Hours:** 11 am-3 & 4-9 pm, Fri-10 pm, Sat 11 am-10 pm, Sun 4 pm-9 pm. Closed: 11/25, 12/25. **Address:** 6863 W 91st St 66212 **Location:** On US 169, just e. **Parking:** on-site.

JOSE PEPPERS BORDER GRILL & CANTINA **Phone:** 913/341-5673 (72)

Mexican
$6-$13

Traditional Mexican entrees offer much in the way of creativity, and several dishes are presented in large portions. You will find your old standbys available, such as fajitas and chimichangas, as well as more creative dishes such as the chili relleno platter and the Pollo Magnifico. You will enjoy the elegant, but casual ambience. Casual dress. **Bar:** Full bar. **Reservations:** not accepted. **Hours:** 11 am-10 pm, Fri & Sat-11 pm. Closed: 11/25, 12/25. **Address:** 10316 Metcalf Ave 66212 **Location:** I-435, exit 79 (Metcalf Ave/US 169), 0.6 mi n; in strip mall, set back to west from street. **Parking:** on-site.

K.C. MASTERPIECE BARBECUE & GRILL **Phone:** 913/345-2255 (73)

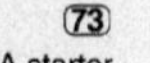

American
$6-$25

Featuring a large menu, this family-friendly restaurant caters to those seeking excellent barbecue. A starter of tasty onion straws often leads into a great plate of ribs. Casual dress. **Bar:** Full bar. **Reservations:** not accepted. **Hours:** 11 am-10 pm, Fri & Sat-11 pm, Sun-9:30 pm. Closed: 11/25, 12/25. **Address:** 10985 Metcalf Ave 66210 **Location:** I-435, exit 79 (Metcalf Ave/US 169), just se. **Parking:** on-site.

THE LONGBRANCH STEAKHOUSE **Phone:** 913/642-2042 (67)

Steak
$5-$20

This restaurant appears to be a rollicking place no matter what time of day you visit. They serve good burgers, iced coffee if you ask, and other tavern-style fare such as steak, sandwiches and salad. The server staff is friendly and helpful. Casual dress. **Bar:** Full bar. **Reservations:** accepted. **Hours:** 11 am-11 pm, Sun 4 pm-10 pm. Closed: 11/25, 12/25. **Address:** 9095 Metcalf Ave 66212 **Location:** I-435, exit 79 (Metcalf Ave/US 169), 1.5 mi n. **Parking:** on-site.

SUSHI GIN **Phone:** 913/649-8488 (70)

Japanese
$7-$20

The extensive menu shows good variety, including 25 appetizers and offerings from the sushi bar. Carry-out and catering services are available. Several combination plates are appealing. The dining room is cozy. Casual dress. **Bar:** Full bar. **Reservations:** not accepted. **Hours:** 11:30 am-2 & 5-9 pm, Fri & Sat-9:30 pm. Closed major holidays; also Sun. **Address:** 9559 Nall Ave 66207 **Location:** I-435, exit 77 (Nall Ave), 1 mi n. **Parking:** on-site.

PRAIRIE VILLAGE pop. 22,072 (See map and index starting on p. 456)

WHERE TO DINE

CAFE PROVENCE **Phone:** 913/384-5998 (54)

French
$8-$38

The cozy cafe's food is excellent and elegantly presented. Treat yourself to excellent flavors and textures, including very rich sauces and soups; the bouillabaisse is quite good. Casual dress. **Bar:** Full bar. **Reservations:** suggested. **Hours:** 11 am-2:30 & 5-10 pm. Closed major holidays; also Sun. **Address:** 3936 W 69th Terr 66208 **Location:** Downtown; in Prairie Village Shopping Center. **Parking:** on-site.

SHAWNEE pop. 47,996 (See map and index starting on p. 456)

COURTYARD BY MARRIOTT *Book great rates at AAA.com* **Phone:** (913)631-8800 (71)

Hotel
$152-$186 All Year

Address: 17250 Midland Dr 66217 **Location:** I-435, exit 5 (Midland Dr), just w. **Facility:** Smoke free premises. 90 units. 87 one-bedroom standard units, some with whirlpools. 3 one-bedroom suites. 3 stories, interior corridors. *Bath:* combo or shower only. **Parking:** on-site. **Terms:** cancellation fee imposed. **Amenities:** video games (fee), high-speed Internet, dual phone lines, voice mail, irons, hair dryers. **Pool(s):** heated indoor. **Leisure Activities:** whirlpool, exercise room. **Guest Services:** valet and coin laundry, wireless Internet. **Business Services:** meeting rooms, business center.

CALL &M

AAA Benefit:
Members save a minimum 5% off the best available rate.

(See map and index starting on p. 456)

HAMPTON INN-SHAWNEE *Book great rates at AAA.com* **Phone:** (913)248-1900 72

Hotel
$99-$149 All Year

Address: 16555 Midland Dr 66217 **Location:** I-435, exit 5 (Midland Dr), just se. **Facility:** 127 one-bedroom standard units, some with whirlpools. 4 stories, interior corridors. *Bath:* combo or shower only. **Parking:** on-site. **Terms:** 1-7 night minimum stay, cancellation fee imposed. **Amenities:** dual phone lines, voice mail, irons, hair dryers. **Pool(s):** heated indoor. **Leisure Activities:** whirlpool, exercise room. **Guest Services:** valet laundry, wireless Internet. **Business Services:** meeting rooms, PC.

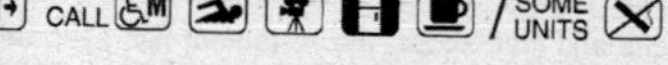

AAA Benefit:
Members save up to 10% everyday!

—— WHERE TO DINE ——

BARLEY'S BREWHAUS **Phone:** 913/268-5160 51

American
$7-$27

Nearby microbreweries provide 99 varieties of draft beer at the relaxing restaurant, which is comparable to a sports bar but has a more upscale atmosphere and better offerings of pasta, pizza, steaks, sandwiches and creative salads. Hardwood floors, neon lights and pool tables off to the side add to the mood. Friendly servers are efficient. A good selection of cigars is available in the full-service bar. Casual dress. **Bar:** Full bar. **Reservations:** not accepted. **Hours:** 11 am-11 pm, Fri & Sat-1 am, Sun-midnight. **Address:** 16649 Midland Dr 66217 **Location:** I-435, exit 5 (Midland Dr), just e. **Parking:** on-site.

American Jazz Museum / © Don Smetzer / Alamy

This ends listings for the Kansas City Vicinity.
The following page resumes the alphabetical listings of cities in Missouri.

KEARNEY—See Kansas City p. 486.

KIMBERLING CITY—See Branson p. 433.

KIMMSWICK pop. 94

—— WHERE TO DINE ——

BLUE OWL RESTAURANT & BAKERY **Phone:** 636/464-3128

American
$7-$12

Tucked amid a village of antique and craft shops, the restaurant has been delighting palates since 1985. Owner-chef Mary Hostetter prepares quiche, croissants, soups, salads, sandwiches and specials. Save room for the luscious desserts made in the on-premises bakery. More than 25 kinds of pies are served each day, as are widely varied cakes and cookies. Casual dress. **Reservations:** not accepted. **Hours:** 10 am-3 pm, Sat & Sun-5 pm. Closed major holidays; also Mon. **Address:** 6116 2nd St 63052 **Location:** Center. **Parking:** on-site.

KINGDOM CITY pop. 121

COMFORT INN *Book great rates at AAA.com* **Phone:** 573/642-7745

Hotel
Rates not provided

Address: 3207 County Rd 211 65262 **Location:** I-70, exit 148 (US 54), just sw. **Facility:** 59 one-bedroom standard units, some with whirlpools. 2 stories (no elevator), interior corridors. *Bath:* combo or shower only. **Parking:** on-site. **Amenities:** irons, hair dryers. **Pool(s):** heated indoor. **Leisure Activities:** whirlpool, exercise room. **Guest Services:** wireless Internet. CALL / SOME UNITS

FREE expanded continental breakfast and high-speed Internet

KIRKSVILLE pop. 16,988

COMFORT INN BY CHOICE HOTELS *Book at AAA.com* **Phone:** 660/665-2205

Motel
Rates not provided

Address: 2209 N Baltimore 63501 **Location:** Jct US 63 and SR 6, just s. **Facility:** Smoke free premises. 46 one-bedroom standard units. 2 stories (no elevator), interior corridors. **Parking:** on-site, winter plug-ins. **Amenities:** high-speed Internet, irons, hair dryers. **Leisure Activities:** whirlpool. **Guest Services:** wireless Internet. CALL

SUPER 8-KIRKSVILLE *Book at AAA.com* **Phone:** (660)665-8826

Motel
$56-$80 All Year

Address: 1101 Country Club Dr 63501 **Location:** On US 63 and SR 6. **Facility:** 61 one-bedroom standard units. 3 stories (no elevator), interior corridors. **Parking:** on-site, winter plug-ins. **Amenities:** high-speed Internet, safes (fee), hair dryers. **Leisure Activities:** limited exercise equipment. **Guest Services:** coin laundry, wireless Internet. ASK / SOME UNITS FEE

—— WHERE TO DINE ——

CHINA PALACE **Phone:** 660/627-8888

Chinese
$5-$11

The locally popular restaurant features a Hunan cuisine in its daily buffet for lunch and dinner. The rice pudding and fried bananas are very good. The relaxed decor has an upscale feel that business people and families enjoy. Casual dress. **Bar:** Beer & wine. **Reservations:** accepted. **Hours:** 11 am-9:30 pm, Fri & Sat-10:30 pm. Closed major holidays. **Address:** 124 N Franklin St 63501 **Location:** On the Square. **Parking:** on-site.

IL SPAZIO BREWERY, PUB & RESTAURANT **Phone:** 660/665-8484

American
$7-$19

The comfortably casual restaurant offers a pleasant surprise with its contemporary decor and sophisticated touches. Menu selections are ambitious. Casual dress. **Bar:** Full bar. **Reservations:** accepted. **Hours:** 11 am-10 pm, Sun-9 pm. Closed: 11/25, 12/25. **Address:** 215 W Washington St 63501 **Location:** At Washington and S Main sts. **Parking:** on-site.

THOUSAND HILLS DINING LODGE **Phone:** 660/665-7119

Continental
$5-$19

This restaurant offers a very pleasant dining experience because of its beautiful view of the scenic lake, valley and surrounding woods. The menu features prime rib, steak and lobster, shrimp, and turtle cheesecake. And you'll enjoy the relaxed ambience. Casual dress. **Bar:** Full bar. **Reservations:** suggested. **Hours:** Open 3/1-12/15 & 2/15-2/28; 4 pm-8 pm, Wed-Fri to 9 pm, Sat 11 am-9 pm, Sun 8 am-8 pm; Fri from 11 am 5/24-9/1. **Address:** 20431 State Hwy 157 63501 **Location:** Jct US 63 N, 3.3 mi w on SR 6; jct SR 157, 2.5 mi s to lake; in Thousand Hills State Park. **Parking:** on-site.

KIRKWOOD—See St. Louis p. 562.

LAKE OZARK pop. 1,489

THE LODGE OF FOUR SEASONS GOLF RESORT AND SPA SHIKI

Book great rates at AAA.com

Phone: (573)365-3000

Resort Hotel

$89-$329 3/1-10/31
$79-$279 11/1-2/28

Address: 315 Four Seasons Dr 65049 **Location:** US 54B, 2.5 mi to CR HH, then 2.5 mi w. **Facility:** A top golf resort, as well as home to one of the Midwest's top spa facilities; landscaped grounds are luscious and expansive. 357 units. 294 one-bedroom standard units. 8 one-bedroom suites, some with kitchens. 55 condominiums. 1-4 stories, interior/exterior corridors. **Parking:** on-site and valet. **Terms:** check-in 4 pm, 3 day cancellation notice-fee imposed. **Amenities:** high-speed Internet, dual phone lines, voice mail, irons, hair dryers. *Some:* DVD players, honor bars. **Dining:** 6 restaurants. **Pool(s):** 2 outdoor, heated outdoor, heated indoor/outdoor. **Leisure Activities:** whirlpools, limited beach access, 2 lighted tennis courts, recreation programs in summer, hiking trails, jogging, playground, exercise room, spa, volleyball. *Fee:* boats, marina, fishing, charter fishing, pontoon, parasailing, scenic cruises in-season, golf-54 holes, trap shooting, cinema with nightly feature film. **Guest Services:** valet laundry, airport transportation-Lee C Fine Memorial Airport, area transportation-within resort, wireless Internet. **Business Services:** conference facilities, business center.

/ SOME UNITS

THE RESORT AT PORT ARROWHEAD

Book great rates at AAA.com

Phone: 573/365-2334

Hotel

Rates not provided

Address: 3080 Bagnell Dam Blvd 65049 **Location:** 2.6 mi s of Bagnell Dam. **Facility:** 209 units. 205 one-bedroom standard units, some with whirlpools. 2 one- and 2 two-bedroom suites, some with whirlpools. 2-3 stories, interior/exterior corridors. *Bath:* combo or shower only. **Parking:** on-site. **Terms:** check-in 4 pm. **Amenities:** voice mail, irons, hair dryers. *Some:* DVD players, safes. **Pool(s):** 2 outdoor, heated indoor. **Leisure Activities:** whirlpools, miniature golf, recreation programs in summer, bocci, gazebo, exercise room, shuffleboard. **Guest Services:** valet and coin laundry, airport transportation-Lee C. Fine Memorial & Grand Glaize Memorial airports, area transportation-within 5 mi, wireless Internet. **Business Services:** conference facilities, PC. **Free Special Amenities:** **newspaper and high-speed Internet.**

CALL / SOME UNITS FEE

The following lodgings were either not evaluated or did not meet AAA rating requirements but are listed for your information only.

HOLIDAY SHORES

Phone: 573/348-3438

fyi

Not evaluated. **Address:** 15 Orville Rd 65065. Facilities, services, and decor characterize a mid-scale property.

PORT ELSEWHERE

Phone: 573/365-4077

fyi

Not evaluated. **Address:** 100 Elsewhere Dr 65049. Facilities, services, and decor characterize a mid-scale property.

WHERE TO DINE

BENTLEY'S RESTAURANT

Phone: 573/365-5301

Steak
$17-$24

The restaurant's English pub atmosphere makes it a nice spot in which to savor an English-cut prime rib that's good enough to put this place in locals' highest regard. The casual dining room affords a pleasant view of the forest up close and the lake in the distance. Ozark trout amandine centers on farm-raised trout from nearby Gravois Mills, Mo. This place is rightly known for its outstanding desserts. Formally dressed staffers deliver polished service with a friendly country flair. Casual dress. **Bar:** Full bar. **Reservations:** suggested, weekends. **Hours:** 5 pm-10 pm. Closed: 11/25, 12/25; also Sun. **Address:** 3100 Bagnell Dam Blvd 65049 **Location:** On US 54 business route; 2 mi s of Bagnell Dam Blvd. **Parking:** on-site.

J. B. HOOKS

Phone: 573/365-3255

Seafood
$9-$33

Community Bridge and the Lake of the Ozarks are clearly visible from the large windows along one wall of the comfortable blufftop restaurant's dining room. Flavorful Greek, classic Caesar and honey mustard salads are favorite lighter meals, while popular entrees include preparations of ocean and freshwater fish, shellfish and steak. Minimalist decor characterizes the spot, which also has a dining patio. A limited number of choices lines the lunch menu. Casual dress. **Bar:** Full bar. **Reservations:** not accepted. **Hours:** 11 am-9 pm, Fri & Sat-10 pm. Closed: 11/25, 12/25. **Address:** 2260 Bagnell Dam Blvd 65049 **Location:** On US 54 business route, 0.7 mi w from jct US 54. **Parking:** on-site.

LI'L RIZZO'S

Phone: 573/365-3003

Italian
$6-$20

Li'l Rizzo's features a scenic view of the lake, a relaxed atmosphere, and a good selection of pasta, beef and seafood. They also serve domestic and imported beers and wine by the glass. Patio seating is available, weather permitting. Casual dress. **Bar:** Full bar. **Reservations:** not accepted. **Hours:** 11 am-10 pm; Fri & Sat-11 pm 5/25-9/7. Closed: 11/25, 12/24, 12/25. **Address:** 434 Horseshoe Bend Pkwy 65049 **Location:** On CR HH, 2.1 mi w of jct US 54B. **Parking:** on-site.

LAMAR pop. 4,452

SUPER 8-LAMAR

Book at AAA.com

Phone: (417)682-6888

Hotel

$57-$80 All Year

Address: 45 SE 1st Ln 64759 **Location:** Jct US 71 and 160. **Facility:** 57 one-bedroom standard units, some with whirlpools. 2 stories (no elevator), interior corridors. *Bath:* combo or shower only. **Parking:** on-site. **Amenities:** irons, hair dryers. **Pool(s):** heated outdoor. **Leisure Activities:** limited exercise equipment. **Guest Services:** coin laundry, wireless Internet. **Business Services:** meeting rooms, business center. ASK / SOME UNITS FEE

LAURIE pop. 663

WHERE TO DINE

DAL'S

Phone: 573/374-0922

American

$3-$8

In a small town on the west side of Lake of the Ozarks, this casual spot employs cordial, competent waitresses to serve its popular country comfort foods. One option is breakfast, which is served anytime the restaurant is open. Pancakes, French toast, Belgian waffles, omelets and eggs are among the extensive choices. Lunch options include several sandwiches, including the highly recommended Reuben, and a few platters, such as the super tenderloin platter. Photos of customers line the front wall. Casual dress. **Reservations:** not accepted. **Hours:** 6 am-2 pm. Closed: 11/25; also 12/24-1/4. **Address:** 601 N Hwy 5 65038 **Location:** Jct SR 135, just s. **Parking:** on-site.

LEBANON pop. 12,155

BEST WESTERN WYOTA INN

Book great rates at AAA.com

Phone: (417)532-6171

Hotel

$77-$100 All Year

Address: 1221 Mill Creek Rd 65536 **Location:** I-44, exit 130, just nw. **Facility:** 52 one-bedroom standard units. 1-2 stories (no elevator), exterior corridors. **Parking:** on-site, winter plug-ins. **Amenities:** irons, hair dryers. *Some:* high-speed Internet. **Pool(s):** outdoor. **Guest Services:** valet and coin laundry, wireless Internet. **Business Services:** PC. **Free Special Amenities: continental breakfast and high-speed Internet.**

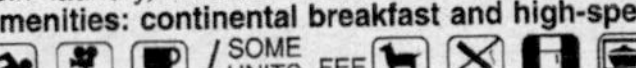

AAA Benefit:

Members save up to 20%, plus 10% bonus points with rewards program.

HAMPTON INN

Book great rates at AAA.com

Phone: (417)533-3100

Hotel

$99-$124 All Year

Address: 930 Ivey Ln 65536 **Location:** I-44, exit 127, just sw. **Facility:** 68 one-bedroom standard units, some with whirlpools. 3 stories, interior corridors. *Bath:* combo or shower only. **Parking:** on-site. **Terms:** 1-7 night minimum stay, cancellation fee imposed. **Amenities:** video games (fee), voice mail, irons, hair dryers. **Pool(s):** outdoor. **Leisure Activities:** exercise room. **Guest Services:** valet laundry, wireless Internet. **Business Services:** meeting rooms, PC.

CALL / SOME UNITS

AAA Benefit:

Members save up to 10% everyday!

HOLIDAY INN EXPRESS

Book at AAA.com

Phone: (417)532-1111

Hotel

$99-$106 All Year

Address: 1955 W Elm St 65536 **Location:** I-44, exit 127, just n. **Facility:** 62 one-bedroom standard units, some with whirlpools. 3 stories, interior corridors. **Parking:** on-site. **Amenities:** dual phone lines, voice mail, irons, hair dryers. **Pool(s):** heated indoor. **Guest Services:** valet laundry, wireless Internet. **Business Services:** meeting rooms, PC.

ASK / SOME UNITS FEE

The following lodging was either not evaluated or did not meet AAA rating requirements but is listed for your information only.

SUPER 8

Phone: 417/588-2574

Not evaluated. **Address:** 1831 W Elm St 65536 **Location:** I-44, exit 127, just nw. Facilities, services, and decor characterize an economy property.

WHERE TO DINE

CORNERSTONE SUBS & PIZZA

Phone: 417/588-3616

American

$3-$15

Bustling at lunchtime, the establishment prepares tasty pizza and sandwich selections. The atmosphere is decidedly "no frills". Casual dress. **Reservations:** not accepted. **Hours:** 10:30 am-8 pm, Fri-9 pm. Closed major holidays; also Sun. **Address:** 399 S Jefferson Ave 65536 **Location:** At Jefferson Ave and Hayes St. **Parking:** on-site.

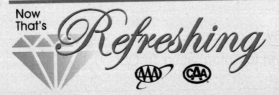

LEE'S SUMMIT—See Kansas City p. 486.

LICKING pop. 1,471

SCENIC RIVERS INN **Phone:** 573/674-4809

Motel

$54-$60 All Year

Address: 209 S Hwy 63 65542 **Location:** On US 63. **Facility:** 50 one-bedroom standard units, some with whirlpools. 2 stories (no elevator), exterior corridors. *Bath:* combo or shower only. **Parking:** on-site. **Terms:** office hours 7 am-11 pm, cancellation fee imposed. **Amenities:** hair dryers. **Pool(s):** heated indoor. **Leisure Activities:** whirlpool, exercise room. **Guest Services:** coin laundry, wireless Internet. ASK / SOME UNITS FEE

LINN pop. 1,354

SETTLE INN & SUITES *Book at AAA.com* **Phone:** (573)897-9903

Hotel

$79-$99 All Year

Address: 1639 US Hwy 50 E 65051 **Location:** 1 mi e of jct US 50 and SR 89. **Facility:** 43 units. 41 one-bedroom standard units, some with whirlpools. 2 one-bedroom suites. 2 stories, interior corridors. *Bath:* combo or shower only. **Parking:** on-site. **Amenities:** high-speed Internet, voice mail, irons, hair dryers. **Leisure Activities:** exercise room. **Guest Services:** coin laundry, wireless Internet. **Business Services:** meeting rooms, business center. ASK / SOME UNITS FEE

LOUISIANA pop. 3,863

WHERE TO DINE

EAGLE'S NEST **Phone:** 573/754-9888

American

$5-$25

Good food is offered at this trendy spot in the historic downtown area; coffees, teas, pastries and wines are available in addition to the specialty menu items. Casual dress. **Bar:** Full bar. **Reservations:** suggested, weekends. **Hours:** 7 am-2 & 5-9 pm, Sat 8 am-3 & 5-9 pm, Sun 9:30 am-2 pm. Closed: 1/1, 11/25, 12/25. **Address:** 221 Georgia St 63353 **Location:** Just s of jct SR 54 and 79; at SR 79 and Georgia St. **Parking:** street.

MACON pop. 5,538

COMFORT INN *Book at AAA.com* **Phone:** (660)395-8000

Hotel

$75-$80 All Year

Address: 1821 N Missouri St 63552 **Location:** Jct US 36 and 63. **Facility:** 62 one-bedroom standard units, some with whirlpools. 3 stories, interior corridors. *Bath:* combo or shower only. **Parking:** on-site. **Amenities:** high-speed Internet, safes (fee), irons, hair dryers. **Pool(s):** heated indoor. **Leisure Activities:** whirlpool, exercise room. **Guest Services:** coin laundry, wireless Internet. **Business Services:** meeting rooms, business center.
ECO ASK CALL / SOME UNITS

SUPER 8 *Book at AAA.com* **Phone:** (660)385-5788

Hotel

$64 All Year

Address: 203 E Briggs Dr 63552 **Location:** Jct US 36 and 63. **Facility:** 59 one-bedroom standard units. 3 stories (no elevator), interior corridors. **Parking:** on-site. **Amenities:** safes (fee), hair dryers. **Guest Services:** wireless Internet. **Business Services:** PC.
ASK / SOME UNITS FEE

WHERE TO DINE

THE LONG BRANCH RESTAURANT **Phone:** 660/385-4600

American

$6-$18

You'll find good home-style family dining at the Long Branch, which offers a daily buffet with several choices of entrees including fried chicken, pork chops, baked stuffed green peppers as well as salad, soup, vegetables and dessert. Friendly service. Casual dress. **Bar:** Full bar. **Reservations:** accepted. **Hours:** 11 am-9 pm, Sat from 7 am, Sun 7 am-8 pm. Closed: 1/1, 12/25. **Address:** 28855 Sunset Dr 63552 **Location:** On Outer Rd S; at US 36 and Long Branch Lake exit. **Parking:** on-site.

PEAR TREE SUB STOP **Phone:** 660/385-1500

American

$4-$18

Guests unwind in the cozy dining room over a fresh sandwich, pizza or any of a number of "extras". Casual dress. **Reservations:** not accepted. **Hours:** 10:30 am-9 pm. Closed major holidays; also Sun. **Address:** 1206 N Missouri St 63552 **Location:** Jct US 36 and 63, just s. **Parking:** on-site.

MAPLEWOOD—See St. Louis p. 562.

MARSHALL pop. 12,433

COMFORT INN-MARSHALL STATION *Book great rates at AAA.com* **Phone:** (660)886-8080

AAA SAVE

Hotel

$95-$125 8/12-2/28

$77-$115 3/1-8/11

Address: 1356 W College St 65340 **Location:** On US 65, 2 mi w. **Facility:** 58 one-bedroom standard units, some with whirlpools. 3 stories, interior corridors. *Bath:* combo or shower only. **Parking:** on-site. **Amenities:** voice mail, irons, hair dryers. **Pool(s):** heated indoor. **Leisure Activities:** whirlpool. **Guest Services:** coin laundry, wireless Internet. **Business Services:** meeting rooms. **Free Special Amenities: expanded continental breakfast and local telephone calls.**
/ SOME UNITS

MARSHFIELD pop. 5,720

HOLIDAY INN EXPRESS **Book at AAA.com** **Phone:** 417/859-6000

Hotel
Rates not provided

Address: 1301 Banning St 65706 **Location:** I-44, exit 100 (SR 38), on southeast corner. **Facility:** 58 one-bedroom standard units, some with whirlpools. 2 stories (no elevator), interior corridors. **Parking:** on-site. **Amenities:** high-speed Internet, irons, hair dryers. **Pool(s):** outdoor. **Guest Services:** coin laundry, wireless Internet. **Business Services:** PC.
CALL / SOME UNITS FEE

WHERE TO DINE

LA HACIENDA **Phone:** 417/859-7605

Mexican
$5-$12

Friendly servers at this spot quickly deliver such traditional Mexican favorites as enchiladas, chimichangas, fajitas and burritos. La Hacienda's specialty is margaritas, and the salsa and tortillas are homemade. Connected to an RV park, the restaurant offers outdoor patio seating. Casual dress. **Bar:** Full bar. **Reservations:** not accepted. **Hours:** 11 am-9 pm. **Address:** 1150 Spur Dr, #16 65706 **Location:** I-44, exit 100 (SR 38), just se. **Parking:** on-site.

MARYLAND HEIGHTS—See St. Louis p. 562.

MARYVILLE pop. 10,581

COMFORT INN **Book at AAA.com** **Phone:** 660/562-2002

Hotel
Rates not provided

Address: 2817 S Main St 64468 **Location:** On Business Rt US 71; just n of US 71 Bypass. **Facility:** 50 one-bedroom standard units. 2 stories (no elevator), interior corridors. **Parking:** on-site, winter plug-ins. **Amenities:** voice mail, safes (fee), irons, hair dryers. **Pool(s):** heated indoor/outdoor. **Leisure Activities:** whirlpool. *Fee:* game room. **Guest Services:** wireless Internet. **Business Services:** PC. / SOME UNITS

HOLIDAY INN EXPRESS HOTEL & SUITES **Book at AAA.com** **Phone:** (660)562-9949

Hotel
$89-$139 All Year

Address: 2929 S Main St 64468 **Location:** On Business Rt US 71; just n of US 71 Bypass. **Facility:** 59 units. 40 one-bedroom standard units. 19 one-bedroom suites, some with whirlpools. 3 stories, interior corridors. *Bath:* combo or shower only. **Parking:** on-site. **Amenities:** high-speed Internet, voice mail, irons, hair dryers. **Pool(s):** heated indoor. **Leisure Activities:** whirlpool, exercise room. **Guest Services:** valet and coin laundry, wireless Internet. **Business Services:** meeting rooms, PC. ASK CALL / SOME UNITS

SUPER 8 **Book at AAA.com** **Phone:** (660)582-8088

Hotel
$55-$61 All Year

Address: 222 Summit Dr 64468 **Location:** On Business Rt US 71; just n of US 71 Bypass. **Facility:** 32 one-bedroom standard units. 2 stories (no elevator), interior corridors. **Parking:** on-site. **Amenities:** safes (fee), irons, hair dryers. **Guest Services:** wireless Internet.
ASK / SOME UNITS FEE

WHERE TO DINE

LA BONITA MEXICAN RESTAURANT **Phone:** 660/562-2229

Mexican
$7-$23

This inviting restaurant serves traditional favorites such as burritos, chalupas, chimichangas, enchiladas and much more. Also available is a children's menu and a wide variety of Mexican sodas. Casual dress. **Bar:** Beer only. **Reservations:** accepted. **Hours:** 11 am-10 pm, Fri & Sat-10:30 pm, Sun-9 pm. Closed: 11/25, 12/25. **Address:** 2717 S Main St 64468 **Location:** On Business Rt US 71, just n of US 71 Bypass. **Parking:** on-site.

NAPOLIS ITALIAN RESTAURANT **Phone:** 660/582-3451

Italian
$6-$15

Diners head to this casual, family-friendly dining atmosphere to enjoy pizza, homemade pastas and other classic Italian dishes. Casual dress. **Bar:** Full bar. **Reservations:** accepted. **Hours:** 11 am-9:30 pm, Fri & Sat-10:30 pm. Closed: 7/4; also Mon. **Address:** 2805 S Main St 64468 **Location:** On Business Rt US 71, just n of US 71 Bypass. **Parking:** on-site. CALL

MEHLVILLE—See St. Louis p. 565.

MEXICO pop. 11,320

BEST WESTERN TEAL LAKE INN *Book great rates at AAA.com*

Phone: (573)582-0700

Hotel

$70-$100 All Year

Address: 3602 S Clark St 65265 **Location:** Jct US 54 and 54 S business route, 1.4 mi n. **Facility:** 48 one-bedroom standard units, some with whirlpools. 2 stories (no elevator), interior corridors. *Bath:* combo or shower only. **Parking:** on-site. **Amenities:** voice mail, irons, hair dryers. *Some:* high-speed Internet. **Pool(s):** heated indoor. **Leisure Activities:** whirlpool, limited exercise equipment. **Guest Services:** wireless Internet. **Business Services:** PC. **Free Special Amenities: full breakfast and high-speed Internet.** / SOME UNITS

AAA Benefit: Members save up to 20%, plus 10% bonus points with rewards program.

COUNTRY HEARTH INN & SUITES *Book at AAA.com*

Phone: (573)582-0055

Hotel

$50-$100 All Year

Address: 900 Vance Rd 65265 **Location:** Jct Business Rt US 54 S and 54 Bypass. **Facility:** 61 one-bedroom standard units, some with whirlpools. 2 stories (no elevator), interior corridors. *Bath:* combo or shower only. **Parking:** on-site. **Amenities:** safes (fee), irons, hair dryers. **Pool(s):** heated indoor. **Leisure Activities:** whirlpool, exercise room. **Guest Services:** wireless Internet. **Business Services:** meeting rooms. CALL / SOME UNITS

MINER pop. 1,056

BEST WESTERN COACH HOUSE INN *Book great rates at AAA.com*

Phone: (573)471-9700

Hotel

$75-$150 All Year

Address: 220 S Interstate Dr 63801 **Location:** I-55, exit 67, just ne. **Facility:** 64 units. 54 one- and 10 two-bedroom suites, some with kitchens (no utensils). 2 stories, interior corridors. *Bath:* combo or shower only. **Parking:** on-site. **Amenities:** high-speed Internet, irons, hair dryers. **Pool(s):** outdoor. **Leisure Activities:** exercise room. *Fee:* game room. **Guest Services:** valet and coin laundry, wireless Internet. **Business Services:** meeting rooms, PC. **Free Special Amenities: expanded continental breakfast and high-speed Internet.**

CALL / SOME UNITS FEE

AAA Benefit: Members save up to 20%, plus 10% bonus points with rewards program.

DRURY INN SUITES - SIKESTON *Book at AAA.com*

Phone: (573)472-2299

Hotel

$90-$159 All Year

Address: 2608 E Malone Ave 63801 **Location:** I-55, exit 67, just sw. **Facility:** 153 units. 135 one-bedroom standard units. 18 one-bedroom suites. 5 stories, interior corridors. *Bath:* combo or shower only. **Parking:** on-site. **Terms:** cancellation fee imposed. **Amenities:** dual phone lines, voice mail, irons, hair dryers. **Pool(s):** heated indoor/outdoor. **Leisure Activities:** whirlpool, exercise room. **Guest Services:** valet and coin laundry, wireless Internet. **Business Services:** meeting rooms, business center. / SOME UNITS

PEAR TREE INN-SIKESTON *Book at AAA.com*

Phone: (573)471-4100

Hotel

$70-$134 All Year

Address: 2602 E Malone Ave 63801 **Location:** I-55, exit 67, just sw. **Facility:** 80 units. 78 one-bedroom standard units. 2 one-bedroom suites. 4 stories, interior corridors. *Bath:* combo or shower only. **Parking:** on-site. **Terms:** cancellation fee imposed. **Amenities:** high-speed Internet, dual phone lines, voice mail, irons, hair dryers. **Pool(s):** heated indoor/outdoor. **Leisure Activities:** whirlpool, exercise room. **Guest Services:** valet and coin laundry, wireless Internet. **Business Services:** meeting rooms, PC. CALL / SOME UNITS

WHERE TO DINE

LAMBERT'S CAFE

Phone: 573/471-4261

American

$8-$16

Diners who settle in at the friendly, energetic and fun cafe can expect their dinner rolls to be thrown to them from almost anywhere in the restaurant. Examples of down-home country food include chicken and dumplings, ribs and seafood. Servers pleasantly bring out seconds, thirds and more. Casual dress. **Reservations:** not accepted. **Hours:** 10:30 am-9 pm. Closed: 11/25, 12/24, 12/25. **Address:** 2305 E Malone Ave 63801 **Location:** I-55, exit 67, 1 mi w on US 62. **Parking:** on-site.

MOBERLY pop. 11,945

BEST WESTERN MOBERLY INN *Book great rates at AAA.com*

Phone: (660)263-6540

Hotel

$68-$116 All Year

Address: 1200 Hwy 24 E 65270 **Location:** Jct US 24 and 63 business route. **Facility:** 98 units. 88 one-bedroom standard units. 10 one-bedroom suites. 1-2 stories (no elevator), interior/exterior corridors. **Parking:** on-site. **Amenities:** high-speed Internet, voice mail, irons, hair dryers. **Pool(s):** outdoor. **Guest Services:** valet and coin laundry, wireless Internet. **Business Services:** meeting rooms, PC. **Free Special Amenities: full breakfast and high-speed Internet.**

CALL / SOME UNITS

AAA Benefit: Members save up to 20%, plus 10% bonus points with rewards program.

WHERE TO DINE

THE BRICK — **Phone:** 660/263-1414

American
$4-$8

This casual eatery prepares classic comfort food with a touch of flair. Orchard pie is an excellent choice. Casual dress. **Reservations:** accepted. **Hours:** 6:30 am-2 pm. Closed: 11/25, 12/25. **Address:** 107 N Williams St 65270 **Location:** At N Williams and Rollins sts; downtown. **Parking:** street.

MOUND CITY pop. 1,193

MOUND CITY SUPER 8 *Book great rates at AAA.com* — **Phone:** 660/442-4000

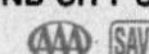

Hotel
Rates not provided

Address: 109 W 8th St 64470 **Location:** I-29, exit 84, just e. **Facility:** 43 one-bedroom standard units, some with whirlpools. 2 stories (no elevator), interior corridors. *Bath:* combo or shower only. **Parking:** on-site. **Amenities:** high-speed Internet, hair dryers. **Pool(s):** heated indoor. **Leisure Activities:** whirlpool. **Guest Services:** coin laundry, wireless Internet. **Free Special Amenities: continental breakfast and high-speed Internet.**

/ SOME UNITS FEE

MOUNTAIN GROVE pop. 4,574

WHERE TO DINE

THE HAYLOFT RESTAURANT — **Phone:** 417/926-6200

American
$5-$13

Travelers can join the locals in the eatery, which offers small-town charm, a pleasant atmosphere and plenty of comfort food. Casual dress. **Reservations:** accepted. **Hours:** 10:30 am-8 pm, Fri & Sat-9 pm, Sun-2:30 pm. Closed major holidays. **Address:** 503 N Main St 65711 **Location:** 0.9 mi s on SR 95. **Parking:** on-site.

CALL

NEOSHO pop. 10,505

BEST WESTERN BIG SPRING LODGE *Book great rates at AAA.com* — **Phone:** (417)455-2300

Hotel
$70 All Year

Address: 1810 Southern View Dr 64850 **Location:** 0.9 mi e of jct US 60 and 71. **Facility:** 63 one-bedroom standard units, some with whirlpools. 3 stories, interior corridors. *Bath:* combo or shower only. **Parking:** on-site. **Amenities:** irons, hair dryers. **Pool(s):** outdoor. **Leisure Activities:** sauna, exercise room. **Guest Services:** coin laundry, wireless Internet. **Business Services:** meeting rooms, PC.

/ SOME UNITS FEE

Best Western

AAA Benefit:
Members save up to 20%, plus 10% bonus points with rewards program.

FREE expanded continental breakfast and high-speed Internet

NEVADA pop. 8,607

COUNTRY INN & SUITES BY CARLSON *Book at AAA.com* — **Phone:** 417/667-9292

Hotel
Rates not provided

Address: 2520 E Austin Blvd 64772 **Location:** US 71, exit Camp Clark, just w. **Facility:** Smoke free premises. 45 units. 38 one-bedroom standard units, some with whirlpools. 7 one-bedroom suites. 2 stories, interior corridors. *Bath:* combo or shower only. **Parking:** on-site. **Amenities:** voice mail, irons, hair dryers. **Pool(s):** heated indoor. **Leisure Activities:** whirlpool, exercise room. **Guest Services:** coin laundry, wireless Internet. **Business Services:** meeting rooms.

CALL

WHERE TO DINE

CASA AZTECA — **Phone:** 417/667-4771

Mexican
$5-$12

Colorful murals depicting lively Mexican scenes cover the walls. Hearty portions of favorite dishes fill guests' plates. Casual dress. **Bar:** Beer only. **Hours:** 11 am-10 pm, Fri & Sat-11 pm. Closed major holidays. **Address:** 117 Centennial Blvd 64772 **Location:** Just n of jct US 71 business route and 54. **Parking:** on-site.

NIXA pop. 12,124

SUPER 8 *Book at AAA.com* — **Phone:** (417)725-0880

Hotel
$54-$61 All Year

Address: 418 Massey Blvd 65714 **Location:** 0.5 mi n of jct SR 14 and 160; US 65, 4.7 mi w on SR 14, then 0.4 mi n on SR 160. **Facility:** 60 one-bedroom standard units, some with whirlpools. 2 stories (no elevator), interior corridors. *Bath:* combo or shower only. **Parking:** on-site. **Amenities:** hair dryers. *Some:* irons. **Pool(s):** outdoor. **Leisure Activities:** limited exercise equipment. **Guest Services:** coin laundry, wireless Internet. **Business Services:** meeting rooms, fax.

ASK CALL / SOME UNITS FEE

NORTH KANSAS CITY—See Kansas City p. 487.

OAK GROVE (JACKSON COUNTY)—See Kansas City p. 488.

O'FALLON—See St. Louis p. 565.

OSAGE BEACH pop. 3,662

DOGWOOD HILLS RESORT
Book at AAA.com

Phone: (573)348-1735

Hotel

$52-$114 3/1-11/13

Address: 1252 State Hwy KK 65065 **Location:** 0.5 mi n, off US 54. **Facility:** 59 one-bedroom standard units, some with kitchens. 2-3 stories (no elevator), exterior corridors. **Parking:** on-site. **Terms:** open 3/1-11/13, check-in 4 pm, cancellation fee imposed. **Amenities:** irons, hair dryers. *Some:* high-speed Internet. **Pool(s):** outdoor. **Leisure Activities:** whirlpool. *Fee:* golf-18 holes. **Guest Services:** wireless Internet. **Business Services:** meeting rooms, PC.

ASK / SOME UNITS FEE

HOLIDAY INN EXPRESS
Book at AAA.com

Phone: (573)302-0330

Hotel

$119-$149 3/1-10/31

$109-$139 11/1-2/28

Address: 4533 Hwy 54 65065 **Location:** On US 54, just n of Grand Glaize Bridge. **Facility:** Smoke free premises. 60 one-bedroom standard units, some with whirlpools. 3-4 stories, interior corridors. *Bath:* combo or shower only. **Parking:** on-site. **Terms:** cancellation fee imposed. **Amenities:** voice mail, irons, hair dryers. **Pool(s):** heated indoor. **Guest Services:** valet laundry, wireless Internet. **Business Services:** PC.

ASK CALL FEE / SOME UNITS

SCOTTISH INNS
Book at AAA.com

Phone: (573)348-3123

Motel

$50-$95 3/1-9/6

$50-$75 9/7-2/28

Address: 5404 Hwy 54 65065 **Location:** 1 mi w of Grand Glaize Bridge. **Facility:** 23 one-bedroom standard units. 2 stories (no elevator), interior/exterior corridors. **Parking:** on-site, winter plug-ins. **Terms:** check-in 4 pm, 3 day cancellation notice-fee imposed. **Amenities:** hair dryers. **Pool(s):** outdoor. **Guest Services:** wireless Internet.

ASK / SOME UNITS

TAN-TAR-A RESORT GOLF CLUB, MARINA & INDOOR WATER PARK
Book at AAA.com

Phone: (573)348-3131

Resort Hotel

$85-$185 All Year

Address: 494 Tantara Dr 65065 **Location:** US 54, 2 mi w on SR KK. Located in a secluded area. **Facility:** Expansive grounds surround this rustic resort; located on 370 acres on the banks of Lake of the Ozarks. 899 units. 731 one-bedroom standard units, some with kitchens and/or whirlpools. 141 one-, 26 two- and 1 three-bedroom suites, some with kitchens and/or whirlpools. 1-8 stories, interior/exterior corridors. *Bath:* combo or shower only. **Parking:** on-site. **Terms:** check-in 4 pm, 3 day cancellation notice-fee imposed. **Amenities:** high-speed Internet, voice mail, irons, hair dryers. *Some:* dual phone lines. **Pool(s):** 2 outdoor, heated indoor. **Leisure Activities:** whirlpools, waterslide, rental boats, rental paddleboats, fishing, 2 lighted tennis courts, jogging, playground, exercise room, spa, volleyball. *Fee:* marina, waterskiing, golf-27 holes, miniature golf, horseback riding. **Guest Services:** valet and coin laundry, wireless Internet. **Business Services:** conference facilities, business center.

ASK / SOME UNITS

The following lodging was either not evaluated or did not meet AAA rating requirements but is listed for your information only.

ROBINS RESORT

Phone: 573/348-2275

fyi

Not evaluated. **Address:** 4935 Robins Cir 65065 **Location:** Jct US 54, 2 mi s on Passover Rd. Facilities, services, and decor characterize a mid-scale property.

WHERE TO DINE

THE BRASS DOOR

Phone: 573/348-9229

American

$14-$27

If you're searching for an early-evening sun-drenched dinner or a quiet, romantic supper, you'll find just what you're looking for at this very nice steak and seafood restaurant. Choose the rainbow trout or prime rib—both are delicious. Good service too. Casual dress. **Bar:** Full bar. **Reservations:** suggested. **Hours:** 5 pm-9 pm, Fri & Sat-10 pm. Closed: 11/25, 12/25. **Address:** 5167 US 54 65065 **Location:** On US 54, 0.5 mi w of Grand Glaize Bridge. **Parking:** on-site.

MICHAEL'S STEAK CHALET & SWISS VILLAGE

Phone: 573/348-3611

Steak

$19-$38

Affording views of the lake, the secluded restaurant prepares a wonderful assortment of steaks and seafood. Casual dress. **Bar:** Full bar. **Reservations:** not accepted. **Hours:** 5 pm-9 pm, Fri & Sat-10 pm. Closed major holidays; also Sun & Mon. **Address:** 1440 Swiss Village Rd 65065 **Location:** Just w of jct US 54 and SR KK, 1.3 mi n on Swiss Village Rd (Lake Rd 54-59). **Parking:** on-site.

ON THE RISE BAKERY & BISTRO

Phone: 573/348-4224

American

$7-$12

The atmosphere in the contemporary bistro is casual and comfortable. A variety of coffees and teas is served with a good selection of dishes presented in generous portions. Casual dress. **Bar:** Beer & wine. **Reservations:** not accepted. **Hours:** 7 am-3 pm. Closed: 1/1, 11/25, 12/24, 12/25; also Mon & Tues. **Address:** 5439 Hwy 54 65065 **Location:** 1 mi w of Grand Glaize Bridge. **Parking:** on-site.

PICKLED PETE'S SPORTS BAR & GRILL **Phone:** 573/302-8800

American
$7-$18

The locally popular sports bar/restaurant offers a very good variety of sandwiches, entrees, pastas, soups and salads as well as appetizer favorites including "Fried Pete's," a.k.a. fried pickles! Also featured are an entertainment area and outdoor dining in season. Casual dress. **Bar:** Full bar. **Reservations:** not accepted. **Hours:** 11 am-11 pm. Closed: 11/25, 12/25. **Address:** 5276 Hwy 54 65065 **Location:** 1 mi w of Grand Glaize Bridge. **Parking:** on-site.

THE POTTED STEER **Phone:** 573/348-5053

American
$23-$32

Locals who dine at this restaurant favor the deep-fried lobster, but the salads with fresh ingredients and delicious homemade dressings are so good that you may want to make a meal of the salad. The restaurant also offers a lake view and superb service. Casual dress. **Bar:** Full bar. **Reservations:** not accepted. **Hours:** Open 3/15-11/26; 5:30 pm-10 pm, Fri & Sat from 5 pm. Closed: Sun & Mon. **Address:** 5085 Hwy 54 65065 **Location:** On US 54, 0.3 mi sw of Grand Glaize Bridge. **Parking:** on-site.

VISTA GRANDE **Phone:** 573/348-1231

Mexican
$4-$16

Generous servings of tasty, hot food is what Vista Grande is known for locally. A few American items complement the mostly Spanish choices, including the usual suspects of tacos, enchiladas and burritos. Servers are cheerful and competent in this comfortable establishment, which displays Mexican knick-knacks and folk decor. Casual dress. **Bar:** Full bar. **Reservations:** not accepted. **Hours:** 11 am-10 pm; to 9 pm in winter. Closed: 1/1, 11/25, 12/24, 12/25. **Address:** 4579 Hwy 54 65065 **Location:** On US 54, 1 mi e of Grand Glaize Bridge; across from Factory Outlet Village. **Parking:** on-site.

OVERLAND—See St. Louis p. 566.

OZARK pop. 9,665

AMERICAS BEST VALUE INN *Book at AAA.com* **Phone:** 417/581-8800

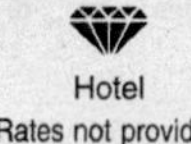

Hotel
Rates not provided

Address: 299 N 20th 65721 **Location:** US 65, exit SR 14, just w to 20th St, then just s. **Facility:** 60 units. 59 one-bedroom standard units. 1 one-bedroom suite. 2 stories (no elevator), interior/exterior corridors. **Parking:** on-site. **Amenities:** high-speed Internet. **Pool(s):** outdoor. **Guest Services:** coin laundry, wireless Internet. / SOME UNITS FEE

BARNAGAIN BED & BREAKFAST **Phone:** (417)581-2276

Bed & Breakfast
$129-$159 All Year

Address: 904 W Church St 65721 **Location:** Jct US 65 and SR 14, 1.3 mi e on US 65 business route, just w on Church St. Located in a quiet area. **Facility:** A Victorian farmhouse and 1922 dairy barn have been converted into lodging quarters in a peaceful country setting near a stream and hiking trail. 4 units. 3 one-bedroom standard units, some with whirlpools. 1 two-bedroom suite with kitchen. 1 story, exterior corridors. **Parking:** on-site. **Terms:** check-in 4 pm, age restrictions may apply, 7 day cancellation notice-fee imposed. **Amenities:** video library, hair dryers. *Some:* irons. **Pool(s):** outdoor. **Leisure Activities:** bicycles, hiking trails, exercise room, horseshoes, game room. **Guest Services:** complimentary laundry, wireless Internet.
ASK CALL

WHERE TO DINE

LAMBERT'S CAFE **Phone:** 417/581-7655

American
$9-$18

Lamberts is housed in a rustic building with flags representing the military services adorning the walls. They serve wholesome home-style food in a bustling atmosphere. Servers toss rolls across the room to those brave enough to try this form of delivery! Casual dress. **Reservations:** not accepted. **Hours:** 10:30 am-9 pm. Closed: 1/1, 11/25, 12/24, 12/25. **Address:** 1800 W State Hwy J 65721 **Location:** Jct US 65, CR J and CC. **Parking:** on-site. CALL

RIVERSIDE INN **Phone:** 417/581-7051

American
$17-$48

A fine dining restaurant nestled in the trees and on the banks of a small river, this eatery appeals to those looking for a wonderful contemporary dining experience while surrounded by the allure of the past. The restaurant was built in the early 1900s when fried chicken and the trimmings were the only things on the menu. Today fried chicken is still served but many steak, seafood and chicken dishes have been added. Casual dress. **Bar:** Full bar. **Reservations:** suggested. **Hours:** 5:30 pm-9 pm, Fri & Sat-10 pm. Closed: 7/4, 12/24, 12/25; also Sun & Mon. **Address:** 2629 N Riverside Rd 65721 **Location:** US 65, 1 mi e on SR 14, 0.3 mi n on 3rd St, then 1 mi e. **Parking:** on-site.

PACIFIC pop. 5,482 (See map and index starting on p. 526)

COMFORT INN *Book great rates at AAA.com* **Phone:** (636)257-4600 38

SAVE

Hotel
$79-$119 All Year

Address: 1320 Thornton St 63069 **Location:** I-44, exit 257, just ne. **Facility:** 70 one-bedroom standard units, some with whirlpools. 3 stories, interior corridors. *Bath:* combo or shower only. **Parking:** on-site. **Amenities:** high-speed Internet, voice mail, irons, hair dryers. **Pool(s):** heated indoor. **Leisure Activities:** sauna, whirlpool, exercise room. **Guest Services:** coin laundry, wireless Internet. **Business Services:** meeting rooms, business center. **Free Special Amenities: full breakfast and newspaper.** / SOME UNITS FEE

(See map and index starting on p. 526)

QUALITY INN NEAR SIX FLAGS *Book great rates at AAA.com* Phone: (636)257-8400 

Hotel
$69-$109 All Year

Address: 1400 W Osage St 63069 **Location:** I-44, exit 257, just se. **Facility:** 46 units. 45 one-bedroom standard units. 1 one-bedroom suite. 2-3 stories (no elevator), interior/exterior corridors. *Bath:* combo or shower only. **Parking:** on-site. **Amenities:** irons, hair dryers. **Pool(s):** heated indoor. **Guest Services:** wireless Internet. **Business Services:** meeting rooms. **Free Special Amenities: continental breakfast and high-speed Internet.**

/ SOME UNITS FEE

PARKVILLE—See Kansas City p. 488.

PERRYVILLE pop. 7,667

AMERICAS BEST VALUE INN *Book great rates at AAA.com* Phone: (573)547-1091

Motel
$60-$76 3/1-8/31
$55-$70 9/1-2/28

Address: 1500 Liberty St 63775 **Location:** I-55, exit 129 (SR 51). **Facility:** 60 one-bedroom standard units, some with whirlpools. 2 stories (no elevator), interior corridors. **Parking:** on-site, winter plug-ins. **Terms:** 3 day cancellation notice. **Amenities:** irons, hair dryers. **Pool(s):** outdoor. **Leisure Activities:** pavilion, grills. **Guest Services:** coin laundry, wireless Internet. **Free Special Amenities: continental breakfast and high-speed Internet.** / SOME UNITS FEE

SUPER 8 PERRYVILLE *Book at AAA.com* Phone: (573)517-7888

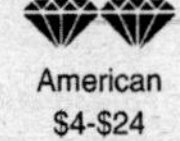

Hotel
$72-$104 All Year

Address: 1119 Vincent Dr 63775 **Location:** I-55, exit 129 (SR 51), just w, then just s. **Facility:** 64 units. 58 one-bedroom standard units, some with whirlpools. 6 one-bedroom suites with whirlpools. 3 stories, interior corridors. *Bath:* combo or shower only. **Parking:** on-site. **Amenities:** safes (fee), irons, hair dryers. *Some:* dual phone lines. **Pool(s):** heated indoor. **Leisure Activities:** whirlpool, exercise room. **Guest Services:** coin laundry, wireless Internet. **Business Services:** meeting rooms, PC.

ASK CALL / SOME UNITS

— WHERE TO DINE —

TRACTORS CLASSIC AMERICAN GRILL Phone: 573/547-1868

American
$4-$24

On the town square, the charming establishment is locally popular for its creative yet comfortable menu selections. Casual dress. **Bar:** Full bar. **Reservations:** not accepted. **Hours:** 11 am-9 pm, Fri & Sat-10 pm. Closed major holidays; also Sun. **Address:** 15 W St. Joseph St 63775 **Location:** I-55, exit 129 (SR 51), 1 mi n to W St. Joseph St, then 1 mi e; in town square. **Parking:** street.

PEVELY pop. 3,768

— WHERE TO DINE —

BOBBY TOM'S BAR-B-QUE Phone: 636/475-3400

American
$4-$11

From the wood stacked on the front porch to the tender, flavorful barbecue, guests appreciate the offerings of the tidy, comfortable roadside establishment. Casual dress. **Reservations:** not accepted. **Hours:** 11 am-8 pm, Sun-6 pm. Closed major holidays; also Mon. **Address:** 1620 Hwy Z 63070 **Location:** I-55, exit 180 (SR Z), just e. **Parking:** on-site. CALL

PLATTE CITY—See Kansas City p. 488.

PLEASANT HILL pop. 5,582

MULBERRY HILL BED & BREAKFAST Phone: (816)540-3457

Bed & Breakfast
$79-$135 All Year

Address: 226 N Armstrong St 64080 **Location:** Jct SR 7, just w on Myrtle St. **Facility:** Smoke free premises. 5 one-bedroom standard units, some with whirlpools. 3 stories (no elevator), interior corridors. **Parking:** on-site. **Terms:** check-in 4 pm, age restrictions may apply, 7 day cancellation notice-fee imposed. **Amenities:** video library, DVD players, hair dryers. **Leisure Activities:** whirlpool. **Guest Services:** wireless Internet. ASK

POPLAR BLUFF pop. 16,651

COMFORT INN BY CHOICE HOTELS *Book great rates at AAA.com* Phone: (573)686-5200

Hotel
$90-$110 All Year

Address: 2582 N Westwood Blvd 63901 **Location:** 1.3 mi s from jct US 60 E. **Facility:** 58 one-bedroom standard units. 3 stories, interior corridors. *Bath:* combo or shower only. **Parking:** on-site. **Amenities:** voice mail, safes (fee), irons, hair dryers. **Pool(s):** heated outdoor. **Guest Services:** valet and coin laundry, wireless Internet. **Business Services:** meeting rooms, PC.

CALL / SOME UNITS FEE

DRURY INN-POPLAR BLUFF Book at AAA.com Phone: (573)686-2451

Hotel
$80-$119 All Year

Address: 2220 N Westwood Blvd 63901 **Location:** On US 67, 1.4 mi s from jct US 60 E. **Facility:** 78 one-bedroom standard units. 3 stories, interior corridors. **Parking:** on-site. **Terms:** cancellation fee imposed. **Amenities:** high-speed Internet, dual phone lines, voice mail, irons, hair dryers. **Pool(s):** heated indoor/outdoor. **Leisure Activities:** whirlpool, exercise room. **Guest Services:** valet and coin laundry, wireless Internet. **Business Services:** meeting rooms, business center.

HOLIDAY INN Book at AAA.com Phone: (573)776-1200

Hotel
$69-$169 All Year

Address: 2781 N Westwood Blvd 63901 **Location:** On US 67. **Facility:** 117 units. 114 one-bedroom standard units, some with whirlpools. 3 one-bedroom suites. 4 stories, interior corridors. *Bath:* combo or shower only. **Parking:** on-site. **Amenities:** high-speed Internet, voice mail, irons, hair dryers. **Pool(s):** heated indoor. **Leisure Activities:** whirlpool, exercise room. *Fee:* game room. **Guest Services:** valet and coin laundry, wireless Internet, beauty salon. **Business Services:** conference facilities, business center.

SUPER 8 Book at AAA.com Phone: (573)785-0176

Hotel
$60-$70 All Year

Address: 2831 N Westwood Blvd 63901 **Location:** On US 67, 0.8 mi s from jct US 60 E. **Facility:** 63 one-bedroom standard units. 2 stories (no elevator), interior corridors. **Parking:** on-site. **Terms:** cancellation fee imposed. **Amenities:** voice mail, safes, hair dryers. *Some:* irons. **Guest Services:** wireless Internet. **Business Services:** PC.

WHERE TO DINE

EL ACAPULCO AUTHENTIC MEXICAN RESTAURANT Phone: 573/776-7000

Mexican
$4-$12

The pleasing, family-owned-and-operated establishment offers a pleasant atmosphere and Mexican favorites. Casual dress. **Bar:** Full bar. **Reservations:** accepted. **Hours:** 11 am-10 pm, Fri & Sat-10:30 pm. Closed major holidays. **Address:** 2260 N Westwood Blvd 63901 **Location:** On US 67, 1.4 mi s of jct US 60 E. **Parking:** on-site.

MAYA'S MEXICAN GRILL Phone: 573/785-7966

Mexican
$5-$13

Lively and casual atmosphere within a colorful setting. Large menu selection, including vegetarian options. Casual dress. **Bar:** Full bar. **Reservations:** not accepted. **Hours:** 11 am-10 pm, Fri & Sat-10:30 pm. Closed major holidays. **Address:** 940 S Westwood Blvd 63901 **Location:** Jct SR 53, 0.3 mi ne on US 67. **Parking:** on-site.

POTOSI pop. 2,662

POTOSI SUPER 8 Book at AAA.com Phone: (573)438-8888

Hotel
$60-$77 All Year

Address: 820 E High St 63664 **Location:** Jct SR 8 and 21. **Facility:** 49 one-bedroom standard units, some with whirlpools. 2 stories (no elevator), interior/exterior corridors. **Parking:** on-site. **Amenities:** high-speed Internet, safes (fee), hair dryers. **Guest Services:** coin laundry, wireless Internet. **Business Services:** meeting rooms, PC, fax.

REPUBLIC pop. 8,438

AMERICINN LODGE & SUITES OF REPUBLIC Book at AAA.com Phone: (417)732-5335

Hotel
$85-$90 All Year

Address: 950 Austin Ln 65738 **Location:** I-44, exit 67, 4.4 mi s to SR 174 (flashing red light/4-way stop), then 0.7 mi e to Highland Park Town Center; just nw of jct US 60, SR 413 and 174. **Facility:** 47 units. 45 one- and 2 two-bedroom standard units, some with whirlpools. 2 stories, interior corridors. *Bath:* combo or shower only. **Parking:** on-site. **Amenities:** high-speed Internet, voice mail, irons, hair dryers. **Pool(s):** heated indoor. **Leisure Activities:** whirlpool, exercise room. **Guest Services:** coin laundry, wireless Internet. **Business Services:** meeting rooms, PC.

RICHMOND HEIGHTS—See St. Louis p. 566.

RIDGEDALE—See Branson p. 433.

RIVERSIDE—See Kansas City p. 490.

ROCHEPORT pop. 208

WHERE TO DINE

LES BOURGEOIS BLUFFTOP BISTRO Phone: 573/698-2300

American
$7-$30

On a beautiful blufftop overlooking the Missouri River, this restaurant prepares beef, seafood and pasta dishes with fresh local produce. Wines are provided by the neighboring vineyard, which has the same owners as the restaurant. Casual dress. **Bar:** Full bar. **Reservations:** accepted. **Hours:** 11 am-9 pm, Sun-3 pm. Closed: 1/1, 11/25, 12/25; also Mon. **Address:** 12847 W Hwy BB 65279 **Location:** I-70, exit 115, 1.5 mi n, then just w. **Parking:** on-site.

ROLLA pop. 16,347

BAYMONT INN & SUITES *Book great rates at AAA.com* **Phone:** (573)364-7000

Hotel
$76-$95 All Year

Address: 1801 Martin Springs Dr 65401 **Location:** I-44, exit 184, just sw. **Facility:** 69 one-bedroom standard units, some with whirlpools. 3 stories, interior corridors. *Bath:* combo or shower only. **Parking:** on-site. **Amenities:** high-speed Internet, safes (fee), irons, hair dryers. **Pool(s):** heated indoor. **Leisure Activities:** whirlpool, exercise room. **Guest Services:** coin laundry, wireless Internet. **Business Services:** PC. **Free Special Amenities: continental breakfast and high-speed Internet.**

CALL / SOME UNITS FEE

BEST WESTERN COACHLIGHT *Book great rates at AAA.com* **Phone:** (573)341-2511

Motel
$70-$155 All Year

Address: 1403 Martin Springs Dr 65401 **Location:** Jct I-44 and Business Rt 44 S, exit 184. **Facility:** 88 one-bedroom standard units. 2 stories (no elevator), exterior corridors. **Parking:** on-site. **Amenities:** safes (fee), irons, hair dryers. **Pool(s):** outdoor. **Guest Services:** coin laundry, wireless Internet. **Business Services:** meeting rooms, PC, fax. **Free Special Amenities: expanded continental breakfast and high-speed Internet.**

/ SOME UNITS FEE

AAA Benefit: Members save up to 20%, plus 10% bonus points with rewards program.

COMFORT SUITES *Book at AAA.com* **Phone:** (573)368-4300

Hotel
$96-$180 All Year

Address: 1650 Old Wire Outer Rd 65401 **Location:** I-44, exit 184, 0.4 mi nw. **Facility:** Smoke free premises. 73 units. 62 one-bedroom standard units, some with whirlpools. 11 one-bedroom suites, some with efficiencies. 3 stories, interior corridors. *Bath:* combo or shower only. **Parking:** on-site, winter plug-ins. **Terms:** cancellation fee imposed. **Amenities:** high-speed Internet, dual phone lines, voice mail, safes (fee), irons, hair dryers. **Pool(s):** heated indoor. **Leisure Activities:** sauna, whirlpool, exercise room. **Guest Services:** valet and coin laundry, wireless Internet. **Business Services:** conference facilities, business center. ASK CALL

DRURY INN-ROLLA *Book at AAA.com* **Phone:** (573)364-4000

Hotel
$70-$114 All Year

Address: 2006 N Bishop Ave 65401 **Location:** I-44, exit 186 (US 63), just ne. **Facility:** 61 one-bedroom standard units. 2 stories (no elevator), interior corridors. **Parking:** on-site. **Terms:** cancellation fee imposed. **Amenities:** high-speed Internet, voice mail, irons, hair dryers. **Pool(s):** outdoor. **Leisure Activities:** limited exercise equipment. **Guest Services:** valet laundry, wireless Internet. **Business Services:** meeting rooms, PC.

ASK / SOME UNITS

HAMPTON INN *Book great rates at AAA.com* **Phone:** (573)308-1060

Hotel
$86-$159 All Year

Address: 2201 N Bishop Ave 65401 **Location:** I-44, exit 186 (US 63), just n. **Facility:** 70 one-bedroom standard units, some with whirlpools. 3 stories, interior corridors. *Bath:* combo or shower only. **Parking:** on-site. **Terms:** 1-7 night minimum stay, cancellation fee imposed. **Amenities:** video games (fee), high-speed Internet, dual phone lines, voice mail, irons, hair dryers. **Pool(s):** heated outdoor. **Guest Services:** valet and coin laundry, wireless Internet. **Business Services:** PC.

CALL / SOME UNITS

AAA Benefit: Members save up to 10% everyday!

HOLIDAY INN EXPRESS HOTEL & SUITES *Book at AAA.com* **Phone:** 573/426-2900

Hotel
Rates not provided

Address: 1610 Old Wire Outer Rd 65401 **Location:** I-44, exit 184, just nw. **Facility:** Smoke free premises. 80 one-bedroom standard units, some with whirlpools. 3 stories, interior corridors. *Bath:* combo or shower only. **Parking:** on-site. **Amenities:** video library, high-speed Internet, dual phone lines, voice mail, irons, hair dryers. *Some:* DVD players, CD players. **Pool(s):** heated indoor. **Leisure Activities:** whirlpool, exercise room. **Guest Services:** valet and coin laundry, wireless Internet. **Business Services:** meeting rooms, business center.

CALL / SOME UNITS

SUPER 8 - ROLLA - MO UNIV OF SCIENCE & TECHNOLOGY *Book great rates at AAA.com* **Phone:** (573)426-6688

Hotel
$60-$90 All Year

Address: 1641 Martin Springs Dr 65401 **Location:** I-44, exit 184, just sw. **Facility:** 64 one-bedroom standard units, some with whirlpools. 3 stories, interior corridors. *Bath:* combo or shower only. **Parking:** on-site, winter plug-ins. **Amenities:** high-speed Internet, voice mail, irons, hair dryers. **Pool(s):** heated outdoor. **Leisure Activities:** exercise room. **Guest Services:** coin laundry, wireless Internet. **Free Special Amenities: expanded continental breakfast and high-speed Internet.**

CALL / SOME UNITS

WHERE TO DINE

GORDOZ **Phone:** 573/364-2780

American
$6-$25

Steaks and seafood are prominent selections and daily specials reflect an Italian flair at this casual eatery, which occupies a shopping plaza setting. Casual dress. **Bar:** Full bar. **Reservations:** accepted. **Hours:** 11 am-2 & 5-9 pm, Fri-9:30 pm, Sat 4:30 pm-9:30 pm. Closed: 5/31, 11/25, 12/25; also Sun. **Address:** 1212B Hwy 72 E 65401 **Location:** SR 72 at Salem Ave; in 72 Center Shopping Plaza. **Parking:** on-site.

JOHNNY'S HICKORY PIT **Phone:** 573/364-4838

American
$7-$14

In a neat red-brick building just east of the major north-south corridor through town, the small restaurant is in a busy commercial area that borders on a residential neighborhood. The menu features an excellent variety of smoked, barbecued ham, pork and beef dishes. A must are the hickory-smoked ribs—they're so tender they fall off the bone. They're dry-rubbed, smoked and served with the house barbecue sauce. The great food and friendly servers make for an enjoyable dining experience. Casual dress. **Bar:** Beer & wine. **Reservations:** not accepted. **Hours:** 11 am-8 pm, Fri & Sat-9 pm. Closed: 1/1, 11/25, 12/25. **Address:** 201 Hwy 72 W 65401 **Location:** 1 mi s on US 63, then 0.3 mi e on SR 72. **Parking:** on-site.

KYOTO JAPANESE RESTAURANT **Phone:** 573/341-2939

Japanese
$6-$20

Crisp, fresh, light and bright are words that may come to mind when entering Kyoto because the dining room is decorated with lots of natural light-colored wood. This observation will be enhanced when you see the food - which is also crisp, fresh, light and bright as is typical for authentic Japanese restaurants. Casual dress. **Bar:** Beer & wine. **Reservations:** accepted. **Hours:** 11 am-2:30 & 4:30-9:30 pm, Fri & Sat-10 pm. Closed: Sun & week of July 4th. **Address:** 1002 N Bishop Ave 65401 **Location:** At 11th St. **Parking:** on-site.

SIRLOIN STOCKADE **Phone:** 573/364-7168

Regional Steak
$6-$9

The steakhouse lines up buffet items, including pizza, tacos, soups, salads and desserts, providing both excellent variety and a good value. Rotating theme nights might allow for the sampling of sushi, barbecue and seafood. The buffet also may serve to complement a quality steak. Rolls are baked several times daily. Casual dress. **Reservations:** not accepted. **Hours:** 11 am-9 pm. Closed: 11/25, 12/25. **Address:** 1401 Martin Springs Dr 65401 **Location:** Jct I-44 and Business Rd 44, exit 184. **Parking:** on-site.

WASABI **Phone:** 573/341-1200

Asian
$6-$20

The sushi rolls at Wasabi are prepared by a skilled chef, and the other menu items comprise varieties of beef, pork and chicken prepared in classic Korean and Japanese styles. Intimate table dividers form a practical, yet still romantic, dinner experience. Casual dress. **Bar:** Beer & wine. **Reservations:** accepted. **Hours:** 11 am-2:30 & 5-9 pm, Fri & Sat-9:30 pm. Closed major holidays; also Mon. **Address:** 1011 Kingshighway St 65401 **Location:** I-44, exit 184, 0.7 mi e. **Parking:** on-site.

ZENO'S STEAK HOUSE **Phone:** 573/364-1301

Steak
$5-$21

You'll appreciate the comfortable, sophisticated atmosphere at Zeno's. The steaks and prime rib are cooked to perfection. They also offer Italian and seafood dishes. Without reservations you may have to wait, but the food won't disappoint. Casual dress. **Bar:** Full bar. **Reservations:** accepted. **Hours:** 7 am-8 pm, Fri & Sat-9 pm. Closed: 12/25. **Address:** 1621 Martin Springs Dr 65402 **Location:** I-44, exit 184; in Zeno's Motel. **Parking:** on-site.

ST. ALBANS (See map and index starting on p. 526)

— WHERE TO DINE —

THE GARDENS AT MALMAISON **Phone:** 636/458-0131 (29)

Traditional French
$17-$28

This sophisticated restaurant is known for sustaining French country dining at its dressy casual best with a tempting array of meals and seasonal specialties. Entrées feature classic French cuisine as well as a few Italian favorites. The signature appetizer is a mushroom creation served in a puff pastry treasure chest that looks as good as it tastes. For dessert, the St. Albans ice cream confection is a treat for the eyes as well as the palate. Prix fixe selections are available. Dressy casual. **Bar:** Full bar. **Reservations:** suggested. **Hours:** 5 pm-10 pm; hours may vary. Closed major holidays; also Tues & Wed. **Address:** 3519 St. Albans Rd 63073 **Location:** Jct SR 100 and CR T, 3.5 mi n to St. Albans entrance, 2 mi to village. **Parking:** on-site. **Historic**

ST. ANN—See St. Louis p. 566.

ST. CHARLES—See St. Louis p. 567.

ST. CLAIR pop. 4,390

BUDGET LODGING *Book great rates at AAA.com* **Phone:** (636)629-1000

Motel
$69-$79 All Year

Address: 866 S Outer Rd W 63077 **Location:** I-44, exit 240, just w. **Facility:** 60 units. 59 one-bedroom standard units. 1 one-bedroom suite with whirlpool. 1-2 stories (no elevator), exterior corridors. **Parking:** on-site, winter plug-ins. **Amenities:** video library, hair dryers. *Some:* DVD players, CD players, dual phone lines, irons. **Pool(s):** outdoor. **Leisure Activities:** charcoal grill, picnic area. **Guest Services:** coin laundry, wireless Internet. **Business Services:** meeting rooms. **Free Special Amenities: expanded continental breakfast and high-speed Internet.**

/ SOME UNITS FEE

ST. JOSEPH pop. 73,990

BEST WESTERN CLASSIC INN *Book great rates at AAA.com* **Phone:** (816)232-2345

Motel
$70-$80 3/1-9/30
$60-$70 10/1-2/28

Address: 4502 SE US 169 64507 **Location:** I-29, exit 44, just e. **Facility:** 52 one-bedroom standard units, some with whirlpools. 2 stories (no elevator), exterior corridors. *Bath:* combo or shower only. **Parking:** on-site, winter plug-ins. **Amenities:** high-speed Internet, irons, hair dryers. **Pool(s):** outdoor. **Leisure Activities:** sauna, exercise room. **Guest Services:** wireless Internet. **Business Services:** PC. **Free Special Amenities: continental breakfast and high-speed Internet.**

CALL / SOME UNITS FEE

AAA Benefit: Members save up to 20%, plus 10% bonus points with rewards program.

COMFORT SUITES *Book at AAA.com* **Phone:** (816)232-6557

Hotel
$81-$110 All Year

Address: 917 N Woodbine Rd 64506 **Location:** I-29, exit 47, just sw. **Facility:** Smoke free premises. 65 units. 64 one-bedroom standard units, some with whirlpools. 1 one-bedroom suite with whirlpool. 3 stories, interior corridors. *Bath:* combo or shower only. **Parking:** on-site. **Amenities:** voice mail, safes (fee), irons, hair dryers. *Some:* dual phone lines. **Pool(s):** heated indoor. **Leisure Activities:** whirlpool, exercise room. **Guest Services:** valet and coin laundry, wireless Internet. **Business Services:** meeting rooms, PC. ASK CALL

DAYS INN *Book great rates at AAA.com* **Phone:** (816)279-1671

Motel
$66-$86 All Year

Address: 4312 Frederick Blvd 64506 **Location:** I-29, exit 47, just e. **Facility:** 100 one-bedroom standard units. 2 stories (no elevator), exterior corridors. **Parking:** on-site. **Amenities:** hair dryers. *Some:* irons. **Pool(s):** outdoor. **Guest Services:** wireless Internet. **Business Services:** meeting rooms. **Free Special Amenities: continental breakfast and high-speed Internet.**

/ SOME UNITS

DRURY INN & SUITES-ST. JOSEPH *Book at AAA.com* **Phone:** (816)364-4700

Hotel
$75-$149 All Year

Address: 4213 Frederick Blvd 64506 **Location:** I-29, exit 47, just e. **Facility:** 132 units. 121 one-bedroom standard units. 11 one-bedroom suites. 4 stories, interior corridors. **Parking:** on-site. **Terms:** cancellation fee imposed. **Amenities:** high-speed Internet, dual phone lines, voice mail, irons, hair dryers. **Pool(s):** heated indoor. **Leisure Activities:** whirlpool, exercise room. **Guest Services:** valet and coin laundry, wireless Internet. **Business Services:** meeting rooms, business center.

ASK CALL / SOME UNITS

HAMPTON INN BY HILTON *Book great rates at AAA.com* **Phone:** 816/390-9300

Hotel
Rates not provided

Address: 3928 Frederick Blvd 64506 **Location:** I-29, exit 47, just w. **Facility:** 60 one-bedroom standard units. 4 stories, interior corridors. *Bath:* combo or shower only. **Parking:** on-site. **Amenities:** voice mail, irons, hair dryers. *Some:* high-speed Internet. **Pool(s):** heated indoor. **Leisure Activities:** whirlpool. **Guest Services:** valet laundry, wireless Internet. **Business Services:** PC.

CALL / SOME UNITS

AAA Benefit: Members save up to 10% everyday!

MUSEUM HILL BED AND BREAKFAST **Phone:** 816/387-9663

Historic Bed & Breakfast
$120-$160 All Year

Address: 1102 Felix St 64501 **Location:** I-229, exit Edmond St northbound; exit Felix St southbound; downtown. **Facility:** Expect a unique experience at this well-maintained inn, where you'll find wonderfully landscaped grounds. Meeting space is available. Smoke free premises. 4 one-bedroom standard units, some with whirlpools. 2 stories (no elevator), interior corridors. *Bath:* combo or shower only. **Parking:** street. **Terms:** age restrictions may apply, 14 day cancellation notice-fee imposed. **Amenities:** hair dryers. **Leisure Activities:** *Fee:* massage. **Guest Services:** wireless Internet. **Business Services:** meeting rooms.

RAMADA AND MONKEY COVE WATERPARK *Book at AAA.com* **Phone:** (816)233-6192

Hotel
$87-$149 All Year

Address: 4016 Frederick Ave 64506 **Location:** I-29, exit 47, just w. **Facility:** 159 units. 153 one-bedroom standard units. 6 one-bedroom suites, some with whirlpools. 2 stories (no elevator), interior corridors. **Parking:** on-site. **Terms:** check-in 4 pm. **Amenities:** voice mail, safes (fee), irons, hair dryers. *Some:* high-speed Internet. **Dining:** Whiskey Creek Wood Fire Grill, see separate listing. **Pool(s):** heated indoor. **Leisure Activities:** whirlpool, waterslide, exercise room. **Guest Services:** valet and coin laundry, wireless Internet. **Business Services:** conference facilities, PC.

ST. JOSEPH HOLIDAY INN-RIVERFRONT *Book at AAA.com* **Phone:** (816)279-8000

Hotel
$85-$105 All Year

Address: 102 S Third St 64501 **Location:** I-229, exit Edmond St northbound; exit Felix St southbound; downtown. **Facility:** 169 units. 168 one-bedroom standard units. 1 one-bedroom suite. 6 stories, interior corridors. *Bath:* combo or shower only. **Parking:** on-site. **Terms:** cancellation fee imposed. **Amenities:** voice mail, irons, hair dryers. *Some:* high-speed Internet. **Pool(s):** heated indoor. **Leisure Activities:** sauna, whirlpool, exercise room. **Guest Services:** valet and coin laundry, area transportation, wireless Internet. **Business Services:** conference facilities, business center.

STONEY CREEK INN *Book at AAA.com* **Phone:** (816)901-9600

Hotel
$85-$175 All Year

Address: 1201 N Woodbine Rd 64506 **Location:** I-29, exit 47, just w to Woodbine Rd. **Facility:** Smoke free premises. 129 units. 127 one-bedroom standard units, some with whirlpools. 2 one-bedroom suites with whirlpools. 3 stories, interior corridors. *Bath:* combo or shower only. **Parking:** on-site. **Terms:** 2-3 night minimum stay - seasonal, cancellation fee imposed. **Amenities:** high-speed Internet, voice mail, irons, hair dryers. *Some:* video games (fee), dual phone lines. **Pool(s):** heated indoor/outdoor. **Leisure Activities:** whirlpool, exercise room. *Fee:* game room. **Guest Services:** valet and coin laundry, area transportation, wireless Internet. **Business Services:** conference facilities, business center.

— WHERE TO DINE —

BARBOSAS' **Phone:** 816/233-4970

Mexican
$4-$13

The dining room carries out a Romanesque-Gothic motif. Among creative dishes are chicken mole and chiles rellenos. Other choices include fajitas, burritos, tostadas, enchiladas and fideos, as well as children's favorites. Casual dress. **Bar:** Full bar. **Reservations:** accepted. **Hours:** 11 am-9 pm, Fri & Sat-10 pm. Closed major holidays; also Sun & Mon. **Address:** 906 Sylvanie St 64506 **Location:** Downtown. **Parking:** on-site.

BOUDREAUX'S LOUISIANA SEAFOOD & STEAK **Phone:** 816/387-9911

Cajun
$6-$21

On the menu is gumbo, jambalaya, Creole oysters, crawfish and plenty of other varieties of fish and seafood along with steaks and some of the area's best fried chicken. Casual dress. **Bar:** Full bar. **Reservations:** not accepted. **Hours:** 11 am-9 pm, Fri & Sat-11 pm. Closed major holidays; also Sun. **Address:** 224 N 4th St 64502 **Location:** I-229, exit Edmond St, just ne; downtown. **Parking:** street.

FREDRICK INN STEAK HOUSE & LOUNGE **Phone:** 816/364-5151

American
$5-$23

The busy lunch crowd at this restaurant testifies to its popularity. They have an excellent variety of choices on the menu, including prime rib, seafood, fresh veggies, salad and homemade dessert, and very good service by friendly, attentive servers. Casual dress. **Bar:** Full bar. **Reservations:** suggested, weekends. **Hours:** 11 am-9 pm, Sat 4 pm-10 pm. Closed major holidays; also Sun. **Address:** 1627 Frederick Ave 64501 **Location:** I-29, exit 47, 2.5 mi w. **Parking:** on-site.

LA DOLCE VITA AT 36TH STREET RESTAURANT **Phone:** 816/364-1565

American
$6-$25

Delicious steak and fresh vegetables make an excellent combination for dinner at this restaurant. The upscale, traditional decor creates an inviting, friendly environment. The varied menu including homemade cheesecake completes the dining experience. Casual dress. **Bar:** Full bar. **Reservations:** accepted. **Hours:** 11 am-10 pm, Fri & Sat-11 pm. Closed major holidays; also Sun. **Address:** 501 N Belt Hwy 64506 **Location:** I-29, exit 47, 0.3 mi w to US 169, then 0.3 mi s. **Parking:** on-site.

RIB CRIB BBQ AND GRILL **Phone:** 816/279-7422

American
$6-$16

Most guests need extra napkins to tackle the ribs, brisket, ham, pork and chicken selections. The menu also lists sandwiches and wraps, along with tempting sides and large desserts. The decor is decidedly Western. Casual dress. **Bar:** Beer only. **Reservations:** not accepted. **Hours:** 11 am-10 pm. Closed major holidays. **Address:** 3704 Faraon St 64506 **Location:** I-29, exit 47, just sw. **Parking:** on-site.

WHISKEY CREEK WOOD FIRE GRILL **Phone:** 816/676-1298

American
$9-$22

Guests can watch as their steak is cooked over a wood-burning fire and throw peanut shells on the floor at this fun, casual steakhouse. The menu's wide variety includes chicken, pasta and barbecue dishes. A rustic theme evokes the wild, wild West. Casual dress. **Bar:** Full bar. **Reservations:** accepted, except Fri & Sat. **Hours:** 11 am-10 pm, Fri & Sat-11 pm. Closed: 11/25, 12/25. **Address:** 4016 Frederick Ave 64501 **Location:** I-29, exit 47, just w; in Ramada and Monkey Cove Waterpark. **Parking:** on-site.

Destination St. Louis

pop. 348,189

Let the Gateway to the West be your access to excitement.

Bike or stroll in expansive Forest Park; cheer on the Cardinals; take the tram to the top of the city's most interesting "arch"-itectural feature, which offers an outstanding view; or check out the entertainment venues at downtown's historic Laclede's Landing.

© Gibson Stock Photography

Laclede's Landing, St. Louis.
(See listing page 210)

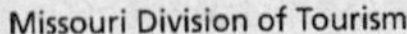

Missouri Division of Tourism

St. Louis Cardinals.

Places included in this AAA Destination City:

Missouri Division of Tourism

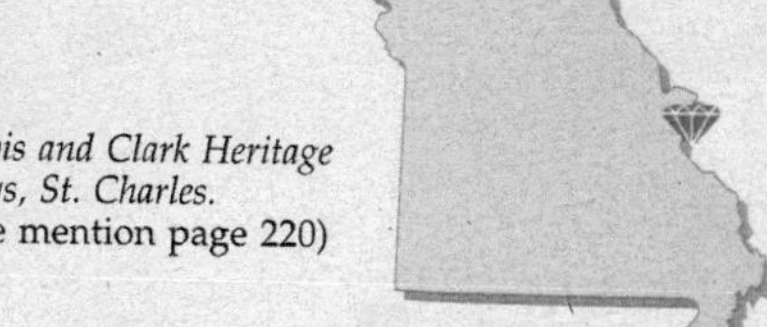

Lewis and Clark Heritage Days, St. Charles.
(See mention page 220)

Missouri Division of Tourism

St. Louis Storytelling Festival.

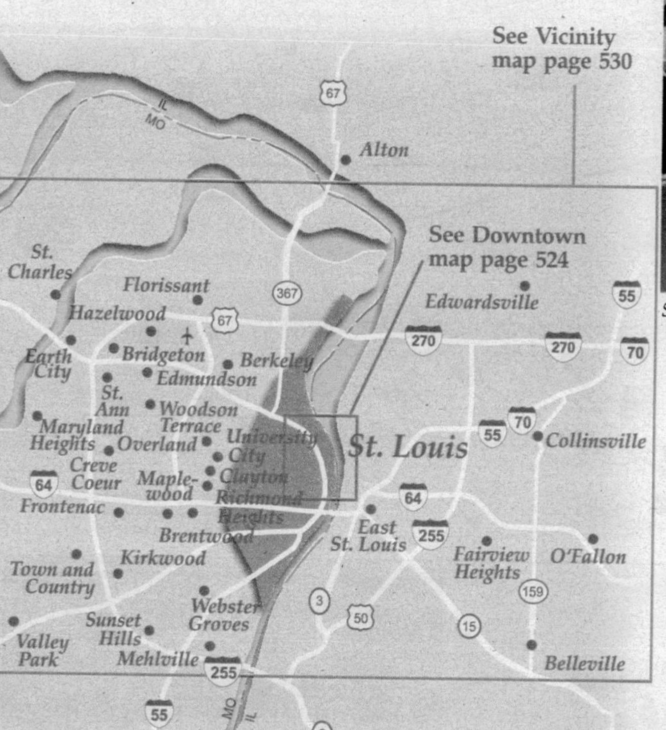

© Gateway Arch Riverfront

The Gateway Arch, St. Louis.
(See listing page 209)

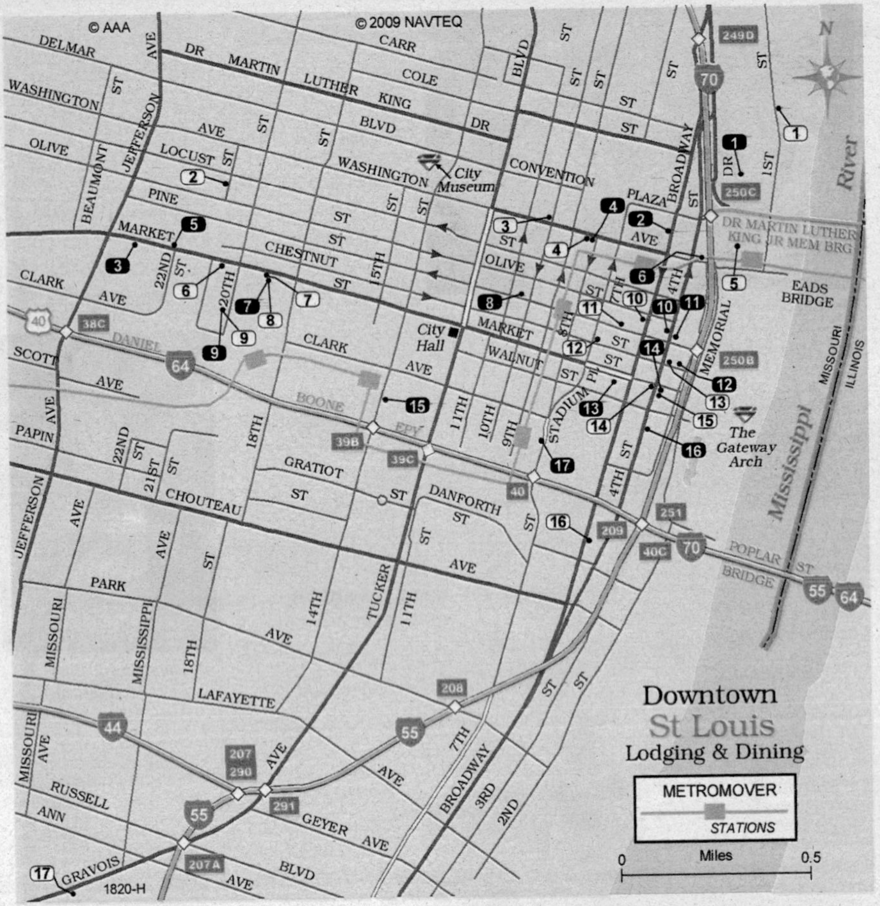

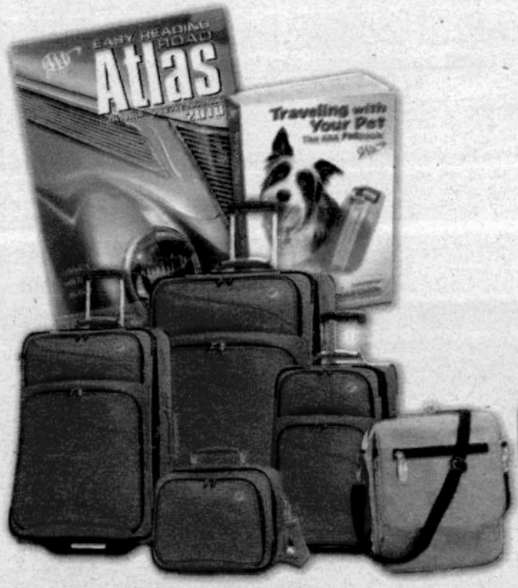

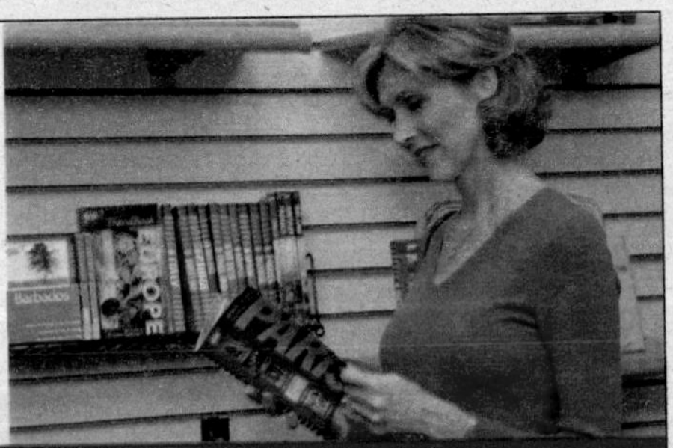

Downtown St Louis Lodging & Dining

METROMOVER
STATIONS

Miles 0 0.5

© AAA © 2009 NAVTEQ

Downtown St. Louis

This index helps you "spot" where approved lodgings and restaurants are located on the corresponding detailed maps. Lodging daily rate range is for comparison only and show the property's high season. Restaurant rate range is a combination of lunch and/or dinner. Turn to the listing page for more detailed rate information and consult display ads for special promotions.

DOWNTOWN ST. LOUIS

Map Page	OA	Lodgings	Diamond Rated	High Season	Page
1 / p. 524	AAA	**Four Seasons Hotel St. Louis**	◆◆◆◆◆	$195-$3000 SAVE	540
2 / p. 524		Drury Inn & Suites-St. Louis-Convention Center	◆◆◆	$90-$204	538
3 / p. 524	AAA	**Courtyard by Marriott Downtown**	◆◆◆	$149-$169 SAVE	538
4 / p. 524	AAA	**Renaissance Grand & Suites Hotel St. Louis** - see color ad p 542	◆◆◆◆	$159-$199 SAVE	541
5 / p. 524		Pear Tree Inn - St. Louis/Union Station	◆◆◆	$85-$159	541
6 / p. 524	AAA	**Hampton Inn-Gateway Arch**	◆◆◆	$89-$199 SAVE	540
7 / p. 524	AAA	**St. Louis Union Station Marriott** - see color ad p 543	◆◆◆◆	$189-$199 SAVE	543
8 / p. 524		Omni Majestic Hotel	◆◆◆	$179-$349	541
9 / p. 524		Drury Inn-St. Louis/Union Station	◆◆◆	$100-$189	540
10 / p. 524		Hilton-St. Louis Downtown	◆◆◆	$99-$189	540
11 / p. 524	AAA	**Crowne Plaza St. Louis Downtown**	◆◆◆	$169-$189 SAVE	538
12 / p. 524	AAA	**Hyatt Regency St. Louis Riverfront**	◆◆◆	$79-$349 SAVE	541
13 / p. 524	AAA	**Hilton St. Louis at the Ballpark**	◆◆◆	$109-$259 SAVE	540
14 / p. 524	AAA	**Drury Plaza Hotel-St. Louis At the Arch**	◆◆◆	$105-$289 SAVE	540
15 / p. 524	AAA	**Sheraton St. Louis City Center Hotel & Suites**	◆◆◆	$109-$429 SAVE	543
16 / p. 524	AAA	**Millennium Hotel St. Louis** - see color ad p 538	◆◆	$99-$299 SAVE	541
17 / p. 524	AAA	**The Westin St. Louis**	◆◆◆◆	$119-$399 SAVE	544

Map Page	OA	Restaurants	Diamond Rated	Cuisine	Meal Range	Page
1 / p. 524		Al's Restaurant	◆◆◆	American	$28-$80	544
2 / p. 524		St. Louis Brewery Tap Room	◆	American	$7-$15	545
3 / p. 524		Mosaic Modern Fusion	◆◆◆	Fusion	$7-$16	545
4 / p. 524		An American Place	◆◆◆◆	American	$18-$38	544
5 / p. 524		Hannegan's	◆◆	American	$8-$23	544
6 / p. 524		Harry's Restaurant & Bar	◆◆◆	Continental	$10-$27	545
7 / p. 524		Hard Rock Cafe	◆◆	American	$8-$27 SAVE	545
8 / p. 524		Station Grille	◆◆◆	American	$11-$40	545
9 / p. 524	AAA	**Lombardo's Trattoria**	◆◆◆	Italian	$8-$25	545
10 / p. 524		Kemoll's Italian Restaurant	◆◆◆	Italian	$17-$44	545
11 / p. 524		Charlie Gitto's Downtown	◆◆	Italian	$16-$42	544
12 / p. 524	AAA	**Mike Shannon's Steaks & Seafood**	◆◆◆	Steak	$9-$50	545
13 / p. 524		Red Bar & Kitchen	◆◆◆	American	$7-$22	545
14 / p. 524	AAA	**Tony's**	◆◆◆◆	Italian	$20-$40	546
15 / p. 524	AAA	**Carmine's Steak House**	◆◆◆	Steak	$19-$55	544
16 / p. 524		Broadway Oyster Bar	◆	Traditional Cajun	$8-$16	544
17 / p. 524		Hodak's Restaurant & Bar	◆◆	American	$5-$14	545

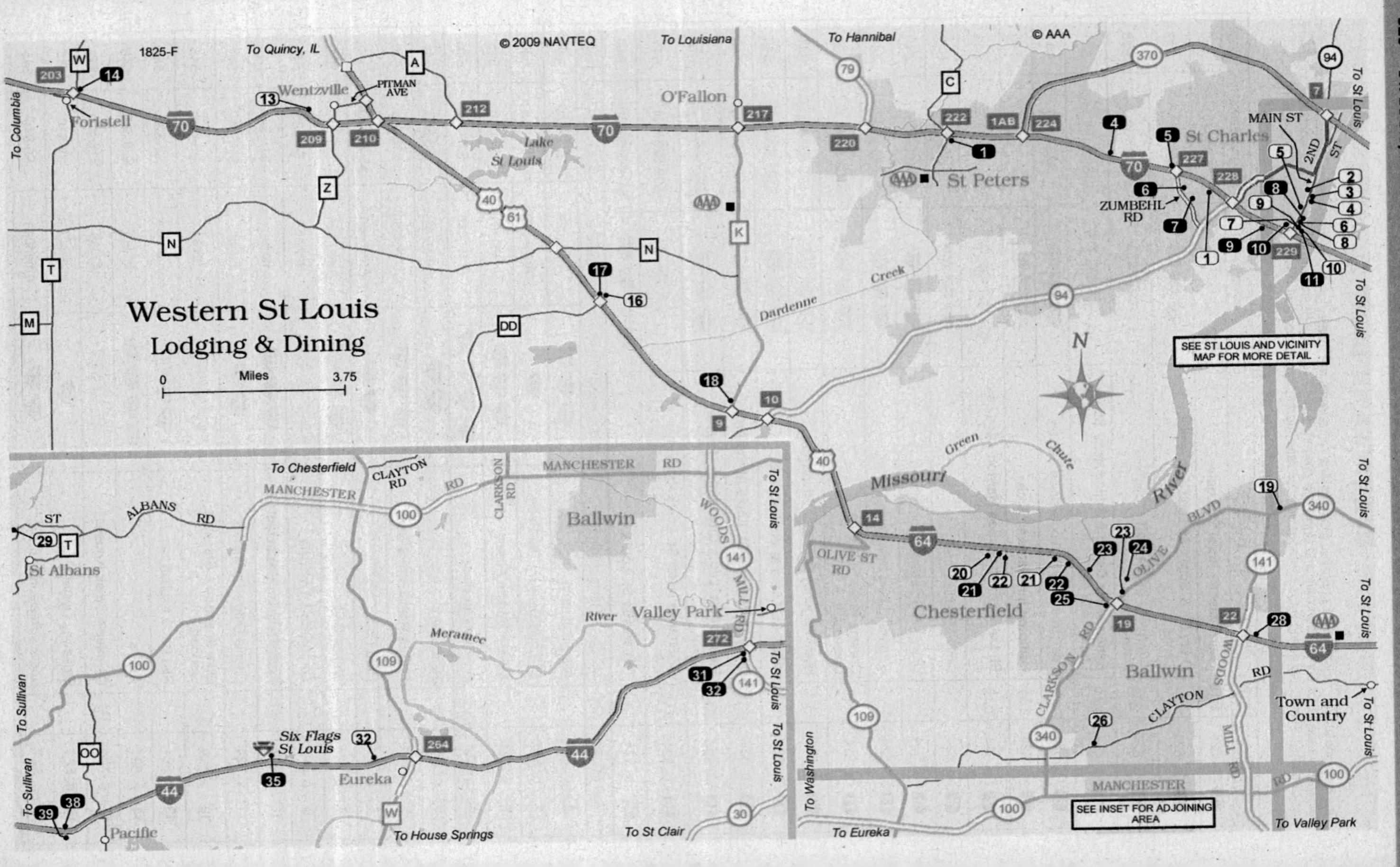
Western St Louis
Lodging & Dining
Miles
0
3.75
1825-F
© 2009 NAVTEQ
© AAA
SEE ST LOUIS AND VICINITY MAP FOR MORE DETAIL
SEE INSET FOR ADJOINING AREA
To Columbia
To Quincy, IL
To Louisiana
To Hannibal
To St Louis
To Chesterfield
To Sullivan
To House Springs
To St Clair
To Washington
To Eureka
To Valley Park
Foristell
Wentzville
PITMAN AVE
O'Fallon
St Peters
St Charles
MAIN ST
2ND ST
ZUMBEHL RD
Lake St Louis
Dardenne Creek
Missouri River
Green Chute
OLIVE ST RD
OLIVE BLVD
Chesterfield
Ballwin
CLARKSON RD
CLAYTON RD
WOODS MILL RD
MANCHESTER RD
Town and Country
ST ALBANS RD
St Albans
Valley Park
Meramec River
Six Flags St Louis
Eureka
Pacific

St. Louis Western Area

This index helps you "spot" where approved lodgings and restaurants are located on the corresponding detailed maps. Lodging daily rate range is for comparison only and show the property's high season. Restaurant rate range is a combination of lunch and/or dinner. Turn to the listing page for more detailed rate information and consult display ads for special promotions.

ST. PETERS

Map Page	OA	Lodging	Diamond Rated	High Season	Page
1 / p. 526		Drury Inn St. Peters	◆◆	$85-$169	569

ST. CHARLES

Map Page	OA	Lodgings	Diamond Rated	High Season	Page
4 / p. 526	AAA	**Hampton Inn-St Charles**	◆◆◆	$69-$129 SAVE	567
5 / p. 526		Super 8	◆	$69-$99	567
6 / p. 526		Red Roof Inn	◆◆	$40-$77	567
7 / p. 526		TownePlace Suites by Marriott	◆◆	$80-$98	568
8 / p. 526	AAA	**Country Inn & Suites By Carlson**	◆◆◆	$120-$152 SAVE	567
9 / p. 526	AAA	**Embassy Suites St. Louis-St. Charles**	◆◆◆	$109-$199 SAVE	567
10 / p. 526		Comfort Suites-St. Charles	◆◆◆	Rates not provided	567
11 / p. 526	AAA	**Ameristar St. Charles Casino Resort & Spa**	◆◆◆◆	$119-$699 SAVE	567

Map Page	OA	Restaurants	Diamond Rated	Cuisine	Meal Range	Page
1 / p. 526		Mr. Steak	◆◆	American	$8-$25	568
2 / p. 526		Lewis and Clark's An American Restaurant & Public House	◆◆	American	$7-$20	568
3 / p. 526		Trailhead Brewing Company	◆◆	American	$8-$20	569
4 / p. 526	AAA	**The New Mother-in-Law House Restaurant**	◆◆	American	$7-$20	568
5 / p. 526		Magpie's	◆◆	American	$6-$22	568
6 / p. 526		The Landmark Buffet	◆◆	American	$9-$18	568
7 / p. 526		Pearl's Oyster Bar	◆◆	Creole	$7-$34	569
8 / p. 526		The Falcon Diner	◆◆	American	$7-$25	568
9 / p. 526		Amerisports Bar & Grill	◆◆	American	$7-$20	568
10 / p. 526		47 Port Street Grill	◆◆◆	American	$15-$25	568

FORISTELL

Map Page	OA	Lodging	Diamond Rated	High Season	Page
14 / p. 526	AAA	**Best Western West 70 Inn**	◆◆	$67-$72 SAVE	560

O'FALLON

Map Page	OA	Lodgings	Diamond Rated	High Season	Page
17 / p. 526		Hilton Garden Inn St. Louis/O'Fallon	◆◆◆	$79-$169	565
18 / p. 526		Staybridge Suites O'Fallon	◆◆◆	$91-$137	565

Map Page	OA	Restaurant	Diamond Rated	Cuisine	Meal Range	Page
16 / p. 526		J. Buck's Restaurant	◆◆◆	American	$8-$26	566

CHESTERFIELD

Map Page	OA	Lodgings	Diamond Rated	High Season	Page
21 / p. 526		Hampton Inn & Suites-Chesterfield	◆◆◆	$89-$99	554
22 / p. 526	AAA	**Hilton Garden Inn**	◆◆◆	$75-$149 SAVE	554
23 / p. 526		Doubletree Hotel & Conference Center St. Louis	◆◆◆	$79-$159	554
24 / p. 526		Homewood Suites by Hilton	◆◆◆	$89-$149	554

CHESTERFIELD (cont'd)

Map Page	OA	Lodgings (cont'd)	Diamond Rated	High Season	Page
25 / p. 526		Drury Plaza Hotel-Chesterfield	◆◆◆	$90-$299	554

Map Page	OA	Restaurants	Diamond Rated	Cuisine	Meal Range	Page
19 / p. 526		El Maguey	◆◆	Mexican	$5-$14	555
20 / p. 526		Villa Farotto Vineyards	◆◆◆	Italian	$8-$33	555
21 / p. 526		Annie Gunn's	◆◆◆	Regional American	$8-$38	555
22 / p. 526		East Coast Pizza	◆	American	$6-$10	555
23 / p. 526		Yia Yia's Euro Bistro	◆◆◆	Northern Continental	$9-$25	555

TOWN AND COUNTRY

Map Page	OA	Lodging	Diamond Rated	High Season	Page
28 / p. 526		Courtyard by Marriott St. Louis/Maryville	◆◆◆	$125-$139	569

VALLEY PARK

Map Page	OA	Lodgings	Diamond Rated	High Season	Page
31 / p. 526		Hampton Inn-St. Louis Southwest	◆◆◆	$94-$124	570
32 / p. 526		Drury Inn & Suites-St. Louis Southwest	◆◆◆	$80-$179	570

EUREKA

Map Page	OA	Lodging	Diamond Rated	High Season	Page
35 / p. 526		Holiday Inn at Six Flags	◆◆◆	$129-$299	559

Map Page	OA	Restaurant	Diamond Rated	Cuisine	Meal Range	Page
32 / p. 526		Poor Richard's	◆◆	American	$6-$15	559

PACIFIC

Map Page	OA	Lodgings	Diamond Rated	High Season	Page
38 / p. 526	AAA	**Comfort Inn**	◆◆◆	$79-$119 SAVE	514
39 / p. 526	AAA	**Quality Inn Near Six Flags**	◆	$69-$109 SAVE	515

WENTZVILLE

Map Page	OA	Restaurant	Diamond Rated	Cuisine	Meal Range	Page
13 / p. 526		Stefanina's	◆◆	Italian	$5-$15	571

BALLWIN

Map Page	OA	Restaurant	Diamond Rated	Cuisine	Meal Range	Page
26 / p. 526		Charlotte's Rib BBQ	◆◆	American	$6-$15	552

ST. ALBANS

Map Page	OA	Restaurant	Diamond Rated	Cuisine	Meal Range	Page
29 / p. 526		The Gardens at Malmaison	◆◆◆	Traditional French	$17-$28	518

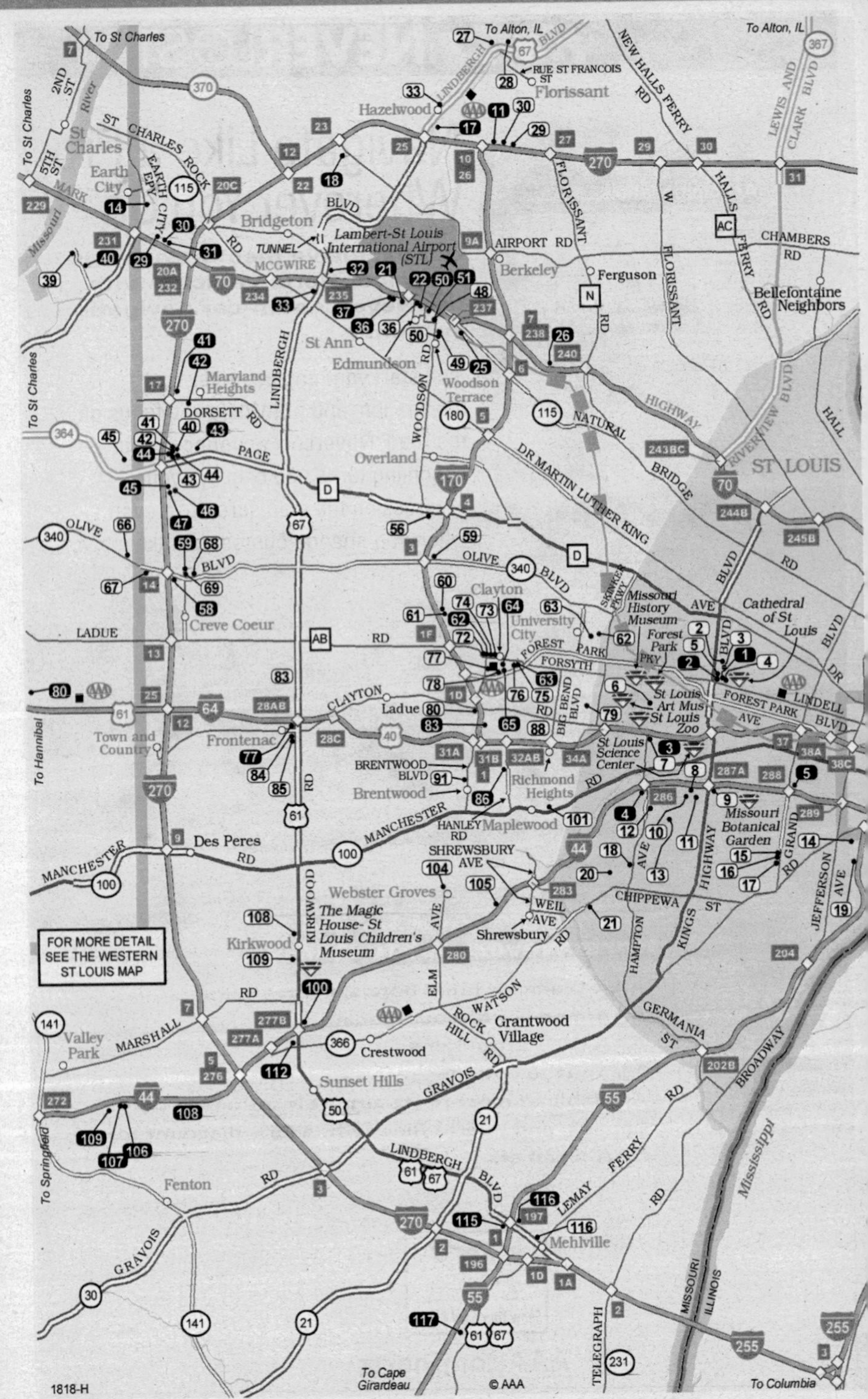

To St Charles
To Alton, IL
To Alton, IL
LINDBERGH BLVD
RUE ST FRANCOIS ST
Florissant
NEW HALLS FERRY RD
LEWIS AND CLARK BLVD
2ND ST
5TH ST
St Charles
ST CHARLES ROCK
Hazelwood
Earth City
EARTH CITY EPY
MARK
Missouri
River
Bridgeton
BLVD
RD
TUNNEL
Lambert-St Louis International Airport (STL)
MCGWIRE
AIRPORT RD
Berkeley
FLORISSANT
W FLORISSANT
Ferguson
HALLS FERRY RD
CHAMBERS RD
Bellefontaine Neighbors
St Ann
Edmundson
WOODSON RD
Woodson Terrace
LINDBERGH
Maryland Heights
DORSETT RD
To St Charles
PAGE
Overland
NATURAL BRIDGE
HIGHWAY
RIVERVIEW BLVD
HALL
ST LOUIS
DR MARTIN LUTHER KING
OLIVE
BLVD
OLIVE BLVD
Clayton
University City
SKINKER PKWY
Missouri History Museum
AVE
BLVD
Cathedral of St Louis
BLVD
DR
Creve Coeur
LADUE
RD
FOREST PARK
FORSYTH
Forest Park
PKY
BIG BEND BLVD
St Louis Art Mus
St Louis Zoo
FOREST PARK AVE
LINDELL BLVD
To Hannibal
CLAYTON
Ladue
RD
Town and Country
Frontenac
St Louis Science Center
BRENTWOOD BLVD
Brentwood
Richmond Heights
RD
HANLEY RD
Maplewood
MANCHESTER
Missouri Botanical Garden
Des Peres
RD
MANCHESTER
SHREWSBURY AVE
AVE
GRAND
RD
HIGHWAY
KINGS
JEFFERSON
AVE
Webster Groves
WEIL AVE
CHIPPEWA ST
Shrewsbury
RD
HAMPTON
The Magic House- St Louis Children's Museum
KIRKWOOD RD
Kirkwood
ELM AVE
FOR MORE DETAIL SEE THE WESTERN ST LOUIS MAP
WATSON
ROCK HILL RD
Grantwood Village
GERMANIA ST
RD
Valley Park
MARSHALL
Crestwood
Sunset Hills
GRAVOIS
BROADWAY
Mississippi
RD
FERRY
LEMAY
RD
To Springfield
Fenton
RD
LINDBERGH BLVD
Mehlville
GRAVOIS
MISSOURI
ILLINOIS
TELEGRAPH
To Cape Girardeau
© AAA
To Columbia
1818-H

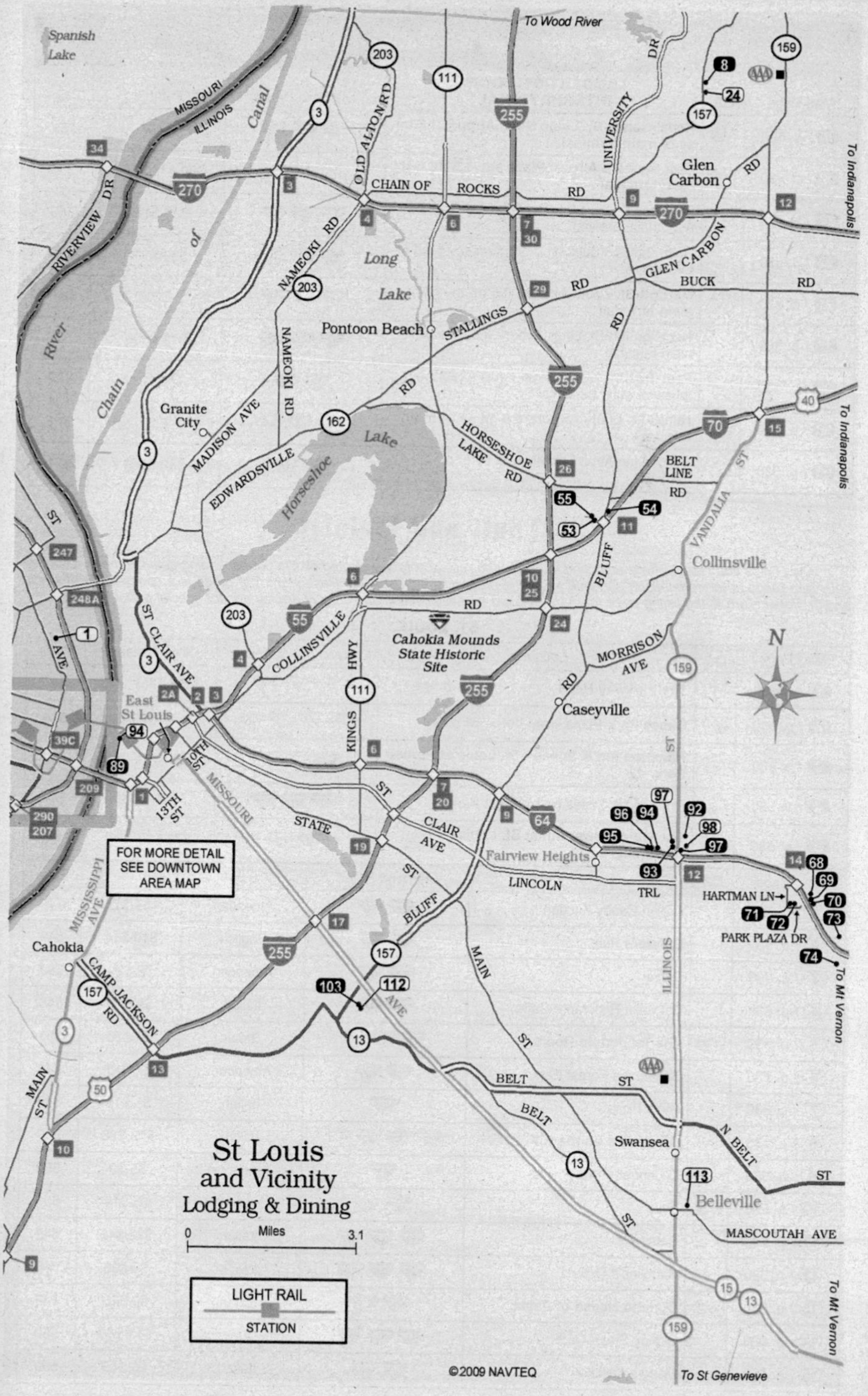
St Louis
and Vicinity
Lodging & Dining
0 Miles 3.1
LIGHT RAIL
STATION
FOR MORE DETAIL SEE DOWNTOWN AREA MAP
To Wood River
To Indianapolis
To Indianapolis
To Mt Vernon
To Mt Vernon
To St Genevieve
Spanish Lake
Granite City
Pontoon Beach
Glen Carbon
Collinsville
Caseyville
Fairview Heights
East St Louis
Cahokia
Swansea
Belleville
Cahokia Mounds State Historic Site
Long Lake
Horseshoe Lake
Chain of Rocks Rd
Glen Carbon Rd
Buck Rd
Stallings Rd
Horseshoe Lake Rd
Belt Line Rd
Collinsville Rd
Morrison Ave
St Clair Ave
State St
Lincoln Trl
Hartman Ln
Park Plaza Dr
Mascoutah Ave
N Belt St
©2009 NAVTEQ

Airport Accommodations

Map Page	OA	LAMBERT-ST. LOUIS INTERNATIONAL	Diamond Rated	High Season	Page
25 / p. 530		**Renaissance St. Louis Hotel Airport, 1.5 mi se of main terminal**	♦♦♦	$161-$197 SAVE	552
32 / p. 530		**Best Western Airport Plaza Inn, 1.5 mi from main terminal**	♦♦	$80-$120 SAVE	553
33 / p. 530		Embassy Suites St. Louis Airport, 1.5 mi sw from main terminal	♦♦♦	$89-$179	553
22 / p. 530		Drury Inn-St. Louis Airport, 0.5 mi se of main terminal	♦♦♦	$80-$194	558
21 / p. 530		**Marriott-St. Louis Airport, 0.5 mi sw from main terminal**	♦♦♦	$170-$208 SAVE	558
37 / p. 530		Hampton Inn-St. Louis Airport, 0.5 mi sw of main terminal	♦♦♦	$79-$159	566
36 / p. 530		Pear Tree Inn by Drury-St. Louis Airport, 0.5 mi sw of main terminal	♦♦	$70-$139	566
50 / p. 530		**Hilton St. Louis Airport, 0.8 mi se of main terminal**	♦♦♦	$79-$209 SAVE	571
51 / p. 530		Holiday Inn Airport Hotel, 1 mi se of main terminal	♦♦	$89-$169	571

St. Louis and Vicinity

This index helps you "spot" where approved lodgings and restaurants are located on the corresponding detailed maps. Lodging daily rate range is for comparison only and show the property's high season. Restaurant rate range is a combination of lunch and/or dinner. Turn to the listing page for more detailed rate information and consult display ads for special promotions.

ST. LOUIS

Map Page	OA	Lodgings	Diamond Rated	High Season	Page
1 / p. 530		**The Parkway Hotel** - see color ad p 548	♦♦♦	$117-$269 SAVE	547
2 / p. 530		**Chase Park Plaza** - see color ad p 546	♦♦♦♦	$229-$479 SAVE	546
3 / p. 530		**Hampton Inn & Suites - St. Louis at Forest Park**	♦♦♦	$89-$169 SAVE	547
4 / p. 530		Drury Inn & Suites Near Forest Park	♦♦♦	$95-$229	547
5 / p. 530		**The Water Tower Inn at St. Louis University**	♦♦	$75-$89 SAVE	548

Map Page	OA	Restaurants	Diamond Rated	Cuisine	Meal Range	Page
1 / p. 530		Crown Candy Kitchen	♦♦	American	$4-$7	549
2 / p. 530		Dressel's Pub	♦♦	English	$10-$14	549
3 / p. 530		Duff's	♦♦	American	$8-$20	549
4 / p. 530		Bar Italia Ristorante-Caffe	♦♦	Italian	$9-$25	548
5 / p. 530		**The Tenderloin Room**	♦♦♦	Steak	$8-$36	551
6 / p. 530		Boathouse Forest Park	♦♦	American	$7-$15	548
7 / p. 530		Imo's Pizza	♦	Italian	$5-$15	549
8 / p. 530		**Giovanni's on the Hill**	♦♦♦♦	Italian	$17-$38	549
9 / p. 530		O'Connell's Pub	♦	American	$5-$9	550
10 / p. 530		**Zia's**	♦♦	Italian	$6-$19	551
11 / p. 530		Dominic's	♦♦♦	Italian	$22-$42	549
12 / p. 530		Bartolino's Osteria	♦♦♦	Italian	$9-$36	548
13 / p. 530		**Cunetto House of Pasta**	♦♦	Italian	$8-$20	549
14 / p. 530		Sidney Street Cafe	♦♦♦	New American	$18-$30	550
15 / p. 530		Mangia Italiano	♦♦	Italian	$6-$16	550

Map Page	OA	Restaurants (cont'd)	Diamond Rated	Cuisine	Meal Range	Page
16 / p. 530		King & I Restaurant	◆◆	Thai	$9-$17	550
17 / p. 530		Pho Grand Vietnamese Restaurant	◆◆	Vietnamese	$7-$11	550
18 / p. 530		Brazie's Ristorante	◆◆	Southern Italian	$6-$29	549
19 / p. 530		Frazer's	◆◆	American	$8-$24	549
20 / p. 530		Trattoria Marcella	◆◆◆	Italian	$11-$19	551
21 / p. 530		Ted Drewe's Frozen Custard	◆	American	$1-$8	551

EDWARDSVILLE, IL

Map Page	OA	Lodging	Diamond Rated	High Season	Page
8 / p. 530	AAA	**Country Hearth Inn & Suites**	◆◆◆	$100-$140 SAVE	573

Map Page	OA	Restaurant	Diamond Rated	Cuisine	Meal Range	Page
24 / p. 530		Bull & Bear Grill & Bar	◆◆	American	$8-$17	573

FLORISSANT

Map Page	OA	Lodging	Diamond Rated	High Season	Page
11 / p. 530	AAA	**Hampton Inn-St. Louis Northwest**	◆◆◆	$79-$129 SAVE	560

Map Page	OA	Restaurants	Diamond Rated	Cuisine	Meal Range	Page
27 / p. 530		Fresh Italy	◆◆	Italian	$8-$15	560
28 / p. 530		Ruiz Mexican Restaurant	◆◆	Mexican	$7-$18	560
29 / p. 530	AAA	**Yacovelli's Restaurant**	◆◆	Italian	$11-$20	560
30 / p. 530		The Barn Deli	◆	Deli	$5-$8	560

EARTH CITY

Map Page	OA	Lodging	Diamond Rated	High Season	Page
14 / p. 530		Residence Inn St. Louis Airport/Earth City	◆◆◆	$144-$164	558

HAZELWOOD

Map Page	OA	Lodgings	Diamond Rated	High Season	Page
17 / p. 530		La Quinta Inn Hazelwood	◆◆	Rates not provided	561
18 / p. 530		La Quinta Inn St. Louis (Airport)	◆◆	Rates not provided	561

Map Page	OA	Restaurant	Diamond Rated	Cuisine	Meal Range	Page
33 / p. 530		Village China Wok	◆	Chinese	$5-$10	561

EDMUNDSON

Map Page	OA	Lodgings	Diamond Rated	High Season	Page
21 / p. 530	AAA	**Marriott-St. Louis Airport** - see color ad p 547	◆◆◆	$170-$208 SAVE	558
22 / p. 530		Drury Inn-St. Louis Airport	◆◆◆	$80-$194	558

Map Page	OA	Restaurant	Diamond Rated	Cuisine	Meal Range	Page
36 / p. 530		Lombardo's Restaurant	◆◆◆	Italian	$7-$20	559

BERKELEY

Map Page	OA	Lodgings	Diamond Rated	High Season	Page
25 / p. 530	AAA	**Renaissance St. Louis Hotel Airport**	◆◆◆	$161-$197 SAVE	552
26 / p. 530	AAA	**Hilton Garden Inn St. Louis Airport**	◆◆◆	$79-$189 SAVE	552

BRIDGETON

Map Page	OA	Lodgings	Diamond Rated	High Season	Page
29 / p. 530		StudioPlus-St Louis-Earth City	◆◆	$59-$74	554
30 / p. 530	AAA	**Courtyard by Marriott - Airport/Earth City**	◆◆◆	$119-$139 SAVE	553

BRIDGETON (cont'd)

Map Page	OA	Lodgings (cont'd)	Diamond Rated	High Season	Page
31 / p. 530	AAA	**SpringHill Suites by Marriott - St. Louis Airport/Earth City**	♦♦♦	$114-$129 SAVE	553
32 / p. 530	AAA	**Best Western Airport Plaza Inn**	♦♦	$80-$120 SAVE	553
33 / p. 530		Embassy Suites St. Louis Airport	♦♦♦	$89-$179	553

ST. ANN

Map Page	OA	Lodgings	Diamond Rated	High Season	Page
36 / p. 530		Pear Tree Inn by Drury-St. Louis Airport	♦♦	$70-$139	566
37 / p. 530		Hampton Inn-St. Louis Airport	♦♦♦	$79-$159	566

MARYLAND HEIGHTS

Map Page	OA	Lodgings	Diamond Rated	High Season	Page
40 / p. 530	AAA	**Harrah's Casino & Hotel**	♦♦♦	$79-$399 SAVE	563
41 / p. 530		Hampton Inn St. Louis/Westport - see color ad p 563	♦♦	$69-$144	563
42 / p. 530		Drury Inn & Suites-St. Louis-Westport	♦♦	$75-$159	563
43 / p. 530		Courtyard by Marriott-Westport	♦♦♦	$119-$139	562
44 / p. 530	AAA	**Sheraton Westport Plaza Tower**	♦♦♦	Rates not provided SAVE	564
45 / p. 530	AAA	**Doubletree Hotel St. Louis at Westport**	♦♦♦	$85-$189 SAVE	562
46 / p. 530		Staybridge Suites	♦♦♦	$79-$189	564
47 / p. 530		Residence Inn by Marriott - Westport	♦♦♦	$152-$186	564

Map Page	OA	Restaurants	Diamond Rated	Cuisine	Meal Range	Page
39 / p. 530		Eat UP! Buffet	♦♦	American	$9-$24	564
40 / p. 530		Pujols 5 Westport Grill	♦♦	American	$7-$18	565
41 / p. 530		Dierdorf & Harts Steakhouse	♦♦♦	Eastern Steak	$18-$43	564
42 / p. 530		Trainwreck Saloon Westport	♦♦	American	$7-$15	565
43 / p. 530		Ozzie's Restaurant & Sports Bar	♦♦	American	$6-$22	564
44 / p. 530		The Drunken Fish Sushi Bar and Lounge	♦♦	Japanese	$9-$24	564
45 / p. 530		Balducci's Winefest Restaurant & Bar	♦♦	Italian	$5-$11	564

WOODSON TERRACE

Map Page	OA	Lodgings	Diamond Rated	High Season	Page
50 / p. 530	AAA	**Hilton St. Louis Airport**	♦♦♦	$79-$209 SAVE	571
51 / p. 530		Holiday Inn Airport Hotel	♦♦	$89-$169	571

Map Page	OA	Restaurants	Diamond Rated	Cuisine	Meal Range	Page
48 / p. 530		Oakland Park Restaurant	♦♦	American	$7-$24	571
49 / p. 530		Erio's Restaurant	♦	Italian	$5-$10	571
50 / p. 530		Yesterday's	♦	American	$4-$16	571

COLLINSVILLE, IL

Map Page	OA	Lodgings	Diamond Rated	High Season	Page
54 / p. 530		Drury Inn-St. Louis/Collinsville	♦♦	$85-$159	572
55 / p. 530		Super 8-Collinsville	♦	$60-$90	572

Map Page	OA	Restaurant	Diamond Rated	Cuisine	Meal Range	Page
53 / p. 530		Zapata's Mexican Restaurant & Cantina	♦♦	Mexican	$6-$15	573

CREVE COEUR

Map Page	OA	Lodgings	Diamond Rated	High Season	Page
58 / p. 530		Drury Inn & Suites-Creve Coeur	◆◆◆	$90-$174	557
59 / p. 530		Courtyard by Marriott-Creve Coeur	◆◆◆	$139-$149	557

Map Page	OA	Restaurants	Diamond Rated	Cuisine	Meal Range	Page
66 / p. 530		Kobe Steak House of Japan	◆◆◆	Japanese	$6-$27	557
67 / p. 530		La Bonne Bouchee Westgate Center	◆◆	French	$8-$15	557
68 / p. 530		Il Bellagio City Place	◆◆◆	Italian	$10-$36	557
69 / p. 530		Bristol Bar & Seafood Grill	◆◆◆	Seafood	$10-$30	557

CLAYTON

Map Page	OA	Lodgings	Diamond Rated	High Season	Page
62 / p. 530	AAA	**Seven Gables Inn**	◆◆◆	Rates not provided SAVE	556
63 / p. 530	AAA	**The Ritz-Carlton, St. Louis**	◆◆◆◆	$159-$525 SAVE	555
64 / p. 530	AAA	**Crowne Plaza St. Louis-Clayton**	◆◆◆	$99-$299 SAVE	555
65 / p. 530	AAA	**Sheraton Clayton Plaza Hotel**	◆◆◆	Rates not provided SAVE	556

Map Page	OA	Restaurants	Diamond Rated	Cuisine	Meal Range	Page
72 / p. 530		Cardwell's in Clayton	◆◆◆	American	$6-$25	556
73 / p. 530		BARcelona Tapas Restaurant	◆◆◆	Spanish	$10-$15	556
74 / p. 530		Portabella	◆◆◆	Italian	$8-$27	556
75 / p. 530	AAA	**The Grill**	◆◆◆◆	American	$16-$40	556
76 / p. 530		Luciano's Trattoria	◆◆◆	Italian	$8-$40	556
77 / p. 530		Dominic's Trattoria	◆◆◆	Italian	$9-$25	556
78 / p. 530		Remy's Kitchen & Wine Bar	◆◆◆	Regional Continental	$6-$20	557
79 / p. 530		Jimmy's On the Park Cafe Bistro & Bar	◆◆◆	American	$9-$30	556
80 / p. 530		Yen Ching	◆◆	Chinese	$7-$16	557

O'FALLON, IL

Map Page	OA	Lodgings	Diamond Rated	High Season	Page
68 / p. 530		Country Inn & Suites By Carlson	◆◆	$75-$110	575
69 / p. 530		Extended StayAmerica-St. Louis-O'Fallon	◆◆	$79-$89	575
70 / p. 530		Suburban Extended Stay Hotel	◆◆	Rates not provided	576
71 / p. 530		Days Inn O'Fallon	◆◆	$50-$69	575
72 / p. 530		Candlewood Suites	◆◆◆	$84-$139	575
73 / p. 530		Hilton Garden Inn Green Mount/O'Fallon	◆◆◆	$89-$159	575
74 / p. 530		Drury Inn & Suites-O'Fallon	◆◆◆	$90-$184	575

FRONTENAC

Map Page	OA	Lodging	Diamond Rated	High Season	Page
77 / p. 530		Hilton St. Louis Frontenac	◆◆◆	$99-$289	561

Map Page	OA	Restaurants	Diamond Rated	Cuisine	Meal Range	Page
83 / p. 530	AAA	**Kreis Restaurant**	◆◆◆	Steak	$25-$64	561
84 / p. 530		Brio Tuscan Grille	◆◆◆	Regional Italian	$12-$30	561
85 / p. 530		Canyon Cafe	◆◆◆	Southwestern	$7-$22	561

TOWN AND COUNTRY

Map Page	OA	Lodging	Diamond Rated	High Season	Page
80 / p. 530	AAA	**St. Louis Marriott West** - see color ad p 537	◆◆◆	$170-$208 SAVE	569

RICHMOND HEIGHTS

Map Page	OA	Lodging	Diamond Rated	High Season	Page
83 / p. 530		Residence Inn By Marriott-St. Louis Galleria	◆◆◆	$139-$159	566

Map Page	OA	Restaurant	Diamond Rated	Cuisine	Meal Range	Page
88 / p. 530		Harvest	◆◆◆	New American	$18-$28	566

BRENTWOOD

Map Page	OA	Lodging	Diamond Rated	High Season	Page
86 / p. 530		SpringHill Suites by Marriott	◆◆◆	$149-$169	552

Map Page	OA	Restaurant	Diamond Rated	Cuisine	Meal Range	Page
91 / p. 530		Frank Papa's Ristorante	◆◆◆	Italian	$12-$25	552

EAST ST. LOUIS, IL

Map Page	OA	Lodging	Diamond Rated	High Season	Page
89 / p. 530	AAA	**Casino Queen Hotel**	◆◆◆	$110-$130 SAVE	573

Map Page	OA	Restaurant	Diamond Rated	Cuisine	Meal Range	Page
94 / p. 530	AAA	**Prime Steakhouse**	◆◆◆	American	$15-$35	573

FAIRVIEW HEIGHTS, IL

Map Page	OA	Lodgings	Diamond Rated	High Season	Page
92 / p. 530	AAA	**Four Points by Sheraton**	◆◆◆	Rates not provided SAVE	574
93 / p. 530		Drury Inn & Suites-Fairview Heights	◆◆◆	$85-$164	574
94 / p. 530		Comfort Suites	◆◆◆	$89-$99	574
95 / p. 530		Hampton Inn by Hilton	◆◆◆	$94-$119	574
96 / p. 530		Fairfield Inn by Marriott	◆◆	$90-$100	574
97 / p. 530	AAA	**Ramada Inn Fairview Heights**	◆◆	$67-$81 SAVE	574

Map Page	OA	Restaurants	Diamond Rated	Cuisine	Meal Range	Page
97 / p. 530		Houlihan's	◆◆◆	American	$7-$22	574
98 / p. 530		Lotawata Creek Southern Grill	◆◆	Regional American	$10-$23	575

KIRKWOOD

Map Page	OA	Lodging	Diamond Rated	High Season	Page
100 / p. 530	AAA	**Best Western Kirkwood Inn**	◆◆	$100-$120 SAVE	562

Map Page	OA	Restaurants	Diamond Rated	Cuisine	Meal Range	Page
108 / p. 530		Sunset 44	◆◆◆	American	$8-$32	562
109 / p. 530	AAA	**Citizen Kane's**	◆◆◆	American	$18-$33	562

BELLEVILLE, IL

Map Page	OA	Lodging	Diamond Rated	High Season	Page
103 / p. 530	AAA	**The Shrine Hotel** - see color ad p 222	◆◆	$70-$85 SAVE	572

Map Page	OA	Restaurants	Diamond Rated	Cuisine	Meal Range	Page
112 / p. 530	AAA	**The Shrine Restaurant** - see color ad p 222	◆◆	American	$6-$14	572
113 / p. 530		The Pie Pantry	◆	American	$5-$12	572

FENTON

Map Page	OA	Lodgings	Diamond Rated	High Season	Page
106 / p. 530		Drury Inn & Suites-Fenton	◆◆◆	$80-$170	559

FENTON (cont'd)

Map Page	OA	Lodgings (cont'd)	Diamond Rated	High Season	Page
107 / p. 530		Pear Tree Inn by Drury-Fenton	◆◆	$55-$119	559
108 / p. 530		TownePlace Suites by Marriott	◆◆	$107-$131	559
109 / p. 530		Holiday Inn Express Hotel & Suites	◆◆◆	$76-$129	559

SUNSET HILLS

Map Page	OA	Lodging	Diamond Rated	High Season	Page
112 / p. 530	AAA	**Holiday Inn-Southwest & Viking Conference Center**	◆◆◆	$99-$139 SAVE	569

MEHLVILLE

Map Page	OA	Lodgings	Diamond Rated	High Season	Page
115 / p. 530	AAA	**Americas Best Value Inn**	◆◆	$50-$70 SAVE	565
116 / p. 530		Holiday Inn South County Center	◆◆◆	$116-$156	565
117 / p. 530		Holiday Inn St. Louis-South I-55	◆◆◆	$84-$139	565

Map Page	OA	Restaurant	Diamond Rated	Cuisine	Meal Range	Page
116 / p. 530		Gingham's Homestyle Restaurant	◆	American	$4-$11	565

OVERLAND

Map Page	OA	Restaurant	Diamond Rated	Cuisine	Meal Range	Page
56 / p. 530		Mandarin House Restaurant	◆◆	Chinese	$6-$17	566

UNIVERSITY CITY

Map Page	OA	Restaurants	Diamond Rated	Cuisine	Meal Range	Page
59 / p. 530		Nobu's Japanese Restaurant	◆◆	Japanese	$7-$22	570
60 / p. 530		House of India	◆◆	Indian	$8-$14	570
61 / p. 530		Mai Lee Restaurant	◆◆	Asian	$5-$11	570
62 / p. 530		Seki Fine Japanese Cuisine & Sushi Bar	◆◆	Japanese	$6-$25	570
63 / p. 530	AAA	**Blueberry Hill**	◆◆	American	$6-$12	570

MAPLEWOOD

Map Page	OA	Restaurant	Diamond Rated	Cuisine	Meal Range	Page
101 / p. 530		Monarch Restaurant	◆◆◆	International	$19-$33	562

WEBSTER GROVES

Map Page	OA	Restaurants	Diamond Rated	Cuisine	Meal Range	Page
104 / p. 530		Llywelyn's Pub	◆◆	Irish	$8-$15	571
105 / p. 530		Big Sky Cafe	◆◆◆	Regional American	$14-$24	570

▼ See AAA listing p 569 ▼

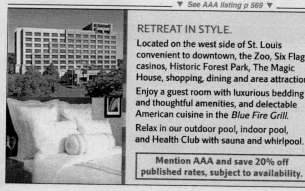

DOWNTOWN ST. LOUIS (See map and index starting on p. 524)

COURTYARD BY MARRIOTT DOWNTOWN

Book great rates at AAA.com

Phone: (314)241-9111 3

AAA Benefit: Members save a minimum 5% off the best available rate.

Hotel

$149-$169 All Year

Address: 2340 Market St 63103 **Location:** I-64/US 40, exit 39, just n on Jefferson Ave, then just e. **Facility:** Smoke free premises. 151 units. 139 one-bedroom standard units. 12 one-bedroom suites. 4 stories, interior corridors. *Bath:* combo or shower only. **Parking:** on-site. **Terms:** cancellation fee imposed. **Amenities:** high-speed Internet, voice mail, irons, hair dryers. **Pool(s):** heated indoor. **Leisure Activities:** whirlpool, exercise room. **Guest Services:** valet and coin laundry, wireless Internet. **Business Services:** meeting rooms, business center. **Free Special Amenities: full breakfast and high-speed Internet.**

ECO CALL / SOME UNITS

CROWNE PLAZA ST. LOUIS DOWNTOWN

Book great rates at AAA.com

Phone: (314)621-8200 11

Hotel

$169-$189 All Year

Address: 200 N 4th St 63102 **Location:** I-70, exit 250B (Stadium/Memorial Dr), just w; at 4th and Pine sts. **Facility:** 440 units. 346 one-bedroom standard units. 79 one- and 15 two-bedroom suites. 29 stories, interior corridors. *Bath:* combo or shower only. **Parking:** on-site (fee) and valet. **Terms:** cancellation fee imposed. **Amenities:** video games (fee), CD players, high-speed Internet, dual phone lines, voice mail, irons, hair dryers. **Pool(s):** outdoor. **Leisure Activities:** exercise room. **Guest Services:** valet and coin laundry, wireless Internet. **Business Services:** conference facilities, business center. **Free Special Amenities: high-speed Internet.**

/ SOME UNITS

DRURY INN & SUITES-ST. LOUIS-CONVENTION CENTER

Book at AAA.com

Phone: (314)231-8100 2

Hotel

$90-$204 All Year

Address: 711 N Broadway 63102 **Location:** I-70, exit 250B (Stadium/Memorial Dr), at convention center. **Facility:** 178 units. 144 one-bedroom standard units. 34 one-bedroom suites. 6 stories, interior corridors. **Parking:** on-site. **Terms:** cancellation fee imposed. **Amenities:** high-speed Internet, voice mail, irons, hair dryers. **Pool(s):** heated indoor. **Leisure Activities:** whirlpool, exercise room, game room. **Guest Services:** valet and coin laundry, wireless Internet. **Business Services:** meeting rooms, PC. ASK / SOME UNITS

▼ See AAA listing p 541 ▼

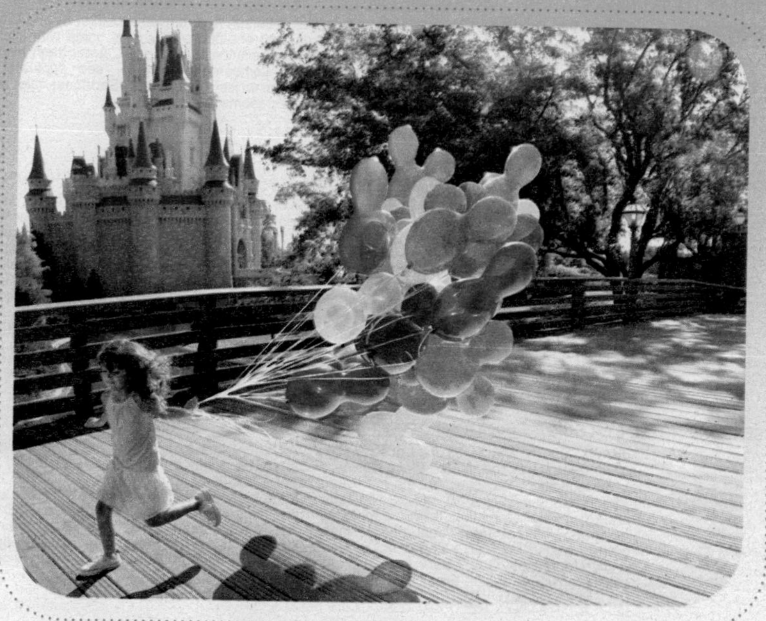

(See map and index starting on p. 524)

DRURY INN-ST. LOUIS/UNION STATION Book at AAA.com Phone: (314)231-3900 9

Hotel

$100-$189 All Year

Address: 201 S 20th St 63103 **Location:** Just e of Jefferson Ave; between Market St and Clark Ave. **Facility:** 177 units. 171 one-bedroom standard units. 6 one-bedroom suites, some with kitchens. 7 stories, interior corridors. **Parking:** on-site. **Terms:** cancellation fee imposed. **Amenities:** high-speed Internet, voice mail, irons, hair dryers. **Dining:** Lombardo's Trattoria, see separate listing. **Pool(s):** heated indoor. **Leisure Activities:** whirlpool, exercise room. **Guest Services:** valet and coin laundry, wireless Internet. **Business Services:** meeting rooms, business center.

ASK / SOME UNITS

DRURY PLAZA HOTEL-ST. LOUIS AT THE ARCH Book great rates at AAA.com Phone: (314)231-3003 14

AAA SAVE

Historic Hotel

$105-$289 All Year

Address: 4th & Market Sts 63102 **Location:** I-70, exit 250B (Stadium/Memorial Dr), just w on Pine St to Broadway, just s to Walnut St, just e to 4th St, then just n. **Facility:** Elaborate public areas featuring crystal chandeliers and upscale appointments. Bathrooms with marble walls and large guest units with upscale design. 355 units. 299 one-bedroom standard units, some with whirlpools. 56 one-bedroom suites, some with whirlpools. 4-10 stories, interior corridors. *Bath:* combo or shower only. **Parking:** on-site (fee). **Terms:** cancellation fee imposed. **Amenities:** high-speed Internet, dual phone lines, voice mail, irons, hair dryers. **Dining:** Carmine's Steak House, see separate listing. **Pool(s):** heated indoor. **Leisure Activities:** whirlpools, exercise room. **Guest Services:** valet and coin laundry, wireless Internet. **Business Services:** meeting rooms, business center. **Free Special Amenities: full breakfast and high-speed Internet.**

CALL / SOME UNITS

FOUR SEASONS HOTEL ST. LOUIS Book great rates at AAA.com Phone: (314)881-5800 1

AAA SAVE

Hotel

$195-$3000 All Year

Address: 999 N 2nd St 63102 **Location:** I-70, exit 250A, just s, 1.1 mi e, then just s. Connected through breezeway to Lumiere Place Casino. **Facility:** The infinity pool provides spectacular views of the surrounding area; guest rooms and baths feature luxurious appointments. 200 units. 186 one-bedroom standard units. 10 one-, 3 two- and 1 three-bedroom suites. 19 stories, interior corridors. **Parking:** on-site and valet. **Terms:** cancellation fee imposed. **Amenities:** DVD players, CD players, high-speed Internet (fee), dual phone lines, voice mail, safes, honor bars, irons, hair dryers. **Pool(s):** heated outdoor. **Leisure Activities:** whirlpools, children's weekend recreational programs, exercise room, spa. **Guest Services:** valet laundry, wireless Internet. **Business Services:** conference facilities, business center. **Free Special Amenities: newspaper.**

CALL / SOME UNITS

HAMPTON INN-GATEWAY ARCH Book great rates at AAA.com Phone: (314)621-7900 6

AAA SAVE

Hotel

$89-$199 All Year

Address: 333 Washington Ave 63102 **Location:** I-70, exit 250B (Stadium/Memorial Dr), just sw. **Facility:** Smoke free premises. 190 one-bedroom standard units. 17 stories, interior corridors. *Bath:* combo or shower only. **Parking:** on-site (fee). **Terms:** 1-7 night minimum stay, cancellation fee imposed. **Amenities:** video games (fee), high-speed Internet, dual phone lines, voice mail, irons, hair dryers. **Pool(s):** heated indoor. **Leisure Activities:** whirlpool, exercise room. *Fee:* game room. **Guest Services:** valet and coin laundry, wireless Internet. **Business Services:** meeting rooms, business center. **Free Special Amenities: expanded continental breakfast and high-speed Internet.**

HILTON ST. LOUIS AT THE BALLPARK Book great rates at AAA.com Phone: (314)421-1776 13

AAA SAVE

Hotel

$109-$259 All Year

Address: One S Broadway 63102 **Location:** Between Walnut and Market sts. **Facility:** 675 units. 668 one-bedroom standard units. 6 one- and 1 two-bedroom suites. 22-25 stories, interior corridors. *Bath:* combo or shower only. **Parking:** on-site (fee) and valet. **Terms:** check-in 4 pm, 1-7 night minimum stay, cancellation fee imposed. **Amenities:** dual phone lines, voice mail, irons, hair dryers. *Fee:* video games, high-speed Internet. **Pool(s):** heated indoor. **Leisure Activities:** saunas, whirlpool, exercise room. **Guest Services:** valet and coin laundry, wireless Internet. **Business Services:** conference facilities, business center. **Free Special Amenities: newspaper.**

CALL / SOME UNITS FEE

HILTON-ST. LOUIS DOWNTOWN Book great rates at AAA.com Phone: (314)436-0002 10

Historic Hotel

$99-$189 All Year

Address: 400 Olive St 63102 **Location:** I-70, exit 249C/251C (6th St) to N Broadway to Olive St. **Facility:** Located in the Historical Merchants Laclede Building, this hotel has been restored to its turn-of-the-century ambiance. 195 units. 194 one-bedroom standard units, some with whirlpools. 1 one-bedroom suite with efficiency and whirlpool. 8 stories, interior corridors. *Bath:* combo or shower only. **Parking:** on-site (fee) and valet. **Terms:** 1-7 night minimum stay, cancellation fee imposed. **Amenities:** video games (fee), high-speed Internet, dual phone lines, voice mail, irons, hair dryers. **Leisure Activities:** whirlpool, exercise room. **Guest Services:** valet laundry, wireless Internet. **Business Services:** meeting rooms, business center.

CALL / SOME UNITS FEE

(See map and index starting on p. 524)

HYATT REGENCY ST. LOUIS RIVERFRONT Book great rates at AAA.com

Phone: (314)655-1234 

Hotel

$79-$349 All Year

Address: 315 Chestnut St 63102 **Location:** I-70, exit 250B (Stadium/Memorial Dr); at 4th and Chestnut sts. Located across from Gateway Arch. **Facility:** 910 units. 907 one-bedroom standard units. 3 one-bedroom suites. 18 stories, interior corridors. *Bath:* combo or shower only. **Parking:** on-site (fee) and valet. **Terms:** cancellation fee imposed. **Amenities:** voice mail, irons, hair dryers. *Fee:* video games, high-speed Internet. **Dining:** Red Bar & Kitchen, see separate listing. **Guest Services:** valet laundry, wireless Internet. **Business Services:** conference facilities, business center.

CALL / SOME UNITS

HYATT HOTELS & RESORTS

AAA Benefit: Ask for the AAA rate and save 10%.

MILLENNIUM HOTEL ST. LOUIS Book great rates at AAA.com

Phone: (314)241-9500 16

Hotel

$99-$299 All Year

Address: 200 S 4th St 63102 **Location:** Jct Market St, just s. **Facility:** 780 one-bedroom standard units, some with whirlpools. 10-28 stories, interior corridors. **Parking:** on-site (fee). **Amenities:** dual phone lines, voice mail, irons, hair dryers. *Fee:* video games, high-speed Internet. *Some:* DVD players, CD players. **Dining:** 2 restaurants. **Pool(s):** heated outdoor, heated indoor. **Leisure Activities:** bicycles, exercise room. **Guest Services:** valet and coin laundry, area transportation-within 3 mi, wireless Internet. **Business Services:** conference facilities, business center. (See color ad p 538)

/ SOME UNITS

OMNI MAJESTIC HOTEL Book at AAA.com

Phone: (314)436-2355 8

Historic Hotel

$179-$349 3/1-12/11

$159-$329 12/12-2/28

Address: 1019 Pine St 63101 **Location:** Jct N Broadway, just w; at 10th St. **Facility:** This is a charming 1913 European-style hotel offering personal service in a professional atmosphere. 91 units. 88 one-bedroom standard units. 2 one- and 1 two-bedroom suites with whirlpools, some with kitchens (no utensils). 9 stories, interior corridors. **Parking:** valet. **Terms:** cancellation fee imposed. **Amenities:** dual phone lines, voice mail, honor bars, irons, hair dryers. **Guest Services:** valet laundry, area transportation, wireless Internet. **Business Services:** meeting rooms, business center.

ASK FEE / SOME UNITS FEE

PEAR TREE INN - ST. LOUIS/UNION STATION Book at AAA.com

Phone: (314)241-3200 5

Hotel

$85-$159 All Year

Address: 2211 Market St 63103 **Location:** I-64/US 40, exit 39, just n on Jefferson Ave, then just e. **Facility:** 239 units. 229 one-bedroom standard units. 10 one-bedroom suites. 11 stories, interior corridors. **Parking:** on-site. **Terms:** cancellation fee imposed. **Amenities:** dual phone lines, voice mail, irons, hair dryers. **Pool(s):** heated indoor. **Leisure Activities:** whirlpool, exercise room. **Guest Services:** valet and coin laundry, wireless Internet. **Business Services:** meeting rooms, PC.

ASK / SOME UNITS

RENAISSANCE GRAND & SUITES HOTEL ST. LOUIS Book great rates at AAA.com

Phone: (314)621-9600 4

Hotel

$159-$199 All Year

Address: 800 Washington Ave 63101 **Location:** Jct N Broadway, just w; jct 8th St. Located across from America's Center Convention Complex. **Facility:** The hotel occupies two historic buildings in the heart of downtown, both offering elegant accommodations, modern amenities and enhanced services. Smoke free premises. 1073 units. 883 one-bedroom standard units. 190 one-bedroom suites. 21-25 stories, interior corridors. *Bath:* combo or shower only. **Parking:** on-site (fee) and valet. **Terms:** check-in 4 pm, cancellation fee imposed. **Amenities:** high-speed Internet (fee), dual phone lines, voice mail, irons, hair dryers. **Dining:** 2 restaurants, also, An American Place, see separate listing. **Pool(s):** heated indoor. **Leisure Activities:** saunas, whirlpools. **Guest Services:** valet laundry, wireless Internet. **Business Services:** conference facilities, business center. (See color ad p 542)

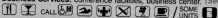

RENAISSANCE. HOTELS & RESORTS

AAA Benefit: Members save a minimum 5% off the best available rate.

▼ See AAA listing p 541 ▼

(See map and index starting on p. 524)

ST. LOUIS UNION STATION MARRIOTT Book great rates at AAA.com **Phone:** (314)621-5262 7

AAA SAVE

Classic Hotel

$189-$199 All Year

Address: 1 St. Louis Union Station 63103 **Location:** I-64, exit 38C eastbound; exit 39A westbound, just n on N Jefferson Ave, then 0.5 mi e on Market St. **Facility:** Built in 1894 and once the largest/busiest station in the world, history buffs might request a room in the original train track section, as well as take advantage of the guided tours. Smoke free premises. 539 units. 532 one-bedroom standard units. 7 one-bedroom suites. 5-6 stories, interior corridors. *Bath:* combo or shower only. **Parking:** on-site (fee) and valet. **Terms:** cancellation fee imposed. **Amenities:** high-speed Internet (fee), dual phone lines, voice mail, irons, hair dryers. *Some:* DVD players. **Dining:** Station Grille, see separate listing. **Pool(s):** outdoor. **Leisure Activities:** saunas, exercise room. **Guest Services:** valet laundry, wireless Internet. **Business Services:** conference facilities, business center. *(See color ad below)*

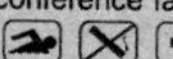  / SOME UNITS

Marriott HOTELS & RESORTS

AAA Benefit:

Members save a minimum 5% off the best available rate.

SHERATON ST. LOUIS CITY CENTER HOTEL & SUITES Book great rates at AAA.com **Phone:** (314)231-5007 15

AAA SAVE

Hotel

$109-$429 All Year

Address: 400 S 14th St 63103 **Location:** I-64, exit 39B (14th St) eastbound, just n; exit 40A westbound, just n, just w on Clark Ave, then just s. **Facility:** Smoke free premises. 288 units. 147 one-bedroom standard units, some with whirlpools. 135 one- and 6 two-bedroom suites, some with whirlpools. 13 stories, interior corridors. *Bath:* combo or shower only. **Parking:** on-site (fee) and valet. **Terms:** cancellation fee imposed. **Amenities:** dual phone lines, voice mail, irons, hair dryers. *Fee:* video games, high-speed Internet. *Some:* CD players. **Pool(s):** heated indoor. **Leisure Activities:** whirlpool, sun deck, exercise room. **Guest Services:** valet and coin laundry, wireless Internet. **Business Services:** conference facilities, business center.

AAA Benefit:

Members get up to 15% off, plus Starwood Preferred Guest® bonuses.

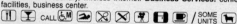

(See map and index starting on p. 524)

THE WESTIN ST. LOUIS Book great rates at AAA.com **Phone:** (314)621-2000 17

AAA SAVE

Historic Hotel

$119-$399 All Year

Address: 811 Spruce St 63102 **Location:** I-64, exit 39C eastbound, just n on 11th St, then just e; exit 40A westbound, just n, just e on Clark Ave, just s on 8th St, then just w. Adjacent to Busch Stadium. **Facility:** Rehabilitated warehouse offering strong design elements with luxurious, ultra-modern and upscale appointments. Smoke free premises. 255 units. 240 one-bedroom standard units. 15 one-bedroom suites. 5-7 stories, interior corridors. *Bath:* combo or shower only. **Parking:** on-site (fee) and valet. **Terms:** cancellation fee imposed. **Amenities:** high-speed Internet (fee), voice mail, safes, honor bars, irons, hair dryers. *Some:* DVD players, CD players. **Leisure Activities:** spa. **Guest Services:** valet laundry, wireless Internet. **Business Services:** conference facilities, business center. **Free Special Amenities: newspaper.**

CALL / SOME UNITS

The following lodging was either not evaluated or did not meet AAA rating requirements but is listed for your information only.

HOTELUMIERE **Phone:** 314/881-7800

fyi

Not evaluated. **Address:** 999 N 2nd St 63102 **Location:** Just n of jct Dr Martin Luther King Jr. Facilities, services, and decor characterize a mid-scale property.

WHERE TO DINE

AL'S RESTAURANT **Phone:** 314/421-6399 1

American

$28-$80

Al's Restaurant offers fine dining with elegant rooms and polished, professional service. The server recites dinner choices and displays meat choices on a chilled silver charger. The filet mignon with peppercorn and cognac cream sauce is very good. Dressy casual. **Bar:** Full bar. **Reservations:** suggested. **Hours:** 5 pm-9:30 pm. Closed major holidays; also Sun & Mon. **Address:** 1200 N 1st St 63102 **Location:** 1.1 mi n from I-44/55/66; just w of Riverfront. **Parking:** on-site and valet.

AN AMERICAN PLACE **Phone:** 314/418-5800 4

American

$18-$38

High-quality decor adorns this historical, elegant dining room. Many original elements of this former 1917 hotel lobby—including an elaborate ceiling, marble walls and large columns—as well as elegant draperies and glorious potted palms set the stage for an innovative menu of great American foods. A daily changing menu identifies the farmers, ranchers and fishermen who provide excellent products found in local and regional markets. Dressy casual. **Bar:** Full bar. **Reservations:** suggested. **Hours:** 5 pm-10 pm, Fri & Sat-11 pm. Closed: 1/1, 11/25, 12/25; also Sun & Mon. **Address:** 822 Washington Ave 63101 **Location:** Jct N Broadway, just w; jct 8th St; in Renaissance Grand & Suites Hotel St. Louis. **Parking:** valet.

BROADWAY OYSTER BAR **Phone:** 314/621-8811 16

Traditional Cajun

$8-$16

This restaurant is one of a very few eateries in the downtown area offering Cajun and Creole cuisine. The strong smell of spicy cooking and nightly live music reflect a New Orleans Mardi Gras influence. A courtyard beer garden is available for outdoor dining in the summer season. Casual dress. Entertainment. **Bar:** Full bar. **Reservations:** accepted. **Hours:** 11 am-10 pm, Fri & Sat-11 pm. Closed: 1/1, 11/25, 12/24, 12/25. **Address:** 736 S Broadway 63102 **Location:** I-64, exit 40B, just w on Cerre St, then just s. **Parking:** street.

CARMINE'S STEAK HOUSE **Phone:** 314/241-1631 15

AAA

Steak

$19-$55

Conveniently close to the Gateway Arch and Busch Stadium, the restaurant's dining room offers a bright, upscale setting for enjoying beef that's been aged a minimum of twenty-one days. In addition to some eight or more cuts of beef, the menu lists chicken, lamb, pork chops, veal and seafood. The preparations are not complex or complicated but it is delicious. Dressy casual. **Bar:** Full bar. **Reservations:** suggested. **Hours:** 4 pm-10 pm, Fri & Sat-11 pm, Sun-9 pm. Closed major holidays. **Address:** 20 S 4th St 63102 **Location:** I-70, exit 250B (Stadium/Memorial Dr), just w on Pine St to Broadway, just s to Walnut St, just e to 4th St, then just n; in Drury Plaza Hotel-St. Louis At the Arch. **Parking:** on-site. CALL

CHARLIE GITTO'S DOWNTOWN **Phone:** 314/436-2828 11

Italian

$16-$42

This bustling restaurant prepares fine Italian cuisine, including an exemplary toasted ravioli that shouldn't be passed over. Casual dress. **Bar:** Full bar. **Reservations:** accepted. **Hours:** 11 am-10 pm, Fri & Sat-11 pm. Closed: 1/1, 11/25, 12/25; also Sun. **Address:** 207 N 6th St 63101 **Location:** At 6th and Pine sts. **Parking:** street. CALL

HANNEGAN'S **Phone:** 314/241-8877 5

American

$8-$23

In a replica of the US Senate dining room, the casual restaurant is splashed in unusual decor. Longtime favorites include the 20-ounce double-rib pork chop with peppercorn sauce and deep-dish blackberry pie. The signature dish is Senate bean soup made from the authentic recipe used in the U.S. Senate dining room. Casual dress. **Bar:** Full bar. **Reservations:** accepted. **Hours:** 11 am-10 pm, Fri & Sat-11 pm. Closed: 11/25, 12/24, 12/25; also 1st week of Jan. **Address:** 719 N 2nd St 63102 **Location:** Just n of Gateway Arch; in Laclede's Landing. **Parking:** street.

(See map and index starting on p. 524)

HARD ROCK CAFE

Phone: 314/621-7625 (7)

American
$8-$27

Rock 'n' roll memorabilia decorates the walls of the popular theme restaurant. Live music on the weekends contributes to the bustling atmosphere. On the menu is a wide variety of American cuisine—from burgers and sandwiches to seafood, steaks and pasta. Casual dress. **Bar:** Full bar. **Reservations:** accepted. **Hours:** 11 am-midnight, Fri & Sat-1 am. Closed: 11/25, 12/25. **Address:** 450 St. Louis Union Station 63103 **Location:** Inside Union Station. **Parking:** on-site (fee).

HARRY'S RESTAURANT & BAR

Phone: 314/421-6969 (6)

Continental
$10-$27

A longtime favorite of the business crowd, the casually sophisticated restaurant is decidedly masculine. Regional produce factors into such dishes as blue crab-encrusted Atlantic salmon and sauteed shrimp linguine. Casual dress. **Bar:** Full bar. **Reservations:** suggested. **Hours:** 11 am-3 & 5-10 pm, Sat from 5 pm; Easter & Mother's Day for brunch. Closed major holidays; also Sun. **Address:** 2144 Market St 63104 **Location:** Just w of Union Station. **Parking:** on-site.

HODAK'S RESTAURANT & BAR

Phone: 314/776-7292 (17)

American
$5-$14

Consider among the city's best, the restaurant's fried chicken packages well in a good-value four-piece platter with fries and coleslaw. Reasonably priced weekday luncheon specials center on everything from hot dogs to rib-eye steak. Casual dress. **Bar:** Full bar. **Reservations:** not accepted. **Hours:** 10 am-10 pm, Fri & Sat-11 pm. Closed major holidays. **Address:** 2100 Gravois Rd 63104 **Location:** I-55, exit 207/290C; corner of McNair, exit toward Gravois Rd/I-44 W/12th St ramp, then just w. **Parking:** street.

KEMOLL'S ITALIAN RESTAURANT

Phone: 314/421-0555 (10)

Italian
$17-$44

Accented with an Old European ambiance, each dining room offers an elegant atmosphere for enjoying a fine dining experience and smooth service. A local legend, the restaurant is known for its fresh artichoke antipasto. The extensive wine list is well balanced in price and variety. Garage parking is available off Pine Street. Dressy casual. **Bar:** Beer & wine. **Reservations:** suggested. **Hours:** 5 pm-9 pm. Closed major holidays; also Sun. **Address:** 1 Metropolitan Square 63102 **Location:** Jct Olive St, just s on Broadway; on ground floor of Metropolitan Square Building. **Parking:** on-site.

LOMBARDO'S TRATTORIA

Phone: 314/621-0666 (9)

AAA

Italian
$8-$25

A sophisticated atmosphere punctuates the restaurant, which is a nice place for celebrating special occasions. Creative entrees show pleasant presentation. Casual dress. **Bar:** Full bar. **Reservations:** suggested. **Hours:** 11 am-10 pm, Fri-11 pm, Sat 4 pm-11 pm, Sun 4 pm-9 pm. Closed major holidays. **Address:** 201 S 20th St 63103 **Location:** Just e of Jefferson Ave; between Market St and Clark Ave; in Drury Inn-St. Louis/Union Station. **Parking:** valet.

MIKE SHANNON'S STEAKS & SEAFOOD *Menu on AAA.com*

Phone: 314/421-1540 (12)

AAA

Steak
$9-$50

Sports lovers and others will appreciate the classic decor, solid service and great steaks at Mike Shannon's, two blocks from Busch Stadium. Some of the best beef and fresh seafood in St. Louis, as well as plenty of sports memorabilia, can be found here. Dressy casual. **Bar:** Full bar. **Reservations:** suggested. **Hours:** 11 am-11 pm, Sat from 5 pm, Sun 5 pm-10 pm. Closed major holidays. **Address:** 620 Market St 63101 **Location:** Corner of 7th and Market sts. **Parking:** street.

MOSAIC MODERN FUSION

Phone: 314/621-6001 (3)

Fusion
$7-$16

Enjoy an array of hot and cold tapas-style offerings that are perfect for sharing. House favorites include the frisee and warm goat cheese salad, the fresh seared ahi tuna, the pulled Korean barbecue pork-apple, and the dulce de leche dessert. Red lighting and tall booths provide intimacy, creating the perfect spot for a romantic date. An extensive wine list is available. Casual dress. **Bar:** Full bar. **Reservations:** suggested. **Hours:** 11 am-4 & 5-10 pm, Thurs & Fri-11 pm, Sat 5 pm-11 pm. Closed: 12/25; also Sun. **Address:** 1001 Washington Ave 63101 **Location:** Jct 10th and Washington sts. **Parking:** on-site and valet. CALL M

RED BAR & KITCHEN

Phone: 314/655-1234 (13)

American
$7-$22

Patrons can settle into plush and often bustling surroundings in the lobby restaurant. Fresh twists on favorites are served in an eye-appealing style. Casual dress. **Bar:** Full bar. **Reservations:** accepted. **Hours:** 6 am-10 pm. **Address:** 315 Chestnut St 63102 **Location:** I-70, exit 250B (Stadium/Memorial Dr); at 4th and Chestnut sts; in Hyatt Regency St. Louis Riverfront. **Parking:** on-site (fee) and valet.

ST. LOUIS BREWERY TAP ROOM

Phone: 314/241-2337 (2)

American
$7-$15

As the name might imply, the restaurant's dining room occupies a working brewery. At least 10 fresh beers, which diners can watch being brewed on the premises through a picture window, are on tap at all times. Those interested in tasting more than one house brew should order the Schlafly Sampler, which includes six, five-ounce samples. Casual dress. **Bar:** Full bar. **Reservations:** not accepted. **Hours:** 11 am-10 pm, Fri & Sat-midnight, Sun noon-9 pm. Closed major holidays. **Address:** 2100 Locust St 63103 **Location:** Jct N 21st St. **Parking:** on-site.

STATION GRILLE

Phone: 314/802-3460 (8)

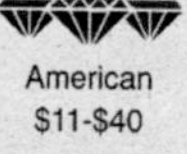

American
$11-$40

For almost 100 years, many a rail journey began or ended at the historic Union Station in downtown St. Louis. Today, diners can enjoy a gastronomic excursion in the warm setting of the Station Grill, which is housed in the historic railroad hotel at the entrance to Union Station. A variety of meats are paired with fresh, seasonal vegetables, and traditional desserts are worth a taste. Dressy casual. **Bar:** Full bar. **Reservations:** suggested. **Hours:** 6:30 am-2 & 5-10 pm. **Address:** 1 St. Louis Union Station 63103 **Location:** I-64, exit 38C eastbound; exit 39A westbound, just n on N Jefferson Ave, then 0.5 mi e on Market St; in Hyatt Regency St. Louis At Union Station. **Parking:** on-site (fee) and valet.

(See map and index starting on p. 524)

TONY'S Menu on AAA.com **Phone:** 314/231-7007 (14)

Italian
$20-$40

Patrons enjoy fine dining in an intimate, candlelit setting. The formal service features tableside finishing of a varied cuisine that incorporates regional and Continental influences. Dishes are often prepared with rich cream sauces. Semi-formal attire. **Bar:** Full bar. **Reservations:** suggested. **Hours:** 5:30 pm-10:30 pm, Sat 5 pm-11 pm. Closed major holidays; also Sun. **Address:** 410 Market St 63102 **Location:** I-70, exit 250B (Stadium/Memorial Dr), just w on Pine St, just s on Broadway, then just e. **Parking:** valet.

ST. LOUIS pop. 348,189 (See map and index starting on p. 530)

BEST WESTERN ST. LOUIS INN Book great rates at AAA.com **Phone:** (314)416-7639

Hotel
$60-$89 3/1-8/31
$55-$65 9/1-2/28

Address: 6224 Heimos Industrial Park Dr 63129 **Location:** I-55, exit 193, just e on Meramec Bottom Rd, then just n. **Facility:** 85 one-bedroom standard units, some with whirlpools. 3 stories, interior corridors. *Bath:* combo or shower only. **Parking:** on-site. **Amenities:** irons, hair dryers. **Pool(s):** heated indoor. **Leisure Activities:** exercise room. **Guest Services:** valet and coin laundry, wireless Internet. **Business Services:** meeting rooms, PC. **Free Special Amenities: full breakfast and high-speed Internet.**

/ SOME UNITS FEE

AAA Benefit:
Members save up to 20%, plus 10% bonus points with rewards program.

CHASE PARK PLAZA Book great rates at AAA.com **Phone:** (314)633-3000 (2)

Historic Hotel
$229-$479 All Year

Address: 212-232 N Kingshighway Blvd 63108 **Location:** I-64, exit 36 (Kingshighway Blvd), 0.8 mi n. **Facility:** A legendary hotel offering a contemporary blend of charm and sophistication, rising in stately grandeur. Catering to business and leisure travelers. 338 units. 131 one-bedroom standard units. 194 one- and 13 two-bedroom suites, some with kitchens and/or whirlpools. 8-11 stories, interior corridors. *Bath:* combo or shower only. **Parking:** on-site (fee) and valet. **Terms:** 3 day cancellation notice-fee imposed. **Amenities:** high-speed Internet (fee), dual phone lines, voice mail, safes, honor bars, irons, hair dryers. **Dining:** 4 restaurants, also, The Tenderloin Room, see separate listing. **Pool(s):** heated outdoor. **Leisure Activities:** spa. *Fee:* cinemas. **Guest Services:** valet laundry, wireless Internet, beauty salon, barber shop, shoeshine. **Business Services:** conference facilities, business center. *(See color ad below)*

   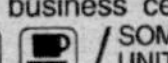   / SOME UNITS

(See map and index starting on p. 530)

DRURY INN & SUITES NEAR FOREST PARK Book at AAA.com Phone: (314)646-0770 4

Hotel
$95-$229 All Year

Address: 2111 Sulphur Ave 63139 **Location:** I-44, exit 286, just s. **Facility:** 164 units. 142 one-bedroom standard units, some with whirlpools. 22 one-bedroom suites. 5 stories, interior corridors. *Bath:* combo or shower only. **Parking:** on-site. **Terms:** cancellation fee imposed. **Amenities:** voice mail, irons, hair dryers. **Dining:** Bartolino's Osteria, see separate listing. **Pool(s):** heated indoor/outdoor. **Leisure Activities:** whirlpool, exercise room. **Guest Services:** valet and coin laundry, wireless Internet. **Business Services:** meeting rooms, business center.

ASK CALL / SOME UNITS

HAMPTON INN & SUITES - ST. LOUIS AT FOREST PARK Book great rates at AAA.com Phone: (314)655-3993 3

AAA SAVE

Hotel
$89-$169 All Year

Address: 5650 Oakland Ave 63110 **Location:** I-64, exit 34C, just s, then just e. **Facility:** Designated smoking area. 126 one-bedroom standard units. 6 stories, interior corridors. *Bath:* combo or shower only. **Parking:** on-site. **Terms:** 1-7 night minimum stay, cancellation fee imposed. **Amenities:** high-speed Internet, voice mail, irons, hair dryers. **Pool(s):** heated indoor. **Leisure Activities:** whirlpool, exercise room. **Guest Services:** valet laundry, wireless Internet. **Business Services:** meeting rooms, business center. **Free Special Amenities: expanded continental breakfast and high-speed Internet.**

CALL / SOME UNITS

AAA Benefit:
Members save up to 10% everyday!

THE PARKWAY HOTEL Book great rates at AAA.com Phone: (314)256-7777 1

AAA SAVE

Hotel
$117-$269 All Year

Address: 4550 Forest Park Blvd 63108 **Location:** I-64, exit 36 (Kingshighway Blvd), 0.6 mi n, then just e. Adjacent to Barnes-Jewish Hospital. **Facility:** Smoke free premises. 220 units. 218 one-bedroom standard units. 2 one-bedroom suites. 8 stories, interior corridors. *Bath:* combo or shower only. **Parking:** on-site (fee). **Terms:** check-in 4 pm, cancellation fee imposed. **Amenities:** high-speed Internet, dual phone lines, voice mail, irons, hair dryers. *Some:* DVD players, CD players. **Leisure Activities:** exercise room. **Guest Services:** valet and coin laundry, wireless Internet. **Business Services:** meeting rooms, business center. *(See color ad p 548)*

CALL / SOME UNITS FEE

FREE newspaper and high-speed Internet

▼ See AAA listing p 558 ▼

(See map and index starting on p. 530)

THE WATER TOWER INN AT ST. LOUIS UNIVERSITY **Phone:** 314/977-7500 5

Hotel
$75-$89 All Year

Address: 3545 Lafayette Ave 63104 **Location:** I-44, exit 288 (Grand Blvd), just n, then just e; in University Salus Center located at St. Louis University. **Facility:** 62 one-bedroom standard units. 6 stories, interior corridors. *Bath:* combo or shower only. **Parking:** on-site. **Amenities:** high-speed Internet, voice mail, irons, hair dryers. **Leisure Activities:** exercise room. **Guest Services:** valet and coin laundry, wireless Internet. **Business Services:** meeting rooms, administrative services. **Free Special Amenities: continental breakfast and high-speed Internet.** / SOME UNITS

The following lodging was either not evaluated or did not meet AAA rating requirements but is listed for your information only.

MOONRISE HOTEL **Phone:** 314/721-1111

fyi
Boutique Hotel

Did not meet all AAA rating requirements for locking devices in some guest rooms at time of last evaluation on 07/23/2009. **Address:** 6177 Delmar Blvd 63112 **Location:** I-64, exit 38A, 2.4 mi on Forest Park Pkwy, 0.4 mi n on Skinner Blvd, then just e; in "The Loop". Facilities, services, and decor characterize an upscale property.

WHERE TO DINE

BAR ITALIA RISTORANTE-CAFFE **Phone:** 314/361-7010 4

Italian
$9-$25

The creative and colorful cuisine of this restaurant is served in a casual, sidewalk cafe atmosphere. In addition to pasta dishes, the menu lists fresh seafood, steaks and chicken entrees. Casual dress. **Bar:** Full bar. **Reservations:** suggested. **Hours:** 11:30 am-10 pm, Fri & Sat-11 pm. Closed major holidays; also Mon. **Address:** 13 Maryland Plaza 63108 **Location:** I-64, exit 36 (Kingshighway Blvd), 1 mi n, then just e. **Parking:** street.

BARTOLINO'S OSTERIA **Phone:** 314/644-2266 12

Italian
$9-$36

Family owned and operated for over 40 years, the restaurant has been a local favorite thanks to its generous portions of traditional Italian fare. Veal, fresh seafood, chicken, pasta and homemade desserts line the menu. In 2008, the restaurant moved to a new location, which offers a casually upscale setting, plus outdoor seating. Casual dress. **Bar:** Full bar. **Reservations:** accepted. **Hours:** 11 am-10 pm, Sat & Sun from 4 pm. Closed major holidays. **Address:** 2103 Sulphur Ave 63139 **Location:** I-44, exit 286, just s; in Drury Inn & Suites Near Forest Park. **Parking:** on-site. CALL

BOATHOUSE FOREST PARK **Phone:** 314/367-2224 6

American
$7-$15

During warm weather, patrons head to the patio to enjoy cold drinks, live music and beautiful lakeside sunsets. Patrons' dogs are welcomed to take a seat beside patio tables, where they're given their own water bowl and treats. When temperatures drop, guests head inside to enjoy relaxing meals and tasty hot cocoa by the large stone fireplace. Casual dress. **Bar:** Full bar. **Reservations:** suggested. **Hours:** 11 am-10 pm, Fri & Sat-midnight, Sun 10 am-10 pm. Closed: 4/4, 11/25. **Address:** 6101 Government Dr 63110 **Location:** I-64, exit 34D (Hampton Ave), just n , just w on Wells Dr, then just n; in Forest Park. **Parking:** on-site.

▼ *See AAA listing p 547* ▼

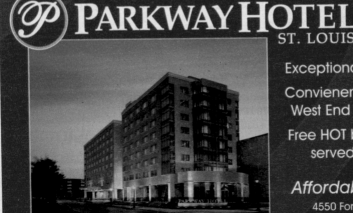

(See map and index starting on p. 530)

BRAZIE'S RISTORANTE

Phone: 314/481-5464 (18)

Southern Italian
$6-$29

You'll enjoy this family-owned and operated restaurant featuring traditional fare of sandwiches, pasta, salad and soup that are freshly prepared and imaginatively seasoned. The setting has a pleasant atmosphere, relaxing decor and friendly service. Casual dress. **Bar:** Full bar. **Reservations:** suggested. **Hours:** 11 am-9 pm, Fri & Sat-10 pm, Sun & Mon 5 pm-9 pm. Closed major holidays. **Address:** 3073 Watson Rd 63139 **Location:** I-44, exit 286 (Hampton Ave), 1 mi s, just e on Arsenal St, then just nw. **Parking:** on-site.

CROWN CANDY KITCHEN

Phone: 314/621-9650 (1)

American
$4-$7

A local tradition, the soda fountain opened in 1913. This place makes all its own ice cream and still practices the confectionery art. Sandwiches, soups, hot dogs and chili are among choices, but the soda fountain is the reason for visiting. Casual dress. **Hours:** 10:30 am-8 pm, Fri & Sat-10 pm, Sun 11 am-6 pm; to 10 pm, Sun 11 am-8 pm in summer. Closed major holidays. **Address:** 1401 St. Louis Ave 63106 **Location:** I-70, exit 248B eastbound, just se on 11th St, then just e; exit westbound, just nw on Branch St, just s on 13th St, then just sw. **Parking:** street. **Classic Historic**

CUNETTO HOUSE OF PASTA

Phone: 314/781-1135 (13)

Italian
$8-$20

Since 1972 this casual, family-run eatery has served a lengthy list of Italian favorites in generous portions. The menu includes pasta, chicken, veal, seafood and beef selections. Reservations are not accepted for dinner, and it's not unusual to have quite a wait at peak hours. Casual dress. **Bar:** Full bar. **Reservations:** accepted, for lunch. **Hours:** 11 am-2 & 5-10 pm, Fri-11 pm, Sat 5 pm-11 pm. Closed major holidays; also Sun. **Address:** 5453 Magnolia Ave 63139 **Location:** I-44, exit 286, 0.7 mi s on Hampton Ave, 0.4 mi e on Columbia Ave, just s on Sublette Ave, then just e. **Parking:** on-site.

DOMINIC'S

Phone: 314/771-1632 (11)

Italian
$22-$42

Patrons enjoy elegant dining and sophisticated service with tableside preparation at this establishment. The varied menu includes pleasing presentations of chicken, pasta and fresh seafood entrées as well as an extensive wine list. Service is prompt and attentive. Dressy casual. **Bar:** Full bar. **Reservations:** suggested. **Hours:** 5 pm-10 pm, Fri & Sat-11 pm. Closed major holidays; also Sun. **Address:** 5101 Wilson Ave 63110 **Location:** I-44, exit 287 (Kingshighway Blvd), just s, just w on Shaw Ave, then 2 blks s on Hereford St. **Parking:** valet and street.

DRESSEL'S PUB

Phone: 314/361-1060 (2)

English
$10-$14

Dressel's, renowned for its stew, soup and homemade, deep-fried potato chips, also offers sandwiches and salads. This place appeals to the university crowd and theater-goers. Its cozy atmosphere features pictures of literary and musical greats, plus a sidewalk cafe that's open in season. Casual dress. **Bar:** Full bar. **Reservations:** not accepted. **Hours:** 11 am-11:15 pm, Sun-10:45 pm. Closed: 11/25, 12/25. **Address:** 419 N Euclid Ave 63108 **Location:** I-64, exit 36 (Kingshighway Blvd), 1.2 mi n, just e on McPherson Ave, then just n. **Parking:** street.

DUFF'S

Phone: 314/361-0522 (3)

American
$8-$20

You'll discover festive dining at Duff's, which is quite popular with local residents and business people. They feature creative pasta, chicken, steak, seafood entrees and brunch on Saturday and Sunday. Choose either the rustic indoor area with wood floors and brick walls or the outdoor cafe covered in a canopy of lush foliage in the summer season. Casual dress. **Bar:** Full bar. **Reservations:** accepted. **Hours:** 11 am-10 pm, Fri-11 pm, Sat 10 am-11 pm, Sun 10 am-10 pm. Closed: 11/25, 12/25; also Mon except 5/31 & 9/6. **Address:** 392 N Euclid Ave 63108 **Location:** I-64, exit 36 (Kingshighway Blvd), 1.2 mi n, just e on McPherson Ave, then just s. **Parking:** on-site.

FRAZER'S

Phone: 314/773-8646 (19)

American
$8-$24

The stylish, creative menu is the star at this restaurant. A nice variety of pasta, pizza, seafood, pork, chicken, beef and sandwiches are the flavorful offerings. All desserts are made in-house. The setting features a relaxed, comfortable dining area. Casual dress. **Bar:** Full bar. **Reservations:** suggested. **Hours:** 11 am-10 pm, Fri-11 pm, Sat 5 pm-11 pm. Closed major holidays; also Sun. **Address:** 1811 Pestalozzi St 63118 **Location:** I-55, exit 206C (Arsenal St), just w, just n on Lemp Ave, then just e. **Parking:** street.

GIOVANNI'S ON THE HILL

Phone: 314/772-5958 (8)

Italian
$17-$38

Located in "The Hill," patrons will discover fine dining in an unpretentious yet elegant setting at this restaurant, featuring tableside preparations of locally renowned and innovative pasta, veal, lamb and seafood cuisine. Dressy casual. **Bar:** Full bar. **Reservations:** suggested. **Hours:** 5 pm-11 pm, Sat-midnight. Closed major holidays; also Sun. **Address:** 5201 Shaw Ave 63110 **Location:** I-44, exit 287 (Kingshighway Blvd), just s, then just w. **Parking:** valet and street.

IMO'S PIZZA

Phone: 314/644-5480 (7)

Italian
$5-$15

Original St. Louis-style pizza is said to have begun with Ed Imo's distinctive recipe, which includes square-cut pieces of thin crispy crust, tomato sauce and provolone cheese. This place is nothing fancy, but the pizza's hard to beat. Casual dress. **Reservations:** not accepted. **Hours:** 10 am-midnight, Fri & Sat-1 am. Closed: 1/1, 11/25, 12/25. **Address:** 1000 Hampton Ave 63110 **Location:** I-64/US 40, exit 34D (Hampton Ave), just se. **Parking:** on-site.

(See map and index starting on p. 530)

KING & I RESTAURANT — **Phone:** 314/771-1777 (16)

Thai
$9-$17

Authentic, well-prepared Thai cuisine is complemented by Chinese and vegetarian selections at this family-owned restaurant. Specials include pad thai, kai tom kha, chicken satay and pik seafood. The warm, romantic atmosphere features seating on the floor. Casual dress. **Bar:** Full bar. **Reservations:** not accepted. **Hours:** 11 am-2:30 & 5-9:30 pm, Fri-10 pm, Sat noon-3 & 5-10 pm, Sun noon-3 & 5-9:30 pm. Closed: 7/4, 11/25, 12/25; also Mon & 7/5-7/10. **Address:** 3157 S Grand Ave 63118 **Location:** I-44, exit 288 (Grand Ave), 1 mi s. **Parking:** street.

MANGIA ITALIANO — **Phone:** 314/664-8585 (15)

Italian
$6-$16

Featuring eclectic decor, casual charm, and a menu offering a number of specialty items, the restaurant is located amongst unique shops and restaurants in a quirky but established south city area. Casual dress. **Bar:** Full bar. **Hours:** 11:30 am-10 pm, Fri & Sat-10:30 pm, Sun 10:30 am-10 pm. Closed: 1/1, 11/25, 12/25. **Address:** 3145 S Grand Ave 63118 **Location:** I-64/US 40, exit Grand Ave, 1.5 mi s. **Parking:** street.

O'CONNELL'S PUB — **Phone:** 314/773-6600 (9)

American
$5-$9

Daily specials might include Reubens, barbecue rib tips or fish and chips. Casual dress. **Bar:** Full bar. **Reservations:** not accepted. **Hours:** 11 am-midnight, Sun noon-10 pm. Closed major holidays; also week of 7/4. **Address:** 4652 Shaw Ave 63110 **Location:** I-44, exit 287A (Kingshighway Blvd S), just s, then just e. **Parking:** on-site.

PHO GRAND VIETNAMESE RESTAURANT — **Phone:** 314/664-7435 (17)

Vietnamese
$7-$11

Since 1990, through the medium of food, the Trinh family has been sharing the warmth and tradition of their homeland with a growing circle of friends and fans who are drawn to Pho Grand for a taste of Vietnam. Your taste might include Cha Gio (a deep fried Vietnamese egg roll) and Mi Xao Mem (stir fried soft egg noodles with assorted meats and vegetables) or one of the many aromatic and flavorful soups. Try the robust Cafe Sua Da (iced coffee with sweetened condensed milk). Casual dress. **Bar:** Beer & wine. **Hours:** 11 am-9:30 pm, Fri & Sat-10:30 pm. Closed major holidays; also Tues. **Address:** 3195 S Grand Ave 63118 **Location:** I-44, exit 288, 1.2 mi s. **Parking:** street.

SIDNEY STREET CAFE — **Phone:** 314/771-5777 (14)

New American
$18-$30

Near the Anheuser-Busch Brewery in the Benton Park residential neighborhood, the casually upscale bistro presents a frequently changing menu of contemporary American fare. Parking for guests is provided in a lot across the street. Dressy casual. **Bar:** Full bar. **Reservations:** suggested. **Hours:** 5 pm-9:30 pm, Fri & Sat-10:30 pm. Closed major holidays; also Sun & Mon. **Address:** 2000 Sidney St 63104 **Location:** I-44, exit 289 (Jefferson Ave), just s, just e on Russell Blvd, 0.5 mi s on McNair Ave, then just e. **Parking:** on-site and street. **Historic**

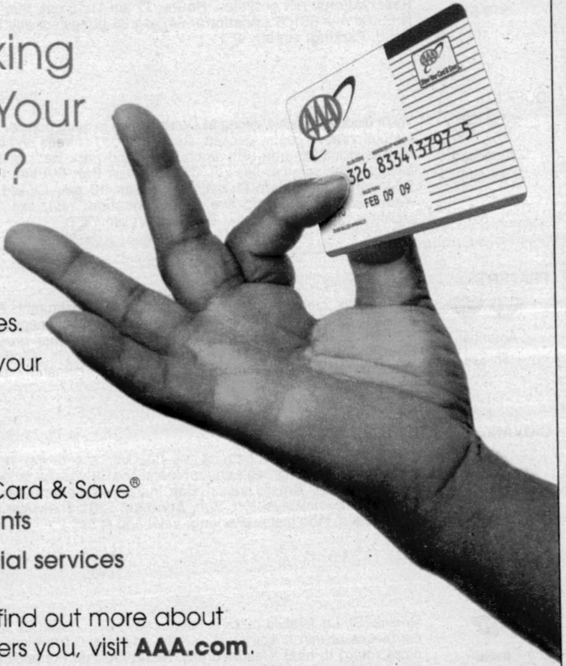

(See map and index starting on p. 530)

TED DREWE'S FROZEN CUSTARD

Phone: 314/481-2652 (21)

American
$1-$8

Folks in St. Louis stand in line for the eatery's specialty custard, no matter what the season. Limited parking and standing room only are just a part of the experience that has been a local tradition since 1931. Casual dress. **Reservations:** not accepted. **Hours:** Open 3/1-1/1 & 2/14-2/28; 11 am-10 pm; seasonal hours vary. Closed: 1/1, 11/25, 12/25. **Address:** 6726 Chippewa St 63109 **Location:** I-44, exit Laclede Station Rd, just e on Wilshusen Ave, just n on Murdoch Ave, just w on Lansdowne Ave, just e on Jamieson Ave, then just ne. **Parking:** on-site.

THE TENDERLOIN ROOM

Phone: 314/361-0900 (5)

Steak
$8-$36

The restaurant is legendary in the area. The longtime owner-operator gives character to the elegant, Old World dining room. On the menu are steaks, seafood specialties and fresh seasonal salads. Dressy casual. **Bar:** Full bar. **Reservations:** suggested. **Hours:** 11 am-2 & 5-10 pm, Sat & Sun from 5 pm. **Address:** 232 N Kingshighway Blvd 63108 **Location:** I-64, exit 36 (Kingshighway Blvd), 0.8 mi n; in Chase Park Plaza. **Parking:** valet. CALL

TRATTORIA MARCELLA

Phone: 314/352-7706 (20)

Italian
$11-$19

The popularity of Trattoria Marcella means you'd better call early for your reservation and then be prepared to be a part of a full house when you dine. The happy chorus of your fellow diners will set a festive tone for your enjoyment of rustic Italian dishes prepared with fresh-picked herbs, crisp vegetables and mushrooms straight-from-the-field, all depending on the time of the year. Dressy casual. **Bar:** Full bar. **Reservations:** suggested. **Hours:** 5 pm-10 pm, Fri & Sat-11 pm. Closed major holidays; also Sun & Mon. **Address:** 3600 Watson Rd 63109 **Location:** I-44, exit 286 (Hampton Ave), 0.5 mi s, then 1.2 mi sw; jct Pernod Ave. **Parking:** on-site.

ZIA'S *Menu on AAA.com*

Phone: 314/776-0020 (10)

Italian
$6-$19

In the Italian neighborhood of "The Hill," the restaurant serves reliable Italian food, such as chicken spiedini. Casual dress. **Bar:** Full bar. **Reservations:** not accepted. **Hours:** 11 am-10 pm, Fri & Sat-10:30 pm. Closed major holidays; also Sun. **Address:** 5256 Wilson Ave 63110 **Location:** I-44, exit 287 (Kingshighway Blvd), just s to Shaw Ave, 0.4 mi w to Wilson Ave, then just s. **Parking:** street.

The following restaurants have not been evaluated by AAA but are listed for your information only.

ADRIANA'S

Phone: 314/773-3833

fyi

Not evaluated. This small, always-crowded lunch place serves huge, tasty Sicilian-inspired sandwiches. **Address:** 5101 Shaw Blvd 63110

THE DRUNKEN FISH SUSHI BAR AND LOUNGE

Phone: 314/367-4222

fyi

Not evaluated. The cozy, contemporary and sophisticated restaurant serves sushi and other Japanese specialties. **Address:** 1 Maryland Plaza Dr 63108 **Location:** I-64, exit 36 (Kingshighway Blvd), 1 mi n, then just e.

KOPPERMAN'S DELICATESSEN

Phone: 314/361-0100

fyi

Not evaluated. The menu features kosher-style fare, including overstuffed sandwiches and imported foods. **Address:** 386 N Euclid Ave 63108 **Location:** I-64, exit 36 (Kingshighway Blvd), 1.2 mi n, just e on McPherson Ave, then just s.

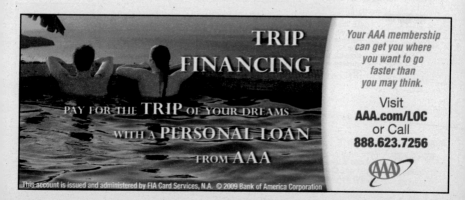

The St. Louis Vicinity

BALLWIN pop. 31,283 (See map and index starting on p. 526)

WHERE TO DINE

CHARLOTTE'S RIB BBQ — **Phone:** 636/394-3332 — 26

American
$6-$15

Patrons can sit back and enjoy the Western-themed eatery, which serves appetizers, salads and a wide range of barbecue favorites, including sugar-cured ham, ribs, brisket, catfish and pork steaks, to name a few. Save room for one of the homemade desserts. Casual dress. **Bar:** Beer & wine. **Reservations:** not accepted. **Hours:** 11 am-9 pm, Sun noon-8 pm. Closed: 4/4, 11/25, 12/25; also Mon. **Address:** 15467 Clayton Rd 63011 **Location:** SR 141, 3.2 mi w; in Claymont Center. **Parking:** on-site. CALL

BERKELEY pop. 10,063 (See map and index starting on p. 530)

HILTON GARDEN INN ST. LOUIS AIRPORT — Book great rates at AAA.com — **Phone:** (314)521-6444 — 26

Hotel
$79-$189 All Year

Address: 4450 Evans Place Dr 63134 **Location:** I-70, exit 240, just nw. **Facility:** Smoke free premises. 136 units. 123 one-bedroom standard units, some with whirlpools. 13 one-bedroom suites. 3 stories, interior corridors. *Bath:* combo or shower only. **Parking:** on-site. **Terms:** check-in 4 pm, 1-7 night minimum stay, cancellation fee imposed. **Amenities:** high-speed Internet, voice mail, irons, hair dryers. **Pool(s):** heated indoor. **Leisure Activities:** whirlpool, exercise room. **Guest Services:** valet and coin laundry, airport transportation-Lambert-St. Louis International Airport, wireless Internet. **Business Services:** meeting rooms, business center.

CALL

Hilton Garden Inn
AAA Benefit:
Members save 5% or more everyday!

RENAISSANCE ST. LOUIS HOTEL AIRPORT — Book great rates at AAA.com — **Phone:** (314)429-1100 — 25

Hotel
$161-$197 All Year

Address: 9801 Natural Bridge Rd 63134 **Location:** I-70, exit 237 (Natural Bridge Rd), just n; I-170, exit 6 (Natural Bridge Rd), just n. **Facility:** Smoke free premises. 393 units. 388 one-bedroom standard units. 5 one-bedroom suites. 12 stories, interior corridors. *Bath:* combo or shower only. **Parking:** on-site (fee) and valet. **Terms:** cancellation fee imposed. **Amenities:** high-speed Internet (fee), dual phone lines, voice mail, irons, hair dryers. *Some:* CD players. **Pool(s):** outdoor, heated indoor. **Leisure Activities:** whirlpool, exercise room. **Guest Services:** valet laundry, airport transportation-Lambert-St. Louis International Airport, area transportation-within 2 mi, wireless Internet. **Business Services:** conference facilities, business center. **Free Special Amenities: newspaper and preferred room (subject to availability with advance reservations).**

/ SOME UNITS FEE

RENAISSANCE HOTELS & RESORTS
AAA Benefit:
Members save a minimum 5% off the best available rate.

BRENTWOOD pop. 7,693 (See map and index starting on p. 530)

SPRINGHILL SUITES BY MARRIOTT — Book great rates at AAA.com — **Phone:** (314)647-8400 — 86

Hotel
$149-$169 All Year

Address: 1231 Strassner Dr 63144 **Location:** I-64, exit 32A (Hanley Rd), 0.5 mi s, then just w. **Facility:** Smoke free premises. 123 one-bedroom standard units. 6 stories, interior corridors. *Bath:* combo or shower only. **Parking:** on-site. **Terms:** cancellation fee imposed. **Amenities:** high-speed Internet, voice mail, irons, hair dryers. **Pool(s):** heated indoor. **Leisure Activities:** exercise room. **Guest Services:** valet and coin laundry, wireless Internet. **Business Services:** meeting rooms, business center.

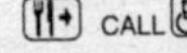   

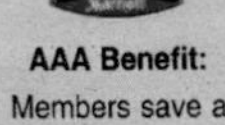

AAA Benefit:
Members save a minimum 5% off the best available rate.

WHERE TO DINE

FRANK PAPA'S RISTORANTE — **Phone:** 314/961-3344 — 91

Italian
$12-$25

Attractively priced country Italian fare is dished in generous portions. The casual fine-dining establishment includes a wine cellar. Casual dress. **Bar:** Full bar. **Reservations:** suggested. **Hours:** 5 pm-10 pm, Fri & Sat-11 pm. Closed: major holidays, 12/24; also Sun. **Address:** 2241 S Brentwood Blvd 63144 **Location:** I-64, exit 31A westbound, 0.7 mi s; exit 31 eastbound, 0.6 mi s. **Parking:** on-site. CALL

BRIDGETON pop. 15,550 (See map and index starting on p. 530)

BEST WESTERN AIRPORT PLAZA INN *Book great rates at AAA.com* Phone: (314)731-3800 

Hotel
$80-$120 All Year

Address: 4530 N Lindbergh Blvd 63044 **Location:** I-70, exit 235B, just e. **Facility:** 170 units. 2 stories (no elevator), interior corridors. *Bath:* combo or shower only. **Parking:** on-site. **Amenities:** voice mail, irons, hair dryers. **Pool(s):** outdoor. **Leisure Activities:** exercise room. **Guest Services:** valet and coin laundry, airport transportation-Lambert-St. Louis International Airport, area transportation-within 5 mi, wireless Internet. **Business Services:** conference facilities, business center. **Free Special Amenities: expanded continental breakfast and early check-in/late check-out.**

CALL / SOME UNITS

AAA Benefit:
Members save up to 20%, plus 10% bonus points with rewards program.

COURTYARD BY MARRIOTT - AIRPORT/EARTH CITY *Book great rates at AAA.com* Phone: (314)209-1000 (30)

Hotel
$119-$139 All Year

Address: 3101 Rider Tr S 63044 **Location:** I-70, exit 231B (Earth City Expwy), just n, then 0.8 mi e. **Facility:** Smoke free premises. 121 units. 115 one-bedroom standard units, some with whirlpools. 6 one-bedroom suites. 3 stories, interior corridors. *Bath:* combo or shower only. **Parking:** on-site. **Terms:** cancellation fee imposed. **Amenities:** high-speed Internet, voice mail, irons, hair dryers. **Pool(s):** heated indoor. **Leisure Activities:** whirlpool, exercise room. **Guest Services:** valet and coin laundry, wireless Internet. **Business Services:** meeting rooms, PC.

ECO / SOME UNITS

AAA Benefit:
Members save a minimum 5% off the best available rate.

EMBASSY SUITES ST. LOUIS AIRPORT *Book great rates at AAA.com* Phone: (314)739-8929 (33)

Hotel
$89-$179 All Year

Address: 11237 Lone Eagle Dr 63044 **Location:** I-70, exit 235A (Lindberg Blvd/US 67), just s, then just w. **Facility:** 159 one-bedroom suites. 6 stories, interior corridors. *Bath:* combo or shower only. **Parking:** on-site. **Terms:** 1-7 night minimum stay, cancellation fee imposed. **Amenities:** voice mail, irons, hair dryers. *Fee:* video games, high-speed Internet. **Pool(s):** heated indoor. **Leisure Activities:** sauna, whirlpool, exercise room. **Guest Services:** valet and coin laundry, area transportation, wireless Internet. **Business Services:** meeting rooms, business center.

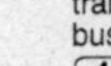     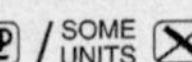 / SOME UNITS

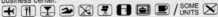

AAA Benefit:
Members save 5% or more everyday!

SPRINGHILL SUITES BY MARRIOTT - ST. LOUIS AIRPORT/EARTH CITY *Book great rates at AAA.com* Phone: (314)739-9991 (31)

Hotel
$114-$129 All Year

Address: 3099 Rider Tr S 63044 **Location:** I-70, exit 231B (Earth City Expwy), 0.5 mi n, then 0.9 mi e. **Facility:** Smoke free premises. 117 one-bedroom standard units. 4 stories, interior corridors. *Bath:* combo or shower only. **Parking:** on-site. **Terms:** cancellation fee imposed. **Amenities:** video games (fee), high-speed Internet, voice mail, irons, hair dryers. **Pool(s):** heated indoor. **Leisure Activities:** exercise room. **Guest Services:** valet and coin laundry, wireless Internet. **Business Services:** meeting rooms, business center. **Free Special Amenities: expanded continental breakfast and high-speed Internet.**

CALL

AAA Benefit:
Members save a minimum 5% off the best available rate.

(See map and index starting on p. 530)

STUDIOPLUS-ST LOUIS-EARTH CITY Book at AAA.com Phone: (314)209-1011 29

Extended Stay Hotel
$59-$74 All Year

Address: 3125 Rider Tr S 63045 **Location:** I-70, exit 231B (Earth City Expwy), just n, then 0.7 mi e **Facility:** 73 one-bedroom standard units with kitchens. 3 stories, interior corridors. *Bath:* combo c shower only. **Parking:** on-site. **Terms:** office hours 7 am-11 pm, cancellation fee imposed **Amenities:** voice mail, irons. **Leisure Activities:** whirlpool, exercise room. **Guest Services:** coi laundry, wireless Internet. ASK / SOME UNITS FEE

CHESTERFIELD pop. 46,802 (See map and index starting on p. 526)

DOUBLETREE HOTEL & CONFERENCE CENTER ST. LOUIS Book great rates at AAA.com Phone: (636)532-5000 23

Hotel
$79-$159 All Year

Address: 16625 Swingley Ridge Rd 63017 **Location:** I-64, exit 19A (Chesterfield Pkwy), 0.5 mi w. **Facility:** 223 units. 221 one-bedroom standard units. 2 one-bedroom suites. 12 stories, interior corridors. *Bath:* combo or shower only. **Parking:** on-site. **Terms:** 1-7 night minimum stay, cancellation fee imposed. **Amenities:** dual phone lines, voice mail, irons, hair dryers. **Pool(s):** outdoor, heated indoor. **Leisure Activities:** sauna, whirlpool, 15 tennis courts (9 indoor, 2 lighted), racquetball courts, jogging, basketball, volleyball. *Fee:* massage. **Guest Services:** valet laundry, area transportation, wireless Internet. **Business Services:** conference facilities, business center.
FEE FEE / SOME UNITS

DOUBLETREE® HOTELS·SUITES·RESORTS·CLUBS
AAA Benefit:
Members save 5% or more everyday!

DRURY PLAZA HOTEL-CHESTERFIELD Book at AAA.com Phone: (636)532-3300 25

Hotel
$90-$299 All Year

Address: 355 Chesterfield Center E 63017 **Location:** I-64/US 40, exit 19B (Clarkson Rd/Olive Blvd) jct I-64/US 40 and Clarkson Rd; southwest corner. **Facility:** 274 units. 223 one-bedroom standard units. 51 one-bedroom suites, some with whirlpools. 10 stories, interior corridors. *Bath:* combo o shower only. **Parking:** on-site. **Terms:** cancellation fee imposed. **Amenities:** voice mail, irons, hai dryers. **Pool(s):** heated indoor/outdoor. **Leisure Activities:** whirlpool, exercise room. **Guest Services** valet and coin laundry, wireless Internet. **Business Services:** meeting rooms, business center.
ASK CALL M / SOME UNITS

HAMPTON INN & SUITES-CHESTERFIELD Book great rates at AAA.com Phone: (636)530-0770 21

Hotel
$89-$99 All Year

Address: 5 McBride and Son Center Dr 63005 **Location:** I-64/US 40, exit 17 (Boones Crossing), just e. **Facility:** 120 units. 90 one-bedroom standard units. 30 one-bedroom suites with efficiencies, some with whirlpools. 3 stories, interior corridors. *Bath:* combo or shower only. **Parking:** on-site. **Terms:** check-in 4 pm, 1-7 night minimum stay, cancellation fee imposed. **Amenities:** video games (fee), voice mail, irons, hair dryers. *Some:* DVD players, dual phone lines. **Pool(s):** heated indoor. **Leisure Activities:** whirlpool, exercise room. *Fee:* game room. **Guest Services:** valet and coin laundry, area transportation, wireless Internet. **Business Services:** meeting rooms, PC. / SOME UNITS

Hampton Inn & Suites
AAA Benefit:
Members save up to 10% everyday!

HILTON GARDEN INN Book great rates at AAA.com Phone: (636)532-9400 22

Hotel
$75-$149 All Year

Address: 16631 Chesterfield Grove Rd 63005 **Location:** I-64, exit 19A (Chesterfield Pkwy), 0.5 mi w on N Outer 40 Dr to Chesterfield Pkwy N, 0.8 mi on Chesterfield Airport Rd to Baxter Rd, then 0.3 mi. **Facility:** 100 one-bedroom standard units. 4 stories, interior corridors. *Bath:* combo or shower only. **Parking:** on-site. **Terms:** 1-7 night minimum stay, cancellation fee imposed. **Amenities:** high-speed Internet, dual phone lines, voice mail, irons, hair dryers. **Pool(s):** heated indoor. **Leisure Activities:** whirlpool, exercise room. **Guest Services:** valet and coin laundry, area transportation-within 5 mi, wireless Internet. **Business Services:** meeting rooms, business center. **Free Special Amenities: high-speed Internet.**
CALL M / SOME UNITS

Hilton Garden Inn
AAA Benefit:
Members save 5% or more everyday!

HOMEWOOD SUITES BY HILTON Book great rates at AAA.com Phone: (636)530-0305 24

Extended Stay Hotel
$89-$149 All Year

Address: 840 N Chesterfield Pkwy W 63017 **Location:** I-64, exit 20 (Chesterfield Pkwy), 1 mi n. **Facility:** 145 units. 140 one- and 5 two-bedroom suites with efficiencies. 3 stories, interior corridors. *Bath:* combo or shower only. **Parking:** on-site. **Terms:** 1-7 night minimum stay, cancellation fee imposed. **Amenities:** video games (fee), high-speed Internet, dual phone lines, voice mail, irons, hair dryers. *Some:* DVD players. **Pool(s):** heated outdoor. **Leisure Activities:** exercise room. **Guest Services:** valet and coin laundry, area transportation, wireless Internet. **Business Services:** meeting rooms, business center.
/ SOME UNITS FEE

AAA Benefit:
Members save 5% or more everyday!

(See map and index starting on p. 526)

WHERE TO DINE

ANNIE GUNN'S — **Phone:** 636/532-7684 (21)

Regional American $8-$38

Traditional barbecue reflects creative gourmet twists in this laid-back Irish pub. Favorites include smoked pork chops grilled with barbecue glaze and bread pudding. The delightful mixed field green salad is served with toasted pine nuts. The popular restaurant is often busy so waiting for a table is not unusual. Casual dress. **Bar:** Full bar. **Reservations:** suggested. **Hours:** 11 am-10:30 pm, Fri & Sat-11:30 pm, Sun-9 pm. Closed major holidays; also Mon. **Address:** 16806 Chesterfield Airport Rd 63005 **Location:** I-64, exit 19A (Chesterfield Pkwy), 0.4 mi w to Chesterfield Pkwy, just s to Chesterfield Airport Rd, then 1 mi w. **Parking:** on-site.

EAST COAST PIZZA — **Phone:** 636/536-7888 (22)

American $6-$10

The family-owned and operated eatery serves New York pizza with daily made hand-tossed dough and homemade pizza sauce. Philadelphia cheese steak and other sandwiches, as well as soups and spaghetti, are other delicious options. Casual dress. **Bar:** Beer & wine. **Reservations:** accepted. **Hours:** 11 am-10 pm, Fri & Sat-11 pm, Sun-9 pm. Closed: 4/4, 11/25, 12/25. **Address:** 17304 Chesterfield Airport Rd 63005 **Location:** At Chesterfield Commons Shopping Center. **Parking:** on-site.

EL MAGUEY — **Phone:** 314/878-5988 (19)

Mexican $5-$14

One of a chain of restaurants, this place prepares all the favorites, including tacos, burritos, enchiladas and, of course, chips and salsa. Patrons won't go home hungry. Casual dress. **Bar:** Beer only. **Reservations:** accepted. **Hours:** 11 am-10 pm. Closed major holidays. **Address:** 13377 Olive Blvd 63017 **Location:** Just e of SR 141; in Woodchase Shopping Plaza. **Parking:** on-site. CALL M

VILLA FAROTTO VINEYARDS — **Phone:** 636/519-0048 (20)

Italian $8-$33

Contemporary and classy, this sophisticated trendy spot comes highly recommended by local businesses; you won't be disappointed. Casual dress. **Bar:** Full bar. **Reservations:** accepted. **Hours:** 11 am-10 pm, Fri-11 pm, Sat 4 pm-11 pm, Sun 4 pm-9 pm. Closed: 11/25, 12/25. **Address:** 17417 Chesterfield Airport Rd 63005 **Location:** I-64, exit 17, 0.3 mi on Boones Crossing St, then 0.4 mi w. **Parking:** on-site.
CALL M

YIA YIA'S EURO BISTRO — **Phone:** 636/537-9991 (23)

Continental $9-$25

Among examples of European-style cuisine that reflects a Mediterranean flair are oak-fired pizza, piadini and pasta favorites. Dressy casual. **Bar:** Full bar. **Reservations:** suggested. **Hours:** 11 am-10 pm, Fri & Sat-11 pm, Sun 10 am-9 pm. Closed: 7/4, 12/25. **Address:** 15601 Olive Blvd 63017 **Location:** I-64, exit 20 (Chesterfield Pkwy), just ne. **Parking:** on-site.

The following restaurant has not been evaluated by AAA but is listed for your information only.

GIANFABIO RISTORANTE/IL FORNO CAFE — **Phone:** 636/532-6686

fyi

Not evaluated. The establishment features both traditional and West Coast-style Italian cuisine. **Address:** 127 Hilltown Village Center 63017

CLAYTON pop. 13,900 (See map and index starting on p. 530)

CROWNE PLAZA ST. LOUIS-CLAYTON *Book great rates at AAA.com* — **Phone:** (314)726-5400 (64)

AAA SAVE

Hotel $99-$299 All Year

Address: 7750 Carondelet Ave 63105 **Location:** I-64, exit 32B (Hanley Rd), 1.3 mi n, then just w. **Facility:** 250 one-bedroom standard units, some with whirlpools. 2-8 stories, interior corridors. *Bath:* combo or shower only. **Parking:** on-site (fee) and valet. **Amenities:** video games (fee), CD players, high-speed Internet, dual phone lines, voice mail, honor bars, irons, hair dryers. *Some:* safes. **Pool(s):** heated indoor/outdoor. **Leisure Activities:** sauna, exercise room, game room. **Guest Services:** valet and coin laundry, airport transportation-Lambert-St. Louis International Airport, area transportation-within Clayton & Galleria, wireless Internet. **Business Services:** conference facilities, business center. **Free Special Amenities: newspaper and high-speed Internet.**

/ SOME UNITS

THE RITZ-CARLTON, ST. LOUIS *Book great rates at AAA.com* — **Phone:** (314)863-6300 (63)

AAA SAVE

Hotel $159-$525 3/1-12/31 $139-$525 1/1-2/28

Address: 100 Carondelet Plaza 63105 **Location:** I-64, exit 32B (Hanley Rd), 1.2 mi n, then just e. **Facility:** A luxury hotel with elegant public areas paneled in African Makore mahogany with original oil paintings, marble floors and oriental rugs. Smoke free premises. 300 units. 265 one-bedroom standard units. 35 one-bedroom suites, some with whirlpools. 18 stories, interior corridors. *Bath:* combo or shower only. **Parking:** on-site (fee) and valet. **Terms:** check-in 4 pm, cancellation fee imposed. **Amenities:** dual phone lines, voice mail, safes, honor bars, irons, hair dryers. *Fee:* video games, high-speed Internet. *Some:* DVD players. **Dining:** The Grill, see separate listing. **Pool(s):** heated indoor. **Leisure Activities:** saunas, whirlpool, steamroom, sun deck. *Fee:* massage. **Guest Services:** valet laundry, wireless Internet. **Business Services:** conference facilities, business center. **Free Special Amenities: newspaper.**

24 / SOME UNITS FEE

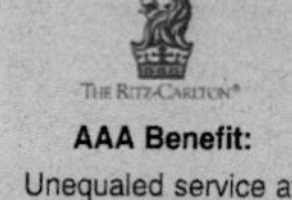

AAA Benefit: Unequaled service at Special Member Savings.

(See map and index starting on p. 530)

SEVEN GABLES INN Phone: 314/863-8400 62

Historic Boutique Hotel
Rates not provided

Address: 26 N Meramec Ave 63105 **Location:** I-64, exit 31 (Brentwood Blvd), 1.3 mi on, just e on Bonhomme Ave, then just n. **Facility:** The 1926 Tutor-style inn offers a variety of guest room types and sizes. There is no elevator at this multi-level property. Designated smoking area. 32 one-bedroom standard units. 3 stories (no elevator), interior corridors. **Parking:** on-site (fee) and valet. **Amenities:** voice mail, irons, hair dryers. **Guest Services:** wireless Internet. **Business Services:** meeting rooms, PC. **Free Special Amenities: continental breakfast and high-speed Internet.**

SHERATON CLAYTON PLAZA HOTEL Book great rates at AAA.com Phone: 314/863-0400 65

Hotel
Rates not provided

Address: 7730 Bonhomme Ave 63105 **Location:** I-64, exit 31 (Brentwood Blvd), 1.3 mi n, then 0.7 mi e. **Facility:** Smoke free premises. 259 units. 245 one-bedroom standard units. 12 one- and 2 two-bedroom suites. 16 stories, interior corridors. *Bath:* combo or shower only. **Parking:** on-site (fee) and valet. **Amenities:** video games (fee), dual phone lines, voice mail, irons, hair dryers. **Pool(s):** heated indoor. **Leisure Activities:** sun deck, exercise room. **Guest Services:** valet and coin laundry, airport transportation-Lambert-St. Louis International Airport, area transportation-within 5 mi, wireless Internet, beauty salon. **Business Services:** conference facilities, business center. **Free Special Amenities: local telephone calls and newspaper.**

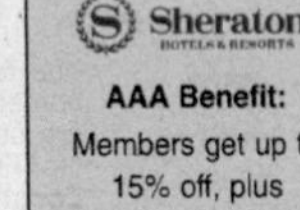

AAA Benefit: Members get up to 15% off, plus Starwood Preferred Guest® bonuses.

/ SOME UNITS

WHERE TO DINE

BARCELONA TAPAS RESTAURANT Phone: 314/863-9909 73

Spanish
$10-$15

At this favorite spot, guests should be prepared for high-energy atmosphere and great food. A lengthy menu of "little bites" is designed to facilitate sampling many plates and sharing with friends. Dressy casual. **Bar:** Full bar. **Reservations:** accepted. **Hours:** 11 am-11 pm, Sun 5 pm-10 pm. Closed: 11/25, 12/25. **Address:** 34 N Central Ave 63105 **Location:** Just n of Forsyth Blvd. **Parking:** on-site and valet.

CALL

CARDWELL'S IN CLAYTON Phone: 314/726-5055 72

American
$6-$25

Cardwell's offers creative, superb cuisine prepared with a subtle flair in a casually elegant atmosphere. The menu includes tasty fare like five-onion soup, roasted rack of lamb and pepper-grilled New York strip, along with pasta and salads. A well-rounded wine list is offered. Dressy casual. **Bar:** Full bar. **Reservations:** suggested. **Hours:** 11:30 am-2:30 & 5:30-10 pm, Fri & Sat-11 pm. Closed major holidays; also Sun. **Address:** 8100 Maryland Ave 63105 **Location:** I-64, exit 31A (Brentwood Blvd), 1.6 mi n on Brentwood Blvd. **Parking:** street.

DOMINIC'S TRATTORIA Phone: 314/863-4567 77

Italian
$9-$25

Sophisticated without being stuffy, the restaurant is on the ground floor of a multi-story building. Favorite preparations of pasta, veal, chicken, beef and fish all are complemented by the complete wine list. Service is professional and efficient. Dressy casual. **Bar:** Full bar. **Reservations:** suggested. **Hours:** 11 am-2 & 5-10 pm, Sat 5 pm-10:30 pm. Closed major holidays; also Sun. **Address:** 200 S Brentwood Blvd 63105 **Location:** I-64/US 40, exit 31A (Brentwood Blvd), 1.1 mi n to Bonhomme; in Park Tower Building. **Parking:** on-site.

THE GRILL Phone: 314/863-6300 75

American
$16-$40

Fresh interpretations of classic cuisine combine the finest ingredients with creative techniques. Beef and seafood dishes anchor the menu, complemented by lamb, poultry and pork. The dessert menu features traditional classics like chocolate souffle and creme brulee. The atmosphere merges refinement with comfort. Dressy casual. **Bar:** Full bar. **Reservations:** suggested. **Hours:** 6 pm-10 pm. Closed: Sun & Mon. **Address:** 100 Carondelet Plaza 63105 **Location:** I-64, exit 32B (Hanley Rd), 1.2 mi n, then just e; in The Ritz-Carlton, St. Louis. **Parking:** on-site (fee) and valet.

JIMMY'S ON THE PARK CAFE BISTRO & BAR Phone: 314/725-8585 79

American
$9-$30

The casual restaurant's specialties reflect fine contemporary cuisine, including light and tasty flash-fried spinach and tenderloin Anthony. Live jazz fills the air Friday and Saturday nights, as well as Saturday and Sunday afternoons. Casual dress. **Bar:** Full bar. **Reservations:** suggested. **Hours:** 11:30 am-10 pm, Fri & Sat-10:30 pm, Sun 10 am-2 & 5-9 pm, Mon 5 pm-10 pm. Closed major holidays. **Address:** 706 DeMun Ave 63105 **Location:** I-64, exit 34B (Clayton/Skinker), 0.6 mi w on Clayton Rd, then 0.5 mi n. **Parking:** on-site.

LUCIANO'S TRATTORIA Phone: 314/863-9969 76

Italian
$8-$40

Sophistication marks the warm, contemporary atmosphere at Luciano's. Fresh seasonal ingredients go into preparations of pasta, seafood, veal and wood-fired pizzas. For dessert, the tiramisu is a classic. Dressy casual. **Bar:** Full bar. **Reservations:** suggested. **Hours:** 11 am-2 & 5-10:30 pm, Fri & Sat-11 pm, Sun 4 pm-9 pm. Closed major holidays. **Address:** 172 Carondelet Pl 63105 **Location:** I-64, exit 32B (Hanley Rd), 1.2 mi n, then just e; in The Plaza. **Parking:** on-site (fee) and valet. CALL

PORTABELLA Phone: 314/725-6588 74

Italian
$8-$27

Portabella's has enhanced the traditional menu of pasta and mushrooms—appetizers and entrees—with light touches and splendid accents. Its atmosphere is understated elegance, and its wine list is extensive. Valet service is available after 6 pm. Dressy casual. **Bar:** Full bar. **Reservations:** suggested. **Hours:** 11:30 am-2 & 5:30-10 pm, Fri-11 pm, Sat 5:30 pm-11 pm, Sun 5 pm-9 pm. Closed: 7/4, 11/25, 12/25. **Address:** 15 N Central Ave 63105 **Location:** I-64, exit 31A (Brentwood Blvd), 1.6 mi n, just e on Maryland Ave, then just s. **Parking:** valet and street.

(See map and index starting on p. 530)

REMY'S KITCHEN & WINE BAR

Phone: 314/726-5757 (78)

Regional Continental $6-$20

Gourmet cuisine with Mediterranean accents is served in a friendly and energetic atmosphere. The menu includes both large and small plates, designed for sampling and sharing multiple courses. Casual dress. **Bar:** Full bar. **Reservations:** suggested. **Hours:** 11:30 am-2 & 5:30-10 pm, Fri-11 pm, Sat 5:30 pm-11 pm. Closed major holidays; also Sun. **Address:** 222 S Bemiston Ave 63105 **Location:** I-64, exit 32B (Hanley Rd), 1 mi n, just w on Bonhomme Ave, then just s. **Parking:** on-site.

YEN CHING

Phone: 314/721-7507 (80)

Chinese $7-$16

This locally popular restaurant has a casual, relaxed decor and authentic cuisine. Families and business people enjoy this eatery, although it has limited parking. The Yen Ching beef and chicken choices are good, as is the glazed banana dessert. Casual dress. **Bar:** Full bar. **Reservations:** suggested, weekends. **Hours:** 11:30 am-2 & 5-9:30 pm, Fri-10:30 pm, Sat 5 pm-10:30 pm, Sun 4:30 pm-9 pm. Closed: 11/25, 12/25. **Address:** 1012 S Brentwood Blvd 63117 **Location:** I-64/US 40, exit 31A (Brentwood Blvd), 0.4 mi n. **Parking:** on-site.

The following restaurant has not been evaluated by AAA but is listed for your information only.

CAFÉ NAPOLI

Phone: 314/863-5731

fyi

Not evaluated. Classic Italian dishes are served in large portions. **Address:** 7754 Forsyth Blvd 63105 **Location:** I-64, exit 32B (Hanley Rd), 1 mi n, then just w.

CREVE COEUR pop. 16,500 (See map and index starting on p. 530)

COURTYARD BY MARRIOTT-CREVE COEUR *Book great rates at AAA.com*

Phone: (314)993-0515 (59)

Hotel $139-$149 All Year

Address: 828 N New Ballas Rd 63146 **Location:** I-270, exit 14 (Olive Blvd), 0.5 mi e to New Ballas Rd, then just n. **Facility:** Smoke free premises. 154 units. 141 one-bedroom standard units. 13 one-bedroom suites. 2-4 stories, interior corridors. *Bath:* combo or shower only. **Parking:** on-site. **Terms:** cancellation fee imposed. **Amenities:** video games (fee), high-speed Internet, dual phone lines, voice mail, irons, hair dryers. **Pool(s):** heated indoor. **Leisure Activities:** whirlpool, exercise room. **Guest Services:** valet and coin laundry, wireless Internet. **Business Services:** meeting rooms, business center.

CALL / SOME UNITS

AAA Benefit: Members save a minimum 5% off the best available rate.

DRURY INN & SUITES-CREVE COEUR *Book at AAA.com*

Phone: (314)989-1100 (58)

Hotel $90-$174 All Year

Address: 11980 Olive Blvd 63141 **Location:** I-270, exit 14 (Olive Blvd). **Facility:** 187 units. 155 one-bedroom standard units. 32 one-bedroom suites. 8 stories, interior corridors. *Bath:* combo or shower only. **Parking:** on-site. **Terms:** cancellation fee imposed. **Amenities:** high-speed Internet, dual phone lines, voice mail, irons, hair dryers. **Pool(s):** heated indoor. **Leisure Activities:** whirlpool, exercise room. **Guest Services:** valet and coin laundry, wireless Internet. **Business Services:** meeting rooms, business center. ASK CALL / SOME UNITS

WHERE TO DINE

BRISTOL BAR & SEAFOOD GRILL

Phone: 314/567-0272 (69)

Seafood $10-$30

All seafood is a great catch, and fresh fish is grilled over a mesquite-wood fire. Because attention is paid to seasonal ingredients, the menu is printed each day. A warm, sophisticated atmosphere draws the local corporate crowd. Casual dress. **Bar:** Full bar. **Reservations:** suggested. **Hours:** 11 am-10 pm, Fri-10:30 pm, Sat 4:30 pm-10:30 pm, Sun 10 am-2 & 4:30-9 pm. Closed: 12/25. **Address:** 11801 Olive Blvd 63141 **Location:** I-270, exit 14 (Olive Blvd), 0.5 mi e. **Parking:** on-site.

IL BELLAGIO CITY PLACE

Phone: 314/994-1080 (68)

Italian $10-$36

Rich contemporary decor characterizes the casual, fine-dining atmosphere. Formal service appeals to business, special occasion and casual diners. Dressy casual. **Bar:** Full bar. **Reservations:** accepted. **Hours:** 11 am-10 pm, Fri & Sat-11 pm. Closed major holidays; also Sun. **Address:** 11631 Olive Blvd 63141 **Location:** I-270, exit 14 (Olive Blvd), 0.6 mi e. **Parking:** on-site.

KOBE STEAK HOUSE OF JAPAN

Phone: 314/434-2600 (66)

Japanese $6-$27

Patrons often visit the popular casual spot for special occasions. The menu focus is on steak, chicken and seafood. Casual dress. **Bar:** Full bar. **Reservations:** suggested. **Hours:** 5:30 pm-9 pm, Thurs & Fri 11:30 am-2 & 5-10 pm, Sat 4:30 pm-10 pm, Sun 4:30 pm-8:30 pm. **Address:** 12521 Olive Blvd 63141 **Location:** I-270, exit 14 (Olive Blvd), 0.7 mi w; in Dierbergs Heritage Place Shopping Center. **Parking:** on-site.

LA BONNE BOUCHEE WESTGATE CENTER

Phone: 314/576-6606 (67)

French $8-$15

A cafe-like decor sets the stage for casual, quiet dining with fabulous, yet simple, meals. Most days, only one meat and one fish entree are offered. Otherwise, diners opt for salads, quiche, soups, sandwiches and other light fare. The bakery offers many European cakes and fresh pastries. Casual dress. **Bar:** Full bar. **Reservations:** accepted. **Hours:** 7 am-9 pm, Sun 8:30 am-1:30 pm, Mon 7 am-3 pm. Closed major holidays. **Address:** 12344 Olive Blvd 63141 **Location:** I-270, exit 14 (Olive Blvd), 0.3 mi w; in Westgate Center. **Parking:** on-site.

EARTH CITY (See map and index starting on p. 530)

RESIDENCE INN ST. LOUIS AIRPORT/EARTH CITY Book great rates at AAA.com **Phone:** (314)209-0995 14

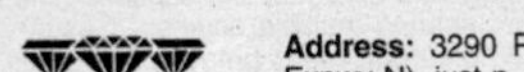

Extended Stay Hotel

$144-$164 All Year

Address: 3290 Rider Tr S 63045 **Location:** I-70, exit 231B (Earth City Expwy N), just n, then just e. **Facility:** Smoke free premises. 104 units. 40 one-bedroom standard units, some with efficiencies or kitchens. 42 one- and 22 two-bedroom suites, some with efficiencies or kitchens. 4 stories, interior corridors. *Bath:* combo or shower only. **Parking:** on-site. **Terms:** cancellation fee imposed. **Amenities:** high-speed Internet, dual phone lines, voice mail, irons, hair dryers. **Pool(s):** heated indoor. **Leisure Activities:** whirlpool, exercise room, sports court. **Guest Services:** valet and coin laundry, area transportation, wireless Internet. **Business Services:** meeting rooms, PC.

CALL

/ SOME UNITS FEE

AAA Benefit:

Members save a minimum 5% off the best available rate.

EDMUNDSON pop. 840 (See map and index starting on p. 530)

DRURY INN-ST. LOUIS AIRPORT Book at AAA.com **Phone:** (314)423-7700 22

Hotel

$80-$194 All Year

Address: 10490 Natural Bridge Rd 63134 **Location:** I-70, exit 236 (Lambert Airport), just s, then just e. **Facility:** 172 units. 162 one-bedroom standard units. 10 one-bedroom suites. 6 stories, interior corridors. *Bath:* combo or shower only. **Parking:** on-site. **Terms:** cancellation fee imposed. **Amenities:** high-speed Internet, voice mail, irons, hair dryers. **Pool(s):** heated indoor. **Leisure Activities:** whirlpool, exercise room. **Guest Services:** valet and coin laundry, wireless Internet. **Business Services:** meeting rooms, PC.

ASK CALL / SOME UNITS

MARRIOTT-ST. LOUIS AIRPORT Book great rates at AAA.com **Phone:** (314)423-9700 21

AAA SAVE

Hotel

$170-$208 All Year

Address: 10700 Pear Tree Ln 63134 **Location:** I-70, exit 236 (Lambert Airport), just s. **Facility:** Smoke free premises. 601 units. 598 one-bedroom standard units. 3 one-bedroom suites. 3-9 stories, interior corridors. *Bath:* combo or shower only. **Parking:** on-site (fee). **Terms:** cancellation fee imposed. **Amenities:** high-speed Internet (fee), voice mail, irons, hair dryers. *Some:* CD players. **Pool(s):** outdoor, heated indoor/outdoor. **Leisure Activities:** whirlpool. **Guest Services:** valet and coin laundry, airport transportation-Lambert-St. Louis International Airport, wireless Internet. **Business Services:** conference facilities, business center. *(See color ad p 547)*

24 / SOME UNITS

Marriott HOTELS & RESORTS

AAA Benefit:

Members save a minimum 5% off the best available rate.

(See map and index starting on p. 530)

WHERE TO DINE

LOMBARDO'S RESTAURANT — **Phone:** 314/429-5151 (36)

Italian
$7-$20

A longtime and well-respected restaurant family, the Lombardos have been serving fine food since 1934. Warm and sophisticated decor, fine service and an atmosphere suitable for business and special occasion dining characterize this place. Casual dress. **Bar:** Full bar. **Reservations:** accepted. **Hours:** 11 am-10 pm, Sat from 5 pm. Closed: 11/25, 12/25; also Sun. **Address:** 10488 Natural Bridge Rd 63134 **Location:** I-70, exit 236 (Lambert Airport), just se. **Parking:** on-site.

EUREKA pop. 7,676 (See map and index starting on p. 526)

HOLIDAY INN AT SIX FLAGS — Book at AAA.com — **Phone:** (636)938-6661 (35)

Hotel
$129-$299 3/1-9/5
$99-$229 9/6-2/28

Address: 4901 Six Flags Rd 63025 **Location:** I-44, exit 261 (Allenton Rd). **Facility:** 179 units. 167 one- and 12 two-bedroom standard units. 1-3 stories, interior/exterior corridors. *Bath:* combo or shower only. **Parking:** on-site. **Terms:** check-in 4 pm. **Amenities:** video games (fee), high-speed Internet, voice mail, irons, hair dryers. **Pool(s):** heated indoor. **Leisure Activities:** sauna, whirlpool, exercise room, shuffleboard. *Fee:* game room. **Guest Services:** valet and coin laundry, area transportation, wireless Internet. **Business Services:** meeting rooms, PC.

WHERE TO DINE

POOR RICHARD'S — **Phone:** 636/938-4666 (32)

American
$6-$15

Since 1998, the restaurant has served basic pub fare, including the ever-popular chicken wings. Casual dress. **Bar:** Full bar. **Reservations:** not accepted. **Hours:** 11 am-midnight, Sun noon-11 pm. Closed: 4/4, 11/25, 12/25. **Address:** 108A Hilltop Village Center 63025 **Location:** I-44, exit 264, 1 mi w; in Hilltop Village Center. **Parking:** on-site.

FENTON pop. 4,360 (See map and index starting on p. 530)

DRURY INN & SUITES-FENTON — Book at AAA.com — **Phone:** (636)343-7822 (106)

Hotel
$80-$170 All Year

Address: 1088 S Highway Dr 63026 **Location:** I-44, exit 274 (Bowles Ave), just se. **Facility:** 139 units. 127 one-bedroom standard units. 12 one-bedroom suites. 4 stories, interior corridors. **Parking:** on-site. **Terms:** cancellation fee imposed. **Amenities:** high-speed Internet, dual phone lines, voice mail, irons, hair dryers. **Pool(s):** heated indoor/outdoor. **Leisure Activities:** whirlpool, exercise room. **Guest Services:** valet and coin laundry, wireless Internet. **Business Services:** meeting rooms, business center.

HOLIDAY INN EXPRESS HOTEL & SUITES — Book at AAA.com — **Phone:** (636)349-4444 (109)

Hotel
$76-$129 All Year

Address: 1848 Bowles Ave 63026 **Location:** I-44, exit 274A (Bowles Ave), just s. Located in a commercial area. **Facility:** Smoke free premises. 76 units. 73 one-bedroom standard units, some with whirlpools. 3 one-bedroom suites with whirlpools. 3 stories, interior corridors. *Bath:* combo or shower only. **Parking:** on-site, winter plug-ins. **Amenities:** high-speed Internet, voice mail, irons, hair dryers. *Some:* DVD players, dual phone lines. **Pool(s):** heated indoor. **Leisure Activities:** exercise room. **Guest Services:** valet and coin laundry, wireless Internet. **Business Services:** meeting rooms, PC, fax.

PEAR TREE INN BY DRURY-FENTON — Book at AAA.com — **Phone:** (636)343-8820 (107)

Hotel
$55-$119 All Year

Address: 1100 S Highway Dr 63026 **Location:** I-44, exit 274 (Bowles Ave), just s. **Facility:** 104 one-bedroom standard units. 3 stories, interior corridors. **Parking:** on-site. **Terms:** cancellation fee imposed. **Amenities:** voice mail, irons, hair dryers. **Pool(s):** outdoor. **Guest Services:** valet laundry, wireless Internet.

TOWNEPLACE SUITES BY MARRIOTT — Book great rates at AAA.com — **Phone:** (636)305-7000 (108)

Extended Stay Hotel
$107-$131 All Year

Address: 1662 Fenton Business Park Ct 63026 **Location:** I-44, exit 275 westbound; exit 274 eastbound to S Highway Dr, just s. **Facility:** Smoke free premises. 95 units. 69 one-bedroom standard units with kitchens. 4 one- and 22 two-bedroom suites with kitchens. 3 stories, interior corridors. *Bath:* combo or shower only. **Parking:** on-site. **Terms:** cancellation fee imposed. **Amenities:** voice mail, irons, hair dryers. **Pool(s):** outdoor. **Leisure Activities:** exercise room. **Guest Services:** valet and coin laundry, wireless Internet. **Business Services:** business center.

AAA Benefit:
Members save a minimum 5% off the best available rate.

WHERE TO DINE

BANDANA'S BAR-B-Q — **Phone:** 636/305-8855

Barbecue
$5-$16

The real wood-pit smoker produces tasty meats. Try a Southern favorite: hot boiled peanuts on the side. Casual dress. **Bar:** Beer & wine. **Reservations:** not accepted. **Hours:** 11 am-9 pm, Fri & Sat-10 pm. Closed: 11/25, 12/25. **Address:** 1160 S Highway Dr 63026 **Location:** I-44, exit 274 (Bowles Ave), just s. **Parking:** on-site.

(See map and index starting on p. 530)

The following restaurant has not been evaluated by AAA but is listed for your information only.

POOR RICHARD'S **Phone:** 636/349-3438

fyi Not evaluated. Since 1998, the restaurant has been serving basic pub fare, including its ever-popular chicken wings. **Address:** 960 Brookwood Center 63026 **Location:** I-44, exit 274 (Bowles Ave).

FLORISSANT pop. 50,497 (See map and index starting on p. 530)

HAMPTON INN-ST. LOUIS NORTHWEST Book great rates at AAA.com **Phone:** (314)839-2200 11

AAA SAVE

Hotel
$79-$129 All Year

Address: 55 Dunn Rd 63031 **Location:** I-270, exit 26B (Graham Rd/Hanley Rd), just nw. Located in a commercial area. **Facility:** 126 one-bedroom standard units. 4 stories, interior corridors. *Bath:* combo or shower only. **Parking:** on-site. **Terms:** 1-7 night minimum stay, cancellation fee imposed. **Amenities:** video games (fee), voice mail, irons, hair dryers. **Pool(s):** outdoor. **Leisure Activities:** exercise room. **Guest Services:** valet laundry, wireless Internet. **Business Services:** meeting rooms, business center. **Free Special Amenities: newspaper and high-speed Internet.** / SOME UNITS

AAA Benefit:
Members save up to 10% everyday!

WHERE TO DINE

THE BARN DELI **Phone:** 314/838-3670 30

Deli
$5-$8

Built in the early 1870s as a farm barn, the building has been converted to retail space including this laid-back deli, a hidden treasure. Lining the menu are taste-tempting soups, salads, sandwiches and sweets. The signature barn nut pie features pecans on a cheesecake filling in a pie-dough crust. Casual dress. **Bar:** Beer & wine. **Reservations:** accepted. **Hours:** 11 am-3 pm. Closed major holidays; also Sun. **Address:** 180 Dunn Rd 63031 **Location:** I-270, exit 26B (Graham Rd/Hanley Rd), just n on Graham Rd, then just w. **Parking:** on-site.

FRESH ITALY **Phone:** 314/830-0600 27

Italian
$8-$15

Homemade food makes the wait worthwhile at the cozy and comfortable neighborhood establishment. Casual dress. **Bar:** Beer & wine. **Reservations:** not accepted. **Hours:** 4 pm-9 pm, Fri & Sat-10 pm. Closed major holidays; also Mon. **Address:** 119 Florissant Oaks Plaza 63031 **Location:** I-270, exit 25 (Lindbergh Blvd), 2 mi n; in Florissant Oaks Plaza. **Parking:** on-site.

RUIZ MEXICAN RESTAURANT **Phone:** 314/838-3500 28

Mexican
$7-$18

The city's oldest Mexican restaurant is run by the Ruiz family's third generation. Popular with locals, it serves enchiladas, tamales made from scratch, fajitas with tender rib eye and great margaritas. Casual dress. **Bar:** Full bar. **Reservations:** accepted. **Hours:** 11 am-10 pm, Sun-9 pm. Closed major holidays. **Address:** 901 N Hwy 67 (Lindbergh Blvd) 63031 **Location:** I-270, exit 25 (Lindbergh Blvd), 2.1 mi n. **Parking:** on-site.

YACOVELLI'S RESTAURANT **Phone:** 314/839-1000 29

AAA

Italian
$11-$20

One of the area's oldest names in the restaurant industry, Yacovelli's has been in continuous operation since 1919. Specializing in a varied cuisine of prime rib, steak, seafood, fried chicken and Italian gourmet, this place offers a fine dining experience in a comfortable and relaxed atmosphere. Casual dress. **Bar:** Full bar. **Reservations:** suggested, weekends. **Hours:** 4 pm-9 pm, Fri & Sat-10 pm, Sun-8 pm. Closed: 11/25, 12/25; also Mon & Tues. **Address:** 407 Dunn Rd 63031 **Location:** I-270, exit 26B (Graham Rd/Hanley Rd), just n. **Parking:** on-site.

FORISTELL pop. 331 (See map and index starting on p. 526)

BEST WESTERN WEST 70 INN Book great rates at AAA.com **Phone:** (636)673-2900 14

AAA SAVE

Hotel
$67-$72 All Year

Address: 12 Hwy W 63348 **Location:** I-70, exit 203 (CR W), just n. Located near a truck stop. **Facility:** 58 one-bedroom standard units. 2 stories (no elevator), interior corridors. **Parking:** on-site. **Amenities:** high-speed Internet, voice mail, irons, hair dryers. **Pool(s):** outdoor. **Guest Services:** coin laundry, wireless Internet. **Business Services:** meeting rooms, PC. **Free Special Amenities: expanded continental breakfast and high-speed Internet.**

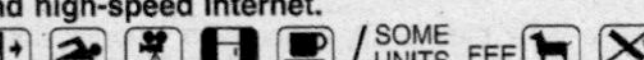

AAA Benefit:
Members save up to 20%, plus 10% bonus points with rewards program.

FRONTENAC pop. 3,483 (See map and index starting on p. 530)

HILTON ST. LOUIS FRONTENAC *Book great rates at AAA.com* **Phone:** (314)993-1100 77

Hotel
$99-$289 All Year

Address: 1335 S Lindbergh Blvd 63131 **Location:** I-64, exit 28A (S Lindbergh Blvd), just s. **Facility:** 263 units. 224 one-bedroom standard units. 39 one-bedroom suites. 2-3 stories, interior corridors. *Bath:* combo or shower only. **Parking:** on-site. **Terms:** 1-7 night minimum stay, cancellation fee imposed. **Amenities:** dual phone lines, voice mail, irons, hair dryers. *Some:* high-speed Internet (fee). **Pool(s):** outdoor. **Leisure Activities:** exercise room. **Guest Services:** valet laundry, area transportation, wireless Internet, barber shop. **Business Services:** conference facilities, business center.

CALL / SOME UNITS

AAA Benefit:
Members save 5% or more everyday!

— WHERE TO DINE —

BRIO TUSCAN GRILLE **Phone:** 314/432-4410 84

Regional Italian
$12-$30

While the atmosphere is casual, upscale Tuscan villa-style decor lends a sophisticated touch to the dining experience. Both lunch and dinner offer all the attentiveness a diner expects. From the garlic, spinach and artichoke dip starter to beef, chicken, veal, seafood and homemade pasta entrees, there is a selection to satisfy all tastes. Among specialties are home-made mozzarella, crisp flat breads and wood-fired oven-baked pizza, in addition to a selection of steak. Dressy casual. **Bar:** Full bar. **Reservations:** accepted. **Hours:** 11 am-10 pm, Fri & Sat-11 pm. Closed: 11/25, 12/25. **Address:** 1601 S Lindbergh Blvd 63131 **Location:** I-64/US 40, exit 28A (S Lindbergh Blvd), just s; at Plaza Frontenac. **Parking:** on-site.

CANYON CAFE **Phone:** 314/872-3443 85

Southwestern
$7-$22

Enjoy a gourmet take on tacos, quesadillas, fajitas and enchiladas at this casually upscale cantina. House specialties include dishes featuring Spanish, Mexican, Native American and Southwestern influences, like applewood-smoked pecan salmon, chile-rubbed sirloin and carne asada. Patio seating is a pleasant option in warm weather. Casual dress. **Bar:** Full bar. **Reservations:** suggested. **Hours:** 11 am-9 pm, Wed & Thurs-10 pm, Fri & Sat-11 pm. Closed: 11/25, 12/25. **Address:** 1707 S Lindbergh Blvd, Suite 2 63131 **Location:** I-64/US 40, exit 28A (S Lindbergh Blvd), just s; at Plaza Frontenac. **Parking:** on-site.

KREIS RESTAURANT **Phone:** 314/993-0735 83

Steak
$25-$64

A fine dining institution since the 1930s, the restaurant exudes a classic English hunt-club atmosphere with a lively business crowd on weeknights. Known for its prime rib, steak and fresh seafood, this place also prepares German dishes. Dressy casual. **Bar:** Full bar. **Reservations:** suggested, weekends. **Hours:** 5 pm-10 pm, Sat-10:30 pm, Sun 4:30 pm-9 pm. Closed major holidays. **Address:** 535 S Lindbergh Blvd 63131 **Location:** I-64/US 40, exit 28B (N Lindbergh Blvd), 0.8 mi n. **Parking:** on-site.

HAZELWOOD pop. 26,206 (See map and index starting on p. 530)

LA QUINTA INN HAZELWOOD *Book at AAA.com* **Phone:** 314/731-4200 17

Hotel
Rates not provided

Address: 318 Taylor Rd 63042 **Location:** I-270, exit 25B (N Lindbergh Blvd), just s. **Facility:** 99 units. 95 one-bedroom standard units, some with kitchens. 4 one-bedroom suites. 4 stories, interior corridors. **Parking:** on-site. **Amenities:** video games (fee), voice mail, irons, hair dryers. *Some:* high-speed Internet. **Leisure Activities:** exercise room. **Guest Services:** valet and coin laundry, wireless Internet. **Business Services:** meeting rooms. / SOME UNITS FEE

LA QUINTA INN ST. LOUIS (AIRPORT) *Book at AAA.com* **Phone:** 314/731-3881 18

Hotel
Rates not provided

Address: 5781 Campus Ct 63042 **Location:** I-270, exit 23 (McDonnell Blvd), just s, just w on Campus Pkwy, then just n. Located in a commercial area. **Facility:** 104 units. 103 one-bedroom standard units. 1 one-bedroom suite. 2-3 stories, interior corridors. **Parking:** on-site. **Amenities:** video games (fee), voice mail, irons, hair dryers. *Some:* high-speed Internet. **Pool(s):** outdoor. **Leisure Activities:** exercise room. **Guest Services:** valet and coin laundry, area transportation, wireless Internet. **Business Services:** meeting rooms, PC.

/ SOME UNITS

— WHERE TO DINE —

VILLAGE CHINA WOK **Phone:** 314/838-5995 33

Chinese
$5-$10

The lunch and dinner buffets at this popular dining spot offer an array of traditional Chinese dishes as well as such American options as pizza and wings. An a la carte menu is also available. Casual dress. **Bar:** Beer & wine. **Reservations:** not accepted. **Hours:** 11 am-9 pm, Fri & Sat-10 pm, Sun-9 pm. Closed: 11/25. **Address:** 7541 N Lindbergh Blvd 63042 **Location:** I-270, exit 25 (US 67/Lindbergh Blvd), 0.6 mi n. **Parking:** on-site. CALL

KIRKWOOD pop. 27,324 (See map and index starting on p. 530)

BEST WESTERN KIRKWOOD INN *Book great rates at AAA.com* **Phone:** (314)821-3950 100

SAVE

Hotel

$100-$120 All Year

Address: 1200 S Kirkwood Rd 63122 **Location:** I-44, exit 277B (Lindbergh Blvd), just n. **Facility:** Designated smoking area. 112 one-bedroom standard units. 6 stories, interior corridors. **Parking:** on-site. **Amenities:** voice mail, safes, irons, hair dryers. *Some:* high-speed Internet. **Pool(s):** heated outdoor. **Leisure Activities:** playground, exercise room. **Guest Services:** valet and coin laundry, wireless Internet. **Business Services:** meeting rooms, business center. **Free Special Amenities: expanded continental breakfast and high-speed Internet.**

/ SOME UNITS FEE

Best Western

AAA Benefit:

Members save up to 20%, plus 10% bonus points with rewards program.

WHERE TO DINE

CITIZEN KANE'S *Menu on AAA.com* **Phone:** 314/965-9005 109

American

$18-$33

Steak reigns so supreme in this house that even the soup selection includes steak soup. However, the menu also offers fish and fowl choices. Entrees come with soup, salad and a vegetable. Professional, polished service avoids being overly personal. Casual dress. **Bar:** Full bar. **Reservations:** suggested. **Hours:** 5 pm-9 pm, Fri & Sat-10 pm. Closed: 11/25, 12/25; also Sun & Mon. **Address:** 133 W Clinton Pl 63122 **Location:** I-44, exit 277B (Lindbergh Blvd), 1.2 mi n, then just w. **Parking:** on-site.

SUNSET 44 **Phone:** 314/965-6644 108

American

$8-$32

The restaurant sustains a casually elegant atmosphere and light, airy decor. In addition to nightly specials, preparations on the seasonally changing, award-winning menu may include Italian beef tenderloin, Atlantic salmon and crab cakes. Service is friendly, casual and efficient. Casual dress. **Bar:** Full bar. **Reservations:** suggested. **Hours:** 11:30 am-2 & 4:30-9 pm, Fri-10 pm, Sat 4:30 pm-10 pm, Sun 10 am-1 & 4:30-8 pm, Mon 4:30 pm-9 pm. Closed: 12/25. **Address:** 118 W Adams Ave 63122 **Location:** I-44, exit 277B (Lindbergh Blvd), 1.7 mi n, then just w; in Adams Place Plaza. **Parking:** on-site.

MAPLEWOOD pop. 9,228 (See map and index starting on p. 530)

WHERE TO DINE

MONARCH RESTAURANT **Phone:** 314/644-3995 101

International

$19-$33

The sophisticated establishment offers both casual bistro and fine-dining experiences. International cuisine shows French overtones. Monarch's two distinct menus change seasonally, and a five-course tasting menu is offered. Dressy casual. **Bar:** Full bar. **Reservations:** suggested. **Hours:** 5 pm-11:30 pm. Closed major holidays; also Sun & Mon. **Address:** 7401 Manchester Rd 63143 **Location:** I-44, exit 285, 1 mi nw on Southwest Ave, then just w; jct Sutton Blvd. **Parking:** on-site. CALL

MARYLAND HEIGHTS pop. 25,756 (See map and index starting on p. 530)

COURTYARD BY MARRIOTT-WESTPORT *Book great rates at AAA.com* **Phone:** (314)997-1200 43

Hotel

$119-$139 All Year

Address: 11888 Westline Industrial Dr 63146 **Location:** I-270, exit 16A (Page Ave), 0.8 mi e on Lackland Rd, just w, just n on Westport Plaza Dr, then just e. **Facility:** Smoke free premises. 149 units. 137 one-bedroom standard units. 12 one-bedroom suites. 3 stories, interior corridors. *Bath:* combo or shower only. **Parking:** on-site. **Terms:** cancellation fee imposed. **Amenities:** video games (fee), high-speed Internet, voice mail, irons, hair dryers. **Pool(s):** heated indoor. **Leisure Activities:** whirlpool, exercise room. **Guest Services:** valet and coin laundry, wireless Internet. **Business Services:** meeting rooms, business center.

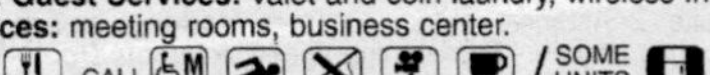

AAA Benefit:

Members save a minimum 5% off the best available rate.

DOUBLETREE HOTEL ST. LOUIS AT WESTPORT *Book great rates at AAA.com* **Phone:** (314)434-0100 45

SAVE

Hotel

$85-$189 All Year

Address: 1973 Craigshire Rd 63146 **Location:** I-270, exit 16A (Page Ave), just e to Lackland Rd, then 0.4 mi sw on Lackland and Craigshire rds. **Facility:** 327 one-bedroom standard units. 11 stories, interior corridors. *Bath:* combo or shower only. **Parking:** on-site. **Terms:** 1-7 night minimum stay, cancellation fee imposed. **Amenities:** dual phone lines, voice mail, irons, hair dryers. *Fee:* video games, high-speed Internet. **Pool(s):** heated indoor. **Leisure Activities:** whirlpool, exercise room. **Guest Services:** valet laundry, airport transportation-Lambert-St. Louis International Airport, area transportation-Westport Plaza, wireless Internet. **Business Services:** conference facilities, business center. **Free Special Amenities: newspaper and preferred room (subject to availability with advance reservations).**

AAA Benefit:

Members save 5% or more everyday!

(See map and index starting on p. 530)

DRURY INN & SUITES-ST. LOUIS-WESTPORT *Book at AAA.com* **Phone:** (314)576-9966 42

Hotel
$75-$159 All Year

Address: 12220 Dorsett Rd 63043 **Location:** I-270, exit 17 (Dorsett Rd), just e. **Facility:** 125 units. 119 one-bedroom standard units. 6 one-bedroom suites. 4 stories, interior corridors. **Parking:** on-site. **Terms:** cancellation fee imposed. **Amenities:** high-speed Internet, voice mail, irons, hair dryers. **Pool(s):** outdoor. **Leisure Activities:** exercise room. **Guest Services:** valet and coin laundry, wireless Internet. **Business Services:** meeting rooms, business center.

ASK / SOME UNITS

HAMPTON INN ST. LOUIS/WESTPORT *Book great rates at AAA.com* **Phone:** (314)298-7878 41

AAA Benefit:
Members save up to 10% everyday!

Hotel
$69-$144 All Year

Address: 2454 Old Dorsett Rd 63043 **Location:** I-270, exit 17 (Dorsett Rd), just e, then just n. **Facility:** 122 one-bedroom standard units. 5 stories, interior corridors. **Parking:** on-site. **Terms:** 1-7 night minimum stay, cancellation fee imposed. **Amenities:** voice mail, irons, hair dryers. **Pool(s):** outdoor. **Leisure Activities:** exercise room. **Guest Services:** valet laundry, area transportation, wireless Internet. **Business Services:** meeting rooms, PC. ***(See color ad below)***

/ SOME UNITS

HARRAH'S CASINO & HOTEL *Book great rates at AAA.com* **Phone:** (314)770-8100 40

Hotel
$79-$399 All Year

Address: 777 Casino Center Dr 63043 **Location:** I-70, exit 231A (Earth City Expwy S), 1 mi s, then 1.2 mi nw. **Facility:** Contemporary unit decor in bold building with modern architecture which is part of casino complex. Adjacent restaurants are within same building complex. 502 units. 466 one-bedroom standard units. 36 one-bedroom suites, some with whirlpools. 8-11 stories, interior corridors. *Bath:* combo or shower only. **Parking:** on-site and valet. **Terms:** check-in 4 pm, cancellation fee imposed. **Amenities:** dual phone lines, voice mail, safes, irons, hair dryers. *Some:* DVD players, CD players. **Dining:** 6 restaurants, also, Eat UP! Buffet, see separate listing. **Leisure Activities:** exercise room. **Guest Services:** valet laundry, airport transportation-Lambert-St. Louis International Airport, area transportation-area hotels, wireless Internet. **Business Services:** conference facilities, business center. **Free Special Amenities: early check-in/late check-out.**

CALL / SOME UNITS

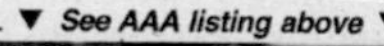

(See map and index starting on p. 530)

RESIDENCE INN BY MARRIOTT - WESTPORT *Book great rates at AAA.com* **Phone:** (314)469-0060 47

Extended Stay Hotel
$152-$186 All Year

Address: 1881 Craigshire Rd 63146 **Location:** I-270, exit 16A (Page Ave), 0.8 mi e, just w on Lackland Rd, just s on Craig Rd, then just w. **Facility:** Smoke free premises. 127 units. 95 one-bedroom standard units with kitchens. 32 two-bedroom suites with kitchens. 2 stories (no elevator), exterior corridors. *Bath:* combo or shower only. **Parking:** on-site. **Terms:** cancellation fee imposed. **Amenities:** high-speed Internet, dual phone lines, voice mail, irons, hair dryers. **Pool(s):** outdoor. **Leisure Activities:** whirlpool, exercise room, sports court. **Guest Services:** valet and coin laundry, wireless Internet. **Business Services:** meeting rooms, business center.

/ SOME UNITS FEE

AAA Benefit:
Members save a minimum 5% off the best available rate.

SHERATON WESTPORT PLAZA TOWER *Book great rates at AAA.com* **Phone:** 314/878-1500 44

Hotel
Rates not provided

Address: 900 Westport Plaza 63146 **Location:** I-270, exit 16A (Page Ave), 0.8 mi e; exit Lackland Rd, just w, then just n. Located in Westport Plaza Shopping Center. **Facility:** Smoke free premises. 210 one-bedroom standard units. 12 stories, interior corridors. *Bath:* combo or shower only. **Parking:** on-site. **Amenities:** dual phone lines, voice mail, irons, hair dryers. *Fee:* video games, high-speed Internet. **Pool(s):** heated indoor. **Leisure Activities:** sauna, exercise room. **Guest Services:** valet laundry, airport transportation-Lambert-St. Louis International Airport, wireless Internet. **Business Services:** conference facilities, business center. **Free Special Amenities: room upgrade (subject to availability with advance reservations).**

CALL / SOME UNITS

Sheraton HOTELS & RESORTS

AAA Benefit:
Members get up to 15% off, plus Starwood Preferred Guest® bonuses.

STAYBRIDGE SUITES *Book at AAA.com* **Phone:** (314)878-1555 46

Extended Stay Hotel
$79-$189 All Year

Address: 1855 Craigshire Rd 63146 **Location:** I-270, exit 16A (Page Ave), 0.8 mi e, exit Lackland Rd, 1 mi w, 0.4 mi s on Craig Rd, then just e. **Facility:** 106 units. 58 one- and 48 two-bedroom suites with kitchens. 2 stories (no elevator), interior/exterior corridors. **Parking:** on-site. **Terms:** cancellation fee imposed. **Amenities:** video library (fee), DVD players, CD players, high-speed Internet, voice mail, irons, hair dryers. **Pool(s):** outdoor. **Leisure Activities:** whirlpool, exercise room, sports court. **Guest Services:** complimentary and valet laundry, area transportation, wireless Internet. **Business Services:** meeting rooms, business center.

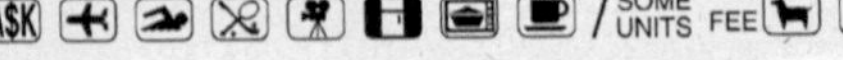
ASK / SOME UNITS FEE

WHERE TO DINE

BALDUCCI'S WINEFEST RESTAURANT & BAR **Phone:** 314/576-5024 45

Italian
$5-$11

A family tradition since 1887, locally owned and operated, Balducci's is locally popular. Menu offers toasted ravioli, quiche, pasta, pizza and a good selection of salads and sandwiches. Casual dress. **Bar:** Full bar. **Reservations:** accepted. **Hours:** 11 am-9 pm, Fri-10 pm, Sat 5 pm-10 pm, Sun 5 pm-9 pm. Closed major holidays. **Address:** 12527 Bennington Pl 63146 **Location:** I-270, exit 16B (Page Ave W), 0.5 mi w to Bennington Pl, then 0.3 mi n. **Parking:** on-site.

DIERDORF & HARTS STEAKHOUSE **Phone:** 314/878-1801 41

Eastern Steak
$18-$43

Owned by former St. Louis Cardinal football players Dan Dierdorf and Jim Hart, this restaurant proves they know food as well as they knew football. The finest quality beef and fresh seafood are prepared to perfection and served in a dining room with upscale, masculine decor. Dressy casual. **Bar:** Full bar. **Reservations:** suggested. **Hours:** 5 pm-10 pm, Fri & Sat-10:30 pm. Closed major holidays. **Address:** 311 Westport Plaza 63146 **Location:** I-270, exit 16A (Page Ave), 0.8 mi e; exit Lackland Rd, just w, then 0.5 mi n on Craig Rd; in Westport Plaza Shopping Center. **Parking:** on-site.

THE DRUNKEN FISH SUSHI BAR AND LOUNGE **Phone:** 314/275-8300 44

Japanese
$9-$24

The trendy bistro's lengthy menu of sushi and cocktails attracts a loyal following. Specialties include a variety of rolls as well as teriyaki, tempura and noodle dishes. Casual dress. **Bar:** Full bar. **Reservations:** accepted. **Hours:** 11 am-2 & 5-10 pm, Tues & Wed-11 pm, Thurs & Fri-midnight, Sat 5 pm-midnight, Sun 5 pm-10 pm. Closed: 1/1, 11/25, 12/25. **Address:** 639 Westport Plaza 63146 **Location:** I-270, exit 16A (Page Ave), 0.8 mi e; exit Lackland Rd, just w, then 0.5 mi n on Craig Rd; in Westport Plaza Shopping Center. **Parking:** on-site.

EAT UP! BUFFET **Phone:** 314/770-8100 39

American
$9-$24

A feast for the eyes and the stomach, the expansive buffet features a variety of cuisines sure to satisfy anyone's palate. There are stations for Asian, Italian and American classics, plus a carving station and salad bar. The array of desserts will tempt the sweet tooth. Casual dress. **Bar:** Beer & wine. **Reservations:** not accepted. **Hours:** 7-10 am, 11-3 & 5-9:30 pm, Sat 7-10 am, 11-3 & 4:30-10:30 pm, Sun 7:30 am-3 & 5-9:30 pm. **Address:** 777 Casino Center Dr 63043 **Location:** I-70, exit 231A (Earth City Expwy S), 1 mi s, then 1.2 mi nw; in Harrah's Casino & Hotel. **Parking:** on-site. CALL

OZZIE'S RESTAURANT & SPORTS BAR **Phone:** 314/434-1000 43

American
$6-$22

Ozzie's offers a wide variety of salad, grilled chicken, fajitas, pasta, appetizers and soup. The sporty, enjoyable atmosphere becomes louder when a popular game is being played. Families, business professionals and couples like this place. Casual dress. **Bar:** Full bar. **Reservations:** accepted. **Hours:** 11 am-10 pm, Thurs-11 pm, Fri & Sat-midnight. Closed: 12/25. **Address:** 645 Westport Plaza Dr 63146 **Location:** I-270, exit 16A (Page Ave), 0.8 mi e; exit Lackland Rd, just w, then 0.5 mi n on Craig Rd; in Westport Plaza Shopping Center. **Parking:** on-site.

(See map and index starting on p. 530)

PUJOLS 5 WESTPORT GRILL — Phone: 314/878-6767 (40)

American
$7-$18

Named after St. Louis Cardinals great Albert Pujols, this sports-themed dining establishment presents a varied menu that includes steaks, pizza and seafood. Casual dress. **Bar:** Full bar. **Reservations:** accepted. **Hours:** 11 am-10 pm, Fri & Sat-11 pm. Closed: 12/25. **Address:** 342 Westport Plaza 63146 **Location:** I-270, exit 16A (Page Ave), 0.8 mi e, exit Lackland Rd, just w, then 0.5 mi n on Craig Rd; in Westport Plaza Shopping Center. **Parking:** on-site.

TRAINWRECK SALOON WESTPORT — Phone: 314/434-7222 (42)

American
$7-$15

The menu at this casual eatery lists bison burgers, sandwiches, steaks, ribs, chicken and salads. Outdoor seating is available in season. The non-smoking area is 75 percent at lunch, 50 percent at dinner and nonexistent after 10 pm, when the kitchen closes and the bar crowd flocks in to listen to live music. Patrons must be 21 or older after 9 pm. Casual dress. **Bar:** Full bar. **Reservations:** not accepted. **Hours:** 11 am-10 pm. Closed major holidays; also Sun. **Address:** 314 Westport Plaza 63146 **Location:** I-270, exit 16A (Page Ave), 0.8 mi e, exit Lackland Rd, just w, then 0.5 mi n on Craig Rd; in Westport Plaza Shopping Center. **Parking:** on-site.

MEHLVILLE pop. 28,822 (See map and index starting on p. 530)

AMERICAS BEST VALUE INN — Book great rates at AAA.com — Phone: (314)894-9449 (115)

AAA SAVE

Hotel
$50-$70 All Year

Address: 6602 S Lindbergh Blvd 63123 **Location:** I-55, exit 197 (Lindbergh Blvd), just w, just s on Rusty Rd, then just e on Feth St. **Facility:** 95 one-bedroom standard units, some with whirlpools. 3 stories, interior corridors. **Parking:** on-site. **Terms:** cancellation fee imposed. **Amenities:** high-speed Internet, voice mail, hair dryers. **Pool(s):** outdoor. **Leisure Activities:** limited exercise equipment, game room. **Guest Services:** valet and coin laundry, wireless Internet. **Business Services:** meeting rooms. **Free Special Amenities: continental breakfast and high-speed Internet.**

/ SOME UNITS

HOLIDAY INN ST. LOUIS-SOUTH I-55 — Book at AAA.com — Phone: (314)894-0700 (117)

Hotel
$84-$139 All Year

Address: 4234 Butler Hill Rd 63129 **Location:** I-55, exit 195 (Butler Hill Rd), just e, then just s. **Facility:** 163 units. 161 one-bedroom standard units. 2 one-bedroom suites. 2 stories (no elevator), interior/exterior corridors. *Bath:* combo or shower only. **Parking:** on-site. **Terms:** cancellation fee imposed. **Amenities:** video games (fee), high-speed Internet, dual phone lines, voice mail, irons, hair dryers. **Pool(s):** outdoor, heated indoor. **Leisure Activities:** whirlpool, exercise room, shuffleboard. *Fee:* game room. **Guest Services:** valet and coin laundry, wireless Internet. **Business Services:** meeting rooms, PC. ASK / SOME UNITS FEE

HOLIDAY INN SOUTH COUNTY CENTER — Book at AAA.com — Phone: (314)892-3600 (116)

Hotel
$116-$156 All Year

Address: 6921 S Lindbergh Blvd 63125 **Location:** I-55, exit 197 (Lindbergh Blvd), just e. **Facility:** 149 one-bedroom standard units. 4 stories, interior corridors. *Bath:* combo or shower only. **Parking:** on-site. **Terms:** cancellation fee imposed. **Amenities:** video games (fee), dual phone lines, voice mail, irons, hair dryers. *Some:* high-speed Internet. **Pool(s):** heated indoor. **Leisure Activities:** whirlpool, exercise room. **Guest Services:** valet and coin laundry, wireless Internet. **Business Services:** conference facilities, PC. ASK / SOME UNITS

WHERE TO DINE

GINGHAM'S HOMESTYLE RESTAURANT — Phone: 314/487-2505 (116)

American
$4-$11

Enveloped in a country atmosphere, the locally popular restaurant features warm, family-friendly dining. The menu lists a variety of home-style meals, including pancakes, omelets, burgers, sandwiches and homemade pies. Seniors love this place. Casual dress. **Reservations:** not accepted. **Hours:** 24 hours. Closed: 11/25, 12/25. **Address:** 7333 S Lindbergh Blvd 63125 **Location:** I-55, exit 197 (Lindbergh Blvd), 0.5 mi e. **Parking:** on-site.

O'FALLON pop. 46,169 (See map and index starting on p. 526)

HILTON GARDEN INN ST. LOUIS/O'FALLON — Book great rates at AAA.com — Phone: (636)625-2700 (17)

Hotel
$79-$169 All Year

Address: 2310 Technology Dr 63368 **Location:** US 40/61, exit 6 (Wing Haven Blvd/CR DD), just ne; I-70, exit 216 (Bryan Rd), 4.2 mi s. **Facility:** 122 one-bedroom standard units. 3 stories, interior corridors. *Bath:* combo or shower only. **Parking:** on-site. **Terms:** 1-7 night minimum stay, cancellation fee imposed. **Amenities:** video games (fee), high-speed Internet, dual phone lines, voice mail, irons, hair dryers. **Pool(s):** heated indoor. **Leisure Activities:** whirlpool, exercise room. **Guest Services:** valet and coin laundry, area transportation, wireless Internet. **Business Services:** meeting rooms, business center.

CALL / SOME UNITS

STAYBRIDGE SUITES O'FALLON — Book at AAA.com — Phone: (636)300-0999 (18)

Extended Stay Hotel
$91-$137 All Year

Address: 1155 Technology Dr 63368 **Location:** I-64/US 40, exit 9 (CR K), just nw. **Facility:** 97 units. 45 one-bedroom standard units with efficiencies. 40 one- and 12 two-bedroom suites with efficiencies. 3 stories, interior corridors. *Bath:* combo or shower only. **Parking:** on-site. **Amenities:** DVD players, high-speed Internet, dual phone lines, voice mail, irons, hair dryers. **Pool(s):** heated outdoor. **Leisure Activities:** exercise room. **Guest Services:** complimentary laundry, area transportation, wireless Internet. **Business Services:** meeting rooms, business center.

ASK CALL / SOME UNITS FEE

(See map and index starting on p. 526)

WHERE TO DINE

J. BUCK'S RESTAURANT — Phone: 636/329-0070 (16)

American
$8-$26

Sophisticated and contemporary decor distinguishes this sleek setting, which celebrates some of baseball's greats. The menu lines up fresh and innovative offerings. Casual dress. **Bar:** Full bar. **Reservations:** accepted. **Hours:** 11 am-10 pm. Closed: 11/25, 12/25; also Sun. **Address:** 1165 Technology Dr 63368 **Location:** I-64/US 40, exit 9 (CR K), just nw. **Parking:** on-site.

OVERLAND pop. 16,838 (See map and index starting on p. 530)

WHERE TO DINE

MANDARIN HOUSE RESTAURANT — Phone: 314/427-8070 (56)

Chinese
$6-$17

Mandarin House has been a locals' favorite since 1978. Its menu is extensive, offering many specialties in addition to the traditional favorites, including some Korean dishes. The spacious setting features an attractive entry with an small indoor stream complete with a bridge and mini-pagoda. Casual dress. **Bar:** Full bar. **Reservations:** accepted. **Hours:** 11 am-2 & 5-9 pm, Fri & Sat-10 pm, Sun 11 am-2 & 4:30-9 pm. Closed major holidays. **Address:** 9150 Overland Plaza 63114 **Location:** I-170, exit 4 (Page Ave), just w; in Overland Plaza Shopping Center. **Parking:** on-site.

RICHMOND HEIGHTS pop. 9,602 (See map and index starting on p. 530)

RESIDENCE INN BY MARRIOTT-ST. LOUIS GALLERIA *Book great rates at AAA.com* — Phone: (314)862-1900 (83)

Extended Stay Hotel
$139-$159 All Year

Address: 1100 McMorrow Ave 63117 **Location:** I-170, exit 1C (Brentwood Blvd) northbound; exit 1D southbound, just s, just e on Galleria Pkwy, then just s. **Facility:** Smoke free premises. 152 units. 114 one-bedroom standard units with kitchens. 28 one- and 10 two-bedroom suites with kitchens. 2 stories (no elevator), exterior corridors. *Bath:* combo or shower only. **Parking:** on-site. **Terms:** cancellation fee imposed. **Amenities:** high-speed Internet, voice mail, irons, hair dryers. **Pool(s):** heated outdoor. **Leisure Activities:** exercise room, sports court. **Guest Services:** valet and coin laundry, wireless Internet. **Business Services:** meeting rooms, PC.

ECO CALL / SOME UNITS FEE

Residence Inn Marriott
AAA Benefit:
Members save a minimum 5% off the best available rate.

WHERE TO DINE

HARVEST — Phone: 314/645-3522 (88)

New American
$18-$28

Food is king at the sophisticated restaurant. Fresh seasonal and local ingredients are used in innovative American cuisine. The menu changes frequently, but the level of creativity does not. Dressy casual. **Bar:** Full bar. **Reservations:** suggested. **Hours:** 5:30 pm-9:30 pm, Fri & Sat-10 pm, Sun 5 pm-9 pm. Closed major holidays; also Mon. **Address:** 1059 S Big Bend Blvd 63117 **Location:** I-64, exit 33B, just n. **Parking:** on-site.

ST. ANN pop. 13,607 (See map and index starting on p. 530)

HAMPTON INN-ST. LOUIS AIRPORT *Book great rates at AAA.com* — Phone: (314)429-2000 (37)

Hotel
$79-$159 All Year

Address: 10820 Pear Tree Ln 63074 **Location:** I-70, exit 236 (Airport Dr), just sw. **Facility:** 99 one-bedroom standard units. 5 stories, interior corridors. *Bath:* combo or shower only. **Parking:** on-site. **Terms:** 1-7 night minimum stay, cancellation fee imposed. **Amenities:** high-speed Internet, voice mail, irons, hair dryers. **Pool(s):** outdoor. **Leisure Activities:** exercise room. **Guest Services:** valet laundry, wireless Internet. **Business Services:** meeting rooms, business center.

/ SOME UNITS

Hampton Inn
AAA Benefit:
Members save up to 10% everyday!

PEAR TREE INN BY DRURY-ST. LOUIS AIRPORT *Book at AAA.com* — Phone: (314)427-3400 (36)

Hotel
$70-$139 All Year

Address: 10810 Pear Tree Ln 63074 **Location:** I-70, exit 236 (Airport Dr), just sw. **Facility:** 153 one-bedroom standard units. 4 stories, interior corridors. **Parking:** on-site. **Terms:** cancellation fee imposed. **Amenities:** high-speed Internet, voice mail, irons, hair dryers. **Pool(s):** outdoor. **Leisure Activities:** exercise room. **Guest Services:** valet and coin laundry, wireless Internet. **Business Services:** meeting rooms, PC. ASK / SOME UNITS

WHERE TO DINE

BANDANA'S BAR-B-Q — Phone: 314/426-9955

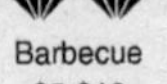

Barbecue
$5-$10

The real wood-pit smoker produces tasty meats. Guests might want to try hot boiled peanuts, a Southern favorite, as a side item. Casual dress. **Bar:** Beer & wine. **Reservations:** not accepted. **Hours:** 11 am-10 pm. Closed: 11/25, 12/25. **Address:** 10800 Pear Tree Ln 63074 **Location:** I-70, exit 236 (Airport Dr), just sw. **Parking:** on-site. CALL

ST. CHARLES pop. 60,321 (See map and index starting on p. 526)

AMERISTAR ST. CHARLES CASINO RESORT & SPA Book great rates at AAA.com

Phone: (636)940-4300 11

Hotel
$119-$699 All Year

Address: One Ameristar Blvd 63301 **Location:** I-70, exit 229B, just n on I-70 business route, then just e. **Facility:** Spacious guest rooms include two 36-inch flat-panel televisions, a honor bar and upscale furnishings. This is one of the finest hotels in the area. 397 units. 395 one-bedroom standard units, some with whirlpools. 2 one-bedroom suites with whirlpools. 25 stories, interior corridors. *Bath:* combo or shower only. **Parking:** on-site and valet. **Terms:** cancellation fee imposed. **Amenities:** video games (fee), voice mail, safes, honor bars, irons, hair dryers. **Dining:** 4 restaurants, also, Amerisports Bar & Grill, Pearl's Oyster Bar, see separate listings, entertainment. **Pool(s):** heated indoor/outdoor. **Leisure Activities:** whirlpools, exercise room, spa, game room. **Guest Services:** valet laundry, wireless Internet. **Business Services:** conference facilities, business center.

CALL / SOME UNITS

COMFORT SUITES-ST. CHARLES Book at AAA.com

Phone: 636/949-0694 10

Hotel
Rates not provided

Address: 1400 S 5th St 63301 **Location:** I-70, exit 229 (5th St), just ne. **Facility:** Smoke free premises. 71 units. 69 one-bedroom standard units, some with whirlpools. 2 one-bedroom suites, some with whirlpools. 3 stories, interior corridors. *Bath:* combo or shower only. **Parking:** on-site. **Amenities:** high-speed Internet, voice mail, safes (fee), irons, hair dryers. **Pool(s):** heated indoor. **Leisure Activities:** exercise room. **Guest Services:** coin laundry, wireless Internet. **Business Services:** business center. / SOME UNITS

COUNTRY INN & SUITES BY CARLSON Book great rates at AAA.com

Phone: (636)724-5555 8

Hotel
$120-$152 All Year

Address: 1190 S Main St 63301 **Location:** I-70, exit 229A (5th St S), to S Main St, then 0.7 mi ne. **Facility:** 86 units. 67 one-bedroom standard units, some with whirlpools. 19 one-bedroom suites. 3 stories, interior corridors. *Bath:* combo or shower only. **Parking:** on-site. **Amenities:** high-speed Internet, dual phone lines, voice mail, irons, hair dryers. **Pool(s):** heated indoor. **Leisure Activities:** whirlpool, adjacent to Katy Trail, rental bicycles, exercise room. **Guest Services:** valet and coin laundry, wireless Internet. **Business Services:** meeting rooms, business center. **Free Special Amenities: newspaper and high-speed Internet.**

/ SOME UNITS FEE

EMBASSY SUITES ST. LOUIS-ST. CHARLES Book great rates at AAA.com

Phone: (636)946-5544 9

Hotel
$109-$199 All Year

Address: Two Convention Center Plaza 63303 **Location:** I-70, exit 229A (5th St S), just s to Veterans Memorial Pkwy, then just w. Adjacent to St. Charles Memorial Convention Center. **Facility:** 296 one-bedroom suites, some with whirlpools. 12 stories, interior corridors. *Bath:* combo or shower only. **Parking:** on-site. **Terms:** 1-7 night minimum stay, cancellation fee imposed. **Amenities:** high-speed Internet (fee), dual phone lines, voice mail, safes, irons, hair dryers. **Pool(s):** heated indoor. **Leisure Activities:** whirlpool, exercise room, spa. **Guest Services:** valet and coin laundry, area transportation-within 3 mi, wireless Internet. **Business Services:** conference facilities, business center. **Free Special Amenities: full breakfast and newspaper.**

/ SOME UNITS

AAA Benefit:
Members save 5% or more everyday!

HAMPTON INN-ST CHARLES Book great rates at AAA.com

Phone: (636)947-6800 4

Hotel
$69-$129 All Year

Address: 3720 W Clay St 63301 **Location:** I-70, exit 225 (Cave Springs), 0.5 mi e. **Facility:** 123 one-bedroom standard units. 4 stories, interior corridors. *Bath:* combo or shower only. **Parking:** on-site, winter plug-ins. **Terms:** 1-7 night minimum stay, cancellation fee imposed. **Amenities:** video games (fee), voice mail, irons, hair dryers. *Some:* dual phone lines. **Pool(s):** heated indoor. **Leisure Activities:** whirlpool, exercise room. **Guest Services:** valet laundry, wireless Internet. **Business Services:** meeting rooms, business center. **Free Special Amenities: expanded continental breakfast and high-speed Internet.**

/ SOME UNITS

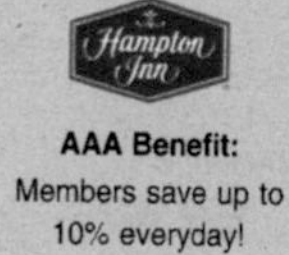

AAA Benefit:
Members save up to 10% everyday!

RED ROOF INN Book at AAA.com

Phone: (636)947-7770 6

Hotel
$40-$77 All Year

Address: 2010 Zumbehl Rd 63303 **Location:** I-70, exit 227 (Zumbehl Rd), just se. Located in busy commercial area adjacent to interstate. **Facility:** 108 one-bedroom standard units. 2 stories (no elevator), exterior corridors. *Bath:* combo or shower only. **Parking:** on-site. **Amenities:** video games (fee), voice mail. *Some:* irons, hair dryers. **Guest Services:** wireless Internet.

ASK CALL / SOME UNITS

SUPER 8 Book at AAA.com

Phone: (636)946-9992 

Hotel
$69-$99 All Year

Address: 3040 W Clay St 63301 **Location:** I-70, exit 227 (Zumbehl Rd), 0.3 mi w. **Facility:** 52 one-bedroom standard units. 3 stories, interior corridors. **Parking:** on-site. **Amenities:** high-speed Internet, irons, hair dryers. **Pool(s):** heated indoor. **Guest Services:** wireless Internet.

ASK / SOME UNITS

(See map and index starting on p. 526)

TOWNEPLACE SUITES BY MARRIOTT *Book great rates at AAA.com* **Phone:** (636)949-6800 **7**

Extended Stay Hotel
$80-$98 All Year

Address: 1800 Zumbehl Rd 63303 **Location:** I-70, exit 227 (Zumbehl Rd), 0.6 mi s, then just se. Adjacent to Zumbehl Crossing Shopping Center. **Facility:** Smoke free premises. 95 units. 69 one-bedroom standard units with kitchens. 4 one- and 22 two-bedroom suites with kitchens. 3 stories, interior corridors. *Bath:* combo or shower only. **Parking:** on-site. **Terms:** cancellation fee imposed. **Amenities:** voice mail, irons, hair dryers. *Some:* safes. **Pool(s):** outdoor. **Leisure Activities:** exercise room. **Guest Services:** valet and coin laundry, wireless Internet. **Business Services:** PC. / SOME UNITS FEE

AAA Benefit:
Members save a minimum 5% off the best available rate.

WHERE TO DINE

47 PORT STREET GRILL **Phone:** 636/940-4471 **10**

American
$15-$25

Located at the gaming complex, the restaurant fosters a fine-dining atmosphere in a tasteful, intimate room of cherry wood, natural wood tables and etched glass. For starters, try the spring rolls. Valet parking is validated for diners by well-informed, professional staff. Casual dress. **Bar:** Full bar. **Reservations:** suggested. **Hours:** 5 pm-10 pm, Fri & Sat-11 pm. Closed: Sun & Mon. **Address:** 1260 S Main St 63301 **Location:** I-70, exit 228 (First Capitol), 1.3 mi ne. **Parking:** on-site.

AMERISPORTS BAR & GRILL **Phone:** 636/940-4935 **9**

American
$7-$20

Guests eat up not only the delicious ribs, which are cooked in a wood-fired oven, but also the state-of-the-art audio/video system, which features a 34-foot video wall. Casual dress. **Bar:** Full bar. **Reservations:** accepted. **Hours:** 4 pm-11 pm, Sat 11 am-1 am, Sun 11 am-11 pm. **Address:** One Ameristar Blvd 63301 **Location:** I-70, exit 229B, just n on I-70 business route, then just e; in Ameristar St. Charles Casino Resort & Spa. **Parking:** on-site. CALL

THE FALCON DINER **Phone:** 636/940-4955 **8**

American
$7-$25

The contemporary, retro-style diner specializes in Midwestern favorites. The menu lists appetizers, soups, salads, barbecue, seafood, pasta, sandwiches, burgers and breakfast items. Casual dress. **Bar:** Full bar. **Reservations:** not accepted. **Hours:** 7 am-3 am, Fri & Sat 24 hours. **Address:** 1260 S Main St 63301 **Location:** I-70, exit 228 (First Capitol), 1.3 mi ne. **Parking:** on-site. CALL

THE LANDMARK BUFFET **Phone:** 636/940-4470 **6**

American
$9-$18

Among the generous options onboard the glittering casino riverboat are prime rib, steak, crab legs and shrimp. The restaurant is popular with gamblers, but the international buffet is a good enough draw on its own. Casual dress. **Bar:** Beer & wine. **Reservations:** not accepted. **Hours:** 11 am-2 & 4-9:30 pm, Sat & Sun 9:30 am-2:30 & 4-9:30 pm. **Address:** 1260 S Main St 63301 **Location:** I-70, exit 228 (First Capitol), 1.3 mi ne. **Parking:** on-site.

LEWIS AND CLARK'S AN AMERICAN RESTAURANT & PUBLIC HOUSE **Phone:** 636/947-3334 **2**

American
$7-$20

Located in the Historic Main Street District, Lewis and Clark's features a good variety of prime rib, seafood and pasta dishes as well as Mexican and Creole food. The building dates back to the mid-1800s and its third-floor balcony is quite popular. Casual dress. **Bar:** Full bar. **Reservations:** accepted. **Hours:** 11 am-10 pm, Fri & Sat-11 pm. Closed: 12/25. **Address:** 217 S Main St 63301 **Location:** In historic Old Town. **Parking:** street.

MAGPIE'S **Phone:** 636/947-3883 **5**

American
$6-$22

The circa 1821 building is cozy and casual. On the eclectic menu are daily specials, as well as soups, salads, quiche, crepes, sandwiches, steaks, chicken, fish and homemade desserts. Outdoor seating is available in season. Casual dress. **Bar:** Full bar. **Reservations:** not accepted. **Hours:** 11 am-3 pm, Wed-Sat also 5 pm-9 pm; to 3 pm in winter. Closed major holidays. **Address:** 903 S Main St 63301 **Location:** Downtown; in historic Old Town. **Parking:** street. **Historic**

MR. STEAK **Phone:** 636/946-7444 **1**

American
$8-$25

The long-time family-owned and operated business offers no pretentions, just good food in a comfortable atmosphere. Casual dress. **Reservations:** not accepted. **Hours:** 10:30 am-10 pm, Sun-9 pm. Closed: 11/25, 12/25. **Address:** 2731 Veterans Memorial Pkwy 63303 **Location:** I-70, exit 228 (First Capitol), 1 mi w on service road (Bogey Rd). **Parking:** on-site.

THE NEW MOTHER-IN-LAW HOUSE RESTAURANT *Menu on AAA.com* **Phone:** 636/946-9444 **4**

AAA

American
$7-$20

Regardless of how you feel about going to YOUR mother-in-law's house, you'll enjoy coming to this one because it is a casual and welcoming place to enjoy house-made comfort foods. An island in the middle of the dining room is the salad bar featuring over a dozen recipes gathered from family and friends of owner, Donna Hafer. Casual dress. **Bar:** Full bar. **Reservations:** suggested, weekends. **Hours:** 11 am-2:30 & 5:30-9:30 pm, Mon-2:30 pm. Closed: 1/1, 11/25, 12/25; also Sun. **Address:** 500 S Main St 63301 **Location:** Main St at Tomkins; in historic Old Town. **Parking:** street. **Historic**

(See map and index starting on p. 526)

PEARL'S OYSTER BAR

Phone: 636/940-5565 (7)

Creole
$7-$34

Exhibition-style cooking is applied to preparations of fresh, Southern-style seafood, as well as offerings from the raw bar. Casual dress. **Bar:** Full bar. **Reservations:** accepted, weekdays. **Hours:** 5 pm-11 pm, Fri & Sat-1 am. Closed: Tues & Wed. **Address:** One Ameristar Blvd 63301 **Location:** I-70, exit 229B, just n on I-70 business route, then just e; in Ameristar St. Charles Casino, Resort & Spa. **Parking:** on-site.

CALL

TRAILHEAD BREWING COMPANY

Phone: 636/946-2739 (3)

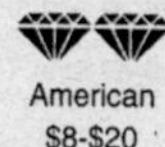

American
$8-$20

Nothing fancy here—just good old-fashioned hamburgers, sandwiches, fries and one of the favorites: chili. Casual dress. **Bar:** Full bar. **Reservations:** accepted. **Hours:** 11 am-10 pm, Fri & Sat-11 pm. **Address:** 921 S Riverside Dr 63301 **Location:** Downtown; in historic Old Town. **Parking:** street.

ST. PETERS pop. 51,381 (See map and index starting on p. 526)

DRURY INN ST. PETERS

Phone: (636)397-9700 (1)

Hotel
$85-$169 All Year

Address: 170 Mid Rivers Mall Dr 63376 **Location:** I-70, exit 222 (Mid Rivers Mall Dr), just se. Adjacent to Mid Rivers Mall. **Facility:** 135 units. 129 one-bedroom standard units. 6 one-bedroom suites. 6 stories, interior corridors. *Bath:* combo or shower only. **Parking:** on-site. **Terms:** cancellation fee imposed. **Amenities:** high-speed Internet, voice mail, irons, hair dryers. **Pool(s):** heated indoor. **Leisure Activities:** whirlpool, exercise room. **Guest Services:** valet and coin laundry, wireless Internet. **Business Services:** meeting rooms, PC, fax.

ASK CALL / SOME UNITS

SUNSET HILLS pop. 8,267 (See map and index starting on p. 530)

HOLIDAY INN-SOUTHWEST & VIKING CONFERENCE CENTER *Book great rates at AAA.com*

Phone: (314)821-6600 (112)

AAA SAVE

Hotel
$99-$139 All Year

Address: 10709 Watson Rd 63127 **Location:** I-44, exit 277B, just s. **Facility:** 209 one-bedroom standard units, some with whirlpools. 4 stories, interior corridors. *Bath:* combo or shower only. **Parking:** on-site. **Terms:** check-in 4 pm. **Amenities:** dual phone lines, voice mail, irons, hair dryers. *Some:* CD players. **Pool(s):** outdoor, heated indoor. **Leisure Activities:** whirlpool, exercise room. *Fee:* game room. **Guest Services:** valet and coin laundry, area transportation-within 5 mi, wireless Internet. **Business Services:** conference facilities, business center. **Free Special Amenities: newspaper and high-speed Internet.**

/ SOME UNITS FEE

TOWN AND COUNTRY pop. 10,894 (See maps and indexes starting on p. 526, 530)

COURTYARD BY MARRIOTT ST. LOUIS/MARYVILLE *Book great rates at AAA.com*

Phone: (314)514-7300 (28)

Hotel
$125-$139 All Year

Address: 511 Maryville University Dr 63141 **Location:** I-64, exit 23 (Maryville Centre Dr) eastbound; exit 22 westbound, just n. Adjacent to Maryville University. **Facility:** Smoke free premises. 122 units. 116 one-bedroom standard units, some with whirlpools. 6 one-bedroom suites. 3 stories, interior corridors. *Bath:* combo or shower only. **Parking:** on-site. **Terms:** cancellation fee imposed. **Amenities:** video games (fee), high-speed Internet, dual phone lines, voice mail, irons, hair dryers. **Pool(s):** heated indoor. **Leisure Activities:** whirlpool, exercise room. **Guest Services:** valet and coin laundry, area transportation, wireless Internet. **Business Services:** meeting rooms, PC.

CALL / SOME UNITS

AAA Benefit:
Members save a minimum 5% off the best available rate.

ST. LOUIS MARRIOTT WEST *Book great rates at AAA.com*

Phone: (314)878-2747 (80)

AAA SAVE

Hotel
$170-$208 All Year

Address: 660 Maryville Centre Dr 63141 **Location:** I-64, exit 23 (Maryville Centre Dr), just n. **Facility:** Smoke free premises. 299 one-bedroom standard units. 8 stories, interior corridors. **Parking:** on-site. **Terms:** check-in 4 pm, cancellation fee imposed. **Amenities:** voice mail, irons, hair dryers. *Some:* dual phone lines. **Pool(s):** outdoor, heated indoor. **Leisure Activities:** sauna, whirlpool, hiking trails, jogging, exercise room. **Guest Services:** valet and coin laundry, area transportation-within 3 mi, wireless Internet. **Business Services:** conference facilities, business center. *(See color ad p 537)*

CALL / SOME UNITS

Marriott
HOTELS & RESORTS

AAA Benefit:
Members save a minimum 5% off the best available rate.

UNIVERSITY CITY pop. 37,428 (See map and index starting on p. 530)

WHERE TO DINE

BLUEBERRY HILL — **Phone:** 314/727-4444 (63)

American
$6-$12

A St. Louis area landmark nestled along the St. Louis Walk of Fame, the restaurant is filled with pop culture memorabilia and is famous for serving delicious hamburgers, jerk chicken, vegetarian specials, trout almondine, soups, chili, salads, sandwiches and all-day breakfast items. The menu includes a superb beer selection. Darts, pinball machines, video games and a photo booth entertain guests before and after the meal. Casual dress. Entertainment. **Bar:** Full bar. **Reservations:** accepted. **Hours:** 11 am-1:30 am, Sun-midnight. **Address:** 6504 Delmar Blvd 63130 **Location:** I-170, exit 2 (Delmar Blvd), 2.9 mi e; in The Loop. **Parking:** street. **Historic**

St. Louis landmark filled with pop culture memorabilia

HOUSE OF INDIA — **Phone:** 314/567-6850 (60)

Indian
$8-$14

A lengthy list of tasty, traditional Indian cuisine is standard fare at this pleasantly casual eatery. Lamb, chicken and seafood selections line the menu, but the tandoor dishes, curries and vegetarian options are popular selections. A lunch buffet is offered every day. Casual dress. **Bar:** Beer & wine. **Reservations:** accepted. **Hours:** 11:30 am-2:30 & 5-10 pm, Sun-9 pm. Closed: 7/4, 9/6, 12/25. **Address:** 8501 Delmar Blvd 63124 **Location:** I-170, exit 2 (Delmar Blvd), just e. **Parking:** on-site.

MAI LEE RESTAURANT — **Phone:** 314/993-3754 (61)

Asian
$5-$11

The winner of many local "best of" awards, this casual cafe draws a crowd for its comprehensive menu of Vietnamese cuisine. Chinese fare is featured as well. Casual dress. **Bar:** Beer & wine. **Reservations:** required. **Hours:** 11 am-9 pm, Fri & Sat-10 pm. Closed major holidays; also Mon. **Address:** 8440 Delmar Blvd 63124 **Location:** I-170, exit 2 (Delmar Blvd), just e; in Delcrest Plaza. **Parking:** on-site.

NOBU'S JAPANESE RESTAURANT — **Phone:** 314/997-2303 (59)

Japanese
$7-$22

Specializing in fresh seafood, the restaurant employs several different techniques in the preparation of their meals. Sushi, sashimi and tempura plus the more common fried and grilled methods are used. You might want to consider a combination dinner which includes miso soup, salad with peanut oil dressing and steamed rice plus the entree of your choice. Dramatic lacquered trays provide the palate on which the food is displayed. Casual dress. **Bar:** Beer & wine. **Reservations:** suggested, weekends. **Hours:** 11:30 am-2 & 5-9:30 pm, Fri-10 pm, Sat 5 pm-10 pm, Sun 5 pm-9 pm. Closed major holidays; also Mon & week of 7/4. **Address:** 8643 Olive Blvd 63132 **Location:** I-170, exit 3A (Olive Blvd), just e. **Parking:** on-site.

SEKI FINE JAPANESE CUISINE & SUSHI BAR — **Phone:** 314/726-6477 (62)

Japanese
$6-$25

An extensive list of authentic Japanese cuisine includes sushi and sashimi options, plus teriyaki, tempura and noodle dishes. The cozy dining room can be crowded at peak dining hours. Casual dress. **Bar:** Beer & wine. **Reservations:** accepted. **Hours:** 11:30 am-2:30 & 5:30-9:45 pm, Fri-10:15 pm, Sat noon-2:45 & 5:30-10:15 pm, Sun 5 pm-9:45 pm. Closed: 11/25, 12/25; also Mon. **Address:** 6335 Delmar Blvd 63130 **Location:** I-170, exit 2, 3 mi e; in The Loop. **Parking:** street.

VALLEY PARK pop. 6,518 (See map and index starting on p. 526)

DRURY INN & SUITES-ST. LOUIS SOUTHWEST *Book at AAA.com* — **Phone:** (636)861-8300 (32)

Hotel
$80-$179 All Year

Address: 5 Lambert Drury Pl 63088 **Location:** I-44, exit 272 (SR 141), just sw. **Facility:** 175 units. 145 one-bedroom standard units. 30 one-bedroom suites. 7 stories, interior corridors. *Bath:* combo or shower only. **Parking:** on-site. **Terms:** cancellation fee imposed. **Amenities:** high-speed Internet, voice mail, irons, hair dryers. **Pool(s):** heated indoor/outdoor. **Leisure Activities:** whirlpool, exercise room. **Guest Services:** valet and coin laundry, wireless Internet. **Business Services:** meeting rooms, PC. ASK / SOME UNITS

HAMPTON INN-ST. LOUIS SOUTHWEST *Book great rates at AAA.com* — **Phone:** (636)529-9020 (31)

Hotel
$94-$124 All Year

Address: 9 Lambert Drury Pl 63088 **Location:** I-44, exit 272 (SR 141), just sw. **Facility:** 92 one-bedroom standard units. 4 stories, interior corridors. *Bath:* combo or shower only. **Parking:** on-site. **Terms:** 1-7 night minimum stay, cancellation fee imposed. **Amenities:** high-speed Internet, voice mail, irons, hair dryers. **Pool(s):** outdoor. **Leisure Activities:** exercise room. **Guest Services:** valet laundry, wireless Internet. **Business Services:** PC. / SOME UNITS

AAA Benefit:
Members save up to 10% everyday!

WEBSTER GROVES pop. 23,230 (See map and index starting on p. 530)

WHERE TO DINE

BIG SKY CAFE — **Phone:** 314/962-5757 (105)

Regional American
$14-$24

Revitalized American fare is on the cafe's menu, meaning comfort foods are prepared with flair. Many small plates are offered, making sampling multiple courses possible, and an award-winning wine list is a highlight. An attractive patio allows for outdoor dining amid casually upscale decor. Casual dress. **Bar:** Full bar. **Reservations:** suggested. **Hours:** 5:30 pm-9:30 pm, Fri-10:30 pm, Sat 5 pm-10:30 pm, Sun 4:30 pm-9 pm. Closed major holidays; also Mon. **Address:** 47 S Old Orchard Ave 63119 **Location:** I-44, exit 282 (Murdoch Rd/Laclede Station Rd), just s, just nw on Murdoch Rd, just w on Big Bend Blvd, then just s. **Parking:** on-site.

(See map and index starting on p. 530)

LLYWELYN'S PUB

Phone: 314/962-1515 (104)

Irish
$8-$15

Examples of traditional pub fare include shepherd's pie, Irish stew, fish and chips, Welsh potato chips, Welsh rarebit and pub pretzels. Casual dress. **Bar:** Full bar. **Reservations:** not accepted. **Hours:** 11 am-9 pm, Fri & Sat-10 pm, Sun noon-9 pm. Closed: 7/4, 11/25, 12/25. **Address:** 17 W Moody St 63119 **Location:** 1 blk n of Lockwood St; between Elm and N Gore sts. **Parking:** on-site.

WENTZVILLE pop. 6,896 (See map and index starting on p. 526)

WHERE TO DINE

STEFANINA'S

Phone: 636/327-5800 (13)

Italian
$5-$15

Since 1995, this casual restaurant on the north frontage road along I-70 has served traditional Italian favorites and a few Sicilian specialties. Pizza is the most popular menu item. Casual dress. **Bar:** Full bar. **Reservations:** not accepted. **Hours:** 11 am-9 pm, Fri & Sat-10 pm. Closed major holidays. **Address:** 762 W Pearce Blvd 63385 **Location:** I-70, exit 208 (Pearce Blvd), just n, then 1 mi e. **Parking:** on-site.

WOODSON TERRACE pop. 4,189 (See map and index starting on p. 530)

HILTON ST. LOUIS AIRPORT *Book great rates at AAA.com*

Phone: (314)426-5500 (50)

Hotel
$79-$209 All Year

Address: 10330 Natural Bridge Rd 63134 **Location:** I-70, exit 236 (Lambert Airport), 0.5 mi se. **Facility:** 397 one-bedroom standard units, some with whirlpools. 4-9 stories, interior corridors. *Bath:* combo or shower only. **Parking:** on-site (fee). **Terms:** 1-7 night minimum stay, cancellation fee imposed. **Amenities:** high-speed Internet (fee), dual phone lines, voice mail, irons, hair dryers. **Pool(s):** heated indoor. **Leisure Activities:** exercise room. **Guest Services:** valet laundry, airport transportation-Lambert-St Louis International Airport, area transportation-within 5 mi, wireless Internet. **Business Services:** conference facilities, business center. **Free Special Amenities: newspaper.**

SOME UNITS

HOLIDAY INN AIRPORT HOTEL *Book at AAA.com*

Phone: (314)427-4700 (51)

Hotel
$89-$169 All Year

Address: 4505 Woodson Rd 63134 **Location:** I-70, exit 236 (Lambert Airport), 0.6 mi e on Natural Bridge Rd, then just s. **Facility:** 158 one-bedroom standard units. 5 stories, interior corridors. *Bath:* combo or shower only. **Parking:** on-site. **Amenities:** video games (fee), voice mail, irons, hair dryers. **Dining:** Oakland Park Restaurant, see separate listing. **Pool(s):** heated outdoor. **Leisure Activities:** exercise room. **Guest Services:** valet and coin laundry, area transportation, wireless Internet. **Business Services:** conference facilities, business center.

ASK SOME UNITS

WHERE TO DINE

ERIO'S RESTAURANT

Phone: 314/423-1555 (49)

Italian
$5-$10

At the longtime family-owned-and-operated business, expect straightforward Italian fare served in a comfortable atmosphere. Pizza, subs and pasta dishes line the menu. Casual dress. **Bar:** Beer & wine. **Reservations:** not accepted. **Hours:** 11 am-9 pm, Fri & Sat-10:30 pm, Sun 4 pm-9 pm. Closed major holidays; also Mon. **Address:** 4434 Woodson Rd 63134 **Location:** I-70, exit 236 (Lambert Airport), 0.6 mi e on Natural Bridge Rd, then just s. **Parking:** on-site.

OAKLAND PARK RESTAURANT

Phone: 314/656-1660 (48)

American
$7-$24

The Italian chef creates American cuisine with his homeland flair. The restaurant is best known for steaks and ribs. Casual dress. **Bar:** Full bar. **Reservations:** accepted. **Hours:** 6-10:30 am, 11-1 & 5-9:30 pm, Sat & Sun 6 am-10:30 & 5-9 pm. **Address:** 4505 Woodson Rd 63134 **Location:** I-70, exit 236 (Lambert Airport), 0.6 mi e on Natural Bridge Rd, then just s; in Holiday Inn Airport Hotel. **Parking:** on-site. CALL

YESTERDAY'S

Phone: 314/423-5677 (50)

American
$4-$16

On the menu is a good selection of appetizers, soups, salads, pizzas and sandwiches, as well as chicken, shrimp, fish and steak entrees. Casual dress. **Bar:** Full bar. **Reservations:** not accepted. **Hours:** 11 am-midnight. Closed: 12/25. **Address:** 4412-16 Woodson Rd 63134 **Location:** I-70, exit 236 (Lambert Airport), 0.6 mi e on Natural Bridge Rd, then just s. **Parking:** on-site.

Nearby Illinois

ALTON pop. 30,496

COMFORT INN *Book at AAA.com*

Phone: 618/465-9999

Hotel
Rates not provided

Address: 11 Crossroads Ct 62002 **Location:** Off SR 3, jct SR 140. **Facility:** 62 one-bedroom standard units, some with whirlpools. 3 stories, interior corridors. *Bath:* combo or shower only. **Parking:** on-site. **Amenities:** high-speed Internet, safes (fee), irons, hair dryers. **Pool(s):** heated indoor. **Guest Services:** coin laundry, wireless Internet. **Business Services:** business center.

CALL FEE SOME UNITS

SUPER 8 Book at AAA.com **Phone:** (618)465-8885

Hotel
$70-$75 All Year

Address: 1800 Homer Adams Pkwy 62002 **Location:** On SR 111, 1.8 mi e of jct US 67. Located in a commercial area. **Facility:** 62 one-bedroom standard units. 3 stories (no elevator), interior corridors. **Parking:** on-site. **Amenities:** safes (fee), irons, hair dryers. **Guest Services:** wireless Internet.
ASK CALL FEE / SOME UNITS FEE

WHERE TO DINE

CASTELLI'S MOONLIGHT RESTAURANT **Phone:** 618/462-4620

Italian
$7-$24

Since 1937, patrons have enjoyed the casual atmosphere and homemade specialties here. The Roman house salad with creamy Italian dressing and the "talk-n-chic" fried chicken are notable hits in this cozy and friendly eatery convenient for travelers. Casual dress. **Bar:** Full bar. **Hours:** 11 am-2 & 4-9 pm, Fri-10 pm, Sat 4 pm-10 pm, Sun 11 am-9 pm, Mon 4 pm-9 pm. Closed: 11/25, 12/25. **Address:** 3400 Fosterburg Rd 62002 **Location:** Jct SR 3/140/111, 0.4 mi e, then 1.2 mi n. **Parking:** on-site.

TONY'S RESTAURANT & THIRD STREET CAFE **Phone:** 618/462-8384

Steak
$8-$25

Close to the banks of the Mississippi River, this eatery occupies a building that once housed a popular department store. The building is now home to a restaurant with several dining rooms, each with different levels of sophistication and elegance. Patrons can select from pasta, pizza, steak and seafood, as well as a wide variety of cheesecake desserts. Casual dress. **Bar:** Full bar. **Reservations:** suggested. **Hours:** 4:30 pm-10 pm, Sun 4 pm-9 pm. Closed: 4/4, 12/24, 12/25; also Mon. **Address:** 312 Piasa St 62002 **Location:** US 67, just n of jct SR 100. **Parking:** on-site.

BELLEVILLE pop. 41,410 (See map and index starting on p. 530)

THE SHRINE HOTEL Book great rates at AAA.com **Phone:** (618)397-1162 103

AAA SAVE

Hotel
$70-$85 All Year

Address: 451 S Demazenod Dr 62223 **Location:** I-255, exit 17A, 1 mi e on SR 15; in Shrine of Our Lady of the Snows Complex. Located on grounds of National Shrine. **Facility:** Smoke free premises. 78 one-bedroom standard units. 2 stories, interior corridors. *Bath:* combo or shower only. **Parking:** on-site. **Amenities:** irons, hair dryers. **Dining:** restaurant, see separate listing. **Leisure Activities:** gazebo & picnic tables, hiking trails, playground, exercise room. **Guest Services:** coin laundry, wireless Internet. **Business Services:** conference facilities, PC. *(See color ad p 222)*
/ SOME UNITS

FREE expanded continental breakfast and high-speed Internet

WHERE TO DINE

THE PIE PANTRY **Phone:** 618/277-4140 113

American
$5-$12

The courtyard of this 100-year-old carriage house with a cobblestone floor, antique furniture, large skylights and high beamed ceiling is striking. The pie is the definite show stopper though, and is an excellent ending to any meal you choose here. Casual dress. **Reservations:** accepted. **Hours:** 7 am-3 pm, Sun 8 am-2 pm. Closed major holidays. **Address:** 310 E Main St 62220 **Location:** I-64, exit 12, 6 mi s on SR 159, then just e. **Parking:** on-site.

THE SHRINE RESTAURANT **Phone:** 618/397-6700 112

AAA

American
$6-$14

Homemade soup and a varied salad bar that includes a pasta station are favorites at the casual family restaurant, which is known for its comfort foods. The setting, on the grounds of the National Shrine for which it is named, is beautiful and serene. Casual dress. **Bar:** Full bar. **Hours:** 11 am-8 pm, Fri & Sat-9 pm, Sun 10 am-8 pm. Closed: 11/25, 12/25. **Address:** 442 S Demazenod Dr 62223 **Location:** I-255, exit 17A, 1 mi e on SR 15; in Shrine of Our Lady of the Snows Complex; in The Shrine Hotel. **Parking:** on-site. *(See color ad p 222)*

COLLINSVILLE pop. 24,707 (See map and index starting on p. 530)

DRURY INN-ST. LOUIS/COLLINSVILLE Book at AAA.com **Phone:** (618)345-7700 54

Hotel
$85-$159 All Year

Address: 602 N Bluff Rd 62234 **Location:** I-55/70, exit 11 (SR 157), just n. **Facility:** 123 one-bedroom standard units. 4 stories, interior corridors. **Parking:** on-site. **Terms:** cancellation fee imposed. **Amenities:** high-speed Internet, dual phone lines, voice mail, irons, hair dryers. **Pool(s):** heated indoor. **Leisure Activities:** exercise room. **Guest Services:** valet and coin laundry, wireless Internet. **Business Services:** meeting rooms, business center.
ASK CALL / SOME UNITS

SUPER 8-COLLINSVILLE Book at AAA.com **Phone:** (618)345-8008 55

Hotel
$60-$90 All Year

Address: 2 Gateway Dr 62234 **Location:** I-55/70, exit 11 (SR 157), just n. **Facility:** 62 one-bedroom standard units. 3 stories (no elevator), interior corridors. *Bath:* combo or shower only. **Parking:** on-site, winter plug-ins. **Amenities:** safes (fee), irons, hair dryers. **Guest Services:** wireless Internet.
ASK FEE / SOME UNITS

(See map and index starting on p. 530)

—— WHERE TO DINE ——

BANDANA'S BAR-B-Q

Phone: 618/344-4476

Barbecue

$5-$12

The hickory smoke taste in the ribs, pork, chicken, turkey and beef brings patrons back time and again. Of the four basic sauces, the hot Memphis style is for those who prefer spicy. For a different flavor, deep-fried corn on the cob is interesting. Casual dress. **Bar:** Beer & wine. **Reservations:** not accepted. **Hours:** 11 am-9 pm, Fri & Sat-10 pm. Closed: 11/25, 12/25. **Address:** 4 Commerce Dr 62234 **Location:** I-55/70, exit 11 (SR 157), just n. **Parking:** on-site.

ZAPATA'S MEXICAN RESTAURANT & CANTINA

Phone: 618/343-1337 (53)

Mexican

$6-$15

Authentic Mexican entrees of burritos, fajitas and chiles rellenos are sure to please the casual diner. The camarones diablo are a great shrimp offering with a little spice. Casual dress. **Bar:** Full bar. **Hours:** 11 am-10 pm, Fri-11 pm, Sat noon-11 pm, Sun noon-10 pm. Closed: 4/4, 11/25, 12/25. **Address:** 8 Eastport Plaza Dr 62234 **Location:** I-55/70, exit 11 (SR 157), just nw. **Parking:** on-site. CALL

EAST ST. LOUIS pop. 31,542 (See map and index starting on p. 530)

CASINO QUEEN HOTEL

Phone: (618)874-5000 (89)

Hotel

$110-$130 All Year

Address: 200 S Front St 62201 **Location:** I-55, exit 2A, 0.6 mi n on River Park Dr, then just w. Metrolink stop in parking lot. **Facility:** The hotel's large guest rooms feature comfortable seating, fine quality bedding, elegant baths and large flat-panel TVs. 157 units. 150 one-bedroom standard units, some with whirlpools. 7 one-bedroom suites with whirlpools. 7 stories, interior corridors. *Bath:* combo or shower only. **Parking:** on-site and valet. **Terms:** age restrictions may apply, cancellation fee imposed. **Amenities:** video games (fee), high-speed Internet, dual phone lines, voice mail, irons, hair dryers. **Dining:** 2 restaurants, also, Prime Steakhouse, see separate listing. **Pool(s):** heated indoor. **Leisure Activities:** exercise room. **Guest Services:** valet laundry, area transportation-downtown lodgings, wireless Internet. **Business Services:** conference facilities. **Free Special Amenities: newspaper and high-speed Internet.**

CALL / SOME UNITS

—— WHERE TO DINE ——

PRIME STEAKHOUSE

Phone: 618/874-5000 (94)

American

$15-$35

The intimate and elegant atmosphere is just the beginning of your dining experience. From aged beef of chateaubriand for two to filet mignon to rack of lamb and fresh seafood selections, you are sure to find a tempting selection. Various pasta and vegetarian dishes complete the entree selections. Wonderful appetizers and desserts are offered for the start of your meal or for a great ending. Casual dress. **Bar:** Full bar. **Reservations:** suggested. **Hours:** 5 pm-9 pm. **Address:** 200 S Front St 62201 **Location:** I-55, exit 2A, 0.6 mi n on River Park Dr, then just w; in Casino Queen Hotel. **Parking:** on-site and valet. CALL

EDWARDSVILLE pop. 21,491 (See map and index starting on p. 530)

COUNTRY HEARTH INN & SUITES *Book great rates at AAA.com*

Phone: (618)656-7829 (8)

Hotel

$100-$140 All Year

Address: 1013 Plummer Dr 62025 **Location:** I-270, exit 9, 3 mi on SR 157. **Facility:** Smoke free premises. 39 one-bedroom standard units, some with whirlpools. 3 stories, interior corridors. *Bath:* combo or shower only. **Parking:** on-site. **Terms:** cancellation fee imposed. **Amenities:** voice mail, irons, hair dryers. *Some:* DVD players (fee), CD players. **Leisure Activities:** patio, gazebo, exercise room. **Guest Services:** valet and coin laundry, wireless Internet. **Business Services:** PC. **Free Special Amenities: full breakfast and high-speed Internet.**

CALL

—— WHERE TO DINE ——

BULL & BEAR GRILL & BAR

Phone: 618/655-9920 (24)

American

$8-$17

The casual restaurant features a masculine sports theme and has a universal menu offering steaks, ribs, chicken, seafood, large salads, pizza, pasta and some Southwestern grilled items. The service is prompt and laid-back. Casual dress. **Bar:** Full bar. **Reservations:** accepted. **Hours:** 11 am-midnight, Fri & Sat-1 am, Sun-11 pm. Closed major holidays. **Address:** 1071 S SR 157 62025 **Location:** I-270, exit 9, 3 mi n. **Parking:** on-site.

FAIRVIEW HEIGHTS pop. 15,034 (See map and index starting on p. 530)

COMFORT SUITES Book at AAA.com **Phone:** (618)394-0202 94

Hotel
$89-$99 All Year

Address: 137 Ludwig Dr 62208 **Location:** I-64, exit 12 (SR 159), just n to Ludwig Dr, then 0.4 mi w. **Facility:** Smoke free premises. 71 one-bedroom standard units, some with whirlpools. 3 stories, interior corridors. *Bath:* combo or shower only. **Parking:** on-site. **Terms:** check-in 4 pm. **Amenities:** high-speed Internet, dual phone lines, voice mail, safes (fee), irons, hair dryers. **Pool(s):** heated indoor. **Leisure Activities:** exercise room. **Guest Services:** valet and coin laundry, wireless Internet. **Business Services:** business center.

ASK CALL &M / SOME UNITS FEE

DRURY INN & SUITES-FAIRVIEW HEIGHTS Book at AAA.com **Phone:** (618)398-8530 93

Hotel
$85-$164 All Year

Address: 12 Ludwig Dr 62208 **Location:** I-64, exit 12 (SR 159). **Facility:** 142 units. 126 one-bedroom standard units. 16 one-bedroom suites. 4 stories, interior corridors. *Bath:* combo or shower only. **Parking:** on-site. **Terms:** cancellation fee imposed. **Amenities:** video library, DVD players, high-speed Internet, dual phone lines, voice mail, irons, hair dryers. **Pool(s):** heated indoor/outdoor. **Leisure Activities:** whirlpool, exercise room. **Guest Services:** valet and coin laundry, wireless Internet. **Business Services:** meeting rooms, PC.

ASK / SOME UNITS

FAIRFIELD INN BY MARRIOTT Book great rates at AAA.com **Phone:** (618)398-7124 96

Hotel
$90-$100 All Year

Address: 140 Ludwig Dr 62208 **Location:** I-64, exit 12 (SR 159), 1 mi nw. **Facility:** Smoke free premises. 63 one-bedroom standard units. 3 stories, interior corridors. *Bath:* combo or shower only. **Parking:** on-site, winter plug-ins. **Terms:** cancellation fee imposed. **Amenities:** irons, hair dryers. **Pool(s):** heated indoor. **Leisure Activities:** whirlpool. **Guest Services:** valet laundry, wireless Internet. **Business Services:** PC.

CALL &M / SOME UNITS

AAA Benefit: Members save a minimum 5% off the best available rate.

FOUR POINTS BY SHERATON Book great rates at AAA.com **Phone:** 618/622-9500 92

AAA SAVE

Hotel
Rates not provided

Address: 319 Fountains Pkwy 62208 **Location:** I-64, exit 14, just n. **Facility:** Smoke free premises. 120 units. 117 one-bedroom standard units, some with whirlpools. 3 one-bedroom suites with whirlpools. 4 stories, interior corridors. *Bath:* combo or shower only. **Parking:** on-site. **Amenities:** video games (fee), high-speed Internet, voice mail, irons, hair dryers. *Some:* dual phone lines. **Pool(s):** heated indoor. **Leisure Activities:** whirlpool. **Guest Services:** valet laundry, wireless Internet. **Business Services:** conference facilities, business center. **Free Special Amenities: local telephone calls and high-speed Internet.**

CALL &M FEE / SOME UNITS

FOUR POINTS BY SHERATON

AAA Benefit: Members get up to 15% off, plus Starwood Preferred Guest® bonuses.

HAMPTON INN BY HILTON Book great rates at AAA.com **Phone:** (618)397-9705 95

Hotel
$94-$119 All Year

Address: 150 Ludwig Dr 62208 **Location:** I-64, exit 12 (SR 159), 1 mi nw. **Facility:** 61 one-bedroom standard units. 3 stories, interior corridors. *Bath:* combo or shower only. **Parking:** on-site. **Terms:** 1-7 night minimum stay, cancellation fee imposed. **Amenities:** voice mail, irons, hair dryers. **Pool(s):** heated indoor. **Leisure Activities:** whirlpool, exercise room. **Guest Services:** valet laundry, wireless Internet. **Business Services:** PC.

CALL &M / SOME UNITS

AAA Benefit: Members save up to 10% everyday!

RAMADA INN FAIRVIEW HEIGHTS Book great rates at AAA.com **Phone:** (618)632-4747 97

AAA SAVE

Hotel
$67-$81 All Year

Address: 6900 N Illinois St 62208 **Location:** I-64, exit 12 (SR 159), just n. **Facility:** 158 one-bedroom standard units, some with whirlpools. 5 stories, interior corridors. *Bath:* combo or shower only. **Parking:** on-site. **Amenities:** voice mail, irons, hair dryers. **Pool(s):** outdoor, heated indoor. **Leisure Activities:** exercise room. *Fee:* game room. **Guest Services:** valet and coin laundry, wireless Internet. **Business Services:** conference facilities, PC. **Free Special Amenities: expanded continental breakfast and high-speed Internet.**

/ SOME UNITS FEE

WHERE TO DINE

HOULIHAN'S **Phone:** 618/397-9242 97

American
$7-$22

This busy eatery provides a comfortable atmosphere for gathering with friends or family. Menu favorites include the goat cheese bruschetta, stuffed chicken and the triple berry cobbler. Casual dress. **Bar:** Full bar. **Reservations:** accepted. **Hours:** 11 am-10 pm, Fri & Sat-11 pm. Closed: 12/25. **Address:** 15 Ludwig Dr 62208 **Location:** I-64, exit 12 (SR 159), just n to Ludwig Dr, then just w. **Parking:** on-site. CALL &M

(See map and index starting on p. 530)

LOTAWATA CREEK SOUTHERN GRILL

Phone: 618/628-7373 98

Regional American
$10-$23

Traditional Southern food served in a casual setting is what you'll find, along with lots of country-fried items and blackened Cajun fare. The quality is consistently high, especially among the hand-cut beef, homemade bread and dessert. Casual dress. **Bar:** Full bar. **Reservations:** not accepted. **Hours:** 11 am-10 pm, Fri & Sat-11 pm. Closed: 11/25, 12/25. **Address:** 311 Salem Pl 62208 **Location:** I-64, exit 12 (SR 159), just n. **Parking:** on-site. CALL

O'FALLON pop. 21,910 (See map and index starting on p. 530)

CANDLEWOOD SUITES *Book at AAA.com*

Phone: (618)622-9555 72

Extended Stay Hotel
$84-$139 5/29-3/31
$84-$129 4/1-5/28

Address: 1332 Park Plaza Dr 62269 **Location:** I-64, exit 14 (US 50), just s on Lincoln Hwy, 0.5 mi w on Hartman Ln, then just n on 2nd entrance to Park Plaza Dr. **Facility:** 79 units. 63 one-bedroom standard units with efficiencies. 16 one-bedroom suites with efficiencies. 4 stories, interior corridors. *Bath:* combo or shower only. **Parking:** on-site. **Amenities:** video library, DVD players, high-speed Internet, voice mail, irons, hair dryers. **Leisure Activities:** exercise room. **Guest Services:** complimentary laundry, wireless Internet. **Business Services:** business center.
ASK CALL / SOME UNITS FEE

COUNTRY INN & SUITES BY CARLSON *Book at AAA.com*

Phone: (618)622-8600 68

Hotel
$75-$110 All Year

Address: 116 Regency Park Dr 62269 **Location:** I-64, exit 14 (US 50), just n. **Facility:** 66 units. 61 one-bedroom standard units, some with whirlpools. 5 one-bedroom suites. 3 stories, interior corridors. *Bath:* combo or shower only. **Parking:** on-site, winter plug-ins. **Amenities:** high-speed Internet, voice mail, safes, irons, hair dryers. **Pool(s):** heated indoor. **Leisure Activities:** whirlpool, exercise room. **Guest Services:** coin laundry, wireless Internet. **Business Services:** meeting rooms, PC.
CALL / SOME UNITS

DAYS INN O'FALLON *Book at AAA.com*

Phone: (618)628-9700 71

Hotel
$50-$69 All Year

Address: 1320 Park Plaza Dr 62269 **Location:** I-64, exit 14 (US 50), just s, 0.3 mi e, then just n. **Facility:** 63 one-bedroom standard units, some with whirlpools. 3 stories, interior corridors. *Bath:* combo or shower only. **Parking:** on-site. **Amenities:** high-speed Internet, irons, hair dryers. **Pool(s):** heated indoor. **Leisure Activities:** exercise room. **Guest Services:** valet and coin laundry, wireless Internet. **Business Services:** meeting rooms, PC.
ASK / SOME UNITS FEE

DRURY INN & SUITES-O'FALLON *Book at AAA.com*

Phone: (618)624-2211 74

Hotel
$90-$184 All Year

Address: 1118 Central Park Dr 62269 **Location:** I-64, exit 16, just s. **Facility:** 180 units. 144 one-bedroom standard units, some with whirlpools. 36 one-bedroom suites. 7 stories, interior corridors. *Bath:* combo or shower only. **Parking:** on-site, winter plug-ins. **Terms:** cancellation fee imposed. **Amenities:** voice mail, irons, hair dryers. **Pool(s):** heated indoor/outdoor. **Leisure Activities:** whirlpool, exercise room. **Guest Services:** valet and coin laundry, wireless Internet. **Business Services:** meeting rooms, business center.
ASK CALL / SOME UNITS

EXTENDED STAYAMERICA-ST. LOUIS-O'FALLON *Book at AAA.com*

Phone: (618)624-1757 69

Extended Stay Hotel
$79-$89 All Year

Address: 154 Regency Park Dr 62269 **Location:** I-64, exit 14 (US 50), just w to Regency Park Dr, then 0.4 mi s. **Facility:** 89 one-bedroom standard units with efficiencies. 3 stories, interior corridors. *Bath:* combo or shower only. **Parking:** on-site. **Terms:** office hours 7 am-11 pm, cancellation fee imposed. **Amenities:** high-speed Internet, voice mail, irons. **Guest Services:** coin laundry, wireless Internet. ASK CALL / SOME UNITS FEE

HILTON GARDEN INN GREEN MOUNT/O'FALLON *Book great rates at AAA.com*

Phone: (618)624-4499 73

Hotel
$89-$159 All Year

Address: 360 Regency Park Dr 62269 **Location:** I-64, exit 16, just nw. **Facility:** 128 units. 101 one-bedroom standard units, some with whirlpools. 27 one-bedroom suites. 4 stories, interior corridors. *Bath:* combo or shower only. **Parking:** on-site. **Terms:** 1-7 night minimum stay, cancellation fee imposed. **Amenities:** high-speed Internet, voice mail, irons, hair dryers. **Pool(s):** heated indoor. **Leisure Activities:** whirlpool, jogging, exercise room. **Guest Services:** valet and coin laundry, wireless Internet. **Business Services:** conference facilities, business center.
CALL / SOME UNITS

Hilton Garden Inn

AAA Benefit:

Members save 5% or more everyday!

SETTLE INN & SUITES *Book great rates at AAA.com*

Phone: (618)624-6060

Hotel
$69-$149 All Year

Address: 1100 Eastgate Dr 62269 **Location:** I-64, exit 19B (SR 158), 0.5 mi n, then just sw. Located in a semi-rural area. **Facility:** 96 one-bedroom standard units, some with whirlpools. 2 stories (no elevator), interior corridors. **Parking:** on-site. **Amenities:** high-speed Internet, safes (fee), irons, hair dryers. **Pool(s):** outdoor. **Leisure Activities:** whirlpool. **Guest Services:** coin laundry, wireless Internet. **Business Services:** meeting rooms, PC. **Free Special Amenities: full breakfast and high-speed Internet.** / SOME UNITS

(See map and index starting on p. 530)

SUBURBAN EXTENDED STAY HOTEL *Book at AAA.com* **Phone:** 618/589-3696 

Extended Stay Hotel

Rates not provided

Address: 148 Regency Park Dr 62269 **Location:** I-64, exit 14 (US 50), 0.5 mi e. **Facility:** 89 units. 81 one-bedroom standard units with efficiencies. 8 one-bedroom suites with efficiencies. 3 stories, interior corridors. *Bath:* combo or shower only. **Parking:** on-site. **Amenities:** high-speed Internet, voice mail, irons, hair dryers. **Leisure Activities:** exercise room. **Guest Services:** coin laundry, wireless Internet. **Business Services:** business center. / SOME UNITS

WHERE TO DINE

THIP'S THAI CUISINE **Phone:** 618/632-8500

Thai

$7-$19

The authentic, family-run place is very popular with locals. Its dining room sports modest decor. Casual dress. **Bar:** Full bar. **Reservations:** not accepted. **Hours:** 11 am-9:30 pm. Closed: 7/4, 11/25, 12/25. **Address:** 701 W US Hwy 50 62269 **Location:** I-64, exit 16, 1 mi n on N Greenmount Rd, then just e. **Parking:** on-site.

Daniel Boone Home, Defiance / Missouri Division of Tourism

This ends listings for the St. Louis Vicinity.
The following page resumes the alphabetical listings of cities in Missouri.

ST. PETERS—See St. Louis p. 569.

ST. ROBERT pop. 2,760

BAYMONT INN & SUITES FT. LEONARD WOOD-ST. ROBERT *Book at AAA.com*

Phone: (573)336-5050

Hotel
$80-$153 All Year

Address: 139 Carmel Valley Way 65584 **Location:** I-44, exit 161, just nw. **Facility:** 70 one-bedroom standard units, some with kitchens and/or whirlpools. 4 stories, interior corridors. *Bath:* combo or shower only. **Parking:** on-site. **Amenities:** high-speed Internet, dual phone lines, voice mail, safes (fee), irons, hair dryers. *Some:* DVD players. **Pool(s):** heated indoor. **Leisure Activities:** exercise room. **Guest Services:** valet and coin laundry, wireless Internet. **Business Services:** meeting rooms, PC. ASK / SOME UNITS FEE

BEST WESTERN MONTIS INN *Book great rates at AAA.com*

Phone: (573)336-4299

Hotel
$75-$85 All Year

Address: 14086 Hwy Z 65584 **Location:** I-44, exit 163, just s. **Facility:** 41 one-bedroom standard units. 2 stories (no elevator), exterior corridors. **Parking:** on-site, winter plug-ins. **Amenities:** irons, hair dryers. *Some:* high-speed Internet. **Pool(s):** outdoor. **Guest Services:** coin laundry, wireless Internet. **Business Services:** PC. **Free Special Amenities: continental breakfast and high-speed Internet.** / SOME UNITS FEE

AAA Benefit:
Members save up to 20%, plus 10% bonus points with rewards program.

COMFORT INN *Book at AAA.com*

Phone: 573/336-3553

Hotel
Rates not provided

Address: 103 St. Robert Blvd 65584 **Location:** I-44, exit 161, just nw. **Facility:** 70 one-bedroom standard units, some with whirlpools. 3 stories, interior corridors. *Bath:* combo or shower only. **Parking:** on-site. **Amenities:** high-speed Internet, voice mail, safes (fee), irons, hair dryers. *Some:* DVD players, dual phone lines. **Pool(s):** heated indoor. **Leisure Activities:** whirlpool, exercise room. **Guest Services:** valet and coin laundry, wireless Internet. **Business Services:** PC. CALL / SOME UNITS

HAMPTON INN ST. ROBERT/FT. LEONARD WOOD *Book great rates at AAA.com*

Phone: (573)336-3355

Hotel
$76-$199 All Year

Address: 103 St. Robert Plaza Dr 65584 **Location:** I-44, exit 161, just nw. **Facility:** 80 one-bedroom standard units, some with whirlpools. 3 stories, interior corridors. *Bath:* combo or shower only. **Parking:** on-site. **Terms:** 1-7 night minimum stay, cancellation fee imposed. **Amenities:** video games (fee), high-speed Internet, voice mail, irons, hair dryers. **Pool(s):** outdoor. **Leisure Activities:** exercise room. **Guest Services:** valet and coin laundry, wireless Internet. **Business Services:** meeting rooms, PC. ECO CALL / SOME UNITS

AAA Benefit:
Members save up to 10% everyday!

HOLIDAY INN EXPRESS-ST. ROBERT *Book at AAA.com*

Phone: 573/336-2299

Hotel
Rates not provided

Address: 114 Vickie Lynn Ln 65584 **Location:** I-44, exit 161, just s, then 0.3 mi e on frontage road. **Facility:** Smoke free premises. 52 one-bedroom standard units. 2 stories (no elevator), interior corridors. **Parking:** on-site. **Amenities:** video library, dual phone lines, voice mail, irons, hair dryers. *Some:* high-speed Internet. **Pool(s):** heated indoor. **Leisure Activities:** exercise room. **Guest Services:** valet and coin laundry, wireless Internet. **Business Services:** business center. / SOME UNITS

MAINSTAY SUITES *Book at AAA.com*

Phone: (573)451-2700

Extended Stay Hotel
$92-$160 All Year

Address: 227 St. Robert Blvd 65584 **Location:** I-44, exit 159, 0.8 mi nw. **Facility:** 77 units. 50 one-bedroom standard units with efficiencies. 24 one- and 3 two-bedroom suites with efficiencies. 4 stories, interior/exterior corridors. *Bath:* combo or shower only. **Parking:** on-site. **Amenities:** DVD players, high-speed Internet, voice mail, irons, hair dryers. *Some:* dual phone lines. **Pool(s):** outdoor. **Leisure Activities:** exercise room. **Guest Services:** valet and coin laundry, wireless Internet. **Business Services:** business center. ECO ASK / SOME UNITS FEE

MICROTEL INN & SUITES *Book at AAA.com*

Phone: (573)336-7705

Hotel
$60-$80 All Year

Address: 562 Old Route 66 65584 **Location:** I-44, exit 161 westbound to Business Loop 44/Old Route 66, 0.9 mi w; exit 159 eastbound, 0.4 mi se. **Facility:** 66 one-bedroom standard units, some with whirlpools. 3 stories, interior corridors. *Bath:* combo or shower only. **Parking:** on-site. **Amenities:** high-speed Internet (fee), voice mail. *Some:* irons. **Leisure Activities:** exercise room. **Guest Services:** coin laundry, wireless Internet. **Business Services:** meeting rooms, PC. ASK CALL / SOME UNITS FEE

ST. ROBERT/FT. WOOD FAIRFIELD INN BY MARRIOTT Book great rates at AAA.com

Phone: (573)336-8600

Hotel
$80-$98 All Year

Address: 131 St. Robert Blvd 65584 **Location:** I-44, exit 161, just nw. **Facility:** Smoke free premises. 79 one-bedroom standard units, some with whirlpools. 3 stories, interior corridors. *Bath:* combo or shower only. **Parking:** on-site. **Terms:** cancellation fee imposed. **Amenities:** high-speed Internet, voice mail, irons, hair dryers. **Pool(s):** heated indoor. **Leisure Activities:** whirlpool, exercise room. **Guest Services:** valet laundry, wireless Internet. **Business Services:** PC.

CALL / SOME UNITS

AAA Benefit:
Members save a minimum 5% off the best available rate.

WHERE TO DINE

AUSSIE JACK'S

Phone: 573/336-2447

Australian
$7-$19

An Australian influence punctuates such casually comfortable favorites as Toowoomba chicken, a charbroiled chicken breast topped with Monterey Jack cheese, bacon and sauteed mushrooms. Other popular choices include the 12-ounce campfire rib-eye and the decadent crocodile sundae, which is topped with whipped cream and candied pecans covered in caramel sauce. Casual dress. **Bar:** Full bar. **Reservations:** not accepted. **Hours:** 11 am-10 pm, Fri & Sat-11 pm, Mon & Tues 4 pm-10 pm. Closed: 1/1. **Address:** 141 St. Robert Blvd 65584 **Location:** I-44, exit 161, just nw. **Parking:** on-site.

MEDITERRANEAN GRILL

Phone: 573/336-4378

Continental
$9-$25

This place is usually busy at lunchtime thanks to its buffet offering Mediterranean and Italian dishes. It's a great opportunity to sample a lot of different, unique items, from chicken Parmesan to hummus, gyros and baklava. Specialty pizzas also line the menu. Casual dress. **Bar:** Full bar. **Reservations:** not accepted. **Hours:** 11 am-9:30 pm, Fri & Sat-10:30 pm, Sun-9 pm. **Address:** 379 Hwy Z 65584 **Location:** I-44, exit 161, just s. **Parking:** on-site. CALL

SEOUL GARDEN

Phone: 573/336-2023

Asian
$9-$22

A variety of menu offerings hail from traditional Japanese and Korean cooking styles, and a full sushi bar offers creative specialty rolls. The miso soup is fantastic. Private alcoves for nearly every table contribute to a cozy atmosphere. Casual dress. **Reservations:** not accepted. **Hours:** 11 am-9 pm. Closed: Sun. **Address:** 626 Old Historic Route 66 65584 **Location:** I-44, exit 161 westbound to Business Loop 44/Old Route 66, then 0.9 mi w; exit 159 eastbound, 0.7 mi se. **Parking:** on-site. CALL

The following restaurant has not been evaluated by AAA but is listed for your information only.

SWEETWATER BAR-B-QUE

Phone: 573/336-8830

fyi

Not evaluated. A tiny gem of the Ozarks, the restaurant invites guests to cozy up with real wood-pit-smoked barbecue and fixings. **Address:** 14076 Hwy 2 65584 **Location:** I-44, exit 163, just se.

STE. GENEVIEVE pop. 4,476

MAIN STREET INN B & B

Phone: (573)883-9199

Historic Bed & Breakfast
$105-$170 All Year

Address: 221 N Main St 63670 **Location:** Jct Main and Washington sts; in historic downtown. **Facility:** Originally built in 1882 as a hotel, this B&B features spacious public areas and rooms enhanced by fine country antiques. Smoke free premises. 7 one-bedroom standard units, some with whirlpools. 3 stories (no elevator), interior/exterior corridors. *Bath:* combo or shower only. **Parking:** street. **Terms:** age restrictions may apply, 7 day cancellation notice-fee imposed. **Amenities:** video library, hair dryers. *Some:* DVD players. **Guest Services:** wireless Internet.

ASK / SOME UNITS

WHERE TO DINE

ANVIL RESTAURANT & SALOON

Phone: 573/883-7323

American
$5-$17

The charming, circa 1850 establishment originally was a hardware store. Pork chops, fried chicken, burgers and sandwiches, along with homemade desserts, are served daily. Casual dress. **Bar:** Full bar. **Reservations:** accepted. **Hours:** 11 am-8 pm, Fri & Sat-9 pm. Closed major holidays. **Address:** 46 3rd St 63670 **Location:** In historic downtown. **Parking:** street.

OLD BRICK HOUSE

Phone: 573/883-2724

American
$5-$20

This restaurant is situated in the first brick structure built west of the Mississippi, circa 1780. It's well-known for its fried chicken, but the baked chicken au vin and prime rib are also superb. The buffet lunch attracts a loyal following. Business people and visitors alike enjoy this popular no-frills eatery. Casual dress. **Bar:** Full bar. **Reservations:** suggested. **Hours:** 8 am-9 pm, Sat from 11 am, Sun 11 am-7 pm. Closed major holidays. **Address:** 90 S 3rd St 63670 **Location:** 3rd and Market sts; center. **Parking:** on-site and street. **Historic**

SALEM pop. 4,854

HOLIDAY INN EXPRESS — *Book at AAA.com*

Phone: (573)729-4700

Hotel
$95-$167 All Year

Address: 1200 S Main St (Hwy 19) 65560 **Location:** Jct SR 19 and 32-72. **Facility:** 65 one-bedroom standard units. 4 stories, interior corridors. *Bath:* combo or shower only. **Parking:** on-site. **Amenities:** high-speed Internet, voice mail, irons, hair dryers. **Pool(s):** heated indoor. **Leisure Activities:** whirlpool, exercise room. **Guest Services:** valet and coin laundry, wireless Internet. **Business Services:** meeting rooms, PC.

ASK CALL / SOME UNITS

SEDALIA pop. 20,339

BEST WESTERN STATE FAIR INN — *Book great rates at AAA.com*

Phone: (660)826-6100

AAA SAVE

Hotel
$72-$149 All Year

Address: 3120 S Limit Ave 65301 **Location:** Jct US 50, 1.5 mi s on US 65. **Facility:** 117 units. 114 one-bedroom standard units. 3 one-bedroom suites. 2 stories (no elevator), interior/exterior corridors. *Bath:* combo or shower only. **Parking:** on-site, winter plug-ins. **Amenities:** voice mail, irons, hair dryers. *Some:* high-speed Internet. **Pool(s):** heated indoor. **Leisure Activities:** whirlpool, shuffleboard. *Fee:* game room. **Guest Services:** valet and coin laundry, wireless Internet. **Business Services:** conference facilities, PC. **Free Special Amenities: full breakfast and early check-in/late check-out.**

/ SOME UNITS

Best Western

AAA Benefit:
Members save up to 20%, plus 10% bonus points with rewards program.

COMFORT INN SEDALIA STATION — *Book at AAA.com*

Phone: (660)829-5050

Hotel
$80-$124 All Year

Address: 3600 W Broadway 65301 **Location:** On US 50, 1 mi w of US 65. **Facility:** 76 one-bedroom standard units, some with whirlpools. 3-4 stories, interior corridors. *Bath:* combo or shower only. **Parking:** on-site. **Amenities:** CD players, high-speed Internet, irons, hair dryers. **Pool(s):** heated indoor. **Leisure Activities:** whirlpool. **Guest Services:** valet and coin laundry, wireless Internet. **Business Services:** meeting rooms, PC.

ASK / SOME UNITS

HOLIDAY INN EXPRESS & SUITES Book at AAA.com Phone: (660)826-4000

Hotel
$110-$160 All Year

Address: 4001 W Broadway 65301 **Location:** Jct US 50 and Main St. **Facility:** Smoke free premises. 76 one-bedroom standard units. 3 stories, interior corridors. *Bath:* combo or shower only. **Parking:** on-site. **Amenities:** high-speed Internet, dual phone lines, voice mail, irons, hair dryers. **Pool(s):** heated indoor. **Leisure Activities:** whirlpool, exercise room. **Guest Services:** valet and coin laundry, wireless Internet. **Business Services:** meeting rooms, business center.

ASK CALL

HOTEL BOTHWELL, AN ASCEND COLLECTION HOTEL Book at AAA.com Phone: 660/826-5588

Classic Hotel
Rates not provided

Address: 103 E 4th St 65301 **Location:** Corner of 4th and S Ohio sts; downtown. **Facility:** A tastefully restored historic hotel which allows guests to enjoy authentic "railroad hotel" rooms all the way up to spacious and elegant suites. Smoke free premises. 48 units. 45 one- and 3 two-bedroom standard units, some with whirlpools. 7 stories, interior corridors. *Bath:* combo or shower only. **Parking:** on-site. **Amenities:** CD players, voice mail, irons, hair dryers. **Leisure Activities:** sauna, exercise room. **Guest Services:** valet and coin laundry, wireless Internet. **Business Services:** meeting rooms, business center. / SOME UNITS FEE

WHERE TO DINE

EL TAPATIO MEXICAN RESTAURANT Phone: 660/827-5553

Mexican
$7-$13

The popular, family-run restaurant nurtures a lively and colorful atmosphere. Live entertainment on weekends. Casual dress. **Bar:** Full bar. **Reservations:** accepted. **Hours:** 10 am-9 pm, Fri & Sat-10 pm. Closed: 7/4, 11/25, 12/24, 12/25. **Address:** 1705 W Broadway 65301 **Location:** Jct US 50 and 65, just e. **Parking:** on-site. CALL

KEHDE'S BARBEQUE Phone: 660/826-2267

American
$6-$20

Unique inside and out, featuring railroad memorabilia. Expect large portions and friendly hometown service. Casual dress. **Bar:** Beer only. **Reservations:** accepted. **Hours:** 11 am-9 pm. Closed major holidays; also Tues. **Address:** 1915 S Limit Ave 65301 **Location:** US 65, 0.7 mi s of jct US 50. **Parking:** on-site.

PATRICIA'S MEXICAN RESTAURANT AND MORE Phone: 660/827-4141

Mexican
$6-$11

Patricia's has a rustic decor that is light and airy and offers patio dining in season. The menu features Southwestern meals and sandwiches, and the fruit chimichanga is one of the more unusual desserts. The server staff is friendly and efficient. Casual dress. **Bar:** Full bar. **Reservations:** not accepted. **Hours:** 10:30 am-9 pm, Fri & Sat-10 pm. Closed major holidays; also Mon. **Address:** 3000 S Limit Ave 65301 **Location:** On US 65, 0.7 mi s of jct US 50. **Parking:** on-site.

SHELL KNOB pop. 1,393

WHERE TO DINE

THE STEAK INN Phone: 417/858-6814

Steak
$8-$25

Cedar and etched-glass accents combine with a glossy flagstone floor to evoke a warm, rustic atmosphere. For a touch of spring, the garden room may be just the ticket. Locals frequent this place for its salad bar and because they can watch their steak being grilled. Casual dress. **Bar:** Full bar. **Reservations:** not accepted. **Hours:** Open 3/1-12/31 & 2/14-2/28; 5 pm-9 pm; hours may vary in winter. Closed: 1/1, 11/25, 12/24, 12/25; also Mon. **Address:** S Hwy 39 65747 **Location:** 0.3 mi s of bridge. **Parking:** on-site.

SIKESTON pop. 16,992

COMFORT INN & SUITES Book great rates at AAA.com Phone: (573)472-0197

AAA SAVE

Hotel
$80-$180 All Year

Address: 109 Matthews Ln 63801 **Location:** I-55, exit 67, just sw. **Facility:** 64 one-bedroom standard units, some with whirlpools. 3 stories, interior corridors. *Bath:* combo or shower only. **Parking:** on-site. **Amenities:** high-speed Internet, voice mail, irons, hair dryers. **Pool(s):** heated indoor. **Leisure Activities:** whirlpool, exercise room. **Guest Services:** valet and coin laundry, wireless Internet. **Business Services:** meeting rooms, business center.

/ SOME UNITS

WHERE TO DINE

JEREMIAH'S RESTAURANT & LOUNGE Phone: 573/472-4412

American
$10-$35

The exterior is basic, but the atmosphere inside is pleasant, warm and inviting. On the menu are fine steak, chicken, seafood and pasta selections. Dressy casual. **Bar:** Full bar. **Reservations:** suggested. **Hours:** 5 pm-10 pm. Closed: Sun. **Address:** 102 N Kingshighway St 63801 **Location:** Corner of E Malone and N Kingshighway sts; downtown. **Parking:** on-site.

SMITHVILLE—See Kansas City p. 490.

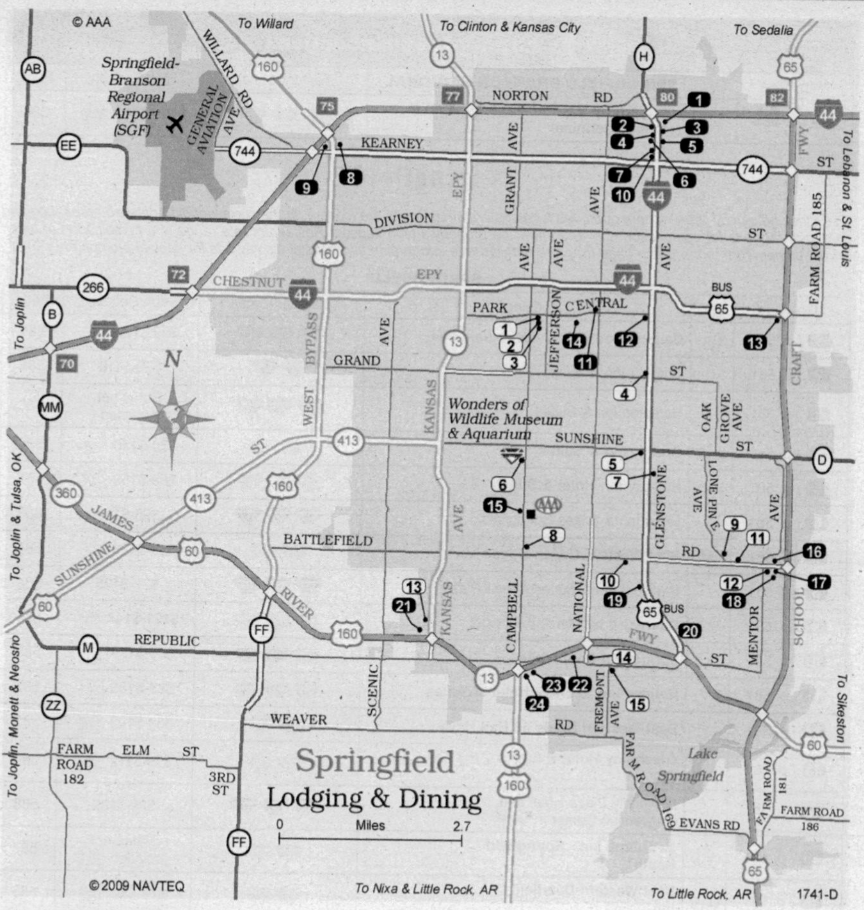

© AAA

To Willard | To Clinton & Kansas City | To Sedalia | To Lebanon & St. Louis | To Joplin | To Joplin & Tulsa, OK | To Joplin, Monett & Neosho | To Sikeston | To Nixa & Little Rock, AR | To Little Rock, AR

Springfield-Branson Regional Airport (SGF)

Wonders of Wildlife Museum & Aquarium

Lake Springfield

Springfield
Lodging & Dining

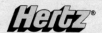

0 Miles 2.7

© 2009 NAVTEQ

1741-D

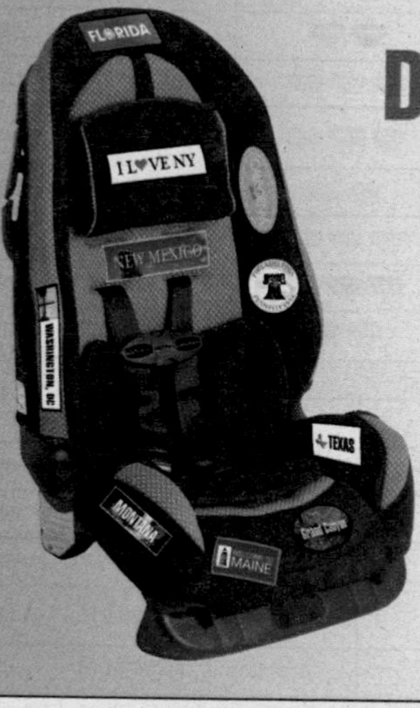

Airport Accommodations

Map Page	OA	SPRINGFIELD-BRANSON REGIONAL	Diamond Rated	High Season	Page
9 / p. 581	AAA	**Courtyard by Marriott Airport, 1.8 mi e from main terminal**	◆◆◆	$121-$147 SAVE	586

Springfield

This index helps you "spot" where approved lodgings and restaurants are located on the corresponding detailed maps. Lodging daily rate range is for comparison only and show the property's high season. Restaurant rate range is a combination of lunch and/or dinner. Turn to the listing page for more detailed rate information and consult display ads for special promotions.

SPRINGFIELD

Map Page	OA	Lodgings	Diamond Rated	High Season	Page
1 / p. 581	AAA	**Candlewood Suites Springfield I-44**	◆◆◆	$99-$129 SAVE	585
2 / p. 581		Comfort Inn & Suites	◆◆	$70-$110	585
3 / p. 581		Hampton Inn & Suites	◆◆◆	Rates not provided	586
4 / p. 581	AAA	**Quality Inn & Suites**	◆◆	$70-$120 SAVE	587
5 / p. 581	AAA	**Holiday Inn Hotel & Suites**	◆◆◆	$89-$159 SAVE	587
6 / p. 581		Drury Inn & Suites-Springfield	◆◆◆	$95-$184	586
7 / p. 581	AAA	**Best Western Coach House Inn**	◆◆	$69-$129 SAVE	584
8 / p. 581		Baymont Inn & Suites Airport Plaza	◆◆◆	$77-$135	584
9 / p. 581	AAA	**Courtyard by Marriott Airport**	◆◆◆	$121-$147 SAVE	586
10 / p. 581	AAA	**Springfield Doubletree**	◆◆◆	$89-$179 SAVE	588
11 / p. 581	AAA	**Holiday Inn Express Hotel & Suites**	◆◆◆	$99-$169 SAVE	587
12 / p. 581	AAA	**Best Western Route 66 Rail Haven**	◆◆	$69-$129 SAVE	585
13 / p. 581	AAA	**Greenstay Hotel & Suites** - see color ad p 587	◆◆	$79-$112 SAVE	586
14 / p. 581		University Plaza Hotel and Convention Center	◆◆◆	$89-$189	588
15 / p. 581	AAA	**La Quinta Inn - Springfield South**	◆◆	Rates not provided SAVE	587
16 / p. 581	AAA	**Best Western Deerfield Inn**	◆◆	$74-$80 SAVE	585
17 / p. 581	AAA	**Comfort Inn**	◆◆	$74-$109 SAVE	585
18 / p. 581		Days Inn Battlefield	◆◆	$68-$87	586
19 / p. 581	AAA	**Clarion Hotel & Conference Center**	◆◆◆	$80-$100 SAVE	585
20 / p. 581	AAA	**Baymont Inn & Suites** - see color ad p 584	◆◆◆	$79-$149 SAVE	584
21 / p. 581	AAA	**Quality Inn & Suites**	◆◆	$85-$129 SAVE	587
22 / p. 581	AAA	**Candlewood Suites South**	◆◆◆	$99-$129 SAVE	585
23 / p. 581		Comfort Suites Medical District	◆◆◆	$94-$150	586
24 / p. 581		Sleep Inn of Springfield	◆◆	$80-$90	588

Map Page	OA	Restaurants	Diamond Rated	Cuisine	Meal Range	Page
1 / p. 581		Nonna's Italian American Cafe	◆◆	Italian	$6-$14	589
2 / p. 581		Gallery Bistro	◆◆◆	American	$14-$27	588
3 / p. 581		Maria's Mexican Restaurant	◆◆	Mexican	$8-$12	589
4 / p. 581		Anton's Coffee Shop	◆	American	$6-$7	588
5 / p. 581		Nearly Famous Deli & Pasta House	◆◆	Italian	$6-$15	589
6 / p. 581		Hemingway's Blue Water Cafe	◆◆	American	$7-$16	588

Map Page	OA	Restaurants (cont'd)	Diamond Rated	Cuisine	Meal Range	Page
7 / p. 581		Ocean Zen	3 diamonds	Pacific Rim	$7-$25	589
8 / p. 581		Valentine's	2 diamonds	American	$4-$25	589
9 / p. 581		Schultz & Dooley's III	2 diamonds	American	$5-$10	589
10 / p. 581		J Parrino's Pasta House & Bar	2 diamonds	Italian	$5-$20	588
11 / p. 581		Metropolitan Grill	3 diamonds	Mediterranean	$8-$24	589
12 / p. 581		Pasta Express	1 diamond	American	$5-$7	589
13 / p. 581		Garbo's Pizzeria	2 diamonds	Italian	$6-$12	588
14 / p. 581		Mr Yen's	2 diamonds	Chinese	$6-$14	589
15 / p. 581		The Argentina Steakhouse	3 diamonds	Argentine	$6-$42	588

SPRINGFIELD pop. 151,580 (See map and index starting on p. 581)

BAYMONT INN & SUITES *Book great rates at AAA.com* **Phone:** (417)889-8188 **20**

Hotel
$79-$149 All Year

Address: 3776 S Glenstone Ave 65804 **Location:** On US 60. **Facility:** 106 units. 102 one-bedroom standard units, some with whirlpools. 4 one-bedroom suites, some with whirlpools. 4 stories, interior corridors. *Bath:* combo or shower only. **Parking:** on-site. **Amenities:** high-speed Internet, dual phone lines, voice mail, irons, hair dryers. **Pool(s):** heated indoor. **Leisure Activities:** whirlpool, exercise room. **Guest Services:** valet and coin laundry, wireless Internet. **Business Services:** PC. *(See color ad below)*

CALL / SOME UNITS FEE

FREE expanded continental breakfast and high-speed Internet

BAYMONT INN & SUITES AIRPORT PLAZA *Book at AAA.com* **Phone:** (417)447-4466 **8**

Hotel
$77-$135 1/1-2/28
$75-$135 3/1-12/31

Address: 2445 N Airport Plaza Ave 65803 **Location:** I-44, exit 77, just se. **Facility:** 92 one-bedroom standard units, some with whirlpools. 3 stories, interior corridors. *Bath:* combo or shower only. **Parking:** on-site. **Amenities:** high-speed Internet, voice mail, irons, hair dryers. *Fee:* video games, safes. **Pool(s):** heated indoor. **Leisure Activities:** whirlpool, exercise room. **Guest Services:** valet and coin laundry, wireless Internet. **Business Services:** meeting rooms, business center.

ASK  / SOME UNITS FEE

BEST WESTERN COACH HOUSE INN *Book great rates at AAA.com* **Phone:** (417)862-0701 

Hotel
$69-$129 All Year

Address: 2535 N Glenstone Ave 65803 **Location:** I-44, exit 80A, just s. **Facility:** 130 units. 129 one-bedroom standard units, some with whirlpools. 1 one-bedroom suite with whirlpool. 1 story, exterior corridors. **Parking:** on-site. **Amenities:** DVD players, high-speed Internet, irons, hair dryers. **Pool(s):** 2 outdoor. **Leisure Activities:** playground. **Guest Services:** coin laundry, wireless Internet. **Business Services:** meeting rooms, PC. **Free Special Amenities: expanded continental breakfast and high-speed Internet.** / SOME UNITS FEE

AAA Benefit:
Members save up to 20%, plus 10% bonus points with rewards program.

▼ *See AAA listing above* ▼

(See map and index starting on p. 581)

BEST WESTERN DEERFIELD INN Book great rates at AAA.com Phone: (417)887-2323 16

Hotel
$74-$80 3/1-10/31
$70-$74 11/1-2/28

Address: 3343 E Battlefield St 65804 **Location:** US 65, exit Battlefield St, just w. **Facility:** 103 one-bedroom standard units, some with whirlpools. 3 stories, interior corridors. **Parking:** on-site. **Amenities:** irons, hair dryers. **Pool(s):** heated indoor. **Leisure Activities:** exercise room, game room. **Guest Services:** valet laundry, wireless Internet. **Business Services:** meeting rooms, PC. **Free Special Amenities: expanded continental breakfast and high-speed Internet.**
/ SOME UNITS FEE

AAA Benefit: Members save up to 20%, plus 10% bonus points with rewards program.

BEST WESTERN ROUTE 66 RAIL HAVEN Book great rates at AAA.com Phone: (417)866-1963 12

Classic Historic Motel
$69-$129 All Year

Address: 203 S Glenstone Ave 65802 **Location:** I-44, exit 80A, 3 mi s. **Facility:** Ask about the 1950s theme rooms at this historic Route 66 property with contemporary room appointments. 92 units. 87 one-bedroom standard units, some with whirlpools. 5 one-bedroom suites. 1 story, exterior corridors. **Parking:** on-site. **Terms:** 3 day cancellation notice. **Amenities:** irons, hair dryers. *Some:* DVD players, high-speed Internet. **Pool(s):** outdoor. **Leisure Activities:** whirlpool. **Guest Services:** valet laundry, wireless Internet. **Business Services:** PC, fax. **Free Special Amenities: expanded continental breakfast and high-speed Internet.**
CALL / SOME UNITS

AAA Benefit: Members save up to 20%, plus 10% bonus points with rewards program.

CANDLEWOOD SUITES SOUTH Book great rates at AAA.com Phone: (417)881-8500 22

Extended Stay Hotel
$99-$129 All Year

Address: 1035 E Republic Rd 65807 **Location:** US 60, exit National Ave, just s. **Facility:** 83 units. 61 one-bedroom standard units with efficiencies. 22 one-bedroom suites with efficiencies. 4 stories, interior corridors. *Bath:* combo or shower only. **Parking:** on-site. **Amenities:** video library, DVD players, CD players, high-speed Internet, dual phone lines, voice mail, irons, hair dryers. **Leisure Activities:** barbecue grill, gazebo, exercise room. **Guest Services:** complimentary laundry, wireless Internet. **Business Services:** meeting rooms, business center. **Free Special Amenities: local telephone calls and high-speed Internet.**
CALL / SOME UNITS FEE

CANDLEWOOD SUITES SPRINGFIELD I-44 Book great rates at AAA.com Phone: (417)866-4242 1

Extended Stay Hotel
$99-$129 All Year

Address: 1920 E Kerr St 65803 **Location:** I-44, exit 80A, just e to Evergreen St. **Facility:** 83 units. 61 one-bedroom standard units with efficiencies. 22 one-bedroom suites with efficiencies. 4 stories, interior corridors. *Bath:* combo or shower only. **Parking:** on-site. **Amenities:** video library, DVD players, CD players, high-speed Internet, dual phone lines, voice mail, irons, hair dryers. **Leisure Activities:** pool privileges, gazebo and grill, exercise room. **Guest Services:** valet and coin laundry, wireless Internet. **Business Services:** meeting rooms, business center. **Free Special Amenities: local telephone calls and high-speed Internet.**
CALL / SOME UNITS FEE

CLARION HOTEL & CONFERENCE CENTER Book great rates at AAA.com Phone: (417)883-6550 19

Hotel
$80-$100 All Year

Address: 3333 S Glenstone Ave 65804 **Location:** On US 60 (James River Expwy), 0.5 mi n. **Facility:** 192 units. 188 one-bedroom standard units. 4 one-bedroom suites, some with whirlpools. 2 stories (no elevator), interior corridors. *Bath:* combo or shower only. **Parking:** on-site. **Amenities:** voice mail, safes, irons, hair dryers. **Pool(s):** heated outdoor. **Leisure Activities:** exercise room. **Guest Services:** valet and coin laundry, airport transportation-Springfield-Branson Regional Airport, wireless Internet. **Business Services:** conference facilities, business center. **Free Special Amenities: full breakfast and high-speed Internet.**
CALL / SOME UNITS FEE

COMFORT INN Book great rates at AAA.com Phone: (417)520-6200 17

Hotel
$74-$109 All Year

Address: 3370 E Battlefield Rd 65804 **Location:** US 65, exit Battlefield Rd, just w. **Facility:** 107 one-bedroom standard units, some with whirlpools. 2 stories, interior corridors. *Bath:* combo or shower only. **Parking:** on-site, winter plug-ins. **Amenities:** high-speed Internet, voice mail, safes (fee), irons, hair dryers. **Pool(s):** heated outdoor. **Leisure Activities:** whirlpool, exercise room, basketball. **Guest Services:** valet and coin laundry, airport transportation-Springfield-Branson Regional Airport, wireless Internet. **Business Services:** meeting rooms, business center. **Free Special Amenities: full breakfast and high-speed Internet.** / SOME UNITS

COMFORT INN & SUITES Book at AAA.com Phone: (417)869-8246 2

Hotel
$70-$110 All Year

Address: 2815 N Glenstone Ave 65803 **Location:** I-44, exit 80A, just s. **Facility:** 78 one-bedroom standard units. 3-4 stories, interior corridors. **Parking:** on-site. **Amenities:** high-speed Internet, voice mail, safes (fee), irons, hair dryers. **Pool(s):** heated indoor. **Leisure Activities:** whirlpool, exercise room. **Guest Services:** valet and coin laundry, wireless Internet. **Business Services:** meeting rooms, PC. ASK CALL / SOME UNITS

(See map and index starting on p. 581)

COMFORT SUITES MEDICAL DISTRICT Book at AAA.com Phone: (417)887-8500 23

Hotel
$94-$150 5/1-2/28
$88-$140 3/1-4/30

Address: 310 E Monastery St 65810 **Location:** SR 60 (James River Frwy), 5.7 mi w to Campbell St, 0.4 mi s to Republic Rd, then just w. **Facility:** Smoke free premises. 87 one-bedroom standard units. 4 stories, interior corridors. *Bath:* combo or shower only. **Parking:** on-site. **Amenities:** high-speed Internet, dual phone lines, voice mail, irons, hair dryers. *Some:* DVD players. **Pool(s):** heated indoor. **Leisure Activities:** whirlpool, exercise room. **Guest Services:** coin laundry, wireless Internet. **Business Services:** meeting rooms, business center.

COURTYARD BY MARRIOTT AIRPORT Book great rates at AAA.com Phone: (417)869-6700 9

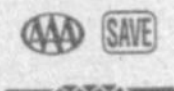

Hotel
$121-$147 All Year

Address: 3527 W Kearney 65803 **Location:** I-44, exit 75 (US 160 W Bypass), just se to SR 744, then just w. **Facility:** Smoke free premises. 142 units. 138 one-bedroom standard units, some with whirlpools. 4 one-bedroom suites. 3 stories, interior corridors. *Bath:* combo or shower only. **Parking:** on-site. **Terms:** cancellation fee imposed. **Amenities:** video games (fee), dual phone lines, voice mail, irons, hair dryers. *Some:* high-speed Internet. **Pool(s):** heated indoor. **Leisure Activities:** whirlpool, gazebo, courtyard, exercise room. **Guest Services:** valet and coin laundry, airport transportation-Springfield Branson Regional Airport, wireless Internet. **Business Services:** meeting rooms, PC. **Free Special Amenities: newspaper.**

CALL / SOME UNITS FEE

COURTYARD Marriott

AAA Benefit:
Members save a minimum 5% off the best available rate.

DAYS INN BATTLEFIELD Book at AAA.com Phone: (417)882-9484 18

Hotel
$68-$87 11/1-2/28
$66-$85 3/1-10/31

Address: 3260 E Montclair St 65804 **Location:** US 65, exit Battlefield Rd, just w to Moulder Ave, then just sw. **Facility:** Smoke free premises. 54 one-bedroom standard units. 2 stories (no elevator), interior corridors. *Bath:* combo or shower only. **Parking:** on-site. **Amenities:** hair dryers. **Pool(s):** outdoor. **Guest Services:** wireless Internet. **Business Services:** fax.

ASK CALL / SOME UNITS

DRURY INN & SUITES-SPRINGFIELD Book at AAA.com Phone: (417)863-8400 6

Hotel
$95-$184 All Year

Address: 2715 N Glenstone Ave 65803 **Location:** I-44, exit 80A (Glenstone Ave), just s. **Facility:** 110 units. 95 one-bedroom standard units, some with whirlpools. 15 one-bedroom suites with whirlpools. 5 stories, interior corridors. *Bath:* combo or shower only. **Parking:** on-site. **Terms:** cancellation fee imposed. **Amenities:** high-speed Internet, voice mail, irons, hair dryers. **Pool(s):** heated indoor/outdoor. **Leisure Activities:** whirlpool, exercise room. **Guest Services:** valet and coin laundry, wireless Internet. **Business Services:** meeting rooms, PC.

ASK CALL / SOME UNITS

GREENSTAY HOTEL & SUITES Book great rates at AAA.com Phone: (417)863-1440 13

Hotel
$79-$112 All Year

Address: 222 N Ingram Mill Rd 65802 **Location:** I-65, exit Chesnut Expwy, just sw. **Facility:** 99 one-bedroom standard units. 2 stories (no elevator), interior/exterior corridors. **Parking:** on-site. **Amenities:** dual phone lines, voice mail, irons, hair dryers. **Pool(s):** outdoor. **Leisure Activities:** exercise room. **Guest Services:** valet laundry, wireless Internet. **Business Services:** meeting rooms, PC. *(See color ad p 587)*

/ SOME UNITS FEE

FREE expanded continental breakfast and high-speed Internet

HAMPTON INN & SUITES Book great rates at AAA.com Phone: 417/869-5548 3

Hotel
Rates not provided

Address: 2750 N Glenstone Ave 65803 **Location:** I-44, exit 80A (Glenstone Ave), just s. **Facility:** 89 units. 64 one-bedroom standard units. 25 one-bedroom suites. 3 stories, interior corridors. *Bath:* combo or shower only. **Parking:** on-site. **Amenities:** video games (fee), voice mail, irons, hair dryers. **Pool(s):** heated indoor. **Leisure Activities:** whirlpool, exercise room. **Guest Services:** valet and coin laundry, wireless Internet. **Business Services:** meeting rooms, business center.

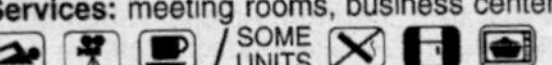

AAA Benefit:
Members save up to 10% everyday!

(See map and index starting on p. 581)

HOLIDAY INN EXPRESS HOTEL & SUITES *Book great rates at AAA.com* **Phone:** (417)862-0070 11

Hotel
$99-$169 All Year

Address: 1117 E St. Louis St 65806 **Location:** Just w of National Ave. **Facility:** 120 units. 117 one-bedroom standard units. 3 one-bedroom suites. 4 stories, interior corridors. *Bath:* combo or shower only. **Parking:** on-site. **Amenities:** high-speed Internet, dual phone lines, voice mail, irons, hair dryers. **Pool(s):** heated outdoor. **Leisure Activities:** whirlpools, exercise room. **Guest Services:** valet and coin laundry, wireless Internet. **Business Services:** meeting rooms, business center. **Free Special Amenities: expanded continental breakfast and newspaper.**

/ SOME UNITS

HOLIDAY INN HOTEL & SUITES *Book great rates at AAA.com* **Phone:** (417)865-8600 5

Hotel
$89-$159 All Year

Address: 2720 N Glenstone Ave 65803 **Location:** I-44, exit 80A, just se. **Facility:** 188 units. 166 one- and 4 two-bedroom standard units. 18 one-bedroom suites, some with whirlpools. 6 stories, interior corridors. *Bath:* combo or shower only. **Parking:** on-site. **Amenities:** video games (fee), voice mail, irons, hair dryers. *Some:* high-speed Internet. **Pool(s):** heated indoor. **Leisure Activities:** whirlpool, exercise room. **Guest Services:** valet and coin laundry, airport transportation-Springfield-Branson National Airport, wireless Internet. **Business Services:** conference facilities, business center. **Free Special Amenities: newspaper.**

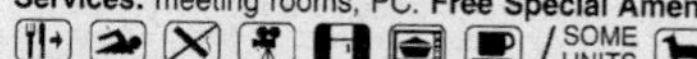

/ SOME UNITS

LA QUINTA INN - SPRINGFIELD SOUTH *Book great rates at AAA.com* **Phone:** 417/890-6060 15

Hotel
Rates not provided

Address: 2535 S Campbell Ave 65807 **Location:** Jct Battlefield Rd and Campbell Ave, 0.5 mi n. **Facility:** Smoke free premises. 61 one-bedroom standard units, some with whirlpools. 3 stories, interior corridors. *Bath:* combo or shower only. **Parking:** on-site. **Amenities:** video games (fee), high-speed Internet, dual phone lines, voice mail, safes, irons, hair dryers. **Pool(s):** heated indoor. **Leisure Activities:** whirlpool, exercise room. **Guest Services:** coin laundry, wireless Internet. **Business Services:** meeting rooms, PC. **Free Special Amenities: full breakfast and high-speed Internet.**

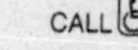

/ SOME UNITS

QUALITY INN & SUITES *Book great rates at AAA.com* **Phone:** (417)888-0898 21

Hotel
$85-$129 All Year

Address: 3930 S Overland Ave 65807 **Location:** US 60 (James River Expwy), exit Kansas Expwy, just n to Chesterfield Blvd, then just w. Adjacent to Chesterfield Village. **Facility:** 50 one-bedroom standard units, some with whirlpools. 2 stories (no elevator), interior corridors. *Bath:* combo or shower only. **Parking:** on-site. **Amenities:** high-speed Internet, voice mail, safes (fee), irons, hair dryers. **Pool(s):** heated indoor. **Leisure Activities:** exercise room. **Guest Services:** valet and coin laundry, wireless Internet. **Business Services:** meeting rooms, PC. **Free Special Amenities: expanded continental breakfast and high-speed Internet.**

CALL / SOME UNITS FEE

QUALITY INN & SUITES *Book great rates at AAA.com* **Phone:** (417)869-0001 4

Hotel
$70-$120 All Year

Address: 2745 N Glenstone Ave 65803 **Location:** I-44, exit 80A, just sw. **Facility:** 102 units. 95 one-bedroom standard units. 7 one-bedroom suites, some with whirlpools. 2-3 stories (no elevator), interior/exterior corridors. **Parking:** on-site. **Amenities:** voice mail, irons, hair dryers. **Pool(s):** outdoor. **Leisure Activities:** exercise room. **Guest Services:** coin laundry, wireless Internet. **Business Services:** meeting rooms, PC.

/ SOME UNITS FEE

▼ See AAA listing p 586 ▼

(See map and index starting on p. 581)

SLEEP INN OF SPRINGFIELD Book at AAA.com Phone: (417)886-2464 24

Hotel
$80-$90 3/1-10/31
$75-$85 11/1-2/28

Address: 233 El Camino Alto 65810 **Location:** US 60 (James River Expwy), exit Campbell Ave, just se. **Facility:** 104 one-bedroom standard units, some with whirlpools. 3 stories, interior corridors. *Bath:* combo or shower only. **Parking:** on-site. **Amenities:** voice mail, irons, hair dryers. **Pool(s):** heated indoor. **Leisure Activities:** whirlpool. **Guest Services:** valet laundry, wireless Internet. **Business Services:** meeting rooms. ASK / SOME UNITS FEE

SPRINGFIELD DOUBLETREE Book great rates at AAA.com Phone: (417)831-3131 10

AAA SAVE

Hotel
$89-$179 All Year

Address: 2431 N Glenstone Ave 65803 **Location:** I-44, exit 80A, just s. **Facility:** 201 units. 197 one-bedroom standard units. 4 one-bedroom suites. 11 stories, interior corridors. **Parking:** on-site. **Terms:** 1-7 night minimum stay, cancellation fee imposed. **Amenities:** voice mail, irons, hair dryers. **Pool(s):** heated indoor/outdoor. **Leisure Activities:** whirlpool, exercise room. **Guest Services:** valet and coin laundry, airport transportation-Springfield-Branson Regional Airport, wireless Internet. **Business Services:** conference facilities, business center. **Free Special Amenities: newspaper and high-speed Internet.**
CALL / SOME UNITS FEE

DOUBLETREE
HOTELS·SUITES·RESORTS·CLUBS
AAA Benefit:
Members save 5% or more everyday!

UNIVERSITY PLAZA HOTEL AND CONVENTION CENTER Book at AAA.com Phone: (417)864-7333 14

Hotel
$89-$189 All Year

Address: 333 John Q Hammons Pkwy 65806 **Location:** 0.5 mi e on St. Louis St. **Facility:** Smoke free premises. 271 units. 238 one-bedroom standard units. 33 one-bedroom suites. 9 stories, interior corridors. *Bath:* combo or shower only. **Parking:** on-site. **Terms:** 3 day cancellation notice. **Amenities:** video games (fee), voice mail, irons, hair dryers. *Some:* high-speed Internet. **Pool(s):** heated outdoor, heated indoor. **Leisure Activities:** whirlpool, exercise room. **Guest Services:** valet and coin laundry, area transportation, wireless Internet, beauty salon. **Business Services:** conference facilities, business center.
CALL / SOME UNITS FEE

WHERE TO DINE

ANTON'S COFFEE SHOP Phone: 417/869-7681 4

American
$6-$7

Breakfast served all day has been a tradition since 1974 in the basic, no-frills eatery. Daily chalkboard specials complement an extensive selection of omelets, sandwiches, burgers and salads. Casual dress. **Reservations:** not accepted. **Hours:** 6 am-2 pm, Sun from 8 am. Closed major holidays; also Tues. **Address:** 937 S Glenstone Ave 65802 **Location:** I-44, exit 80A, 3 mi s at Grand Ave. **Parking:** on-site and street.

THE ARGENTINA STEAKHOUSE Phone: 417/886-8010 15

Argentine
$6-$42

The kitchen staff—all trained and certified chefs from Buenos Aires—cooks many of the steak, chops, chicken, seafood and pasta selections over a parrilla, the traditional Argentinean open fire pit. Dressy casual. **Bar:** Full bar. **Reservations:** suggested. **Hours:** 11 am-2 & 5-9 pm, Fri & Sat-10 pm. Closed: 1/1, 12/25; also Sun. **Address:** 1410 E Republic Rd 65804 **Location:** US 60 (James River Expwy), 2.7 mi w. **Parking:** on-site.

GALLERY BISTRO Phone: 417/866-0440 2

American
$14-$27

The restaurant's contemporary cuisine includes a large selection of beef, seafood and pasta entrees. Pan-seared Alaskan halibut with risotto is a nice choice. Creme caramel over fresh berries makes a light, pleasant ending. Casual dress. **Bar:** Full bar. **Reservations:** suggested. **Hours:** 5 pm-10 pm, Fri & Sat-11 pm. Closed major holidays; also Sun. **Address:** 221 E Walnut St 65806 **Location:** Just sw of Jefferson Ave. **Parking:** street.

GARBO'S PIZZERIA Phone: 417/883-9010 13

Italian
$6-$12

The pleasant, casual setting offers a variety of selections, including the signature pizzas, which are great. Casual dress. **Bar:** Full bar. **Reservations:** not accepted. **Hours:** 11 am-9 pm, Fri & Sat-10 pm. Closed major holidays. **Address:** 2101 W Chesterfield Blvd, Bldg C 65807 **Location:** US 60 (James River Expwy), exit Kansas Expwy, just w; in Chesterfield Village. **Parking:** on-site.

HEMINGWAY'S BLUE WATER CAFE Phone: 417/891-5100 6

American
$7-$16

The restaurant celebrates the sea with an atmosphere inspired by American author and saltwater fishing legend Ernest Hemingway. Buffets are virtual feasts with so many selections that diners could return repeatedly and not duplicate a meal. Casual dress. **Bar:** Full bar. **Reservations:** accepted. **Hours:** 7 am-10 pm, Sun 9 am-5 pm. Closed: 12/25. **Address:** 1935 S Campbell 65807 **Location:** Business Rt US 65, 2 mi w on US 60 (Sunshine St); in south end of Bass Pro Shops Outdoor World. **Parking:** on-site.

J PARRINO'S PASTA HOUSE & BAR Phone: 417/882-1808 10

Italian
$5-$20

The casual, fresh and delightful cafe offers much to tempt the palate. The menu lists a wide variety of appetizers, with an even wider array of pastas. Specialty entrees also are a satisfying choice. Casual dress. **Bar:** Full bar. **Reservations:** suggested, weekends. **Hours:** 11 am-10 pm, Fri & Sat-11 pm, Sun-9 pm. Closed: 1/1, 11/25, 12/25. **Address:** 1550 E Battlefield Rd 65804 **Location:** US 65, exit Battlefield Rd, 2.8 mi w; in Galleria Shopping Center. **Parking:** on-site.

(See map and index starting on p. 581)

MARIA'S MEXICAN RESTAURANT

Phone: 417/831-9339 (3)

Mexican
$8-$12

Located in bustling downtown, this cozy dining room provides a nice view of the street as well as the open kitchen and bar area activity. Established in 1997, this is one of the most popular Mexican restaurants in town, known for its twists on traditional Mexican dishes. Popular items include the burrito and queso de cabra, a goat cheese and chorizo dip. A house margarita, made with an impressive variety of tequilas, complements any menu item. Casual dress. **Bar:** Full bar. **Reservations:** not accepted. **Hours:** 11 am-10 pm, Fri & Sat-11 pm. Closed major holidays. **Address:** 406 South St 65806 **Location:** Jct South and Walnut sts; downtown. **Parking:** street.

METROPOLITAN GRILL

Phone: 417/889-4951 (11)

Mediterranean
$8-$24

Appropriate for both sophisticated and casual meals, this pleasant restaurant delivers a fresh and creative approach both in its food and atmosphere. Casual dress. **Bar:** Full bar. **Reservations:** accepted. **Hours:** 4 pm-10 pm, Fri-11 pm, Sat 5 pm-11 pm, Sun 5 pm-9 pm. Closed major holidays. **Address:** 2931 E Battlefield Rd 65804 **Location:** 0.6 mi w of jct US 65. **Parking:** on-site.

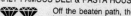

MR YEN'S

Phone: 417/881-1061 (14)

Chinese
$6-$14

The visual feast begins upon arrival, when diners gaze around at the red-tile roof, gardens, fountains and striking, pagoda-style architecture. Featured is a variety of Chinese dishes, as well as live lobster that can be selected from a large tank. On weekends from 11 am to 3 pm, diners can select from a dim sum menu with 30 items brought to the table. Casual dress. **Bar:** Full bar. **Reservations:** suggested, weekends. **Hours:** 11 am-10 pm, Fri & Sat-11 pm. **Address:** 4117 S National Ave 65807 **Location:** US 60 (James River Expwy), 1.3 mi w of Business Rt US 65, exit National Ave, just s to Kingsley, then just w. **Parking:** on-site.

NEARLY FAMOUS DELI & PASTA HOUSE

Phone: 417/883-3403 (5)

Italian
$6-$15

Off the beaten path, the quiet, unassuming restaurant has a simple exterior, but it's wise not to judge the book by its cover. Since 1976, this place has served such tasty foods as delicatessen sandwiches, soups, pasta dishes and homemade desserts with beverages ranging from soft drinks and espresso to wine and cocktails. Staff members seem to enjoy what they do, and that attitude carries over into the service they provide. Casual dress. **Bar:** Full bar. **Reservations:** not accepted. **Hours:** 11 am-9 pm, Fri & Sat-10 pm. Closed major holidays; also Sun. **Address:** 2708 S Glenstone Ave 65804 **Location:** In Brentwood Shopping Center; across from Battlefield Mall. **Parking:** on-site.

NONNA'S ITALIAN AMERICAN CAFE

Phone: 417/831-1222 (1)

Italian
$6-$14

A casual dining room and good food await diners at Nonna's. Traditional pasta dishes, as well as steak and chicken entrees, line the menu. Casual dress. **Bar:** Full bar. **Reservations:** accepted. **Hours:** 11 am-10 pm, Sun & Mon-9 pm. Closed major holidays. **Address:** 306 South Ave 65806 **Location:** At McDaniel St; downtown. **Parking:** on-site.

OCEAN ZEN

Phone: 417/889-9596 (7)

Pacific Rim
$7-$25

The restaurant serves fresh seafood and sushi in a trendy, ocean-theme dining room. Casual dress. **Bar:** Full bar. **Reservations:** accepted. **Hours:** 11 am-3 & 4:30-10 pm, Fri & Sat-11 pm. Closed: 11/25, 12/25. **Address:** 600 E Battlefield Rd 65807 **Location:** 6.5 mi w of US 65. **Parking:** on-site.

PASTA EXPRESS

Phone: 417/890-1345 (12)

American
$5-$7

Although the establishment bustles at lunchtime, it manages to prepare tasty dishes in short order. Casual dress. **Reservations:** not accepted. **Hours:** 11 am-9 pm. Closed major holidays; also Sun. **Address:** 3250 E Battlefield Rd 65804 **Location:** US 65, exit Battlefield Rd; in Fox Grape Plaza. **Parking:** on-site.
CALL

RIB CRIB BBQ AND GRILL

Phone: 417/866-6677

American
$6-$20

Most guests need extra napkins to tackle the ribs, brisket, ham, pork and chicken selections. The menu also lists sandwiches and wraps, along with tempting sides and large desserts. The decor is decidedly Western. Casual dress. **Bar:** Beer only. **Reservations:** not accepted. **Hours:** 11 am-10 pm. Closed: 11/25, 12/25. **Address:** 1640 N Glenstone Ave 65804 **Location:** I-44, exit 80A, 2 mi s. **Parking:** on-site.

SCHULTZ & DOOLEY'S III

Phone: 417/655-1222 (9)

American
$5-$10

The bar and hamburger business focuses on freshness in its ground beef, produce and baked items. Also of note are the old-fashioned milkshakes. The atmosphere is warm and casual. Casual dress. **Bar:** Full bar. **Reservations:** not accepted. **Hours:** 11 am-10 pm, Fri & Sat-11 pm. Closed: 11/25, 12/25. **Address:** 2916 S Lone Pine 65804 **Location:** 0.8 mi w of US 65; in Battlefield Tower Shopping Center. **Parking:** on-site.
CALL

VALENTINE'S

Phone: 417/891-9700 (8)

American
$4-$25

Minimalist decor adds a touch of contemporary sophistication to the casual establishment. On the menu is a good selection of appetizers, salads, steaks, pasta, seafood, chicken and sandwiches. Casual dress. **Bar:** Full bar. **Reservations:** accepted. **Hours:** 11 am-9 pm, Fri-10 pm, Sat 10 am-10 pm, Sun 10 am-9 pm. Closed: 11/25, 12/25. **Address:** 2902-B S Campbell St 65807 **Location:** At Battlefield Rd and Campbell St; in Imperial Plaza. **Parking:** on-site. CALL

ZIGGIE'S CAFE

Phone: 417/447-1607

American
$7-$15

Lending to the warm, cheerful atmosphere is a mix of contemporary decor and memorabilia. A good variety of menu selections includes salads, pastas, charbroiled items, burgers and sandwiches. Casual dress. **Reservations:** accepted. **Hours:** 24 hours. **Address:** 853 N Glenstone Ave 65802 **Location:** I-44, exit 80A, 2 mi s. **Parking:** on-site.

(See map and index starting on p. 581)

ZIGGIE'S CAFE **Phone:** 417/883-0900

American
$7-$15

Popular with locals and visitors alike, the restaurant serves breakfast 24 hours a day. Also on the menu is a wide variety of standard Midwestern comfort foods, including wonderful fried chicken. On Wednesdays, dessert is free. Casual dress. **Reservations:** accepted. **Hours:** 24 hours. **Address:** 2222 S Campbell St 65807 **Location:** 0.4 mi s from jct S Campbell and W Sunshine sts. **Parking:** on-site.

SULLIVAN pop. 6,351

BAYMONT INN *Book at AAA.com* **Phone:** (573)860-3333

Hotel
$99 All Year

Address: 275 N Service Rd W 63080 **Location:** I-44, exit 225. **Facility:** 67 one-bedroom standard units, some with whirlpools. 3 stories, interior corridors. *Bath:* combo or shower only. **Parking:** on-site. **Amenities:** voice mail, irons, hair dryers. **Pool(s):** heated indoor. **Leisure Activities:** whirlpool, exercise room. **Guest Services:** coin laundry, wireless Internet. **Business Services:** meeting rooms, PC. ASK / SOME UNITS

COMFORT INN *Book great rates at AAA.com* **Phone:** 573/468-7800

Hotel
Rates not provided

Address: 736 S Service Rd W 63080 **Location:** I-44, exit 225, just sw. **Facility:** Smoke free premises. 59 one-bedroom standard units, some with whirlpools. 3 stories, interior corridors. *Bath:* combo or shower only. **Parking:** on-site. **Amenities:** high-speed Internet, voice mail, irons, hair dryers. **Pool(s):** heated indoor. **Leisure Activities:** whirlpool, exercise room. **Guest Services:** coin laundry, wireless Internet. **Business Services:** meeting rooms, PC. **Free Special Amenities: full breakfast and newspaper.** / SOME UNITS FEE

WHERE TO DINE

EL NOPAL **Phone:** 573/860-5214

Mexican
$6-$12

Authentic Mexican food is served in a lively dining room featuring bright colors. Local favorites include the variety of burritos and such house specialties as carnitas and shrimp tacos. Combination plates, which feature mix-and-match menu items, make for quick meals at lunch or dinner. In the evening, the atmosphere gets more raucous thanks to the bar/lounge. Casual dress. **Bar:** Full bar. **Reservations:** not accepted. **Hours:** 11 am-10 pm, Fri & Sat-10:30 pm. **Address:** 148 S Service Rd 63080 **Location:** I-44, exit 225, just ne. **Parking:** on-site.

SUNRISE BEACH pop. 368

The following lodging was either not evaluated or did not meet AAA rating requirements but is listed for your information only.

LAKEVIEW RESORT **Phone:** 573/374-5555

fyi
Cottage

Did not meet all AAA rating requirements for viewports/peepholes in some guest rooms at time of last evaluation on 08/03/2009. **Address:** 328 Lakeview Resort Blvd 65079 **Location:** Jct CR MM and CR TT, 1.3 mi ne. Facilities, services, and decor characterize a mid-scale property.

SUNSET HILLS—See St. Louis p. 569.

TOWN AND COUNTRY—See St. Louis p. 569.

TRENTON pop. 6,216

HYDE MANSION BED & BREAKFAST INN **Phone:** 660/359-5631

Bed & Breakfast
Rates not provided

Address: 418 E 7th St 64683 **Location:** Just e of jct Main and 7th sts, then just e from courthouse. Located in a quiet residential area. **Facility:** Smoke free premises. 6 one-bedroom standard units. 2 stories (no elevator), interior corridors. *Bath:* combo or shower only. **Parking:** on-site. **Terms:** check-in 4 pm. **Amenities:** hair dryers. *Some:* DVD players. **Leisure Activities:** limited exercise equipment. **Guest Services:** wireless Internet.

TRENTON KNIGHTS INN *Book at AAA.com* **Phone:** (660)359-2988

Hotel
$66-$79 All Year

Address: 1845A E 28th St 64683 **Location:** US 65, 1 mi n of jct SR 6 and US 65. **Facility:** 34 one-bedroom standard units. 2 stories (no elevator), interior corridors. *Bath:* combo or shower only. **Parking:** on-site. **Terms:** check-in 4 pm. **Guest Services:** wireless Internet. ASK / SOME UNITS FEE

WHERE TO DINE

WASHINGTON STREET FOOD & DRINK COMPANY **Phone:** 660/359-9800

American
$6-$18

Well-designed contemporary decor complements the laid-back atmosphere, where diners sit down to good preparations of beef, chicken and seafood. Casual dress. **Bar:** Full bar. **Reservations:** accepted. **Hours:** 11 am-10 pm, Fri & Sat-10:30 pm, Sun-9 pm. Closed: 1/1, 12/25. **Address:** 1843 E 28th St 64683 **Location:** US 65, 1 mi n of jct SR 6 and US 65. **Parking:** on-site.

TROY pop. 6,737

SUPER 8-TROY Book at AAA.com

Hotel
$72-$99 3/1-10/1
$65-$89 10/2-2/28

Phone: (636)528-688

Address: 28 Turnbull Tr 63379 **Location:** Jct US 61 and SR 47, just w. **Facility:** 70 one-bedroo standard units, some with whirlpools. 3 stories, interior corridors. *Bath:* combo or shower onl **Parking:** on-site. **Amenities:** video library, DVD players, high-speed Internet, dual phone lines, safe (fee), irons, hair dryers. **Pool(s):** heated indoor. **Leisure Activities:** whirlpool, exercise room. **Gues Services:** coin laundry, wireless Internet. **Business Services:** PC.

ASK / SOME UNITS

UNION pop. 7,757

SUPER 8 Book at AAA.com

Hotel
$78-$125 All Year

Phone: (636)583-880

Address: 1015 E Main St 63084 **Location:** I-44, exit 247 (US 50), 4.7 mi w; just w of jct SR 47 **Facility:** 50 one-bedroom standard units, some with whirlpools. 3 stories, interior corridors. *Bath* combo or shower only. **Parking:** on-site. **Terms:** cancellation fee imposed. **Amenities:** safes (fee) irons, hair dryers. **Pool(s):** heated indoor. **Guest Services:** coin laundry, wireless Internet.

ASK CALL / SOME UNITS FEE

UNIVERSITY CITY—See St. Louis p. 570.

VALLEY PARK—See St. Louis p. 570.

WARRENSBURG pop. 16,340

COMFORT INN WARRENSBURG STATION Book at AAA.com

Hotel
$70-$120 All Year

Phone: (660)429-4848

Address: 609 E Russell Ave 64093 **Location:** Jct US 50 and SR 13, just s to Russell Ave, then 0.8 mi e. **Facility:** 78 one-bedroom standard units, some with whirlpools. 3-4 stories, interior corridors. *Bath* combo or shower only. **Parking:** on-site. **Amenities:** high-speed Internet, voice mail, irons, hair dryers. **Pool(s):** heated indoor. **Leisure Activities:** whirlpool, exercise room. **Guest Services:** coin laundry, wireless Internet. **Business Services:** meeting rooms, PC.

ASK CALL / SOME UNITS

HOLIDAY INN EXPRESS Book at AAA.com

Hotel
$89-$119 All Year

Phone: (660)747-3000

Address: 626 E Russell Ave 64093 **Location:** Jct US 50 and SR 13, just s to Russell Ave, then 0.8 mi e. **Facility:** 82 one-bedroom standard units. 3 stories, interior corridors. *Bath:* combo or shower only. **Parking:** on-site. **Amenities:** high-speed Internet, dual phone lines, voice mail, irons, hair dryers. *Some:* DVD players, CD players. **Pool(s):** heated indoor. **Leisure Activities:** whirlpool, exercise room. *Fee:* game room. **Guest Services:** valet and coin laundry, wireless Internet. **Business Services:** meeting rooms, PC. ASK CALL / SOME UNITS

WHERE TO DINE

HERO'S RESTAURANT & PUB

American
$6-$17

Phone: 660/747-3162

Sports, Hollywood and political heroes are central to the wealth of memorabilia. The menu offers something for everyone, with homemade onion rings and fries being a popular speciality. Casual dress. **Bar:** Full bar. **Reservations:** accepted. **Hours:** 11 am-10 pm, Fri & Sat-11 pm, Sun-9 pm; Sunday brunch. Closed: 11/25, 12/25; also for dinner 12/24. **Address:** 107 W Pine St 64093 **Location:** Downtown. **Parking:** street.

PLAYERS RESTAURANT & LOUNGE

American
$5-$17

Phone: 660/747-2115

You'll enjoy the sports bar and grill atmosphere and very good selection of menu items at Players. The meals and sandwiches are hot, tasty and appetizingly presented, and the servers are fast, efficient and friendly. Some Italian and Greek dishes. Casual dress. **Bar:** Full bar. **Reservations:** not accepted. **Hours:** 11 am-10 pm, Fri & Sat-11 pm. Closed major holidays. **Address:** 627 E Russell Rd 64093 **Location:** Jct US 50 and SR 13, just s to Russell Rd, then 0.8 mi e. **Parking:** on-site.

WARRENTON pop. 5,281

WHERE TO DINE

BREWSKIES

American
$5-$15

Phone: 636/456-7678

Popular with the local crowd, the downtown restaurant presents a menu that lists something for almost everyone. A warm, lived-in atmosphere prevails. Casual dress. **Bar:** Full bar. **Reservations:** not accepted. **Hours:** 6:30 am-9 pm. Closed major holidays; also Sun. **Address:** 209 E Main St 63383 **Location:** Downtown. **Parking:** street.

WARSAW pop. 2,070

PARKFIELD INN Book at AAA.com

Hotel
$59-$125 All Year

Phone: (660)438-2474

Address: 151 N Dam Access Rd 65355 **Location:** 1 mi n on US 65, then just w. **Facility:** 57 units. 49 one- and 8 two-bedroom standard units, some with whirlpools. 2 stories, interior corridors. *Bath:* combo or shower only. **Parking:** on-site. **Amenities:** high-speed Internet, irons, hair dryers. **Pool(s):** heated indoor. **Leisure Activities:** whirlpool. **Guest Services:** coin laundry, wireless Internet. **Business Services:** meeting rooms. ASK CALL / SOME UNITS

WASHINGTON pop. 13,243

BRICK INN BED & BREAKFAST — **Phone:** 636/390-3264

Bed & Breakfast
$109-$159 All Year

Address: 516 W 3rd 63090 **Location:** Jct SR 47 and 3rd St, 1 mi nw. **Facility:** Smoke free premises. 4 units. 3 one-bedroom standard units. 1 one-bedroom suite. 2 stories, interior corridors. *Bath:* combo or shower only. **Parking:** on-site. **Terms:** 7 day cancellation notice-fee imposed. **Amenities:** hair dryers. *Some:* DVD players, CD players, high-speed Internet. **Leisure Activities:** whirlpool. **Guest Services:** wireless Internet. / SOME UNITS

SLEEP INN & SUITES *Book at AAA.com* — **Phone:** (636)390-8877

Hotel
$90-$160 All Year

Address: 2621 E 5th St 63090 **Location:** I-44, exit 251, 8.5 mi w on SR 100. **Facility:** Smoke free premises. 71 one-bedroom standard units, some with whirlpools. 3 stories, interior corridors. *Bath:* combo or shower only. **Parking:** on-site. **Terms:** cancellation fee imposed. **Amenities:** high-speed Internet, voice mail, safes (fee), irons, hair dryers. **Pool(s):** heated indoor. **Leisure Activities:** whirlpool, exercise room. **Guest Services:** valet and coin laundry, wireless Internet. **Business Services:** meeting rooms. ASK / SOME UNITS FEE

SUPER 8 WASHINGTON *Book at AAA.com* — **Phone:** (636)390-0088

Hotel
$77-$125 All Year

Address: 2081 Eckelkamp Ct 63090 **Location:** I-44, exit 251, 10 mi w on SR 100, just s of SR 100 and 47. **Facility:** 51 one-bedroom standard units, some with whirlpools. 2 stories (no elevator), interior corridors. *Bath:* combo or shower only. **Parking:** on-site. **Terms:** cancellation fee imposed. **Amenities:** safes (fee), irons, hair dryers. *Some:* high-speed Internet. **Leisure Activities:** limited exercise equipment. **Guest Services:** coin laundry, wireless Internet.
ASK / SOME UNITS FEE

WHERE TO DINE

AMERICAN BOUNTY RESTAURANT — **Phone:** 636/390-2150

New American
$8-$24

In a restored 1858 brick home facing the Missouri River, chef/owner Brian Manhardt and his wife, Tina, prepare sophisticated cuisine with an emphasis on regional dishes reflecting the produce of the Missouri Valley. Plate presentations are a delight. Seafood, pork, lamb and steak selections are prepared with creativity and flair. Service is friendly and energized. Casual dress. **Bar:** Full bar. **Reservations:** suggested, weekends. **Hours:** 5 pm-9 pm, Sun noon-7 pm. Closed major holidays; also Mon. **Address:** 430 W Front St 63090 **Location:** Jct SR 47 and 100, 0.7 mi w on SR 100, 1.3 mi n on Jefferson St, then 0.4 mi w. **Parking:** street. **Historic**

CHICO'S CANTINA — **Phone:** 636/390-9393

Mexican
$5-$16

The attractive facility allows for sidewalk dining in season. Diners relax in the colorful setting to savor meals prepared with fresh ingredients. Casual dress. **Bar:** Full bar. **Reservations:** accepted. **Hours:** 11 am-10 pm, Fri & Sat-11 pm, Sun-9 pm. Closed major holidays. **Address:** 2000 Phoenix Center Dr 63090 **Location:** 0.9 mi e of jct SR 100 and 47; on SR 100; in Phoenix Center. **Parking:** on-site.

WEBSTER GROVES—See St. Louis p. 570.

WENTZVILLE—See St. Louis p. 571.

WESTON—See Kansas City p. 490.

WEST PLAINS pop. 10,866

SUPER 8-WEST PLAINS *Book at AAA.com* — **Phone:** (417)256-8088

Hotel
$55-$70 All Year

Address: 1210 Porter Wagoner Blvd 65775 **Location:** On US 63B, 0.8 mi s of jct US 63. **Facility:** 49 one-bedroom standard units. 2 stories (no elevator), interior corridors. **Parking:** on-site. **Amenities:** safes (fee), irons, hair dryers. **Guest Services:** wireless Internet.
ASK / SOME UNITS FEE

WOODSON TERRACE—See St. Louis p. 571.

Washita Battlefield National Historic Site, Cheyenne © Tom Bean

Oklahoma Orientation

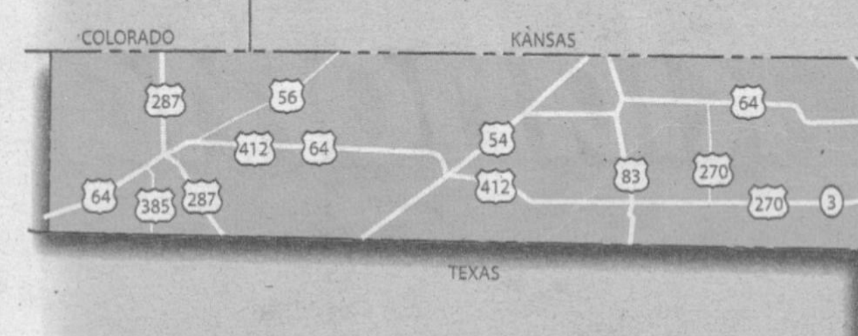

Oklahoma City (see p. 607)

The Oklahoma City Vicinity (see p. 627)

Tulsa (see p. 644)

The Tulsa Vicinity (see p. 663)

Map To Destinations

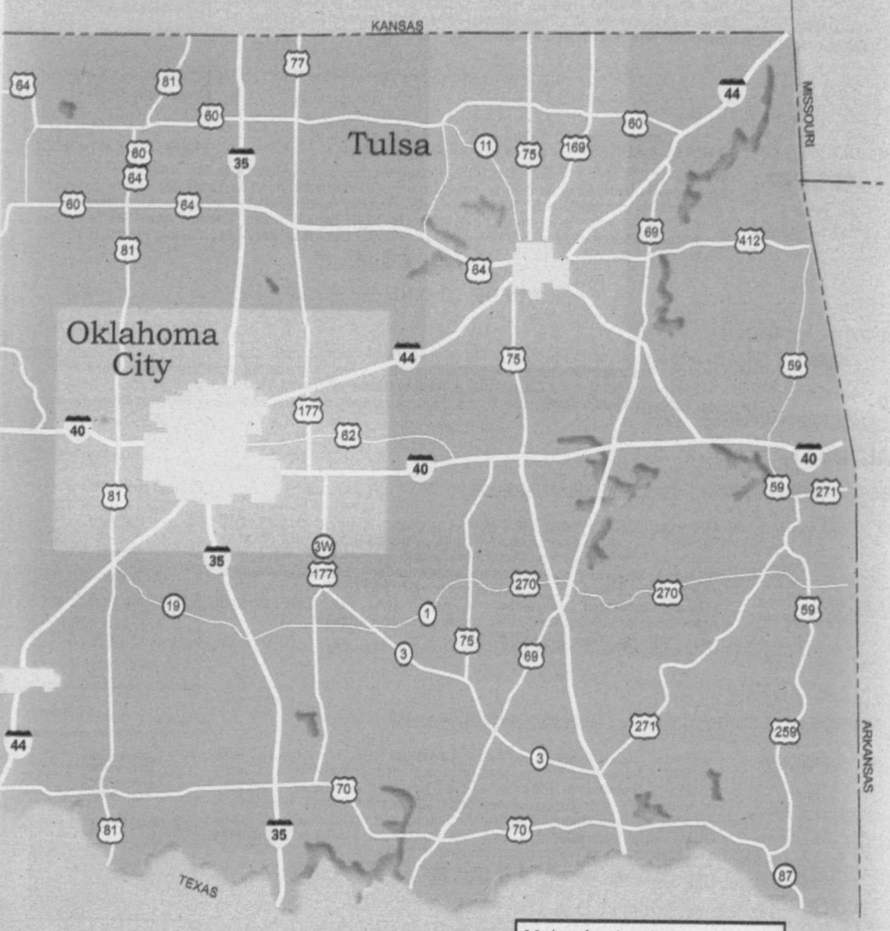

Major destinations are color-coded to index boxes, which display vicinity communities you will find listed within that destination's section of the book.
Cities outside major destination vicinities are listed in alphabetical order throughout the book.
Use the Comprehensive City Index at the back of this book to find every city's listing locations.

ADA pop. 15,691

BEST WESTERN RAINTREE MOTOR INN

Book great rates at AAA.com

Phone: (580)332-6262

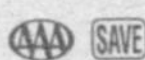

Hotel
$80-$89 All Year

Address: 1100 N Mississippi Ave 74820 **Location:** 1.5 mi n on US 377/SR 99. **Facility:** 39 one-bedroom standard units. 2 stories (no elevator), exterior corridors. **Parking:** on-site. **Amenities:** high-speed Internet, irons, hair dryers. **Pool(s):** heated indoor. **Guest Services:** wireless Internet. **Business Services:** PC. **Free Special Amenities: expanded continental breakfast and high-speed Internet.** / SOME UNITS

AAA Benefit:
Members save up to 20%, plus 10% bonus points with rewards program.

HOLIDAY INN EXPRESS HOTEL & SUITES

Book at AAA.com

Phone: (580)310-9200

Hotel
$114-$152 All Year

Address: 1201 Lonnie Abbott Blvd 74820 **Location:** Just e of jct Mississippi Ave. **Facility:** Smoke free premises. 84 units. 82 one-bedroom standard units. 2 one-bedroom suites. 3 stories, interior corridors. *Bath:* combo or shower only. **Parking:** on-site. **Terms:** cancellation fee imposed. **Amenities:** high-speed Internet, voice mail, irons, hair dryers. **Pool(s):** heated indoor. **Leisure Activities:** exercise room. **Guest Services:** coin laundry, wireless Internet. **Business Services:** meeting rooms, business center. ASK CALL

WHERE TO DINE

JD'S CAFE & CAFETERIA

Phone: 580/332-9750

American
$5-$10

JD's features a good menu selection of family-style meals such as roast beef, mashed potatoes, corn and apple cobbler. The restaurant has a friendly and courteous staff that's attentive to your needs while dining, and a wholesome environment. Casual dress. **Reservations:** accepted. **Hours:** 5 am-8:30 pm; 11 am-2 pm cafeteria. Closed: 11/25, 12/25; also Sun & Mon. **Address:** 911 N Broadway 74820 **Location:** Center. **Parking:** on-site.

ALTUS pop. 21,447

BEST WESTERN ALTUS

Book great rates at AAA.com

Phone: (580)482-9300

Hotel
$49-$99 All Year

Address: 2804 N Main St 73521 **Location:** 2 mi n on US 283. **Facility:** 100 one-bedroom standard units. 2 stories (no elevator), exterior corridors. **Parking:** on-site. **Amenities:** video games (fee), voice mail, irons, hair dryers. **Pool(s):** heated indoor/outdoor. **Leisure Activities:** whirlpool, exercise room. **Guest Services:** valet and coin laundry, wireless Internet. **Business Services:** meeting rooms, PC. **Free Special Amenities: local telephone calls and high-speed Internet.**

AAA Benefit:
Members save up to 20%, plus 10% bonus points with rewards program.

HAMPTON INN & SUITES ALTUS

Book great rates at AAA.com

Phone: (580)482-1273

Hotel
$99-$159 All Year

Address: 3601 N Main St 73521 **Location:** 2.2 mi n on US 283. **Facility:** 83 one-bedroom standard units. 3 stories, interior corridors. *Bath:* combo or shower only. **Parking:** on-site. **Terms:** 1-7 night minimum stay, cancellation fee imposed. **Amenities:** voice mail, irons, hair dryers. **Pool(s):** heated indoor. **Leisure Activities:** whirlpool, exercise room. **Guest Services:** valet and coin laundry, wireless Internet. **Business Services:** meeting rooms, business center. CALL / SOME UNITS

AAA Benefit:
Members save up to 10% everyday!

ANADARKO pop. 6,645

WHERE TO DINE

K.I.G. CUE BAR-B-CUE

Phone: 405/247-2454

Barbecue
$6-$13

Patrons can sample from the daily all-you-can-eat buffet or order from the menu. Casual dress. **Reservations:** accepted. **Hours:** 11 am-8 pm, Fri & Sat-9 pm, Wed-6 pm. Closed: 11/25, 12/25; also Sun & Mon. **Address:** 1315 E Central Blvd 73005 **Location:** 0.5 mi e of jct SR 8. **Parking:** on-site.

ARDMORE pop. 23,711

BEST WESTERN INN *Book great rates at AAA.com* **Phone:** (580)223-7525

Hotel
$80-$86 3/1-10/31
$70-$76 11/1-2/28

Address: 136 Holiday Dr 73401 **Location:** I-35, exit 32, 0.5 mi se. **Facility:** 55 one-bedroom standard units, some with whirlpools. 2 stories (no elevator), interior corridors. **Parking:** on-site. **Amenities:** irons, hair dryers. *Some:* high-speed Internet. **Pool(s):** outdoor. **Guest Services:** valet and coin laundry, wireless Internet. **Business Services:** meeting rooms, PC. **Free Special Amenities: expanded continental breakfast and high-speed Internet.**

SOME UNITS FEE

AAA Benefit: Members save up to 20%, plus 10% bonus points with rewards program.

HOLIDAY INN *Book at AAA.com* **Phone:** (580)223-7130

Hotel
$99-$125 All Year

Address: 2705 W Broadway 73401 **Location:** I-35, exit 31A, just e. **Facility:** 169 units. 167 one-bedroom standard units, some with whirlpools. 2 one-bedroom suites. 2 stories (no elevator), exterior corridors. **Parking:** on-site, winter plug-ins. **Terms:** cancellation fee imposed. **Amenities:** voice mail, irons, hair dryers. **Pool(s):** outdoor. **Leisure Activities:** playground, exercise room. **Guest Services:** valet and coin laundry, wireless Internet. **Business Services:** meeting rooms, PC.

ASK SOME UNITS

LA QUINTA INN ARDMORE *Book at AAA.com* **Phone:** 580/223-7976

Hotel
Rates not provided

Address: 2432 Veterans Blvd 73401 **Location:** I-35, exit 33, just e. **Facility:** 64 one-bedroom standard units. 2 stories (no elevator), exterior corridors. **Parking:** on-site, winter plug-ins. **Amenities:** high-speed Internet, voice mail, irons, hair dryers. **Pool(s):** heated outdoor. **Leisure Activities:** whirlpool, exercise room. **Guest Services:** valet and coin laundry, wireless Internet. **Business Services:** PC. SOME UNITS

SHILOH MORNING INN **Phone:** (580)223-9500

Bed & Breakfast
$159-$299 All Year

Address: 2179 Ponderosa Rd 73401 **Location:** 2.1 mi n of jct US 177 and SR 199, 0.8 mi w. Located in a quiet area; gated property. **Facility:** A view of the sunrise can be seen from guest room balconies at this inn located in the country. Smoke free premises. 9 units. 8 one-bedroom standard units. 1 cottage. 2 stories (no elevator), interior corridors. *Bath:* combo or tub only. **Parking:** on-site. **Terms:** check-in 4 pm, 2 night minimum stay - weekends, age restrictions may apply, 7 day cancellation notice-fee imposed. **Amenities:** video library, DVD players, hair dryers. *Some:* voice mail. **Leisure Activities:** hiking trails. **Guest Services:** wireless Internet. **Business Services:** meeting rooms.

CALL SOME UNITS

SPRINGHILL SUITES BY MARRIOTT *Book great rates at AAA.com* **Phone:** (580)226-7100

Hotel
$125-$153 All Year

Address: 2501 Centennial Dr N 73401 **Location:** I-35, exit 33, just se. **Facility:** Smoke free premises. 80 one-bedroom standard units. 3 stories, interior corridors. *Bath:* combo or shower only. **Parking:** on-site. **Terms:** cancellation fee imposed. **Amenities:** video games (fee), high-speed Internet, voice mail, irons, hair dryers. **Pool(s):** heated indoor. **Leisure Activities:** whirlpool, exercise room. **Guest Services:** valet and coin laundry, wireless Internet. **Business Services:** meeting rooms, PC.

AAA Benefit: Members save a minimum 5% off the best available rate.

WHERE TO DINE

BUDRO'S RIB JOINT **Phone:** 580/223-2272

Barbecue
$5-$18

In addition to barbecue beef and pork dishes, the menu lists a good selection of steak, catfish and chicken. Casual dress. **Bar:** Beer only. **Hours:** 11 am-11 pm. Closed major holidays. **Address:** 1606 McLish 73401 **Location:** I-35, exit 31A, 0.8 mi e. **Parking:** on-site.

POLO'S MEXICANO **Phone:** 580/226-7656

Mexican
$5-$12

Traditional preparations are served in ample portions. Fajitas are the signature dish. Casual dress. **Hours:** 11 am-9 pm. Closed: 11/25, 12/25. **Address:** 2610 W Broadway 73401 **Location:** I-35, exit 31A, just e. **Parking:** on-site.

SIRLOIN STOCKADE **Phone:** 580/226-6281

Regional Steak
$6-$9

The steakhouse lines up buffet items, including pizza, tacos, soups, salads and desserts, providing both excellent variety and a good value. Rotating theme nights might allow for the sampling of sushi, barbecue and seafood. The buffet also may serve to complement a quality steak. Rolls are baked several times daily. Casual dress. **Reservations:** not accepted. **Hours:** 11 am-9 pm. Closed: 11/25, 12/25. **Address:** 1217 N Commerce 73401 **Location:** 1 mi n of jct US 77 and SR 199. **Parking:** on-site.

TWO FROGS GRILL Phone: 580/226-3764

American
$6-$18

Food that will make your mouth water is served in a casual and fun atmosphere. The relaxed feel from the moment you step through the door tells you that this is one place to hop on into and fill your tank. Casual dress. **Bar:** Full bar. **Hours:** 11 am-10 pm, Sun-9 pm. Closed: 12/25. **Address:** 2646 W Broadway 73401 **Location:** I-35, exit 31A, just se. **Parking:** on-site.

BARTLESVILLE pop. 34,748

HAMPTON INN *Book great rates at AAA.com* **Phone:** (918)333-4051

Hotel
$94-$129 All Year

Address: 130 SE Washington Blvd 74006 **Location:** 0.8 mi n of jct US 60 and 75. **Facility:** 67 one-bedroom standard units. 3 stories, interior corridors. *Bath:* combo or shower only. **Parking:** on-site. **Terms:** 1-7 night minimum stay, cancellation fee imposed. **Amenities:** dual phone lines, voice mail, irons, hair dryers. **Pool(s):** heated indoor. **Leisure Activities:** sauna, whirlpool, exercise room. **Guest Services:** valet and coin laundry, wireless Internet. **Business Services:** meeting rooms, business center.

/ SOME UNITS

AAA Benefit:
Members save up to 10% everyday!

MICROTEL INN & SUITES OF BARTLESVILLE *Book at AAA.com* **Phone:** (918)333-2100

Hotel
$69-$99 All Year

Address: 2696 SE Washington Blvd 74006 **Location:** 1.4 mi s of jct US 60 E. **Facility:** 56 one-bedroom standard units, some with whirlpools. 3 stories, interior corridors. *Bath:* combo or shower only. **Parking:** on-site. **Terms:** cancellation fee imposed. **Amenities:** voice mail, irons, hair dryers. **Leisure Activities:** limited exercise equipment. **Guest Services:** coin laundry, wireless Internet.

ASK CALL / SOME UNITS FEE

WHERE TO DINE

GOLDIES PATIO GRILL **Phone:** 918/335-5507

American
$6-$15

The menu comprises grilled items, chicken, sandwiches and steak, but this place is best known for its excellent charbroiled burgers. The decor incorporates 1950s and '60s memorabilia. Casual dress. **Hours:** 11 am-9 pm. Closed major holidays. **Address:** 201 SE Washington 74006 **Location:** 1.1 mi n of jct US 60 and 75. **Parking:** on-site.

MONTANA MIKE'S **Phone:** 918/333-2666

Steak
$7-$20

This steakhouse offers a dining experience for the whole family. A rustic look with Western appointments characterizes the dining room. Although it's hard to go wrong with a hearty steak of USDA Choice aged beef, guests also can try smoked, fire-grilled chicken breast, chicken-fried steak, baby back ribs and other selections. Casual dress. **Bar:** Full bar. **Hours:** 11 am-9 pm, Fri & Sat-10 pm. Closed: 11/25, 12/25. **Address:** 3825 SE Adams 74006 **Location:** 1 mi n of center. **Parking:** on-site.

RIB CRIB BBQ AND GRILL **Phone:** 918/333-6200

Barbecue
$6-$15

Most guests need extra napkins to tackle the ribs, brisket, ham, pork and chicken selections. The menu also lists sandwiches and wraps, along with tempting sides and large desserts. The decor is decidedly Western. Casual dress. **Bar:** Beer only. **Hours:** 11 am-10 pm. Closed: 11/25, 12/25. **Address:** 2077 SE Washington Blvd 74006 **Location:** 1.4 mi s of jct US 60 and 75. **Parking:** on-site.

BIG CABIN pop. 293

SUPER 8-BIG CABIN *Book at AAA.com* **Phone:** (918)783-5888

Motel
$60-$68 All Year

Address: 30954 S Hwy 69 74301 **Location:** I-44, exit 283, just ne. **Facility:** 62 one-bedroom standard units. 1-2 stories (no elevator), interior/exterior corridors. **Parking:** on-site, winter plug-ins. **Amenities:** hair dryers. **Pool(s):** heated indoor. **Leisure Activities:** whirlpool. **Guest Services:** coin laundry, wireless Internet. ASK / SOME UNITS FEE

BIXBY—See Tulsa p. 663.

BLACKWELL pop. 7,668

BEST WESTERN BLACKWELL INN *Book great rates at AAA.com* **Phone:** (580)363-1300

AAA SAVE

Hotel
$85-$93 All Year

Address: 4545 W White Ave 74631 **Location:** I-35, exit 222, just ne. **Facility:** 62 one-bedroom standard units. 3 stories, interior corridors. *Bath:* combo or shower only. **Parking:** on-site. **Amenities:** high-speed Internet, voice mail, irons, hair dryers. **Pool(s):** heated indoor. **Leisure Activities:** whirlpool. **Guest Services:** coin laundry, wireless Internet. **Business Services:** PC. **Free Special Amenities: expanded continental breakfast and high-speed Internet.**

/ SOME UNITS FEE

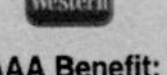

AAA Benefit:
Members save up to 20%, plus 10% bonus points with rewards program.

COMFORT INN *Book great rates at AAA.com* **Phone:** (580)363-7000

Hotel
$75-$100 All Year

Address: 1201 N 44th St 74631 **Location:** I-35, exit 222, just ne. **Facility:** Smoke free premises. 60 one-bedroom standard units. 2 stories (no elevator), interior corridors. *Bath:* combo or shower only. **Parking:** on-site. **Amenities:** irons, hair dryers. *Some:* high-speed Internet. **Pool(s):** heated indoor. **Guest Services:** wireless Internet. **Business Services:** meeting rooms. **Free Special Amenities: early check-in/late check-out and high-speed Internet.**

/ SOME UNITS FEE

BROKEN ARROW—See Tulsa p. 663.

CATOOSA—See Tulsa p. 665.

CHICKASHA pop. 15,850

BEST WESTERN INN *Book great rates at AAA.com* **Phone:** (405)224-4890

Hotel
$64-$85 All Year

Address: 2101 S 4th St 73018 **Location:** I-44, exit 80, just nw. **Facility:** 150 units. 145 one-bedroom standard units. 5 one-bedroom suites. 2 stories (no elevator), interior/exterior corridors. **Parking:** on-site. **Terms:** check-in 4 pm. **Amenities:** high-speed Internet, irons, hair dryers. **Pool(s):** heated indoor. **Leisure Activities:** whirlpool, limited exercise equipment. *Fee:* game room. **Guest Services:** valet and coin laundry, wireless Internet. **Business Services:** meeting rooms, PC.

/ SOME UNITS FEE

AAA Benefit:
Members save up to 20%, plus 10% bonus points with rewards program.

FREE local telephone calls and high-speed Internet

CHOCTAW—See Oklahoma City p. 627.

CLAREMORE—See Tulsa p. 665.

CLINTON pop. 8,833

HAMPTON INN *Book great rates at AAA.com* **Phone:** (580)323-4267

Hotel
$106-$125 All Year

Address: 2000 Lexington Ave 73601 **Location:** I-40, exit 65, just ne. **Facility:** 68 one-bedroom standard units. 3 stories, interior corridors. *Bath:* combo or shower only. **Parking:** on-site. **Terms:** 1-7 night minimum stay, cancellation fee imposed. **Amenities:** high-speed Internet, voice mail, irons, hair dryers. **Pool(s):** heated indoor. **Leisure Activities:** whirlpool, exercise room. **Guest Services:** valet and coin laundry, wireless Internet. **Business Services:** meeting rooms, business center.

CALL / SOME UNITS

AAA Benefit:
Members save up to 10% everyday!

WHERE TO DINE

WONG'S RESTAURANT **Phone:** 580/323-4588

Chinese
$4-$13

The extensive menu at Wong's features Cantonese and Szechuan selections with many American dishes including pork, beef, shrimp and chicken samplings. The friendly, family-style atmosphere is casual and relaxed. Service is efficient and prompt. Casual dress. **Bar:** Beer only. **Hours:** 11 am-10 pm. Closed: 11/25, 12/25; also Mon. **Address:** 712 Opal Ave 73601 **Location:** I-40, exit 65A, 0.5 mi n, then just e. **Parking:** on-site. CALL

DAVIS pop. 2,610

DAVIS MICROTEL INN & SUITES-TREASURE VALLEY CASINO **Phone:** 580/369-3223

Hotel
$78-$140 All Year

Address: 12252 Ruppe Rd 73030 **Location:** I-35, exit 55, just e. **Facility:** 59 units. 55 one-bedroom standard units. 4 one-bedroom suites. 3 stories, interior corridors. *Bath:* combo or shower only. **Parking:** on-site. **Terms:** check-in 4 pm, cancellation fee imposed. **Amenities:** high-speed Internet, voice mail, irons, hair dryers. **Pool(s):** heated indoor. **Leisure Activities:** sauna, whirlpool, exercise room, game room. **Guest Services:** coin laundry, wireless Internet. **Business Services:** meeting rooms, PC. ASK CALL / SOME UNITS

DEL CITY—See Oklahoma City p. 627.

DUNCAN pop. 22,505

HAMPTON INN Book great rates at AAA.com Phone: (580)255-1700

Hotel
$89-$169 All Year

Address: 2301 N Hwy 81 73533 **Location:** Center. **Facility:** 78 one-bedroom standard units, some with whirlpools. 4 stories, interior corridors. *Bath:* combo or shower only. **Parking:** on-site. **Terms:** 1-7 night minimum stay, cancellation fee imposed. **Amenities:** high-speed Internet, voice mail, irons, hair dryers. **Pool(s):** heated indoor. **Leisure Activities:** exercise room. **Guest Services:** valet and coin laundry, wireless Internet. **Business Services:** meeting rooms, business center.

CALL / SOME UNITS

AAA Benefit:
Members save up to 10% everyday!

DURANT pop. 13,549

BEST WESTERN MARKITA INN Book great rates at AAA.com Phone: (580)924-7676

Hotel
$86-$100 All Year

Address: 2401 W Main St 74701 **Location:** Just w of US 69/75 and 70. **Facility:** 62 units. 61 one-bedroom standard units, some with whirlpools. 1 one-bedroom suite with whirlpool. 2 stories (no elevator), exterior corridors. *Bath:* combo or shower only. **Parking:** on-site. **Amenities:** high-speed Internet, irons, hair dryers. **Pool(s):** outdoor. **Guest Services:** coin laundry, wireless Internet. **Business Services:** meeting rooms, PC. **Free Special Amenities: local telephone calls and high-speed Internet.**

/ SOME UNITS

AAA Benefit:
Members save up to 20%, plus 10% bonus points with rewards program.

COMFORT INN & SUITES Book at AAA.com Phone: 580/924-8881

Hotel
Rates not provided

Address: 2112 W Main St 74701 **Location:** Just e of jct US 75/69 and 70. **Facility:** 62 one-bedroom standard units, some with whirlpools. 2 stories (no elevator), interior corridors. *Bath:* combo or shower only. **Parking:** on-site. **Amenities:** high-speed Internet, irons, hair dryers. **Pool(s):** outdoor. **Guest Services:** valet and coin laundry, wireless Internet. **Business Services:** meeting rooms, PC.

/ SOME UNITS

HAMPTON INN & SUITES DURANT Book great rates at AAA.com Phone: (580)924-0300

Hotel
$89-$129 All Year

Address: 3199 Shamrock Ln 74701 **Location:** Just ne of jct US 70 and University Pl. **Facility:** Smoke free premises. 79 one-bedroom standard units, some with whirlpools. 4 stories, interior corridors. *Bath:* combo or shower only. **Parking:** on-site. **Terms:** 1-7 night minimum stay, cancellation fee imposed. **Amenities:** high-speed Internet, voice mail, irons, hair dryers. **Pool(s):** heated outdoor. **Leisure Activities:** whirlpool, exercise room. **Guest Services:** valet and coin laundry, wireless Internet. **Business Services:** meeting rooms, business center.

CALL / SOME UNITS

AAA Benefit:
Members save up to 10% everyday!

EDMOND—See Oklahoma City p. 627.

ELK CITY pop. 10,510

BEST WESTERN ELK CITY INN Book great rates at AAA.com Phone: (580)225-2331

Hotel
$110-$150 All Year

Address: 2015 W 3rd St 73644 **Location:** I-40, exit 41 westbound, 4 mi nw; exit 32 eastbound, 5 mi ne. **Facility:** 40 one-bedroom standard units. 2 stories (no elevator), exterior corridors. **Parking:** on-site. **Amenities:** irons, hair dryers. **Pool(s):** indoor. **Guest Services:** wireless Internet. **Business Services:** PC. **Free Special Amenities: continental breakfast and high-speed Internet.**

/ SOME UNITS

AAA Benefit:
Members save up to 20%, plus 10% bonus points with rewards program.

— WHERE TO DINE —

PORTOBELLO GRILLE Phone: 580/225-3744

Italian
$6-$20

This casual restaurant has a nice selection of Italian dishes but offers other options for those not in the mood for Italian. Diners can choose to sit in the lounge area, which boasts a sports bar theme. Casual dress. **Bar:** Full bar. **Hours:** 11 am-9 pm, Fri & Sat-10 pm. Closed major holidays; also Sun. **Address:** 301 N Eastern Ave 73644 **Location:** I-40, exit 40, just ne. **Parking:** on-site.

EL RENO—See Oklahoma City p. 628.

ENID pop. 47,045

BAYMONT INN & SUITES-ENID   Book at AAA.com   **Phone:** 580/234-6800

Hotel

Rates not provided

Address: 3614 W Owen K Garriott Rd 73703 **Location:** 2 mi w of jct US 81. **Facility:** 60 one-bedroom standard units, some with whirlpools. 2 stories (no elevator), interior corridors. *Bath:* combo or shower only. **Parking:** on-site. **Amenities:** voice mail, safes (fee), irons, hair dryers. **Pool(s):** heated indoor. **Leisure Activities:** whirlpool, limited exercise equipment. **Guest Services:** coin laundry, wireless Internet. **Business Services:** meeting rooms, PC.

CALL / SOME UNITS FEE

HOLIDAY INN EXPRESS HOTEL & SUITES   Book at AAA.com   **Phone:** 580/237-7722

Hotel

Rates not provided

Address: 4702 W Owen K Garriott Rd 73703 **Location:** 2.3 mi w of jct US 81. **Facility:** 78 units. 75 one-bedroom standard units, some with whirlpools. 3 one-bedroom suites with whirlpools. 3 stories, interior corridors. *Bath:* combo or shower only. **Parking:** on-site. **Amenities:** high-speed Internet, voice mail, safes, irons, hair dryers. *Some:* DVD players. **Pool(s):** heated indoor. **Leisure Activities:** whirlpool, exercise room. **Guest Services:** valet and coin laundry, wireless Internet. **Business Services:** meeting rooms, business center. / SOME UNITS

WHERE TO DINE

RIB CRIB BBQ AND GRILL   **Phone:** 580/237-7333

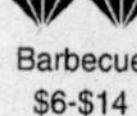

Barbecue

$6-$14

Most guests need extra napkins to tackle the ribs, brisket, ham, pork and chicken selections. The menu also lists sandwiches and wraps, along with tempting sides and large desserts. The decor is decidedly Western. Casual dress. **Bar:** Beer only. **Hours:** 11 am-10 pm. Closed: 11/25, 12/25. **Address:** 4901 W Owen K Garriott Rd 73703 **Location:** Center. **Parking:** on-site.

EUFAULA pop. 2,639

BEST WESTERN EUFAULA INN   Book great rates at AAA.com   **Phone:** (918)689-5553

Hotel

$80-$100 All Year

Address: 1300 Birkes Rd 74432 **Location:** 0.7 mi ne of jct US 69 and SR 9. **Facility:** Smoke free premises. 50 one-bedroom standard units, some with whirlpools. 2 stories, interior corridors. *Bath:* combo or shower only. **Parking:** on-site. **Amenities:** voice mail, irons, hair dryers. **Pool(s):** heated indoor. **Leisure Activities:** exercise room. **Guest Services:** coin laundry, wireless Internet. **Business Services:** meeting rooms, business center. **Free Special Amenities: local telephone calls and high-speed Internet.**

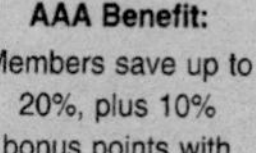

AAA Benefit:

Members save up to 20%, plus 10% bonus points with rewards program.

GLENPOOL—See Tulsa p. 666.

GROVE pop. 5,131

BEST WESTERN TIMBER RIDGE INN   Book great rates at AAA.com   **Phone:** (918)786-6900

Hotel

$87 All Year

Address: 120 W 18th St 74344 **Location:** Just w of jct US 59. **Facility:** Smoke free premises. 46 one-bedroom standard units, some with whirlpools. 2 stories (no elevator), interior/exterior corridors. *Bath:* combo or shower only. **Parking:** on-site. **Amenities:** irons, hair dryers. **Pool(s):** outdoor. **Guest Services:** coin laundry, wireless Internet. **Business Services:** business center. **Free Special Amenities: early check-in/late check-out and high-speed Internet.**

/ SOME UNITS FEE

AAA Benefit:

Members save up to 20%, plus 10% bonus points with rewards program.

WHERE TO DINE

RIB CRIB BBQ AND GRILL   **Phone:** 918/786-5400

Barbecue

$6-$14

Most guests need extra napkins to tackle the ribs, brisket, ham, pork and chicken selections. The menu also lists sandwiches and wraps, along with tempting sides and large desserts. The decor is decidedly Western. Casual dress. **Bar:** Beer only. **Hours:** 11 am-10 pm. Closed: 11/25, 12/25. **Address:** 1801 Main St 74344 **Location:** Center. **Parking:** on-site.

GUTHRIE—See Oklahoma City p. 629.

GUYMON pop. 10,472

BEST WESTERN GUYMON HOTEL & SUITES *Book great rates at AAA.com* **Phone:** (580)338-0800

Hotel
$64-$130 All Year

Address: 1102 NE 6th St (Hwy 54) 73942 **Location:** Just s of jct US 64. **Facility:** 70 one-bedroom standard units, some with efficiencies and/or whirlpools. 3 stories, interior/exterior corridors. *Bath:* combo or shower only. **Parking:** on-site. **Amenities:** high-speed Internet, voice mail, irons, hair dryers. *Some:* DVD players. **Leisure Activities:** exercise room. **Guest Services:** coin laundry, wireless Internet. **Business Services:** meeting rooms, business center.

CALL / SOME UNITS FEE

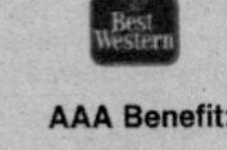

AAA Benefit:
Members save up to 20%, plus 10% bonus points with rewards program.

FREE full breakfast and high-speed Internet

COMFORT INN & SUITES *Book at AAA.com* **Phone:** (580)338-0831

Hotel
$80-$90 All Year

Address: 501 5th St (Hwy 54 E) 73942 **Location:** Just s of jct US 64. **Facility:** 51 units. 49 one-bedroom standard units, some with whirlpools. 2 one-bedroom suites. 3 stories, interior corridors. *Bath:* combo or shower only. **Parking:** on-site. **Amenities:** DVD players, high-speed Internet, voice mail, irons, hair dryers. **Pool(s):** heated indoor. **Leisure Activities:** whirlpool, exercise room. **Guest Services:** coin laundry, wireless Internet. **Business Services:** meeting rooms, PC.

ASK / SOME UNITS FEE

GUYMON SUPER 8 *Book great rates at AAA.com* **Phone:** (580)338-0507

Hotel
$70-$100 All Year

Address: 1201 Hwy 54 E 73942 **Location:** Jct US 54 and 64. **Facility:** 59 one-bedroom standard units, some with whirlpools. 2 stories (no elevator), interior corridors. *Bath:* combo or shower only. **Parking:** on-site, winter plug-ins. **Amenities:** irons, hair dryers. **Guest Services:** coin laundry, wireless Internet. **Business Services:** meeting rooms, PC. **Free Special Amenities: full breakfast and high-speed Internet.** / SOME UNITS FEE

WHERE TO DINE

NAIFEH'S STEAKHOUSE **Phone:** 580/338-5355

Steak
$6-$20

You'll enjoy the relaxed, casual atmosphere, friendly and attentive service, and tasty, family-style food at Naifeh's. Steaks are their specialty, but the catfish, cheesecake and pecan pie are also good. The home-style decor complements the environment. Casual dress. **Reservations:** suggested, weekends. **Hours:** 11 am-8:30 pm. Closed major holidays; also Sun & Mon. **Address:** 704 NE 12th St 73942 **Location:** 0.8 mi n on US 64. **Parking:** on-site.

HENRYETTA pop. 6,096

GREEN COUNTRY INN **Phone:** 918/652-9988

Motel
$45-$58 All Year

Address: 2004 Old Hwy 75 W 74437 **Location:** I-40, exit 237, just ne. **Facility:** 41 one-bedroom standard units. 1 story, exterior corridors. **Parking:** on-site, winter plug-ins. **Amenities:** hair dryers. **Pool(s):** outdoor. **Guest Services:** wireless Internet.

/ SOME UNITS FEE

IDABEL pop. 6,952

COMFORT SUITES *Book at AAA.com* **Phone:** (580)286-9393

Hotel
$80-$100 All Year

Address: 400 SE Lincoln Rd 74745 **Location:** Just s of jct US 70 and 259. **Facility:** Smoke free premises. 60 one-bedroom standard units, some with whirlpools. 2 stories, interior corridors. *Bath:* combo or shower only. **Parking:** on-site. **Amenities:** dual phone lines, voice mail, irons, hair dryers. **Pool(s):** outdoor. **Leisure Activities:** whirlpool, exercise room. **Guest Services:** coin laundry, wireless Internet. **Business Services:** meeting rooms, business center.

ASK / SOME UNITS FEE

JENKS—See Tulsa p. 666.

LAWTON pop. 92,757

BAYMONT INN & SUITES *Book great rates at AAA.com* **Phone:** 580/353-5581

Hotel
Rates not provided

Address: 1203 NW 40th St 73505 **Location:** I-44, exit 39A, 3.7 mi w. **Facility:** Smoke free premises. 72 one-bedroom standard units, some with whirlpools. 3 stories, interior corridors. *Bath:* combo or shower only. **Parking:** on-site. **Amenities:** video games (fee), voice mail, irons, hair dryers. *Some:* fax. **Pool(s):** heated indoor. **Leisure Activities:** exercise room. **Guest Services:** coin laundry, wireless Internet. **Business Services:** PC. **Free Special Amenities: full breakfast and newspaper.**

/ SOME UNITS

BEST WESTERN HOTEL & CONVENTION CENTER *Book great rates at AAA.com* **Phone:** (580)353-0200

Hotel
$94-$110 3/1-11/18
$94-$99 11/19-2/28

Address: 1125 E Gore Blvd 73501 **Location:** I-44, exit 37, just e. **Facility:** 145 units. 141 one-bedroom standard units, some with whirlpools. 4 one-bedroom suites. 2 stories, interior/exterior corridors. *Bath:* combo or shower only. **Parking:** on-site, winter plug-ins. **Amenities:** high-speed Internet, voice mail, irons, hair dryers. **Dining:** nightclub. **Pool(s):** 2 outdoor, heated indoor. **Leisure Activities:** sauna, lighted tennis court, exercise room. **Guest Services:** valet and coin laundry, airport transportation-Lawton Municipal Airport, area transportation-within 3 mi, wireless Internet. **Business Services:** conference facilities, business center.

/ SOME UNITS

Best Western

AAA Benefit:
Members save up to 20%, plus 10% bonus points with rewards program.

FREE full breakfast and high-speed Internet

FAIRFIELD INN & SUITES BY MARRIOTT *Book great rates at AAA.com* **Phone:** (580)248-5500

Hotel
$103-$125 All Year

Address: 201 SE 7th St 73501 **Location:** I-44, exit 37, just sw. **Facility:** Smoke free premises. 84 one-bedroom standard units, some with whirlpools. 4 stories, interior corridors. *Bath:* combo or shower only. **Parking:** on-site. **Terms:** cancellation fee imposed. **Amenities:** voice mail, irons, hair dryers. *Some:* CD players. **Pool(s):** heated outdoor. **Leisure Activities:** whirlpool, exercise room. **Guest Services:** valet and coin laundry, wireless Internet. **Business Services:** meeting rooms, business center.

CALL / SOME UNITS

AAA Benefit:
Members save a minimum 5% off the best available rate.

HAMPTON INN & SUITES *Book great rates at AAA.com* **Phone:** (580)355-8200

Hotel
$114-$144 All Year

Address: 2610 NW Cache Rd 73505 **Location:** I-44, exit 39A (Cache Rd), 2 mi w. **Facility:** 86 one-bedroom standard units. 4 stories, interior corridors. *Bath:* combo or shower only. **Parking:** on-site. **Terms:** 1-7 night minimum stay, cancellation fee imposed. **Amenities:** high-speed Internet, voice mail, irons, hair dryers. *Some:* DVD players. **Pool(s):** heated indoor. **Leisure Activities:** whirlpool, exercise room. **Guest Services:** valet and coin laundry, wireless Internet. **Business Services:** meeting rooms, business center.

/ SOME UNITS

AAA Benefit:
Members save up to 10% everyday!

HOLIDAY INN EXPRESS HOTEL & SUITES *Book at AAA.com* **Phone:** 580/248-4446

Hotel
Rates not provided

Address: 209 SE Interstate Dr 73501 **Location:** I-44, exit 37, just sw. **Facility:** 99 one-bedroom standard units. 4 stories, interior corridors. *Bath:* combo or shower only. **Parking:** on-site. **Amenities:** high-speed Internet, voice mail, irons, hair dryers. **Pool(s):** outdoor. **Leisure Activities:** whirlpool, exercise room. **Guest Services:** valet and coin laundry, wireless Internet. **Business Services:** meeting rooms, business center.

CALL / SOME UNITS

The following lodging was either not evaluated or did not meet AAA rating requirements but is listed for your information only.

SPRINGHILL SUITES BY MARRIOTT **Phone:** 580/248-8500

fyi

Not evaluated. **Address:** 3 SE Interstate Dr 73501 **Location:** I-44, exit 37, just w. Facilities, services, and decor characterize a mid-scale property.

AAA Benefit:
Members save a minimum 5% off the best available rate.

WHERE TO DINE

BIANCO'S — Phone: 580/353-9543

Italian
$6-$12

This place's style, which hasn't changed much from when it first became family owned in 1952, is in keeping with its good food, which reflects that great flavor is ageless. There's nothing fancy here, but diners can look forward to well-prepared Italian dishes served in an intimate, nostalgic setting. Casual dress. **Bar:** Full bar. **Hours:** 11 am-9 pm. Closed major holidays; also Sun. **Address:** 113 N 2nd St 73507 **Location:** Just n of jct Gore Blvd. **Parking:** on-site.

GOLDEN CHINA — Phone: 580/248-9889

Chinese
$4-$10

All of the expected beef, poultry, pork, vegetable and seafood dishes are served in a casual, relaxed setting. Casual dress. **Hours:** 11 am-2:30 & 4-9:30 pm, Fri & Sat 11 am-10 pm, Sun 11 am-9 pm. Closed: 11/25, 12/25. **Address:** 2512 NW Cache Rd 73505 **Location:** I-44, exit 39A, 2 mi w. **Parking:** on-site.

LOCUST GROVE pop. 1,366

BEST WESTERN LOCUST GROVE INN & SUITES — *Book great rates at AAA.com* — **Phone:** (918)479-8082

AAA SAVE

Hotel
$72-$200 All Year

Address: 106 Holiday Ln 74352 **Location:** Just nw of jct US 412 and SR 82. **Facility:** 50 units. 42 one-bedroom standard units, some with whirlpools. 8 one-bedroom suites. 2 stories, interior corridors. *Bath:* combo or shower only. **Parking:** on-site. **Amenities:** high-speed Internet, voice mail, irons, hair dryers. **Pool(s):** outdoor. **Leisure Activities:** whirlpool, exercise room. **Guest Services:** valet and coin laundry, wireless Internet. **Business Services:** meeting rooms, business center. **Free Special Amenities: continental breakfast and high-speed Internet.**

/ SOME UNITS FEE

AAA Benefit:
Members save up to 20%, plus 10% bonus points with rewards program.

MARIETTA pop. 2,445

WHERE TO DINE

MCGEHEES CATFISH RESTAURANT — **Phone:** 580/276-2751

Regional American
$5-$14

Of course, this restaurant serves farm-raised and delicious catfish, but it's also well-known for freshly made coleslaw and hush puppies, steak and hamburgers. The rustic Western decor creates a family-friendly atmosphere. Casual dress. **Hours:** 5 pm-8:30 pm, Sat & Sun from 1 pm. Closed: 11/25, 12/25; also Mon-Wed. **Address:** 407 W Broadway 73448 **Location:** I-35, exit 15, 1.5 mi w, then 3.5 mi sw, follow signs. **Parking:** on-site.

MCALESTER pop. 17,783

AMERICINN LODGE & SUITES OF MCALESTER — *Book at AAA.com* — **Phone:** (918)426-1300

Hotel
$105-$170 All Year

Address: 609 S George Nigh Expwy 74501 **Location:** 1 mi s on US 69. **Facility:** Smoke free premises. 56 units. 55 one-bedroom standard units, some with whirlpools. 1 one-bedroom suite with whirlpool. 3 stories, interior corridors. *Bath:* combo or shower only. **Parking:** on-site. **Amenities:** video library, DVD players, high-speed Internet, voice mail, irons, hair dryers. **Pool(s):** heated indoor. **Leisure Activities:** whirlpool, exercise room. **Guest Services:** valet and coin laundry, wireless Internet. **Business Services:** PC. CALL

BEST WESTERN INN OF MCALESTER — *Book great rates at AAA.com* — **Phone:** (918)426-0115

Hotel
$89-$129 All Year

Address: 1215 George Nigh Expwy 74502 **Location:** 3 mi s on US 69. **Facility:** 61 one-bedroom standard units. 2 stories (no elevator), exterior corridors. **Parking:** on-site. **Amenities:** high-speed Internet, irons, hair dryers. **Pool(s):** outdoor. **Guest Services:** valet laundry, wireless Internet. **Business Services:** PC. **Free Special Amenities: continental breakfast and high-speed Internet.**

/ SOME UNITS

AAA Benefit:
Members save up to 20%, plus 10% bonus points with rewards program.

COMFORT SUITES — *Book at AAA.com* — **Phone:** (918)302-0001

Hotel
$108-$130 All Year

Address: 650 George Nigh Expwy 74501 **Location:** 1.2 mi s on US 69. **Facility:** Smoke free premises. 80 units. 79 one-bedroom standard units, some with whirlpools. 1 one-bedroom suite with kitchen. 3 stories, interior corridors. *Bath:* combo or shower only. **Parking:** on-site. **Amenities:** high-speed Internet, dual phone lines, voice mail, irons, hair dryers. **Pool(s):** outdoor. **Leisure Activities:** whirlpool, exercise room. **Guest Services:** valet and coin laundry, wireless Internet. **Business Services:** meeting rooms, PC. ASK / SOME UNITS

HAPPY DAYS HOTEL — **Phone:** 918/429-0910

AAA SAVE

Hotel
Rates not provided

Address: 1400 S George Nigh Expwy 74501 **Location:** 3.3 mi s on US 69. **Facility:** Smoke free premises. 61 units. 60 one-bedroom standard units. 1 two-bedroom suite with whirlpool. 2 stories (no elevator), interior corridors. *Bath:* combo or shower only. **Parking:** on-site. **Amenities:** high-speed Internet, irons, hair dryers. **Pool(s):** outdoor. **Guest Services:** valet and coin laundry, wireless Internet. **Business Services:** PC. **Free Special Amenities: expanded continental breakfast and high-speed Internet.** / SOME UNITS

HOLIDAY INN EXPRESS HOTEL & SUITES *Book at AAA.com* **Phone:** (918)423-1118

Hotel
$99-$159 All Year

Address: 1811 Peaceable Rd 74501 **Location:** 1.2 mi s on US 69. **Facility:** Smoke free premises. 99 one-bedroom standard units. 4 stories, interior corridors. *Bath:* combo or shower only. **Parking:** on-site. **Amenities:** video games (fee), high-speed Internet, voice mail, irons, hair dryers. **Pool(s):** heated outdoor. **Leisure Activities:** whirlpool, exercise room. **Guest Services:** valet and coin laundry, wireless Internet. **Business Services:** meeting rooms, business center.

ASK CALL

WHERE TO DINE

GIA COMO'S RESTAURANT **Phone:** 918/423-2662

Italian
$14-$26

This restaurant features well-prepared, generous portions of traditional Italian meals in a friendly, warm, family-style atmosphere. The steaks are also good, and the staff provides pleasant, prompt service. The spumoni ice cream is worth a taste. Casual dress. **Bar:** Beer only. **Reservations:** suggested, weekends. **Hours:** 11:30 am-9 pm. Closed major holidays; also Sun & Mon. **Address:** 501 S George Nigh Expwy 74501 **Location:** 2 mi e on US 69. **Parking:** on-site.

MEERS

WHERE TO DINE

THE MEERS STORE & RESTAURANT **Phone:** 580/429-8051

American
$4-$16

The down-home barbecue ribs choice is the signature dish at the Meers Store, which is located in a historic grocery store in an old mining town. The burgers are popular too. The atmosphere is rustic and friendly to families. Casual dress. **Bar:** Beer only. **Hours:** 10:30 am-8 pm; hours vary in winter. Closed: 11/25, 12/25. **Address:** 26005 State Hwy 115 73507 **Location:** I-44, exit 45, 12 mi nw, follow signs on SR 49 and 17. **Parking:** on-site.

MIAMI pop. 13,704

HAMPTON INN *Book great rates at AAA.com* **Phone:** (918)541-1500

Hotel
$79-$149 All Year

Address: 115 Deacon Turner Rd 74354 **Location:** I-44, exit 313, just w. **Facility:** 74 one-bedroom standard units. 3 stories, interior corridors. *Bath:* combo or shower only. **Parking:** on-site. **Terms:** 1-7 night minimum stay, cancellation fee imposed. **Amenities:** high-speed Internet, voice mail, irons, hair dryers. **Pool(s):** heated indoor. **Leisure Activities:** exercise room. **Guest Services:** coin laundry, wireless Internet. **Business Services:** meeting rooms, business center.

CALL / SOME UNITS

AAA Benefit:
Members save up to 10% everyday!

MICROTEL INN & SUITES *Book great rates at AAA.com* **Phone:** (918)540-3333

Hotel
$61-$105 All Year

Address: 2015 E Steve Owens Blvd 74355 **Location:** I-44, exit 313, just w. **Facility:** 60 one-bedroom standard units, some with whirlpools. 2 stories (no elevator), interior corridors. *Bath:* combo or shower only. **Parking:** on-site. **Amenities:** voice mail. *Some:* irons, hair dryers. **Pool(s):** heated indoor. **Leisure Activities:** whirlpool, exercise room. **Guest Services:** coin laundry, wireless Internet. **Business Services:** meeting rooms, PC. **Free Special Amenities: continental breakfast and high-speed Internet.**

/ SOME UNITS FEE

WHERE TO DINE

MONTANA MIKE'S **Phone:** 918/542-8808

Steak
$7-$20

This steakhouse offers a dining experience for the whole family. A rustic look with Western appointments characterizes the dining room. Although it's hard to go wrong with a hearty steak of USDA Choice aged beef, guests also can try smoked, fire-grilled chicken breast, chicken-fried steak, baby back ribs and other selections. Casual dress. **Bar:** Full bar. **Hours:** 11 am-9 pm, Fri & Sat-10 pm. Closed: 11/25, 12/25. **Address:** 840 N Main 74354 **Location:** Just n of jct 1st St. **Parking:** on-site.

MIDWEST CITY—See Oklahoma City p. 629.

MOORE—See Oklahoma City p. 631.

MUSKOGEE pop. 38,310

COMFORT INN *Book at AAA.com* **Phone:** (918)682-3724

Hotel
$110-$160 All Year

Address: 3133 Azalea Park Dr 74401 **Location:** Jct US 62 and 69, just sw. **Facility:** 54 one-bedroom standard units, some with whirlpools. 2 stories (no elevator), interior corridors. *Bath:* combo or shower only. **Parking:** on-site. **Terms:** 3 night minimum stay - seasonal, 3 day cancellation notice. **Amenities:** high-speed Internet, voice mail, irons, hair dryers. **Pool(s):** outdoor. **Leisure Activities:** exercise room. **Guest Services:** coin laundry, wireless Internet. **Business Services:** business center.

ASK / SOME UNITS

HAMPTON INN *Book great rates at AAA.com* **Phone:** 918/682-2587

Hotel
Rates not provided

Address: 3100 Military Blvd 74401 **Location:** Just se of jct US 62 and 69. **Facility:** 64 one-bedroom standard units, some with whirlpools. 3 stories, interior corridors. *Bath:* combo or shower only. **Parking:** on-site. **Amenities:** high-speed Internet, dual phone lines, voice mail, irons, hair dryers. **Pool(s):** heated indoor. **Leisure Activities:** sauna, whirlpool, exercise room. **Guest Services:** valet and coin laundry, wireless Internet. **Business Services:** business center.
/ SOME UNITS

AAA Benefit:
Members save up to 10% everyday!

HOLIDAY INN EXPRESS HOTEL & SUITES *Book at AAA.com* **Phone:** (918)687-4224

Hotel
$110-$199 All Year

Address: 2701 W Shawnee 74401 **Location:** Just se of jct US 62 and 69. **Facility:** 70 one-bedroom standard units, some with whirlpools. 3 stories, interior corridors. *Bath:* combo or shower only. **Parking:** on-site. **Amenities:** high-speed Internet, voice mail, irons, hair dryers. **Pool(s):** heated indoor. **Leisure Activities:** sauna, whirlpool, exercise room. **Guest Services:** coin laundry, wireless Internet. **Business Services:** meeting rooms, business center.
ASK CALL

LA QUINTA INN & SUITES MUSKOGEE *Book great rates at AAA.com* **Phone:** (918)687-9000

AAA SAVE

Hotel
$69-$179 All Year

Address: 3031 Military Blvd 74401 **Location:** Just se of jct US 62 and 69. **Facility:** Smoke free premises. 69 one-bedroom standard units, some with whirlpools. 3 stories, interior corridors. *Bath:* combo or shower only. **Parking:** on-site. **Amenities:** high-speed Internet, voice mail, irons, hair dryers. *Some:* dual phone lines. **Pool(s):** heated indoor. **Leisure Activities:** whirlpool, exercise room. **Guest Services:** coin laundry, wireless Internet. **Business Services:** meeting rooms, PC. **Free Special Amenities: continental breakfast.** / SOME UNITS

WHERE TO DINE

CHINA KING SUPER BUFFET **Phone:** 918/686-9888

Chinese
$6-$8

The buffet lines up a large variety of entrees, soups, egg rolls and desserts. Casual dress. **Hours:** 11 am-9 pm, Fri & Sat-9:30 pm. Closed: 11/25, 12/25. **Address:** 231 W Shawnee Ave 74401 **Location:** 2.2 mi e of jct US 69 and 62. **Parking:** on-site.

MAHYLON'S **Phone:** 918/686-7427

Barbecue
$5-$11

This restaurant's rustic, log cabin atmosphere with knotty pine walls and high ceilings is the perfect setting for their hickory-smoked barbecue dishes. They serve good-sized portions of barbecue chicken, pork and beef in a traditional plate presentation. Casual dress. **Bar:** Beer only. **Reservations:** not accepted. **Hours:** 11 am-9 pm. Closed major holidays; also Sun & Mon. **Address:** 3301 Chandler Rd 74403 **Location:** Off Muskogee Tpke, exit Chandler Rd, 1.2 mi w. **Parking:** on-site.

MISS ADDIE'S TEA ROOM **Phone:** 918/682-1506

American
$6-$25

Located in a restored drugstore dating to 1915, Miss Addie's features fresh ingredients, good flavors, pleasant service, bright ambience and a pianist Friday and Saturday. The ever changing menu offers steak, fresh salmon, shrimp provencal and Saturday brunch. Casual dress. **Bar:** Full bar. **Reservations:** accepted. **Hours:** 11 am-9 pm, Fri & Sat-9:30 pm; Saturday brunch. Closed: 1/1, 11/25, 12/24, 12/25; also Sun. **Address:** 821 W Broadway 74401 **Location:** At 9th St and Broadway; downtown. **Parking:** on-site and street.

SPEEDWAY GRILLE **Phone:** 918/687-6552

American
$3-$6

There's nothing fancy here, just good, old-fashioned hamburgers, sandwiches, french fries and one of the favorites, chili. Casual dress. **Hours:** 5:30 am-3 pm, Sat-2:30 pm. Closed major holidays; also Sun. **Address:** 2010 W Okmulgee Ave 74401 **Location:** 0.6 mi e of jct US 69. **Parking:** on-site.

NORMAN—See Oklahoma City p. 631.

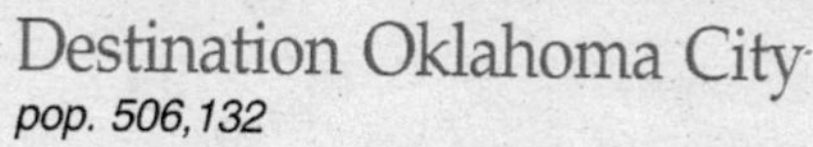

Destination Oklahoma City

pop. 506,132

The Wild West. American Indians, oil wells, bucking broncos and undaunted cowboys paint a picture of the lives led by those who called the land west of the Mississippi River home.

Today Oklahoma City celebrates its Old West heritage with American Indian festivals, rodeos and a wagonload of national and international horse shows.

Oklahoma City CVB

Lake Hefner, Oklahoma City. (See mention page 268)

© Gibson Stock Photography

Oklahoma City skyline.

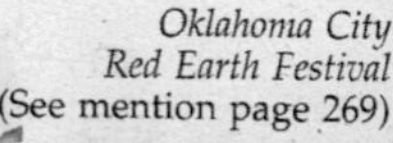

Oklahoma City Red Earth Festival (See mention page 269)

Oklahoma City Red Earth Festival

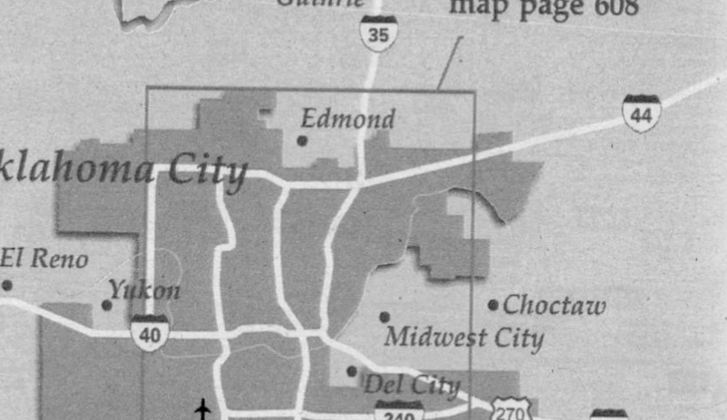

Civic Center Music Hall, Oklahoma City. (See mention page 269)

Oklahoma City CVB

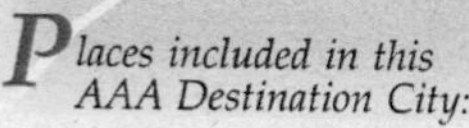

Places included in this AAA Destination City:

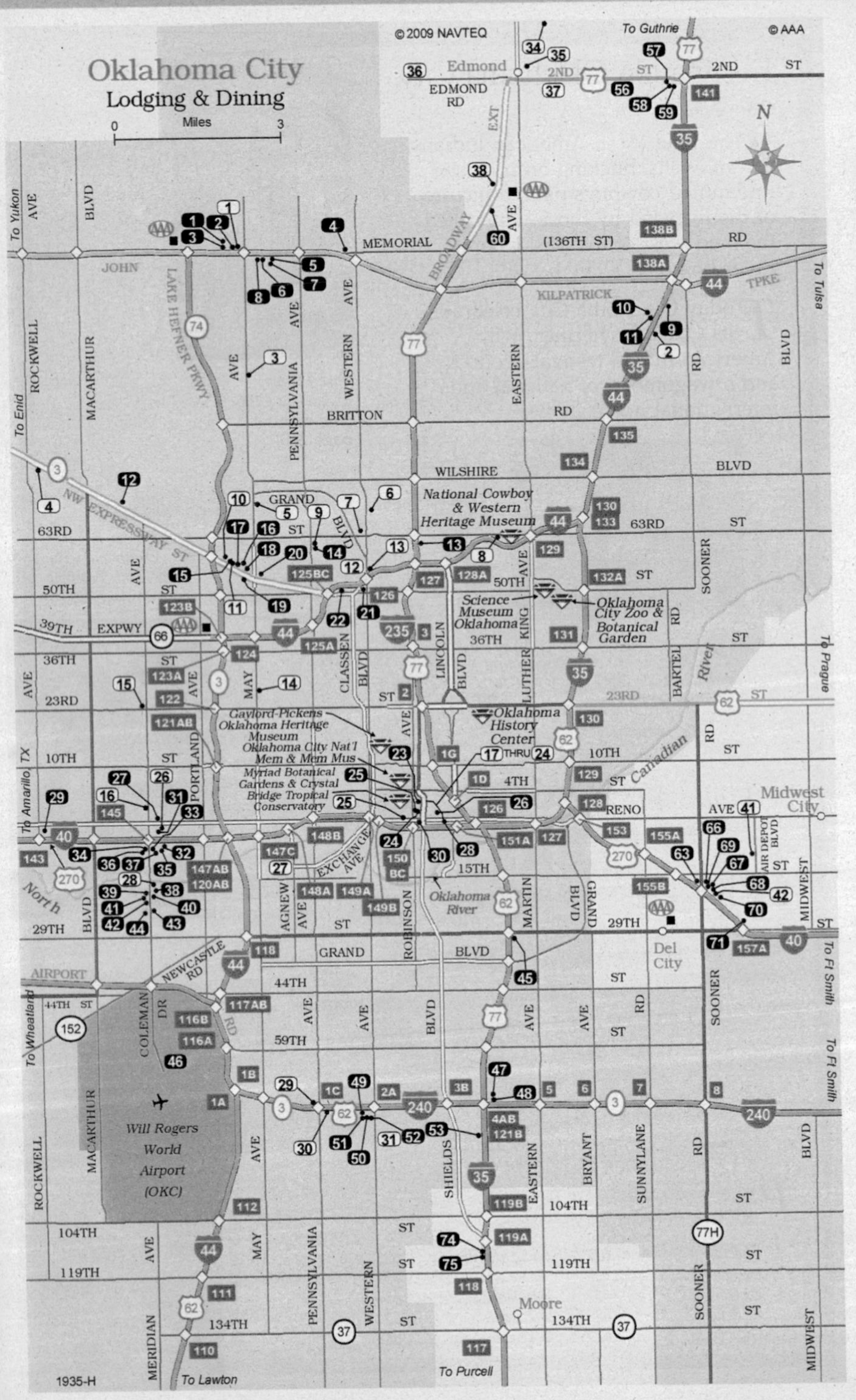
Oklahoma City
Lodging & Dining
0 Miles 3
© 2009 NAVTEQ
© AAA
To Guthrie
Edmond
To Yukon
To Enid
To Tulsa
To Prague
To Amarillo, TX
To Wheatland
To Ft Smith
To Lawton
To Purcell
National Cowboy & Western Heritage Museum
Science Museum Oklahoma
Oklahoma City Zoo & Botanical Garden
Gaylord-Pickens Oklahoma Heritage Museum
Oklahoma City Nat'l Mem & Mem Mus
Myriad Botanical Gardens & Crystal Bridge Tropical Conservatory
Oklahoma History Center
Will Rogers World Airport (OKC)
Midwest City
Del City
Moore
Oklahoma River
North Canadian River
1935-H

Airport Accommodations

Map Page	OA	WILL ROGERS WORLD	Diamond Rated	High Season	Page
39 / p. 608	AAA	**Embassy Suites, 3.5 mi n of terminal**	◆◆◆	$109-$209 SAVE	616
46 / p. 608	AAA	**Four Points by Sheraton Oklahoma City, just n of terminal**	◆◆◆	Rates not provided SAVE	616
43 / p. 608	AAA	**Governors Suites Hotel, 2 mi n of terminal**	◆◆◆	$69-$99 SAVE	616
41 / p. 608		Hampton Inn OKC Airport, 3.5 mi n of terminal	◆◆◆	$119-$149	618
40 / p. 608	AAA	**Hyatt Place Oklahoma City Airport, 3.5 mi n of terminal**	◆◆◆	$79-$209 SAVE	619
42 / p. 608		Wingate Inn, 3.5 mi n of terminal	◆◆◆	Rates not provided	622

Oklahoma City and Vicinity

This index helps you "spot" where approved lodgings and restaurants are located on the corresponding detailed maps. Lodging daily rate range is for comparison only and show the property's high season. Restaurant rate range is a combination of lunch and/or dinner. Turn to the listing page for more detailed rate information and consult display ads for special promotions.

OKLAHOMA CITY

Map Page	OA	Lodgings	Diamond Rated	High Season	Page
1 / p. 608		Hilton Garden Inn Oklahoma City North Quail Springs	◆◆◆	$89-$169	618
2 / p. 608		La Quinta Inn & Suites-Quail Springs	◆◆◆	$89-$229	619
3 / p. 608		SpringHill Suites by Marriott	◆◆◆	$98-$120	622
4 / p. 608	AAA	**Best Western Memorial Inn & Suites**	◆◆◆	$85-$99 SAVE	613
5 / p. 608		Comfort Inn & Suites Quail Springs	◆◆◆	$80-$109	614
6 / p. 608		Fairfield Inn by Marriott-Quail Springs	◆◆	$86-$105	616
7 / p. 608		Courtyard by Marriott	◆◆◆	$116-$142	615
8 / p. 608		Hampton Inn by Hilton-Quail Springs	◆◆◆	$99-$119	617
9 / p. 608		Sleep Inn & Suites	◆◆	$79-$140	621
10 / p. 608	AAA	**Comfort Inn North**	◆◆	$70-$125 SAVE	614
11 / p. 608		Econo Lodge	◆◆	Rates not provided	616
12 / p. 608		La Quinta Inn & Suites Oklahoma City (Northwest Expressway)	◆◆◆	$49-$114	619
13 / p. 608	AAA	**Best Western Broadway Inn & Suites**	◆◆◆	$90-$120 SAVE	613
14 / p. 608	AAA	**Waterford Marriott Hotel**	◆◆◆◆	$152-$186 SAVE	622
15 / p. 608		Oklahoma City Marriott	◆◆◆	$153-$187	619
16 / p. 608	AAA	**Comfort Inn at Founders Tower**	◆◆	$89-$109 SAVE	614
17 / p. 608		Country Inn & Suites By Carlson, Oklahoma City-NW Express	◆◆◆	$76-$107	615
18 / p. 608		Crowne Plaza Hotel	◆◆◆	$79-$179	616
19 / p. 608	AAA	**Hampton Inn NW**	◆◆◆	$95-$129 SAVE	617
20 / p. 608		Holiday Inn Express Hotel & Suites Penn Square	◆◆◆	Rates not provided	618
21 / p. 608		Sleep Inn & Suites	◆◆	$60-$150	621
22 / p. 608		Courtyard by Marriott-NW	◆◆◆	$107-$131	615
23 / p. 608	AAA	**Skirvin Hilton** - see color ad p 621	◆◆◆◆	$149-$269 SAVE	620

OKLAHOMA CITY (cont'd)

Map Page	OA	Lodgings (cont'd)	Diamond Rated	High Season	Page
24 / p. 608	AAA	**Renaissance Oklahoma City Convention Center, Hotel & Spa**	◆◆◆◆	$179-$219 SAVE	619
25 / p. 608	AAA	**Sheraton Oklahoma City**	◆◆◆	Rates not provided SAVE	620
26 / p. 608		Hampton Inn & Suites Oklahoma City-Bricktown	◆◆◆	$119-$139	617
27 / p. 608	AAA	**Residence Inn by Marriott-Oklahoma City West**	◆◆◆	$161-$197 SAVE	620
28 / p. 608	AAA	**Residence Inn by Marriott**	◆◆◆	$179-$219 SAVE	620
29 / p. 608		Homewood Suites Oklahoma City-West	◆◆◆	$95-$149	618
30 / p. 608	AAA	**Courtyard by Marriott-Downtown/Bricktown**	◆◆◆	$161-$197 SAVE	615
31 / p. 608	AAA	**Best Western Saddleback Inn & Conference Center** - see color ad p 614	◆◆◆	$89-$159 SAVE	613
32 / p. 608	AAA	**Comfort Inn**	◆◆	$74-$109 SAVE	614
33 / p. 608		La Quinta Inn Oklahoma City (Airport)	◆◆◆	$49-$125	619
34 / p. 608		Hilton Garden Inn Oklahoma City Airport	◆◆◆	$89-$179	618
35 / p. 608		Courtyard by Marriott Airport	◆◆◆	$107-$131	615
36 / p. 608	AAA	**Sleep Inn**	◆◆	$60-$80 SAVE	621
37 / p. 608		Holiday Inn Express Hotel & Suites	◆◆◆	$89-$159	618
38 / p. 608		Candlewood Suites Hotel	◆◆	$104-$124	613
39 / p. 608	AAA	**Embassy Suites**	◆◆◆	$109-$209 SAVE	616
40 / p. 608	AAA	**Hyatt Place Oklahoma City Airport**	◆◆◆	$79-$209 SAVE	619
41 / p. 608		Hampton Inn OKC Airport	◆◆◆	$119-$149	618
42 / p. 608		Wingate Inn	◆◆◆	Rates not provided	622
43 / p. 608	AAA	**Governors Suites Hotel**	◆◆◆	$69-$99 SAVE	616
44 / p. 608	AAA	**Country Inn & Suites By Carlson, Oklahoma City Airport**	◆◆◆	$99-$159 SAVE	615
45 / p. 608		Super 8 Bricktown	◆	Rates not provided	622
46 / p. 608	AAA	**Four Points by Sheraton Oklahoma City**	◆◆◆	Rates not provided SAVE	616
47 / p. 608		Fairfield Inn by Marriott Crossroads Mall	◆◆	$98-$120	616
48 / p. 608		Residence Inn by Marriott Oklahoma City South-Crossroads Mall	◆◆◆	$170-$208	620
49 / p. 608		Holiday Inn Express	◆◆	$80-$85	618
50 / p. 608		Quality Inn	◆◆	$60-$90	619
51 / p. 608	AAA	**Best Western Barsana Hotel & Suites**	◆◆◆	$81-$146 SAVE	613
52 / p. 608		Hampton Inn & Suites	◆◆◆	$82-$89	617
53 / p. 608		Baymont Inn	◆◆	$39-$89	613

Map Page	OA	Restaurants	Diamond Rated	Cuisine	Meal Range	Page
1 / p. 608		Abuelo's The Flavor of Mexico	◆◆◆	Mexican	$6-$17	622
2 / p. 608		Charly's Restaurant	◆	American	$4-$8	624

Map Page	OA	Restaurants (cont'd)	Diamond Rated	Cuisine	Meal Range	Page
3 / p. 608		Papa Dio's Italian Restaurant & Wine Bar	◆◆	Italian	$6-$23	625
4 / p. 608		Hunan Wok Restaurant	◆	Chinese	$5-$11	625
5 / p. 608		La Baguette Bistro Casual Restaurant & Bakery	◆◆	French	$7-$23	625
6 / p. 608		Charlie Newton's	◆◆◆	American	$11-$33	624
7 / p. 608		The Coach House	◆◆◆◆	American	$15-$55	624
8 / p. 608		The County Line Barbecue	◆◆	American	$7-$19	624
9 / p. 608		Bellini's Ristorante & Grill	◆◆◆	Italian	$8-$48	622
10 / p. 608		Beverly's Pancake House	◆◆	American	$5-$12	623
11 / p. 608		J W's Steakhouse	◆◆◆	Steak	$18-$38	625
12 / p. 608	AAA	**Pearl's Oyster Bar**	◆◆	Seafood	$6-$18	625
13 / p. 608		Deep Fork Grill	◆◆	Continental	$8-$34	624
14 / p. 608		Ted's Cafe Escondido	◆◆	Mexican	$8-$14	626
15 / p. 608	AAA	**Gopuram, Taste of India**	◆◆	Indian	$6-$15	624
16 / p. 608	AAA	**Cimarron Steak House**	◆◆	Steak	$6-$22	624
17 / p. 608		Mantel Wine Bar & Bistro	◆◆◆	American	$9-$35	625
18 / p. 608		Abuelo's The Flavor of Mexico	◆◆◆	Mexican	$6-$17	622
19 / p. 608		Bricktown Brewery	◆◆	American	$6-$16	623
20 / p. 608	AAA	**Nonna's Euro-American Ristorante and Bar**	◆◆◆	American	$11-$42	625
21 / p. 608		Mickey Mantle's Steakhouse	◆◆◆	Steak	$20-$35	625
22 / p. 608		Chelino's Mexican Restaurant	◆◆	Mexican	$6-$13	624
23 / p. 608		Coach's BBQ Pizza & Brewery	◆◆	Barbecue	$7-$16	624
24 / p. 608		Bourbon Street Cafe	◆◆	Cajun	$6-$20	623
25 / p. 608		LaLuna Mexican Cafe	◆◆	Mexican	$6-$15	625
26 / p. 608	AAA	**Trapper's Fishcamp & Grill**	◆◆	American	$7-$23	626
27 / p. 608		Cattlemen's Steakhouse	◆◆	Steak	$8-$25	623
28 / p. 608		Golden Palace	◆◆	Chinese	$5-$12	624
29 / p. 608		Aloha Garden Restaurant	◆◆	Chinese	$5-$11	622
30 / p. 608		Hunan Chinese Restaurant	◆	Chinese	$6-$8	625
31 / p. 608		Ted's Cafe Escondido	◆◆	Mexican	$8-$14	626

EDMOND

Map Page	OA	Lodgings	Diamond Rated	High Season	Page
56 / p. 608	AAA	**Best Western Edmond Inn & Suites**	◆◆	$86-$91 SAVE	627
57 / p. 608		Holiday Inn Express Hotel & Suites	◆◆◆	$114-$159	627
58 / p. 608	AAA	**Fairfield Inn & Suites by Marriott**	◆◆◆	$103-$125 SAVE	627
59 / p. 608		Hampton Inn	◆◆◆	$87-$175	627
60 / p. 608		Sleep Inn & Suites	◆◆	$80-$145	628

Map Page	OA	Restaurants	Diamond Rated	Cuisine	Meal Range	Page
34 / p. 608		Ted's Cafe Escondido	2 diamonds	Mexican	$9-$16	628
35 / p. 608		Papa Dino's Pizza	1 diamond	Pizza	$3-$7	628
36 / p. 608		House of Hunan	2 diamonds	Chinese	$4-$22	628
37 / p. 608		Alvarado's	2 diamonds	Mexican	$5-$15	628
38 / p. 608		Coach's BBQ, Pizza & Brewery	2 diamonds	Barbecue	$7-$16	628

DEL CITY

Map Page	OA	Lodging	Diamond Rated	High Season	Page
63 / p. 608		La Quinta Inn Oklahoma City East (Del City)	2 diamonds	$45-$95	627

MIDWEST CITY

Map Page	OA	Lodgings	Diamond Rated	High Season	Page
66 / p. 608		Holiday Inn Express Hotel & Suites	3 diamonds	$99-$169	630
67 / p. 608	AAA	**Sheraton Midwest City Hotel at the Reed Conference Center**	3 diamonds	Rates not provided SAVE	630
68 / p. 608		Hampton Inn	3 diamonds	$104-$129	630
69 / p. 608	AAA	**Comfort Inn & Suites**	3 diamonds	$85-$131 SAVE	629
70 / p. 608		Hawthorn Suites	3 diamonds	$105-$125	630
71 / p. 608	AAA	**Best Western Midwest City Inn & Suites**	3 diamonds	$95-$115 SAVE	629

Map Page	OA	Restaurants	Diamond Rated	Cuisine	Meal Range	Page
41 / p. 608		Chequers Restaurant & Pub	2 diamonds	American	$5-$10	631
42 / p. 608		Primo's d' Italia	2 diamonds	Italian	$8-$16	631

MOORE

Map Page	OA	Lodgings	Diamond Rated	High Season	Page
74 / p. 608	AAA	**Best Western Green Tree Inn & Suites**	2 diamonds	$85-$99 SAVE	631
75 / p. 608		Comfort Inn & Suites	2 diamonds	$75-$125	631

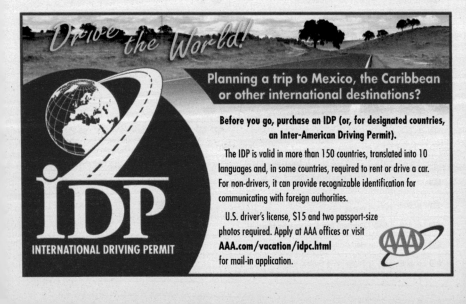

OKLAHOMA CITY pop. 506,132 (See map and index starting on p. 608)

BAYMONT INN Book at AAA.com Phone: (405)631-8661 53

Hotel
$39-$89 All Year

Address: 8315 I-35 S 73149 **Location:** I-35, exit 121A (82nd St), just sw. **Facility:** 121 units. 120 one-bedroom standard units. 1 one-bedroom suite. 2 stories (no elevator), exterior corridors. **Parking:** on-site. **Amenities:** voice mail, irons, hair dryers. *Some:* high-speed Internet. **Pool(s):** outdoor. **Guest Services:** coin laundry, wireless Internet. **Business Services:** meeting rooms.

FEE / SOME UNITS FEE FEE

BEST WESTERN BARSANA HOTEL & SUITES Book great rates at AAA.com Phone: (405)601-1200 51

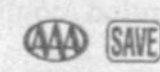

Hotel
$81-$146 All Year

Address: 7701 CA Henderson Blvd 73139 **Location:** I-240, exit 2A, just sw. **Facility:** Smoke free premises. 64 units. 62 one-bedroom standard units, some with whirlpools. 2 one-bedroom suites. 3 stories, interior corridors. *Bath:* combo or shower only. **Parking:** on-site. **Amenities:** high-speed Internet, voice mail, irons, hair dryers. **Pool(s):** heated indoor. **Leisure Activities:** exercise room. **Guest Services:** coin laundry, wireless Internet. **Business Services:** meeting rooms, PC. **Free Special Amenities: full breakfast and high-speed Internet.**

CALL

AAA Benefit:
Members save up to 20%, plus 10% bonus points with rewards program.

BEST WESTERN BROADWAY INN & SUITES Book great rates at AAA.com Phone: (405)848-1919 13

Hotel
$90-$120 All Year

Address: 6101 N Santa Fe 73118 **Location:** I-44, exit 127, just e on 63rd St, then just s. **Facility:** 96 one-bedroom standard units, some with whirlpools. 3 stories, interior corridors. **Parking:** on-site. **Amenities:** voice mail, irons, hair dryers. **Pool(s):** outdoor. **Leisure Activities:** whirlpool. **Guest Services:** valet and coin laundry, wireless Internet. **Business Services:** meeting rooms, PC. **Free Special Amenities: local telephone calls and high-speed Internet.**

/ SOME UNITS FEE

AAA Benefit:
Members save up to 20%, plus 10% bonus points with rewards program.

BEST WESTERN MEMORIAL INN & SUITES Book great rates at AAA.com Phone: (405)286-5199 4

Hotel
$85-$99 All Year

Address: 1301 W Memorial Rd 73114 **Location:** John Kilpatrick Tpke, exit Western Ave, just nw. **Facility:** 60 one-bedroom standard units, some with whirlpools. 3 stories, interior corridors. *Bath:* combo or shower only. **Parking:** on-site. **Amenities:** high-speed Internet, voice mail, irons, hair dryers. **Pool(s):** heated indoor. **Leisure Activities:** whirlpool, exercise room. **Guest Services:** valet and coin laundry, wireless Internet. **Business Services:** meeting rooms, business center. **Free Special Amenities: full breakfast and high-speed Internet.**

CALL / SOME UNITS FEE

AAA Benefit:
Members save up to 20%, plus 10% bonus points with rewards program.

BEST WESTERN SADDLEBACK INN & CONFERENCE CENTER Book great rates at AAA.com Phone: (405)947-7000 31

Hotel
$89-$159 All Year

Address: 4300 SW 3rd St 73108 **Location:** I-40, exit 145 (Meridian Ave), just ne. **Facility:** 220 one-bedroom standard units. 3 stories, interior/exterior corridors. **Parking:** on-site. **Amenities:** high-speed Internet, voice mail, safes, irons, hair dryers. *Some:* DVD players, CD players. **Pool(s):** outdoor. **Leisure Activities:** sauna, whirlpool, exercise room. **Guest Services:** valet and coin laundry, airport transportation-Will Rogers World Airport, area transportation-within 5 mi, wireless Internet. **Business Services:** conference facilities, business center. *(See color ad p 614)*

/ SOME UNITS FEE

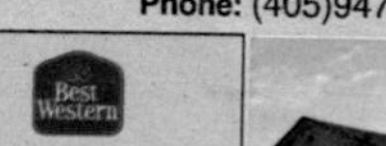

AAA Benefit:
Members save up to 20%, plus 10% bonus points with rewards program.

FREE full breakfast and high-speed Internet

CANDLEWOOD SUITES HOTEL Book at AAA.com Phone: (405)680-8770 38

Extended Stay Hotel
$104-$124 All Year

Address: 4400 River Park Dr 73108 **Location:** I-40, exit 145 (Meridian Ave), 1.1 mi s. **Facility:** 122 units. 98 one-bedroom standard units with efficiencies. 24 one-bedroom suites with kitchens. 3 stories, interior corridors. *Bath:* combo or shower only. **Parking:** on-site. **Terms:** cancellation fee imposed. **Amenities:** video library, DVD players, high-speed Internet, voice mail, irons, hair dryers. **Leisure Activities:** exercise room. **Guest Services:** valet and coin laundry.

ASK CALL / SOME UNITS FEE

(See map and index starting on p. 608)

COMFORT INN Book great rates at AAA.com **Phone:** (405)943-4400 32

Hotel
$74-$109 All Year

Address: 4240 W I-40 Service Rd 73108 **Location:** I-40, exit 145 (Meridian Ave), just e on south frontage road. **Facility:** 50 one-bedroom standard units. 2 stories (no elevator), interior/exterior corridors. *Bath:* combo or shower only. **Parking:** on-site. **Amenities:** high-speed Internet, irons, hair dryers. **Pool(s):** outdoor. **Leisure Activities:** exercise room. **Guest Services:** coin laundry, wireless Internet. **Business Services:** PC. **Free Special Amenities: expanded continental breakfast and high-speed Internet.** / SOME UNITS

COMFORT INN & SUITES QUAIL SPRINGS Book at AAA.com **Phone:** (405)286-2700 5

Hotel
$80-$109 All Year

Address: 13501 N Highland Park Blvd 73120 **Location:** John Kilpatrick Tpke, exit May Ave, just e on south frontage road. **Facility:** Smoke free premises. 68 one-bedroom standard units, some with whirlpools. 4 stories, interior corridors. *Bath:* combo or shower only. **Parking:** on-site. **Amenities:** high-speed Internet, voice mail, irons, hair dryers. **Pool(s):** heated indoor. **Leisure Activities:** exercise room. **Guest Services:** valet and coin laundry, wireless Internet. **Business Services:** meeting rooms, business center. ASK CALL

COMFORT INN AT FOUNDERS TOWER Book great rates at AAA.com **Phone:** (405)810-1100 16

Hotel
$89-$109 All Year

Address: 5704 Mosteller Dr 73112 **Location:** 0.5 mi e of jct SR 3 and 74. **Facility:** Smoke free premises. 51 one-bedroom standard units, some with whirlpools. 3 stories, interior corridors. *Bath:* combo or shower only. **Parking:** on-site. **Amenities:** high-speed Internet, dual phone lines, voice mail, irons, hair dryers. **Leisure Activities:** exercise room. **Guest Services:** valet and coin laundry, wireless Internet. **Business Services:** business center. **Free Special Amenities: expanded continental breakfast and high-speed Internet.**

COMFORT INN NORTH Book great rates at AAA.com **Phone:** (405)478-7282 10

Hotel
$70-$125 All Year

Address: 4625 NE 120th St 73131 **Location:** I-35, exit 137 (122nd St), just sw. **Facility:** 60 one-bedroom standard units, some with whirlpools. 2 stories (no elevator), interior corridors. *Bath:* combo or shower only. **Parking:** on-site. **Terms:** cancellation fee imposed. **Amenities:** voice mail, irons, hair dryers. **Pool(s):** heated indoor. **Leisure Activities:** whirlpool, exercise room. **Guest Services:** coin laundry, wireless Internet. **Business Services:** meeting rooms, PC.
/ SOME UNITS FEE

▼ See AAA listing p 613 ▼

(See map and index starting on p. 608)

COUNTRY INN & SUITES BY CARLSON, OKLAHOMA CITY AIRPORT *Book great rates at AAA.com* **Phone:** (405)605-8300 44

AAA SAVE

Hotel
$99-$159 All Year

Address: 2415 S Meridian Ave 73108 **Location:** I-40, exit 145 (Meridian Ave), 1.3 mi s. **Facility:** Smoke free premises. 102 units. 67 one-bedroom standard units, some with whirlpools. 35 one-bedroom suites. 4 stories, interior corridors. *Bath:* combo or shower only. **Parking:** on-site. **Terms:** cancellation fee imposed. **Amenities:** high-speed Internet, irons, hair dryers. **Pool(s):** heated indoor. **Leisure Activities:** whirlpool, exercise room. **Guest Services:** valet and coin laundry, airport transportation-Will Rogers World airport, wireless Internet. **Business Services:** meeting rooms, business center. **Free Special Amenities: full breakfast and high-speed Internet.**

CALL

COUNTRY INN & SUITES BY CARLSON, OKLAHOMA CITY-NW EXPRESS *Book at AAA.com* **Phone:** (405)843-2002 17

Hotel
$76-$107 All Year

Address: 3141 Northwest Expwy 73112 **Location:** 0.4 mi e of jct SR 74 and 3. **Facility:** 80 units. 68 one-bedroom standard units. 12 one-bedroom suites, some with whirlpools. 10 stories, interior corridors. *Bath:* combo or shower only. **Parking:** on-site. **Terms:** cancellation fee imposed. **Amenities:** high-speed Internet, dual phone lines, voice mail, irons, hair dryers. **Pool(s):** outdoor. **Leisure Activities:** exercise room. **Guest Services:** valet and coin laundry. **Business Services:** meeting rooms, business center. ASK / SOME UNITS FEE

COURTYARD BY MARRIOTT *Book great rates at AAA.com* **Phone:** (405)418-4000 7

Hotel
$116-$142 All Year

Address: 13511 Highland Park Blvd 73120 **Location:** John Kilpatrick Tpke, exit May Ave, just e on south frontage road. **Facility:** Smoke free premises. 110 units. 109 one-bedroom standard units, some with whirlpools. 1 one-bedroom suite with whirlpool. 4 stories, interior corridors. *Bath:* combo or shower only. **Parking:** on-site. **Terms:** cancellation fee imposed. **Amenities:** high-speed Internet, dual phone lines, voice mail, irons, hair dryers. **Pool(s):** heated indoor/outdoor. **Leisure Activities:** whirlpool, exercise room. **Guest Services:** valet and coin laundry, wireless Internet. **Business Services:** meeting rooms, business center.

AAA Benefit: Members save a minimum 5% off the best available rate.

COURTYARD BY MARRIOTT AIRPORT *Book great rates at AAA.com* **Phone:** (405)946-6500 35

Hotel
$107-$131 All Year

Address: 4301 Highline Blvd 73108 **Location:** I-40, exit 145 (Meridian Ave), just e on south frontage road. **Facility:** Smoke free premises. 149 units. 137 one-bedroom standard units. 12 one-bedroom suites. 3 stories, interior corridors. *Bath:* combo or shower only. **Parking:** on-site. **Terms:** cancellation fee imposed. **Amenities:** high-speed Internet, dual phone lines, voice mail, irons, hair dryers. **Pool(s):** heated outdoor. **Leisure Activities:** whirlpool, exercise room. **Guest Services:** valet and coin laundry, wireless Internet. **Business Services:** meeting rooms, business center. / SOME UNITS

AAA Benefit: Members save a minimum 5% off the best available rate.

COURTYARD BY MARRIOTT-DOWNTOWN/BRICKTOWN *Book great rates at AAA.com* **Phone:** (405)232-2290 30

AAA SAVE

Hotel
$161-$197 All Year

Address: 2 W Reno Ave 73102 **Location:** Gaylord and Reno aves; downtown. **Facility:** Smoke free premises. 225 units. 213 one-bedroom standard units, some with whirlpools. 12 one-bedroom suites. 8 stories, interior corridors. *Bath:* combo or shower only. **Parking:** on-site (fee) and valet. **Terms:** cancellation fee imposed. **Amenities:** video games (fee), high-speed Internet, dual phone lines, voice mail, safes, irons, hair dryers. **Pool(s):** heated indoor. **Leisure Activities:** whirlpool, exercise room. **Guest Services:** valet and coin laundry, wireless Internet. **Business Services:** meeting rooms, business center. **Free Special Amenities: newspaper.**

CALL / SOME UNITS FEE

AAA Benefit: Members save a minimum 5% off the best available rate.

COURTYARD BY MARRIOTT-NW *Book great rates at AAA.com* **Phone:** (405)848-0808 22

Hotel
$107-$131 All Year

Address: 1515 Northwest Expwy 73118 **Location:** I-44, exit 125C westbound; exit 125B eastbound, just e. **Facility:** Smoke free premises. 122 units. 118 one-bedroom standard units, some with whirlpools. 4 one-bedroom suites. 4 stories, interior corridors. *Bath:* combo or shower only. **Parking:** on-site. **Terms:** cancellation fee imposed. **Amenities:** high-speed Internet, voice mail, irons, hair dryers. **Pool(s):** heated indoor. **Leisure Activities:** whirlpool, exercise room. **Guest Services:** valet and coin laundry, wireless Internet. **Business Services:** meeting rooms, PC.

CALL / SOME UNITS FEE

AAA Benefit: Members save a minimum 5% off the best available rate.

(See map and index starting on p. 608)

CROWNE PLAZA HOTEL Book at AAA.com Phone: (405)848-4811 18

Hotel
$79-$179 All Year

Address: 2945 Northwest Expwy 73112 **Location:** 0.5 mi e of jct SR 74 and 3. **Facility:** Smoke free premises. 215 units. 213 one-bedroom standard units. 2 one-bedroom suites, some with whirlpools. 9 stories, interior/exterior corridors. *Bath:* some combo or shower only. **Parking:** on-site. **Terms:** cancellation fee imposed. **Amenities:** video games (fee), dual phone lines, voice mail, irons, hair dryers. **Pool(s):** outdoor. **Leisure Activities:** whirlpool, exercise room. **Guest Services:** valet laundry, wireless Internet. **Business Services:** meeting rooms, business center.

ASK / SOME UNITS FEE FEE

ECONO LODGE Book at AAA.com Phone: 405/478-0400 11

Hotel
Rates not provided

Address: 12001 N I-35 Service Rd 73131 **Location:** I-35, exit 137, just sw. **Facility:** 65 one-bedroom standard units. 2 stories (no elevator), exterior corridors. **Parking:** on-site, winter plug-ins. **Amenities:** irons, hair dryers. **Pool(s):** outdoor. **Guest Services:** coin laundry, wireless Internet.

/ SOME UNITS FEE

EMBASSY SUITES Book great rates at AAA.com Phone: (405)682-6000 39

Hotel
$109-$209 All Year

Address: 1815 S Meridian Ave 73108 **Location:** I-40, exit 145 (Meridian Ave), 1 mi s. **Facility:** 236 one-bedroom suites. 6 stories, interior corridors. **Parking:** on-site. **Terms:** 1-7 night minimum stay, cancellation fee imposed. **Amenities:** video games (fee), voice mail, irons, hair dryers. **Dining:** nightclub. **Pool(s):** heated indoor. **Leisure Activities:** sauna, whirlpool, exercise room. *Fee:* game room. **Guest Services:** valet and coin laundry, airport transportation-Will Rogers World Airport, wireless Internet. **Business Services:** meeting rooms, business center.

/ SOME UNITS FEE

EMBASSY SUITES HOTELS
AAA Benefit:
Members save 5% or more everyday!

FAIRFIELD INN BY MARRIOTT CROSSROADS MALL Book great rates at AAA.com Phone: (405)634-9595 47

Hotel
$98-$120 All Year

Address: 1101 E I-240 Service Rd 73149 **Location:** I-240, exit 4C eastbound; exit 5 westbound, 0.8 mi w. **Facility:** Smoke free premises. 81 one-bedroom standard units. 3 stories, interior corridors. *Bath:* combo or shower only. **Parking:** on-site. **Terms:** cancellation fee imposed. **Amenities:** voice mail, irons, hair dryers. **Pool(s):** heated indoor. **Leisure Activities:** whirlpool. **Guest Services:** valet laundry, wireless Internet. **Business Services:** PC.

/ SOME UNITS

FAIRFIELD INN Marriott
AAA Benefit:
Members save a minimum 5% off the best available rate.

FAIRFIELD INN BY MARRIOTT-QUAIL SPRINGS Book great rates at AAA.com Phone: (405)755-8686 6

Hotel
$86-$105 All Year

Address: 13520 Plaza Terr 73120 **Location:** John Kilpatrick Tpke, exit May Ave, just e on south frontage road. **Facility:** Smoke free premises. 63 one-bedroom standard units. 3 stories, interior corridors. *Bath:* combo or shower only. **Parking:** on-site. **Terms:** cancellation fee imposed. **Amenities:** voice mail, irons, hair dryers. **Pool(s):** heated indoor. **Leisure Activities:** whirlpool. **Guest Services:** valet laundry, wireless Internet. **Business Services:** PC.

/ SOME UNITS

FAIRFIELD INN Marriott
AAA Benefit:
Members save a minimum 5% off the best available rate.

FOUR POINTS BY SHERATON OKLAHOMA CITY Book great rates at AAA.com Phone: 405/681-3500 46

Hotel
Rates not provided

Address: 6300 Terminal Dr 73159 **Location:** I-40, exit 145 (Meridian Ave), 4 mi s. **Facility:** Smoke free premises. 117 units. 116 one-bedroom standard units. 1 one-bedroom suite. 2 stories (no elevator), interior corridors. *Bath:* combo or shower only. **Parking:** on-site. **Amenities:** video games (fee), dual phone lines, voice mail, irons, hair dryers. *Some:* fax. **Pool(s):** heated outdoor. **Leisure Activities:** exercise room. **Guest Services:** valet and coin laundry, airport transportation-Will Rogers World Airport, wireless Internet. **Business Services:** meeting rooms, business center.

/ SOME UNITS FEE

FOUR POINTS BY SHERATON
AAA Benefit:
Members get up to 15% off, plus Starwood Preferred Guest® bonuses.

GOVERNORS SUITES HOTEL Phone: (405)682-5299 43

Hotel
$69-$99 3/1-8/31
$62-$82 9/1-2/28

Address: 2308 S Meridian Ave 73108 **Location:** I-40, exit 145 (Meridian Ave), 1.2 mi s. **Facility:** 50 units. 45 one-bedroom standard units. 5 one-bedroom suites with whirlpools, some with efficiencies (no utensils). 3 stories, interior corridors. **Parking:** on-site. **Amenities:** voice mail, irons, hair dryers. **Pool(s):** outdoor. **Leisure Activities:** whirlpool, steamroom, exercise room. **Guest Services:** coin laundry, wireless Internet. **Business Services:** meeting rooms, business center.

/ SOME UNITS

(See map and index starting on p. 608)

HAMPTON INN & SUITES *Book great rates at AAA.com*

Phone: (405)602-3400 52

Hotel
$82-$89 All Year

Address: 920 SW 77th St 73139 **Location:** I-240, exit 2A, just s. **Facility:** Smoke free premises. 90 one-bedroom standard units, some with whirlpools. 4 stories, interior corridors. *Bath:* combo or shower only. **Parking:** on-site. **Terms:** 1-7 night minimum stay, cancellation fee imposed. **Amenities:** high-speed Internet, voice mail, irons, hair dryers. **Pool(s):** heated outdoor. **Leisure Activities:** exercise room. **Guest Services:** valet and coin laundry, wireless Internet. **Business Services:** meeting rooms, business center. CALL

HAMPTON INN & SUITES OKLAHOMA CITY-BRICKTOWN *Book great rates at AAA.com*

Phone: (405)232-3600 26

Hotel
$119-$139 All Year

Address: 300 E Sheridan Ave 73102 **Location:** Just e of jct Mickey Mantle Blvd. **Facility:** Smoke free premises. 200 units. 193 one-bedroom standard units, some with whirlpools. 7 one-bedroom suites. 9 stories, interior corridors. *Bath:* combo or shower only. **Parking:** on-site (fee). **Terms:** 1-7 night minimum stay, cancellation fee imposed. **Amenities:** high-speed Internet, voice mail, irons, hair dryers. **Pool(s):** heated indoor. **Leisure Activities:** whirlpool, exercise room. **Guest Services:** valet and coin laundry, wireless Internet. **Business Services:** meeting rooms, business center. CALL / SOME UNITS

HAMPTON INN BY HILTON-QUAIL SPRINGS *Book great rates at AAA.com*

Phone: (405)752-7070 8

Hotel
$99-$119 All Year

Address: 13500 Plaza Terr 73120 **Location:** John Kilpatrick Tpke, exit May Ave, just e on south frontage road. **Facility:** 63 one-bedroom standard units. 3 stories, interior corridors. *Bath:* combo or shower only. **Parking:** on-site, winter plug-ins. **Terms:** 1-7 night minimum stay, cancellation fee imposed. **Amenities:** voice mail, irons, hair dryers. **Pool(s):** heated indoor. **Leisure Activities:** whirlpool. **Guest Services:** valet laundry, wireless Internet. **Business Services:** PC. / SOME UNITS

HAMPTON INN NW *Book great rates at AAA.com*

Phone: (405)947-0953 19

Hotel
$95-$129 All Year

Address: 3022 Northwest Expwy 73112 **Location:** Jct SR 3A and May Ave. **Facility:** 97 one-bedroom standard units, some with whirlpools. 5 stories, interior corridors. *Bath:* combo or shower only. **Parking:** on-site. **Terms:** 1-7 night minimum stay, cancellation fee imposed. **Amenities:** high-speed Internet, voice mail, irons, hair dryers. *Some:* dual phone lines. **Pool(s):** heated indoor. **Leisure Activities:** exercise room. **Guest Services:** valet laundry, wireless Internet. **Business Services:** meeting rooms, PC. **Free Special Amenities: full breakfast and high-speed Internet.** / SOME UNITS

(See map and index starting on p. 608)

HAMPTON INN OKC AIRPORT **Phone:** (405)682-2080 41

Hotel
$119-$149 All Year

Address: 1905 S Meridian Ave 73108 **Location:** I-40, exit 145 (Meridian Ave), 1 mi s. **Facility:** 134 one-bedroom standard units. 3 stories, interior corridors. **Parking:** on-site. **Terms:** 1-7 night minimum stay, cancellation fee imposed. **Amenities:** video games (fee), high-speed Internet, voice mail, irons, hair dryers. **Pool(s):** outdoor. **Leisure Activities:** exercise room. **Guest Services:** valet laundry, wireless Internet. **Business Services:** meeting rooms, PC.

/ SOME UNITS

AAA Benefit:
Members save up to 10% everyday!

HILTON GARDEN INN OKLAHOMA CITY AIRPORT **Phone:** (405)942-1400 34

Hotel
$89-$179 All Year

Address: 801 S Meridian Ave 73108 **Location:** I-40, exit 145 (Meridian Ave), just sw. **Facility:** 161 units. 137 one-bedroom standard units. 24 one-bedroom suites. 6 stories, interior corridors. *Bath:* combo or shower only. **Parking:** on-site. **Terms:** 1-7 night minimum stay, cancellation fee imposed. **Amenities:** high-speed Internet, dual phone lines, voice mail, irons, hair dryers. **Pool(s):** heated outdoor. **Leisure Activities:** whirlpool, exercise room. **Guest Services:** valet and coin laundry, area transportation, wireless Internet. **Business Services:** meeting rooms, business center.

CALL / SOME UNITS

Hilton Garden Inn

AAA Benefit:
Members save 5% or more everyday!

HILTON GARDEN INN OKLAHOMA CITY NORTH QUAIL SPRINGS **Phone:** (405)752-5200 1

Hotel
$89-$169 All Year

Address: 3201 N 137th St 73134 **Location:** John Kilpatrick Tpke, exit May Ave, 0.4 mi w on north service road. **Facility:** Smoke free premises. 113 one-bedroom standard units. 3 stories, interior corridors. *Bath:* combo or shower only. **Parking:** on-site. **Terms:** 1-7 night minimum stay, cancellation fee imposed. **Amenities:** high-speed Internet, voice mail, irons, hair dryers. **Pool(s):** heated indoor. **Leisure Activities:** whirlpool, exercise room. **Guest Services:** valet and coin laundry, wireless Internet. **Business Services:** meeting rooms, business center.

CALL

Hilton Garden Inn

AAA Benefit:
Members save 5% or more everyday!

HOLIDAY INN EXPRESS **Phone:** (405)631-3111 49

Hotel
$80-$85 All Year

Address: 7601 CA Henderson Blvd 73139 **Location:** I-240, exit 2A, just s. **Facility:** 64 one-bedroom standard units. 3 stories, interior corridors. *Bath:* combo or shower only. **Parking:** on-site. **Terms:** cancellation fee imposed. **Amenities:** voice mail, irons, hair dryers. **Pool(s):** heated indoor. **Leisure Activities:** whirlpool. **Guest Services:** valet laundry, wireless Internet. **Business Services:** PC.

ASK / SOME UNITS

HOLIDAY INN EXPRESS HOTEL & SUITES **Phone:** (405)948-3366 37

Hotel
$89-$159 All Year

Address: 4400 Highline Blvd 73108 **Location:** I-40, exit 145 (Meridian Ave), just se. **Facility:** 83 units. 81 one-bedroom standard units. 2 one-bedroom suites. 3 stories, interior corridors. *Bath:* combo or shower only. **Parking:** on-site. **Terms:** cancellation fee imposed. **Amenities:** dual phone lines, voice mail, irons, hair dryers. **Leisure Activities:** exercise room. **Guest Services:** valet and coin laundry, wireless Internet. **Business Services:** meeting rooms, business center.

ASK / SOME UNITS

HOLIDAY INN EXPRESS HOTEL & SUITES PENN SQUARE **Phone:** 405/848-1500 20

Hotel
Rates not provided

Address: 2811 Northwest Expwy 73112 **Location:** 0.7 mi e of jct SR 3 and 74. **Facility:** 76 one-bedroom standard units, some with whirlpools. 3 stories, interior corridors. *Bath:* combo or shower only. **Parking:** on-site. **Amenities:** dual phone lines, voice mail, irons, hair dryers. **Pool(s):** heated indoor. **Leisure Activities:** exercise room. **Guest Services:** valet and coin laundry, wireless Internet. **Business Services:** meeting rooms, PC.

CALL / SOME UNITS

HOMEWOOD SUITES OKLAHOMA CITY-WEST **Phone:** (405)789-3600 29

Extended Stay Hotel
$95-$149 All Year

Address: 6920 W Reno Ave 73127 **Location:** Just e of jct Rockwell Ave. **Facility:** 90 units. 44 one-bedroom standard units with efficiencies. 46 one-bedroom suites with efficiencies. 3 stories, interior corridors. *Bath:* combo or shower only. **Parking:** on-site. **Terms:** 1-7 night minimum stay, cancellation fee imposed. **Amenities:** video games (fee), high-speed Internet, dual phone lines, voice mail, irons, hair dryers. *Some:* DVD players. **Pool(s):** heated outdoor. **Leisure Activities:** whirlpool, exercise room, sports court. **Guest Services:** valet and coin laundry, wireless Internet. **Business Services:** meeting rooms, business center.

CALL / SOME UNITS

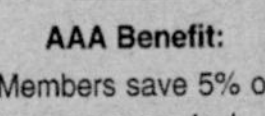

AAA Benefit:
Members save 5% or more everyday!

(See map and index starting on p. 608)

HYATT PLACE OKLAHOMA CITY AIRPORT *Book great rates at AAA.com* **Phone:** (405)682-3900 40

Hotel
$79-$209 All Year

Address: 1818 S Meridian Ave 73108-1718 **Location:** I-40, exit 145 (Meridian Ave), 1 mi s. **Facility:** Smoke free premises. 126 one-bedroom standard units. 6 stories, interior corridors. *Bath:* combo or shower only. **Parking:** on-site. **Terms:** cancellation fee imposed. **Amenities:** video games (fee), dual phone lines, voice mail, safes, irons, hair dryers. **Pool(s):** heated outdoor. **Leisure Activities:** exercise room. **Guest Services:** valet laundry, airport transportation-Will Rogers World Airport, wireless Internet. **Business Services:** meeting rooms, business center. **Free Special Amenities: continental breakfast and high-speed Internet.**

HYATT PLACE
AAA Benefit:
Ask for the AAA rate and save 10%.

LA QUINTA INN & SUITES OKLAHOMA CITY (NORTHWEST EXPRESSWAY) *Book at AAA.com* **Phone:** (405)773-5575 12

Hotel
$49-$114 All Year

Address: 4829 Northwest Expwy 73132-5215 **Location:** 1.9 mi w of jct SR 3 and 74. **Facility:** 119 units. 113 one-bedroom standard units. 6 one-bedroom suites. 6 stories, interior corridors. *Bath:* combo or shower only. **Parking:** on-site. **Amenities:** video games (fee), high-speed Internet, voice mail, irons, hair dryers. *Some:* dual phone lines. **Pool(s):** heated outdoor. **Leisure Activities:** whirlpool, exercise room. **Guest Services:** valet and coin laundry, wireless Internet. **Business Services:** meeting rooms. ASK / SOME UNITS

LA QUINTA INN & SUITES-QUAIL SPRINGS *Book at AAA.com* **Phone:** (405)755-7000 2

Hotel
$89-$229 All Year

Address: 3003 W Memorial Rd 73134 **Location:** John Kilpatrick Tpke, exit May Ave, just nw. **Facility:** 96 one-bedroom standard units, some with whirlpools. 3 stories, interior corridors. *Bath:* combo or shower only. **Parking:** on-site. **Amenities:** high-speed Internet, dual phone lines, voice mail, irons, hair dryers. *Some:* CD players. **Pool(s):** heated indoor. **Leisure Activities:** whirlpool, putting green, exercise room. **Guest Services:** valet and coin laundry, wireless Internet. **Business Services:** meeting rooms, business center.
ASK CALL / SOME UNITS

LA QUINTA INN OKLAHOMA CITY (AIRPORT) *Book at AAA.com* **Phone:** (405)942-0040 33

Hotel
$49-$125 All Year

Address: 800 S Meridian Ave 73108 **Location:** I-40, exit 145 (Meridian Ave), just se. **Facility:** 168 units. 167 one-bedroom standard units. 1 one-bedroom suite with kitchen. 2 stories (no elevator), interior/exterior corridors. *Bath:* combo or shower only. **Parking:** on-site. **Amenities:** video games (fee), voice mail, irons, hair dryers. **Pool(s):** outdoor. **Leisure Activities:** exercise room. **Guest Services:** valet laundry, wireless Internet. **Business Services:** meeting rooms, PC.
ASK / SOME UNITS

OKLAHOMA CITY MARRIOTT *Book great rates at AAA.com* **Phone:** (405)842-6633 15

Hotel
$153-$187 All Year

Address: 3233 Northwest Expwy 73112 **Location:** Just e of jct SR 3 and 74. **Facility:** Smoke free premises. 354 units. 352 one-bedroom standard units. 2 one-bedroom suites. 16 stories, interior corridors. *Bath:* combo or shower only. **Parking:** on-site. **Terms:** cancellation fee imposed. **Amenities:** high-speed Internet (fee), voice mail, irons, hair dryers. **Dining:** J W's Steakhouse, see separate listing. **Pool(s):** heated indoor/outdoor. **Leisure Activities:** whirlpool, exercise room. **Guest Services:** valet and coin laundry. **Business Services:** conference facilities, business center.
/ SOME UNITS

Marriott HOTELS & RESORTS
AAA Benefit:
Members save a minimum 5% off the best available rate.

QUALITY INN *Book at AAA.com* **Phone:** (405)632-6666 50

Hotel
$60-$90 All Year

Address: 7800 CA Henderson Blvd 73139 **Location:** I-240, exit 2A, just s. **Facility:** 149 one-bedroom standard units. 2 stories (no elevator), exterior corridors. *Bath:* combo or shower only. **Parking:** on-site. **Amenities:** safes (fee), irons, hair dryers. **Pool(s):** outdoor. **Guest Services:** coin laundry, wireless Internet. **Business Services:** meeting rooms.
ASK / SOME UNITS FEE

RENAISSANCE OKLAHOMA CITY CONVENTION CENTER, HOTEL & SPA *Book great rates at AAA.com* **Phone:** (405)228-8000 24

Hotel
$179-$219 All Year

Address: 10 N Broadway Ave 73102 **Location:** Sheridan and Broadway aves; downtown. **Facility:** Located in the heart of downtown and within walking distance of Bricktown, this upscale, well-appointed hotel is also near the interstate. Smoke free premises. 311 units. 258 one-bedroom standard units. 53 one-bedroom suites, some with whirlpools. 15 stories, interior corridors. *Bath:* combo or shower only. **Parking:** on-site (fee) and valet. **Terms:** cancellation fee imposed. **Amenities:** dual phone lines, voice mail, honor bars, irons, hair dryers. *Fee:* video games, high-speed Internet. **Pool(s):** heated indoor. **Leisure Activities:** sauna, whirlpool, exercise room, spa. **Guest Services:** valet and coin laundry, wireless Internet. **Business Services:** conference facilities, business center. **Free Special Amenities: newspaper.**
CALL / SOME UNITS

AAA Benefit:
Members save a minimum 5% off the best available rate.

(See map and index starting on p. 608)

RESIDENCE INN BY MARRIOTT Book great rates at AAA.com **Phone:** (405)601-1700 28

Extended Stay Hotel
$179-$219 All Year

Address: 400 E Reno Ave 73104 **Location:** Just se of jct Joe Carter Ave; in Bricktown. **Facility:** Smoke free premises. 151 units. 17 one-bedroom standard units. 117 one- and 17 two-bedroom suites. 6 stories, interior corridors. *Bath:* combo or shower only. **Parking:** on-site. **Terms:** cancellation fee imposed. **Amenities:** high-speed Internet, dual phone lines, voice mail, irons, hair dryers. **Pool(s):** heated outdoor. **Leisure Activities:** whirlpools, tennis court, exercise room, sports court. **Guest Services:** valet and coin laundry, wireless Internet. **Business Services:** meeting rooms, business center. **Free Special Amenities: expanded continental breakfast and newspaper.**

CALL / SOME UNITS

AAA Benefit: Members save a minimum 5% off the best available rate.

RESIDENCE INN BY MARRIOTT OKLAHOMA CITY SOUTH-CROSSROADS MALL Book great rates at AAA.com **Phone:** (405)634-9696 48

Extended Stay Hotel
$170-$208 All Year

Address: 1111 E I-240 Service Rd 73149 **Location:** I-240, exit 4C eastbound, 0.4 mi nw; exit 5 westbound, 0.8 mi nw. **Facility:** Smoke free premises. 90 units. 37 one-bedroom standard units with efficiencies. 35 one- and 18 two-bedroom suites, some with efficiencies or kitchens. 3 stories, interior corridors. *Bath:* combo or shower only. **Parking:** on-site. **Terms:** cancellation fee imposed. **Amenities:** dual phone lines, voice mail, irons, hair dryers. *Some:* high-speed Internet. **Pool(s):** heated indoor. **Leisure Activities:** whirlpool, exercise room. **Guest Services:** valet and coin laundry, wireless Internet. **Business Services:** meeting rooms, PC.

/ SOME UNITS FEE

AAA Benefit: Members save a minimum 5% off the best available rate.

RESIDENCE INN BY MARRIOTT-OKLAHOMA CITY WEST Book great rates at AAA.com **Phone:** (405)942-4500 27

Extended Stay Hotel
$161-$197 All Year

Address: 4361 W Reno Ave 73107 **Location:** I-40, exit 145 (Meridian Ave), 0.3 mi n, then just e. **Facility:** Smoke free premises. 136 units. 98 one-bedroom standard units with kitchens. 38 one-bedroom suites with kitchens. 2 stories (no elevator), exterior corridors. **Parking:** on-site. **Terms:** cancellation fee imposed. **Amenities:** voice mail, irons, hair dryers. *Some:* DVD players. **Pool(s):** outdoor. **Leisure Activities:** exercise room, sports court. **Guest Services:** valet and coin laundry, wireless Internet. **Business Services:** meeting rooms, business center. **Free Special Amenities: full breakfast and high-speed Internet.**

/ SOME UNITS FEE

AAA Benefit: Members save a minimum 5% off the best available rate.

SHERATON OKLAHOMA CITY Book great rates at AAA.com **Phone:** 405/235-2780 25

Hotel
Rates not provided

Address: One N Broadway Ave 73102 **Location:** Sheridan and Broadway aves; downtown. **Facility:** Smoke free premises. 396 units. 393 one-bedroom standard units. 3 one-bedroom suites with kitchens, some with whirlpools. 15 stories, interior corridors. *Bath:* combo or shower only. **Parking:** on-site (fee) and valet. **Amenities:** voice mail, irons, hair dryers. *Fee:* video games, high-speed Internet. *Some:* dual phone lines. **Pool(s):** outdoor. **Leisure Activities:** exercise room. **Guest Services:** valet laundry, wireless Internet, beauty salon. **Business Services:** conference facilities, business center.

/ SOME UNITS

AAA Benefit: Members get up to 15% off, plus Starwood Preferred Guest® bonuses.

SKIRVIN HILTON Book great rates at AAA.com **Phone:** (405)272-3040 23

Historic Hotel
$149-$269 All Year

Address: 1 Park Ave 73102 **Location:** Just n of jct Robinson Ave; downtown. **Facility:** Modern conveniences are plentiful throughout the three architecturally impressive towers built in 1911 and restored in 2007. Smoke free premises. 225 units. 204 one-bedroom standard units. 21 one-bedroom suites, some with whirlpools. 14 stories, interior corridors. *Bath:* combo or shower only. **Parking:** on-site (fee) and valet. **Terms:** 1-7 night minimum stay, cancellation fee imposed. **Amenities:** high-speed Internet (fee), voice mail, safes, irons, hair dryers. **Pool(s):** heated indoor. **Leisure Activities:** whirlpool, exercise room. **Guest Services:** valet laundry, wireless Internet. **Business Services:** conference facilities, business center. *(See color ad p 621)*

24 CALL / SOME UNITS FEE

Hilton

AAA Benefit: Members save 5% or more everyday!

(See map and index starting on p. 608)

SLEEP INN *Book great rates at AAA.com*

Phone: (405)946-1600 

Hotel
$60-$80 All Year

Address: 4620 Enterprise Way 73128 **Location:** I-40, exit 145 (Meridian Ave), just sw. **Facility:** Smoke free premises. 56 one-bedroom standard units. 3 stories, interior corridors. *Bath:* combo or shower only. **Parking:** on-site. **Amenities:** voice mail, irons, hair dryers. **Pool(s):** heated indoor. **Leisure Activities:** exercise room. **Guest Services:** valet and coin laundry, wireless Internet. **Business Services:** PC. **Free Special Amenities: full breakfast and high-speed Internet.**

SLEEP INN & SUITES *Book at AAA.com*

Phone: (405)286-5400 21

Hotel
$60-$150 All Year

Address: 5200 N Classen Cir 73118 **Location:** I-44, exit 125, just s. **Facility:** Smoke free premises. 55 one-bedroom standard units, some with whirlpools. 4 stories, interior corridors. *Bath:* combo or shower only. **Parking:** on-site. **Terms:** cancellation fee imposed. **Amenities:** high-speed Internet, voice mail, safes (fee), irons, hair dryers. **Pool(s):** heated indoor. **Leisure Activities:** whirlpool, exercise room. **Guest Services:** valet and coin laundry. **Business Services:** business center.

ASK CALL

SLEEP INN & SUITES *Book at AAA.com*

Phone: (405)478-9898 9

Hotel
$79-$140 All Year

Address: 12024 122nd St 73131 **Location:** I-35, exit 137 (122nd St), just e. **Facility:** 69 one-bedroom standard units, some with whirlpools. 3 stories, interior corridors. *Bath:* combo or shower only. **Parking:** on-site. **Amenities:** high-speed Internet, voice mail, irons, hair dryers. **Pool(s):** heated indoor. **Leisure Activities:** whirlpool, exercise room. **Guest Services:** coin laundry, wireless Internet. **Business Services:** PC. ASK / SOME UNITS

SPRINGHILL SUITES OKLAHOMA CITY AIRPORT *Book great rates at AAA.com*

Phone: (405)604-0200

Hotel
$134-$164 All Year

Address: 510 S Macarthur Blvd 73128 **Location:** I-40, exit 144, just ne. **Facility:** Smoke free premises. 100 one-bedroom standard units. 4 stories, interior corridors. *Bath:* combo or shower only. **Parking:** on-site. **Terms:** cancellation fee imposed. **Amenities:** high-speed Internet, voice mail, irons, hair dryers. **Pool(s):** heated indoor. **Leisure Activities:** whirlpool, exercise room. **Guest Services:** TV in common area, valet and coin laundry, wireless Internet. **Business Services:** meeting rooms, business center.

CALL / SOME UNITS FEE

AAA Benefit:
Members save a minimum 5% off the best available rate.

FREE expanded continental breakfast and high-speed Internet

▼ See AAA listing p 620 ▼

(See map and index starting on p. 608)

SPRINGHILL SUITES BY MARRIOTT *Book great rates at AAA.com* **Phone:** (405)749-1595 3

Hotel
$98-$120 All Year

Address: 3201 W Memorial Rd 73134 **Location:** John Kilpatrick Tpke, exit May Ave, 0.4 mi w on north service road. **Facility:** Smoke free premises. 128 one-bedroom standard units. 6 stories, interior corridors. *Bath:* combo or shower only. **Parking:** on-site. **Terms:** cancellation fee imposed. **Amenities:** video games (fee), high-speed Internet, voice mail, irons, hair dryers. *Some:* dual phone lines. **Pool(s):** outdoor. **Leisure Activities:** exercise room. **Guest Services:** valet and coin laundry, wireless Internet. **Business Services:** meeting rooms, PC.

AAA Benefit:
Members save a minimum 5% off the best available rate.

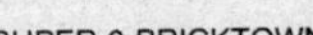

SUPER 8 BRICKTOWN *Book at AAA.com* **Phone:** 405/677-1000 45

Motel
Rates not provided

Address: 3030 S I-35 73129 **Location:** I-35, exit 124B northbound; exit 125A southbound, just n on service road. **Facility:** 98 one-bedroom standard units. 2 stories (no elevator), exterior corridors. **Parking:** on-site. **Amenities:** voice mail, hair dryers. *Some:* irons. **Guest Services:** coin laundry, wireless Internet. **Business Services:** fax. / SOME UNITS FEE

WATERFORD MARRIOTT HOTEL *Book great rates at AAA.com* **Phone:** (405)848-4782 14

Hotel
$152-$186 All Year

Address: 6300 Waterford Blvd 73118 **Location:** I-44, exit 125A, 1.4 mi n. Located in a corporate and residential area. **Facility:** Splendid landscaping and elegant public areas characterize this Marriott. Smoke free premises. 197 units. 196 one-bedroom standard units. 1 one-bedroom suite with whirlpool. 9 stories, interior corridors. *Bath:* combo or shower only. **Parking:** on-site and valet. **Terms:** cancellation fee imposed. **Amenities:** video games (fee), voice mail, irons, hair dryers. *Some:* dual phone lines. **Pool(s):** heated outdoor. **Leisure Activities:** saunas, whirlpool, exercise room. *Fee:* massage. **Guest Services:** valet laundry, wireless Internet. **Business Services:** conference facilities, business center. / SOME UNITS

Marriott HOTELS & RESORTS

AAA Benefit:
Members save a minimum 5% off the best available rate.

WINGATE INN *Book at AAA.com* **Phone:** 405/682-3600 42

Hotel
Rates not provided

Address: 2001 S Meridian Ave 73108 **Location:** I-40, exit 145 (Meridian Ave), 1.1 mi s. **Facility:** 99 one-bedroom standard units, some with whirlpools. 4 stories, interior corridors. *Bath:* combo or shower only. **Parking:** on-site. **Amenities:** video games (fee), high-speed Internet, dual phone lines, voice mail, safes, irons, hair dryers. **Pool(s):** heated indoor. **Leisure Activities:** sauna, whirlpool, exercise room. **Guest Services:** valet laundry, wireless Internet. **Business Services:** meeting rooms, business center. / SOME UNITS

WHERE TO DINE

ABUELO'S THE FLAVOR OF MEXICO **Phone:** 405/235-1422 18

Mexican
$6-$17

The upscale restaurant's menu incorporates top-quality steaks and traditional Mexican dishes. Casual dress. **Bar:** Full bar. **Hours:** 11 am-10 pm, Fri & Sat-11 pm; to 9 pm in winter. Closed: 11/25, 12/25. **Address:** 17 E Sheridan Ave 73104 **Location:** Just w of jct Oklahoma Ave. **Parking:** on-site (fee).

ABUELO'S THE FLAVOR OF MEXICO **Phone:** 405/755-2680 1

Mexican
$6-$17

Well-prepared dishes include shredded beef burritos, grilled chicken and other Mexican favorites. Plenty of attractive plants, murals and statues decorate the upscale dining room. Casual dress. **Bar:** Full bar. **Hours:** 11 am-10 pm, Fri & Sat-11 pm. Closed: 11/25, 12/25. **Address:** 3001 W Memorial Rd 73134 **Location:** John Kilpatrick Tpke, exit May Ave, just n. **Parking:** on-site.

ALOHA GARDEN RESTAURANT **Phone:** 405/686-0288 29

Chinese
$5-$11

The locally popular Aloha Garden offers a nice selection on its luncheon and dinner buffet, which includes large portions and is a good value. You may also order from the menu that offers American dishes in addition to Chinese offerings. Pleasant, friendly service. Casual dress. **Bar:** Full bar. **Reservations:** accepted. **Hours:** 11 am-9 pm, Fri & Sat-9:30 pm, Sun-8 pm. Closed: 7/4, 11/25, 12/25. **Address:** 2219 SW 74th St, #105 73159 **Location:** I-240, exit 1C, just nw; in Walnut Square Shopping Center. **Parking:** on-site.

BAKER ST. PUB & GRILL **Phone:** 405/751-1547

English
$5-$13

A long bar, pool table and darts promote the same casual Old English theme that weaves through the menu. Beer-battered cod with tartar sauce and malt vinegar helps hunger pangs subside, as do the varied sandwiches, salads and Mexican items. Casual dress. **Bar:** Full bar. **Hours:** 11 am-2 am. **Address:** 2701 W Memorial 73134 **Location:** John Kilpatrick Tpke, exit Penn Ave, just w. **Parking:** on-site.

BELLINI'S RISTORANTE & GRILL **Phone:** 405/848-1065 9

Italian
$8-$48

Next to underground parking, the restaurant is appointed in upscale decor and treats patrons to nicely presented and prepared Italian fare. Dressy casual. **Bar:** Full bar. **Reservations:** accepted. **Hours:** 11 am-9 pm, Fri & Sat-10 pm. Closed: 11/25, 12/25. **Address:** 6305 Waterford Blvd 73118 **Location:** I-44, exit 125A, 1.4 mi n. **Parking:** on-site.

(See map and index starting on p. 608)

BEVERLY'S PANCAKE HOUSE

Phone: 405/848-5050 (10)

American

$5-$12

Hearty portions and a good selection keep locals returning to this pancake house. As expected, breakfast is popular. Casual dress. **Hours:** 24 hours. **Address:** 3315 Northwest Expwy 73112 **Location:** 0.4 mi e of jct SR 3 and 74. **Parking:** on-site.

BOURBON STREET CAFE

Phone: 405/232-6666 (24)

Cajun

$6-$20

Patrons might think they've stepped into New Orleans, due to the lively jazz music and bustling atmosphere. Menu selections include seafood, pasta, chicken and steak, all prepared in the expected Cajun tradition. Casual dress. **Bar:** Full bar. **Hours:** 11 am-9:30 pm, Fri & Sat-11 pm. Closed: 11/25, 12/25. **Address:** 100 E California Ave 73104 **Location:** Just n of jct Reno and Oklahoma aves; in Bricktown. **Parking:** on-site (fee).

BRICKTOWN BREWERY

Phone: 405/232-2739 (19)

American

$6-$16

Bricktown Brewery is nestled in the city's historic, restored-warehouse district. The two-story warehouse was built before statehood (1903) and has a rustic atmosphere. The menu includes delicious roasted salmon steak, barbecue copperhead and chicken pot pie. Casual dress. **Bar:** Full bar. **Hours:** 11 am-10 pm, Fri & Sat-midnight, Sun noon-8 pm. Closed: 11/25, 12/25. **Address:** 1 N Oklahoma Ave 73104 **Location:** Near downtown; at Sheridan and Oklahoma aves. **Parking:** on-site (fee).

CATTLEMEN'S STEAKHOUSE

Phone: 405/236-0416 (27)

Steak

$8-$25

Located in the historic stockyards city, Cattlemen's Steakhouse has been an Oklahoma tradition since 1910. They offer freshly cut beef of the finest grade, cooked to your specification. And you'll find the server staff friendly and attentive. Casual dress. **Bar:** Full bar. **Hours:** 6 am-10 pm, Fri & Sat-midnight. Closed: 11/25, 12/25. **Address:** 1309 S Agnew Ave 73108 **Location:** I-40, exit 148A, 0.8 mi s. **Parking:** on-site.

CHARLESTON'S RESTAURANT

Phone: 405/681-0055

American

$9-$23

This casual dining spot boasts a friendly, club-like atmosphere. Fine steak and seafood, as well as hardwood-grilled dishes, are at the heart of the menu. The noteworthy baked potato soup is rich with onions and bacon bits. Casual dress. **Bar:** Full bar. **Hours:** 11 am-9 pm, Fri & Sat-10 pm. Closed: 11/25, 12/25. **Address:** 1429 SW 74th St 73159 **Location:** I-240, exit 1C, just nw. **Parking:** on-site.

CHARLESTON'S RESTAURANT

Phone: 405/721-0060

American

$9-$23

This casual dining spot boasts a friendly, club-like atmosphere. Fine steak and seafood, as well as hardwood-grilled dishes, are at the heart of the menu. The noteworthy baked potato soup is rich with onions and bacon bits. Casual dress. **Bar:** Full bar. **Reservations:** accepted. **Hours:** 11 am-10 pm, Fri & Sat-11 pm, Sun-9 pm. Closed: 11/25, 12/25. **Address:** 5907 Northwest Expwy 73132 **Location:** Just w of jct MacArthur Blvd. **Parking:** on-site.

(See map and index starting on p. 608)

CHARLESTON'S RESTAURANT Phone: 405/681-6686

American
$9-$24

This casual dining spot boasts a friendly, club-like atmosphere. Fine steak and seafood, as well as hardwood-grilled dishes, are at the heart of the menu. The noteworthy baked potato soup is rich with onions and bacon bits. Casual dress. **Bar:** Full bar. **Reservations:** accepted. **Hours:** 11 am-10 pm, Fri & Sat-11 pm. Closed: 11/25, 12/25. **Address:** 2000 S Meridian Ave 73102 **Location:** I-40, exit 145 (Meridian Ave), 1.1 mi s. **Parking:** on-site.

CHARLIE NEWTON'S **Phone:** 405/840-0115 (6)

American
$11-$33

The subdued, yet elegant, dining room is a nice setting in which to savor one of a superb array of tastefully prepared entrees. Diverse selections ensure diners enjoy a memorable experience. Dressy casual. **Bar:** Full bar. **Reservations:** suggested. **Hours:** 5:30 pm-9:30 pm, Fri & Sat-10 pm. Closed major holidays; also Sun. **Address:** 1025 NW 70th St 73116 **Location:** I-44, exit 126, 1.2 mi n. **Parking:** on-site.

CHARLY'S RESTAURANT **Phone:** 405/475-9944 (2)

American
$4-$8

A variety of popular American dishes are prepared for lunch and dinner. This place also is a favorite for breakfast. Casual dress. **Hours:** 6 am-10 pm. Closed: 11/25, 12/25. **Address:** 12000 N I-35 73149 **Location:** I-44, exit 137, just e. **Parking:** on-site.

CHELINO'S MEXICAN RESTAURANT **Phone:** 405/235-3533 (22)

Mexican
$6-$13

In the Bricktown area, the restaurant makes seating available on the terrace as well as in a festive dining room. Casual dress. **Bar:** Full bar. **Reservations:** not accepted. **Hours:** 11 am-10 pm, Fri & Sat-11 pm, Sun-9 pm. Closed: 11/25, 12/25. **Address:** 15 E California Ave 73104 **Location:** Just w of Oklahoma Ave. **Parking:** on-site (fee).

CIMARRON STEAK HOUSE **Phone:** 405/948-7778 (16)

AAA

Steak
$6-$22

The steaks served here are naturally aged and cut on the premises, then mesquite-broiled for a good flavor. They also serve ribs, pork chops and seafood. Pleasant service is provided in a Western decor and atmosphere. Live entertainment offered Saturday. Casual dress. **Bar:** Full bar. **Reservations:** accepted, except Fri & Sat. **Hours:** 11 am-10 pm, Fri & Sat-11 pm. Closed: 11/25, 12/25. **Address:** 201 N Meridian Ave 73107 **Location:** I-40, exit 145 (Meridian Ave), 0.5 mi n. **Parking:** on-site.

THE COACH HOUSE **Phone:** 405/842-1000 (7)

American
$15-$55

This cottage-style restaurant—with its high, arched windows and stone exterior—is warm and inviting. Rich, dark woods in the interior adds to the elegance. The artful presentation of skillfully prepared cuisine contributes to a dining extravaganza. Dressy casual. **Bar:** Full bar. **Reservations:** suggested. **Hours:** 11:30 am-2 & 6-10 pm, Sat from 6 pm. Closed major holidays; also Sun. **Address:** 6437 Avondale Dr 73116 **Location:** I-44, exit 126, 0.8 mi to Avondale Dr, then just nw. **Parking:** on-site.

COACH'S BBQ PIZZA & BREWERY **Phone:** 405/232-6224 (23)

Barbecue
$7-$16

Baby back ribs, rib-eye, pizza and assorted other dishes make up the menu. Large windows overlook Bricktown Ball Field, allowing for great views from many tables. A balcony is available by reservation during events. Casual dress. **Bar:** Full bar. **Hours:** 11 am-10 pm, Fri & Sat-11 pm. Closed: 11/25, 12/25. **Address:** 20 S Mickey Mantle Dr 73104 **Location:** Just n of jct Reno Ave. **Parking:** on-site (fee).

THE COUNTY LINE BARBECUE **Phone:** 405/478-4955 (8)

American
$7-$19

Slow-smoked barbecue and prime rib dishes are served in the 1930s roadhouse atmosphere of the Oklahoma County Line Restaurant. The interior is decorated with Western memorabilia, and the server staff is attentive and prompt. The baby back ribs are great. Casual dress. **Bar:** Full bar. **Hours:** 11 am-9 pm, Fri & Sat-10 pm. Closed: 1/1, 11/25, 12/24, 12/25. **Address:** 1226 NE 63rd St 73111 **Location:** I-44, exit 129 (ML King Ave), 0.6 mi w. **Parking:** on-site.

DEEP FORK GRILL **Phone:** 405/848-7678 (13)

Continental
$8-$34

The favorites among Deep Fork Grill's good selection are cedar-plank salmon, chili-lacquered chicken salad, fresh seafood, certified Angus beef steak and housemade desserts. The quiet, intimate, romantic atmosphere suits businesspeople and couples. Casual dress. **Bar:** Full bar. **Reservations:** suggested, weekends. **Hours:** 11 am-10 pm, Fri-11 pm, Sat 5 pm-11 pm, Sun 10:30 am-10 pm. Closed major holidays. **Address:** 5418 N Western Ave 73118 **Location:** I-44, exit 126, just n. **Parking:** on-site and valet.

GOLDEN PALACE **Phone:** 405/686-1511 (28)

Chinese
$5-$12

Guests can sample Chinese or Vietnamese dishes from the menu or buffet or opt for the Mongolian barbecue. The food is enjoyable. Casual dress. **Bar:** Beer only. **Reservations:** not accepted. **Hours:** 11 am-9:30 pm, Sun-8:30 pm. Closed: 1/1, 11/25, 12/25. **Address:** 1500 S Meridian Ave 73108 **Location:** I-40, exit 145 (Meridian Ave), 1 mi s. **Parking:** on-site.

GOPURAM, TASTE OF INDIA *Menu on AAA.com* **Phone:** 405/948-7373 (15)

AAA

Indian
$6-$15

Although the exterior, which sits in a strip shopping center, is nondescript, the interior is loaded with charm. Indian cultural decorations set the mood to transfer you to another part of the world. The authentic cuisine and extensive menu are a world diner's delight. Casual dress. **Bar:** Full bar. **Hours:** 11 am-10 pm. **Address:** 4559 NW 23rd St 73127 **Location:** I-44, exit 122, 1.3 mi w; in Windsor Hills Shopping Center. **Parking:** on-site.

(See map and index starting on p. 608)

HUNAN CHINESE RESTAURANT

Phone: 405/685-5288 (30)

Chinese
$6-$8

The all-you-can-eat buffet, which lines up a nice sampling of dishes, is most diners' preferred method o assembling a meal. Casual dress. **Hours:** 11 am-9 pm. Closed: 11/25, 12/25. **Address:** 1506 SW 74th S 73159 **Location:** I-240, exit 1C, just se. **Parking:** on-site.

HUNAN WOK RESTAURANT

Phone: 405/722-8996 (4)

Chinese
$5-$11

Many returning patrons choose from the buffet or the Mongolian barbecue. Both are equally good and have a nice variety of choices. Casual dress. **Hours:** 11 am-10 pm. Closed: 11/25, 12/25. **Address:** 6812 Northwest Expwy 73132 **Location:** 3.4 mi w of jct SR 3 and 74. **Parking:** on-site.

J W'S STEAKHOUSE

Phone: 405/842-6633 (11)

Steak
$18-$38

You won't go wrong by choosing the prime rib or garlic filet mignon at J W's. The menu has a very good selection of fresh seafood, pork and beef, and meals are well-prepared. The restaurant has an elegant, intimate atmosphere with Southwestern decor. Dressy casual. **Bar:** Full bar. **Reservations:** suggested. **Hours:** 5 pm-10 pm. Closed major holidays; also Sun. **Address:** 3233 Northwest Expwy 73112 **Location:** Just e of jct SR 3 and 74; in Oklahoma City Marriott. **Parking:** on-site.

LA BAGUETTE BISTRO CASUAL RESTAURANT & BAKERY

Phone: 405/840-3047 (5)

French
$7-$23

La Baguette's delicious, creative food belies its modest surroundings. Entrees offered: chicken, duck, pork, beef tenderloin, lamb and seafood—all delicious. The choices from their in-house bakery are also excellent, rich and flavorful. Pleasant service. Casual dress. **Bar:** Full bar. **Reservations:** accepted. **Hours:** 8 am-10 pm, Fri & Sat-11 pm, Sun 9:30 am-2:30 pm. Closed major holidays. **Address:** 7408 N May Ave 73116 **Location:** I-44, exit 124, 2.3 mi n. **Parking:** on-site.

LALUNA MEXICAN CAFE

Phone: 405/235-9596 (25)

Mexican
$6-$15

Good-size portions and all the expected Mexican standbys are available. Service is relaxed and casual. Casual dress. **Bar:** Full bar. **Hours:** 11 am-9 pm, Fri & Sat-9:30 pm. Closed: 1/1, 11/25, 12/25; also Sun. **Address:** 409 W Reno Ave 73102 **Location:** Just ne of jct Walker Ave. **Parking:** on-site.

MANTEL WINE BAR & BISTRO

Phone: 405/236-8040 (17)

American
$9-$35

This upscale restaurant serves attractive dishes that burst with flavor. Reservations are suggested due to space limitations in the dining room and small waiting area. Dressy casual. **Bar:** Full bar. **Reservations:** suggested. **Hours:** 11 am-10 pm, Fri & Sat-11 pm, Sun 5 pm-9 pm. Closed major holidays. **Address:** 201 E Sheridan Ave 73104 **Location:** Just ne of jct Mickey Mantle Blvd. **Parking:** on-site.

MICKEY MANTLE'S STEAKHOUSE

Phone: 405/272-0777 (21)

Steak
$20-$35

Patrons can expect tender steak selections served amid tasteful memorabilia spanning Mickey Mantle's career. A nice selection of desserts is available to those who save room. Casual dress. **Bar:** Full bar. **Reservations:** suggested. **Hours:** 5 pm-10 pm, Fri & Sat-11 pm. Closed major holidays. **Address:** 7 Mickey Mantle Dr 73104 **Location:** Just n of jct Reno Ave and Mickey Mantle Blvd; in Bricktown. **Parking:** on-site and valet.

NONNA'S EURO-AMERICAN RISTORANTE AND BAR

Phone: 405/235-4410 (20)

American
$11-$42

You'll find upscale decor and furnishings and a nice selection of Euro-American dishes at the restaurant, which is also known for quality treats from the bakery. Dressy casual. **Bar:** Full bar. **Reservations:** suggested. **Hours:** 11 am-2 & 5-10 pm. Closed: 11/25, 12/25; also Sun. **Address:** 1 Mickey Mantle Dr 73104 **Location:** Just n of jct Reno Ave. **Parking:** valet.

PAPA DIO'S ITALIAN RESTAURANT & WINE BAR

Phone: 405/755-2255 (3)

Italian
$6-$23

You'll discover creative and tasty dishes and an upbeat atmosphere at Papa Dio's, which has an upscale side where there is more of a fine-dining atmosphere with soft candlelight. The veal parmigiana, mozzarella sticks and cheesecake are very good. Casual dress. **Bar:** Full bar. **Hours:** 4 pm-9:30 pm, Fri-10 pm, Sat 4:30 pm-10 pm, Mon 4:30 pm-9 pm. Closed major holidays; also Sun. **Address:** 10712 N May Ave 73120 **Location:** SR 74, exit Hefner Rd, 0.6 mi e, then just se. **Parking:** on-site.

PEARL'S OYSTER BAR *Menu on AAA.com*

Phone: 405/848-8008 (12)

Seafood
$6-$18

Pearl's features entree selections of seafood such as trout and catfish as well as chicken, pork chops and steak dishes, many with Cajun-style spiciness. The upbeat-tempo atmosphere creates a fun dining experience with pleasant and attentive service. Casual dress. **Bar:** Full bar. **Hours:** 11 am-10 pm, Fri & Sat-11 pm, Sun-9 pm. Closed: 11/25, 12/25. **Address:** 5641 N Classen Blvd 73118 **Location:** 0.4 mi n of jct NW Expwy. **Parking:** on-site.

RIB CRIB BBQ AND GRILL

Phone: 405/616-7800

Barbecue
$6-$14

Most guests need extra napkins to tackle the ribs, brisket, ham, pork and chicken selections. The menu also lists sandwiches and wraps, along with tempting sides and large desserts. The decor is decidedly Western. Casual dress. **Bar:** Beer only. **Hours:** 11 am-10 pm. Closed: 11/25, 12/25. **Address:** 401 SW 74th St 73139 **Location:** I-240, exit 3B, just n. **Parking:** on-site.

See map and index starting on p. 608)

RIB CRIB BBQ AND GRILL — **Phone:** 405/917-7400

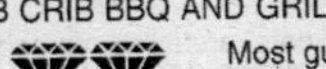

Barbecue
$6-$14

Most guests need extra napkins to tackle the ribs, brisket, ham, pork and chicken selections. The menu also lists sandwiches and wraps, along with tempting sides and large desserts. The decor is decidedly Western. Casual dress. **Bar:** Beer only. **Hours:** 11 am-10 pm. Closed: 11/25, 12/25. **Address:** 1223 S Meridian Ave 73108 **Location:** I-40, exit 145 (Meridian Ave), 0.5 mi s. **Parking:** on-site.

RON'S HAMBURGERS & CHILI — **Phone:** 405/943-7667

American
$4-$6

Although Ron's Hamburgers & Chili's name gives indicators of its strengths—varied hamburgers and savory chili—the menu also throws in a few tasty surprises. Casual dress. **Hours:** 10:30 am-8 pm. Closed: 11/25, 12/25; also Sun. **Address:** 4723 N May Ave 73112 **Location:** I-44, exit 124, 0.4 mi n. **Parking:** on-site.

SHORTY SMALL'S — **Phone:** 405/947-0779

Barbecue
$7-$19

Focusing on ribs, fried catfish, sandwiches and cheesecake, this restaurant is popular with the locals. The rustic and nostalgic atmosphere is family-oriented, and the feel is casual, hectic and sometimes noisy. Casual dress. **Bar:** Full bar. **Reservations:** not accepted. **Hours:** 11 am-10 pm. Closed: 12/25. **Address:** 4500 W Reno Ave 73127 **Location:** I-40, exit 145 (Meridian Ave), just n. **Parking:** on-site.

TED'S CAFE ESCONDIDO — **Phone:** 405/635-8337 (31)

Mexican
$8-$14

The Oklahoma City favorite is frequently busy but handles large crowds efficiently to prevent them from being a distraction. Casual dress. **Bar:** Beer only. **Hours:** 11 am-10 pm, Fri & Sat-10:30 pm. Closed major holidays. **Address:** 8324 S Western Ave 73159 **Location:** I-240, exit 2A, 0.8 mi s. **Parking:** on-site.

TED'S CAFE ESCONDIDO — **Phone:** 405/848-8337 (14)

Mexican
$8-$14

Ted's is a free-standing Mexican restaurant with the exterior of a typical stucco facade. The restaurant is a local family favorite, serving a variety of Mexican dishes. Casual dress. **Bar:** Beer only. **Hours:** 10:45 am-10 pm, Fri & Sat-10:30 pm, Sun 11 am-8 pm. Closed major holidays. **Address:** 2836 NW 68th St 73116 **Location:** I-44, exit May Ave, 2.4 mi n to 68th St, then just e. **Parking:** on-site.

TRAPPER'S FISHCAMP & GRILL — ***Menu on AAA.com*** — **Phone:** 405/943-9111 (26)

American
$7-$23

Evocative of a rustic lodge, the dining room sports hunting and fishing equipment and some mounted game on the walls. Choices on the menu range from beef to seafood. Casual dress. **Bar:** Full bar. **Hours:** 11 am-10 pm. Closed: 11/25, 12/25. **Address:** 4300 W Reno Ave 73107 **Location:** I-40, exit 145 (Meridian Ave), 0.3 mi n, then just e. **Parking:** on-site.

ZIO'S ITALIAN KITCHEN — **Phone:** 405/680-9999

Italian
$8-$13

The warm, comfortable atmosphere and Old World decor complement the menu. Meals are a good value, and so is the service. This small chain specializes in Italian cuisine, including oven-baked pizzas and pasta dishes. Guests are encouraged to get creative with their pizzas by mixing and matching from a list of 24 toppings. Particularly tempting dishes are Artichoke spinach pasta, chicken parmigiana, and Shrimp Limone. Casual dress. **Bar:** Full bar. **Hours:** 11 am-10 pm, Fri & Sat-11 pm. Closed: 12/25. **Address:** 2305 S Meridian Ave 73108 **Location:** I-40, exit 145 (Meridian Ave), 1.2 mi s. **Parking:** on-site.

The Oklahoma City Vicinity

CHOCTAW pop. 9,377

— WHERE TO DINE —

OLD GERMANY RESTAURANT Menu on AAA.com Phone: 405/390-864

German
$6-$29

You'll enjoy Old World-style food and environment here. Sit in the Bavarian room, Black Forest Chalet o Wine Cellar and have jager schnitzel (grilled pork loin), wiener schnitzel (breaded veal) or a variety o German sausages. Weekends offer live music. Casual dress. **Bar:** Full bar. **Reservations:** accepted **Hours:** 11 am-2 & 5-9 pm. Closed major holidays; also Sun & Mon. **Address:** 15920 SE 29th St 7302 **Location:** I-40, exit 166, 3 mi n, then 1 mi e. **Parking:** on-site.

DEL CITY pop. 22,128 (See map and index starting on p. 608)

LA QUINTA INN OKLAHOMA CITY EAST (DEL CITY) Book at AAA.com Phone: (405)672-0067 63

Hotel
$45-$95 All Year

Address: 5501 Tinker Diagonal Rd 73115-4613 **Location:** I-40, exit 156A (Sooner Rd), just nw. **Facility:** 105 units. 102 one-bedroom standard units. 3 one-bedroom suites. 3 stories, interior/exterio corridors. *Bath:* combo or shower only. **Parking:** on-site. **Amenities:** video games (fee), voice mail, irons, hair dryers. **Pool(s):** outdoor. **Guest Services:** coin laundry, wireless Internet.
ASK / SOME UNITS

EDMOND pop. 68,315 (See map and index starting on p. 608)

BEST WESTERN EDMOND INN & SUITES Book great rates at AAA.com Phone: (405)216-0300 56

Hotel
$86-$91 All Year

Address: 2700 E 2nd St 73034 **Location:** I-35, exit 141, 1.1 mi w. Located in a quiet area. **Facility:** Smoke free premises. 60 one-bedroom standard units, some with whirlpools. 2 stories (no elevator), interior corridors. *Bath:* combo or shower only. **Parking:** on-site. **Amenities:** irons, hair dryers. **Pool(s):** heated indoor. **Leisure Activities:** whirlpool, exercise room. **Guest Services:** wireless Internet. **Business Services:** meeting rooms, PC. **Free Special Amenities: local telephone calls and high-speed Internet.** / SOME UNITS FEE

FAIRFIELD INN & SUITES BY MARRIOTT Book great rates at AAA.com Phone: (405)341-4818 58

Hotel
$103-$125 All Year

Address: 301 Meline Dr 73034 **Location:** I-35, exit 141, just w. **Facility:** Smoke free premises. 90 units. 87 one-bedroom standard units, some with whirlpools. 3 one-bedroom suites. 3 stories, interior corridors. *Bath:* combo or shower only. **Parking:** on-site. **Terms:** cancellation fee imposed. **Amenities:** high-speed Internet, voice mail, irons, hair dryers. *Some:* CD players. **Pool(s):** heated indoor. **Leisure Activities:** whirlpool, exercise room. **Guest Services:** valet and coin laundry, wireless Internet. **Business Services:** meeting rooms, business center. **Free Special Amenities: expanded continental breakfast and high-speed Internet.**
CALL / SOME UNITS

HAMPTON INN Book great rates at AAA.com Phone: (405)844-3037 59

Hotel
$87-$175 All Year

Address: 300 Meline Dr 73034 **Location:** I-35, exit 141, just w. **Facility:** 71 one-bedroom standard units, some with whirlpools. 3 stories, interior corridors. *Bath:* combo or shower only. **Parking:** on-site. **Terms:** 1-7 night minimum stay, cancellation fee imposed. **Amenities:** voice mail, irons, hair dryers. **Pool(s):** heated indoor. **Leisure Activities:** whirlpool, exercise room. **Guest Services:** valet laundry, wireless Internet. **Business Services:** meeting rooms, PC.
/ SOME UNITS

HOLIDAY INN EXPRESS HOTEL & SUITES Book at AAA.com Phone: (405)844-3700 57

Hotel
$114-$159 All Year

Address: 3840 E 2nd St 73034 **Location:** I-35, exit 141, just w. **Facility:** Smoke free premises. 80 units. 77 one-bedroom standard units, some with whirlpools. 3 one-bedroom suites. 3 stories, interior corridors. *Bath:* combo or shower only. **Parking:** on-site. **Amenities:** video games (fee), high-speed Internet, dual phone lines, voice mail, irons, hair dryers. **Pool(s):** heated indoor. **Leisure Activities:** whirlpool, exercise room. **Guest Services:** valet and coin laundry, wireless Internet. **Business Services:** meeting rooms, business center. ASK / SOME UNITS

See map and index starting on p. 608)

LEEP INN & SUITES *Book at AAA.com* **Phone:** (405)844-3000 60

Hotel
$80-$145 All Year

Address: 3608 S Broadway Extension 73013 **Location:** John Kilpatrick Tpke, 1.5 mi n on US 77. **Facility:** 100 units. 94 one-bedroom standard units, some with whirlpools. 6 one-bedroom suites, some with whirlpools. 3 stories, interior corridors. *Bath:* combo or shower only. **Parking:** on-site. **Amenities:** voice mail, safes (fee), irons, hair dryers. *Some:* high-speed Internet, dual phone lines. **Pool(s):** heated indoor. **Leisure Activities:** whirlpool, exercise room. **Guest Services:** valet and coin laundry, wireless Internet. **Business Services:** meeting rooms, PC.

ASK CALL / SOME UNITS

WHERE TO DINE

LVARADO'S **Phone:** 405/359-8860 37

Mexican
$5-$15

Traditional Mexican dishes are served in a relaxed setting. The basic decor and seating match the restaurant's theme. Casual dress. **Bar:** Beer only. **Hours:** 11 am-9 pm, Fri-10 pm. Closed: 11/25, 12/25; also Sun. **Address:** 1000 E 2nd St 73034 **Location:** I-35, exit 141, 2.3 mi w. **Parking:** on-site.

CHARLESTON'S RESTAURANT **Phone:** 405/478-4949

American
$8-$22

This casual dining spot boasts a friendly, club-like atmosphere. Fine steak and seafood, as well as hardwood-grilled dishes, are at the heart of the menu. The noteworthy baked potato soup is rich with onions and bacon bits. Casual dress. **Bar:** Full bar. **Reservations:** accepted. **Hours:** 11 am-9 pm, Fri & Sat-10 pm. Closed: 11/25, 12/25. **Address:** 3409 S Broadway, Suite 400 73013 **Location:** John Kilpatrick Tpke, 1.5 mi n on US 77. **Parking:** on-site.

COACH'S BBQ, PIZZA & BREWERY **Phone:** 405/359-2222 38

Barbecue
$7-$16

Although gourmet pizza and barbecue dishes get the marquee billing, other dishes here are equally well prepared. Casual dress. **Bar:** Full bar. **Hours:** 11 am-10 pm, Fri & Sat-11 pm. Closed: 11/25, 12/25. **Address:** 3005 S Broadway 73013 **Location:** John Kilpatrick Tpke, 1.5 mi n on US 77. **Parking:** on-site.

GOLDIES PATIO GRILL **Phone:** 405/348-1555

American
$6-$15

The menu comprises grilled items, chicken, sandwiches and steak, but this place is best known for its excellent charbroiled burgers. The decor incorporates 1950s and '60s memorabilia. Casual dress. **Hours:** 11 am-9 pm. Closed major holidays. **Address:** 834 W Danforth Rd 73013 **Location:** Center. **Parking:** on-site.

HOUSE OF HUNAN **Phone:** 405/330-1668 36

Chinese
$4-$22

The House of Hunan's extensive menu features pork, chicken and shrimp entrees served with vegetables and fried rice. The restaurant offers a casual, family-dining atmosphere. Service is prompt and attentive. They will also deliver meals to motels. Casual dress. **Bar:** Full bar. **Reservations:** accepted. **Hours:** 11 am-9 pm, Fri-10 pm, Sat noon-10 pm, Sun noon-9 pm. Closed: 7/4, 11/25, 12/25. **Address:** 2137 W Edmond Rd 73034 **Location:** 1.4 mi w of US 77 on 2nd St (Edmond Rd); in Oakbrook Center. **Parking:** on-site.

PAPA DINO'S PIZZA **Phone:** 405/330-4999 35

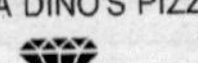

Pizza
$3-$7

The restaurant's appearance is modest, but guests come back again and again for good pizza and calzones. Casual dress. **Bar:** Beer only. **Hours:** 11 am-9 pm, Fri & Sat-10 pm. Closed: 11/25, 12/25. **Address:** 119 N University Dr 73034 **Location:** Just n of jct US 77. **Parking:** on-site.

RIB CRIB BBQ AND GRILL **Phone:** 405/715-2200

Barbecue
$6-$9

Most guests need extra napkins to tackle the ribs, brisket, ham, pork and chicken selections. The menu also lists sandwiches and wraps, along with tempting sides and large desserts. The decor is decidedly Western. Casual dress. **Hours:** 11 am-10 pm. Closed: 11/25, 12/25. **Address:** 720 S Broadway 73013 **Location:** Center. **Parking:** on-site.

TED'S CAFE ESCONDIDO **Phone:** 405/810-8337 34

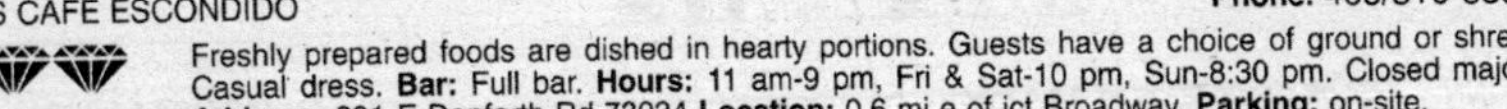

Mexican
$9-$16

Freshly prepared foods are dished in hearty portions. Guests have a choice of ground or shredded beef. Casual dress. **Bar:** Full bar. **Hours:** 11 am-9 pm, Fri & Sat-10 pm, Sun-8:30 pm. Closed major holidays. **Address:** 801 E Danforth Rd 73034 **Location:** 0.6 mi e of jct Broadway. **Parking:** on-site.

EL RENO pop. 16,212

BEST WESTERN HENSLEY'S *Book great rates at AAA.com* **Phone:** (405)262-6490

Hotel
$80-$100 All Year

Address: 2701 S Country Club Rd 73036 **Location:** I-40, exit 123, just s. **Facility:** 60 one-bedroom standard units. 2 stories (no elevator), exterior corridors. **Parking:** on-site, winter plug-ins. **Amenities:** irons, hair dryers. *Some:* high-speed Internet. **Pool(s):** outdoor. **Leisure Activities:** playground. **Guest Services:** wireless Internet. **Free Special Amenities: full breakfast and high-speed Internet.**

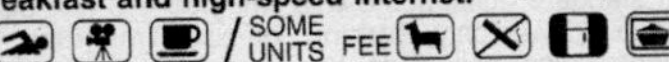

AAA Benefit:
Members save up to 20%, plus 10% bonus points with rewards program.

MOTEL 6 *Book great rates at AAA.com*

Phone: 405/262-606

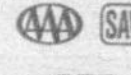

Hotel
Rates not provided

Address: 1506 Domino Dr 73036 **Location:** I-40, exit 123, just ne. **Facility:** 64 one-bedroom standar units. 3 stories, interior corridors. *Bath:* combo or shower only. **Parking:** on-site. **Amenities:** high speed Internet, voice mail. **Pool(s):** outdoor. **Guest Services:** coin laundry. **Business Services:** PC **Free Special Amenities: local telephone calls and high-speed Internet.**

/ SOME UNITS FEE

WHERE TO DINE

MONTANA MIKE'S

Phone: 405/422-110C

Steak
$7-$20

This steakhouse offers a dining experience for the whole family. A rustic look with Western appointments characterizes the dining room. Although it's hard to go wrong with a hearty steak of USDA Choice agec beef, guests also can try smoked, fire-grilled chicken breast, chicken-fried steak, baby back ribs and other selections. Casual dress. **Hours:** 11 am-9 pm, Fri & Sat-10 pm. Closed: 11/25, 12/25. **Address:** 1609 SW 27th St 73036 **Location:** I-40, exit 123, just ne. **Parking:** on-site.

GUTHRIE pop. 9,925

BEST WESTERN TERRITORIAL INN *Book great rates at AAA.com*

Phone: (405)282-8831

Hotel
$84-$99 All Year

Address: 2323 Territorial Tr 73044 **Location:** I-35, exit 157, just sw. **Facility:** 84 one-bedroom standard units. 2 stories (no elevator), interior corridors. *Bath:* combo or shower only. **Parking:** on-site. **Amenities:** voice mail, irons, hair dryers. **Pool(s):** outdoor. **Guest Services:** wireless Internet. **Business Services:** PC. **Free Special Amenities: expanded continental breakfast and high-speed Internet.**

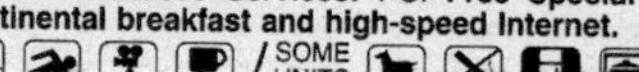

AAA Benefit:
Members save up to 20%, plus 10% bonus points with rewards program.

SLEEP INN & SUITES *Book at AAA.com*

Phone: (405)260-1400

Hotel
$83-$135 All Year

Address: 414 Heather Rd 73044 **Location:** I-35, exit 157, just nw. **Facility:** 78 units. 77 one-bedroom standard units, some with whirlpools. 1 one-bedroom suite with whirlpool. 3 stories, interior corridors. *Bath:* combo or shower only. **Parking:** on-site. **Amenities:** voice mail, safes (fee), irons, hair dryers. **Pool(s):** heated indoor. **Leisure Activities:** whirlpool, limited exercise equipment. **Guest Services:** coin laundry, wireless Internet. **Business Services:** meeting rooms, PC.

ASK CALL / SOME UNITS

WHERE TO DINE

STABLES CAFE

Phone: 405/282-0893

Barbecue
$5-$15

First a livery and feed store when built in 1890, the renovated building now houses a restaurant that serves great-tasting barbecue and steaks. Nostalgic advertisements for beverages, bread, soap and the like lend to the decor. Casual dress. **Hours:** 11 am-9 pm, Fri & Sat-10 pm. Closed major holidays. **Address:** 223 N Division 73044 **Location:** I-35, exit 157, 1.8 mi w. **Parking:** on-site.

MIDWEST CITY pop. 54,088 (See map and index starting on p. 608)

BEST WESTERN MIDWEST CITY INN & SUITES *Book great rates at AAA.com*

Phone: (405)737-6060 71

Hotel
$95-$115 All Year

Address: 6701 Tinker Diagonal 73110 **Location:** I-40, exit 157A, just nw. **Facility:** 69 one-bedroom standard units, some with whirlpools. 3 stories, interior corridors. *Bath:* combo or shower only. **Parking:** on-site. **Amenities:** high-speed Internet, voice mail, irons, hair dryers. **Pool(s):** heated indoor. **Leisure Activities:** exercise room. **Guest Services:** valet and coin laundry, wireless Internet. **Business Services:** business center. **Free Special Amenities: full breakfast and high-speed Internet.** / SOME UNITS

AAA Benefit:
Members save up to 20%, plus 10% bonus points with rewards program.

COMFORT INN & SUITES *Book great rates at AAA.com*

Phone: (405)733-1339 69

Hotel
$85-$131 All Year

Address: 5653 Tinker Diagonal Rd 73110 **Location:** I-40, exit 156A (Sooner Rd), just n. **Facility:** 78 units. 75 one-bedroom standard units. 3 one-bedroom suites with whirlpools. 4 stories, interior corridors. *Bath:* combo or shower only. **Parking:** on-site. **Amenities:** high-speed Internet, dual phone lines, voice mail, irons, hair dryers. **Pool(s):** heated indoor. **Leisure Activities:** exercise room. **Guest Services:** valet and coin laundry, wireless Internet. **Business Services:** meeting rooms, PC. **Free Special Amenities: expanded continental breakfast and high-speed Internet.**

/ SOME UNITS

(See map and index starting on p. 608)

HAMPTON INN Book great rates at AAA.com Phone: (405)732-5500 68

Hotel
$104-$129 All Year

Address: 1833 Center Dr 73110 **Location:** I-40, exit 156A (Sooner Rd), just ne. **Facility:** 101 units. 97 one-bedroom standard units. 4 one-bedroom suites with whirlpools. 3 stories, interior corridors. *Bath:* combo or shower only. **Parking:** on-site. **Terms:** 1-7 night minimum stay, cancellation fee imposed. **Amenities:** high-speed Internet, dual phone lines, voice mail, irons, hair dryers. **Pool(s):** heated indoor. **Leisure Activities:** whirlpool, exercise room. **Guest Services:** valet and coin laundry, wireless Internet. **Business Services:** meeting rooms, business center.

/ SOME UNITS

AAA Benefit:
Members save up to 10% everyday!

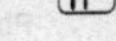

HAWTHORN SUITES Book at AAA.com Phone: (405)737-7777 70

Hotel
$105-$125 All Year

Address: 5701 Tinker Diagonal Rd 73110 **Location:** I-40, exit 156A (Sooner Rd), just n. **Facility:** 80 one-bedroom standard units. 4 stories, interior corridors. *Bath:* combo or shower only. **Parking:** on-site. **Terms:** 3 day cancellation notice. **Amenities:** high-speed Internet, voice mail, irons, hair dryers. *Some:* dual phone lines. **Pool(s):** heated indoor. **Leisure Activities:** exercise room. **Guest Services:** valet and coin laundry, wireless Internet. **Business Services:** meeting rooms, business center.

ASK CALL / SOME UNITS FEE

HOLIDAY INN EXPRESS HOTEL & SUITES Book at AAA.com Phone: (405)736-1000 66

Hotel
$99-$169 All Year

Address: 1700 S Sooner Rd 73110 **Location:** I-40, exit 156A (Sooner Rd), just n. **Facility:** 87 one-bedroom standard units, some with whirlpools. 4 stories, interior corridors. *Bath:* combo or shower only. **Parking:** on-site. **Amenities:** high-speed Internet, dual phone lines, voice mail, irons, hair dryers. **Pool(s):** heated indoor. **Leisure Activities:** whirlpool, exercise room. **Guest Services:** valet and coin laundry, wireless Internet. **Business Services:** meeting rooms, business center.

ASK / SOME UNITS

SHERATON MIDWEST CITY HOTEL AT THE REED CONFERENCE CENTER Book great rates at AAA.com Phone: 405/741-7333 67

AAA SAVE

Hotel
Rates not provided

Address: 5750 Will Rogers Rd 73110 **Location:** I-40, exit 156A (Sooner Rd), just ne. **Facility:** Smoke free premises. 151 units. 149 one-bedroom standard units. 2 one-bedroom suites. 5 stories, interior corridors. *Bath:* combo or shower only. **Parking:** on-site. **Amenities:** video games (fee), high-speed Internet, dual phone lines, voice mail, irons, hair dryers. **Pool(s):** heated indoor. **Leisure Activities:** whirlpool, exercise room. **Guest Services:** valet and coin laundry, wireless Internet. **Business Services:** conference facilities, PC. **Free Special Amenities:** newspaper.

24 / SOME UNITS FEE FEE

Sheraton HOTELS & RESORTS

AAA Benefit:
Members get up to 15% off, plus Starwood Preferred Guest® bonuses.

(See map and index starting on p. 608)

WHERE TO DINE

CHEQUERS RESTAURANT & PUB

Phone: 405/736-6944 (41)

American
$5-$10

Menu choices—which include Mexican, pasta, steak and seafood dishes—suit many tastes. Casual dress. **Bar:** Full bar. **Hours:** 11 am-10 pm, Fri & Sat-11 pm. Closed: 7/4, 12/25. **Address:** 1009 S Air Depot 73110 **Location:** I-40, exit 156B, 1.4 mi n. **Parking:** on-site.

PRIMO'S D' ITALIA

Phone: 405/736-9090 (42)

Italian
$8-$16

The extensive menu includes both traditional Italian dishes and assorted pizzas. Casual dress. **Bar:** Full bar. **Reservations:** accepted. **Hours:** 10:30 am-10 pm. Closed: 11/25, 12/25. **Address:** 5661 Tinker Diagonal Rd 73110 **Location:** I-40, exit 156A (Sooner Rd), just ne. **Parking:** on-site.

RIB CRIB BBQ AND GRILL

Phone: 405/737-4500

Barbecue
$6-$14

Most guests need extra napkins to tackle the ribs, brisket, ham, pork and chicken selections. The menu also lists sandwiches and wraps, along with tempting sides and large desserts. The decor is decidedly Western. Casual dress. **Bar:** Beer only. **Hours:** 11 am-10 pm. Closed: 11/25, 12/25. **Address:** 1821 S Douglas Blvd 73130 **Location:** I-40, exit 159A (Sooner Rd), 0.7 mi ne. **Parking:** on-site.

RON'S HAMBURGERS & CHILI

Phone: 405/733-7667

American
$4-$6

Although Ron's Hamburgers & Chili's name gives indicators of its strengths—varied hamburgers and savory chili—the menu also throws in a few tasty surprises. Casual dress. **Hours:** 10:30 am-8 pm. Closed: 11/25, 12/25; also Sun. **Address:** 351 N Air Depot, Suite A 73110 **Location:** I-40, exit 156B, 2.3 mi n. **Parking:** on-site.

MOORE pop. 41,138 (See map and index starting on p. 608)

BEST WESTERN GREEN TREE INN & SUITES *Book great rates at AAA.com*

Phone: (405)912-8882 (74)

AAA SAVE

Hotel
$85-$99 All Year

Address: 1811 N Moore Ave 73160 **Location:** I-35, exit 118, just n on westbound frontage road. **Facility:** 64 units. 55 one-bedroom standard units. 9 one-bedroom suites, some with efficiencies (no utensils). 3 stories, interior corridors. *Bath:* combo or shower only. **Parking:** on-site. **Amenities:** high-speed Internet, voice mail, irons, hair dryers. **Pool(s):** heated indoor. **Leisure Activities:** whirlpool, exercise room. **Guest Services:** coin laundry, wireless Internet. **Business Services:** meeting rooms, PC. **Free Special Amenities: continental breakfast and high-speed Internet.**

/ SOME UNITS FEE

Best Western

AAA Benefit:
Members save up to 20%, plus 10% bonus points with rewards program.

COMFORT INN & SUITES *Book at AAA.com*

Phone: (405)912-1400 (75)

Hotel
$75-$125 All Year

Address: 1809 N Moore Ave 73160 **Location:** I-35, exit 118, just nw. **Facility:** 58 one-bedroom standard units. 3 stories, interior corridors. *Bath:* combo or shower only. **Parking:** on-site. **Amenities:** high-speed Internet, irons, hair dryers. **Pool(s):** heated indoor. **Leisure Activities:** whirlpool. **Guest Services:** wireless Internet. **Business Services:** PC.

ASK / SOME UNITS

WHERE TO DINE

ROYAL BAVARIA BREWHAUS & RESTAURANT *Menu on AAA.com*

Phone: 405/799-7666

AAA

German
$6-$25

Located just outside town in the peaceful, rolling countryside, the Royal Bavaria Brewhaus serves great-tasting, authentic German cuisine. Casual dress. **Bar:** Full bar. **Hours:** 5:30 pm-9:30 pm, Sat from 4 pm, Sun 4 pm-8:30 pm. Closed: 11/25, 12/25; also Mon. **Address:** 3401 S Sooner Rd 73165 **Location:** I-240, exit 8, 6 mi s. **Parking:** on-site.

NORMAN pop. 95,694

COMFORT INN & SUITES NORMAN *Book at AAA.com*

Phone: (405)701-5200

Hotel
$80-$169 All Year

Address: 840 Copperfield Dr 73019 **Location:** I-35, exit 110, 0.4 mi sw, off west service road. **Facility:** Smoke free premises. 73 one-bedroom standard units, some with whirlpools. 3 stories, interior corridors. *Bath:* combo or shower only. **Parking:** on-site. **Amenities:** high-speed Internet, voice mail, irons, hair dryers. **Pool(s):** heated indoor. **Leisure Activities:** whirlpool, exercise room. **Guest Services:** valet and coin laundry, wireless Internet. **Business Services:** meeting rooms, business center. ASK CALL

COUNTRY INN & SUITES BY CARLSON *Book at AAA.com* **Phone:** (405)360-0240

Hotel
$82-$174 All Year

Address: 960 Ed Noble Pkwy 73072 **Location:** I-35, exit 108B (Lindsey St), just nw. **Facility:** Smoke free premises. 77 units. 58 one-bedroom standard units. 19 one-bedroom suites, some with whirlpools. 3 stories, interior corridors. *Bath:* combo or shower only. **Parking:** on-site. **Amenities:** high-speed Internet, voice mail, irons, hair dryers. **Pool(s):** heated indoor. **Leisure Activities:** whirlpool, exercise room. **Guest Services:** valet and coin laundry, wireless Internet. **Business Services:** meeting rooms, business center. ASK CALL / SOME UNITS

COURTYARD BY MARRIOTT NORMAN *Book great rates at AAA.com* **Phone:** (405)701-8900

Hotel
$116-$142 All Year

Address: 770 Copperfield Dr 73072 **Location:** I-35, exit 110, 0.4 mi sw, off west service road. **Facility:** Smoke free premises. 113 units. 107 one-bedroom standard units, some with whirlpools. 6 one-bedroom suites. 3 stories, interior corridors. *Bath:* combo or shower only. **Parking:** on-site. **Terms:** cancellation fee imposed. **Amenities:** CD players, high-speed Internet, dual phone lines, voice mail, irons, hair dryers. **Pool(s):** heated indoor. **Leisure Activities:** whirlpool, exercise room. **Guest Services:** valet and coin laundry, wireless Internet. **Business Services:** meeting rooms, business center.

CALL

AAA Benefit: Members save a minimum 5% off the best available rate.

ECONO LODGE *Book great rates at AAA.com* **Phone:** (405)364-5554

AAA SAVE

Motel
$65-$90 All Year

Address: 100 SW 26th Dr 73069 **Location:** I-35, exit 109 (Main St), just se. **Facility:** 44 one-bedroom standard units. 2 stories (no elevator), exterior corridors. **Parking:** on-site, winter plug-ins. **Amenities:** irons, hair dryers. **Guest Services:** wireless Internet. **Business Services:** PC. **Free Special Amenities: continental breakfast and high-speed Internet.** / SOME UNITS FEE

EMBASSY SUITES NORMAN - HOTEL & CONFERENCE CENTER *Book great rates at AAA.com* **Phone:** (405)364-8040

AAA SAVE

Hotel
$109-$299 All Year

Address: 2501 Conference Dr 73069 **Location:** 0.7 mi n of jct 24th Ave NW and Robinson. **Facility:** 283 one-bedroom suites, some with whirlpools. 10 stories, interior corridors. *Bath:* combo or tub only. **Parking:** on-site and valet. **Terms:** 1-7 night minimum stay, cancellation fee imposed. **Amenities:** dual phone lines, voice mail, safes, irons, hair dryers. *Fee:* video games, high-speed Internet. *Some:* DVD players (fee). **Pool(s):** heated indoor. **Leisure Activities:** whirlpool, exercise room. **Guest Services:** valet and coin laundry, wireless Internet. **Business Services:** conference facilities, business center. **Free Special Amenities: full breakfast and newspaper.** CALL / SOME UNITS FEE

AAA Benefit: Members save 5% or more everyday!

FAIRFIELD INN BY MARRIOTT *Book great rates at AAA.com* **Phone:** (405)447-1661

Hotel
$99-$121 All Year

Address: 301 Norman Center Ct 73072 **Location:** I-35, exit 109 (Main St), just sw. **Facility:** Smoke free premises. 76 one-bedroom standard units. 3 stories, interior corridors. *Bath:* combo or shower only. **Parking:** on-site. **Terms:** cancellation fee imposed. **Amenities:** voice mail, irons, hair dryers. **Pool(s):** heated indoor. **Leisure Activities:** whirlpool. **Guest Services:** valet laundry, wireless Internet. **Business Services:** PC. / SOME UNITS

AAA Benefit: Members save a minimum 5% off the best available rate.

HAMPTON INN *Book great rates at AAA.com*

Phone: 405/366-2100

Hotel
Rates not provided

Address: 309 Norman Center Ct 73072 **Location:** I-35, exit 109 (Main St), just sw. **Facility:** 61 one-bedroom standard units, some with whirlpools. 2 stories, interior corridors. *Bath:* combo or shower only. **Parking:** on-site. **Amenities:** voice mail, irons, hair dryers. **Pool(s):** heated indoor. **Leisure Activities:** sauna, exercise room. **Guest Services:** valet laundry, wireless Internet. **Business Services:** meeting rooms, PC.

CALL / SOME UNITS

AAA Benefit: Members save up to 10% everyday!

HILTON GARDEN INN *Book great rates at AAA.com*

Phone: (405)579-0100

Hotel
$99-$209 All Year

Address: 700 Copperfield Dr 73072 **Location:** I-35, exit 110, 0.5 mi sw, off west service road. **Facility:** 121 one-bedroom standard units. 3 stories, interior corridors. *Bath:* combo or shower only. **Parking:** on-site. **Terms:** 1-7 night minimum stay, cancellation fee imposed. **Amenities:** high-speed Internet, voice mail, irons, hair dryers. **Pool(s):** heated outdoor. **Leisure Activities:** whirlpool, exercise room. **Guest Services:** valet and coin laundry, wireless Internet. **Business Services:** meeting rooms, business center.

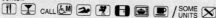

CALL / SOME UNITS

Hilton Garden Inn

AAA Benefit: Members save 5% or more everyday!

LA QUINTA INN & SUITES OKLAHOMA CITY (NORMAN) *Book at AAA.com*

Phone: (405)579-4000

Hotel
$79-$129 All Year

Address: 930 Ed Noble Dr 73072 **Location:** I-35, exit 108B (Lindsey St), just nw. **Facility:** 117 units. 113 one-bedroom standard units. 4 one-bedroom suites. 4 stories, interior corridors. *Bath:* combo or shower only. **Parking:** on-site. **Amenities:** video games (fee), high-speed Internet, voice mail, irons, hair dryers. *Some:* dual phone lines. **Pool(s):** outdoor. **Leisure Activities:** whirlpool, exercise room. **Guest Services:** valet and coin laundry, wireless Internet. **Business Services:** meeting rooms, PC.

ASK CALL / SOME UNITS

MONTFORD INN & COTTAGES

Phone: (405)321-2200

Bed & Breakfast
$99-$239 All Year

Address: 322 W Tonhawa 73069 **Location:** I-35, exit 109 (Main St), 2.1 mi e to University Blvd, then just n. **Facility:** Near downtown shops and restaurants and the University of Oklahoma, the inn offers a porch, a flower and herb garden and rooms with fireplaces. Smoke free premises. 16 units. 10 one-bedroom standard units, some with whirlpools. 4 one-bedroom suites with whirlpools. 2 cottages. 2 stories (no elevator), interior/exterior corridors. **Parking:** on-site. **Terms:** check-in 4 pm, 5 day cancellation notice-fee imposed. **Amenities:** video library, DVD players, irons, hair dryers. *Some:* CD players. **Guest Services:** valet laundry, wireless Internet. **Business Services:** meeting rooms.

ASK / SOME UNITS

RESIDENCE INN BY MARRIOTT *Book great rates at AAA.com*

Phone: (405)366-0900

Extended Stay Hotel
$134-$164 All Year

Address: 2681 Jefferson St 73072 **Location:** I-35, exit 108A, just se. **Facility:** Smoke free premises. 126 units. 96 one- and 30 two-bedroom standard units with kitchens. 2 stories (no elevator), exterior corridors. *Bath:* combo or shower only. **Parking:** on-site. **Terms:** cancellation fee imposed. **Amenities:** voice mail, irons, hair dryers. **Pool(s):** outdoor. **Leisure Activities:** whirlpool, exercise room, sports court. **Guest Services:** valet and coin laundry, area transportation, wireless Internet. **Business Services:** meeting rooms, PC.

/ SOME UNITS FEE

AAA Benefit: Members save a minimum 5% off the best available rate.

WHERE TO DINE

CHARLESTON'S RESTAURANT

Phone: 405/360-0900

American
$8-$22

This casual dining spot boasts a friendly, club-like atmosphere. Fine steak and seafood, as well as hardwood-grilled dishes, are at the heart of the menu. The noteworthy baked potato soup is rich with onions and bacon bits. Casual dress. **Bar:** Full bar. **Reservations:** accepted. **Hours:** 11 am-9 pm, Fri & Sat-10 pm. Closed: 11/25, 12/25. **Address:** 300 Ed Noble Pkwy 73072 **Location:** I-35, exit 109 (Main St), just sw. **Parking:** on-site.

COACH'S BBQ, STEAKS & PIZZA & BREWERY

Phone: 405/360-5726

American
$5-$11

The restaurant's hickory-smoked barbecue dishes are excellent, and the freshly made pizzas are superb. Plus, diners can sample several home-brewed beers, view Heisman Trophies on display and watch sports on TV while they eat. Casual dress. **Bar:** Full bar. **Hours:** 11 am-10 pm, Thurs-Sat to 11 pm. Closed: 11/25, 12/25. **Address:** 102 W Main St 73069 **Location:** Downtown. **Parking:** on-site.

GOLDIES PATIO GRILL

Phone: 405/329-6363

American
$6-$15

The menu comprises grilled items, chicken, sandwiches and steak, but this place is best known for its excellent charbroiled burgers. The decor incorporates 1950s and '60s memorabilia. Casual dress. **Hours:** 11 am-9 pm. Closed major holidays. **Address:** 1310 E Alameda St 73071 **Location:** Just s of jct Main St and 12th Ave NE. **Parking:** on-site.

LA BAGUETTE RESTAURANT & BAKERY Phone: 405/329-5822

French
$4-$10

La Baguette serves an appetizing array of French pastries, fruit tarts and delicious European tortes. The chocolate mousse cake is rich and flavorful. The marble-top coffee bar and artwork are reminiscent of a French bistro with a light, airy atmosphere. Casual dress. **Hours:** 7 am-9 pm, Sun 9 am-2 pm, Mon 7 am-6 pm. Closed major holidays. **Address:** 924 W Main St 73069 **Location:** I-35, exit 109 (Main St), 1.6 mi e. **Parking:** on-site.

LEGEND'S RESTAURANT Phone: 405/329-8888

Continental
$6-$22

A quiet, elegant atmosphere envelops the restaurant, which specializes in a variety of daily-made homemade desserts. Casual dress. **Bar:** Full bar. **Hours:** 11 am-10 pm, Fri & Sat-11 pm, Sun 10 am-10 pm. Closed major holidays. **Address:** 1313 W Lindsey St 73069 **Location:** I-35, exit 108B (Lindsey St), 1 mi e. **Parking:** on-site.

MISAL OF INDIA BISTRO Phone: 405/579-5600

Indian
$7-$20

Lining the popular restaurant's menu is a wide assortment of chicken, lamb, beef and vegetable dishes, many of which are prepared in a tandoor. Casual dress. **Bar:** Full bar. **Hours:** 11 am-3 & 5-10 pm, Fri & Sat-11 pm. Closed: 11/25, 12/25. **Address:** 580 Ed Noble Pkwy 73072 **Location:** I-35, exit 109 (Main St), 0.7 mi s on west service road. **Parking:** on-site.

RIB CRIB BBQ AND GRILL Phone: 405/573-7900

Barbecue
$6-$14

Most guests need extra napkins to tackle the ribs, brisket, ham, pork and chicken selections. The menu also lists sandwiches and wraps, along with tempting sides and large desserts. The decor is decidedly Western. Casual dress. **Bar:** Full bar. **Hours:** 11 am-10 pm. Closed: 11/25, 12/25. **Address:** 1131 Rambling Oaks Dr 73072 **Location:** I-35, exit 110, just w. **Parking:** on-site.

VAN'S PIG STANDS Phone: 405/364-0600

Barbecue
$3-$11

Don't let the modest exterior and seating prevent you from trying this flavorful barbecue that you can watch being prepared; they've been in business since 1930 for a good reason. Casual dress. **Reservations:** not accepted. **Hours:** 11 am-9 pm, Fri & Sat-10 pm. **Address:** 320 N Porter Ave 73069 **Location:** I-35, exit 110, 2.5 mi e to US 77 (Porter Ave), then 0.5 mi s. **Parking:** on-site.

SHAWNEE pop. 28,692

DAYS INN-SHAWNEE *Book great rates at AAA.com* Phone: (405)275-6720

AAA SAVE

Motel
$70-$90 All Year

Address: 5107 N Harrison 74804 **Location:** I-40, exit 186, just n. **Facility:** 52 one-bedroom standard units. 2 stories (no elevator), interior corridors. **Parking:** on-site, winter plug-ins. **Amenities:** hair dryers. **Guest Services:** valet laundry, wireless Internet. **Free Special Amenities: expanded continental breakfast and high-speed Internet.** / SOME UNITS

HAMPTON INN BY HILTON *Book great rates at AAA.com* Phone: (405)275-1540

Hotel
$79-$109 All Year

Address: 4851 N Kickapoo 74801 **Location:** I-40, exit 185, just se. **Facility:** 64 one-bedroom standard units. 3 stories, interior corridors. *Bath:* combo or shower only. **Parking:** on-site. **Terms:** 1-7 night minimum stay, cancellation fee imposed. **Amenities:** voice mail, irons, hair dryers. **Pool(s):** heated indoor. **Leisure Activities:** whirlpool. **Guest Services:** valet laundry, wireless Internet. **Business Services:** PC. / SOME UNITS

AAA Benefit:
Members save up to 10% everyday!

HOLIDAY INN EXPRESS HOTEL & SUITES *Book at AAA.com* Phone: (405)275-8880

Hotel
$99-$119 All Year

Address: 4909 N Union 74804 **Location:** I-40, exit 186, just nw. **Facility:** 99 units. 97 one-bedroom standard units. 2 one-bedroom suites. 4 stories, interior corridors. *Bath:* combo or shower only. **Parking:** on-site. **Terms:** cancellation fee imposed. **Amenities:** high-speed Internet, voice mail, irons, hair dryers. *Some:* DVD players. **Pool(s):** outdoor. **Leisure Activities:** whirlpool, exercise room. **Guest Services:** valet and coin laundry, wireless Internet. **Business Services:** meeting rooms, business center. ASK / SOME UNITS

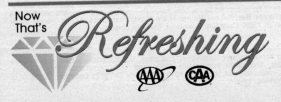

LA QUINTA INN & SUITES *Book great rates at AAA.com* **Phone:** (405)275-7930

Hotel

$79-$155 All Year

Address: 5401 Enterprise Ct 74804 **Location:** I-40, exit 186, just ne. **Facility:** 79 units. 75 one-bedroom standard units, some with whirlpools. 4 one-bedroom suites. 3 stories, interior corridors. *Bath:* combo or shower only. **Parking:** on-site. **Amenities:** high-speed Internet, voice mail, irons, hair dryers. **Pool(s):** heated indoor. **Leisure Activities:** whirlpool, exercise room. **Guest Services:** coin laundry, wireless Internet. **Business Services:** meeting rooms, business center. **Free Special Amenities: expanded continental breakfast and high-speed Internet.**

CALL / SOME UNITS

WHERE TO DINE

BILLY BOY BBQ **Phone:** 405/275-2040

American

$4-$10

Family-owned since 1972, Billy Boy's specializes in very good barbecue dishes served in enormous helpings. They also serve shrimp, chicken, steak and sandwiches. This place is a bright, clean and casual restaurant with hometown-style service. Casual dress. **Hours:** 11 am-8:30 pm. Closed major holidays; also Sun. **Address:** 120 W MacArthur St 74801 **Location:** I-40, exit 186, 1.5 mi s to MacArthur St, then 0.7 mi w. **Parking:** on-site.

YUKON pop. 21,043

BEST WESTERN INN & SUITES YUKON *Book great rates at AAA.com* **Phone:** (405)265-2995

Hotel

$84-$144 All Year

Address: 11440 W I-40 Service Rd 73099 **Location:** I-40, exit 138, just sw. **Facility:** 69 units. 68 one-bedroom standard units, some with whirlpools. 1 one-bedroom suite with efficiency. 2 stories, interior/exterior corridors. *Bath:* combo or shower only. **Parking:** on-site. **Amenities:** dual phone lines, voice mail, irons, hair dryers. *Some:* high-speed Internet. **Pool(s):** heated indoor. **Leisure Activities:** whirlpool, exercise room. **Guest Services:** valet and coin laundry, wireless Internet. **Business Services:** meeting rooms, PC. *(See color ad below)* / SOME UNITS FEE

Best Western

AAA Benefit:

Members save up to 20%, plus 10% bonus points with rewards program.

FREE full breakfast and high-speed Internet

▼ See AAA listing above ▼

COMFORT SUITES

Hotel

$86-$150 All Year

Book at AAA.com

Phone: (405)577-6500

Address: 11424 NW 4th St 73099 **Location:** I-40, exit 138, just nw. **Facility:** Smoke free premises. 72 units. 69 one- and 3 two-bedroom suites, some with whirlpools. 4 stories, interior corridors. *Bath:* combo or shower only. **Parking:** on-site. **Amenities:** high-speed Internet, voice mail, irons, hair dryers. **Pool(s):** heated indoor. **Leisure Activities:** whirlpool, exercise room. **Guest Services:** coin laundry, wireless Internet. **Business Services:** meeting rooms, business center.

ASK / SOME UNITS FEE

HAMPTON INN

Hotel

$94-$104 All Year

Book great rates at AAA.com

Phone: (405)350-6400

Address: 1351 Canadian Ct 73099 **Location:** I-40, exit 136, just ne. **Facility:** 73 one-bedroom standard units, some with whirlpools. 3 stories, interior corridors. *Bath:* combo or shower only. **Parking:** on-site. **Terms:** 1-7 night minimum stay, cancellation fee imposed. **Amenities:** voice mail, irons, hair dryers. *Some:* dual phone lines. **Pool(s):** heated indoor. **Leisure Activities:** exercise room. **Guest Services:** valet and coin laundry, wireless Internet. **Business Services:** meeting rooms, PC.

/ SOME UNITS

AAA Benefit:

Members save up to 10% everyday!

LA QUINTA INN & SUITES

Hotel

Rates not provided

Book at AAA.com

Phone: 405/494-7600

Address: 11500 W I-40 73099 **Location:** I-40, exit 138, just s. **Facility:** 80 one-bedroom standard units, some with whirlpools. 3 stories, interior corridors. *Bath:* combo or shower only. **Parking:** on-site. **Amenities:** voice mail, irons, hair dryers. **Pool(s):** heated indoor. **Leisure Activities:** whirlpool, exercise room. **Guest Services:** wireless Internet. **Business Services:** meeting rooms, business center.

CALL / SOME UNITS

WHERE TO DINE

ALFREDO'S MEXICAN CAFE

Mexican

$7-$12

Phone: 405/354-4343

Prompt servers satisfy diners with a good selection of entrees. The popular lunch spot has a well-lit dining room that offers a good window view. Casual dress. **Hours:** 11 am-9 pm, Fri & Sat-9:30 pm, Sun-8 pm. Closed: 11/25, 12/25. **Address:** 1751 Garth Brooks Blvd, Suite 110 73099 **Location:** I-40, exit 136, just se. **Parking:** on-site.

PRIMO'S D'ITALIA **Phone:** 405/350-9090

Italian
$6-$18

Guests can expect generous portions of freshly prepared dishes. Among menu selections are prime rib, seafood pasta and pizza. Casual dress. **Bar:** Full bar. **Reservations:** suggested. **Hours:** 11 am-9 pm, Fri-Sun to 10 pm. Closed: 11/25, 12/25. **Address:** 1215 Garth Brooks Blvd, Suite C 73099 **Location:** I-40, exit 136, just n. **Parking:** on-site.

RIB CRIB BBQ AND GRILL **Phone:** 405/354-2828

Barbecue
$6-$14

Most guests need extra napkins to tackle the ribs, brisket, ham, pork and chicken selections. The menu also lists sandwiches and wraps, along with tempting sides and large desserts. The decor is decidedly Western. Casual dress. **Bar:** Beer only. **Hours:** 11 am-10 pm. Closed: 11/25, 12/25. **Address:** 1750 Garth Brooks Blvd 73099 **Location:** I-40, exit 136, just s. **Parking:** on-site.

Oklahoma City National Memorial & Museum / © Michael Snell / Alamy

This ends listings for the Oklahoma City Vicinity.
The following page resumes the alphabetical listings of cities in Oklahoma.

OKMULGEE pop. 13,022

BEST WESTERN OKMULGEE *Book great rates at AAA.com* **Phone:** (918)756-9200

Hotel
$75-$89 All Year

Address: 3499 N Wood Dr 74447 **Location:** Just n of jct US 75 and SR 56. **Facility:** 50 one-bedroom standard units, some with kitchens and/or whirlpools. 2 stories, interior corridors. *Bath:* combo or shower only. **Parking:** on-site, winter plug-ins. **Amenities:** high-speed Internet, voice mail, irons, hair dryers. **Pool(s):** outdoor. **Leisure Activities:** exercise room. **Guest Services:** coin laundry, wireless Internet. **Business Services:** meeting rooms, business center. **Free Special Amenities: expanded continental breakfast and high-speed Internet.**
/ SOME UNITS FEE

Best Western
AAA Benefit: Members save up to 20%, plus 10% bonus points with rewards program.

WHERE TO DINE

SIRLOIN STOCKADE **Phone:** 918/756-4440

Regional Steak
$6-$9

The steakhouse lines up buffet items, including pizza, tacos, soups, salads and desserts, providing both excellent variety and a good value. Rotating theme nights might allow for the sampling of sushi, barbecue and seafood. The buffet also may serve to complement a quality steak. Rolls are baked several times daily. Casual dress. **Reservations:** not accepted. **Hours:** 11 am-9 pm. Closed: 11/25, 12/25. **Address:** 130 S Wood Dr 74447 **Location:** Between E 6th and E 7th sts. **Parking:** on-site.

OWASSO—See Tulsa p. 666.

PAULS VALLEY pop. 6,256

COMFORT INN & SUITES *Book at AAA.com* **Phone:** (405)207-9730

Hotel
$90-$100 All Year

Address: 103 S Humphrey Blvd 73075 **Location:** I-35, exit 72, just e. **Facility:** 64 one-bedroom standard units, some with whirlpools. 3 stories, interior corridors. *Bath:* combo or shower only. **Parking:** on-site. **Terms:** cancellation fee imposed. **Amenities:** high-speed Internet, voice mail, irons, hair dryers. **Pool(s):** heated indoor. **Leisure Activities:** exercise room. **Guest Services:** coin laundry, wireless Internet. **Business Services:** meeting rooms.
ASK CALL / SOME UNITS

DAYS INN *Book great rates at AAA.com* **Phone:** (405)238-7548

Hotel
$78 All Year

Address: 2606 W Grant Ave 73075 **Location:** I-35, exit 72, just e. **Facility:** 53 one-bedroom standard units. 2 stories (no elevator), interior corridors. **Parking:** on-site. **Amenities:** hair dryers. **Guest Services:** wireless Internet. **Free Special Amenities: continental breakfast and high-speed Internet.** / SOME UNITS

PONCA CITY pop. 25,919

COMFORT INN & SUITES *Book great rates at AAA.com* **Phone:** (580)765-2322

Hotel
$81 All Year

Address: 3101 N 14th St 74604 **Location:** I-35, exit 214, 3 mi n on US 77. **Facility:** 59 units. 58 one-bedroom standard units, some with whirlpools. 1 one-bedroom suite. 3 stories, interior corridors. *Bath:* combo or shower only. **Parking:** on-site. **Amenities:** high-speed Internet, voice mail, irons, hair dryers. **Pool(s):** heated indoor. **Leisure Activities:** whirlpool, limited exercise equipment. **Guest Services:** valet and coin laundry, wireless Internet. **Business Services:** meeting rooms, business center.
CALL / SOME UNITS FEE

FAIRFIELD INN BY MARRIOTT *Book great rates at AAA.com* **Phone:** (580)765-3000

Hotel
$89-$99 All Year

Address: 3405 N 14th St 74601 **Location:** 3.4 mi n on US 77. **Facility:** Smoke free premises. 63 one-bedroom standard units. 3 stories, interior corridors. *Bath:* combo or shower only. **Parking:** on-site. **Terms:** cancellation fee imposed. **Amenities:** irons, hair dryers. **Pool(s):** heated outdoor. **Leisure Activities:** whirlpool, exercise room. **Guest Services:** valet laundry, wireless Internet. **Business Services:** PC.
/ SOME UNITS

AAA Benefit: Members save a minimum 5% off the best available rate.

WHERE TO DINE

HUNAN CHINESE RESTAURANT **Phone:** 580/765-6716

Chinese
$6-$8

Locals enjoy the buffet, which is well stocked with a selection of entrees and side items. Casual dress. **Hours:** 11 am-9:30 pm. Closed major holidays. **Address:** 2800 N 5th St 74601 **Location:** Just nw of jct 14th and Prospect sts. **Parking:** on-site.

POTEAU pop. 7,939

BEST WESTERN TRADERS INN *Book great rates at AAA.com* **Phone:** (918)647-4001

 SAVE

Hotel
$75-$85 All Year

Address: 3111 N Broadway 74953 **Location:** Just s of jct US 69 Bypass and US 59 and 271. **Facility:** 75 one-bedroom standard units, some with whirlpools. 2 stories (no elevator), exterior corridors. *Bath:* combo or shower only. **Parking:** on-site. **Amenities:** irons, hair dryers. *Some:* high-speed Internet. **Pool(s):** outdoor. **Guest Services:** coin laundry, wireless Internet. **Business Services:** meeting rooms, PC. **Free Special Amenities: local telephone calls and high-speed Internet.**

/ SOME UNITS

AAA Benefit:
Members save up to 20%, plus 10% bonus points with rewards program.

DAYS INN & SUITES *Book at AAA.com* **Phone:** (918)647-3510

Hotel
$94-$98 All Year

Address: 1702 N Broadway 74953 **Location:** Center. **Facility:** 62 one-bedroom standard units, some with whirlpools. 3 stories, interior corridors. *Bath:* combo or shower only. **Parking:** on-site. **Terms:** 10 day cancellation notice. **Amenities:** high-speed Internet, voice mail, irons, hair dryers. **Pool(s):** outdoor. **Leisure Activities:** whirlpool, limited exercise equipment. *Fee:* massage. **Guest Services:** valet laundry, wireless Internet. **Business Services:** meeting rooms, PC.

ASK / SOME UNITS

PRYOR pop. 8,659

COMFORT INN & SUITES *Book great rates at AAA.com* **Phone:** 918/476-6660

SAVE

Hotel
Rates not provided

Address: 307 Mid America Dr 74361 **Location:** 5 mi s on US 69. **Facility:** 64 units. 62 one-bedroom standard units, some with whirlpools. 2 one-bedroom suites with efficiencies and whirlpools. 3 stories, interior corridors. *Bath:* combo or shower only. **Parking:** on-site. **Amenities:** high-speed Internet, voice mail, irons, hair dryers. **Pool(s):** heated indoor. **Leisure Activities:** whirlpool, exercise room. **Guest Services:** coin laundry, wireless Internet. **Business Services:** meeting rooms, business center. **Free Special Amenities: continental breakfast and high-speed Internet.**

/ SOME UNITS

WHERE TO DINE

GOLDIES PATIO GRILL **Phone:** 918/825-3313

American
$6-$15

The menu comprises grilled items, chicken, sandwiches and steak, but this place is best known for its excellent charbroiled burgers. The decor incorporates 1950s and '60s memorabilia. Casual dress. **Hours:** 11 am-9 pm. Closed major holidays. **Address:** 21 SE 8th St 74361 **Location:** Center. **Parking:** on-site.

ROLAND pop. 2,842

CHEROKEE CASINO INN **Phone:** 918/427-1000

Hotel
$49-$59 All Year

Address: 207 W Cherokee Blvd 74954 **Location:** I-40, exit 325, just ne. **Facility:** 44 one-bedroom standard units. 2 stories (no elevator), interior corridors. *Bath:* combo or shower only. **Parking:** on-site. **Amenities:** hair dryers. **Pool(s):** outdoor. **Guest Services:** coin laundry, wireless Internet. **Business Services:** meeting rooms. ASK / SOME UNITS

SALLISAW pop. 7,989

WHERE TO DINE

CAPORALES **Phone:** 918/774-0604

Mexican
$5-$9

Dishes with straightforward appeal are served in an open, unadorned dining room. Casual dress. **Bar:** Beer only. **Hours:** 11 am-9 pm. Closed: 7/4, 11/25, 12/25; also Sun. **Address:** 1600 S Tatham Ave 74955 **Location:** I-40, exit 308 (US 59), 0.4 mi n. **Parking:** on-site.

The following restaurant has not been evaluated by AAA but is listed for your information only.

SHAD'S CATFISH HOLE RESTAURANT **Phone:** 918/775-5801

fyi

Not evaluated. The restaurant is known for hearty portions and flavorful catfish in an area that recognizes good catfish. **Address:** Applegate Cove Rd 74955 **Location:** I-40, exit 308 (US 59), 7.2 mi s.

SAND SPRINGS—See Tulsa p. 667.

SAPULPA—See Tulsa p. 668.

SAVANNA pop. 730

CANDLELIGHT INN & SUITES **Phone:** (918)548-3676

AAA SAVE
Hotel
$75-$90 All Year

Address: Hwy 69 74565 **Location:** 1.5 mi sw of jct US 69 and Indian Creek Tpke. **Facility:** 33 one-bedroom standard units. 1 story, interior corridors. *Bath:* combo or shower only. **Parking:** on-site. **Terms:** 3 day cancellation notice. **Amenities:** high-speed Internet, voice mail, irons, hair dryers. **Guest Services:** coin laundry. **Free Special Amenities: expanded continental breakfast and high-speed Internet.** / SOME UNITS

SAYRE pop. 4,114

AMERICINN LODGE & SUITES OF SAYRE *Book at AAA.com* **Phone:** 580/928-2700

Hotel
Rates not provided

Address: 2405 S El Camino Rd 73662 **Location:** I-40, exit 20, just n. **Facility:** 45 units. 44 one-bedroom standard units, some with whirlpools. 1 one-bedroom suite with whirlpool. 2 stories (no elevator), interior corridors. *Bath:* combo or shower only. **Parking:** on-site. **Amenities:** high-speed Internet, hair dryers. *Some:* irons. **Pool(s):** heated indoor. **Leisure Activities:** sauna, whirlpool. **Guest Services:** coin laundry. **Business Services:** meeting rooms, PC.
CALL / SOME UNITS FEE

SEMINOLE pop. 6,899

BEST WESTERN SEMINOLE INN & SUITES *Book great rates at AAA.com* **Phone:** (405)382-3139

AAA SAVE
Hotel
$87-$98 All Year

Address: 1525 N Milt Phillips Ave 74868 **Location:** 0.5 mi s of jct US 377, SR 9 and 99. **Facility:** 52 one-bedroom standard units, some with whirlpools. 3 stories, interior corridors. *Bath:* combo or shower only. **Parking:** on-site. **Amenities:** high-speed Internet, voice mail, irons, hair dryers. **Pool(s):** heated indoor. **Leisure Activities:** exercise room. **Guest Services:** valet and coin laundry, wireless Internet. **Business Services:** PC. **Free Special Amenities: expanded continental breakfast and high-speed Internet.** / SOME UNITS FEE

AAA Benefit:
Members save up to 20%, plus 10% bonus points with rewards program.

WHERE TO DINE

THE CATFISH ROUND-UP **Phone:** 405/382-7957

American

$7-$10

You'll find prompt and friendly service, a relaxed, casual atmosphere and a good selection of offerings at the Catfish Round-Up, which specializes in fried catfish dishes. Sugar-coated donut balls and hot rolls are included with your selection. Casual dress. **Hours:** 11 am-9 pm. Closed: 1/1, 11/25, 12/25. **Address:** Hwy 99 74868 **Location:** I-40, exit 200, just se. **Parking:** on-site.

SHAWNEE—See Oklahoma City p. 634.

STILLWATER pop. 39,065

FAIRFIELD INN BY MARRIOTT *Book great rates at AAA.com* **Phone:** (405)372-6300

Hotel

$86-$106 All Year

Address: 418 E Hall of Fame Ave 74075 **Location:** Just w of jct US 177 (Perkins Rd). **Facility:** Smoke free premises. 64 one-bedroom standard units. 3 stories, interior corridors. *Bath:* combo or shower only. **Parking:** on-site, winter plug-ins. **Terms:** cancellation fee imposed. **Amenities:** irons, hair dryers. **Pool(s):** heated indoor. **Leisure Activities:** whirlpool. **Guest Services:** valet laundry, wireless Internet. **Business Services:** PC. / SOME UNITS

AAA Benefit:

Members save a minimum 5% off the best available rate.

HAMPTON INN & SUITES *Book great rates at AAA.com* **Phone:** (405)743-1306

Hotel

$109-$169 All Year

Address: 717 E Hall of Fame Ave 74075 **Location:** Just e of jct US 177 (Perkins Rd). **Facility:** 81 units. 73 one-bedroom standard units. 8 one-bedroom suites, some with whirlpools. 3 stories, interior corridors. *Bath:* combo or shower only. **Parking:** on-site. **Terms:** 1-7 night minimum stay, cancellation fee imposed. **Amenities:** video games (fee), high-speed Internet, voice mail, irons, hair dryers. **Pool(s):** heated outdoor. **Leisure Activities:** whirlpool, exercise room. **Guest Services:** valet and coin laundry, wireless Internet. **Business Services:** meeting rooms, business center. *(See color ad below)* CALL / SOME UNITS

AAA Benefit:

Members save up to 10% everyday!

FREE expanded continental breakfast and high-speed Internet

▼ See AAA listing above ▼

WHERE TO DINE

GOLDIES PATIO GRILL — **Phone:** 405/372-6700

American
$6-$15

The menu comprises grilled items, chicken, sandwiches and steak, but this place is best known for its excellent charbroiled burgers. The decor incorporates 1950s and '60s memorabilia. Casual dress. **Bar:** Beer only. **Hours:** 10:45 am-9 pm. Closed major holidays. **Address:** 508 E Hall of Fame Ave 74075 **Location:** Just w of jct US 177 (Perkins Rd). **Parking:** on-site.

JOSEPPI'S ITALIAN KITCHEN — **Phone:** 405/624-8037

Italian
$5-$16

Italian dishes, pizza and salad are served in the lively, energetic restaurant. Casual dress. **Bar:** Full bar. **Hours:** 11 am-10 pm, Fri & Sat-11 pm, Sun-9 pm. Closed: 11/25, 12/25. **Address:** 223 E Hall of Fame Ave 74075 **Location:** Just w of jct US 177 (Perkins Rd). **Parking:** on-site.

KYOTO JAPANESE RESTAURANT — **Phone:** 405/377-8168

Japanese
$6-$23

Kyoto's features delightful hibachi-style cooking and a fresh-sushi bar with Japanese chefs. Try the Kyoto dragon roll—it's a unique combination of eel, crabmeat, cucumbers, avocados and shrimp. Two tatami rooms are available for private parties. Casual dress. **Bar:** Full bar. **Reservations:** suggested. **Hours:** 11 am-10 pm, Sun-9 pm. Closed: 1/1, 11/25, 12/25. **Address:** 2021 N Boomer Rd 74075 **Location:** 1.9 mi n of SR 51. **Parking:** on-site.

MEXICO JOE'S — **Phone:** 405/372-1169

Mexican
$5-$11

The lively, upbeat restaurant presents a menu that lists a nice selection of traditional fare. Casual dress. **Hours:** 11 am-10 pm, Fri & Sat-11 pm, Sun-9 pm. Closed: 11/25, 12/25. **Address:** 311 E Hall of Fame Ave 74075 **Location:** Just w of jct US 177 (Perkins Rd). **Parking:** on-site.

RIB CRIB BBQ AND GRILL — **Phone:** 405/372-1900

Barbecue
$6-$14

Most guests need extra napkins to tackle the ribs, brisket, ham, pork and chicken selections. The menu also lists sandwiches and wraps, along with tempting sides and large desserts. The decor is decidedly Western. Casual dress. **Bar:** Beer only. **Hours:** 11 am-10 pm. Closed: 11/25, 12/25. **Address:** 103 S Perkins Rd 74074 **Location:** Center. **Parking:** on-site.

SIRLOIN STOCKADE — **Phone:** 405/624-1681

Regional Steak
$6-$9

The steakhouse lines up buffet items, including pizza, tacos, soups, salads and desserts, providing both excellent variety and a good value. Rotating theme nights might allow for the sampling of sushi, barbecue and seafood. The buffet also may serve to complement a quality steak. Rolls are baked several times daily. Casual dress. **Reservations:** not accepted. **Hours:** 11 am-9 pm. Closed: 11/25, 12/25. **Address:** 208 N Perkins Rd 74074 **Location:** On US 177, just s of jct E Hall of Fame Ave. **Parking:** on-site.

STROUD pop. 2,758

WHERE TO DINE

THE ROCK CAFE — **Phone:** 918/968-3990

American
$5-$15

Located on historic Route 66, the café is on the National Register of Historic Places. A rustic decor and bustling service define the cozy ambiance. A diverse menu includes hearty breakfasts, burgers, Reubens, jagersnitzal and alligator burgers. Casual dress. **Reservations:** not accepted. **Hours:** 6 am-9 pm. Closed: 11/25, 12/25. **Address:** 114 W Main St 74079 **Location:** Center. **Parking:** on-site. **Historic**

TAHLEQUAH pop. 14,458

BEST WESTERN TAHLEQUAH INN — **Phone:** 918/458-1818

Hotel
Rates not provided

Address: 3296 S Muskogee Ave 74464 **Location:** 0.7 mi w of jct US 62, SR 10, 51 and 82. **Facility:** 42 one-bedroom standard units, some with whirlpools. 2 stories, interior corridors. *Bath:* combo or shower only. **Parking:** on-site. **Amenities:** high-speed Internet, irons, hair dryers. **Pool(s):** heated indoor/outdoor. **Leisure Activities:** exercise room. **Guest Services:** wireless Internet. **Business Services:** meeting rooms, business center. **Free Special Amenities: local telephone calls and high-speed Internet.** / SOME UNITS

AAA Benefit:
Members save up to 20%, plus 10% bonus points with rewards program.

COMFORT INN & SUITES *Book at AAA.com* — **Phone:** 918/431-0600

Hotel
Rates not provided

Address: 101 Reasor St 74464 **Location:** Just se of jct US 62, SR 10, 51 and 82. **Facility:** 58 one-bedroom standard units, some with whirlpools. 3 stories, interior corridors. **Parking:** on-site. **Amenities:** high-speed Internet, voice mail, irons, hair dryers. **Pool(s):** heated indoor. **Leisure Activities:** whirlpool, limited exercise equipment. **Guest Services:** coin laundry, wireless Internet. **Business Services:** business center. / SOME UNITS

HOLIDAY INN EXPRESS *Book at AAA.com* — **Phone:** (918)456-7800

Hotel
$90-$149 All Year

Address: 701 Holiday Dr 74464 **Location:** 1.2 mi e on SR 51 from jct US 62. **Facility:** 62 units. 58 one-bedroom standard units. 4 one-bedroom suites with whirlpools. 2 stories, interior corridors. *Bath:* combo or shower only. **Parking:** on-site. **Terms:** check-in 4 pm, cancellation fee imposed. **Amenities:** voice mail, irons, hair dryers. **Pool(s):** outdoor. **Leisure Activities:** exercise room. **Guest Services:** wireless Internet. **Business Services:** PC.

WHERE TO DINE

EL ZARAPE

Mexican
$4-$12

Phone: 918/456-0708

A local favorite for Mexican cuisine, the restaurant presents a varied menu of well-prepared choices. Service is prompt. Simple furnishings decorate the dining area. Casual dress. **Bar:** Beer only. **Hours:** 11 am-9 pm. Closed major holidays; also Sun. **Address:** 701 E Downing St 74464 **Location:** Just w of jct US 62 and SR 82. **Parking:** on-site.

THACKERVILLE pop. 404

BEST WESTERN RED RIVER INN & SUITES *Book great rates at AAA.com* **Phone:** 580/276-5001

Hotel
Rates not provided

Address: 21 Blackjack Rd 73459 **Location:** I-35, exit 1, 1.1 mi n on E Service Rd. **Facility:** Smoke free premises. 60 one-bedroom standard units, some with whirlpools. 3 stories, interior corridors. *Bath:* combo or shower only. **Parking:** on-site. **Amenities:** irons, hair dryers. **Pool(s):** outdoor. **Leisure Activities:** exercise room. **Guest Services:** coin laundry, wireless Internet. **Business Services:** meeting rooms, business center. **Free Special Amenities: expanded continental breakfast and high-speed Internet.** CALL

AAA Benefit:
Members save up to 20%, plus 10% bonus points with rewards program.

WINSTAR MICROTEL INN & SUITES **Phone:** 580/276-4487

Hotel
Rates not provided

Address: Rt 1, Box 682 73459 **Location:** I-35, exit 1, 1.2 mi n on E Service Rd. **Facility:** 100 one-bedroom standard units, some with whirlpools. 3 stories, interior corridors. *Bath:* combo or shower only. **Parking:** on-site. **Amenities:** voice mail, irons, hair dryers. **Pool(s):** heated indoor. **Leisure Activities:** whirlpool, exercise room. **Guest Services:** coin laundry, wireless Internet. **Business Services:** meeting rooms, PC. / SOME UNITS

WINSTAR WORLD CASINO HOTEL *Book at AAA.com* **Phone:** 580/276-3100

fyi

Hotel
$99-$229 All Year

Too new to rate. **Address:** One World Way 73459 **Location:** I-35, exit 1. **Amenities:** 395 units, restaurant, coffeemakers, pool. **Terms:** cancellation fee imposed.

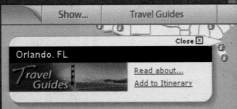

Destination Tulsa

pop. 393,049

Tulsa, nicknamed the "Green Country," has an abundance of parks where visitors can explore nature trails or eat a picnic lunch.

River Parks is the site of more than 25 annual festivals; Tulsa's spirited shindigs include American Indian powwows, art shows and myriad music festivals featuring bluegrass, blues, gospel, jazz and reggae performers.

The "Golden Driller," Tulsa.

Indian powwow, Tulsa.

Art Deco buildings, Tulsa.

Prayer Tower at Oral Roberts University, Tulsa. (See listing page 283)

Places included in this AAA Destination City:

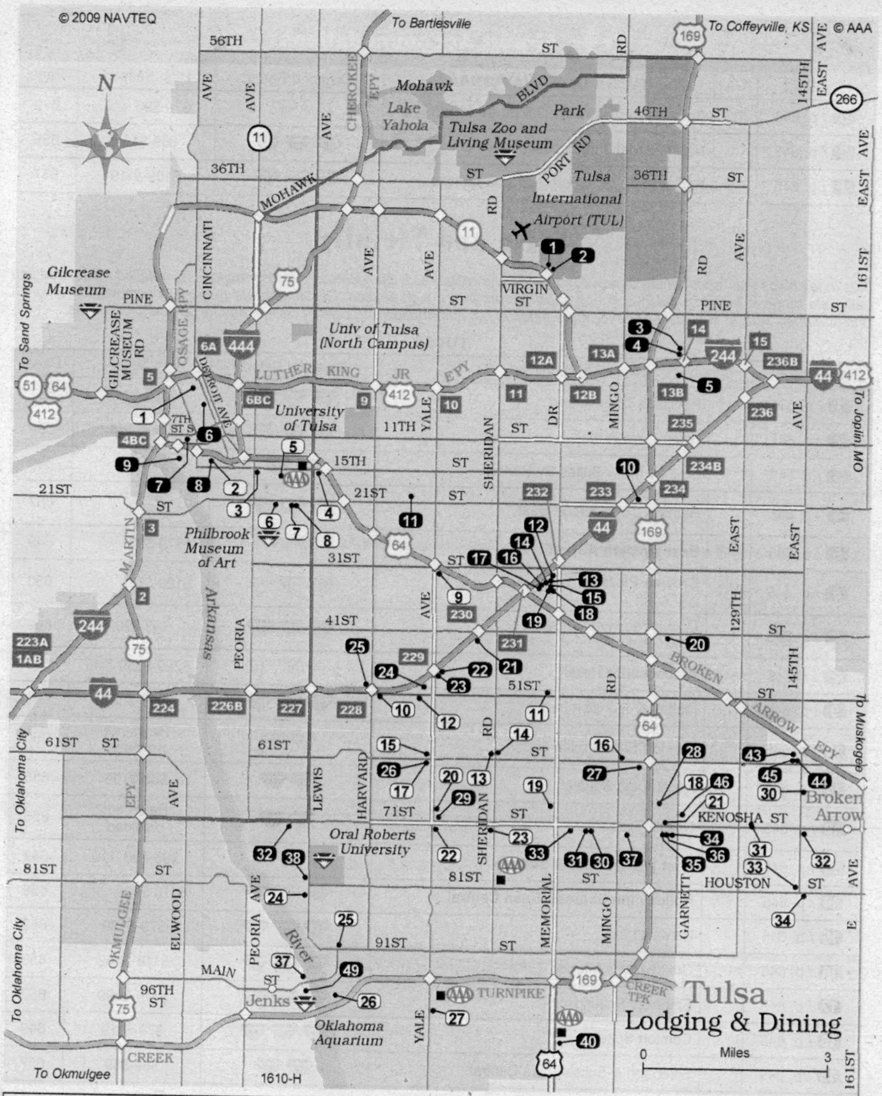

© 2009 NAVTEQ © AAA

Tulsa Lodging & Dining

Miles 0 3

Airport Accommodations

Map Page	OA	TULSA INTERNATIONAL	Diamond Rated	High Season	Page
5 / p. 645	AAA	**Best Western Airport, 3.5 mi se of terminal**	◆◆	$70-$90 SAVE	649
2 / p. 645		Hilton Garden Inn, opposite terminal	◆◆◆	$69-$154	655
1 / p. 645		Radisson Tulsa Airport, opposite terminal	◆◆◆	$109-$119	657

Tulsa and Vicinity

This index helps you "spot" where approved lodgings and restaurants are located on the corresponding detailed maps. Lodging daily rate range is for comparison only and show the property's high season. Restaurant rate range is a combination of lunch and/or dinner. Turn to the listing page for more detailed rate information and consult display ads for special promotions.

TULSA

Map Page	OA	Lodgings	Diamond Rated	High Season	Page
1 / p. 645		Radisson Tulsa Airport	◆◆◆	$109-$119	657
2 / p. 645		Hilton Garden Inn	◆◆◆	$69-$154	655
3 / p. 645		Country Inn & Suites By Carlson	◆◆	$79-$85	650
4 / p. 645		Ramada Tulsa Airport East	◆◆◆	Rates not provided	657
5 / p. 645	AAA	**Best Western Airport**	◆◆	$70-$90 SAVE	649
6 / p. 645	AAA	**Crowne Plaza Tulsa -** see color ad p 650	◆◆◆	$129-$169 SAVE	650
7 / p. 645		Doubletree Hotel Tulsa Downtown	◆◆◆	$95-$209	652
8 / p. 645	AAA	**Ambassador Hotel**	◆◆◆	$209-$339 SAVE	649
9 / p. 645		McBirney Mansion Inn	◆◆◆	$225-$325	656
10 / p. 645		Comfort Suites-Tulsa Airport	◆◆	Rates not provided	650
11 / p. 645		Inn At Expo Square	◆◆	$63-$100	656
12 / p. 645		Quality Suites	◆◆	Rates not provided	656
13 / p. 645	AAA	**Best Western Inn & Suites**	◆◆◆	$85-$90 SAVE	649
14 / p. 645	AAA	**Holiday Inn Express-Tulsa Central**	◆◆◆	$110-$120 SAVE	656
15 / p. 645		Hampton Inn	◆◆◆	$79-$129	652
16 / p. 645		Courtyard by Marriott Tulsa	◆◆◆	$116-$142	650
17 / p. 645		Embassy Suites Hotel	◆◆◆	$119-$199	652
18 / p. 645		Comfort Suites	◆◆◆	$79-$119	649
19 / p. 645		Sleep Inn & Suites Tulsa Central	◆◆	$69-$89	657
20 / p. 645		Radisson Tulsa	◆◆◆	Rates not provided	657
21 / p. 645		La Quinta Inn & Suites Tulsa Central	◆◆◆	Rates not provided	656
22 / p. 645		Tulsa Select Hotel	◆◆◆	$60-$129	658
23 / p. 645		Red Roof Inn	◆◆	$50-$100	657
24 / p. 645		Baymont Inn & Suites Tulsa	◆◆	Rates not provided	649
25 / p. 645	AAA	**Best Western Trade Winds Central Inn**	◆◆	$70-$75 SAVE	649
26 / p. 645		Doubletree Hotel At Warren Place	◆◆◆	$89-$99	652
27 / p. 645	AAA	**Sleep Inn & Suites Tulsa South**	◆◆	$90 SAVE	657
28 / p. 645	AAA	**Renaissance Tulsa Hotel & Convention Center**	◆◆◆◆	$176-$215 SAVE	657

TULSA (cont'd)

Map Page	OA	Lodgings (cont'd)	Diamond Rated	High Season	Page
29 / p. 645	AAA	**Hyatt Place Tulsa/Southern Hills**	◆◆◆	$79-$199 SAVE	656
30 / p. 645		Fairfield Inn by Marriott-Tulsa/Woodland Hills	◆◆	$98-$120	652
31 / p. 645		Holiday Inn Express	◆◆	Rates not provided	655
32 / p. 645		Tulsa Marriott Southern Hills	◆◆◆	$188-$230	658
33 / p. 645	AAA	**Hampton Inn & Suites-Woodland Hills - see color ad p 654**	◆◆◆	$89-$102 SAVE	654
34 / p. 645		Staybridge Suites	◆◆◆	$139-$169	658
35 / p. 645		SpringHill Suites by Marriott	◆◆◆	$116-$142	658
36 / p. 645		Residence Inn by Marriott	◆◆◆	$134-$164	657
37 / p. 645		Candlewood Suites	◆◆◆	$89-$119	649
38 / p. 645		Hilton Tulsa Southern Hills	◆◆◆	$89-$199	655
40 / p. 645		Hampton Inn & Suites Tulsa South-Bixby	◆◆◆	Rates not provided	654

Map Page	OA	Restaurants	Diamond Rated	Cuisine	Meal Range	Page
1 / p. 645		Caz's Chowhouse	◆◆	American	$6-$17	659
2 / p. 645		The Chalkboard	◆◆◆	Mediterranean	$10-$36	659
3 / p. 645		Chimi's Mexican Food	◆◆	Mexican	$6-$15	659
4 / p. 645		Brothers Houligan	◆◆	American	$4-$15	658
5 / p. 645		Te Kei's	◆◆◆	Asian	$7-$21	661
6 / p. 645		McGill's	◆◆◆	Steak	$8-$27	660
7 / p. 645		Fleming's Prime Steakhouse & Wine Bar	◆◆◆	Steak	$19-$40	659
8 / p. 645		Polo Grill	◆◆◆◆	Continental	$11-$49	661
9 / p. 645		Celebrity Restaurant	◆◆	Steak	$7-$60	659
10 / p. 645		Bodeans Seafood Restaurant	◆◆◆	Seafood	$8-$38	658
11 / p. 645		Royal Dragon	◆◆	Chinese	$7-$14	661
12 / p. 645		The Green Onion	◆◆◆	Continental	$7-$25	660
13 / p. 645		Ti Amo Restaurante	◆◆◆	Italian	$7-$24	662
14 / p. 645		La Roma Pizza	◆	Pizza	$5-$10	660
15 / p. 645		McGill's	◆◆◆	Steak	$9-$33	660
16 / p. 645		Brothers Houligan	◆◆	American	$4-$15	658
17 / p. 645		Warren Duck Club	◆◆◆	Continental	$10-$48	662
18 / p. 645		Cyprus Grille	◆◆◆	Mediterranean	$10-$38	659
19 / p. 645		Cosmo-Sophisticated Sandwiches Coffee Bar	◆◆	Deli	$6-$13	659
20 / p. 645		Mahogany Prime Steakhouse	◆◆◆	Steak	$17-$40	660
21 / p. 645		Abuelo's The Flavor of Mexico	◆◆◆	Mexican	$7-$19	658
22 / p. 645		The French Hen	◆◆◆	Continental	$7-$38	659
23 / p. 645		Mexicali Border Cafe	◆◆	Mexican	$6-$14	660
24 / p. 645		Chimi's Mexican Food	◆◆	Mexican	$6-$15	659
25 / p. 645		Pepper's Grill	◆◆	Tex-Mex	$6-$16	661
26 / p. 645		Michael Fusco's Riverside Grill	◆◆◆	American	$17-$47	661

Map Page	OA	Restaurants (cont'd)	Diamond Rated	Cuisine	Meal Range	Page
27 / p. 645		The Bistro At Seville	3 diamonds	American	$7-$29	658

BROKEN ARROW

Map Page	OA	Lodgings	Diamond Rated	High Season	Page
43 / p. 645		Clarion Hotel	3 diamonds	$80-$100	663
44 / p. 645		Hampton Inn-Broken Arrow	3 diamonds	$89-$109	663
45 / p. 645		Comfort Inn	2 diamonds	$65-$89	663
46 / p. 645		Homewood Suites by Hilton Tulsa South	3 diamonds	$99-$159	664

Map Page	OA	Restaurants	Diamond Rated	Cuisine	Meal Range	Page
30 / p. 645		Stone Mill BBQ and Steakhouse	2 diamonds	Barbecue	$7-$21	664
31 / p. 645		Ted's Cafe Escondido	2 diamonds	Mexican	$7-$14	664
32 / p. 645		China Star	2 diamonds	Chinese	$4-$11	664
33 / p. 645		Jake's Cafe	2 diamonds	American	$5-$9	664
34 / p. 645		Big Daddys All American BBQ	1 diamond	Barbecue	$4-$8	664

JENKS

Map Page	OA	Lodging	Diamond Rated	High Season	Page
49 / p. 645		Holiday Inn Express Hotel & Suites	3 diamonds	$99-$159	666

Map Page	OA	Restaurant	Diamond Rated	Cuisine	Meal Range	Page
37 / p. 645		Los Cabos Mexican Grill & Cantina	2 diamonds	Mexican	$7-$20	666

TULSA pop. 393,049 (See map and index starting on p. 645)

AMBASSADOR HOTEL *Book great rates at AAA.com* **Phone:** (918)587-8200 **8**

AAA SAVE

Historic Hotel

$209-$339 All Year

Address: 1324 S Main St 74119 **Location:** Jct 14th and Main sts. **Facility:** Although the property boasts a historic background, the decor is modern with some upscale appointments. Smoke free premises. 55 units. 47 one-bedroom standard units. 8 one-bedroom suites with whirlpools. 9 stories, interior corridors. *Bath:* combo or shower only. **Parking:** on-site and valet. **Terms:** cancellation fee imposed. **Amenities:** dual phone lines, voice mail, safes, irons, hair dryers. **Dining:** The Chalkboard, see separate listing. **Leisure Activities:** exercise room. **Guest Services:** valet laundry, airport transportation-Tulsa International Airport, area transportation-within 5 mi, wireless Internet. **Business Services:** meeting rooms, PC. **Free Special Amenities: newspaper and high-speed Internet.** / SOME UNITS

BAYMONT INN & SUITES TULSA *Book at AAA.com* **Phone:** 918/488-8777 **24**

Hotel

Rates not provided

Address: 4530 E Skelly Dr 74135 **Location:** I-44, exit 229 (Yale Ave/SR 66), just s, then w. **Facility:** 101 units. 98 one-bedroom standard units. 3 one-bedroom suites. 4 stories, interior corridors. *Bath:* combo or shower only. **Parking:** on-site. **Amenities:** video games (fee), voice mail, irons, hair dryers. **Pool(s):** outdoor. **Leisure Activities:** exercise room. **Guest Services:** coin laundry, wireless Internet. **Business Services:** meeting rooms. / SOME UNITS

BEST WESTERN AIRPORT *Book great rates at AAA.com* **Phone:** (918)438-0780 **5**

AAA SAVE

Hotel

$70-$90 All Year

Address: 222 N Garnett Rd 74116 **Location:** I-244, exit 14 (Garnett Rd), just s. **Facility:** 106 units. 105 one-bedroom standard units. 1 one-bedroom suite with whirlpool. 2 stories (no elevator), exterior corridors. **Parking:** on-site. **Amenities:** irons, hair dryers. *Some:* high-speed Internet. **Pool(s):** outdoor. **Leisure Activities:** exercise room. **Guest Services:** coin laundry, airport transportation-Tulsa International Airport, wireless Internet. **Business Services:** meeting rooms, business center. **Free Special Amenities: expanded continental breakfast and high-speed Internet.** / SOME UNITS FEE

AAA Benefit: Members save up to 20%, plus 10% bonus points with rewards program.

BEST WESTERN INN & SUITES *Book great rates at AAA.com* **Phone:** (918)858-2100 **13**

AAA SAVE

Hotel

$85-$90 All Year

Address: 3212 S 79th E Ave 74145 **Location:** I-44, exit 231 eastbound; exit 232 (Memorial Dr) westbound, just sw. **Facility:** 62 one-bedroom standard units, some with whirlpools. 3 stories, interior corridors. *Bath:* combo or shower only. **Parking:** on-site. **Amenities:** high-speed Internet, dual phone lines, voice mail, irons, hair dryers. **Pool(s):** heated indoor. **Leisure Activities:** sauna, limited exercise equipment. **Guest Services:** valet and coin laundry, wireless Internet. **Business Services:** business center. **Free Special Amenities: expanded continental breakfast and high-speed Internet.** / SOME UNITS

AAA Benefit: Members save up to 20%, plus 10% bonus points with rewards program.

BEST WESTERN TRADE WINDS CENTRAL INN *Book great rates at AAA.com* **Phone:** (918)749-5561 **25**

Hotel

$70-$75 All Year

Address: 3141 E Skelly Dr 74105 **Location:** I-44, exit 228 (Harvard Ave), on northwest frontage road. **Facility:** 164 one-bedroom standard units, some with whirlpools. 2 stories (no elevator), interior/exterior corridors. **Parking:** on-site, winter plug-ins. **Amenities:** video games (fee), voice mail, irons, hair dryers. **Dining:** nightclub, entertainment. **Pool(s):** outdoor. **Leisure Activities:** exercise room. **Guest Services:** valet and coin laundry, airport transportation-Tulsa International Airport, wireless Internet. **Business Services:** meeting rooms, business center. **Free Special Amenities: expanded continental breakfast and newspaper.** / SOME UNITS

AAA Benefit: Members save up to 20%, plus 10% bonus points with rewards program.

CANDLEWOOD SUITES *Book at AAA.com* **Phone:** (918)294-9000 **37**

Extended Stay Hotel

$89-$119 All Year

Address: 10008 E 73rd St S 74133 **Location:** Just sw of jct 71st St and 101st E Ave. **Facility:** 72 units. 51 one-bedroom standard units with efficiencies. 21 one-bedroom suites with kitchens. 3 stories, interior corridors. *Bath:* combo or shower only. **Parking:** on-site. **Terms:** check-in 4 pm, cancellation fee imposed. **Amenities:** video library, DVD players, high-speed Internet, dual phone lines, voice mail, irons, hair dryers. **Leisure Activities:** exercise room. **Guest Services:** complimentary and valet laundry, wireless Internet. **Business Services:** meeting rooms, business center. ASK CALL / SOME UNITS FEE

COMFORT SUITES 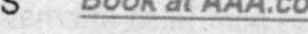 *Book at AAA.com* **Phone:** (918)622-6300 **18**

Hotel

$79-$119 3/1-8/31
$69-$99 9/1-2/28

Address: 8039 E 33rd St S 74145 **Location:** I-44, exit 231 eastbound; exit 232 (Memorial Dr) westbound. **Facility:** Smoke free premises. 63 units. 60 one-bedroom standard units, some with whirlpools. 3 one-bedroom suites with whirlpools. 3 stories, interior corridors. *Bath:* combo or shower only. **Parking:** on-site. **Amenities:** high-speed Internet, dual phone lines, voice mail, safes, irons, hair dryers. **Pool(s):** heated indoor. **Leisure Activities:** whirlpool, exercise room. **Guest Services:** valet and coin laundry, wireless Internet. **Business Services:** meeting rooms, business center. ASK CALL

(See map and index starting on p. 645)

COMFORT SUITES-TULSA AIRPORT *Book at AAA.com* **Phone:** 918/628-0900 10

Hotel
Rates not provided

Address: 1737 S 101st E Ave 74128 **Location:** I-44, exit 233 eastbound; exit 233B westbound, follow signs. **Facility:** Smoke free premises. 57 one-bedroom standard units, some with whirlpools. 2 stories (no elevator), interior corridors. *Bath:* combo or shower only. **Parking:** on-site. **Amenities:** safes (fee), irons, hair dryers. **Pool(s):** heated indoor. **Leisure Activities:** whirlpool, exercise room. **Guest Services:** valet laundry, wireless Internet.

COUNTRY INN & SUITES BY CARLSON *Book at AAA.com* **Phone:** (918)234-3535 3

Hotel
$79-$85 All Year

Address: 1034 N Garnett Rd 74116 **Location:** I-244, exit 14 (Garnett Rd), just n. **Facility:** 48 units. 36 one-bedroom standard units, some with whirlpools. 12 one-bedroom suites, some with whirlpools. 2 stories (no elevator), interior corridors. **Parking:** on-site. **Amenities:** irons, hair dryers. **Pool(s):** heated outdoor. **Guest Services:** valet and coin laundry, wireless Internet. **Business Services:** PC.

ASK / SOME UNITS

COURTYARD BY MARRIOTT TULSA *Book great rates at AAA.com* **Phone:** (918)660-0646 16

Hotel
$116-$142 All Year

Address: 3340 S 79th E Ave 74145 **Location:** I-44, exit 231 (31st St) eastbound; exit 232 westbound, just s, then just w. **Facility:** Smoke free premises. 122 units. 116 one-bedroom standard units, some with whirlpools. 6 one-bedroom suites. 3 stories, interior corridors. *Bath:* combo or shower only. **Parking:** on-site. **Terms:** cancellation fee imposed. **Amenities:** high-speed Internet, voice mail, irons, hair dryers. **Pool(s):** heated indoor. **Leisure Activities:** whirlpool, exercise room. **Guest Services:** valet and coin laundry, wireless Internet. **Business Services:** meeting rooms, business center.

CALL

COURTYARD Marriott

AAA Benefit:
Members save a minimum 5% off the best available rate.

CROWNE PLAZA TULSA *Book great rates at AAA.com* **Phone:** (918)582-9000 6

AAA SAVE

Hotel
$129-$169 All Year

Address: 100 E 2nd St 74103 **Location:** Jct 2nd St and Boston; downtown. **Facility:** 455 units. 450 one-bedroom standard units. 5 one-bedroom suites. 14 stories, interior corridors. *Bath:* combo or shower only. **Parking:** on-site (fee) and valet. **Terms:** 14 day cancellation notice. **Amenities:** CD players, voice mail, irons, hair dryers. *Fee:* video games, high-speed Internet. **Pool(s):** heated indoor/outdoor. **Leisure Activities:** exercise room, spa. **Guest Services:** valet and coin laundry, airport transportation-Tulsa International Airport, wireless Internet. **Business Services:** conference facilities, business center. *(See color ad below)*

CALL / SOME UNITS FEE

▼ See AAA listing above ▼

(See map and index starting on p. 645)

DOUBLETREE HOTEL AT WARREN PLACE Book great rates at AAA.com Phone: (918)495-1000 26

Hotel
$89-$99 All Year

Address: 6110 S Yale Ave 74136 **Location:** I-44, exit 229 (Yale Ave/SR 66), 1.3 mi s. **Facility:** 370 units. 364 one-bedroom standard units. 6 one-bedroom suites, some with whirlpools. 9 stories, interior corridors. *Bath:* combo or shower only. **Parking:** on-site and valet. **Terms:** 1-7 night minimum stay, cancellation fee imposed. **Amenities:** dual phone lines, voice mail, irons, hair dryers. **Dining:** Warren Duck Club, see separate listing. **Pool(s):** heated indoor. **Leisure Activities:** saunas, whirlpool, jogging, exercise room. **Guest Services:** valet laundry, area transportation, wireless Internet. **Business Services:** conference facilities, business center.

CALL / SOME UNITS FEE

DOUBLETREE HOTELS·SUITES·RESORTS·CLUBS
AAA Benefit:
Members save 5% or more everyday!

DOUBLETREE HOTEL TULSA DOWNTOWN Book great rates at AAA.com Phone: (918)587-8000 7

Hotel
$95-$209 All Year

Address: 616 W 7th St 74127 **Location:** Jct 7th St and Houston. **Facility:** 417 units. 404 one-bedroom standard units, some with whirlpools. 13 one-bedroom suites, some with whirlpools. 17 stories, interior corridors. **Parking:** on-site (fee). **Terms:** 1-7 night minimum stay, cancellation fee imposed. **Amenities:** dual phone lines, voice mail, irons, hair dryers. **Pool(s):** heated indoor. **Leisure Activities:** whirlpool, exercise room. *Fee:* game room. **Guest Services:** valet and coin laundry, wireless Internet. **Business Services:** conference facilities, business center.

/ SOME UNITS FEE

DOUBLETREE HOTELS·SUITES·RESORTS·CLUBS
AAA Benefit:
Members save 5% or more everyday!

EMBASSY SUITES HOTEL Book great rates at AAA.com Phone: (918)622-4000 17

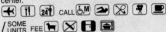

Hotel
$119-$199 All Year

Address: 3332 S 79th E Ave 74145 **Location:** I-44, exit 231 eastbound; exit 232 (Memorial Dr) westbound, just sw. **Facility:** 244 units. 4 one-bedroom standard units. 232 one- and 8 two-bedroom suites, some with whirlpools. 9 stories, interior corridors. **Parking:** on-site. **Terms:** 1-7 night minimum stay, cancellation fee imposed. **Amenities:** video games (fee), dual phone lines, voice mail, irons, hair dryers. **Pool(s):** heated indoor. **Leisure Activities:** whirlpool, exercise room. **Guest Services:** valet and coin laundry, wireless Internet. **Business Services:** conference facilities.

/ SOME UNITS FEE

AAA Benefit:
Members save 5% or more everyday!

FAIRFIELD INN BY MARRIOTT-TULSA/WOODLAND HILLS Book great rates at AAA.com Phone: (918)252-7754 30

Hotel
$98-$120 All Year

Address: 9020 E 71st St 74133 **Location:** US 169, exit E 71st St, 1 mi w. **Facility:** Smoke free premises. 64 one-bedroom standard units. 3 stories, interior corridors. *Bath:* combo or shower only. **Parking:** on-site. **Terms:** cancellation fee imposed. **Amenities:** irons, hair dryers. **Pool(s):** heated indoor. **Leisure Activities:** whirlpool. **Guest Services:** valet laundry, wireless Internet. **Business Services:** PC.

/ SOME UNITS

AAA Benefit:
Members save a minimum 5% off the best available rate.

HAMPTON INN Book great rates at AAA.com Phone: (918)663-1000 15

Hotel
$79-$129 All Year

Address: 3209 S 79th E Ave 74145 **Location:** I-44, exit 231 eastbound; exit 232 (Memorial Dr) westbound, just sw. **Facility:** 148 units. 136 one-bedroom standard units. 12 one-bedroom suites. 4 stories, interior corridors. *Bath:* combo or shower only. **Parking:** on-site. **Terms:** 1-7 night minimum stay, cancellation fee imposed. **Amenities:** video games (fee), voice mail, irons, hair dryers. **Pool(s):** heated outdoor. **Leisure Activities:** exercise room. **Guest Services:** valet laundry, wireless Internet. **Business Services:** meeting rooms, PC.

/ SOME UNITS

Hampton Inn
AAA Benefit:
Members save up to 10% everyday!

Hard Rock
HOTEL & CASINO

(See map and index starting on p. 645)

HAMPTON INN & SUITES TULSA SOUTH-BIXBY   Book great rates at AAA.com   Phone: 918/394-2000   40

Hotel

Rates not provided

Address: 8220 E Regal Pl 74133 **Location:** Just e of jct Memorial Rd. **Facility:** Smoke free premises. 102 one-bedroom standard units. 4 stories, interior corridors. *Bath:* combo or shower only. **Parking:** on-site. **Amenities:** video games (fee), high-speed Internet, voice mail, irons, hair dryers. **Pool(s):** heated indoor. **Leisure Activities:** sauna, whirlpool, exercise room. *Fee:* game room. **Guest Services:** valet and coin laundry, wireless Internet. **Business Services:** meeting rooms, business center.

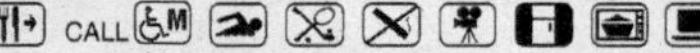

AAA Benefit:

Members save up to 10% everyday!

HAMPTON INN & SUITES-WOODLAND HILLS   Book great rates at AAA.com   Phone: (918)294-3300   33

Hotel

$89-$102 All Year

Address: 7141 S 85th E Ave 74133 **Location:** 1.2 mi w of jct US 169, exit 71st St. **Facility:** 74 units. 47 one-bedroom standard units. 27 one-bedroom suites, some with efficiencies and/or whirlpools. 4 stories, interior corridors. *Bath:* combo or shower only. **Parking:** on-site. **Terms:** check-in 4 pm, 1-7 night minimum stay, cancellation fee imposed. **Amenities:** video library, high-speed Internet, dual phone lines, voice mail, irons, hair dryers. *Some:* DVD players. **Pool(s):** outdoor. **Leisure Activities:** whirlpool, exercise room. **Guest Services:** valet and coin laundry, wireless Internet. **Business Services:** meeting rooms, business center. *(See color ad below)* / SOME UNITS

AAA Benefit:

Members save up to 10% everyday!

FREE expanded continental breakfast and high-speed Internet

(See map and index starting on p. 645)

HILTON GARDEN INN *Book great rates at AAA.com* Phone: (918)838-1444 **2**

Hotel
$69-$154 All Year

Address: 7728 E Virgin Ct 74115 **Location:** SR 11, exit airport terminal. **Facility:** 120 one-bedroom standard units. 3 stories, interior corridors. *Bath:* combo or shower only. **Parking:** on-site. **Terms:** 1-7 night minimum stay, cancellation fee imposed. **Amenities:** video games (fee), high-speed Internet, dual phone lines, voice mail, irons, hair dryers. **Pool(s):** heated indoor. **Leisure Activities:** whirlpool, exercise room. **Guest Services:** valet and coin laundry, wireless Internet. **Business Services:** meeting rooms, business center.

/ SOME UNITS

Hilton Garden Inn
AAA Benefit:
Members save 5% or more everyday!

HILTON TULSA SOUTHERN HILLS *Book great rates at AAA.com* Phone: (918)492-5000 **38**

Hotel
$89-$199 All Year

Address: 7902 S Lewis Ave 74136 **Location:** I-44, exit 227, 3 mi s. Opposite Oral Roberts University. **Facility:** 285 units. 277 one-bedroom standard units, some with whirlpools. 8 one-bedroom suites, some with whirlpools. 11 stories, interior corridors. *Bath:* combo or shower only. **Parking:** on-site. **Terms:** 1-7 night minimum stay, cancellation fee imposed. **Amenities:** high-speed Internet (fee), dual phone lines, voice mail, irons, hair dryers. **Pool(s):** heated indoor. **Leisure Activities:** exercise room. **Guest Services:** valet laundry, wireless Internet. **Business Services:** conference facilities, business center.

/ SOME UNITS FEE

Hilton
AAA Benefit:
Members save 5% or more everyday!

HOLIDAY INN EXPRESS *Book at AAA.com* Phone: 918/459-5321 **31**

Hotel
Rates not provided

Address: 9010 E 71st St 74133 **Location:** US 169, exit 71st St, 1 mi w. **Facility:** Smoke free premises. 64 one-bedroom standard units. 3 stories, interior corridors. *Bath:* combo or shower only. **Parking:** on-site, winter plug-ins. **Amenities:** dual phone lines, voice mail, irons, hair dryers. **Pool(s):** heated indoor. **Leisure Activities:** whirlpool. **Guest Services:** valet laundry, wireless Internet. **Business Services:** PC.

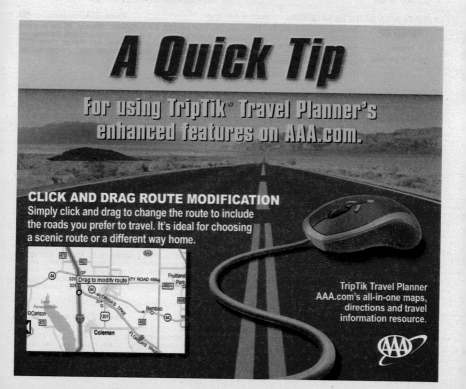

/ SOME UNITS

(See map and index starting on p. 645)

HOLIDAY INN EXPRESS-TULSA CENTRAL *Book great rates at AAA.com* **Phone:** (918)665-4242 14

Hotel
$110-$120 All Year

Address: 3215 S 79th E Ave 74145 **Location:** I-44, exit 231 eastbound; exit 232 (Memorial Dr) westbound, just sw. **Facility:** 62 one-bedroom standard units, some with whirlpools. 3 stories, interior corridors. *Bath:* combo or shower only. **Parking:** on-site. **Terms:** cancellation fee imposed. **Amenities:** high-speed Internet, dual phone lines, voice mail, irons, hair dryers. **Pool(s):** heated outdoor. **Leisure Activities:** sauna, exercise room. **Guest Services:** valet and coin laundry, wireless Internet. **Business Services:** business center.

CALL / SOME UNITS

FREE expanded continental breakfast and high-speed Internet

HYATT PLACE TULSA/SOUTHERN HILLS *Book great rates at AAA.com* **Phone:** (918)491-4010 29

Hotel
$79-$199 All Year

Address: 7037 S Zurich Ave 74136 **Location:** I-44, exit 229 (Yale Ave/SR 66), 3 mi s to 71st St, then just e. **Facility:** Smoke free premises. 126 one-bedroom standard units. 6 stories, interior corridors. *Bath:* combo or shower only. **Parking:** on-site. **Terms:** cancellation fee imposed. **Amenities:** voice mail, irons, hair dryers. **Pool(s):** outdoor. **Leisure Activities:** exercise room. **Guest Services:** valet laundry, wireless Internet. **Business Services:** meeting rooms, business center. **Free Special Amenities: continental breakfast and high-speed Internet.**

CALL

AAA Benefit:
Ask for the AAA rate and save 10%.

INN AT EXPO SQUARE *Book at AAA.com* **Phone:** (918)858-3775 11

Hotel
$63-$100 All Year

Address: 4531 E 21st St 74114 **Location:** Just w of 21st St and Yale Ave. **Facility:** 82 one-bedroom standard units. 3 stories, interior corridors. *Bath:* combo or shower only. **Parking:** on-site. **Terms:** 30 day cancellation notice. **Amenities:** video games (fee), voice mail. **Guest Services:** wireless Internet. **Business Services:** meeting rooms, PC. ASK / SOME UNITS FEE

LA QUINTA INN & SUITES TULSA CENTRAL *Book at AAA.com* **Phone:** 918/665-2630 21

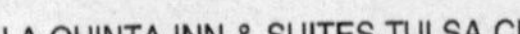

Hotel
Rates not provided

Address: 6030 E Skelly Dr 74135 **Location:** I-44, exit 230, just s. **Facility:** 105 units. 86 one-bedroom standard units. 19 one-bedroom suites, some with whirlpools. 4 stories, interior corridors. **Parking:** on-site. **Amenities:** high-speed Internet, dual phone lines, voice mail, irons, hair dryers. *Some:* DVD players. **Pool(s):** outdoor. **Leisure Activities:** exercise room. **Guest Services:** valet and coin laundry, wireless Internet. **Business Services:** meeting rooms, business center.

/ SOME UNITS

MCBIRNEY MANSION INN **Phone:** (918)585-3234 9

Historic Bed & Breakfast
$225-$325 All Year

Address: 1414 S Galveston Ave 74127 **Location:** US 64 and SR 51, exit Denver Ave, 0.5 mi sw. **Facility:** Nestled on nicely landscaped grounds, the mansion overlooks the Arkansas River. Smoke free premises. 6 units. 5 one-bedroom standard units, some with whirlpools. 1 one-bedroom suite with whirlpool. 4 stories (no elevator), interior/exterior corridors. *Bath:* combo or shower only. **Parking:** on-site. **Terms:** age restrictions may apply, 8 day cancellation notice-fee imposed. **Amenities:** video library, voice mail, irons, hair dryers. *Some:* DVD players. **Leisure Activities:** hiking trails. **Guest Services:** valet laundry, wireless Internet. **Business Services:** meeting rooms. ASK

MICROTEL INN & SUITES *Book great rates at AAA.com* **Phone:** (918)234-9100

Hotel
$65-$80 All Year

Address: 16518 E Admiral Pl 74116 **Location:** I-44, exit 238 (161st Ave), just s. **Facility:** 46 one-bedroom standard units, some with whirlpools. 3 stories, interior corridors. *Bath:* combo or shower only. **Parking:** on-site. **Amenities:** irons, hair dryers. **Guest Services:** coin laundry, wireless Internet. **Free Special Amenities: continental breakfast and high-speed Internet.**

/ SOME UNITS

POST OAK LODGE **Phone:** 918/425-2112

Hotel
Rates not provided

Address: 5323 W 31st St N 74127 **Location:** 0.7 mi w of jct Apache/41st St. **Facility:** Smoke free premises. 60 one-bedroom standard units. 2 stories (no elevator), interior corridors. **Parking:** on-site. **Amenities:** video library, voice mail, irons, hair dryers. *Some:* DVD players. **Pool(s):** heated outdoor. **Leisure Activities:** whirlpools, fishing, hiking trails, exercise room, basketball, horseshoes, volleyball. **Guest Services:** wireless Internet. **Business Services:** conference facilities, business center.

/ SOME UNITS

QUALITY SUITES *Book at AAA.com* **Phone:** 918/858-9625 12

Hotel
Rates not provided

Address: 3112 S 79th E Ave 74145 **Location:** I-44, exit 232 (Memorial Dr), just sw. **Facility:** 69 one-bedroom standard units, some with whirlpools. 2 stories, interior/exterior corridors. *Bath:* combo or shower only. **Parking:** on-site. **Amenities:** high-speed Internet, voice mail, irons, hair dryers. **Pool(s):** heated indoor. **Leisure Activities:** whirlpool, limited exercise equipment. **Guest Services:** valet and coin laundry, wireless Internet. **Business Services:** PC.

/ SOME UNITS

(See map and index starting on p. 645)

RADISSON TULSA Book at AAA.com Phone: 918/627-5000 20

Hotel
Rates not provided

Address: 10918 E 41st St 74146 **Location:** Just e of US 169. **Facility:** 325 units. 323 one-bedroom standard units. 2 one-bedroom suites with whirlpools. 11 stories, interior corridors. *Bath:* combo or shower only. **Parking:** on-site. **Amenities:** dual phone lines, voice mail, irons, hair dryers. *Some:* fax. **Pool(s):** heated outdoor, heated indoor. **Leisure Activities:** sauna, whirlpool, exercise room. **Guest Services:** valet laundry, area transportation, wireless Internet. **Business Services:** conference facilities, business center. / SOME UNITS

RADISSON TULSA AIRPORT Phone: (918)835-9911 1

Hotel
$109-$119 All Year

Address: 2201 N 77th E Ave 74115 **Location:** SR 11, exit airport terminal. **Facility:** 172 one-bedroom standard units. 2 stories (no elevator), interior corridors. **Parking:** on-site. **Amenities:** dual phone lines, voice mail, irons, hair dryers. *Some:* high-speed Internet. **Pool(s):** outdoor. **Leisure Activities:** exercise room. **Guest Services:** valet laundry, wireless Internet. **Business Services:** conference facilities, PC. ASK / SOME UNITS FEE

RAMADA TULSA AIRPORT EAST Book at AAA.com Phone: 918/437-7660 4

Hotel
Rates not provided

Address: 1010 N Garnett Rd 74116 **Location:** I-244, exit 14 (Garnett Rd), just n. **Facility:** 158 one-bedroom standard units. 2 stories (no elevator), interior corridors. *Bath:* combo or shower only. **Parking:** on-site. **Amenities:** high-speed Internet, dual phone lines, voice mail, irons, hair dryers. **Pool(s):** heated indoor. **Leisure Activities:** playground, exercise room. *Fee:* game room. **Guest Services:** valet laundry, wireless Internet. **Business Services:** meeting rooms, business center. CALL / SOME UNITS FEE

RED ROOF INN Book at AAA.com Phone: (918)622-6776 23

Motel
$50-$100 All Year

Address: 4717 S Yale Ave 74135 **Location:** I-44, exit 229 (Yale Ave), just s. **Facility:** 101 one-bedroom standard units, some with whirlpools. 3 stories, exterior corridors. *Bath:* combo or shower only. **Parking:** on-site. **Terms:** cancellation fee imposed. **Amenities:** irons, hair dryers. **Pool(s):** heated outdoor. **Guest Services:** coin laundry, wireless Internet. **Business Services:** PC. ASK / SOME UNITS

RENAISSANCE TULSA HOTEL & CONVENTION CENTER Book great rates at AAA.com Phone: (918)307-2600 28

AAA SAVE
Hotel
$176-$215 All Year

Address: 6808 S 107th E Ave 74133 **Location:** Just ne of jct US 169 and 71st St. **Facility:** Water cascading over a rock wall and a stream winding through the lobby create a scenic and serene ambience at this upscale hotel. Smoke free premises. 300 units. 265 one-bedroom standard units. 35 one-bedroom suites, some with whirlpools. 9 stories, interior corridors. *Bath:* combo or shower only. **Parking:** on-site and valet. **Terms:** cancellation fee imposed. **Amenities:** high-speed Internet (fee), dual phone lines, voice mail, safes, irons, hair dryers. **Dining:** Cyprus Grille, see separate listing. **Pool(s):** heated indoor. **Leisure Activities:** sauna, whirlpool, exercise room. **Guest Services:** valet and coin laundry, wireless Internet. **Business Services:** conference facilities, business center. **Free Special Amenities: newspaper.** CALL / SOME UNITS

AAA Benefit:
Members save a minimum 5% off the best available rate.

RESIDENCE INN BY MARRIOTT Book great rates at AAA.com Phone: (918)250-4850 36

Extended Stay Hotel
$134-$164 All Year

Address: 11025 E 73rd St 74133 **Location:** US 169, exit 71st St, just e. **Facility:** Smoke free premises. 90 units. 37 one-bedroom standard units with efficiencies. 35 one- and 18 two-bedroom suites, some with efficiencies or kitchens. 3 stories, interior corridors. *Bath:* combo or shower only. **Parking:** on-site. **Terms:** cancellation fee imposed. **Amenities:** dual phone lines, voice mail, irons, hair dryers. **Pool(s):** heated indoor. **Leisure Activities:** whirlpool, exercise room, sports court. **Guest Services:** valet and coin laundry, wireless Internet. **Business Services:** meeting rooms, PC. / SOME UNITS FEE

AAA Benefit:
Members save a minimum 5% off the best available rate.

SLEEP INN & SUITES TULSA CENTRAL Book at AAA.com Phone: (918)663-2777 19

Hotel
$69-$89 3/1-8/31
$59-$79 9/1-2/28

Address: 8021 E 33rd St S 74145 **Location:** I-44, exit 231 eastbound; exit 232 (Memorial Dr) westbound, just sw. **Facility:** 66 units. 63 one-bedroom standard units, some with whirlpools. 3 one-bedroom suites. 3 stories, interior corridors. *Bath:* combo or shower only. **Parking:** on-site, winter plug-ins. **Amenities:** voice mail, safes, irons, hair dryers. **Pool(s):** heated indoor. **Leisure Activities:** sauna, whirlpool, limited exercise equipment. **Guest Services:** valet and coin laundry, wireless Internet. **Business Services:** business center. ASK / SOME UNITS FEE

SLEEP INN & SUITES TULSA SOUTH Book great rates at AAA.com Phone: (918)249-8100 27

AAA SAVE
Hotel
$90 All Year

Address: 10143 E 62nd St S 74133 **Location:** Just w of jct US 169 and 61st St. **Facility:** Smoke free premises. 65 one-bedroom standard units, some with whirlpools. 3 stories, interior corridors. *Bath:* combo or shower only. **Parking:** on-site. **Terms:** cancellation fee imposed. **Amenities:** high-speed Internet, voice mail, irons, hair dryers. **Pool(s):** heated indoor. **Leisure Activities:** sauna, whirlpool, exercise room. **Guest Services:** coin laundry, wireless Internet. **Business Services:** PC. **Free Special Amenities: expanded continental breakfast and high-speed Internet.**

(See map and index starting on p. 645)

SPRINGHILL SUITES BY MARRIOTT *Book great rates at AAA.com* **Phone:** (918)254-1777 35

Hotel
$116-$142 All Year

Address: 11015 E 73rd St S 74133 **Location:** Just se of jct US 169 and 71st St. **Facility:** Smoke free premises. 76 one-bedroom standard units. 3 stories, interior corridors. *Bath:* combo or shower only. **Parking:** on-site. **Terms:** cancellation fee imposed. **Amenities:** dual phone lines, voice mail, irons, hair dryers. **Pool(s):** heated indoor. **Leisure Activities:** whirlpool, exercise room. **Guest Services:** valet and coin laundry, wireless Internet. **Business Services:** business center.

AAA Benefit:
Members save a minimum 5% off the best available rate.

STAYBRIDGE SUITES *Book at AAA.com* **Phone:** (918)461-2100 34

Extended Stay Hotel
$139-$169 All Year

Address: 11111 E 73rd St 74133 **Location:** Just se of jct US 169 and 71st St. **Facility:** Smoke free premises. 85 units. 52 one-bedroom standard units with efficiencies. 26 one- and 7 two-bedroom suites with efficiencies. 4 stories, interior corridors. **Parking:** on-site. **Amenities:** high-speed Internet, voice mail, irons, hair dryers. **Pool(s):** heated outdoor. **Leisure Activities:** sauna, whirlpool, exercise room, sports court. **Guest Services:** complimentary and valet laundry, wireless Internet. **Business Services:** meeting rooms, business center.

ASK CALL / SOME UNITS FEE

TULSA MARRIOTT SOUTHERN HILLS *Book great rates at AAA.com* **Phone:** (918)493-7000 32

Hotel
$188-$230 All Year

Address: 1902 E 71st St 74136 **Location:** I-44, exit 227 (Lewis Ave), 2 mi s; jct 71st St and Lewis Ave. **Facility:** Smoke free premises. 383 units. 379 one-bedroom standard units, some with kitchens. 4 one-bedroom suites. 11 stories, interior corridors. **Parking:** on-site, winter plug-ins. **Terms:** check-in 4 pm, cancellation fee imposed. **Amenities:** video games (fee), voice mail, irons, hair dryers. *Some:* dual phone lines. **Pool(s):** heated indoor. **Leisure Activities:** saunas, whirlpool, exercise room, spa. **Guest Services:** valet laundry, wireless Internet. **Business Services:** conference facilities, business center.

/ SOME UNITS FEE FEE FEE

Marriott HOTELS & RESORTS

AAA Benefit:
Members save a minimum 5% off the best available rate.

TULSA SELECT HOTEL *Book at AAA.com* **Phone:** (918)622-7000 22

Hotel
$60-$129 All Year

Address: 5000 E Skelly Dr 74135 **Location:** I-44, exit 229 (Yale Ave/SR 66); on south frontage road. **Facility:** 313 units. 305 one-bedroom standard units. 8 one-bedroom suites, some with whirlpools. 4 stories, interior/exterior corridors. **Parking:** on-site. **Terms:** check-in 4 pm, cancellation fee imposed. **Amenities:** video games (fee), high-speed Internet, voice mail, irons, hair dryers. *Some:* dual phone lines. **Pool(s):** heated outdoor. **Leisure Activities:** exercise room. **Guest Services:** valet and coin laundry, area transportation, wireless Internet. **Business Services:** meeting rooms, business center.

ASK / SOME UNITS FEE FEE FEE

WHERE TO DINE

ABUELO'S THE FLAVOR OF MEXICO **Phone:** 918/249-1546 21

Mexican
$7-$19

The upscale and artistically decorated restaurant presents a menu of well-prepared and attractively presented dishes. Casual dress. **Bar:** Full bar. **Reservations:** not accepted. **Hours:** 11 am-10 pm, Fri & Sat-11 pm. Closed: 11/25, 12/24, 12/25. **Address:** 10909 E 71st St S 74133 **Location:** Just e of jct US 169. **Parking:** on-site.

THE BISTRO AT SEVILLE **Phone:** 918/296-3000 27

American
$7-$29

Seafood, steak, pasta and chicken dishes are among the bistro's varied menu offerings. Dressy casual. **Bar:** Full bar. **Reservations:** suggested. **Hours:** 11 am-10 pm. Closed: 11/25, 12/25. **Address:** 10021 S Yale Ave 74145 **Location:** Jct 101st St. **Parking:** on-site.

BODEANS SEAFOOD RESTAURANT **Phone:** 918/743-3861 10

Seafood
$8-$38

On the menu are several fresh seafood choices, as well as a nice selection of steaks. The attentive, knowledgeable staff provides service in a comfortable yet formal manner. Casual dress. **Bar:** Full bar. **Reservations:** accepted. **Hours:** 11 am-10 pm, Sat from 5 pm, Sun 5 pm-9 pm. Closed major holidays. **Address:** 3376 E 51st St 74105 **Location:** I-44, exit 228 (Harvard Ave), just se. **Parking:** on-site.

BROTHERS HOULIGAN **Phone:** 918/747-1086 4

American
$4-$15

This popular eatery is known for great-tasting food, generous portions and attentive service. Among favorites are varied steak choices, hamburgers, chili and chicken-fried steak. Casual dress. **Bar:** Full bar. **Hours:** 11 am-10 pm, Fri & Sat-11 pm. Closed major holidays; also Sun. **Address:** 2508 E 15th St 74104 **Location:** Just e of jct Lewis Ave. **Parking:** on-site.

BROTHERS HOULIGAN **Phone:** 918/254-1086 16

American
$4-$15

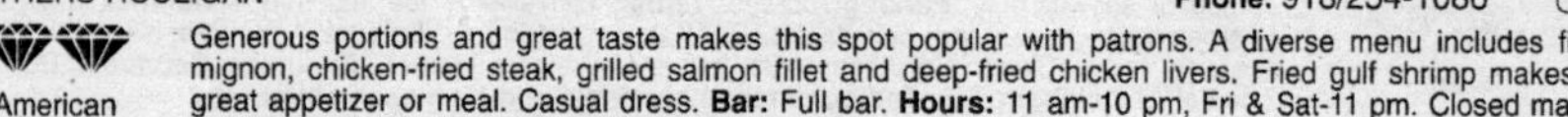

Generous portions and great taste makes this spot popular with patrons. A diverse menu includes filet mignon, chicken-fried steak, grilled salmon fillet and deep-fried chicken livers. Fried gulf shrimp makes a great appetizer or meal. Casual dress. **Bar:** Full bar. **Hours:** 11 am-10 pm, Fri & Sat-11 pm. Closed major holidays; also Sun. **Address:** 9701 E 61st St 74133 **Location:** 0.5 mi w of jct US 169. **Parking:** on-site.

(See map and index starting on p. 645)

CAZ'S CHOWHOUSE

Phone: 918/588-2469 (1)

American
$6-$17

Creativity and attention to presentation are evident at this restaurant. Ingredients are fresh, and servers are conscientious. Casual dress. **Bar:** Full bar. **Hours:** 11 am-9 pm, Fri-10 pm, Sat 5 pm-10 pm. Closed: 11/25, 12/25; also Sun & Mon. **Address:** 18 E Brady St 74103 **Location:** Just w of jct N Boston Ave. **Parking:** on-site.

CELEBRITY RESTAURANT

Phone: 918/743-1800 (9)

Steak
$7-$60

An area institution for more than 30 years, the restaurant presents a concise selection of well-prepared items in a semi-formal atmosphere that caters to couples and businesspeople. Caesar salad is a notable specialty. Dressy casual. **Bar:** Full bar. **Reservations:** suggested, evenings. **Hours:** 11 am-2 & 5-9 pm, Fri & Sat-10 pm. Closed major holidays; also Sun. **Address:** 3109 S Yale Ave 74135 **Location:** Jct 31st St and Yale Ave; on southeast corner. **Parking:** on-site.

THE CHALKBOARD

Phone: 918/582-1964 (2)

Mediterranean
$10-$36

The restaurant is equally well-suited for a business lunch or romantic dinner with well-prepared and presented entrées and a nice selection of wines. Dressy casual. **Bar:** Full bar. **Reservations:** accepted. **Hours:** 6:30-10 am, 11-2:30 & 5-10 pm, Fri & Sat-10:30 pm, Sun-9 pm. **Address:** 1324 S Main St 74105 **Location:** Jct 14th and Main sts; in Ambassador Hotel. **Parking:** on-site.

CHARLESTON'S RESTAURANT

Phone: 918/749-3287

American
$8-$22

This casual dining spot boasts a friendly, club-like atmosphere. Fine steak and seafood, as well as hardwood-grilled dishes, are at the heart of the menu. The noteworthy baked potato soup is rich with onions and bacon bits. Casual dress. **Bar:** Full bar. **Reservations:** accepted. **Hours:** 11 am-10 pm, Fri & Sat-11 pm, Sun-9 pm. Closed: 11/25, 12/25. **Address:** 3726 S Peoria Ave 74136 **Location:** I-44, exit 226B, 1.6 mi n. **Parking:** on-site.

CHARLESTON'S RESTAURANT

Phone: 918/495-3511

American
$8-$22

This casual dining spot boasts a friendly, club-like atmosphere. Fine steak and seafood, as well as hardwood-grilled dishes, are at the heart of the menu. The noteworthy baked potato soup is rich with onions and bacon bits. Casual dress. **Bar:** Full bar. **Hours:** 11 am-10 pm, Fri & Sat-11 pm. Closed: 11/25, 12/25. **Address:** 6839 S Yale Ave 74136 **Location:** I-44, exit 229 (Yale Ave), 3 mi s. **Parking:** on-site.

CHIMI'S MEXICAN FOOD

Phone: 918/298-1570 (24)

Mexican
$6-$15

The locally popular Chimi's features a good menu selection of traditional, well-prepared dishes. This large, busy restaurant has a casual atmosphere and a well-coordinated Mexican theme. The server staff is prompt and cordial. Casual dress. **Bar:** Full bar. **Hours:** 11 am-10 pm, Fri & Sat-11 pm. Closed: 11/25, 12/25. **Address:** 8144 S Lewis Ave 74137 **Location:** I-44, exit 227 (Lewis Ave), 2 mi s at 81st St. **Parking:** on-site.

CHIMI'S MEXICAN FOOD

Phone: 918/587-4411 (3)

Mexican
$6-$15

A good menu selection is offered at Chimi's, which is quite popular with local residents. This large, busy, rustic restaurant features a casual atmosphere as the backdrop for its traditional, well-prepared dishes. Service is friendly and attentive. Casual dress. **Bar:** Full bar. **Hours:** 11 am-10 pm, Fri & Sat-11 pm. Closed: 11/25, 12/25. **Address:** 1304 E 15th St 74120 **Location:** At Peoria Ave; center. **Parking:** on-site.

COSMO-SOPHISTICATED SANDWICHES COFFEE BAR

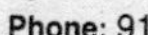

Phone: 918/459-0497 (19)

Deli
$6-$13

Although the menu lists a good assortment of specific sandwiches and salads, patrons can chart their own course by creating their own from the list of ingredients. Sofa seating in the dining area invites relaxing with a favorite book, meal and beverage. Casual dress. **Bar:** Full bar. **Hours:** 9:30 am-9 pm. Closed: 11/25, 12/25. **Address:** 6746 Memorial Dr 74133 **Location:** Just n of jct 71st St. **Parking:** on-site.

CYPRUS GRILLE

Phone: 918/307-2600 (18)

Mediterranean
$10-$38

Entrees provide both visual and taste appeal. Everything from soups to desserts shows wonderful taste and presentation. Dressy casual. **Bar:** Full bar. **Reservations:** suggested. **Hours:** 6 am-2 & 5:30-10 pm, Sat & Sun from 7 am. **Address:** 6808 S 107th E Ave 74133 **Location:** Just ne of jct US 169 and 71st St; in Renaissance Tulsa Hotel & Convention Center. **Parking:** on-site.

FLEMING'S PRIME STEAKHOUSE & WINE BAR

Phone: 918/712-7500 (7)

Steak
$19-$40

The warm, clubby atmosphere is the ideal setting for perfectly grilled steaks and seafood. Side dishes come in hearty portions, and salads are fresh and crisp. More than 100 wine selections are available. Dressy casual. **Bar:** Full bar. **Reservations:** accepted. **Hours:** 5 pm-10 pm, Fri & Sat-10:30 pm, Sun-9 pm. Closed: 11/25, 12/25. **Address:** 1976 Utica Square 74114 **Location:** US 64, exit Utica Ave, s to 21st St, then just e. **Parking:** on-site.

THE FRENCH HEN

Phone: 918/492-2596 (22)

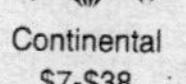

Continental
$7-$38

A nice casual diner restaurant or casual business meeting place, serving a broad variety of American dishes. There are windows on three sides of the restaurant, which all face a courtyard, in which the restaurant is situated. The subdued lighting lends itself to the relaxing environment and the service is prompt and efficient. Dressy casual. **Bar:** Full bar. **Reservations:** suggested. **Hours:** 11 am-2 & 4-10 pm, Fri-11 pm, Sat 4 pm-11 pm. Closed major holidays; also Sun. **Address:** 7143 S Yale Ave 74136 **Location:** I-44, exit 229 (Yale Ave), 1.8 mi s. **Parking:** on-site.

GOLDIES PATIO GRILL

Phone: 918/743-2188

American
$6-$15

The menu comprises grilled items, chicken, sandwiches and steak, but this place is best known for its excellent charbroiled burgers. The decor incorporates 1950s and '60s memorabilia. Casual dress. **Hours:** 10:45 am-8 pm, Fri & Sat-9 pm. Closed major holidays. **Address:** 5200 S Lewis Ave 74136 **Location:** I-44, exit 227 (Lewis Ave), just s. **Parking:** on-site.

(See map and index starting on p. 645)

GOLDIES PATIO GRILL **Phone:** 918/747-2007

American
$6-$15

The menu comprises grilled items, chicken, sandwiches and steak, but this place is best known for its excellent charbroiled burgers. The decor incorporates 1950s and '60s memorabilia. Casual dress. **Hours:** 10:45 am-8 pm, Fri & Sat-9 pm. Closed major holidays. **Address:** 2005 E 21st St 74114 **Location:** Just w of jct US 64 and SR 51. **Parking:** on-site.

GOLDIES PATIO GRILL **Phone:** 918/494-0330

American
$6-$15

The menu comprises grilled items, chicken, sandwiches and steak, but this place is best known for its excellent charbroiled burgers. The decor incorporates 1950s and '60s memorabilia. Casual dress. **Bar:** Beer only. **Hours:** 10:45 am-8 pm, Fri & Sat-9 pm. Closed major holidays. **Address:** 6121 E 61st St 74136 **Location:** Just w of jct Sheridan Rd. **Parking:** on-site.

GOLDIES PATIO GRILL **Phone:** 918/747-4546

American
$6-$15

The menu comprises grilled items, chicken, sandwiches and steak, but this place is best known for its excellent charbroiled burgers. The decor incorporates 1950s and '60s memorabilia. Casual dress. **Hours:** 10:45 am-9 pm. Closed major holidays. **Address:** 4401 E 31st St 74135 **Location:** Just w of jct Yale Ave. **Parking:** on-site.

THE GREEN ONION **Phone:** 918/481-3338 12

Continental
$7-$25

This nice casual dining restaurant or casual business meeting place, serves a broad variety of American dishes and some Italian dishes. There is a small dance floor and entertainment is provided in the evenings. The subdued lighting lends itself to the relaxing environment and the service is prompt and efficient. Casual dress. Entertainment. **Bar:** Full bar. **Reservations:** suggested. **Hours:** 11 am-2 & 5-10 pm, Fri & Sat-10:30 pm, Sun-2 pm. Closed major holidays. **Address:** 4532 E 51st St 74135 **Location:** I-44, exit 229 (Yale Ave), just s to 51st St, then just w. **Parking:** on-site.

HIDEAWAY PIZZA **Phone:** 918/366-4777

Pizza
$5-$14

The restaurant is a favorite spot for pizza lovers who like a wide variety of topping choices. Casual dress. **Bar:** Beer only. **Hours:** 11 am-9:30 pm, Fri & Sat-10:30 pm. Closed: 11/25, 12/25. **Address:** 8222 E 103rd St 74133 **Location:** Just e of jct Memorial Rd. **Parking:** on-site.

HIDEAWAY PIZZA **Phone:** 918/270-4777

Pizza
$5-$14

Locals flock to this place for pizza, including a good selection of out-of-the-ordinary choices. Casual dress. **Bar:** Beer only. **Hours:** 11 am-10 pm, Fri & Sat-11 pm. Closed: 11/25, 12/25. **Address:** 7877 E 51st St 74145 **Location:** 1.2 mi w of jct US 169. **Parking:** on-site.

HIDEAWAY PIZZA **Phone:** 918/492-4777

Pizza
$5-$14

Locals flock to this place for pizza, including a good selection of out-of-the-ordinary choices. Casual dress. **Bar:** Beer only. **Hours:** 11 am-9:30 pm, Fri & Sat-10:30 pm. Closed: 11/25, 12/25. **Address:** 8204 S Harvard Ave 74137 **Location:** Just s of jct 81st St. **Parking:** on-site.

LA ROMA PIZZA **Phone:** 918/491-6436 14

Pizza
$5-$10

La Roma's is a family-owned restaurant specializing in Mediterranean cuisine, homemade pizza with fresh ingredients and authentic Lebanese dishes. They have a casual, serve-yourself atmosphere. All desserts are made in-house and taste great. Casual dress. **Bar:** Beer only. **Hours:** 11 am-2 & 5-8 pm, Fri & Sat-9 pm. Closed: Sun. **Address:** 6027 S Sheridan Rd 74145 **Location:** I-44, exit 230, 2 mi s. **Parking:** on-site.

MAHOGANY PRIME STEAKHOUSE **Phone:** 918/494-4043 20

Steak
$17-$40

The house specialty is well-prepared, high-quality steak. Included in the selection of sides is fresh, flavorful corn. Dressy casual. **Bar:** Full bar. **Reservations:** suggested. **Hours:** 5 pm-10 pm, Fri & Sat-11 pm, Sun-9 pm. Closed: 12/25. **Address:** 6823 S Yale Ave 74136 **Location:** I-44, exit 229 (Yale Ave), 2.8 mi s. **Parking:** on-site.

MCGILL'S **Phone:** 918/742-8080 6

Steak
$8-$27

The restaurant is a good choice for a fine-dining experience centered on great-tasting steak, seafood and prime rib. Dressy casual. **Bar:** Full bar. **Reservations:** suggested. **Hours:** 11 am-10 pm, Fri-11 pm, Sat 5 pm-11 pm, Sun 4 pm-9 pm. Closed: 11/25, 12/25. **Address:** 1560 E 21st St 74114 **Location:** Just w of Utica Ave. **Parking:** on-site.

MCGILL'S **Phone:** 918/388-8080 15

Steak
$9-$33

Well-prepared entrees are made with enhanced flavors and presented attractively. The dining room has upscale appointments but is casual enough to make everyone comfortable. Dressy casual. **Bar:** Full bar. **Reservations:** suggested. **Hours:** 11 am-10 pm, Sat from 5 pm, Sun 4 pm-9 pm. Closed: 11/25, 12/25. **Address:** 6058 S Yale Ave 74136 **Location:** I-44, exit 229 (Yale Ave), 1.3 mi s. **Parking:** on-site.

MEXICALI BORDER CAFE **Phone:** 918/481-1114 23

Mexican
$6-$14

A bar at the entry lends to the lively atmosphere that lures patrons to the Mexican cafe. Casual dress. **Bar:** Full bar. **Hours:** 11 am-10 pm. Closed major holidays. **Address:** 7104 S Sheridan Rd 74133 **Location:** Just w of jct 71st St. **Parking:** on-site.

(See map and index starting on p. 645)

MICHAEL FUSCO'S RIVERSIDE GRILL

Phone: 918/394-2433 (26)

American
$17-$47

Fresh seafood, beef, poultry and pasta are equally well-prepared and served in this refined restaurant. A nice selection of wine is available, and attractive, delicious desserts are a wonderful way to finish the dining experience. Dressy casual. **Bar:** Full bar. **Reservations:** accepted. **Hours:** 11 am-2:30 & 5-10 pm. Closed major holidays; also Sun. **Address:** 9912 Riverside Pkwy 74137 **Location:** Just n of jct 101st St. **Parking:** on-site.

PEPPER'S GRILL

Phone: 918/296-0592 (25)

Tex-Mex
$6-$16

Guests don't come to the grill for anything fancy. Instead, they clamor for large portions of tasty Tex-Mex. Casual dress. **Bar:** Full bar. **Hours:** 11 am-10 pm, Fri & Sat-11 pm. Closed major holidays. **Address:** 2809 E 91st St 74137 **Location:** Just e of jct Riverside Pkwy. **Parking:** on-site.

POLO GRILL

Phone: 918/744-4280 (8)

Continental
$11-$49

This restaurant sports a stone front with a red English phone booth located just outside the entrance. A favorite spot for business lunches and dinners, the menu is dominated by beef entrées. Casual dress. Entertainment. **Bar:** Full bar. **Reservations:** suggested. **Hours:** 11 am-10 pm, Fri & Sat-11 pm. Closed major holidays; also Sun. **Address:** 2038 Utica Ave 74114 **Location:** US 64, exit Utica Ave, just s to 21st St, then just e. **Parking:** on-site.

RIB CRIB BBQ AND GRILL

Phone: 918/828-0010

Barbecue
$6-$14

Most guests need extra napkins to tackle the ribs, brisket, ham, pork and chicken selections. The menu also lists sandwiches and wraps, along with tempting sides and large desserts. The decor is decidedly Western. Casual dress. **Bar:** Beer only. **Hours:** 11 am-10 pm. Closed: 11/25, 12/25. **Address:** 3022 S Garnett Rd 74129 **Location:** Just ne of jct 31st St. **Parking:** on-site.

RIB CRIB BBQ AND GRILL

Phone: 918/447-1400

Barbecue
$6-$14

Most guests need extra napkins to tackle the ribs, brisket, ham, pork and chicken selections. The menu also lists sandwiches and wraps, along with tempting sides and large desserts. The decor is decidedly Western. Casual dress. **Bar:** Beer only. **Hours:** 11 am-10 pm. Closed: 11/25, 12/25. **Address:** 3232 W Skelly Dr 74104 **Location:** I-44, exit 223C, just se. **Parking:** on-site.

RIB CRIB BBQ AND GRILL

Phone: 918/742-2742

Barbecue
$6-$14

Most guests need extra napkins to tackle the ribs, brisket, ham, pork and chicken selections. The menu also lists sandwiches and wraps, along with tempting sides and large desserts. The decor is decidedly Western. Casual dress. **Bar:** Beer only. **Hours:** 11 am-10 pm. Closed: 11/25, 12/25. **Address:** 1601 S Harvard Ave 74112 **Location:** Just n of jct 21st St. **Parking:** on-site.

RIB CRIB BBQ AND GRILL

Phone: 918/492-8627

Barbecue
$6-$14

Most guests need extra napkins to tackle the ribs, brisket, ham, pork and chicken selections. The menu also lists sandwiches and wraps, along with tempting sides and large desserts. The decor is decidedly Western. Casual dress. **Bar:** Beer only. **Hours:** 11 am-10 pm. Closed: 11/25, 12/25. **Address:** 8040 S Yale Ave 74136 **Location:** Just n of jct 81st St. **Parking:** on-site.

RIB CRIB BBQ AND GRILL

Phone: 918/663-4295

Barbecue
$6-$14

Most guests need extra napkins to tackle the ribs, brisket, ham, pork and chicken selections. The menu also lists sandwiches and wraps, along with tempting sides and large desserts. The decor is decidedly Western. Casual dress. **Bar:** Beer only. **Hours:** 11 am-10 pm. Closed: 11/25, 12/25. **Address:** 5025 S Sheridan Rd 74145 **Location:** Just n of jct 51st St. **Parking:** on-site.

RON'S HAMBURGERS & CHILI

Phone: 918/496-4328

American
$4-$6

Although Ron's Hamburgers & Chili's name gives indicators of its strengths—varied hamburgers and savory chili—the menu also throws in a few tasty surprises. Casual dress. **Hours:** 11 am-8:30 pm. Closed: 11/25, 12/25. **Address:** 8201 S Harvard Ave 74105 **Location:** I-44, exit 228 (Harvard Ave), 3.5 mi s. **Parking:** on-site.

RON'S HAMBURGERS & CHILI

Phone: 918/250-7667

American
$4-$6

Although Ron's Hamburgers & Chili's name gives indicators of its strengths—varied hamburgers and savory chili—the menu also throws in a few tasty surprises. Casual dress. **Bar:** Full bar. **Hours:** 11 am-8:30 pm, Sun-3 pm. Closed: 11/25, 12/25. **Address:** 7119 S Mingo Rd 74133 **Location:** 0.6 mi w of jct US 169. **Parking:** on-site.

ROYAL DRAGON

Phone: 918/664-2245 (11)

Chinese
$7-$14

The well-stocked buffet bar is a favorite for the restaurant's regular patrons. Casual dress. **Hours:** 11 am-10 pm. Closed: 11/25. **Address:** 7837 E 51st St 74145 **Location:** 1.2 mi w of jct US 169. **Parking:** on-site.

TE KEI'S

Phone: 918/382-7777 (5)

Asian
$7-$21

Attractive, artistic and distinctive decor, along with diverse Asian dishes, are hallmarks of this place. Dressy casual. **Bar:** Full bar. **Reservations:** accepted. **Hours:** 11 am-10 pm, Fri & Sat-11 pm. Closed major holidays. **Address:** 1616 S Utica Ave 74104 **Location:** 0.4 mi s of jct US 64/SR 51. **Parking:** on-site.

(See map and index starting on p. 645)

TI AMO RESTAURANTE

Phone: 918/499-1919 (13)

Italian

$7-$24

Attractive presentations and ample portions set the restaurant's traditional Italian food apart. Casual dress. **Bar:** Full bar. **Reservations:** suggested. **Hours:** 11 am-2 & 5-9 pm, Fri-10 pm, Sat 5 pm-10 pm, Sun 11 am-9 pm. Closed: 11/25, 12/25. **Address:** 6024A S Sheridan Rd 74145 **Location:** Just n of jct 61st St. **Parking:** on-site.

WARREN DUCK CLUB

Phone: 918/497-2158 (17)

Continental

$10-$48

The intimate, sophisticated restaurant is ideally suitable for special occasions and business get-togethers. The menu features well-prepared American, Italian and European selections, including the signature duck. Dressy casual. **Bar:** Full bar. **Reservations:** suggested. **Hours:** 6 am-2 & 5-10 pm. **Address:** 6110 S Yale Ave 74136 **Location:** I-44, exit 229 (Yale Ave/SR 66), 1.3 mi s; in DoubleTree Hotel At Warren Place. **Parking:** on-site.

ZIO'S ITALIAN KITCHEN

Phone: 918/250-5999

Italian

$8-$13

The warm, comfortable atmosphere and Old World decor complement the menu. Meals are a good value, and so is the service. This small chain specializes in Italian cuisine, including oven-baked pizzas and pasta dishes. Guests are encouraged to get creative with their pizzas by mixing and matching from a list of 24 toppings. Particularly tempting dishes are Artichoke spinach pasta, chicken parmigiana, and Shrimp Limone. Casual dress. **Bar:** Full bar. **Reservations:** accepted. **Hours:** 11 am-10 pm, Fri & Sat-11 pm. Closed: 12/25. **Address:** 7111 S Mingo Rd 74133 **Location:** 0.6 mi w of jct US 169. **Parking:** on-site.

The Tulsa Vicinity

BIXBY pop. 13,336

WHERE TO DINE

RIB CRIB BBQ AND GRILL

Phone: 918/369-4799

Barbecue
$6-$14

Most guests need extra napkins to tackle the ribs, brisket, ham, pork and chicken selections. The menu also lists sandwiches and wraps, along with tempting sides and large desserts. The decor is decidedly Western. Casual dress. **Bar:** Beer only. **Hours:** 11 am-10 pm. Closed: 11/25, 12/25. **Address:** 12850 S Memorial Ave 74008 **Location:** Just n of jct 131st St. **Parking:** on-site.

BROKEN ARROW pop. 74,859 (See map and index starting on p. 645)

BEST WESTERN KENOSHA INN *Book great rates at AAA.com*

Phone: (918)251-2795

AAA SAVE

Hotel
$76-$86 All Year

Address: 1200 E Lansing St 74012 **Location:** 0.4 mi nw of jct SR 51 and Kenosha (71st St). **Facility:** 44 one-bedroom standard units, some with whirlpools. 2 stories (no elevator), interior corridors. **Parking:** on-site. **Terms:** 3 day cancellation notice. **Amenities:** irons, hair dryers. *Some:* high-speed Internet. **Pool(s):** heated outdoor. **Leisure Activities:** exercise room. **Guest Services:** wireless Internet. **Business Services:** PC. **Free Special Amenities: local telephone calls and high-speed Internet.**

/ SOME UNITS

AAA Benefit:
Members save up to 20%, plus 10% bonus points with rewards program.

CLARION HOTEL *Book at AAA.com*

Phone: (918)258-7085 43

Hotel
$80-$100 All Year

Address: 2600 N Aspen Ave 74012 **Location:** Just s of jct SR 51. **Facility:** 196 units. 193 one-bedroom standard units. 3 one-bedroom suites, some with kitchens. 4 stories, interior corridors. **Parking:** on-site. **Terms:** cancellation fee imposed. **Amenities:** voice mail, irons, hair dryers. *Some:* high-speed Internet. **Pool(s):** heated outdoor. **Leisure Activities:** exercise room. **Guest Services:** coin laundry, wireless Internet. **Business Services:** meeting rooms, PC.

ASK / SOME UNITS FEE

COMFORT INN *Book at AAA.com*

Phone: (918)258-8585 45

Hotel
$65-$89 All Year

Address: 2301 W Concord St 74012 **Location:** Just sw of jct SR 51 and Aspen Ave (145th St). **Facility:** Smoke free premises. 50 one-bedroom standard units, some with whirlpools. 2 stories (no elevator), interior/exterior corridors. *Bath:* combo or shower only. **Parking:** on-site, winter plug-ins. **Amenities:** voice mail, irons, hair dryers. **Pool(s):** heated indoor. **Leisure Activities:** limited exercise equipment. **Guest Services:** valet and coin laundry, wireless Internet. **Business Services:** PC.

ASK

HAMPTON INN-BROKEN ARROW *Book great rates at AAA.com*

Phone: (918)251-6060 44

Hotel
$89-$109 All Year

Address: 2300 W Albany St 74012 **Location:** Just sw of jct SR 51 and Aspen Ave (145th St). **Facility:** 80 one-bedroom standard units, some with whirlpools. 4 stories, interior corridors. *Bath:* combo or shower only. **Parking:** on-site, winter plug-ins. **Terms:** 1-7 night minimum stay, cancellation fee imposed. **Amenities:** high-speed Internet, dual phone lines, voice mail, irons, hair dryers. **Pool(s):** heated indoor. **Leisure Activities:** exercise room. **Guest Services:** valet and coin laundry, wireless Internet. **Business Services:** meeting rooms, business center.

CALL / SOME UNITS

Hampton Inn

AAA Benefit:
Members save up to 10% everyday!

HOLIDAY INN EXPRESS HOTEL & SUITES *Book at AAA.com*

Phone: (918)355-3200

Hotel
$105-$169 All Year

Address: 2201 N Stone Wood Cir 74012 **Location:** I-64/51, exit Elm Pl, just ne of jct SR 51 and Elm Pl. **Facility:** 120 units. 114 one-bedroom standard units. 6 one-bedroom suites with whirlpools. 3 stories, interior corridors. *Bath:* combo or shower only. **Parking:** on-site. **Terms:** check-in 4 pm, cancellation fee imposed. **Amenities:** high-speed Internet, voice mail, irons, hair dryers. *Some:* video games, dual phone lines. **Pool(s):** heated indoor. **Leisure Activities:** whirlpool, miniature golf, exercise room. *Fee:* game room. **Guest Services:** valet and coin laundry, wireless Internet. **Business Services:** meeting rooms, business center.

ASK CALL / SOME UNITS

(See map and index starting on p. 645)

HOMEWOOD SUITES BY HILTON TULSA SOUTH *Book great rates at AAA.com* **Phone:** (918)392-7700 46

Extended Stay Hotel
$99-$159 All Year

Address: 4900 W Madison Pl 74012 **Location:** Just ne of jct 71st St and Garnett Ave. **Facility:** 99 units. 41 one-bedroom standard units with efficiencies. 55 one- and 3 two-bedroom suites with efficiencies. 4 stories, interior corridors. *Bath:* combo or shower only. **Parking:** on-site. **Terms:** 1-7 night minimum stay, cancellation fee imposed. **Amenities:** high-speed Internet, voice mail, irons, hair dryers. **Pool(s):** heated outdoor. **Leisure Activities:** whirlpool, exercise room, sports court. **Guest Services:** valet and coin laundry, wireless Internet. **Business Services:** meeting rooms, business center.

CALL / SOME UNITS FEE

HOMEWOOD SUITES Hilton

AAA Benefit:
Members save 5% or more everyday!

WHERE TO DINE

BAMBOO GARDEN **Phone:** 918/369-7863

Chinese
$3-$6

Large portions of a good variety of classic favorites line the menu in the modest restaurant. Casual dress. **Hours:** 11 am-9 pm. Closed: 11/25, 12/25; also Sun. **Address:** 8210 S Elm Pl 74011 **Location:** Just n of jct 131st St. **Parking:** on-site.

BIG DADDYS ALL AMERICAN BBQ **Phone:** 918/439-4460 34

Barbecue
$4-$8

Modest decor may hide the fact that locals lay claim to this place as a favorite for good barbecue. Casual dress. **Hours:** 11 am-9 pm. Closed: 11/25, 12/25; also Sun & Mon. **Address:** 201 W Houston St 74012 **Location:** Just e of jct Aspen Ave (145th St). **Parking:** on-site.

CHINA STAR **Phone:** 918/258-8899 32

Chinese
$4-$11

Assorted seafood preparations are among offerings of varied Chinese favorites. Many locals enjoy the buffet choices. Casual dress. **Hours:** 11 am-9 pm, Fri & Sat-9:30 pm. Closed: 11/25, 12/25. **Address:** 803 N Aspen Ave 74012 **Location:** 1.4 mi s of SR 51. **Parking:** on-site.

DOOLEYS ANGUS INN **Phone:** 918/258-2333

American
$9-$24

Great tasting steaks, chops and chicken are served in the converted main-street drugstore. Portions are ample, and service is friendly. Casual dress. **Bar:** Full bar. **Hours:** 4:30 pm-9 pm, Fri & Sat-10 pm. Closed: 11/25, 12/25; also Sun. **Address:** 201 S Main St 74012 **Location:** Center. **Parking:** on-site.

GOLDIES PATIO GRILL **Phone:** 918/455-6128

American
$6-$15

The menu comprises grilled items, chicken, sandwiches and steak, but this place is best known for its excellent charbroiled burgers. The decor incorporates 1950s and '60s memorabilia. Casual dress. **Hours:** 10:45 am-9 pm. Closed major holidays. **Address:** 1912 S Elm Pl 74012 **Location:** Just s of jct 91st St. **Parking:** on-site.

JAKE'S CAFE **Phone:** 918/258-7710 33

American
$5-$9

The menu and decor are reminiscent of a 1950s diner. Freshness and hearty portions contribute to the popularity of the breakfast items. Casual dress. **Hours:** 6 am-8 pm, Sat & Sun 7 am-2 pm, Mon 6 am-2 pm. **Address:** 626 S Aspen Ave 74012 **Location:** 1.5 mi s of jct SR 51. **Parking:** on-site.

RIB CRIB BBQ AND GRILL **Phone:** 918/258-1559

Barbecue
$6-$14

Most guests need extra napkins to tackle the ribs, brisket, ham, pork and chicken selections. The menu also lists sandwiches and wraps, along with tempting sides and large desserts. The decor is decidedly Western. Casual dress. **Bar:** Beer only. **Hours:** 11 am-10 pm. Closed: 11/25, 12/25. **Address:** 121 W Kenosha St 74012 **Location:** Just e of jct Elm Pl. **Parking:** on-site.

RON'S HAMBURGERS & CHILI **Phone:** 918/451-7667

American
$4-$6

Although Ron's Hamburgers & Chili's name gives indicators of its strengths—varied hamburgers and savory chili—the menu also throws in a few tasty surprises. Casual dress. **Hours:** 11 am-8 pm. Closed: 11/25, 12/25; also Sun. **Address:** 1913 E Elm Pl 74012 **Location:** Just s of jct 91st St. **Parking:** on-site.

STONE MILL BBQ AND STEAKHOUSE **Phone:** 918/258-4227 30

Barbecue
$7-$21

Rustic decor sets the mood for freshly prepared steaks and barbecue. Hearty portions may make dessert a stretch. Casual dress. **Hours:** 11 am-9 pm, Fri & Sat-10 pm. Closed: 11/25, 12/25. **Address:** 2000 W Reno Ave 74012 **Location:** 0.5 mi s of jct SR 51. **Parking:** on-site.

TED'S CAFE ESCONDIDO **Phone:** 918/254-8337 31

Mexican
$7-$14

This busy restaurant is popular because of attentive service, large portions, good value and tasty dishes. The tradition at Ted's Cafe includes complimentary chips, salsa, spicy vegetables and flour taco shells. Casual dress. **Bar:** Full bar. **Hours:** 11 am-10 pm. Closed major holidays. **Address:** 3202 W Kenosha St 74012 **Location:** Just e of jct 129th St. **Parking:** on-site.

CATOOSA pop. 5,449

HARD ROCK HOTEL & CASINO TULSA Book great rates at AAA.com

Phone: (918)384-7800

Resort Hotel
$119-$139 All Year

Address: 777 W Cherokee St 74015 **Location:** I-44, exit 240A, just nw. **Facility:** The property features an 18-hole championship golf course, onsite casino and several dining choices. 356 units. 327 one-bedroom standard units. 29 one-bedroom suites with whirlpools. 7 stories, interior corridors. *Bath:* combo or shower only. **Parking:** on-site and valet. **Terms:** check-in 4 pm, cancellation fee imposed. **Amenities:** high-speed Internet, dual phone lines, voice mail, safes, irons, hair dryers. **Dining:** 5 restaurants, also, McGill's, see separate listing. **Leisure Activities:** exercise room. *Fee:* golf-18 holes. **Guest Services:** valet laundry, airport transportation-Tulsa International Airport, wireless Internet. **Business Services:** conference facilities, business center. (See color ad p 653)

SOME UNITS

FREE newspaper and high-speed Internet

—— WHERE TO DINE ——

MCGILL'S

Phone: 918/384-7500

Steak
$8-$33

This sophisticatedly decorated fine-dining restaurant is limited in size, making reservations a wise idea. Dressy casual. **Bar:** Full bar. **Reservations:** suggested. **Hours:** 11 am-2:30 & 5-10 pm, Fri & Sat-11 pm. **Address:** 777 W Cherokee St 74015 **Location:** I-44, exit 240A, just nw; in Hard Rock Hotel & Casino Tulsa. **Parking:** on-site and valet.

MOLLY'S

Phone: 918/266-7853

American
$13-$35

Nestled beside a river just off historic Route 66, Molly's is an unusual restaurant housed in a log cabin featuring mounted wildlife and leather rawhide chairs in a casual, rustic atmosphere. Diners will find a good menu selection and pleasant service. Casual dress. **Bar:** Full bar. **Hours:** 4 pm-10 pm. Closed: 1/1, 12/25; also Sun. **Address:** 3700 N Hwy 66 74015 **Location:** I-44, exit 241, 3.6 mi n. **Parking:** on-site.

CLAREMORE pop. 15,873

CLAREMORE MOTOR INN Book great rates at AAA.com

Phone: (918)342-4545

Motel
$44-$89 All Year

Address: 1709 N Lynn Riggs Blvd 74017 **Location:** 1.2 mi n on SR 66. **Facility:** 29 one-bedroom standard units. 2 stories (no elevator), interior/exterior corridors. **Parking:** on-site. **Amenities:** high-speed Internet. *Some:* DVD players (fee), hair dryers. **Guest Services:** wireless Internet. **Business Services:** meeting rooms, PC. **Free Special Amenities: continental breakfast and high-speed Internet.** SOME UNITS FEE

COMFORT INN CLAREMORE Book at AAA.com

Phone: (918)343-3297

Hotel
$62-$95 All Year

Address: 1720 S Lynn Riggs Blvd 74017 **Location:** 1.6 mi s on SR 66. **Facility:** 58 one-bedroom standard units. 2 stories (no elevator), interior corridors. **Parking:** on-site, winter plug-ins. **Amenities:** irons, hair dryers. **Pool(s):** outdoor. **Guest Services:** wireless Internet. **Business Services:** meeting rooms, PC. ASK SOME UNITS FEE

MICROTEL INN & SUITES Book at AAA.com

Phone: (918)343-2868

Hotel
$72-$79 All Year

Address: 10600 E Mallard Lake Rd 74017 **Location:** 2.6 mi s on SR 66. **Facility:** 57 one-bedroom standard units, some with whirlpools. 3 stories, interior corridors. *Bath:* combo or shower only. **Parking:** on-site. **Amenities:** *Some:* irons, hair dryers. **Pool(s):** outdoor. **Leisure Activities:** whirlpool. **Guest Services:** valet laundry, wireless Internet. **Business Services:** PC. ASK SOME UNITS FEE

SUPER 8 Book great rates at AAA.com

Phone: (918)341-2323

Hotel
$59-$99 All Year

Address: 1100 E Will Rogers Blvd 74017 **Location:** I-44, exit 255, just w. **Facility:** 40 one-bedroom standard units, some with whirlpools. 2 stories, interior/exterior corridors. **Parking:** on-site. **Terms:** cancellation fee imposed. **Amenities:** high-speed Internet, irons, hair dryers. *Some:* DVD players. **Guest Services:** coin laundry, wireless Internet. **Business Services:** PC. **Free Special Amenities: expanded continental breakfast and high-speed Internet.** SOME UNITS FEE

—— WHERE TO DINE ——

GOLDIES PATIO GRILL

Phone: 918/342-3744

American
$6-$15

The menu comprises grilled items, chicken, sandwiches and steak, but this place is best known for its excellent charbroiled burgers. The decor incorporates 1950s and '60s memorabilia. Casual dress. **Hours:** 10:45 am-9 pm. Closed major holidays. **Address:** 967 W Will Rogers Blvd 74017 **Location:** Center. **Parking:** on-site.

HAMMETT HOUSE RESTAURANT *Menu on AAA.com* **Phone:** 918/341-7333

American
$7-$23

Hammett House has a casual style and family atmosphere with daily specials and a great variety of home-style American dishes. They also serve homemade pie and freshly baked rolls. The server staff is attentive, friendly and efficient. A regionally known dining establishment for over 30 years. Casual dress. **Bar:** Beer only. **Hours:** 11 am-9 pm. Closed: 11/25, 12/25; also Mon. **Address:** 1616 W Will Rogers Blvd 74017 **Location:** On SR 88; adjacent to Will Rogers Memorial Park. **Parking:** on-site.

RIB CRIB BBQ AND GRILL **Phone:** 918/283-4600

Barbecue
$6-$14

Most guests need extra napkins to tackle the ribs, brisket, ham, pork and chicken selections. The menu also lists sandwiches and wraps, along with tempting sides and large desserts. The decor is decidedly Western. Casual dress. **Bar:** Beer only. **Hours:** 11 am-10 pm. Closed: 11/25, 12/25. **Address:** 1736 S Lynn Riggs Blvd 74017 **Location:** Center. **Parking:** on-site.

GLENPOOL pop. 8,123

BEST WESTERN GLENPOOL/TULSA *Book great rates at AAA.com* **Phone:** (918)322-5201

Hotel
$85-$90 All Year

Address: 14831 S Casper St 74033 **Location:** I-44, exit 224, 9.5 mi s on US 75. **Facility:** 64 one-bedroom standard units, some with whirlpools. 2 stories (no elevator), exterior corridors. **Parking:** on-site, winter plug-ins. **Terms:** cancellation fee imposed. **Amenities:** high-speed Internet, voice mail, irons, hair dryers. **Pool(s):** outdoor. **Guest Services:** coin laundry, wireless Internet. **Business Services:** PC. **Free Special Amenities: expanded continental breakfast and high-speed Internet.** / SOME UNITS FEE

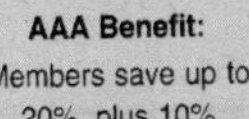

AAA Benefit:
Members save up to 20%, plus 10% bonus points with rewards program.

JENKS pop. 9,557 (See map and index starting on p. 645)

HOLIDAY INN EXPRESS HOTEL & SUITES *Book at AAA.com* **Phone:** (918)296-7300 49

Hotel
$99-$159 All Year

Address: 150 Aquarium Dr 74037 **Location:** Just s of jct Main St and Riverfront Dr. **Facility:** Smoke free premises. 76 units. 72 one-bedroom standard units, some with kitchens and/or whirlpools. 4 one-bedroom suites. 4 stories, interior corridors. *Bath:* combo or shower only. **Parking:** on-site. **Amenities:** high-speed Internet, voice mail, irons, hair dryers. **Pool(s):** heated indoor. **Leisure Activities:** sauna, whirlpool, exercise room. **Guest Services:** valet and coin laundry, wireless Internet. **Business Services:** meeting rooms, business center. ASK

WHERE TO DINE

LOS CABOS MEXICAN GRILL & CANTINA **Phone:** 918/298-2226 37

Mexican
$7-$20

The popular grill and cantina turns out tasty, freshly prepared Mexican favorites. Casual dress. **Bar:** Full bar. **Hours:** 11 am-10 pm, Fri & Sat-11 pm. Closed: 11/25, 12/25. **Address:** 300 Riverwalk Terr 74037 **Location:** Just n of jct Main St. **Parking:** on-site.

OWASSO pop. 18,502

BEST WESTERN OWASSO INN & SUITES *Book great rates at AAA.com* **Phone:** (918)272-2000

Hotel
$76-$80 All Year

Address: 7653 N Owasso Expwy 74055 **Location:** Just ne of jct US 169 and 76th St. **Facility:** 62 units. 60 one-bedroom standard units, some with whirlpools. 2 one-bedroom suites. 2 stories, interior/exterior corridors. *Bath:* combo or shower only. **Parking:** on-site, winter plug-ins. **Terms:** cancellation fee imposed. **Amenities:** voice mail, irons, hair dryers. **Pool(s):** outdoor. **Leisure Activities:** exercise room. **Guest Services:** valet and coin laundry, wireless Internet. **Business Services:** meeting rooms. **Free Special Amenities: continental breakfast and high-speed Internet.** / SOME UNITS

AAA Benefit:
Members save up to 20%, plus 10% bonus points with rewards program.

CANDLEWOOD SUITES *Book great rates at AAA.com* **Phone:** (918)272-4334

Extended Stay Hotel
$80-$100 All Year

Address: 11699 E 96th St N 74055 **Location:** 0.4 mi nw of jct US 169. **Facility:** Smoke free premises. 88 units. 76 one-bedroom standard units with efficiencies. 12 one-bedroom suites with efficiencies. 3 stories, interior corridors. *Bath:* combo or shower only. **Parking:** on-site. **Terms:** cancellation fee imposed. **Amenities:** video library, DVD players, high-speed Internet, voice mail, irons, hair dryers. **Leisure Activities:** exercise room. **Guest Services:** valet and coin laundry, wireless Internet. **Business Services:** meeting rooms, business center.

CALL / SOME UNITS FEE

FREE high-speed Internet

HAMPTON INN & SUITES TULSA NORTH OWASSO Book great rates at AAA.com

Phone: (918)609-6700

Hotel

$99-$139 All Year

Address: 9009 N 121st Ave E 74055 **Location:** Just e of jct Garnett Rd. **Facility:** Smoke free premises. 103 one-bedroom standard units, some with whirlpools. 4 stories, interior corridors. *Bath:* combo or shower only. **Parking:** on-site.. **Terms:** 1-7 night minimum stay, cancellation fee imposed. **Amenities:** voice mail, safes, irons, hair dryers. **Pool(s):** heated indoor. **Leisure Activities:** sauna, whirlpool, exercise room. **Guest Services:** valet and coin laundry, wireless Internet. **Business Services:** meeting rooms, business center.

CALL / SOME UNITS

AAA Benefit:

Members save up to 10% everyday!

HOLIDAY INN EXPRESS Book at AAA.com

Phone: 918/274-4100

Hotel

Rates not provided

Address: 7551 N Owasso Expwy 74055 **Location:** Just se of jct US 169 and 76th St. **Facility:** 60 units. 58 one-bedroom standard units. 2 one-bedroom suites with whirlpools. 3 stories, interior corridors. *Bath:* combo or shower only. **Parking:** on-site. **Amenities:** high-speed Internet, dual phone lines, voice mail, irons, hair dryers. *Some:* DVD players. **Pool(s):** heated indoor. **Leisure Activities:** sauna, whirlpool, exercise room. **Guest Services:** valet and coin laundry, wireless Internet. **Business Services:** meeting rooms, business center. / SOME UNITS

WHERE TO DINE

GOLDIES PATIO GRILL

Phone: 918/272-8501

American

$6-$15

The menu comprises grilled items, chicken, sandwiches and steak, but this place is best known for its excellent charbroiled burgers. The decor incorporates 1950s and '60s memorabilia. Casual dress. **Hours:** 10:45 am-8 pm, Fri & Sat-9 pm. Closed major holidays. **Address:** 8591 N Owasso Expwy 74055 **Location:** Just e of jct US 169. **Parking:** on-site.

RIB CRIB BBQ AND GRILL

Phone: 918/376-2600

Barbecue

$6-$14

Most guests need extra napkins to tackle the ribs, brisket, ham, pork and chicken selections. The menu also lists sandwiches and wraps, along with tempting sides and large desserts. The decor is decidedly Western. Casual dress. **Bar:** Beer only. **Hours:** 11 am-10 pm. Closed: 11/25, 12/25. **Address:** 8551 N 129th E Ave 74055 **Location:** Just s of jct E 86th St N. **Parking:** on-site.

RON'S HAMBURGERS & CHILI

Phone: 918/272-6996

American

$4-$6

Although Ron's Hamburgers & Chili's name gives indicators of its strengths—varied hamburgers and savory chili—the menu also throws in a few tasty surprises. Casual dress. **Hours:** 11 am-8 pm. Closed: 11/25, 12/25. **Address:** 9100 N Garnett Rd 74055 **Location:** Just n of jct US 169 and 86th St. **Parking:** on-site.

SAND SPRINGS pop. 17,451

BEST WESTERN SAND SPRINGS INN & SUITES Book great rates at AAA.com

Phone: (918)245-4999

Hotel

$70-$90 All Year

Address: 211 S Lake Dr 74063 **Location:** US 64 and 412, exit 81st W Ave, just sw. **Facility:** 51 one-bedroom standard units, some with whirlpools. 2 stories (no elevator), interior/exterior corridors. *Bath:* combo or shower only. **Parking:** on-site, winter plug-ins. **Terms:** cancellation fee imposed. **Amenities:** voice mail, safes, irons, hair dryers. **Pool(s):** outdoor. **Leisure Activities:** exercise room. **Guest Services:** coin laundry, wireless Internet. **Business Services:** PC. **Free Special Amenities: continental breakfast and high-speed Internet.**

AAA Benefit:

Members save up to 20%, plus 10% bonus points with rewards program.

HAMPTON INN-TULSA/SAND SPRINGS Book great rates at AAA.com

Phone: 918/245-8500

Hotel

Rates not provided

Address: 7852 W Parkway Blvd 74127 **Location:** Off US 64 and 412, exit 81st W Ave, just nw. **Facility:** 71 one-bedroom standard units, some with whirlpools. 3 stories, interior corridors. *Bath:* combo or shower only. **Parking:** on-site. **Amenities:** video games (fee), high-speed Internet, dual phone lines, voice mail, irons, hair dryers. **Pool(s):** heated indoor. **Leisure Activities:** sauna, whirlpool, exercise room. **Guest Services:** valet and coin laundry, wireless Internet. **Business Services:** meeting rooms, business center. / SOME UNITS

AAA Benefit:

Members save up to 10% everyday!

WHERE TO DINE

RIB CRIB BBQ AND GRILL

Phone: 918/241-5200

Barbecue

$6-$14

Most guests need extra napkins to tackle the ribs, brisket, ham, pork and chicken selections. The menu also lists sandwiches and wraps, along with tempting sides and large desserts. The decor is decidedly Western. Casual dress. **Bar:** Beer only. **Hours:** 11 am-10 pm. Closed: 11/25, 12/25. **Address:** 450 W Wekiwa Rd 74063 **Location:** Just w of jct SR 97. **Parking:** on-site.

RON'S HAMBURGERS & CHILI

Phone: 918/245-6010

American
$4-$6

Although Ron's Hamburgers & Chili's name gives indicators of its strengths—varied hamburgers and savory chili—the menu also throws in a few tasty surprises. Casual dress. **Hours:** 10:30 am-8 pm. Closed: 11/25, 12/25; also Sun. **Address:** 233 S Adams Rd 74063 **Location:** Just s of jct Charles Page Blvd. **Parking:** on-site.

SAPULPA pop. 19,166

— WHERE TO DINE —

RIB CRIB BBQ AND GRILL

Phone: 918/248-6800

Barbecue
$6-$14

Most guests need extra napkins to tackle the ribs, brisket, ham, pork and chicken selections. The menu also lists sandwiches and wraps, along with tempting sides and large desserts. The decor is decidedly Western. Casual dress. **Bar:** Beer only. **Hours:** 11 am-10 pm. Closed: 11/25, 12/25. **Address:** 705 S Mission St 74066 **Location:** Center. **Parking:** on-site.

WAGONER pop. 7,669

THE CANEBRAKE

Phone: 918/485-1810

Hotel
$159-$349 All Year

Address: 33241 E 732nd Rd 74467 **Location:** 1.7 mi n of jct SR 51 and S 330th Rd. **Facility:** Smoke free premises. 16 one-bedroom standard units, some with whirlpools. 2 stories (no elevator), exterior corridors. *Bath:* combo or shower only. **Parking:** on-site. **Terms:** 7 day cancellation notice-fee imposed. **Amenities:** video library, DVD players, CD players, hair dryers. **Dining:** The Canebrake Kitchen, see separate listing. **Leisure Activities:** fishing, hiking trails, yoga instruction, volleyball. *Fee:* massage. **Guest Services:** wireless Internet. **Business Services:** meeting rooms.

ASK CALL / SOME UNITS

— WHERE TO DINE —

THE CANEBRAKE KITCHEN

Phone: 918/485-1810

AAA
American
$12-$34

The restaurant serves what owners term "new age American with an ethnic flair" cuisine. An exhibition kitchen allows diners a view of the dish preparation. Casual dress. **Bar:** Full bar. **Reservations:** suggested. **Hours:** 5:30 pm-9 pm; Sunday brunch 10 am-2 pm. Closed: Mon & Tues. **Address:** 33241 E 732nd Rd 74467 **Location:** 1.7 mi n of jct SR 51 and S 330 Rd; in The Canebrake. **Parking:** on-site.

Discoveryland!, Sand Springs / © Christian Heeb

This ends listings for the Tulsa Vicinity.
The following page resumes the alphabetical listings of cities in Oklahoma.

VINITA pop. 6,472

HOLIDAY INN EXPRESS HOTEL & SUITES *Book at AAA.com* Phone: (918)256-4900

Hotel
$99-$129 All Year

Address: 232 S 7th St 74301 **Location:** I-44, exit 289, 0.7 mi nw. **Facility:** 60 one-bedroom standard units, some with whirlpools. 3 stories, interior corridors. *Bath:* combo or shower only. **Parking:** on-site. **Amenities:** high-speed Internet, dual phone lines, voice mail, irons, hair dryers. **Pool(s):** heated indoor. **Leisure Activities:** whirlpool, exercise room. **Guest Services:** coin laundry, wireless Internet. **Business Services:** meeting rooms, PC.

ASK CALL / SOME UNITS

WAGONER—See Tulsa p. 668.

WEATHERFORD pop. 9,859

BEST WESTERN MARK MOTOR HOTEL *Book great rates at AAA.com* Phone: (580)772-3325

Hotel
$80-$170 All Year

Address: 525 E Main St 73096 **Location:** I-40, exit 82, 0.5 mi n. **Facility:** 63 units. 61 one-bedroom standard units. 2 two-bedroom suites with kitchens. 2 stories (no elevator), exterior corridors. *Bath:* combo or shower only. **Parking:** on-site, winter plug-ins. **Amenities:** voice mail, irons, hair dryers. *Some:* high-speed Internet. **Pool(s):** outdoor. **Guest Services:** wireless Internet. **Business Services:** PC. *(See color ad below)*

/ SOME UNITS

AAA Benefit: Members save up to 20%, plus 10% bonus points with rewards program.

FREE full breakfast and high-speed Internet

▼ See AAA listing above ▼

COMFORT INN & SUITES Book great rates at AAA.com Phone: (580)772-9100

AAA SAVE

Hotel
$75-$115 All Year

Address: 1311 E Main St 73096 **Location:** I-40, exit 82, on north side. **Facility:** 71 one-bedroom standard units, some with kitchens (no utensils) and/or whirlpools. 4 stories, interior corridors. *Bath:* combo or shower only. **Parking:** on-site. **Amenities:** high-speed Internet, irons, hair dryers. **Pool(s):** heated indoor. **Leisure Activities:** exercise room. **Guest Services:** coin laundry, wireless Internet. **Business Services:** meeting rooms, business center.

CALL / SOME UNITS

HOLIDAY INN EXPRESS HOTEL & SUITES Book great rates at AAA.com Phone: (580)774-0400

AAA SAVE

Hotel
$100-$110 All Year

Address: 3825 E Main St 73096 **Location:** I-40, exit 84, just nw. **Facility:** Smoke free premises. 65 one-bedroom standard units. 2 stories, interior corridors. *Bath:* combo or shower only. **Parking:** on-site. **Amenities:** high-speed Internet, dual phone lines, voice mail, irons, hair dryers. **Pool(s):** heated indoor. **Guest Services:** valet and coin laundry, wireless Internet. **Business Services:** meeting rooms, PC. **Free Special Amenities: expanded continental breakfast and high-speed Internet.**

CALL FEE / SOME UNITS

WHERE TO DINE

NEW YOUNG CHINA Phone: 580/774-2845

Chinese
$4-$8

Patrons can choose from the lunch or dinner buffet or select from the many choices on the menu. Orders also are available for carryout. Casual dress. **Hours:** 11 am-9:30 pm, Sun-9 pm. Closed: 11/25, 12/25. **Address:** 205 W Main St 73096 **Location:** I-40, exit 82, 1 mi n. **Parking:** on-site.

T-BONE STEAK HOUSE Phone: 580/772-6329

Steak
$6-$20

Slow-cooked, smoked prime rib, flavorful steaks and bacon-wrapped charbroiled shrimp are excellent choices here. A sports-bar motif is featured on one side; a beautiful brick fireplace dominates the other side of the warm, inviting atmosphere. Casual dress. **Bar:** Full bar. **Hours:** 5 pm-10 pm. Closed: 11/25, 12/25; also for dinner 12/24. **Address:** 1805 E Main St 73096 **Location:** I-40, exit 82, 1 mi e on north frontage road. **Parking:** on-site.

WEST SILOAM SPRINGS

BEST WESTERN STATE LINE LODGE Book great rates at AAA.com Phone: (918)422-4444

AAA SAVE

Hotel
$85-$89 All Year

Address: 273 S Hwy 59 74338 **Location:** Jct US 59 and 412. **Facility:** 50 one-bedroom standard units, some with whirlpools. 2 stories, interior corridors. **Parking:** on-site. **Amenities:** high-speed Internet, voice mail, safes (fee), irons, hair dryers. **Pool(s):** heated indoor. **Leisure Activities:** exercise room. **Guest Services:** coin laundry, wireless Internet. **Business Services:** meeting rooms, PC. **Free Special Amenities: expanded continental breakfast and high-speed Internet.**

/ SOME UNITS

 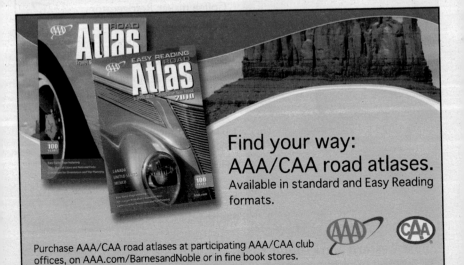
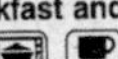

AAA Benefit:
Members save up to 20%, plus 10% bonus points with rewards program.

WOODWARD pop. 11,853

HOLIDAY INN EXPRESS HOTEL & SUITES *Book great rates at AAA.com* **Phone:** (580)774-0400

Hotel
$100-$110 All Year

Address: 3825 E Main St 73096 **Location:** I-40, exit 84, just nw. **Facility:** Smoke free premises. 65 one-bedroom standard units. 2 stories, interior corridors. *Bath:* combo or shower only. **Parking:** on-site. **Amenities:** high-speed Internet, dual phone lines, voice mail, irons, hair dryers. **Pool(s):** heated indoor. **Guest Services:** valet and coin laundry, wireless Internet. **Business Services:** meeting rooms, PC. **Free Special Amenities: expanded continental breakfast and high-speed Internet.**

CALL FEE / SOME UNITS

NORTHWEST INN **Phone:** 580/256-7600

Hotel
$85-$119 All Year

Address: Hwy 270 S & 1st St 73802 **Location:** 1.4 mi s of jct US 183 and 270, SR 3 and 34. **Facility:** 124 one-bedroom standard units. 2 stories (no elevator), interior/exterior corridors. **Parking:** on-site. **Amenities:** irons, hair dryers. **Pool(s):** heated indoor. **Leisure Activities:** billiards, table tennis, exercise room. **Guest Services:** valet and coin laundry, wireless Internet. **Business Services:** meeting rooms, PC. **Free Special Amenities: full breakfast and high-speed Internet.**

/ SOME UNITS FEE

The following lodging was either not evaluated or did not meet AAA rating requirements but is listed for your information only.

HAMPTON INN & SUITES WOODWARD **Phone:** 580/254-5050

fyi

Not evaluated. **Address:** 2814 Williams Ave 73801. Facilities, services, and decor characterize a mid-scale property.

AAA Benefit:
Members save up to 10% everyday!

WHERE TO DINE

K-BOB'S STEAKHOUSE **Phone:** 580/256-9413

Steak
$7-$18

The steakhouse prepares a great variety of plump, juicy fillets. A fireplace opens up into both dining rooms, and antique clocks decorate the walls. Rustic wagon-wheel chandeliers illuminate the room. Casual dress. **Hours:** 11 am-9 pm. Closed: 11/25, 12/25. **Address:** 270 NW Highway St 73801 **Location:** US 183 and 270 at Anderson Rd. **Parking:** on-site.

YUKON—See Oklahoma City p. 635.

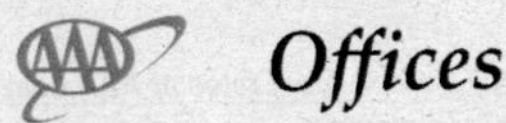

Offices

Cities with main offices are listed in **BOLD TYPE** and toll-free member service numbers in *ITALIC TYPE*.
All are closed Saturdays, Sundays and holidays unless otherwise indicated.
The addresses, phone numbers and hours for any AAA/CAA office are subject to change.
The type of service provided is designated below the name of the city where the office is located:

- ✚ Auto travel services, including books and maps, and on-demand TripTik® routings.
- ● Auto travel services, including selected books and maps, and on-demand TripTik® routings.
- ■ Books/maps only, no marked maps or on-demand TripTik® routings.
- ▲ Travel Agency Services, cruise, tour, air, car and rail reservations; domestic and international hotel reservations; passport photo services; international and domestic travel guides and maps; travel money products; and International Driving Permits. In addition, assistance with travel related insurance products including trip cancellation, travel accident, lost luggage, trip delay and assistance products.
- ✪ Insurance services provided.
- ✖ Car Care Plus Facility provides car care services.

AAA NATIONAL OFFICE: 1000 AAA DRIVE, HEATHROW, FLORIDA 32746-5063, (407) 444-7000

ARKANSAS

CABOT—AAA MISSOURI, 1102 S PINE, 72023. WEEKDAYS (M-F) 8:30-5:30. (501) 843-9090. ✪

CONWAY—AAA MISSOURI, 603 COURT ST # 2, 72032. WEEKDAYS (M-F) 9:00-5:30. (501) 327-9222. ✪

CONWAY—AAA MISSOURI, 930 WINGATE D-1, 72032. WEEKDAYS (M-F) 8:30-5:30. (501) 327-0233, *(800) 822-7705.* ✪

FAYETTEVILLE—AAA MISSOURI, 4262 FRONTAGE RD, 72703. WEEKDAYS (M-F) 8:30-5:30. (479) 444-9222, *(800) 822-5356.* ✚✪

FORT SMITH—AAA MISSOURI, 1401 S WALDRON RD, 72903. WEEKDAYS (M-F) 9:00-5:30, SAT 9:00-1:00. (479) 452-2010, *(800) 622-7389.* ✪

HOT SPRINGS—AAA MISSOURI, 227 HOBSON AVE, 71913. WEEKDAYS (M-F) 9:00-5:30. (501) 624-1222. ✪

LITTLE ROCK—AAA MISSOURI, 1604 MERRILL DR STE D, 72211. WEEKDAYS (M-F) 9:00-5:30. (501) 224-8700. ✪

LITTLE ROCK—AAA MISSOURI, 9116 RODNEY PARHAM RD, 72205. WEEKDAYS (M-F) 8:30-5:30, SAT 9:00-1:00. (501) 223-9222, *(800) 632-6808.* ✚▲✪

NORTH LITTLE ROCK—AAA MISSOURI, 4718 JFK BLVD, 72116. WEEKDAYS (M-F) 9:00-5:30. (501) 771-9100. ✪

KANSAS

LAWRENCE—AAA ALLIED GROUP INC, 3514 CLINTON PKY #L, 66047. WEEKDAYS (M-F) 9:00-6:00, SAT 9:00-3:00. (785) 843-1600, *(800) 234-1442.* ✚▲✪

MANHATTAN—AAA ALLIED GROUP INC, 321 SOUTHWIND RD, 66503. WEEKDAYS (M-F) 8:30-5:30, SAT 9:00-3:00. (785) 776-3131, *(800) 579-9470.* ✚▲✪

OLATHE—AAA MISSOURI, 13849C MUR-LEN, 66062. WEEKDAYS (M-F) 9:00-5:30. (913) 764-5300. ✪

OVERLAND PARK—AAA MISSOURI, 10600A METCALF, 66212. WEEKDAYS (M-F) 8:30-5:30, SAT 9:00-1:00. (913) 649-2280, *(800) 422-6375.* ✚▲✪

SHAWNEE—AAA MISSOURI, 15810 B SHAWNEE MSN PKY, 66217. WEEKDAYS (M-F) 8:30-5:30, SAT 9:00-1:00. (913) 248-1627, *(866) 222-2288.* ✚▲✪

TOPEKA—AAA ALLIED GROUP INC, 1223 SW WANAMAKER, 66604. WEEKDAYS (M-F) 8:00-6:00, SAT 9:00-3:00. (785) 233-0222, *(866) 245-6222.* ✚▲✪

WICHITA—AAA ALLIED GROUP INC, 7724 E CENTRAL STE 100, 67206. WEEKDAYS (M-F) 9:00-6:00, SAT 9:00-3:00. (316) 685-5241, *(800) 759-7222.* ✚▲✪

WICHITA—AAA ALLIED GROUP INC, 2110 N MAIZE RD STE 400, 67212. WEEKDAYS (M-F) 9:00-6:00, SAT 9:00-3:00. (316) 942-0008, *(800) 789-4222.* ✚▲✪

MISSOURI

ARNOLD—AAA MISSOURI, 3510 JEFFCO BLVD STE 103, 63010. WEEKDAYS (M-F) 9:00-5:30. (636) 464-6222. ✪

BALLWIN—AAA MISSOURI, 15480 CLAYTON RD STE 215, 63011. WEEKDAYS (M-F) 9:00-5:30. (636) 227-7100. ✪

BALLWIN—AAA MISSOURI, 15425 MANCHESTER RD #32, 63011. WEEKDAYS (M-F) 9:00-5:30, SAT 9:00-1:00. (636) 394-0052. ✪

BLUE SPRINGS—AAA MISSOURI, 710 W MAIN ST STE H, 64015. WEEKDAYS (M-F) 9:00-5:30. (816) 224-9559. ✪

BRANSON—AAA MISSOURI, 500 W MAIN #102B, 65616. WEEKDAYS (M-F) 9:00-5:30. (417) 334-3222, *(800) 972-8222.* ✪

BRIDGETON—AAA MISSOURI, 12462 ST CHARLES ROCK RD, 63044. WEEKDAYS (M-F) 9:00-5:30, SAT 9:00-1:00. (314) 291-6357. ✪

CAPE GIRARDEAU—AAA MISSOURI, 1903 BROADWAY, 63701. WEEKDAYS (M-F) 8:30-5:30, SAT 9:00-1:00. (573) 334-3038, *(800) 922-0941.* ✚▲✪

CHESTERFIELD—AAA MISSOURI, 15510 OLIVE BLVD STE 202, 63017. WEEKDAYS (M-F) 9:00-5:30 (SAT BY APPOINTMENT ONLY). (636) 532-9229. ✪

CLAYTON—AAA MISSOURI, 8235 FORSYTH BLVD, 63105. WEEKDAYS (M-F) 9:00-5:30, SAT 9:00-1:00. (314) 862-8021. ✚▲✪

COLUMBIA—AAA MISSOURI, 108-6 E GREEN MEADOWS RD, 65203. WEEKDAYS (M-F) 8:30-5:30. (573) 449-4490. ✪

COLUMBIA—AAA MISSOURI, 313 S PROVIDENCE RD, 65203. WEEKDAYS (M-F) 8:30-5:30. (573) 874-1909. ✪

COLUMBIA—AAA MISSOURI, 2101 W BROADWAY #D, 65203. WEEKDAYS (M-F) 8:30-5:30, SAT 9:00-1:00. (573) 445-8426, *(800) 822-5567.* ✚▲✪

CREVE COEUR—AAA MISSOURI, 13035 OLIVE BLVD STE 101, 63141. WEEKDAYS (M-F) 9:00-5:30, SAT 9:00-1:00. (314) 434-5555. ✪

FARMINGTON—AAA MISSOURI, 725B MAPLE VALLEY DR, 63640. WEEKDAYS (M-F) 9:00-5:30, SAT 9:00-1:00. (573) 756-4299, *(800) 922-7471.* ✪

FLORISSANT—AAA MISSOURI, 8194 N LINDBERGH BLVD, 63031. WEEKDAYS (M-F) 9:00-5:30, SAT 9:00-1:00. (314) 838-9900, *(800) 477-2224.* ✚▲✪

GLADSTONE—AAA MISSOURI, 104 NE 72ND ST STE C, 64118. WEEKDAYS (M-F) 9:00-5:30. (816) 436-8800. ✪

INDEPENDENCE—AAA MISSOURI, 4201 S NOLAND RD #Y, 64055. WEEKDAYS (M-F) 8:30-5:30, SAT 9:00-1:00. (816) 373-1717, *(800) 722-6978.* ✚▲✪

JEFFERSON CITY—AAA MISSOURI, 703 EASTLAND DR, 65101. WEEKDAYS (M-F) 9:00-5:30. (573) 761-1500. ✪

JEFFERSON CITY—AAA MISSOURI, 757A W STADIUM BLVD, 65109. WEEKDAYS (M-F) 8:30-5:30, SAT 9:00-1:00. (573) 634-3322, *(800) 438-5222.* ✚✪

JOPLIN—AAA MISSOURI, 2639 E 32ND ST #D, 64804. WEEKDAYS (M-F) 8:30-5:30, SAT 9:00-1:00. (417) 624-2000, *(800) 822-9132.* ✚✪

KANSAS CITY—AAA MISSOURI, 3245 BROADWAY, 64111. WEEKDAYS (M-F) 9:00-5:30, SAT 9:00-1:00. (816) 931-5252, *(800) 345-4283.* ✚▲✪

KANSAS CITY—AAA MISSOURI, 7679 NW PRAIRIE VIEW RD, 64151. WEEKDAYS (M-F) 8:30-5:30, SAT 9:00-1:00. (816) 455-4900, *(866) 222-8800.* ✚▲✪

KIRKSVILLE—AAA MISSOURI, 516 N BALTIMORE, 63501. WEEKDAYS (M-F) 8:30-5:30. (660) 665-3737, *(800) 922-7117.* ✪

LEBANON—AAA MISSOURI, 525A E ELM ST, 65536. WEEKDAYS (M-F) 9:00-5:30. (417) 588-3151. ✪

LIBERTY—AAA MISSOURI, 810 W LIBERTY DR, 64068. WEEKDAYS (M-F) 9:00-5:30. (816) 781-9999. ✪

MOBERLY—AAA MISSOURI, 213 N WILLIAMS, 65270. WEEKDAYS (M-F) 8:30-5:30. (660) 263-8844. ✪

O'FALLON—AAA MISSOURI, 844 BRYAN RD, 63366. WEEKDAYS (M-F) 9:00-5:30. (636) 272-1365. ✪

O'FALLON—AAA MISSOURI, 2277 HWY K, 63368. WEEKDAYS (M-F) 9:00-5:30, SAT 9:00-1:00. (636) 272-2362. ✚ ▲ ✪

POPLAR BLUFF—AAA MISSOURI, 2725 N WESTWOOD STE 4, 63901. WEEKDAYS (M-F) 9:00-5:30. (573) 785-1408. ✪

RAYTOWN—AAA MISSOURI, 9812 E 87TH ST, 64138. WEEKDAYS (M-F) 9:00-5:30. (816) 353-3205. ✪

ROLLA—AAA MISSOURI, 602 W 6TH ST STE B, 65401. WEEKDAYS (M-F) 9:00-5:30, SAT 9:00-1:00. (573) 364-1117, *(800) 822-1454.* ✪

SAINT LOUIS—AAA MISSOURI, 3917 LINDELL BLVD, 63108. WEEKDAYS (M-F) 9:00-5:30, SAT 9:00-1:00. (314) 531-0700, *(800) 315-3222.* ✚ ✪

SAINT LOUIS—AAA MISSOURI, 9948 KENNERLY CTR PLZ, 63128. WEEKDAYS (M-F) 9:00-5:30, SAT 9:00-1:00. (314) 849-6663. ✪

SAINT LOUIS—AAA MISSOURI, 12901 N FORTY DR, 63141. WEEKDAYS (M-F) 9:00-5:30, SAT 9:00-1:00. (314) 523-7350, *(800) 222-7623.* ● ▲ ✪

SAINT LOUIS—AAA MISSOURI, 9005 WATSON, 63126. WEEKDAYS (M-F) 9:00-5:30, SAT 9:00-1:00. (314) 962-2282, *(800) 986-4222.* ✚ ▲ ✪

SEDALIA—AAA MISSOURI, 1204 WINCHESTER, 65301. WEEKDAYS (M-F) 8:30-5:30, SAT 9:00-1:00. (660) 826-1800, *(800) 822-8692.* ✚ ▲ ✪

SPRINGFIELD—AAA MISSOURI, 2552 S CAMPBELL #B, 65807. WEEKDAYS (M-F) 8:30-5:30, SAT 9:00-1:00. (417) 882-8040, *(800) 922-7350.* ✚ ▲ ✪

ST. CHARLES—AAA MISSOURI, 1046 COUNTRY CLUB RD, 63303. WEEKDAYS (M-F) 9:00-5:30 (SAT BY APPOINTMENT ONLY). (636) 946-2229. ✪

ST. CHARLES—AAA MISSOURI, 6173 MID RIVERS MALL DR, 63304. WEEKDAYS (M-F) 9:00-5:30. (636) 477-0222. ✪

ST. JOSEPH—AAA MISSOURI, 1301 VILLAGE DR, 64506. WEEKDAYS (M-F) 9:00-5:30, SAT 9:00-1:00. (816) 233-1377, *(800) 863-4222.* ✪

ST. PETERS—AAA MISSOURI, 591 MID RIVERS MALL DR, 63376. WEEKDAYS (M-F) 9:00-5:30, SAT 9:00-1:00. (636) 279-2299, *(800) 983-4222.* ✚ ▲ ✪

WASHINGTON—AAA MISSOURI, 1053 WASHINGTON SQ, 63090. WEEKDAYS (M-F) 9:00-5:30, SAT 9:00-12:00 (SUMMER HOURS SAT 9-1). (636) 239-6791, *(800) 922-2451.* ✚ ▲ ✪

WILDWOOD—AAA MISSOURI, 16942 MANCHESTER RD, 63040. WEEKDAYS (M-F) 9:00-5:30 (SAT BY APPOINTMENT ONLY). (636) 273-4256. ✪

OKLAHOMA

ARDMORE—AAA OKLAHOMA, 1505 N COMMERCE #103, 73401. WEEKDAYS (M-F) 8:30-5:00. (580) 223-5170, *(800) 499-5170.* ✚ ▲ ✪

BARTLESVILLE—AAA OKLAHOMA, 112 SE FRANK PHILLIPS BLV, 74003. WEEKDAYS (M-F) 8:30-5:30. (918) 337-3737, *(800) 688-2701.* ✚ ▲ ✪

BETHANY—AAA OKLAHOMA, 6818 NORTHWEST 23RD, 73008. WEEKDAYS (M-F) 8:30-5:00 (SAT BY APPOINTMENT ONLY). (405) 787-9595. ✪

BIXBY—AAA OKLAHOMA, 8222 E 103RD ST S STE 101, 74133. WEEKDAYS (M-F) 8:30-5:30 (SAT BY APPOINTMENT ONLY). (918) 364-8222. ✪

BROKEN ARROW—AAA OKLAHOMA, 3746 S ELM PL, 74011. WEEKDAYS (M-F) 8:30-6:00. (918) 455-4764, *(800) 380-6443.* ✚ ▲ ✪

BROKEN ARROW—AAA OKLAHOMA, 2604 W KENOSHA STE 221, 74012. WEEKDAYS (M-F) 9:00-5:00 (SAT BY APPOINTMENT ONLY), FRI 9:00-4:30. (918) 251-8877. ✪

CHOUTEAU—AAA OKLAHOMA, 114 W MAIN, 74337. WEEKDAYS (M-F) 8:30-5:30 (SAT BY APPOINTMENT ONLY). (918) 476-6001. ✪

CLAREMORE—AAA OKLAHOMA, 445 S BRADY, 74017. WEEKDAYS (M-F) 8:30-5:30 (SAT BY APPOINTMENT ONLY). (918) 341-2100. ✪

COLLINSVILLE—AAA OKLAHOMA, 11400 N GARNETT RD STE A, 74021. WEEKDAYS (M-F) 8:30-5:30 (SAT BY APPOINTMENT ONLY). (918) 371-7800. ✪

DEL CITY—AAA OKLAHOMA, 4605 SE 29TH ST, 73115. WEEKDAYS (M-F) 8:30-5:30. (405) 670-1474. ✚ ▲ ✪

DURANT—AAA OKLAHOMA, 628 BRYAN DR, 74701. WEEKDAYS (M-F) 8:30-5:30 (SAT BY APPOINTMENT ONLY). (580) 924-2100. ✪

EDMOND—AAA OKLAHOMA, 16620 N WESTERN AVE, 73012. WEEKDAYS (M-F) 8:30-5:30 (SAT BY APPOINTMENT ONLY). (405) 340-5222. ✪

EDMOND—AAA OKLAHOMA, 3222 SOUTH BLVD, 73013. WEEKDAYS (M-F) 8:30-6:00. (405) 348-8281, *(888) 841-9127.* ✚ ▲ ✪

ENID—AAA OKLAHOMA, 215 W OWEN GARRIOTT # 1B, 73701. WEEKDAYS (M-F) 8:30-5:30 (SAT BY APPOINTMENT ONLY). (580) 242-7100. ✪

LANGLEY—AAA OKLAHOMA, 1792 N HIGHWAY 82, 74301. WEEKDAYS (M-F) 8:30-5:30 (SAT BY APPOINTMENT ONLY). (918) 782-4091. ✪

LAWTON—AAA OKLAHOMA, 7009 NW CACHE RD SUITE A, 73505. WEEKDAYS (M-F) 9:00-5:00 (SAT BY APPOINTMENT ONLY). (580) 536-9100. ✪

MCALESTER—AAA OKLAHOMA, 319 S 6TH ST, 74501. WEEKDAYS (M-F) 9:00-5:00, FRI 9:00-4:00. (918) 426-1104. ✪

MOORE—AAA OKLAHOMA, 104 SE THIRD, 73160. WEEKDAYS (M-F) 9:00-5:00 (SAT BY APPOINTMENT ONLY). (405) 799-2870. ✪

MUSKOGEE—AAA OKLAHOMA, 1021 W OKMULGEE ST, 74401. WEEKDAYS (M-F) 8:30-5:30. (918) 683-0341, *(800) 259-9299.* ✚ ▲ ✪

NORMAN—AAA OKLAHOMA, 430 W MAIN ST, 73069. WEEKDAYS (M-F) 8:30-5:30 (SAT BY APPOINTMENT ONLY). (405) 801-3353. ✪

NORMAN—AAA OKLAHOMA, 1017 24TH AVE NW, 73069. WEEKDAYS (M-F) 8:30-5:30. (405) 360-7771, *(877) 314-3489.* ✚ ▲ ✪

OKLAHOMA CITY—AAA OKLAHOMA, 3557 W MEMORIAL RD, 73134. WEEKDAYS (M-F) 8:30-6:00. (405) 753-9777, *(888) 434-2270.* ✚ ▲ ✪

OKLAHOMA CITY—AAA OKLAHOMA, 8013 S WESTERN AVE STE C, 73139. WEEKDAYS (M-F) 9:00-5:00 (SAT BY APPOINTMENT ONLY). (405) 604-5600. ✪

OKLAHOMA CITY—AAA OKLAHOMA, 3625 NW 39TH ST, 73112. WEEKDAYS (M-F) 8:30-6:00, SAT 9:00-1:00. (405) 717-8200, *(800) 926-9922.* ✚ ▲ ✪

OWASSO—AAA OKLAHOMA, 8506 N 128 E AVE, 74055. WEEKDAYS (M-F) 8:30-5:00 (SAT BY APPOINTMENT ONLY). (918) 272-4700. ✪

SAND SPRINGS—AAA OKLAHOMA, 658 E CHARLES PAGE BLVD, 74063. WEEKDAYS (M-F) 8:00-6:00 (SAT BY APPOINTMENT ONLY). (918) 245-8884. ✪

SKIATOOK—AAA OKLAHOMA, 747 WILL ROGERS BLVD #A, 74070. WEEKDAYS (M-F) 9:00-5:30. (918) 396-7542. ✪

TAHLEQUAH—AAA OKLAHOMA, 209 W CHOCTAW, 74464. WEEKDAYS (M-F) 8:30-5:30 (SAT BY APPOINTMENT ONLY). (918) 456-5835. ✪

TULSA—AAA OKLAHOMA, 10051 S YALE STE 106, 74137. WEEKDAYS (M-F) 8:30-6:00. (918) 296-9600, *(888) 222-7611.* ✚ ▲ ✪

TULSA—AAA OKLAHOMA, 11609 E 31ST ST, 74146. WEEKDAYS (M-F) 8:30-5:30 (SAT BY APPOINTMENT ONLY). (918) 949-4080. ✪

TULSA—AAA OKLAHOMA, 6808 S MEMORIAL STE 208, 74133. WEEKDAYS (M-F) 8:30-5:30 (SAT BY APPOINTMENT ONLY). (910) 872-7100. ✪

TULSA—AAA OKLAHOMA, 4103 E 31ST ST, 74135. WEEKDAYS (M-F) 8:30-5:00 (SAT BY APPOINTMENT ONLY). (918) 712-8003. ✪

TULSA—AAA OKLAHOMA, 6944 S LEWIS, 74136. WEEKDAYS (M-F) 9:00-5:00. (918) 488-1002. ✪

TULSA—AAA OKLAHOMA, 2121 E 15TH ST, 74104. WEEKDAYS (M-F) 8:30-6:00. (918) 748-1000, *(800) 222-2582.* ✚ ▲ ✪

TULSA—AAA OKLAHOMA, 4924 S MEMORIAL DR, 74145. WEEKDAYS (M-F) 8:30-5:00 (SAT BY APPOINTMENT ONLY). (918) 663-7600. ✪

TULSA—AAA OKLAHOMA, 8013 S SHERIDAN RD, 74133. WEEKDAYS (M-F) 8:30-6:00, SAT 9:00-1:00. (918) 496-0496, *(800) 745-5222.* ✚ ▲ ✪

Metric Equivalents Chart

TEMPERATURE

To convert Fahrenheit to Celsius, subtract 32 from the Fahrenheit temperature, multiply by 5 and divide by 9.
To convert Celsius to Fahrenheit, multiply by 9, divide by 5 and add 32.

Celsius °		Fahrenheit °
100	**BOILING**	**212**
37		100
35		95
32		90
29		85
27		80
24		75
21		70
18		65
16		60
13		55
10		50
7		45
4		40
2		35
0	**FREEZING**	**32**
-4		25
-7		20
-9		15
-12		10
-15		5
-18		0
-21		-5
-24		-10
-27		-15

ACRES

1 acre = 0.4 hectare (ha) 1 hectare = 2.47 acres

MILES AND KILOMETERS

Note: A kilometer is approximately 5/8 or 0.6 of a mile.
To convert kilometers to miles multiply by 0.6.

Miles	Kilometers	Kilometers	Miles
15	24.1	30	18.6
20	32.2	35	21.7
25	40.2	40	24.8
30	48.3	45	27.9
35	56.3	50	31.0
40	64.4	55	34.1
45	72.4	60	37.2
50	80.5	65	40.3
55	88.5	70	43.4
60	96.6	75	46.6
65	104.6	80	49.7
70	112.7	85	52.8
75	120.7	90	55.9
80	128.7	95	59.0
85	136.8	100	62.1
90	144.8	105	65.2
95	152.9	110	68.3
100	160.9	115	71.4

LINEAR MEASURE

Customary	Metric
1 inch = 2.54 centimeters	1 centimeter = 0.4 inches
1 foot = 30 centimeters	1 meter = 3.3 feet
1 yard = 0.91 meters	1 meter = 1.09 yards
1 mile = 1.6 kilometers	1 kilometer = .62 miles

LIQUID MEASURE

Customary	Metric
1 fluid ounce = 30 milliliters	1 milliliter = .03 fluid ounces
1 cup = .24 liters	1 liter = 2.1 pints
1 pint = .47 liters	1 liter = 1.06 quarts
1 quart = .95 liters	1 liter = .26 gallons
1 gallon = 3.8 liters	

WEIGHT

If You Know:	Multiply By:	To Find:
Ounces	28	Grams
Pounds	0.45	Kilograms
Grams	0.035	Ounces
Kilograms	2.2	Pounds

PRESSURE

Air pressure in automobile tires is expressed in kilopascals. Multiply pound-force per square inch (psi) by 6.89 to find kilopascals (kPa).

24 psi = 165 kPa 28 psi = 193 kPa
26 psi = 179 kPa 30 psi = 207 kPa

GALLONS AND LITERS

Gallons	Liters	Gallons	Liters
5	19.0	12	45.6
6	22.8	14	53.2
7	26.6	16	60.8
8	30.4	18	68.4
9	34.2	20	76.0
10	38.0	25	95.0

Liters	Gallons	Liters	Gallons
10	2.6	40	10.4
15	3.9	50	13.0
20	5.2	60	15.6
25	6.5	70	18.2
30	7.8	80	20.8
35	9.1	90	23.4

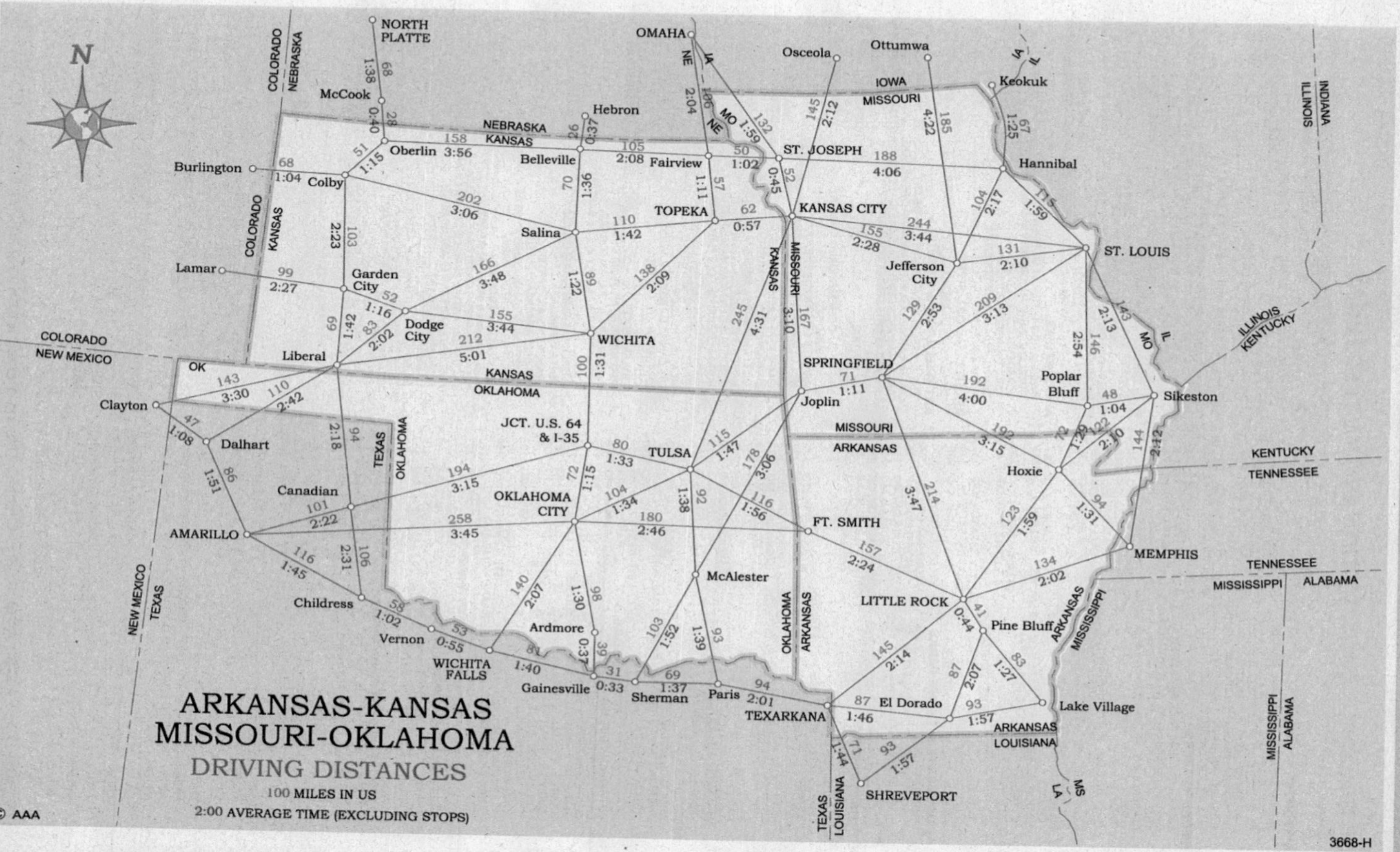
ARKANSAS-KANSAS
MISSOURI-OKLAHOMA
DRIVING DISTANCES
100 MILES IN US
2:00 AVERAGE TIME (EXCLUDING STOPS)
© AAA
3668-H
N
NORTH PLATTE
McCook
Oberlin
Burlington
Colby
Hebron
Belleville
Fairview
OMAHA
Osceola
Ottumwa
Keokuk
ST. JOSEPH
Hannibal
KANSAS CITY
TOPEKA
Salina
ST. LOUIS
Jefferson City
Lamar
Garden City
Dodge City
WICHITA
Liberal
SPRINGFIELD
Joplin
Poplar Bluff
Sikeston
Clayton
Dalhart
JCT. U.S. 64 & I-35
TULSA
Hoxie
Canadian
OKLAHOMA CITY
FT. SMITH
AMARILLO
MEMPHIS
McAlester
Childress
LITTLE ROCK
Pine Bluff
Ardmore
Vernon
WICHITA FALLS
Gainesville
Sherman
Paris
TEXARKANA
El Dorado
Lake Village
SHREVEPORT

Points of Interest Index

Index Legend

NB....national battlefield
NBP....national battlefield park
NC....national cemetery
NF....national forest
NHM....national historic(al) monument
NHP....national historic(al) park
NHS....national historic(al) site
NL....national lakeshore
NME....national memorial
NMO....national monument
NMP....national military park
NP....national park
NRA....national recreation area
NR....national river
NS....national seashore
NWR....national wildlife refuge
PHP....provincial historic(al) park
PHS....provincial historic(al) site
PP....provincial park
SF....state forest
SHM....state historic(al) monument
SHP....state historic(al) park
SHS....state historic(al) site
SME....state memorial
SP....state park
SRA....state recreation area

GEM: Points of Interest Offering a *Great Experience for Members*®

EXHIBITS & COLLECTIONS-INDIAN

EXHIBITS & COLLECTIONS-MUSIC

EXHIBITS & COLLECTIONS-RELIGIOUS ITEMS

EXHIBITS & COLLECTIONS-REVOLUTIONARY WAR

EXHIBITS & COLLECTIONS-SCIENCE

MUSEUMS